D0054310

the SUN·COAST chronicles

the SUN·COAST chronicles

Four Bestselling Mystery Novels Complete in One Volume

Evidence of Mercy

Justifiable Means

Ulterior Motives

Presumption of Guilt

Terri Blackstock

Inspirational Press
New York

Previously published as four separate volumes:

EVIDENCE OF MERCY
Copyright © 1995 by Terri Blackstock.

JUSTIFIABLE MEANS
Copyright © 1996 by Terri Blackstock.

ULTERIOR MOTIVES
Copyright © 1996 by Terri Blackstock.

PRESUMPTION OF GUILT
Copyright © 1997 by Terri Blackstock.

First Inspirational Press edition published in 1999.

Inspirational Press
A division of BBS Publishing Corporation
386 Park Avenue South
New York, NY 10016

Inspirational Press is a registered trademark of BBS Publishing Corporation.

Published by arrangement with Zondervan Publishing House.

Published in association with the literary agency of Alive Communications, 1465 Kelly Johnson Blvd., Suite 320, Colorado Springs, CO 80920.

Library of Congress Catalog Card Number: 98-75435

ISBN: 0-88486-237-2

Printed in the United States of America.

Contents

EVIDENCE OF MERCY

This book and all those to follow it
are lovingly dedicated to
the Nazarene

Acknowledgments

SPECIAL THANKS TO Chip Anderson, of Anderson's Optique in Jackson, Mississippi, for showing me his magic; to Carla Nowell, physical therapist at Methodist Hospital in Jackson, Mississippi, for helping me find authenticity; to Ellis Warren, pilot, for talking me through my landing; to Larry Morgan, aircraft mechanic, and Lane Smith, general genius, for helping me create my disasters; to the Cockrells and many others at First Baptist Church in Jackson, Mississippi, for their powerful prayers; to Greg Johnson, for sharing the vision; to the Phillips-Corry Class, for leading me to the brink of awakening.

And to Ken, my spiritual leader, for helping me decide where to go from there.

Prologue

HE HAD WAITED for a new moon, for he needed the cover of darkness. Tonight was perfect. Dressed in black, he knew it would be virtually impossible for anyone to see him. The airport guard who patrolled the small building in the wee hours would never notice that anything improper was going on right beneath his nose. Not as long as he was swift and quiet.

Checking once again to make sure no one was near, he crept across the tarmac, past the private planes lined up like a military fleet, squinting to read the number and name on each fuselage.

Solitude was the fourth from the right, just as he'd expected.

With one more quick look around, he bent down and duckwalked under the plane, found the wheel well, and shone his small flashlight to find the spot he needed. Calmly he pulled the tool he'd brought out of his pocket, made the necessary adjustment, then flicked off the light.

It had taken less than thirty seconds to create the catastrophe that would finally make things right. Grinning, he hurried quietly back across the tarmac then broke into a jog for a mile beyond the airport until he reached his car. He'd parked it far enough away so he wouldn't be heard back at the airport as he cranked it. He pulled into the street, keeping his lights off. Laughing out loud, he headed home, eager for the satisfaction he would feel the next time *Solitude* was flown.

Then there would be one less obstacle between him and his prize—and one more victory to show who was really in control.

1

SOLITUDE—THE PERFECT name for the toy that defined Jake Stevens, not because he liked being alone. He didn't. He'd always found it better to be surrounded by the right kind of people, and Jake had a knack for collecting friends just like he collected brandy snifters from the cities he'd traveled to. But the only way to be completely autonomous was to be unattached. It was a credo Jake lived by, and it meant that he knew the value of his own solitude. At the top of the pyramid that was Jake's life, there was only one person—the one he smiled at in the mirror every morning. At thirty-nine, he was just where he'd wanted to be at this point in his life. Unfettered and financially fluid, he had the world by the tail, and today he was going to bag it and take it home.

Ignoring the doorman who greeted him, he trotted down the steps in front of the Biltmore. At the bottom of the steps, his red Porsche idled as the valet got out. "Hey, put the top down, will ya?" Jake called down.

The kid, who looked no more than eighteen, knew exactly how to do it, and as the top began to buzz back, Jake's attention was snatched away by the blonde on her way up the steps. She was college aged, probably twenty years his junior, but he'd never found that to be a problem. Tipping his sunglasses, he gave her that engaging grin that had always worked for him before.

She smiled back, as they always did, and slowed her step as he came toward her.

"I'm not usually this blunt, Ma'am, but I've learned over the years that if I let an opportunity slip by me, I sometimes never get it again. And you are, by far, the most beautiful woman I've laid eyes on since I pulled into St. Clair yesterday."

She laughed, as though she'd heard the line before, but it didn't seem to hurt his chances. "I'm Sarah," she said. "Are you staying in the hotel?"

"Yes," he said, "and if I had time, I'd turn around and escort you right back inside. But alas—" He threw his hand dramatically over his heart and sighed heavily as she laughed again. "I have to be somewhere—to look at a plane I'm thinking about buying." He waited a beat for her to be sufficiently impressed, and when her eyebrows lifted slightly, he went on. "Now, I don't want you to think I'm the kind of guy who hits on every woman he sees, but do you think, by any chance, you'd care to meet a lonely transplanted Texan for drinks later? I can call you when I get back."

He knew he wasn't imagining the sparkle in her eye, for he'd seen it many times before. "I'm in room 323," she answered. "But if I'm not there, I'll probably be out by the pool."

The pool, he thought with a grin. *Perfect.* "I'll call as soon as I get back."

"You haven't told me your name yet."

"Oh, yeah," he said. "Jake. Jake Stevens."

But already he'd forgotten hers. The room number was all that really mattered. Waving, he trotted the rest of the way down the steps. Tossing a five-dollar bill at the valet, he slid behind the wheel.

Florida was great, he told himself as he pulled onto Highway 19. Opportunities everywhere he looked. It was pure luck that he'd gotten transferred here. He only wished he could spend less time house hunting and more time playing in the few days he had left before he had to report to work.

He pulled up to a stoplight and leaned his head back on the headrest, letting the morning rays of sunlight beat down on his face. The wind was picking up, haphazardly blowing his hair. *I should stop somewhere and get a haircut,* he thought, glancing into his mirror. But it didn't look so bad a little longer, and the women seemed to like it. Idly, he decided to wait.

The stoplight didn't change, and he started to get irritated. Traffic often made him feel out of control, and there was nothing he hated worse.

He glanced around at the billboards that dominated the four corners and saw one for his favorite cognac, another for a restaurant near Honeymoon Island, a third for the outlet mall, a fourth for a television station.

The light still hadn't changed, and he began to perspire. He flicked on the air conditioner, knowing that it would do little to combat the heat with the top down, but Jake had never been one to let logic interfere with his quest for comfort.

When the light flashed green, Jake stepped on the accelerator and flicked on the radio. The wind in his ears made it impossible to hear, so finally he turned it off and tried to concentrate instead on the new toy he was going to buy—a Piper Arrow PA 28. Just what he needed to make life complete.

Once he had it, he would finally have everything he wanted.

The wind was too strong for a leisurely afternoon test flight, and Lynda Barrett wished she'd scheduled it for another day . . . another month . . . another year. But this fellow Jake Stevens was her first potential buyer, and she had already delayed showing him the plane as long as she dared; she didn't have the luxury of waiting any longer. The maddening thing about listing something for sale is that, sooner or later, someone will buy it.

Lynda stood on the wing of the Piper, gently polishing the name she'd had painted on the side when she'd bought it two years ago. *Solitude.* This plane was her escape, her refuge from the pressures of her job as an attorney. She would rather have sold her home, her father's home, and everything else either of them owned than the plane.

But she had tried selling both houses, and there hadn't been any buyers. Now the only way she could see to get a start on paying off the enormous debts her father had bequeathed her was to sell her favorite possession—the only thing she had that anyone seemed to want to buy.

The wind picked up, blowing an empty paper cup across the tarmac. Her eyes followed it—until she saw Gordon Addison leaning against the wall of the hangar, smoking a cigarette. He was watching her the way he always did, with that narrow-eyed look that gave her chills. He hadn't spoken to her in weeks, not since she'd come up with her fifth excuse not to go out with him. He was the one thing about this airport she wouldn't miss when she sold her plane.

Moving to the other side of the wing so he couldn't see her so easily, she looked into the wind and ran her fingertips over the cold, smooth metal of the fuselage. She remembered the day she bought *Solitude.* It had meant that she'd finally risen above the humdrum existence of her parents—whose lives consisted of "Jeopardy" and macaroni-and-cheese. Lynda had had a plan—to have more, to do more, to *be* more. Buying the plane had meant that she had finally arrived.

As her love for the plane had grown, she had begun casting off friends, as though they exceeded the weight limit of the baggage she could carry. She had shaken off her hobbies, her clubs, and her church in order to free up more time to spend in the cockpit. The cockpit she was about to sell. Where would she anchor herself once the plane was gone?

Shaking off her quicksand depression, Lynda went back to polishing the plane. The prospective buyer would be here any minute, and she supposed she should be practicing some kind of sales pitch. She did need the money after all. But somewhere in the back of her mind, she knew she was still hoping some miracle would keep her from having to go through with the sale.

She heard the sound of a car and turned around. Across the tarmac, a red Porsche was weaving through the parked planes, as if the driver had a perfect right to drive wherever he pleased. Lynda stopped polishing and watched as he made his way toward her.

The man who got out was in his late thirties and sported a dark tan and designer clothes that mocked his attempt to look casual. He grinned up at her, a cocky grin that set her instantly on guard. "This isn't a parking lot," she called down.

"It's okay," he said. "I parked here yesterday when I looked at the plane, and nobody objected. I'm Jake Stevens."

The confidence with which he uttered his name riled her, and she resisted the urge to say, "Oh, *well.* Since you're Jake Stevens—"

Climbing down, she eyed him more closely. He was too good-looking, too self-assured, and probably had too much money. The combination made her dislike him instantly.

Grudgingly, she extended her hand. "I'm Lynda Barrett."

"I figured as much," he said. "Did Mike tell you I came yesterday?"

"Yes. He said you'd want to take a test flight today."

"I wanted to take one yesterday, but he had a problem with it."

"He runs the airport," she said, "but he doesn't own this plane. I do, and I was in court."

"So he said." He took off his Ray Bans and dropped them into his shirt pocket, as if by showing her his "mesmerizing" eyes he might soften her mood a bit. "No problem, though. Today's as good a day as any."

"Not really," she said, looking into the breeze. "The wind's a little stronger than I like."

"Not for me. I can handle it."

The ego behind his words made her grin slightly. "Of course you can. So, Lindbergh, any questions you wanted to ask about the plane?"

He cocked his head at her barb. "No, but I might have a few about its owner."

"Such as."

"Such as, where you get your attitude?"

"*My* attitude?" She breathed a laugh and shook her head, her comeback forming on the tip of her tongue. But something stopped her. *No need to make him angry,* she told herself. *Unfortunately, this is business.* Sighing, she took a stab at honesty. "Look, I guess I'm just having a little trouble with this. I'm not looking forward to selling my plane."

"I don't blame you." Walking under the Piper, he checked the wing flaps and glanced back at her. "I looked it over pretty well yesterday. You've really maintained it."

"I spend all my spare time taking care of it," she said. She watched him drain a little fuel from the wing sump and fought the proprietary urge to tell him to keep his hands off her plane. "Did Mike let you see the log books?"

"Yeah, and the maintenance records. He was able to answer most of my questions, but he didn't really know why you were selling it."

Lynda's stomach tightened. "Financial reasons."

"Your law practice isn't doing well?"

"My practice is fine, thank you."

Frowning, he turned back to her. "Excuse me for asking, but before I sink a wad into a plane like this, I need to know the real reason you want to sell."

"I told you the real reason."

"Okay, okay. Don't get so hot. Save it for something worthwhile."

It was his type that she hated she finally realized, and this guy fit every macho stereotype she could think of. "You're pretty sure of yourself, aren't you?"

"Sometimes." Grinning, he checked the engine sump and the oil, and Lynda watched, shaking her head at his arrogance.

The attitude, she thought. Her attitude was coming back again, filling her with bitterness, and somehow she had to fight it. Taking a deep breath, she tried to change the subject. "How long have you been flying?"

"About twenty years," he said. "Right now I fly a 747 for TSA Airlines."

Lynda raised her eyebrows. "Then why would you want your own plane? I'd think you'd be tired of flying when you aren't working."

Jake went to the propellers and ran his hands along the blades. "Flying for work and flying for pleasure are two different things. There's nothing like leaving the world behind and being up there all alone without anybody telling you where to go."

Lynda looked up at the sky and realized that, finally, they had found common ground. "It's a sanctuary," she said quietly. "If my church could blueprint that feeling, they'd pack the pews every Sunday."

He looked around the prop, eyeing her narrowly. "Oh, no. You're not one of those, are you?"

"Those what?"

"Those flower-selling, tract-passing, baloney-flinging religion junkies."

She couldn't decide whether to be offended or not. "Do you mean Christians?"

"Whatever they call themselves," he said, turning back to the plane. "I attract them, you know. They flock to me in airports like I'm wearing a sign that says, 'Try me. I'll believe anything.'"

"I've never sold flowers or passed out tracts or flung baloney, and you certainly don't attract me. At the moment, the only thing I'm trying to sell you is my plane."

Chuckling slightly, he touched the name painted on the side. "I like what you named it. *Solitude.* It fits me. I think I'll keep the name."

"You haven't even decided to buy it yet."

"No, but I'm really interested. It's the best I've found for the money."

"You'd better fly it first. It's a big step down from a 747 to a single engine."

"No kidding."

"You might not like it."

His grin returned. "You're trying to talk me out of it, aren't you?"

"No, of course not."

He stepped up onto the wing, opened the door, and turned back to her. "Come on, get in. Let's see what she can do."

Reluctantly Lynda followed him up and slipped into the seat next to him. She attributed the feeling of dread taking hold of her heart to her despair that she might have to surrender the plane today.

2

"AM I MAKING you nervous?" Jake glanced at her as he pitched the plane downward then pulled back up, like a Thunderbird performing for his fans.

"I always get nervous when my life is in the hands of a psychopath." Gripping the edge of her gray vinyl seat, she closed her eyes as he dove again. "You know, you won't get a good feel for the ride if you keep showboating."

He laughed and brought it back up. "I'd forgotten how much lighter this feels. I love the hands-on quality instead of everything being so automatic. The pilot is in complete control."

"I knew you were one of those control types."

He laughed. "Don't tell me you're not. You wouldn't own a plane like this if you didn't like being in control."

She looked out the window and saw the airport growing smaller below them. "I don't fly for control," she said quietly.

"Then why do you?"

"Because unless I'm in the company of an aspiring stunt pilot who asks a lot of questions, I can think up here. Reflect."

"So how long have you been hiding up here in your Piper?"

She shot him a look. "I've had the plane for two years if that's what you mean. The best two years of my life."

He chuckled. "You almost sound like you're talking about a husband."

"Oh, no. A plane can give a lot more pleasure than grief. Not like a husband at all."

"Those are the words of a bitter woman. You must be divorced."

His presumptions amazed her. "Actually, I've never been married. And I'm not bitter. Just smart." Her eyes trailed back out the window, and she wished he'd hurry and land so they could get this transaction over with.

"Me either," he said. "I try not to strap on anything I can live without."

Lynda laughed out loud, surprising him. "You've got to be kidding. You could live without that Porsche you drove up in or that Rolex on your wrist or that diamond cluster on your finger? Those are not the trappings of a man who likes to keep things simple."

"Hey, I never said I don't like a little self-indulgence now and then. Besides, we were talking about spouses, not possessions."

"We were talking about keeping things simple," she said. "I'm just pointing out your contradictions."

He was getting annoyed, and something about that pleased her. "It's not a contradiction to want a few material things. I'm a firm believer in going after whatever makes you happy."

"Is that what all those things do? Make you happy?"

"Don't I look like a happy guy?"

She smiled, unable to help herself. "But owning a plane would make you happier?"

"You got it, darlin'. It made you happy, didn't it?"

"Yeah," she whispered. "It did most of the time." That melancholy fell over her again, and she tried to steer her mind from imagining what life would be without *Solitude.*

"I'd like to close the deal as soon as possible," Jake said, cutting into her thoughts. "When we land, we can discuss the particulars."

She sighed. "I guess the sooner the better. Are you ready to land now?"

"Sure," he said. "I've seen what I need to see."

Taking the radio mike from its hook, she held it to her mouth. "St. Clair Unicom—Cherokee 1-0-1-2 Delta. We're ready to land, Mike."

Mike's voice crackled in their headphones. "All clear, Lynda. No traffic reported. Runway 4."

She glanced at Jake as he began to fly parallel to the right side of the runway. "I'll land, if you want me to."

"I've got it," he said.

She watched out the window as he boxed around the airport and began his descent, and her heart grew heavier. Absently, her fingertips stroked the soft gray cloth of the seats that were so comfortable to her, and she wondered if she'd ever find another sanctuary that was quite as fulfilling. Jake was getting a real bargain, and she was the big loser. She almost wished she hadn't cleaned the charcoal carpet last week or polished the instrument panel or vacuumed the cloth ceiling. All those things only contributed to the comfort and luxury of the quiet cabin. If it had been dirty or ragged or badly maintained, maybe he wouldn't have wanted it.

Jake reached for the lever to release the landing gear, and a short whirring sound followed as it started lowering. But the sound was too short, and Lynda shot a look at the instruments.

"Is there something wrong with these lights?" Jake asked.

Lynda checked the gear indicator lights. According to them, the landing gear hadn't gone down. She leaned up and grabbed the lever. Nothing happened.

"I heard them go down before," Jake said. "Didn't you hear it?"

"It didn't sound right," Lynda said. "Either they're jammed, or the light's not working. Pull up."

She waited as Jake aborted the landing and climbed again. "I'll check the circuit breaker," she said. "Keep trying the lever."

Jake tried again and failed, as Lynda pressed on the circuit breaker marked "gear."

"It seems okay," she said, maintaining her calm. "Let me pump it down manually."

Gripping the hand pump between the seats, she tried to pump it down by hand, but the light still wouldn't come on.

"Here, let me," he said, trying to move her hand.

"Something's wrong," she said, surrendering it. "The pump moves too easily, and nothing happens."

Jake tried it, his face growing tense. "It has to be a busted hose, or there'd be more resistance."

"No," she argued. "It can't be. It just can't."

But she couldn't think of anything else it could be, and as panic began to rise inside her, she tried it again.

There was nothing Mike Morgan hated worse than a hotdogger playing with a plane as though it were a paper kite. Aggravated, he watched out the window as the plane feigned a landing, then pulled up at the last minute.

It couldn't be Lynda flying, he told himself, sitting in his makeshift control tower that looked more like a concession booth. Lynda had too much respect for her plane. It had to be the arrogant guy who belonged to that red Porsche. Grabbing his microphone, he called up to the plane to put a stop to this.

"Cherokee 1-2 Delta—St. Clair Unicom. What's with the touch-and-go's, Lynda?"

He waited for an answer, and when he didn't get one, he pushed the button again. "Lynda? Do you read me?"

Finally, he heard her voice. "We're having a little problem with our landing gear, Mike. We're not sure whether it's down or not."

"Oh, no," he said to himself then glanced out at the plane circling overhead.

"Mike, we're going to do a flyby. Could you come out and see if the gear's down?"

Mike grabbed his binoculars with his left hand and pressed the button again with his right. "Affirmative, Lynda."

Then dashing through the glass doors, he tried to see just how much trouble they were really in.

Cherokee 1-2 Delta—St. Clair Unicom. You reading me, Lynda?"

"1-2 Delta." Bracing herself, Lynda looked over at Jake, whose temples glistened with perspiration. "How does it look, Mike?"

"Worse than we thought, guys. The landing gear is only partially down, and one looks like it's down further than the other."

Jake swore, and Lynda closed her eyes and tried to let the news sink in.

"We can't even do a smooth belly landing if it's *partially* down!" Jake said. "And if it's not locked all the way down, it could squirrel all over the place."

"Even if it's locked where it is, we'll land lopsided," she said. "We'll lose a wing and cart-wheel."

Jake grabbed the microphone out of her hand. "Mike, could you see any oil?"

"I was just getting to that," Mike said. "It looks like there could be oil streaming down the belly behind the gear. Did you try to pump it manually?"

Lynda and Jake exchanged worried looks, and Lynda took the mike back. "We tried, Mike. It has to be a loose hose."

Jake snatched the microphone again. "Mike, we're gonna have to take our chances and land with what we've got."

"No!" Lynda shouted. "We could crash! My plane would be destroyed."

"Not to mention its passengers!" he shouted back at her. "But there isn't enough fuel for us to stay up here long enough for a miracle, so unless you've got any better ideas. . . ."

Viciously, Lynda tried the hand pump again and then the automatic lever, as if the plane might have healed itself in the last few minutes.

Finally giving up, she took the mike back. "It won't go up *or* down, Mike. He's right. We don't have any choice."

"I'm so glad you agree," Jake said caustically.

Lynda ignored him.

"I don't see any alternative either, Lynda," Mike admitted. "This could be bad. The wind isn't gonna help any. This crosswind could be a nightmare."

"Yeah," she said, "and if the gear isn't down all the way, then our brakes aren't working, either. And the fire hazard. . . ."

Jake jerked the mike back. "If we had a choice, Mike, we'd sure find another way. But we don't. Are you ready for us or not?"

"No, not yet," Mike said. "It'll take some preparation. Just stand by, and I'll get back to you."

Silence followed, and Jake set the microphone back on its hook and continued circling the airport.

For a moment, neither of them spoke.

It was the closest Lynda had ever been to death, yet she didn't feel the peace she had always thought she'd feel. She wasn't ready to die—not mentally, emotionally, or spiritually. Wasn't there supposed to be a warning so good-byes could be said, apologies made, and affairs put in order? She just wasn't supposed to take off into the sky on a morning test flight and then never come back down.

"I hope somebody moves my Porsche," Jake said, eyeing the small airport below them.

Again, Lynda was amazed. "We're about to crash, and all you care about is your car?"

His expression betrayed his growing anger. "You're the one who cared more about your plane surviving than the people in it."

"Hey, *I'm* in it. I'm not crazy about the prospect of death either!"

Wiping his forehead with the back of his sleeve, he said, "Look, we don't have time for this. We have to get ready, whether we like it or not. I'll land the plane. I have more experience with emergencies."

"You don't have experience with *this plane,* Lindbergh. The weight's different, and you don't have a feel for it. You might bring it down too hard, and with this crosswind—"

"How many real emergency landings have you ever made?" he cut in.

"None. But I know—"

"I've had two," he said. "*I'm* landing the plane."

"This is no time for ego!"

"You're right. It's not."

Livid, they stared at each other, neither wanting to back down. Suddenly, the cabin seemed too small for both of them, and she wished she could put more space between them. If she could just breathe. . . .

On the verge of tears, she said, "All right, maybe you *are* more experienced. You land it, and I'll cut off the engine and the fuel. We'll need to shut everything off before we touch down. This is gonna take both of us."

Cursing, Jake tried the pump again, his hands trembling. When it was obvious how hopeless it was, he sent another expletive flying and slammed his hand into the instrument panel. "Piece of trash! Don't you ever check your landing gear?"

"Of course I do," she said. "I've never had any problem with it at all! I just had an annual three months ago, and everything was fine."

"A pilot should know every inch of his plane!"

"I didn't notice *you* sticking your head up the wheel well on the preflight!"

"It's *your* plane." He wiped his forehead again. "Are you sure you weren't just trying to unload it on some poor soul before you had to foot some major repair bills?"

Her mouth fell open. "I didn't even want to sell it! If my father hadn't died and left me a mountain of debts, you wouldn't even be here!"

"Lucky me."

Again, thick silence filled the cabin, and she told herself she wouldn't cry. She couldn't do what had to be done if her eyes were blurry with tears. "Look, we have to try to get this plane down without either of us getting killed. Now, if we could just—"

"Cherokee 1-2 Delta," the radio cut in. "St. Clair Unicom."

Lynda took the microphone. "1-2 Delta. Go ahead, Mike."

"We're trying to clear the runway, but we need a little time to clear the tarmac, too, so no other planes are damaged. Just hang on for a few minutes. You have plenty of fuel, don't you?"

"Enough to blow us to kingdom come," Jake muttered.

She sighed and checked the gauge. "About forty minutes' worth."

"Well," Mike said, "it won't hurt to burn some of that off to cut down on the fire hazard. While we're waiting, is there anyone either of you would like for us to contact? Jake?"

Jake hesitated for a moment, racking his brain for someone who would care. The little blonde on the steps came to mind, but he only remembered her room number, not her name. He thought of his boss, but in case things came out all right, he was afraid of the conclusions the airline might draw about the crash landing.

Dismally, he realized that there really wasn't anyone.

"Jake?" Mike prompted. "Do you read me?"

Jake took the mike. "Nobody, okay? I don't want you to contact anybody."

He couldn't escape the long look Lynda gave him.

"Lynda?"

Jake handed the mike to her and saw the emotion pulling at her face. "Yes," she said quietly. "Contact Sally Crawford at 555-2312. Tell her to cancel all my appointments for this afternoon. But you don't have to do it now, Mike. Wait until . . . afterward, so she won't have to sweat this out."

Jake gaped at her. "Cancel your *appointments?*"

Her face turned rock hard, and she didn't answer him.

"Don't you have a mother or a lover or somebody?" he asked.

"No."

"So the closest person to you is your secretary? That's pretty pathetic."

Her face reddened. "Who do you think *you* are? At least I had somebody to call. What about *your* mother or a close friend or even an enemy or two? Surely you must have a couple of women somewhere who'd be interested in knowing you're about to buy the farm!"

His jaw popped. "Both of my parents are dead. And I'd rather admit there was no one than to hide behind some secretary and all those important appointments."

"If I wanted someone, I could have someone. There are plenty—" Her voice cracked, and she cut herself off, unable to go on. Tears came to her eyes, making her angrier, and she struggled to hold them back.

"But right now there's no one who cares that you're probably about to die. You're just as alone as I am."

"There are worse things than dying alone!" Lynda threw back at him.

"Are there?" His voice softened by degrees, and as he looked out the window at the activity on the tarmac below them, he said, "Right now it seems to me that the worst thing in the world is. . . ."

"What?" she asked. "What is the worst thing in the world?"

"Dying with a total stranger."

The reality of that concept knocked the breath from her, and she fought the conflicting feelings assaulting her. As her first tears fell, they were both quiet, embroiled in battle with their own raging thoughts.

Her tears softened him, and finally, he let out a long, weary breath. "You're right, you know. There're at least three women who would like to see me burn."

"They probably have good reason," she whispered.

"Yeah, probably. I guess if you condemn a man for not wanting to tie himself to one woman for life, I deserve what I get."

"Life isn't really that long, though, is it?"

"Not lately," he said.

He looked out the window, searching the area around the airport. "If we could just find a pasture or something to land in. If we landed in the dirt, it would cut down on the fire hazard."

"The joys of flying in this part of Florida. Nothing but pavement and swamp. And the swamp has too many trees for a water landing."

"It might not be so bad if the gas tank weren't so low. I think I could get us down on the belly, maybe without cartwheeling, but the sparks could start a fire."

"Maybe they won't," she whispered with her last vestige of hope.

"Maybe not," Jake whispered. "I've still got a lot of living to do."

3

ON THE GROUND, Mike looked at the plane through his binoculars again, wishing for a miracle. But the landing gear was still unevenly dropped and only partially down. Dropping the binoculars around his neck, he waved an arm, directing the planes that were moving, one by one, from their parked positions on the tarmac. The red Porsche sat right in the way, and for a moment, he thought of driving it out to the middle of Runway 4 so that Jake would have to run over it himself. It would be poetic justice.

Then he quelled the thought and checked to see whether the keys were in the ignition. Waving to one of the men nearby, he said, “Get this car out of the way, will you?”

Sirens drew closer, and he ran to the end of the building and parted the growing crowd of spectators to direct the fire trucks onto the tarmac. Three of them whizzed past him, lights flashing. Then there were the ambulances—one, two, three, four—and he realized with a sinking stomach that they were preparing for additional casualties on the ground.

He started back to the planes taxiing out of the way and saw a van pull in behind him. It was a media van with the call letters *WTTV* on the side. The van slowed beside him, and a reporter he recognized from the six o’clock news jumped out. “We heard on the police radio that there’s a plane about to crash.” He pointed up to the plane circling overhead. “Is that it?”

“Stay back,” Mike ordered as he kept walking. “Don’t get any closer to the runway and move the van.”

“Man, I need it right here.”

“I’m telling you, when that plane hits the ground, it’s liable to blow from here to Montana. Don’t say I didn’t warn you!”

“Have you been in contact with the pilots?” the reporter asked.

But Mike didn’t answer. He had too much work to do.

The trees beyond the airport were greener than Lynda thought they should be in September, probably because they’d had so much rain this summer. She wondered now why she hadn’t noticed that stark, clear color before. Only now was she even aware that those trees existed. Of course, this landing was different. This time the plane might not stop until it reached them.

Between two lines of those trees, one on either side of the street leading to the small airport, she saw a convoy of vehicles that looked as small as toy cars heading to the gates. A shiver went through her. “Are those fire trucks?”

“And ambulances. Just waiting for us to hit bottom.”

“Don’t be so cynical. They’re there to help us.”

“There may not be anything left to help.” He tore his eyes away from the small square airport and checked the gauges. Lynda followed his eyes and noted that they’d used up half of their fuel already.

“If you’ve already given up, maybe I should land the plane after all.”

“No. If there’s a chance of getting us out of this alive, I’m the one who can do it.”

Disgusted, she gaped at him. “Has it ever occurred to you that you’re not the final authority in all this?”

“No? Then who is?”

“Oh, that’s right,” she said. “You don’t believe in God. You’ve got the world all figured out.”

“I’m not into myths,” he said. “I like facts. And what is there to figure out, really? You’re born, you live, you die. End of story.”

“It’s *not* the end of the story,” she said. “There’s an afterlife.”

He laughed then and shook his head. “Wouldn’t that be convenient?”

She bristled. “Convenient?”

“Yeah. Tell yourself a little lie just before you crash, and maybe you’ll feel better about giving it all up.”

She opened her mouth to argue but changed her mind and wearily leaned back. “Believe what you want. You’re not worth trying to convince.”

The steady, muffled hum of the engine became the only sound in the cabin again, and their eyes strayed to the concrete square below them where mechanics, pilots, and staff ran up and down the tarmac. Half of the planes had been moved already, and the other half taxied out in a single stream of traffic, like toy planes strung together and dragged by a toddler. It looked orderly and peaceful from here, not at all like a rushed attempt to prepare for a tragedy.

The air seemed thinner now than she remembered it being before, and she longed to roll a window down as she would in a car. But even if that had been a reasonable thing to do at 10,000 feet, moving 100 miles per hour, the windows weren't built to budge. The vessel that had once been her refuge was now just a cage.

Jake seemed to be struggling with his own thoughts. Swallowing, he wiped his brow and glanced at her. "So how long since your father died?"

Wondering where that question had come from, Lynda reluctantly answered, "Three months."

"I'm sorry," he said quietly.

It was true that losing her father had been tough, but she couldn't say it was the death itself that had grieved her. Instead, it was the "what-might-have-been's" that had assaulted her when she'd buried him. The relationship they could have had. The one she had been too busy to maintain.

"You don't want to talk about it," he said quietly. "No problem. I'm just trying to get our minds off this."

She shook her head. "It's all right. I just can't think right now. It's so quiet up here—so *normal.* The engine's running like a charm; everything's intact. It's hard to believe that this landing is gonna do us in. But look at them down there. *They* know it. That's why they're hurrying around, getting ready for the worst case."

"Yeah," he said, "and none of them knows the first thing about us."

She turned back to him, and saw the first trace of vulnerability she'd seen. "Would it make any difference if they did?"

"There might be some comfort in knowing there was somebody down there who had a stake in whether we made it through this."

"It wouldn't help us land any smoother," she whispered.

"I don't know," he said. "It might."

Why his words frightened her, she wasn't sure. "Are you saying you'd take more care in the landing if you knew someone cared about you? That just because neither of us has close attachments, it doesn't *matter* if we crash?"

"No! I don't have a death wish."

"Well, that's the second time you've said something pretty negative about our landing. I'm starting to get really scared that you might just give up and let us die. Is that what you're saying?"

"Of course not! I don't *know* what I'm saying, okay? I just wish. . . ." His voice trailed off, and he found it difficult to center his thoughts. "I mean, doesn't this make you feel . . . something? Incomplete? Regret?"

A still, small voice reminded her what she knew—or what she had once known—about completion, about regret. The memories were vague from lack of use, and she couldn't share them with him for fear that he would mock her and throw the words back in her face.

"You *must* feel that way," he said. "I mean here you are in a busted plane called *Solitude,* telling your secretary to cancel your appointments. Not the makings of a full life."

The voice in her heart died, and she let her old, human voice speak instead. "You have a lot of room to talk."

"I know. Maybe I'm thinking that if I can figure you out, I can figure me out."

"Hey, there's nothing wrong with me. I'm a loner, okay? I have everything I need."

"Do you?" he asked.

"Yes. No surprises, no letdowns. No one to disappoint me."

"So you've eliminated the lows. But that also means there are no highs."

Those words might have been her own. But the ego part of her, the part that held pride to her breast like a shield, dismissed them. "That's why I fly."

"A woman who spends all her free time alone in an airplane strikes me as someone who's hiding from something."

"Oh, brother," she groaned. "You've got a lot of nerve, you know that? Driving up in your yup-mobile with your diamonds flashing and your arrogance dripping off you like cheap cologne—How dare you make any judgments about me?"

"I'm not. I'm making an observation."

Furious, she jerked the microphone off its hook. "Come in, Mike. This is Cherokee 1-2 Delta. I'm ready to land right now! Do you read me?"

Jake grabbed her arm. "What do you think you're doing?"

But Mike's answer came quickly. "Negative, Lynda. We're not ready."

"How long are you going to keep us up here?"

"Until we've taken every precaution! Do not land until I give you the go-ahead! Do you read me?"

Lynda wiped away another tear. "Loud and clear."

Slamming the radio down, she covered her face and told herself to calm down. She was letting this man dig at her in the painful, bruised places she'd been shielding for so long, and suddenly she wished she could just be alone to face her life—and her death.

"Look, I'm sorry," Jake said quietly. "I didn't mean to send you off the deep end."

"Just shut up, will you? You're not making this any easier. If you're so interested in figuring someone out, maybe you should do a little *self*-analysis. Why are *you* all alone in the world?"

He hesitated only a moment, and his voice was flat when he answered. "Simple. Because I'm a selfish pig."

"Now, there's an unexpected revelation. I guess fear of death brings out the truth."

"Too much maybe," he said sullenly. "Too late."

She let those words sink in and wondered if *she'd* gotten to the point of honesty yet. Had she missed the chances she'd had to face the truth? Would she get another chance?

That small voice prompted her again to tell him it wasn't too late, but the voice was growing more distant and easier to ignore.

"We're going to make it, you know," Jake said. "Together, we can do this. We're both experienced pilots, and neither of us wants to die."

She tried to imagine the plane landing carefully, easily, and without incident, but the possibility seemed too remote. "But neither of us has tried to land metal to pavement with no brakes in a crosswind."

"Talk about looking at the bright side," he muttered. He glanced at her. "You're shaking."

"So are you," she pointed out.

"I'm scared."

Lynda wasn't sure why those two matter-of-fact words, uttered by such a tough, hard man would shake her so, but she wilted and surrendered to her tears. "I'm scared, too," she whispered.

He reached over and took her hand, and something about that touch comforted her. Their eyes met, a moment of connection, where she thought she knew him, and he thought he knew her, a moment when they ceased to be strangers.

"Cherokee 1-2 Delta—St. Clair Unicom. Come in, Lynda."

Jake let go of her hand, and she grabbed the mike, bracing herself. "1-2 Delta. Go ahead, Mike. Are you ready for us?"

"Affirmative. You can land now, guys," Mike said softly. "Just watch that crosswind, and be careful. I wish I could offer you something in the way of advice, but you know what to do. I'll be praying for you guys down here."

Lynda swallowed and wiped her eyes. "Yeah. Thank you, Mike."

She put the radio back on its hook and looked at Jake, who was staring dully out the window. His face was empty, drained, and for a moment she thought he might cry too. She wished he would so that she could fully surrender to her own emotions and wilt outwardly the way she was wilting inside.

Finally, he looked at her, reached across to touch her face, and whispered, "Are you ready?"

"Yeah," she said. "You?"

"As ready as I'll ever be, I guess." He checked the gauges, then said, "Once we're on short final and know we've got the runway made, kill the engine and cut all the switches. And if you can, unlatch the door so we can get out fast."

In a gesture that surprised her, he leaned over and tested her seat belt then checked his own. "All right," he said. "Here goes."

The plane descended smoothly like any other craft coming in on any other day, but Mike knew that the moment it touched down the problems would begin. He eyed the rolling cameras and the reporter with his microphone in hand, waiting to get every gory frame.

The ambulances were in place, ready to speed to the scene, and the fire trucks were standing by. Mike felt a wave of dizziness and shook it away, telling himself this was no time for panic. There was too much that had to be done.

He brought the binoculars to his eyes as the plane narrowed the distance between the sky and the runway, and under his breath, he prayed for a miracle.

The plane touched down, sending a spray of sparks as it scraped down the runway—too fast, like a speedboat on an open sea. When it fishtailed, Mike dropped the binoculars.

For several seconds that stretched into eternity, the plane cartwheeled across the runway, rolling and sliding, breaking a wing here, losing the tail there, leaving pieces in its wake, until it finally rolled to a deadly halt on its side.

The ambulances and fire trucks launched across the runways. Stricken with dread and terror, Mike ran toward what was left of the plane.

4

ACROSS TOWN IN the law offices of Schilling, Martin and Barrett, Sally Crawford rushed to type the three motions that Lynda needed ready for court the next morning. As much as she managed to accomplish each day, it was clear to her that Lynda needed a second secretary. Sometimes things moved so fast that she had to run just to stay in place.

But it was tough convincing a workaholic that you were working too hard. As long as Sally's fingers flew across that keyboard, and the phone calls were answered, and the motions were filed, and the appointments were made, and the office ran smoothly, Lynda was happy.

She shouldn't complain, Sally admitted as she punched in the command to *print* then swiveled in her chair and began stacking the papers that had to be ready before the mail boy came around to empty the "out" baskets.

The phone buzzed; she picked it up. "Lynda Barrett's office."

"Sally, there's a Paige Varner here to see Lynda."

"Lynda's not in," Sally told the receptionist who intercepted visitors as they came in. "Take a message, and I'll have Lynda call her." Hanging up, she saw that the printer was finished, and she pulled out the pages.

The phone buzzed again. "Lynda Barrett's office."

"Sally, she says she's left messages, and Lynda hasn't called. She's pretty upset—"

Sally moaned. "All right. Send her back. I'll talk to her."

She hung up and sat for a moment, staring at the phone, wondering what excuse she'd use to cover for Lynda this time. The plain, simple truth was that Paige Varner's was a *pro bono* case, and it wasn't exactly one of Lynda's top priorities.

She saw the elevator doors open, and Paige bolted off, clutching her three-year-old daughter, Brianna, on her hip. Paige's eyes were swollen and red as she cast Sally a frantic look and started toward her.

Sally got up to meet her. "Hello, Paige. Lynda's not here."

"I've *got* to talk to her," Paige said, starting to cry. "We've got to *do* something. He tried to kidnap Brianna!"

"Who?" Sally asked, leading her to a chair and making her sit down. Brianna's feet hit the floor, but Paige pulled her into her lap, unable to let her go.

"Her father," she said. "Do we have a court date yet? If we do, I can make plans to leave the state, so he won't know where we are—"

"Calm down," Sally said, stooping in front of her. "Now start over. Take a deep breath and tell me what happened."

Paige didn't want to take time to start over, but she tried. "Her day-care teacher called me at work and told me that Keith was there claiming that I told him to pick her up."

"Wait a minute. Don't you have a restraining order?"

"Yes!" Paige cried. "But it's *worthless!* We're not safe here! I have to talk to Lynda. If she can get us a court date, then I can get that over with and get out of town, before he takes her, or comes after me again, or—"

The phone rang, and Sally stood up reluctantly. "I'm sorry, Paige. I have to get that."

Paige covered her eyes and nodded.

Sally went back to her desk and grabbed the phone, praying it was Lynda. "Lynda Barrett's office."

"Is this Sally Crawford?"

Sally glanced at Paige. Brianna was wiping her mother's tears, and Paige was whispering to her. "Yes."

"This is Mac Lowery. I'm a mechanic at the St. Clair Airport. I'm afraid there's been an accident."

5

FOR A MOMENT, as the fog slowly cleared, Lynda lay still, trying to find some clarity to hang her thoughts on. The plane had hit belly to pavement, she remembered, and had slid for what had seemed like miles, breaking into fragments, crumpling, shattering, rolling—

Now the plane was on its side, and she hung sideways in her seat, still clamped by the seat belt that cut mercilessly into her shoulder and hipbones. Trying to get her head upright, wincing at the stab of pain in her ribs and the cracking pain in her head, she released the latch and slid from her seat against the back of the one next to her.

Pain seared through her, and she looked down to find the source of it. Shards of glass had lodged in her arm, her thigh, and her stomach. With bloody hands that seemed to belong to someone else, she tried to pull one out.

But then she saw him.

All clarity returned as she reached for Jake, still strapped into the bottom of his seat, which had broken off from its back. Twisted, unconscious, and soaked with blood, he lay limp under the bashed instrument panel.

"Jake!" Her voice sounded hollow and distant, as if it came from someone else as she tried to reach for him. "Jake, are you all right?"

But he didn't stir.

Panic shook her as the first hint of smoke reached her senses—then, with dim relief, she heard sirens. But they sounded too far away, and there was no time to wait!

Forcing herself to move despite her pain, she managed to free Jake from his seat belt then grabbed under his arms and, with all her might, slid him two feet back toward the door. Praying that it would open, she disengaged the latch. The door swung down, providing a hatch no more than a yard above the ground.

The smoke was growing thicker as the sirens came closer. Lynda half-fell out the opening. Then with every ounce of energy she could gather, pulled Jake behind her, ignoring her own fuzzy thoughts about his limpness and the blood soaking into her clothes.

The moment he dropped onto the pavement, she struggled to her feet beside the plane, grabbed his arms, and dragged him across the dirt as far away from the plane as she could before collapsing beside him.

She heard tires screeching and people yelling; suddenly she was aware of movement around her. Closing her eyes, she surrendered to the paramedics as they lifted her onto a gurney then ran with her like war medics taking her out of the line of fire. A vague protest formed in her mind that they should leave her and save Jake, but that thought evaporated as a loud, vacuum sound—*whoosh*—split the air.

She opened her eyes—her plane was engulfed in quiet flames that spread to cover the place where she and Jake had lain only moments before. *It should be loud,* she thought, *like a lightning bolt from God.* Instead, this explosion had been a quiet one, almost gentle, as it worked its violence on the plane.

As the paramedics hurried her along, she glimpsed another group of medics carrying Jake. He was still limp on the gurney, and blood glistened on that expensive shirt and those slacks that had been so perfectly creased such a short time ago. The paramedics set her down and, blocking her view, bent over her with stethoscopes and an IV. "No!" she cried, trying to move them out of her way. "Help him! He's bleeding!"

"So are you."

"No, take him first! Please!"

"He's in good hands," the lead paramedic said in a steady voice, trying to calm her. "*You're* my concern right now." He took her vitals, barking out numbers that meant little to her. Still, she strained to see around him. "Is he—is he—alive?"

They were busy attaching the IV, talking to each other over her, shouting and exchanging orders.

And then she saw the urgency on the faces of the other group of paramedics, and someone shouted, "Talk to him! He's going into shock!"

"Jake, can you hear me?" someone asked him. "Jake, you've got to hold on. We're getting you to the hospital."

"We're losing him!" one of the others shouted.

"Oh, no, God, please!" She lost sight of him as the EMTs crowded around him, desperately trying to bring him back. She saw someone bring the defibrillator, and heard the desperate counting and the "Clear!" then the shock that jolted his body.

She lost sight of him again as her paramedics loaded her into the ambulance, and she tried to sit up to see through the doors before they closed them. "Please! I've got to know if he's—"

But the doors shut, and the ambulance accelerated away.

Lynda didn't remember when she had lost consciousness, but when she woke, she was in a hospital room, the cold antiseptic smell stirring her back to life.

A woman she didn't know stood over her, shining a light in her eyes. "How are you feeling?"

Lynda squinted against the light and jerked her face away. "Am I in the hospital?"

"That's right," the woman said. "You just got out of surgery."

"Surgery?"

The woman nodded. "And judging by what you've been through, I'd say you're extremely lucky. You're scratched and cut up pretty good, and you broke a couple of ribs, but you're going to be fine." The woman patted her shoulder gently then said, "I'll go tell the doctor you're awake."

Lynda squeezed her eyes shut and tried to find some clarity. Images rushed through her mind: the plane hitting the ground; the horror of impact after impact; the sight of Jake strapped in his seat . . . Jake drenched in blood . . . Jake not responding. . . . He was dead. It was her punishment, she told herself—although she wasn't sure at the moment what she was being punished for. A thick, smothering shroud of guilt draped itself over her.

Tears oozed from her eyes. She squeezed them shut and, under her breath, tried to bargain with God for Jake's life.

The door swung open. Two doctors came in, followed by the nurse, who rushed to Lynda's side when she saw her tears. "Lynda, you're going to be all right," one of the doctors said gently. "You had some internal bleeding, and we had to remove your spleen. I know it's been traumatic for you—but try to understand this: You're going to be okay. Please try to calm down."

Hiccuping her sobs, she reached up and grabbed the doctor's coat with her good hand. "Is he . . . dead?"

"Is who dead?"

"Jake!" she shouted.

"Doctor, the other crash victim," the nurse said. "He was brought in with her."

The second doctor took her hand, and she gripped it with all the urgency she felt as he leaned over her. "I just left him, Lynda," he said. "He's still in surgery. His condition is critical, but—"

"He's alive?" she asked, almost sitting up. "Jake's alive?"

"We almost lost him," he said. "But we think he's going to pull through."

"Oh, thank God," she cried, wilting back down.

The doctor checked the monitors attached to her then whispered a few instructions to the nurse as Lynda tried to catch her breath. When she was able, she grabbed the doctor's coat again. "I want to see him. The minute he's out of surgery I need to see him."

"That won't be possible today," he said gently. "And even tomorrow, if he regains consciousness, he'll be in ICU. That means no visitors."

"Please," she said. "You can bend a few rules, can't you? Let me see him for five minutes. That's all."

The two doctors exchanged looks, and finally, one shrugged. "We'll see what we can do. No promises. But right now there are several people out in the waiting room anxious to see you. Are you up to any visitors?"

She covered her face with a hand and tried to stop her tears. "Uh, who's out there?"

The nurse pulled a pad from her pocket, flipped a few pages, and said, "Mike somebody. And Sally—she said she's your secretary. And your pastor and a few people who said you used to go to their church. . . ."

"Um, I'd like to talk to Mike first," she whispered.

"All right," the nurse said, "but just for a few minutes, okay? You don't realize how weak you are, but you will as soon as you start seeing people."

Lynda already felt too weak to talk, but there were things she needed to say to Mike. Things that couldn't wait.

6

THE POLICE STATION smelled like stale cigarettes and three-day-old sweat, and the noise level was worse than the day-care center where Brianna spent each day. Paige bent and picked up the child, holding her close and felt that familiar surge of shame that she hadn't been able to shelter her from the ugly realities of life.

"It's okay, Brianna," she whispered, kissing the child's forehead. "We're going to get one of these policemen to help us."

"Are they putting Daddy in jail, Mommy?"

Paige hesitated. "I don't know, honey. We'll see. Do you want them to?"

"Yes," she whispered with timid honesty.

Paige made her way to the big desk where people waited in line to file complaints, trying to blink back the tears that threatened her eyes again.

A plane crash. It couldn't be real, yet it was. Lynda had been in a plane crash.

She closed her eyes and tried to fight off the abject terror that her lawyer could die—or might, in fact, already be dead. Sally had said that Lynda was still alive, but she'd been in such a panic that Paige wasn't sure it was true.

The person at the front of the line left the desk, and Paige counted the people in front of her. She was fourth in line. Any minute now it would be her turn, and someone would tell her what to do.

Brianna laid her head on Paige's shoulder, and Paige realized that the child hadn't had her nap today. She was tired. She should be home, safe in her own room, resting to a Barney tape, instead of waiting in a police station to find a way to keep her father from getting close to her.

Lynda had known ways and had made lots of promises, but Paige couldn't depend on her now. Those tears surfaced again, and she told herself that she should stop thinking so much of herself. Lynda's plane crash was a tragedy, but Paige could only deal with one tragedy at a time.

At last her turn came, and she tried to steady her voice as she faced the uniformed woman behind the desk. "My name's Paige Varner. I have a restraining order against my ex-husband, Keith Varner, but today he tried to take our daughter from her day care. I went to my lawyer first, but she was in an accident today. . . ." Her voice trailed off, and she waited for a response.

The officer casually dropped her pencil and leaned forward, elbows on her desk. "Mrs. Varner, we can't arrest someone for violating a restraining order unless we witness the violation."

"What do you mean, witness it? Who has to witness it?"

"You're supposed to call the police when it happens, and when they arrive, they have to see him there. If he leaves, it's out of our hands."

Paige gripped Brianna tighter, incredulous. "But that's ridiculous! I wasn't there! The restraining order is supposed to keep him away from her, too."

"You should have had the teachers call 911. Next time, you need to call us as soon as he shows up, and if the officers get there while he's still there—"

"Next time?" Paige shouted. "There's not supposed to *be* a next time. You people are supposed to protect me from that!"

"We can only do what the law allows."

"Then what's the use in having a restraining order? He can still do anything he wants!"

"You do have recourse," the woman said, as if talking to a child. "You need to file a motion for order to show cause."

"A what?"

The woman sighed. "Mrs. Varner, did you say you have a lawyer?"

"Yes, but—" She stopped, pinched the bridge of her nose, and tried to temper her voice again. "I can't reach her right now. And no one else will represent me because I—I don't have much money. Do I have to have a lawyer to do this?"

"It would help. Then a judge would review it and decide whether to arrest him or summon him back to court. But usually, if there was no violence involved, and if he didn't threaten you in any way, the judge doesn't opt for jail time."

"Threaten?" Paige asked. "You don't think it's threatening for him to show up at her school and tell her teacher that I told him to pick her up? Do we have to wait until he attacks one of us again or until he kidnaps her and takes her so far—"

"I'm just telling you your options, Ma'am. Now, if I were you, I'd contact my lawyer right away."

"But if there's no guarantee he'll even be put in jail. . . ." Frustrated, she half turned away. "You don't know my husband. He'll just get madder and then come after me. And he's smart. He probably already knows that he can't be arrested unless he's caught. That's why he's getting so bold."

The woman behind the desk softened a little. "Look, I can give you the name of a shelter for battered women. We could get you in there tonight if you want."

Paige thought about that for a moment. Her mind was too muddled, and she couldn't think.

"Mommy, I want to go home," Brianna said.

"Just a minute, honey." Wiping her face, she tried to take a deep breath. "He knows where the shelter is. He told me that if I ever went there, he'd drag me out."

"But he *can't* know, Mrs. Varner. It's a very well-kept secret. He was probably just trying to scare you."

"You don't know him. He has ways of finding things out."

"Mrs. Varner, every woman in that shelter has an angry man looking for her. You just have to trust the staff to know how to handle these things."

"I can't trust anyone," Paige said dismally.

"Well, here's the number anyway if you change your mind." The officer handed Paige a piece of paper. "Good luck, Mrs. Varner."

But as Paige carried Brianna back to their car, she realized she was going to need a lot more than luck. What she really needed now was Lynda.

I have to tell you," Mike said as he approached Lynda's bed, "for a few minutes there I didn't think I was ever going to see that smile again." He pulled a chair up to her bed and sat down. "So how do you feel?"

"Like I've been spared," she whispered.

He leaned his elbows on his knees and rested his chin on his hand. "It *was* a miracle, you know. When I saw that plane hit the ground, I didn't see any way in the world either one of you would make it. Who could have believed you both would?"

"Jake's not even out of surgery yet, much less out of the woods."

"Yeah, but he has a lot of people praying for him out there."

"Really?" she asked, sitting partially up. "Who?"

"Some of the people here from your church."

"My church." Wearily, she wilted back down. "I'm surprised they remember me; it's been so long since I darkened the doorstep."

She looked at the man she had known for the last two years, the man with whom she had talked airplanes and flight reports and weather, the man who was as close a friend as she had. Only now did she realize how little they really knew about each other.

"Mike, I want to thank you."

"For what?"

"For offering to pray for us today," she whispered.

Tears came to his eyes, and he struggled to blink them back. "What else was I gonna do, Lynda?"

"Oh, I don't know. Stay busy. Throw up your hands. All I know is that I wasn't doing much praying up there. Yours are the ones that got answered."

As long as he was still breathing, Jake figured he was alive, even if he couldn't manage to open his eyes or move an inch or speak.

There was something in his mouth impeding his speech and something else holding his eyelids down.

Panic struck him, and he wanted to sit up, cry out, run away, but his body wouldn't cooperate.

He could hear quiet voices around him, a steady beeping of machinery, and he felt hands probing. . . .

The crash, he thought. He had survived the crash.

Or had he?

Panic seized him, and he opened his mouth to cry out, but something in his throat choked him. Concentrating all his effort on the task of clearing his mouth, he lifted his hand—but he moved it only an inch or two before he felt something sting and someone laying it back down.

"Calm down, Jake," a soft voice said. "You're going to be okay. Just rest."

He struggled to open his eyes but failed. Once more he tried to cry out, but the voice was back again. "Don't try to talk, Jake. There's a tube in your throat. Tomorrow you can talk if you want."

But Jake's panic needed answers, and it needed answers now. He tried to formulate a question to ask but found that his mind was too fuzzy. Then the voices seemed to fade farther away, as numbness crept like mercy through his limbs.

And soon he forgot about those questions and surrendered instead to the darkness.

7

THE RAIN BEGAN as Paige drove home from the police station, her brain reeling from the injustice of the system that left her entirely on her own. But it wasn't the first time she hadn't known where to turn.

She turned on her windshield wipers and tried to concentrate on the slippery road. The last thing she needed now was an accident. Lynda's was bad enough.

Then again, maybe a four-car crash on the highway was just what she should expect. Maybe she deserved all she'd been going through. Maybe, as Keith had said so many times, Paige was petty and selfish and stupid. Maybe she had brought all this misery on herself.

Lightning flashed, followed by a quick clap of thunder, and she touched Brianna's knee to reassure her. What did it really matter what Paige deserved, she argued. It was what Brianna deserved that mattered. Brianna deserved peace and she deserved safety and she deserved security and stability. She didn't deserve a father who could sing her a lullaby one minute and crack her mother's jaw the next.

The child was just drifting off to sleep as Paige turned onto their street and glanced ahead to her house halfway up the road. It would be good finally to get home, make Brianna a bowl of soup, and put her to bed for her nap.

Then she saw it: Keith's car in the driveway.

Slamming her foot on the accelerator, she flew past the house, skidded around the corner, and headed as far away from the neighborhood as she could.

Her breath came in gasps as she watched her rearview mirror for a sign of him. Terror clutched at her heart. Where could she go to be safe? Not home—he was there, sitting in her house, waiting for her.

Trembling, she pulled into a Walmart parking lot and groped for her purse. Grabbing out two quarters, she circled to a pay phone on the edge of the lot. Afraid to get out of the car, she inched as close as she could to the phone then rolled her window down. The rain poured in, soaking her arm as she reached for the receiver. Quickly she dialed 911.

"You've got to help me!" she cried when the dispatcher answered. "I have a restraining order against my ex-husband, but he's in my house waiting for me right now. You have to send an officer out immediately. They have to see him there!"

She rattled off the address, then restated the urgency. When she'd hung up, she tried to catch her breath.

She'd go back, she told herself. She'd go back to make sure they got him. If he was still there, maybe she'd go in and try to reason with him. Maybe that would hold him there until they came.

But what if it didn't? What if he took Brianna?

No. She couldn't risk it. Instead, she would drive by the house to make sure he was still there. Then she would watch from the corner, and when the police came, she could follow them into the driveway.

The rain pounded harder against the roof of the car, and the wind whipped more viciously, but Brianna stayed asleep as Paige, weeping softly, made her way back to the neighborhood and turned up her street. Holding her breath, she peered through the rain-blurred windshield to see if his car was still in her driveway.

He was gone.

Slamming the heel of her hand against her steering wheel, she cried harder. This was *hopeless!* He was out there somewhere, looking for her. . . .

And the women's shelter would be the first place he'd look if she didn't come home. He'd told her more than once that he knew where all of them were, and if she ever went there, he'd go after her and make her sorry.

Leaving the street as fast as she could, she went back to the Walmart parking lot and dug through her wallet for money. She had thirty dollars and an ATM card. There might be fifty more in her account if her checkbook balance were right. That was enough for a hotel room, she told herself, trying to calm down. It would get her through until tomorrow.

She took a few deep breaths, trying to calm down, scanned the roads nearby to make sure he was nowhere in sight, and then pulled back into the street. *Don't even think about tomorrow right now,* she cautioned herself. *All you can deal with is one day at a time.*

8

THE CREAK OF her hospital room door woke Lynda from her shallow sleep. Squinting her eyes open, she watched the plump nurse come in, her nylons making a brushing sound as she walked and her white Reeboks squeaking on the floor. It was the same nurse who had attended to her the last time she'd awakened—Jill something—and Lynda watched her set down her tray of medications and flick on the dim light over Lynda's head.

"How are you feeling?" the nurse asked in a voice loud enough to wake the comatose patients on the floor above her. "Any pain?"

"Some," Lynda mumbled.

"Well, that's expected." Pulling a thermometer out of her pocket, she covered it with plastic and shoved it into Lynda's mouth. "If I had as many stitches in me as you have, I'd be hurting, too. The doctor said they pulled half the plane's windshield out of you." She took the thermometer, made a notation on Lynda's chart, then adjusted the IV. "We've given you something for pain, but if it's worn off, I can give you more."

Lynda moaned. "No wonder I've slept most of the day. No, I don't want any more." She watched the nurse wrap the blood pressure cuff around her arm. "Jill, do you know if Jake is out of surgery yet?"

Jill stared at her watch for a few seconds then slipped the cuff off again. "As a matter of fact, he is," she said, making another notation. "He's still critical, though. I don't have any of the details."

Lynda tried to sit up. "I want to see him."

"Sorry." The nurse gently pushed her back down. "He's still in ICU. No visitors."

"But I'm not a visitor. I was in that crash with him. It was my plane."

Jill snapped her chart shut and put it back in the pocket at the foot of Lynda's bed. "He isn't even conscious yet. Wait until tomorrow, and we'll see if we can get you permission to visit him. But not tonight, Lynda. Besides, you're still too weak to get out of bed."

"No, I feel fine. I just want to make sure he's all right."

"I'm sorry, Lynda. You'll just have to take our word for it tonight."

Lynda closed her eyes as the nurse left and tried in vain to steer her thoughts to something besides Jake's life. What weren't they telling her? Critical. What did that mean?

She tried to turn over, but a cut down her leg made it uncomfortable, so she shifted to her other side. The sheets were rough beneath her skin, and she wondered why they couldn't manage to get sheets that covered the whole bed, instead of those stupid half sheets that folded halfway down, overlapping another one that covered the end. It made changing the beds easier, she supposed, but that didn't help the patient's comfort any, especially when the patient was covered with cuts and scrapes. She longed for her own smooth sheets and the big bed she had shopped for a month to find.

She was so uncomfortable she might *never* fall back to sleep, and what good was lying here when Jake could be dying? If she could just see him, maybe she could relax tonight and let go of the guilt that was causing more pain than her broken ribs. If the only way to see him was to sneak through the halls and slip into ICU, she was willing to give it a try.

Making the decision almost as quickly as the thought came to her mind, she sat up and moved her feet over the side of the bed. The checkerboard floor was cold beneath her feet, and she felt a wave of vertigo as she sat up. Fighting it, she stood slowly. Her muscles strained, and she touched the place on her abdomen where her spleen had been removed. The pain in her head got worse, and she stood still a moment, waiting for the dizziness to pass.

Steadying herself with a hand against the brick wall, she put one foot in front of the other, stepping carefully until she reached the door. Already she felt soul weary, but she knew that ICU was just one floor up. If she could just get to the elevator. . . .

Opening the door, she peered up the corridor. A visitor was going into another room, but she saw no one else. She closed the door behind her and took a barefoot step up the hall.

Miraculously, a wheelchair sat parked against the wall. Mumbling a "Thank you, Lord," she dropped into it. For a moment, she tried to catch her breath, but then, fearing she'd be caught if she didn't hurry, she grabbed the wheels and tried to push herself along.

Her left arm was stiff and sore, and pain stabbed through her ribs, making her perspire, but she pushed on nonetheless, passing the nurse's station without being noticed. She made it past the waiting room, where two or three people sat watching television, and breathed another "thank you" that none of them knew her.

Waiting anxiously beside the elevator, Lynda glanced up the hall. Nurse Jill stepped out into the hall from someone's room, and Lynda turned her head away. The elevator doors opened, and quickly she rolled on.

She pressed the button for the next floor up and waited, trying to fight the pain sending clouds circling through her head. The elevator stopped and she got off, careful to avoid the nurses clustered at the coffee pot near the elevator.

She was growing fatigued, and she pushed more slowly, wondering whether she'd made a mistake. But the doubts fled when she caught sight of the glass doors to the Intensive Care Unit.

A sign warned against unauthorized personnel entering ICU, and she knew that in the wheelchair she'd never get through that door and to Jake's bed. Taking a deep breath and bracing herself against the pain, she got to her feet.

Slowly, she opened the door and slipped inside.

A nurse was on the phone, and another one bent over a monitor. Stepping carefully, and battling the dizziness threatening her again, she made her way past them.

A little girl lay in an oxygen tent behind one curtain, and further down she saw an old man. She reached out to steady herself against the wall and checked a file on a door. Heather Nelson and then Lawrence Sims—

She froze as she came to the next room. Inside was a man with a bandaged face lying still on his bed, tubes and wires attaching him to the monitors and machines that hummed and beeped.

She searched for the name on the file on his door.

Jake Stevens.

A sob choked her, and she stumbled into the room. He was as still and pale as death. A bandage covered one eye and half his face, and large patches of skin were scraped from his arm, his hand. . . .

"Jake?" she whispered.

He didn't stir. Muffling another sob, she stood over him, thinking how carefree and healthy he had looked this morning, driving up in his Porsche and irritating her with that lethal grin.

"Jake, I'm so sorry." Clutching the bed rail, she leaned over him. "I don't know how—"

"What are you doing here?"

The voice startled her, and she swung around and saw one of the nurses she'd seen outside, a black woman, standing in the doorway. "How did you get in here?"

"I—I had to see him," Lynda wept. "I had to."

Instantly, the nurse was at her side. "It's all right, child," she said, putting her arms around her and guiding her back to the door. "You're the lady who was in the crash with him, aren't you?"

Unable to speak, Lynda nodded her head.

"Honey, I'm so sorry," the nurse said, taking her to her wheelchair and lowering her into it. "But you shouldn't be out of your room. You should be in bed. Jake will still be here tomorrow."

"Will he?" Lynda asked, looking up at her. "He looks like—like he may not make it."

"Looks can be deceiving," the nurse said. "I don't know you, but I'd say you've probably looked better yourself."

"But he's still . . . unconscious. What if he doesn't wake up? And what's wrong with his face? It's all bandaged."

"He was in a plane crash, darlin'. His face is the least of his problems."

Lynda grabbed the nurse's arm and started to stand, her face pleading for the truth. "Just tell me if—if he's expected to die."

The woman gently lowered her back to the chair. "I can't lie to you. It could go either way. But if he makes it through tonight, I'll feel a lot better about his chances tomorrow."

Finally leaning back, Lynda wailed into her hands.

"I'm gonna take you back to your room now, darlin', and tomorrow, if he wakes up, I'll make sure you get to see him. My name's Abby, and you can call me anytime tomorrow to get a report."

Lynda couldn't talk as the nurse rolled her back to the elevator.

9

PAIGE LAY STILL as she heard a car door slam in front of her motel room. Footsteps passed her door, and then she heard the door to the next room open and a woman's shrill laughter.

It wasn't Keith. She turned onto her side and looked at her daughter, sleeping only in her underwear since they hadn't brought any extra clothes with them. The child slept soundly. Why not? She feared her father, but she didn't understand that her father was stalking them, threatening to take her from her mother and make her little life one nightmare after another, just as Paige's marriage had been.

What was he doing right now? Was he still waiting at her house, expecting Paige to breeze in and confront him? Or was he at his own apartment, devising another way of getting close to Brianna, inventing more lies about Paige's being an unfit mother, a child abuser, and a general danger to society?

"What am I gonna do?" she whispered to the darkness.

Brianna muttered a string of nonsense words under her breath. Turning on her side, Paige pulled her daughter against her. "It's okay, sweetheart," she said softly. "Mommy's here."

Brianna's breathing settled back into a peaceful rhythm, and Paige checked the clock. Only three hours before she had to be at work, she thought. What was she going to do with Brianna? She couldn't take her to day care again. Keith could come back and intimidate Brianna's teachers into handing her over. No, she couldn't take that chance. But she couldn't call in sick, either. She'd used up all her sick days earlier in the year when Keith had broken her arm and blackened both eyes. The shame of going to work like that had kept her home until makeup could disguise her bruises. But there were no sick days left.

There was no choice, she told herself. She would take Brianna to work with her. Brianna could sit on the floor and color as Paige typed; maybe if she explained it to her boss, he would understand. Maybe, just this once, fate would have a little mercy on her.

10

SOMEONE HAD DRIVEN a stake through his temples, Jake thought as he opened the eye that wasn't bandaged. And if his pain was any indication, that someone had done the same through his cheekbone, his neck, down his arms, and across his shoulders.

Had some woman's angry boyfriend or husband beaten him to a pulp? Had he been in a car accident?

He opened his eye, and a cruel, blaring light forced him to close it. Confused, feeling the beginnings of panic, he squinted the eye open and tried again to orient himself. Before his eye was able to make out the room, his other senses detected the smell of iodine and alcohol, a soft beeping, and the electrical hum of machinery. Focusing, he saw the white walls of intensive care, the camera in the corner with which he was monitored, and the impressive machinery around his bed.

Yes, he thought through the haze in his brain. He'd been in an accident. But not a car crash.

A plane crash.

Catching his breath as the horror of his landing came back to him, he tried to sit up, but something held him down, and the pain stabbing through his face and head warned him not to try again.

His throat felt as if he'd swallowed a bucket of sand. He needed a drink, he thought desperately. He needed a drug. He needed to die.

"He's waking up!"

He looked up to see a pale, skinny nurse standing over him on one side, and a man with a stethoscope on the other.

"Jake, can you hear me?" the man asked in a voice so loud it thundered through his brain. "Jake, you're in the hospital."

No kidding, he thought, but when he tried to speak, his throat rebelled. The nurse set something cold against his lips, something wet—ice chips—and he opened his mouth gratefully and let the cold water ooze into his throat.

"How long?" he asked in a raspy whisper.

"Since the crash?" she asked. "Almost twenty-four hours. How do you feel?"

He thought of the worst hangover he'd ever had and decided it was a mere annoyance compared to this. "My head," he said, raising a lead-heavy hand to touch the bandage covering his eye.

"You have a gash down your face, Jake," the man said gently. "Your eye was pretty badly injured."

Jake looked up at him with horror. "My eye?"

"Yes. Do you have any feeling in your legs yet?"

His legs. There was no pain in his legs, he realized for the first time. They were numb. He tried to slide his leg up, to feel his toes, but it wouldn't move. Closing his eye, he wished he could block this out, that he could have stayed asleep, never to wake up and face the ways his body was failing him.

"Jake?"

"Tell me about my legs," he whispered, looking up at them with dread.

The doctor laid his hand on his shin. "Can you feel me touching you, Jake?"

"Yes!" he blurted, as if that proved that things weren't as bad as they seemed. "I feel pressure. Weight."

"That could be a good sign," he admitted weakly. "We need to run some tests." He started listing orders for the nurse, but Jake grabbed the sleeve of his coat and stopped him.

"What's broken?" he asked desperately. "My legs? My neck?"

It was obvious the doctor wasn't ready to be pinned down. "No broken bones, Jake, but you have deep lacerations in several places. The numbness is probably a blessing, considering the pain you might be feeling."

"I don't need any blessings like this," he bit out. "Besides, my head is enough to do me in."

"Well, if you need a stronger painkiller—"

"Yes," he cut in. "I need it."

"All right." But he didn't rush off for a hypodermic, as Jake had hoped. "Jake, your chart says you're new in town and no relatives have been notified. Is there anyone we could call for you?"

He thought of the one relative he still had, the one he'd woven stories about to make his past sound charmed, the one he had pretended was dead. "No," he said finally. "The last thing I need is people crying over me, waiting like vultures to see if the new me will have any resemblance to the old one."

"It wouldn't be like that, Jake," the nurse said. "You need the support of people who love you."

"I've never needed it before," he whispered as he closed his eye to dismiss them. "And I'm not about to start needing it now."

"If you'd wanted a vacation, Lynda, all you had to do was say so." Sally Crawford pulled a chair up to Lynda's bed and set the bag she'd brought on the table in front of her. "I could use one, too, but you don't see me crashing a plane to get one."

Lynda was tired—her sleep last night had been restless and plagued with nightmares—but she managed to smile at her secretary. "Looks like I'm gonna get a longer vacation than I need. That blasted doctor said I have to stay out at least a month. Honestly, I feel like I'll be as good as new in a few days, but—"

"Lynda, you have injuries you can't even see. You have to let yourself recover. Besides, I'll be in the office taking care of the day-to-day stuff."

"But I have cases pending. Court dates. . . ."

"Some of them can be postponed, and the ones that can't are going to be divided among the partners and associates. We went over all of them this morning. Your cases are in good hands."

Lynda sank back onto her pillow. "Well, I guess that's something."

"There's just one thing."

Lynda looked up. "What?"

"The Paige Varner case. No one wanted it."

"No one?" she asked.

"There's no money in it," Sally reminded her. "And it's a real shame because she came in yesterday all upset because her husband had shown up at her daughter's day care and tried to take her."

Lynda closed her eyes. "It's my fault. I've been putting her off."

"You've been busy. When you reach for a handout, you have to wait your turn."

That had, indeed, been her philosophy, Lynda admitted, but hearing it now, she didn't like the way it sounded. "She can't help not having any money. And that man. The restraining order obviously hasn't scared him at all. I was afraid it wouldn't. He's fearless. He'd *have* to be—he's suing *her* for custody, claiming *she's* the one who's abusive."

"She's anxious to get the case resolved so she can leave the state."

"I know. The judge has ordered her to stay in town until after court. Do you have her file with you?" Sally reached for her briefcase and pulled it out, and Lynda took it. "So nobody wanted her, huh?"

"I'll just tell her she'll have to find another attorney."

"No, she's tried." She studied the file for a moment, then glanced at Sally again. "Sally, am I really that mercenary?"

"How mercenary?" Sally asked, not following.

"So mercenary that I would push this case to the bottom of my priority list just because the hours I spent on it weren't billable?"

"Lynda, you did what anybody would do."

Lynda sighed and closed the file. "I'm keeping this case," she said. "I'll handle it."

"But Lynda!"

"It'll be all right," she said. "Just call Paige and tell her to come by to see me here."

Sally held back her protest, but her disapproval was apparent. "All right, Lynda. If you say so. I'm gonna go now. You look like you need some rest. A lot of it."

Lynda dropped the file onto the table next to her. "You think *I* look bad. You should see the other guy." But the words weren't said in humor, and that haunted look passed over her eyes again. "At least he's alive. I've been calling ICU every hour. As far as I know, he's still not awake, though."

"They're saying he may never walk again."

Lynda snapped a look back to Sally. Slowly, she sat up. "What? Where did you hear that?"

"On the news," Sally said. "Last night they did a report about the crash. Apparently he has a spinal cord injury, and he lost one eye."

Lynda brought her hands up to cover her face and sank back into her pillow. "Abby said his face was the least of his problems, but I didn't know. . . ."

"All things considered, Lynda, he's lucky to be alive."

Lynda tried to take in a deep, cleansing breath and slid her hands down her face. "Yeah," she whispered. "I guess we have to look at it that way. I just don't understand."

"Understand what?"

"Why *I* wasn't hurt worse. My legs are fine. I only broke a couple of ribs and lost my spleen. He almost died, and it wasn't even his plane!"

"Lynda, stop beating yourself up. If you'd been hurt worse, do you think it would have taken away from his injuries?"

Sally didn't understand, Lynda thought dismally. Nobody could understand.

Sally seemed at a loss for anything else that would comfort her, so she opened Lynda's bag. "Well, anyway, I got you everything you wanted from home. If you need me to go back, I'll be happy to."

"No," she said, without even checking the bag's contents, "this should be enough. Thanks, Sally."

Sally slapped her thighs. "No problem. I'll get in touch with Paige as soon as I can. And you call if you need me. Everything will be back to normal in no time, okay?"

"Yeah," Lynda whispered, but as she watched Sally leave the room, she wasn't sure that normal would ever be good enough again.

Jake wished he'd stayed asleep.

And frankly, he didn't know why he hadn't. What was the use in waking up, just so he could listen to the doctor tell him again of the gash that had maimed his face and destroyed one eye? And that was just the beginning.

"Tell me about my back and my legs, Doctor. Tell me why I can't move."

Dr. Randall—a man in his mid-fifties who had more lines on his face than a street map of Tampa—leaned wearily over Jake's bed rail and seemed to consider his words carefully. This was going to be a tough one, Jake thought. When a doctor grew that thoughtful and hesitant about giving a prognosis, the most obvious question was, "How soon should I buy my burial plot?" But Jake feared the news might even be worse than death.

"You have lower lumbar compression, Jake, due to the impact of the crash, and that's led to a condition called spinal shock," the doctor said carefully. "It's caused paralysis in your legs. You can count yourself fortunate, though. If the compression had been higher, you wouldn't have use of your arms, either."

"So I'm supposed to breathe a sigh of relief because I'm a paraplegic and not a quadriplegic?"

The doctor accepted his cynicism with patience. "Let me finish, Jake. The paralysis could be temporary. You have a gash on your back, too, and a lot of swollen tissue. The steroids we're giving you are to keep the swelling down so it won't cause any more nerve damage. And until we get that swelling down, there's no way to tell how much of the damage is permanent."

Jake fought the furious tears burning his eyes. "Bottom line, Doc. Am I ever gonna walk again or not?"

Dr. Randall rubbed his eyes, leaving them red. "We can't know that for several days. Maybe longer."

"But what do you *think?*"

The truth seemed to take more out of the doctor than he had to give. "I don't know, Jake. We've been successful with a drug that we think regenerates the nerve cells, and we've started you on it today, in your IV. It all depends on the extent of the nerve damage. We just have to be patient and hope for the best. Meanwhile, you'll start working with the physical therapist and occupational therapist this morning to keep your joints and muscles working."

"I can't move," Jake scoffed. "How can I work my muscles or joints?"

"They'll do it for you. But Jake. . . ." He touched Jake's arm, forcing him to look up at him. "As hard as your therapy is going to be, you have to cooperate. Those therapists are going to get you functioning as well as possible, but you have to work really hard. Harder than you've ever worked before."

"I don't want to work at being a functional invalid," Jake countered. "I'd rather just give it all up."

"Well, that's not one of your choices," Dr. Randall said, still kindly. "You flat-lined in the ambulance, but the paramedics brought you back. And later, when the worst part of this is behind you, you're going to be glad they did."

"They should have let me die," he said through dry, cracked lips. "I don't want to be here. I don't want to do this."

"No one ever does, Jake," the doctor told him. "But you're going to."

"What about *her?*" he asked. "The plane's owner. Did she make it?"

"Yes, she survived," Randall assured him.

"Is she paralyzed, too?"

The doctor seemed to know where this was going. "No. She broke some ribs, damaged her spleen, but she was lucky."

Jake's face reddened. "Terrific," he bit out. "And I'm lying flat on my back." Gritting his teeth, he slammed his fist on the bed. "It wasn't even my plane!"

"There'll be anger, Jake," the doctor said. "But you'll get through it. You'll need support. Call all of your family and friends to rally around you. Don't underestimate how much they can help."

Jake didn't respond, for the tears were blurring the one eye he had left, constricting his throat, making him so angry he could have killed someone if he'd just had a weapon.

Family, he scoffed bitterly. Friends.

Didn't the doctor realize that he didn't want anyone to see him like this?

Dr. Randall left him then with the monitors and machines humming in his room, with the IV dripping through a tube in his arm, with the nasogastric tube in his nose draining the bile that kept rising.

Who would have believed it when he'd gotten up yesterday morning, all enthusiasm and hope?

He wished he'd never decided to buy a plane of his own; he wished he'd never picked up the aviation magazine that had advertised the Piper in its classified ads; he wished he'd never met Lynda Barrett.

It seemed like a year ago that he came bouncing down the steps of the Biltmore, introducing himself to the blonde—now he couldn't even remember her room number—and riding off in his Porsche. He wondered whether anyone had contacted the manager of the Biltmore to get his stuff or called the moving company about storing his furniture. Was anyone watching his car?

But who? It wasn't as if he had anyone here he could call. He was new in town and completely alone. Flat on his back or not, he was on his own.

The thought sent rage spiraling up inside him, anger that he didn't know how to direct. Why had this happened to him? Why not her? *She* was the one who'd taken *him* up in a busted plane.

As if in answer to his thoughts, the nurse who'd been hovering over him all morning came to his door. "Jake, is it all right if Lynda Barrett visits you for just a minute? If you're not up to it, I'll send her away."

Jake looked at the door with his remaining good eye, welcoming the opportunity to feed his anger. "Yeah," he said bitterly. "Send her in. She might as well get a good look."

The nurse hesitated a moment, then disappeared. In a few moments, she was back, wheeling Lynda in a wheelchair. He gave her a once-over—she was stitched and bruised, too, but both eyes were intact, and her legs, crossed at the ankles, looked as healthy as his had looked yesterday.

"Hi, Jake," she whispered almost timidly. "How do you feel?"

He looked at the ceiling. "How do you think I feel?"

She took that gracefully. "Probably pretty bad." She watched as the nurse stepped out of the room to give them some privacy, then wheeled herself closer to the bed. "Jake, I'm so sorry."

"Not as sorry as I am."

She swept her eyes down his body, and they lingered on his legs. "We didn't know if you'd make it. I prayed all night that you would."

"What for? So I could lie here like a vegetable for the rest of my life?"

"I know how you must feel—"

"Do you?" he asked with exaggerated surprise. "Do you really? Tell me how you know how I feel, Lynda. Have you ever been paralyzed? Have you ever had the sight cut out of your eye? Have you had your face maimed beyond recognition? How do you know how I feel?"

She only gaped at him for a moment, and her fragile expression crumbled. "Okay, I don't know. But you survived, Jake. Just like I did. We both could have died in that crash, but we didn't."

He turned his head to look at her now. "Are you kidding me? I'm supposed to be happy that I'm useless as a human being instead of dead?" Disgusted, he looked at the ceiling again. "Why did you come in here anyway? What do you want?"

For a moment, she couldn't speak. "Just . . . I just wanted to see if you were all right."

"Well, I'm not. Satisfied?"

It was clear that she hadn't expected this reaction from him, and he wondered if she'd expected them to bond from the trauma. Were they supposed to be best friends now and compare notes on what they remembered of the crash and eat lunch together and play cards? Didn't she realize that the very sight of her made him lament the day he'd laid eyes on her?

She covered her mouth and started to cry. "I guess I shouldn't have come. I'll go now."

"Yeah," he said. "You need to nurse those poor cracked ribs. I'd call the nurse, but I can't move."

At that, Lynda sprang to her feet. He watched her reach unsteadily for the rail, and with a look of furious determination made softer by the tears on her face, she grabbed the remote control with the nurse's call button from his bed table and thrust it into his hand. "That's one less thing you can feel sorry for yourself about," she said. Then, grabbing the handles of her chair, she walked carefully out of the room, pushing it in front of her.

Jake watched her go, his bitter anger at her for surviving intact fading as his indignation at her attitude grew.

Abby, the nurse who had found Lynda in Jake's room the night before, came upon her again, sitting in her wheelchair in the hall of ICU, weeping bitterly into her hands. Stooping in front of her, Abby tried to raise her face.

"Are you all right, child?"

Sucking back her sobs, Lynda looked up at her. "Jake just said some things—"

"He's hurtin', darlin'. Don't put any stock in what he says. When people hurt, they say all sorts of things."

But her assurance didn't help. This was bigger than words. "You want me to push you back to your room, honey?"

Lynda couldn't answer. "I went there to comfort him, and he just made me so mad—" She broke off and covered her face again. "I told him he felt sorry for himself. How could I *say* that?"

"You're human," Abby said. "Girl, I've been spit on, slapped, kicked, cursed, screamed at, puked on—and as much as I pride myself on keeping my cool, I have been known to say some nasty things, just because I'm human. You aren't even getting paid for listening to it. You can't expect to grit your teeth and smile through it. That takes something bigger than either one of us."

Reaching into her pocket, she pulled out a tissue, and Lynda wiped her eyes.

"You know where I go when I can't take much more, and I feel that old dark side of Abby taking over?"

"Where?"

"The chapel. It's on this floor. I'll take you there if you want me to, child. Maybe you'll find some peace there."

Lynda nodded. "Yes, that's where I need to go."

"Fine." Abby got to her feet and pushed her out of the ICU doors. "When I get off tonight, how 'bout I come by your room and wash your hair? I'll bet you're a pretty brunette when you don't look like you've lost a fight with a grizzly."

Lynda managed to smile under the tissue. "That would be great. I have trouble lifting my arms."

They reached the double doors to the small chapel, and Abby pushed her inside. The room was dimly lit with candles at the corners of the altar, and it was only big enough for three small pews on either side of the wide aisle.

Abby rolled her to the front and then in a more reverent voice, said, "There's a phone here at the back, honey. You call me when you're ready—extension 214—and I'll have someone come get you."

"Thank you," Lynda whispered.

Abby smiled, then closed the doors on her way out.

Lynda sat still for a moment, staring at the cross behind the small lectern and then behind that, at the stained glass window. A white dove was etched into the glass, flying down to the shoulder of a silhouette kneeling in a pool of water.

This is my son, in whom I am well pleased. God's words echoed through her mind, their very praise an indictment of her own actions.

Tears stung her eyes, and she sat before the altar, wishing to be judged, ready to be condemned. "I don't know what to say to him," she confessed aloud. "I don't even know what to say to you."

It had been too long since she'd had a serious heart-to-heart with God, too long since she'd sat in his presence. Now she felt her inadequacy like a verdict.

Awkwardly, she tried to thank him for her survival, but Jake's injuries limited her gratitude. And then she thought of the plane she had loved so much, destroyed in a matter of minutes, leaving her to face the solitude of her life without it.

As her own thoughts condemned her, she looked up to the window again.

. . . in whom I am well pleased . . .

It was from the New Testament, she thought quickly, but she couldn't remember where. It had been too long since she'd read her Bible, and now she wasn't even sure where she'd put it.

But she didn't have to recall the reference to know what it meant to her.

God wasn't pleased with *her.* How could he be when she'd made a god of an airplane, an altar of her job, and an idol of her own ego? How could he smile on her when she'd spoken to a sick man the way she had today or when she'd ignored the needs of a poor battered wife who depended on her?

The truth was that she'd just quit caring. She hadn't cared about her relationship with God or her friends or her family. She hadn't cared about anything except her job and that plane. Not in a long time.

Like Peter after he'd denied Christ, she wept bitterly, brokenly, not expecting God to recognize or comfort her, not expecting his peace—

But suddenly it came.

Her tears slowed, her sobbing stopped, and she looked up at the dove on the window and felt his slow, warm, forgiving embrace welcoming her home.

Instead of remorse, she felt hope. Instead of shame, she felt purpose. It *wasn't* too late.

For a moment, she sat still in her wheelchair, her head bowed, her eyes closed. For the first time in she couldn't remember how long, she listened.

And God spoke.

In that still, small voice that could be so easily ignored, so quickly forgotten, so often dismissed as nothing more than an idle thought, he reminded her to whom she belonged.

And with that reminder came a flood of determination finally to do something about it.

But what?

She thought of Abby, offering to wash her hair after working a twelve-hour shift, because she couldn't lift her own arms. That was faith in action, wasn't it? It was giving of yourself when you got nothing back. It was stretching out of that comfort zone, even when you got cursed at.

The new Lynda would do better, she promised as she sat before that altar. She would stretch. She would grow.

And filled with a renewed spirit and a peace that gave her strength, she felt a sudden urgency to go back to her room and get started.

11

SHE WASN'T DEAD. He had been there when the plane crashed. He'd been standing at the fence, watching like a curious spectator as the plane circled overhead and the ground crews scurried around in a panic. It had made the news on all three local channels and even got a mention on CNN.

He had watched as the plane descended at the end, had held his breath as it had spun. He'd seen both wings breaking off, metal flying, glass breaking—and he'd been sure that he'd succeeded, that it was impossible for anyone to survive that.

But the paramedics had moved too quickly, and when the plane had ignited, she was out of its range. He had watched, troubled, as the ambulances blared past him, carrying both passengers to the hospital.

Still, he'd seen the blood, and he had believed that the injuries would be too great, that she would die en route or on the operating table or later in her room.

But no. She was not only still alive, but she was also doing well. No lasting impairment. No permanent damage.

It was a failure. But it would not be repeated. Next time, she would not escape.

All he could do now was bide his time and wait until the right moment. It would come soon enough. And then his problems would be over.

Then he could finally get on with his life.

12

THE ORDERLY WHO came to get Lynda from the chapel had a cautious, compassionate demeanor, and Lynda wondered with some embarrassment if Abby had warned him of her emotional state. As he wheeled her toward the elevator, he made light conversation.

"It's gonna rain again today, looks like. And, of course, I left my umbrella in the car. Isn't that always where it is when you need it? But I don't get off till three. Maybe I'll miss the storm."

The elevator doors opened, and he wheeled her on. "Oh, I was supposed to tell you that there's somebody here to see you. She's down in the first-floor lobby."

"Who?" Lynda asked, straining her sore neck to look up at him.

"I didn't get her name," he said. The doors opened, and he rolled her off. "She couldn't come up because she has a kid with her. They won't let her past the first floor. I told her you would call down when you were back in your room."

Paige. Lynda grabbed the wheel to stop the chair and looked up at him. "I have to go down," she said. "I have to go see her."

"Are you sure you're up to it?" the orderly asked her. "You look tired."

"I'm fine," she said. "Really. It's important."

An alarm sounded, and two nurses bolted around the desk, running toward an emergency. "I can't take you," he said. "I have to help with this."

"It's okay. I can make it. Go ahead."

The orderly rushed off behind the nurses, and quickly Lynda rolled back onto the elevator, ignoring the pain in her ribs when she used her arms. One crowd of people on the cramped elevator commiserated about a grandfather and a heart attack; another couple at the back cried softly and whispered together. *Pain all around me,* Lynda thought. *Pain and desperation. How can I have floated through it for so long, not seeing any of it?*

The moment the doors opened, she saw Paige across the plush maroon-and-gray lobby and pushed toward her. She was sitting on the couch, rocking Brianna back and forth gently. Her clothes were rumpled and wrinkled, and her eyes were swollen, as if she hadn't slept in days.

"Paige?"

Paige looked up quickly. "Lynda!" She sprang to her feet and rushed to help her. "Oh, I didn't expect them to send you down here! I was going to call you when you got back to your room. Oh, I'm so glad you're alive! I didn't see how you'd survive, and when I called Sally today, and she told me—"

"It could have been so much worse," Lynda cut in, smiling at the child whose thumb had gravitated to her mouth at the sight of the bruised, cut-up woman wheeling toward her. "I'm really doing pretty well. How are you, Brianna?"

The little blonde girl took her thumb out of her mouth. "Fine. Did you hurt yourself?"

"Yes, a little. But I'll be better soon."

"Did you fall down?"

"Way down."

"Did it hurt?"

"Bad. But I'm okay."

"But you look . . . terrible," Paige said. "I mean, not really terrible. . . . Just . . ."

"Like I've been in a plane crash? That's okay, Paige. I'm just happy to be alive."

Tears came to Paige's eyes, and she sank to the couch again. "I'm happy you are, too, Lynda. For really selfish reasons."

"What's wrong?"

Using her fingers, Paige combed her fine blonde hair back from her face and held it in a ponytail. "Keith was at my house when I went home last night," she blurted. "He was in there waiting. I saw his car in the driveway, and I kept going. I haven't been back."

"Did you call the police?"

She let the ponytail go, and her hair fell around her face again. "I called, but he was gone before they got there. I can't believe they have to catch him violating the order. Do they think he's stupid enough to be caught?"

"Where did you go, Paige?"

"To a motel. But I don't have much money left, and then this morning—" Her voice broke off, and she covered her mouth. Sensing her mother's despair, Brianna climbed onto Paige's lap and put her arms around her mother's neck to comfort her. The sweet gesture only made Paige wilt more.

Lynda pulled Brianna gently away. "Honey, see that book over there? Why don't you go get it and look at the pictures?"

"The Winnie the Pooh one or the Barney one?" Brianna asked.

"Barney," Lynda said.

The child considered that for a moment. "No, Pooh."

Lynda smiled faintly as Brianna gave her mother one last look, then scurried to the table with the books. Paige watched her every step of the way.

"Then what, Paige?" Lynda asked. "What happened this morning?"

"I couldn't take her back to day care, because he had been there yesterday. I was afraid he'd take her, Lynda, so I took her to work with me. And my boss came in and saw her, and he—he fired me."

"You lost your job?"

"Yes," she cried softly. "I might have all of forty dollars left to my name, and I'm afraid to go home." She looked at Lynda, her eyes pleading. For what, Lynda suspected even Paige didn't know.

Lynda took Paige's hand. "Sally told you that I'm keeping your case, didn't she?"

Paige nodded. "Yes."

"As soon as I get back to the room, I'll call her and get her to file a motion to get us before a judge so we can tell him Keith violated his order—"

"No," Paige cut in. "That won't do any good. It'll just make him mad."

"It doesn't matter, Paige. If he realizes he won't get away with it—"

"*If* they put him in jail, he'll get out in a couple of days. He'll come after me, Lynda. I'm afraid of him. All I want is my court date so we can get the custody hearing over with and have his visitation denied so I can take Brianna someplace where he'll never find us—"

A man walked past the place Brianna sat reading. Springing from her seat, Paige dashed to her daughter. "Brianna, honey, bring the book and sit by me."

"Okay." Brianna followed her mother back to the couch and climbed up next to her. Paige put her arm around her, as if only by touching the child could she be assured of her safety. Weary, Lynda realized that a court date could still be weeks away, and the woman had no livelihood and was living in terror. If Lynda hadn't left so much of her case to chance, it might have been over by now.

Lynda dropped her head into her hand, wrestling with the emotions she knew were on her face. "Paige, I hope you'll forgive me for letting you down."

"Letting me down?" Paige asked. "You haven't let me down. You're the only lawyer who would take me."

"No," Lynda said. "I *have* let you down. I could have pressed for a court date earlier. I could have paid more attention to your case."

Paige was silent for a moment, obviously confused about what to say.

"I want to make it up to you," Lynda whispered. "I've just been in the chapel, trying to sort things out, and I'm starting to see that I haven't been a very nice person."

Paige shook her head adamantly. "No, you're the greatest, Lynda. I don't know what I would have done without you."

"That's sweet," Lynda said, but she wasn't buying. "I want to help you for real this time. Somehow I feel like if I do, I'll be helping myself, too."

"But you *are* helping me."

"No," Lynda said. "Not really. But that can change. I want you to stay at my house."

Paige caught her breath. "No, I couldn't. Lynda, representing me for free is enough of an imposition."

"It's not an imposition. It's a favor," Lynda said. "Please, I want you to. My house is just sitting there, and Keith will never think to look for you there. I'll get Sally to get you some money out of my account, so you won't have to worry about your job *or* about Keith until we get into court."

Paige was stunned. "But that's too much, Lynda. You don't have to do this."

"Yes, I do," Lynda said. "Please, Paige."

"But why? I'm just a client. You hardly even know me."

Lynda paused and tried to find the right words. "Because your hair doesn't need washing."

Paige breathed a laugh. "What?"

"It's something I can do, Paige. Something besides sitting here and worrying about you. Please."

Paige stared at her for a moment as fresh tears came to her eyes. "I can't believe you'd do this."

"Then it's yes?"

Paige shrugged and looked down at her daughter. "Yes, I guess so."

"Then I'll go call Sally right now. She has a key, and she can let you into the house. There's food there, but she'll get you some money out of my account, so you can get anything else you need. Meanwhile, I'll make some phone calls. We'll get someone to go to your house and get your clothes and whatever else you need. Just don't tell anyone where you are. If anyone needs you, they can go through me or Sally." When Paige still didn't respond, she asked, "Does this sound all right to you?"

Paige surrendered and relaxed, her gratitude evident on her face. "Yes," she whispered. "Thank you."

As Lynda rode the elevator back up to her room to call Sally, she told herself that she should have offered Paige this kind of help weeks ago. It wouldn't have hurt her at all, and it would have made a world of difference in the young woman's life.

She only hoped she had the fortitude now to finish what she was starting.

Two hours later, Lynda was still on the phone when Sally came into her room. She whispered that she was on hold, and Sally set her hands on her plump hips and glared at her. "The nurse told me that she's calling the doctor to fink on you. She said you'd been either out of your room or on the phone all day. Lynda, if you don't stop this, you'll never recover."

Lynda put her hand over the receiver. "It takes my mind off my ribs. Did you get Paige situated?"

"Of course I did," she said. "I got her the money and gave her the key. I put them in one of the guest rooms, in case you ever get out of here. But at the rate you're working, that's not looking good. Who are you holding for?"

"Steve McRae."

"Keith's attorney? Oh, good. He ought to be a big help. He's the one trying to take that beautiful little girl away from her mother."

"He needs a warning," Lynda said. The Muzak on the phone stopped as someone picked it up, and Lynda raised a hand to silence Sally.

"Lynda?" the attorney asked in a voice that seemed a little too cordial.

"Yes, it's me," she said. "I need to talk to you about your client, Keith Varner."

"What a relief to hear your voice," he said. "I saw the crash on the news last night. I have to admit, I thought it would be a while before I'd hear from you again."

"Sorry," Lynda said in a saccharine voice. "No such luck. I am still in the hospital, which gives me all the time in the world to work on Paige Varner's case. And I called to tell you to warn your client that his harassment has got to stop."

"What harassment?"

"For starters, he tried to take Brianna from day care, despite the restraining order, and he broke into Paige's home—"

"Give me a break, Lynda," the man cut in, dropping the cordiality. "You know as well as I do that he has a key. It was his home."

"*Was* being the key word. She was granted possession of the house in their divorce, and the restraining order stated that he wasn't to come near it. And as for Brianna, until we see him in court, he isn't to go near her either."

"Put yourself in his place," the man said. "He hasn't seen his daughter in over a month."

"You're right. Not since he bashed her mother's head into the wall and knocked her out."

"Her word against his. He contends that *she* knocked *him* out when he was defending the child from one of Paige's rampages."

Lynda saw now what she was dealing with. "I'll have him arrested, Steve. If he comes near her again, I'll use every resource I have to get him locked up. Tell him."

The man sighed. "Anything else?"

"Yes. I'm going to appeal to the judge for a court date as soon as possible. I won't let you keep dragging this out."

"No need," the man said. "I got a date this afternoon. Despite what you might think, we're anxious to bring this to a head, too. It's October 14."

"That's six weeks away!" she said. "We need it earlier."

"Too bad. That's as early as we could get it."

She sank back onto her pillow and closed her eyes. "Six weeks is a long time, Steve. Tell your client that he'd better be on his best behavior during that time because I plan to pull out all the stops when we get into court."

"Good luck," he said. "You're gonna need it."

She heard the phone click in her ear, and slowly she dropped it back in its cradle and collapsed into her pillow.

"Good going," Sally said. "You told him." She looked at the color draining from Lynda's face and said, "Now will you get some rest? Paige and Brianna are safe, you have a court date, Keith's hand has been slapped—All is well with the world. Please, just get some rest before the nurses convince the doctor to sedate you."

"All right, Sally," she said, already feeling herself slipping away. "Maybe for a minute."

That night, true to her word, Abby came down from ICU with a cart made especially for washing hair and had Lynda lie down with her head over the small tub full of warm water. Gently, carefully, she washed Lynda's hair, methodically pulling more tiny chips of glass from her scalp as she did.

"It's a wonder you could sleep with all this glass in you and your hair all matted like this," she said. "Wasn't it hurtin' you?"

"Sure, it was," Lynda said. "But I thought the pain was just from the cuts." She closed her eyes as Abby poured more warm water over her head. "I thought they got all the glass out in surgery."

"No, child," Abby said. "It's hard to get it all, and the nurses don't have that kind of time when they're on duty. But we'll get every piece tonight if I have to work on it till my shift tomorrow."

Lynda opened her eyes and gazed up at the woman. "Why would you do this?"

Abby smiled. "Because it needs doin'. We're supposed to wash each other's feet, but I figure washin' hair is just as good."

The tear that rolled from Lynda's eye disappeared into the water Abby poured over her hair.

13

THERE WAS LITTLE relief for Jake in being moved out of ICU to a private room on the orthopedic floor. He was still flat on his back, unable to sit up or stand, unable to take care of his own bodily functions without help, and his hope of being released from this place was as dismal as his hope for the rest of his life.

But the Clinitron bed they laid him in gave him some degree of comfort. For one thing, it reduced the likelihood of bedsores. It felt something like a waterbed, except that air was continually pumping through it, making it conform to his shape and weight. And this room had a television so that he could keep remembering what normal people's lives were like while he contemplated what he'd do now that his would never be normal again. And he had a phone—a reminder that he had no one to call.

At least no one in Florida.

He looked at it, wondering whether anyone in Texas had heard of his accident. He doubted it. As far as they knew, he was living it up, as he'd always done. If they could see him now.

He picked up the phone and tried to remember the number of someone—anyone—who might care what had happened to him. What about Sheila—red, flowing hair, big green eyes. She'd been in love with him forever and had followed him around like a devoted puppy, even when he'd shunned her. He'd broken her heart, finally, and sent her on her way. But she would never get over him. She would want to know about this accident.

He dialed her number and waited as it rang, wondering what to say to her. Would she be glad to hear from him? Would she fly to Florida to visit him?

Quickly, he hung the phone back up. She might. He couldn't take that chance. He couldn't let her see him like this. *No* one could see him like this. Not yet. Not until the bandages came off and he could see how extensive the scarring was. Then he would decide.

Loneliness filled him like a disease, further darkening the black places in his heart. Jake Stevens wasn't used to being alone. What he wouldn't give for someone he *could* talk to without fearing how that person would see him.

And then he thought of that little truck stop in Slapout, Texas, where Doris waited tables each day, always naively hopeful that one of the truck drivers who came through would be the one to rescue her from her own loneliness and shame, make an honest woman of her, and provide her with the white picket fence and the little pink house that she had done nothing to earn on her own.

He wondered if she'd found her dream man yet among the regulars who came and went. He wondered if she'd been able to forgive him for running away from her himself, putting her behind him like forgotten garbage. Maybe she'd realized somewhere along the way that he'd had a life to make for himself and that he'd had to make it without letting her pull him down.

Maybe *she* would care that he lay here now, unable to run anymore.

He reached for the phone, called information, and got the number of the truck stop. With a trembling hand, he punched in the number.

"May I speak to Doris, please?"

On hold, he waited long, threatening moments, wanting to hang up. Finally, he heard her familiar voice, though it had grown raspier and deeper from cigarette smoke and booze.

"Yeah, hello?"

Jake swallowed, almost hanging up, but finally forced himself to speak.

"Mama? It's me. Jake."

Silence.

"Did you hear me, Mama?"

"I heard you," she said. "What do you want?"

If it was possible for his heart to fall further, it did. "I know it's been a long time. I've just been real busy, and—"

"Busy gettin' rich," she said. "I know why you haven't called. It's because you were afraid you'd have to let go of a few bucks if you talked to me. What made you call me now?"

He thought of telling her that he was lying in the hospital, that his charmed world hadn't been so charmed, that it had all come crashing down, that he didn't know if things would ever be the same. But something told him it wouldn't make any difference. He had never been there for her, though he could have been. Why did he expect her to be here for him now?

"Answer me, Jake. What do you want?"

"I just wanted to see how you were."

"Oh, I'm great," she rasped. "I just got a secondhand stove put in since mine has been out of commission for ten months. And my trailer is fallin' apart, but hey, at least it's a roof over my head. May not be a fancy condo like you've got . . ."

He didn't know whether to offer her money or an apology, but that old anger that he'd nursed since childhood began to fill him again, keeping him from offering either.

"Look, I'm sorry I bothered you. You might as well get back to work."

"Yeah, I think I will. I can't afford to miss any tips. It's not like I have anybody to take up the slack if I can't pay my rent, is there?"

The click in his ear startled him, and for a moment, he held the phone to his ear as the dial tone hummed out its indifference. Then, as his face reddened, he hung up and lay glaring at the ceiling, trying hard to push the stark self-recriminations out of his mind. He'd been good at it before, but that was when he'd had life to keep him busy. There was always a party somewhere. Always a woman. Always a drink that could make him forget.

Until now.

He flung the telephone across the room, and it crashed with a final, protesting ring. There would be no parties now and no relief from his despair. But he didn't need his mother, and he didn't need his friends. They would all only let him down in the long run.

Mommy, is this gonna be our house?"

Paige smiled at her daughter, who sat on the floor playing with some of the blocks a police officer had gotten from their house, along with most of their clothes. "No, sweetheart. We're just staying here for a while."

"Until that lady gets well?"

She left the spaghetti she was cooking and bent down to her daughter. "Maybe. I don't know how long we'll be here. But it's nice, isn't it? It's a lot better than that old motel room."

"But why can't we go home?"

"Because. . . ." She lowered herself to the floor to put herself at eye level with the child and met her big, innocent eyes. There was so much Brianna didn't understand, and Paige didn't know how to explain it to her. How could she tell her that her father was a threat to them, that she feared for her life around him, that she feared for Brianna? "Because it has bugs," she said finally.

Brianna's face twisted. "Bugs? What kind of bugs?"

"The gross kind," Paige said. "A man's spraying so they'll go away, but it's gonna take a while."

"You mean spiders and stink bugs?"

Brianna might never want to go back into the house if she made it sound too horrible. "No. Roly-polies and grasshoppers. But this man is getting them out."

"Oh." Brianna got quiet, and Paige could almost see the wheels turning as the child imagined her bedroom full of roly-polies and grasshoppers. She hoped it didn't give her nightmares. She got up and went back to the spaghetti sauce simmering on the stove.

"Mommy?"

She looked back at Brianna.

"Can I keep just some of them? In a jar with holes in the top?"

She laughed out loud and realized it was the first time in weeks. "Yes, sweetheart. You sure can."

Jake, are you up to seeing that insurance guy?" Beth, Jake's nurse in orthopedics, asked him later that day. "I told him it was your first day in the private room and that you weren't up to seeing anybody, so if you don't want to, I'll nix it right now."

Jake looked irritably at her. "What insurance guy?"

"Something about the plane."

Jake had nothing better to do, and he'd grown so tired of being alone that he had actually been lying here wishing Lynda would come by. But after the way he'd treated her yesterday, he didn't really expect her back.

"Yeah, all right," he said. "Tell him to come in."

Beth disappeared, and Jake waited until a man in a dark suit came into his room and introduced himself as Rick Malone, investigator for the company that covered Lynda's plane.

"I just want to ask you a few questions," Malone said.

"About the crash?" Jake asked. "I would think the condition of the plane pretty much tells the whole story."

Malone consulted his notes, disregarding the comment. "Mr. Stevens, could you tell me if you or Miss Barrett did a preflight inspection of the plane?"

"Of course," Jake said. "I did it myself. I never fly without a preflight."

"And everything looked fine?"

"It looked perfect. And the day before I had really given the plane a once-over. I checked everything. I was thinking of buying it, you know. I wanted to make sure I wasn't missing anything. It was the best-maintained plane I'd ever seen for its age."

Malone plunked down, as if too tired to stand. "Is there anything you could tell me about Miss Barrett's behavior that day? Did she seem nervous, jumpy?"

Jake frowned. "What are you getting at?"

"I just want to know how she acted, Mr. Malone. Did she seem to behave normally?"

"How do I know if she was normal? It was the first time I'd met her. But yeah, I'd say she was pretty normal. She wasn't crazy about selling her plane. That was obvious."

"Did she suggest you test fly it alone? Or balk at going up with you?"

Jake thought for a moment. "No. She mentioned something about the crosswind, but I really don't think she would have let me go up alone."

"Did she mention her financial condition?"

Jake stared incredulously at him. "You don't think *Lynda* had anything to do with this."

Malone shifted in his seat. "We've been on the site since the crash yesterday," Malone said. "And we've found evidence that a hose was partially cut so the hydraulic pressure would pull it completely apart as soon as the landing gear was lowered."

Jake sat silently for a moment, trying to make sense of that. "It could have torn—"

"There's more. We've gone over all of the airport's security videos, and on the night before the crash, it caught someone tampering with that plane."

"Who?"

"We can't tell exactly," Malone said. "All we were able to make out was a penlight around the wheel well and the vague shape of someone under the plane. We can't rule out that the plane's owner might have set up the crash to collect the insurance."

Jake was getting angry. "Let me get this straight," he said. "You think she would sabotage her own plane and stage her own crash just to get the money when she could just as easily have sold it to me for full market value?"

"Maybe she didn't plan to fly with you," Malone said. "Or she didn't anticipate such a dangerous landing. After all, she did survive."

Jake gaped at him for a moment, unable to believe what he was hearing. "That is the most ludicrous thing I've ever heard. Lynda Barrett had nothing to do with that crash. She was as surprised as I was when the landing gear didn't go down. And she was scared to death. She could easily have *died* in that crash. What good would the insurance money have done her then?"

"All we know is that somebody did it."

"Then stop trying to pin this on her and find out who really did it and why." He struggled to sit up, but dropped down, defeated. "And when you do," he said through his teeth, "you tell me who they are. If it's the last thing I do, I'll make sure they pay."

14

"I DON'T *BELIEVE* this." Lynda sat in a vinyl chair that hadn't been made for comfort, watching the parking lot below through her hospital room window as the insurance investigator cut between the cars. "He thought *I* had something to do with the crash."

"Don't sweat it," Mike said from where he sat by Lynda's bed. "Between Jake and me, we convinced him you didn't. But the question is, who did?"

She turned back to Mike, the light from outside casting a shadow on one side of her face. "Why would *any*body want to sabotage my plane, Mike? Wouldn't they know that the next time I flew it—?"

Mike only looked helplessly at her.

"That's it, isn't it? Someone was trying to kill me."

"Maybe. Maybe not. It could have been a random act."

"Were any of the other planes tampered with?"

"No. We've inspected all of them and checked back over the videotapes for anything out of the ordinary. It looks like it was just your plane."

She leaned back in the chair and looked out the window again. "How could I have made such an enemy and not known it?"

"I can't believe you did," Mike said. "Maybe it *was* random, Lynda. Random acts of violence happen all the time. People break into houses randomly, shoot at passing cars—"

"Some world we live in, huh?"

"You're right; it's not a pleasant thought—but it's better than thinking someone tried to kill you."

"What if they're still trying?" she whispered. She felt fear rising inside. "I mean, they failed, didn't they? What if they haven't given up?"

Mike got up and came to lean against the windowsill. "Think, Lynda. Is there anyone in your life who hates you enough to want to kill you?"

"Well, I didn't *know* there was, but obviously—"

"Not so obviously. I mean, yes, there's somebody out there who was trying to get his kicks, but that doesn't mean he's after you."

"Kicks?" she whispered. "Causing a plane crash gave him his kicks?"

"There's a lot of evil around us, Lynda. We don't have to let it consume us."

"What if we don't have a choice?" she whispered. "They're probably going to let me go home tomorrow. Am I gonna be a sitting duck? And what about Paige and Brianna? They're staying in my house."

"If he'd wanted *you,* whoever it is, he could have found you at home before, don't you think? That's what makes me think it's random."

Lynda shrugged, unconvinced.

"Anyway, the two cops who are working on it are planning to come by and talk to you today. If there *is* someone after you, they can get to the bottom of it." He leaned over and pressed a gentle kiss on her forehead and wiped a stray tear off her cheek. "It'll be okay."

"I just need some time alone to think about it, I guess."

"I'm going," he said. "But first, I want to tell you that the cops who are investigating this are Tony Danks and Larry Millsaps. Larry's a buddy of mine from church. I've known him for years. You can trust him."

She felt some comfort in that. "Thank you, Mike," she whispered.

The two people assigned to rehabilitate Jake—Allie Williams, a 120-pound dynamo who approached occupational therapy with a determination that rivaled Jake's determination to sink into depression, and Buzz Slater, a former paraplegic who'd become a physical therapist after learning to walk again himself—didn't seem to care that Jake's head was still on the verge of bursting with pain or that nausea was hiding just below the surface, waiting to assault him at any given moment. Since he awoke from the accident, their hands had been all over him, poking and prodding, flexing and massaging, despite his venomous verbal resistance.

Nothing he said daunted them, no insult offended them, at least not enough to make them leave him alone. Every two hours they came in and turned him over, massaged him, and bent him this way and that until finally he'd vowed to learn how to turn *himself* over just to get a little peace.

"That's not all you'll learn to do today," Allie said brightly as she wheeled a gurney into the room. "Today you're going to the tilt table in the rehab room. We're going to get you sitting up, so you can get out of bed."

That sounded easy enough, and Jake was almost hopeful as they wheeled him down the hallway, flat on his back to the big room where a dozen or more people like him worked—on mats, in a pool, on parallel bars, with walkers.

He didn't object when they transferred him to the flat table, but when they began strapping him down, he got worried. "What are the straps for?"

"To keep you from sliding off, Jake," Buzz said. "You've been flat for three days. We have to get you upright gradually. You may have some problems."

But Jake couldn't imagine ever having problems being upright. "Try me," he said.

They finished strapping him on then slowly began to tilt him up.

He felt a cold sweat prickling his skin; his head pounded. Though the table inched upward at a snail's pace, he grew increasingly dizzy, nauseous, weak. . . .

"I'm gonna pass out!"

Instantly, they lowered him flat again.

"That's all right, Jake," Allie said. "You made it to thirteen degrees."

Jake looked at her. "That's all? Why did I react like that?"

"It's called orthostatic hypotension. You've been lying down for a while, so your circulation is weak. Your blood pressure drops when you're upright. We just have to keep trying it, getting a little higher each time, until you get through it. Ready to go again?"

He wanted to scream out that he wasn't, but instead he said, "No. I'm thirsty."

"We can give you some ice chips," Allie said, "but you won't be able to keep anything else down."

She put an ice chip in Jake's mouth, then allowed a few seconds for it to melt. "Ready now?"

Jake cursed as the table tilted again. As the blood drained to pool in his feet, the world threatened to turn black.

"Just get through this, Jake," Buzz said when he was flat again. "After this, we'll start you on traction."

Two hours later, they wheeled him back to his room in time for the bland lunch that awaited him, the lunch he couldn't eat. His skull felt as if it had intercepted the pain from all the places on his body that he couldn't feel. His stomach was empty but still threatened to turn on him, and the worst part was that for all his work, he'd only made it up to twenty degrees on the tilt table. At this rate, he'd be flat on his back for the rest of his life.

And the traction had been another nightmare. They had hooked him to the pulleys and turned the machine on, making it pull for twenty seconds, then release for five, then pull again. . . .

Jake's hope as he endured the pain was that the pulleys would relieve the compression in his spine, free the nerves to function again, and bring the feeling back into his legs. But when the exercise was over, he was as numb from his hips down as he had been when he'd gotten here. It would take time, Buzz told him. Lots of time.

And time was something he had more than enough of. He had all the time in the world and absolutely nothing to do with it but endure more torture, more terror, more disappointment.

Yanking at the sheet the nurse had laid over him, he tried to fling it off the bed, but it was attached somewhere. Instead, he grabbed a glass of watery tea and hurled it across the room. It shattered and left a stain on the wall, but that did nothing to appease Jake's rage.

Lynda heard a crash as she reached the door of Jake's room. Stepping out of her wheelchair, she pushed the door open. A tray of food flew against the wall, and plates and food and a cup went crashing to the floor.

"Jake! What are you—?"

She ducked out of the way of the plastic pitcher.

Jake's face was red, and his bandage was wet with tears. Randomly, he reached for something else to throw. The phone book sailed across the room and then the tissue box. When he grabbed the phone he had already broken the other day and tried to yank off the cord, she dove for him.

"Stop it!" she cried, wrestling the phone from him and grabbing his flailing arms. "Jake, stop it!"

He fought for a moment more, and then, sobbing and cursing, finally gave up and let his arms fall across his face.

Lynda stood next to the bed, staring down at him, feeling helpless. Where were the people who loved this man? Where were the ones who could fight this battle with him? Was there really no one?

But there *was* someone, Lynda thought, succumbing to her own tears. *She* was here, and Jake needed her probably more than he'd ever needed anyone in his life.

She leaned over him and slid her hands to his shoulders. Somehow as he sobbed and shook and wailed, she got her arms around him, and suddenly he was clutching her like someone hanging from a cliff, about to fall to his death.

Maybe she was the only one who could pull him back.

He held her while he wept out his last ounces of strength while she cried against the bandage on his face.

"It's okay, Jake," she whispered. "I promise it's going to be all right."

But they were empty words. She could make no such promises.

When his grief had run out of strength for the moment, he loosened his arms.

Slowly, she let go of him.

He looked like a little boy in a broken man's body, she thought as she stroked his hair back from his damp forehead. Tears still rolled slowly down his temple, but he was too exhausted to wipe them away.

She stroked his forehead until his wet eye finally closed, until she felt the last ounce of fight seep out of him, until she heard his breathing settle into a relaxed cadence.

When she was sure he was sleeping, she went to get someone to clean up the mess he'd made.

But she didn't leave him until someone from her floor came and forced her to.

For it was only now that she realized just how alone he was. As much as he might hate her, she was all he had.

15

HE FINGERED THE newspaper photo of the crashed plane, still amazed that anyone had survived. It should have been a sure thing. He'd snipped the hose with such precision, leaving it partially intact so that it wouldn't be noticed on the preflight. When the landing gear engaged, the pressure in the line was certain to tear it the rest of the way. The gear would go partially down without locking—a deadly combination of problems. They should have been the last ones she would ever encounter.

But Lynda Barrett had a way of getting around sure things.

He clenched his jaw in frustration as he picked up the phone and dialed the number he had memorized for the hospital. He'd gotten daily updates on her condition, posing as a reporter one day, an uncle the next, a deacon another. The nurses had been unusually forthcoming, probably because her injuries were so minor. She'd be going home soon, he'd been told. Now he just had to find out when.

He asked for the nurse's station on her floor then waited as he was transferred. After a few rings, someone answered.

"Third floor nurse's station. Sarah McNair speaking."

"Sarah!" he said as though he knew her. "How's it going?"

She hesitated, trying to place his voice. "Fine."

He grinned. He loved throwing people off guard.

"Listen, this is Bob Schilling, Lynda Barrett's law partner. I just tried calling her room, but the line was busy. I wonder if you can tell me yet if she's had any word on when she might be released."

"Uh . . . just a second. I'll check."

He waited as she left the phone. She was back in just a moment. "I'm sorry, but there's no word yet. We may keep her a couple more days. Would you like for me to transfer you to her room?"

"No need. I'll drop by to see her this afternoon. You gave me what I needed for now. Thanks a lot, Sarah."

He hung up, frowning, and wondered whether he should make his move now, rather than waiting until she returned home.

But how?

He checked his watch. Three hours before he had to be at work. Time enough to pay the hospital a visit, check out the possibilities, and formulate a plan. If he played his cards right and caught her while she was sleeping, he might even be able to get into her room to see if she is on an IV. Maybe he could inject it with something—aspirin to thin her blood, maybe. Or he could grind up some of his blood-pressure pills. Maybe enough to make hers crash. Maybe this crash she wouldn't survive.

One way or another, he was going to get her out of his way. Lynda Barrett's luck was about to run out.

16

HE KNEW THEY were cops the minute he spotted them. It was probably the sports coats that tipped him off, he thought; cops always wore coats to cover the guns strapped under their armpits. Or maybe it was the way they walked, with that quick, arrogant stride, as though they didn't exist on the same plane as everyone else. Then the radio blaring in their unmarked car confirmed it.

Were they here to talk to Lynda? he wondered. Had they realized yet that the crash was not an accident?

Curious, he sped up to join the two men where they waited for the elevator. Rubbing his hand over the slick hair he'd combed back, he tried to assess them over the frames of his glasses.

One of them, the dark-haired one who stood at least four inches above him, flashed him a smile. He hoped they'd never seen his picture before. The last thing he needed was to be identified before he even got to her room.

The elevator doors opened, and he followed them on.

"Which floor?" the blonde cop asked the other one.

"She's on three; he's on four. You want to talk to her first?"

"Might as well," he said, punching the button. "How about you? Where are you going?"

For a moment he didn't realize they were addressing him. "Uh . . . three."

"We may not be able to talk to him," the tall one said. "They're saying he's in pretty bad shape."

"We need to, man. Our hands are tied until we do."

The bell rang, and the number three flashed above them. The doors opened, and they all stepped off.

He looked both ways up the hall, as if trying to figure out which way to go. The two cops headed for the nurse's station. Taking out their badges, they flashed them to the first nurse they approached.

"Hi, Ma'am. I'm Larry Millsaps, St. Clair Police Department. This is my partner Tony Danks. Could you tell us Lynda Barrett's room number, please?"

He made a mental note of their names. He might need to know them later.

"Lynda's in 413. Down that hall and to the left."

"Thanks a lot." They started in the direction she was pointing.

He stepped into the waiting area and watched as they disappeared into her room.

What were they up to? Until now, the crash had been ruled an accident, at least according to the television. They couldn't know that someone had sabotaged the plane, could they? No—they were here for something else.

He eyed the room next to hers; there was a name on the door. But the room on the other side of hers appeared to be empty. Checking behind him to make sure no one was watching, he went into the vacant room.

The bathroom door was on the side adjacent to Lynda's room. The door was closed. He remembered being in a hospital once that had rooms that adjoined through the bathroom, and carefully, he turned the knob.

The door opened quietly, and he peered in. Another door was on the other side. It must open into Lynda's room.

Grinning, he went in and pressed his ear against the door. He couldn't hear, so he hesitated a moment weighing the risk and then turned the knob.

The door opened silently, and he heard her voice.

Perfect. If he could get this close, he could wait until she was alone. Maybe he could wait until she slept, then put a pillow over her face. That way he wouldn't have to worry about IVs and blood thinners. He could take care of her with his bare hands and make sure that he did the job right this time.

Then, as quickly as the thought had come, he realized how absurd it was. The cops had seen him. If she were found smothered in her bed, wouldn't they consider everyone who'd been on the floor a suspect? Of course, they'd still have to find him and identify him, but it was too risky. When he finally took her out, he needed an alibi. He needed to be far enough away that they could never pin it on him.

For now, just listening was enough. Maybe he'd hear what he needed to hear.

17

"YOU'RE THE PILOT," Larry told Lynda as she sat up in bed, all bruised and scraped and stitched, like a mad scientist's experiment. "Maybe you can help us figure out what kind of person might know enough about planes to cut exactly the right hose."

Lynda shrugged. "A mechanic, I suppose. I'm not sure *I* would have even known which hose to cut."

Tony paced to the window and looked down on the parking lot. "What we're trying to determine is whether we're dealing with someone who's very familiar with planes or someone who didn't know what he was doing and just got lucky."

"Lucky, huh?" Lynda said in a dull, flat voice, and Larry wished Tony had chosen a better word.

"See, Lynda," Larry threw in, "it was difficult to determine if there was anything else tampered with, since the fire destroyed so much, but from what the NTSB can tell us, that was the only hose that was cut. It seems pretty deliberate. Calculated. Like someone who knew planes well had done it."

Lynda agreed. "It would have to be someone who's done a lot of work on airplanes."

Larry shot Tony a look. "So I guess that narrows down our hunt to someone with a background in aircraft mechanics or maintenance or maybe someone who had built planes."

"Did you interview all the guys who work at the airport?"

"We're in the process of doing it now. The problem is, we aren't having any luck finding anyone who has a vendetta against you."

Pulling her robe tighter around her, Lynda got out of bed and went to the dresser across the room. "I've been racking my brain since yesterday to think of anyone who might hate me. Maybe people whose cases I lost or didn't get along with or people I've been rude to." She let her voice trail off and tried to blink back the tears as she pulled a small notebook out of the drawer. Pulling out a piece of paper with a short list on it, she handed it to them. "These people wouldn't put me on their top-ten list of favorite people. But I can't see *any* of them doing something so deadly. I felt guilty even putting their names down."

"Anything would help at this point," Larry said, examining the list. "So who's this first guy?"

"Jack Gild. A client whose business was being sued, and I lost the case. He had to file bankruptcy, and he lost his home. He was really angry."

"What kind of business was it?"

"He repaired medical equipment. He was real mechanical, but I don't know if he knew about airplanes."

"What about this one? Doug Chastain?"

She sighed. "That was a client I dropped because he was so hard to get along with. I should have stuck it out, but I cut him loose before we went to trial, and it might have hurt his case."

"Did he make any threats?"

"No, not to my face. He really didn't seem like the violent type. He just had an attitude."

"What were his charges?"

"Arson. He and some friends got drunk and set a girl's yard on fire, just for kicks. Unfortunately, the house caught fire, too."

"How old is he?"

"Maybe twenty."

"What's he doing now?"

She shrugged. "I don't know. He served a little time, but I haven't kept up with him. And that third name, Gordon Addison. Well, I feel silly even putting it down. It's a pilot who's asked me out several times, but I didn't go. He has a tremendous ego, so I thought maybe. . . ."

"That he might try to get even for his hurt pride?"

She winced. "Actually, it's ridiculous. Just mark him off. Talk about egos. I'm as bad as he is if I could imagine him being that torn up over my rejecting him."

"We'll just question him like we're questioning everybody. He won't know you gave us his name."

"All right." She sank back down on her bed. "This is the hardest thing I've ever done."

"It might save your life. Try to think of more names, Lynda. It's possible that your plane was picked randomly, that all of this had nothing to do with you specifically, but until we can determine that for sure, I think we have to assume it was someone going after you."

She went back to her bed and sat back on the pillows. "It's just so unbelievable."

"It always is when something like this happens."

"But who would want me dead?"

"Like he said," Tony suggested, "it may not be you at all. In fact, it's occurred to us that it could have been someone after Jake."

"But it wasn't his plane."

"Maybe someone knew he was looking at it. We're going to talk to him next."

Lynda's face changed. "I don't know if that's a good idea."

"Why not?"

"He's . . . having a real hard time. He's depressed. Really depressed. I don't know if he can take any pressure right now, especially if you're planting the seed in his mind that someone may have done this to him deliberately."

"It's a long shot," Larry said. "But we have to ask. Don't worry. We'll try to be sensitive. But sometimes it's helpful for someone in his position to have a chance to brainstorm with us. It gives them back a little control. If they know something's being done—"

"But nothing really *is* being done, is it?" she asked quietly. "I mean, you don't know who it is, so you can't do any more than I can."

"But we can keep digging until we reach the bottom," Larry told her. "And that's exactly what we intend to do."

Lynda stared into space for a while after they had left, wondering whether, indeed, someone wanted her or Jake dead and why. It was crazy. It was amazing. It was unlikely.

Yet it had happened.

She heard a knock and thought the detectives had forgotten something. "Come in."

Gordon Addison, one of the men whose names she had put on the list, stepped inside.

"Gordon!" she said, every muscle in her body tensing.

He smiled—which may have been, she realized, the first time she'd ever seen that expression on his face. "I didn't know if it was appropriate for me to come," he said stiffly. "But I wanted to bring you some flowers and tell you you're missed at the airport."

Her heartbeat accelerated as she took the flowers wrapped in tissue paper and tried to look grateful. "You shouldn't have, Gordon. But thanks. That's so sweet."

"How do you feel?"

"Better," she said. "I'm expecting to get out soon."

"Great. That's good news."

An awkward silence settled between them, and she looked down at the flowers, as if studying the petals.

"Well," he said, finally. "You look tired. I'll go. I just wanted to bring those by."

She swallowed. "Thank you. Really."

She watched as he left the room, and when the door closed behind him, she let out a deep breath and wilted back on her pillow. She should be ashamed, she thought. All he'd ever done to her was ask her out then act hurt because she wouldn't go. He wasn't a killer. Didn't the flowers prove that he was only trying to be nice?

But *someone* had tried to kill her. Someone who'd gotten into the airport. Someone who knew airplanes. Someone who had a vendetta. That made it hard to be anything less than suspicious of someone like Gordon, who met those criteria as well as anyone.

Finally, she picked up the phone, hoping she could catch Larry and Tony in Jake's room.

18

JAKE WAS SO relieved to have visitors that forced his therapists to postpone his torture for an hour that he would have told the cops anything just to keep them there.

But for the life of him, he couldn't come up with the name of anyone who might want him dead.

"Think," Larry said. "You had looked at the plane the day before. Who knew about that?"

Jake shrugged. "Well, a few people. There's the first officer I fly with sometimes. We had a few drinks the night before while he was laid over. And there was the woman I met in a club that night . . . and some of her friends. . . ."

"Can you name them?"

He moaned. "The pilot is Frank Adkins. But as for the others, I can't even remember the name of the woman I was with. I'm not very good with names. Besides, why would someone who'd just met me want me dead?"

"You tell us," Tony said.

Jake was getting tired of this. "Nobody wants me dead, okay? It was *her* plane."

"Well, that's what we're thinking, too," Tony said. "But we just thought we'd try. If you think of anybody, maybe you could give us a call."

"Sure," Jake said, watching him set his card down on the bedside table. "If I come up with any valets I didn't tip enough or any gas-station attendants I might have offended, I'll let you guys know."

"And we might call you, if we think of any questions you might be able to answer."

"I'm not going anywhere," Jake assured them. "Look, you find that guy, okay? You find whoever it is and tell him what he did to me. He may not have wanted me dead, but you can sure bet that I'd love to see *him* dead. And if I ever get the chance—"

"We have to find him first," Tony said.

The door opened, and Abby stuck her head in. "Jake, Lynda was trying to call your room, darlin', but the phone wasn't working."

Jake glanced at it sitting cracked and lopsided on his table. "What did she want?"

Abby came in further. "Are you gentlemen from the police department?"

"Yes," Larry said.

"Well, she said to tell you that as soon as you left, one of the guys she put on her list visited her. Gordon somebody. He just left."

Tony and Larry looked at each other. "We'd better go," Tony said.

"Yeah." Larry patted Jake's arm and mumbled, "Take care."

Abby followed them out, and Jake watched the door close behind them then let out a labored breath. He wondered if the cops' questions had frightened Lynda. She was probably scared to death, and he couldn't really say he blamed her. He wondered if the guy who'd done this to them would really have the guts to show up here.

She'd given them a list, they'd said. Her paranoia about people she'd insulted, offended, or defeated almost amused him, but it really wasn't funny. She was struggling to think of people who had reason to be irritated with her since she couldn't think of anyone who hated her outright.

On the other hand, there were plenty of people who hated him. Women whose hearts he'd broken, men whose women he'd stolen, people he'd walked on, stepped on, kicked in the teeth—

Even his own mother.

He shoved the thought out of his mind.

Frustrated, he tried to sit up and move his legs, as if he could jump off the bed and run as fast as he could from his own thoughts, but they wouldn't budge. Finally, he gave up in a sweat and collapsed back into the pillows.

Why hadn't he just died?

Maybe it wasn't too late. Maybe if he just kept his eyes open for an opportunity, he would find a way to do just that.

If there was a hell for people like him, it couldn't be any worse than this.

Lynda saw the vacuous look in Jake's eye when she came to his room hours later. It was a haunting look, a look that spoke of defeat and self-loathing, that said he would throw the towel in if only he had a towel and knew where to throw it.

He seemed unwilling to look her in the eye now. She wondered if he were beating himself up for holding her and crying against her yesterday. He was probably surprised she had let him, after the way he had treated her. He had just finished throwing things at her, for pete's sake, as if doing her further harm could somehow relieve him of his own injuries.

But Jake Stevens didn't seem like the type to let anyone see him so unveiled, so vulnerable. And she could tell he didn't like it.

"Did you talk to Larry and Tony?" she asked.

"The cops? Yeah, I talked to them. Did they catch up with the guy who visited you?"

"I don't know," she said. "I never heard."

"They seem to know what they're doing. Maybe they'll find whoever did this. I just wish I could get out and look for him myself. You don't know how many times I've dreamed of getting my hands around his throat and showing him just what he did to me."

The words startled her, but then she realized that she had had the same fantasy. "I just want to know why he did it. What if we had died?"

She saw the raw pain growing more pronounced on his face. Covering his bandage with his wrist, he lay quietly for a moment. "Funny," he said finally. "I've been more concerned with the consequences of living."

He was back, she thought, that man who had been broken, vulnerable, and honest yesterday. Taking a chance, she reached down and touched his hand and moved it away from his face to make him look at her. "What do you mean?"

When he looked up, she knew the barrier was gone. This was Jake, the man so full of pain that he couldn't contain his grief or his rage, the man she liked more than the one he often pretended to be. "I mean if I'm paralyzed, I'll lose my pilot's license. Even in the best-case scenario—if my legs do start working again—I've still lost an eye. Which means I'm out of a job. There's disability, of course, or I could take a desk job. But TSA has a policy against keeping pilots who are damaged goods. And did I mention the fact that my face has a gash the size of the San Andreas Fault? The Elephant Man didn't have anything on me."

When she couldn't find the words to take his pain away, she squeezed his hand. And he squeezed back. It was something, she thought.

Trying to lighten the mood, she said, "No, but what's *really* wrong?"

He shot her a look that said she was crazy, but when he saw the grin in her eyes, he began to laugh softly. "Maybe I just need a hobby," he said facetiously.

"Sure," she teased. "You should take up woodworking or something."

"I'm actually thinking about taking up jogging. I hear there's a great running track on the roof of this building. And if running doesn't boost your spirits, you can always jump."

Her grin faded. "That's not funny."

His smile died as well. "No, it isn't. Don't mind me. I'm just fantasizing."

"You don't need to fantasize about suicide, Jake. That's not the answer."

She saw the mist welling in his eye as he looked away. "Then what is? The doctors told me I'll never take a step again. So tell me what good physical therapy will do me."

"None," she admitted, "if you go into it determined to fail. Besides, I know they've told you that there's a chance you could walk again. I've asked them myself."

"All right," Jake conceded. "A slim chance. A next-to-nothing chance. And judging by the way my legs are lying here like limbs on a corpse, I'd say the chances are even slimmer than that."

"And what odds would they have given either of us for surviving that crash? Probably none, Jake. And they sure wouldn't have bet on my being able to go home tomorrow, less than a week after the crash."

"They're letting you out?" he asked, his gears suddenly shifted.

She wondered at his choice of words. Did he consider this a prison? "Yes. Only because I have someone at home who can help me out."

"Yeah? Who's that?"

"A client of mine who needed a place to stay. But my point is that—"

"Well, if that's the criteria, I guess I'll grow old here."

She forgot what she was saying, and for a moment, just looked at him. "You're going to be all right, Jake. And if you need anything—I could go by your hotel room and bring you all your things. Or go to the store for you. I could sneak you in a hamburger. . . ."

Jake looked up at the ceiling, his face expressionless. "Get off it, Lynda. You're gonna leave here without looking back, just like I'd do."

"No, I'm not," she said. "I'm going to visit you every day."

He moved his angry eyes back to her. "Why?"

"Because, I . . . I want to."

He let go of her hand. "I don't need your pity," he said as his lips began to tremble. "And I don't need your visits. We hardly even know each other, and we sure don't owe each other anything."

"Jake, there's no way I'm going to forget that you're lying in here. And pity is the last thing I feel for you. I'm not the one moaning about how you'll never walk again and how you need to get to the roof so you can jump off."

"What if I don't want you to come?"

"Tough," she said. "I'm coming, anyway."

For a moment, he seemed at a loss for a reply. Finally, he muttered,

"I'll believe it when I see it."

"Good."

There was a thick silence between them as they stared at each other, and finally his eyes softened infinitesimally. He reached for her hand again and held it in front of his face, as if examining it. "Are you sure it's safe for you to be at home?"

Instantly her courage deflated, and she felt like a broken, injured, frightened woman again. "I hope so. Mike seems convinced that no one's after me personally, that it was just some random act, that it could just as easily have been one of the other planes on the tarmac that night."

"And what do you think?"

She sighed. "I think I'll go along with his theory. I have to go on with my life, after all. And if there is someone after me, maybe having the police snoop around will deter him."

"Pretty optimistic, considering what you've been through."

"Yeah, well . . ." She looked down at their hands, clasped on his chest and felt a surge of warmth that there was someone who cared. "I'll be okay." Taking a deep breath, she redirected her thoughts. "Anyway, back to my offer. Do you want me to do anything for you when I get out?"

He considered that and realized there wasn't anyone else he could ask. And there were loose ends of his life to be tied up. Loose ends that he'd tried to handle by phone until now. "Yeah," he admitted finally. "There are a few things you could do once you get on the outside."

19

THE LIGHT ASSAULTED Jake with jackhammer force as Allie, his occupational therapist, threw open his drapes the next morning.

"I like them closed," he muttered.

"Don't be silly. You can't lie here in the dark all day. You need sunlight to motivate you."

"Motivate me to do what? Roll over? I've gotten real good at that already."

"Nope," she said. "You're going to sit up today. We're gonna get you in a wheelchair if it kills you."

"It might," he said, getting angry. "We've only gotten to twenty degrees without me passing out or puking all over the place, remember?"

"Buzz is bringing a special wheelchair that reclines. We'll move you up as slowly as we need to. And to help with the circulation, I brought you these TEDS."

She held up a pair of stockings, and Jake moaned. "Forget it. I'm not wearing those. There's got to be a limit to the humiliation."

"Oh, yes, you are." She uncovered his legs and began to work a stocking over one foot. "And then we're going to wrap the legs tight with Ace bandages. It'll help you fight the orthostasis, so we can get you sitting up." As she spoke, she worked the tight stocking up his calf then propped his foot on her shoulder as she pulled it over his knee. "Tonight we're gonna start you on sequential compression stockings to keep the blood from pooling in your legs while you're asleep."

"If I could kick, I'd send you flying," he gritted as she got the stocking up his thigh.

"If you could kick, none of this would be necessary."

He lay on his back, miserable, as she fought the other stocking up then began wrapping both legs so tightly that he imagined his face turning red. He was almost glad he couldn't feel them.

"I have this theory about Mary Poppins," he told her through his teeth.

"Mary Poppins?"

"Yeah. You remind me of her. I hated her even when I was a kid. I've always thought she was a child abuser, leading those kids into all sorts of danger, introducing them to bums and no-accounts, playing with their heads. She was probably an occupational therapist before she was a nanny."

Allie looked undaunted. "Well, I did finish Torture 101 at the top of my class."

She finished wrapping just as Buzz came in followed by two orderlies, pushing a black monstrosity on two wheels.

"Hey, Jake," he said, just as cheerfully as Allie. "You ready to go for a ride?"

"You people are crazy. If I don't pass out in the first ten seconds—"

"When you start feeling faint, we'll lay you back for a few minutes," Buzz said. "This chair reclines to whatever angle we need. It'll be slow going, but we've got to get you sitting up before we can get on with serious therapy."

There was nothing he could do to stop them, so Jake braced himself as they surrounded his bed.

"All right now, on the count of three," Buzz said. "We're going to lift you carefully into the chair, lying flat. Our goal is just to get into it for a few minutes. Are you ready?"

Jake couldn't answer, but it was just as well. At the count of three, they lifted him into the chair.

Allie was all business now as she adjusted the recline of the chair and moved his foot rests to elevate his feet then carefully positioned them. Then she gave Buzz the signal to begin raising him up. "Easy, easy . . . How do you feel, Jake?"

He couldn't find words to describe the agony of dizziness and nausea. Sweat dripping from his chin, he muttered, "Sick."

"He's pale. Let him down," she said, and they lowered him flat again.

"Imagine how bad it'll be when it's moving," he whispered.

"You'll get over it, Jake. Come on now. Let's try it again."

He groaned as they pulled him back up. "Talk about motivation," he said, breathing hard. "I'm starting to feel some. I'm wanting real bad to move these feet so I can ram them through your teeth."

Buzz suppressed his grin. "Well, we all have to have goals. But if it's any consolation, I've been there. I was in a bad car wreck when I was nineteen, and I had injuries real similar to yours." He held out his hands, as if he might burst into a shave-and-a-haircut routine. "And look at me now."

"Yeah, well, I'm not nineteen, and they told me I may never walk again."

"They told me that, too, man. But with hard work, I overcame it. That's why I went into physical therapy. I'm gonna do everything I can for you, too. Trust me. You do what we say, try really hard, and I promise you, if we don't have you walking within a few months, you'll at least be able to function within your disability."

Jake looked down at the wheelchair beneath him and realized for the first time that he truly was disabled now. He was one of those people he got impatient with in stores because they took up too much room in the aisles and slowed him down. He was one of those people who had to be boarded first on airplanes and needed special attention getting off. He was one of those people he had always looked at with an air of superiority, an air that said, "Sorry you're disabled, pal, but you're in my way."

Disabled. The word hung in his heart like a fish hook, and that familiar, fighting anger spread through him like an infectious disease.

"After we get you up higher," Allie said gently, "I can take you for a ride. You're probably ready to get out of this room on something besides a gurney, aren't you?"

He had seen a Stephen King movie once where a deranged nurse had wheeled her victim into walls, down stairs, and dumped him out into a heap on the floor when she was finished with him.

"No thanks," he muttered.

As if in punishment, they began raising him up again until his stomach churned.

By the time they had worked him up to forty-five degrees, Jake was exhausted.

"I—I think we damaged something," he grunted after they moved him back to his bed. "My head feels like it's about to burst."

"That's normal, Jake. At least now you know that you don't have to lie on your back all the time. You can sit up, and you can get out of bed. We may get you all the way up tomorrow. And before you know it, we can change you to a lighter-weight chair, and you can get in and out of it by yourself. After that, we may be able to send you home."

Home, Jake thought with a sinking heart. Where was that? He'd sold his condo in Houston, and everything he owned was here, except his car, which he couldn't drive. He didn't have a job, a place to live, or any friends to speak of.

And he might as well not have any family.

As Allie and Buzz left, he dropped his head back on the pillows. Home, he thought. What had once been such a given, such an expected element in his life was now something he didn't have. He was not only disabled, but he was also homeless. He didn't even want to think of all the biases he'd once had against homeless people.

He had no idea where home would be when he was released from here. At least he wouldn't be released for months and months. But that thought, his greatest comfort, was also his greatest fear.

20

"YOU DIDN'T HAVE to come get me," Lynda told Paige the next morning when she met her in the lobby. "I could have had Sally bring me home."

"Well, that would be silly," Paige said. "Sally has plenty of work to do, and I'm just sitting there in your house."

Lynda looked down at the child sitting on the lobby floor, playing with a puzzle. She looked so safe today, so secure. "Paige," Lynda said with a heavy sigh, "we need to talk."

Paige's face took on a guarded look, and she started twisting her hair into a pony tail. "Okay."

Lynda sat down on the couch and glanced around, making sure no one could overhear. No one sat nearby. "Paige, they've found out that someone sabotaged my plane and caused my crash."

"How awful!" she said.

"Yeah, it's pretty awful," Lynda said. "But the really awful part is that this person might have been trying to kill me. We don't know."

Paige twisted her hair harder. "Do you know who it could be?"

Lynda shook her head dolefully. "I've thought and thought. But the bottom line is, if someone is out to get me, then anyone with me is also in danger."

Paige let her hair fall. "You want us to move out."

"No, that's not what I want. I just wanted you to know the danger. You have to know that living in my house might be putting you and Brianna in jeopardy."

Paige considered her child for a moment, then brought her gaze back to Lynda. "Are you scared?"

Lynda tried to find honest words to express what she felt. "I think . . . that maybe . . ." She failed and tried again. "I don't know. It could have been just a fluke that he picked my plane. But that's really just what I want to believe. If I'm wrong . . ."

Paige sat slowly back down on the couch, the look on her face telling Lynda that she couldn't take much more. "You don't need the stress of having us around anyway."

"I'd love to have you around, Paige. You know that's not it. And if you still want to stay, you can. You just had to know."

For a moment, she watched Paige's big blue eyes wrestle with the decision. Other visitors waited on the couches or milled through the lobby. The elevator bell kept ringing every few seconds, and on the intercom doctors were paged and codes were recited. In the corner across the room, a television was on, and a few children sat transfixed in front of it.

When Paige finally brought her eyes back to Lynda, Lynda fully expected Paige to thank her, then say that she would find another place to stay. But Lynda had underestimated the girl's desperation.

"Well, Lynda, I guess I see it like this. If I go home, I'm in absolute, inevitable danger. And if I stay with you, I may be in danger—but I may not. And since I don't see any other possibilities right now, I think Brianna and I will stay."

Lynda hadn't realized how much she had hoped Paige would say that until she heard the words. "Good," she said. "I'm glad." She reached out and squeezed Paige's hand. "We're in God's hands, Paige. I believe that. We're going to be all right."

And as they left the hospital, Lynda believed it more than ever.

21

TODAY. SHE WAS going home today. Thanking the nurse who'd given him the information, he hung up the phone, leaned back, and laughed.

So much for patience. He didn't have to wait even one more day.

But he had a lot of work to do if he was going to take care of things tonight. He'd heard every word that she'd said to the police that day in her hospital room, and the knowledge empowered him, even while it created a new urgency. He had to do this quickly before they managed to stop him.

Grabbing his car keys, he dashed out of his apartment, his spirits higher and more hopeful than they had been since the day of the crash.

22

THE AIRPORT LOOKED just the same as it had the morning of the crash, and as Paige pulled her car into a parking place facing the fence—and beyond that, the runway—Lynda found herself reliving that morning. It had been windy, like this, and she remembered thinking she should have postponed the test flight. If only she had. But that wouldn't have helped, would it? The crash would have happened anyway the next time she took the plane up, and she might not have survived the landing if she'd been alone.

"Are you all right?" Paige asked quietly.

Lynda shook herself out of her reverie. "Yeah. Fine. It's just kind of weird, coming here after what happened."

Paige crossed her arms over the steering wheel. "Is it really necessary? I mean, I'm sure Jake's car is fine."

"I just have to get his hotel key out of it," she said. "And I want to get Mike to move it someplace where Jake doesn't have to worry about it."

Paige checked the back seat where Brianna was sound asleep in her car seat, and she patted Lynda's hand. "You go on in and do what you need to. I don't want to wake her up. Take your time, okay?"

"Okay." Wincing against the pain in her ribs when she twisted, Lynda got out of the car and went inside.

The small airport was just as she remembered: the blue couches forming a square in the middle of the floor; the line of vending machines against one wall; the posters of exotic places; the rest rooms; the tall desk that looked like a concession stand but was really Mike's version of a control tower.

Mike sat there now, sipping on coffee and going over paperwork. He looked up when she started toward him.

"Lynda!" Spilling his coffee, he blotted it up quickly then came around the desk to meet her. "What in the world are you doing here?"

She hugged him, careful not to test her ribs, and he led her to a seat and made her sit down. "They sprang me this morning."

"You should have called me," he said. "I would have picked you up. Are you okay? Do you need a wheelchair? I have three."

She couldn't help being amused. "Mike, relax. I'm fine. I may look like Frankenstein's daughter, but I'm really okay."

"But you aren't supposed to drive this soon after your surgery, are you? And shouldn't you be at home—?"

She touched his arm to stem his rambling. "I didn't drive. I have a friend out in the car waiting for me. I just came to make some arrangements about Jake's car and get some things out of it for him."

"Oh. Well, okay. I have it parked in the hangar."

Getting to her feet, she tried to look stronger than she was. "Do you have the keys?"

"Yeah. He left them in the ignition that day. I locked it up and put the keys in my safe." He hurried around behind the desk and unlocked the safe.

"Here they are." He handed them to her. "I'll walk out to the hangar with you."

"No," she said. "It's okay. You need to stay here. Who knows? Somebody's landing gear might fail."

He hesitated then looked at the controls behind his desk and realized she was right. "All right," he said. "Are you sure you'll be all right?"

"I'll be great."

She pushed through the glass door of the airport, and the wind immediately whipped her hair into her face. Shoving it back, she peered across the concrete to Runway 4. She wasn't sure exactly where her plane had ended up—the crash was such a blur to her now—but she remembered waking up and seeing Jake crushed and twisted and bleeding, and she remembered sliding him to the door. . . .

Shivering, she started to the hangar.

It was open, as it usually was this time of day, and planes sat lined up, waiting to be flown. There was a big space where she had occasionally parked *Solitude,* and tears came to her eyes. But she reminded herself that she hadn't come here to mourn, and she blinked the tears away. She had things to take care of.

She saw the red Porsche parked at the back of *Solitude*'s empty space, and slowly she started toward it.

"Lynda? How are you doing?"

She looked up; one of the mechanics was standing on the wing of a plane. "Hi, Mac. I'm great."

"You sure look a lot better than I expected you would after I saw that plane hit."

She smiled. "It'll take a lot more than a little ole plane crash to get me down."

He laughed. "It's good to have you back."

But her smile faded. She wasn't back. Not really.

She went to Jake's car and unlocked the door, but as she did, she heard footsteps behind her. She turned and saw Gordon Addison.

Though she waved, a shiver went through her again; quickly, she got into the car and locked it shut. Trembling, she looked back at him through the windshield, wondering whether he knew she had given his name to the police or whether they'd caught him leaving the hospital and interrogated him about why he'd come. He was standing half in the shadow of his plane, staring at her as if surprised to see her. That look frightened her, and she found it hard to breathe. She had to calm down. He probably wasn't the one who'd done this to her, and she had no reason to be frightened. Besides, there were witnesses all around them here in the hangar—mechanics and maintenance people, other pilots—and he couldn't do anything to her here.

When he disappeared behind his plane, she calmed down. He wasn't going to approach her. She was just being paranoid.

She tried to relax in the sleek interior of Jake's car, smelling the spearmint scent of the gum he kept on the dashboard. Opening his glove compartment, she found the hotel key just where he'd told her it would be. She pulled it out, along with the hairbrush he kept there, the sunglasses, and the ID tag that identified him as a TSA employee.

Putting them into the bag she'd brought with her, she looked around for anything else he might like to have. There was an aviation magazine on the passenger's seat—probably the same one in which he'd seen her classified ad—and she stuffed it into the bag to throw away. She flipped down the visor over the driver's seat and saw his checkbook. Slipping it out of the pocket that held it, she dropped it into the bag, and looked around for anything else. Only the gum, she thought, and he might like that.

She got out, opened the small trunk, and saw some of the bigger items he'd put there during his move—things he'd decided to bring to Florida himself rather than turning them over to the movers since he might need them before he found a place to live—and she took out what she thought she could carry and made a mental note to ask Mike to unload the other things and take them to Jake. The more personal items he had around him, the better he would feel.

Taking one last inventory, she reached for the trunk, wincing at the pain in her ribs, and closed it.

She jumped, startled—Gordon Addison stood leaning against the car, staring at her with his arms crossed. "You scared me, Gordon."

"What did you tell the police?" he asked.

She swallowed and looked toward the plane where Mac had been working. He was gone.

"What do you mean?" she asked, starting to back away.

He stayed where he was. "They came here this morning asking all kinds of questions. Where I was the night before the crash, what my relationship with you is, why I came to the hospital yesterday—"

"Well, they interviewed everybody here. They weren't singling you out."

He pushed away from the car then, the frown on his face revealing a deeper anger than she could hear in his voice. "I want to know what you told them."

"I told them something about everybody here, Gordon. Not just you." Again, she searched around for Mac or one of the other mechanics, and though she could hear some of them on the other side of the hangar, none was in sight.

"If you think I had anything to do with that crash—"

"Of course not," she cut in. "What reason would you possibly have?"

As if he turned that question over in his mind, he left it unanswered.

Lynda started to walk away. She half expected him to catch up with her, grab her, and stop her, but as she stepped out into the wind again, she turned back. He hadn't moved from where he was standing, and he was watching her.

With more energy than she could spare, she walked faster until she was all the way to Paige's car.

Later that night after Paige had cooked her the best meal she'd had since her mother died, Lynda walked outside to sit on the massive deck attached to the back of her house. The cool night air felt good on her face as she lay on a white wicker chaise lounge chair and gazed up into the stars. Somewhere, under these same stars, an enemy lurked with deadly intention. God knew who it was.

Maybe it wasn't Gordon Addison at all, she thought. Maybe it was some kid caught in a game, and now that he'd seen the results of his actions, he was remorseful and repentant. Maybe it *was* just an accident.

Or maybe not.

But the face of Gordon Addison, angry and pensive, staring at her in the hangar today still chilled her.

Across the deck, a cricket chirped, and she could hear the sound of the leaves in the oak tree whispering over her head. The breeze had grown cooler while she was in the hospital, but she knew it wouldn't stay that way for long. Soon the temperature would rise, and it would feel like summer again. Summer didn't let go easily in Florida.

The back door opened, spilling light out, and Paige looked startled. "Oh, I'm sorry. I didn't know you were out here. I was just going to take the garbage out, but I'll do it later."

"No, it's all right," Lynda said. "I was just thinking."

Paige set the garbage bag in the vinyl can next to the deck and took a step toward the chair. "Really, if you want to be alone . . ."

"Sit down, Paige," she whispered. "Brianna's asleep, everything's put away—you deserve to rest."

"Oh, I'm not tired. Really. I love doing household things. And I'm so thankful that you've given us a place to stay."

"You don't have to wait on me hand and foot just because you're grateful. I think I'm getting a lot more out of this deal than you are."

Paige was quiet for a moment. "I just want you to see that I'm . . . decent. I don't want you to think I'm just trash."

"Why would I think that?"

Paige had trouble meeting her eyes. "I don't know. That's what people think about women who have to hide from their ex-husbands. Things like this don't happen to 'nice people.'"

Lynda touched her hand and made her meet her eyes. "I've *never* thought you were trash, Paige. If anyone is, it's me, for not giving your case the priority it deserved."

"Well, why would you? I couldn't pay—"

"That doesn't matter," Lynda said. "You needed help, and I just became another problem."

Paige walked out to the railing of the deck and leaned back against it. She sighed and rubbed her eyes wearily. "Sometimes, I look back on the dreams I had growing up and all the promises I made myself, and I can't figure out how I got into all this."

"What promises, Paige?"

Paige turned her back to Lynda and looked out over the night. "Promises that I'd have a different kind of life when I grew up." She laughed softly, but there was no joy in the sound. "You know, the picket-fence promises. The ones about the knight in shining armor who would protect me instead of threatening me."

Lynda tried to listen beyond Paige's words. "Paige, did you come from an abusive home?"

Paige was silent for a while, and Lynda wondered if she'd heard her at all. When she finally spoke again, her evasion told Lynda what Paige couldn't. "Keith seemed like just the kind of man I needed. Strong and smart—have I told you that he has a genius IQ?"

The turn in the conversation surprised Lynda, but she tried to follow it. "Really?"

"Yeah. But he still keeps failing. He's a computer whiz, but he has trouble keeping a job because of his temper. I think he expected to really be somebody. But his IQ hasn't helped him much. That only adds to all that anger boiling inside him. I really don't think he means to let his temper blow up the way it does. He's just so used to being in control. Every time I leave him, it just sends him into a rage."

"You've left him before?"

Paige turned back. "Yeah, a few times."

Lynda sat up. "And you went back?"

Paige turned to the night again. "He convinced me to, every time. Told me how sorry he was, that he'd change, that he'd never lay a finger on me again. He really did love me, Lynda. I know he did. And I worried about him. Nobody understands him like I do."

Lynda got up then and went to stand beside Paige. She turned Paige to face her and saw Paige's tears. "You sound like you still love him."

Paige shrugged. "I just get so mixed up. Sometimes I hate him, and sometimes. . . ."

"But he hurt you, Paige. He hurt Brianna. How could you find any rationale for that?"

"He never means to, Lynda. It just . . . happens."

Lynda tried hard to keep her expression from revealing her amazement—or her judgment. "Paige, abusive husbands kill their wives all the time. They kill their children."

"I know that," she said. "That's why I'm here. That's why we're divorced. I'm just trying to explain to you why I'm in this position. I'm not stupid, you know. Things happen to people sometimes that are out of their control."

"I know that more than anyone." She reached out to stroke Paige's hair and wished she had the wisdom that Paige needed right now. "But Paige, you did what you had to do to protect yourself and your daughter. It took a lot of courage, but you did it. Don't back down now."

"I'm not," she said adamantly. "Besides, Brianna's scared to death of him. Whenever I get weak and think of going back, I remember that."

Lynda stared at her, wanting to blurt out that she was crazy if she'd even considered going back to Keith, that she needed to go to counseling and get help, and that she needed to step back and start looking at things realistically.

But then she realized that Paige didn't need to be condemned right now. She needed patience and understanding. And she needed someone she could count on. Maybe that was the reason God had forced Lynda to rearrange her priorities: so that she'd be here for Paige. Not as a judge but as a friend.

She only hoped she had the grace to put friendship ahead of her own personal biases.

23

THE FIVE-GALLON bug sprayer was perfect for the job. He screwed off the top, pulled the sprayer cord out, and dropped in the funnel he'd brought. Then, careful not to spill any, he poured the gasoline out of the can with the "J.R.'s Auto Repair" logo on the side.

That should be enough gas, he thought, checking his watch. It was after midnight. Lynda should be asleep by now since it was her first day home from the hospital. She was probably zonked out, what with those internal injuries and those painful broken ribs. She should thank him for putting her out of her misery.

He loaded the bug sprayer and the empty gas can into his car and drove across town to Lynda's house; he had located it days ago by simply looking up the address in the phone book. Turning down the exclusive street lined with groomed palm trees and extravagant homes, he did a drive-by, checking out the lights in the neighbors' houses, making sure there were no late-night walkers, no dogs liable to bark, no policemen staked out in parked cars.

He slowed when he reached Lynda's house, a two story Tudor style that reminded him of a miniature castle, and he thought how ironic that she had that whole house to herself when there were entire families living out of cars. She deserved whatever he gave her.

And it looked like the perfect night. No lights had been left on. The garage door was closed, and even the porch light was off. It would be easy to steal through the shadows and do what he had to do.

He drove the car around the block and parked at a vacant lot he'd found earlier. Quietly, he got out, pulled the empty gas can and the sprayer full of gasoline out with him, and cut through the trees separating the yards.

Her backyard was the third from the vacant lot. He slipped into her yard and saw the deck that would be the first to ignite. Quietly, he laid the empty gas can in the grass, close enough to the house to be found later but far enough away to escape harm. Stealing closer to the house, he began pumping the trigger on the sprayer and doused the side of the deck with gas.

The fumes reached his nostrils, satisfying him, and when he finished the deck, he ran a stream along the walls of the house, then turned up the side between the house and the garage, and kept spraying.

He sprayed until he ran out of fuel, and still there was no sign that Lynda had awakened. It was all falling perfectly into place.

Reaching into his pocket, he pulled out the matches he'd brought. All he had to do now was light it.

And then his problems would go up in flames.

24

ACROSS THE STREET, Curtis McMillan, an eighty-year-old retired judge, awoke from a sound sleep. It happened more and more often these days, this middle-of-the-night wake-up call, when he knew that going back to sleep would be next to impossible.

Careful not to wake Lizzie, who didn't have that problem and had slept like a baby since he'd met her his senior year of high school, he reached for his robe and slippers and padded into the kitchen.

Without turning on the light, he got a glass out of the cabinet and scuffed to the sink for water. Next to the sink were his glasses; shoving them on with his free hand, he brought the glass of water to his lips.

His eyes focused on the night outside the window and the shadows of windblown trees dancing on Lynda Barrett's house across the street. Poor woman, he thought. Bless her soul. He hoped she was recovering quickly and would be home soon. The crash was such a tragedy.

He set the glass down and started to head toward the den to see if any late-night movies worth watching were on, but as he turned, a movement outside caught his eye.

It was different from the shadows of trees. It moved more deliberately, more methodically, and he cupped his hands on the glass and peered out more earnestly.

It was a prowler, he thought, someone trying to break into Lynda's house.

His heart began pounding, as if he'd climbed that flight of stairs at the courthouse, and calling out, "Lizzie!" he reached for the phone.

He heard his wife stirring as he punched out 911. Just as the dispatcher answered, the perimeter of the house went up in flames, draping the walls like neon paint.

And he couldn't see the prowler any more.

By now, Lizzie was in the kitchen, and the dispatcher was waiting.

"It's a fire at 422 West Evan Street," Curtis blurted, and Lizzie looked quickly out the window and threw her hand over her mouth. "It's arson," he said. "I saw a prowler, and then it went up in flames."

"Oh, Curtis!" Lizzie shouted.

"It's okay," he said then to both the dispatcher and his wife. "Thank God nobody's home."

Lynda rested more soundly that night than she had since her plane crashed, tucked in her own bed on the second floor of her own home. The soft percale sheets on her queen-sized bed were a wonderful contrast to the hospital sheets, and as she snuggled down under her Laura Ashley comforter, she felt welcomed by the items around her she had grown to love: the antique furniture she had collected a piece at a time, the finely crafted vases with silk flower arrangements, the oriental rug on her hardwood floor, the small baskets of potpourri scattered around the room, and her favorite art hung in strategic places on her papered walls.

She had worked hard for these comforts, and as she slipped into the depths of sleep, she had a sweet contentment that all would be well.

But sometime just after midnight, a whining sound outside startled her. Disoriented, she sat up, looking around, hearing it more clearly. A siren . . . no, two or three sirens, right here on her street. She scrambled out of bed, but the moment her feet touched the floor she felt the heat and caught the faint smell of smoke.

"Paige!" Grabbing the pillow from her bed and holding it to her face, she ran down the hall to the guest bedroom where mother and daughter slept. "Paige, get up! There's a fire!"

Paige sat up and rubbed her eyes. "What?"

"The house is on fire! Get Brianna!"

As though a light had come on in her brain, Paige grabbed the child and began to cough. The smoke was more dense on this side of the house; Lynda was choking on it as well. Grabbing another pillow and wrestling it out of its case, she tossed the case at Paige. "Here, cover Brianna's face with this!"

"The floor's hot!" Paige shouted, and Brianna started to cry.

"We've got to get out!" Lynda cried as Paige followed her into the hall.

Lynda reached the top of the stairs in a half-dozen frantic strides then immediately jumped back; long, reaching flames were climbing the carpeted stairs and lapping against the wall. "We'll have to go out the window!" she shouted, pushing them toward the other end of the second floor. "Hurry, before the floor collapses!"

Two of the windows they passed were engulfed in flames from the outside, but at the far end of the house, the flames hadn't yet taken hold. Lynda threw open the window. "Climb out there on the roof. Hurry!"

Brianna's screams went up two octaves as she saw the flames licking their way up the side of the house. But holding her tightly, with the pillowcase pressed over the child's face, Paige climbed out and ran to the edge of the roof. Lynda followed her, ignoring the pain shooting through her ribs, pulling at her stitches, but she couldn't fight the dizziness beginning to take hold.

"How will we get down?" Paige screamed.

Only then did Lynda see the flashing lights of three fire trucks in front of her house. Someone shouted, "There's someone on the roof!"

In seconds, a ladder had been elevated to lift them down, out of the grasping hands of the flames.

They hadn't even reached the ground when the roof they'd been standing on caved in.

And so did Lynda. Covering her face in horror, she got off of the ladder and slid down to sit in the dirt, watching through her fingers as her house and everything she owned surrendered to the fire.

Brianna's wailing only echoed what was in Lynda's own heart as paramedics rushed to examine them. Lynda was just too tired and too stunned to express it herself.

"I'm so sorry, Lynda," a voice said above her as the paramedics put her on oxygen. She looked up into the troubled eyes of Curtis McMillan from across the street, who stood over her in his slippers and robe. "I didn't know you were home! I thought you were still in the hospital—I should have checked. I should have called."

She pulled the oxygen mask away from her face. "What are you talking about?"

"I woke up around midnight and happened to look out the window. I saw him start the fire, so I called the police, but I told them you weren't in there. I didn't know—"

"Wait a minute," she said. "You saw someone start the fire?"

"Yes," he said. "I thought it was a prowler at first. He was sneaking around your house, and the minute I had 911 on the phone, I saw him light it. The house went up in flames, but I didn't even check to see if you were in there."

"Did he go *into* the house, Judge?" she asked in a shocked whisper.

"I didn't see it if he did. But he must have doused it with gas because the fire caught instantly and circled the house—"

The paramedics were checking her vitals, prodding under her clothes, checking her incisions and her ribs. Impatiently, she shoved them away and got to her feet. "Judge, did you see his face? The color of his hair?"

The old man shook his head with distraught frustration. "He was more or less just a shadow. I only saw him for a second."

Smoke fell like a cloud around them as the flames devoured her house. Waving it away so she could breathe, she grabbed the old judge's arm. "I have to talk to the police," she told the frustrated paramedics. "I'm fine, really. Just let me go."

"But you probably need to go to the hospital! You need to be examined at least!" one of them said.

"In a minute," she said.

Lynda pulled the judge toward one of the trucks to find someone in authority. But as she did, she saw a car approaching, and Tony Danks and Larry Millsaps got out.

Still pulling the judge behind her, she met them at the car. "It was *arson!*" she blurted before they could even get out. "This is Judge Curtis McMillan, my neighbor. He saw the man who did it."

Larry shook the man's hand then somberly studied the house. "Thank God you got out."

"Only because he called." Lynda's face glowed with the orange reflection of the inferno as she gazed back at it. "He called 911. The sirens woke me up." Turning back to Larry, she said, "It's official now. Someone's trying to kill me."

Larry opened his arms and she collapsed against him, crying out her rage and terror as everything she loved burned down behind her.

25

"SO WHAT'S NEXT?" Lynda's voice was weary as she looked across Curtis's kitchen table to the two detectives who had spent the last hour questioning the old couple.

"We follow up on the leads we've got until we apprehend the right person," Tony said.

"You don't *have* any leads," she said in a hoarse voice. "You don't really have a clue who he is, do you?"

Larry leaned forward on the table, meeting her eyes directly. "Here's what we know, Lynda. It's probably a man, between five feet eight and five feet ten, around 180 pounds. We know that he has at least a working knowledge of airplanes—"

"And we have the gas can he used with the name of an auto repair shop on it, even though he didn't leave any fingerprints."

"And you know he wants me dead."

"Yes," Tony admitted. "That does seem to be his goal. Now all we have to do is find someone with a motive. We still need your help for that."

But Lynda couldn't help. Wearily, she got up and went to the same window through which Curtis had seen her house catch fire, and she peered at the smoldering pile of rubble that had once been such a source of pride. Next to the pile the garage still stood, unscathed except for the black scars from the fire that had just begun to penetrate the structure when the fire trucks arrived. Lizzie, who had been tending to a fresh pot of coffee, slid her arm around Lynda. "It'll be all right, honey. These young men aren't going to let anything happen to you."

Lynda didn't respond. Instead, she ambled into the living room where Paige and Brianna sat in a rocking chair. Brianna was asleep, and Paige's smoke-stained face looked numb with shock as she leaned her chin against her daughter's head and stared blankly in front of her.

"Well, I guess the thing to do now is figure out where we're going to go," Lynda said. "At least our cars survived."

"I was just thinking how glad I am that *we* did," Paige whispered, bringing her dull eyes back to Lynda's.

Lynda shook her head, feeling gently—and, she was sure, unintentionally—reproved. What were her lost treasures compared to her life? And Brianna's? "You're right. Once again for some reason, God spared us."

Lizzie squeezed Lynda's shoulder again. "Honey, I've already made up the guest rooms for you. You're going to stay here tonight, all three of you."

"No, Lizzie. That's sweet of you, but I can't do that."

"Why not?"

Her face reddened, and she hugged herself as a shiver ran through her. "Someone's trying to kill me," she said. "I'm not safe. And if I'm in your house, *you're* not safe. I shouldn't even be here now."

Lizzie's eyes drifted to her husband's. Curtis took the baton. "Lynda, don't you think you're safe enough tonight? I mean, he wouldn't dare come back, and besides, how would he know you were here?"

"It's okay," she said, waving off the questions. "I've got an idea. I still have my father's house on the other side of town. I've been trying to sell it, but I'll just have to live there until I can rebuild. It should be safe. Only a few people even know I have that house. If I don't tell anyone where I am . . ." She met Paige's eyes, and saw the despair on her face, the indecision. "Paige, I know you won't want to come with me, but I can give you some money so you can get by until he's caught. You could stay here or get a hotel—"

As if she'd spent the last hour holding them back with a paper-thin wall of resolve, Paige's eyes filled with tears. "Maybe I should just take my chances and go home."

"No," Lynda insisted. "You can't. Paige, we've come this far. Don't let this make you drop your guard."

Paige pinched the bridge of her nose and tried to steady her voice. "I can't keep taking your money, Lynda. I've got to start handling things myself."

"Not until after we go to court, you don't." Lynda stooped in front of her, making Paige meet her eyes. "I know this was traumatic tonight, but don't give up just because some lunatic is out to get me. That has nothing to do with you."

Larry, who had been jotting notes on a pad, looked up at Paige. "What do you mean, take your chances? What's the risk in going home?"

"My ex-husband." Paige swallowed, and a tear dropped from her cheek onto the top of Brianna's head. "He's abusive, and he's suing me for custody of Brianna. Lynda's representing me."

"She's not safe at home," Lynda cut in. "Despite our restraining order, he's tried to take Brianna, and he's broken into her house. That's why she's staying with me."

"I see." Frowning, he got up and paced across the kitchen. "And you don't have anyone else you can stay with?"

Paige shook her head. "My family is in Arizona. But the judge ordered me to stay in town until this court thing is settled."

Tony frowned and stared thoughtfully at Paige, as though flipping through possibilities in his mind. But it was Larry who had the solution. "Listen, Lynda, what if I guaranteed that we'll have someone guarding your father's house, at least for the next couple of days? That way Paige and Brianna could go with you, and you could feel safe. If it isn't common knowledge that you have that house, chances are you'd be okay there anyway."

Lynda was skeptical. "Larry, I know how the police department works. They're not going to waste a man guarding me twenty-four hours a day."

"I'll take care of it," Larry promised. "Even if Tony and I have to take turns on our off-hours, I know I can at least get them to agree to somebody the rest of the time."

Lynda glanced at Tony, who was gaping at Larry, but Larry ignored him. "You both need protecting. You might as well be in the same place so we can kill two birds with one stone."

Lynda smirked. "Somehow that cliché isn't very comforting to me right now."

"Sorry," Larry smiled. "So what do you say?"

Lynda turned her worried eyes back to Paige. "Paige, this is up to you. I can't ask you to put your life and your daughter's life in jeopardy to stay with me."

The turmoil on Paige's face told Lynda what a struggle this was. Then Paige wiped her eyes and settled her troubled gaze on Lynda. "Who'll take care of you if I'm not there? I promised. You just got out of the hospital. The doctor said—"

"Paige, I'll be fine. For heaven's sake, I just scaled the roof and got out of a burning house. I can take care of myself. I've done it for a long time."

Paige dropped her head back on the chair. "This nightmare just keeps getting worse."

They waited for her decision, not prodding her, and finally, she took a deep breath and tried to steady her voice. "I guess we'll stay in a hotel. But . . . I swear I'll pay you back someday, Lynda. I know it's hard to believe, but—"

"It's not hard to believe, Paige. But I don't care about the money right now. That's not important."

"I feel like I'm letting you down or taking advantage of you, and you've been so nice to me."

Stooping down in front of the rocking chair, Lynda stroked Brianna's sleeping head. "You aren't letting me down, Paige," she said softly. "You're protecting your daughter. I think you've made the right decision. And when they catch this guy, you can stay with me again."

Paige turned her worried face to Tony and Larry. "Do you promise you'll guard her? You won't let anything happen to her?"

"I promise," Larry said. "And we'll take you to the motel tonight to make sure you get there safely."

Tony didn't look too happy about all the promises Larry was making on his behalf, but he didn't argue.

Lynda's father's house sat at the end of a dead-end street; a thickly wooded area separated it from the other two houses back up the road. Looking out the living room window, Lynda realized that she'd never thought of her parents' house in terms of safety before. She had only seen it as too small, too old, too mundane for an up-and-coming young lawyer.

The furniture was worn and faded, hopelessly outdated. From the rickety rocker in the corner to the recliner that had provided the only comfort her father had been able to find in his last days, she had been ashamed of it all.

Now it was all she had.

And coming here from a position of vulnerability and fear, she found some comfort in that it was so secluded and so familiar.

Larry touched her shoulder, and she jumped. "Sorry," she said, embarrassed. "I guess I'm a little jumpy."

"Can't say I blame you." Stepping closer to the window, he peered out. "Well, one thing's for sure. No cars will be coming here by accident. If anyone comes this far up the street, they're looking for something."

Lynda glanced across the street; in the moonlight, she saw only one edge of the empty car backed into the wooded lot where Larry would be spending the rest of the night.

Turning away from the window, she looked back over the stale-smelling house she hadn't walked into in weeks. "It's pretty dusty in here. No wonder it hasn't sold."

Larry looked around. "It's homey. I like it."

"I used to hate it," she said pensively. "I couldn't wait to get away from here. My folks turned the garage into a little apartment for me when I started college since we couldn't afford for me to live on campus. It was a little more freedom, but I still felt so trapped here."

For a moment, she let melancholy creep in as she surveyed the living room where her parents used to spend so much time—her mother crocheting, her father reading the paper and watching "Jeopardy" at the same time, each occasionally blurting out an answer that often was right. The standing joke around the house was that someday her father's ship would come in by way of a stint on "Jeopardy," where he was certain to win. But he'd never made it.

Shaking off her thoughts, she sank wearily onto the gold-and-green plaid couch.

"Where's the linen closet?" Larry asked.

She gave him a questioning look. "At the end of the hall. Why?"

"I'm going to make a bed up for you," he said. "I don't think you want to sleep on a bare mattress."

"No, I can do it," she said, getting up. "Really."

"Sit down," he ordered gently. "I've had broken ribs before. And you're not in any shape to be up at this hour, much less dressing beds. Now, which bedroom do you want?"

She looked toward the hall for a moment, trying to decide. "The guest room. I don't think I can sleep in my father's room yet."

"How long has he been . . .?" The word fell off, and Lynda took a deep breath.

"Just three months."

"I'm sorry," Larry said. "Looks like a run of bad times for you."

"It could be worse," she whispered. "I thought it was bad luck that I hadn't sold this house, but now I see that God was saving it for me."

"No subtlety there, huh?"

Remembering what Mike had told her about Larry being a believer, she smiled as he left the room, and she heard him in the guest room, shaking out sheets and blankets, stepping around the bed. Was changing beds a part of his job description?

After a few minutes, he came out. "All done. You get some sleep now, and I'll be right out there in my car. No one's gonna get past me, so just relax. And tomorrow, I'll take you to the doctor to get checked out, just to make sure you didn't hurt yourself getting out of the house."

"I'm fine," she assured him, "but I need to go by the hospital anyway. I need to visit Jake."

"Then you can do both." He picked up the cellular phone he'd made her bring in from her car. "Now since you don't have a phone hooked up here, use this if you need to call anyone. I've got one in my car, too, and I've punched my number in here already. If you need me, all you have to do is punch the memory button and the number 1."

"Okay," she said, taking the phone. "Thanks."

He looked reluctant to leave her, and she knew it was because she looked so fragile. Lifting her chin and trying to look a little tougher, she said, "You don't have to worry about me, Larry. I'm really fine."

He sat down across from her, fixing his soft, green eyes on her. "You know, Lynda, you've survived two really narrow brushes with death in the last few days. You've seen two pretty obvious miracles, so maybe we'll get a couple more to help you out."

Lynda sighed. "I'm starting to wonder."

"About what?"

She swallowed, knowing that the thoughts raging through her mind bordered on blasphemy. "I just . . . sometimes wonder if God's really working in this. I mean . . . it's just all so bizarre. Why is he letting this person do these things to me? Is he trying to teach me something, or is he just turning his head, or is it Satan?"

"I personally don't like to attribute a whole lot to Satan," Larry said. "I believe God is in control. And he's working on this. I can tell."

She got up, trying not to cry, and turned her back to him. "Then why doesn't he just strike this person dead and keep him from terrorizing me anymore?"

"Because God doesn't work that way," Larry said. "If he did, Tony and I would be out of a job."

Lynda tried to laugh, but it didn't come easily. Taking a deep breath, she turned back around. "Thank you for watching over me, Larry. I feel better knowing you're out there."

"No problem," he said, getting up. "Call if you need me."

Lynda could only nod mutely as he went out the door and locked her in.

Across town, in a hotel room that was nicer—because Lynda had insisted on it—than the cheap motel Paige had stayed in just days before, Paige lay next to her sleeping daughter and stared up at the ceiling.

She heard the elevator ring, and her stomach tightened as she listened to the doors open and the footsteps in the hallway and then a door opening halfway down the hall. Relieved, she let out her breath.

Too many noises, she thought. Too many strange people around her. Too many reasons to be afraid.

She got up, went to the window, and peeked out between the crack in the curtains. Down in the parking lot, a trucker with a cigarette in his mouth walked around his eighteen wheeler, a huge rig that took up the whole back edge of the lot.

Everyone was suspect. Anyone could have set that fire. Anyone could have almost killed her and Lynda and Brianna tonight.

It was ironic that she had been staying with Lynda only to get out of danger in the first place.

Helpless, she dropped down onto the bed and closed her eyes against the tears assaulting her. How was she ever going to find peace in her life again? Would she spend the rest of her life running with Brianna, relying on the kindness of others? Even if she proved that Keith's allegations about her being an unfit mother were a lie and was allowed to keep custody of Brianna, wouldn't she still have to fear him for the rest of her life? Wouldn't he be able to track her down wherever she went?

Seeking comfort, she mouthed a clichéd prayer that she feared fell on deaf ears. "God, if you're listening—please help us."

Brianna jerked, and her face twisted in her sleep. As she muttered something incoherent, Paige began stroking her daughter's forehead. Was she dreaming about fire? Or about her father? Or was it some new nightmare, the next one, that her little mind was working through?

"It isn't fair," Paige whispered, not certain if she still addressed God or the black space around her. "She's too little to fear for her life. She's just a baby."

Brianna rolled over, found her mother, and snuggled in next to her.

And as Paige held her closely, that powerful maternal love that could fix boo-boos and scare away monsters washed over her, and she knew that whatever happened—whatever she had to do—she would protect her daughter.

26

STILL FLAT ON his back, Jake stared mindlessly at the television screen as Harry Smith interviewed someone in Washington about a bill being debated in the Senate. It didn't affect him, he thought, touching the bandage on his eye that had been changed this morning. Nothing affected him any more—he didn't have a job or a home or a life. He might as well not even exist for all the hope he had.

CBS broke for a commercial. After a detergent ad, the local news came on for an update. He reached for the remote control to change the channel as the anchor told about a fire in the exclusive Willow Heights area last night.

"Police suspect arson. The home belonged to local attorney Lynda Barrett, who—"

Jake dropped the remote control and tried to raise himself up. Dizziness assaulted him, and he dropped back down, straining to listen.

"—was involved in the plane crash at St. Clair Airport earlier this week. Sources told Channel 16 News that there is evidence that the crash was the result of foul play, and that this may have been a second attempt on Barrett's life. Barrett and two houseguests escaped the fire, but we have no word yet on whether they sustained any injuries."

Amazed, Jake groped for the buzzer to ring for his nurse. In moments, she was in the doorway. "What is it, Jake?"

"Do you have Lynda's number?" he asked.

"No, but I can look it up."

"You can't look it up!" he threw back. "Her house burnt down last night! Do you have her number at work?"

"Her house burnt down? Are you sure?"

"I saw it on the news," he said, breathing hard. "Was she—was she brought in here last night?"

"Well . . . I don't know. I can go check." She walked further into the room and peered at the television screen. "Do you think somebody's really trying to kill her?"

"Without a doubt," Jake said. "Just—get me a phone book. And a phone that works. I'll pay for the one I broke. And see if anybody knows anything."

The nurse hurried in, pulled the phone book from the drawer in Jake's table, and handed it to him. "Who are you calling?"

"Her office. Maybe her secretary can tell me where she is."

"I'll go see if she's checked in here," she said, scurrying out of the room.

27

CURTIS MCMILLAN SAT at his kitchen window, looking across at the neighbors clustering in Lynda's yard, marveling at how thoroughly, and how quickly, the fire had destroyed her home. He had watched all morning, trying to remember exactly what he'd seen, so that some detail that could help the police might come back to him. But there were no details. It had been too dark and had happened too fast.

He saw a car drive by, slow down in front of the skeleton of the house, then pull over on the side of the road. Curtis wondered if he was another reporter—there had been so many around early this morning. But as he got out, he saw that he didn't carry a camera or a notepad, and for a moment, he just stood and looked at the structure, as if stricken by what had happened. Then, slowly, he headed toward one of the clusters of neighbors.

"You should come away from that window, Curtis," Lizzie said. "You're getting obsessed with it."

Curtis glanced back at her over his shoulder. She was knitting—something for Brianna, he suspected. She had really taken to that little girl last night.

"It's not obsession, Lizzie," he said. "It's just that I don't remember when there's been this much excitement around here. People coming and going . . . Investigators, fire inspectors, reporters . . ."

His eyes strayed out the window again, and he saw that the man was questioning the neighbors, and one of them was pointing toward the McMillan's house. Was he asking who had reported the fire? Or something about Lynda?

The man started to cross the street toward his house, and Curtis stood up. Something about his walk looked familiar . . . and he was the right size . . . but he couldn't swear it wasn't just his imagination groping for the culprit, trying to make up for what he hadn't seen last night. But in all his years on the bench, he'd had many cases where the perpetrator of a crime had been caught returning to the scene. Could this be . . . ?

The doorbell rang, and Lizzie jumped up. "I'll get it. Probably another reporter."

But Curtis didn't think so. He went to stand behind her, and she opened the door slightly. "Yes?"

The man flashed a smile that made Curtis uncomfortable. "Excuse me, but I'm John Hampton, a close friend and coworker of Paige Varner, the woman who was staying with Lynda Barrett. I saw her and her daughter on the news this morning—that they were in the fire. I wanted to check on them, and one of the neighbors told me you might know where I could reach them."

Lizzie stiffened and started to close the door. "I'm sorry. I don't know where they are."

"Well, you must have heard them discussing it last night. Didn't they mention anybody they could stay with?"

Lizzie stepped aside, and Curtis came to the door. "Paige and Brianna are fine," he said. "No one was hurt."

"Well—are they still with Lynda?"

"I wouldn't know," he said. "Who did you say you are?"

"John Hampton, sir." He reached out and shook the old man's hand. "Don't you know where either of them is?"

"I'm afraid I can't help you." Curtis started to close the door, and the man backed away.

"All right," he said. "Well—thanks, anyway."

He backed down the steps, but Lizzie and Curtis kept staring at him through the narrowing opening in the door.

Lizzie closed it all the way and locked it. "Get the tag number, Lizzie," Curtis said as he headed for the phone.

Lizzie rushed to the window and squinting, whispered the numbers out loud as the man drove off down the street. Then, quickly, she scribbled them down. "Do you think he's the one you saw last night?"

"I can't say," Curtis told her, dialing the police station. "All I know is he's the right size. He could be the one. We'll just let the police decide."

Larry's eyes felt like sand by ten o'clock that morning, and he hoped his third cup of coffee would finally clear his fatigue. He poured it into the styrofoam cup, then went back to the table where Tony sat with their captain, going over the few things they did have on the Lynda Barrett case.

"I'll make sure she has a round-the-clock watch for at least a few days, but I can't do it indefinitely, guys. We just don't have enough manpower."

Larry pulled up a chair and sat down, rubbing his eyes. "Well, maybe he'll slip up soon."

The door opened, and one of the uniformed officers stuck his head in. "Call for you guys. It's Judge McMillan. Says he has a lead on the Barrett case."

Larry slid his chair back. "That's Curtis. He's our eyewitness," he told the captain. "I'll take it."

He closed the door behind him and went out to his desk. Picking up the phone, he said, "Millsaps, here. Whatcha got, Judge?"

"A man was just by here looking for Paige and Lynda," Curtis said. "He said his name is John Hampton, and he insisted that he had to know how to reach them. Now I may be jumping to conclusions, but I thought you—"

"You didn't tell him anything, did you?"

"No, of course not."

"John Hampton, huh?" Larry asked, jotting down the name. "Can you give me a description?"

"About five-eight, 180 pounds," Curtis said. "He may be just what he said he was, of course—a concerned friend—but one can never be sure. Lizzie got his license number just in case."

Larry sat back hard in his chair, smiling. "Tell her if I were there I'd kiss her. What's the number?" He wrote it down. "Thanks, Judge. If he comes back, you call me. Meanwhile, we'll find out who this sucker is, and if he's involved, you can bet we'll pick him up."

He hung up, tore off the page with the license number, and turned to the computer on his desk. "Lucy, go in there and get Tony," he said, punching the numbers onto the keyboard to start a search. "Tell him I may have something."

He waited a few seconds as the computer searched, and just as the license number surfaced, Tony reached Larry's desk.

"What is it?"

"A guy showed up at Judge McMillan's house, looking for Paige and Lynda. They got his tag number."

He watched as the information scrolled down the screen then finally stopped on a name. "Well, he lied about his name. That's a bad sign."

"Who is it?" Tony asked, leaning on the desk.

"Says the car belongs to Keith A. Varner."

"Varner. Isn't that Paige's name?"

"Yep." Punching a command on the keyboard, Larry started a cross-search for any information he could find on the man. "That's her ex-husband, all right. We show a restraining order against him."

"But that doesn't make sense," Tony said. "Paige wasn't anywhere near that plane. And last night their daughter was with her. Would he deliberately burn down a house with his child in it?"

"He would if he's a nut case." Larry pressed the button for a printout, then tore it out of his printer. "Happens all the time. I say we pick him up."

"For what?" Tony asked.

"For questioning. We can't prove he was there when the house burned, but we can at least find out where he was and why he's looking for Paige when he's not supposed to go near her."

"All right," Tony said. "Let's go."

28

KEITH VARNER WASN'T used to being told what to do, and when Larry and Tony found him sleeping in his apartment and insisted that he come with them for questioning, he hadn't taken it well. Now he sat in the interrogation room waiting for his lawyer, trying to be a little more cooperative since he was beginning to see that he had no choice.

"I was looking for my little girl," Keith told Larry. "There's no law against that, is there?"

"No, but there's a law against arson, pal."

"I told you I was at work last night. Ask anybody."

"We did. We found out that you work alone on the bank's computer system. You're not that closely supervised. You could have left at any time and come back."

Keith dropped his face helplessly into his palm. "What would you guys do? You're sitting at home watching the news on television; you hear about some fire, and all of a sudden you see your only child right in the middle of the whole thing." He looked up at them. "I freaked, okay? I didn't care about that stupid restraining order. I just cared that my Brianna was okay. And I *still* haven't found out if she is."

"She's fine," Larry said. "And your concern is moving, especially considering that her mother feels the need to hide from you to protect that same child."

"Give me a break!" Keith shouted, slapping the table and springing to his feet. "It's the oldest trick in the book. There's probably a restraining order and an abuse accusation for every custody case that's brought to court. You guys have been around. You know how things work!"

Tony glanced at the notes he'd found in Paige's and Keith's files. "Says here that Paige called just the other day because you had broken into her home. She also alleged that you tried to take the child from her school."

Keith sat back down and leaned forward, fixing his eyes on theirs as if they could understand. "I just had to know she was okay. I wanted to see her, make sure she was clean, didn't have any bruises, that sort of thing. Paige may come across as a sweet, mousy little thing, but she can be violent when you cross her, and she tends to be real selfish. She's neglected my daughter before. And if I broke into her house, why didn't I get arrested?"

Neither Larry nor Tony made any response.

"It's her word against mine. You won't show one violation of that restraining order against me. Look in the file. Do you see one?"

"That just means the police department didn't catch you in the act."

He leaned his elbows on the table. "As I recall, you're innocent until proven guilty. I'm telling you, boys, this is a war. She'll stop at nothing to keep me from getting custody, so she's going around staging crises to make her look like the victim. She deserves an Oscar."

The door burst open, and Keith's lawyer, a spit-and-polish yuppie who'd been too successful for his own—or anyone else's—good, rushed into the room. "What's going on here, gentlemen?"

Larry shot Tony a look that said the production was about to begin. He'd never liked Steve McRae, first because he was a smart aleck who thought he had all the answers and expected everyone else to acknowledge it, and second, because he'd gotten too many criminals off on technicalities, after the police department had spent hours of legwork making an arrest. With a bored, markedly unimpressed expression, Larry muttered, "We were just questioning your client about his whereabouts last night."

"They think I torched the lawyer's house," Keith said, like a kid telling his mommy of all the wrongs done against him. "Can you believe that? I wouldn't be surprised if Paige gave them the idea herself. Great strategy. Make me out to be the culprit, and it'll still be in the judge's head by the time we have the hearing."

McRae set his briefcase down on the desk but didn't sit. "Is my client under arrest?"

Larry glanced at Tony, knowing there wasn't cause. His restraining order didn't prohibit him from going to the site of a burned-down house, and as far as they could document, he hadn't gone near Paige or Brianna. At least not today. "Not at this time, no."

"Then I'd suggest you release him immediately, gentlemen."

"We could get a warrant. Search his house. Lock him up."

"Not without evidence," his attorney said. "And unless I've read the report wrong, the only evidence you have is that he asked one of the neighbors where his daughter is. Am I missing something?"

Larry rolled his eyes and breathed a heavy sigh.

"He fits the description of the arsonist," Tony said. "We have a witness, you know."

"No way," Keith said.

All eyes in the room turned back to him. "What's that?" Larry asked.

What Larry had at first thought was fear instantly became indignation. "I said, *no way.* Did someone tell you they saw *me* there last night? Could they pick me out in a lineup? Could they describe what I was wearing?"

Neither of the cops answered, and after a moment, McRae began to chuckle. "You know, if you guys would stop wasting time bringing in innocent fathers, you might get a little police work done. Now, if you're finished with him . . ."

Tony swept his hand in a be-my-guest gesture, indicating that Keith was free to go. Keith got up and with a mocking grin, extended his hand to Larry for a facetious handshake. Larry made no move to take his hand. "It's been fun, guys."

"Hasn't it, though?" Larry muttered.

Keith headed for the door. Still within hearing range of the two cops, he said, "If somebody's really trying to kill that woman, and Paige is still staying with her, that means she's putting my daughter into direct, unnecessary danger. Isn't there something I can do about that before this guy tries again?"

"There sure is," McRae told him. "We'll go back to my office now and put our heads together."

Larry waited until the men were gone, then glanced back at Tony. "I think he's lying."

Tony shook his head. "I don't see it, Larry. He could just be a father who cares about his little girl."

"His wife is hiding from him. Doesn't that tell you something?"

"It tells me that both their stories are convincing, and either one could be a lie. When custody of a child is involved, sometimes the parents take desperate measures. You know that."

"Sometimes they will," Larry agreed. "Even to the point of killing her lawyer?"

"Why her lawyer?" Tony asked. "Why not Paige herself?"

"He almost did, last night."

"Well, the crash had nothing to do with Paige. Your theory is kind of scattering all over the place, Larry. I say we get back to the facts. Stick to what we know for sure."

"All we know for sure," Larry said, "is that there was a crash and a fire, and Lynda almost died in both of them. And that if we don't do something soon, chances are, there's going to be another attempt."

"Then let's get out there and find the guy," Tony said.

29

THE PHYSICAL STRAIN of the night before had taken its toll on Lynda as had the stark loneliness. Outside, a policeman whom she hadn't met guarded her house in Larry's place. Fighting soreness and fatigue, she got up and went to the washer to drop in the pajamas she had worn here last night, the only clothes she had escaped with. Today, she wore an old T-shirt of her father's and a ragged pair of her old jeans that she'd found in one of the closets.

She wondered what Paige and Brianna were going to do for clothes. Mrs. McMillan had given Paige a housedress to wear last night, but it wasn't something Paige would want to be seen wearing in public. And Brianna had nothing but the big T-shirt she'd worn to bed last night for pajamas.

Larry had left a note under Lynda's door before he'd left that morning with the phone number and room number of the hotel where Paige was staying. Now Lynda dialed the hotel, hoping she'd catch Paige there.

"Hello?" Paige's voice was soft, tentative.

"Paige? It's just me."

"Lynda!" she said, breathing more freely. "How are you feeling?"

"A little tired and a little sore. But very much alive."

"Yeah, me, too. I keep trying to be thankful."

"I was thinking," Lynda said. "We all need clothes. Do you think it would be too much trouble for you to take my credit card this afternoon and buy us all something to wear?"

"I'll be glad to go shop for you, but we're fine," Paige said. "Really. We don't need anything—"

"Come on, Paige," Lynda insisted. "Everything was burned. You can't wear the same thing every day for the rest of your life."

"But it isn't your responsibility to pay for replacements. I can go to the Salvation Army or something."

Lynda moved her phone to the other ear, as if that would help her make her point more clearly. "My house was insured, Paige. I'll get compensated for it. Please. I want you to buy enough clothes for several days for both of you. Socks, underwear, shoes, clothes—everything."

Paige still wouldn't budge. "I still have some things at my own house."

"Not enough. Admit it, Paige. Most of your clothes were at my house."

Paige hesitated. "Okay. I guess they were."

"Come on. Let me do this. Help me assuage some of this guilt."

"Guilt? What do you have to feel guilty for?"

"Everything," she insisted. "Don't make me recite the list. Just buy some clothes."

"All right," Paige said with a chuckle. "Maybe just a few things."

Lynda smiled weakly. "Good."

"So what time are you due for your doctor's appointment?"

"Three o'clock," Lynda said. "They said Larry or Tony will take me." She breathed a soft, sad laugh. "Isn't this amazing? I'm practically trapped here in this house that I've been trying desperately to get rid of and can't go anywhere without police protection." Her voice broke off, and tears filled her eyes. Her voice betrayed her despair as she whispered, "Who would have ever thought I'd be in this position?"

"It's gonna be okay," Paige said, too quickly and without conviction.

And as Lynda surrendered to the emotions she'd been storing up, she realized how ironic it was that this woman whom she had vowed to comfort and protect was now comforting her instead.

An hour later from the offices of Schilling, Martin, and Barrett, Sally Crawford dialed the number of Lynda's cellular phone.

"Hello?"

"You're not going to believe this," Sally blurted. "Are you ready?"

Lynda hesitated, and Sally realized with a tinge of guilt that Lynda couldn't take many more surprises. "What is it?" she asked in a hoarse, hollow voice.

"Keith Varner just filed a motion with the court to get temporary custody of Brianna pending the hearing"

"What? That's ludicrous! He's wasting his time."

"I don't know," Sally said. "He's basing it on the fire last night, Lynda. He saw Brianna and Paige on the television coverage, and now he's saying that Paige has put Brianna in jeopardy."

"You've got to be kidding."

Sally wagged her head, as though Lynda could see her. "The hearing's tomorrow. If you're not up to meeting him in court, maybe Bill or Andy can fill in."

"No," she said quickly. "I'll be there."

"Are you sure, Lynda?"

"Dead sure," she said. "Call me back if you need me. I'm keeping the cellular close by."

"Are you sure you don't want to tell me where you are, Lynda? I could do some shopping for you, or whatever. You know you can trust me."

"Of course I do. But knowing could put you in danger," Lynda told her. "It's best if no one knows. Besides, I'm not sure the office phone isn't bugged. If you need to give me something, I'll meet you somewhere. And be careful, okay? This lunatic might follow anyone who knows me, hoping they'll lead him to me. I don't want you getting caught in the crossfire."

"Reassuring thought," Sally said. "Maybe I need to get a gun. So have there been any leads yet?"

"None that I know of." She paused. "Sally, you're the one who has to deal with the tempers of all the irate clients. Have there been any angry enough to kill me?"

"Not even close. Most of your clients are pretty happy."

"Well, one of them isn't. Would you do me a favor and pull up a list of all the cases I lost in the past—say, three years? Or even cases I may have won but didn't win big. You know, low awards, that sort of thing."

"Will do," Sally said. "I'll call you as soon as I get it. Hey, Lynda, take it easy, okay? You sound really tired."

"What can I say? It's been a rough week."

"Are you sure you're all right?"

"Well, I'm safe. I'm being guarded twenty-four hours a day, at least for a while."

Sally heard a doorbell ring on Lynda's end.

"Sally, I've got to go. Somebody's here."

The phone clicked, and Sally hung up, hoping that whoever stood at Lynda's door wasn't bringing more trouble.

Lynda saw Larry Millsaps through the peephole in the front door and let him in. "I thought it must be you. I'm almost ready to go."

"No hurry." Larry came in and closed the door behind him.

"Sorry about the outfit," she said, slipping on a pair of sandals. "I found these shoes in my old closet. They must be ten years old. And the clothes are my father's. All I had when I got here were the pajamas I was wearing."

"You look fine. Uh—before we go . . . can I talk to you for a minute?"

Lynda stopped what she was doing and braced herself. "Sure. What is it, Larry?"

He looked dead tired, and Lynda realized he hadn't slept all night. "I thought you should know that Keith Varner was caught hanging around your house today, asking questions about where Paige and Brianna are. Apparently, he saw them both on the news."

"Oh, no."

"Judge McMillan called and reported it, and we picked Keith up for questioning. We had to consider the possibility that he could have set the fire."

"Keith? But that still wouldn't explain the crash—Paige wasn't anywhere near it," Lynda said quickly. "And besides, why would he try to kill his own daughter?"

"Good question," Larry said. "One that probably lets him off the hook. His answers were reasonable when we got right down to it."

"You let him go, didn't you?"

"Had to. That hotshot lawyer of his rode in on his white horse, and we didn't really have any evidence against him. And it's possible that he *was* just trying to make sure his kid was all right."

"You didn't tell him where they are."

"No, of course not. We didn't give him a clue."

Lynda pulled out a chair and slowly fell into it. "He's assuming she's still with me."

"How do you know?"

"Because I was just on the phone with Sally, and she told me that his lawyer has filed a motion for a temporary hearing to get custody of Brianna pending the final hearing. He thinks she's in danger."

Larry plopped into a chair and rubbed the stubbled jaw that was in desperate need of a shave. "I thought this might happen. He was already talking about it when he left."

"He won't get her," Lynda assured him. "I'll be there myself. I have all of Paige's medical records already, showing fractures and injuries that he caused. Oh, if only formal charges could have been filed against him for violating his restraining order, so I'd have something concrete to mention in court."

"Sorry. So far, all he's guilty of is looking for his daughter. We can't arrest him for that. Chances are that's all he's done."

Lynda shook her head. "Except beat and terrorize his wife. I don't know how much more Paige can take." Lynda took a deep breath and tried to think like a lawyer. "Part of this is probably his attempt to draw her out or make me tell in court where she is. If he accuses her of putting Brianna in danger by staying with me, then he thinks I have to tell him where she is to prove she's not. But it won't work. I know every judge in this town. If I tell them she's not staying with me, they'll believe me."

"Problem is, McRae knows them, too." Larry gestured to the phone. "You want to call Paige and break the news before we go? I can talk to her if she has any questions."

"She's not there," Lynda said glumly. "I asked her to do a little shopping for us. I'll take the phone with me. She's supposed to call when she gets back to the room."

30

JAKE HAD TRIED all day long to reach Lynda or find out how she was, but the people at her office had been deliberately vague. Though he could understand their caution, he had been desperate for information.

Now she stood before him, keeping her promise to visit him even though she was on the tail end of her second trauma in a week—a fact that moved him more than he cared to admit. She looked pale and bruised and weak, but she was, nevertheless, one of the most beautiful sights he'd ever seen.

But it wouldn't do to tell her that, so he hid his feelings behind flippancy. "You look worse than I do," he said.

"Thanks." She walked closer to the bed and leaned on the rail to look down at him.

"Sit down, Lynda," he said quietly. "You don't need to stand for my benefit. I can see you fine if you sit."

Acquiescing, she pulled a chair across the floor and sat down. Her eyes were tired and dejected, and he longed to see in them the fiery spirit he had grown accustomed to.

Without thinking, he reached out and took her hand. Closing her eyes, she brought his hand to her face and squeezed it. For an instant, it made him feel needed, as if his existence gave her strength, as if he had some purpose other than lying flat in this bed. "You're in trouble, Lynda," he whispered.

"Tell me about it."

He could see from her eyes that she wasn't taking this lightly. "What did the doctor say?"

"He said not to do any more leaping from two-story buildings for a while."

"I'm serious."

She smiled. "I'm okay. Just tired and sore. He told me to get plenty of rest and try not to exert myself."

"So, what are you doing in here?"

She closed her other hand over his and looked down at it. "Visiting a friend."

He wanted to tell her how much he appreciated it, how it changed his day, but something inside him kept him from saying it.

"Have they found out who did this? Do they have any promising leads?"

"They're working hard on it," she said. "I guess I can't complain."

"But it could happen again. Are they protecting you?"

"Yes," she said. "Twenty-four hours a day. Larry's right outside."

As if to take the focus off her, she stood and leaned on his bed rail again. "So how are *you* doing?"

"Not so good today," he said. "I've had visions of you wasting away somewhere from smoke inhalation or living in some homeless shelter or making yourself an open target for some insane sniper."

He could see that his concern pleased her. "I should have called," she said. "I guess I didn't realize it was all over the news."

He grinned. "That's okay. My phone was kind of broken anyway, remember? They replaced it today."

She laughed softly, and he joined her as his eyes swept over her. It felt good having her so close, and he wondered if it were Lynda Barrett he was growing attached to or just the idea of having anyone he could touch.

To be honest, he really couldn't say.

"So how was physical therapy today?" she asked.

"Oh, peachy," he said. "My therapists are a laugh a minute. We're still working on getting me upright."

"You have to start somewhere, Jake."

He breathed a laugh. "What's the point?"

She thought about that for a second. "Don't you want to sit up?"

He shrugged. "I'm just trying to be realistic. It's such a simple thing, but when I try it, my system goes haywire." He fixed his eyes on the ceiling. "I'm trying to accept. That's what the shrink told me to do."

"You're not being realistic *or* accepting," she argued gently. "Realistically, you've got your whole life ahead of you. All you can do is work with what you have and make it the best it can be. And pray. Hard. I've been praying for you, Jake."

"No offense, Lynda, but if there is a God, it doesn't look like he's on your side."

Instead of the fight he expected, she wilted. The defeated look that crossed her face startled him, and he hated himself for putting it there. Lowering herself back into her chair, she said, "Maybe you're right."

He frowned. "So you're backing down from your beliefs now?"

She shook her head, and he saw the tears reddening her eyes. "No," she said. "I'm not backing down. I guess I'm just confused. Is God really dealing with me through all this? Maybe it's just a really loud wake-up call."

She saw the emotion cross his face, and finally, he whispered, "I'm sorry, Lynda. I didn't mean to upset you. I was just trying to rile you—to see some of that famous Barrett passion in your face again."

She kept those haunted eyes on him for a moment, but finally, the humor in what he'd said seeped in, and a rueful grin returned to her face. "I'm still going to pray for you, Jake. I'm going to pray that you'll stop being a jerk."

He smiled.

"I'm also going to pray for your therapy," she said. "Maybe if you get more mobile, you'll have a better disposition."

"Don't waste your time praying for me," he said. "I've got this under control."

"Is that why you can't sit up?" she asked. "Is it better to keep telling yourself that you'll never walk?"

That question irritated him, but she didn't seem to care. He let go of her hand. "Do you think I *want* to lie here like this?"

"No, I don't," she said, standing up again. "So don't do it. Work hard and do what the therapists tell you, and stop thinking how this is the end of your life. Start thinking of it as a beginning."

"The beginning of *what?*"

"The beginning of your learning how to be a human being." When he gave her a surprised look, she went on. "You know, you weren't my idea of a terrific guy when you had functioning legs and a flawless face."

"So you think being paralyzed is going to build character?" he asked, growing angrier. "Hey, I didn't need to have my world ripped out from under me to know how to be a human being."

She looked regretful. Setting her elbow on his rail, she dropped her forehead into her palm. "I'm sorry, Jake. I need to learn how to keep my mouth shut. I really didn't come here to lambaste you." She slid her hand down her face and lifted her brows as she gazed at him over her fingertips. "I was really just trying to get that famous Stevens passion back in your eyes."

He didn't find that amusing, as she had. For a moment, he was quiet, focusing his eye on the ceiling to keep from meeting hers. When he spoke again, his voice was lower. "I'm not a charity case. I don't even know why you're here. Tell the truth," he said glumly. "They hired you to give me an aerobic workout, didn't they? You come in here, get my blood boiling, then leave. It's probably covered under my health insurance."

"Right," she said with a wink. "It's all a clever conspiracy. And they wanted to find a lawyer to get your blood boiling because we're so good at it."

He smiled now. "I thought so."

"Oh, I almost forgot," she said. "I went by your hotel on the way home yesterday and got all your stuff and paid your bill and checked you out. Luckily, your things were still in my trunk when the fire hit. The garage was all that was left standing. Larry Millsaps left the boxes at the nurse's station since I'm not supposed to carry anything heavy. They'll be bringing them in later. Maybe you'll feel better having your own things."

"I don't know," he said. "I was getting kind of attached to these air-conditioned gowns." He smiled and squeezed her hand. "I appreciate your doing that for me. What about my car?

"It's been parked at the airport since the crash," she said. "It's just fine, locked in the hangar until you're ready to move it."

"Terrific," he said. "I hope it's safer than your plane was."

"We'll move it wherever you want."

Jake looked at her, his eye soft, searching. "Do you feel guilty about the accident or what? Why are you doing all this for me?"

"Because I care about you," she admitted with great effort.

"Why? You hardly know me, and what you knew before the accident, you didn't even like."

"I see a lot of potential there," she said with a coy smile.

He didn't find that amusing. "Well, I hate to disappoint you, Lynda, but crippled and half-blind, the only potential I'm likely to reach is the potential for suicide."

Her face changed. "That's the second time you've mentioned that, Jake. You don't mean it, and when you say it, I feel just as threatened as I felt after the fire last night."

"Why would that be a threat to you?" he asked.

"Because I've started getting attached to you, Jake, and I don't let go of my friends that easily." Tears came to her eyes, and she blinked them back. "I had you figured for a guy with at least a little bit of integrity," she said quietly. "The guy who landed my plane wasn't a coward."

"The guy who *crashed* your plane did what he had to do. But don't worry. It's not like I have a gun under my pillow or a knife in the drawer. I can't get out of bed to hurl myself out the window, and I don't have free access to the drugs they're giving me. I'm trapped here for now."

"If I can go out there and fight for my life, Jake, you can do it in here. And if you think I'm going to sympathize with your fantasy to rig up a noose, then you need to call a neurologist because you have brain damage, too."

Someone knocked on the door, but Jake only kept staring at her, his own misty eye taking seriously the fire he had restored to hers.

He heard the door open. "Sorry to interrupt. How are you, Jake?"

Finally breaking the lock he had on her eyes, Jake saw Larry and nodded.

"I'm gonna have to take you on home, Lynda," Larry said. "Tony has a suspect in custody. He thinks he might be the one who's been after you. I have to get to the station to question him."

"Really?" Lynda wiped her eyes. "Who is it?"

"One of the guys on your list," he said. "Doug Chastain."

"Doug?" she asked. "But—what evidence is there?"

Jake frowned. "Who is this guy?"

Larry checked the notes he'd jotted when Tony had called. "He's a mechanic who lives in the area, and he already has one prior arson conviction. We traced the gas can we found back to where he works."

"You're kidding," Lynda said.

Larry tried to hurry her to the door. "This might be the guy, Lynda."

Her face suddenly hopeful, she turned back to Jake. "I'll be back tomorrow, Jake," she said. "And I'll call you tonight and let you know what they come up with. That is, if you don't break your phone between now and then."

He nodded again but didn't speak until she was almost out the door. "Hey, Lynda? Be careful, okay?"

"You, too."

Jake got her meaning. He only wished he had a choice.

31

"BRACE YOURSELF," TONY told Larry as he rushed into the precinct. "He's in an even worse mood than he was when we interviewed him yesterday. He got a tad bit offended when I told him he was under arrest."

Larry watched the twenty-year-old kid through the one-way glass. Yesterday, when they'd interviewed him at home, Larry had been suspicious, but he'd talked himself out of considering the kid a suspect since he had no experience with airplanes. It was feasible that he could have started the fire, but could he have rigged the crash in such an expert way? "What have you got on him?"

"Besides his prior arson conviction and his mechanic experience and the gas can we found with the name of his employer on it, we found gas stains in the carpet in his trunk. Fresh ones. You could still smell the fumes. And his alibi is weak."

Larry stepped closer to the glass. There was a tattoo of a bald eagle covering most of Doug's upper arm, and his hair was doused with mousse and spiked to stand straight up on his head. He wore a black T-shirt with the sleeves rolled up to his shoulders and a general expression of readiness to curse the next cop who crossed him.

"So what's his alibi?"

"Says he was at home. No witnesses."

They opened the door, and the kid burst out of his seat. "You might as well let me out of here," he spat out. "I didn't do it."

Larry gave him a long, considering look as the kid sneered back at him. Finally, he reached across the table to shake his hand. "I'm Larry Millsaps," he said, then withdrew his hand when the kid rejected it. "Why don't you calm down, Doug? My partner here can be a little gruff sometimes, but I just want to ask you a few questions."

"I already answered the main one," the kid said. "I didn't do it!"

"Didn't do what?"

"I didn't set her house on fire! They keep asking me if I had a grudge against her, if I was in the area last night, if I was near the airport when that crash happened—I'm telling you morons, I've never even been *down* that street, and I wouldn't know how to get to that airport. I was sitting at home last night. Reading."

Larry's eyebrows lifted. Somehow he couldn't picture this kid reading. "Reading what?"

The kid threw up his hands. "What is it? You don't think I can read?"

"You don't look like the type who stays at home and reads."

"Yeah? Well, you don't look like the type who gets out of work by pinning crimes on innocent people." He sat back and cocked his head arrogantly. "I was reading *Hamlet.* You got a problem with that?"

"Yeah? Who wrote it?"

"You tell me," the kid challenged. "You're the one with all the answers. What do you do? Go down the list of ex-cons in the area and assign one of them to each crime that comes down?"

"We found a gas can that belongs to your employer," Tony said less patiently.

"Yeah? Well, maybe *he* did it! Were my fingerprints on it?"

Neither Tony nor Larry answered, but they both knew that no fingerprints had been found on the gas can. The arsonist must have been wearing gloves.

"How do you explain the gas stains in your trunk?" Larry asked.

Doug mouthed a curse. "I mow yards on weekends, okay? I always take extra gas in case I run out. I'd have been more careful not to spill some if I'd known somebody was gonna be sniffing around trying to pin something on me."

"What do you carry it in?"

He looked from Larry to Tony then back again. "In a can, okay? Probably a J.R.'s Auto Repair can. We have them all over the shop. People stop by and borrow them all the time. Lots of people have them."

Larry only watched him as he rambled, giving him enough rope to hang himself.

The kid realized what was going on and crossed his arms obstinately. Flopping back into his chair, he said, "I'm not talking anymore without a lawyer."

"Do you have one?"

"Sure, man," he said facetiously. "Got one on retainer."

"You don't have one, do you?"

"So appoint one," the kid said through his teeth. "Only don't appoint that witch whose house burnt down because she'll string me along and dump me at the last minute. Besides, there's somebody out there still trying to kill her. I don't want to be around her."

Tony shot Larry a telling look, and Larry nodded.

The door opened, and one of the officers stuck his head in. "Tony, can I see you a minute?"

Larry watched his partner leave the room then turned back to the kid. "I'll have an attorney appointed, but he won't do you any good if you're not telling the truth."

"You don't want the truth, man. You want a scapegoat."

The door opened again, and Tony stepped back in. "I just got an interesting bit of information." He pulled out a chair and set his foot on it. Leaning on his knee, he looked down at the kid. "Seems somebody you work with called your house three times last night, and you weren't home."

"So I didn't feel like talking," Doug said, his face reddening. "I'm taking a night class at the college, and I had to read *Hamlet.* I swear. You can call and check. Search my house. You'll find my Shakespeare book."

Tony shot Larry a skeptical look.

Doug slammed his hand on the table. "Hey, man, last time I checked, it wasn't a crime to unplug your phone!"

"No, it isn't. And neither is going to the Monroe Street Lounge, where several people saw you earlier last night."

Larry breathed an incredulous laugh. "Still want to stick to your story about being at home reading?"

"You asked me where I was when the fire started. I was at home. So I had a few drinks earlier. That's no crime either."

"And it just slipped your mind?"

For a moment, Doug sat still, his face a study in belligerence and hatred, but finally, he leaned forward and clasped his hands in front of his face. "Go ahead and get that lawyer," he said. "I'm not saying another friggin' word."

32

THE RADIO NEWS blared in the background as Keith Varner checked out the suit he would wear in court tomorrow. He would look like a competent businessman when he faced the judge, he thought, and Paige would play the role of a stringy-haired waif about to have a nervous breakdown. And the lawyer—he chuckled for a moment at the thought that she was going to appear in court to represent Paige. When he'd seen her on the news after the fire, she'd looked like someone who'd been beaten up. He could just see the judge's reaction to her propping herself up in the courtroom—complete with bruises and scrapes and the stitches that held her together—fighting for Paige. Her very presence would be all the argument he needed that she herself was in danger and, therefore, Brianna was in danger. By tomorrow night, he'd have Brianna at home.

He went into the empty bedroom in his apartment, kicked aside the piles of dirty laundry, and considered where he would put the child's bed. There, in the corner. Once the judge awarded him temporary custody, he'd ask him if he could get her bed from her home. That way she'd be comfortable with him. He just hoped she didn't cry all night like the last time he had her.

But that he blamed on Paige. She had filled the child's head full of lies, and until he got that woman out of his daughter's life, he would never get Brianna to bond with him. He had so many plans for them. She would learn to be dependent on him, to obey and respect him, to need him. . . .

He went back into his small den, knocked the newspapers out of his chair and onto the floor, and flicked on the television. Maybe there was another hint about where they were. Maybe they'd have something about the sheriff department's pitiful hunt for the arsonist.

He listened through two murders, a rally for a local politician, a mail fraud scam that had been uncovered.

"—and in other news, an arrest was made today in the Lynda Barrett case—"

He leaned forward and turned it up, watching carefully as the film clip showed the mechanic being led through the precinct in handcuffs. Flopping back on his couch, Keith began to laugh. It was perfect. They were off his trail. They were hanging it on that poor bozo he'd heard Lynda name that day in her hospital room. It had been easy to find him, and using the gas can to lead them to where Chastain worked was ingenious. Now Lynda Barrett had a false sense of security. He loved it.

Now there would be another chance, he thought with a smile. If he didn't convince the judge to give him Brianna tomorrow, he could still make sure he got Lynda Barrett out of the way before the real hearing. It would take a host of angels to keep her alive the next time.

33

THE TELEPHONE RANG, and Lynda pulled it out of her jeans pocket, which was baggy enough to carry several small appliances. "Hello?"

"I hope I didn't wake you."

It was Paige, and Lynda smiled at the sound of her voice. The house was getting awfully quiet. She abandoned the stack of books she'd been sorting through in the closet and sat down on the closest chair. "I just woke up a few minutes ago, and I've been sorting through some things to see if my dad left a Bible somewhere."

"Any luck?"

"No. I know he had one, though. He used to wave it at me all the time."

She could hear Paige's soft laughter. "I'll go buy you one if you want."

Lynda sighed. "No, that's okay. I'll get one the next time Larry or Tony takes me somewhere."

"Well, it doesn't look like that'll be necessary any more. The guy they picked up? Looks like he's the one."

Lynda caught her breath. "Really? How do you know?"

"They called me a little while ago. Larry said you were tired when he brought you home and were probably sleeping, so he asked me to give you a couple of hours and then tell you. They shot his alibi to pieces, found gas stains in his car—it's him, Lynda. We're home free."

Lynda leaned back in the chair. "No more guards? No more surprises?"

"Nope. They called the guard back to the precinct over an hour ago. Look out the window."

Lynda got up and pulled the curtain back. For the first time since she'd come here last night, there was no one watching her from across the street. A chill went through her, and she had the fleeting sensation of standing on the edge of a cliff, leaning, leaning, with nothing to catch her when she fell. "They're gone."

"That's right. You don't need them now."

Lynda allowed the news to sink in for a moment. "I knew he didn't like me when I resigned from his case, but I didn't think he'd come back to kill me."

"Well, at least he's behind bars. And we can come and go as we please. The only thing we have to fear is this hearing tomorrow."

Lynda pushed aside her uneasiness and tried instead to concentrate on tomorrow. "This is perfect, Paige. Keith's motion is based on your putting Brianna in danger by being with me. That whole premise has just been shot into a million pieces. Once I tell the judge that I'm not in danger any longer, his theory is shot. And then I'll tell the court that your whereabouts are confidential due to Keith's threats and leave it at that. In fact, if you want to check out of the hotel right now, you can come here. It's probably okay now."

"I don't know," Paige said. "He's assuming I'm still with you."

"But he doesn't know where I am."

"I told you, Lynda. He's smart. He figures out ways to get information."

"He's not *that* smart. He's just conditioned you to think so. But even if he did find out, he's not as likely to hassle you knowing I'm here as he might be if you were alone. I mean, I'm the one who's going to pull out all the stops when we finally get to trial. He won't want to give me any more ammunition to throw at him."

Paige hesitated. "Even if you're right, I still think I should stay here tonight. If for some reason the judge asks you point blank if I'm staying with you, you can say no."

Lynda sighed. "You're right, I guess. But how about tomorrow?"

"Are you sure you want us there?"

She heard the smile in Lynda's voice. "Of course I want you. I need company. I'm at my wit's end."

"Okay, then," she said. "Tomorrow. And about that Bible. Why don't I buy you one and bring it when I bring all the clothes I got for you?"

"Where's Brianna?"

"Watching "Barney." It's almost over."

Lynda looked down at the junk she'd begun sorting through. "Paige, if you would do that, it would be such a lifesaver. Use the credit card I gave you last night. I'll call the store and find out what translations they have and tell them what I want. Just ask the clerk when you get there. By the way, do you have one?"

"A Bible? Well . . . somewhere . . . at home."

"Buy yourself one, too," she said. "On me. A little thank-you for taking such good care of me. And get Brianna something, too."

"Lynda, you don't have to do that."

"Yes, I do," Lynda whispered. "And you have to let me."

A few minutes later Lynda dialed her office number. "Do me a favor," she told Sally. "Go back a couple of years and dig up Doug Chastain's file. I need to refresh my memory about his case."

"I heard they'd arrested him," Sally said. "Thank goodness. You want me to bring it to you along with the other papers I need to give you for tomorrow?"

"Yeah," she said. "We can meet this afternoon."

"Are you going to tell me where you are yet?"

Lynda considered it a moment and realized she didn't yet feel safe enough to tell anyone where she was. "No, I'll just meet you somewhere. Call me on my cellular phone before you leave work today."

"Are you supposed to be driving?" Sally asked.

Lynda hesitated. "Well . . . no. But it can't be helped."

"Yes, it can. I can bring them to you."

"Just humor me," Lynda said. "I'll get over it. It'll sink in eventually that I'm not being hunted."

"All right," Sally said with resignation. "Do you want to come to the office?"

"No. I don't think I'm up to seeing everybody yet. How about the Jackson Street Post Office? Then I can just have Paige meet me there too with some stuff she's picking up."

Sally let out a ragged breath. "All right. But I'll be so glad when all this is over."

"You think *you* will."

Paige drove up just as Lynda finished signing some papers Sally needed her to sign. Saying good-bye to her secretary, she got out of her car and got into Paige's.

Paige handed her the Bible, still in its box. "They were expensive," she said. "You should have just ordered me a paperback one."

"I wanted you to have that one," she said. "Did they put your name on it like I told them?"

Paige opened her box and took out her leather-bound Bible. Running her hand across the name engraved in gold, she said, "Yeah, they sure did." Her eyes were misty when she looked up at Lynda. "That may be the sweetest thing anybody's ever bought me."

"Well, make it worthwhile. Read it."

Paige leaned over and planted a kiss on Lynda's cheek. "You're a real friend."

"I'm trying," she said. "But I've got a lot of catching up to do."

34

"ARE YOU SURE you should be here today, Lynda?" Judge Albert Stacey set his elbows on the conference table, assessing her with deep concern. Keith and his lawyer sat on one side of the table, and Lynda sat alone on the other.

She tried to smile, but it was difficult. The long walk through the building had been tiring, and she'd encountered several bouts with dizziness since she'd been here. Everywhere she went, people stared, especially those who knew her. She hadn't even tried to hide the bruises and scrapes on her face. "I feel fine, your honor. And I had to be here today. This motion Mr. McRae is filing is ridiculous and a waste of the court's time."

The judge turned to Keith's lawyer. "Well, I've reviewed the motion, and my understanding is that your client is concerned about the safety of this child since she was involved in the fire at Miss Barrett's the other night. Am I reading that correctly?"

"Yes, Judge. Mr. Varner feels that his ex-wife has deliberately risked the child's life by staying in the same home with Miss Barrett, even after so many attempts have been made on her life."

"Excuse me," Lynda cut in. "Be specific, please. How many attempts?"

McRae sat back in his chair with a look that said she was walking proof of his case. "You tell us."

Rather than telling him anything, she addressed the judge. "Your honor, there were two attempts made on my life. The first was the plane crash I was involved in last week, and the second was, obviously, the fire two nights ago. Paige was staying in my house while I was in the hospital, primarily because she became convinced that the restraining order she had filed against Mr. Varner was not going to stop him from breaking into her home or trying to remove their child from school. At that time no one realized that anyone was after me. It wasn't until after the fire the first night I was home that we realized that."

The judge turned back to McRae. "So what's the problem exactly? How did Mrs. Varner endanger her daughter's life? Are you saying *she* started the fire or knew it was going to happen?"

"Of course not, your honor."

Keith couldn't stay quiet any longer. "I'm saying that for all I know she's still staying with her, even though she's aware that someone's out to get her."

"Your honor," Lynda said, calling his attention back to her side of the table. "May I?"

He gestured for her to go ahead with her explanations, and she took a deep breath. "First of all, I can assure you that Paige Varner and Brianna are safe and that they have been in no danger—except perhaps from Mr. Varner—since the fire. In fact, they're here in the building as we speak but chose not to come into the hearing because she feared the child would be traumatized by seeing her father."

"Oh, for crying out—"

The judge's stern look silenced Keith, who gave a disgusted look at the ceiling, as if calling on some unknown entity in the plaster to come to his aid.

"Secondly," Lynda went on, "the police have a suspect in custody. They captured him yesterday, and he's in jail awaiting his own hearing."

"Really?" the judge asked, eyebrows raised. "Well, I know that's good news for you."

"Extremely good news, your honor."

Keith rolled his eyes. "So a guy was arrested. He could get out on bond within the week if he's the right guy in the first place. How can I be assured that my child is safe?"

Lynda answered the question for him. "Your honor, I can assure you that it's my priority to keep those two safe as well. In fact, that's why theirs is the only case I've kept since my accident and why I came here, against doctor's orders, to make sure the rights of Mrs. Varner and her daughter are adequately protected."

Judge Stacey studied the motion in front of him, and McRae seized the moment of silence to speak up. "Judge, my client is also concerned with the mother's neglect of the child, her inability to support that child, and her past abuses. Mrs. Varner has lost her job and left her home, and my client worries about her mental stability and her capacity to provide Brianna with what she needs. He's concerned about their whereabouts, as I'm sure you would be if your own children disappeared."

"Well, your honor, I can answer that as well," Lynda spoke up. "For the duration of this crisis—and it is a crisis, sir, whenever a battered wife goes into hiding—I am helping my client and her daughter financially. I won't allow them to go without. For the time being, I've recommended that she remain in hiding."

The judge sat back in his chair. "Well, I'm satisfied that the child is in capable hands and that she's being cared for. As for the allegations of neglect and abuse on either side of this case, that remains to be proven in the appropriate hearing. That's not what this hearing is about. I hereby rule that the child shall remain with her mother until the trial."

Keith cursed, and his lawyer grabbed his arm, trying to shut him up, but he burst out of his chair and started for the door.

Lynda waited until he was gone then turned back to the judge with a little smile, knowing he made note of the volatile temper. She hoped he was the judge assigned to the custody hearing. "Thank you, your honor."

Patting her hand, he got to his feet. "Quite impressive that you would come to court in your condition, Lynda. It speaks to your conviction that the child is in the right place." He leaned over the table and whispered, "And I trust you."

"I appreciate that, sir. Would you like to confer with Mrs. Varner?"

"No, that won't be necessary."

She watched him disappear through the door that led to his chambers and picking up the few papers she'd been able to carry in with her, she went back to the conference room where she'd left Paige.

Paige jumped when the door opened then wilted with relief when she saw it was Lynda.

"What happened?"

"We won," Lynda said. "I told you."

"Oh, thank God." She drew Brianna into a crushing hug. "Where is he? Is he still in the building?"

"No, he's gone. He rushed out cussing and ranting. I'm glad you weren't there."

"Me, too." Propping her chin on Brianna's head, she said, "Are you sure we can win next time, Lynda? He's not going to pull a fast one on us and trip us up, is he? He's always been able to do that with me."

The worry in Paige's eyes touched Lynda. "He won't trip me up, Paige. I'll have so much against him, he won't know what hit him. We'll get everyone who's ever seen him lose his temper into that courtroom. I'll have documentation of every trip to the emergency room, every neighbor who heard him yelling through the walls, every call to 911. I won't leave anything to chance."

Paige's lips trembled as she took it all in. "It's Brianna's life at stake here," she whispered, "but if I have to trust anyone to fight for it, I trust you."

35

KEITH CRUISED THROUGH the courthouse parking garage, looking for Paige's white car. He found it on the third level.

He stopped his car right behind it. The door-lock buttons were down, he could see. He glanced around to see whether there was anyone nearby who might see him when he got out.

Someone was pulling into an empty space a few cars down. And two people across the aisle stood talking beside one of their cars.

He took a piece of paper off the seat next to him, folded it to look like a note, and got out the switchblade he carried in his pocket. Leaving his car idling, he stepped out and glanced at the others in the garage. He still hadn't been noticed.

He set the blank note under her windshield wiper, so it would look as if that was his purpose then pretended to drop his keys. Bending over, he opened his switchblade then slashed her front tire. Still stooped, he went to the back one and stabbed it, too.

He drove around until he found a parking place on the other side of that level from which he'd be able to see her come to her car.

It would take more than a judge to keep him from being with his daughter.

36

PAIGE HELD BRIANNA'S hand as they stepped off the elevator into the parking garage. Trying to remember where she had parked her car, she let her eyes sweep over the colors until she came to the white Chevette parked across the garage.

The car parked next to hers began to pull out as she approached, leaving the space next to her car empty. Her step slowed—through that open space, she saw that both tires on that side of her car were flat.

She froze.

She heard a car start across the garage and caught a glimpse of pastel blue pulling out—the color of Keith's car.

Her heart stopped and she dropped her purse, spilling out her car keys, a lipstick, some change. Abandoning it, she grabbed Brianna and bolted back toward the elevator.

Brianna started to cry, but over the child's sobs Paige heard tires screeching. The elevator was taking too long. She scanned the area for a door to the stairway. Quickly, she headed toward it and shoved it open. It clanged shut behind her as she tore down the stairs.

Above her, just beyond the door, she heard a car door slam and footsteps running. The door above her opened, and she heard the click of shoes taking the steps faster than she could move.

Her foot slipped, and she stumbled, skinning her shin against the metal railing. Brianna's screams went up an octave. Reaching out to grab the rail with her free hand, Paige steadied herself and took the next flight down.

But he was right behind her, closing in. "You can't get away from me, Paige!" he shouted, his voice echoing in the stairwell.

As if she only now realized what they were running from, Brianna's shrieks grew more piercing, reverberating through the stairwell. Her little arms tightened desperately around her mother's neck. Struggling to breathe, Paige threw herself at a door on one of the landings.

But just as her fingers grazed the handle, Keith grabbed her shirt and flung her against the wall. He reached for Brianna, but the child fought and struggled and screamed. Bracing herself against the wall, Paige kicked him with all her might.

He fell back, cursing, then rallied and grabbed her hair. He jerked her off-balance, trying to get his arm between her and the child. Then he shoved her back and kicked her feet out from under her. Losing her grip on the child, Paige fell back, stumbling down four stairs and landing on her back.

"Mommmmeeee!" The child's terror rang through the stairwell, echoing off the walls. Keith grabbed her, and she bit his arm and kicked him with her sharp little shoe. He recoiled long enough for her to reach her mother again and attach herself in another strangling grip.

Suddenly the door one flight below them burst open. Startled, Keith let them go and took a step backward, then turned and fled back up the steps.

"Help me!" Paige cried, stumbling down the stairs. She fell into the building and collapsed as a crowd formed around her, Brianna still screaming at the top of her lungs, clinging for dear life to her mother.

It took twenty minutes to quiet the child's screaming, but she trembled for the next two hours as Lynda and Larry sat with Paige and Brianna, trying to calm them both.

"I searched the whole garage and all around the courthouse, Paige," Larry said. "He's gone."

"Can't you—can't you arrest him?"

"We have to find him first."

"What if he finds *me* first?" Paige shouted. "Who would have ever thought he'd try to snatch her out of my hands right here at the courthouse?"

"He's getting desperate," Lynda said. "He's liable to do anything."

"He'll go to every hotel in the city until he finds my car—if I can manage to drive it again after what he did to my tires. He'll find us. I know he will."

"No, he won't," Lynda said through her teeth. "You're coming home with me. I'll send someone to change the tires, and we'll get your car later. But you don't need to be alone."

"What's happening to us?" Paige cried, sopping her tears with a wadded tissue. "Everywhere I turn, there's danger. How am I ever going to protect her? Feel her. She's still shaking."

Lynda laid her hands on the child and felt the shiver. "She must have been pretty scared when she saw him."

"Well, what do you expect? To have him burst out of nowhere like that and start grabbing her—What is he trying to do to her? Doesn't he realize that a child shouldn't ever have to be that afraid?"

Lynda stroked back Paige's hair where it was matted to her wet face. "It's going to be okay, Paige. Come on. Larry's following us home now."

Wearily, Paige got up, shifted Brianna more securely to her hip, and with a troubled, miserable expression, regarded Larry. "You have a gun, don't you?"

"Of course I have a gun. I'm a cop."

"But—you would use it if you had to, wouldn't you?"

"That's my job, Paige. Don't worry. I'm not going to let anything happen to you."

Her face was pale as they started out of the room. "Larry, do you think I should get a gun?"

Lynda watched Larry's face, for she had wondered the same thing herself. "No, Paige, I don't. Too many accidents happen. Too many people rely on them when their tempers flare. Too many people die because there was a gun too readily available. And I sure don't recommend it with a child in the house."

"That's what I thought you'd say." But as they walked to Larry's unmarked car, Paige whispered to Lynda, "If I had the money, I'd buy one anyway. And the next time Keith sprang up out of nowhere, I'd be ready."

Larry was quiet later that day as he and Tony prowled St. Clair in their unmarked car, working on a cocaine case that they were close to breaking. The sheriff's department was too small for any of its detectives to specialize in one area, so Larry didn't know from one week to the next what kind of crime he'd be assigned to.

It gave the job some diversity, which he supposed was a plus. But the minus was that they slapped a file closed so quickly the moment they had someone booked that he was never able to get a sense of closure.

"What's on your mind?" Tony asked, glancing over at him as he drove.

He shrugged. "I don't know. I was just thinking about that Doug Chastain kid. Did I tell you we found a Shakespeare book in his apartment?"

"Three times. Why is that bothering you so?"

He sighed. "I didn't say it was bothering me. I just stated a fact. He really is enrolled in night school. And his phone *was* unplugged."

Tony rubbed his chin in disbelief. "So you think a guy who reads *Hamlet* can't burn down a house? Is this another one of your bleeding-heart theories?"

"No," Larry returned. "But I don't want to assume somebody's guilty just because he has an attitude and a weird haircut. Especially when his alibi could be true."

"*Part* of his alibi. The other part was a lie. And what about his mechanic skills and the gas stains and the arson conviction and the gas can? You think some Shakespeare book clears up all that evidence?"

"No, I don't." He took in a deep breath and shifted in his seat. "I just feel uneasy about things. Like maybe we closed the case too fast."

"We have an assignment board full of unsolved cases, Larry. Neither one of us has time to dwell on long shots."

"Well, I'd feel better if we could pick up Keith Varner again. Slap an assault charge on him."

"There are deputies working on it, buddy."

Larry was quiet for a few moments. "You just should have seen how scared they were to-day. The little kid and Paige. Even Lynda. I wish there was something definitive we could do."

Tony only chuckled. "Lighten up, pal. They'll be fine."

37

PAIGE TUCKED HER sleeping child into bed in the master bedroom then pulled back the curtain and peered out the front window.

The street was dark, and she wasn't sure she would even know if someone sat out there, watching, waiting. What if Keith had discovered where they were? What if he were just biding his time, waiting until her guard was down to pounce again and snatch Brianna from her hands?

She was getting crazy, she told herself, but she wished the police would go back to guarding the house again. But police never guarded battered, frightened mothers or abused children. They didn't consider the threats wrathful husbands made to be as serious as attempted murder. Paige didn't see the difference.

Sighing, she closed the curtain and went through the living room to the back door. Through the window, she saw Lynda sitting on the patio with her head resting against the back of her chair, staring up into the stars.

Quietly, she opened the door and stepped outside. "Lynda, are you okay?"

Lynda offered a weak smile. "I'm fine, Paige. Sit down."

"I don't know." Crossing her arms, Paige gazed across the yard to the woods behind the fence. "I feel too vulnerable out here. I think I'd rather stay closed up inside."

"I felt that way at first, too. But I love sitting outside at night, and I decided not to let Doug Chastain take that away from me. You shouldn't let Keith."

"All right." Still watching the shadows beyond the yard, Paige took the padded swing across from Lynda and began to move gently back and forth. "I've been so jumpy today since the run-in with him. It feels good to relax."

"It does, doesn't it?"

Crickets chirped in the yard, signaling that fall was approaching, and Lynda smiled. "Those crickets remind me of college."

"College? Why? Did you study them?"

Lynda laughed. "Crickets? No. But every fall, the library seemed to be full of them. Especially at night. I'd be there studying, and those crickets would be chirping as loud as you could imagine, and I'd look for them so I could throw them outside. I don't know why they bothered me so much."

Paige closed her eyes against the cool breeze whispering through her hair. "I always meant to go to college. When I married Keith, he promised I could. But every time I brought it up, he nipped it in the bud."

"Well, maybe you could try it now."

Paige shook her head. "No, I'd never make it through. I'm not smart enough."

"Smart enough?" Lynda asked. "Paige, you have as much upstairs as anyone I know."

Paige didn't seem to buy it. "Besides, now I have to worry about making ends meet. It's not easy supporting a child alone. The whole time we've been divorced, I haven't gotten one penny of child support from Keith. But I don't really want it. I don't want him having anything at all to do with Brianna." Hugging herself, Paige scanned the fence.

"I think God's with you on this, Paige."

Paige chuckled softly. "Oh, really? Why?"

"Call it deductive reasoning. You've come through more narrow escapes than I have. You do believe in God, don't you?"

Paige sighed. "I guess so. I wish I had as much faith as you."

"Where do you get the idea that I have more than you?"

Paige considered that for a moment. "Well, you live a real decent life, Lynda. You're a good example. Like you really believe."

"Why?" Lynda asked honestly. "Because I don't have a criminal record, I only let a curse word fly when I'm really mad, my name is on a church roster, and I have a pro-life sticker on my bumper? Is that my example?"

"No," Paige said. "Because you took Brianna and me in, and you gave us money, and clothes. . . ."

Lynda sighed. "That's nothing, Paige. With my income, I should be ashamed for all I *haven't* done."

Paige was amazed. "Lynda, you just don't know. Other people aren't like that. Even family."

Lynda grew quiet for a moment, and Paige diverted her eyes, knowing she'd said too much.

"Paige, you never talk much about your family. Why?"

"Not much to tell," she said without conviction. "They live in Arizona."

"But have you contacted them to tell them what's going on? Do they know you're in trouble?"

"Oh, Lynda. They don't care."

Lynda sat up straighter. "Don't care? How do you know?"

Paige blinked back the tears pushing into her eyes. "Lynda, you have to know my mother. She's lived with my father for thirty years, and no matter how bad things get, she believes in sticking it out. No matter who gets hurt."

Lynda sat quietly, weighing the implications of what Paige had just said and decided to take a chance. "Paige, were you abused when you were a child?"

Paige looked into the trees for a moment, struggling to keep her face free of emotion, but it wasn't easy, and finally, she covered her face with a hand and squeezed her eyes shut, but the tears pressed out anyway. "I won't let Brianna live that way," she whispered. "I'm not like my mother. I can't turn my head, and I can't keep bouncing back."

Lynda moved across to sit on the swing next to Paige, reached out for her, and pulled her into a hug, and Paige laid her head against Lynda's shoulder and wept like a child.

"Is that why you married Keith? To get away from home?"

She nodded. "He ended up being so much like my father. I thought his temper was just normal because that's the way things always were at home, too. But it's not normal, is it?"

"No," Lynda said. "It's not normal. It's criminal."

Paige wept for a moment longer until she heard Brianna crying through the door she'd left open, and sucking in a deep breath, she got to her feet. "Brianna's crying," she said quickly, wiping her face. "I guess I'll go lie down with her." Paige could see the helplessness on Lynda's face, and she wished she hadn't burdened her with this. "Good night, Lynda."

"Good night."

Paige hurried into the master bedroom where Brianna, in the throes of a dream, cried out in her sleep. Lying down beside her, Paige stroked her face and comforted her. "Shhh. Mommy's here. Nothing's going to hurt you."

As she held her, she felt the terror seeping out of her.

For a while, she lay still in the dark, thinking about the fears that plagued her daughter, and that stalked her as well. They were real fears—fear for her life, fear of losing her child, fear of harm coming to either of them. She had never expected to live in such fear once she left her father's home.

Despair settled into her heart like a slow-moving disease, but as she drifted toward sleep, she thought she heard a voice: *"Shhh. I'm here. Nothing's going to hurt you."*

And even as she sank into sleep, she realized that the voice, the promise, and the feeling of peace warming through her felt as tangible as that little girl curled up against her chest.

38

THE CROWD IN the bar where Keith had decided to brood was thinning out, and men and women had begun to couple off with a frenzied desperation, as if going home alone was tantamount to social suicide.

But it wasn't his reputation that worried Keith tonight; rather, it was that he'd driven into the parking lot of his apartment building today to see three sheriff's cars. He didn't have to be Einstein to figure out that they were looking for him.

Never one to linger too long when trouble was brewing, Keith had turned his car around before they could spot him and had headed to this obscure bar across town where people knew him only by his first name.

He'd been drinking for hours, and his head had begun to throb. He needed to lie down somewhere.

Sliding off the bar stool he'd been propped on for the past several hours, he stumbled toward the door, catching the chairs as he passed to steady himself. He heard laughter outside as he fell out into the night and saw a couple of intoxicated men pawing at a woman who cackled loudly enough to wake the dead. Though they weren't looking at him, he suspected that the laughter was directed at him anyway, and he set his eyes on his car and concentrated on getting to it.

Again, laughter erupted behind him, and he swung around, letting a string of expletives tear from his mouth. One of the men cursed back at him and started toward him, and Keith opened his car door and fell behind the wheel.

He heard the man's fist hit his trunk, and groping to get his key into the ignition, he started the car. The man was banging on it now, and the woman's abrasive laughter split the night again.

Cursing because his hands were so maddeningly slow to cooperate, he got the car into gear and took off through the dirt.

Looking in his rearview mirror, he saw the man shouting obscenities at him. Keith rolled down his window and yelled back, "You can't touch me! I'm invincible!"

But that invincibility was meaningless if he couldn't prove it to someone. He wished he knew where Paige was tonight, so he could burst into her house, jerk her out of bed, and remind her who the man of the family is. He would show her what all her whining and running had gotten her. He would teach her how to show a little respect.

The idea became more attractive to him as he wove and zigzagged through town, heading toward the neighborhood where he had lived with her. Maybe she and Brianna were home. Maybe she had run out of money and been forced to go home, and he could walk in and surprise her. . . .

The street was dark, and he chuckled under his breath and tried to focus his blurry vision on the house as he got closer. There were no lights on and no cars in the garage. Blast it all, she wasn't home. She was still hiding.

He thought about pulling into the driveway and going in, just to rest for a few minutes until his head quit hurting. But that voice inside his head that remained the slightest bit rational reminded him that a world of trouble would fall on him if he were caught here after what had happened today. No, he had to keep driving. He had to go home.

He ran over a corner curb making the turn off her street and felt his car bounce and screech as he accelerated. His eyes were growing heavy, and his head was hammering, but somehow he kept driving.

By rote he made his way home and pulled into his parking lot, making a cursory inspection through his blurred vision; he saw no squad cars. Satisfied, he pulled into a space. They'd forgotten about him by now, he thought with relief. That was the thing about the St. Clair Sheriff's Department. If you weren't there the first time they looked for you, chances were, they wouldn't be back. Not on a stupid charge like approaching his wife at the courthouse.

His parking job was crooked, but at least he didn't hit the car next to him. He cut off the engine and got out, stumbling toward his apartment while he searched his key chain for the apartment key.

When he heard a car door slam, he didn't bother to look. His head hurt too badly, and he had to find that key—

"Police! Hold it right there! You're under arrest!"

Keith cursed again and turned around, his hands limp at his sides as he glared at Larry Millsaps, who held a gun on him as if he'd just caught him robbing a bank. "You gotta be kiddin'."

Larry came up behind him and threw him against a car next to him, which wasn't difficult since he could barely stand as it was.

"What're the charges?"

"Assault, contempt of court, and whatever else we can hang on you."

Jerking him up, Larry threw him into the back seat of the unmarked car as he read him his rights, and Keith decided that he didn't care where Larry took him or for what reason, as long as there was a place there to lay his head.

There was no outside light to indicate that it was morning, but the sounds of echoing doors and yelling men sliced through Keith's brain with machete force. His head still pounded, but forcing himself to open his eyes, he looked around and tried to orient himself.

And then he remembered that he was in jail.

The reason escaped him, however, and clutching his head, he sat up on the side of his cot and tried to think. Had he gotten into a fight last night? Had they pulled him over for drunk driving? Had it been for driving by Paige's house?

Paige. It was something about Paige. The haze over his brain seemed to clear as he recalled the incident in the parking garage yesterday when he'd tried to take Brianna. What had Paige told them?

Fury rose up inside him, intense enough to propel him to the cell bars. "Hey!" he shouted up the corridor. "Hey! I want to talk to my lawyer!"

An inmate several cells down yelled for him to shut up, but he turned up the volume a few decibels. "I want a lawyer, do you hear me? I have the right to a lawyer!"

He heard someone coming then, a linebacker in a guard's uniform, and he backed a few steps away from the bars. "Are you gonna let me call my lawyer?"

The man leveled hateful, bloodshot eyes on him as he stuck the key in the lock and opened the door. "Come on, Varner."

Keith hesitated. "Are you—am I gonna call my lawyer now?"

The man smirked. "What do you think? That I'm gonna smash your face in as soon as you step over this line?"

Keith didn't like the question, so he offered no answer.

The man's grin faded. "Get out here, Varner. You're wasting my time."

He felt nauseous as he stepped out of the cell, and the guard escorted him to the telephone.

Two hours later, standing in front of a judge who might or might not let him out on bail, Keith did as he was told and let his lawyer do the talking.

"It was all a misunderstanding, your honor. My client and his ex-wife are in the middle of a custody dispute. She's tried pinning things on him before to stack the deck in her favor, but this takes the cake."

The judge didn't seem all that interested. "Says here that he vandalized her car, assaulted her, and tried to take the child against the orders of the court. Is it or is it not true?"

"No, your honor," McRae said. "All that happened is that they happened to be parked on the same level in the parking garage. He hadn't seen his child in over a month, and when he saw them coming across the garage, he was overcome with the desire to see her and approached her. He never dreamed she would interpret it as a threat right there in the courthouse parking lot."

The judge propped his chin in his hand, as if he'd heard it all a million times and didn't know if he could stay awake for one more.

"His ex-wife saw him and assuming incorrectly that he planned to take the child, took off running down the stairs. Unfortunately, she slipped and fell on the way down, and when my client heard her scream, he went to see if she was all right. She milked the incident for everything it was worth, your honor, and made it look as if he had assaulted her, which couldn't be farther from the truth. Judge, I ask that you drop these charges so that we won't waste any more of your time."

The judge studied the paperwork on his desk. "Is his ex-wife in the courtroom?"

McRae made a helpless gesture. "We weren't able to reach her or her attorney. My guess is that they are reluctant to stand before you with such a blatant lie."

The judge assessed Keith, who was tired and unshaven. "I'm divorced, myself, Mr. Varner, and I know how difficult it is to be without your children. But your ex-wife must have a restraining order for a reason."

"I told you, Judge. She's stacking her deck so she'll win permanent custody."

The judge rubbed his head, as if he nursed a headache of his own and then in a half-audible voice, said, "All right then. I'll give him the benefit of the doubt." He leaned forward then and pointed a finger at Keith. "But I won't do it again. If I see you back in this courtroom for any reason, Mr. Varner, you'll go to jail. Do you understand me?"

"Yes sir."

"All right." Banging the gavel, he moved on to the next case.

Trying to look humble and sincere, Keith left the courtroom. But inside he was dancing; he'd gotten away with it again.

His lawyer brooded as he drove him home, which aggravated Keith. He wasn't in the mood for this silent treatment. His head still hurt, and he wanted to take something and go to bed for a few hours before he had to go to work. When they reached Keith's apartment building, Keith started to get out.

"Hey, Keith," McRae said, stopping him. "No more antics, huh? You almost ruined your case."

"I didn't do anything," Keith said.

McRae breathed a disbelieving laugh. "This is me you're talking to. I know what you did, and it was stupid. And if you do anything like it again, you're going to have to find yourself a new lawyer."

"Okay, so it was stupid. I lost my head."

"Don't lose it again."

Keith got out then leaned back in the door. "Relax. It's going to be all right. We'll still win the case. Paige won't be able to fight back much longer."

McRae frowned back at him. "What do you mean by that?"

"Just that you should trust me," Keith said. "I've got this under control."

39

THE MADDENING THING about having his own clothes in his room was that Jake couldn't put them on. Allie had told him that he'd have to be sitting upright before he could learn to dress himself, and even though she'd offered to do it for him, he'd declined. He liked the gowns, he told her. She believed him—which just proved how naive she was.

The truth was that he couldn't stand the thought of a woman doing something so personal as dressing him. Already Jake had little dignity left. The things they had to do for him were things he'd always taken for granted. Now he'd never take anything for granted again.

That morning they had put him in that monstrosity of a wheelchair again, and he'd persuaded them to leave him in it; the longer he sat upright, the easier it would become. He was up to sixty degrees now, and he was determined to conquer this particular obstacle. But it was taking too much time.

Rolling carefully toward the closet, he tried to reach a coat hanger, but it was just out of reach. Looking around in the closet where the nurses had put all of the things Lynda had gotten out of his hotel room, he found a tennis racket. Carefully, he slipped it into the triangle of the hanger and lifted it off the rod.

He dropped the racket then bent the hanger into a straight piece of wire with a hook at one end, and slipped it into the waistband of his sweat pants. If he could just hook that waistband over his foot and work it up to the point where his arms could reach, maybe he could actually get them on.

He broke out in a sweat as he maneuvered the pants with the hanger, trying to hook them over, missing, then trying again. The waistband of the sweat pants kept collapsing when it hit his feet, and the hanger offered little control, but he kept trying.

And trying.

And trying.

But it was too difficult, and finally, he gave up and flung both the pants and the hanger across the room. Slamming his hands down on the wheelchair armrests, he let out a raging curse.

A knock sounded on the door, and he cursed again, hoping it wasn't Lynda. It was bad enough that she saw him as a helpless invalid, but he didn't relish the idea of her catching him in this stupid chair, reclined back the way he was, wearing that degrading hospital gown that covered only his thighs, revealing the stupid stockings and Ace bandages wrapped the length of his legs.

The door opened, and Mike, the guy from the airport, stuck his head in. "Hey, Jake. Is it a bad time?"

Jake breathed a sigh of relief. "No, come on in."

Mike stepped tentatively into the room, wearing the same look of awkwardness most people did when they saw him. "I thought I'd come by and see how you are doing."

"Terrific," Jake said, throwing up his hands. "I'm great. How are you?"

Mike went to the chair across from Jake and started to turn it around but saw the sweat pants lying at the foot of it. Bending down, he picked them up. "You want me to hang these up for you?"

Jake swallowed. "You can throw them out the window for all I care."

Mike's eyebrows rose. "Tired of them?"

Jake laughed sarcastically. "Yeah, that's it. I'm sick of them."

Mike sat down and was quiet for a moment, and Jake knew he wasn't making it easy on him. "Thought you might want some of your stuff," Mike said, holding out a box of Jake's things that were in the trunk of his car. Lynda thought you might want it, but I thought I'd make sure. If you don't need any of it, I could just put it back."

Jake considered it for a moment, wishing that he had some means of taking care of these things himself. "Uh, just put it back in the trunk. It's okay."

"All right," Mike said. "You know, it's really good to see you sitting up."

Jake gave a dry laugh. "Not all the way up."

"You're getting there."

"Maybe."

Mike shifted. "When I think how close you came to going up in that plane's explosion—I still don't know how she got you out."

Jake frowned. "How who got me out?"

"Lynda," Mike said. "The plane was on its side, and you were strapped into your seat. Somehow, she unfastened you and pulled you through the door then dragged you away, even before we could get there. The plane went up seconds later."

"She did that? With broken ribs, spleen damage, and cuts all over her? How?"

Mike smiled. "I guess somebody was helping her. Maybe there was a reason you weren't supposed to die."

Jake couldn't exactly swallow that. "Well, if you think of one, you let me know. Right now, I'm not looking toward some great purpose. All I want to do is get my pants on."

Mike looked down at the sweat pants he was holding. "These? Hey, man, I could help you with these." He got up and came to stand at Jake's feet, but Jake shook his head.

"No, that's all right. I don't need them."

"But you'll feel a hundred times better if you don't have to wear that gown. No offense man, but I don't think that's your look."

Jake grinned, then eyed the pants again. "If you could just get them over my feet and up to where I can reach them—"

"No problem." Mike slipped the pants over Jake's feet and slid them up his legs. As soon as Jake could reach them, Mike let him take over.

It took some effort, but Jake worked them under his hips and all the way up.

"Would you look at that?" Jake asked. "I look almost normal now."

Mike went to the closet. "Which shirt do you want?"

"Give me that Far Side T-shirt," Jake said, pulling the gown off over his head and tossing it to the bottom of the closet.

Mike handed him the shirt, and Jake pulled it on and tucked it in.

He looked down at himself and smiled. "Man, that feels better."

"It sure looks better," Mike said.

Jake looked up at Mike, gratitude in his eyes. "I owe you one, buddy."

"Well, then, we may as well run up the tab. I can come by tonight and help you change again if you want. Or drop by on my way to work in the morning."

"No need," Jake said. "I'll ask my PT. He just wasn't here this morning, and my OT is a woman. I think I'll be fine. Either that, or I won't take these off again."

Mike laughed and relaxed back in his chair, feeling like he knew Jake better already.

40

"I CAN'T BELIEVE my eyes," Lynda said later that day. "You're sitting up and dressed and everything."

Jake looked up at her from his wheelchair by the window, trying not to look quite so glad that she was here. "Yeah, but let me tell you. It's no picnic."

Lynda took the chair across from him. "When did this happen?"

"This morning. I got up to sixty degrees, so they left me here. I threw my usual tantrum, called them names, and threatened lawsuits, but they left me anyway."

He could see that she wasn't sure if he was kidding or not. "Don't you want to sit up?" she asked.

He shrugged. "It's not as simple as that, Lynda. Sitting up is a major ordeal. If I ever get all the way up, I'll never take it for granted again."

Her face softened. "I'm sorry, Jake. I didn't mean to be insensitive."

Now he felt like a heel. "It's okay. Actually, I asked them to leave me in the chair. I wanted to look out the window."

Lynda peered out at the parking lot below them. "So how is it?"

"Makes me feel more like a prisoner, frankly," he said quietly. "I'm stuck in here, and there's a whole world still out there."

"A whole bunch of cars, anyway. Oh, look. Is that a red Porsche parked over there? It looks just like yours."

Jake struggled upward to see it. "Where?"

"In that last row, off by itself."

Jake spotted it, and his face changed. "Yeah, it does look like mine. What do you know?"

"Me?" she asked with a grin. "Nothing. I don't know anything."

He looked up at her, his eye narrowing and saw her teasing grin. "Lynda, that wouldn't be mine—"

She nodded slowly. "I had Mike move it today. He said he came in and saw you."

Jake gazed hungrily down at the car. "He didn't tell me he brought my Porsche."

"It's a surprise," she said. "We were going to wait until you could see it out the window, but here you are."

His smile faded, and a look of longing came over his face—not for the car but for the life he'd had when he could drive it.

Lynda looked down at his chair. "Does this thing roll easily?"

"It's supposed to," he said.

"Then how about if I take you for a walk? We can go say hello to the car."

Jake grinned. "I'd like that. But what about your ribs? You're not supposed to push anything heavy, are you?"

"I'm doing a lot better," she said. "I'm getting my strength back. Don't worry."

"I don't want you hurting yourself for me, Lynda."

"Would I do that?"

"Of course you would. You already have."

"What does that mean?"

Jake's look was soft as he met her eyes. "Mike told me how you pulled me out of the plane. Nobody told me. I don't know how I thought I'd gotten out, but it never occurred to me that you'd done it."

"You would have done the same thing for me."

She started pushing him toward the door, and he mulled those words over. *Would* he have done the same thing? If she had been unconscious and he'd been the one awake, would he have risked his life to take the time to save her?

He doubted it. And if he *had,* he no doubt would have told her about it the moment she came to. He didn't like doing things he didn't get credit for.

But she'd done it and then hadn't mentioned it; she probably counted her heroism as such a natural thing that it hadn't occurred to her to tell him.

Shaking off the thoughts, he tried to be flip again. "So—has anybody tried to kill you today?"

She smiled. "Not today. I think it's all over now that they have Doug locked up. I'm starting to relax a little."

"So you feel pretty sure he did it?"

She was quiet for a moment. "Well—I still find it hard to believe. I mean, it's just weird that he would try something like that after all this time. But I guess things fester. Who knows what prison was like for him? Maybe he spent the whole time plotting his revenge on me."

As she spoke, she pushed him down the long hall and onto the elevator then to the first floor and through the courtyard where patients were scattered about under trees and strolled down sidewalks while the Florida sun shone down warmly and the autumn breeze cooled.

"How do you feel?" she asked after a moment.

Jake was smiling. "Fine," he said. "I'm feeling just fine."

"We can go back in any time you want."

"Not yet," he said. "I really do want to see my car."

She pushed him out onto the parking lot and through the rows of cars. He closed his eyes and let the sun beat down on his face and thought how good it was to be out of that controlled, air-conditioned environment.

When he opened his eyes again, he saw his car. Slowly, he smiled. "Not a scratch on it."

"No, it looks pretty good, for a Porsche."

He laughed as they got closer, and he touched the fender with featherlight fingers, as if greeting a cherished lover. "Man, what I wouldn't give to sit in it again."

Lynda's smile faded. "Well—I could go try to find an orderly who'd be willing to lift you in."

Jake shook his head. "No. I can't sit all the way up, remember? I'll save it for later."

The look she gave him was sweet and surprised. "Jake? Do you realize that's the first positive thing I've heard you say?"

"That I can't sit up?"

"No, that you'll save it for later. You know you're getting better, don't you?"

He sighed. "I guess so. I'm just not very optimistic about how much better I can get." He rolled to the window of the car, peered in at the plush, sleek seats that used to feel so natural beneath him. "Thanks for bringing it here, Lynda. It made the effort of sitting up worth it."

"Good," she said. "I'll leave it here for a while, so you can look out and see it any time you want."

He smiled. "That'll be good."

She wheeled him back to the courtyard where other patients and family members milled around. They found a shady place under a tree, and she sat down on a bench opposite him. Jake relaxed and looked up at the sky. It was cobalt blue, cloudless, a perfect day for flying. He wondered if he'd ever be able to experience that feeling again.

"Do you miss flying?" he asked her.

She nodded. "Yeah. I miss it pretty bad."

"What are you gonna do about your plane? Get another one?"

"No. I was going to sell that one, remember?"

He brought his gaze back to her. "But you loved it so much."

"Maybe too much. Anyway, I've kind of reconciled myself to giving it up for a while."

"What a waste," he said, his gaze returning to the sky. "You can fly and don't want to while I'd give my right arm to fly—and can't."

Lynda followed his gaze to the sky.

"They replaced me, you know," he went on. "I got flowers from my boss at TSA. I called him to thank him, and he said that he'd had to find a replacement. He said they were looking into a supervisory job on the ground if I wanted it, but I told him no thanks."

"Well, couldn't you at least consider it?"

"Right now, I'm not up to considering anything. I don't want to take a desk job, and I don't want to be on disability, and I don't want to be grounded for the rest of my life."

"You can get a medical waiver to fly with one eye, Jake, if you get use of your legs back. Maybe you can't fly for TSA, but you'll be able to fly again someday."

"But I loved my job." His voice caught, and he let out a heavy breath. "I guess I thought that maybe . . . by some miracle . . ." His words fell off, and she saw the tears gather in his eye as he shook the thought away.

After a moment, as if one dread reminded him of another, he spoke again. "We're having the unveiling Monday."

"What unveiling?"

He pointed to the bandage on his face. "The bandages. They're taking them off for good."

"Jake, that's wonderful."

Those tears seemed to well deeper. "Is it? I have a gash that goes through my eye to my cheekbone, Lynda. It was bad enough to blind me. I don't even know how many stitches I have. Do you honestly think I'm looking forward to seeing myself?"

"It'll be okay. You have good doctors."

"It doesn't matter how good they are if I have only one eye and a mug that would terrify children." He looked away, as though doing so could divert her attention from his tears. "You know, I was a good-looking guy. Women liked me. It was my greatest strength."

"I guess that's a matter of opinion."

"What? You didn't think I was good-looking?" he asked skeptically.

"Oh, there is no question that you were. But that wasn't your greatest strength. It never is. Maybe you needed to stop relying on your looks so you could find what you're really made of."

He felt his face reddening. "In other words, I was arrogant about my looks, so I needed to lose my face? Is that what you're saying?"

"No. What I am saying is that looks are just temporary, anyway. Don't you think it's time you go deeper into yourself to discover other strengths?"

"Wow," he said. "What did the doctor do? Ask you to prepare me for looking like the Elephant Man? Did he tell you to teach me to be beautiful on the inside?"

"No. Your face is going to be fine, Jake. You lost an eye. But you can still see. You're not blind."

"I'm blind enough to lose my job even if I get my legs back! What am I gonna do for a living?"

"Not everyone who works in the airline industry is a pilot, Jake—there are other positions, even at TSA. And if that doesn't appeal to you, you'll find something, Jake! You're an intelligent man. It's going to be all right."

Her reassurances seemed to make him angrier, and he looked off into the trees and shook his head dolefully. "Sometimes I wish I could have your kind of naivete."

"I'm not naive," she said. "In fact, I think I'm pretty savvy." She touched his hand, and he recoiled. "Jake, look at me."

He moved his disgusted gaze back to her. "What?"

"You're scared, but it'll be all right. In fact, I'll be here when they take the bandages off if you want. Do you want me to be here?"

He breathed a sarcastic laugh. "Yeah. You can give me another pep talk like this one after I see myself. You always make me feel so much better."

"I'm sorry, Jake," she said. "I haven't been trying to depress you, really. Do you want me there?"

His shoulders wilted, and he rubbed his forehead. "Yeah, I guess so," he said quietly. "I'll probably need somebody in my corner."

"Okay, I'll be here. And you'll see. You're probably even better looking now than you were before."

"Yeah," he said, not believing a word. "The scar will give me character, right?"

"Right. I happen to really like men with scars."

"Yeah, sure," he said. "I didn't notice any scars on that detective friend of yours."

She frowned. "Who, Larry?"

"Yeah, *Larry.*"

For a moment, she stared at him blankly, and he hated himself for sounding like a jealous lover. He wasn't jealous. He was just . . . curious. "So you two are getting pretty close, aren't you?"

She seemed to struggle with the smile creeping across her face. "There's something about having a maniac trying to kill you that makes you depend on the detective on the case. Call me crazy. I don't think I'll be seeing that much of him now, though, since they caught the guy."

She couldn't tell if Jake accepted that or not or if he even wanted to. Finally she stood up. "Are you ready to go back in?"

"Yeah," he said. "I have a hot date with Oprah. Can't miss that."

"Do you want me to bring you some books Monday? Or a radio? Or a hamburger?"

"Why don't we get these bandages off first, and then I'll decide if I have an appetite."

She looked down at him, wishing for the right words. "Are you that scared, Jake?"

He thought for a moment then said honestly, "Scareder than I was when we were about to crash. On Monday, I might just hit bottom."

41

WEARING HIS SHADED glasses and a fake mustache with his hair moussed back, Keith pulled into the parking lot outside the Schilling Building where Lynda worked and slowly drove through it, searching for her car. If only he could find it, he could wait for her to come out then follow her to wherever she was staying now. He could get her out of the picture once and for all and find Paige and Brianna in the bargain.

But her car wasn't there. It wasn't going to happen today. He tried not to let it discourage him.

But the clock was ticking, and recent developments hadn't helped his case any. If he knew Lynda Barrett, she'd find some way to use his arrest against him in court, even though he'd gotten off. She was slick that way. That's why she was dangerous. He never should have shown up that day at Brianna's school, but after the crash, he'd felt so sure he wouldn't meet with any resistance. If Paige didn't have a lawyer to run to, she would start feeling defeated and give in.

He'd always made her give in before. All those visits to the emergency room when he'd convinced her to tell the doctors that she had fallen down the stairs or been in a car accident or a dozen other creative stories he'd come up with, she had always complied.

Until Brianna had gotten hurt.

That, he admitted now, was his biggest mistake, but it wasn't as if it was all his fault. They'd been arguing, he and Paige, and she'd mouthed off to him, forcing him to crack her with a backhand across the face. Brianna had started crying—that loud, shrill, eardrum-piercing screaming that drove him up the wall—and someone *had* to shut her up.

It was his duty as a father to teach her to control herself.

But, as usual, Paige had gone off the deep end. And Lynda Barrett had empowered her to leave him, once and for all, and take his little girl.

But if he could get rid of Lynda now, he knew he could reason with Paige again. She *knew* he was a better parent. He made more money and could give Brianna nicer things. He could teach her self-control, teach her right from wrong. He could discipline her much more effectively than Paige, who let her run wild most of the time. And he was certain that he loved her more.

All he had to do was catch up with Lynda. She would have to report to work sooner or later, and when she did, he would be waiting. What he would do then he wasn't sure, but he knew something would come to him.

For a while, he drove around town—as he did every day before he reported to work—looking through parking lots of hotels and apartments, driving through neighborhoods and parks, looking for Paige's or Lynda's car, searching for his daughter's tawny head among the children at playgrounds.

He had even called Lynda's secretary, pretending he was an insurance investigator looking for her, but the woman wouldn't tell him a thing. When he'd asked her when she expected Lynda to return to work, she'd said maybe another week or two, possibly sooner.

He thought as he drove: What *would* he do when he finally caught up with her? She had escaped the crash and the fire, so this time his attack needed to be swift and vicious. And certain.

A bomb.

A slow smile came to his face as he flipped through the possibilities. It was easier to buy dynamite than a gun, and he knew enough about engines to rig it to her car. All he needed was a few ingredients and a window of time to plant it in the right place. Then it would be all over.

Turning the car around, he headed for the interstate. He'd have to buy the dynamite out of town, so the cops couldn't trace it to him after the fact. While he was at it, he should probably get a gun, too. Then if he discovered where they were all staying before Lynda returned to work, he could try one more time to get her out of the way.

One more time was all he would need.

42

THE BIG CHURCH that had once been like a home to Lynda was still warm and welcoming, but in many ways she felt like the Prodigal Son, covered with mud and pig slop, starving and remorseful as she returned to her Father's house.

At her side was Paige, holding Brianna on her hip, looking a little awkward and nervous as they stepped through the side door of the church and entered the hallway where the Sunday school classes were.

Paige's step slowed, and Lynda saw the trepidation on her face. "I hate to leave her. I know this sounds crazy, but what if somehow Keith found out we were coming? Or sees our car here? He's smart, Lynda. What if he comes to her class and takes her?"

Lynda knew she couldn't promise that nothing would happen, not when Paige had encountered so many surprises already. "I really wanted you to come to the adult class with me, Paige," said Lynda, "but I understand your fear and wanting to stay with Brianna."

"I think it's more important right now for *her* to be in Sunday school," Paige said. "Do you think they'd let me stay with her? I could help with the other kids."

She had half expected Paige to flee back home. This idea was at least better than that. "I'm sure it'll be all right," she said. "They always need help in the preschool area." She followed the signs to the class for three-year-olds and looked inside. A few children were already there, playing with blocks, coloring, and banging on the piano in the corner of the room. Lynda didn't know the teacher, and sadly she realized that a whole new group of people had become family members in the church in her absence. Maybe it wasn't even her family any more.

The teacher welcomed Brianna with delight and immediately interested her in some Play-Doh, and Lynda waited as Paige explained that she didn't want to leave her.

The teacher embraced Paige as an answered prayer. "My assistant just had a baby, and I didn't know how I was going to handle the class today. Come on over here, and you can help me get the glue out for the projects."

Satisfied that Paige was welcome, Lynda left the room and drifted back up the hallway, wondering if her class was still meeting in the same place. Despair and humility fell over her as she went up the hall, against the crowd beginning to get thicker and realized that the few people she did recognize didn't notice her.

And then she saw Brother Tommy, the pastor who'd once had such faith in her, the man who'd come to visit her in the hospital, who'd started a prayer vigil for her the moment he'd heard of the crash.

Like the Prodigal Son, she was transformed by the joy in his eyes, and he cut through the crowd, arms outstretched to meet her.

"It's so good to see you, Lynda." He hugged her carefully, as if he feared breaking her. "I've been waiting for you to come back."

Sadly, she looked around her. "I don't even know anyone any more."

"Sure you do," he said. "Come on. I'll go with you to your class. They'll be glad to see how their prayers have been answered."

The class met in the same place it had for years, and by the time the hour was over, Lynda felt accepted back into the family. When she met Paige and Brianna outside the sanctuary before the worship service, she felt so full of God's Spirit that she had no doubt some of it would spill over onto Paige.

43

ACROSS ST. CLAIR, Keith Varner worked at his kitchen table with the background noise of a broadcast church service filling the dead air in his apartment. He had all the ingredients laid out on the table in front of him: fuse wires, needle-nose pliers, ten pounds of Power Prime Dynamite, a blasting cap—everything he would need to blow Lynda to kingdom come.

All he would need was a few minutes under her car, and he could tape the bomb to her gas tank, wire it to the starter, and then get back and wait.

He could see it now. The explosion, the fire, the ambulances that would get there too late, and the media reports. And then he'd get a call from his lawyer saying that the court date had been postponed until Paige was able to find another lawyer. Only she wouldn't be able to get another lawyer because she had no money, and then she'd have to make a choice: either go into court to represent herself or give Brianna to him without a fight. And if she chose to represent herself, it would be a joke. Paige was not an articulate person, and she froze whenever she had to speak in front of a crowd. She would stutter and stammer and hem and haw, but she wouldn't make her case as clearly as he and his attorney would. It wouldn't take anything for the judge to rule that Keith was the better parent to have custody of his daughter. It was practically a done deal.

All he had to do was make sure that—once he caught up with Lynda Barrett—she would be taken out of the picture once and for all. And if he could get her when she was parked in her office parking lot, maybe she would have Paige's file and all of the evidence against him in her briefcase. That, too, would go up in flames.

He heard the choir on television singing the "Hallelujah Chorus," and with a round of laughter, he joined in.

He had an awful lot to be thankful for.

44

JAKE WAS SITTING upright in bed when Lynda got there on Monday morning, and she stopped and smiled at him before coming all the way into the room. "You look like sitting up comes more naturally now, Jake," she said. "Are the nausea and dizziness gone?"

"Yes, thanks to those two sadistic slave drivers who wouldn't let me rest until I was upright." He grinned slightly then and added, "Actually, I'm pretty thankful for them."

"So am I."

She came further into the room and set down the bag of magazines and books she'd brought him. "So have you heard from the doctor yet?"

His grin faded. "I'm told he's in the building, but he hasn't made it by yet." He breathed a sardonic laugh. "Amazing. Getting this bandage off seems like a matter of life and death to me, and to him it's just routine."

"It's going to be all right, Jake. I know it is. Have they prepared you at all? I mean, you've seen yourself when they changed the bandages, haven't you?"

"They wouldn't let me. The hospital shrink convinced the doctor that I couldn't handle it. When they took my eye out after the crash, they put in an implant and attached it to the muscles. They told me it doesn't look like an eye at all. In fact, they said it looks like the inside of my mouth. Talk about bloodshot."

Lynda stepped closer to the bed, realizing that this might be more grim than she'd expected. "I guess I figured they had already put an artificial eye in."

"No, they can't do that for another three weeks or so. Most of the swelling has to go down. Plus, they have to make the eye. The guy who makes them and installs them is coming by this morning, too, to fill me in on the gory details."

"The guy who makes them puts them in?" she asked, cringing. "Is he a doctor?"

"Nope. An optician."

"An optician in the operating room?"

"Apparently there's no surgery involved," he said. He glanced up at her and noted the dour expression on her face. "Hey, if you don't want to stay, I understand. In fact, I'm not too thrilled about anybody seeing this but me."

"I'm staying," she said firmly. "You're going to need somebody here. It's just—I didn't realize they did it that way."

Groping for something to get both their minds off the dread, she glanced at the untouched breakfast tray beside his bed. "Aren't you going to eat?"

He shook his head. "Can't. I don't have much appetite today."

"But Jake, you're losing so much weight."

"And you think that'll detract from my good looks?" he asked sarcastically.

"Well, it won't help your therapy. You need your strength."

"I can't eat," he bit out. "Period. So give it a rest."

"Fine."

He reached over to his bed table and pulled out the mirror he shaved with. As he gazed into it, Lynda realized that the bandage allowed him to imagine his eye still intact and his scars perfectly healed. After it came off, however, there would be no imagining.

"Did you know I was in a calendar once?" he asked quietly.

"A calendar? What kind?"

"It was a calendar that the Chamber of Commerce in Houston put together—Houston's eligible bachelors. I was August. For a couple of years, people recognized me wherever I went. I had women lined up. I even got fan mail."

She wasn't impressed. "And are you better for the experience?"

He thought for a moment. "All I know is I didn't have a scar down my face, and my baby blues were intact. Small things, I know, but they meant a lot to me."

The catch in his voice reminded her how hypercritical it was for her to pass judgment on his vanity, when she had lost so little in comparison. "They're not small things, Jake," she whispered. "It's got to be a trauma. But you know, don't you, that no matter what your face looks like under that bandage, they can do plastic surgery? They're doing great things now. And artificial eyes look real."

"Yeah," he whispered without conviction. "I keep telling myself that."

She was about to name all the celebrities she knew who'd had false eyes when the door opened, cutting off her thoughts.

"Good morning, Jake," the doctor said, coming into the room followed by an entourage of others. "Are you ready to get that bandage off?"

"Ready as I'll ever be."

"Great." The doctor was too cheerful, and Lynda wished he would make this a little easier, acknowledge Jake's suffering, offer him reassurances. As the doctor approached, she started to step away from the bed, but Jake caught her hand.

"No. Stay here."

"Okay," she said.

The doctor sat on the edge of the bed and got the scissors out of his pocket. "Jake, I'd like you to meet Dan Cirillo. He's the one who's going to be making your eye."

Jake shook his hand.

"Have they explained to you that you shouldn't be shocked when you see your eye, Jake?" Dan asked.

"Yeah, they warned me."

"It's not going to be pretty, but we'll put a patch over it until we can put a prosthesis in. After that, you'll be almost as good as new."

"Unless TSA has changed its policy about pilots having vision in both eyes, I won't be good as new." Turning back to the doctor, he said, "Let's get this over with."

Lynda held her breath as the doctor began to work the tape off Jake's face. She felt his hand tightening, and she squeezed back, wishing there were more she could do.

The doctor got the tape off and slowly began to peel the gauze away from Jake's face.

She saw the gash down his eyebrow, the black, blood-caked stitches that had been cleaned and sterilized with yellow iodine whenever the bandage had been changed. Now it was clear just how deep the gash on his face had been, deep enough to require several layers of stitches, and deep enough to destroy his eye.

"Yes, that's healing nicely," the doctor said in a pleasant voice as he worked the bandage further down. "When I saw that gash originally, I didn't know how well we'd be able to repair it. But this looks very nice."

But Lynda knew Jake's heart was going to be broken. The doctor uncovered his damaged eye, and she saw the small scar down the center of his eyelid, where it had been severed.

"Can you open that eye now, Jake?"

Jake opened it slowly, and it came only halfway up. In the socket was a pinkish-clear implant that looked nothing like an eye.

Perspiration beaded on her temples, and she tried to fight the tears threatening her. She couldn't cry. Whatever she did, she had to be positive. She had to smile.

The rest of the bandage peeled down easily, and finally, the doctor rolled it up and handed it to a nurse. Then, leaning in, he examined the gash. "Let me take these stitches out before I let you have a look," he said, reaching for another pair of scissors the nurse handed him. As he snipped, he kept talking. "The healing looks good, Jake. If you opt for plastic surgery later on, after it all heals, you can do a lot to get rid of this scar. For now, though, it looks like you lost a bad fight."

He finished snipping the stitches, pulled them out, and then cleaned the scar. "What do you think, guys?" the doctor asked. "Better than we expected?"

The others in the room concurred with scripted enthusiasm, but Lynda was silent.

The doctor got up, and Dan took his place to examine the eyelid.

Jake's hand still clung to hers.

"Most of this swelling should be gone in a couple of weeks, Jake. When that happens, you can come by my office, and we'll make you a new eye."

Jake looked up at him. "Come by your office? Will I be out by then?"

"Oh, you'll be going home in a few days, Jake," the doctor said as he made a notation on his chart. "You're doing fine. You're sitting up now, so there's no reason we should keep you here. You'll have to come back every day for therapy, of course, but there's no reason you have to stay here."

Ambivalence was written all over Jake's face. "Doc, I can hardly get around in that chair. Do you really think I'm capable of going home and taking care of myself?"

"Dr. Randall seems to think so, and he's ordered Allie to start concentrating on that a lot in the next few days," he said. "And we certainly don't mean to send you home alone. You'll need someone with you at first, to help you, and of course, you can't drive yourself back and forth to the hospital for therapy."

Lynda saw the emotional struggle on his face.

"So this is it?" Jake said. "You're accepting that I am like I am for good? You're not going to give me any more hope of getting better—or any more help?"

"There's plenty of hope, Jake, and we'll be helping you every day. We haven't given up on you."

She saw how desperately he struggled not to let go of his tenuous emotions, and finally, he looked up at Dan again. "So is this eye gonna wander all over the place? Are people going to know which eye not to look at when they talk to me?"

"It shouldn't," he said. "Artificial eyes have come a long way, Jake. They tend to move pretty well, especially if the initial surgery is done right. It looks like this was."

"Pretty well?"

"They satisfy most people who have them," he said. "But there are some methods to get more precise movement with the other eye. Most people don't think they need them after they see how well the eye moves, but for people who are on television, or say, models, we might go that extra mile and install a peg in the back of the eye that helps kick it around. Either way, the eye is going to be very similar to your other one. Most people won't realize you have a prosthesis."

Jake wasn't buying any of it, and Lynda had to admit that she wasn't either.

"So—are you ready to see?" the doctor asked.

Jake let go of her hand and took the mirror the doctor offered him. Slowly, he brought it to his face.

For a moment, he showed no expression as he saw the scar cutting down his face, the still-swollen socket where his eye used to be, the red conformer in the place of his eyeball, the black-and-blue bruising covering his forehead and most of his cheek.

"Not bad, huh?" the doctor asked.

Jake couldn't speak.

"It's not finished, Jake," Lynda whispered. "You have to give it time."

She saw the tear forming in his swollen eye, and felt some relief that he could still make tears. His face began to redden, and she realized that he was about to break down. She turned back to the doctor and the others. "Can you give him a little time alone?"

"Sure," the doctor said, patting his leg. "Jake, you give us a call if you have any problems. Lynda, here's the eye patch. It's easy to put on. Ring for a nurse if you have any problems with it."

Jake stayed silent as they left and kept staring blankly into the mirror.

"Do you want me to go, too, Jake?"

He didn't answer her, but his face grew redder, and he began to tremble.

"Jake?"

His face twisted, and his knuckles turned white as he gripped the mirror's handle. Suddenly, he hurled it across the room. It crashed against the wall.

"Stop it, Jake!" Lynda shouted.

But he didn't stop, and when he reached out and turned over the table beside his bed sending a cup of water, a plastic pitcher, a box of tissues, and the telephone crashing onto the floor, she covered her ears. "Jake, I know you're upset, but—"

His face still raging red, he scooted to the side of his bed, pushed his legs off, and acted as though he would stand on them and walk out on sheer anger.

"Jake, stop it!" she said, trying to hold him back, but he shook her away. "You know you can't do that! Jake, you'll fall!"

Gritting his teeth, he tried with all his might to stand on his feet, but they only hung there limply, brushing the floor without life.

The rolling tray of food sat next to his bed, and he swung his arm and sent it toppling over, too, his breakfast spilling onto the floor with a crash that reverberated throughout the room. Righting it, Lynda began to cry. Finally, she swung around to him, her hands in fists at her side. "Who cares about your stupid face!" she screamed.

He froze then and brought his tormented gaze up to her, staring at her with greater, deeper pain than she'd ever seen in anyone. Catching her breath, she cried, "It's not what matters, Jake! There's so much more to you!"

"That's easy for you to say," he said through his teeth. "Your face was only bruised!"

"And yours has a scar! It's not the end of the world, Jake! Your face has nothing to do with who you are!"

"Get out of my room," he said, trying to pull his legs back up. She reached over to help him, but he pushed her away again. "Just get out!"

Muffling her sobs, she ran from the room, not knowing what to do, where to go, how to help. For now, any help she offered was futile. Jake was hitting bottom, and there was nothing she could do to pull him back up. Not now. Not yet.

Instead of going home, Lynda found refuge in the prayer room and prayed that Jake's heart, so freshly broken, would start to seek God's face, instead of his own.

Jake couldn't remember weeping as hard as he wept that day. Now he knew the meaning of "gnashing of teeth." His teeth were gnashing, his heart was bleeding, and he didn't know where to turn.

No one could comfort him. No one. He would never be comforted again.

He wept over his distorted face and the legs that refused to move and his life that had been so prosperous and busy and content before. He wept over his loneliness, his isolation, despite how self-inflicted it was. And he wept over having no place to go even though he would be released in a few days. Where would he go when he couldn't even walk, and his face might frighten strangers? Was there a halfway house for maimed invalids?

Not for the first time he wished he'd died in the crash.

Jake Stevens, who always had so much control over his life, who was unfettered and uncommitted, who had all the money he needed, and who won friends and influenced women wherever he went, was now broken, alone, and homeless.

And there was no hope.

From the depths of his despair, from some place he didn't know existed inside of him, he cried out to God in fury. *I don't even know if you're up there, God, but I need a miracle.*

Did God hear him? He didn't know. But in that faithless moment of brokenness when he'd been sure that he was talking to thin air, he decided to believe that God had indeed heard him. He had no other choice.

45

JAKE WORE THE patch the next day, even though he was despondent and still refused to eat. He put forth little effort in therapy. He had determined that he was going to die even if it took every ounce of the strength he had remaining. Nothing mattered any more.

When Lynda knocked on his door, he was surprised. After yesterday, he had expected never to see her again. "What are you doing here?" he asked.

She stayed in the doorway, leaning against the wall. "I wanted to see how you are. I worried about you all night."

"I'm still here," he said. He swallowed and struggled with the apology on the tip of his tongue. "I figured I scared you off yesterday. Thought you wouldn't come back."

She started slowly toward him. "I never even considered staying away," she said. "You're not going to run me off just because you have a bad day."

"All my days are bad," he said.

She came to his bedside where he was sitting up. "You know, the way you reacted yesterday wasn't surprising. I might have done the same thing."

"Would you?" he asked sarcastically but without much fervor. "I would have thought you'd take it real philosophically. It's just a face, they're just legs, it was just my life."

"No," she said. "I wouldn't have felt that way at all. I'd be as mad as you were. I might not have the strength you had to throw things and knock things over, but I'd have been just as mad. You know, for somebody who has to stay in one spot, you sure did a lot of damage."

"Yeah," he said without humor. "Funny how much strength you can come up with when you don't care anymore."

"You do care, Jake. You know you do."

He fixed his sight on the ceiling. "Nope. That's where you're wrong."

Crossing her arms as if warding off his chill, she got up and stepped closer to the bed. "Well, anyway—I kind of like that patch. It gives you an air of mystery."

He kept staring at the ceiling. A tear fell to his cheek and rolled to his chin. "I'm gonna give little kids nightmares and old ladies heart attacks everywhere I go."

"No, you're not, Jake. They'll be fascinated, especially when you tell them the scar is the result of a plane crash."

He met her eyes directly for the first time that day. "Do you think the artificial eye is going to look just like mine?"

"I think so, Jake. They said it would."

"How can it?" he asked helplessly.

"I don't know how, but it can. Trust them."

He wiped the tear off his face and looked at the ceiling again. "I wonder if this is as good as it gets."

"Of course not. There are still several layers of stitches in there. There's a lot of swelling." She reached out and touched his injured cheek with her fingertips. "It'll go down," she whispered. "When these bruises clear, you'll see."

He took in a deep breath and caught her hand in his fist. Another tear dropped out, and he whispered, "No one back home would even recognize me. Not even my mother."

Lynda was confused. "Didn't you say your parents had both died?"

He let go of her hand then and covered his face, and a sob overtook him, then another, and another, until he wilted against her.

She sat next to him on the bed and held him, and she felt his arms closing around her, felt the despair, the loneliness, and the regrets wash out of him as he wept.

"I have a mother," he whispered. "I lie about her. But I have one."

"Jake, why haven't you told me? She should be here. I would have called her."

"She wouldn't have come," he said with certainty. "There's a lot of bad blood between us. She hates me."

"She can't hate you," Lynda said. "Mothers don't hate their sons."

"They do when their sons go years without seeing them, pretend they don't exist, and are too stingy to give a dime to help them out." He caught another sob, and his body shook with the force of it.

She pulled back to search his face. "But, Jake . . ."

"I'm being punished," he said, pointing to his injured face. "That's what all this is about. Before the crash, there was a lot of ugliness inside of me. Now I'm wearing it on the outside, too."

Lynda just held him tighter.

"I'll call your mother for you, Jake," she offered softly. "I'll talk to her. Does she know you're here?"

He shook his head. "She doesn't know anything about the crash. As far as she knows, I'm still living high, looking good, and trying to forget where I came from."

Someday she wanted to know just where that was, where Jake Stevens came from, but for now she was more concerned with where he was right now.

"Don't call her," he said. "I've got enough scars to last me a lifetime. I don't need any more."

"You need your mother, Jake. I'd give anything if mine were still alive and could be here with me one more time. There's so much I'd say to her."

"She *won't come,* Lynda."

"She needs to have the chance to decide that for herself."

"Fine, then," he said. "Call her. You'll see. She's the only Doris Stevens in Slapout, Texas. Just don't get your hopes up. Her tongue can slice right through you."

"I've survived worse," she whispered. "And so have you."

He crumpled in tears again and breathing a deep sob, shook his head viciously. "No, I haven't. I haven't survived. Not at all."

And as they clung to each other, Lynda searched for a way to make Jake see that it wasn't the end, it wasn't the worst, and he wasn't alone.

She would be here for him no matter how bad things got because in a strange way that she wasn't able to understand just yet, his despair had become her own. And she was determined to find a way to change it into joy.

"May I speak to Doris Stevens?"

The woman who had answered the phone didn't respond but just put the phone down, and Lynda hoped that she had gone to get Jake's mother. It hadn't been easy to track her down. First Lynda had called information, only to find that they didn't have a listing for Doris Stevens, so she had tried the Slapout post office. The postal clerk knew Doris and had explained that she was listed in the phone book under her initials, H. D. Stevens. Graciously, she gave Lynda the number then told her to try Grady's Truck Stop if she wasn't home. That was where Doris worked, she said.

Now she waited, listening to the noise of the crowd in the background, and hoping that Doris would be able to hear her. She had practiced all the way home from the hospital what she would say, but now that the moment had come, she had forgotten all of it.

"Hello?"

Lynda's heart skipped a beat. "Is this Doris Stevens?"

"Yeah, who wants to know?"

"My name is Lynda Barrett. I live in St. Clair, Florida. Ms. Stevens, I've gotten to know your son, Jake. He's here and—"

"Whatever he's done, I had nothin' to do with it."

Lynda hesitated. "Ms. Stevens, why do you think he's done anything?"

"Because he's got a heart of ice, that's why. I ain't seen the man in eight years. He got to be a big-shot pilot, and now he's ashamed of me. Well, you know what? I don't care. I'm ashamed of him, too."

This was harder than Lynda had imagined. "Ms. Stevens, Jake's been in an accident. A plane crash."

"What?"

The voice came through louder, clearer now, and she imagined the woman clutching the phone tighter. "That's right. About three weeks ago."

"Three weeks?" She hesitated, and then in a softer voice said, "That's about when he called me. He didn't tell me nothin' about no plane crash."

Lynda didn't know what to say to that. Why would Jake have called her and not told her that he was lying in the hospital? "He was injured badly, Ms. Stevens. He has a bad back injury that has caused paralysis in his legs."

"He can't walk?"

"No. There is a possibility that the paralysis will go away, though. They think when the swelling goes down, the feeling may come back. But there's no guarantee. And he also had a severe cut to his face and lost an eye."

Doris muttered an expletive then asked in a wobbly voice, "So what do you want from me?"

The question took Lynda by surprise. "Nothing. I just thought you'd want to know that your son is in the hospital in a lot of pain. Ms. Stevens, he's absolutely alone. He apparently doesn't know many people here—"

"What is he doin' there, anyway? I thought he lived in Houston."

She couldn't believe that Jake hadn't told his mother he was moving. "He was in the process of moving here when this happened. Ms. Stevens—he needs you."

She laughed then, a bitter, cold laugh. "Oh, yeah? Well, where was he when I needed him? Huh?"

"I don't know."

"Yeah, well, neither do I. Is there a lawsuit involved here? Is he suin' somebody?"

Until now, the thought had never occurred to her that Jake could sue her. Deciding against telling her that it was her plane and that she had been in the same crash, she said, "No, not that I know of."

"Then there's no money involved?"

"No. I haven't heard him suggest suing, at all."

"Then there's no need in my comin', is there?"

She didn't want to believe that Jake's mother was mercenary enough to see dollar signs in Jake's accident, so she chose to believe that it was a question of how she would finance the trip. "Uh—if you don't have the money, I'd be happy to send you a plane ticket."

The woman hesitated. "I wouldn't have a place to stay."

"I'd pay for your hotel, too," she said. "Will you come, Ms. Stevens?"

Again a pause. "What's the weather like there this time of year?"

"It's fine. Nice."

"Nice enough to go to the beach?"

She closed her eyes. Surely she wasn't looking at this as an opportunity to take a free vacation. "I don't know, Ms. Stevens."

"How close are you to Disney World?"

Reality began closing in on her. "I would think your time would be spent with Jake. Don't you care about his condition?"

"Let me tell you something," the woman spat back. "I raised that ingrate by myself with no help from anybody. I was there for him until the day he skipped town without lookin' back. When I was strugglin' and needed a hand, he wasn't there for me. So now, when he can't walk and can't see, I'm supposed to welcome him back with open arms so I can wait on him hand and foot? What's in it for me?"

For a moment, Lynda was quiet. "Maybe the knowledge that you did everything you could for your son?"

"I already did that," she said. "I don't owe him nothin' more."

Slowly Lynda set the phone back in its cradle and rested her face on her palm. No wonder he had lied about his mother. No wonder he hadn't visited her. Their relationship was an endless cycle of blame and selfishness and anger, a cycle that Lynda wasn't wise enough to break.

But what would she tell Jake? That his mother wouldn't come unless there was a monetary settlement involved or a trip to Disney World or nice weather for sunbathing?

How could a mother have such contempt for her son?

"Are you crying, Miss Lynda?"

Lynda turned around and saw Brianna standing in the doorway, looking up at her with big, curious eyes.

"Come here."

Brianna came slowly toward her. "Why are you crying?"

"Because somebody just made me real sad." She pulled Brianna into her lap, and the child kept gazing at her.

"Did somebody hit you?"

"No."

"Did they try to take you?"

She realized then that Brianna was going down the list of things that made her sad, and Lynda felt a twofold rush of sorrow. Closing her eyes against the tears, she dropped her face to Brianna's crown. "No, Brianna, no one tried to take me. I'm sad for someone else."

"So they won't have to be?" she asked, as if trying to understand this new concept of surrogate sorrow.

She smiled. "Something like that."

Brianna laid her head against Lynda's chest, as if she knew that sitting still might be of some comfort to her, and finally, she looked up at her again. "Do you like to color?"

Lynda smiled. "Yeah. Yeah, I do."

Brianna slid out of her lap. "Come on, then."

And Lynda realized that the child's simple therapy might be just what she needed right now.

46

IT FELT LIKE a burning, tingling sensation, just on the outside of his big toe. Nothing to get excited about.

But Jake got excited anyway. He jerked the sheets off his legs and peered down at his feet.

He'd been so exhausted when he'd gotten back from rehab today—where they'd forced him to work despite his indifference—that he had almost forgotten the scar and his eye. Maybe now he was just imagining the sensation. Maybe he just wanted to feel it so badly.

But it felt real, and his surprise gave birth to a fragile hope.

He started to call the nurse but changed his mind. What if he told the nurses, and they assured him it was just a side effect from the traction they'd had him on in the rehab room? What if he found out that it was nothing?

He focused all his concentration and every ounce of his energy into that big toe, willing it to move. But it lay still, dead, not getting the messages his brain was sending.

Was this no different than the pressure he felt when he was touched or pulled? Was it without meaning?

He heard Lynda's familiar rat-tat-a-tat-tat knock on the door and called, "Come in."

She came into the room all cheer and sunshine, and he debated whether to tell her what he felt.

"Hi," she said.

"Hi." He kept staring at his foot.

"How'd your rehab go today?"

"Good."

She followed his gaze to his toe. "What are you looking at, Jake?"

He didn't answer for a moment then finally looked up at her. "My toe," he said. "I've been feeling some pain in it. Kind of a burning."

She caught her breath and with wide eyes, went to stand at the foot of his bed. Touching the toes on both feet, she asked, "Can you feel this?"

His eyes grew wider. "Just on that toe. But I feel you touching that toe!"

She was trying to hold back her excitement, just as he was. "Have you tried to move it?"

"I was trying," he said. "It hasn't budged."

"Well, try again. Come on, Jake. Move it."

Silence fell over the room as he found his concentration again, and as though he could telekinetically move the toe, he stared down at it.

"Was that a twitch?" she asked finally. "I thought I saw a twitch!"

Jake wasn't sure. He tried again, and this time the toe moved an eighth of an inch.

"You did it!" Lynda cried, jumping up and slinging a fist through the air. "Oh, Jake, you moved it!"

He started to laugh, and she ran around the bed and hugged him.

"Call somebody before I forget how," he said.

With trembling hands, she found the button that called for the nurse.

It was definitely cause for celebration, Dr. Randall said when he finally made it to the hospital to examine Jake. It might mean that Jake could get his legs back.

But for all his newfound hope, Jake couldn't escape the doctor's qualifier that it didn't mean he'd get all his feeling back, or get movement in his leg or the rest of his foot. But this was something.

Torn between exhilaration and frustration, he asked Lynda to take him out of the hospital.

Glad to be asked for anything, she wheeled him outside where night had already descended, and the stars lit up the sky with a magnificent brilliance. Jake leaned his head back and looked up, taking it all in.

Lynda had gotten quiet, and he could see that something was on her mind. Maybe there was something she didn't want to tell him. When they got to a small park near the hospital, she locked his wheels and sat down on a bench facing him.

He met her eyes squarely. "What's wrong, Lynda?"

"Nothing. Why do you think something's wrong?"

"I could read it in your mood swings today," he said. "As happy as we got, something kept bringing you down."

He studied her face for a moment. "She won't come, will she?"

Lynda couldn't deny it. "No."

He took in a deep, ragged breath. "It's okay," he said, trying not to look crestfallen. "I told you it would be that way. What did she say?"

He saw the turmoil on her face and realized that it must be bad, too bad for her to relate to him. He almost wished he hadn't asked. "She's just . . . busy right now."

Jake looked into the breeze and thought about the last time he'd seen his mother. He wondered if she had changed, or if the years of hard work, cigarette smoke, and nights spent in the truck stop flirting with the patrons had aged her. "When you told her about my injuries . . . What did she say?"

"She was shocked," Lynda said. "She said you had called her since the crash, and you didn't say anything about it."

"She didn't seem all that receptive." He could see by her face that she knew what he meant. "There's a lot of water under our bridge, Lynda," he went on. "I haven't been proud of where I came from, and I haven't been particularly proud of her. I've said and done some hateful things. She has a reason for hating me."

As he spoke, he felt exposed, open, as transparent as he'd ever been in his life. But Lynda had already seen farther into him than anyone else ever had. "I think you're changing, Jake."

He breathed a laugh. "Oh, yeah? You think so?"

She smiled. "I don't think the old Jake would ever have admitted guilt."

"Well, I've had a lot of time to think about it over the last few weeks."

Her smile faded. "Have you been thinking about going home, Jake?"

He averted his eyes again and studied the trunk of the tree next to him. "Home where? I've thought of going back to Texas to finish my therapy there. There are people there I could probably stay with. That is, if they aren't too repulsed by me. I haven't even told them I've been hurt."

She wasn't sure why that disappointed her. "Is that what you want to do?" she asked.

He sighed. "I don't know. It honestly feels like I'm somebody else now. Like the Jake Stevens they all knew is dead. And here I am in his useless shell, trying to figure out who I am now. And nothing against all my friends, but most of them are kind of—self-centered. I can't see them wanting to help out an invalid."

"You're not an invalid," she said. "You're just in transition. You need time."

Something about that sweet declaration made his heart soften, and he smiled at her. She leaned forward, her big, round eyes drilling into his, and he wondered how she had managed to make him risk more honesty with her than he'd ever risked with anyone else. Even himself.

"I had an idea," she said. "But I don't know how you'll feel about it."

"What?"

She averted her eyes and studied her hands. "I've been staying at my father's house, and there's a garage apartment there that used to be mine. It's got a small kitchen, a refrigerator, and a bathroom, and it's pretty comfortable." She made herself meet his gaze. "I was thinking that . . . maybe when they release you . . . you could stay there. I could take care of all your meals, transport you back and forth to the hospital for your therapy every day, and help you in whatever way you needed. But you'd still have your privacy."

A lump the size of Wyoming formed in his throat, and he gaped at her, not believing that he'd heard her right. "I couldn't, Lynda. That's too much of an imposition. You're recovering, too. The last thing you need is somebody like me in your way."

"You won't be in the way. You'd have your own place. You won't have to worry about rent or food or anything for a while. I have someone else staying with me, a client of mine and her daughter. She's hiding from her abusive ex-husband until we can get into court. Between his shenanigans and the stuff that's already happened to me, we're both a little paranoid. It might be nice to have a man around the house."

The word "man" shook him, for he hadn't thought of himself as a man in a long time. "Not that I'd be of any use if anything happened," he said. "I guess I could run over somebody in my wheelchair, but it's not like I can defend you."

She smirked. "I don't know, Jake. You were pretty dangerous the other day. If you had something to throw—"

He took it as it was intended and chuckled softly.

"Besides, we don't need defending," she said. "Her ex doesn't know where we are, and the guy who was after me is still in jail. Your presence will just lend a little stability."

She didn't mean it, he thought. She was just saying that to make him feel needed, but he had to admit he appreciated it. She was giving him the option of keeping his dignity, his masculinity. She was offering him a home, temporary though it might be.

It was better than any other option he had.

She saw his reticence. "Come on, Jake. Say yes if for no other reason than to appease my conscience. It was my plane that crashed. Let me make it up to you as much as I can."

Tears came to his eyes, and he struggled to hold them back. "You don't have to buy my forgiveness," he whispered after a moment.

"That's not what I'm doing," she said. "The truth is neither your feet nor your hair needs washing, so I can do this instead."

"What?"

She smiled. "Never mind. Just say yes."

He sighed. "You're going to regret it."

"No," she said with a smile. "I don't think I will."

47

THE SOUND OF his heels echoed through the old, musty judicial building as Keith checked the sign on each door, looking for the county clerk's office. He was tired of waiting. He'd spent most of several days watching the parking lot at Lynda's law firm, but she hadn't been there yet. Then he'd tried to get her forwarding address by sending something to her old address with a note to the post office to return it with her new one. But the address they had returned was to a post office box. He had even tried staking out the post office, but he hadn't been able to be there all the time, and if she'd checked her box, he'd missed her.

But he wasn't stupid. He had resources, and he knew how to use them. And he was going to start with public records. It had been worth the drive to St. Petersburg where the county records were kept, and though he didn't know what he was looking for, he was sure he'd know when he found it. His goal for now was to find every public record that existed on Lynda or her family. Something there would have to give him a clue.

He found the office and went into the dimly lit room that looked as if it could use a good electrician to update the wiring. A young couple was there getting a marriage license. Smirking, he leaned on the counter and thought of telling the poor guy to save his fifteen bucks and run like the wind. But the kid was young—too young to be reasoned with, old enough to make mistakes that would ruin his life. Just like Keith had been when he and Paige had stood there, giggling like this couple and anticipating the life they were planning together.

But that was before he'd learned what a shrew she was.

Now, on the battleground of their marriage, his daughter had become the spoils. Didn't Paige realize what her obstinance was going to cost her? Didn't she understand that when he got through with her, she'd have nothing left? Least of all Brianna.

The couple blushed over their finished license, and Keith flashed them a saccharine, congratulatory smile then winked at the lady behind the desk. "Cute kids," he said as they left the room.

"Yes, they are," she said. "I hope everything works out for them."

"I'm sure it will," he said. "We've been married for ten years now, and we're as happy as the day we came in here to get our license."

"Oh, that's nice."

"Yes. Course, I realize that not everybody is as lucky as I am, but we work at it, you know? Teamwork. It's the only way."

He could have sworn her eyes were twinkling as she smiled up at him. "That's so rare these days. Frankly, I worry about every couple that comes in here. I pray for them."

"Good for you," he said. "Good for you."

She cleared off the papers she'd had them sign and stuck them in the appropriate bins. "Now, what can I do for you?"

"I need to look up some public records."

"All right," she said, grabbing a form out of another bin. "Just fill this out, and I'll show you how to find them. What exactly are you looking for? A person or a property?"

"A person, but that might lead me to real estate."

"That's fine. And what is the last name of the person you're looking for?"

He almost gave her Lynda's last name then realized that there had been too much publicity about the attempts on her life. "Barnett," he said finally. "Frank Barnett."

"All right," she said, taking the form back and checking the fake signature. "Just follow me. We have A through J in this room."

She took him to a huge room full of volumes of public records for Pinellas County and led him to a computer where she showed him how to find the name of the person he was looking for, see the list of documents the county had on that person, and determine what volume the record was in.

He thanked her profusely then waited as she left him alone.

The moment he typed in Lynda's name, two listings came up. Quickly he jotted down where to find her birth certificate and the documents pertaining to her property. There was no record of a marriage license or a divorce or any judgments against her or any other documents.

Leaving the computer, he found the book with her birth certificate and flipped through it until he found her name. There she was.

As if he'd found some crucial bit of information, he stared down at it with a smile and quickly jotted down both parents' names and her birthdate in case he ever needed it.

The documents on her house would be useless now; the house was burned, so she wouldn't be going back. He went back to the computer and typed in her mother's name.

A list of records emerged, and he jotted down the number of the book that had records on her property. He scanned the list again, looking for anything else he could use and saw her death certificate.

Dead end, he thought, clearing the screen.

He punched in her father's name. Again, he jotted down the property book and came across another death certificate.

Frustrated, he sat back in the chair.

All right, he told himself, *don't give up yet. There's got to be something here.*

Looking down at his note paper, he noticed a connection. One of the numbers on the list of Lynda's properties matched the book number for the property on both of Lynda's parents. Had she inherited their home? If so, it surely wasn't the one that had burned down—that one had been far too new and expensive.

He flew to that book, pulled it out, and shuffled through the pages until he came to what he was looking for—A house on the other side of town, bought forty years ago; ownership had been transferred to Lynda three months ago upon the death of her father!

He banged his fist on the table then waved it over his head in exhilaration. This was it! It had to be. She was staying in her father's home, and he had found her! Paige and Brianna were probably there with her!

He slammed the book shut but didn't bother to put it back. Quickly, he went back to the computer, cleared the screen so no one would link him to her, and headed out without another word to the clerk.

48

IT HAD BEEN months since the garage apartment had even been opened and years since it had been used for more than storage. With Paige's help, Lynda cleaned all of the junk out of it then set about scrubbing. A thick layer of dust had settled over every piece of furniture, and the bedspread and sheets and curtains all smelled musty. She gathered them all up to wash while Paige vacuumed the mattress and couch, the recliner, and the carpet, which really didn't look so bad considering how old it was.

"Does this Jake person know about me?" Paige asked in a slightly troubled voice as she worked.

"Yes. I told him last night."

"Mmmm." She coiled the cord on the vacuum cleaner then got her bucket from Brianna, who was sitting in the empty bathtub, "scrubbing it" with a dry brush. "So you say he's paralyzed? He can't walk?"

"No, he can't. What's the matter, Paige?"

Paige shrugged. "I don't know." She started to say something, stopped, then tried again.

"What is it, Paige? What's on your mind?"

Paige leaned back against a wall and looked down at her feet. "I was thinking. Maybe it's time we went on home."

"Home? Are you serious?"

"Well, yeah. I mean, Jake's coming, and you won't be alone any more."

"But Paige, what about Keith?"

Paige thought that over for a moment. "He's probably cooled down by now. His rages don't usually last that long. He's probably feeling real bad about what he did, and when he gets like that—sorry and all—he can be okay. Maybe I don't have to be afraid of him."

Lynda wanted to scream at her that she was being stupid, but if her time with Jake had taught her anything, it was that she had to learn diplomacy. "Paige, if you go back home and have any contact with him at all, it could ruin our case. And it could get you killed."

When Paige covered her face with her hand, Lynda stepped closer. Removing Paige's hand and making the young woman look at her, she said, "Paige, what's really wrong?"

"I don't know. Maybe I'm just homesick. And with Jake coming—I don't know; I'm just not very comfortable around men."

"But you weren't uncomfortable with Larry or Tony."

"I didn't have to be *alone* with them much. Besides, I knew they were protecting me."

"Well, think of Jake as protecting you, too. And you're not really going to be alone with him. I'll be here."

"Yeah, but you'll be going back to work soon." She caught herself and tried to rally. "I'm sorry. You're helping me, so you have every right to help him, too. It's awfully nice of you. I'm sure he needs help. I'll get over it."

"But will you get over it here or at home?"

Paige met Lynda's eyes, and Lynda saw the struggle there. "You'd hate me if I went back home, wouldn't you?"

"No, Paige, but I think *you* would hate you."

"But I'm not considering taking him back. Not at all. I just miss things being familiar."

Lynda sat down and studied the carpet for a moment, trying to find the right words. "Paige, familiarity has a lot of power. That's why you went back to Keith all those times before. It probably had a lot to do with familiarity, didn't it?"

Paige nodded.

"And if you let familiarity cause you to put yourself in danger again, don't you think that when—not if, but when—Keith shows up, he'll be able to convince you one way or another to take him back for that same familiarity?"

"Maybe, but—"

"Paige, he might take Brianna this time and go so far that you'd never see her again. The court date isn't that far off. He's bound to be getting desperate."

Paige's face changed, and she glanced into the bathroom at Brianna, who was singing the theme from "Barney." When she looked back at Lynda, she whispered, "You're right. Absolutely."

Lynda got up and faced Paige head on. "Paige, Jake's paralyzed. Why would you be worried about what he might do?"

"That's the crazy part. I know he won't hurt me if he's your friend, and I know he couldn't if he wanted to. But—men are so unpredictable to me. I never knew what to expect with Keith. Just when I thought I had all my bases covered, he'd show me that I didn't."

"You have them covered now, Paige. Right?"

Her sigh suggested she wasn't sure. "Maybe being around Jake is what I need now. Maybe he'll restore my faith in men."

Lynda wished she could say that was possible, but she wasn't so sure. "Well—he's a little scary-looking right now. He has a patch over his eye and a big scar down his cheek, and he's not the most pleasant person to be around because he's so angry about his injuries. But I've watched him change since I met him. In big ways. And he's going to keep changing. He'll have to if he's going to make it. But he'd never hurt you or Brianna. More likely, he'll keep absolutely to himself, and you won't see him at all except to take him meals."

Paige regarded Brianna, still sitting in the empty bathtub. "I guess I should realize how lucky I am," she said. "I have my legs, both eyes, and I have Brianna." She smiled and turned back to Lynda. "And I have you. So does he. Because of that, I promise to make him feel welcome here."

"Thank you, Paige. I knew I could count on you."

49

KEITH KNEW BETTER than to drive down her street; it looked like a dead end. Instead, he parked his car a couple of blocks away in a small church parking lot and walked into the thick woods that lined one side of the street, except where it had been cleared for houses. There were only about three houses on the street, two right at the entrance and one secluded down at the dead end. He worked his way quietly through the woods, trying not to be seen.

There was someone outside at the first house he passed, a man working in the garden, so he assumed that wasn't the house. He crept forward until he had a clear view across the street and read the numbers on the opposite house. That wasn't it, either.

So it must be the one at the far end of the street. He stole through the trees and came up to the cyclone fence that defined the property. But there was no sign of any of them. He needed to get around front to see if he could identify one of their cars.

He was just about to risk stepping out of the woods when the back door opened. Keith froze.

He saw his little girl bounce out, and his heart melted.

It had been so long since he'd seen Brianna happy. The last few times she'd been screaming her lungs out, after all those ideas Paige had put into her head about him. But once he got her, he would manage to erase those ideas and turn them back on Paige. Then Brianna would be just as happy with him as she was now without him.

He trembled with anticipation as she walked out into the yard, talking to her doll as she went, and he poised himself to act the moment she came close enough. He could reach over the fence, grab her, and have her out of here before Paige even knew she was gone.

He wished he'd brought some candy or something to keep her quiet until they got away.

But then Paige came out with a broom and started sweeping the back porch. That was her, always cleaning, as if she couldn't stand to sit still.

Well—too bad. He would grab Brianna anyway, whether Paige saw or not. Maybe he could get out of there before she could get to the phone—

No. That was ludicrous. He'd be arrested before he got his car started. And he'd probably wind up in jail. This time, McRae would probably wash his hands of him, and he wouldn't have an advocate in court, and that lady lawyer would convince the judge that he was dangerous.

Quietly, he sat down on the ground behind a bush and watched, waiting for Paige to go back in and for Brianna to come near the fence. His only hope was to take her when Paige wasn't watching, so he'd have a head start in getting away.

But that wasn't going to happen today.

Paige said something to the child, and Brianna turned and frolicked in behind her mother. The door closed.

He didn't move. Maybe they would come back out. Maybe Brianna would stray out here alone. . . .

He heard another door close, one he couldn't see from this position and then a car door. In seconds, he heard the car in the driveway starting.

They were leaving!

Jumping up, he ran through the trees back toward his car parked at the little church, hoping to catch up with them and follow them. But by the time he was behind the wheel, they were nowhere in sight.

Cursing his luck, he slammed his hand against the wheel. Didn't it always happen this way? Fate just kept working against him.

But it wouldn't forever. Sooner or later, something had to give. He thought of the possibilities, now that he knew where they were living. He couldn't set this house on fire because Brianna might be hurt. And if he installed the car bomb here, Brianna might be in the car or nearby when it blew up. No, he couldn't do anything that might put her in danger again. But he could watch the house; he could follow Lynda and, when she got to where she was going, fix a little surprise in her car. Or, if he kept watching, sooner or later Paige would take her eyes off Brianna and he could grab her. Either way, when the chance came, he would be there.

Time was running out, and he was getting anxious. But he was several steps ahead of the game already.

And he intended to win.

50

THE MORNING JAKE was to be released Lynda gave the garage apartment one final inspection. It was clean now, and she'd moved things around to accommodate his wheelchair. While the room wasn't as luxurious as he was probably used to, it was certainly better than a hospital room. She sat down in her father's recliner, which she'd asked Larry to move out here for Jake, and looked around at the small rooms her father had so lovingly built for her.

She had never forgotten the ribbon-cutting ceremony her parents had had for her the day she'd moved into the room. Her father had made a little speech in which he told her that while this room signified her independence from her parents, its proximity to the house symbolized that no matter how independent she grew or how far away she moved, she would always belong to them. Always.

As she sat here now, breathing the familiar scents and absorbing the warm colors and textures, she missed her parents. As much as she'd wanted to believe she was independent when she'd moved into this room, she had been far from it. Her parents had helped her to take her first leap out of the nest gracefully. They had made it easy for her, until she'd learned to fly on her own.

In many ways, Jake was like she had been then. She would have to teach him that he could be independent and that he could make it on his own. But she also wanted to teach him who he belonged to. And she surprised herself—she who had been so long without darkening the doorway of a church—with the fervency of her desire that Jake understand this.

She bowed her head and whispered a heartfelt prayer that this room would be blessed and that God would change Jake here. Then she got out the Bible she had bought especially for him and slipped it into the drawer of the end table beside the recliner. She wouldn't mention it; he would have to discover it for himself. She only hoped she would be able to help him understand the truth of its message.

She couldn't preach to him or force him. All she could do was pray for him.

Jake's life—both physical and spiritual—was in God's hands.

Allie walked beside Jake's wheelchair as he left the hospital, letting him push the wheels to move it along. He couldn't believe they were sending him home like this, still unable to walk. Oh, Allie had taught him how to function well enough in day-to-day activities, and now that he could sit all the way up and had this smaller, more maneuverable chair, he was much more capable. But he still didn't like it. Hospitals are supposed to heal people, not teach them how to cope with their brokenness.

But the alternative—*staying* in the hospital—was worse. He'd rather be going away somewhere, even if it wasn't home.

Lynda had brought the car to the front entrance. She had dressed up for the occasion, he saw, and had pulled her hair up in a loose chignon. He wondered why she'd bothered.

"Do you need help getting in, Jake?" she asked.

He wasn't sure whether he did or not but decided not to accept it anyway. "I can do it," he said, sidling his chair up to the open car door.

"You can do it, Jake," Allie said, not offering a hand to help. "Just use your arms and your stomach."

He could feel them all holding their breath as he got his arms into position then slid his body onto the car seat.

As if he'd just completed some Olympic feat, they all congratulated him. He felt like a toddler who'd just gone to the potty by himself, and the idea of such pathetic enthusiasm worsened his mood.

Lynda closed his door and got into the driver's side, but Allie came to his window. Jake lowered it.

"Just because you're going home doesn't mean you can neglect your therapy, Jake. I want you back here at nine tomorrow, and Lynda can just plan to leave you for six hours or so. We'll see if we can get some more of your toes to burn."

He smiled in spite of himself; he liked the sound of that. "I'll be here."

And as they drove away from the hospital, Jake wasn't sure whether to consider it a beginning or an ending. To him, it seemed as though he left the old Jake back there in the morgue, and he didn't yet know who the new Jake was.

51

A BUTTERFLY LIT on Keith's shoulder, and he waved it away and peered between two bushes to the yard where Brianna played. Paige had set up a little tea party for her, and she had all her dolls in attendance. He smiled as she talked aloud to her friends and herself like a little princess to her courtiers.

But as always, Paige was right there, hovering over her. Calculating the distance to his car, which he'd parked on the closest street behind Lynda's house through the woods, he tried to decide whether he should chance jumping the fence and grabbing Brianna. Sweat broke out on his forehead, and he wiped it on his sleeve. He would have the advantage of surprise. Paige would probably be stunned long enough for him to get Brianna. It would probably take less than ten seconds to get back over the fence and maybe another thirty to get back to his car. By the time Paige stopped screaming and got to the phone, he would have blended into the cars on the main road a mile or so away.

The butterfly flitted across the fence and lit in some wildflowers growing in an old, untended garden. Keith watched Brianna laughing with one of her dolls and then pouring more invisible tea and offering it a cup.

He heard a car pull up in the front, and his heartbeat accelerated. "Lynda's home," Paige said as she got up. "I'll be in front, okay, Brianna?"

Brianna nodded indifferently as Paige went around between the garage and the house, and a slow smile came to Keith's lips. Was Brianna really alone?

He straightened and stepped through the bushes, watching his child with hungry, anxious eyes. He watched the butterfly flit over to the table where she sat.

"Mommy, it's a butterfly!" she said, her voice soft so that she wouldn't frighten it away.

It fluttered off, and Brianna got up and followed it. It lit in a piece of grass, and she bent over, trying to coax it onto her finger, but it flew a little further. As if it were in cahoots with Keith, it led her closer, closer, closer to the fence until she was almost close enough to reach.

Keith stepped into her view and touched the fence, whispering, "Brianna."

She looked up at him, stunned. The butterfly flew away.

His heart hammered, and his hands shook; there was so little time before Paige came back.

"Come closer, honey," he whispered, leaning over the fence. "Come give Daddy a kiss."

Her bottom lip began to tremble, and she backed away, farther out of his reach.

"Brianna, I said to come here," he said more firmly. "Now."

She started to cry and looked around for her mother, who was nowhere in sight.

He was getting angry now. This wasn't working out like he'd planned. Gritting his teeth, he whispered, "Brianna, I told you to come here right now! I'm your daddy!"

He started to lunge over the fence, but Brianna screamed and lit out across the yard.

Cursing, Keith realized he'd gone too far; he'd never catch her before she made it to the front yard. Afraid of being caught, he tore back through the woods to his car.

Lynda had just gotten Jake into the apartment and introduced him to Paige when they heard the scream.

Paige dashed outside and found Brianna almost to the garage apartment already, shrieking. "What is it, honey? What's wrong?"

"Daddy! Daddy! He's gonna take me!" she screamed.

Paige stepped back into the doorway, looking helplessly at Lynda. "No, honey. Daddy can't get you here."

"It's him!" Brianna screamed.

"It's me, isn't it?" Jake asked. "She saw me coming in, and I scared her."

Paige wasn't sure. "Honey, that's not Daddy. That's a nice man named Jake. Remember I told you he was going to live here? Remember we got the room fixed up for him?"

Hiccuping her sobs, Brianna refused to look up.

Paige looked apologetically at Jake. "She's—terrified of men. If you knew her father you'd know why. I'm so sorry."

"It's all right," he said. "I make a pretty scary first impression."

"I'll take her in," Paige said and quickly hurried back toward the house.

The silence in their wake was palpable, and Lynda turned back to Jake, trying to find the words that would make him feel less like an intruder. "Not exactly the welcome I had planned for you. I'm sorry, Jake."

He tried to take it philosophically. "Hey, I told you I'd frighten little kids. It's no surprise. Look, if this is gonna be a problem, they were here first."

"It'll be all right," Lynda assured him. "She's just been through an awful lot lately. Her father tried to fight her out of Paige's arms at the courthouse just a few days ago. It was terrifying to her. It's not the way you look, Jake; it's the fact that you're a man."

But Jake wasn't buying it. "It's okay, Lynda. Really, I can handle this."

She sighed. "We're having dinner at seven. Paige has been doing the cooking. She made a special dinner just for you."

"Maybe I'd better just eat here."

"Out of the question. You have to have dinner with us tonight."

"It might spoil your appetite," he said sardonically. "That is, if it doesn't send the kid into hysterics again."

"She'll be all right," Lynda said. "Come on. We all need to get used to each other."

"Bet you never dreamed you'd have a houseful of wounded souls, did you?"

"Recovering souls," she amended with a smile. "And I couldn't be happier to have all of you here. It's about time I had someone besides my secretary in my life." It seemed like so long ago that they'd had the argument in the plane about the emptiness in both their lives, but Jake remembered and smiled slightly.

She went to the portable intercom she had bought just for him. "I haven't had the phones hooked up yet. I'll get someone here eventually, I guess. I'm just a little jumpy about having strangers here. Anyway, if you need anything, just press this button, and I'll hear you in the house."

"I won't need anything."

"Well, the kitchen's stocked, the refrigerator's full, there are towels in the bathroom. . . . Oh, and I had some special rails put into the tub, so you shouldn't have any trouble getting in. I can't think of anything else."

"It's real comfortable, Lynda," he said softly. "Thank you."

Her smile was genuine. "I'll see you at seven, Jake. And if you don't show up, I'm coming after you."

Brianna was still crying when Lynda went back into the house. Paige held her close and rocked her, but the child hadn't calmed down at all. "Is she all right?" Lynda asked.

"She's scared to death," Paige said. "She's shaking worse than she was at the courthouse."

Lynda sat down next to them and stroked the tiny child's hair. "Do you think it was Jake?"

"I don't know, Lynda. I think she must have caught a glimpse of him after he got out of the car. She probably thought he was Keith for a split second, and it freaked her out."

"Brianna, were you afraid of that man we were with?"

Brianna hiccuped another sob. "It was Daddy."

"No, honey," Lynda said. "That was Jake. And he might look a little scary with that patch over his eye and that wheel chair, but he's a really nice man. You're going to like him."

But Brianna was still trembling and crying softly, and Paige tried to loosen the child's clutch so she could see her face. "Honey, you didn't finish your tea party. Do you want to go out and get your dolls?"

"No!" Terror twisted the child's face, and she threw her arms more tightly around Paige's neck. "Daddy's there!"

Paige sighed with frustration and glanced at Lynda. "No, he's not, sweetheart. That's just Jake, and we have to be nice to him because he needs our help."

But the child couldn't be convinced. "I'll go out and get her dolls, Paige," Lynda said. "She'll be all right. She just has to get to know him."

"Yeah," Paige said, though her voice lacked conviction. "Look, we'll give it a try, but if she goes off the deep end when he comes over for dinner tonight, I think I'll just take her to McDonald's or something."

"Of course," Lynda said. "I don't want her to be afraid."

She went outside, feeling more despondent than she had hoped to feel on Jake's homecoming day. She gathered up the dolls then dropped down wearily on the porch swing with her arms full.

What was she going to do? The last thing Jake needed was for someone to be afraid of him, reinforcing the fears he had of being too repulsive to go out in public.

And the last thing Brianna needed was more terror in her life. They had all been through enough. Lynda just wondered when the ripples of all this tragedy would finally settle down.

In the apartment, Jake rolled around in his chair, unpacking the few belongings he'd brought with him from the hospital. Lynda had already brought over most of his things in the past few days, and they had been all neatly put away.

Quietly, he opened each drawer in the big room, exploring the contents, taking mental inventory of where she'd put his socks, his shirts, his underwear. Then he came to the end table with the Bible.

He smiled as if he had expected as much but closed the drawer without taking it out.

He rolled to the window and looked out at the driveway, to the red Porsche that Lynda had moved here from the hospital just yesterday. It had been well protected; there wasn't a scratch on it.

Rolling to the door, he went outside, hoping the child wasn't anywhere near a window; he didn't want to frighten her again. But he needed to get to his car, to smell the leather of the seats, feel the wheel in his hands. . . .

He rolled down the driveway, opened the driver's door, and aligned his chair so that he could pull himself into the seat.

It felt different than he remembered—cramped, tight, but he put his hands on the wheel nonetheless and imagined himself driving through town that day he'd gone to the airport. He'd been on top of the world. He hadn't realized then how far he had to fall.

But it wasn't the car that was different now. *He* was different.

And now he couldn't drive this car. He might never be able to again. Even if he could by some miracle have it redesigned so that a paraplegic could drive it by hand, it wasn't big enough to fit his wheelchair into. Besides that, it was a look-at-me car, a car that screamed that an eligible bachelor was inside, looking for a good time.

He didn't want anyone to look at him now, and he didn't feel so eligible any more, and he had more important things on his mind lately than having a good time.

Like an old girlfriend who didn't fit into his life anymore, the car felt uncomfortable, awkward, useless.

Grief washed over him, grief at the things he was leaving behind. The car, the job, the fast friends, the money . . .

And what was left of him was something he couldn't quite relate to, something he couldn't quite identify.

"If I'd known I was going to be left with just my character," he whispered to no one, "I'd have worked harder at building some."

But there was none there, at least none that he could put his finger on. He was helpless and hopeless and heartless. And he didn't want to be any of those things.

Cursing, he pulled himself out of the car and back into the chair, slammed the door, and went back inside.

He should count his blessings, he told himself sardonically. At least he *had* a Porsche, even if he couldn't drive it. And a houseful of great furniture, even though it was in storage and he had no place to put it. And a little black book full of names of women he couldn't call.

His anger faded as his despair grew, and he found himself grasping for the real positives, the ones that might add up to just a little bit of hope.

He was able to sit up.

He could still see out of one eye.

He could move his toe.

He had a temporary place to live.

Little things. But they were all he had. And he'd better get used to them, he thought, for he would probably never have the big things again.

52

WHEN BRIANNA HAD cried herself to sleep, Paige laid her down on the couch and went to help Lynda prepare dinner. She watched as Lynda bustled around nervously, looking distraught, too preoccupied to notice Paige's help. Whenever Lynda passed the kitchen window, which looked out toward the garage apartment, she peered out, as if to catch a glimpse of Jake.

"What's wrong, Lynda?" Paige asked finally.

"Nothing," Lynda said. "Why do you think something's wrong?"

"Well, you've been awfully preoccupied."

Lynda stopped what she was doing and looked out the window again. "I saw him go out to his car and get into it," she whispered.

Paige frowned. "He can't drive—can he?"

"No. He just went out and sat in it for a while. You'd have had to know him before to understand. He loved that car. When we were in that plane knowing we were about to crash, he was actually worried about who would take care of his car."

"You were going to crash, and he was worried about his *car?*"

"Yeah. And it was so sad to watch him roll out there just to sit in it. Maybe I shouldn't have brought the car here."

Paige didn't know what to say. It seemed so silly to her to grieve over a car when there was so much else to mourn. "So—do you think he'll come over at seven?"

"I don't know," Lynda said. "I hope so. He needs to be around people."

"But the thing with Brianna—I wouldn't blame him if he stayed locked in there forever after that. That was so embarrassing."

"I still don't understand it," Lynda said. "I mean, he has that scar and everything, but it's not that bad."

"That's because you're used to it," Paige cut in. "We're not. It's the whole picture. The scar, the patch, the wheelchair. It's going to take some time."

"But he's still a man. Inside he's just like you and me. Just because of a scar on his face—"

"You're right," Paige said. "Absolutely right. But this isn't a rational thing. It kind of took me by surprise, and it obviously jolted Brianna. I'm ashamed of myself for saying that, Lynda, but I'm going to get over it. I'm sure once I get to know him I won't even notice those things."

Weary from the emotional toll the day had taken on her, Lynda sighed and dropped into a chair. "Maybe when he gets his artificial eye it'll be easier."

"Oh," Paige said, "I'm sure I'll get used to him before that."

"I mean other people," Lynda said. "I want him to be able to go out in public—to the store, to a movie, to church—without people staring at him." But Lynda knew that if it were up to Jake, he might not ever count himself healed enough to blend normally with the public.

"Does he go to your church?" Paige asked.

"No. In fact, I just met him the day of the crash."

"*Really?* All this time I thought the two of you had known each other forever. I mean, the way you kept visiting him, and the way you took him in—"

"No. He's all alone. He doesn't have anybody. You know, almost dying with somebody is quite an intimate experience. It bonds you somehow."

"Yeah." Paige smiled. "I've had that experience myself."

Lynda realized that she referred to the fire, and she smiled. "Yeah, you have, haven't you? Then you understand. I can't help caring about Jake. Even if he's totally opposite from me, and he's belligerent and moody." She went to stir the pot on the stove and then wiped her hands on a towel. "I have a theory about Jake. I think maybe God is refining him."

"What does that mean?"

"Do you know how they used to refine silver?" Lynda asked.

Paige laughed. "No, not that I recall."

"Well, I heard it in Sunday school a long time ago. The silversmith hammered the silver into little pieces and then melted them. And he stayed with it the whole time, making sure it wasn't damaged in the fire. But as the silver melted, the impure metals rose to the top. He removed it from the fire, scraped off the impurities, and saw a blurry image of himself in the silver. Then he put it back on the fire and did the whole thing again. He did it seven times, each time scraping off another layer of impurities, until he saw his clear reflection in the silver. God does that with us, too."

"Scrapes off the impurities?"

"Yes. But he also puts us through the fire. What you're going through with Keith is your fire, Paige. And what I'm going through. And what Jake's going through."

Paige tried to follow. "So you think he's making these things happen so he can get the impurities out of us?"

"Maybe he didn't *make* them happen, but he's using them," Lynda said. "And with each trial, we get stronger and purer. And he sees more of his reflection in us."

"But people don't always get closer to God when they suffer."

"True," Lynda said. "Sometimes we cling to those impurities, and we're impossible to refine. But I think God keeps working on us. And sometimes he has to take everything we've got to make us notice him."

Paige was quiet for a moment, and finally she looked up at Lynda. "Is that what you think he's done with Jake?"

Her eyes drifted to the window again. "I think that's what he's done with *me,*" she whispered. "Whatever he's doing with Jake, that's between Jake and God. All I know is that whether God caused or allowed the crash to happen, it happened, and here we all are in this house together. And I don't think it's an accident."

Jake struggled to get himself into the tub and onto the bench that Lynda had left there for him so that he could take a shower. But once he got there and turned on the water, pleasure burst through him. He hadn't had a private shower since he'd gone into the hospital. An orderly had taken him into one in a wheelchair every day for the last couple of weeks, and he'd felt degraded and embarrassed to let a stranger help him with such intimate needs. Now he was on his own, and as difficult as it was, it was worth the effort.

Getting out, his hand slipped on the rail and he fell, but he quickly pulled himself back up into his chair. He could do this, he told himself. He could take care of himself. He didn't need nurses and aides and orderlies to wait on him hand and foot.

He rolled back into the bedroom and gathered his clothes from the drawer. Allie had been working with him to teach him to dress himself, but it was still difficult getting pants legs up, and putting the socks on was almost too much. He looked around, wondering where Lynda had put his Birkenstocks.

And then he felt it.

That burning sensation again, spreading *throughout* his toes and down the bottom of his foot!

He wiggled the toe that he'd managed to move the other day then concentrated on moving the other ones. For a moment, they resisted and just lay there, motionless. But he kept trying, kept focusing, kept watching—

His little toe twitched.

"Yes!" he shouted, feeling as if he could leap out of the chair and dance a jig on the coffee table. He moved the toe again and then with great effort, managed to bend the middle three toes slightly.

Tears welled in his eyes, and he looked up at the ceiling. "Thank you," he whispered brokenly. "Thank you."

He couldn't bear to put shoes on those feet, for he wanted to show Lynda what he could do. He glanced at the clock—almost seven. She probably wouldn't mind if he barged in a little early.

Humming a tune, he finished getting ready. Leaving his feet bare, he rolled out across the patio to one of the back doors of the house.

Lynda had seen him burst out of his apartment and race in his wheelchair across the concrete, and now, before she had even made it to the door, he was banging urgently.

She threw it open and saw the joy on his face. "I moved them," he said. "The other toes. I moved all of them. Look!"

She caught her breath and looked down at his bare feet and saw the infinitesimal twitch of his toes. A small movement but as significant as kicking the winning field goal in the Super Bowl. "Oh, Jake!" she said, throwing her arms around him. "Paige, come look! He's moving his toes!"

Paige came to the door and looked down at them, not sure what it meant. "Does this mean you'll be able to walk again?"

"It might," Lynda said.

"I'll walk," Jake told her. "I know I will. I'm gonna throw myself into my rehab and work with everything I've got."

"Do you have feeling in your other foot?" Paige asked.

"Not yet. But I will."

It was one of the first purely positive things Lynda had ever heard from Jake, so she didn't dash his hopes by reminding him that there were still no guarantees.

He came into the kitchen and closed his eyes as he breathed deeply of the smell of the turkey baking in the oven, the homemade dressing baking beside it, and the vegetables on the stove. "And to think I didn't believe in heaven. It was right here in this kitchen all along."

Lynda smiled. "Heaven smells a lot better than this," she said. "But I think you're gonna like it." She stirred the peas then turned back to him. "How are you doing over there? Is everything going all right?"

"I've hit a few rough spots," he said. "But all in all, it's good to be free of that hospital." He looked down at his toes again, wiggled them slightly and then threw his head back and laughed. "I can't believe this. I never thought I'd feel anything there again."

He saw Paige's face change from amusement to concern as she looked past him to the doorway, and quickly he followed her gaze. Brianna stood there, clutching her blankie to her cheek and looking sleepily into the kitchen.

For a moment, they all held their breath as she assessed Jake.

"Who are you?" Brianna asked calmly.

He glanced up at Paige then back at the child. "I'm Jake," he said in as calm a voice as he could. He extended his hand gently, as if coaxing a deer to eat out of it. "Who are you?"

"Brianna," she said, taking his hand and shaking it. As she stepped closer, she regarded the patch on his eye. "Are you a pirate?"

He laughed. "No. I just hurt my eye, and I have to wear this until it gets better."

"Like a Band-Aid?"

Lynda smiled; Paige just looked confused.

"What is this?" Brianna asked, touching the wheel on his chair.

"It's a wheelchair," he said. "I hurt my legs, too, and I can't walk. So I ride around in this."

Brianna's eyes lit up. "Is it fun?"

He smiled. "Well—"

"Can I ride?"

He looked up at Paige, surprised, and a slow smile came to his face. "Well, sure." Patting his leg, he said, "Hop up."

Brianna climbed onto his lap, and he began to roll her around in circles. She giggled as if she had a new toy then looked up at him and pointed to the scar. "How'd you get your boo-boo?"

He stopped and looked at Lynda again, his smile fading. "I had a real bad cut."

"I have a Band-Aid if it hurts. A Garfield one."

He smiled down at her. "It's not so bad."

"Can we ride some more?"

It was as if he'd been validated, accepted by the world and by life; he did not, after all, repulse this little child. As he rode her into the living room, Lynda looked back at Paige.

"Well, what do you think of that?"

Paige shook her head. "Weird."

"Well, I'm grateful. Children are so resilient."

"And so unpredictable," Paige whispered. "I don't get it. She was petrified this afternoon."

"Well, maybe the nap did it. Maybe she was just irritable when she saw him, and he took her by surprise."

"Guess so," Paige said. "But I never would have dreamed she'd warm up to him this fast." She watched, flabbergasted, as he tipped the chair back, almost making Brianna fall out, and she clutched him tightly and giggled with delight.

That night, Lynda led Jake out onto the patio as Paige put Brianna to bed, and they sat side by side, looking out over the yard.

"I told you you weren't repulsive," she said with a smile.

"That sure was one quick turnaround. I'll never understand children."

"Who knows what set her off today? It doesn't really matter now, though." She caught him looking down at his foot, wiggling the toes again. "I think you've gotten more movement just in the last few hours."

"I have," he said. "And unless I'm imagining it, I'm starting to feel that burning on the bottom of my other foot."

"Really?" she asked. "Jake, maybe the swelling's going down. Maybe the traction's helping. Maybe—" Her voice trailed off as she saw him look distractedly out across the yard and rub his top lip with his finger. "What's wrong?"

"Do you think I'm getting my hopes up too high? I mean, it's such a little bit of feeling."

"It has to start somewhere."

"But what if it doesn't go any further? What if—"

"Hey—I was just starting to enjoy the positive, upbeat Jake. Give yourself a chance to be happy before you start knocking yourself down again."

His smile returned like a gift, and he started to laugh quietly. "Who would have thought?"

"What?"

"That day when I looked at your plane, who would have ever thought that we'd be sitting here, actually friends?"

"I sure didn't."

He raised his eyebrows. "Was I that bad?"

"Pretty bad," she admitted. "I knew your type."

"Yeah, well, you were probably right." He looked up at the stars sprinkled across the sky. "Do you think I'll ever look normal again?"

She smiled. "When you get your eye, Jake, you'll probably start knocking the ladies dead again. I dread it, actually. I hate to see you revert to your old self."

"My old self seems a long way away," he said softly. "I don't know if I'll ever find him again."

53

KEITH WAS GLAD there were no street lights on this deadend street; the darkness gave him the perfect cover. Ever since he'd left Brianna that afternoon, he'd been watching his back, waiting for a uniformed car to squeal up behind him, lights flashing.

Why it hadn't happened he wasn't sure, but he knew he didn't have much more time. The court date was fast approaching, and with every day that passed, Lynda Barrett would find more and more evidence against him. Already she had all of the medical reports, and she probably had records of all of Paige's calls to the police. And McRae had warned him that she was getting depositions from neighbors who claimed to have witnessed things. The idiots ought to mind their own business instead of sticking their noses into things they didn't understand.

He was getting desperate either to take Lynda out or grab Brianna and run. Either way would bring about the same result. All he wanted was his daughter.

He crept closer to the house and saw the cars in the driveway: a red Porsche that he recognized as belonging to that paralyzed pilot who was still in the hospital, Lynda's BMW, and Paige's old Chevette with new, unslashed tires. He smiled and laughed softly as he slipped his knife from his pocket. Releasing the blade, he started toward the car to slash the tires again—then caught himself. Not a good idea. If he didn't manage to get Brianna tonight, Paige would know he'd been here. As much as he'd like for her to know she hadn't bested him, he couldn't take that chance yet.

She'd figure that out for herself anyway—when he disappeared with Brianna.

He stole through the front yard, glancing from one window to another. All of the curtains were drawn, but he saw a light on in two of the rooms. One of them, he guessed, was the living room, but the other, dimmer one, probably came from a bedroom.

Knowing that Brianna always slept with a nightlight, he stole toward it and checked the screen to see if it was locked. It was, but it was plastic screen—easy enough to cut if he could be sure he wouldn't be heard. He wondered if the window was locked. From here, it looked as if it was.

The idea of cutting a section out of the glass big enough to slip his hand through and unlock the window was quickly discarded; the section he cut would likely fall in and shatter on the floor. No, he couldn't do anything that stupid.

Quietly he made his way to the front door, tested the knob, and found it locked. Not giving up, he went around to the side of the house, saw the garage apartment, and wondered whether it was empty. Maybe he could hide in there until he had the chance to catch Brianna.

He pulled a silver fingernail file from his pocket, preparing to try to pick the lock.

Voices.

He froze.

They were coming from the back patio just around the corner of the house. Two voices. A man's and a woman's.

For a moment he couldn't breathe, and he stood motionless like a bobcat caught in headlights, trying to decide which way to go.

Finally, he slipped around the garage apartment into the woods surrounding the fence. Once hidden by the bushes and shadows of the trees, he tried to figure out who was outside. But it was too dark; he could barely see the two forms on the patio. They were talking quietly. The woman was Lynda, he thought. Brianna must be inside, then.

But this man, whoever he is, certainly changed the equation a bit. Is he one of those cops who'd picked him up, here because Brianna had told them he'd been here today? Were they setting a trap for him?

Panic gripped him. Turning, he jogged silently back through the woods and came out on the block behind Lynda's house. Hurrying back to his car, he flipped through all the possibilities.

But by the time he'd settled in behind the wheel, he'd decided that he was just being paranoid. After all, even though he hadn't gone home today, they could have caught up with him at work if they'd been after him. Still, he'd better stay away for a few days, just until the heat died down.

Work, he grimaced, checking his watch. He had to get back before someone noticed he was gone. He needed to keep this job—at least until one way or another he managed to get Brianna. Then he could quit and flee the state before Paige caught up with them.

He would show her. He would show all of them. And somehow he'd make Paige sorry she'd ever filed those divorce papers.

54

"I'VE GOT TO get to the hospital fast!" Skidding his chair across the kitchen floor, Jake grabbed Lynda's purse and keys off of the table. "My left foot is burning!"

If not for the look of unadulterated joy on his face, Lynda would have been alarmed. "Jake, slow down. I'm coming."

"Didn't you hear me?" he asked. "The *other* foot. It's burning!"

She caught her breath and grabbed his chair, stopping him halfway down the driveway. He turned back to her impatiently. "Are you telling me that you have feeling in *both* feet now?" she asked.

"Yes!" he said. "Now come on! I want to get to the hospital."

Laughing, she grabbed her keys from him and ran to get into her car. By the time she'd started the engine, he was already inside, folding up his chair and slipping it in behind his seat. "Jake, do you think this means—"

"You bet it does. I'm gonna walk."

"But—are you sure?"

When he met her gaze, she realized how good hope looked on him. "As sure as I can be. I'm gonna walk, Lynda. I know it."

She was quiet as they drove to the rehab wing of the hospital, possibilities flitting through her mind. As they drove, she prayed that he wouldn't be disappointed, that his hopes wouldn't be shattered, that this new burning sensation did indeed mean that something was happening. Something permanent.

She got out of the car to help him when they reached the hospital, and when he was in his chair, he checked his watch. "You want me to give you a call when I'm finished?"

"That'll be fine," she said. "Do you think it'll be several hours?"

He nodded with certainty. "I'm gonna work today until either I stand on these feet or collapse trying."

"Jake, don't push it. You've come a long way. There's no need to get impatient now."

"Don't worry about it," he said with a grin and started inside.

She caught up to him. "Don't you want me to take you in?"

"Nope," he said. "I can take it from here."

She stopped and watched him moving farther away from her. "Don't do anything stupid, okay?"

"Like what?"

"Like—throwing away your chair or something. You're going to give this time, aren't you?"

"As little as possible," he said.

She got back into the car and sat at the wheel for a moment, praying with all her heart that his expectations weren't in vain.

But Jake wasn't known for his patience or for his emotional resilience in the face of disappointment.

Buzz and Allie were pleased with the new sensations in his feet, but as Jake might have expected, his doctor was a little more reserved. "We've got to be patient, Jake," he said. "Don't expect too much too soon."

"But can't I expect anything at all, Doc? I mean, this all means *something,* doesn't it?"

Dr. Randall could have made a killing as a poker player, for his expression never betrayed a thought. "Well—your swelling has probably gone down significantly, which would help with the spinal shock. And the traction is, no doubt, helping with the compression. There's certainly cause for hope, Jake. But I have to emphasize that there are no guarantees."

"Give me odds, Doc. What are the chances that I'll walk again?"

The doctor wasn't about to go that far. "I can't do that, Jake. If I gave you terrific odds, and this is as much feeling as you ever get back, you'd never forgive me."

"But if you were inclined to give me odds, you're saying they'd be terrific?"

The doctor laughed. "I didn't say that."

"But they *are* terrific, aren't they?"

"They're hopeful, Jake. They're better than they were when you came in. But there still are no guarantees."

"Yeah, well, I can live with that," Jake said. "I've been through enough in the last few weeks to know that nothing comes with guarantees. Not life, not health, nothing. In fact, *you* could walk out of here right now and meet with a terrible accident and never walk again. So essentially, you and I have the same guarantee."

Dr. Randall smirked. "Thank you, Jake, for pointing that out to me. I appreciate it."

"No problem. I give as good as I get."

Dr. Randall laughed again and patted Jake's leg. Jake thought he felt it.

"Allie and Buzz are putting you in the pool today. It should be a nice change of pace."

"What will that do?" Jake asked. "Increase circulation? Help with motor coordination?"

"Well, it does a number of things. Today you'll just float and do some resistance exercises with your arms. The lack of gravity sometimes makes it easier for people to stand when they're ready, but you're not ready for that yet. We'll just take it a step at a time."

But Jake decided he *was* ready. When they took him to the pool and moved him from the chair into a harness seat that would lift him mechanically and lower him into the water by a chain, he saw the parallel bars in the pool and immediately knew what they were there for. People used them to balance . . . to stand . . .

To walk.

The water felt like liquid heaven, and as he slid into it, he let his upper body relax. Allie helped him float then ordered him to push his arms against the water.

She stood waist deep, and he tried to determine where the water would have come on him. He was six-two, and she was only five-seven or so. If it came halfway up her ribcage, it was probably waist deep for him.

He kept at the arm exercises the doctor had told him about for as long as he could but didn't want to tire himself out. He would need his arm muscles when he stood. "Can we go to the parallel bars?" he asked Allie finally.

Grinning, she shot Buzz a look. "Jake, we were just going to float today."

"Come on, Allie. Just let me see what my feet will do without gravity."

"I say we take him over there," Buzz said.

Allie's grin grew more mischievous. "Truth is, I have been wondering just how much function you might have in those feet."

"Then let's go."

They helped him over to the bars, and Jake grabbed one on each side of him. The weight of his legs made them float to the bottom, and for the first time since the accident, he was in a standing position, upright, his height towering above Allie and even above Buzz.

"Can you feel your feet touching the bottom?" Allie asked.

He barely felt the smooth bottom of the pool and looked down at his limp legs. "Sort of."

"Now, see if you can let your weight rest on your legs. Use your gluteus," Buzz said. "That's the trick. You have to hold your torso up with your glutes."

He felt his face reddening as he put every ounce of concentration he had into tightening his gluteals, and he looked down at his body. His legs weren't taking the weight, and his stomach was trying to arch outward. He tightened more and felt his body aligning more normally, but it was still only his arms that held him up. His legs were useless.

But Allie and Buzz didn't see the futility of it, and he saw that they were pleased by the smiles on their faces as they checked the alignment of his legs and feet to his torso.

"This is good, Jake," Buzz said, standing in front of him. "Real good. You have the muscular strength to stand, even if your legs aren't cooperating."

"What good are the muscles if I can't use them to do what I want?"

"You *will* be able to get them to do what you want, Jake. It's happening a little at a time, but we're seeing a lot of progress. So are you, and you know it."

He let his arms relax a little, and his body collapsed into the water. Allie caught him.

Defeated, he let her pull him into a float, but he feared the weight of his disappointment would drown him completely. And he almost didn't care if it did.

Something was wrong. It wasn't like Brianna not to want to go outside. But since the day Jake had moved in and Brianna had run in screaming that her daddy was trying to get her, she had absolutely refused to set foot through the back door, with or without her mother. Paige was getting frustrated; they'd been too cooped up in the house, and she wanted Brianna to get some fresh air.

"Honey, why can't we go out there? I'll be right there with you. There's a fence and everything. Nothing's going to happen to you."

Brianna's bottom lip puckered out, and she looked worriedly through the door. "No, Mommy. I don't want to."

"But why? Just tell Mommy why."

"Daddy's out there."

"He's not, honey. He doesn't even know where we are. How could he be out there?"

Brianna shrugged, but she didn't accept Paige's logic. Paige realized that regardless of what had originally triggered it, Brianna's fear was real, not imaginary, and she couldn't dismiss it. Stooping in front of her daughter, she got to eye level with her. "Brianna, tell Mommy why you think Daddy is out there."

"Because he is," she said, and big tears filled her eyes. "He's waiting for me."

"How could he be?"

The question confused the child, and she didn't answer, just wiped her eyes and smeared the tears across her temples.

"That day you thought you saw Daddy, it was Jake. He scared you, and you thought he was your daddy. But it wasn't him."

"Yes, it was," Brianna said. "I was chasing the butterfly, and he told me to come with him."

"The butterfly?"

"No, Daddy!" Brianna was getting upset now, and Paige pulled her into a hug.

"It's okay, honey. We don't have to go out. You don't have to cry."

Brianna hiccuped a sob and nodded her head, as though that would be fine with her.

But Paige couldn't understand what the problem was, and later that afternoon as Brianna napped, Paige stepped out into the backyard and looked around at the perimeter of the fence. There was nothing but woods that backed up to the fence and no trails. No one would be there by accident. If there had been someone there, he would have been there deliberately.

Had Brianna really seen someone?

She wanted to dismiss the possibility, as she had so quickly done when it had first come up, but she realized now that Brianna had never really demonstrated a fear of Jake except for that first meeting. And she wasn't entirely sure that Brianna had even seen Jake at that point.

Had Brianna been trying to tell her something all along, something that she had refused to believe?

She looked through the trees again, shivering with the sense that she was being watched, that someone was out there. Someone dangerous.

Had Keith found them? Had he approached Brianna in the back yard?

Starting to tremble, she backed into the house. Quickly, she bolted the door then ran to the front and checked the lock. In the master bedroom, she locked the door that opened to the patio.

By the time she was back in the kitchen, she heard a car door. Lynda was back with Jake.

Breathing a huge sigh of relief, she rushed outside.

Jake was getting into his wheelchair with a hang-dog look on his face, and Lynda was decidedly sober, too. But Paige hardly noticed.

"Thank goodness you're both home."

"What is it?" Lynda asked.

"Keith," she said breathlessly. "You know how Brianna keeps insisting that her father is in the backyard?"

Lynda waited for Jake to move away from the car door then closed it. "Yeah."

"Maybe he was."

Lynda stopped cold. "You think Keith was back there? When? How?"

"I don't know," she said. "But I'm scared. What if Brianna wasn't imagining it? What if he really was back there? I mean, she's obviously terrified of something, and it isn't Jake because she warmed right up to him that night. But she still won't go outside."

Lynda stood still, thinking for a moment. "Maybe we ought to give Larry a call."

Jake pulled the house key out of his pocket and quietly opened his apartment door.

"Jake?" Paige asked before he could go in.

He looked back at her over his shoulder. "Yeah?"

"Would you mind . . . coming into the house for a while? Just for security. Until we hear from Larry? I'd feel better if there were a man around."

He looked stunned by the request. "Who are you worried about? Me or you?"

She didn't understand the question and glanced at Lynda for help. "I'm just scared, Jake. I was hoping—"

"So you think I need a couple of women to protect me?"

She looked stricken. "No. I wanted you to protect us."

"Nice try," he said, rolling over the threshold and pivoting at the door. "But I think I'll stay here."

He closed the door hard, and Paige jumped. "What's wrong with him?"

Lynda sighed. "He had these grand delusions of walking today, I think. It didn't happen. He's really depressed."

"But I really meant it, Lynda. I'd feel better with a man in the house. Why did he twist what I was saying?"

"Because he truly doesn't feel that he can offer us any protection. In his own mind, he's useless, so he thinks he's useless to everyone else, too."

"Oh, for heaven's sake." As if she had no more time to dwell on Jake's problems, Paige headed inside. "I need to go in and check on Brianna."

Lynda gave Jake's door one last glance then followed her in. "I'll call Larry," she said.

55

KEITH KNEW BETTER than to come back, especially in the daytime, but the obsession that kept him from sleeping, eating, or thinking drove him to take chances.

In the three days since he'd tried to grab her, Brianna's face had haunted him day and night: the fear in her eyes when she'd spotted him; the way she'd backed away; the shrill scream that had startled him and sent him running through the woods. . . .

She'd been brainwashed, and he had to put a stop to it. He couldn't allow her mother to poison her mind against her own father. It would take some time to get those thoughts out of her mind and win back her trust. But once he had her in his possession, he would have all the time in the world. He would tell her that Paige was dead, that she'd been in a car wreck or something. She'd get over it quickly; kids are like that. Resilient.

He moved quietly through the trees, again approaching the fence around Lynda's house. He had to be bolder if he was going to succeed. He hadn't gotten many breaks lately. Even his lawyer was turning against him.

He took his usual place, sitting on the ground against a tree, hidden behind two bushes, between which he had a clear view of the back door. He still seethed from the call he'd gotten from McRae that day, asking him whether he'd found where Paige was staying and whether he'd approached the child without permission.

"I don't *need* permission," Keith had said. "She's my kid. I'm her father, and no judge is ever going to tell me I can't see her."

"Does that mean you did show up at their place and threaten the kid?" McRae asked.

"How would I know where they're staying?"

McRae had thought about that for a moment. "You're a smart man, Keith. Did you or didn't you find them?"

He'd been amused at McRae's assessment of him; he always enjoyed it when people found out this night-shift employee had some brains. For a moment, he'd entertained the thought of telling him how he'd found Lynda's house, but then he realized that it wouldn't pay to brag. McRae was liable to resign from the case, and then where would he be?

So he'd lied and told McRae that he didn't have a clue where they were, but that if some guy had approached his daughter, he wanted the police to find out who it was. He'd even suggested filing another motion for temporary custody since she still seemed to be in danger, but McRae had rejected it. Court was only two weeks away, he said. He wasn't going back before the judge on Keith's behalf until the trial.

But Keith could see the writing on the wall. McRae was pulling back, losing faith in him. If Keith couldn't depend on him anymore, then he couldn't depend on the justice system to get Brianna. He could only count on himself.

And in just two weeks he would have to go into court and face Lynda Barrett. Unless something happened to her in the meantime.

So he was back here, waiting for a glimpse of Brianna, praying for another chance to grab her. This time he wouldn't botch it.

And if he couldn't reach Brianna, then he'd bide his time until he caught Lynda leaving and rush to his car to follow her.

He heard the side door open; he got to his feet, still crouched low, and moved until he could see who was coming out. It was Lynda, all dressed up, as though she was going to church, but she was alone.

Perfect. He took off through the trees. If he could make it to his car and follow her, he could plant his little surprise under her gas tank while her car was in the church parking lot. Talk about hellfire and brimstone.

Laughing breathlessly, he fired up his car and drove up the block and around the corner. He pulled over and waited.

Today was the day. Lynda would be taken out, Paige would be homeless and without representation, and his court case would be in the bag. Piece of cake. Even McRae would have to give him credit for working things out.

He saw the car come to the end of the street, stop, and then turn right. He waited until it was far enough away so she couldn't see him. Then he began to follow.

56

"I THOUGHT YOU were going to invite Jake," Paige said as Lynda turned the corner.

"I did. Last night and again this morning. He wasn't interested."

"He should go anyway," Paige said. "After all you're doing for him . . ."

Lynda looked at her thoughtfully. "Is that why you're coming with me? Because you feel you owe me something?"

Paige looked embarrassed, as though she'd just stuck her foot in her mouth. "No, of course not. I told you, I need to get Brianna back in church. You've made it easier. It's not always so easy to walk into a new church by yourself."

Lynda wasn't sure she believed her. "I didn't mean to strong-arm you into going with me or to make you feel guilty if you didn't. It's just that what they teach there is the most important thing in the world." She glanced into the rearview mirror as she merged into the next lane. "I just wish Jake would have come. He needs to hear that message more than anything."

Paige didn't respond, and Lynda wondered whether she agreed.

They pulled into the parking lot of the church, waiting behind a few cars looking for parking places as cars from the earlier service left. Three security guards in the parking lot helped to direct traffic. She glanced in her rearview mirror again to see if she was holding anyone up.

A pale blue car slowed at the entrance to the parking lot, hesitated, and then drove on. The car looked familiar, but many of the cars here looked familiar.

They parked and went into the church, and again, Paige opted to stay in Brianna's class with her. She was starting to learn where everything was and what was expected of her, and the teacher seemed glad to see her.

As she went to her class, Lynda hoped that Paige would also seize the chance to be ministered to. She wasn't sure that the foundation of Paige's faith was any stronger than Jake's was.

57

OUTSIDE, KEITH CIRCLED the church, trying to decide what to do. He had seen Paige and Brianna in the car with Lynda, so he could forget about the bomb, at least for today. He wanted Lynda dead, and if Paige had to go, too, the more the merrier. But he didn't want his little girl to die.

Besides, even after the traffic died down, the security guards remained in the parking lot like sentinels guarding the cars.

Continuing past the church, he pulled into an empty space in the parking lot of a closed jewelry store. For a moment, he just sat and thought, trying to sort out the possibilities.

Brianna was in that church somewhere now. Probably since she was a visitor and the teachers didn't know the family, no one would protest if her own father showed up to get her.

On the other hand, if she went into hysterics and started screaming like she had the other day, they would call the police. And this time there would be witnesses.

Still, there was no harm in going in to check things out. Then he could make a plan. He reached into the glove compartment for the fake mustache and thick glasses he'd used the day he bought the dynamite. Then, walking at a brisk pace as though he knew where he was going, he went in the back door of the church, hoping to avoid the Christian "welcome wagon" that always seemed to be on the lookout for visitors.

He ducked into a men's room at the end of the hall and wet his hair so he could comb it back. It wasn't him anymore, he thought, looking into the mirror. It was someone else—someone who couldn't be identified.

He went back into the hallway. There seemed to be classrooms further down the hall. He saw the babies through a glass window in the nursery nearby. The kids seemed to get older as he walked on until finally, he came to the three-year-olds' room.

He passed the door quickly without looking in for fear of startling Brianna if she saw him. But then he turned back and peered in from the side.

He saw his little girl working a puzzle at a table near the door. His heart began to race.

Just a few steps away, he thought. All he would have to do is wait till the teacher had her back to him, take a few steps inside the door, and grab Brianna before she had the chance to scream. He could have her in his car before anyone noticed she was gone.

He stepped closer, trying to see inside to where the teacher was. He saw two of them, and they both had their backs to him. It was perfect.

"I'm finished!" Brianna said, popping the last piece into the puzzle. "Mommy, come look."

He jumped back, startled, as the teachers turned around. One of them was Paige.

What was she doing here? Didn't they have classes for adults? Did they let just anybody teach these children?

His heart sank, and he quickly found the closest door and jogged back to his car.

When he got in, he hit his steering wheel and let out a loud curse.

Today wasn't going to be the day after all, he thought, cranking his engine and screeching away. But tomorrow had to be. Time was running out.

58

IF THERE WAS a bright side to a boring Sunday, it was that Paige had cooked a meal fit for a prince. Jake sat quietly at the table, reminded of his days as a child when one of his friends—Jimmy Anderson—used to go to church every Sunday then come home and eat a big, sit-down meal with his parents. Jake had envied him. Doris always used Sunday mornings to catch up on her sleep, and then they feasted on sandwiches or canned ravioli on paper plates. At the time, Jake had believed that it was the meal he envied, but now he realized that it had been more than that—it was the good mood everyone seemed to bring home from church, the structure of having a reason to get all dressed up, and the camaraderie of sitting down together at the table. He'd shared that meal with the Andersons a time or two when he'd shown up to play at exactly the right moment, but when Doris had found out, she'd forbidden him to go anymore.

"They look down their noses at us," she had said. "And when you eat with them, it's like saying that your own mother won't feed you. You can eat at home if you're hungry."

Well, his mother couldn't stop him now.

But the conversation today was awkward, and he could see that Lynda was struggling to pull him out of his melancholy. He admired her for the attempt; he just wasn't sure that anyone could do it. Even though he'd spent the night wallowing in depression, he'd still hoped that when he woke this morning, he'd have more feeling in his feet and legs than he'd had yesterday. But he'd been disappointed again.

"Brianna likes her Sunday School class," Paige said. "Don't you, Brianna?"

Brianna nodded and finished her mouthful of potatoes. "Are we going back tonight?"

Paige gave Lynda a questioning look.

"If you want to," Lynda said. "I'm going, and I'd love for you to go with me."

"Can we go every day?"

Paige laughed. "No, honey. They don't have it every day."

Brianna looked perplexed at that.

"So what did they teach you in there?" Jake asked for the sake of conversation.

"About Jesus making people well." Her eyes brightened, and she began to get excited. "And there was this guy like you, Jake, and he couldn't walk, only they didn't have wheelchairs then—"

"She asked," Paige interjected with a smile.

"But he was lying down by the beautiful gate, the man was—"

"The name of the gate was Beautiful," Paige clarified.

"And you know what happened?"

"What?" Jake asked, getting uncomfortable.

"Some of Jesus' friends came and told the man to stand up, only he couldn't stand up, but they took his hand like this—" She slid down from her chair and went to take Jake's hand to demonstrate. "And he said—what did he say, Mommy?"

"Rise and walk," Paige said.

"Yeah!" Brianna said. "He said, 'Rise and walk,' and you know what the man did?"

Jake withdrew his hand and took a deep breath. He didn't want to know what the man had done. He didn't care because it had nothing to do with him. But the child waited beside him, bursting with excitement, and he knew she wouldn't back down until he took the bait. "What?"

"He got right up, and he could walk!"

Jake glanced at Lynda, who was smiling proudly at the child's enthusiasm, and he wondered if they'd rehearsed it in the car. He didn't like being talked about behind his back, and in his opinion, the story they'd chosen was particularly cruel. He didn't appreciate it.

"That story is in Acts, isn't it? And who gave him the power to do that, Brianna?" Lynda prompted.

"Jesus!" she said. "Jake, why don't you do it?" When he didn't answer, she shook his arm. "Jake?"

"I heard you," he said, staring down at his food. "I heard every word." He looked up at

Lynda and Paige. "Nice try. If I recall, there are stories in there about people's eyes being gouged out, too. You want to lay one of those on me?"

"Jake, come on," Lynda said. "We didn't plan this."

Jerking his napkin out of his lap, he threw it on the table and started to back out of his place.

"Jake, what's a matter?" Brianna asked in her high-pitched voice.

"Nothing's the matter," he said, glaring at Lynda again. "You know, it's reprehensible to use a child to deal a low blow like that."

Lynda's face showed the full force of her anger. "Oh, right. Riding home in the car today, I asked Paige what we could do to really twist the knife in you. We came up with that story, and Paige said, 'I know! Let's use Brianna!' It was a clever plan, Jake, only you're too smart for us."

Confused at the exchange, Brianna sat back down, still looking at Jake, and said softly, "I asked Jesus to make you walk. Didn't I, Mommy?"

Paige put a protective arm around her daughter. "Yes, honey. You sure did." Her voice hardened, and she leered at Jake. "She told the whole class about you, Jake, and we all prayed for you. I don't know how you can turn this into some kind of conspiracy."

A host of emotions did battle on his face. "I don't need your prayers."

"Well, you're getting them anyway," Lynda said. "Powerful ones. Jesus said that children's angels always see the face of God." She looked at Brianna. "That means that God listens extra carefully to the prayers of children."

Jake, too, looked at the baffled child staring up at him with those big, questioning eyes.

"If that's the case," he said, "then where was God when her dad was abusing her? If God's paying special attention to the children, why do so many of them have to suffer?"

And Lynda knew that they weren't just talking about Brianna any more. They were talking about Jake.

Trying with all her might to fight her anger instead of Jake, she lowered herself back into her chair. "God got her out of there, didn't he? He used her mother to protect her."

"Why didn't he protect her before anything ever happened?"

She hesitated. "I don't know. There's a lot of evil in this world, Jake. God didn't cause it. And we don't know how he's working in suffering children's lives. We don't even know how he's working in our lives."

"Then you're contradicting yourself again, Lynda. Out of one side of your mouth, you tell me this beautiful idea about children having angels with access to God. And out of the other side, you say that it really doesn't make that much difference because God can't protect us from evil."

"I didn't say that he couldn't. God can do anything."

"Oh, I see. He just won't."

Paige's hand came down hard on the table, startling them all. "That's not what she said, Jake, and you know it!"

"It *is* what she said."

Lynda started to speak, but Paige stopped her. "You have a lot of nerve, you know that?" she said. "All she's done is take care of you, be a friend to you, feed you, give you a place to live—and you still keep throwing her kindness back in her face!"

"Paige, it's all right," Lynda said quietly.

"No, it isn't!" she said. "And as for God, he *has* protected Brianna. He's protected me, too. He gave us Lynda, and a place to live, and a means to get away from Keith. And he even made it so I didn't have to worry about money or a job or anything while I'm waiting to go to court. And I know he's going to take care of that, too. I know because he's taken care of everything else." Tears choked her, and she stopped, trying to steady her voice. "You know, you're not just blind in that one eye. You're blind in both eyes if you can't see that God is providing for you, too. If he didn't care, you'd still be in the hospital right now, and everybody would be trying to figure out what to do with you!"

Brianna started to cry. Picking her up and hugging her close, Paige went on. "Or worse. You could be just like you were before the accident, walking around on two good legs with two good eyes, worshiping that Porsche of yours and in all your vanity and arrogance, be even more blind and crippled than you are now!"

Lynda collapsed back into her chair and covered her face, uttering a silent prayer that whatever happened, the outcome of this wouldn't be as bad as she anticipated.

Paige stormed from the room, carrying Brianna, and silence fell over them as Jake sat motionless in his wheelchair, avoiding Lynda's eyes.

She rubbed her hands down her face and looked at him over her fingertips. "Jake, I'm sorry."

He started rolling his chair toward the door. "I think I'd better go now."

"But you didn't finish eating."

"I'm not hungry," he said quietly and left the house.

Back in his room, Jake pulled himself onto the bed and lay flat, looking up at the ceiling. Tears rolled down his temples, and he wondered why he felt as if he were drowning in that waist-deep pool with legs that served only as cement weights to pull him under. Why did he try to pull everyone else down with him?

Restless, he sat up, wiped his face, and pushed his legs over the side of the bed. His eyes strayed to the drawer in the table beside his chair where she'd put that Bible. He pulled it out and began flipping through it.

Acts, she'd said. He found the book then turned the pages, looking at the topic headings for the one about the crippled man being healed. He was almost surprised when he found it.

He began to read the third chapter aloud:

One day Peter and John were going up to the temple at the time of prayer—at three in the afternoon.

Now a man crippled from birth was being carried to the temple gate called Beautiful, where he was put every day to beg from those going into the temple courts.

When he saw Peter and John about to enter, he asked them for money.

Peter looked straight at him, as did John. Then Peter said, "Look at us!"

So the man gave them his attention, expecting to get something from them.

Then Peter said, "Silver or gold I do not have, but what I have I give you. In the name of Jesus Christ of Nazareth, walk."

Taking him by the right hand, he helped him up, and instantly the man's feet and ankles became strong.

He jumped to his feet and began to walk. Then he went with them into the temple courts, walking and jumping, and praising God. When all the people saw him walking and praising God, they recognized him as the same man who used to sit begging at the temple gate called Beautiful, and they were filled with wonder and amazement at what had happened to him.

Jake stopped reading as tears dropped onto the pages of the Bible, and he wondered why that passage affected him so. It was just a story. But it was *his* story. He could have been the man who'd "been put" at the gate to beg. In many ways, he was "put" here to beg from Lynda for the food and the shelter he needed. His pain was the same as that of the man who was so desperate, so alone that he had to cry out to everyone who passed to help him.

Funny how quickly pride could vanish when you were desperate.

His eyes strayed out the window to that red Porsche sitting like an indictment in the driveway, and he knew that Paige was right. In some ways, he had been just as crippled before the accident as he was now. He clenched his teeth. He'd rather be figuratively crippled than physically crippled any day.

He looked back at the Bible. Why had Peter and John cared about the man? Why hadn't they just stepped over him and forgotten him? Why hadn't they averted their eyes? Why hadn't they just thrown money at him?

He didn't know the answer, any more than he knew why Lynda had helped him. And Paige was right. He continually threw her kindness back in her face. It was a hobby, challenging her beliefs, but he'd learned already that he wasn't going to shake them. Lynda knew what she believed. He, on the other hand, didn't have a clue.

But as the afternoon passed, he continued to read. Maybe he would find out.

When someone knocked on his door two hours later, he'd already finished the entire book of Acts and had turned back to Matthew. But he didn't want Lynda to know it yet. Closing the book, he stuck it back into the drawer then went to answer the door.

Paige stood there, her arms crossed in front of her, and she gave a stab at smiling. "Hi."

"Hi," he said.

She swallowed and looked down at her hands. "I just came to tell you I'm sorry. I shouldn't have blown up at you like that."

"Yes, you should have," he said. "You were absolutely right, and it needed to be said. I owe you an apology."

For a moment, she seemed unsure if he was mocking her. "Really?"

"Really," he said. "It's all right, Paige."

She laughed softly. "And I was so nervous about coming over here. I figured you'd never speak to me again, but I wanted you to come for supper. It's just leftovers, but you liked what we had today. It was cut a little short, but—"

"I'll be there," he said. "Is Brianna up?"

"Yeah," she said. "She just woke up from her nap."

"Maybe I'll come over in a little while and play with her. Let her know I'm not a total jerk. Maybe thank her for praying for me."

"She'd like that."

He closed the door and sat for a moment, surprised at how good it felt to make someone smile.

Maybe the day wasn't turning out so badly after all.

59

THE BURNING HAD spread partially up Jake's calves by the next morning. Allie and Buzz didn't want to put him in the pool again so soon, but when he managed to move one foot at the ankle, they gave in to his pleading.

Determined that he would stand this time, he moved between the parallel bars, got his feet into place, and tightened his gluteals.

"That's good," Allie said. "Real good."

"Just watch the knees," Buzz told him. "Keep the stomach from bowing out. Easy now."

Focusing hard, Jake got his knees to lock. It took a moment for him to realize that he was standing. He looked up at them with something close to terror in his eyes.

"I'm doing it. I'm standing!"

He would have paid money for the look on Allie's face as she realized that he really was.

"Buzz, he is. He's standing!"

"All right, Jake. Let's see how long you can do it."

Already he felt the energy seeping out of him, and he knew he couldn't hold the position for long. "I feel so heavy," he said. "And wobbly." He looked up at the joy in both their faces. "But this is the beginning, isn't it? I'm gonna walk again."

"Looks like it, man," Buzz said. "I'd bet money on it."

His PT's confidence was what Jake had waited weeks to hear, but now that he had, exhaustion kicked in, and he deflated like a balloon losing its air.

"That's okay," Allie assured him. "You were up for about thirty seconds. That's great."

"But you're sure it means I'll walk."

"It means you'll be able to get around on your legs. You might need crutches or a cane or walker, but—"

"No," Jake cut in. "I'm going to walk on my own. You'll see. It's gonna happen."

No one tried to dampen that enthusiasm as he worked toward doing that for the rest of the day.

Jake decided not to tell Lynda about his progress; he wanted to surprise her when he took his first steps. When the doctor declared that Jake's eye was healed enough to have his prosthesis put in, he decided not to tell her about that, too. It would be more rewarding to see the surprise on her face. After she dropped him off at the hospital for therapy, he got Buzz to drive him to the optical center where he'd be fitted for his eye.

He was mildly surprised as he wheeled himself into the shop with hundreds of pairs of glasses on the walls and posters that advertised contact lenses. "I thought this place would seem more—medical," he told the receptionist. "I didn't know you could pick up an eye like you'd get a pair of lenses."

"Well, there's a little more to it," she said, pushing his chair into the back room where Dan Cirillo, the optician, waited. "But probably not as much as you'd imagined."

He wasn't expecting to have the eye made while he waited, but that was Dan's intention. After they'd taken the impression of his socket, Jake waited for the wax model of his eye to be made, and sat in front of the optician and allowed him to use his other eye as a model while he painted a little disk to match Jake's iris. When that was done, the wax model was ready to try on, and Dan checked its fit.

Jake thought it odd that he couldn't feel it. Pulling it back out as easily as he would a contact lens, Dan said, "Okay—go on back to therapy for a few hours, and by the time you're done, your eye should be ready."

Buzz brought Jake back that afternoon, and Dan greeted him with a plastic, painted model. "So what do you think?" he asked.

Jake cringed. "No way. That's not gonna look normal."

"Wait and see."

Dan put the eye in, then tested the movement. "It's perfect," he said. "It moves right along with your other one. I think you're really gonna be happy with this."

He handed Jake a mirror, and bracing himself, Jake brought it to his face. The eye looked identical to his other one, and he felt a rising sense of relief that the man in the mirror looked more like the Jake he used to know than he had since the crash.

He blinked, testing it and then moved his eyes back and forth to see how it felt.

"What do you think?"

Jake's smile spoke volumes. "I think I'm amazed."

Jake wasn't wearing his patch when Lynda picked him up that afternoon, and she gaped at him as he got into the car. "Jake, why didn't you tell me?"

His grin almost split his face. "I wanted to surprise you."

She couldn't stop staring. "Look at me. I can't even tell which eye is false. It looks just like your other one!"

Still grinning, he leaned over and planted a quick kiss on her lips. The look on her face told him she was stunned, and he began to laugh. "It's back. The old mesmerizing charm. I hypnotized you with my baby blues, didn't I?"

"Well, I—"

He kissed her again. "See? I've still got it."

Shaking her head, she started to laugh. "It's like a whole personality change."

"It's hope, darlin'," he said, leaning back in his seat. "Just pure, colorful hope. I might just wind up with a life after all, now that I don't make people cringe when they look at me."

Still laughing, she started the car. "So are there any other surprises?"

"You mean, am I gonna lay one on you again? I don't know," he teased. "If I were you, I'd keep my guard up."

He enjoyed the pink color that faded across her cheekbones as she drove and realized what a joy it would be when she finally did learn of the other surprise he hadn't told her. He had stood outside the pool this afternoon on both feet without holding his weight up with his arms. He was ready to walk, he thought. It was just a matter of time. In a very few days, maybe he'd be able to walk out to the car when Lynda came to get him. The look on her face would almost make all the misery he'd gone through worth it.

60

WHEN LYNDA ANNOUNCED that she was going back to work on the following Monday to prepare for Paige's deposition a few days later, Paige was concerned. Lynda still had yellow bruises on her cheekbone and forehead, and last night Paige had caught a glimpse of Lynda dressing. Black bruises still colored her ribcage, and Paige could only imagine the pain that Lynda had been suffering without complaining since the crash.

"You know, I could go with you and help you," Paige said as she worked on getting breakfast ready, so at least Lynda wouldn't have to leave on an empty stomach. "I could bring Brianna something to occupy her, and—"

"Paige, what do you think I have Sally for? She can help me."

"I'm just worried about you. It's too soon to be going back."

"The doctor said it's all right. Besides, we go to court in two weeks. I have to be ready."

"But you could prepare for the deposition at home. Why do you have to go in?"

"There are things I can do better there, Paige. I want to document every infraction Keith has ever had in his life, and I need to be there to get it all put together the way the judge likes it. McRae's had some run-ins with this judge, which may play in our favor as long as I don't do anything to neutralize that advantage, so I'm going to do everything I can to please him in court. I have to contact all of the witnesses and meet with them. With time running out, I can't afford not to be on top of this."

Paige felt like a heel for being the cause of this.

"But are you sure you feel up to it?"

"I'll be fine, Paige."

"All right," Paige said, giving up.

"Will you be all right here with Jake?"

"Yeah," Paige said. "I don't know what it is, but his mood seems to be changing lately. I think we'll get along fine."

61

"FINALLY!" KEITH WHISPERED to himself when he saw Lynda's car pull into her parking space beside her office building. He had figured that she'd probably be back to work today since it was Monday and she had to prepare for the hearing. He'd been sitting in his car across the street for a couple of hours already, waiting for her to make her appearance. His homemade bomb, wrapped in a leather pouch, sat on the seat next to him.

He had already decided that her personal space was in the perfect location—far enough to the side of the building that the security guard couldn't see it easily. Besides, as Keith had noticed for the past two hours, the guard stayed in his little office inside the building most of the time, watching television and talking on the phone. Keith could slip under her car, plant his package, and rig some wires, and the guard would never know. He could do it quickly; he'd been practicing.

Then all it would take was one turn of the key. . . . Keith made an exploding noise and then laughed as Lynda got out of her car and headed into the building.

He waited until she'd had enough time to get on the elevator, then grabbed his package and got out of his car. The security guard was nowhere in sight. Looking down and walking fast, as if he knew exactly where he was going, he reached her car, looked around casually to make sure no one was watching and then got down on the ground and slid under it.

On his back, he unwrapped the bomb, pulled the duct tape out of his front pocket, and peeled off a long piece. He tore it off with his teeth, taped it to the gas tank, and then peeled off some more. When the bomb was taped securely enough to stay put, he inched forward on his shoulder blades and wired the bomb to the starter.

The guard still hadn't resurfaced when Keith stood up slowly beside the car. He hurried to the sidewalk, then slowed to a leisurely pace and cut across the street to his own car again.

Should he get out of the area or stick around and watch? The temptation was too great. He got back into his car, got comfortable, and prepared to wait as long as he needed to see the result of his planning and cleverness.

62

THE WALL OF noise that assaulted Lynda when she got off the elevator startled her into a near coronary—until she realized that it was just her co-workers shouting "Surprise!"

Pressing her hand over her heart, she stepped back onto the elevator, and Sally grabbed the doors to stop them from closing. "It's a welcome back, Lynda!"

Lynda covered her mouth then and started to laugh, allowing Sally to pull her into the circle of her friends and associates. "You guys wouldn't do that if you knew how many surprises I've had in the last few weeks!"

Barraged with welcomes and pats on the back, she let them sweep her to the staff lounge where they had donuts and drinks and a "Welcome Back, Lynda" cake.

When the celebration was over and she wound up back in her office with Sally, she settled back in her chair and relaxed. "Gosh, it's good to be back."

"We're just so glad you're alive," Sally told her.

Lynda pulled Sally into a tight hug. "You've been a life-saver, holding down the fort the way you have. I really appreciate it."

Sally took a deep breath. "Well, it'll be nice helping you get caught up. I'll admit, it's been a little hard juggling everything. Are you ready to dive into this mess?"

Lynda looked over the stacks of mail, messages, and papers on her desk. "I really need to get some things done on Paige's case first. Then we'll tackle the stack."

"All right." Sally shuffled the papers around and pulled out her pen and notepad. "Shoot."

And as Lynda started doing what she did best, she felt as if the world were realigning itself, and things were on their way to getting back to normal.

Jake helped Paige with the breakfast dishes as Brianna sat on a stool at the sink, "washing" the plates but getting more suds on herself than she did on the dishes.

He'd been quiet ever since Paige had told him that Lynda had gone to work today, but he couldn't pinpoint what bothered him about it the most. That she might not be physically ready to dive back into work yet? That she hadn't told him? That she wouldn't be the one to drive him to the hospital for therapy today? Or was it simply that she wasn't here, and he missed her?

"As soon as you're ready to go, I'll change Brianna's clothes and take you," Paige said.

Jake shrugged. "No hurry. Buzz and Allie don't expect me today until ten o'clock." He rolled his chair up to Brianna's stool and asked, "Why don't you and I go outside and get some fresh air, Brianna?"

Brianna's little smile faded, and she shook her head and kept scrubbing a plate. "No."

Paige stopped what she was doing and shot Jake a look.

"Why not?" Jake asked.

"Cause." It was a simple answer, but in Brianna's mind, it probably covered it all.

"Cause why?"

"Daddy might come."

"She just insists that he's been out there," Paige said quickly. "That day you got here, when she started screaming, I thought she was just mixed up. That she thought you were her daddy . . ."

"But she sure wasn't afraid of me later."

"Yeah, that's been bothering me, too." She walked to the back door and peered out the window into the back yard. "Maybe he really was here."

To Jake, that seemed unlikely. Why would anyone take that chance? It would be crazy, coming here and talking to Brianna. If he were caught, it would show everyone, including the judge, that Keith lacked any kind of judgment, that he was willing to break the law, and that he was unpredictable—and dangerous. "Hey, Brianna, what if I go out there with you?" he asked. "Your mom and I want some fresh air. We could all go. Nobody's gonna take you with all of us out there."

From her stool, Brianna looked down at him then thoughtfully considered her mother.

When her eyes moved back to Jake, she said in her borderline baby voice, "You won't leave me? Even if he comes, you won't let him get me?"

"Of course not," Jake said. "But your mom will never let him get you, either."

"He's strong," she said matter-of-factly as she slipped off the stool. "He can push her down."

As Brianna scurried through the house to find her shoes, Jake and Paige exchanged troubled looks.

In seconds, Brianna reappeared with her shoes.

Paige's eyebrows rose. "Are we going out?"

"Only if Jake comes."

"I'm coming, kiddo." But as Brianna put on her shoes, he looked up at Paige and asked, "Why would that make her feel safer?"

"Because you're a man," Paige said. "I guess she thinks Keith is more of a threat to me than he is to you."

As Jake let that sink in, Brianna ran to get her dolls. They followed her out the door, then watched as her gaze gravitated to the back corner of the yard. Timidly, she took a few steps into the grass.

Paige followed her gaze to the area beyond the fence where it would be easy for anyone to hide.

"What's on the other side of those woods?" Jake asked behind her.

"A street with a few houses." She glanced back at him. "You think he was here, too, don't you?"

"I don't know, Paige."

Feeling sick, Paige settled onto the swing as Brianna set her babies around the picnic table and began talking to herself.

"I can't believe this," Paige whispered. "When I married him, I thought he was a dream come true. I thought he was my escape. But three days after we got married, his temper exploded, and I found out I'd just traded one nightmare for another."

"Did he hit you that soon?"

"No. If he had, I probably would have left. But he broke things and yelled a lot. I started trying to walk on eggshells just to keep from setting him off. But it's like he doesn't think straight. There is no reasoning with him. Keith has a whole different way of viewing the world than most people."

"So why did you stay with him?"

She considered that for a moment. "You have to understand him. He had been this brilliant kid raised in foster homes with no one who ever really got that involved with him. He had never had anyone of his own or anyone he could trust, and I had this stupid idea that if I just proved myself to him he'd settle down."

"When did he start hitting you?"

"When I was five months pregnant with Brianna." Her eyes filled, and she blinked back the tears. "And there I was with this little baby on the way . . . and my only real option was to go back to my family—which wasn't an option at all. Besides, I wanted Brianna to have a father. And I wanted to give her a home. I kept thinking that once he saw her, he'd love her so much that he'd change. If not for me, for her."

"Did you ever leave him before now?"

"Sure I did," she said. "Several times. But he always talked me into coming back. You have to understand; we were in the military. He wasn't home half the time, so I told myself that I could manage the times he was. When I'd leave him, we'd be stuck in some town where I had no friends, no help." She swallowed. "I owe a lot to Lynda. If she hadn't been willing to take my case and give me advice, I don't know if I would have had the courage to leave him for good, even after he hurt Brianna. I don't know why it's so hard for me to stick to my guns."

Jake's eyes strayed to the child playing at the table then scanned the trees on the perimeter of the yard. "Did you say he was in the military?"

"Yes. The Navy."

"No wonder he was gone so much."

"Yeah. He'd be out on that aircraft carrier for weeks at a time. I wouldn't even hear from him. It was so peaceful."

"Aircraft carrier?" Jake cut in. "What did he do?"

"He was an aircraft mechanic," she said. "On the ships, they—"

"Wait a minute." Jake stopped her and sat straighter. "Did you say he was an *aircraft* mechanic?"

"Yes. He ..." Her voice trailed off as she saw his reaction, and she realized what he was thinking.

"Does Lynda know this?"

"Well, she knows he was in the Navy. I don't think she ever asked what he did there. Jake, you don't think—"

"Paige, was Keith ever a suspect in the plane crash?"

Paige gaped at him. "I don't know. But anyway, they caught the guy who did that."

True, Jake thought, they had. Yet he couldn't dismiss the uneasy feeling that had gripped him. "I'm just saying—what if they were wrong? What if they got the wrong guy? I mean, if Keith knows airplanes, he would know exactly what to do to sabotage Lynda's plane. The cops may have overlooked it because you don't think of airplanes when you think of the Navy."

"But why would he do that? To get Brianna, he would have to get *me* out of the way, not Lynda—and I wasn't anywhere near Lynda that day." She thought back to the day that had erupted so horribly, starting the bizarre chain of events that had brought her to where she was now. "As a matter of fact, he went to the day care that morning trying to get Brianna. That's when this whole thing started."

"Doesn't that seem coincidental? That Lynda and I crashed the same morning that he started aggressively trying to take Brianna? Whoever sabotaged our plane did it the night before the crash. He could have been anticipating that Lynda would be out of the way, so that when he kidnapped Brianna, you'd have no one to help you."

Paige's face slowly drained of its color. "No, it can't be. Keith would do a lot of things. Sinister, mean things. But I can't believe he'd kill somebody."

"When they questioned him about the fire, you thought he could, didn't you?"

She got up, unable to sit still. "No. I mean yes. I was confused, but—Brianna was in that house. Of course, he didn't know that at the time." She turned back to Jake. "Keith *can't* be the one. He can't be. Because if he is, then the guy they've got locked up is the wrong guy. And Keith is still loose."

"Waiting to hit again."

The thought chilled her. Rushing across the grass, she picked Brianna up. "Come on, honey. We're going in." Abandoning the dolls, she took her into the house.

"Mommy, I want to play!"

"No, honey." She stepped back as Jake followed them in. Then she let Brianna down, closed the door, and bolted it. "We have to come in now."

"Paige, I think it's okay if she plays—"

"No!" Paige ran her trembling hands through her hair. "Brianna said he was here, and he was, Jake. He found out where we are, and he's been watching us! He's going to do something! I have to stop him!"

He watched her run frantically around the house, looking for something. Brianna stood watching her, not moving, and her thumb gravitated to her mouth. "Lynda took the cellular phone, didn't she? We haven't gotten a phone hooked up yet, Jake. Can I use the one in your car?"

"Sure," he said. "Who are you calling?"

She was out the door before he could get an answer. Pulling Brianna onto his lap, he rolled out after her.

She was already in the car dialing. After a moment's wait, she said in a shaky voice, "This is Paige Varner. I need to speak to Larry Millsaps, please." She closed her eyes and shook her head, apparently not liking the answer she received. "Then I'll speak to Tony Danks. Well, when will they be back? Do you know how I can reach them?"

She wilted and covered her face. "No, they can't call me back. Look, this is an emergency. Tell them to come to Lynda Barrett's house as soon as possible. And tell them I think they've got the wrong guy!"

Hanging up, she breathed a quick sob. "I'm going there."

"Where?"

"To the police department. I'm going to wait there until they get back. We're not safe here, Jake. You come with me."

"No," he said. "I'll stay in case Lynda comes home."

"Oh, no!" Paige wailed. "*She's* in danger, too. If he would mess up her plane and burn down her house, he'll do anything. If she's at work, she's a sitting duck. He knows where to find her!"

"All right," Jake said, trying to calm her. "I'll stay here and call her, and you take Brianna and go to the police station. Don't worry. I'll make sure Lynda's careful, and Tony and Larry will take care of the rest."

Sucking in a deep breath and wiping her face, she carried Brianna to her car.

Jake was dialing Lynda's office before Paige was out of the driveway, but the receptionist put him on hold for what seemed an eternity. When she came back, she told him that Lynda's line was busy. Would he like to hold, call back, or leave a message?

"Let me try her secretary," he said.

"Her line's busy, too. But she could call you back."

"Look, have her call me, but tell her it's an emergency. Tell her not to move until she talks to me. Did you get that?"

"Yes, sir."

"I mean it. This is very serious. Tell her to call me on my car phone at this number. Do you have a pen?"

He rattled off the number, and the woman jotted it down. "I'll give her the message, Mr. Stevens."

Jake cut the phone off and sat still a moment, wondering whether Paige had overreacted, and whether his own concern had caused her to. If this were all just a wild tangent. . . .

Somehow, he didn't think it was.

He sat beside his car for twenty minutes or so, waiting for Lynda to call him back, and finally he dialed the number again.

"She's in a meeting, Mr. Stevens," the receptionist said. "I gave her the message, but—"

"Did she see it, or did you just put it on her desk?"

"Well—I gave it to Sally and told her it was urgent. But she was already in the meeting."

"How could she be in a meeting if she was on the phone before?"

"I guess she hung up and went before I could get back there."

He wanted to reach through the phone and throttle the woman. "Look, I don't *care* if she's in a meeting. Get her out."

"I can't do that, sir. It's a partners' meeting, and I've been given instructions to—"

"Then transfer me to Sally!"

He waited as he was put on hold, realizing what Paige must have gone through all those months before she was one of Lynda's priorities.

"Lynda Barrett's office."

It was Sally, and he breathed a sigh of relief. "Sally, this is Jake Stevens."

"Jake, I got your message. What's going on?"

"It's a long story. Is there any way you can get Lynda out of that meeting for an emergency?"

"Well, I suppose I could, but—"

"Then do it! Tell her to call me ASAP! I'm sitting out here by my car so I can take the call. Here's the number."

When he hung up, he waited, his heart racing. If only he could do something besides sit. If he could just get into this car and drive to her office.

Minutes ticked by, but the phone didn't ring. And he had no intention of going inside until it did.

Lynda couldn't have been more relieved when Sally got her out of the meeting. The sheer act of sitting still was making her ache all over, and her head throbbed from all the questions her partners and associates kept flinging at her about the cases they had taken over for her. And it was all time she could have spent working on Paige's case or catching up on her correspondence.

Sally gave her a once-over as she came out, laden down with papers. "Are you feeling okay? You look pale."

"I'm a little tired. What's wrong?"

"I got you out because Jake has been calling. He says it's an emergency. You'd better call him. He's waiting at his car. Here's the number."

Frowning, she took it. "Did he say what's wrong?"

"Nope."

"Okay, I'll call him," she said, heading for her office. "Hold all my calls."

She hurried into her office and dialed the number. Jake answered on the first ring.

"Hello?"

"Jake, it's Lynda. What's going on?"

"Lynda, Paige and I were talking, and we hit on something I think you should know about."

"What?"

"Did you know that Keith Varner used to be an aircraft mechanic?"

She caught her breath. "No he wasn't!"

"Yes, he was. In the Navy," he said. "He worked on airplanes on an aircraft carrier."

"Are you sure?"

"Dead sure. Paige said it herself."

There was a moment of silence, and finally, Lynda blew out an unsteady breath. "Jake, they had him. After the fire and again after the assault. They had him twice, but they let him go. It was him all the time."

"Yeah. Some poor guy is sitting in the slammer right now for something he didn't do, and this lunatic is still out there. Probably waiting for another opportunity. Or at least we have to assume for your safety as well as Paige's and Brianna's, that that's true."

She felt dizzy, and for a moment, she considered asking him to hold while she splashed cold water on her face.

"Where's Paige? How's she taking this?"

"The way you might expect, just short of hysterical. She decided to take Brianna and go to the sheriff's department to talk to Larry and Tony."

"Good. That was smart."

"But I'm worried about you."

She swallowed and reached for her car keys. "Frankly, *I'm* worried about me. Look, I'm coming home. I'm not feeling that terrific anyway. I'll just call it a day."

The relief was clear in Jake's voice. "All right. I'll see you soon. Lynda?"

"Yeah."

"Be careful, huh?"

She sat for a moment after he'd hung up, trying to organize her thoughts. She wasn't going to panic.

Picking up the phone, she buzzed Sally's desk. "Sally, would you get me all those files I need to look at for Paige's case? I'm going home, and I'll take those with me."

"Sure thing."

She looked up the number of the police station, dialed it, and asked for either of the two detectives.

Neither Larry nor Tony was in, and they couldn't be reached.

As she sank back into her chair, Sally breezed in with the files. "Lynda, are you sure you're all right?"

"Yeah. Sally, Jake's just run across some information that makes him think Keith Varner caused our crash and that he burned down my house."

Sally's eyes widened. "Paige's husband?"

"Yeah. And to tell you the truth, I think he's right. It all makes sense." She was trembling as she got to her feet. "I'm going home, but if Larry or Tony calls, tell one or both of them to call me on the cellular phone. I have to talk to them."

"Okay."

Lynda reached for the stack of files that contained the depositions from all the witnesses, all the emergency-room reports, and all the police complaints and stories from neighbors. But Sally put out a hand to stop her.

"This is too heavy for you," she said. "Give me the keys, and I'll go drop them in the car for you so you won't have to carry them."

Lynda managed a smile. "That would be great." She tossed her the keys. "I have a few other things I need to do before I leave."

"I'll be right back," Sally said and flitted out of the room.

Lynda sat and thought for a moment then decided not to wait for Larry and Tony. She would go straight to the DA, even before going home to Jake. Picking up the phone, she dialed the district attorney's number and told him she was coming right over.

Preoccupied, she got on the elevator and rode it down, hoping to intercept Sally in the parking lot.

The security guard was waiting just outside the elevator door when she got off.

"Sally said she'd bring your car up to the door, Miss Barrett, so you wouldn't have to walk."

Lynda smiled wanly. "That was sweet of her. All I wanted her to—"

A sound like the end of the world shook the building, breaking out the front windows and knocking her to her knees. The security guard threw himself against her, covering her from the flying glass with his body.

"No!" she screamed as she hit the floor, but it was too late. She'd already seen the glow that bathed the parking lot in a weird, unearthly light and the smoke that billowed across the lot as if shot from a hose. She knew without the slightest doubt that a car in the parking lot had just exploded.

And she knew without looking whose car it was.

63

STRUGGLING TO HER feet, Lynda crunched across the shattered glass and through the ruined door toward the flames, but the security guard caught up to her on the sidewalk.

"You have to stay back!" he shouted.

"But Sally's in there!" She tried to push him away, but he held her more tightly, and finally, the fight turned to mourning as she collapsed into his arms, covering her face with her hands, watching through her fingers as the flames devoured the car.

Already a crowd was spilling out of the building, and she heard sirens.

"They've got to get her out!" she cried.

But the guard wouldn't let her go. "She's dead, Miss Barrett. There's no way she could have survived that."

Lynda shook free of him again. "But it was my car! It was meant for me!"

She collapsed on the ground and immediately friends surrounded her as the parking lot filled with emergency vehicles.

Paige paced the floor at the police precinct, waiting for Larry or Tony to come back in or call. She couldn't just stay here, she told herself. Keith was still loose out there. He could try to hurt Lynda or even Jake again. He could burn the house down—or worse.

Grabbing Brianna from the dirty floor where she'd been looking at a book, she went back to the precinct desk and tapped the arm of the uniformed deputy who had helped her earlier. "I have to go," she said. "Please tell Tony or Larry when they come in that Keith Varner is the one who's been after Lynda Barrett. Please. They have to arrest him."

The man had already checked Paige's situation out in the computer. He knew that she'd complained about her ex several times. He also knew they were embroiled in a custody battle, and he'd seen enough to know that such spouses would do whatever it took to discredit the other. He jotted down the note disinterestedly then slipped it in a stack. "They'll get the message."

Paige could see that he wasn't counting it as urgent. "I'm telling you if you don't do something, somebody might die. He's out there."

"Call us if anything comes up," he said.

Cursing under her breath, Paige gave up.

"Where are we going, Mommy?" Brianna asked as they headed out the door.

Paige sighed. "I don't know. Maybe to Lynda's office."

"Good. I like Miss Lynda's office."

"Okay," Paige said. "That's where we'll go then."

Brianna was quiet as they drove, as though she knew that her mother needed time to think.

But the moment Paige turned onto the law firm's street and saw the fire trucks and police cars surrounding the parking lot, her heart leapt in fear. Forced to stop in the line of traffic, she rolled down her window and stretched as far out as she could to see what the problem was.

A car alongside the building was on fire.

Terror ripped through her, and she covered her mouth, muffling a scream.

Brianna started to cry. "What's the matter, Mommy?"

But Paige didn't answer, for as the traffic began to move, she saw the car that was burning.

Lynda's car.

Trembling, she pulled out of the line of traffic, did a quick U-turn, and headed back to the house as fast as she could, trying with all her heart to fight the certainty that Lynda was dead.

64

KEITH HAD WATCHED and waited from three blocks away, knowing that the moment the car went up, he'd know it. And he'd been right.

He hadn't expected it to happen so soon. He'd figured he would have to spend a few more hours sitting in his car watching, but she had made it easy on him.

He laughed now as he drove to the house where his wife and daughter were hiding. Paige was defenseless now, both in court and out. Brianna was his. All he had to do was tie up these loose ends.

Boldly, he turned down the street that he hadn't dared to drive down before and passed the trees he had hidden in as he had stalked them over the last week.

But Paige's car wasn't in the driveway. Only the red Porsche sat there—the car that hadn't been moved since he'd first noticed it.

Disappointed, he turned around at the dead end and left the street. Okay. So he would park and watch for her to come home, then. And the moment she did, he would grab Brianna before Paige could get inside. There would be nothing she could do. Absolutely nothing.

65

"It's Keith Varner." Lynda's voice was dull and without inflection. "He did it."

Larry had just shown up on the scene after getting the urgent message from Lynda—one that had to be delivered by another detective since he and Tony had been working on an undercover case in which they couldn't carry their radios. "What?"

"He was an aircraft mechanic in the Navy. It's him, Larry. He's the one who's been trying to kill me. I thought you had the right guy behind bars! I never would have let Sally go out there if I'd known—"

"You didn't know. You couldn't have known. You don't even know now."

"Then explain this!" she screamed at him. "Something seems to go up in flames everywhere I go! If the guy you've got in jail is the right one, then why did this happen? I'm telling you, it's Keith! He's crazy!"

Larry looked up at the other officers who were filling out reports. "Put out an APB on Keith Varner. If he did it, we'll know it soon enough."

"Do you honestly think you're just going to go get him? He's not sitting at home waiting for the police!" Lynda shouted.

"We'll find him. Just calm down."

"I *can't* calm down! My secretary is dead in my place! She was my friend!" She collapsed in tears, then shook her head, trying to pull herself together. In a cracked, high-pitched voice, she said, "I have to tell her family. They can't hear this from just anyone."

"Well, you'd better do it soon," Larry said. "Before the authorities tell them."

"Would you—would you take me?"

"Sure." He took a deep breath, then walked her to his car and set her inside. Then he turned and gave a few more instructions to the deputies still on the scene.

As they pulled away, Lynda glanced back at the crowd that had formed around the parking lot. Another gruesome sight they would never forget. Another incident Lynda Barrett had escaped.

She didn't know how many more she could take. Especially not at this cost.

66

KEITH GOT TIRED of waiting and decided to park his car in his usual spot on the street behind Lynda's house and cut through the woods. Then he would sneak up on the back of the house, look through the windows, and find out whether anyone was home.

He made his way to the fence enclosing the back yard, the same place where he'd talked to Brianna just a few days ago. Satisfied that no one was near, he climbed the fence and cut across the yard.

Boldly, he crossed the patio and peered into the kitchen window. The lights were off. He moved past the back kitchen door and looked through the living-room window. No one was there.

Stepping quietly, he made his way down the length of the house to the other back door, the one that went into the master bedroom. Peering through the glass pane in the door, he saw that the bed was made and the lights were off.

So they were gone. He tested the door that led into the bedroom. Locked. Going back to the kitchen door, he tested it, too.

The house was empty. When Paige came home, it would be just the two of them—and Brianna. He found a comfortable seat behind the house and waited for Paige.

Jake heard the screeching tires as Paige pulled into the driveway; as quickly as he could, he pushed himself out of the recliner and into his wheelchair. He rolled to the door—but even before he could turn the knob, he heard Brianna scream.

Through the door's window, he saw that a man had grabbed Brianna out of Paige's car and that Paige was fighting and clawing and kicking him with all her might.

His heart jumped, and he twisted the knob, ready to burst through the door and defend her—until he was hit with the crushing realization that there was nothing he could do. He couldn't walk or fight or defend anyone.

For a moment, he sat stunned, watching Paige fight for her life, watching as the man—he assumed it was Keith Varner—held Brianna roughly around her waist with one arm, and with the other pulling Paige by the hair to the door, making her unlock it. "You have ten minutes to pack everything she has here," he said through his teeth. "And then I'll decide what to do with you."

Jake roused himself, knowing that regardless of his limitations, Paige and Brianna needed his help. Flying back to the small kitchenette, he pulled the biggest knife he could find from the drawer, set it in his lap, and headed back to the door.

He heard the house door slam. He hoped that, with all the screaming inside, Keith wouldn't hear him if he went out and tried to reach his car phone. Jake guessed that they were in the bedroom at the back of the house, getting Brianna's things.

As quietly as he could, he opened the door and rolled out onto the driveway.

Paige's screams still sounded from inside the house, and something crashed. Jake's hands trembled as he opened his car door as quietly as he could then slipped inside. Pulling the door shut, he checked to make sure that Keith had not heard him. Apparently he hadn't.

He dialed 911 and keeping his voice barely above a whisper, told the dispatcher that Paige and Brianna were being held hostage inside the house and that Keith was dangerous. When he told them it was the home of Lynda Barrett, the dispatcher hesitated.

"Barrett? The same woman whose car blew up today?"

Jake clutched the phone. "What?"

"Is it the Lynda Barrett who works in the Schilling building?"

For a moment he couldn't find his voice. "Yes," he said. "What happened to her car?"

"Uh—there was an accident. An explosion."

Trying to steady his breath, he said, "Was she—was she killed?"

"There was one death in the accident," the woman confirmed hurriedly. "Do you think the person in the house could be a suspect in the explosion?"

Jake felt as if he were falling, falling, and there was nothing he could grab to stop his fall.

"Sir? Can you hear me?"

"Yes," he breathed. "Yes, it's him. Hurry, or he'll kill them."

He punched the "end" button on the phone then sat still, trying to grasp everything she had said. Explosion. Lynda's car. One death.

For a moment, he considered putting his key in the ignition, turning on the car, and ramming it headfirst into the house. Maybe he could get rid of Keith and himself in one quick action.

It was too much.

Not Lynda. She couldn't be dead.

He covered his face with his hand, too shocked to weep or scream. It had to be a mistake. She wouldn't die on him just like that. She would fight and survive. Somehow she'd make it.

So caught up was he in the turmoil of his raging thoughts that he didn't hear a car pull into the driveway behind him. But he jumped when he heard the car door slam and wrenched his neck to see. Lynda was walking toward the house, and a car was backing out of the driveway.

He flung the door open and almost fell out. "Lynda! You're alive!"

She looked pale, and there were red circles under her eyes. "Yeah," she said, and tears came to her eyes again as she reached for him. "Sally's dead."

He wanted to fling himself at her, hug her, but there wasn't time. "He's in there, Lynda. He has Paige and Brianna."

"What? Who?"

"Keith! He caught her getting out of her car and dragged them in. I've called the police."

Lynda stood shocked for a moment, then turned frantically toward the street, lifting a hand—but the car was already gone. Jake pulled himself into his chair then rolled around a corner of the house where Keith couldn't see him if he looked out. Lynda followed him.

"That was Larry who dropped me off! I should have made him stay, but he had a lead on where Keith was—" She looked around for a weapon then saw the knife Jake clutched in his hand. "But surely the dispatcher will let him know—"

"We can't wait," Jake said. "We have to do something! I think they're in the bedroom getting Brianna's things. If we can figure out where they are, when the police get here they can go in another door and surprise him."

Lynda nodded. "I'll go look."

A shadow of frustration crossed Jake's face. He wanted to go. But he couldn't.

"Be careful," he said.

Lynda crept along the side of the house. Peering around the corner nearest the bedroom, she saw them.

Keith stood in front of the screen door that opened to the patio. He held Brianna with one arm while he pointed a gun at Paige. She was on her knees, throwing clothes into a suitcase. Lynda could hear Brianna screaming. And through it, their voices.

"Please," Paige begged. "Just put her down, Keith. Let her go!"

"Shut up," Keith snarled. He grabbed Paige and pulled her up. "Now, where's the rest of her stuff?"

"The living room," Paige choked out. "Her dolls are in the living room."

As soon as they were out of sight, Lynda dashed back around the house to where Jake waited.

"They're headed for the living room," she whispered.

Something else crashed inside the house, and Lynda jumped. Brianna's blood-curdling scream cut through the air.

"He'll kill them," she whispered loudly. "He's insane. What are we going to do?"

"First, we're gonna calm down," he whispered. "And we're gonna think."

"I can get in through the back way," she whispered. "The door to the master bedroom."

"And do what? You don't have a gun. And even if you did, you couldn't use it."

"Then what do you suggest?"

"Let me go in that way," he said. "You wait here then create a diversion at the front of the house when the police get here."

She looked at his functionless legs, at his wheelchair. "No, I can't let you do it."

There was another crash, and Brianna's screaming stopped short. From the house came nothing but dead silence.

"That's it! I won't let him take another of my friends!" Throwing down her purse, she sprang toward the kitchen door.

"Lynda, stop!" he said in a loud hiss.

But she burst through the door before he could reach her. "Stop it!" she screamed. "Let them go and take me instead! I'm the one you really want!" The door slammed shut behind her.

For a moment, Jake sat frozen. He thought of going in after her, giving the fight everything he had. But that wouldn't help anyone. In the distance, he could hear sirens, but they were still too far away. Lynda's purse lay on its side on the ground; he reached for it and dug for her house key. Gripping the knife, he rolled around the back of the house, through the dirt so he wouldn't make noise. As the sirens got louder, he unlocked the master bedroom door and rolled inside.

He heard Keith cursing at Lynda, and Paige starting to scream again; things crashed and fell. Outside, the sirens seemed to have disappeared; had they gone the wrong way?

What if it was all up to him?

Grasping for help, Jake closed his eyes. *If you're up there, God, I could use a hand. Just make my body function well enough to help them.*

In the living room, Lynda tried to breathe, but Keith's arm was brutally tight against her throat. Paige's face was bleeding where he'd hit her, and Brianna sat hunched under a table with her arms covering her head.

"At least let Brianna go," Paige was crying. "Please, Keith. She's your *daughter!* If you really loved her you wouldn't make her watch this!"

"You don't know the first thing about love," he bit out. "She needs to know what kind of a tramp her mother is. She needs to see how weak you are. And she needs to see you dead, so she won't keep expecting you to rescue her when I take her. That way we can start a new life together, and she can depend on me, and I can clear her mind of all the brainwashing you've done."

Lynda struggled to loosen his hold on her. "You won't get away with this," she said. "You think they'll let you keep that child after you've killed two more people? They'll never let you out of here with her."

"Who won't?"

"The police!" she shouted, but Keith just grinned down at her insanely.

"The police are idiots. They already had me twice, and they let me go."

"Don't you hear the sirens?"

For the first time, he listened. The sirens were loud now and sounded as if they were right outside the house. Venomous rage reddened his face. "Then I have nothing more to lose, do I?"

Throwing Lynda down, he grabbed Paige's hair and put his gun to her head.

The doorbell rang, and a loud banging followed. "Police department! Open up!"

The gun fired, and Paige collapsed. Lynda screamed and dove for Brianna, who clung desperately to her, shivering. Keith kicked Paige, and when she recoiled, it was clear that she hadn't been shot. Thankful, Lynda tried to catch her breath and whispered to Brianna, "She's all right, sweetheart. Mommy's all right."

"The next shot goes through the door!" Keith shouted. "And then I'll kill both women!"

"We just want to talk to you, Varner!"

Lynda recognized the voice outside the door—Larry. She prayed that he hadn't come too late.

"Where's the phone?" Keith asked, sweat beading on his face as he looked from one side of the room to the other. "I can talk to 'em—negotiate."

"We don't have one!" Lynda threw back. "We used the cellular phone in my car, but you blew it up!"

"Shut up!" Keith bellowed and kicked over the table they sat under.

It didn't take another gunshot to tell Jake that there was no more time. If he were going to act, he had to do it now. Opening the bedroom door as quietly as he could, he wheeled into the hallway, holding the knife in his fist.

Keith picked up Paige again by the hair and arm, and as she struggled to free herself, Keith's hold tightened and Paige let out a muffled scream.

"In the name of God, let her *go!*" Lynda cried. "Think of Brianna. Look what you're doing to her!"

Jake silently wheeled to the corner where the hall joined the living room. Staying as far back as he could, he saw Brianna crouched beside Lynda. Keith stood nearby, still holding Paige with both arms. He let her go, and she fell to the floor. Bending down, he reached out to touch Brianna.

Curling into a tighter ball, she strained away from him.

"Brianna, it's just Daddy," he said in a quiet voice. "I'm not gonna hurt you again. Don't you believe me?"

Jake's gaze narrowed to the revolver hanging in Keith's hand, muzzle toward the ground, as he reached for Brianna with the other.

Slowly, Jake came out of the shadows and began to move across the carpet.

Tears started down Keith's face as he touched Brianna's hair. She hunched her shoulders higher, and her mouth grew even wider in terror, but her heaving sobs were silent.

First Lynda then Paige caught sight of Jake moving across the carpet in his wheelchair, and they froze, not certain what to do.

"It's not too late, Keith," Lynda said, keeping her timbre steady and low, trying to draw Keith's attention. "You can change your life. You can be the father she needs. Just let her go for now."

Keith dropped his head and began to weep; the gun slipped slightly in his loosening grasp.

Jake pushed his wheels gently one more time, easing closer to Keith's side, holding his breath to avoid any sound that would give him away—

And swung his arm with all the strength and speed he could muster. He hit the gun, sending it bouncing several feet away across the carpet, then swung back to grab Keith's wrist and twist it behind his back, forcing him to his knees. "Didn't know I was here, did you, pal?" Jake asked through gritted teeth. "Recognize me? I'm the guy you maimed in the plane crash."

Keith couldn't move; the strength Jake had built in his arms over the past few weeks was overpowering. "Let me go!" he screamed, but Jake forced him forward until his face rested on the floor. Paige scrambled after the gun and stood up, aiming it at her ex-husband.

"Take her out, Lynda!" Paige shouted. "I don't want her to see me kill her father."

Lynda grabbed Brianna and rushed for the kitchen door. Paige waited until they were out of the room before she pulled the hammer back. "I could pull this trigger right now!" she said through her teeth, "and they'd call it self-defense. I'd be a hero for ridding the world of you. And my daughter could finally learn what it's like to live without terror."

Keith struggled against Jake's grip and tried to look up at her. "You won't do it. Brianna would always blame you—"

"Shut up!" she cried.

There was the sound of splintering wood, and the front door burst open. Larry lunged into the room then stopped when he saw Paige holding the gun on Keith.

"Paige, give me the gun," he said.

Paige shook her head. "Stay back. Jake, move away."

Reluctantly, Jake let Keith go and slowly rolled backward.

Her face was red and streaked with tears. "If I blew you away," she said, her voice trembling, "it would be for all the pain you've caused Brianna. All the nightmares. All the trauma. It would be for her peace of mind." The gun began to shake.

"Send him to jail, Paige," Jake said carefully. "Don't let him die knowing he finally broke you."

Her face twisted as she struggled between the emotion of the moment and the hope of the future. Finally, she breathed in and out deeply, her breath catching as her tears flowed anew. "He's right, Keith," she said. "You're not going to break me. You're just going to rot in prison."

When she lowered the gun, the house filled with deputies. Larry handcuffed Keith, jerked him to his feet, and took him away.

67

AS LOW AS Lynda's life had gotten in the past few weeks, she was certain that Sally's funeral was the lowest point yet. As if even God mourned her passing, the sky opened up with torrential rains that morning, and it stormed throughout the day. Lynda sat between Paige and Jake, holding hands with each of them, trying to rein back the tears that had controlled her since the day of the explosion. Even Keith's confession and guilty plea to felony murder had not relieved the pain.

She watched Sally's parents weep over their daughter. Sally had been close to them, even though they lived several hours away.

"At least she didn't leave a husband and children," Lynda heard someone whisper behind her.

Lynda quelled the urge to turn around and tell them that Sally had had many people who'd loved her, that she'd had as much of a family as most people had, and that her being single didn't make it any easier to say good-bye.

The car ride home was quiet, and when they had been back at the house for a while, Paige came out of her room with her bags packed.

Lynda had known they were going back home today, but she'd tried to put it out of her mind. Now there was nothing she could do but face it.

Dropping the bag, Paige reached out to hug Lynda. As they clung together like sisters, Lynda realized that, for the first time in her life, she didn't feel like an only child.

"I'm gonna miss you," Lynda whispered.

Paige wiped her tears. "Me, too. I don't know how I'll ever thank you for what you've done for us."

Lynda tried to smile. "Well, for starters—I need a new secretary." Tears rushed into her eyes again as she got the words out. "And frankly, I don't think I can get used to someone new right now. How about taking Sally's job?"

Paige seemed confused, wary. "Do you really mean it?"

"I sure do."

"But how do you know I'm qualified?"

"You can do anything," Lynda said. "I have a lot of faith in you."

Again, they embraced, then Lynda stooped to kiss Brianna. The child had been quiet and withdrawn since the scene with her father, but she'd already expressed her wish to go back to "school" soon. Paige thought it was a good idea to get her life back to normal as soon as possible.

Jake offered Brianna a final ride on his lap as they hurried through the rain to the car, and Lynda smiled sadly as he hugged the child who had brought him so far, gave her a quick kiss on the cheek, and then helped her into the car.

The rain poured harder as the car pulled away, but neither Lynda nor Jake made a move to go inside.

"Are you all right?" he asked when the car was out of sight.

Lynda was still gazing in the direction they had gone as raindrops mixed with the tears on her face. "I was just thinking."

"About what?"

"That day in the plane," she said. "When they asked us if we had anyone to contact. Neither of us had anyone, really."

"You had Sally."

"Sally the secretary," she whispered. "But not Sally the friend, not then. I didn't really have any close friends then. I thought I was happy, all alone."

"We've both come a long way."

She looked down at him, saw how wet his hair was getting, how soaked his clothes, but he didn't seem to mind. He wasn't the same man who had gotten out of his Porsche that day wearing his designer clothes, expecting crowds to part and women to swoon. "I like having people to love," she said.

He nodded, swallowed, and she knew that the mist in his eyes had nothing to do with the rain. "I like it, too."

For a moment, they smiled at each other as the rain dripped down their faces, and finally, she said, "It's going to be awfully quiet around here without them."

"Well, I'll see what I can do about making a little more noise."

She wiped her tears. "You'll have to eat my cooking now."

"I've been keeping it a secret, but I'm a pretty talented cook myself," he said. "As a matter of fact, I was thinking of making my special Texas stew for you tonight. Paige left all the ingredients in there. I already checked."

Slowly, the despair left Lynda's eyes, and she began to smile. "Then we'd better get busy peeling potatoes. You do have potatoes in your stew, don't you?"

"Among lots of other things, which shall remain secret."

"Well, I've survived four brushes with death in the last few weeks. I guess one more won't hurt me."

His smile faded. "That's not really funny," he said softly. "Matter of fact, it's downright chilling when you think about it."

"You're telling me." Looking around at the trees surrounding her house, she rubbed her arms and shivered. "Let's go in before we get sick and your chair starts to rust."

"I'd better change clothes first," he said. "If I don't, I'll ruin your kitchen floor."

"All right," she said. "I'll meet you in the kitchen."

She went back into the quiet house and felt the assault of silence again. But it wasn't so bad because she knew Jake was coming. Quickly she changed out of her wet clothes and towel-dried her hair.

When she went back into the kitchen, he was already at the table, peeling potatoes.

The sight of him there stirred her. Feeling awkward, she pulled out a chair and sat next to him. There were things she needed to say, things he needed to hear.

"We haven't talked much about that day," she said. "It's been kind of busy, and Sally's been on my mind. And we were all worried about Brianna. . . ."

"Yeah. There hasn't been much time for reflection, has there?"

She looked down at the table, tracing the pattern of the wood grain with her fingertip. "I've been meaning to thank you."

"For what?"

"For coming to the rescue when Keith was here. My bursting into the house was really stupid. If you hadn't come in when you did—"

"I got lucky," he said. "If he had turned around and seen me coming, things could have turned out a lot differently."

"No, I think you would have been able to defend us even then. I didn't realize how strong you are, Jake. Even without your legs, you overpowered him. He couldn't fight you."

He smiled, but that smile quickly faded. "I just kept remembering that morning, when Brianna agreed to go outside because I was with her. I realized that she *expected* me to protect her. My legs weren't a factor to her. If I was to help her, then they couldn't be a factor to me, either."

She leaned on the table and faced him squarely. "Did you learn anything from that, Jake?"

His smile was subtle, but it reached all the way through her. "I think I did."

He didn't have to explain. She already knew that whatever he had learned, it was miles ahead of where he'd been before the plane crash.

"The important thing," he said, returning to his work, "is that that slimeball is behind bars." He finished peeling a potato then grew still for a moment, staring down at it.

"What's wrong?" she asked quietly.

He shrugged. "I was just thinking. That day when I called the police about Keith being in the house. They told me about the car blowing up, and said there had been a death."

Stillness.

"You thought it was me."

His facial muscles shifted with emotions he could not have named. "I was so glad when you walked up."

For a moment their eyes locked, and she wanted to reach out and hold him, cling to him. She had done it before when he'd needed comforting. But this was different.

This was more dangerous.

This was more important.

He reached out and took her hand, and squeezing it tightly, brought it to his lips. "You're a miracle, you know that?"

Coming from a man who didn't believe in miracles, that statement overwhelmed her. She saw the way his eyes misted as he gazed openly at her without the barriers of pride or humor, with only the honest glisten of pure affection.

Was he going to kiss her? Did she want him to?

She wasn't sure.

When he let her hand go and picked up his paring knife again, she breathed a sigh of both relief and disappointment. For as much as she'd feared that moment of truth between them, she regretted that it was over before it even started.

68

DAVID LETTERMAN WAS almost over when Jake started getting ready for bed. Turning off the lamp and leaving only the light of the television, he glanced out the window to see whether Lynda's light was still on. It wasn't. Was she sleeping? Or was she lying awake, struggling with her grief, needing the same kind of comfort she'd offered him more than once?

And then he saw movement in the darkness on the patio and realized she was sitting out there alone, her feet pulled up and her arms hugging her knees. Moonlight played on her hair and touched her face, and he wondered why he hadn't been struck by how pretty she was the first time he'd met her. She was beautiful to him now.

Wanting to be close to her, he rolled out his door. Lynda looked up at him as he came around the house.

In the moonlight, he could see that she'd been crying. How did one soothe a grief like this one? How did you offer comfort when there was none?

"Need company?" he asked softly, rolling up beside her.

She smiled. "Yeah, I could use some."

He remembered the old days when he would have eagerly held a woman with tears on her face—but it would only have been so that he could use his hundred-dollar-an-ounce charm to work her vulnerability to his favor. It had been so easy for him, then, to make them trust him, count on him, believe in him—then to walk away without looking back the next morning.

Things had changed. Nothing was that easy anymore. He knew that all the introspection of the past weeks had given birth to something new in his life: a conscience. And he didn't think of Lynda the way he'd thought about any other woman in his life.

"I was just thinking about Sally," she whispered.

"Not beating yourself up again, I hope."

She looked out into the shadows of her yard. "I was thinking how unfair it is that she should die because of Keith's vendetta against me."

He turned his chair to face her, then reached out and took her hand in both of his. "Well, call me selfish if you have to, but I'm not going to feel guilty for being glad you weren't in that car."

"What could make a man want to kill?" she asked. "How could he have believed it would set anything right? Didn't he understand that he lost Brianna because of his violence in the first place?"

"He must by now, or he wouldn't have confessed and pled guilty."

Lynda shook her head. "No, I don't think he did that because he understands. I think he did that because McRae dropped his case, and he wasn't getting a lot of sympathy from his public defender."

Jake thought about that for a moment. "Not to mention the little fact that he was caught red-handed holding you all hostage, and he'd admitted, to all of us, that he'd done the other things."

"I think it was more a matter of defeat than regret," Lynda said. "He knew he couldn't win."

"Well, I guess our revenge is in knowing that he's behind bars and that he'll probably never see his daughter again."

She shook her head slowly. "I'm not supposed to want revenge."

"Why not?"

She looked up into the stars as new tears rolled down her cheek. "I'm supposed to pray for my enemies. I'm supposed to love them."

"Yeah, well, 'supposed to' is a long way from being able to. Look at all he did to you. Look what he did to me. I can't forgive him for that. I don't want to. But if I ever get the chance to meet him alone—"

"You won't," she whispered. "He'll probably get the death penalty. Unless I do something . . . say something. . . ."

"Lynda, you can't."

Her sudden surrender to her tears surprised him, but without giving it a second thought, he gathered her up and pulled her against him. She closed her arms around his neck and wept against his shoulder, and he found himself weeping with her—*for* her. And he remembered how *she* had held *him* when he'd wept, how right it had felt, how much it had comforted him, how it had seemed like light seeping into the darkened chambers of his heart. That, more than her heroics in the plane, had probably saved his life.

"I came out here to pray for him," she whispered. "I made up my mind that I would. But I'm having trouble. It's the hardest thing I've ever done."

She wilted against his chest, and he stroked her hair. "It's okay, Lynda. It doesn't matter."

"It *does* matter."

"Why? Tell me why it matters."

She sat up then, breaking his hold on her and looked him squarely in the eyes. He reached up to wipe her tears away with the back of his fingers.

"It matters because Christ forgave me."

"Forgave you for what? What terrible thing have you ever done?"

"Oh, Jake," she cried. "I do terrible things all the time. And the morning of the crash when we were in that plane, knowing we could die the minute we landed, I just sat there. I didn't care what would happen to you if you'd died. I didn't even try to tell you what I knew. What could save you. But he didn't turn his back on either of us. He forgave me and let me start over. He let me see—"

"Lynda, you couldn't have saved me if you'd tried. I thought I had all the answers. Maybe I still think that. I was a creep then, and I'm probably still a creep, and you were justified in how you felt about me in that plane."

She shook her head. "You don't think it's important because you don't believe. But I do. And I want to obey now, but if it means forgiving Keith . . ."

"Keith Varner hasn't asked for your forgiveness."

"That doesn't matter. I still have to forgive him. And I hate myself for not being able to do it."

Later that night, when she had gone back into the house and lay awake in bed, staring at the ceiling and wrestling the monsters of memory and despair, Lynda tried to tell herself that she *could* forgive Keith, that maybe she already had. But as she drifted into a shallow sleep, she dreamed about cars blowing up and planes crashing and houses burning and about that panic that comes right before death between realizing it's going to happen and surrendering to it. Like a running theme through those images, Keith appeared here and there, laughing, cursing, escaping. . . .

She awoke in a cold sweat and looked around at the room full of distorted shadows; she had left the lamp on. Trembling, she reached for her radio and turned it on. Maybe the noise would block out the fears, override the terror.

But her heart was beating too wildly for her to go back to sleep, so she got up and wandered around the quiet house. What if the dream were a warning? He is smart, after all. What if he *had* found some way to escape?

She went back to her bedroom; the dresser mirror caught her reflection as she passed, and she stopped to study it. She wasn't the same person she'd been before the crash. She was different. More fragile in some ways, tougher in others.

Would she ever stop being afraid?

Sitting down on the end of her bed, she pressed her face into her hands and tried with all her heart to pray for peace of mind. But the words wouldn't come, and she found herself unable to pray, unable to ask for help, unable to surrender.

She thought of going to Jake's door and waking him up, but the idea seemed crazy. She would have to wait until morning. And then, perhaps she'd look into counseling. Maybe she needed professional help. Maybe she needed her preacher to teach her to pray again. Maybe she needed a gun and a security system and a bodyguard.

Maybe none of this was really over yet.

69

"I WISH I'D killed him."

Paige's words would have surprised Lynda if she hadn't struggled with the same thought herself. Paige sat at her new desk—Sally's desk—with dark circles under her eyes, indicating that she hadn't been able to sleep either.

"I had the chance," Paige added quietly.

"Don't say that," Lynda whispered without much conviction as she sank into the chair across from Paige's desk. "You did the right thing. The only thing you could have done."

"Brianna's still having nightmares."

"Aren't we all?"

Paige's tired eyes met Lynda's, and she shook her head. "The DA asked me to testify at Keith's sentencing. It's amazing that he confessed and didn't even try to negotiate away the death penalty. I think maybe he really wants to die."

"The DA called me, too," Lynda said.

"So I guess, indirectly I have another chance." Paige propped her chin on her hand. "I keep having visions of sitting up there in front of him, telling the judge to give him the chair while he watches me with those persuasive, hurt eyes. He'd be so shocked that I went through with it."

"So are you going to?"

Paige shrugged, despair evident on her face. "I don't think I can."

Lynda was quiet, not questioning, for she knew the dilemma.

"He's Brianna's father. I don't want her growing up with that kind of stigma. And I guess when I come right down to it, I don't want that guilt. I don't even know if I believe in the death penalty."

Lynda was quiet for a moment. "I used to be against it right across the board. But now I'm not so sure. I've never been the victim before." She thought that over for a moment, hating herself for not being able to choose one side of the line or the other. "I guess it's time I decided what I really believe."

"Are you going to testify?"

"I don't know," Lynda whispered. "The judge's pre-sentencing investigation has already probably told him all he needs to know. My testimony wouldn't make that much difference." She sighed. "Maybe I'm just wimping out. I don't know what to do."

Paige accepted that. "Jake probably will."

Yes. That would be his way of getting some measure of revenge. She almost hoped he did.

But the reality of that hope only drew her deeper into a pit of depression that seemed impossible to escape.

Lynda didn't sleep for the three nights before the day she was to testify at the sentencing, and that morning as she drove Jake to the courthouse, she still wasn't sure whether she would even go in when she got there.

Her dejection hadn't escaped Jake's notice, and reaching across the seat, he stroked her hair. "You don't have to do this, you know."

Lynda nodded. "I don't know if I will." She glanced over at him. "Do you think I'm a coward?"

"No, Lynda. When I think about you, a lot of different words come to mind, but coward isn't one of them. I don't think it's fear that's keeping you from wanting to testify."

"Then what is it?"

"Indecision, maybe? Those people in there want to know how we, the victims, feel about what should happen to Keith Varner. And you can't really tell them if you don't know yourself."

She reached the courthouse and pulled into a parking place then sat there for a moment, making no move to get out. "But you're sure, aren't you, Jake? You think he should be put to death."

Jake's face hardened slightly. "I'd do it myself if I could."

She dropped her head back on her headrest and stared at the courthouse—the same building where Keith had attacked Paige and tried to take Brianna such a short time ago. She remembered Brianna's terror that day—and on another day, cowering under a table. . . .

"Let's go in," she said quietly.

Jake shot her a surprised look. "Really? You're going to testify? What are you going to say?"

"I'll decide when I get in there," she said.

Jake got his wheelchair out of the back and slipped into it, and she followed him in. The building seemed too warm, and she found it hard to breathe. At the entrance, a few reporters rushed toward them with questions about their testimony, but they both threw out "No comment," and kept walking.

By the time they reached the courtroom, Lynda felt as if she might hyperventilate. Jake glanced back at her and noticed the perspiration on her temples and above her lip, and he handed her a handkerchief. "You okay?"

She sat down next to him. "Yeah. Fine."

The DA spotted them and came toward them. At the same time, the door at the front of the courtroom opened, and the bailiffs brought Keith in.

His eyes were bloodshot and he hadn't shaved. He searched the room frantically. Lynda knew he was looking for Paige, but when his gaze rested on her, her heart jolted.

All her anger rushed back in a tidal wave of memory, and she thought again about Brianna and Sally. Yes, he deserved death. And he deserved to hear her say it.

Why then did she still feel so divided? Could she really get up there and say what the DA wanted her to say?

Standing up, she pushed past the DA and Jake. "I'm sorry," she said. "I can't do this."

Jake caught her arm, and the DA looked crestfallen. "Lynda, what's wrong?"

Tears came to her eyes, and she glanced back at Keith, whose back was to her now. "I just don't know what I believe anymore," she whispered harshly. "And I can't sit up there and say something if I'm not sure." She looked down at Jake, expecting condemnation, but all she saw was concern. "You do what you have to do, Jake. Call me when it's over, and I'll come back to get you."

And before he could respond or the DA could talk her out of it, she shot out of the room.

At home, Lynda sat in the quiet, trying to decide why she was so angry with herself. Was it because she thought she'd wimped out or because she hadn't? Or was it even deeper? Did it have to do with this forgiveness issue that had plagued her since Keith's arrest?

Praying for her enemies had always seemed so logical, so easy—when she'd had no enemies. Loving had been a breeze—when she'd never really hated.

Now she was being tested. She had been tested before, but those other tests she had failed, and God had taught her through that failure how fruitless she was to his kingdom. How useless.

And if she'd learned anything in the past few weeks, it was that the only true joy she'd found was in being obedient to him. Maybe that was why her heart was so heavy now. Maybe it was because she was resisting.

Pulling her feet up onto the couch and wrapping her arms around her knees, she dropped her head into the circle of her arms and tried to pray again.

But this time, instead of praying for her fears and her trauma and her decisions, she prayed for Keith.

And as she did, his tremendous guilt became real to her, as did his grief. He had lost his wife and his daughter. Even though he'd caused those losses, that didn't change the level of pain he suffered. She didn't pray for his release or for some miraculous acquittal—for she knew that God was a just God and that crimes held consequences. Instead, she prayed for a change of heart, for light in his darkness, and for his salvation.

And she prayed that God would help her find a way to forgive him.

The moment she ended the prayer, she felt a great weight lifted off her, and peace replaced it.

A car door slammed. Through the window, she could see Jake getting out of a car. The car backed out of her driveway, and Jake rolled toward the door.

She opened it before he knocked. "Who brought you home?"

"One of the guys from the DA's office," he said. "Are you all right?"

She smiled, probably for the first time since Sally's funeral. "Yeah. I think I am."

Jake came inside, and he gazed at her for a long moment. "I was the last witness to testify, so they gave it to the jury right afterward. They agreed unanimously on the death penalty. The judge accepted their recommendation, Lynda. He got death."

She pulled out a chair and sat down slowly. "I figured he would." She let out a long breath. "It sure didn't take long."

"No, the jury wasn't out very long," he said. A slow, gentle smile changed his expression. "You really are better, aren't you? What happened?"

"I had a long talk with the Lord," she said. "And we got a few things straightened out."

"That's good." Then, as he gazed at her, he saw the pain return to her eyes. "What is it?"

She let out a deep, ragged breath. "I have to go see him," she whispered.

"What?"

"You heard me," she said. "I have to."

He rolled closer, as if by touching her he could chase away this madness. Taking her hand, he said, "Lynda, you can't. No one expects you to do this. Probably not even God."

"You're wrong," she whispered. "I think God does expect it. And I'm going."

"What will it prove?"

"I don't know," she said. "Maybe nothing."

Jake looked out the window, and she saw the intense struggle on his face as he groped to understand. "This is crazy, Lynda. I want you to think about it."

"I already have," she said. "I'm going tomorrow, before they transfer him to the state penitentiary."

He gaped at her again, his face a study in disgusted bewilderment, but after a moment, that look faded, and he sank back in his chair. "You can't be talked out of this?"

"No," she said. "If I could, I would have talked myself out of it already. It's not something I *want* to do, Jake, believe me; it's something I *have* to do. I was going to let a man die unsaved once before—I can't do it again. That's as clear to me as it was to you when you testified today."

Silence screamed out between them as he stared at her, and finally, he broke it. "All right," he said finally. "But I'm going with you."

Back in his apartment that night, Jake searched the New Testament for the reasons Lynda might have chosen to pray for her enemy, to visit him in prison. As he read through Matthew, Mark, Luke, and finally John, he saw it there over and over. This was why, then, she felt that God wanted her to go, why it was so important to her.

When she'd left the courthouse that day, she'd been confused about what she believed. She must have come home and decided. And tonight, rather than depressed, she seemed centered, peace-filled, and eager to do what she'd decided to do.

He lay awake for a long time that night, thinking back over Lynda's active concern for him and for Paige and Brianna, her determination to do God's will even when it meant sacrifice, and the way she had made him feel less like a shell of a human and more like a man with a spirit. A man with a soul.

And as he reflected on those things, that slow, deep, burning ache began to spread farther up his legs.

He lay there, knowing what it meant, knowing that maybe it would help him to finally take that first step. . . .

Tomorrow, he thought. Maybe he would do it tomorrow.

But first, he would keep his word to Lynda. First he would go with her to see Keith.

Because Keith had not yet been transported to the state penitentiary—that event was scheduled for the next day—the visitation room at the St. Clair Correctional Institute was not the maximum security sort where plexiglass separated them. Instead, Lynda used her attorney's credentials to meet with him on a day that wasn't a visiting day, so the room was empty. The fact that she and Jake were his victims complicated things somewhat—but Lynda had known the warden for years, so he allowed the visit to take place with the stipulation that two of his burliest guards would stand watch over them, just in case Keith tried anything.

It was clear from the disappointment on his face as they brought him in that Keith probably had expected Paige and Brianna. His face twisted in a vile sneer at the sight of Lynda in the chair across the table from him, and Jake in his wheelchair beside her. Muttering a curse, he pulled a chair out and dropped into it.

"You've got a lot of nerve coming here."

Lynda had gotten up early that morning and prayed that God would give her the words she needed when she came face-to-face with Keith, but now she found her courage faltering. "I know we're the last ones you expected to see, Keith. But we're not the reasons you're in prison. You're the reason."

"I did what I had to do for my kid!" he said, hammering a fist on the table. "And if you weren't such a bleeding heart fool, you'd see that Paige drove me to this, and you helped her. You're as much to blame for that plane crash and that woman's death as I am!"

"Wait a minute, Varner!" Jake blurted, but Lynda touched his hand to quiet him, and he flopped back, rubbing his temple and gritting his teeth. Jake had had enough. It had been all he could do to come in with a facade of civility, but Lynda knew he was aching to hurl himself across the table and shut Keith up once and for all.

"I didn't come here to answer your accusations, Keith," she said. "I don't even care what you think of me."

"Then what *did* you come for?"

Looking at this angry, hostile, deluded man, his face rigid with hate, Lynda suddenly felt a deep compassion for him, a compassion that she couldn't explain, for it wasn't something she had pulled out of any human part of her. She leaned on the table, getting closer to him. "I came here because you're going to die, Keith. But I wanted you to know that you don't have to die alone. It wasn't too late for the thief being executed next to Christ on the cross, and it isn't too late for you."

Reaching into her bag, which the guards had thoroughly searched at the door, she withdrew the Bible she had brought for Keith. "This is for you, Keith. I hope you'll read it."

He stared down at it, raw but undefined emotion tugging at his face, and for a moment, she thought he was going to take it. But suddenly that stricken look changed to potent rage, and he ripped the Bible out of her hands, spat on it, and flung it hard against the wall.

The guards rushed to grab Keith, and fury shot through Lynda as she sprang to her feet. For a second, she thought of rushing around the table and unleashing all the rage she'd been harboring for weeks. But she held herself still, and soon a quiet and unexpected peace fell over her. The rage vanished, and instead she felt a deep, abysmal sorrow for him. "I'll pray for you, Keith," she said.

Then she turned and strode from the room.

Jake had been ready to lambaste Keith Varner, the man who had crippled him, with every curse he knew. But seeing Lynda's reaction, he felt suddenly humbled. Without another look at the prisoner, he turned his chair around and followed her out.

When they were back in the car, Jake touched her shoulder and made her look at him. "Are you all right?"

"I'm fine," she said. "Really. I feel good."

He couldn't quite understand that, for he had expected her to be crushed. "But you hoped for a turnaround, didn't you? I mean, didn't you at least go in there thinking that he'd take the Bible?"

She thought about that for a moment. "That was between Keith and God. All I know is that I did what I was supposed to do." Sighing, she started her car. "Maybe he'll pick that Bible up and take it with him, after all."

"But probably he won't."

She smiled sadly. "But he had the chance, Jake."

Jake thought he understood that on some primitive level. She had given Varner the chance to change, even though he didn't deserve it. In that way, she had been like Christ to him.

Just as she had been like Christ to Jake.

"Have you forgiven him?" he asked, amazed.

She thought about that for a long moment. "Let's just say I'm working on it."

Silently, he watched her face with appreciation and deep contemplation as she drove. Self-conscious, she finally shot him a questioning look. "Why are you staring at me like that?"

He sighed and leaned his head back. "I was just thinking. God and I aren't on real familiar terms. Maybe you could pray for me that I'd get my legs back all the way."

"I thought you didn't believe," she said.

He hesitated then said, "Yeah, well. I've seen a lot of evidence lately. Maybe I'm changing my mind."

She smiled. "I pray for your legs all the time, Jake."

"But tomorrow is going to be a real important day. I haven't told you this, but I've been standing."

She almost ran off the road but managed to pull over. Gaping at him across the seat, she asked, "Really? By yourself?"

"Well, I used the parallel bars, but I've been standing on my legs. I'm getting more feeling every day."

"Why haven't you *told* me?"

"I wanted it to be a surprise," he said. "I had this fantasy of ambling out to the car one day when you came to pick me up. But I'm really nervous about tomorrow. I'm going to try to walk, and I couldn't keep it to myself anymore."

"Oh, Jake, can I be there? Can I watch? What time are you planning to get on the bars?"

He almost told her then faltered. He couldn't take the disappointment if he failed in front of her. So he lied. "Probably around ten. They'll put me on traction for a while first and then warm up my muscles."

"I'll be there at ten," she said. "Oh, Jake, this is wonderful!" Reaching across the seat, she hugged him, and he closed his eyes and held her a moment longer than he needed to.

When she pulled back, their eyes locked, and for a fleeting moment, he realized that he would be willing to give up the opportunity to walk tomorrow in exchange for the courage to lean over and kiss her like he had the day he'd gotten his eye. But he'd just been playing then, and this was serious.

Something stopped him.

Fear? The great Jake, who had never met a woman he couldn't charm? The same Jake who had once practiced womanizing with as much devotion as Lynda practiced her faith?

He let her go, and she drove back to the house in quiet. When they pulled into the driveway, she cut off the engine and sat still for a moment. "Well, I guess I'll see you tomorrow."

He caught her hand as she reached for the car door, and she turned to look at him. Her face was expectant as he held her gaze, and his heart sprinted wildly in his chest, anticipating, hoping. . . .

Finally, he leaned forward and kissed her. And at the gentle, sweet touch of her lips, he felt the world settling back on its axis, righting itself and everything around him falling into place.

When he broke the kiss, she looked up at him, soft, humble, surprised.

He touched her face, as if it were something precious, priceless. "Good night," he said quietly.

She leaned forward then slowly and pressed a soft kiss on his scar. He closed his eyes and found her lips again, and this time the kiss was more startling, more telling. When at last it ended, he pulled back and gazed at her, seeing the emotion clearly written on her face.

"Good night," she whispered.

He sat still as she opened the door, slipped out, and started to the house. But before she went inside, she looked back at him.

And there was a sweet, unguarded smile on her face.

Jake found it hard to sleep that night. What had happened between them haunted him—and not in a completely positive way. It didn't make sense. In his "old life," if he'd been attracted to a woman for this long, he would have had more than a passing intimacy with her by now.

This was the first time he'd stopped at just one kiss and the first time he had ever lain awake thinking about one. It was the first time he'd felt such a dependence on another human being, a painful but sweet, heartrending need for her smile, her touch, her presence.

It was frightening. It was frustrating. It was exciting. And it was hard to believe, for no one he knew had had more experience than he had with women. But strangely, he felt as though this was his first experience. As though only now, at age thirty-nine, he was learning the true value of a woman.

As he was learning the true value of himself.

He lay in bed, fighting the searing pain growing more pronounced in his calves—the pain they told him was temporary—and told himself that maybe some good had come from the accident after all. Maybe he was discovering the powerful essence of life, now that the trappings had been taken away.

He sat up in bed, too restless to sleep and thought about tomorrow. What if his legs rebelled and refused to cooperate with him? What if the progress he'd made was as far as he'd ever go? What if he remained a paraplegic for the rest of his life?

For the first time since the crash, Jake admitted that if that happened, he could live with it. He was alive, after all, and things were looking pretty good.

He got into his wheelchair and rolled around the tiny apartment for a little while then restlessly went outside. It was late, and he could hear the crickets chirping and the toads croaking. The wind was strong, whipping through the trees and ruffling his hair, and in the distance, he heard an owl hoot.

It was beginning to feel more like autumn; the wind was brisk and cool as it whispered through the leaves. It never got very cold here, he'd been told, and he wondered what it was like in Texas right now. Was it cool? Were the leaves falling?

He wondered whether autumn was still his mother's favorite time of year.

The moment Doris Stevens came into his mind, his optimism deflated, and he was confronted with all the unfinished business of his past. Before he could clean up his present life, he suddenly realized he would need to clean up his past one. He had skeletons to lay to rest, dirt to wash away, and peace to make.

Going back into his apartment, he picked up the phone that had at last been connected and dialed the number he remembered from so many years ago, the number that had been his in Texas when he'd been nothing more than a poor waitress's illegitimate son. How far he had run to escape that image.

He put the phone to his ear and waited as it rang once, twice, three times. . . .

"Hello?"

The voice was the familiar one he'd had such contempt for before, with its nasal twang and its hoarse brusqueness. Now, it just sounded pleasantly familiar.

"Mama?"

She was silent as he held his breath, then finally said, "Jake?"

That she didn't reject him immediately, as she had so many times before, gave him hope.

"I know it's late, Mama, but I thought you might still be up."

"I just got in from work," she said carefully.

Silence again.

"I heard about your legs. That woman called me."

"Lynda," he said, smiling. "Yeah. She's been looking out for me."

"So . . . how are you doing?"

"I'm fine," he said. "I'm out of the hospital. I'm getting a little feeling back, and I've been able to stand some. I'm gonna walk again, Mama. I know I am."

He could hear the tinge of emotion in her voice when she whispered, "That's good."

Encouraged by the few words, he decided to say what he'd called to say. His voice trembled. "Mama, I know I've been a pretty crummy son all these years. I don't blame you for feeling the way you do about me."

Quiet again and then, "What is it you want from me, Jake?"

Tears misted his eyes. "Your forgiveness."

"My what?"

"I want you to forgive me, Mama. I turned my back on you."

"You were ashamed of me."

"I was ashamed of me, too," he whispered. "Where we came from, where we lived—"

"I *still* live here," she said.

He closed his eyes. "I know, Mama. But I'm not ashamed anymore. I just want to start fresh. I want to do what's right."

"And what would that be, Jake?" his mother asked.

He wasn't sure, and as a tear rolled from his eye and down his scarred cheek, he floundered for some gesture that would make it right. But he had nothing now. Not a job, not a home of his own, not even a plan.

Yet he had a greater sense of the rightness of the direction in his life now than he'd ever had when there was more money in his bank account than he could spend.

"My car," he said suddenly. "I want to give you my car. It's a Porsche, Mama. You probably don't want a Porsche, but you could sell it."

The idea seemed absurd almost the moment he'd said it, but Doris wasn't laughing. "You'd give me your car?"

"Sure," he said. "It's paid for, and it's fairly new. You could get a lot for it."

"But—what if you start drivin' again?"

"I *will* start driving again, sooner or later. But when I do, I won't want to drive that." He hadn't realized that he felt that way until the words were already out of his mouth.

She was quiet again. He knew that this was as awkward for her as it was for him. He was paying her off, in a sense, or at least it seemed that way—as if the Porsche were a bribe to accept him as her son again. But that was all right. It was a start.

"All right," she said. "I'll take it."

He smiled and restrained the urge to laugh. "Okay, Mama. I can either send you a plane ticket, and you can drive it back, or I can sell it here myself and send you the money."

She thought about it for a moment. "I'll come there and get it. Who knows? I might like to drive it a while."

His eyes welled deeper. "Good. I'd like to see you."

"I'm not being greedy, you know," she said quickly. "I'm thinkin' of this as punitive damages. For all the grief you've given me. And all the years I gave to you before you threw them back in my face. Do you understand that?"

"If I didn't, I wouldn't have made the offer."

"You're not gonna back out now, are you?"

"No, Mama," he said. "I'll have the ticket delivered to you tomorrow. One way. Maybe you can stay awhile, on me. I have someone here I'd like for you to meet."

70

SINCE SHE'D DROPPED Jake off at the hospital that morning, Lynda had been praying. She had pled with God, arguing how vital it was that Jake walk again, that he needed a miracle to nudge him along, that he needed to see God working in his life, that he needed to know he had a future.

But as she drove back to the hospital at ten to be there when he tried to take his steps, she realized that God was aware of all of that already. Jake was in God's hands, and God knew much better than she what he needed.

Still, she held her breath as she made her way to the rehab room, where a dozen patients worked on several levels of therapy, each deeply engrossed in the torture required to make one tiny bit of progress.

Jake wasn't in sight.

She looked around for Allie or Buzz but didn't see either of them.

"Excuse me," she said, catching a therapist as he passed. "I was supposed to meet Jake Stevens here. Have you seen him?"

"Yeah, he was here," he said. "I don't know where he went."

"Well, where are Allie and Buzz?"

"In a meeting, I think. Jake probably took a break."

Lynda was confused. Wasn't ten o'clock supposed to have been his big moment? Had they changed his schedule at the last minute? She went back into the corridor. Jake was nowhere in sight.

Maybe he'd gone to say hello to the nurses in orthopedics. Or maybe his morning therapy hadn't gone well; maybe he'd gotten discouraged and had decided not to make the attempt to walk today. Maybe the doctor had stepped in to postpone the attempt for some reason. Maybe something was wrong.

She had worked up a fair amount of anxiety by the time she decided to go to the fourth floor to see if he'd gone to say hello to his nurses. Abby, the nurse who had cared for him in ICU, was waiting for the elevator when the doors opened.

"Abby, have you seen Jake?"

Abby set her hands on her hips, as though offended. "That's it? No hello? No nothing?"

Lynda laughed softly and hugged her. "I'm sorry. It's good to see you."

Abby pointed up the hall. "He's in the chapel, baby."

Lynda glanced toward the prayer room then brought her troubled eyes back to Abby's. "Is everything all right?"

"I don't know," she said. "I just caught a glimpse of him goin' in. He didn't speak to anybody up here. Just rolled right to that room."

Lynda started toward the prayer room, but Abby stopped her. "Lynda, he's doin' okay, isn't he?"

Lynda didn't know how to answer that. "I don't know, Abby. We'll see."

She hesitated outside the chapel door, bracing herself for whatever she might find inside. Slowly she opened it and stepped into the dark room lit only with candles.

Jake was sitting in his chair near the front row, looking up at the cross on the wall behind the small pulpit.

When she approached him, she saw that his face was tear-stained. "Jake, what's wrong?"

His smile was heavy with emotion. "Nothing's wrong," he whispered.

"Then why are you in here? I thought you were going to the parallel bars at ten. I thought—"

"I lied to you," he said quietly. "I didn't want you to see me fail. I've already been there."

Compassion for his disappointment washed through her, and she sank down on the end of a pew. "Jake, I'm so sorry. But it was just the first try."

He started to laugh then, and she frowned, confused.

"What is it?"

"I did it," he whispered. "I walked."

She drew in a sharp breath. "You did?"

But Jake's smile twisted at the corners as a new wave of emotion came over him; new tears welled in his eyes and rolled down his cheeks. "Four steps, Lynda. I took four steps!"

"Four steps?"

"Yes," he said. "They said I'll be able to get around with a walker soon. Then crutches . . ."

"Oh, Jake," she whispered and reached out for him.

He accepted her embrace and clung to her tightly, laughing softly into her ear as his tears wet her hair.

"But why did you come in here? You looked so sad when I came in."

He drew in a long, shaky breath and looked at that cross again. "I had somebody to thank," he whispered.

She pulled back to look at him, afraid to make any assumptions, yet hoping. . . .

"It wasn't just the walking," he told her. "I'm grateful for that. But it's the other things."

"What other things?"

"The way he reached out and chose me and worked on me and even broke me, just to get me to the place where I could start really living." He wiped the wetness on his face and moved his wet, red eyes to hers. "And for his forgiveness that didn't cost me anything—not even a Porsche."

As he smiled through his tears, she leaned back into the pew, weakened by her glad amazement over what she was hearing.

"And I had to thank him for you," he whispered.

He pulled her against him again, and this time they wept together, for joy, for sadness, for the future, for the past.

It was a while before Jake could speak again. "Do you think God really spared me because he had a plan for me?"

She felt as certain of that as she'd ever been of anything in her life. "I know he did."

His arms tightened around her, and as he looked back at the cross, he laid his head on hers. "If it was just to give me one moment like this, it would all have been worth it."

And though Lynda closed her eyes and thanked God, too, for this very moment, she knew in her heart that there was much more in store for them.

So much more.

Afterword

A YEAR OR so before I wrote this book, I became convicted that my Christian walk had been useless. I had never been available to God, though I had called on him often to get me through my crises (usually self-inflicted). My problem was trust. I thought I believed, I said I believed—but I did nothing to put the belief into action. I was neither hot nor cold, but lukewarm, and absolutely fruitless. One day, someone called to my attention something that Jesus had said: "Not everyone who says to me, 'Lord, Lord,' will enter the kingdom of heaven, but only he who does the will of my father who is in heaven. Many will say to me on that day, 'Lord, Lord, did we not prophesy in your name, and in your name drive out demons and perform many miracles?' Then I will tell them plainly, 'I never knew you. Away from me, you evildoers!'" (Matthew 7:21-23).

These words startled me. Was I one of those whom Jesus didn't really know? I finally realized it was only through my knowing him that he would know me as one of his own. And to know him, I needed an ongoing, active, intimate relationship with him—the kind of relationship I would have with anyone important to me. I don't ignore the people I love, and I don't neglect them, and I don't forget them. I talk to them every day, and care about pleasing them, and work hard to be the person they need me to be. If Jesus Christ is real to me, then I have to treat him as a real person.

Once I recommitted myself to making Christ the center of my life, I decided to make myself available to him in every area of my life. That's when the idea for this book came to me. The characters interested me because their own spiritual battles were so much like my own: Lynda, a lukewarm Christian who would let someone die without witnessing to him; Jake, an agnostic who couldn't give up the pilot's seat in his life until it was taken from him; and Paige, a spiritual infant on the verge of belief, who lacked the faith to make the final plunge. I was interested in their awakenings, their spiritual growth, their lessons, and I hoped their struggles might be something others could relate to.

Fortunately, I've finally begun to learn from the lessons God has taught me. I've learned that true Christianity is about going to him on my knees and asking him to fill up all the empty places inside me with his Holy Spirit. It's about asking him to forgive me and cleanse me of all the things that will destroy me—things like greed, apathy, anger, bitterness, fear, malice, and selfishness—so those places can be filled with him, too. It's about deciding what I *really believe,* then relying on it, totally, completely, in every area of my life. This, I discovered, has little to do with sitting in God's house on Sunday mornings. It has everything to do with *being* God's house, every day of the week.

JUSTIFIABLE MEANS

This book is lovingly dedicated to
the Nazarene

Acknowledgments

SPECIAL THANKS TO all of my AOL friends who shared their expertise with me. I am so grateful for the help of Florida attorneys Michael Cohen, James Mays, Mike Gotschall, and a certain judge who wishes to remain anonymous. Also, many thanks to the cops who answered my endless questions—Lou and Pat and others who didn't want their names published. And a huge thank you to Cathy Logg, Washington state crime reporter, who continues to be a wonderful resource.

I also thank my children—Michelle, Marie, and Lindsey, for not taking it personally when my preoccupied "Uhh-hmms" don't really answer their questions—and my husband, Ken, for keeping the family going even when I'm buried in the pages of another world. Without his powerful prayers, his support, and his constant encouragement, I'd have found an easier job long ago.

But most of all, I thank the One who called me and set me apart, and turned my writing into something that has purpose. He truly is a God of second chances.

1

THE LIGHTS FROM the squad cars were still flashing in the night, illuminating the modest apartment building in alternate shades of blue and black. Larry Millsaps pulled his unmarked Chevy to the curb and glanced at his partner. "So much for having a night off."

Tony Danks nodded bleakly as he scanned the crowd forming on the sidewalk. Officers were already questioning some of the neighbors, and other uniformed cops came and went through the building's front door. "This hasn't happened in—how long?"

Larry grabbed his windbreaker from the backseat and pulled it on over the 9 mm he had holstered under his arm. "Almost a year since the last one."

They got out of the car and pushed through the crowd, not bothering to flash their badges since all of the cops in the small St. Clair Police Department knew the two detectives by sight. They made their way through the crowd into the building. "One a year is too many for me," Larry said. He'd been plagued by the trauma on the young girl's face the last time. There was a look that rape victims wore, a waiflike, haunted look that spoke of violation and soul-deep despair. This one probably would be no different, and he started up the stairs reluctantly, past the other tenants who were watching the open door of the apartment with fascination and dread, waiting for bits and pieces of the drama to be revealed.

There were four cops inside the apartment, two with cameras and one with a camcorder, recording the crime scene just as they'd found it. Lamps were broken, tables overturned, glass shattered . . .

Larry spotted the victim then, sitting alone on a chair in a corner, cocooned in a blanket, her blonde hair wet and stringing in her face and around her shoulders, her pale blue eyes raw and swollen from crying. One of the cops handed him a clipboard with her report on it, then turned his back to her and, in a quiet voice, said, "She showered before she called."

"Figures," Tony whispered.

Larry looked back at the young woman and felt that familiar, unwelcome stirring of frustration and compassion as she glanced hopefully up at him with big, blue, tearful eyes, as if he might offer her some comfort, some hope, some . . . *something.* Her showering would definitely make it tougher to get the evidence they needed, but Larry couldn't say he blamed her. She had been defiled, desecrated, dehumanized, and he couldn't imagine any victim of such abuse *not* wanting to wash the filth away.

"Is she hurt?" he asked.

The uniformed cop nodded. "He had a knife. She has a pretty deep cut on her leg. The ambulance should be here soon."

Larry stepped over the broken glass, the lamp shades on their sides, and skirted around the overturned table until he stood in front of the woman. "Hi, I'm Detective Millsaps." He glanced over his shoulder and saw that Tony was right behind him. "This is my partner, Detective Danks. Are you all right?"

She swallowed hard and whispered, "Yes."

Stooping down to get eye level with her, Larry glanced down at the report the other officer had handed him. "Your name is Melissa Nelson? May I call you Melissa?"

"Yes," she said again.

"Good," he said in a don't-spook-the-victim voice. "And you can call me Larry. He's Tony." He scanned the information the first cop to the scene had compiled, and saw that she was twenty-three years old. He looked into her face again. "Melissa, I know that you've already given your statement, but would you mind telling it one more time? Tony and I will be the ones trying to find the man who did this to you. We really need to hear it firsthand."

A stark, determined look filled her reddened eyes. "Yes. I'll tell it over and over until they catch him," she said through clenched teeth. "I don't care how many times I have to tell it."

"Good. First, could you start with a description of him?"

"I can do better than that," she said, smearing her tears away with a trembling hand. "I can give you his name."

"You know him?" Tony asked, sitting down on an ottoman near her chair.

"Yes. I work with him. His name is Edward Soames, and he lives in some apartments on Fresco Street on the north side of town."

Larry jotted down the street. "Have you given this information to anyone else?"

"Yes," she said. "The first officer I talked to is calling it in." A sob broke her voice, and she gave in to it, then tried to recover. "He probably thought I wouldn't tell anybody, that I'd be too ashamed. That I'd just sit here and deal with it."

Tony took his notepad out of his coat pocket and clicked his pen. "Was this someone you were dating?"

She shot him a disgusted look. "Of course not. I was just sitting here watching television, and he knocked on the door. When I opened it, he pushed his way in. He grabbed me, and . . . I started fighting him with everything I had . . . but it didn't stop him . . ."

"I understand he had a weapon?" Larry asked.

"Yes," she said. "A knife. A switchblade, I think." She opened her blanket, revealing the shorts and T-shirt she wore, and lifted the bloody towel she'd been pressing on her leg. "I thought he was going to kill me."

Larry winced at the sight of the cut. "That's deep. You're going to need stitches. The ambulance should be here soon."

"It just all happened so fast," she went on. "And then he was gone . . . and . . . I didn't know what to do. I was so disgusted, so repulsed . . . I didn't think about the evidence. I just wanted to wash it all away . . . but it's not going to go away . . ."

She was trembling, and Larry feared she was going into shock from loss of blood. He made her press the towel back over the wound. Outside, sirens sounded. He hoped it was the ambulance.

"He . . . he touched that table. His fingerprints are there. And they're on the doorknob. And he had my blood on his shirt when he left . . . it was a . . . a T-shirt with some cartoon on it. And if he's not home, if you need to identify him, there's a picture of him in his office at work. We both work at Proffer Builders, over on Haynes Street. He has a recent picture of himself on his desk, catching a fish or something. You could use that to identify him. My boss, Henry Proffer, could let you in. He's in the book."

Tony jotted rapidly as she spoke, and Larry was amazed at how easy it was to get information out of her. Victims of such trauma were usually confused, disoriented, and too upset to remember details.

"Has he ever threatened you before?"

"No," she said. "Oh, he's come on to me, but I just blew it off. I didn't know he was capable of this."

They heard the paramedics running up the stairs. "Melissa, we'll talk to you later. You go get that leg stitched up and let the doctor examine you."

Larry started to stand up, but she grabbed his coat and looked up at him desperately. "You won't just let this go, will you? You're going to go pick him up, aren't you?"

"Of course. Someone's probably picking him up right now."

The paramedics hustled in, but she kept clinging to Larry's coat. "But what if he didn't go straight home? He probably wouldn't. He would know that someone might be looking for him. You have to find him! He's dangerous, and he'll come after me again."

"We won't rest until we have him behind bars," Larry assured her. "You have my promise. Now show them your leg. She needs stitches, guys, and she's lost a lot of blood."

"Let's get you onto the stretcher," one of the EMTs said, coaxing her out of her chair onto her good leg.

"But behind bars isn't good enough!" she pled through gritted teeth, eyes desperate, in obvious pain as she stood. "You have to keep him there. You have to get a conviction."

"We will."

She glanced frantically around the apartment as they tried to put her on the stretcher. "My word won't be good enough. You'll have to have enough evidence. You can't forget anything!"

Larry frowned. "Our police officers are trained, Melissa. They know what to do."

"But will they dust for fingerprints? Will they look for hair follicles, to prove he was here? They can't just stop with my identification of him!"

The paramedics began to carry her out, even though she hadn't yet lain down. "Please don't let them miss anything," she said. "Find the officer I talked to first. I gave him more details—you need to know them."

"We will, Melissa," Larry said. "Just try to relax. We'll talk to you after the doctor examines you. And I'll let you know the minute we pick him up."

But the look on her face as she finally lay down told him that she would believe it when she saw it. Larry watched the paramedics carry her out. Slowly, he turned back to his partner.

Tony looked pensive, perplexed. "Well, she sure came out of her shell. Coaching us on police procedure? That's a first."

Larry shook his head. "Maybe we just underestimated her because she looks so fragile. She's obviously pretty sharp. And let's face it—botched investigations make headlines. You can't blame her for being careful."

Tony stared at the empty doorway for a moment longer. "Yeah, but careful is one thing. There was something more than careful there. Doesn't feel right."

"You're not suggesting she's lying."

"No," Tony said thoughtfully. "Not exactly. I'm just saying that something doesn't ring true. It was all too easy."

"You could look in her face and tell she was raped," Larry said quietly.

"Unfortunately, facial expressions don't hold much water in court."

"Give me a break, Tony. Are we gonna make a broken, violated woman tap-dance and stand on her head to prove that what she described really happened? There's no reason anyone would want to put herself through all this if it didn't really happen."

"Put herself through what?" Tony asked.

"Through *what?* Are you kidding?" Larry asked. "You think this is fun for her? The interrogations of cops who don't believe her, lawyers who drag her through the mud—"

"Okay, okay," Tony cut in. "Maybe you're right. Obviously, there's plenty of evidence here."

"And there'll probably be a lot more when we find this guy."

"We'll see, buddy," Tony said. "I hope you're right."

Two hours later, after being photographed, stitched, examined, and interrogated by the doctors and social workers who claimed to want to help her, Melissa sat alone in the examining room. She had turned the lights off; now she watched frantically out the window into the parking lot for some sign of Edward Soames.

He's going to kill me, she thought miserably. *If they don't lock him up, he'll kill me.*

But they hadn't locked him up. So far, according to the social worker who'd made some phone calls for her, he hadn't even been picked up. He was still out there somewhere, driving around, no doubt looking for vulnerable women to attack.

She had begged the doctor not to release her—not until Soames was off the streets and in police custody. She was too terrified to stay in that apartment by herself, too plagued with memories—she would get no rest. If she could just stay here overnight, long enough for them to find him, then tomorrow she could face going home.

Reluctantly, the doctor had agreed, but told her that, before they admitted her, a police detective would need to talk to her some more. She didn't know why. She'd already given them more than enough information to find him and arrest him. She'd left nothing to chance. Instead of talking to her, they ought to be out looking for him.

She heard footsteps coming up the hall and looked toward the door. Her doctor ambled into the room, studying her chart. "Okay, Melissa," he said, still in the soft, cautious voice that made her want to scream. "We're going to move you to a room now. Are you sure you want to stay?"

"Will it have a guard?" she asked.

"I'm afraid not. But I'm sure you'll be safe here. They'll have this guy picked up in no time, and you won't have to worry."

She sighed and looked out the window again. A car had just driven up, and a tall, slender man was getting out. Was that him? No, she thought with relief. Not yet.

She stood up, wincing at the pain from the stitched gash on her thigh, and the doctor made her sit back down. "An orderly is bringing a wheelchair. You need to stay off that leg for a while. You don't want to break the stitches. Oh, and I've prescribed something for pain, if you need it."

Her eyes strayed out the window again. "No, I don't want it. I need to stay sharp, just in case." The orderly wheeled the chair in, but she didn't take her eyes from the window. "Does that room have a window over the parking lot?"

The doctor glanced at the orderly. "I don't know. Does it?"

The orderly thought for a moment. "Yeah, I think it does. I can change her to a room that doesn't, if she wants—"

"No," she cut in, getting up on her good leg and transferring her weight to the chair. "I want to be able to see the parking lot. I need to see who's coming."

The doctor shot another look at the orderly. She realized that they thought she was suffering from paranoid delusions, but she didn't care.

The orderly wheeled her out, and the doctor stayed beside her. "Oh, Detective Millsaps called and said that he might not be able to come back by tonight. He said it might be morning before he could make it."

"No," she said quickly. "Tell him to come tonight. Please. I don't care what time it is. I don't think I'll do much sleeping tonight."

"We could give you something to help you."

"No," she said again. "I told you, I need to stay alert. Tell him to come no matter how late it is. Have they found Soames yet?"

"He didn't say."

Tears sprang to her eyes again, and she scanned the hallway as if he might jump out of one of the rooms at any moment. "He's still out there. He's too smart to get caught."

"If he's in St. Clair, they'll find him."

"And what if he's not? What if he's already left town?"

"Then you're safe. You don't have to worry."

But his logic was lost on Melissa, and as they pushed her onto the elevator, she tried not to panic. This was just the beginning, after all; it was too soon to jump to conclusions. Larry what's-his-name had seemed competent. Maybe he would catch him. Maybe Soames would finally be taken off the streets. Maybe women everywhere would be safe from his violence.

It had taken two hours to get the warrant they needed for Soames's arrest, as well as a search warrant to check out his apartment, car, and place of business. Though the paperwork had taken longer than he wanted, Larry had been confident that the uniformed officers would find and apprehend Soames even before the warrant was in Larry's hand. But Soames had managed to evade them so far.

As they walked rapidly between the police squad cars in the parking lot toward their own unmarked car, Tony said, "You have that look on your face, Larry."

"What look?"

"The look that says you know exactly where we're going to find Soames."

"Wish I did, pal. I was thinking we should probably go by his office first and get that picture Melissa told us about. Then we could start with the bars in town. See what turns up."

Tony climbed into the passenger seat and checked his notes as Larry started the car and pulled out into traffic. "Let's see. We have the name of the business owner. We could ask him to meet us there to let us in."

"That's what I was thinking. Meanwhile, if Soames is stupid enough to go home, we have people there waiting for him."

"Sure would help if we had a tag number."

"Yeah. Kind of weird, don't you think? A man that age not having a tag registered to him?"

"Maybe he uses somebody else's car."

"Or maybe he drives a stolen car."

Tony grinned and nodded toward a pay phone coming up on their right. "Pull over. I'll call her boss."

Larry watched, chin propped on his palm, as Tony made the phone call. He tried to calm the rising tide of urgency he felt. But that woman sitting with wet hair stringing around her shoulders, trembling as she hugged her bloody knees to her chest, had gotten under his skin, and he wanted, badly, to give her some peace—right now.

Tony got back into the car. "He said he'd meet us there. Sounded helpful. He said he had the guy's tag number in a file at the office, too."

"Great. Let's go."

2

HENRY PROFFER, A short man with Hulk Hogan arms and a ruddy complexion from years under the harsh Florida sun, was waiting when Larry and Tony reached the small office of Proffer Builders. "Is Soames all right?" he asked. "He didn't have an accident or anything, did he?"

"There was a rape tonight," Larry said as he followed the man in and waited for him to flick on the light. "Another one of your employees—Melissa Nelson. Edward Soames is a suspect."

The man's face drained of color. "Melissa—raped? When? Was it here?"

"No," Tony said. "In her apartment. She said there was a picture of Soames on his desk. We need to use it and look around a little."

Looking disturbed, Henry led them down the hall to a small office. He turned on the light, then stepped back as they walked into the immaculate room. "She said *Soames* raped her? You sure that's what she said?"

"Absolutely. When's the last time you saw him?"

"Well . . . today. Around 4:30 or so. It was just an ordinary day. He's my best architect. He's not a rapist!" Distraught, he watched as they took the picture, studied it, and deposited it in a paper sack.

"Can you tell us anything about Soames? What kind of man he is? Where he likes to go after work? Any abnormal behavior you've noticed with women?"

Henry lowered himself into a chair and raked a hand through his hair. "Well, he seems like a decent guy. He does good work. I've never gotten to know him that well, but I've had no complaints about him." He frowned as he looked up at them again. "Uh . . . what were the other questions? Oh, yeah. Women. Well, he was kind of a flirt. But then, so am I. No crime in that. I wouldn't think he'd have to force himself on anyone. I mean, he never had trouble getting a date. Women like him."

"What about Melissa? Did he ever show any interest in her?"

"Well, sure. I mean, so did I. She's a cute girl. A little too serious, sometimes. She's kind of hard to get to know. Doesn't talk much. Kind of high-strung. You know—jumpy. She's only worked here about a month, so none of us knows her very well."

"She get along with Soames?"

"Well, yeah. I mean, I guess so. I kind of thought she might have a crush on him, tell you the truth. She acted funny around him. You know, tense. Clumsy. That kind of thing."

Larry gave Tony a troubled glance. "You said you had his tag number?" Tony asked.

"Sure," Henry said. Popping out of the chair, he rushed down the hall. Larry followed him.

"This is too much," Henry said when he reached his own office. "I mean, what am I gonna do tomorrow? Is Melissa gonna be back? Is Soames? We're working on a big bid for a new office complex on Highland Drive. I can't do without either of them." He pulled out the file he'd been looking for and flipped through it. "Here it is." He got a pen and jotted the number down. "He drives a dark blue Cherokee. Couple of years old. Oh—and you asked where he liked to hang out. He has a favorite bar over on Triumph Street—you know, over by the Kash 'n' Karry. Steppin' Out, I think it's called."

"Thanks." Taking the paper from him, Larry hurried back up the hall to where Tony was still looking through Soames's things. "Come on, Tony," he said. "I think we've got him."

It took only a few minutes to run the tag number through the police computer.

"Edward J. Pendergrast?" Tony jotted the number down. "What do you think, Larry? Is it someone else's car, or did this guy change his name?"

Larry grabbed the radio mike. "Do me a favor, Jane," he told the desk cop who'd done the search for him. "See what you've got on that name."

The radio crackled. "Will do."

A few minutes later, Jane radioed back. "Hey, Larry. Are you ready for this?"

"Yeah, go ahead."

"Edward J. Pendergrast has a rap sheet. Two rape charges, as well as breaking and entering, and assault with a deadly weapon. In the first case, the grand jury acquitted him of all charges due to lack of evidence. The second one never even got to the grand jury because the judge released him on a technicality. Something about an illegal search and seizure."

Larry glanced at Tony. "You believe this?"

"He obviously changed his name. Got to be him."

"Let's get him," Larry said.

Steppin' Out was a popular bar where young professionals came to mingle and drink and dance after work each night. The parking lot was full of BMWs and Mercedes, Jaguars and Infinities. When they found the dark blue Cherokee, they checked the number. "That's it. That's the number," Larry said, trying to control his rush of adrenaline. "He's inside."

"Did you get a good enough look at that picture to recognize him?"

"I think so. Let's go."

They double-parked behind the Cherokee so that their suspect couldn't make a run for it, then went in and tried to blend into the crowd. The mingling aromas of two-hundred-dollar-an-ounce perfume, cheap aftershave, booze, and cigarette smoke wafted on the air, and the music from the band sent a deafening roar over the voices and laughter around them.

"And they really come here to relax after work?" Larry asked his partner facetiously as they wove through the crowd.

"It's really not such a bad place. You should try it sometime when you're not on duty."

"No, thanks, pal," Larry said. "I prefer to breathe clean air and have a little peace and quiet when I relax."

Tony grinned. It was no secret that Larry never darkened the door of any of the bars in town unless he was on duty and looking for someone. Tony, however, didn't mind stopping in now and then. "Great place to meet women."

"I meet plenty of women," Larry said.

"Right," Tony muttered with a smirk. "At church. That's a surefire setup for disaster. Get involved with Judy Churchgoer, and you've automatically got to start giving up stuff, making commitments, acting like the Pope. No, I'd rather meet someone in a place like this, where nobody really expects anything."

Larry had heard it all before. He concentrated on scanning the faces of the people at the bar.

"See anything?" Tony asked.

"Not yet. You?"

Tony shook his head, then checked the faces at the tables—men with their most seductive smiles, women with their faces tipped up in anticipation. A soft haze of smoke gently floated over their heads, as if it held some magic that would cast a spell on each of them.

"There." Larry grabbed Tony's arm and nodded toward the back corner of the room.

It was the face they had seen in the picture, though it wasn't as happy as it had been when photographed catching a twenty-pound bass. He seemed to be sulking as he sipped on his drink and watched a group of women at the bar. His striped pullover shirt was clean and freshly pressed, as were his khaki trousers. He'd obviously gone home to shower after leaving Melissa's—he must have been quick, since he hadn't been home when they'd tried to pick him up.

"Here goes." They wound their way between tables. Soames saw them coming toward him and straightened.

"Edward Soames?" Larry asked, extending his right hand as if to shake.

Soames looked from one man to the other, then accepted the handshake. "Yeah, that's me."

Larry snapped his handcuffs on Soames's wrist. "I'm Larry Millsaps, with the St. Clair Police Department. I have a warrant for your arrest. Would you come with us, please?"

Soames sprang out of his chair and tried to wrest his hand away. "For what?"

"You're being charged with the rape of Melissa Nelson. You have the right to remain silent . . ." As he rambled off the words that had become second nature, he jerked Soames's other arm in front of him and snapped the second cuff.

Even in the darkness, Soames's face was visibly reddening. "Wait a minute! I didn't touch her! What did she say?"

"If you cannot afford an attorney, one will be appointed . . ."

"This is crazy!" Soames shouted. "I never laid a hand on her! She invited me over, then changed her mind and said she was sick or something. I left! That's all there was to it!"

"That's not what *she* says, pal."

"Then she's a liar! I didn't *do* anything!"

The band stopped playing midsong, letting the chorus die a slow death. The crowd in the bar had already grown suddenly quiet. As Tony frisked him, Soames cursed and searched the faces around him. "Hey, McRae!" he shouted. "I need a lawyer, man! Help me!"

Larry groaned as Steve McRae, a lawyer he had had run-ins with before, hurried through the crowd. "I'm his lawyer. What's going on here?"

"They're arresting me for rape!" Soames whispered harshly. "*Do* something!"

"Do you have a warrant?" the lawyer asked the detectives.

"We sure do, McRae," Tony said, pulling it out of his pocket. "We also have one to search his car and his apartment."

"They're trying to pin a *rape* on me," Soames whispered so that the crowd wouldn't hear. "A rape that never happened."

McRae raised one finger to quiet him. "Don't say a word," he ordered. "Not one word. Calm down and just go with them, and we'll get this all straightened out."

Soames cursed again. His face reddened as they pulled him through the crowd, with McRae following.

"Put him in the car," Larry told Tony. "Radio it in, and I'll start searching his car." He turned back to Soames. "Give me your car keys."

"I'm not giving you anything!" Soames spat out.

"Fine. Then I'll bust a window and unlock it myself."

Soames kicked at some invisible object. "They're in my pocket," he said. "I'm cuffed, remember?"

But before Larry could reach into the man's pocket, Soames slid his own hand in, fished the key chain out, and flung it at him. "You're not gonna find anything in there," he said as Tony pushed his head down and guided him into the unmarked car's backseat. "I'm telling you, she's crazy. You'll find that out yourself. I didn't touch her, man. She started freaking out on me, even pulled a knife on me, and I got out of there."

McRae, the lawyer, leaned into the car. "If you want me representing you, Soames, you're gonna have to shut up, *now!* You and I will talk when you get to the station. You're not gonna tell them anything until I give you permission."

"But I didn't *do* anything, man. I have nothing to hide!"

"That shouldn't be too hard to prove."

Soames wilted back on the seat.

A squad car pulled up, and patrons of the bar spilled out onto the parking lot as Larry got his flashlight and began his search of the car. He checked the glove compartment, handed the registration papers to Tony, then released the trunk latch so that Tony could check inside. Then he bent down and shone his light under the seat.

"Bingo," he said. He stood up and pulled a pair of rubber gloves out of his pockets, slid his hands into them, then bent down again. "We've got something here, Tony."

"What is it?"

"Oh, just a bloody shirt," he said. "With a cartoon on it. And look. A knife."

Tony leaned through the back door, astounded. "You mean he just stuffed them under his seat?"

Larry opened the knife. "Blade's got blood on it. What do you bet it's hers?"

"Why would he be that stupid?"

"Maybe she was right. He banked on her being too ashamed to tell anyone." Larry dropped the shirt into a bag, then the knife into another one. "Is there anything back there?"

"No," Tony said. "The trunk's coming up empty."

Larry slid out of the car and went back to his own. Soames sat in the backseat, his teeth gritted, waiting. "Tell me something, Soames. Why would your car be registered under the name Pendergrast?"

Soames shook his head. "I'm not telling you a thing until I've cleared it with my attorney."

"Fine," Larry said. "Then I guess it's going to be a long night for all of us."

When Soames was booked and locked up, they headed for his apartment. Several tenants came outside at the sight of the fleet of police cars in the parking lot, and Larry assigned one of the officers to question them about Soames. They used his key to get in, then began searching for any sign that a rapist lived there.

The apartment was immaculate, with plush, unblemished furniture and cherrywood tables. Nothing was out of place. The bed was made, all the shoes were put away, and the bathroom was spotless. If there was anything telling here, it would be hidden, Larry decided.

He went through the drawers in the kitchen, looking for anything out of the ordinary. When he found a stack of snapshots, he flipped through them. They were low-quality pictures of women who looked as if they hadn't known they were being photographed, coming in and out of doorways, getting into cars—all photographed from a distance. Carefully, he studied them. A vague reflection on some of them made him wonder if they'd been taken from inside a car.

"Larry!" Tony called from the other room. "Come take a look!"

Larry found Tony in the bedroom closet, where the police photographer was taking pictures of something they'd found on the shelf. "What is it?" Larry asked.

"A bag," Tony said. "It has a pair of binoculars, another knife, and a camera with a night lens."

Larry brandished the stack of photos. "And here's what he was taking pictures of."

Tony glanced through the pictures and looked up at him. "His prey?"

"Could be. Found anything else?"

"Yeah. Our man seems to be into pornography. There's magazines up here that would curl your toes. And videos, too."

"Tag 'em. We'll take 'em all."

When they'd labeled everything that seemed to have any significance for their case, they talked to a few of the tenants standing outside. All of them considered Soames a quiet, secretive kind of guy who went out a lot at night and didn't come in until the wee hours of morning.

When they'd finished searching and removed all of the evidence, they drove back to the precinct. "You ready to hear what he has to say for himself?"

"Sure," Tony said. "This ought to be good."

3

MELISSA DIDN'T FEEL the pain in her leg until she got the phone call from Larry Millsaps, telling her that Edward Soames had been picked up, and that they'd found the bloody shirt and knife under his seat. They had also discovered, Larry said, that Soames had been charged with rape before, under another name. He wouldn't be going anywhere for a long time, Larry predicted.

Only then had Melissa been able to relax enough to notice the stinging pain of her cut and stitches, or to realize how her head hurt and how exhausted she had become. Even so, her mind was still reeling. What if something about the search had been illegal? What if they'd forgotten to read him his rights? What if the doctor's report was too ambiguous? What if some idiot judge let him out on bail?

She almost wished she had taken the painkiller or the sedative the doctor had offered so that she would be able to rest tonight and have her wits about her tomorrow, when she would need them. It wasn't too late—she could still call the nurse and ask for something. The social worker had urged her to take something to help her sleep, so that her mind could release what had happened. But Melissa couldn't afford to release it. She had to keep her facts lined up in her mind, like exhibits in a trial. She had to review them, over and over, so that she could make sure everyone else did their job. Otherwise, something might be overlooked. Someone might drop the ball.

Reluctantly, she moved away from the window, where she'd been watching the parking lot, and lay down on the bed. But sleep didn't come. Morning would be here soon enough. And then, maybe, she could breathe. Then she could make sure that morning was something Edward Soames would never again experience outside a jail cell.

Why did you change your name?" Tony asked Soames, who sat slumped in a chair at the end of the table.

McRae nodded to him, and Soames said, "I didn't think I could get a job if someone found out about my record. I was falsely accused, and I was found innocent. But the stigma of the arrests would have followed me here."

"You weren't found innocent," Larry said. "You were never tried."

"If I wasn't found guilty, I was found innocent," Soames said. "It's in the Bill of Rights."

"You have an interesting history of similar false accusations," Tony said sarcastically. "What a poor, misunderstood guy."

Soames leaned on the table, intent on making them understand. "The first one was some married woman who had a crush on me, and when I rejected her, she came up with this crazy story to get attention. The second one was a girl I'd broken up with. She was trying to get even."

"And this one?"

His lawyer leaned forward. "Tell them what you told me about her invitation today."

Soames nodded. "It's weird. Most of the time, she acts like she doesn't even know I exist. Won't look at me, hardly answers me when I talk to her, gets real nervous around me—"

"A real challenge, huh?" Larry asked.

Soames ignored it and went on. "Today, after my boss leaves, she comes into my office and asks me if I'd like to come over for dinner tonight. She seemed real nervous, but I thought it was cute, you know? And I had plans, but I canceled them. I told her I'd come."

"*She* invited *you,*" Larry repeated doubtfully. "You're sure about that?"

"She *did,* man. I was surprised."

"Were there any witnesses?"

Soames thought for a moment. "The bookkeeper in the office, Gretchen, was still there, but I don't know if she heard it or not. Melissa was talking real low, like she didn't want to be overheard."

Tony wrote the bookkeeper's name down. He couldn't wait to ask her. "So—what time did you tell her you'd be there?"

"I said seven. She said okay, and then went home. Then, I show up about 7:15 or so, and she meets me at the door looking real agitated, and tells me that she's not feeling well. She wants to cancel. I thought she was mad 'cause I was late, so I apologized, but she tells me to leave. I got a little ticked off, since I had canceled a date to come over there, and I thought the least she could have done was call—"

"Ticked off?" Larry cut in. "How ticked off?"

"Just a little hot. Hey, I didn't touch her! I just said something about her jerking me around, that I didn't appreciate it. Next thing I know, she's pulling a knife on me—one of those long carving knives like for a turkey—and waving it at me and screaming for me to get out. So I went. That's absolutely all there was. I never laid a hand on her. I didn't even come more than four feet into her apartment."

"Another false accusation?" Tony asked with mock sincerity.

"That's exactly what it is! And I have no idea why she's out to get me. Why she'd call the police and lie like that."

"You're totally in the dark about this, huh?"

Soames turned his palms up, arms spread wide. "Absolutely. I mean, if we'd gone out or something, and things hadn't gone well, and she wanted revenge . . . well, maybe. But it's like she planned this or something."

"What about the shirt under your seat?"

"What shirt?"

"The shirt with the Far Side cartoon on the front."

"It isn't under my seat," Soames said. "It's in my closet at the office. Sometimes I get dirty on the site, and I change clothes." The perplexed look on his face seemed genuine. "You found it under my seat?"

Tony stared, not missing a nuance of Soames's expression. "So you're saying you didn't put it there? Tell me, how do you explain the blood on it? Or the knife wrapped up in it?"

"What?" Looking astounded, Soames turned to his lawyer. "Man, I'm being framed. I noticed my knife missing from my office this afternoon. She must have taken it."

"So let me get this straight," Larry said. "You're saying that she took your shirt out of your office closet, took your knife, opened a vein to get blood all over it, then stuffed it under your car seat so that when you raped her, she'd have evidence?"

"I didn't *touch* her! She had this planned out before she even invited me to dinner. Don't you see? It's starting to make sense. I still don't know why she'd do it, but she did. Isn't it obvious to you morons?"

"It's not obvious to me," Larry said facetiously, glancing at Tony. "Is it obvious to you?"

"Sounds a little far-fetched," Tony agreed.

Soames was beginning to sweat, and he wiped his forehead with the back of his wrist. "Okay, look. If you just think about it—was the blood dry on the shirt? 'Cause if it had just happened, the blood would be wet."

Larry shook his head. "We didn't pick you up until a couple of hours after she reported it, and she didn't even call until a half hour or so after it happened. The blood would have had time to dry."

"Man, you got to believe me. I'm being set up. The woman's out to get me."

"Just like the other two were?"

Soames slammed his hand on the table. "Yes! Just like the other two. It happens, man. One person falsely accuses you, and then you're easy game for the next one who wants to get even."

"You said she didn't have anything to get even for."

"She doesn't! Hey, I don't know any more than you do what's going through her head. But I do know that she's accusing me just as falsely as the others did."

"Then I'd say you have real bad luck with women," Tony said.

The door opened, and one of the uniforms stuck his head in. "Larry, Tony, there's a call for you. Dr. Jasper. Says he's returning your call."

"I'll take it," Tony said, getting up.

Larry watched Tony leave the room, then got up himself. "We found some interesting things in your apartment, Soames. Wonder if you could explain them to us."

Soames looked uncomfortable. "I got nothing to hide."

"Right. So you have a good explanation for why there were binoculars, a camera, and a knife in a bag in your closet."

"I take them to ball games," Soames said. "I can see better with the binoculars, and I like to take pictures."

"Is that why the only pictures we found were of women who didn't know they were being photographed?"

Soames laughed then. "They were my friends. They all knew I was taking their pictures."

"Yeah? Then you won't mind giving us their names, will you, so we can talk to them."

Soames got quiet again.

"Come on, Soames," Larry said. "What are their names?"

"I'm not gonna subject my friends to your gestapo tactics."

"Do you *know* their names, Soames?"

"His friends have no relation to this case," McRae interjected.

"No, but his prey have a lot of bearing on this. And if he can't give us the names of these unsuspecting women he photographed from his car at night, then we have to make our own assumptions."

Soames turned to his attorney, beseeching him to help him out, and McRae leaned forward. "Okay, you've got your statement from him. I don't think he needs to say any more."

Tony came back in, his face glum, but before he could sit down, Larry said, "Fine, I think we've got enough. Maybe a night in jail will help him get his story straight."

"Steve," Soames pled, "can't you get the arraignment moved up? I don't want to stay in here."

"It's just one night," McRae said. "Tomorrow we can probably get you out on bond."

"I wouldn't hold my breath," Larry said. "When the judge sees the evidence and your record, he's gonna want to throw away the key. 'Course, if you came clean and told the truth, he might cut you a little slack."

"I *am* telling the truth, man!"

"Fine. Stick to your story. It's kind of a hobby of mine, shooting stories like this all to pieces."

Soames was still yelling when Larry and Tony closed the door behind them and walked through the noisy precinct. Several gang members just brought in shouted at the officer who had booked them. Across the room, an abusive husband let out a string of obscenities as he struggled to break free of his handcuffs. Somewhere a baby cried incessantly.

"So what do you think?" Tony asked.

"I think he deserves an Oscar. What do you think?"

"I don't know. I mean, yeah, the evidence is pretty clear, and his record doesn't leave much room for doubt."

"But?"

Tony hesitated, looking out over the chaos of the room. Finally, he brought his eyes back to Larry. "On the phone, that was the doctor who examined Melissa Nelson."

"Yeah, I know. What did he say?"

Tony combed his fingers through his sandy hair. "He says that, based on his examination of her, he can't confirm for certain that a rape occurred."

Larry stared at him for a moment. "Did he say it didn't?"

"No, he couldn't say that. Not for sure."

"Well, we knew that evidence was going to be flimsy because she showered. But what does he call the cut on her leg?"

"Assault, maybe, but not rape."

Larry backed up a step, glaring at his friend. "So what are you saying? Just because some doctor says he can't find evidence, it didn't happen? You *saw* the evidence in this guy's car. You saw his record. You heard what he said in there."

"That's just it," Tony said. "What if it happened just like he said?"

Larry gaped at him. "I can't believe you. You want to make this poor woman regret she ever called us."

"I just don't want to accept either one of these stories at face value," Tony said. "We might be getting a little truth from each of them. It just feels like there's something else going on here, like we're not getting the whole story."

"Well, if anybody's hiding something, we'll find out. This guy's not walking out of *this* jail on a technicality."

4

MELISSA LEFT THE hospital the next morning before the doctor had even come in. In the bright, revealing light of morning, the apartment she had left last night had a look of absurdity: tables still overturned, broken glass still scattered across the floor, the bed still rumpled and unmade.

She stood near the front door, slowly perusing the signs of struggle, the evidence laid out so distinctly, the story it all told. Stepping over the broken, overturned lamp, she went into the bathroom, where bloody towels lay crumpled on the floor. Her eyes strayed to the bathtub, then flitted away, then gravitated back again.

The memory of another bathtub flashed into her mind, and quickly she turned away, bending over the sink to splash cold water on her face. Straightening, she grabbed the hand towel and looked into the mirror. The face staring back at her was tight, as it often was, with worry, urgency, and grief. The worry was something that came and went, alternating with a death-defying courage that sometimes propelled her into decisions she had trouble carrying out. But the grief was ever present, always deep, smothering, sickening, something she could not escape. Maybe there would be an end to it now.

Turning, deliberately keeping her eyes from the bathtub that had ignited those memories, she limped into the bedroom she usually kept so neat. She found something else to wear and quickly changed, careful not to brush the cut on her leg. Then, brushing her long blonde hair with little attention to how the soft waves fell, she flipped through the phone book and found the number of the police station.

Larry Millsaps wasn't in, she learned, and neither was Tony Danks. Edward Soames was still in custody, but his bond hearing was at ten.

Fear burst through her, fear that he would somehow convince the judge that this was all a mistake, that he deserved to, at least, be released on bond. She needed to talk to someone, to find out if one of the prosecutors would be there, or if this was one of those hearings where just the defendant and his lawyer would be present. The court *had* to understand the seriousness of the crime he'd committed! Quickly, she found the number to the DA's office and asked for the attorney working on the case.

No one had even been assigned to it yet.

"But his hearing is scheduled for ten this morning! Won't anyone be there from your office? What if they release him?"

"Judges generally won't release a man charged with rape, Miss Nelson. There's really nothing to worry about."

"He'll come after me if he gets out!" she said, her voice rising. "I'd say there's very certainly something to worry about. I've seen people released on technicalities before. I've seen the justice system fumble. I don't want to be the victim of somebody's mistake!"

"I told you, we'll have someone there."

"But I need to talk to whoever it is. They need to see what he did to me, what he did to my apartment. They need to hear—"

"I'm sure we'll have the police report soon. You gave them a statement, didn't you?"

"Yes, but that's not enough! If I could just talk to someone, so you could see how important it is to keep him locked up!"

"I've got your name and number, Miss Nelson. Once the case is assigned, I'm sure they'll be contacting you. Please relax." The voice on the other end paused, then changed to a softer cadence. "Look, I know you've been through an ordeal. I have the number of a terrific counselor who specializes in rape victims. Why don't you call her this morning and talk to her?"

"I don't need a shrink!" she cried. "I need some peace of mind. I need to know it isn't going to happen again just because he managed to charm some judge into letting him go!"

"Please, Miss Nelson. I know it's hard, but you really have no alternative right now except waiting. I promise someone will contact you."

Melissa slammed the phone down and wiped at the tears forming in her eyes. She couldn't just sit here and wait. She had to go somewhere, do something. She couldn't just let it go.

She searched through the phone book for the name Millsaps, then scanned down the page until she came to Larry. Quickly, she dialed the number, then waited as it rang once, twice, three times . . .

Finally, it was picked up, dropped, and then a rumbly, groggy voice said, "Hello?"

"Uh, Detective Millsaps? This is Melissa Nelson. From . . . last night?"

"Yeah, Melissa," he said. "Are you all right?"

"Yes . . . well, no. Look, I'm sorry I woke you. I wouldn't have, except . . ."

"That's okay. Melissa, what's wrong?"

"It's the bond hearing. It's at ten this morning, and it hasn't even been assigned to anyone in the DA's office yet, and I'm worried he might get out."

Larry sighed. "He won't, Melissa. No way. They have your statement, and I stayed late last night making sure all the paperwork was in order. It's all there."

She brought a trembling hand to her forehead and shoved her bangs back. "It's just—so hard for me to trust the justice system."

His voice was waking up now, and she had the feeling he was sitting up. "I understand why you're jumpy. I probably would be, too. Are you still in the hospital?"

"No, I'm at home," she said. "You know, I'm thinking about moving. Maybe I need a new address. Maybe I just need to leave town until this comes to trial."

"That's up to you," he said, "as long as we can reach you. Are you planning to go in to work today?"

"No," she said quickly. "I don't think I can go back there. It would be too hard to face anyone. And his office is there . . ."

Suddenly she realized that she was babbling like a crazy person, and she had awakened him to do it. "Look, I didn't mean to wake you up. Or, maybe I did, but I shouldn't have. I'm sorry. I'm just a little fragmented. Would you—would you call me when you get to the office today? I'd like to talk to you some more."

"Sure," he said.

"All right, good-bye." But she held the receiver in her hand for a few moments before finally setting it back in its cradle. Then, going to her favorite chair, still stained with a few drops of her blood from last night, she curled up on it and tried to think what to do next.

Larry lay in bed for a while after he hung up, wishing there was something he could do to help this distraught woman. He'd seen the way a crisis like this ate at people, how it tore at the fabric of their security and ripped away their trust in all that was good. She needed an anchor.

He rolled toward his bedside table, fighting the fatigue still clinging to him, and dialed information. Then he sat up and punched in Melissa's number.

"Hello?" Her voice was soft, apprehensive, yet hopeful. He wondered who she'd been expecting.

"Uh, Melissa? This is Larry again. Listen, I was just thinking—would you like to have breakfast somewhere? You obviously need to talk, and I've gotten all the sleep I need."

"Are you sure?"

"Well, yeah."

He could hear the relief in her voice, that someone was taking her seriously. "Yes, that would be great. When?"

"How about an hour? I don't live far from you. I could pick you up." But as quickly as he'd said that, he kicked himself. The last thing a rape victim wanted was another man coming to her apartment. "Or if you'd rather just meet somewhere—"

"No, that's fine," she said. "You can pick me up."

A little surprised, he said, "Okay. I'll see you then."

This time, she didn't sound quite as forlorn as she said good-bye.

5

LARRY WASN'T SURE he would have recognized her if Melissa hadn't been standing in the door of the same apartment where he'd met her the night before. Her hair had been wet and matted then, and she had been curled up in a blanket most of the time, her eyes raw and red, her skin pallid.

But today her hair, a soft baby blonde color, waved down to her shoulders. Soft bangs covered her eyebrows. The skin around her eyes was still red, but their soft blueness was striking even though she wore no makeup. Melissa Nelson wasn't a woman who needed much help from cosmetics, Larry decided. They would only cheapen the effect of the beauty she'd been gifted with.

He noticed also how small she was, no more than five-feet-five against his six-two, and he hated the image that crossed his mind of Soames overpowering her. He supposed they should be thankful that she hadn't been left dead.

"You ready?" he asked.

"Yes," she said. "Come on in. I have to get my purse."

The apartment looked just as he'd left it last night—tables overturned, glass shattered, liquid spilled and congealed on the floor. From the doorway, he could see into the bedroom; nothing had been changed on the bed. Not a pillow had been moved, not a sheet disturbed.

"I—I didn't know if the police had gotten all the evidence they needed," she explained, stepping over some glass and still favoring her left leg. "I thought I'd better leave everything alone until I was sure."

He shook his head. "We finished last night, Melissa. We have film and video of the whole scene, and we got fingerprints and a lot of other routine evidence. I don't think we missed anything."

"But are you sure? If I clean it all up, and you think of something you forgot to look for, it'll be too late."

"Have you found anything you think we missed?" he asked, confused.

"No. I'm just saying there could be something."

Gently, trying not to make her feel stupid, Larry said, "Melissa, it's really okay to start putting things back together. I could help if you want, after breakfast. You can't keep living in this mess, with all these reminders. It would drive you crazy."

"I'm willing to take that chance, if it'll ensure that he gets put away."

"I know you are. You're very brave. But you really have to start thinking of yourself. You may not even know this yet, but you've been traumatized. You need to talk to people who know how to deal with this—even some people who've been through it. It would really help you adjust."

"I'll adjust when I know for sure they aren't going to let him go," she said. She started out the door, limping slightly, and Larry followed her, locking the door behind him. Every case was different, he thought as they went down the stairs. The last rape he'd worked, the woman had not only showered before she'd called the police, but she'd cleaned up her apartment, trying to wipe away any sign that the man had ever been there. But she hadn't been able to scrub away the horrible memories, and finally, she had called the police.

It was odd that Melissa, who had also showered to clean away any bodily memory of the man who'd violated her, had chosen to keep the apartment just as he'd left it. Whether she was incredibly strong, or incredibly paranoid, he wasn't sure..

"How's your leg?" he asked.

"Fine," she said. "It really doesn't hurt much."

Incredibly strong, he decided, with a very high threshold of pain.

At the bottom of the stairs, he noticed a tiny old woman peering through the crack of her partially open door. Dismissing her as a neighbor still curious about last night, he stepped out of the building and pointed to his car parked on the street. "It's not much, but it's paid for."

She smiled, and he realized that he'd never seen that expression on her before. It changed her face, softening the lines around her mouth and eyes.

He opened the door for her, and she got in, careful not to hurt her leg.

"So what do you like to eat?"

"Anything's fine," she said. "I didn't really come to eat."

He cranked the car and pulled out into the traffic. "We'll go to this place I know a couple of blocks away. They have great omelets."

"Fine," she said.

He glanced at her occasionally as he navigated his way through the traffic. She was pretty, he thought, but he had realized that last night. Her eyes gave her face a startling softness and depth. Left alone, undisturbed, what did she think about? What did she like to do—before last night, that is. And how long would it take for her to heal?

"Do you have family around here?" he asked quietly.

She shook her head. "No. My parents live in Pensacola."

"Have you—told them?"

The turmoil in her eyes grieved him. "No, I haven't. I'm not going to. Maybe they won't hear about it."

"Well . . . if this goes to trial, it will be in the paper, and since he's had arrests in other counties, the coverage might reach across the state."

She grew quiet, and her eyes strayed out the window.

"Why don't you want them to know?"

She drew in a deep breath, then let it out slowly. "I don't think they can take it. It would kill them."

"Well, maybe you could get someone to help you tell them. Do you have brothers or sisters?"

She hesitated for a moment, and he saw the tears filling her eyes. "No," she said finally, quietly.

"Well, I could help you, if you want. I'm used to breaking bad news to people."

She brought her eyes back to him. "That must be awful."

He frowned and thought about it for a moment. "It used to be. I used to dread it, and wish someone else would do it for me. But then I realized that not everyone can bring bad news with any sense of compassion. I can. I finally decided that if somebody had to tell them horrible things, it might as well be me. At least I could know it was handled right."

"And what's the right way to tell a couple that their daughter has been raped?" she asked in a monotone.

"Well, I'd tell them first that you were all right. That the man is in custody. Those things should give them some peace. Then I'd let them cry and yell and cuss, if they had to. And then I'd tell them what I do in times of deep tragedy, when I don't know where to turn."

She gazed at him for a long moment. "What do you do?"

"I pray," he said. "I turn to God. And instead of asking 'why,' I ask God what he wants me to do."

Those tears resurfaced again, and she looked down at her hands. "If you've never asked why, it's because you've never experienced a tragedy so deep that it shakes the foundation of everything you've ever believed in your life. Sometimes you *have* to ask why."

"And if there are no answers?"

"Then you make some," she said.

They pulled into the parking lot of the little diner. Neither of them spoke as they got out and went inside. He was a little surprised when she ordered; he hadn't expected her to be able to eat. He was glad she could.

Finally, when the waitress brought their food, he got back to the subject they'd started in the car. "I've been thinking about what you said. About making your own answers. And I thought how convenient that would be if it were possible. But I've found that my own attempts to resolve things never work." He studied her for a moment as he sipped his coffee. "Tell me something, Melissa. Do you pray?"

Her eyes seemed to glaze over, as if she were deep in a memory from years earlier. "I used to," she said. "I used to pray all the time."

"What made you stop?"

"I don't know," she whispered. "Anger, maybe."

"Anger at what?"

She seemed to shake out of her reverie at his question, and looked at him again. "Personal things. Things that went wrong, without any reason. Things that didn't make any sense."

"And you haven't prayed since?"

She hesitated. "Some. But I don't think they were heard. Finally, I gave up."

"I can assure you they were heard."

She shrugged. "Well, maybe they were. They just weren't answered."

"Sometimes the answer is 'wait.' Sometimes we don't want to do that. Sometimes maybe we'd rather trust in our own strength."

"Maybe," she whispered. "Maybe so."

The food came to the table, and he watched as she ate, picking at her food, looking distracted.

"So do you want me to talk to your folks?"

She shook her head. "No. I appreciate it, though. If they hear about it, I guess I'll have some explaining to do. But maybe they won't hear, and then they'll never have to suffer through this. I want to protect them from this if I can."

"But you need their support, Melissa. You can't get it if they don't know."

"I'll be all right," Melissa whispered. "I can do this alone."

He shut up then, realizing that she was not only strong, she was stubborn. And she'd made up her mind.

After a few minutes, she moved her plate away and folded her arms on the table. "Detective Millsaps—"

"Larry," he interrupted. "Please, call me Larry."

"Okay, Larry. I wanted to talk to you about the evidence. What's being done with it?"

He set his fork down and leaned back. "What do you mean?"

"I mean, you're not going to just blow off the hair and fingerprints and everything, and assume that the shirt and knife in his car were enough, are you?"

Larry shook his head. "Of course not. It'll all be used in court. Every bit of it."

"And, you did have a warrant when you arrested him, didn't you?"

Larry nodded. "Search warrants, too." Her questions bothered him. He wasn't used to getting the third degree from a victim. She looked at her watch, and he knew that she was calculating how much time before Soames's bond hearing.

"Will the judge make an immediate decision about whether to release him or keep him?"

"Yes," he said. "And I guarantee he'll keep him. He'd be out of his mind to let Edward Soames back out on the streets."

"Yeah, well, I've seen judges out of their minds before. Outrageous decisions are made in court every day."

"That's one of the hardest things about being a cop. I take 'em in, and they let 'em go. But we have too much evidence on this guy. You really don't have to worry." He hoped he sounded more confident than he felt.

He paid the check, and they went back to the car. "I meant it about helping you clean up your apartment," he said. "I can help you right now."

"No," she said. "I don't want to go home."

"Where do you want to go?" he asked.

Her eyes were determined as she faced him. "I want to go with you to the police station, or you can drop me off at the courthouse."

"The courthouse? Melissa, you don't want to be there. You don't want to see this guy—"

"I have to know," she said. "I have to know that they're not releasing him. Either I can sit in the courtroom and watch the hearing, or I can wait with you until you hear something."

"Or I could take you home and call you when I hear."

"By the time you call me, he could be at my apartment banging my door down," she said. "I won't feel safe until I know for sure."

Larry sighed. "All right then. I guess you can come to the precinct. But I can't stay there all morning. I'll probably get called away."

"That's fine," she said. "I won't bother anyone. I just need a safe place, until there's a decision."

Larry moaned inwardly, anticipating what Tony would say. But he didn't have the heart to force her to go home. He'd already taken this much responsiblity for her; he might as well finish what he'd started.

6

THE PRECINCT SMELLED like a locker room when Larry walked Melissa through, trying to find a place to put her while he worked. The waiting area was filled with what looked like a gang, no doubt waiting to post bail for one of their members. Putting her there would be like throwing a lamb to the wolves. She'd already been through enough.

So he grabbed an empty chair and dragged it around to his desk. "Here," he said.

"Thank you." Checking her watch, she sat down. Larry saw on the wall clock that it was almost ten.

He tried to recover last night's train of thought as he sifted through the paperwork he'd left on his desk. He needed more information on the other rape charges against Soames. Names of women. Circumstances. Maybe he could determine his MO, whether he only went after women he knew, or if those pictures found in his apartment were pictures of potential victims. He needed to get a job history, affiliations, a credit report, anything that would help him trace Soames's steps for the past few years. There might be other women who had been attacked and hadn't reported it—women who might come forward if they knew someone else had filed charges.

Whatever it took, he needed to make sure that the system didn't let Melissa down. She was already, for some reason, very distrustful of it.

"Hey, how're you doing?" It was Tony's voice behind him, and Larry looked up and saw that his partner was addressing Melissa.

"Fine."

"Is, uh, Detective Millsaps here helping you?"

Larry grinned. Tony didn't recognize her. "Tony, this is Melissa Nelson."

Tony's eyebrows shot up. "Oh. From last night?"

"Yeah," Larry said. "She's just waiting here for word about Soames's bond hearing."

"What about it?" Tony asked.

"Whether he's released on bond."

Tony almost laughed, but caught himself. "They're not letting him out."

When Melissa didn't answer, Larry spoke up. "She didn't want to wait at home, just in case. Listen, I need to talk to you about some things."

He excused himself and whisked Tony into the interrogation room.

"What's going on?" Tony asked. "Was she waiting here for us?"

"No. I picked her up."

"You what?"

"She called me this morning, all upset, worried he was going to get out and come after her. I took her to breakfast—"

"Oh, brother," Tony said, shaking his head. "You're nuts, you know that? Larry, you can't go getting involved with victims in the crimes you're investigating. That's crazy!"

"I'm not! She's just scared and paranoid right now. If sitting at my desk makes her feel better, it's fine with me."

"You can't work with her sitting there."

"Watch me." With that, Larry flung the door open and stormed through it.

"All right," Tony said, fast on his heels. "But if she's here, I'm not going to tiptoe around her. She's going to have to answer some questions."

"Ask away," he said. "She'll tell you anything you want to know."

But Tony didn't ask. Instead, he busied himself at his computer, punching the keys hard and deliberately, as if to vent some of the frustration he felt. Larry tried to ignore him, doing his own work on the computer, tracking down the work history of Edward Pendergrast, the names of the other two alleged victims who'd pressed charges against him, and any other information he could find.

After a while, Melissa got up and wandered toward him. "Are you working on my case?" she asked.

"Yes." He gave her a distracted glance, then hit the "print" button. "It seems our man has a couple of other arrests. For the same thing."

Melissa didn't look as surprised as he'd expected. "Can that be mentioned in his hearing? Should you call the DA?"

Larry looked fully at her now, studying her face. "You didn't happen to know his background before, did you? Is that why you're so afraid of things falling through?"

She grew stiffer then, but kept her eyes clearly focused on his. "Of course not. How could I have known? I've barely had a complete conversation with him."

As she talked, Larry noticed Tony behind her. Tony stared at her, glanced back at his computer screen, then shot a look at Larry. "Excuse me a minute," Larry said. "I need to talk to Tony."

"What if your phone rings? What if someone calls about the hearing?"

"I'll hear it," he said. "Don't worry." He crossed the room to Tony's desk. "You have that look on your face," he said quietly. "Like you've got something."

Tony glanced up at him over his shoulder. "I thought I'd check out our little lady. Just to get a better take on her. Take a look at this."

Larry leaned over him and read the skeleton history he'd come up with. "She's got a degree from Florida State. Changed her major to criminal justice after her sophomore year. Graduated summa cum laude. My question is, how did a criminal justice whiz wind up here working as a secretary?"

Larry frowned. "Why would she do that?"

Tony shook his head. "Why don't we ask her?"

Larry straightened. "I will."

The phone was ringing when he got back to his desk, and he snatched it up. "Millsaps."

He listened as the secretary in the DA's office relayed the decision in the hearing. "Thanks. I appreciate it."

He hung up and leaned forward on his desk.

"Did they let him go?" Melissa asked.

He shook his head. "No bond. He's staying."

Relief washed over her, and she leaned back in her chair, finally relaxed. "I can't believe it. I was so worried."

"I know you were." He set his chin on his palm and looked at her for a moment. "Can I ask you something, Melissa?" She was smiling, and he hated to ruin it, but he had to. "We had to do a little research on you, just as a matter of routine. And we were looking at your educational background."

Her smile faded, and she fixed her eyes on him. "What about it?"

"Just seemed odd to me, that's all. You have a degree in criminal justice, of all things."

"Why is that odd?" she asked.

"Well, because you're not working in that field. In fact, I wondered why you'd take a job doing secretarial work."

She glanced away then, avoiding his eyes, and shrugged. "I worked for the FBI for three months after I graduated last spring. Three months was long enough. Now I'm a secretary, until I find something better."

"Why didn't you mention this earlier?"

Her eyebrows shot up, and she gaped at him. "I've been a little bit distracted. The subject didn't come up!" She glared at him, as if trying to determine if he was suggesting that she had covered up, then finally, she came to her feet. "Do you have any more questions for me, Detective? Like why I drive a red car instead of a green one, or why I chose exactly the apartment complex I did? I'm familiar with how a rape case often gets turned on the victim. As you pointed out, I spent a lot of time studying things like that. So go ahead! Take your best shot."

His eyes remained locked with hers, but finally, he shook his head. "I'm not trying to interrogate you, Melissa. I just have to ask about things that seem out of sync."

"And since my job is out of sync, maybe what happened to me last night is too, right?"

"I didn't say that."

"You didn't have to. Call me if you come up with anything else that's out of sync. I'll see if I can explain it to you." With that, she started to limp away from his desk.

Larry lunged out of his chair and caught her arm. "Melissa, I'll take you home. Just wait a minute."

"No, thanks," she said. "I'll get a cab."

He stood there as she hurried from the room, and it was a moment before he realized that Tony was standing next to him.

"She didn't like the question, huh?"

"No, she didn't," Larry said. "And now I feel like the kind of pond scum that makes rape victims sorry they ever report the crime."

"If she can't take the heat—"

Larry spun around, his face furious. "If she can't take the heat, what, Tony? Who really *can* take the heat? Could you? What if you were attacked on the street, and when you reported it, all of a sudden your life and your history became suspect? Would your record stand up to our kind of scrutiny? Would *you* be able to take the heat?"

Tony rolled his eyes. "Man, you've got it bad."

"Give me a break!" he shouted, and some of the others in the busy room stopped what they were doing and looked at him. "I would like to think I have a little compassion for any victim I deal with, so don't go accusing me of preferential treatment just because she's a woman!"

"What are you so hot about?" Tony flung back.

"I'm hot about putting an innocent, wounded, violated woman on the defensive, Tony! That kind of thing always gets to me! I don't know why it doesn't get to you."

"Maybe it's because my gut is telling me that things just aren't fitting into place here."

"So who are you gonna believe? A guy who's been accused of rape before, who's being accused now, who had evidence up to his ears in his car and his apartment—or a woman whose only crime is to be overqualified for her job and who had the audacity to get raped?"

Tony threw his hands up. "All right. You got me. You're right. Now can we please get back to work?"

Larry plopped back down into his chair and turned to his computer. This day was going from bad to worse. And he hadn't had enough sleep last night to deal with any of this.

A couple of hours later, as Larry and Tony were returning from investigating a missing persons report on two seventeen-year-old girls who had apparently run away—and for good reason, judging from the neglectful homes they'd each come from—Larry's mind wandered back to Melissa Nelson. He thought about her indignation that morning, then about their conversation at breakfast. Something had been bothering him about that, something she'd said . . .

". . . you're not going to just blow off the hair and fingerprints . . . and assume that the shirt and knife in his car were enough, are you?"

The hair. That was it. How had she known that they would find follicles of Soames's hair on her bed? Just an assumption, based on what she would have looked for, had she been investigating?

He shoved the question out of his mind. Tony's suspicions—of what, he still wasn't sure—were affecting him. Rubbing his eyes, he glanced at Tony, who was driving. "Did I tell you I ordered the police file on Pendergrast from Santa Rosa County?"

Tony shook his head. "No. I was going to do it this afternoon."

"I asked them to rush it. They said it would be here by tomorrow."

"What's the rush?"

"Well, the grand jury will be hearing the case soon."

"So the DA will ask for it."

Larry breathed a laugh. "Yeah, well, you and I both know that the more we lay the case out for the DA's office, the better chance we have of conviction. I just want to make sure."

"What are you looking for?"

"I don't know," he said. "Anything I can find on the previous arrests. Who the victims were, his MO, exactly why he walked. That kind of thing."

Tony glanced over at him. "Larry, you look like a zombie. How much sleep did you get last night?"

"Couple hours," he said.

"Why don't you go on home? I'll fax the info about these runaways to some other PDs across the state and see what I can come up with. Get some sleep. You're not worth a plugged nickel when you're this tired."

"Thanks a lot." They pulled into the PD parking garage. "I think I'll take you up on it, though."

"Sure you can drive?" Tony asked with a grin.

"Hey, I've functioned with less sleep before. Remember the Barrett case?"

"Yeah. I almost killed you, man. Volunteering us to stake her place out all night after we'd been on duty for over twelve hours already."

"Hey, I did it myself."

"Yep. Another case of a lady in distress. You do dumb things for women, Larry."

"It was dumb to stake out her house?" he asked irritably. "Are you telling me there was no threat?"

Tony grinned and shook his head. "Okay, okay. But breakfast this morning? I don't think that was within the call of duty, pal."

"Just don't worry about it. I'm going home."

"Good," Tony laughed. "And don't come back until you have a better disposition. Or I just might have to kill you after all."

Larry grinned as he headed across the garage to his own car.

7

A KNOCK AT the door woke Larry a few hours after he'd fallen asleep. He stumbled to the door. Tony stood there, the setting sun at his back, grinning as if he enjoyed waking Larry. "Rise and shine! We've got work to do."

Larry shuffled into the kitchen, and Tony followed. "What is it?" Larry asked, measuring out some coffee for the pot.

"A witness in the Nelson case."

Larry swung around. "Really? Who?"

"A woman who lives downstairs. She gave a statement last night that she heard things crashing upstairs in Melissa's apartment. I thought we should talk to her."

"Yeah, okay. Just let me change."

A few minutes later, Larry followed Tony out to the car, wondering whether the appearance of this witness would make Tony give more credence to Melissa's story. "So what else have you been doing today?" he asked.

"Well, I interviewed the people she worked with."

"Who worked with?"

"Your friend Melissa."

Larry shot him a look. "*My* friend?"

Tony grinned. "Well, you seem to be her champion. Anyway, you're not going to like what I found out."

Larry waited. "What?"

"That bookkeeper who was still there when Soames says Melissa asked him to dinner? She confirmed it."

"That she was there?"

"No. She confirmed that Melissa asked him. She heard it. She's apparently a real busybody, and she admitted that when she saw Melissa go into his office, she listened outside the door to see what they were talking about. She heard everything."

Larry tried to absorb that. "You believe her?"

"I don't know. What do you think?"

"Well, she could have a crush on him herself, and want to help him. Maybe he paid her. Who knows?"

"Yeah, well . . . I'm just telling you what she said."

Larry stayed quiet as they approached the apartment building where they'd found Melissa last night. Things looked radically different tonight, without flashing lights everywhere and a crowd of people on the street. "Who are we going to see?"

"A Matilda Berkley," Tony said. "She lives in the first apartment as you come in the door."

"Yeah, I saw her peeking out this morning."

Larry followed Tony in. Before they had even reached her door, it opened. The little old lady Larry had seen that morning stuck her head out. "Hello, officers. I've been expecting you. Won't you come in?"

She seemed delighted to have company, and Larry couldn't help smiling. They introduced themselves, accepted the coffee and cake she'd prepared for them, and sat down, anxious to get to the point. Finally, Larry jumped in.

"Mrs. Berkley, you told the police officers last night in your statement that you heard things crashing upstairs. Could you tell us exactly what time that was?"

"It was seven-thirty, because I was baking, and the timer went off right about that time."

Larry nodded. "Did you see anyone leave the apartment after that?"

Her eyebrows shot up. "No, and I kept waiting. I had my door cracked with the chain still on it, and I was watching the stairs to see who would come down. But until you officers came, nobody came out of that apartment."

Larry frowned. "Are you sure? You didn't just miss him?"

"No. I pretty much see almost everyone who comes and goes in this building. I know everyone here, and I like to make sure the people coming and going are *supposed* to be here.

Especially with Melissa—she's such a lovely girl. She's been so sweet, always checking to see if I need anything, bringing me things from the grocery store when I can't get there myself. I feel kind of protective of her. And last night, after that first gentleman left, I heard all that crashing—"

"Wait a minute," Larry said. "What gentleman?"

"Well, the one who was here to see Melissa. I opened my door and looked out when he came into the building, and he asked me which apartment was hers. He seemed like a decent young man, and I was happy that she had a date. She has so few visitors, you know."

Larry was getting impatient. "Did you or didn't you see him leave?"

"I certainly did. He came down rather quickly and slammed the door going out. I was so disappointed, because I had hoped that maybe he was a suitor. She's a very lonely girl, I think—"

Tony tried this time. "But you say you heard the crashing things *after* he left?"

"Yes. I could tell that something was wrong, and I thought someone must be up there, but I hadn't seen anyone else go up. I guess I should have called the police myself, but I just wasn't sure whether anyone was there with her. It's possible that they had come when I hadn't been listening, so I waited and waited for them to come down, so I could decide what to do. But no one ever did. Not until the police began coming. Would you like some more cake?"

"No. Uh, thanks." Larry turned his troubled eyes to Tony.

Tony sighed. "Mrs. Berkley, are you sure you didn't just get the events mixed up? I mean, maybe you heard the crashing, and *then* saw him leave."

Her chin came up with indignation. "I'm telling you the way it happened. There must have been someone else up there. That first gentleman wasn't there long enough to do anything. I'd say maybe five minutes. But if there was someone else, maybe he went up onto the roof, or got into another apartment . . ." Her eyes grew round as she imagined all the places a culprit could have hidden.

"All the other neighbors were interviewed," Tony explained. "None of them saw anything like that."

She sat back hard on her couch. "Then it doesn't make any sense, does it? It's just downright peculiar. How did he get in and out?"

Tony pulled a picture from his shirt pocket. "Mrs. Berkley, was this the man you saw coming to see Melissa last night?"

She took the picture of Soames that they'd used to identify him last night, and nodded. "Yes, that's him. Nice-looking young man, like I told you."

"And you're sure that he's the same man you saw leaving?"

"Oh, absolutely."

"Did he have anything in his hands?"

"Like what?" she asked.

"Anything at all."

The woman thought for a moment. "No. I don't think so."

"Did he look angry?"

"Well, yes, he did."

"And what did he have on?" Larry asked. "Mrs. Berkley, this is very important. Can you remember what he had on when he arrived?"

"Well, the same thing he had on when he left. One of those striped pullover shirts, like a golf shirt or something, you know? It had red and green and navy stripes that went this way . . ."

Larry glanced at Tony. The same shirt he'd been wearing when they'd picked him up.

"And you're sure he was wearing that when he left?"

"Yes," she said adamantly. "Like I told you, he wasn't up there more than five minutes. He looked just the same when he came back down."

No cartoon T-shirt, Larry thought with confusion. So where had the bloody T shirt come from?

They finished questioning her, thanked her, and left.

As he settled in behind the steering wheel, Tony asked, "Am I the only one who notices that something is a little tilted about this case?" He pulled the car back out onto the street.

"The woman has to be eighty years old. Maybe she's imagining things," Larry said.

"Did she imagine the shirt he was wearing when we picked him up?"

"Well—" Larry sighed, looked out the window, then brought his gaze back to his partner. "Well, how do you explain the crashing *after* Soames had left? Melissa didn't tell us anyone else was involved."

Tony shook his head. "I'm not sure Melissa is telling us the truth, Larry. I know you don't want to hear that, but I'm telling you, things aren't fitting together here."

Larry couldn't deny it. "I just don't get it. What really happened?"

"There's no telling," Tony said. "But the only story we've heard that we've been able to corroborate with witnesses is Soames's story."

Larry rolled his eyes. "Oh, come on. You saw his record. You saw the things in his apartment, the pictures, the bloody shirt under his seat—"

"That's right," Tony said. "I saw them. I'm not saying that he's not a scumbag. I'm just not sure what he really did in this case."

He pulled into a parking space near Larry's apartment and let the car idle for a moment. "Look, what do you say we just sleep on it, and tackle all this fresh tomorrow?"

"Yeah, okay." Larry got out and headed back toward his apartment. But before he reached it, he turned back and walked to his own car. He couldn't just let it go; he wouldn't be able to rest haunted by the possibility that Melissa was lying. He had wanted to check on Melissa anyway, to make sure she was all right. Tony would say that he was obsessing—that if she wasn't a blonde with soulful eyes, he wouldn't be giving this case such attention. But Larry hoped that wasn't true. He'd been on the police force for nine years now, and while many of his colleagues had gotten jaded, he'd worked hard not to. He liked to think that he would always stand up for justice, fairness, and the rights of the victims—especially the more vulnerable victims who needed someone to stand up for them. As tough as Melissa's facade suggested she was, he suspected that she was as vulnerable as any victim he'd ever encountered. Even if there were things about her story that didn't make sense.

He drove back to her apartment building and tried to be quiet as he walked in, to see if anyone could get past Mrs. Berkley without being noticed. But the first stair squeaked beneath his foot, and suddenly the door peeped open, still attached with the chain lock. Mrs. Berkley peered out. He waved. "Hi, Mrs. Berkley. I'm just checking on Melissa."

She pressed the door closed, unlocked the chain, then opened it further. "Good. She's up now. She slept most of the afternoon, but I've heard her moving around up there in the last few minutes. Enjoy your visit."

He smiled uncomfortably and continued up the stairs. A television blared from one of the other apartments on the first floor, and a baby cried in another.

The walls were paper-thin, he thought. Thin enough for Mrs. Berkley to hear everyone who came and went—thin enough to know whether Melissa was alone.

He knocked on Melissa's door. He heard footsteps, then waited while, he assumed, she looked at him through the peephole. After a moment, she opened the door.

"Hi," she said.

She couldn't be lying about this, he thought. Not someone with such pure blue eyes, such porcelain skin, such fine blonde hair . . . "Thought I'd come by and check on you," he said. "See if you were all right after our questions this morning. I felt kind of responsible for making things worse for you."

She sighed wearily. "Is that an apology?"

"No. Actually, we were just doing our job," he said. "I just regret how it made you feel."

"Well, I'm fine." She stepped back and invited him in.

He looked around, and saw that the furniture had been turned upright, the toppled lamps were settled back on the tables again, and the broken glass had been swept into little piles.

"I guess I shouldn't have run out like that," she said. "It just got to me a little. If I hadn't been so tired, I probably would have realized that you had to ask. You're supposed to. I wouldn't expect either of you to just take everything at face value."

He glanced into the bedroom and saw that her bed was unmade and the covers pulled back, as if she'd been sleeping in it. "I hope I didn't wake you."

"No," she said. "I just woke up. I was trying to clean up a little. When I came home this morning, I started to, but I was so exhausted I decided to finish later. So I climbed into bed and fell asleep."

Odd, he thought. Most rape victims wouldn't have gone near the place where they'd been violated, yet Melissa had slept there all afternoon? She was tougher than he'd thought. Either that, or . . .

He tried to shove out of his mind the thought that she might not be telling it all exactly as it had happened, that she was leaving something out, or maybe making something up. Seeing the trouble in her expression, the fatigue on her face, he just couldn't believe that. She'd been traumatized. That much was clear.

"I'll help you, if you want," he said finally.

"Are you sure?"

"Sure," he said, rolling up his sleeves. "Have you eaten?"

"I was thinking of ordering a pizza."

"Great," he said. "My treat. You order it, and I'll see if I can get the rest of this up before it comes."

The misery in her expression lightened as she smiled and limped to the telephone. "You're a lifesaver, Larry. I didn't think I could tackle this myself."

It didn't take him long to scrub the stains out of the carpet and sweep up the rest of the glass, but as he did he kept remembering Mrs. Berkley's insistence that she'd heard the crashing lamps and tables *after* Soames had left.

"Melissa," he asked later, over the pizza, "did you have any other visitors last night, other than Soames?"

"No," she said. "And he wasn't exactly a visitor."

"Someone else from the apartments, maybe? Did a neighbor next door stop in? Anybody?"

"No. Nobody."

He studied the pepperoni on his slice again. "Did I tell you I met Mrs. Berkley?"

Melissa smiled. "She's a sweet lady, isn't she?"

"Tell me about her."

Melissa set her pizza down and wiped her fingers on her napkin. "She's been like a grandmother to me. It's been nice to have her around, since my parents are so far away. She's always baking me cakes and cookies, and telling me wild stories about all the neighbors."

"Wild stories? How do you mean?"

She shrugged. "Oh, you know. She doesn't really have much to do all day, so I think she spends a lot of her time imagining what everyone else is doing. And like anyone who lives in their imagination, she gets her facts mixed up. Just last week, she swore that my next-door neighbor in 2B—a forty-eight-year-old widow—had given birth to a little boy. I told her she couldn't have, that she wasn't pregnant, but Mrs. Berkley insisted. Later I found out that the niece of one of the neighbors on the first floor had a baby boy, and she's been visiting. So someone had a baby, all right; it just wasn't who Mrs. Berkley thought it was."

I knew it, Larry thought. The woman wasn't a competent witness. She was mistaken.

"So what did she tell you?" Melissa asked. "Did she see Soames last night?"

"Yeah, she saw him."

That tense look worked back over Melissa's face. "I thought so. She sees everybody."

"Yeah." He felt sorry now that he'd doubted her, that Tony's suspicions had infected him. Something definitely had happened to her. That haunted look in her eye had come from somewhere. And anyway, he couldn't believe that she would simply make up a story like this and put herself through this ordeal for no good reason. She had studied criminal justice; she had to know what this would cost her in emotional stress once it went to trial. No one would subject themselves to that unless they were telling the truth.

She ignored her pizza now, and he wished he hadn't brought the subject up again. Quiet settled over them, and that sad, grieving look in her eyes touched him. There must be some way to assuage that, he thought.

"Listen," he said, sighing. "You need to get out of this place. Just relax a little. Get your mind off things. What if I took you to a movie?"

She smiled softly. "Is that part of your job description?"

He shook his head. "Consider me off duty. This is just pleasure."

Her smile found its way to her eyes, and it was like sunshine reaching a chilled heart. "I'm assuming you aren't married, Detective?"

He shook his head. "You're assuming right."

"Then I guess it would be nice."

Mrs. Berkley was watching at the bottom of the stairs as they left. "Did you find a babysitter for the baby tonight?" the little woman asked her.

Melissa looked confused, then amused. "I'm not the one who had the baby, Mrs. Berkley. Remember? It was Mrs. Jasper's niece."

"That's right," the woman said. "Well, you two go on and have a nice evening, now. And be careful."

"We will," Melissa said. "And Mrs. Berkley, please keep your door locked."

"I always do," she said, though it stood wide open at the moment. "Good-bye, Detective."

Larry waved good-bye, feeling relieved that their witness's word wasn't worth much. If only he could convince Tony of that.

He could see that the movie had done her good. For two hours, she had been allowed to forget her problems, dismiss Soames from her mind, and pretend that she was someone else in another life. Now, as they flowed with the crowd toward the exit doors, he saw the shadow creeping back over her face, and how she glanced from side to side, as if expecting Soames to come out of nowhere.

Feeling protective, he reached out and took her hand. It was small, ice-cold, trembling slightly. Trying to decide what would help her right now, he asked, "Would you like to go get a cup of coffee?"

"Sounds good," she said.

He took her to a little café with lush plants spilling from windowsills and cascading down walls. A man with a goatee and a ponytail played an acoustic guitar in the corner, and they sat in a booth near the back and talked about the movie, then about favorite movies they'd seen growing up.

"My sister and I used to spend every Saturday afternoon at the movies," Melissa said. "Half our allowance went for that each week. We would laugh and cry—and when we cried, neither of us would look at the other, because we knew not to destroy the mood. Sandy was good about that."

Larry was confused. Hadn't she said she had no siblings? "Where's Sandy now?" he asked carefully.

Her smile faded, and she seemed to grow even paler. "She died. About three years ago." Tears welled in her eyes, turning the rims red as she looked away. Quickly, she changed the subject. "Do you come here a lot?"

Though she tried to look bright, the tears were still in her eyes, making her look even more fragile. "No, I don't come here much. I work a lot at night. It's nice, though."

"My father plays guitar," she said, watching the man in the corner as he strummed. "He used to play and we'd all sing with him. He taught me how to play the ukulele when I was little, but I only knew one song. I tried the guitar, but wasn't willing to practice."

Her rambling reminded him of a hamster on a treadmill, running as fast as it could without moving an inch. It was as if one moment's silence would break her completely. Even so, he listened carefully; each rambling revelation provided another clue to the woman who fascinated him.

"Do you play anything?" she asked. She had skillfully blinked back her tears by now, and she didn't look quite as forlorn. Trying to lighten things, he said, "I play softball. But no instrument."

"Softball, huh? For a team?"

"Yeah. A church team, during the summer. I can't make every game, because I have to work so much. We're not a very good team. We manage to snatch defeat from the jaws of victory pretty regularly."

She smiled—a distant, pensive smile. "I played for a while last summer, when I worked for the FBI."

The subject of her job with the FBI had seemed taboo earlier in the day when he had asked about her criminal justice degree, but now he seized the opportunity to ask the question that had been plaguing him. "Why did you quit? That sounds like an ideal job for a criminal justice major just out of college."

She breathed a laugh that said he was naive. "I was at the very bottom of the totem pole. It was drudgery. Mostly clerical work, and the pay stinks. I hated the job, and when I looked around me at the career FBI agents, I just decided that that's not what I wanted to do for the rest of my life." She looked up at him then, her eyes locked with his, and she smiled a little. "No offense, but criminal justice was a mistake for me. So I quit and took a job doing something else until I could decide what I really wanted to do. I should have just answered your question this morning, but I was upset."

"Why did you move here, though?"

She was getting tense again. "I was having trouble living in Pensacola, with all the memories—I missed my sister, okay?" Her voice cracked. "I thought if I started over someplace else . . ."

"But you graduated from Florida State, in Tallahassee. Why didn't you just stay there?"

"I wanted someplace completely new," she said. "St. Clair seemed like the perfect little town."

"It can be." He made his voice gentle and soft as he reached across the table and touched her hand. "You're not on the witness stand, Melissa."

"I know. It's just—" She smiled slightly, then brought those big eyes up to him again. "You've been so nice to me today, so I wanted to explain. I really don't know if I could have gotten through the day without you. It's weird, too. I mean, this morning, you showed up exactly when I needed you to, when I was about to lose it. And then again tonight, facing that mess—I can't believe you showed up when you did."

"I had you on my mind. I thought you could use a friend. You seemed pretty alone."

She seemed troubled by that thought. Letting go of his hand, she folded her arms across her stomach, looked away, and said, "I haven't had time to make many friends since I moved here."

"Why not?" Larry asked.

"Because . . ." Her voice quivered, and she cleared her throat and tried again. "I guess it's hard for me to get close to people."

He believed it. Melissa seemed like a loner who didn't like to be alone. Much like him.

"I've always found church to be a good place to make friends. It takes a while, but the friends I've made there will last my whole life."

She struggled against tears. "I don't belong in church. Sometimes I'm pretty sure that God is disgusted with me."

"Why?"

She wiped her eyes, smearing her tears. "What's the verse I learned when I was a kid in Bible school? 'He is of purer eyes than to even look upon iniquity.' Sometimes God turns away."

"But why would he turn away from you, Melissa? What happened last night wasn't your choice."

"I know he has, though." Struggling to fight her tears, she said, "There are things that happen, Larry. Horrible things. If God was there—if he was watching, he would stop them. When he doesn't, then I know he isn't even watching."

Larry only stared at her, feeling moisture in his own eyes as his emotions responded to hers. To tell her that she was reacting inappropriately to her own suffering would be insensitive. Who was he to say? He had never been violated in the way she had. He said nothing, unable to find words that weren't trite and pat.

"There was something that happened in my family," she whispered, covering half her face with one hand as she uncovered part of the horror that lay hidden inside her. "Something terrible. And I wanted so much to believe that God would take care of it. But he didn't."

Larry could think of no way to break the silence as he watched her struggle with her grief.

"Maybe I'm the one hiding from God," she said finally. "Maybe I've just moved too far to ever get back. There does come a point when you've moved too far."

Larry reached across the table and pushed back a strand of her hair caught in her tears. "I hope I'm around when God proves to you that you're wrong."

"I wish . . ." she started to say, but her words broke off.

She looked down at her hands as more tears fell; finally, she drew in a deep, cleansing breath. "Can we go now?"

They were quiet as they drove back to her apartment, and when they got there she was out of the car before he had even cut the engine off. Larry hopped out and caught up to her. "Let me walk you up."

She nodded and slowed her step then, and he put his arm around her and escorted her up the steps. Mrs. Berkley's door was open an inch or so as they walked by.

Melissa reached into her purse for her keys when they got to her door, but those tears were still coming, and Larry didn't know what to do for her. He took the key from her hand, opened the door, then stood in front of her for a moment, wondering what he could offer her to relieve the pain. "I know things look dark now," he whispered, "but they're going to get better. And if you need to talk, day or night, you can call me. Remember that."

She wilted as he pulled her into a crushing hug, and her arms closed around his neck. For a while, he just held her there, trying to give her support and hope and help as he felt the force of her sobs shaking her body. Some part of his heart wept with her, and his own eyes filled with tears.

When she pulled back, he touched her face. "Are you going to be all right?"

"Yes," she whispered. "Thank you for the shoulder."

"Anytime. That's what it's there for."

She drew in a long breath and looked up at him. "You make me feel safe."

"Good," he said. "That's my job."

"You do it very well." She smiled and almost laughed then, the kind of laughter that often follows weeping, and took a deep breath. "Good night."

He wanted to kiss her but knew it wouldn't be appropriate. Not the night after she was assaulted, not the moment after she'd found comfort weeping on his shoulder. Instead, he whispered, "Good night."

She went inside and closed the door, and he stood listening as she locked two bolts. He started down the stairs, then stopped and pulled one of his cards out of his wallet. It already included his extension at the precinct, so he turned it over and jotted his home and cellular phone numbers down. Then he went back to her apartment and slipped it under her door.

When he reached the bottom of the stairs, Mrs. Berkley was still peering out of a one-inch opening in her door. "Good night, Mrs. Berkley," he called.

"Good night, Detective Millsaps," she replied with perfect clarity. "Be careful driving home."

Larry frowned all the way out to his car, wondering how she'd remembered his name. Maybe she flowed in and out of confusion, sometimes getting things right, sometimes not. Still, it disturbed him.

Tony was going to hit the ceiling anyway, when he heard what Larry had done with his evening.

8

"YOU'RE LOSING YOUR edge." Tony plopped into the extra chair at Larry's desk.

"What?"

"You heard me. I went by Mrs. Berkley's again today. I wanted to ask her a couple more questions, and she told me something very interesting."

Larry knew where this was going. He leaned back in his chair and waited. "Yeah? What?"

"She told me that you took Melissa Nelson out last night."

"It wasn't a date. And Mrs. Berkley is loony. She floats in and out of reality. We can't count on her story at all."

Tony wouldn't let him change the subject. "Did you or didn't you take Melissa Nelson out last night?"

He shifted uncomfortably. "I went by to see her, okay? I helped her clean up. And she needed to get out of the apartment, so I took her."

"On a date."

Larry stacked some loose papers on his desk. A telephone at the next desk rang. He wished it were his. "Call it what you want, Tony."

Tony leaned forward, fixing his eyes on his partner's. "Tell me the truth, Larry. You were disturbed by what Mrs. Berkley told us, right? And also by the stuff we found out yesterday about Melissa's job. You wanted to get to the bottom of it, and that's why you went to see her last night."

Larry dropped the papers and began rubbing his temples. "Okay, yeah. And I did get to the bottom of it. She didn't like criminal justice, once she started working in it. That happens. She decided to take a job doing clerical work until she could figure out what she wanted to do. And her sister had died, she was having trouble with the memories, and that's why she came here."

"A sister, huh?" Tony pulled a pad out of his pocket and jotted that down.

"What? Do you think she's lying about that, too?"

"Just gonna check," Tony said. "By the way, we have to testify for the grand jury day after tomorrow. Did you know that?"

"Yeah." Larry looked at him again. "And what are you gonna say, Tony? You gonna go in there and tell them that, despite what you saw that night, despite all the evidence we found, you think she's lying?"

Tony breathed a laugh. "Man, I'm telling you again. You're losing your edge. When's the last time I sat on a witness stand and told them whether I thought someone was lying or not? I'm being called to talk about the evidence, not my gut feelings."

"Good. Because your gut feelings are wrong."

A police radio on the hip of an officer nearby blared, adding to the grating noise of a teletype printing out a report.

Tony got up and looked down at his friend. "You're getting involved with her, buddy. And that's a big mistake."

"I don't do things the way you do, Tony. You've known that for a long time. I don't have to account to you or anyone else on this force for my personal life."

"Fine," Tony said. "I hope you don't have to eat those words."

Larry watched Tony go back to his desk, then stared for a while at his blank computer screen. Things had been tense between them ever since they'd met Melissa Nelson, but that wasn't his fault. Tony wanted to victimize the victim, and Larry wasn't going to let him. It was as simple as that.

Still, he thought, it probably would be better if he didn't keep seeing Melissa. Though he would never admit it to Tony, she *was* getting under his skin, and that wasn't good. Later, after the case was laid to rest, maybe he could explore those feelings again.

He got up and went into the interrogation room, the only quiet place in the building. He stared out the window at what he could see of downtown St. Clair. He watched as citizens walked by on the sidewalk, trusting the officers in this building to keep them safe.

Was Tony right? Was he slipping? Was this protective feeling toward Melissa compromising his police work?

Maybe it was, he admitted reluctantly. Starting now, he had to put it behind him. He wouldn't call Melissa Nelson again.

Melissa was trembling, two days later, as she sat on the witness stand in front of the grand jury that would decide whether Edward Soames would stand trial. Under oath, she told them her whole story—the way he'd shown up unexpectedly and shoved his way in, the struggle that had ensued as she'd tried to defend herself, the knife with which he'd cut her, his ultimate violation of her. She cried as she spoke, thankful that he wasn't in the courtroom, since defendants weren't allowed in a grand jury hearing. If he'd been sitting there, it would have been so hard . . .

But his attorney was there, and as he cross-examined her, she tried not to back up or stumble, tried not to sway at all or deviate from what she'd told them at first. When he suggested that she'd had a crush on Soames, she knew her repulsion was apparent on her face. He'd then gone on to badger her about inviting him to dinner—apparently Gretchen at work had testified before her—but his merciless bullying of her had only made him look like another monster, and her a victim suffering further abuse.

By the time they dismissed her, she was weak and exhausted. And the first person she saw outside the courtroom was Larry.

Needing his strong shoulder, she wilted into him, and he slid his arms around her and let her cry. "Are you okay?"

"Yeah," she whispered. "It was just . . . I don't know if they believed me. His lawyer was putting so many lies into their heads." She wiped her eyes and stepped back. "Will you wait with me until they give the verdict? I don't think I can stand to be by myself right now."

"Sure," he said, unable to deny her such a simple and heartfelt request. "I'll wait."

It was a couple of hours before the DA came out of the courtroom and found them sitting together. "Well, we have some good news and some bad news," he said.

Melissa looked up, bracing herself. "Was he indicted?"

"Yes, he was," he said. "But the bad news is that the judge let him out on $100,000 bond, pending trial."

Melissa sprang up. "He did *what?*"

"I'm sorry, Melissa. I tried my best to convince him that it would be dangerous to let him out, but he said that it could take a year for it to come to trial, and he didn't want to lock him up for that amount of time."

"He's getting out? When?"

"Probably today," he said.

Feeling as blindsided as she did by this, Larry stood up beside her. "Melissa," he tried, "you know he'd be crazy to come near you. He knows what the consequences would be."

"He *is* crazy! Don't you people get it? He's going to come after me!"

"No, he won't," the DA said. "The judge laid down very specific instructions. He told him he'd throw him back in jail if he so much as thought about you."

"This man doesn't care what a judge told him!" Melissa insisted, starting to cry. "I'm telling you, this is a big mistake! He could kill me the next time!" She headed back toward the courtroom. "Where's the judge? I have to talk to him!"

Larry grabbed her arm. "Melissa, you can't. There's nothing you can do. But I agree with Sid. I don't think he'll bother you."

"You don't *think?*" she shouted. "Well, what if you're wrong?"

Jerking away from him, she turned and ran toward the door that would take her into the parking garage. Helpless, Larry just let her go.

She spent the rest of the afternoon hunting for a new place to live, then packing all of her belongings and moving. The move would wipe out her savings. And she hadn't yet found another job. But it was the only way she could evade the man who would kill her if he found her.

Now, in her new apartment in a building several blocks away from her old one, she found herself still uneasy. As night had fallen and she'd made the last trip from her old apartment, she'd had the uneasy, panicky feeling that someone was watching her.

She locked the dead bolt, checked every window, then sat on the couch, her back straight, eyes darting about. It *was* safer, she told herself. Much safer. Too afraid to sleep in her bed, which sat right below a window, she tried to sleep on the couch, curled up in a fetal position.

And all night, she clutched a knife in her hand.

9

ACROSS THE STREET, in a phone booth that gave him a perfect view of the second-floor window of Melissa's new apartment, Edward Pendergrast, alias Soames, dialed the long-distance number he'd gotten from information. Keeping an eye on the window, he waited for it to ring once . . . twice . . . three times.

"Hello?"

It was the just-awakened voice of an older woman, probably in her fifties, and he got a mental picture of her right away—martyred, long-suffering, self-righteous. It pleased him to death to bring her in on this now.

"Hello?" she said again.

"Mrs. Nelson?" he asked.

"Yes."

"Is this the Mrs. Nelson who's the mother of Melissa Nelson?"

"Yes," she said tentatively. "Do you know my daughter?"

"Do I know your daughter." He chuckled then, and looked back at the window. "Yeah, I'd say I know your daughter. Listen, I need to get in touch with her. Can you help me?"

The woman hesitated. "Well, I'd be happy to give her a message for you."

"I'd rather call her myself," he said.

Again, hesitation. "Would you like to leave a message? I'll get it to her tomorrow."

He grinned. She probably didn't know that her daughter had just moved. Wouldn't she be surprised to hear why? "Yeah, okay. Give her a message. Tell her an old friend called. She'll know who it is."

"Uh—may I tell her your name?"

"Just tell her that," he said. "Tell her I've been looking for her."

"Would you like to leave a number?"

He smiled. "She knows how to reach me."

He hung up then, and laughed out loud at the conversation that was probably taking place between Melissa's parents. Her father would probably grill her mother over and over on what had been said, then convince her that it had no significance. It was just some prankster. Within minutes, they'd roll over and try to get back to sleep.

But they wouldn't get a lot of sleep tonight.

His grin faded as he stepped out of the phone booth and crossed the street. If there was a weakness in that building, he would find it. And tomorrow, he'd have a huge new surprise for her.

The phone rang again, startling Nancy Nelson awake for the second time that night. She looked over at her husband, who was squinting to read the clock. "Three A.M.," he said.

She reached for the phone. "Hello?"

"Hi. Me again."

It was the voice of the man who'd called earlier—the old friend of Melissa. Covering the phone, she whispered, "It's the same person."

Jim sat up.

"Did you give Melissa my message?" the deep voice asked.

"No," she said. "It was late. I'll tell her tomorrow."

"That's okay," he said. "I've found her."

Something about the way he said that sent chills down her spine. "What do you mean, you've found her?"

"If you talk to her, Mrs. Nelson, tell her that she can't hide."

She caught her breath, and Jim snatched the phone away. "Who is this?" he shouted. "What do you want?"

"Ask Melissa," he said. "She knows what I want."

They heard a *click*, then a dial tone.

Jim got up and turned on the lamp.

"What are you doing?" Nancy asked, getting out of bed and reaching for her robe.

"Calling Melissa," he said.

"But it's three A.M. You'll wake her."

"I don't care," he said. "Something's wrong. She needs to know about this call."

Nancy went to sit beside him on the bed, and he reached for her hand and held it in a reassuring grip as he waited for Melissa to answer.

The ringing was interrupted by three ascending tones and an operator's voice. "I'm sorry. The number you have dialed has been disconnected . . ."

He slowly lowered the receiver. "Disconnected," he said. "Where is she?"

Nancy raked her hand through her hair. "Jim, you don't think—"

Jim got up and went to the closet, flicked on the light. "Get dressed. We're driving down to St. Clair."

"But it's 400 miles!" Nancy said, reaching for the phone. "I'm calling the St. Clair police. She may need help now."

Jim nodded. "If only we knew some of her friends to call. People she works with."

He waited as she got the St. Clair police on the phone and asked them to check on Melissa. When she hung up, she was just as troubled as she had been when she'd called.

"What did they say?" he asked.

Nancy shook her head as she began to get dressed. "They said they'd go check on her and ask her to call us. And they advised us not to make the 400 mile trip until we'd tried to reach her at work. But tomorrow's Saturday, and even if she does have to work, she won't be in for another five hours. Something could happen to her before that."

Nancy threw some clothes into a suitcase while Jim closed and locked the windows. Keys in hand, Jim grabbed the suitcase. "We'll stop at a pay phone and call home every hour or so and see if the police have left a message on our machine," he said.

"Okay," Nancy agreed. Grabbing her purse, she dashed out behind him to the car.

10

THE NEXT DAY, tired from the fitful sleep of the night before, when she'd stirred at every noise—ever aware that she had no phone hooked up with which to call for help if he somehow found her—Melissa went to a pay phone and had the telephone at her new address hooked up with an unlisted number. They gave her the new number and told her it would be on later that day. While she was at the pay phone, she called her parents to tell them her new number.

No one was home, so she left a message, explaining that she'd gotten aggravated at her landlord because of a leaky sink, and had moved to a new apartment. She had also taken a new job, she lied—to keep them from trying to reach her at work—and she'd let them know soon what that number was.

Then she set out to make truth out of her lie, checking the want ads for a job.

It was nine o'clock when the Nelsons pulled over to a pay phone for the fifth time since leaving home and called home for messages. Jim caught his breath when he heard Melissa's voice. "It's her!" he told his wife. "Listen."

Nancy put her ear next to his and listened to their daughter's explanation. Her voice sounded calm, not troubled, and everything made sense. She would be out this morning, she told them, but would call them tonight after her phone was turned on and update them on everything.

As Jim hung up the phone, they fell into each other's arms, laughing with relief. "She's okay!" Nancy cried. "She's fine."

"Now what?" Jim asked. "We're only a couple of hours away from St. Clair. Should we go on? Maybe she needs help moving."

"She didn't leave her address," Nancy said. "We wouldn't know how to find her. Besides, there's no need to let her know how badly we overreacted. Let's just go back home and wait until she calls tonight."

Jim thought that over. "I guess you're right."

The two parents got back into their car and headed back the way they had come.

Melissa managed to find a job doing clerical work for a chemical company, a job that didn't pay very well, but which seemed to be located in a safe place. It was a plus that they would let her start Monday. The sooner, the better, she thought.

It was almost dark when she got home and checked her phone to see if it was on yet. It was, so she dialed her parents' number, then cradled the phone between her ear and shoulder as she began to unpack one of her boxes.

"Hello?" Her mother's voice was always a sweet sound.

"Mom? It's me."

"Melissa, thank heaven! It's so good to hear your voice. We tried calling you last night, but the operator said your phone had been disconnected."

"Didn't you get my message this morning?"

"Yes, but until then . . ." She let her voice trail off and sighed. "Well, we're just glad you're all right. After those phone calls, we were beside ourselves."

Melissa frowned. "What phone calls?"

"Some man called last night. He was really kind of scary. At first he said he was an old friend, but I don't think he was a friend at all."

Melissa could feel the blood draining from her face, and she slowly sat down. "Mom, who was the man?"

"'An old friend' was all he said. We were going to come down and look for you, but then we got your message this morning. Melissa, are you all right?"

She clutched the phone so tight her knuckles were turning white. "Mom, what did he say?"

"The first time, he just asked us if we knew how he could get in touch with you. He said he was an old friend, but he was a little rude, calling so late. But we wouldn't give him your number. Then he hung up, and a little later he called back and told me that he'd found you. He said to tell you you can't hide. Melissa, do you know who he is?"

Melissa swallowed hard, and her heart began to race. He knew who she really was, she thought frantically. He had called her parents.

He had figured it out.

"Melissa?"

She tried to steady her voice. "Mom, it's this guy I worked with." She stopped, tried to regroup her thoughts and manufacture the story as she went. "He kept coming onto me, and when I wouldn't go out with him, he got a little hostile." She closed her eyes and tried to stop trembling. "He's harmless, really. Just annoying. Whatever he says, just ignore it."

"So hostile that you had to change your phone number, your address, your job?"

Her hand was trembling so hard she could hardly hold the phone. Maybe her explanation had been too frightening. She'd have to tone it down. "I told you why I moved, Mom. The manager wouldn't fix my sink. And the job . . . well, it just wasn't what I wanted. None of it had anything to do with him. Mom, did he say anything else?"

"No," Nancy said. "But, Melissa, what is this about your hiding? What was he talking about?"

Dizziness washed over her, along with an overwhelming feeling that she wasn't alone. She looked around slowly, warily, as if he were in the apartment somewhere, listening to this call.

"Melissa?"

"Yeah, Mom. Uh . . ." She tried to backtrack through the conversation, to give the response her mother needed. "I don't know what he was talking about. I told you, he's just some idiot. Probably drank too much and thought he'd get a good laugh." She knew her voice was trembling, and she was giving away too much, alarming her mother.

"Melissa, are you sure you're all right? Maybe you should come home for a while."

"No, I can't, Mom. I have to stay."

Her mother was crying now, and she could hear the subtle difference in her breathing, the grainy sound to her voice. "But this is how it happened before . . ."

As hard as she'd tried to shelter them from this, she was causing them grief anyway.

"Melissa?" Her father had taken the phone, and Melissa knew she couldn't hide anything from him without a Herculean effort. Trying to sound upbeat, she said, "Hi, Dad."

"Honey, I want you to tell me the truth. Is something wrong? Are you in some kind of danger?"

"No," she said. "Really. Everything's fine. I just moved yesterday, so my phone was disconnected. Dad, those phone calls—they're just a guy at work." As she spoke, she broke into a sweat. Slowly, she walked into the bedroom, looked nervously around, then cautiously checked the closet. "It's really no big deal. His pride is hurt because I wouldn't go out with him . . ." The bedroom was empty, so she walked out of it, crossed the living room, and went into the kitchen.

"Melissa, I got a recording device today. I'm going to tape the calls from now on. Maybe you should too."

"Just relax, okay? Stop worrying. I have everything under control."

"Melissa, does this person have something to do with why you moved so suddenly?"

She hated lying to her parents, but she had no choice. "No. I told you. My sink was stopped up, and the manager wouldn't fix it. I got fed up and moved. No big deal."

The kitchen was clear, so she headed for the bathroom. "Dad, I love you. Tell Mom I love her, too. And calm down. I'm sorry about the calls, but they really don't mean anything."

"All right, honey. But if we get any more calls, we're going to . . ."

She stepped cautiously into the bathroom as her father continued to talk. The shower curtain was closed, and she couldn't remember closing it herself. Her heart began to palpitate, and her blouse began to stick to her. Clutching the phone tighter, she grabbed the edge of the curtain and jerked it open.

Empty.

Breathing a sigh of relief, she turned slowly around and leaned against the sink. This was crazy. He couldn't know where she was. He couldn't know *who* she was. It was just a coincidence. The caller was someone else.

"Melissa, did you hear me?"

"Yes, Dad. You said if you got any more call—"

Her voice stopped cold as she looked up and saw the writing on her mirror, big red letters made with the lipstick she had left on the sink that morning. She gasped and jumped back, and her throat constricted.

"Melissa? What is it?"

She couldn't speak, couldn't breathe, couldn't think. For a moment, she only stared at the words, bold and big:

Next time for real.

In a high-pitched, breathless, wavering voice, she managed to get the words out. "Dad, I've got to go. Bathtub—overflowing—"

She turned the phone off and dropped it, then grabbed her purse and her keys and fled the apartment.

11

LARRY WAS EATING a TV dinner and watching the news when a sudden banging on his door startled him. He grabbed his gun, which he'd laid on the table, and approached the door quickly but cautiously, sliding along the wall.

Through the peephole he saw Melissa and threw the door open.

Sobbing hysterically, she grabbed him and spoke so rapidly that he could barely understand her. "Help me! He was there. In my new apartment. I don't know how he found it, but he was in there. He wrote on my mirror, Larry! I'm not safe anywhere!"

He pulled her in and made her sit. Kneeling in front of her, he tried to calm her. "Tell me again. Who was there? Soames?"

"Yes!" she cried. "I moved yesterday, but he found me." She grabbed both of his arms. "He was in my apartment, Larry! He wrote in lipstick on my mirror. And he's been calling my parents! I don't know what to do. There's no place to go!"

Larry got up, pulled on his shoulder holster, slipped his gun into it, then put his windbreaker on. "All right, let's go back over there, and you can show me. What did he write?"

"He wrote, 'Next time for real.' I don't know what he means, Larry. But how could he have gotten in? Nobody knew where I was. Not even you!"

"All right. I'm gonna call Tony and have him meet us there. If we can find proof that he was in your apartment, we'll have him picked up again. This joker's going back to the slammer until his trial."

She was a wreck, Larry thought as they drove back to her building. What if he'd been in her apartment while she was home? What if he was still there now? Would he be that bold? That stupid?

Tony was waiting in his car when they drove up, and he got out and met them at the curb. Melissa was shaking and staring up at the window to her apartment.

"She says he was there," Larry said quietly. "Left a message on her mirror, in lipstick."

"Would he be that reckless?" Tony whispered.

"Looks like he was." He turned back to Melissa. "If you want to wait in the car—"

"No!" she said quickly. "I don't want to be by myself. I'm coming with you. I'll show you where it is."

They opened the door quietly and carefully—not wanting to disturb any fingerprints he might have left—pulled their guns, and went in. Melissa waited by the front door as they searched the apartment. Satisfied that he wasn't there, they came to the bathroom. "Was it in here?"

"Yes," she said, hanging back. "On the mirror."

There was a moment of silence, then Larry asked, "Did you clean it off?"

"What?" She abandoned the front door and went in to see for herself.

The mirror was clean.

"No, it was there! Right there, in big letters!" She gasped and backed out of the bathroom. "Oh, no—he was back! He came back while I was gone. Or maybe he was here all the time! Larry, you have to believe me! He's playing games with me. He was here! Dust for fingerprints! You'll see."

But she could see that Tony didn't believe a word, and Larry looked troubled and confused. "Melissa," Larry said, "are you sure you didn't clean it before you came over? You were upset. You might have—"

"No! I was on the phone with my father, and I dropped the phone. See? Here it is." She picked it up off the floor. "And then I ran out." She turned to Tony. "Please, I'm telling you—he was here. You have to pick him up. You have to get him back in jail, or he'll kill me."

"Is that what it meant—'Next time for real'?" Larry asked. "That he would kill you next time?"

"It must have," she agreed quickly. "And how did he get in here? The windows are all locked. I had the door dead-bolted. And how did he find this apartment? He must have been watching me when I moved out—stalking me."

Tony looked at the mirror again. "Is this the lipstick you said he wrote it with?"

She nodded, and Tony picked up the tube with a piece of tissue, opened it, and rolled the lipstick up. The tip was flat, as if it had been used for writing. Even so, Tony shook his head. "It doesn't make sense. Why would he risk coming back to clean it up? Why would he risk doing it in the first place, when he knows he's the first person we'd think of?"

Melissa felt herself trembling with fear and frustration. "Detective Danks, if I were lying about this, I'd have just written something on there myself, and it would still be there. And anyway, why *would* I lie about this? Why would I set myself up to look like a lunatic? I'm telling you, it happened. He came in, he wrote on my mirror, and then he came back—or maybe he was here the whole time. Only—I looked in every room before I saw the mirror. He wasn't here."

Larry left the bathroom and began looking around the apartment. After a moment, he said, "Tony, come look at this."

Tony and Melissa followed him. He stood at the far end of the hallway, pointing at a rectangular wooden door set into the ceiling. "It's an attic," Tony whispered.

Larry questioned Tony with his eyes. Could Soames be hiding there?

"Have you looked up there?" Larry whispered to Melissa.

"No. I didn't even know it was there."

"Do you have a flashlight?"

"Yes," she said, and ran to get it. When she came back, she saw that they were both preparing to open the ceiling door. "Stand back," Larry said, and pulled out his gun again. Tony did the same. Larry reached up and grabbed the hook on the door, and Tony held his gun aimed at it in one hand, the flashlight in the other.

In one rapid motion, Larry pulled the door down. They held their guns aimed for a moment, but nothing happened. Slowly, carefully, Larry reached up and unfolded the narrow ladder. Tony shone the flashlight through the black hole, revealing how small the space was.

Cautiously, Larry climbed the stairs, still aiming his gun, and stepped onto the board floor of the small crawl space. It was big enough for a man to sit in, he thought, though there was no sign that anyone had been here. He touched the floor, felt the dust, then had an idea. Stepping back onto the ladder so that only half his body intruded into the dark space, he shone the light around on the floor. A thick coating of dust covered it, but where he had just stood the dust clearly showed his footprints. He looked carefully around for any more disturbances in the dust.

There it was—the faint outline of the bottom of a sneaker. Beyond that was a wiped place, as if someone had slid across the floor.

"Tony, there's dust all over the place up here," he called down. "But in one place, it's wiped up. Like somebody was sitting there. And there's a shoe print in the dust."

"Let me see."

They traded places. "I see what you're talking about," Tony said, "but it could just be where the previous tenants had a box or something sitting."

"The edges aren't that clean," Larry said. "Looks to me like someone was sitting there."

Larry watched as Tony crawled farther into the attic, shining the light all around. After a moment, he came back to the opening. "Larry, come up here. You've got to see this."

Larry glanced at Melissa. She stood trembling at the end of the hallway, hugging herself and waiting. As Larry began to climb, she took a few steps closer to the ladder.

Tony was shining the light at a place on the attic floor. It was an opening around one of the inset lights in the ceiling of the bathroom. The plate that had been on the back was missing, as was the bulb, and they could see through the glass covering straight into Melissa's bathroom, to the sink and mirror and the area in front of them.

"Still skeptical?" Larry asked.

Tony shook his head. "He was here, all right," he said in a voice too low for her to hear, "watching her discover what he wrote on the mirror."

"Let's dust the apartment for prints."

"Okay. But what about her? He'll be back."

"She can't stay here tonight," Larry said. "I'll think of something."

They climbed back down, then both hesitated to tell her what they'd found.

"Well?" she asked.

"It looks like he might have been up there while you were here," Larry said. "He probably left because he knew you were going to get help."

The color drained from her face. "But he'll come back! He'll come back!"

"We're going to call the ID techs to come dust for prints, Melissa. As soon as we run it through the computer and make a match, we can get him."

She waited, tense and quiet, as the apartment filled up with police photographers and ID technicians. As they dusted for prints, she sat like a little child waiting to be told her fate.

"He was probably wearing gloves," Larry said. "But maybe not."

"He's smart," Melissa said in a hopeless monotone. "He knows you need evidence. He knows what kind. So as long as he doesn't leave any, he can do whatever he wants."

"We'll pick him up anyway," Larry said. "For questioning. We'll put a little scare into him."

"But can't we just tell the judge he was here? Can't we tell him Soames called my parents?"

"It wouldn't help," Larry said. "Not unless we could prove he was here with a print match."

She ran her fingers through her bangs. "I can't stay here. I don't know where to go."

Larry looked at Tony and saw the censure in his eyes, as if he knew that Larry would jump in and rescue her. Larry didn't let it stop him.

"I could take you to a hotel for the night."

She thought for a moment. "I guess so. I'm just afraid that he'll find me there, too. I can't believe he found me this time, and so soon."

"Look, we'll send someone now to pick him up for questioning. We won't move you until we have him in custody. That way we'll know that he can't follow you."

"All right," she said. "But then what? I can't come back here."

"I'll talk to the manager about letting you put your own dead bolts on the door, so that there isn't an extra key anywhere. And we'll go around and reinforce the windows, make absolutely sure that they can't be broken into. Maybe even put up burglar bars."

"I never thought I'd wind up being a prisoner in my own apartment," she whispered.

"We'll put enough fear into him that he won't come near you. I'll even tell him he's being watched."

"You said that before. But he didn't care."

"He'll care this time. And who knows? Maybe tomorrow we can find a witness who saw him around here. And the pattern of that shoe print was pretty distinctive. If we can find that shoe, maybe it'll be enough evidence to convince a judge he was here."

She nodded without much hope. "I'll go pack a few things," she said, and disappeared to the back.

Larry turned back to Tony. "All right, I know what you're thinking."

"She does have to have a safe place to stay," Tony conceded. "But try not to get too involved."

"Don't worry about it." Larry picked up the phone, dialed the station, and asked to have Soames picked up for questioning.

Melissa came back out with a suitcase, her expression strained and distracted. "You know," he said quietly, "maybe you should go home to Pensacola for a while. Spend some time with your parents."

"No, I can't," she said. "I don't want to drag them into this."

"Into what?" Tony asked.

"Into danger. If he comes after me there—" She stopped and tried to steady her emotions. "My parents still don't know about what happened to me. I can't tell them."

"But won't they hear when it goes to trial?"

She shook her head. "I haven't thought that far in advance. All I know is that they don't have to know yet."

"But if he's calling them, they already are involved."

"I told them it was a prank. I told them my sink was stopped up, and I argued about it with the manager, so I moved. That's all they need to know."

The phone rang, and Larry answered, instead of Melissa. "Yeah? You got him already? He was home?" He shot a look at Tony. "What alibi? Well, how long did she say she'd been there? Well, have you checked *her* out?"

He sighed and rubbed his temples. "Well, take them both in for questioning. And keep them separated, so they don't compare notes. Check her out, to make sure she's not lying for him. Oh, and check to see if she has a roommate or a neighbor, anybody who can confirm how long she's been gone.

"What kind of shoes does he have on, by the way? Yeah, I thought so. Get a picture and a print of the bottom of both shoes, will you? And keep him there until we get there."

He hung up, and Melissa sank down on the couch. "He has an alibi?"

"Some woman he was with. Says he's been with her there in his apartment for the last three hours. But it looks like he's got on our shoes. Anyway, they're keeping him until we can question him, so we have some time to get you to a hotel. He can't follow you."

"All right," she said, grabbing the handle of her suitcase, but Larry took it from her.

"I'll get this," he said. "Are you sure this is all you need?"

She looked around and shivered at the thought that he might have gone through her things. "No," she said. "I'm fine. Let's go."

Larry took her key and locked the door behind them.

12

"WE'VE GOT TO let him go," the officer who had picked up Pendergrast told Tony and Larry when they got back to the precinct. "The woman he was with confirmed his alibi."

Larry glanced into the room where the woman sat. She was several years older than Pendergrast, had garishly dyed hair, and wore cheap, tight clothes. She sat flipping through a magazine, swinging her foot with bored nonchalance and popping her gum. "She's not his type," Larry said.

Tony shrugged. "His type may be anything in a skirt."

"Well, I don't think he found her at that yuppie club you like so much. My guess is he's paying her to be his alibi." He turned back to the cop. "Did you tell her he's been indicted for rape?"

"Yep. She says he's innocent. It really didn't faze her."

"And she insists that he was with her? For how long?"

"Hours."

Tony leaned against his desk and thought that over for a moment. "We don't really know what time he wrote on her mirror. Even with the alibi, he still could have done that. But if Snow White here is telling the truth, he wouldn't have been there to wipe it off while she was coming to find you."

"He's lying," Larry said. "Pendergrast—Soames—whatever his name is, he's lying. And so is the woman."

"Probably. Now prove it."

"The shoe," Larry said, turning back to the cop. "You said his shoe matched the print in the attic?"

"Yeah, but I ran it by the captain. He said it was too weak. Lots of people have that shoe. It might be different if we'd gotten a match on the fingerprints. But just between you and me—" He lowered his voice and looked around to make sure he wasn't being overheard. "That lawyer, McRae, has been raising a huge stink about the department harassing Pendergrast. Says they're thinking about a lawsuit when this is over."

Larry chuckled. "Tell him to stand in line."

"Yeah, well. If it was anybody but McRae. That brutality suit he filed for one of his low life clients a few months ago cost the city a mint."

"Come on," Larry said, disgusted. "It was bogus and McRae knew it. Our guys were trying to restrain an addict so high on PCP he had the strength of a gorilla. That was by the book."

"But besides the money, the bad press hurt. The mayor already called the chief on this, Millsaps. He said if we lock Pendergrast up, it better be on something more than his shoe."

Larry groaned and glanced toward the two-way glass of the interrogation room. "Well, at least we can put some fear into him before we let him go."

McRae and Pendergrast sat talking quietly, their heads together, as Larry and Tony walked in. Pendergrast looked up at them with a smug grin. "Is there a problem, gentlemen?"

Larry propped one foot on a chair and leaned on his knee, fixing his eyes on the man who sat waiting for them to admit defeat. "We're not fooled, Pendergrast. Your little friend in there hasn't convinced us of anything."

"Fine," he said, throwing his arms open. "Then book me. What did you say the charge was? Breaking and entering? Stalking? You do have evidence, don't you? Evidence strong enough to override my alibi?"

Larry gritted his teeth. Ignoring the questions, he said, "We're gonna let you go, Pendergrast."

"Soames," the man corrected.

Larry dropped his foot to the floor and leaned over the table, putting his face inches from Pendergrast. "*I* know who you are, *Pendergrast.* You're a slimy nocturnal rodent who preys on innocent women, and I'm gonna see you put away if it's the last thing I ever do. In the meantime, leave Melissa Nelson alone. Stay away from her, or I'll personally see to it that you regret it for what's left of your pathetic little life. Got that?"

"Is that a threat?" McRae asked.

"You bet it is."

Too disgusted to stay, Larry left the room and headed for his desk. A Federal Express package sat on top of it, its return address from the Santa Rosa County Sheriff's Department. Still seething, he tore it open and pulled out the file on Edward J. Pendergrast.

Tony came out of the interrogation room, smirking as he headed for Larry's desk. "Larry, I think you hurt Pendergrast's feelings. He was downright wounded at what you called him. By the way, are rodents really slimy? I thought they were hairy, but—"

"Take a look at this," Larry cut in, unamused. "Pendergrast's file." Sitting down, he opened it.

Tony grabbed a chair and rolled it over beside him. "Took long enough."

"Yeah, but it's all here. Look at these pictures." Larry picked up one of a young woman with blackened, swollen eyes, a broken jaw, and split, bloody lips. He often saw gruesome pictures, and saw even worse horrors face-to-face at crime scenes, but he never got used to it. And brutality to women always turned his stomach.

He began reading the report. The woman who claimed Pendergrast had raped and beaten her had positively identified him. The report said that he'd been charged and questioned, but that he'd been released due to an illegal search of his apartment.

As if he'd been directly involved in the case, Larry struggled with the indignation rising in his chest.

The next photo showed a full body shot of a woman, her face bruised and cut, her eyes blackened, her lips swollen and bloody, and slashes and bruises up and down her legs and arms. Larry handed the picture to Tony and found the report. In this case, Pendergrast had been acquitted. Despite the victim's insistence that Pendergrast was the man who'd raped and beaten her, the grand jury had felt that there wasn't enough evidence to get a conviction. Anger reddening his face, Larry tossed down the report.

"How could they acquit him? Didn't they see the pictures? She gave a positive ID. How could they ignore that?"

"Apparently there were no fingerprints, no physical evidence at all that he was the one who had done it. Plus he had an alibi," Tony said, reading the report. "The only hard evidence was her identification, but they didn't believe she got a good look at him because it was dark."

"It's the way he looks," Larry said. "He looks too prosperous, too good-looking. If he were a scruffy-looking homeless man with a tattoo, he wouldn't have been acquitted." As he spoke, Larry flipped through the file and found a picture of the girl before the rape. She was pretty and blonde, smiling at the camera, looking nothing like the abused portrait after Pendergrast had made his mark. She looked like a happy young woman with a future. She had probably never even dreamed what would happen to her one day.

"Says here she killed herself shortly after he was acquitted," Tony said matter-of-factly.

"Killed herself?" Larry grabbed back the report, read of the suicide, and felt even sicker as he turned back to her smiling portrait. "What's her name?" he asked wearily.

"Uh . . . Sandra Hayden," Tony said. "She was married, no kids. About twenty-three when it happened." He looked over Larry's shoulder and studied the photo pensively. "I wonder if she killed herself because of the rape."

"Probably," Larry whispered.

Tony flipped further, until he came to the newspaper clipping of her obituary. "Married to Jack Hayden for six months," he read. "Buried in Pensacola where she'd lived all her life."

Larry looked up from the picture. "Did you say Pensacola?" He glanced at the obituary. "That's where Melissa is from."

Tony frowned, trying to put things together. "Pendergrast came from Santa Rosa County. Isn't that near Pensacola?"

"Next county over." Larry read on, intrigued but apprehensive. "Says Sandra Hayden had just started working at a department store in a mall. Noticed the guy following her days before he made a move. He broke in one night when her husband was working the night shift. He apparently beat her and left her for dead." He hesitated, swallowed, then forced himself to go on. "But she woke up after he left, showered and cleaned up everything, then passed out again from loss of blood. She never called the police. Her husband found her near death the next morning and took her to the hospital."

Tony flipped through the file, looking at the other documents. "Here's the police report of her suicide." Larry took it, scanned the contents, then shook his head and dropped it on the desk.

"What?" Tony asked.

Sometimes Larry wished he had a different job. "Her younger sister. That's who found her. She had slit her wrists in the bathtub."

"What a way to say good-bye," Tony muttered.

Larry glanced back at the room where they had interviewed Pendergrast moments ago. "We were too easy on him. He was working us. He knows the system too well."

"He must," Tony agreed. "I can't believe they let him go. We need to talk to Sandra Hayden's family. Find out anything that's not in the report. Anything about him we might need to know. Let me see the obit."

Still deep in his dismal, angry thoughts, Larry slid the newspaper clipping across the desk. "Okay," Tony said, poising his pen to jot down her parents' names. "Nancy and Jim Nelson, of Pensacola."

For a moment the name didn't sink in. It wasn't until Larry watched Tony write it that it penetrated. "Did you say Nelson?" Larry asked, reaching for the obituary.

Tony looked up, the significance of the name finally registering. "What are you thinking?" he asked.

A slow ache began at Larry's temples and spread to his forehead. He took the clipping and began to read. "Sandra was survived by both parents and her younger sister . . ." His voice broke off and the words just waited there like a live grenade.

Tony detonated it. "Melissa Nelson," he said.

Larry felt as if he'd had his body blown up from the inside out. His head throbbed, and he couldn't think.

"Oh, man," Tony said, staring at the words. "I don't believe this."

After a moment, Larry got enough control of his faculties to find his voice. "What does it mean?" he asked in a quietly desperate voice. "Pendergrast rapes and almost kills Melissa's sister. Then he comes after her?"

"Doesn't fit," Tony said, his voice growing less surprised and more excited. "*He* was here first, remember? *She* got a job working where he worked. How could he have orchestrated that?"

"Well, why would *she?*" Larry demanded. "You think a woman who'd seen her sister after she'd been left for dead by some guy would deliberately hang around with him afterward?"

Tony was in his element. This was the kind of mystery he loved to solve, the reason he had become a detective. "All right, let's look at what we've got. This happened three years ago, when Sandra Hayden was twenty-three. Melissa would have been twenty then."

"Right."

"So what *do* we know?" Tony went on, getting to his feet and pacing across the floor as he thought it all out. "We know that Melissa changed her major to criminal justice, right?"

"Yeah, so?"

"Well, maybe that was in response to the fact that the criminal justice system let her down. Or maybe it was out of anger. It's like a person with leukemia who decides to be a doctor. They want to fight the thing that has become their enemy."

Larry hated the high Tony was getting from this. And he hated even more where it was leading.

"So she gets out," Tony continued, "takes a job with the FBI, and uses the resources there to locate the guy who did that to her sister." Tony pointed at the photo.

"Now wait a minute." Larry said, resisting, getting to his feet to relieve his growing tension.

Tony shook his head. "No, listen for a minute. It's just a theory, but it fits. Let's say Melissa was obsessed with finding this guy and getting revenge. Now she knows where Pendergrast is working, what name he's using, everything. So she quits the FBI. You got to admit, that bothered us from the first."

"So you're saying she sought him out, so she could get a job working where he worked?" Larry asked angrily. "Why? To what end?"

Tony studied the picture of Melissa's beaten sister again, then brought his troubled eyes back up to Larry. "What if it was to set up another rape—one with so much evidence that he couldn't walk away from it this time?"

"You're out of your mind," Larry bit out. "She saw what he did to her sister. She would never put herself in the position of letting him do it to her."

"I didn't say she did. I said she set him up. It's the perfect revenge. He winds up getting tried for a crime that he really committed—just not to her—and gets put away. All she has to do is choreograph things a little—plant some evidence here, plant some evidence there. The truth is, this thing might have gone down just like Pendergrast said it did."

"Hold it right there." Larry leaned over his desk, seething. "Look at these pictures. This man is a monster, and you're making *her* out to be the criminal."

"Maybe they're both criminals."

"And what is her crime? Getting raped?"

"No. Lying about it." Some of the other cops were clearly listening, so Tony lowered his voice. "Look, it makes perfect sense." He got up and turned his chair backward and sat back down, but Larry kept standing. "To her, it's justice. He gets put away for something he's really done twice. She makes sure the justice system doesn't drop the ball this time. Just think about it. He probably terrorized her sister until she killed herself, and never served any time for it. Maybe Melissa wanted to set up enough evidence this time that he couldn't go free. Think about the night of the crime. She was so cooperative, so helpful. All the evidence was perfectly laid out—except for one thing. Even knowing all she knows, especially after her sister experienced all of it, she still showered before she could be examined. So that evidence was inconclusive. The doctor couldn't even say for sure there had been a rape at all!"

Larry kicked his chair, and it rolled into the desk next to his. The cop sitting there on the phone jumped. "So how do you explain the lipstick and the prints in the attic?" Larry demanded. "Do you think she set that up, too?"

Tony thought about that. "Probably not. I think Pendergrast may be after her now. If somebody set you up for something you didn't do, you'd probably want to get even, too. In fact, if he's been calling her parents, it sounds like he's put two and two together himself and figured out who she is. The 'next time for real' message could have meant that the next time, he'd really rape her. I'd say your friend is in a lot of danger right now."

Larry grabbed his chair and shoved it viciously behind his desk. "It's a theory, Tony. It's not fact. You have nothing to base it on. Just a feeling."

Tony shook his head. "I'd say, based on Melissa's relationship with one of Pendergrast's previous victims and the fact that she chose to withhold that crucial bit of information from us, I have probable cause for suspicion here. And I can get to the bottom of it, too—unless you're intent on standing in my way."

Larry clenched his jaw. "Hey, I'm in this for the same thing you are. To get to the truth."

Tony nodded. "But you're too involved with this woman. Look at you. Maybe you don't *want* to see the truth. In fact, I'd say this is disturbing you a lot."

"*You're* disturbing me!" Larry shouted. "I've never seen anyone so intent on proving the victim's the criminal. If this elaborate story of yours is anywhere close to the truth, I'll find out!"

"And how do you plan to do that?"

"I'm going to ask her," Larry said.

Tony laughed and shook his head. "Yeah. Like she's really going to confess it to you."

Larry rubbed his temples and started to pace. "I'll start with asking about her sister. She can't deny that. After that, she may tell a story that makes yours look ridiculous. Maybe it happened just like she's told us all along."

"Ask her," Tony agreed. "And then we'll measure her story against the facts, and see which one we believe."

Melissa couldn't relax or assume that Soames didn't know where she was. He seemed to know everything. He always had.

She lay in her hotel room bed, listening to the noises of people in the rooms on either side of her, their televisions blaring, their muffled exchange of voices, their footsteps going up the hallway, the ring of the elevators. All the while, she clutched a knife in her hand—and decided to buy a gun tomorrow.

As night turned into dawn, and her numb, exhausted mind registered the sun peeking between the blinds, she asked God if he was still out there somewhere.

Her only answer was silence.

"I hope I'm around when God proves to you that you're wrong." Larry had sounded so sure when he'd said that, but Melissa knew she *wasn't* wrong. There were some crimes too despicable to atone for, some people who weren't worthy of forgiveness—and she knew herself to be one of them. Not because she was evil, but perhaps because of the way she had *responded* to evil. Now she wished she didn't believe in God at all. It made the void too deep, the expectation of his wrath too dreadful, the separation from his love too gaping.

Even before that separation, though, she had lost all faith in God's ability—or willingness—to protect her. He had failed to protect others, and he would fail her as well. She needed protection, but she wasn't sure it was to be found anywhere. She was a target now—right at the center of the bull's-eye.

13

THERE WAS NO answer when Larry knocked on the hotel room door, and for a moment he felt relieved. Melissa wasn't there. Maybe he could postpone this for a while. He turned to leave, then stopped. Where was she? She'd been terrified to leave the room, knowing that Soames would be back on the streets in a matter of hours.

He glanced up and down the hall, then stepped closer to the door. "Melissa," he called quietly, knocking again. "It's me. Larry."

He heard movement then, and the door cracked open. Over the chain lock, Melissa peered out. "Oh, thank goodness. You scared me to death."

She closed the door and opened the chain lock, letting him in. "I wasn't expecting you," she said. "When you knocked, I was sure he'd found me."

"We did have to let him go," Larry said.

Her skin looked pallid, and her blonde hair was mussed, as if she hadn't given it a thought all day. She wore no makeup, and her blue eyes seemed paler, more fragile. There were shadows under her eyes, and he doubted she had slept last night. He felt drawn protectively toward her, but he held back. "Have you eaten, Melissa?"

"No," she said. "I was afraid to go out, and I didn't want to open the door for room service."

"Why don't we go get something?" he asked. "You'll be safe with me."

She sighed and shoved her hair back from her face. "Well, I guess I can't stay locked up in here forever." She went for her purse and room key, then paused and looked around. "I'm running out of money, anyway. I'll have to go home soon."

He watched soberly, pensively, as she brushed her hair, then turned back to him. She looked so young today, he thought, so delicate, like a China doll precariously balanced on the edge of a shelf.

As they stepped off the elevator, she scanned the lobby. She walked very close to him all the way to his car, then she hurried to get in.

Larry was quiet as he drove her to a little restaurant where they could have some privacy and a corner table mostly hidden from the front door. Maybe she'd be comfortable there.

After they ordered, Melissa seemed to relax; he wondered how long it would last. "You've been a lifesaver, Larry," she said, clasping and unclasping her hands in front of her. "I don't know what I'd do without you."

"I'm just doing my job," he said, wanting to emphasize that before he asked what he needed to ask.

"And it's your job to take victims out to lunch?"

"It's my job to protect them." He looked down at his own hands, then added, "And to ask them questions."

She stiffened a little. "What questions?"

Larry didn't want to ask. He wanted to make her laugh instead, ease her mind, restore to her some peace. Instead, he was going to drag up the worst part of her past and dangle it in front of her like an accusation. But he had no choice. "We got the file on Soames this morning. It seems that he has a history in the Pensacola area."

He noted instantly when she averted her eyes.

"There were two other rapes," he went on.

Melissa's big, pale eyes moved back to his and locked there, waiting. Larry knew she expected what was coming, so he forced the question out.

"Melissa, why didn't you tell me that Soames had raped your sister?"

Melissa gasped—not the reaction he'd expected. "What?"

"Sandra Hayden. She was your sister, right?"

"Yes!" Melissa's face reddened, and she stared at him. "But that wasn't Soames. That was some guy named Pendergrast!"

The waitress came to deliver their food, and Larry stayed quiet until she was gone. Neither of them touched their meal. "Melissa, Soames and Pendergrast are the same guy. Are you trying to tell me that you didn't know that?"

Tears of indignation and horror filled her eyes. "Of course I didn't know that! How could I?"

"Hadn't you seen him? Didn't you know what he looked like?"

"The defendant isn't allowed in a grand jury hearing, unless he testifies," she said in a harsh whisper. "And he didn't. I never saw him in person. I saw pictures, but he had this beard, and he was heavier . . ."

That much was true, Larry thought. The mug shots of Pendergrast had looked different. Still . . .

"There are just some questions, Melissa. Like why you quit your job with the FBI to take a job as a receptionist in an office where your sister's rapist just happened to work."

Two tears escaped and ran down her face as she gaped at him. "What do you think? That I *planned* all this?"

He looked helplessly down at his food. "I just need for you to explain to me why it happened the way it did. *How* it could happen. And why you never told me about your sister."

"Because it's not the kind of thing I like to talk about!" She looked around at the other patrons, then lowered her voice as more tears ran down her face. Her lips seemed to grow redder as she got out the words. "Have you ever found your sister dead? Have you had to make that phone call to your parents? To her husband? Have you spent years wishing you could have helped her, gotten there in time . . ."

Her voice broke off, and she covered her face with both hands. Her shoulders rolled with the force of her quiet sobs, and Larry realized it had been a mistake to bring all this up in a public place. "Look, I'm sorry. I have lousy timing."

She couldn't stop crying, and Larry felt helpless. There was nothing he could do for her in the middle of a restaurant. He motioned for the waitress and asked for take-out boxes. Then, taking the bag with the boxes in it, he ushered Melissa gently out of her seat and back to his car. He set the bag on the seat, then nodded to the park across the street. "Wanna go for a walk and talk about this?"

She was still crying, and he hated himself. Doing his job had never been enough reason, he thought, for making a woman cry. He put his arm around her as they walked, and felt her shoulders shaking as more pain flooded back through her. When they'd reached a cluster of trees that surrounded a park bench, he made her sit down next to him.

"Please believe me," she cried, wiping her face with wet hands. "I didn't know that Soames and Pendergrast were the same person. How could I have known? I left Pensacola because I couldn't stand all the memories. I wanted to get away, and I thought St. Clair was a good choice. I had heard how clean the town was, how warm and friendly, and I thought maybe I could forget here."

"How did you know about the opening at that company?" he asked gently.

"It was in the paper," she said. "I answered an ad. And when I met Pendergrast, it never for a second occurred to me that he could be the same guy. Why should it? There was no indication. Maybe—maybe *he* orchestrated it somehow. He's like that. He stalked Sandy for weeks after they let him off. He drove her completely over the edge. Maybe he was following me, too, but I didn't know it. Maybe he put the ad in to lure me."

That was a stretch, Larry thought. A big one. "You weren't a secretary, Melissa. You had a degree in criminal justice. Why would he think that you'd apply for a job like that?"

"Maybe he talked to some of my friends from school. I had told them I would take a clerical job. Maybe he knew I'd gone to a couple of employment agencies looking for clerical work. I don't know."

Larry leaned his elbows on his knees. Propping his chin on his hands, he watched two squirrels darting up the trunk of a tree. It was so far-fetched, yet there was a gut-deep part of him that wanted to believe her. "You said you were a Christian, Melissa. I want to trust your honesty. I really believe that God put me on this case because you needed someone who wouldn't shoot first and ask questions later." He sat straight and looked her in the eye. "But if you're lying, this is very serious. You wouldn't take advantage of me that way, would you?"

She hesitated a moment, and he couldn't tell whether she was struggling with the lie, or devastated that he would question her sincerity. Either way, her expression grieved him.

"I'm telling the truth, Larry," she said in a dull voice. "If I'd known Soames was Pendergrast, I would never even have come to this town. I wouldn't have gone within a hundred miles of him. I'm scared to death of him. You should have seen what he did to my sister. How he destroyed her—"

She covered her mouth then and bowed under her grief, and Larry pulled her against him. This woman had so much pain inside her, he thought, more than he could imagine. To find her only sister dead, the way she'd found her—and now this.

"Tell me about Sandra," he whispered, hoping it would be therapeutic for her. "What was she like?"

"Sandy," she corrected, laying her head on his shoulder. "She was always happy. Sweet to everyone. She had been married just a few months, and they were delirious." She thought for a moment, then laughed softly through her tears. "We didn't always get along. When we were kids, we fought like sisters do. When I started wearing makeup, I was always 'borrowing' her stuff, and she could never find what she needed. When we got to be the same size, though, she started 'borrowing' my clothes. My poor mother—she was like a referee. But we always worked it out."

"Were you in her wedding?"

She smiled again. "Maid of honor. I'll have to show you the pictures. Sandy was beautiful. I always wanted to look like her. But after Pendergrast—"

Her voice broke off again, and she shook her head dolefully. "After it happened, she never looked the same. Not just the scars. I don't think I ever saw her smile again. There was this dullness in her eyes . . . like she was already dead."

She swallowed, then looked up at him, intent on making him understand. "Her husband worked nights, and sometimes she did, too. But she got off at ten that night, at the mall, and came home. She didn't know he was following her. When she opened her front door, he put a knife to her throat and pushed his way in."

Larry tightened his arms around her.

"Rick found her the next morning when he came home from work. She was almost dead from blood loss, and she had gone into shock. He got her to the hospital."

"Tell me about the hearing," he whispered.

She got that helpless look on her face again, and she stood up, paced a few feet, then leaned back against the tree the squirrels had gone up. "I'll never forget that day they decided to acquit him. Sandy fell apart. We practically had to carry her out of the courtroom. He was out on the street again, and she was petrified. Then he started making phone calls to her, laughing about getting away with it, telling her that he was free to do it again. She was so scared she quit her job, but she still saw him following her sometimes. After a while she didn't leave her house at all, just turned it into a prison for herself. She was locked in—but she wasn't convinced that he was locked out. And she just got more and more depressed, more and more terrified, more and more paranoid . . ."

"What about her husband?"

"Wonderful guy. Totally supportive, trying to help her through it," Melissa said. "He was scared, too, and started trying to prove that Pendergrast was making those calls, that he had followed her, that sort of thing, but Pendergrast was smart. They never could catch him."

A pigeon landed at her feet, pecked a little on the ground, then fluttered away, and her eyes followed it. "Sandy was a Christian, Larry, but toward the end, instead of turning to God, she just lived in fear."

Larry watched the pigeon's progress across the sky, then brought his eyes back to her.

"The attack changed her whole personality," Melissa said. She came back to the bench and sat down, wiping her tears. "Do you think a person who commits suicide can go to heaven?"

Larry looked down at the dirt, uttering a silent prayer that he'd give her the right answer. "I don't know, Melissa. I've never seen anywhere in the Bible where Jesus said that suicide was the unpardonable sin. If Sandy really believed—in her heart, not just in her head—if she truly had faith in what Christ had done for her—"

"She did," Melissa said unequivocally. "But sometimes I lie awake at night, just praying and praying that God has her with him. That there's no more pain for her. That the wounds are all healed. That she's forgiven." She stopped and stared off with a broken look. "But he has no reason to answer my prayers."

The last words were so softly uttered that they were almost inaudible, and Larry touched her chin and made her look at him. "Why not, Melissa?"

"Because I have my own sins," she whispered.

"And you don't think you can be forgiven?"

"Not for these," she whispered, averting her eyes again. "There are criteria for forgiveness, you know. I don't think I've met them."

"Just repentance," he said. "That's all."

"That's all?" she asked, almost laughing at the complex simplicity of it. "Well, that's the problem." She looked into the trees, where the wind was lapping against the leaves, and her hair began to blow into her face. Pushing it back, she said, "When I found her, I couldn't believe she had done it. That she had let him do that to her. That I let her do it to herself."

"Melissa, you couldn't have stopped her. What could you have done?"

"I was late," she whispered, fresh tears rolling down her cheeks. "I was supposed to have been there an hour earlier. But I stopped off somewhere. I didn't go when I should have. She had left the door unlocked for me. Maybe she wanted me to find her before it was too late. Maybe she didn't really want to die. If I'd just gone straight there . . ." She was sobbing now, and he pressed her head against his shoulder, wishing he could comfort her, but fearing that she would find comfort only when she was ready to receive it from God.

"Melissa, is that the sin that you think God can't forgive you for?"

"One of them," she cried. "Maybe I don't even want forgiveness. Maybe I don't even want to come close to God again. If I did . . ."

As a Christian, Larry had counseled many brothers and sisters. As a cop, he'd offered comfort before. But he'd never felt more helpless than he felt right now.

He did know one thing, though. No matter where this took him, he was ready. He just might be the only one who could point Melissa back to God.

14

TONY BANGED A fist into the wall of the interrogation room the next morning and muttered a curse. "You're losing it, Millsaps. You're totally losing your perspective. You need to take yourself off this case now before you get any more involved!"

"What!" Larry shot back. "Just because I'm not drawing the same deductions you are, I'm losing my perspective?"

"Listen to what you're saying!" Tony shouted. "She gives you some sob story about her sister and all these horrible coincidences, and you're buying it right down to the last word. I can't believe you! You really don't think she knew that Soames and Pendergrast were the same guy? You *really* don't think she deliberately got a job there, where he worked, so she could set him up?"

"I just think we need more evidence before we draw *any* conclusions," Larry said through his teeth.

Tony headed for the door, shaking his head, then turned back before opening it. "Know what I think? I think you're stalling. You're letting your feelings for some wounded woman interfere with your professionalism."

Larry slapped his open hand on the table. "That's not true! I'm open to any facts we can find. But the key word is *facts.* So far, all you've got is speculation. You're not open to listening to her side."

"Hey, I've got all the sympathy in the world for her," Tony said. "Her sister was brutalized and driven to suicide. I can imagine how she must feel. But she sat in front of that grand jury and told them that he raped *her.* Our job is to find out: did he, or didn't he? And man, if he didn't, if she lied in an official hearing—"

Larry dropped into a chair and rubbed his forehead. "Look, I want the truth as much as you do. And we'll find it. We're both drawing conclusions—just different ones. You're wrong, Tony. I'm not getting too close to her, I'm not losing my professionalism—"

"Then why are you spending so much time with her?"

"Because whatever Pendergrast did to her, we know that he's probably done it to others, and we know he's dangerous. She's not safe."

Tony hesitated, then nodded. "All right, I'll buy that."

After a long moment of silence, during which neither looked at the other, Tony finally shook his head. "Well, this isn't the only case we've got on our plate. We'd better get back to work."

Reluctantly, Larry got up. But he didn't want to work on any other cases right now. Melissa's was the only one that mattered.

Melissa ventured back to her apartment the next morning, propping herself up with the hope that Pendergrast wouldn't dare come back now that he knew they were on to him. But then, that was his game. That was how he had played it with Sandy. He had always gotten around the police. He always had an alibi.

She wavered from panic to determination as she stopped on the way home and tried to buy a gun, but there was a three-day waiting period. From a pay phone, she called a locksmith to meet her at the apartment and had him change her locks. Then she had him add three more locks to the door and check out the windows. And before he left, she asked him if he'd look in her attic, just to make sure she was alone.

Looking a little perplexed, as though he were dealing with a lunatic, he did as she asked, and assured her no one was there.

The bill was more than she'd counted on, and as she sat in her living room balancing her checkbook after he'd left, she realized that her funds were almost depleted. The job she was supposed to have started today was too much of a risk, so she hadn't reported to work.

Since she had gotten it on the same day that Pendergrast hid in her apartment, it was possible that he had followed her to the interview, too. Now she was faced with another job hunt, and she had to find something soon.

She changed clothes, then locked all the locks on her door and rushed out of the apartment that felt so frightening, so intimidating, and so unsafe despite the measures she'd taken. Breathing freer in the fresh air, she got into her car and headed for the nearest employment agency.

15

EDWARD PENDERGRAST, ALIAS Soames, watched from his car parked down the street as Melissa came back out of her apartment. She'd had a locksmith meet her there, as if that could deter him, and he'd laughed softly as the man had left. Did she think a new lock on the door was going to keep her safe from him, when moving to a whole different apartment hadn't worked?

She got into her car and pulled out into traffic, and he waited to let a few other cars pass, then pulled out behind her. She had gotten away from him for a couple of days, but he wouldn't let it happen again. He owed her big time.

And he always paid his debts.

16

ARMED WITH A temporary job that started the next day, Melissa left the temporary employment agency, located in the St. Clair Mall. As she walked back through the mall toward the entrance near where she'd parked, she glanced frequently over her shoulder, feeling that someone was watching her. For a weekday, the mall was crowded. A group of teenagers—the girls dressed in black and the boys in white shirts and ties—clustered behind her, probably here to sing during the noon hour. Already, she heard another choir somewhere across the mall, singing some classical, doomsdayish song that made the hairs on her neck rise.

Determined not to let her panic drive her today as it had for the past several days, she stopped and got a hamburger, then found one of the few vacant tables and sat down to eat.

As she bit into her burger, she watched random faces in the crowd. No one seemed to be looking at her, pointing, staring. Everyone went about their own business, scurrying here and there, rushing back and forth, coming in and out.

And then she saw a man, his dark hair too familiar, his teal shirt even more familiar. She watched him walk around the food court, never looking her way. She twisted in her chair to follow him—and finally, he turned his head toward her.

Pendergrast!

Stifling the urge to scream, she grabbed her purse and pressed between the tables, toppling over a chair here and a chair there as she went, bumping into people, knocking packages out of hands. When she got to the mall exit nearest her car, she looked back.

He was gone.

She broke into a run and made it to her car. Her hands trembled as she jabbed the key into the ignition, screeched out of her parking space, and pulled back into traffic.

She searched her rearview mirror for a sign of him. Nothing.

Still, he was there, she told herself. He could see her this minute. He was nearby, somewhere, following, watching.

She headed for the police station, desperate to find Larry. Stopping in a no-parking zone, she slammed the gearshift into park and ran inside. The precinct was noisy with cops coming and going, angry prisoners, and telephones ringing on a dozen desks around the big room. She glanced toward Larry's desk but didn't see him.

Pushing to the front of the line, she asked, "Is Larry Millsaps here?"

"No," the desk officer told her. "He's out on a case."

"I have to talk to someone!" she shouted. "He's following me!"

"Who?"

"Pendergrast!" she shouted. "Or—Soames! Edward Soames. Please get in touch with Larry. He was at the mall, watching me—"

"Larry Millsaps?"

"No! Pendergrast!" She burst into tears, then, clutching her forehead, said, "Look, just ask a patrol car or someone to circle the block or something. Check out the cars in the parking lots around here. Look for his car—a dark blue Cherokee—and see if he's still following me. I'm afraid to go home."

She sat and waited for what felt like an hour. Finally, an officer told her that Pendergrast's Cherokee was parked in front of his apartment.

"Of course," she mumbled to herself as she hurried out to her car. He'd have known she'd go to the police station, so he'd have gone straight home, figuring that someone would be looking for him. But Larry would believe her.

Frantic, she drove to an electronics store and bought a Caller ID device to connect to her phone, so that she'd know who was calling her before she answered. Then, from a pay phone, she called the phone company and asked them to hook her up to that service.

At least if he called her, she would have proof. If only she had access to some of the surveillance equipment they used at the FBI. But she didn't, and her money was running out.

She hurried home and locked herself inside the apartment, quickly hooked up the device, then grabbed a knife and sat on her couch facing the door, waiting for the knob to move or the floor to creak.

She had felt so relieved when the temp agency had given her a job to start tomorrow—she'd been so worried about her money running out. Now she wondered if she'd even be able to go. He was trying to terrorize her, just like he'd done Sandy. The worst part was—she was letting him.

I'm not going to let him get away with it, Sandy, she promised. *Even if it costs me everything it cost you, I'm not letting him get away with it.*

The phone rang an hour later, and Melissa checked the Caller ID and saw that the call came from the St. Clair Police Department. Quickly, she answered it. "Hello?"

"Melissa, it's Larry. I had a message that you'd been by. Are you okay?"

"He was following me," she blurted. "At the mall. I saw him."

"I talked to the officer who found his car in the parking lot of his apartment complex. It was the right car. Had his plates. And the engine was cold."

"Larry, it was him! I saw him at the food court. He's not going to leave me alone. I don't know what to do!"

"Is he still calling your parents?"

"Yes," she said. "He called a couple of times yesterday, and I keep trying to assure them that it's just a prankster. But I'm not sure they're convinced. My dad has him on tape. He express mailed the tape to me, and I should get it today. Then you'll see. Oh, and I got Caller ID. If he calls here, I'll know."

"Maybe. Caller ID can't identify calls that come from pay phones or car phones."

She sighed helplessly. "Well, what should I do? I came back here because I don't have enough money to stay in a hotel another night. I had all the locks changed. But I'm not sure that will stop him."

"He's not supernatural, Melissa. If anything happens, call me. I'll keep my cell phone with me just in case."

"Larry, I just want to lead a normal life. I have a new job to start tomorrow. It's just temporary, but it's money. If I don't get any sleep tonight . . ."

"Maybe I'll pay Pendergrast a visit. Put a little more fear into him. Let him know he's being watched."

"Can he be? Watched, I mean?"

"Off and on. But we can't spare the man-hours to put someone on him full-time."

"He knows that," she said, her voice falling to a helpless monotone. She sighed. "I'd appreciate your talking to him, Larry. It might help."

"Meanwhile, bring the tape as soon as you get it, and let me know if anything else happens."

Larry found Pendergrast's blue Cherokee in the parking lot, and he and Tony made their way up to the apartment they had searched just days before. They knocked, but no one answered.

"Now what?" Tony asked. "We can't break the door down. We don't have any evidence that he's done anything wrong."

"We have her word," Larry said.

Tony banged on the door again, waited. "He could be sleeping. Or just sitting in there refusing to answer."

"Maybe he rode somewhere with someone else. Maybe his alleged girlfriend." Larry glanced down at the Cherokee again. "Or maybe he has two cars."

"There aren't two registered to him."

Larry gave Tony a wry look. "Think that would stop him?"

Tony gave up on the door and looked back down at the parking lot. "It's possible. Maybe some of the neighbors have seen him driving something else."

"I'll take the downstairs neighbors," Larry said. "You take the ones upstairs."

Melissa hated to hear her mother cry. Worse than that, she hated to be the cause of it.

"Melissa, he's been calling over and over for the last two days. Hanging up in the wee hours of the morning, saying things like, 'Tell her I'll find her' or 'Someone has to pay.' I called the police last night, and today they found out that the calls have definitely been coming from your area. Melissa, what's going on?"

Her voice was weak when she got the words out. "Mom, he's just a jerk. I'll give him a call and tell him to stop. Maybe tell him I've given his name to the police."

"It's starting up again, isn't it? This nightmare. It's just like with Sandy. Melissa, we're worried about you. You're the only child we have left."

Melissa closed her eyes. "I know, Mom. But I'm fine. Really. I'll come home for a visit soon, and you can see for yourself."

"But you'd tell us if something was wrong, wouldn't you?"

For a moment, Melissa hesitated, wanting more than anything to share this burden with someone. But not at the cost of the pain it would cause her parents. "Of course, Mom," she lied. "Really, it's okay. Just let the machine get the phone for a while, and I'll see what I can do from this end about making him stop. Nothing to be worried about."

Her hand trembled as she hung up the phone. Edward Pendergrast had a plan, a plan that would start—and end—with her.

She went to the window and peered out at the street below, scanning the cars in the parking lot. She didn't see his Cherokee, but it could be anywhere, up the street, around the side of the building.

She checked her window locks again.

The phone rang, startling her. She checked the Caller ID, saw the words, "Out of area." Maybe it was her mother again. Her heart pounded as she picked up the phone on the second ring.

"Hello?"

"Were the windows locked nice and tight?"

She caught her breath and slammed the phone down, then looked toward the windows where she'd stood just moments before, looking down for him, checking the locks—

Trembling, she scrambled around for the note with Larry's cell phone number on it, but couldn't find it. It had to be here somewhere—

There was a sudden, metallic sound. She looked up—and saw the doorknob turning, shaking, heard the sound of some kind of gadget working in the locks. Wanting to scream but unable to find her voice, she grabbed a chair and almost leaped with it across the room, then jammed it under the doorknob. With strength she didn't know she had, not even conscious of the strain on joints and muscles, she shoved a heavy cabinet in front of the door.

Looking frantically around the room for her knife, she saw the piece of paper with Larry's number, lying where she'd been sitting. She snatched up the phone and dialed.

"Millsaps here," he said after the first ring.

"Larry, he's here," she whispered into the phone. "He's trying to get in!"

She heard the urgency in his voice. "Melissa, hang up, and call the dispatcher at 911. A squad car might make it before I can, but I'm on my way."

"All right." Melissa hung up and punched 911, but the phone went dead. Frantic, she punched some buttons and held the phone to her ear, but there was still no dial tone.

Pendergrast must have cut her telephone wire. She sat holding the phone in one hand, the knife in the other, waiting for him to come through the door.

17

BY THE TIME Larry and Tony made it to her apartment, there was no sign of Pendergrast. But the scratch marks around one of her dead-bolt locks made it evident that someone had tried to pick it. After hearing Melissa's story—first with the phone call, then the noise at the door, then the cut telephone wire—Larry suspected that it had all been an attempt to terrorize her. If Pendergrast had wanted her, he could have caught her at the mall. And he wouldn't have warned her with the telephone call today.

But that didn't mean he wouldn't try something more dangerous tomorrow. And Larry and Tony had discovered, when they had questioned some of Pendergrast's neighbors, that one of them remembered seeing him driving an older-model gray Toyota now and then. Which strengthened Melissa's story about seeing Pendergrast at the mall.

Larry knew, now, that he couldn't leave Melissa here alone. She was terrified, and her fears were legitimate.

He paced across her apartment, watching her sit balled up in the same chair she'd been in the first night he'd met her. She'd been terrified then, too.

"She can't stay here," he told Tony.

Tony nodded, obviously concerned—something Larry found gratifying. "Melissa, why don't you go home to your parents? Lay low for a little while?"

"Didn't you hear what I told you?" Melissa asked him. "He knows where they live. He's been calling them. I'm no safer there, and I don't want to drag my parents into danger, too."

"She's right," Larry said. "She has to go somewhere where he can't find her. At least until we can catch him doing something and get him back behind bars."

Tony got up and rubbed his neck. "Shades of the Barrett case."

"What?" Larry asked.

Tony shook his head. "It just reminds me of the Barrett case." Lynda Barrett, a lawyer, had been pursued by someone as deadly, and as sneaky, as Pendergrast. In that case, too, Larry had gone beyond the call of duty to protect a lady in distress—which, as it turned out, had been necessary to save her life. Tony was beginning to agree that it might be necessary in this case, too.

"That's it," Larry said, stopping his pacing and turning back to Tony. "Lynda Barrett. I don't know why I didn't think of it before."

Melissa looked up. "Who's Lynda Barrett?"

Larry started to answer, but Tony cut him off. "What has Lynda got to do with this?"

"Her house," Larry said. "It's perfect. And she has room. We could ask her to let Melissa stay there for a while."

"Larry, you can't be serious," Tony said. "You can't call one victim and ask her to house another victim."

"Would you please stop talking around me like I'm not here?" Melissa demanded. "Who is Lynda Barrett?"

Larry sat down. "She's a lawyer who was being stalked a few months ago. Someone sabotaged the plane she owned, and she crashed—"

"Just the first of several murder attempts," Tony said, as if this proved how foolish Larry's idea was.

"And it almost succeeded," Larry continued. "But her father had died shortly before that, and he had this great little house on a secluded dead-end street. She hid out there."

"Does she still have the house?" Tony asked.

Larry nodded. "Still lives there." He picked up the phone, remembered it was dead, then hung it back up. "I'll call her on my car phone, Melissa. We'll see if she'll take you in for a while."

"But she doesn't know me. She wouldn't just take in a stranger, would she?"

Larry nodded. "She's been where you are. And besides that, she's a Christian."

"She kind of has a hobby of taking in strays," Tony threw in.

"Stray animals?"

"No. Stray people."

Melissa didn't appreciate that label. "Is that what I am?"

Larry smiled. "He's talking about Jake, the guy who lives in her garage apartment. It's a long story." He hurried to the door, then turned back. "Stay with her while I call Lynda, will you, Tony? Meanwhile, Melissa, start packing."

"How can you be so sure she'll take me in?" Melissa asked.

"Trust me," he said. "She will."

It was just getting dark when Melissa followed Larry's car onto Lynda's street. Between Lynda's house and the next one up the street was a long stretch of woods. Larry parked on the street, and Melissa pulled in behind the car in the driveway, then waited as Larry got out and walked across the yard to her car. "This house is secluded and safe," he said as she got out. "He'll never find you here."

The stress apparent on Melissa's face told him that the last thing she needed was to be thrust into a live-in situation with a stranger.

She looked toward the house. Lynda had left the porch light on, and mosquitoes buzzed around the bulb. "You won't have to be here long, Melissa," Larry said. "Pendergrast is going to screw up, and as soon as we can prove that he violated his bond, he'll be back in jail until the trial. Then you'll be safe."

"I just feel like such an intruder," she whispered. "Complete strangers, taking me in. I may even be putting them into danger."

"That's why I thought of Lynda," Larry said. "If anyone can understand your dilemma, she can. You'll see. Come on."

He reached into the backseat for her suitcase, and the door to the garage apartment opened. A tall man stepped out, leaning on two canes.

"Hey, Jake!" Larry said, laughing. "You're walking!"

"Yeah, Lynda didn't tell you?"

Larry stepped nearer to shake his hand, then looked down at his legs. "Well, she said you were a little, but I pictured a step or two now and then. I figured you were in the wheelchair most of the time."

"Nope. Got rid of the thing. I'll be jogging around the block in another month or two."

Larry turned to Melissa, who seemed small, fragile, in comparison to the tall man.

"Jake, this is Melissa Nelson. She's going to be staying with Lynda, too, for a while."

"Lynda told me," he said, taking both canes in his left hand so he could shake. "Nice to meet you, Melissa. Tough times, huh?"

"Yeah," she said quietly.

"Larry probably told you we've been through them ourselves. My legs are a result of them. There was this little plane crash."

Melissa caught her breath. "You were in it?"

"Yeah. But there must have been a team of angels surrounding us, because both Lynda and I came out of it alive. Matter of fact, I'd say we both came out of it better than before."

The back door opened, and a woman with shoulder-length brown hair stepped out. Her eyes lit up at the sight of them, as if she welcomed an old friend. "You must be Melissa," she said, bypassing Melissa's extended hand and hugging her. "I'm Lynda. I was just making up a bed for you. Gosh, it'll be good having a roommate again."

"I really appreciate your taking me in like this," Melissa said.

"Have you eaten?" Lynda asked, looking down at Melissa's small frame. "Jake made a killer stew tonight. Larry, you stay, too. There's plenty for everybody."

Before Melissa could answer, she ushered them all into the house. Supper was already on the table.

An hour later, Larry could see that Melissa was relaxing. She'd been intrigued and reassured by Lynda's own story, told over supper, of being chased by a killer. Lynda explained, too, that she had housed another young woman and her child recently, and had been lonely since they had left. Even with Jake right next door, sharing meals and conversation, Lynda said she missed having a roommate. Larry knew it all made Melissa feel like less of an intruder.

Melissa walked Larry out to his car before he left. The smell of fresh-cut grass wafted on the October breeze, conveying a sense of peace and safety. Larry looked around at the trees, whispering in the night. If any cars came up this street, it would have to be deliberate and wouldn't go unnoticed. Melissa would be safe here.

"You're a genius, Larry," Melissa whispered. "Has anyone ever told you that?"

Larry laughed softly as he leaned back against his car's fender, his hands in the pockets of his windbreaker. "No, actually. They haven't. Why am I a genius?"

"Because I think I can feel safe here. I really do."

Taking her hand, he pulled her closer. "I want you to be safe, Melissa. And I want you to trust me. I'm going to get Pendergrast."

She looked away then, and he could see the weight of worry and fear she carried. It was hard for her to believe that the nightmare would *ever* end. Sometimes, he wasn't sure he believed that himself. Pendergrast had walked before. The system didn't always work.

Her blue eyes looked paler in the moonlight as she scanned the darkness. "It's kind of funny, isn't it?" she asked. "There are times like this, when the world seems so peaceful . . . so quiet . . . You can look around, and breathe in the serenity. You can almost believe that there's nothing evil out there. Anywhere."

"But then reality always hits, doesn't it?"

She sighed. "Under these same stars, Pendergrast is sitting somewhere. Or driving around looking for me. And if not me, then some other woman who thinks there's no evil out there."

He cupped her chin and made her look up at him. "Leave the evil to me, Melissa. You concentrate on the good for a while."

She drew in a ragged breath. "I don't know if I can." When he pulled her closer, she slid her arms around him and laid her head on his shoulder.

Something about that small gesture sent his heart reeling, and he touched her hair, stroking, comforting. What a feeling. This was something he'd been missing. Something he had occasionally prayed for, without expecting it to happen.

Was he losing his perspective, as Tony suggested? Or was he gaining something important? Something God had offered him?

"The truth is," she said in a whisper, "even after this is all over, and Pendergrast is locked up forever, I don't know if I can trust goodness again. I know too much."

"No," he said. "I used to think I knew too much, too. But evil is not going to prevail. That's a promise. It's in the Bible."

"But how do you see through the evil?" she asked, looking up at him. "How do you look past a sister's suicide? How do you look past rape? How do you look past that face that wakes me up in my sleep?"

"You let God fill your life with more of himself, so that he crowds Pendergrast out. You surround yourself with his goodness. When's the last time you went to church?"

She hesitated. "I haven't been since . . . since before Sandy died."

"Will you go with me?"

She stepped out of his arms and turned her back to him. "I don't know if I'm ready for that."

"Why not?" he asked. "How do you get ready? There are no prerequisites."

"It's just that—I don't have anything to wear. And I haven't gone in so long."

Frowning, he turned her around, made her look at him. "Melissa, what are you afraid of? It's just church. It's a good place. It's God's house."

Again, she turned away. He waited for an explanation as she leaned back against the fender next to him. "Larry, what do you think it means to blaspheme?"

The question surprised him. "Blaspheme? Why?"

"I just—think about it sometimes. I remember reading in the Bible somewhere that blasphemy was one of the worst kinds of sins. Maybe *the* worst. And I wonder sometimes just what it is."

He shrugged, wishing he'd come more prepared. "Well, I guess it means denying the deity of Christ. What do you think it means?"

She shook her head. "I don't know. Mocking him, maybe?"

Larry tried to imagine where she was going with this. "Well, I guess that could be a form of blasphemy. Melissa, what does this have to do with your going to church with me?"

She hugged herself and took a couple of steps farther away from him, shaking her head. "I just can't, Larry. I don't think everybody belongs in church. Some people have no business there."

"The church should be open to everyone," he said. "No one should be excluded. Melissa, if you think you're tainted in some way, that God doesn't want you anymore—"

"I can't talk about this," she said, preventing what she sensed he was about to say. "Just—just accept that I'm not ready to go back to church. I can't do it. Not yet."

He let that sink in, then finally said, "All right." The curt tone of his voice made her look up at him, and the pain on her face looked so intense, so deep, that he couldn't help reaching for her again. "Melissa, I care about you. You have the most beautiful smile I think I've ever seen. It lights up my heart every time I see it. But I haven't seen it very often. I want to help you find your smile again."

She met his eyes then as tears rolled down her cheeks, and he touched her face gently and pulled her into a kiss.

It was soft, sweet, gentle, and it tasted of her tears.

When he broke it, he pulled back and looked at her again. "This isn't about police work anymore, Melissa," he whispered. "I'm taking this case very personally."

She smiled. "I don't deserve you."

He laughed softly. "Tell me about it. You probably deserve some hunk who can give you everything."

Her smile grew wider. "That's not what I meant."

He knew what she meant, and he kissed her again, this time sliding his arms around her, holding her as he had long wanted to do, only this time it wasn't for her, for her comfort. It was for him.

"I'd better go," he said finally, dragging in a deep breath and letting her go.

She smiled and looked down at her feet. "Yeah. Thanks for bringing me here, Larry."

"You'll be safe. He doesn't know where you'll be working, and he doesn't know where you live. You can relax a little. Just be careful."

"You, too," she whispered as he got into his car.

He watched her go back into the house before he started his car.

Lynda was putting the finishing touches on the master bedroom when Melissa came back into the house. "I think you'll be comfortable here," Lynda said with a smile. "Paige was. She's the one who stayed here before you."

"But this is the master bedroom," Melissa said. "Lynda, I could just sleep on the couch."

"I don't sleep in here," Lynda said. "It was my parents' room. There are too many memories." She sat down on the bed with a sigh and ran her hand along the smooth bedspread. "My dad hasn't been gone long. Just a few months. I really miss him sometimes. Mom, too, even though she's been gone longer."

Melissa sat down across the bed from her, and looked around the room. On the dresser, there was a silver tray with a brush and comb, and an open box with a tie clip and a key ring. A tie rack hung on the closet door with her father's ties still carefully lined up. "You kept their things."

Lynda smiled. "Yeah. I haven't made myself get rid of anything yet. I used to hate this house and everything in it. I wanted more. And I got more. But when I lost it all, I started to realize how precious all my memories were. I guess I realized that *things* don't fill up your life."

"I have memories," Melissa said. "Of my family. My sister. We were so oblivious."

"Oblivious to what?" Lynda asked gently.

"To what was going to happen." She swallowed hard and cleared her throat. "Sometimes I wish I could go back and dwell on those memories. But the bad ones keep interfering. It's hard for me to be with my parents now, in their home. I keep remembering when my sister was there."

Larry had told Lynda most of Melissa's story, and she reached out and took Melissa's hand. "It's normal to grieve, Melissa. How long has it been?"

She shrugged. "About three years."

"Well, what's just happened to you has probably brought it all back. Stirred it all up." Lynda pulled her feet up beneath her on the bed and fixed her thoughtful, compassionate eyes on her. "It takes time, Melissa. Grief has a way of hanging on."

Melissa dipped her head, unable to meet Lynda's eyes with the intimacy of her tears.

"You'll never be the same," Lynda admitted softly. "The world will never be the same. You'll look back on your life before and it'll seem like some kind of surreal dream."

"It already does," Melissa said. "Like those fuzzy old reels of home movies. All laughter and no pain. Just a dream."

For a moment, there was a gentle silence between them, as if they knew each other well enough to share quiet together. "Larry brought you to Jake and me for a reason, Melissa. We've had to grieve, too. We've both had to plunge headfirst into a new era of our lives—whether we liked it or not. We've both survived."

Melissa wiped her eyes with both hands. "Maybe I'll be a survivor, too. Maybe there's hope."

Later that night, after she had gone to bed, Melissa lay awake trying to sort out all the thoughts in her mind. Why had God blessed her by bringing her here to Lynda, where she truly did feel safe, and cared for, and no longer forsaken?

The sweetness and mercy in it was almost more than she could bear, for she saw nothing in herself that merited it. God shouldn't even be able to look upon her, not after the shame of all the events that had brought her here.

In the darkness, she saw a Bible lying beside the bed, where Lynda had put it. Turning on the dim lamp on the bed table, she opened it. By memory—how long had it been since she had held an open Bible?—she turned to the Beatitudes in Matthew, a passage that had given her so much peace as a child. She had learned the whole passage in vacation Bible school once, but it had been years since she'd recited it, even longer since she'd read it.

Now her eyes fell on the one verse she needed to read tonight. "Blessed are the pure in heart, for they shall see God."

She closed the Bible, realizing how unpure her heart was, how far from seeing God she had come. Her heart had been tainted by events—many of them out of her control, true, but many of them well within it, and God could never be pleased with that.

Feeling the abyss of mourning and emptiness growing deeper inside her, she went to the door of the bedroom that opened onto the patio and gazed out into the darkness.

Lynda and Jake were sitting out there on a swing, snuggled up together, talking softly. It hadn't occurred to her that the two were a couple, but now, as she saw Jake lean over and kiss Lynda gently, she realized that something very special was happening between them.

Something she would probably never experience.

She went back to the big bed and lay staring at the tiles on the ceiling, remembering the way Larry had kissed her tonight. It was no longer just business, he had said. It was personal.

His interest in her sent a warm feeling spiraling through her, but she quickly quelled it and sent it away. She couldn't fall in love with Larry, and he couldn't fall in love with her. Nothing good could come from it. Only pain. Larry needed someone with a pure heart, someone like Lynda, who wasn't plagued with hatred and bitterness. Someone who didn't cling to her anger and injustice like an old, familiar—but lethal—friend.

When this was all over—when the trial ended and Pendergrast was behind bars for good—would she then be able to explore these feelings for Larry?

Something—that fatalistic voice that seemed to drive her these days—told her that she would never get that chance. Larry did have a pure heart, and the last thing he needed was someone like her in his life, separating him from God.

She turned over, adjusted the pillow, and tried to find sleep, but it wouldn't come. It wasn't the threat of Pendergrast that kept her awake. Tonight, it was the threat of what lurked inside herself. The threat of who she had become. How far she had strayed.

But that was why she was here. Lynda took in strays. Lynda, who loved Jake. Lynda, who missed her parents. Lynda, who had a pure heart . . .

There was something comforting in that, and finally, surrendering to her exhaustion, Melissa drifted into a troubled sleep.

18

EDWARD PENDERGRAST WATCHED her apartment until the wee hours of morning, then finally decided that she wasn't coming home. Like the other night, she had disappeared.

His mistake had been in trying to get in, but he hadn't been able to resist. Picturing the fear on her face when he had called to let her know he was watching her had spurred him to frighten her even more.

He chuckled now at the thought. When he'd gone to her door and tried to pick the lock, she'd really gone off the deep end. He had heard her calling that cop, just before he cut the line and took off. And while he was off setting up his latest alibi, she had left the apartment to hide from him.

Despite his frustration that he couldn't find her tonight, Pendergrast at least felt the satisfaction of knowing that she was terrified of him, and that she would be constantly, exhaustingly on alert, listening for sounds, vibrations, clues that he was near. He loved these mind games. If only he could see that fear on her face. That would make it complete.

Tomorrow, he thought, heading home. He'd find her tomorrow. She wouldn't be able to hide for long.

19

THE RED PORSCHE that was blocking Melissa's car in had not been in Lynda's driveway last night. Melissa was sure of it. She stood at Lynda's kitchen window, dressed and ready for work, wondering who the car belonged to. The idea of someone new being here made her a little uneasy. Besides, she had to be at her new job in half an hour, and the car was blocking her way.

"Morning, Melissa. Did you sleep well?"

Melissa turned and saw Lynda, dressed in a blue business suit that completely changed her look from soft to professional. Now she looked like a lawyer.

"Yes," she lied. "I was really comfortable, thanks. You look nice."

Lynda smiled and set her briefcase on the table. "Thanks. I have to be in court this morning. I made biscuits. Are you hungry?"

Melissa shook her head. "No, I'm not hungry." She looked out the window again. "Is someone here? I mean, besides you and Jake?"

"Oh, yeah," Lynda said. "That car belongs to Jake's mother. I don't think she'll be here long. I can get her to move it if you need me to."

Melissa turned from the window. "Jake's mother drives a red Porsche?"

"Yeah, well, it's a long story." She glanced over Melissa's shoulder to the window. "Uh-oh, here they come."

Melissa looked out the window again. Jake was coming out of his apartment with an older woman with platinum blonde hair and black roots, and a cigarette in her mouth. "Brace yourself," Lynda said with a grin as she went to the door. "Doris is never dull."

Jake winked at Lynda as they came in, then he grinned at Melissa. "Hi, Melissa. I'd like you to meet my mother, Doris Stevens."

Melissa stepped toward her, extending a hand. "How are you, Mrs. Stevens?"

The woman shook with the tips of her fingers. "Oh, for heaven's sake, call me Doris," she said in a nasal twang.

"Mama's from Texas," Jake said with a slight smile. "She came to pick up her car, and decided to stay awhile."

"It's a beautiful car," Melissa said.

"My boy gave it to me," the wiry woman said. "And I got a job here, so I may not ever go back to Slapout. That truck stop is gonna have to get used to not havin' me to kick around anymore. I can be kicked around just as good here as I can anywhere in Texas. Besides, I been workin' on my tan."

Melissa didn't know how to answer; the woman's leathery complexion looked as if it had had all the sun it could stand. "It is nice here, isn't it?"

"Hot, though," Doris said. "Well, I'd love to stay and chat, but I have to meet somebody."

"Who, Mama?"

"A customer I met at the diner last night. He's takin' me to breakfast." She tossed a wave at Melissa.

"It was nice meeting you," Melissa said.

"Pleasure," the woman returned, then bounced out to the car.

They all watched through the window as Doris cranked up the sports car and sped out of the driveway.

"What was she doing here so early?" Lynda asked Jake.

"The usual," he said. "Wanted money." He opened the refrigerator door and took out a carton of orange juice.

"And you gave it to her."

He shrugged and reached for three glasses. "She's my mother," he said.

Lynda smiled and turned back to Melissa. "A few months ago, they weren't even on speaking terms. Jake doesn't want to admit it, but that Porsche was a peace offering."

"Not a peace offering," Jake said, pouring into the glasses. "Just an opening."

Melissa smiled and took the glass of orange juice Jake offered her. "I've been seeing a change in her, though," Lynda said. "Slowly but surely. I think the change in Jake has had a lot to do with it."

"Change?" Melissa asked, glancing at Jake. "You mean, your injuries?"

Jake shook his head. "Nope. She means my change of heart. A few months ago I had a lot of bitterness toward my mother. Frankly, I didn't care what happened to her, one way or the other. Now, I can actually say I love her. Of course, it makes her real uncomfortable when I tell her."

"So he told her with the Porsche."

He laughed. "I kind of thought she'd sell it and invest the money in a house or something. But she's had the time of her life driving around town in it. Truth is, it's been kind of good for me to have her back in my life. Humbling."

Lynda couldn't help laughing. "If you knew him before the accident, you'd know what an understatement that is. Jake, there are biscuits in the oven. Melissa, are you sure you don't want any?"

Melissa watched the Porsche pull out of sight, and she set her glass in the sink. "No, I really need to get going. First day on a new job."

Both Jake's and Lynda's expressions sobered, and they glanced at each other. "Listen, you be careful, okay?" Lynda said more seriously. "If you need me . . ." She reached into her purse for a card, and handed it to Melissa. "Here's my office number. Paige Varner is my secretary, and if I'm not there, she can help you."

Jake took the card and jotted his own number on it. "Or call me here. And if I'm not here, I'll be at the hospital in physical therapy."

Melissa blinked back the tears in her eyes. "You guys are so sweet. You don't even know me."

"But we know enough about you to worry," Lynda said. "You know, if you wanted to skip this job and just stay here for a while, you don't have to worry about money. Sometimes it's best just to hide out."

It sounded tempting, but Melissa couldn't forget the bills she had piling up. "That's sweet of you, but I really do need the money," she said. "Thanks anyway. And don't worry. I'll be all right."

But as she left the house, she wasn't sure that she really felt that way.

When Larry came in that morning, running late, he found Tony on the telephone, hunched over his desk with a somber look on his face. Larry had spent the past hour driving around the neighborhood of Pendergrast's apartment. He'd found several gray Toyotas that fit the description of the second car Pendergrast's neighbor had seen him driving, and he had written down the tag number of each of them. Now he was ready to check them all out.

Larry slid into his chair and turned on his computer just as Tony hung up, then looked down at his desk, obviously deep in thought. After a moment, Tony picked up the big manila envelope on his desk, pushed his chair back, and headed for Larry's desk. "What's going on?" Larry asked.

Tony looked down at the envelope he carried. "We need to talk," he said.

"Okay, shoot."

"In private," Tony said.

Something told Larry that this was going to be another one of those conversations he would regret, but he got up and nodded toward the vacant interrogation room.

Tony followed Larry in and plunked the manila envelope down on the table. It was a hot room, kept that way on purpose so that the suspects brought here would be uncomfortable. Now, Larry wished there was a thermostat they could turn down.

"What's that?" he asked, gesturing toward the manila envelope.

Tony sat down on the mahogany tabletop and looked at his friend. "It's some stuff I found out about Melissa."

Larry stiffened. "What kind of stuff?"

When Tony didn't answer right away, Larry picked up the envelope and pulled the contents out. "Her employment file at the FBI?"

"That's right," Tony said. "And her transcript from college. I ordered them a few days ago. Just came this morning. Since then, I've been on the phone with people who knew her."

Larry's face reddened as he pulled out a chair to sit down. "All right. Sounds like you have some kind of bomb to drop."

Tony slid off the table and dropped into a chair. "She's lying, Larry. Right across the board."

Larry felt his defenses swing into place. He shook his head. "Evidence," he said. "You'll need some substantial evidence to prove it to me."

"Okay." Tony reached for her college records and consulted the notes he'd taken. "I spoke to two of her professors in criminal justice at Florida State. They both said the same thing: She had an obsession with her sister's rapist. One of the professors pulled his file on her and described some of the papers she wrote for him. Check these out: One involved how to avoid dropping the ball on search and seizures in rape cases, another one was on forensic evidence to tie rapists to the crime scene. There was one on subsequent crimes of rapists who were set free; one analyzing statistical data on repeat crimes; one on profiles of known rapists, MOs, motivations—"

"Okay, okay," Larry said, getting up and walking to the two-way mirror. He stood in front of his own reflection, but didn't see it. "If your sister was raped and the guy walked, you'd be a little obsessed, too."

"One of her professors said that she showed a lot of promise," Tony went on behind him. "He's the one who helped get her the job at the FBI, and he was surprised when she up and quit just a few months later."

"She decided she didn't like that kind of work."

"He thinks differently."

Larry didn't like where this was going. He turned back to his partner. "Okay. What does he think?"

"He thinks now, and he thought then, that she had an agenda. That she was going to find this guy somehow and catch him at something. He told me all this, and I never uttered a word to him about her rape. Excuse me—about her *alleged* rape." Larry shot him a cutting look. "I just told him that she had been a victim of a crime we were investigating, and I needed some information on her."

"Still doesn't mean anything," Larry said.

"I'm not finished." Tony turned his notes around so that Larry could read them across the table. "This guy—Mark Sullivan. He was her supervisor at the FBI. She had a real peon job—you know, entry level. He said that if she hadn't quit when she did, she probably would have gotten fired."

"What for?"

"She was caught using one of the computer systems when someone was away from their desk. Without clearance, she broke into a program that could track people by their Social Security numbers. Sullivan says he caught her himself, and asked her what she was doing. She tore off the printout, shoved it into her pocket, and told him that she had just borrowed the computer to type something up. She tried to turn it off before he could see what she was doing, but he saw the program and stopped her. Guess who she was doing a search on?"

Larry didn't want to know. He just waited for Tony to finish.

"Edward J. Pendergrast. Mark remembered because he had an uncle named Pendergrast, so it stuck in his memory. He volunteered it before I even asked. I hadn't told him anything about the case."

Larry was beginning to feel sick. "Did she find anything on him?"

"Oh, a thing or two. Like the name he was using now, where he lived, where he worked . . ."

Larry sank back down into a chair and covered his face with his hands. A siren outside blared as a squad car sped out of the garage and past the window.

Tony's voice softened as he said, "One more thing. She said she saw the job advertised in the paper. I called her boss today, and asked him. He said he couldn't remember if he'd advertised or not. He just remembers her coming in with a resumé and asking for a job. He gave me her starting date, though, and I called the newspaper. There wasn't a job advertised for that company anywhere around the time she started working for them."

"Then how did she know there was an opening?"

"He says her resumé was so diverse that she would have fit a lot of the jobs there. It just happened that someone had just had a baby and had resigned. She fit right in. Oh, and he faxed me her resumé. Here it is."

Larry took it. It said nothing about a degree in criminal justice, or a job at the FBI. Instead, it listed bookkeeping, secretarial, and receptionist jobs in other towns. Jobs, he suspected, that could not be verified.

"You've been busy today," Larry said, looking at his partner with tired eyes.

"I felt an urgency," Tony said.

Larry sighed and shoved the papers back across the table. "And what urgency was that?"

Tony rubbed his tired face, putting off saying it. "Last night, when you were with her, worried about her, I could tell that this wasn't just any case. You've got feelings for her."

Larry couldn't meet his eyes.

"Now, I know that you're a Good Samaritan kind of guy, that you always go that extra mile. But I've never seen you so blinded by a pretty face. I've never seen a case where you haven't wanted to find the truth—but you just don't want to see the truth in this one. Not only are you buying into a lie, but you're letting her manipulate you."

Larry couldn't believe what he was hearing. "Tell me something," Larry said, finally meeting Tony's eyes. "Have you ever known me, in all the years we've been partners, to ever try to cover up anything?"

"Never," Tony said.

"And have I ever had a gut feeling about something, and been completely wrong?"

The door opened, and a lieutenant stuck his head in. Both detectives shot him scathing looks, and he shrank back. "Sorry," he said. "I thought the room was empty." He ducked out and closed the door.

Larry turned his angry eyes back to Tony.

"So what's your gut feeling here, Larry?"

Larry sighed. "That—that she's a good person. That she's been victimized. Violated."

Tony leaned forward, his eyes riveting into Larry's. "The question is: Was she raped?"

Larry hesitated again, perspiring a little. Phones rang on the other side of the wall, and printers buzzed. Another siren wailed by the window.

He wished he could be any place in the world but here. "So what do you want to do?"

Tony breathed a mirthless laugh. "What do *I* want to do? We're both go-by-the-book cops, Larry. It's not a question of what I want to do. If I had my way, I'd let Pendergrast go to jail for the rest of his life. With three rape arrests, the guy'll probably wind up there anyway, eventually. But we both know that's not the point here."

"Then what is the point?"

"The point is that perjury is a felony."

"No, it's not," Larry argued. "It's a misdemeanor."

"Not in a grand jury hearing, pal. It's a felony of the third degree. If Melissa Nelson sat on that witness stand and lied to a grand jury—"

Larry couldn't listen to the rest. "I'll find out."

"When?"

"Today!" he said. "Now."

"And what if you don't like what you hear?"

Larry shook his head helplessly, hopelessly. "I already don't like what I hear."

"Can you do the right thing, Larry? Because if you're in too deep with her, if your feelings are going to distort your thinking, I can take over from here. Completely leave you out of it."

"No," Larry said, swallowing back his emotion. "I can't be left out. I have to see this through." He looked up into Tony's eyes. "You don't have to worry about me doing the right thing."

But as he headed out of the interrogation room and back into the symphony of ringing phones, raised voices, and profanities flying from those being booked for assorted crimes, Larry had to ask himself: The right thing for whom?

And he prayed that God would enable Melissa to give him some answers that would clear all this up to both Larry's and Tony's satisfaction. Because if she didn't, he didn't think he'd be able to live with himself—regardless of what he chose to do.

20

THE TEMP AGENCY had assigned Melissa to a busy insurance company. She had been hired to collate and staple what seemed like thousands of booklets—a big step down from the jobs she was qualified to do. But she felt safe in her little cubicle at the back of the big room.

It wasn't quite eleven when her supervisor buzzed her. "There's someone here to see you, Melissa."

Clutching the phone to her ear, Melissa stood up and peered over her cubicle. "For me? Are you sure?"

"Positive," the woman said. "He's been waiting awhile because no one knew who you were. Listen, if you need to take lunch now, go ahead."

She hung up and tried to see over the cubicle again. There were too many people—she couldn't find him. But a terrifying certainty overwhelmed her as she reached for her purse.

Pendergrast had found her.

Was he waiting to surprise her in front of an office full of people? To cause her to react hysterically and to lose this new job? Was this part of his game?

She rushed out of her cubicle, looking for a back exit. Maybe there was one she didn't know about near the rest rooms. She started toward them, walking as fast as she could, rounded a corner in the hallway—and someone grabbed her arm.

She gasped and swung around.

Larry let her go as though she had burned him. "Melissa—it's me."

Tears sprang into Melissa's eyes as she fell into his arms. "Larry! I thought you were Pendergrast. I thought he had found me."

"Shhh. It's okay. How would he have found you?"

"The same way you did," she said. "How *did* you, anyway?"

"I went by your agency," he said. "But my badge carries a lot of clout. He doesn't have one."

She took in a deep breath and wiped her face. "You scared me to death."

"I can see that," he said. "I'm sorry. Come on. Let's go somewhere."

She held his hand and let him lead her back through the maze of cubicles to the front door.

The sunlight assaulted her, making her feel vulnerable and exposed. "I only have an hour for lunch," she said. "But I'm not very hungry." She looked up at Larry, and for the first time noted how sober he looked. "Is everything all right? Did something happen?"

He stared off into the breeze coming from the Gulf just a couple of blocks away. "Let's walk down to the beach."

They were both silent as they walked down the sidewalk that led from the insurance building to the park behind it. Ahead, Melissa could see the Gulf, blue-green and majestic. On the sand near the water, two little girls sat with their parents, giggling as they shared a picnic. They looked like Sandy and her, years ago, when there were still things to laugh about.

She looked up at Larry as they reached the edge of the beach and headed across the sand, their feet leaving indentations behind them. Larry took off his windbreaker and slung it over his shoulder, revealing his shoulder holster. He was pensive, squinting into the breeze coming off the water, watching the waves and the seagulls as though they might give him some peace.

"Larry, what's wrong? You didn't track me down at work for a walk on the beach."

Larry stopped then on a little hill of sand, and dropped onto it, setting his forearms over his knees. "I heard some things today. Things about you. They don't add up with what you've told me."

She didn't sit down. Instead, she stood stiffly over him, looking down with sad eyes. "What did you hear?"

He shook his head and avoided looking at her. "Melissa, Tony's a good cop. He digs. He doesn't leave any stones unturned. And he got some background on you. He talked to your college professors."

"So?"

"So, one of them said that you were obsessed with Sandy's rape. That that was the primary focus of all your studies. That all of your papers had something to do with what happened to her."

"That's true," she admitted. "I did try to apply everything I learned there to her case. It was my only point of reference. There were mistakes made in her case, and I didn't want to make those same kinds of mistakes when I got into law enforcement. I'm not trying to hide it, Larry—she was the main reason I went into criminal justice. The thought of things like that happening all the time was more than I could stand."

"Well, I can relate to that. I feel the same way. But—"

"But what?" She lowered herself onto the sand next to him.

"But that professor seems to think you had a plan. That you were going to get Pendergrast on something. That you were waiting to get even somehow."

Her gaze drifted to the waves lopping over the sand. "That was Dr. Jessup. He was worried about me. Thought I needed counseling."

"Maybe you did."

"No," she said. "I didn't need counseling."

"What did you need, then? Closure?"

The frown on her face betrayed her pain as she brought her eyes back to him. "What are you saying, Larry?"

He couldn't say it. Not yet. He looked away. "Tony also talked to your supervisor at the FBI. He said you were caught using a computer you didn't have clearance to use."

"Give me a break." She rolled her eyes and threw up her hands. "I sat at someone's desk and used their computer for a minute. I didn't break national security, for heaven's sake."

"He said you were looking up information on Pendergrast."

The indignant expression faded. "That's not true."

"Melissa, it is. Tony didn't ask him about Pendergrast. He volunteered it. He remembered the name."

For a moment she stared, incredulous, at him. "Oh, now I get it." Angry, she got up and started walking away.

Larry got to his feet and followed her.

"Melissa, I need answers! I need to know what you're doing."

"I reported a crime, Larry! And now people are digging into my past, trying to make sense of a few years there when nothing really did make any sense. I didn't do anything wrong!"

"Proffer hadn't advertised for that job, Melissa! How did you know about it?"

"I—I didn't! I put my resumé in a lot of places. He's the one who hired me."

"What other places, Melissa? Can you name them?"

"No!" she shouted. "I don't remember!"

"Why not? It's only been a few weeks."

She started to cry and began walking faster, but he kept up with her.

"Melissa, why did you leave your college degree and your FBI work off your resumé? Why did you make up all that bookkeeping and receptionist and secretarial experience?"

"I didn't make them up, *Detective,*" she said, spinning around to face him. "Tell your friend Tony he needs to dig a little deeper. I had several jobs in college. I included them all."

"But you didn't mention the FBI. Or your degree."

"I didn't want him to think I was overqualified!"

"But you *were* overqualified, Melissa. Why would you take a job like that in the same place where your sister's rapist worked?"

"Because I didn't know he was there!"

"According to your FBI supervisor, you did know. That's the kind of information you got off their computer."

She turned and began walking again, then, sobbing, she began to run. Larry kept up with her.

"Melissa, I have to know the truth. I've fought for you. I've defended you. I've taken care of you. Now you have to be straight with me!"

He grabbed her arm, stopping her, and she swung around to face him. Her face was raging red, and she smeared the tears on her face. "All right!" she shouted. "I did know he worked there. I did have a plan. I wanted to be where he was so I could watch him. No one else was doing it! I wanted to keep him from hurting anyone else!"

Trying to catch his breath, Larry took a step back and let her go. "Then why did you lie?"

"Because I knew what conclusions you'd jump to! I knew that you'd believe I set him up. I never dreamed he'd come after me, Larry. I thought I could take care of myself. I thought I was smarter than he was."

He remembered the classes he'd seen lined up on her transcript. "You *do* know how to defend yourself, Melissa. You don't get a law enforcement degree without that."

That guarded look returned, and more tears.

"Why didn't you use it on him?"

"He took me by surprise," she said. "I panicked. He had a knife."

Larry dropped his hands helplessly to his sides. "Melissa, someone heard you invite him over for dinner that night."

Crying harder, she turned away, shaking her head, one hand cupped against her forehead. After a moment, she turned back. "Larry, you saw me after it happened. You gathered the evidence. Are you trying to tell me you believe that I set all this up?"

"I think you could have," Larry admitted. "And I'm not sure I could even blame you. I'm not sure I wouldn't have done exactly the same thing, if I'd lost a sister because of some maniac."

"You think I'm lying."

He fought the tears coming to his own eyes, and looked out over the water again. The sun was directly overhead. "I don't know what to think, Melissa. I'm not judging you. I just have to know what really happened."

"I can't believe this!" She brought both hands to her head now, crying harder. "You're going to do it again, aren't you? You're going to let him go! It doesn't matter that he's followed me, broken into my house, threatened to kill me—you're going to let him keep walking free so that he can rape more women! How could you?"

One part of him wanted to shout that he couldn't, to pull her into his arms and hold her until her crying subsided. But that other part, that part that had been a cop for too long, that part that had sworn to uphold the law, battled with him. "Melissa," he said, his voice growing raspy with emotion, "if you set him up, you're denying his civil rights. That's a crime, too."

"As much a crime as *rape?*" she screamed. "What about *my* rights, Larry? What about my sister's rights, or the other woman he raped? Why is it that all anybody cares about is that monster's rights to go out and terrorize to his heart's content, over and over and over?" She dropped back onto the sand and covered her face with her hands, and Larry sat beside her.

After a moment of watching her cry, he put his arm around her and pulled her against him. She shook with the strength of her weeping, soaking his shirt, but he didn't care. He could understand some of what she felt. But he wasn't sure that understanding would change anything.

"Melissa, I'm not the only one asking questions," he whispered. "Tony's a good cop. A go-by-the-book detective, like me. I took a vow to uphold the law—and that means never covering up a violation of it, even when there was a good reason for it."

"So what do you want to do, Larry? See me go to jail? Is that what this is about? Put the victim in jail, so the criminal won't be harassed anymore? Some justice."

"No, of course that's not what I want. I just want the truth."

"The *truth* is that Edward Pendergrast is a malicious, brutal rapist and that he deserves to live the rest of his life in prison. That's the only truth I care about, Larry. Please don't help him get out of this."

That answer didn't satisfy him. He needed more than a rationale—he needed an honest denial. But he had pushed it as far as he could, considering that there was still a part of him that didn't want to know the truth if the truth would hurt Melissa Nelson.

"I need to go," she said, wiping her face and getting to her feet.

"We didn't eat," he said.

"I'm not hungry."

He got up then, brushing the sand off his pants. She didn't say a word as they walked back to the office.

The silence was devastating. Larry was afraid that this good thing, the thing he had thought was a gift, was fast being taken from him, and he didn't know what to do. He'd never been so confused.

When they reached the building, she went in without a word, without a backward glance. And Larry, feeling more dismal than he'd ever felt, went back to his car, trying to decide where he would go from here.

21

THE BUILDING WAS hazy with smoke, and some wailing country song blared on the juke box. At the bar, several cops from Larry's precinct sat over their beers, commiserating about the day's events. Larry spotted Tony among them and wondered once again what his partner saw in this place.

He cut through the happy-hour crowd and reached Tony at the bar. The bartender looked up. "What'll you have?"

"Nothing," Larry said. "I'm not staying."

Tony glanced up at him. "Must be good, to get you in here."

"I was looking for you," Larry said. "What do you say we go have a bite? Talk."

Tony reached into his pocket, pulled out a couple of bills, and tossed them on the bar. Then, bidding good-bye to some of the others, he followed Larry outside.

The fresh air washed over them, and Larry took a deep breath. "That's real similar to how I picture hell," he said.

Tony chuckled. "You know what they say. One man's heaven—"

"They don't say that," Larry said irritably. "No one ever said that."

Tony got into the passenger side of Larry's car and waited for his partner to get in. "So what's going on?" Tony asked as Larry slipped behind the wheel. "I waited for you to come back all afternoon. Where were you?"

"I had some thinking to do," Larry said. "You could have reached me if you needed to."

Tony kept his eyes on his partner. "Did you talk to her?"

Larry didn't answer right away. Instead, he cranked the car and pulled out into traffic. For a moment, he was quiet.

"Bad news?"

Larry hesitated, then said, "Just suppose—"

Tony moaned. "Larry, police work is not about supposing."

"Yes, it is. To get where we're going, we have to start somewhere. Just suppose that Melissa did lie about part of it."

"All right. Which part?"

"Well, maybe she did know that Pendergrast worked there. Maybe she deliberately got a job there so she could watch him, follow him, that kind of thing. Maybe she figured she could put her law enforcement know-how to work."

"So her job was sort of like an undercover detective?"

"Yeah. Only she was her own client."

Tony's eyes narrowed. "Is that what she told you?"

"I told you, this is supposing. Can you just suppose for a minute?"

"All right," Tony said. "I'm listening."

"Suppose it backfired, and Pendergrast came after her. She expected to be able to defend herself if that happened, but she froze. This man, who had terrorized her sister and her family, who had become this huge monster in her mind, finally came after her, and she couldn't use any of what she knew."

"She knew she shouldn't shower. But she did. How do you explain that?"

"Trauma," Larry said, his face turning red. "Maybe she was so traumatized—"

"She wasn't too traumatized to tell us details about Pendergrast, where we could find the evidence we needed, and what we needed to do to make sure he didn't get off on a technicality."

Larry got quiet again.

"Besides, Larry, when she testified before that grand jury, she didn't tell them any of what you're suggesting. She never said he was the one who had raped her sister. She never said she had hunted him down to catch him at something."

"She wasn't asked, Tony. If this is what happened, she didn't lie on the witness stand. No felony was committed."

"No, it wasn't. *If* this is what happened. But if it's not—if she wasn't really raped, if she really set out to set him up by claiming he did, then she did lie. Did you talk to her or not?"

"Of course I did."

"And?"

"And I believe in my heart that he attacked her. I believe that she is telling the truth about that. And if she only lied about the other part, I guess the question is, what difference does it make? She wasn't under oath when she talked to us about her job and how she got it. She was afraid of how it would look to us if we knew the truth. She knew how apt we were to blame the victim."

"You should start writing screenplays, man. You've got a great imagination."

Larry slammed his hand on the steering wheel. "Why *couldn't* it have happened that way? Why are you so intent on making her out to be the criminal here?"

"And why are you so dead set on defending her?"

"Because I don't think she'd lie to me, Tony. I think when it came right down to it, she couldn't do it."

"She already lied to you, Larry. More than once. How do you know this latest story is the truth? I told you she was manipulating you. What did she do, Larry? Tell you she's in love with you? Make you think that you have a future with her, if you just overlook the obvious?"

"No!" Larry shouted. "As a matter of fact, she isn't even speaking to me right now!"

"Good. Maybe you'll have time to get your head clear."

Larry turned his car around and headed back to the bar where he'd found Tony. Pulling back into the parking space in front, he waited for him to get out.

"You're not going to let this woman ruin our partnership, are you?"

Larry didn't even look at his best friend. "That's up to you, man."

Without another word, Tony got out of the car and slammed the door behind him.

Justice, Melissa thought. Everything she'd done had been done in the name of justice. She lay in her bed in Lynda Barrett's house that night, staring at the ceiling and wondering what Larry was going to do next. Would he turn her in? Would he make her out to be the criminal, just because she had tried to set things right when no one else had cared? The police had let Sandy down, and then the court system had made a mockery out of the whole ordeal. They had torn the heart out of her sister, leaving her without even the will to live.

So Melissa had taken matters into her own hands. She had tried to provide justice when no one else was offering any. But they would never understand.

She got up and went to the glass doors overlooking the patio, and stared out into the night. Lynda and Jake had gone to a movie, and they weren't home yet. They had invited her, but she'd been too upset. This was eating at her, just as it was eating at Larry.

He had wanted her to go to church with him. Was that because he knew how far she'd drifted from God?

She stared up at the stars, searching them, as though she could see God's face, angry and dark, looking down at her. Shivering, she closed the curtains and went back to bed.

But she couldn't hide from him, and her sins shone out like neon signs under God's heaven.

She'd read, many times before, "'Vengeance is mine,' saith the Lord." But she hadn't trusted his vengeance, so she'd tried to provide it herself. Now she could neither face God nor hide from him. Now, when she needed him most. Now, when she was most afraid.

She hugged herself and hunched over, crying again. There had been a time when she could pray as if Christ sat in the room next to her, and he would answer. He had always answered. But after Edward Pendergrast stalked and terrorized her sister, Melissa's prayers had been answered with "No." At least, it had seemed that way. Pendergrast had simply walked away from punishment; what kind of vengeance was that? God had not struck him dead, or made sure that he was locked up. Sandy had been the one to die, instead.

She lay back on the bed, balled up and crying into the pillow. Would God ever forgive her for not trusting him, for taking things into her own hands?

Then she heard, whispering in the back of her mind, the question that reached to the root of the problem. Was she sorry? Would she repent?

No, she thought, sitting up suddenly and wiping her tears away. No, she couldn't repent. She couldn't face the consequences of that choice.

Nor, she realized, could she face having Larry turn her in. But if she left things as they had been this afternoon, he might. She needed to do something.

Maybe, if she just explained to him what she had done and why, he would understand. Maybe he would see that she was right to do what she'd done, and that he had to keep quiet and let things run their course.

Maybe he would even protect her.

Trying to calm herself, she stumbled to the phone and dialed his number.

"Hello?" His voice was deep, quiet, distant.

"Larry?" Her voice broke, and she tried to get control. "Larry, it's Melissa. I was wondering . . . could you come over here? To Lynda's? I really need to talk to you."

He was quiet for a moment. "I'll be right over," he said finally.

She hung up and got dressed again, then sat on the edge of the bed, waiting. *Please, God, let him understand,* she prayed, but then she realized the absurdity of her prayer. Even God didn't understand. She couldn't call on him to be her ally now.

Maybe he had turned his back on her forever.

I need you, anyway, Lord, her heart cried out. *Can you forgive me if I don't repent?*

The answer was clear, inscribed deeply into her heart from years of Sunday school as a child. God only required two things of his sinners. Confession and repentance. It was a simple thing, yet it had never held such dire consequences. She couldn't confess it to God, because if she repented, Pendergrast would walk. Instead, she would confess it to Larry, hoping to make him see the necessity in what she'd done.

Tell him the truth, explain it all—since he'd already figured it out anyway—and plead with him to keep quiet. He had feelings for her, she knew, just as she had feelings for him. Maybe he would support and protect her.

Before long, she heard his car in the driveway and met him at the door. Though Lynda had stressed over and over that she wanted Melissa to make herself at home, Melissa didn't feel right bringing her own company into the home when Lynda wasn't there. So she led him back to the patio and sat down across from him, aware of the look of anticipation in his eyes, the look of hope, as if he expected her to tell him the magic words that would make this whole nasty mess go away.

"I couldn't just leave all this hanging," she said finally, looking down at her trembling hands. "Too much isn't adding up, and you're not stupid. Neither is Tony."

She saw the look of dread fall like a shadow over his face, then she looked away as she said, "You were right. I did know that Pendergrast worked at Proffer Builders. I did deliberately seek him out."

Larry opened his mouth, instinctively wanting to help her, to give her an easy out, to tell her that he believed that she had been working "undercover" to catch Pendergrast at something, and that her plan had backfired when Pendergrast came after her. There had been a rape, and she had not been able to defend herself. Those facts would mean that she hadn't lied to the grand jury, and she would be cleared. But Larry the cop couldn't suggest those facts. Because if they weren't the truth, it would offer her another lie. She had to say it on her own. *Please say it,* he thought.

"I couldn't believe it when they let him go, Larry, and he still knew where Sandy lived, and he was calling her and our parents and saying things . . . Oh, we couldn't prove it was him, but we knew. And Sandy lived in fear. She saw him in crowds, in traffic, in every public place she ever went. And at night, she'd lie awake, listening for him. I don't think she had one good night's sleep after her rape." She stopped, tried to compose herself, then went on. "I found her on a Thursday afternoon, in the bathtub. It was . . . the most awful . . . sight I've ever seen. For six months, I was a basket case. I stayed out of school for a whole year, just grieving and trying to cope with what I'd seen. It still haunts me."

She looked fully at him now, saw the mist of tears in his eyes. "Larry, I had to *do* something. I promised her that day, as I sat there holding her limp hand while I waited for the ambulance." She breathed in a sob, and tried again. "I told her that if it was the last thing I ever did, I'd see that man behind bars for the rest of his life. And I set out to do just that."

She still hadn't incriminated herself, Larry thought. It could still turn out to be what he'd suggested to Tony. It could still be something he could deal with. He waited.

"But Pendergrast disappeared. Just moved one day, and left no forwarding address. I didn't know where he'd gone, and neither did anyone else. It was time for me to go back to school, so I changed my major to the thing that interested me the most—not because of the nobility of the profession, but because it failed so often. I wanted to find out why, and how those failures could be avoided. I knew that I'd get him one day, and when I did, I wanted the system to work. I couldn't allow any mistakes."

"I can understand that," Larry said.

"So I got out, and my first order of business was to find him. I was offered the job at the FBI, and it seemed like a good opportunity to track him down. As soon as I did, I quit and came here."

"And you got a job where he worked."

"That's right," she said weakly.

"Why, Melissa? What did you hope would happen?"

"I wanted to get all the evidence I needed on him—enough to put him behind bars for good this time."

"But he was acquitted. They weren't ever going to try Sandy's case."

"Exactly. So I had to make sure there was another one."

So you followed him and watched him? he wanted to prompt her. *You tried to catch him at something, only he came after you instead?* But he couldn't ask. He couldn't give her that story. If she would just say it on her own . . .

"What did you do, Melissa?"

She got up then, unable to look at him, and walked to the edge of the patio. "I decided to make myself the sacrificial lamb."

"No," he said, his heart plummeting. She didn't mean what he thought. She couldn't.

She turned back to him. "I knew the only way I could make sure I got everything on him I needed was to be his victim." Seeing the look of horror on Larry's face, she took a step toward him. "But it's not what you think. I wasn't really going to let him touch me. I just wanted it to look like he did."

"You did set him up." The words came out in a moan, and he stood and faced her squarely. "Is that what you're telling me?"

She was crying now, and her face twisted. She covered it for a moment, then dropped her hands. "Larry, I was desperate. You have to understand. It was the only way."

"How did you do it?"

"I—did invite him over—and I was terrified. I had planned to have him come in for a while, touch some things, get his fingerprints all over the place. But I lost my nerve, and when he got there, I told him I didn't feel well, and I'd give him a rain check. He got mad and pushed his way in—"

"By force." Larry latched onto those words, thinking maybe, just maybe, Pendergrast *had* done something. Maybe she hadn't lied about all of it. Not the important part.

"Well, not for long. I had a knife, and I threatened him with it. He finally just backed off and left."

Larry's stomach sank. "But your apartment . . ."

"I did all that," she said. "I turned over tables and furniture, broke glasses to make it look like a struggle."

He turned away. "What about the cut on your leg? What about the blood on his shirt in his car?"

She waited a long time before answering that one. "He had an extra change of clothes at work. I took his shirt that day, and got the knife out of his drawer. I cut my hand and got blood all over the shirt, then wrapped the knife up in the shirt and stuck them under his seat. And I got some of the hairs out of the brush he kept in his desk, and put them on my sheets. That night, before I called the police, I cut my leg. Then I showered. In case I was examined, I knew there wouldn't be any physical evidence, and a shower would explain that. And then I called the police, and as I waited, I started to cry, deeper and harder than I had even when I found Sandy dead. I don't think I've ever been more miserable in my life, but I also felt—I don't know—justice. That, finally, something was being done."

She clutched her head as the memory came back. "It was supposed to have been easy. They were supposed to arrest him, put him in jail, take him to trial. The evidence was so conclusive that no jury could have acquitted him. But I never counted on getting involved with a cop who could see right through my story."

Larry sank down into his chair and rested his face in his hands.

"Larry, it could work! Don't you see? He's raped two women, and one of them is dead—and those are only the reported cases, the ones we know about. If he goes to jail because of this, it'll be justice—finally."

Larry looked up at her with a helpless expression. "The defense will crucify you, Melissa. He knows you lied. He knows who you are now. He'll tell them everything you did. They'll find as much evidence as we have. You'll never get away with it."

"But I might!" She sank down next to him and touched his face with her trembling hand. "They won't believe him. Even his own lawyers won't. I'm not asking you to cover up, Larry. I'm just asking you to be quiet. Just don't tell anyone what you've found. Now that I've explained it all, you must understand. Haven't you ever had a case where the end justified the means?"

His face was a study in misery as he stared at her. "Melissa, if the police force operated with that philosophy, we wouldn't even have a court system. We'd just go around shooting everybody who looked guilty. I've always gone by the book. I believe in the system."

"That's because it's never failed you!" she shouted. "Your sister didn't *die* because of it! If she had, you'd have done exactly the same thing!"

He got up again, putting some distance between them, and paced across the patio, rubbing the back of his neck. "I understand why you did it, Melissa. But it's still wrong. You can't plant evidence. You can't lie to a grand jury."

"He had already raped, Larry!" she shouted. "They let him go!"

"But he didn't rape *you!*"

Silence screamed across the night, and she looked up at him with pleading eyes. "If you turn me in, Larry, *I'll* be the one punished, and he'll walk away scot-free. Again! Is that right? You swore to get criminals off the streets. Well, I'm not the criminal, and he's still walking the streets!"

His face twisted with pain as he looked down at her, and finally he sat down next to her and cupped her chin with his hand. "Don't you understand? Even if I did keep quiet, Tony's an inch away from going to the captain with what he knows. Everyone's going to figure it out."

"No, they won't!" she cried. "They may think they've figured it out, they may suggest it in court, but they can't prove it! The jury will just think they're grasping! Another case of the victim being made to look like the criminal." She rose up on her knees and grabbed his arms, making him look at her. "Larry, it could work. The man who raped my sister and caused her to kill herself could be convicted. All I'm asking you to do is *nothing.* Just leave it alone. And get Tony off the track. Come up with a story. You can do it."

He looked at her, saw the goodness, the determination, the torture in her eyes. He had vowed to bring her smile back, but instead he was threatening to send it fleeing forever. His convictions began to wane, and he wondered what would happen if he did just what she was asking—nothing. Maybe Tony would buy the story he'd already suggested tonight. Maybe no one would ever have to know.

God will know.

That voice inside him, the one that always warned him when he began to stray, startled him.

"I'm a Christian," he said. "I don't know if that means a whole lot to you, but it does to me."

"I know," she whispered. "But God promised that he would not leave the guilty unpunished. Maybe this is his way of punishing Pendergrast."

"You know it isn't," Larry said. "God never asks us to sin to accomplish his will. God didn't tell you to lie, or to set up a crime, or to pretend that you're a victim—"

"I *am* his victim!" she cried. "The day my sister died, I became his victim. God knows that!"

"You can't hide behind God on this one, Melissa. And I can't hide this *from* him."

"I'm not asking you to. This is between God and me. Leave it at that. This doesn't have to compromise your faith. God won't blame you for it."

"Melissa, if you believe that," he said sadly, "you're farther from God than I thought. If I lie for you, or cover up, or even withhold information, I'll be accountable. My relationship with Christ depends on *my* heart, not yours. And if I make a choice that I know is apart from his will . . ." His voice cracked, and he couldn't go on.

She covered her mouth again and caught a sob, and she rested her forehead on his knee. He touched the back of her head, then bent down to kiss it. Misery overcame him, blinding him, scorching him, and finally, he whispered, "I've got to go. I have a lot of thinking to do."

"Yeah," she whispered, raising her head. "I guess you do."

She followed him to his car, and before he got in, he lingered there for a moment, looking at her with sad, soft eyes. He reached up and touched her wet cheek, and she set her hand on top of his, held it there for a moment. Finally, he leaned over and kissed her, sweet, long, and sad.

"I'm sorry, Larry," she whispered.

"Yeah," he said, squinting against his own tears. "Me, too."

She watched as he got into his car and pulled out of the driveway. In her heart, she knew that he would never kiss her again.

22

LARRY SAT ON the edge of his bed, staring at the floor as if the facts lined up on it like ceramic tiles.

Fact. He had sworn to get criminals off the street.

Fact. Pendergrast had been charged with two other rapes.

Fact. Pendergrast had managed to beat the law and was still on the streets.

Fact. Pendergrast had broken into Melissa's apartment, called her, and stalked her.

Fact. Pendergrast had threatened to fulfill the lies she'd told about him, and his history indicated that he would do just that.

Fact. Tony knew that something wasn't right in the case.

Fact. Melissa was guilty of lying before a grand jury.

Fact. The penalty for that lie was up to five years in prison.

Fact. Larry was falling in love with her.

That final fact made him cover his eyes with his hand and fall back onto his bed. Tony had warned him. He was getting too involved, too close. He was letting her influence him. Maybe he wasn't even thinking straight.

Even so—could he honestly take the chance of sending her to prison?

He fell to his knees beside his bed and cried out to God to help him with this lose-lose decision—this choice that shouldn't be a choice at all.

He had never meant to care about her, but she had seemed so alone.

He felt God's love, radiating through him like sunlight on a July day, and he knew that love was for Melissa, too. God had a plan for her. But what if it wasn't one that Larry could live with?

"She'll go to prison if I tell what I know!" he cried out to God. "With hookers and drug addicts and thieves. She's so little—she'll never survive.

"And Pendergrast will go free—again! He'll hurt others. You know he will, Lord. That can't happen. He raped Sandy. Lord, help me understand . . ."

His prayer went on into the night, pleading with God, reasoning with him, wrestling with him. The options, both his and God's, whirled through his mind, exhausting him with choices and possibilities, absolutes and shades of gray.

And by the time dawn intruded on the room, Larry had made the choice that he knew he shouldn't make, the choice that would protect the woman he loved. The choice that would be a lie. Wearily, he cried out to God again, "Please forgive me for what I'm about to do!"

But a shadow fell over the room as he spoke, for God wasn't listening anymore. Already, there was a barrier.

Already.

Feeling empty and angry, he got to his feet, exhausted, troubled, miserable, and tried to sort out what he needed to do. He would go to the station and tell Tony that Melissa had confirmed the "supposing" he had done last night. He would say that she had worked undercover to catch Pendergrast at something, but that the tables had turned and he had come after her instead. Her plan had backfired, and she'd been made a victim.

And then he'd call in every favor Tony had ever owed him to convince him to let Larry call the shots on this case. Tony would listen. He'd have to.

Melissa would only have to answer to the DA for not telling everything from the beginning. It would look bad for her, but it wouldn't land her in jail. And any jury would believe it.

Whatever the outcome, it was better than telling the truth.

He showered and got dressed, playing the story over and over in his mind. Tony would believe him. It would make sense. And Tony would never in a million years think that Larry would lie. Not even for a woman.

His spirits remained deflated as he went around the apartment straightening up, keeping busy so that he wouldn't think about principles, or values, or his relationship with God. And then he saw his Bible, lying open on the table where he had been reading from it yesterday. The words were suddenly threatening, whatever they were, and he couldn't bear to see them. He closed it suddenly and set it on the bookshelf where it wasn't as likely to catch his eye.

He couldn't think about what he was doing. All he could do was act—quickly—before his own convictions forced him to change his mind.

23

"*M*ELISSA, DO YOU *think suicide keeps you from heaven?"*

"Why would you ask something like that? Sandy, don't even think that. We're going to put this behind us. One day, it'll all be over, and he'll be in jail, and we'll be able to laugh again—"

"He's not in jail, Melissa. He's still out there. And I feel so dirty."

"You have to trust. You have to have faith."

"Sometimes I just don't have the patience for faith. Prayers take too long to be answered. Maybe I have to take things into my own hands—"

"What do you mean? Going after him? Hurting him somehow?"

No answer.

And then the dream changed scenes, and there were ambulances, police cars, interrogations, coroners, the crowd around the house just like it had been on the night of the rape . . .

Drama upon drama . . .

Then the dream flashed back to little girls on the beach, romping in frothing waves, laughing and splashing each other. It changed to a ballet recital, when Melissa, in awe, had watched Sandy as the star soloist in the spring production, then afterward, when the family had gone out for ice cream, and Sandy had laughed and talked nonstop about all the catastrophes backstage.

Then Melissa stood over a baptismal, watching as her sister gave her testimony, then was baptized—then stepped aside as Melissa, younger but just as touched by the Holy Spirit, did the same.

"Do you feel different, Sandy?" she asked as they climbed the stairs out of the baptismal.

"I feel clean," Sandy said with tears in her eyes. "Reborn. Like this is a beginning."

And then the dream changed again, and the baptismal was a bathtub, and it wasn't the beginning, but the end, and Sandy wasn't born; she was dead.

Melissa woke in a cold sweat, shivering from the force of emotion that had assaulted her even in the dream. Throwing the covers back, she ran to the bathroom and threw up, then sat on the floor waiting for it to happen again.

"I feel dirty, too, Sandy," she whispered. Covering her mouth, she tried to muffle her sobs so she wouldn't wake Lynda. She *was* dirty.

And she was making Larry dirty, too.

She leaned back against the wall and looked up at the ceiling, as if she could see God through it. "Why did she have to die?" she asked.

She sobbed into her knees, hugging them tightly.

After a while, she got up wearily and washed her face, dried it, and looked in the mirror. She didn't like what she saw, so she turned away.

Opening the door that went from her bedroom onto the patio, she went outside and sat on the swing, hugging her knees and looking up at the stars as if being there brought her closer to the Lord. "I've asked Larry to do something horrible," she whispered to God. She covered her face. "How could I ask him to make a choice like that? Who am I, to do that?"

Her muffled sobs came harder.

"Oh, God," she whispered. "Can you ever forgive me? Can you ever make me new again, like when I first knew you?"

Slowly, a strange peace fell over her, as though some heavenly hand were stroking her hair, whispering to her that it would be all right. And for the first time since Sandy's death, Melissa began to feel that, someday, maybe it *would* be all right.

Sliding her hands down her face, Melissa cried out, "Lord, tell me what I have to do."

She wept some more, feeling all her energy draining out of her, but into her mind crept the answer she had sought. There was only one answer.

She had to set things right—for Larry, and for herself—no matter what the consequences were. There was no one left to depend on but God. And somehow, now, she felt that she had the patience Sandy had not had to trust him. He would take care of her. He would forgive her.

She really had no choice. She had tried to do it all herself, and she had spoiled everything.

She wiped her face, tried to pull herself together, and went back into the house. Tiptoeing up the hall, she peered into Lynda's room. Lynda was in her bed, but she was sitting up, looking back at Melissa as if she'd been waiting.

"Lynda?" The word came out hoarse, raspy, on the edge of a sob. "You're awake. I hope I didn't wake you."

Lynda pulled back the covers and patted the bed for Melissa to sit down. "I thought I heard you throwing up. I went to check on you, but you were crying. Something told me you needed to be alone. But I was praying for you."

Melissa breathed a laugh. "Well, that explains it."

"Explains what?" Lynda asked softly. "Melissa, are you all right?"

Though it looked as if she wasn't, Melissa nodded her head. "I'm going to be. But I need your help."

"What do you need?" Lynda asked. "I'll do whatever I can."

"That's good," Melissa said. "Because I'm going to need a lawyer."

24

LARRY COULDN'T MAKE himself go straight to the police station that morning. Instead, he drove by Pendergrast's apartment, looking for either of the two cars Pendergrast was known to drive. The dark blue Cherokee was in its place, and after searching the parking lot in front and back, he finally found the gray Toyota, too.

Larry put his car in park and let it idle as he stared up at the apartment where a rapist slept. Had he been out prowling all night? Was he sleeping now? Some part of him—some uncharacteristic part that he didn't recognize—made him want to kick down the man's door, grab him out of bed, and beat him to a pulp.

But he couldn't do that. He had no grounds, no warrant, no just cause.

He drove to a convenience store on the corner and found a pay phone at the end of the small building. He picked up the receiver and held it for a moment, letting his forehead rest against the phone. What would he tell Melissa? That she was off the hook? That he would lie for her?

His stomach played queasy games with him as he went over the words in his mind. Finally, he dialed Lynda's number. After a few rings, Jake answered.

"Hello?"

"Jake? Larry here. Has Melissa left for work yet?"

"Maybe," Jake said. "She and Lynda are both gone. They weren't even here when I came over for breakfast. Maybe they went out for breakfast."

Out for breakfast. His heart sank. He had been up all night, struggling with the decision to lie for her, and she had hopped out of bed and gone out to eat?

It didn't matter, he told himself. He had to stick to his decision to protect her.

His face was tired and somber when he reached the police station. As usual, it was an acoustical nightmare. Even at this hour, voices were deafening as burglary suspects and joyriders brought in hours ago waited to be booked. Printers were printing, phones were ringing. Tony's computer was on, but his chair was empty. "Where's Tony?" Larry asked one of the other officers.

The officer held a telephone between his ear and shoulder and nodded distractedly toward the interrogation room.

Larry frowned. Who would he be interrogating this early?

He walked around the wall, to the two-way mirror that allowed him to look into the room.

And his heart plummeted.

Tony sat at the table across from two women: Lynda Barrett . . . and Melissa.

"Oh, no," he whispered.

Melissa was talking nonstop, and Tony was taking notes. He saw as she turned back to look at Lynda that she was crying, and Lynda was crying, too. Lynda reached out and took her hand, and he saw her tell Melissa to go on.

She's confessing! he thought. But why? She hadn't given him the chance. Had she believed he was going to turn her in? Had she been afraid of what he might do?

He bolted around the corner and burst into the room. "What's going on here?"

Melissa averted her eyes, but Tony and Lynda looked up. "Larry, sit down," Tony said gently.

"No," he said. "I want to know what's going on."

Tony looked genuinely sorry as he got to his feet. "Melissa called me early this morning, Larry. She wanted to meet with me. She had something to say."

Finally, Melissa looked up, her red, wet eyes locking with Larry's, and he could see in her expression that she had told everything.

"I'm sorry, Larry."

He breathed out a sad, exasperated laugh. "For what?"

Floundering, she looked back at Tony. "Tony, can I have a minute alone with Larry? Just a minute?"

Tony seemed a little more humble than he had the last time Larry had seen him, and he closed his notes and took them with him.

"Do you want me to leave you alone, too, Melissa?" Lynda asked.

Melissa nodded. "It won't take long."

The two left, and for a moment Larry just stood there, staring at her. "You told him."

"I had to."

"Why?" he asked, pulling a chair to face her and dropping into it. "Last night, I told you I was going to think about it—"

"That's why. To keep you from having to."

The words came out on an overpowering wave of emotion. "But I wasn't going to!"

Her face twisted, and she touched his face as tears rolled down her cheeks.

"I never meant to put you in that position," she whispered. "God's been dealing with me, Larry."

He covered her hand with his, holding it against his cheek. "But I was going to protect you. I could have, if you'd just waited."

"And what would that have cost you?"

It had already cost him, but he didn't tell her that. "Melissa, what's it going to cost *you?*"

She tried to look stronger. "Lynda said there's a possibility that there won't be any jail time. It's my first felony, so there's a chance I could get probation, maybe some community service. And if I do get jail time, it may not be prison." Her voice cracked, and she lifted her chin. "Just the county jail for women."

He pulled her into his arms and laid his forehead on her shoulder. "I can't stand that thought," he said.

"I'll be all right," she whispered. "I have to trust God in this, like I should have from the first."

Larry wept harder, but he couldn't tell her that it was because *he* had chosen not to trust God, had in fact deliberately turned away from him, deliberately disobeyed. The fact that he hadn't actually committed the act didn't matter. He had made the choice.

"I want to thank you, Larry."

"For what?"

"For reminding me who's in control."

"But Pendergrast is still out there!" Larry cried.

"I know," she whispered. "But I finally realized last night that Pendergrast can't hide his sins from God. Anymore than I can."

Larry gazed at her, his face twisted and reddening. "You can live with that?"

"I have to," she said, wiping her eyes. "Either I believe in God's power or I don't. Sandy didn't. Maybe it wasn't her fault. Maybe she had just gotten too weak—too tired. But I do, Larry."

He crushed her against him and held her so long that he thought he might never let her go. "I love you, you know."

She smiled through her tears. "Yeah, I think I've known that for some time."

Outside the door in the noisy precinct room where people came and went, Tony leaned against the wall, a baffled look on his face. "I'm amazed," he said. "I mean, I suspected things weren't right all along, but I never dreamed she'd just walk in and confess. Why did she?"

"I suspect it had something to do with Larry," Lynda said.

"But she could have told half the truth and gotten away with it."

Lynda studied his face. "You seem almost troubled that she confessed."

"Well," he said, shaking his head. "I have to admit that I wanted to get to the bottom of it. But now, when I think that she'll be punished, and that thug is going to go free . . . It almost makes me wish I didn't know anything about the law."

Lynda sighed wearily. "I know what you mean. When she told me, I came so close to telling her to stay quiet. But that wouldn't have been right, for either of us. This is between Melissa and God. And she feels she's doing the right thing."

"You see?" Tony said, grimacing. "That's what kills me. All these things you guys do in the name of God. Does she realize she'll go to jail in the name of God?"

"She won't be going in the name of God. She'll be going because of her own wrong decisions," she whispered. "Besides, the state may decide not to prosecute."

"But if they do, she'll probably go to jail. The people in that place—" He looked around the huge room and waved his hand toward some of the criminals being charged with crimes for which they deserved punishment they probably wouldn't get. "She may not even survive it."

"She just has to trust, Tony. If she had trusted God in the beginning, instead of taking things into her own hands, none of this would have happened."

Tony had to agree with at least part of that. His gaze shifting to the interrogation room, he asked, "Did *he* know?"

Lynda shrugged. "I honestly don't know. She didn't tell me, and I didn't want to know. I don't think you really do, either. It's between them."

He moaned and looked up at the ceiling.

"But I do know this much," Lynda said. "She didn't want him to be the one to turn her in."

"Or to cover for her." Tony crossed his arms and leaned his head back against the wall. "Under normal circumstances, nothing on earth would have made Larry lie about a case. But this is different. Something about that woman. Larry hasn't been himself lately."

"Maybe he's in love with her."

"Yeah," Tony said quietly. "Maybe he is." He looked back at Lynda, who looked as tired as he felt. He wondered whether she'd gotten any sleep last night. "Sometimes I wish I'd listened to my mother and become a dentist."

She smiled. "You, too?"

The door opened, and Larry stepped out, his eyes red and glassy. Tony pushed off from the wall, and for a moment, just stood looking at his friend.

"You okay?" he asked finally.

"Yeah."

"You want me to book her, or do you want to?"

Larry struggled with the emotion so clear on his face and rubbed his jaw with rough fingertips. "You do it. But go easy, okay? Don't make a spectacle out of her."

"You know I won't, buddy."

Larry touched Lynda's arm, making her look up at him. "Do what you can for her, Lynda. Don't let her go to jail."

"I'll do my very best."

His face was losing its battle with the feelings coursing through him, so he started briskly across the room.

"Larry?"

Larry turned at Tony's call. "Yeah?"

"Where are you going?"

His mouth trembled as he tried to get the words out. "Out. Something I need to take care of. I'll be back."

"All right, buddy."

And Tony and Lynda watched as Larry fairly ran through the precinct and out the back door.

25

THE PAIN RAGING inside Larry was inescapable and constant. His habitual instinct to turn to God for help, for peace, seemed foreign to him now. He was angry, and there was nowhere to turn.

The bell warning that his gas tank was dangerously low kept ringing until he finally pulled over into a small parking area along a beach. He didn't know how long he'd been driving, but he figured he was somewhere in St. Petersburg. The beach was bare, for the day was overcast, just as his heart seemed to be. He left his car and walked across the sand, staring furiously out at the clouds billowing over the farthest reaches of the Gulf.

She won't survive jail, his mind railed. *She'll never make it. She doesn't know what she's doing.*

He reached a long pier that stretched over the water and started walking toward the seagulls perched on the railing at the end.

It's too much—she'll be punished, and he'll go free.

He walked faster, his sneakers making little sound on the wooden planks. The cool wind whipped harshly through his hair and flapped at his jacket. Overhead, he heard the rustle of wings as a flock of egrets settled on the railing behind him.

He reached the end of the pier, scattering the seagulls, and looked across the water to the clouds beyond. It was majestic, beautiful, but it looked like anger coming home to settle on the water.

God's anger.

Larry's anger.

He began to weep, hard and loud, his anguish catching on the wind and flying off to some unknown place where it wouldn't be heeded. "Why?" he shouted. "Why?"

But there was no answer, just the loud drumming of the waves against the shore, and the ruthless *caw* of the seagulls soaring overhead.

He ran back down the pier, across the sand, and back to the car. He slammed the door and collapsed against the wheel, his head resting on his arms.

Forsaken. That was the word. He had been forsaken. His refuge was gone, and his peace had been shattered. He was alone, by his own choice.

Gritting his teeth against the rage that it had come to this, he started the car and pulled out into traffic, pushing his car to the speed limit and beyond.

But it would never be fast enough.

26

IT WAS NO surprise that the state decided to prosecute, nor was it a surprise that Melissa appeared for her arraignment that afternoon with a guilty plea. The judge wasn't interested, at this point, in why she'd done what she had done. All that mattered was that a crime had been committed. He ordered a presentence investigation by the Department of Corrections, then set the sentencing for a little over two weeks away.

All of the charges against Pendergrast were dropped.

As Melissa rode home from the arraignment with Lynda, she was quiet, preoccupied. "What are you thinking?" Lynda asked. "You're not having regrets, are you?"

Melissa thought that over for a moment. "Not about confessing. But I wish I'd found another way to get him." Her eyes strayed out the window as they drove through downtown, past the Ritz cinema and the hardware store and the newspaper office, all part of the town she had never really gotten a chance to know. "He's out there. He's going to hurt more women. Maybe even kill somebody."

"You're scared, aren't you?"

She moved her eyes back to Lynda. "Wouldn't you be?"

"Absolutely," Lynda said. She reached across the seat and patted Melissa's hand. "I've been there, remember?"

"Yeah." She sighed. "I just keep thinking how much rage he must feel toward me, knowing I lied about him and set him up. A man like him—he won't just sit still for that. He'll get revenge somehow."

"Well, you're more than welcome to stay with me as long as you want. Maybe he'll just let the court system get revenge."

"The court system," she muttered. "I'll go to jail, won't I?"

"Not if there's any way I can convince the judge not to send you there. But I have to tell you. This judge, L. B. Summerfield, is the toughest one I've ever dealt with. When the DOC interviews you for the presentence investigation, you need to tell them everything. Everything about Sandy's rape, how he continued to terrorize her, how he terrorized your family—"

"Does any of that really matter?" Melissa asked. "Everybody acts like it's only what I've done that matters." She looked thoughtfully at Lynda. "Won't the fact that I recanted and confessed have any bearing on his decision? Wouldn't he be more lenient because of that?"

Lynda sighed. "I wish I could say he would. But by law, you can't use recantation as a defense—at least, not in your case. There are some cases where you can—like if you recant during the same official proceeding where you lied—but it won't work for us now. The best we can hope is that your story will be enough."

"Will the DOC be interviewing Pendergrast, too?"

"Yes, thank God. And if they have any sense at all, they'll see him for what he is."

"No, they won't," Melissa said quietly, looking out the window again. "He's too smart. Too convincing. He'll make them think he's the victim."

"They'll look at more than his story, Melissa. They'll look at his history, too. You just have to have faith." She glanced at Melissa as they rounded a corner. "Are you going to call your parents?"

For a moment, Melissa couldn't answer. "I don't know. I guess I'll have to. I mean, I can't very well go to jail and keep it from them. Part of me wants to just wait and see how the hearing comes out. But if I'm sentenced to jail time, I might not get the chance to explain it all to them, to make them understand . . ."

"Tell them before the hearing," Lynda said. "Don't leave them out of this. You're their only child. They need to know."

Melissa wiped her tears away. "I'll think about it."

"Good." They reached the outskirts of her neighborhood. "Are you going to see Larry tonight?"

Melissa's mouth twisted, and she shrugged. "I doubt I'll be seeing him anymore. I mean, I don't blame him. It's not real good for a cop's reputation to be involved with a known felon."

"Melissa, the man cares about you. He's not just going to cut you off because of this. You saw how upset he was this morning."

"Exactly my point."

"Well, if I were a gambler, I'd bet that you're wrong about him. If I know Larry Millsaps, this isn't the end."

She turned down her long street, past the two houses on the corner. When her house, set alone at the end of the dead-end street, came into view, there was a small black Chevy parked in the driveway, and Lynda smiled slowly. "As a matter of fact . . ."

Melissa only frowned, afraid to get her hopes up as they pulled into the driveway next to Larry's car. She got out, looking for him, and in a moment, the door to Jake's apartment opened, and the two men walked out.

It had been a hard day for Larry, Melissa thought. His eyes were red, like hers, and she knew he hadn't gotten much sleep last night. He'd probably been up all night struggling with the decision she had given him to make. And this afternoon, in the courtroom, he had seemed to be in worse shape than she was.

She hated herself for putting him through this. If he'd never met her, if she'd never lied, he'd still be out there doing his job, arresting people and locking them up, going to his church, and enjoying his friends—rather than suffering because of something she had done. Yes, she hated herself.

But Larry cut across the driveway without a word and pulled her into a hug that crushed life back into her.

"It'll be all right," he whispered. "Somehow, it's gonna be all right."

She began to cry against his shoulder, and she saw Lynda and Jake disappear into the house, leaving them alone.

"We have to talk," she said finally, looking up at him. "See—you don't owe me anything. What I deserve is to have you just forget you ever knew me. I would be all right. Really."

He stepped back, framed her face with his hands, and gazed intently into her eyes. "Melissa, that's not going to happen. I'm going through this with you."

"But I don't want you to," she cried. "I don't want you to have to suffer."

"But I am suffering," he said. "I'm suffering because you are. I wish I could move the clock back three years and stop what happened to Sandy, for your sake, but I can't. All I can do is be here with you now. And you have to let me."

She wilted in his arms then, allowing herself to feel the peace and comfort and sustenance he offered, the support she didn't deserve, the grace she hadn't earned. Just like God's love, she thought. For she saw Larry as a gift, sent as a light in the darkness her life had become.

They spent as much time together as they could for the next two weeks, avoiding the subject of the hearing coming up, avoiding mention of the names Soames or Pendergrast, avoiding the topic of jail or hearings, avoiding the media, who had latched onto her story like hungry dogs to a bone. Because notice of her arraignment had appeared in the local paper, Melissa lost her job with the temporary agency. That was part curse and part blessing, Larry decided, since her mind wasn't on work right now, anyway, and she needed this time to prepare. Besides, her interview with the DOC had lasted for two whole days, and it had taken a few days after that for her mental and physical exhaustion from rehashing the whole story to fade.

Larry, too, was interviewed, along with Tony and some of the other cops who'd answered her call that first night. It was apparent to him that they were trying to determine just how much damage had been done with her lie, and how calculated it was. Melissa never asked what he had told them, and when he'd tried to tell her, she'd refused to listen. He didn't owe her an explanation, she told him. But whether they spoke of it or not, the clock was ticking.

He took some vacation days the week of her sentencing, and on that Tuesday, drove her to the beach. They took off their shoes and rolled up their jeans and walked barefoot through the gentle waves at high tide. The sun was just beginning to set, and a cool breeze swept in from the Gulf, whispering through Melissa's hair, the pink-golden rays of the sun making her hair look even lighter.

She slowed her step and kicked at a wave as it frothed around her ankles, then turned toward the breeze and watched the sunset fill the sky with a brilliant array of pinks and golds and yellows. "It's beautiful," she whispered. "Look, Larry. Isn't it beautiful?"

He put his hands on her shoulders and stood behind her, watching the sky. She felt so small beneath his hands. Her head barely reached the indentation of his neck. "Yes," he whispered, kissing the top of her head. "It's beautiful."

"Let's just sit here for a while," she said. "Let's watch it until it goes down."

She sat in the white, dry sand, and he sat beside her, holding her against him as the sun made its grand finale of the day. It took over an hour for it to disappear below the horizon, and in all that time, they didn't utter a word.

Finally, when the pinks and golds had given way to a grayish blue, Melissa scooped up some sand in her hand and watched it fall through her fingers. "I have to call my parents," she said.

"Good. I hoped you would."

"It's not going to be easy," she said, still watching the sand. "In fact, I can't tell them this over the phone. I need to do it in person."

"I'm sure they'll come."

She swallowed and looked up at him. "Will you help me, Larry? Help me tell them, I mean?"

"Of course. I'll tell them *for* you if you want."

"No," she said. "They have to hear it from me. But I'm just not sure I'm strong enough. And I'm not sure they are." Her voice broke off, and Larry pulled her against him.

When she finally pulled herself together and sat up straight again, she drew in a deep, rugged breath. "Let's go. I want to call them now. Maybe they can come tomorrow, and I can spend a few days with them before the hearing."

27

MELISSA HAD TROUBLE getting the words out over the telephone, but she managed to tell her parents that she was in trouble and she needed them. They were already frantic after not being able to reach her since her last vague, evasive phone calls, and the cursory note she'd sent them telling them not to worry hadn't helped. When she tried to tell them where she'd been, she couldn't go on. She handed the phone to Larry.

"Mrs. Nelson?" Larry asked. "This is Larry Millsaps. I'm a friend of Melissa's."

"Is she all right?" Nancy Nelson asked with a quiver in her voice.

"What's going on there?" Jim Nelson threw in from the extension.

"Well, she'd rather talk to you in person. I gathered from her end of the conversation that you're coming tomorrow?"

"Yes. We'll get the earliest flight. We can come tonight if she needs us to."

"No. Tomorrow will be fine."

"Mr. Millsaps, tell us—has she been hurt? Is she sick?"

"No, ma'am. She's not hurt or sick. She's fine."

"But she said she was in trouble!" her mother said.

"Does this have anything to do with—Edward Pendergrast?" her father asked.

Larry looked at Melissa, then closed his eyes. "Why would you ask that?"

"Because of the phone calls. The threats. The way she's been evading our questions. All the secrecy! It's so much like it was with Sandy. Does this have anything to do with him?"

Her mother was crying now. "We've just had a feeling all this time. When that man called us . . . I kept thinking I knew that voice."

Larry put his hand over the phone and whispered, "They want to know if it has anything to do with Pendergrast."

"Oh, no." She took back the phone. "Mom, Dad? Please. This is real important, and I need to talk to you in person. All I can tell you right now is that no one has hurt me. Can you just accept that and wait until we can talk?"

"All right, sweetheart." Her father's voice cracked. "All right. If that's how it has to be."

"Will you be all right until morning?" her mother asked.

"Yes, Mom. I'm in really good hands. I'm staying with a terrific person, a new friend. And Larry's watching over me, too. I didn't mean to scare you. This is not like it was with Sandy. My trouble is of my own making."

Perplexed, her parents were silent for a moment, then finally, her father said, "We'll see you early in the morning. Will you be at the airport?"

She wished she could say yes, but the airport was in Tampa, and she had been ordered not to leave St. Clair until her hearing. "Larry will be meeting you," she said. "He'll bring you to where I'm staying. He's a tall man, about six-two, with dark brown hair . . . good-looking . . ." She smiled slightly, and Larry couldn't help returning it. "You'll like him, Mom."

"Is he someone you're seeing?"

"Yes," she said.

"Well, why haven't you mentioned him?"

"I'll explain everything tomorrow, Mom."

Her mother didn't answer for a moment. "Melissa, I'm so worried about you."

"Please try not to worry, Mom. I'll see you both tomorrow."

Larry had made it a point to drive by Pendergrast's apartment several times a day to check for both cars. If one was missing, he would call Melissa and make sure everything was all right. It didn't appear that Pendergrast had yet figured out where she was staying. Larry had found Pendergrast's car parked at Proffer Builders for the past two days, so he assumed that he had gotten his job back. Everything was back to normal for him, Larry thought bitterly. Meanwhile, Melissa had to tell her parents that she might be going to jail.

Satisfied that Pendergrast was nowhere near Melissa, he drove an hour to the Tampa airport and walked the long walk to the gate where the Nelsons would be coming in. Melissa had described them to him, but somehow he felt that he would know them anyway the moment he saw them.

The plane was just landing as he reached the gate, and he stood by the window, watching, praying silently that they'd manage to take this well. It wouldn't be easy dealing with a jail sentence for their only daughter. God certainly knew it wasn't easy for him.

He watched the passengers come out of the tunnel, searching their faces. And then he saw them. The woman's blonde hair was pulled back in a bun, revealing a little gray around the temples, but it was clear from her blue eyes and the shape of her mouth that she was Melissa's mother.

They both looked younger than he had expected, probably in their late forties, and their eyes were troubled as they scanned the crowd for him.

Slowly, Larry worked his way to them. "Mr. and Mrs. Nelson?" he asked.

"Larry?" Jim Nelson returned.

Larry smiled and shook his hand. "It's nice to finally meet you. Do you need to go to the baggage claim?"

"No," her father said. "It's all in our carry-ons."

"All right. My car's this way."

They walked in silence for a moment. Larry glanced over at them. "Did you have a good flight, Mr. Nelson?"

"Jim," he said. "Call me Jim."

"And call me Nancy," Melissa's mother said. "You're obviously important to our daughter. There's no point in formalities. Have you known her long?"

"Only a few weeks," he said.

"Oh. From what she said last night, I thought it had been longer."

"It seems like longer," he agreed. They came to the escalator, and he stood back and allowed both of them to precede him.

Not much more was said as he led them to his car. When they were on their way, with Jim in front and Nancy in back, Larry could sense Jim studying him. "I know Melissa has something to tell us, and she wants to do it herself, but can you at least tell us where she's living? She has an apartment, doesn't she? Why isn't she in it?"

"She's just been spending a couple of weeks with friends," he said. "It wasn't a good time for her to be alone."

Her mother leaned forward on the seat. "Is she living with you?"

He glanced in the rearview mirror. "No, ma'am. Absolutely not. She's staying with a friend named Lynda Barrett."

Jim looked him over again. "What do you do for a living, Larry?"

Larry hesitated to tell him. "I'm a police officer."

Jim let the words sink in for a moment, then glanced back at his wife.

"How did you two meet?" her mother asked in a voice that was growing more raspy.

He swallowed. "I'll let her tell you about that, if you don't mind."

For the rest of the hour's drive to St. Clair, no one spoke. There was nothing more he could tell them, after all, without treading on Melissa's ground.

Lynda was at work and Jake was at physical therapy when Larry brought the Nelsons to Melissa.

Her parents looked apprehensive as they got out of the car and looked around at the modest little house. The side door to the house opened, and Melissa came out. "Mom. Dad." She ran into their arms, and for a moment, Larry stood back, feeling like an outsider. But he had promised her he would stay.

When the family hug broke, she led them all into the house, and into the living room. Her mother and father huddled together on the couch, waiting for the bomb to drop. "What did you want to tell us, Melissa?" her father asked gently. "Please don't make us wait any longer."

Melissa took Larry's hand and sat down across from them. "All right." She took a deep breath, and looked up at Larry, struggling to find the words. She'd practiced all night and all morning, but now that the time had come, all her scripted words escaped her. How would she tell them?

Mom, Dad, I may be going to jail.

No, she couldn't tell them that yet. She had to start at the beginning.

She cleared her throat. "You know when I quit my job at the FBI, and you were all upset and confused?"

"Yes," her mother said.

"I quit because I'd managed to locate Edward Pendergrast." Her mother gasped, and her father's frown grew deeper. "He was working here in St. Clair under another name," she went on.

"Oh, no," her mother cried, sitting back hard on the couch. "You came here to find him? Why? You should have stayed as far away from him as you could!"

Melissa blinked back the tears in her eyes. "I got a job working where he did."

"What?" her father asked in horror.

"I wanted to set him up," she said. She got to her feet, paced across the living room, and turned back to them. "I thought if I made it look like I'd been his next victim, then this time he'd get convicted. I'd make sure that there were no loose ends. That he wouldn't get off on a technicality this time. That he'd go to prison, where he belongs."

Her father stood slowly. "Are you telling us that you pretended he'd raped you?"

"Yes," she said. "That's exactly what I did. Larry was one of the detectives assigned to the case. He's a good cop."

Her mother was starting to cry. "Melissa, how could you do that? It could have gotten you killed! No wonder Pendergrast started calling us. He was looking for you!"

"Yes, he was," Larry agreed, "and they didn't keep him in jail after his indictment. He was out pending trial."

"Oh, Melissa! Is that why you kept moving?"

Melissa shoved her hair behind her ear. Her hand was trembling. "Yes. I caught him following me a couple of times. And he broke in."

"He was in your house?" her mother whispered.

Melissa nodded. "Nothing happened. I think he was just trying to scare me."

"I brought her here because I knew he wouldn't find her here," Larry cut in. "Lynda's a friend of mine."

"But—you lied, Melissa," her father said. "Is he in on this?" he asked, pointing to Larry.

"No, Dad. The thing is, I confessed two weeks ago."

Larry braced his elbows on his knees and propped his chin on his fist. Melissa kept her eyes on her parents.

"Why?" her father asked.

"Because it wasn't right. I had lied. And lying to a grand jury is a felony."

Jim's face paled, and he sank back down onto the couch. Her mother took his hand. "A felony?" she whispered.

"The actual charge is 'perjury in an official proceeding.' I could get up to five years."

"In prison?" her father asked in horror.

Her mother's face reddened. She covered her mouth, then asked, "What about him? What about that monster?"

Larry saw how Melissa struggled with that answer, so he spoke up. "They dropped all charges against him. They couldn't try him for something that hadn't happened."

"So he's still out there?" her mother asked on a sob. "And *Melissa's* the one who might go to jail?"

Larry nodded. "Unless the judge decides to go easy on her. The sentencing is Friday."

"Only two days from now?" Nancy gasped.

"Lynda's my lawyer," Melissa managed to say in a higher pitched voice. "She's hopeful that I won't have to serve any jail time. But there's no way to know for sure until we get into court. The judge will read all the testimony in the presentencing investigation, and he'll make his decision. All we can do is pray."

Melissa watched the pain distorting her parents' faces, and she broke into a sob. "I wanted you to hear it from me. I wanted you to be here."

Both of her parents got up and drew her into a hug. They all wept as Larry sat alone, wishing he could ease their pain.

28

THURSDAY DAWNED WITH harsh finality—the last day of life as she'd always known it. Tomorrow was Melissa's hearing; tomorrow she would find out if she had a future. She had hoped to sleep late, but she woke just after dawn and lay awake staring at the ceiling.

Tomorrow she could be going to jail.

She closed her eyes and prayed for deliverance, but even as she did, she felt the shame of deserving what she was getting.

The funny thing about God's forgiveness was that the consequences still had to be paid. Not because God necessarily required payment—but because the state did.

Not for the first time, she longed to turn back time, to forget her obsession with making Pendergrast pay. If only she had put him out of her mind and gone on with her life, tried to forget. But such a big part of her hadn't wanted to forget. Feeding her vengeful hatred had somehow sustained her. Now it was doing her in.

Tears rolled down her temples and into her hair as she stared up at the ceiling. The image of Gethsemane flashed through her mind—Jesus weeping the night before his own arrest—the disciples sleeping through it all as Larry and Lynda and Jake all probably were. She closed her eyes and thought of Christ's prayer for deliverance. She, too, had asked for deliverance—had pleaded and bargained for it. But she feared that the price of her disobedience would still have to be paid.

Getting out of bed, she pulled on her robe and went barefoot down the hall. A light was already on in the kitchen, and quietly, she stepped into the doorway. Lynda was sitting at the table reading her Bible. In her white cotton nightgown with little blue flowers, Lynda looked like a little girl, rather than a successful attorney. "Hi," Melissa whispered.

Lynda looked up. "Did I wake you?"

"No. I thought you were still asleep. You don't have to be at the office for two hours, do you?"

"No." Lynda closed her Bible and pulled her knees up under her gown as Melissa sat down. "I'm thinking about taking the morning off."

"Why?"

"Because I'm ready for court tomorrow, and I think somebody needs to get your mind off things."

"I'm okay, really."

Lynda set her chin on her palm. "I'm not sure I am."

"This puts a lot of pressure on you, doesn't it? You're worried."

"I want to do my best for you," Lynda said. "I just don't know—"

Melissa touched her hand to silence her. "It's okay, Lynda. I know you'll do your best, and if things don't work out just right, it's not your fault. It's mine."

Lynda sighed. "I know how scared you are, Melissa."

Melissa couldn't argue.

"I've been scared, too," Lynda went on. "I was just thinking about it, trying to put myself in your place. The sense of dread, of uncertainty. And I kept going back to that morning when Jake was test-flying my plane, about to buy it, and we realized the landing gear wouldn't go down. We had forty minutes to burn fuel before we landed. That gave the airport time to prepare for a crash landing, and it cut down on the fire hazard. But it was the longest forty minutes of my life."

"I can imagine."

"I haven't flown since. It's weird, because I used to fly every day. The fact that I don't have a plane anymore has something to do with that, but I had planned to rent one every now and then and get back up there. It's just been kind of hard to get back in the saddle."

"How about Jake? Has he flown yet?"

"No, not yet," she said. "He hasn't been able to get a medical release yet. He still has a way to go before his legs are a hundred percent. But I don't think he's afraid of it. I think he misses it. Just the feeling of being up there in the clouds, looking down over the world . . . you can forget everything."

"Well, maybe when you're ready, you can take him up."

Lynda looked at her for a moment, and a slow smile dawned across her face. "I just had a wonderful idea."

"What?"

"What if we all went up today? I could rent a plane, if Mike—my friend who runs the St. Clair Airport—has one available. It would be a great treat for Jake, and it would help distract you and Larry."

The thought didn't appeal to Melissa. "No, you and Jake go ahead. This should probably be a private moment for the two of you."

Lynda shook her head. "The more, the merrier. Come on. Let's make a memory today." When Melissa still hesitated, Lynda leaned forward, her eyes wide, as if a thought had just occurred to her. "Unless you're scared. Maybe you don't want to go up with me after what happened the last time I flew."

Melissa laughed softly. "I trust you, Lynda. Even in a plane. I'm not afraid."

"Great. Then let's do it. I'll go call Paige and tell her to cancel my appointments for the morning."

"Are you sure?"

"Absolutely. I'll be in the shower. If Jake comes over, don't tell him what we're planning. I want to surprise him."

"What if he doesn't want to go?"

"He will," Lynda was certain. "He's been chomping at the bit to get back in the sky. Even if he's not the one flying."

The morning air was brisk for Florida, and Jake thought maybe there was hope that he'd experience an autumn here, after all. This time of year, especially during his short morning walks, he missed Texas. He'd never thought much, before, about the colors the leaves turned, the piles of leaves in the yards, the way the wind felt sweeping through the stands at football games. He'd taken a lot for granted before, including his ability to walk without thinking about every step. But he was grateful he could walk at all. Not so long ago, he'd believed that part of his life was over.

Now he started each day with a walk up Lynda's street and around a couple of blocks. It took a long time, for he had to walk slowly, but lately he'd been relying on his canes less and less. His legs were getting stronger, and it was just a matter of time before he'd be a hundred percent. Already he'd come so far since the crash—and he'd come a lot further mentally and spiritually than he had physically.

He wished he could make Melissa see that this tragedy about to reach culmination in her life could be a beginning. That tragedies weren't always a curse. Sometimes they were a blessing. Through human eyes, they could look like the end of the world. But through God's eyes, there were forces at work, plans aligning, miracles taking place.

His breathing grew heavier as he passed the small church not too far from Lynda's street, then the house beside it with a bicycle and a pair of skates in the yard. He should get a bike, he thought, and try riding it for exercise. It would get him farther and help him to build up his legs more. Then maybe, finally, he'd be able to get his medical release and fly again.

His eyes strayed to the sky, clear blue and cloudless, and once again he found that melancholy sweeping over him. Yes, his tragedy had been a blessing. Yes, he realized God's sovereignty in all of it. Yes, he'd been given wonderful gifts as a result of his fall. He had met the woman God had chosen for him—the only woman he'd ever given serious thought to spending the rest of his life with—and that only because he couldn't stand to spend a single moment without her. But Lynda understood the emptiness that still ached inside him whenever he thought of flying. Would he never fly again? Or was God going to give that back to him someday?

He made his way up the street to Lynda's driveway, thankful that he could sit down for a while before he went to physical therapy. He wondered if Melissa was up yet. For her sake, he hoped she slept late, so she wouldn't have to deal with the unmitigated fear she must feel at the idea of what could happen to her in court tomorrow. He'd felt that way the weekend before they'd taken the bandages off of his face. In a way, he had feared prison, too. The prison of living the rest of his life with only one eye, with harsh scarring down his face that would frighten children. But now he could see that even that had carried with it blessings.

He saw Larry's car as he approached Lynda's driveway, and the cop came out of the house, dressed in a pair of jeans and sneakers and a pullover shirt—minus the windbreaker he wore to hide his weapon when he was on duty.

"Hey, Larry," Jake said, reaching for his hand.

Larry looked pale and tired as he shook, and Jake wished he would get some sleep. "How's it going, Jake?"

"Great. You take the day off again?"

"Yeah," Larry said. "I wanted to try to take Melissa's mind off things, but I'm afraid we're just going to feed each other's anxiety. Hey, you wouldn't happen to know what those two are cooking up today, would you?"

Jake glanced toward the window, and saw Lynda looking out. She smiled at him, something that never failed to brighten his day. "What do you mean?"

"I mean, Lynda's taking the morning off, and she's walking around the house like she's about to burst with excitement. She said it was a surprise."

Jake's breathing was returning to normal now. "Oh, yeah? Think it has to do with Melissa's case?"

"No, that was my first question, too. They just said it was a diversion."

"A diversion, huh?" He glanced back toward Lynda again in the window. "Then we're going somewhere?"

"As soon as Melissa finishes showering." Larry lowered his voice. "I told them I wasn't really in the mood for much—and frankly, Melissa doesn't seem to be, either. She's pretty down. But Lynda insisted that it wouldn't take more than a couple of hours."

Jake started for Lynda's door. "Well, I don't know what it could be, but I do know this. When that woman sets her mind to something, you might as well sit back and enjoy wherever it takes you."

An hour later, Jake still seemed confused at where, exactly, Lynda's enthusiasm had carried them. When they pulled into a parking space at the small St. Clair Airport, Jake gave Lynda an uncomfortable look. He hadn't been back here since the crash, and it occurred to her that he might not be ready to see where his life had almost ended.

"What's going on?" he asked quietly.

Lynda squeezed his hand. "I was trying to think of a way to get Melissa and Larry's minds off tomorrow, something that would make a memory, and I thought of this." She leaned toward him on the seat, her eyes big, beseeching. "What do you think, Jake? Are you ready to get back into the sky again?"

For a moment, he stared at her, quiet, expressionless. Finally, he asked, "You rented a plane?"

"Just for the morning. Melissa needs to spend some time with her parents this afternoon. But I thought it was time."

Jake looked out over the tarmac, at the planes lined up, just as they had been the morning of their crash. He had driven his Porsche out onto the tarmac and parked beside the plane he wanted to buy, as if that Porsche gave him privileges that everyone else didn't have, never dreaming how final that short drive would be.

The wind had been blowing hard that day, just as it was today, only that day had been warmer. He remembered Lynda mentioning her concerns about the crosswind, but he'd assured her that he could handle it. He was a commercial pilot, after all. But no amount of training or experience could have prepared him for what happened that day. Now, looking back, he felt like Nebuchadnezzar, proud of how high he'd climbed, arrogant about his own status, believing he was invincible. God had showed them both, he and Nebuchadnezzar, just how dependent on him they were.

He looked at Lynda, remembering the conversation in the cockpit as they'd prepared to land that day. She had been trembling. He took her hand now, and felt the slight tremor again. "Are you sure you can do this? You're not afraid?"

She smiled with only a tinge of uncertainty. "I don't think anybody's out to kill me this time, Jake," she said, referring to the man who had sabotaged her plane. "I've really been wanting to do this. And I've wanted to take you. I can't forget that look you had in your eyes that morning when you were hotdogging in the sky like a Thunderbird."

"You hated me then. You thought I was the most obnoxious man you'd ever met."

"I was right. You were."

Jake grinned and looked at the two in the backseat, who listened with mild amusement. "She called me a psychopath."

"I sure did," she said proudly. "He was really being a jerk, showing off with all these loops and dips. But we had one thing in common. We both loved to fly." She squeezed Jake's hand. "And neither of us has done it since the crash."

Jake's hesitation diminished. Raising his eyebrows at the two in the backseat, he grinned. "Are you guys game?"

Larry shifted uneasily and peered out at a plane that was just taking off on runway 3, where he'd seen the jumbled, charred mass of Lynda's plane after the crash. "I don't know."

Melissa took his hand. "Come on, it'll be fun."

"Really?" he asked. "You want to do this?"

"Sure. It's better than moping around all day and playing all the different scenarios of tomorrow over and over in my mind. This might be my last day as a free woman. I might as well soar a little."

The shadows on Larry's face returned. "Melissa, don't say that. Lynda's a good lawyer."

Her eyes turning serious again, she touched Larry's mouth with her fingertips to hush him. "Anything could happen, Larry. I've cried until my eyes are raw, I've prayed until I've run out of words, and I've had so many regrets . . . I can't do anything about tomorrow right now. So let's just take advantage of today."

He leaned wearily back on the seat. "All right," he said without much enthusiasm. "Let's go fly."

Even though the flight was supposed to be relaxing, Lynda's hands trembled as she waited for Mike Morgan—the airport manager who served as air traffic controller in the small concessionlike booth inside the airport—to clear her to take off.

"Take it easy, now," Jake said, his eyes scanning the controls with some discomfort of his own. "We did a real good preflight check. Everything looked good. There's nothing to worry about."

"I know," she said. "I'm not scared to fly. I was just remembering . . ."

The radio crackled, and Mike gave them the go-ahead. The cabin was quiet except for the changing pitch of the engine as she accelerated down the runway.

The moment the wheels left the ground, Jake began to laugh like a little boy on his first Ferris wheel. "This is great!" he said. "Look how clear the sky is! Oh, man, I've missed this."

"I have too." Lynda relaxed as they gained altitude. She glanced to the backseat where Larry and Melissa sat close together, gazing out the window. "You two okay?"

"Yeah, we're fine," Melissa said quietly.

"As soon as I get my medical release—" Jake started to say, then stopped before he could get the rest out.

Lynda looked over at him, grinning. "That's the first time I've heard you say it so positively, Jake. Till now, you've seemed a little unsure if you ever would."

"I will," he said without question. "And when I do, we're buying another plane."

She looked over at him, her amused eyes searching his face. "We?"

"Yes," he said, returning her grin. "We."

Melissa grinned and winked at Larry. She had known Lynda and Jake were getting serious, but she hadn't known if they had discussed marriage. Judging by the pink flush across Lynda's cheekbones, and the smile on her face as she moved her eyes to the window, this may have been the first time they had.

Beginnings, she thought with a sigh as her smile faded and her eyes drifted back to Larry. Other people had beginnings. She had endings.

Larry noted the sadness that had fallen over her like a thick fog, so he slid his arm around her and pulled her tightly against him. She laid her head on his shoulder, wishing there could be a future for her with him. But that was too much to ask.

If they'd just met under different circumstances . . . If she'd just been more worthy of him . . .

But she knew that, if she had to go to jail, her relationship with Larry would be over. Cops didn't associate with convicts. He would forget about her; she almost hoped he would. He deserved happiness, and she would only bring him sorrow.

A tear dropped to her cheek and she quickly wiped it away. Larry saw her do it, and tipped her face up to his. She saw the trouble in his expression, the despair, the heartache. And she hated herself for putting it there.

Lord, please comfort him. Let him forget quickly. Let him find the person who can make him happy.

But it was hard to imagine any happiness replacing the sorrow in his eyes.

"You know, you were right, that morning we went up," Jake said softly to Lynda, breaking the silence in the plane. "This is a sanctuary. As reverent as a church."

"You have a different perspective now, don't you, Jake?" Lynda asked.

"Yeah," he said. "I thank God every day for that crash. Life has been a struggle since then, but I wouldn't trade a minute of it. Sometimes, you just have to go through hell to find heaven."

Was there a lesson there for her? Melissa wondered. She let the words sink in and tried to find comfort in them as her gaze drifted back out the window. Would there be a life after all this was over? Would there be a heaven at the end of her hell?

She knew that her life would go on, ultimately—but first, she would have to pay for her crime. She had to trust, she told herself. Like Jake, she had to believe that good would come out of it all.

She looked up and met Larry's eyes. He was going through a hell of his own, she thought. She was dragging him through it with her. Slowly, she began to withdraw. She lifted her head from his shoulder and sat straighter.

She saw his confusion as he loosened his hold on her, but he was demanding nothing from her today. He was here to give, and she received.

Thank you for letting him be here now, she prayed silently. Even if it was temporary . . . even if he forgot her . . . it was okay. God had given her this little interlude as a memory to take with her.

It was a memory that would remind her that she hadn't been forgotten or forsaken. God still loved her, in spite of herself. And he would see her through this, whatever happened tomorrow.

29

THE HARSH RAP of the gavel intensified the headache that had plagued Larry since he woke in the early hours of the morning. Melissa, too, looked as though she hadn't slept. He sat next to her, gripping her hand.

Around them in the courtroom, others with criminal charges waited to be called—some who looked as nervous as she, others who'd walked this path many times before. In the midst of it all, Melissa looked like the lady she was. She held her head up, as if she'd come prepared to accept whatever the court decided, and Larry hoped the judge would see into her heart and give her a second chance. The agony of waiting until her case number was called was almost more than he could stand.

He had sat through many days in court in his career, waiting to testify in a case against someone he'd arrested, but it wasn't until now that he realized how coldly impersonal it was. There should be privacy when someone's future was being decided, he thought. There should be quiet, reverence. He thought of the injustice of Melissa's having to sit through all the ugliness, like one of these thugs who deserved what they were going to get.

He looked up as the doors opened, and saw Melissa's parents come into the room. Melissa got to her feet instantly and stepped past Lynda and Jake.

She placed her parents between herself and Lynda with whispered introductions, and Larry could feel the agony these two people felt. They had lost one daughter already, and now, in an attempt to set that right, their only remaining daughter had broken the law. It would kill them if she went to jail, he thought. The brutal injustice of what continued to happen to their family was devastating.

The judge ordered a recess of fifteen minutes, and they all stood up. Melissa's parents embraced her tightly for a small eternity, weeping out their hearts. Larry stood back, feeling out of place, not sure where he fit in this circle of tears.

He tried to avert his eyes, tried not to watch the quiet display of emotion. The courtroom doors opened as people quietly came and went. Idly, Larry scanned the faces, wondering what their stories were, whether they were lawbreakers or hurting family members. A man came in alone and stood in the aisle with his back to them, looking for a seat. Slowly, he turned around.

It took a moment for the face to register in Larry's mind, but suddenly he recognized the one man he'd never considered might be here.

Edward Pendergrast.

Some cross of rage and anguish burst inside Larry's mind.

Pendergrast grinned as their eyes made contact, then, one by one, he regarded the faces in their row until he came to Melissa with her parents, the same parents he'd terrorized before.

Instead of taking a seat, he stood still at the end of their row, that smug grin on his face, that victorious expression of hardened pride, of invincible evil.

Melissa was stunned at the sight of him. Her parents slowly turned and saw him.

Pendergrast lifted his hand in a wave, as if they were all old friends, then slid into a seat across the aisle from them.

Larry's teeth clenched, and his breathing grew heavy. He bolted out of his seat and stepped around Melissa and her parents. Pushing out of the row, he headed toward Pendergrast. But Melissa caught his arm. "Larry, don't. Please—just stay here."

"I can't," he bit out, and kept going.

Pendergrast was enjoying this, and he beamed up at Larry as he approached. "Well, if it isn't ole gullible Detective Millsaps. Believer of beautiful women. Swallows their stories hook, line, and sinker. But all's forgiven, man. There is justice, after all." He held out his hand to shake, but ignoring it, Larry leaned over until his face was square with Pendergrast's.

"Don't talk to me about justice," he said through clenched teeth. "You don't have any business in here."

"Au contraire," Pendergrast said with a laugh. "As the victim of her little fantasy, I'd say I belong here even more than you do. I might even have something to say to the judge."

Larry's face paled, and he glanced back over at Melissa. She'd shown unbelievable composure until now, but since Pendergrast had entered her face had reddened and was twisted into a fragile, on-the-verge expression that made his heart ache. Her parents, too, looked as if they might come undone.

Larry pointed a finger in Pendergrast's face. "I want you to know something, Pendergrast."

"Soames. The name is Soames."

Larry wasn't daunted at his coolness. "I'm going to get you, *Pendergrast,*" he said. "One of these days, I'm going to get you."

"I don't think so, Millsaps. Better men than you have tried."

"Watch me," Larry said. He stepped back across the aisle and bent down to Lynda's ear. "He says he's going to say something. Can he do that?"

She gave Pendergrast a troubled look. "I'm afraid so. The judge will listen to anyone who has something to say about this. The wronged party always has the right to speak."

"Then let me speak," Larry said. "I'll tell them what a good person she is, that she had good reason—"

"No," Lynda said, touching his hand. "I'm sorry, Larry, but I don't think it would help. You're the cop she originally lied to. It would be better if you stayed seated. Melissa does plan to address the court herself. I think that'll be enough."

"But you'll tell the judge about his past record, won't you? You'll tell him about Sandy?"

"It's all in the PSI, Larry. The judge has reviewed all of it."

"But maybe he hasn't made up his mind yet!"

She looked to the front of the room, and swallowed. "I'm going to do what I can, Larry. Please, just try to keep Melissa calm."

Miserably, he pushed further down the row, past her parents, and sat on the other side of Melissa.

Melissa was trembling worse now, and her palms were sweating. He didn't know how she would make it through this. Or how he would. "What did he say?" she asked.

"He's just trying to scare you," he said. "It's intimidation. Just ignore him."

Slipping his arm around her shoulders, Larry pulled her against him and pressed his mouth into her hair. Quietly, he prayed for her, not in words she could hear, but he knew that she knew what he was doing.

The gavel banged twice, making her jump, and the bailiff called out the case code. "Pinellas County versus Melissa Nelson."

Melissa got up, wobbling slightly, and Lynda slipped out of her seat with her files and led her to the judge.

Slipping into the seat she had previously occupied, Larry took her mother's hand, squeezed it. And then Jim Nelson, her father, reached over and took both of theirs. They drew strength from each other's touch as they watched Melissa take a seat at the table in the front of the courtroom.

"Is she going to say anything?" Jim asked him in a whisper.

Larry shook his head. "She wasn't sure when we talked about it, but Lynda wants her to, I think." He glanced over at Pendergrast, who had sat up straighter, as if preparing to go forward himself. Every muscle in Larry's body tightened.

The state attorney addressed the court in routine legalese concerning the findings of the presentencing investigation. When he recommended that the judge give Melissa at least two years in the state penitentiary, Larry closed his eyes.

"Your honor, before you rule on this, there's someone here who would like to address the court."

"Fine," the judge said. "Go ahead."

The state attorney turned back and nodded to Pendergrast. With a solemn look on his face—the look of a fine, upstanding citizen who has been deeply wronged—he made his way to the front of the room.

Melissa started to rise in protest, but Lynda made her sit back down and whispered to her as Melissa's face reddened and her eyes filled with tears.

"Your Honor," Pendergrast said, "I'm Edward Soames, the person this woman accused of raping her. I just wanted to say a few words before you decide on her sentence."

"All right," the judge said, taking off his glasses and fixing his full attention on Pendergrast.

Pendergrast cleared his throat and looked at his feet, looking for all the world like a clean-cut professional man who was nervous coming before the judge. "One day I was a successful architect with a lot of friends, just living life and not bothering anybody, and the next day, because of one lie that someone told about me, I'm branded a rapist, I lost my job, my friends won't talk to me—" His voice seemed to catch, and he stopped, swallowed, and started again. "You see, this all started because I didn't return her interest in me."

Across the room, Melissa's muffled cry interrupted, and the judge glanced at her. Lynda quieted her.

"So she got even," Pendergrast went on. "Now I have to live the rest of my life with this stigma following me around. Even though the charges have been dropped, my friends are still suspicious. She made a mess out of my life, and I didn't do a thing to deserve it." He seemed to get emotional, stopped, and pinched the bridge of his nose. After a moment, he looked up at the judge. "That's—that's all I have to say, Your Honor. Just think about that before you decide on her sentence. Women shouldn't be allowed to just go around ruining people's lives. They shouldn't get away with it."

The judge seemed moved. "Thank you, Mr. Soames."

As Pendergrast turned around to go back to his seat, he got that grin on his face again and glanced back at Larry. He was proud of himself.

Lynda stood up. "Your honor, my client would like to address the court herself. That is, if she can still manage to speak after that classic performance."

"All right," the judge said. "Proceed."

Melissa stood up, her knees shaking. She couldn't stop the sobs still overtaking her. "His name is not Soames," she said. "It's Pendergrast, and he's a liar. He killed my sister—"

The judge, looking disgusted, slapped his hand on the table. "Unless you have a murder conviction to back that up, Miss Nelson, I suggest that you rephrase it. Otherwise I might be led to believe that you haven't learned your lesson."

She covered her mouth and tried to pull herself together. Finally, attempting to speak again, she said, "He caused my sister's suicide. He's a rapist, Your Honor. She wasn't the only one."

He shook his head and began taking notes, as if he'd already dismissed her for making false accusations again.

"Your Honor, I know what I did was wrong. I shouldn't have done it. But I was trying to right things. The court system let my family down, and he was still out there—you just don't know how desperate you can get, when you find your only sister dead in a bathtub, and the guy who ruined her life is still walking the streets, working, living like a normal person—"

She broke down then, covering her face, and collapsed back into her chair, unable to go on.

The judge looked up, waiting for her to go on. It was impossible to tell from his expression whether he was disgusted or sympathetic. "Do you have anything else to say, Miss Nelson?" he asked.

Melissa couldn't answer. She only shook her head and tried to muffle her sobs.

Lynda stood up, obviously shaken that Melissa's speech hadn't been more eloquent, and that she hadn't been able to finish what she'd tried so hard to say. "No, Your Honor. She doesn't."

"Anyone else?"

She hesitated, then turned and glanced back at the three people huddled together in the back. "Yes," she said finally. "One more. Detective Larry Millsaps."

Larry sat still for a moment, not sure he had heard correctly. Finally, prying his hands away from Melissa's mother, he got up and headed to the bench.

Because it was an informal hearing, he stood in front of the judge and began speaking without preamble. "Uh . . . Your Honor," he said, "I've seen a lot of criminals in my day. I deal with them day in and day out. Melissa Nelson is not a criminal. She's an innocent young woman who's been deeply wounded by her sister's rape and suicide. I saw the pictures after Sandy's rape, your honor. They were brutal. And I saw Pendergrast's rap sheet. The very reason he changed his name is that he had these other arrests on his record. Yes, there was a stigma. There always is when one is charged with rape—not once, but twice. Yes, this third charge was false, but if you had lived through what Melissa and her family have lived through, and knew that a rapist was still out on the streets, waiting to terrorize more women, your state of mind wouldn't be the best in the world, either. As a police officer, I can say that Melissa is no threat to anyone. But if you send her to prison—" His voice cracked, and he looked up at the judge, his eyes pleading. "—with people who have committed horrible crimes for which they deserve that kind of punishment, I'm just not sure she can handle it, Your Honor. I'm not sure she'll survive it."

He looked at Melissa, still lost in her pain and grief, then brought his eyes back to the judge. "Look at her, Your Honor. How do *you* think she'll fare in prison? Will any justice really be served by sending her there?"

Unable to think of anything other than getting down on his knees and begging, he uttered, "Thank you," and went back to his seat.

The judge put his glasses back on and began to study his notes again. He scribbled something, frowned, then looked back up at Melissa. Setting his pencil down, he steepled his hands in front of his face.

"Well, we have two drastically different stories from three different people. While I do understand the emotional nature of this case, and perhaps even the reasons behind her actions, I can't condone anyone's calling the police on someone they don't like, for something that that party may or may not have done years ago to someone else. I can't condone anyone sitting before a grand jury and lying. Miss Nelson, this man has not been convicted of a crime. Citizens cannot pin crimes on innocent people, no matter what they may think they deserve, and get away with it. There has to be a punishment for that. I think six months in the Pinellas County Correctional Facility for Women should be enough of an example to anyone else who ever thinks of doing such a thing."

Despite her mother's muffled scream and Melissa's guttural sob, he banged his gavel again.

30

SIX MONTHS. THE words took a moment to penetrate into Larry's mind and sink down into his heart.

Had the judge really given her six months in jail?

Melissa sat stiff, stunned, as the judge continued reading his decision. He heard her mother's muffled, strangled cry. Across the aisle, Pendergrast was laughing.

The rapist was free. Melissa was going to jail.

It didn't compute, wouldn't sink in, and Larry found himself coming to his feet as the bailiffs came to take her away. They weren't giving her time to say good-bye, or to break down and cry, or to prepare for where she was going. She looked quickly back at her parents, then at Lynda, her eyes brimming with apology and remorse. Then her wet eyes connected with Larry's.

It can't be right, his eyes told her. *It's not over!*

But they all knew it was over, as the bailiffs ushered her out of the room.

Stepping on the feet of the people next to him, Larry hurried out of the row, then ran out of the courtroom and around through the back door where she would come out. His breathing came too hard, and he felt light-headed, as if he might pass out. He leaned back against the wall, his mind racing as he tried to find something that made sense.

The rapist free . . . Melissa in jail . . .

A sheriff's car drove up and idled at the door, and in a moment, the door opened. The two bailiffs came out with Melissa between them.

Fortunately, he knew one of them. "Al, let me talk to her for a minute. Just for a minute. What would it hurt?"

His friend glanced around at the sheriff and the others, and they all shrugged. "All right, Larry, but just a minute."

Larry looked at her for a moment, aware of the people standing around them. She was struggling to hold back her tears, but her chin trembled with the effort. Finally, he pulled her into a smothering embrace. "It's okay, Larry," she whispered in a fragile, broken voice. "Really, it is. I expected this."

"But Melissa—"

Her face changed, and her eyes fixed on some point across the street. Larry followed her startled gaze to the man standing there alone, leaning against the building opposite them, grinning and rubbing her nose in his freedom.

Something exploded inside him, and he almost launched across the street with his hands poised to grab Pendergrast by the throat. But Melissa stopped him. "Watch him for me, Larry. Catch him on something, okay? Something real."

He turned back to her. "I promise," he whispered. "And I'll come visit you. First visiting day. I'll be there."

"No, don't," she said. "I don't want you to."

"Why not?"

"Because—I don't want you to see me that way. You don't owe me anything." The bailiffs ushered her toward the back door of the car.

"I'm coming anyway," he said. When she didn't answer, he looked around one of the bailiffs at her car door. "Did you hear me, Melissa? I'll be there!"

She slid in and they slammed the door, and she looked at him through the window. Tears streamed down her face as they got into the front. As the car drove away, she looked down at her hands.

When the car was out of sight, Larry started to cross the street.

Pendergrast was gone, but it felt as if the evil lingered in his wake.

"I'll get him for you, Melissa," Larry whispered, looking up and down the sidewalk for a sign of him. "If it's the last thing I ever do."

31

THE PINELLAS COUNTY Correctional Facility for Women in Clearwater had been finished—after a flood of controversy over how much money the separate facility was costing the state—just six months before, not far from the jail that had housed both men and women for so long. Legislators had insisted that it was needed, due to the growing number of women being convicted of crimes. In her wildest dreams, Melissa had never guessed that it would be her home for six months.

The building still smelled like paint, and the floor down the long hall was polished, but she knew that that appearance of clean comfort was deceiving. Within these air-conditioned walls were other women who had committed crimes. Drug dealers, prostitutes, child abusers, thieves—the reports she'd read about the women imprisoned here had seemed like fantastic stories to her then, stories of dangerous women who'd surrendered to evil in their lives. Now Melissa was one of them.

The corrections officer who oriented her didn't care that hers had not been a violent crime, or that it had been designed to bring justice to someone who deserved it. To her, Melissa was only a number: 6324655. A faceless, nameless, colorless member of the inmate population, to be treated no differently from the women who'd been sent here for acts she couldn't even imagine.

Wearing her prison-issued orange jumpsuit with the words PINELLAS COUNTY CORRECTIONAL FACILITY in black block letters on the back, and carrying an armload of provisions—sheets, a thin pillow, a blanket, and the few things she had been allowed to bring from home in a small paper sack, which had been carefully searched—she followed the CO through the maze of locking doors and meandering hallways. They came to a wall of yellow iron bars. The guard pushed a few buttons, and the wall began to rise.

"You'll be in cellblock C," the big woman said, leading her into the cellblock. "We're putting you with Chloe."

"Chloe?"

"Yeah." The guard gave a cursory glance back at her. "If you start trouble, you'll be put in isolation. Trust me, you won't like it. If she—or anybody else for that matter—makes trouble with you, call a guard. Chloe likes to fight."

Melissa swallowed her terror and tried desperately to keep tears from filling her eyes. "Isn't there someone else, then?"

The woman seemed amused. "What are you looking for? A welcoming committee? Sorry, but our Welcome Wagon has four flat tires. Truth is, the other prisoners usually do harass the new ones, especially when they look as scared as you do."

With a loud bang that reverberated through Melissa's body and made her jump, the doors to cellblock C slammed shut behind them. "The cellblock doors are open certain hours during the mornings and at night, so people can get to their jobs in other parts of the facility. Most of the time, the cell doors are open, too, so inmates are allowed to go in and out of each other's cells. They're locked down at night, and if you want your cell locked during the day when you're in it, you can ask the CO. I wouldn't recommend locking Chloe out, though. She holds grudges."

Melissa followed her down a long hall with metal doors on either side, not at all like the cells with bars she had expected. Women she assumed were prisoners milled around the cellblock, smoking cigarettes and watching her make her way up the hallway.

"Most of the gals are working right now," the guard said. "They'll be back in a couple of hours. Some of them go early and get off early. Some of them play sick every day so they don't have to lift a finger. They get time added onto their sentence when they miss, but that doesn't matter to them, I guess."

Two women standing beside one of the cells turned to see the new addition to the block, and Melissa averted her eyes. Her arms were trembling, and she almost dropped her load. Stopping, she tried to get a better grip, but the CO looked back. "Hurry up, will you?"

She fell back into step behind the CO, breathing heavily and beginning to perspire. The guard stopped at a closed door, opened it, and peered in. A huge black woman who could have played linebacker for the Miami Dolphins lay on the lower bunk, and she turned to look at them as Melissa came in.

"Chloe, this is Melissa," the CO said brusquely. "She's your new cellmate."

"Hi," Melissa said, wishing the corners of her lips would stop trembling.

"I told you I don't want no cellmate."

"Well, you may have noticed that you don't call the shots around here, Chloe," the guard said. She pointed to the small table where Melissa could set her load, but Melissa only stood motionless, paralyzed.

"Oh, I've called some shots," Chloe smarted back. She gave Melissa the once-over, then sat up. "And you can't have the bottom bunk. This is my bunk."

"That's fine," Melissa whispered. "The top's fine." She turned back to the CO, her eyes beseeching her to reconsider and find her a smaller, more compatible cellmate, one who didn't terrify her.

But this was not a college dorm, and no one cared whether they got along or not.

The CO barked off a few final instructions that seemed to bounce around and echo in Melissa's head as she tried to take it all in—the bunk bed that was bolted to the floor, the small sink and toilet on the other side of a half wall, a wooden chair, two metal lockboxes. Beside the bed was a nightstand, also made of metal, with a small drawer. In one corner, Chloe had stacked some boxes that she used for shelves. Torn magazines lay crumpled on them, and a radio, and a little vase with some dead flowers.

"Well, do you?" the CO asked, breaking into her thoughts.

Melissa turned back to the woman. "Uh—beg your pardon?"

The woman smirked. "I asked if you had any questions."

"Uh . . ." She struggled to find some just to keep the CO from leaving her alone with Chloe, but her mind was drawing a blank. "No. I guess not."

The CO left, and Chloe lay back down, ignoring her. Melissa set her things down on the dirty floor, slowly, quietly, carefully, then turned back to Chloe. What did one say to one's prison cellmate? *What're you in for?*

Though it was a pressing question on her mind, she didn't feel free to ask it. It might make Chloe mad, and she might take time to show Melissa how she got her fighting reputation.

"So what're you in for?" the big woman barked.

Melissa tried to think. "Uh—perjury."

"Do *what?* You didn't shoot nobody? Didn't rob nobody? Didn't steal nothin'?"

"No."

"And they put you in *jail?*"

"That's right."

"Abomination!" the big woman said in a voice so gruff it made her jump. "They really are tryin' to fill up this joint, aren't they?"

She turned over then, as if to go to sleep, effectively dismissing Melissa.

Quietly, Melissa got her sheets, pillow, and blanket and threw them on top of the bed, then grabbing her bag, she climbed up the steps at the end of the bed and sat down on her bunk, pulling her knees to her chest and hugging them with her trembling arms.

Tears started to flow immediately, but she bit back her sobs.

Sandy, I can't believe this is happening . . .

And then she looked up at the ceiling, beseeching the Savior who had seemed so forgiving just a few days earlier, when she had decided to confess, when that feeling of peace had flooded her spirit. Had he left her now? Could he even find her here?

If there was good for her in this, or for anyone, she couldn't think what it was just now. Quietly, she opened her bag and pulled out her Bible. It had been dusty when she'd found it under the seat of her car, where she'd left it the last time she'd been to church. She'd have plenty of time now to catch up for all the years that she hadn't been reading it.

She heard the noise of the cellblock door opening down the hall. Voices echoed up the hall, voices of women coming back from their jobs and heading for their cells. She glanced at the open door, wishing she could close it. But it would make noise, and that might disturb Chloe, and she didn't want to have to deal with that just now. She didn't have the courage.

So she sat still, wiping her face and hunched like a little doll on her bunk, waiting for the next shoe to drop, for the next act in this nightmare she had written.

An alarm sounded when it was time to convene in the prison dining room. Melissa felt the bed shake as Chloe awakened and pulled herself up. As the woman stood, Melissa realized she had to be over six feet tall and weighed probably over 230 pounds.

Chloe gave her a cursory glance. "That's supper," she said.

Melissa glanced out the open door and saw the other women ambling by amid shouts, laughs, profane insults. "Uh . . . I'm not really hungry."

"So what you gon' do? Starve? Take it from me, honey. You gon' need your strength."

She felt nauseous at the thought of eating in this atmosphere. That would be all she needed, she thought, to throw up in front of everyone her first day here. If that wouldn't make her look vulnerable, she didn't know what would.

"Do I have to go?" she asked in a raspy voice. "I mean, is it required?"

"No, it ain't required. You can eat in your room, if you have something. But I don't see no food."

"Where—where are you supposed to get it?"

"Your family can bring it. Up to thirty-five pounds every two weeks. Or you can buy some things from the commissary, if you got money." Chloe went to the sink, bent over it, and tossed some water on her face. Drying it on her sleeve, she went on. "There's one hot plate per cell-block, and you got to stand in a long line for it. Ain't worth it, you ask me. I like my meals hot. You know, if you don't eat, you won't sleep tonight. You'll probably keep me up all night blubberin'."

It was true, Melissa realized. It was going to be hard enough to sleep tonight as it was. She hadn't eaten much in the last few days, and she would need her strength here.

Quietly acquiescing, she slid down from the bunk. Chloe stood a good head and shoulders taller, and the look in her eye revealed impatience and a low level of tolerance for Melissa's fragile state.

"So what'd you lie about?"

"What?"

"You said you were here for perjury."

"Oh. I kind of—I set someone up for a crime they didn't commit."

"Who was it? An old boyfriend? Dumped you, so you got him back?"

"No," she said. "It was someone who really had committed that crime earlier. He got off, and I just—I wanted him back in jail."

"Hmmm," Chloe said in that gruff voice. "Too bad you got caught."

"I didn't get caught," she said. "I confessed."

"Say *what?* You mean to tell me you in here because you confessed to somethin' you hadn't even been caught doin'?"

"Yeah, basically."

"Man, I thought I was dumb. How long you got?"

"Six months," she said.

"It'll be the longest six months of your life." She went to the doorway, then looked back, as if waiting.

Melissa looked beyond Chloe to the women streaming by. The looks in their eyes frightened her, and she wondered if they would be able to see her fear.

Chloe stepped out into the stream of women heading for the door, and suddenly Melissa felt even more vulnerable, even more afraid. Following, she stayed as close as she could to Chloe all the way to the dining room.

32

LARRY DIDN'T WANT to hear the doorbell ring that night. He didn't feel like company. He had sat alone in his apartment, with the shades drawn and the lights out, until dusk had fallen. Now it was almost dark in the apartment, but he didn't care.

The bell rang again, and he got up and headed slowly for the door. It was probably Tony, he thought, with some lame invitation to go get a pizza, trying to pick up Larry's spirits. But when he opened the door, Lynda and Jake stood there.

"We just wanted to make sure you're all right," Lynda said.

"Me?" he asked, turning his back on them and going back to his living room. They closed the door and followed him in. "It's Melissa who's not all right."

"She is, Larry," Lynda said. "I checked on her this afternoon. She's okay."

Tears came to his eyes, and he covered his face with his hand and plopped into his chair. Jake went to the couch and sat down, leaning his cane against the arm, but Lynda kept standing.

"Every time I picture her there, I just . . ."

"I know," Lynda whispered. "I'm so sorry. I did everything I could."

"I know, I know," Larry said, cutting her off. "Tony and I didn't help a whole lot. I keep going over and over the things I told the DOC, wondering if something I said tipped the scales, if I could have worded things differently. Maybe I could have said something better, different, at the sentencing. Maybe I didn't plead hard enough."

"You did the best you could, Larry. And as for the DOC, you didn't have a choice. You told them the truth. That's all Melissa wanted you to do. Nothing you said would have made that much difference."

He sighed, then leaned his elbows on his knees and looked down at his feet. "Sometimes it's just so hard to understand. I prayed and prayed, with all my heart. I felt God listening."

"He *was* listening."

"Then why did this happen?" he said through gritted teeth, getting to his feet. He walked to his window, pulled back the blinds, and looked down on the parking lot. The streetlights were on, making it seem even darker in the apartment, but he didn't care. "Why didn't God answer this prayer?"

Jake got up and went to stand behind Larry. With his hand on Larry's shoulder, he said, "I've asked that question myself, buddy. More than once. I'm not smart enough to answer it."

"I don't get it," Larry said. "Why wouldn't God intervene? What purpose could it possibly serve to have Melissa in jail?"

Jake's eyes misted. "I've never been to jail, Larry, but after the crash, when I lay flat on my back, not able to move from my waist down, that was as close to prison as I ever want to get. I lost my job, my friends, my looks . . ."

Larry glanced up at the scar on Jake's cheek. He hardly noticed it anymore.

"I asked over and over what purpose there could have been in that. For the life of me, I couldn't see any good in it. But there was a purpose, Larry. A big one."

"But she's in *jail.* There's *not* a purpose in that!" Larry cried, turning sharply away from Jake and marching to the darkest corner of the room.

Lynda and Jake said nothing. Finally, Larry shrank a little, as if the anger were draining out of him. He turned on the lamp and dropped back into his chair.

After a long silence he said, "I'm sorry, guys. I didn't mean to yell at you. It's just—you're the only ones here to yell at."

"Yell away," Lynda said softly. "It's okay."

He wiped his eyes, then looked at Jake. "I wish I could believe it'll all work out. That good will come of it. That there's a reason. That it makes sense, somehow." He leaned back, studying the ceiling. "See, when I think about it, I do trust God. I do know that he's in control. It's just that sometimes it seems like things are so *out* of control. How can anything good come out of all this?"

"He's God," Lynda said. "He made order out of chaos. He created the universe. He also created Melissa, Larry. He'll take care of her."

Lynda saw Larry's Bible lying on a nearby shelf, picked it up, and flipped through it. "There's a verse in Psalms that I quote to myself, whenever I watch a battered wife go back to her husband, or whenever I have a client who winds up serving time. I didn't know this verse when I was going through all my trouble, but it's important to me now." She found the page, then handed the Bible to Larry. "There it is. Psalm 91. Read the whole chapter when you get time, but for now, just verses 11 and 12."

Larry looked down at the verses. "For he will command his angels concerning you to guard you in all your ways; they will lift you up in their hands, so that you will not strike your foot against a stone."

"That's what he'll do with Melissa, Larry," she whispered.

"Do you think so?" he asked, his pain arguing against this simple expression of faith.

"I know it. She's there because she decided to tell the truth. To right a wrong. God will honor that."

He studied the verses again, and slowly felt his tension and bitterness easing a bit, leaving him only bone tired. "Thanks," he whispered. "I'll hold onto that. I really don't have any choice."

They sat still for a moment, then finally, Lynda stood up. "Would you like to come over and watch a movie with us or something? I could make popcorn."

Larry shook his head. "No, thanks. I have something else I have to do. But I really appreciate you guys. You're good friends."

Lynda hugged him quickly, and then they were gone.

Quiet settled over the house. Returning to his seat, Larry read the whole psalm again, feeling the peace that it held. But behind that peace was a growing sense of guilt. Who was he to feel peace while Melissa was where she was? It was Melissa who deserved to feel peace, not him—not after the decisions he'd made.

He set his Bible back on the shelf, grabbed his keys, and headed out the door.

He hadn't lied to Lynda and Jake. He really did have plans. He was going to watch Pendergrast. As he had promised Melissa, he was going to catch him at something. And he didn't care if he had to give up sleep for the next six months to do it. Somehow, Pendergrast was going to pay.

With God's help—if he still had any right to expect God's help—Larry would be the one to *make* him pay.

33

THE WOMEN SPOKE in low tones and sat where they were supposed to sit at dinner, unwilling to start trouble—and no wonder; guards were everywhere. Still, Melissa felt the eyes of some of the inmates on her, assessing her, testing her for that look of fear she knew she wore like a banner. Chloe sat next to her, saying little to those around her, just scarfing down her meal with a zest that Melissa had not seen in many others.

The food was bland but nutritious, so she ate. She thought back over the meals she'd eaten with Larry, when they had shared deep heart-to-hearts, with Melissa sharing parts of her truths with him and Larry probing for more. The memories of time wasted and time lost brought tears to her eyes, but she blinked them back, desperate not to let anyone here see her crying.

When she'd eaten all she could, she set her napkin back on the tray and waited to be told where to go next.

"They give you an assignment yet?" Chloe asked after she'd polished off her plate.

"Laundry," Melissa said.

"It's hot in there," Chloe said. "They got me in there, too."

Melissa looked over at her roommate. She was a brooding woman, and she still sounded gruff, angry, frightening. But she had made a stab at conversation; that was a hopeful sign.

"You watch TV? You can go to the TV room after dinner."

"No. I'll just stay in the room and read." She couldn't bring herself to call it a cell.

"Look," Chloe said, as if growing weary of the timid act. "Your best bet is to get a look at as much as you can this first day in. See what you're up against. Besides, if you stay in the cell by yourself, I can't promise you'll be safe."

"Well, I can lock it, can't I?"

Chloe grinned and breathed a laugh. "You *are* dumb. Girl, these doors lock from the outside—not the inside."

"Oh." She looked around, noted that more inmates had spotted her. A group across the room to her right were staring at her and whispering among themselves, and to her left others were wrenching their neck to see her. "Then I guess I'll go."

Chloe shook her head at her idiocy, and again Melissa stared down at her food, unable to make eye contact with any of the threatening eyes around her.

The TV room was a big room full of couches and game tables, and a television sat up high in the corner, in a metal box that kept anyone from vandalizing it. The biggest, most ominous inmates among them controlled the station selection, and the others sat around in clusters, talking.

Melissa watched two women get up as soon as they saw Chloe come in, and Chloe ambled over to the chairs they had abandoned and sat down, as if they were understood to be hers.

Melissa hung back at the door, trying not to attract any attention. But it was too late. Two of the women standing near her turned toward her, amused. "You new?"

"Yes," she said quietly.

"Hey, everybody!" one of them shouted. "Check this out!"

All eyes in the room turned to her, and Melissa shrank back against the wall.

"So what's your name, honey?" one of the women, with a pasty complexion and greasy red hair, asked.

"Melissa," she choked out.

"Melissa!" the redhead shouted. "Aw, ain't that pretty!"

"Look, I don't want any trouble." But that was the wrong thing to say. She watched as the COs turned their backs, allowing the harassment to continue, as if she somehow deserved it.

"She don't want no trouble!" the redhead said. "I'll bet a sweet thing like you never expected to end up here. Can't believe a jury would convict you, with that soft hair—" She grabbed a handful of Melissa's hair, but Melissa jerked back. "And them big eyes."

"It wasn't a jury," Melissa choked out.

"Not a jury? A judge then. Didn't you bat them eyes at him and tell him that you were just too delicate to be in here with all us criminal types? So what'd you do, anyway?"

Melissa didn't answer.

"Honey, I asked you a question," the redheaded woman asked, growing more agitated. "I don't sense a lot of respect from you. Didn't you hear what I asked?"

"She's in for child abuse, Red," one woman on the couch piped up. "I heard about her last week on the news. She left her children in the house, then burned it down."

"No, I didn't!" Melissa cried.

"I saw it, honey. That was you."

"Child abuse? Murder? Arson?" the redhead taunted. "No wonder even that soft blonde hair didn't save you."

Tears were coming to her eyes, despite her efforts to hold them back. "It's not true," she whispered. "Please."

Another woman grabbed a handful of her hair and jerked her head back so she was looking up at the ceiling. "Please what?"

"Let me go!" Melissa shouted through her teeth. "I haven't done anything to you!"

"We're just welcomin' you, honey," Red said. "Like we do all the girls." A round of laughter erupted over the room as others got up and started toward her.

"SHUT UP!" Chloe's voice cut like a chain saw through the room, and breath-held silence fell over them as the big woman rose to her full height. "Can't you see I'm tryin' to watch *Wheel of Fortune?*" she belted out. "Let her go so she'll shut up! I been listenin' to her whimperin' all day as it is!"

The inmate dropped her hair, and Melissa rubbed the roots where it had started to tear out of her scalp. She looked at Chloe, waiting for her wrath to fall.

The women scattered slowly, so as not to appear frightened by the big woman, but they left Melissa alone.

Melissa stood at the door a while longer, trying to catch her breath, trying not to cry, not knowing whether to go right or left. Finally, she sat down in an empty chair and fixed her eyes on the television, trying not to provoke anyone else, holding her hands clasped to keep their trembling from showing.

She hadn't expected God to protect her through Chloe, but it seemed he had. The next hurdle, she thought, was to stop being so terrified of her protector. Chloe had rescued her from the others, but she didn't know who would rescue her from Chloe. Maybe she could learn not to make Chloe mad, she thought. Maybe she'd be lucky enough not to be around when someone else did. Maybe she was just going to have to get used to living in abject fear.

Maybe not every day of her six months would pass as slowly as this first day was.

The noises of the jail kept Melissa awake that night, though Chloe had fallen asleep the moment her head hit the pillow. Melissa lay in her cell, staring at the ceiling, listening as doors opened and closed for reasons she didn't know and didn't want to know. Now and then, COs spoke to each other without lowering their voices, and the sounds of hard shoes clicked on the floor.

Somewhere, she heard the sound of someone crying, a sound that was sometimes audible, then muffled, then loud again. She wondered how many inmates lay awake as she was tonight, nursing broken hearts, missing family members, bitterly regretting their mistakes.

She wondered about the dead flowers Chloe kept in the vase on the cardboard shelf.

Her own tears couldn't be held back any longer, and she covered her mouth to keep from giving in to the despair. She didn't want anyone to hear her crying. She didn't want to incite the wrath of the guards, or of Chloe.

She wondered if Pendergrast was laughing at her, rejoicing at the way things had turned out. His crime against Sandy was still being played out, the ripples still rippling. He was still raping their family, and Melissa was one of the victims.

Bitterness swelled within her. Her hands trembling, she reached for the Bible that she'd put under her pillow and clutched it tightly against her chest, like a shield that would keep her from her wayward thoughts. There was someone in the world she hated, and before this ordeal was over, there might be many others.

She couldn't forgive—not yet. It was too hard.

Help me, Lord. Help me to do what I'm supposed to do.

Chloe's heavy breathing ceased for a moment at the gasping sound of her tears, and Melissa turned over and buried her face in her pillow.

"You cryin' up there, ain't you?" Chloe barked.

Melissa didn't answer.

"I told you I didn't want to hear no blubberin'."

"I'm sorry," she whispered. "I was trying to be quiet."

She waited, bracing herself, for Chloe to get up, but the woman didn't move.

"Least you ain't makin' all the racket that other one is. You'd think she lost her best friend. Probably killed her herself."

Melissa didn't answer.

"I find out who that is, she'll have a *reason* to cry tomorrow."

Melissa sat stone still, holding her breath to keep from agitating the big woman.

After a moment, Chloe's deep, heavy breathing returned.

She was asleep for now, and Melissa would do well to let her stay that way.

Lying as still as a log, and just as rigid, Melissa waited for the night to pass.

34

LARRY ATE DINNER in his car the next night. The minute he'd gotten off work, he had headed for Pendergrast's apartment complex. The man's Cherokee wasn't there, so he tried Pendergrast's office. The Cherokee was still sitting there in the gravel parking lot.

He parked behind a low-hanging willow tree and rolled down his window. A heat wave had come through, making temperatures hotter than usual for October, and now, as the sun went down, it seemed hotter than it had been all day. As he bit into the hot dog he'd brought with him, he tried to imagine what Melissa had eaten tonight. Was she still terrified? Was she able to eat at all?

His appetite left him, and he tossed the hot dog back into the bag it had come in and sipped on the drink that was now watery from melted ice.

Please Lord, let me catch him at something tonight.

It wouldn't get Melissa out of jail, but at least he would be able to see some justice being served.

He saw the front door to the office building open, and Pendergrast came out and got into his car.

Larry waited until Pendergrast was a block away and had turned right onto the main road before he cranked his Chevy. Staying back in traffic, he followed him across town to Highland Drive, a brand-new, just-paved road near the mall.

Pendergrast pulled into a site where a building was going up; men were still there working. Pendergrast got out, cut across the dirt, and shouted a few orders to the men around him.

Larry waited about twenty minutes for Pendergrast to go back to his car as the other construction workers split up and headed for their own cars. Larry let three trucks pull between him and Pendergrast, then followed them back to the main road. He trailed as Pendergrast went home, locked his car, and trotted up the steps to his apartment door.

Larry waited.

His cellular phone rang, startling him. He reached for it and clicked it on. "Hello?"

"I knew you were in your car." It was Tony, and Larry braced himself.

"Yeah? So?"

"Did you even go home?"

"I had things to do, okay?"

"Yeah, well, I just wanted to see if you'd want to go get a bite to eat."

"I've already eaten."

"Where are you, man?"

"What difference does it make?"

Pause. "You're at his place, aren't you? You're staking out Pendergrast."

Larry glanced up at the apartment. "I'm off duty. I don't have to account for my time."

"Look—let's go eat, and talk, and then you can go back there if you have to."

"No," Larry said. "I'm staying right here."

"He knows you're gonna be on him, Larry. He's not going to do anything this first couple of weeks. He'd be nuts."

"He *is* nuts."

"Man, you're asking for trouble. You're obsessing. You need to let yourself off the hook, man. Melissa doesn't expect this. She wouldn't want you to suffer just because she's in jail."

Larry rubbed his forehead. "Tony, if you don't have anything more constructive to say, I have to go."

"Look, just be careful, will you? I don't want to break in a new partner."

Larry clicked the phone and tossed it on the seat. Maybe Tony was right. Maybe nothing was going to happen tonight. But one of these days it would, and when it did, he would be there.

An hour or so later, Pendergrast came back out, got into his Cherokee, and pulled out. Larry followed, not optimistic that Pendergrast would commit a crime tonight, since Pendergrast seemed to do his prowling in the other car. Still, he followed him to the bar where they'd first arrested him.

He knew it was going to be a long wait as Pendergrast ambled in. To keep busy, he pulled Pendergrast's rap sheet and file out from under the seat. The two rapes they'd known about had happened very late at night, when the women were alone. It was clear that Pendergrast had known they would be alone, because both had been married, and in both cases he'd come on a night when their husbands had been working. Which meant he'd been watching them for some time. Then, on exactly the right night, he had broken into their homes and overpowered them.

Maybe there's someone he's watching now, he thought.

It was nearing midnight when Larry saw Pendergrast strutting out of the bar with a woman under his arm. Quickly, he cranked the car.

He watched as Pendergrast got behind the wheel and started the car, and thought how he'd love to slap a DUI charge on him. But that wouldn't help. That would keep him behind bars for about an hour.

He followed him to a neighborhood with small stucco houses, and hung back, several houses down with his lights off, as Pendergrast and the woman went inside.

Larry checked his watch. Maybe he should just go on home. This wasn't Pendergrast's typical MO. He didn't date the girls he raped. It was all done anonymously, cruelly, without any warning. He doubted this girl was in any danger.

On the other hand, he couldn't take the chance of leaving, just in case Pendergrast did hurt her.

He almost fell asleep several times, but shook himself awake, forcing himself to stay alert. It was almost three when Pendergrast came back out of the woman's house. He watched the man get into his car and drive off, and then he saw lights being turned off throughout the house. She was all right.

Cranking his car, he followed Pendergrast back to his apartment. It was nearing 3:30 when Pendergrast walked slowly back inside. Larry sat watching for a long moment, waiting for Pendergrast's lights to go off. When they did, at around four, he realized that the man was in for the night and wasn't likely to go out again.

Wearily, he headed for home and fell into his bed, praying that he'd be able to function the next day.

He fell into a troubled sleep, filled with dreams of Melissa being stalked and hounded by inmates and prison guards, being hurt or abused.

When the clock woke him at six A.M., he was soaked with sweat. He sat up abruptly. *God, help her,* he cried in his heart. *Please protect her.*

But the troubled feeling wouldn't leave him as he got ready for church—then changed his mind and decided to resume his stakeout instead. The obsessions he'd been accused of kept growing—more and more intense.

35

LARRY'S EYES WERE getting tired as he wove between cars on the interstate, trying to keep up with Pendergrast in the inconspicuous gray Toyota. He had followed Pendergrast home from work again tonight—as he had last night—watched as he went into a fast-food restaurant for dinner, then home. And just after nine, when Pendergrast had come out again and gotten into the gray Toyota, Larry's adrenaline had begun pumping. Maybe this was what he'd been waiting for.

He almost gave up when he saw Pendergrast turn into the mall parking lot and park outside a Dillards store. Was he going shopping just before closing time?

But Pendergrast didn't get out. Larry parked a few rows away and reached for the infrared binoculars he'd laid on the seat next to him. From where he sat, he had a terrific view of Pendergrast. The man made no move to get out. He was waiting for someone. And it didn't seem likely that he'd have brought the gray Toyota to pick up a girlfriend.

Larry watched as several families spilled out of the store near closing time, and he saw the manager of Dillards lock all but one of the doors as they prepared to close.

Group by group, employees walked out, escorted by a security guard, then dispersed in the parking lot, heading to their separate cars.

Pendergrast sat straighter now. He brought something to his face—binoculars? A camera?

Yes, it was a camera, Larry realized. Probably the camera they'd gotten from his apartment. He had, of course, gotten all of his confiscated things back after the charges against him had been dropped. The camera had a long lens on the front, and Larry guessed it was a night lens. He was taking pictures of the employees coming out. Larry moved his binoculars in the direction Pendergrast was shooting, and saw a young woman who looked about twenty, with long, flowing blonde hair a lot like Melissa's. She passed Pendergrast's car, unaware that she was being watched, and got into her own, which was two spaces down from his. By reflex, Larry reached for his gun and waited for Pendergrast to make a move.

The girl got into her car. The lights came on as she cranked it. Pendergrast did nothing as she pulled out of her space. The moment she was far enough across the parking lot not to see him, Pendergrast's lights came on and he pulled out in the same direction.

Larry followed, keeping his lights off, as his mind reeled. Pendergrast had targeted that young woman as his next victim. Larry's heart pumped triple-time as he followed both cars out into the light stream of traffic.

The young woman took an unfortunate route home—Highland Drive, the newly paved road where new construction was in progress during the day. The same road where Pendergrast had construction projects under way. Now, at night, the road was deserted.

From this distance, Larry couldn't read her tag number. He reached for his night binoculars again and held them to his eyes. Mumbling the numbers back to himself, he pulled the pen out of his pocket and scribbled the numbers on his arm. Tomorrow he could look it up, if it wasn't too late.

He followed as they came to an area of new housing at the end of the long road, and she pulled into an apartment complex only a couple of months old. He held his breath, waiting to see if Pendergrast was going to make a move. Pendergrast, too, pulled into the complex but continued on around the parking area, appearing to be just one more resident looking for his parking space. Larry pulled in near the young woman's car and cut his engine, waiting.

She got out and locked her door. Clutching her purse, she started toward her apartment.

Pendergrast's car came slowly around now, and pulled into a space. Larry watched him as Pendergrast watched her go up the steps and around to her apartment door.

"What are you doing?" Larry whispered as Pendergrast just sat there. Was he going to wait until the lights went off, then break in somehow and attack her? Or was he just watching, planning, for some other time?

After about twenty minutes, Pendergrast cranked his car and pulled out again.

Larry sat still for a moment before following. Then, staying far enough back not to be seen, he followed him back across town to Pendergrast's apartment. Pendergrast parked the Toyota at the far end of the parking lot, locked it, and walked over to his Cherokee. He pulled out, and

Larry followed him to the bar where they'd arrested him. Was he done with the woman for tonight? Was he going back later?

Not willing to take the chance of missing whatever Pendergrast was up to, and risking the life of that young woman in the process, Larry decided he could make it the rest of the night without falling asleep. He had to.

Pendergrast was getting ready to make a move, and when he did, Larry would be there to catch him.

Larry's eyes were raw by the time he made it to the police station the next day. Pendergrast hadn't made a move; instead, he'd left the bar well after midnight with some other woman, and Larry had sat outside that house, waiting for some sign that there was trouble inside. At nearly four A.M., Pendergrast had driven home.

"You look like death warmed over," Tony said as Larry approached his desk. "Have you been sleeping?"

"Not much." Larry sat down and flicked on his computer.

"Are you sick, man?"

"No," Larry said irritably. He punched in the tag number of the car he'd seen the young woman driving last night, and waited.

"What are you doing?"

"He's stalking somebody."

Tony pulled up a chair and straddled it, looking over Larry's shoulder to the computer screen. "Who is?"

"Pendergrast. I followed him last night. He's stalking a woman who works at the mall."

Tony looked confused. "What do you mean, he's stalking her?"

"He's been watching her. He knows when she gets off work, what kind of car she drives, where she lives. He follows her home, and watches her go in."

"Well—does *he* go in?"

"No. He waits and watches, and then he just drives away."

Tony thought that over. "Are you sure he's not just pulling your string? I mean, maybe he realizes you've been following him. Maybe he's just trying to give you something to chew on."

"He doesn't know I'm there."

"How do you know? You've been watching him every night. How do you know he doesn't see you?"

"Because I've been careful, okay?" The name came up on the screen, and Larry sat back in his chair. "Her name is Karen Anderson. She's twenty-one. That's her, all right."

"What are you planning, Larry?"

"To get the captain to put somebody on her twenty-four hours. Maybe warn her what's going on."

"Larry, we can't spare that kind of man-hours. We have work to do."

Larry banged his fist on the desk and swiveled around in his chair. "That *is* our work, man! Keeping a woman from getting raped is just as much a part of our job as it is to clean up the mess afterward. Personally, I'd rather do it before."

Tony backed away slightly and lowered his voice. "But look at the logic, Larry. We know at least a dozen dangerous guys out there right now who are likely to commit a crime at any given time. It doesn't mean we can follow them around every minute of the day just to catch them at it."

"Then this whole system is twisted! If we can't prevent crimes, we might as well not even be here!"

Tony got up. "Look at you, Larry," he said, an edge of anger in his voice. "You're going to drop from exhaustion, and nothing's going to be accomplished. As a matter of fact, you'll probably make some terrible mistake and get yourself killed, just because you're not alert."

"I'm plenty alert."

"Oh, yeah? Your eyes look as bloodshot as a drunk's on Monday morning. And you haven't shaved."

Larry rubbed his jaw. He'd forgotten. "I'm growing a beard."

"In honor of Melissa? Have you taken a vow of self-deprivation until she serves her time?"

Ignoring him, Larry got up and kicked his chair out of his way. "I'm going to talk to the captain," he said.

Tony gave the chair a kick of his own as he went back to his desk.

Sam Richter was a no-nonsense captain who hated wasted time more than anything else in the world. He hated meetings and conferences and telephone calls that took him away from his work. Today, he was in a particularly bad mood because of a frustrating new case. And he was in no mood to listen to Larry's pleas to go off on some wild goose chase to get revenge for his convict girlfriend. The thought thoroughly disgusted him.

"Come on, Captain. I know he's about to strike. I have the name of the victim. We need to put a twenty-four-hour watch on her."

Sam looked at the ceiling, as if trying to find some patience there. "Millsaps, tell me something. When's the last time you slept? Or shaved, for that matter? Or took a bath?"

Larry thought of pleading the fifth, but instead he chose to remain silent.

"That's what I thought. It hasn't been recent." He leaned forward on his desk, his big hand propping up his chin. "Millsaps, I'm going to tell you this one time. Leave that man alone. You've caused him enough trouble. If you keep at it, you're going to get this police department slapped with another lawsuit, and I'm not in the mood to negotiate with that ambulance-chaser of a lawyer again."

"But Captain, you can't ignore what I saw! He's going to strike—I know he is. We can keep another girl from being raped."

"*Another* girl?" Sam asked on a laugh. "Millsaps, there wasn't a *first* rape. At least, not one that we can prove."

Larry burst out of his seat. "You're not buying into that innocence story, are you? How many times have you seen a suspect admit to what he's done? He's pretending he's innocent!"

"He may not be pretending." The captain stood up dismissively and took a file over to his file cabinet. "Millsaps, I know your girlfriend's going to jail really knocked you for a loop. Everybody in the precinct's talking about it."

Larry rolled his eyes and peered out the window to all the activity beyond it. "I should have known."

"But I don't have time to coddle you, man. I don't have any man-hours to devote to making you feel better. About fifteen minutes ago a jogger discovered a body washed up on Peretta Beach, and it turns out she was one of those two seventeen-year-old runaways from St. Clair. Now, I only have two detectives. You and Danks. I need you working on this, not going off on some hunch."

Larry couldn't accept that. "We can do both, Captain. Work on both cases. We can follow the girl, and—"

The captain leaned over his desk. "What part of 'no' don't you understand, Millsaps?"

Larry slapped at the chair he'd been sitting in, knocking it over.

The captain straightened with a look of quiet rage in his eye. "One more word—one more outburst—one more *anything* from you, Millsaps, and you're on suspension. Matter of fact, I just might put you on it, anyway. You're losing your edge, Detective. You're cracking up. I've never seen you behave this way in all the years I've known you. If you come in here like this tomorrow, you can look forward to a long vacation."

Not honoring that with a reply, Larry turned and slammed out of the office. As he bolted across the room, Tony looked up. "Hey, Larry. Wait!"

Larry didn't answer. He fled from the building as fast as he could.

36

THOUGH THE PRISON was air-conditioned, the huge room where they worked on the laundry was sweltering. Tiny vents at the top of the big warehouselike room blew cool air in, but the heat from the irons and the dryers and the steam from the washing machines all filled the room with a humid heat.

Melissa had been there only an hour, and already her hair was soaked with perspiration. Her clothes were sopping wet and sticking to her, and she began to feel dizzy, as if she might faint from the heat.

Behind her, women cursed at each other, but guards who had the misfortune of being assigned to this location didn't bat an eye. They were used to the foul moods and foul mouths of the women who worked here day after day.

She grabbed the next jumpsuit in her basket, laid it on the ironing board, and quickly reached for the iron. Her fingers brushed the hot metal, scalding her flesh, and she jumped back, knocking the iron over.

A CO was at her side in an instant, not to help, but to warn her against wasting time.

Quickly, she picked the iron back up, fighting back the tears in her eyes as her skin began to blister.

Where was the peace she was supposed to feel? Where was the comfort that would chase away the paralyzing, stomach-knotting fear? All she felt was the terror of messing up, the horror of making the wrong person mad, the fear of getting killed in this abyss where they had sent her to teach her not to lie.

She looked across the room and saw her big roommate, Chloe, folding towels with a slow, methodical rhythm. Each night, she lay awake, listening to the rhythm of Chloe's breathing, waiting for the woman to snap and decide that she was angry enough at Melissa to attack her.

But she hadn't. Chloe was a mystery. One minute, she was leering at Melissa as if she could snap her in two, and the next she was leering at the others who looked as if they might like to try. She couldn't decide if the woman was tormentor or protector.

She longed for ice to put on the burn to relieve the pain, but she kept working. She tried to shift her mind away from the pain by wondering where Larry was, whether he was working today, whether he would be coming to visit tomorrow.

She wouldn't be crushed if he didn't come, she told herself. It was best if he didn't. She didn't want him to see her this way.

Her parents would come, and that would probably be all the emotional upheaval she could stand for one day. That she had ever put them in the position of having to visit their child in prison gave her such shame that she wanted to die.

Her mind counted the hours she had been here already. Five days. That meant there were only 177 days to go. 4,248 hours. 254,880 minutes.

Only three days before she'd earn her first visitation privileges.

She needed somthing more constructive to occupy her mind and wished that she had memorized scripture so that she could call on it now when she felt such despair. Maybe that's what she would start doing during her free time in her cell. Maybe it would get her mind off Chloe's bad moods—and her fears that the next moment she might explode like a ticking bomb.

37

THE BACK DOOR to his church was open, as it always was during the week, and Larry stepped into the big corridor, avoiding the choir director and minister of education who were conversing in the hall just outside their offices. Hurrying, he made his way to the small, private prayer room at the back of the building and slipped inside.

It was dark, except for two dim little bulbs at the front of the room. There were four pews, and he slipped into the back one and looked at the small podium on which a big Bible lay open. His sister had gotten married here—it had been a quiet wedding, with just the families in attendance. Katie was shy, and she hadn't wanted a big production made out of something she considered so personal.

That had been a joyous occasion, an occasion when Larry had felt the Holy Spirit's presence so keenly that he'd felt he could reach out and touch his Savior. Now, it seemed like ages since he'd felt that.

He sank into the pew, covering his face, letting out the deep, dark misery in his heart. "Everything's out of control," he whispered to his Creator. "I can't help. I can't change anything. And now I can't even come to you."

The barren loneliness in those words hit him harder than anything else had that day, and he wept into his hands, desperate for some word that would somehow restore him. But there was a wall there—between him and God—a wall he had constructed himself. And he had made no move to break it down. Like Melissa, he'd decided that he wasn't worthy, that his own choices had rendered him unacceptable in God's eyes.

"I was going to lie for her," he whispered, propping his elbows on his knees and looking down at his feet. "You took it out of my hands. I didn't have to do it. But I would have. And I'm just as guilty as if I had."

He wondered whether he'd have felt repentant and remorseful if Melissa hadn't come forward and if he'd gone through with his plan to cover for her—

Yes, he thought unequivocally. He had been miserable about the choice even before he'd made it. It would have eaten at him, just as it did now. That was God's curse—as well as God's blessing.

He looked up at the ceiling, as if he could see God sitting there, judging him. "I don't even know what to say," he cried. "I want to pray for her, plead with you to change things somehow, to get her out of jail, to put Pendergrast away—but how can you hear my prayers when I've turned away?"

He leaned his arms on the pew in front of him and rested his head on them. "Nothing makes sense, Lord. He's going to do it again. To another innocent girl. And it's Melissa in jail instead of him. Help me to understand!"

A verse like an admonition came into his mind:

You do not have in mind the things of God, but the things of men.

He looked up, his face wet and twisted, and wondered why that verse, of all others, had spoken to him just now. It couldn't work to God's glory, he thought, for a beautiful, sweet, broken woman to be in jail. Or for Pendergrast to ruin another life. Those couldn't be "things of God."

Again, the verse played like a chant through his mind, and finally, he broke down and got to his knees. Maybe that *was* God's answer—that Larry *didn't* understand it, and that in fact it wasn't up to him to understand. Who was he to question the mind of God?

Suddenly, an overwhelming remorse fell over him, so deep and heavy that it almost flattened him. He had done exactly as Melissa had done. He had trusted his own solutions rather than God's. He had taken things out of his Father's hands, and with his own limited vision, had decided how things should go. "Please forgive me, Lord. Forgive me for not trusting you. Forgive me for making a decision to lie and cheat, for turning away."

He wept until he was exhausted. Finally, he got up again and sat on the pew, listening, waiting, hearing. His eyes fell on the open Bible, and he slowly got up and went toward it.

The book was open to Luke 22. Aloud, in a trembling voice, he read Jesus' words.

"Simon, Simon, Satan has asked to sift you as wheat. But I have prayed for you, Simon, that your faith may not fail. And when you have turned back, strengthen your brothers."

But he replied, "Lord, I am ready to go with you to prison and to death."

Jesus answered, "I tell you, Peter, before the rooster crows today, you will deny three times that you know me."

Jesus had known that Peter would turn away, that he would lie, and cheat, and run. And even knowing that, he had assured him that his relationship with God would not be ruined. *When* you turn back, Jesus had said. He had known he would. Just as he had known Larry would.

Larry felt that same forgiveness washing over him, cleansing him, filling him with the strength he would need to get through the days ahead. They were no worse than Peter's future had been—no more frightening, no more uncertain. But this was *his* future . . . and Melissa's. And he would need God to get him through it.

He sat back down, amazed and awestruck at the way the Lord had ministered to him, even when he hadn't deserved it—but then he realized that he had *never* deserved it. That was the beauty of grace. God was not dwelling on his past sin. God was looking ahead to how he wanted to use Larry.

"Strengthen your brothers."

Melissa would need strengthening. And he would be there for her.

"Peace I leave with you; my peace I give you. I do not give to you as the world gives. Do not let your hearts be troubled and do not be afraid."

More Scripture he'd memorized, never realizing how much he would need it one day. Now it came to him like an old friend, holding his hand, propping him up.

He sat there for a while longer, in his own private Gethsemane, soaking in the peace of God's love and forgiveness and hope. And knowing that whatever was to happen in the next few hours and days, it was all in the hands of the Almighty God.

An hour later, as Larry and Tony drove in silence in their unmarked car to the beach where the runaway's body had washed up, Tony looked at him. "I took it from the way you burst out of the building a little while ago that the captain nixed your idea."

"He said what you said. Not enough manpower."

"I figured."

"So meanwhile, another girl is going to end up a victim before we act."

"Maybe not."

Larry was bone tired and didn't feel like arguing. But he couldn't let that go. "He's a rapist, Tony. We know it. And now he's stalking another woman. How long before we realize what's going on? What'll it take? Why is everybody so dead set on proving that Pendergrast is a saint?"

"History," Tony said. "We thought he'd done something before, and it turned out he didn't. Nobody else wants egg on their face." Tony looked over at his friend, as if deciding whether to say what was on his mind. "Larry, there are people on the force who think you're losing your edge. They think you snapped when Melissa went to jail. They don't give a lot of credence to your ideas right now."

Larry sat still for a moment, letting it all sink in. Too emotionally exhausted to fight back, he said, "I've been on this force for twelve years, Tony. I've always done my job with a clear head and all the energy and commitment I could give it."

"We know that, Larry. But look at you. You haven't shaved in days, you haven't slept, you're probably not even eating—it's hard to put a lot of stock in what you say when you look like you're about to go over the edge."

"Then ride with me," Larry entreated. "Ride with me tonight, after we're off duty. You'll see. I'll show you."

"Larry, you saw him stake her out once. That doesn't mean he does it every night."

"He might," Larry said. "Ride with me. Just come once and you'll see."

"Man, I need my sleep. So do you."

"All right. Just until the mall closes. Just give me that long, and I'll take you home."

"So what do you hope to accomplish? I mean, even if I come, and he stalks her tonight—"

"Back me up with the captain. Tell him I'm not losing it. Talk him into putting a tail on the girl."

Tony sighed. "I don't even know if he'd listen to me."

"That's my problem. Just come with me. Let me show you."

Tony moaned. "But it's Friday night, man. I have a date."

"Cancel it. Look at the irony here, Tony. We're heading out to the beach to investigate this girl's death—and at the same time, *another* girl's life is in danger, and we won't do anything to stop it."

The look in Larry's eyes was so haunted, so weary, so determined, that Tony found himself agreeing.

"No matter what we find, the girl on the beach is dead. We're not going to bring her back. But what if we had seen somebody preparing to kill her before she died? What if we could have stopped it? Would we have turned our heads and gone on with our other cases?"

Tony thought that over for a long moment. "All right, Larry," he said finally. "But just tonight. And that's only if we're finished with the work on this case by then. After the news reports on this girl's death come out, we might get some call-in leads on the girl who ran away with her. But if we don't have any strong leads on this case, I'll go with you."

The girl who'd been found on the beach was a young blonde who had apparently been raped and beaten to death before she'd been dumped into the Gulf. Larry and Tony hadn't spent much time at the site where she'd washed up; there was little evidence there to collect. Instead, they spent the afternoon talking to her shocked family members and friends. Her best friend, Lisa, who had run away with her and still hadn't been located, had been known to abuse drugs with her. The coroner said that the girl may have been dead for two weeks.

The trail of her killer was cold, and Larry suspected that it would take them out of their jurisdiction. She had probably been thrown in from a boat somewhere out at sea, and it had probably taken several days for her to wash up. They had already spent entire days searching for leads on the girls' whereabouts, and Larry suspected that they would have just as much trouble piecing together the facts surrounding her death.

Since they had no leads, and little information about what had happened to the girls since their disappearance, Tony agreed to ride with Larry that night.

They followed Pendergrast home from work, then ate their own cold burgers in the car, waiting for him to come back out. "I thought of going into the mall and finding her," Larry said. "Telling her to be on her guard."

"That would be a mistake at this point, Larry. You can't alert every girl Pendergrast looks at. The man has never been convicted of anything. If you start going around telling people to look out for this guy because he's a rapist and he's after them, you'll wind up losing your job."

The door to Pendergrast's apartment opened, and he came out into the darkness and headed quietly down the steps.

"He's going to the Toyota," Larry said quietly. "He thinks he's covering his tracks with his Cherokee parked at home."

He cranked the engine, and pulled out without turning on the lights. Across the parking lot, they saw the lights come on in the gray Toyota, and Pendergrast pulled out.

"What do you think?" Larry asked, pulling into traffic several cars behind him. "You want to go to the mall?"

Tony was silent as they followed. "Isn't it a little early? The mall doesn't close for another hour."

"I don't know. Let's see."

"He's turning."

"Going to the mall," Larry said victoriously.

They followed him down the streets that would take them to the mall, and Larry pointed to the Dillards store. "He'll go there," he said. "Watch him."

They watched as he pulled into a parking space not far from the Dillards entrance. Larry and Tony pulled in several aisles over.

"Now what?" Tony asked. "Does he just sit there?"

"Did last night. Just sat there watching and waiting."

Tony absorbed it for a moment. "Maybe it's not just her he's after. Maybe he's just waiting for anybody who looks vulnerable."

"Maybe," Larry said. "He was taking pictures. Looked like he had some kind of night lens on his camera."

"He took pictures of her?"

Larry nodded.

"Hmmm." The light came on in Pendergrast's car, and Tony leaned forward. "Is he getting out?"

"Looks like it." Larry grabbed the handle of his car door. "He's going in. I'll follow him. You stay here in case I lose him and he comes back out."

Tony nodded, and Larry got out and quietly mashed the door shut behind him. He walked several yards behind Pendergrast, several rows over, and waited to let him get inside before he made it to the door.

The lights of the department store assaulted him as he stepped inside, and he looked around to find Pendergrast. He was up ahead, walking through the cosmetics section.

Larry skirted the area, then rode the escalator upstairs. As soon as he got off, he went around to the rail that looked down on the cosmetics area in the center of the store. From here he had a perfect view, and Pendergrast wasn't likely to look up and see him.

He watched as Pendergrast seemed to be studying the men's cologne. After a moment, the girl he'd followed home last night finished with her customer and waited on him.

She was pretty, Larry thought, and younger than she'd seemed last night. She looked just the way Pendergrast liked them: blonde, small, delicate—like Melissa and Sandy.

Larry's stomach tightened into a knot as Pendergrast leaned on the counter, with that charming, drop-your-guard grin that was so deceiving. She was enjoying him, he thought. She was laughing at his flirtations.

After a moment, he paid for the cologne and, with one last comment that made her laugh again, he sauntered away.

What is he doing? Larry asked himself as he watched Pendergrast head back out the door. Did he ask her out? Was this whole thing nothing more than a man getting interested in a woman and pursuing her?

He waited until Pendergrast was gone, then rode the escalator back down and went to the same counter. He saw the display of men's cologne that Pendergrast had purchased and picked up a bottle, himself.

"May I help you?"

He knew by the information in the computer about her, based on her car registration, that she was only twenty. She looked even younger. "Yeah, I was just trying to decide if I wanted this. That guy who was here a minute ago, he bought some, didn't he?"

She smiled. "Yeah. He did."

"Is he a regular customer?"

She shrugged. "I've never seen him before, but he said the scent caught his attention. I tried to interest him in the bath products and shaving cream, too. I'll bet he comes back."

"Why?"

"They usually do. They get one product and they fall in love with it. Or they get such a response from their girlfriends that they can't help wanting all the rest."

Larry smiled. "Do you get many of them hassling you for dates?"

She giggled. "Occupational hazard when you sell men's cosmetics. Here, you want to try some?"

She sprayed the cologne on his arm, rubbed it in, then offered him the back of his wrist to smell.

He nodded. "I like it. But I don't generally wear cologne."

"Your girl will like it."

His grin faded slightly. "She likes me without it."

"Then buy *her* some. I sell women's cologne, too. Over here. You can try some of it—"

He held up his hand to stem her sales pitch, and leaned on the counter. "No, I don't need any today. But just tell me one thing. That guy who was here. Did he ask you out?"

She looked confused at the question. "No. Why?"

"I was just curious. He looked a little old for you."

She was irritated now. "I really don't think that is any of your business. Now, if you'll excuse me, I'm a little busy."

As she walked to the other side of the counter, he thought about telling her that the man who'd just bought cologne from her was a known rapist, that he was stalking her, trying to build trust, but that she couldn't trust him. The phone rang, and as she answered it, Tony's cautions raced through his mind. He couldn't panic her now. Not without more cause.

Sighing, he headed for a different entrance from the one he'd used coming in, and circled through the dark parking lot back to the car, praying Pendergrast would be watching the doors he was closest to and not see him.

The light didn't come on when he opened the door. The mechanics at the precinct had long ago wired his car to keep that from happening. He slid into the driver's seat.

"Where have you been, man?" Tony asked. "He came out ten minutes ago."

"Talking to the girl."

"Oh, no. You didn't."

"He bought something from her. Didn't ask her out, though. He's still sitting there?"

"Yeah. Getting close to closing time. Larry, you didn't tell her who you are, or who he is, did you?"

"Nope."

Tony breathed a sigh of relief.

"We just have to watch," Larry said. "Get a little more to go on. He's trying to establish her trust. Maybe so she'll go with him later."

"But that isn't his normal MO, is it? I mean, he didn't attack women who knew him. He uses the element of surprise, breaks into their homes—"

"Those are just the ones we know about. Besides, they identified him, didn't they? Maybe they had seen him before."

Tony grew quiet.

Customers began leaving, going to their cars, as a security car patrolled the parking lot.

They waited quietly for the employees to scatter.

"Here she comes," Larry said as the young woman came out of the building, along with several other women and a security guard. "Funny how they all have such a sense of security being with that guard, but the minute they pull out of the parking lot they're on their own."

"She has us," Tony said.

"Yeah. Tonight she does."

They watched her car start up, and just as Larry had expected, Pendergrast's lights came on, too. "Time to go," Larry said.

Keeping his lights off, Larry waited until she had pulled to the parking lot's exit. Pendergrast followed.

As they drove down the deserted street, Tony shook his head. "Unfortunate route home."

"Tell me about it. 'Course it depends on your perspective. From his, it's the perfect route."

After a few minutes, they reached the end of the road and she turned into her parking lot. Pendergrast followed, but Larry didn't pull in. This time, he stayed way back, on the side of the street, watching.

Tony brought his infrared binoculars to his eyes and watched her trot up to her apartment. Pendergrast stayed in his car, watching.

Her light was on for several minutes when Pendergrast pulled out of the parking lot and headed back the way he had come.

Larry's heart sank.

"Guess he's not doing anything tonight," Tony said.

"No. He's not ready yet. But I don't think he'll wait a whole lot longer."

Larry started the car but headed in the opposite direction from Pendergrast.

"Where we going?" Tony asked.

"Home," Larry said. "That was the deal. After the mall closes, I take you home."

Tony was quiet for a moment. "You're coming back, aren't you?"

Larry didn't answer.

"Larry, are you gonna stay up all night again watching him?"

"What do you want me to do, Tony? He raped Sandy at three A.M. What if I go home and get some sleep in my nice warm bed, and tomorrow morning the headline in the paper is that a nice, young, innocent blonde woman was raped by an unknown assailant during the night."

"Larry, you can't stay up all night and work all day."

"Then back me up on this," Larry said. "Tell the captain we need to be on this case for a while—then we can just work nights. Tell him what we saw tonight. Tell him I'm not crazy."

Tony sighed. "I'll try. But with this other case—"

"There's no case more important than this one," he said. "Not to me. There's a rapist walking the streets of St. Clair. You tell me what's more important."

Tony didn't answer.

38

THE CAPTAIN DIDN'T come in the next day; he had meetings with the mayor all day long. Larry found himself torn between hurrying through his other cases to get back to Pendergrast and haunting City Hall, hoping to run into the captain. Giving up, he resolved to sacrifice another night's sleep to follow Pendergrast, just in case. Tony, afraid that Larry was about to reach the point of exhaustion, agreed to keep watch with him.

Pendergrast was getting bolder. Tonight, as Larry and Tony watched from across the dark mall parking lot, Pendergrast went into Dillards again. This time they both followed, watching him from two separate vantage points in the department store.

Pendergrast didn't go near the young blonde woman; instead, he watched her from a distance across the store. His fascination with her was clear. He watched her wait on customers, watched her clean the counter, watched her restock merchandise.

When she took a break and walked out into the mall, Pendergrast followed her, with Larry not far behind. She went to the food court and bought some French fries and a drink, then joined some friends at one of the tables. Pendergrast blended into the crowd at one of the vendors, continuing to watch her.

Tonight, Larry thought. *He's going to do something tonight.*

One by one, her friends left to go back to their jobs, leaving the woman alone at the table, and Larry held his breath, waiting, wondering if Pendergrast would approach her now. But he didn't. It wasn't his style. He had shown himself to her only once, so that he would be familiar to her, but not recognizable. He probably didn't want to be identified later.

Two women had identified him already. He had probably learned from those mistakes.

Finally, she threw away her bags and her drink and headed into the ladies' rest room.

Pendergrast followed.

The long hall leading to the rest rooms was dimly lit. Larry had long been aware of it because so many crimes had happened right there, and he had once tried to convince the management to either put an armed guard there or else to close the facility altogether and put a rest room out near the mainstream of mall traffic. But so far they hadn't listened.

Now, he felt helpless as Pendergrast gave her a head start to reach the ladies' room around the corner of the long hall, then started down it himself. Larry couldn't follow without being seen. All he could do was wait, and listen, and pray.

Five minutes later, he saw the woman coming back up the hall. Breathing a sigh of relief, Larry backed into the crowd, becoming invisible. After a few seconds, Pendergrast came back up the hall, his eyes intense as he followed her all the way back to her store. When she was behind her counter again, he headed back to his car.

Tony was already in the car when Larry made his way back. "See anything?" Tony asked.

Larry reached for his infrared binoculars. "He followed her to the bathroom. I thought he was going to act then, but he didn't."

"He's getting hungry," Tony said. "No question. Something's about to happen."

"Poor girl is walking right into this." Larry watched as Pendergrast settled back in his seat, watching the door. "So what did you see?"

Tony shrugged. "Same thing you did. When I saw you following them out of the store, though, I figured you had it under control. So I took the opportunity to take a look in that car of his. The door wasn't locked."

Larry dropped the binoculars and looked at him. "Find anything?"

"Nothing in the front. But when I clicked the release on the trunk, it came open. I found a shovel and a jumbo-sized garbage bag."

Larry's face went pale.

"Doesn't mean anything," Tony went on. "He could have been taking them to clean up a construction site or something. Just because it was big enough to put a body in—"

"You think he's a killer?" Larry asked.

Tony shook his head. "I didn't say that. We can't jump to conclusions."

But Larry already had. "Tony, we know that he's got an obsession. We know he's raped twice before, and my bet is that he's done it more than that. We don't know how many times, or how bad. He almost killed Melissa's sister. Could be that he's stopped someone from talking before." He brought the binoculars back to his eyes. "He broke into Melissa's apartment, wrote on her mirror, hid in her attic. He was probably going to kill her, too."

Tony peered toward the man sitting so inconspicuously in his car. "Yeah, well, you should probably be glad she's locked up. She's probably in the only place she could be safe from him. Hey, if somebody set me up for something I didn't do, I'd want to get even. Put that revenge in the mind of a man who's a maniac already, and you don't know what he's capable of."

"Then you're admitting it," Larry said. "He's a maniac."

Tony didn't answer, but he didn't need to. Larry knew Tony was convinced.

"As it stands," Larry whispered, "he's just going along with business as usual. Setting up his target, moving in for the kill . . ."

"Well, if you're right, he won't get away with it this time." Tony looked at his watch. "Mall closes in an hour."

They waited, watching, as Pendergrast waited, watching.

An hour later, when the employees began to come out, they saw Karen Anderson among them. This time, however, she wasn't alone as she separated from the group and headed for her car. There was a man with her. They watched as she got into her car, and the man got in on the other side.

"She's giving this guy a ride home," Tony said, cranking the car but leaving the lights off. "What's Pendergrast doing?"

"He's cranking up," Larry said, watching him through the binoculars. "He's going to follow, anyway."

They followed quietly as she took her usual route home. Pendergrast drove about a quarter of a mile behind her, and Larry and Tony, with their lights still off, followed a good distance behind him. When they reached her apartments, they parked on the street again. The man got out with her, and the two of them headed up to her apartment.

Pendergrast didn't wait. As if angry, he sped back out of the parking lot and headed back up the way they had come, past the construction sites. Larry and Tony struggled to keep him in their view as they turned the car around and followed. Halfway up Highland Drive, Pendergrast turned onto a dirt road and disappeared among the trees. Tony stepped on the brakes.

"Where's he going? Should I follow him?"

"No. We don't know where that road goes. Besides, there's only room for one car. If he turns around and comes back, he'll see us. Let's just wait."

So they waited, holding their breath, for Pendergrast to return. After about twenty minutes, he did.

They followed him back to his apartment. When his lights went off after twenty minutes, they assumed that he'd gone to bed. Quickly they drove back to the dirt road down which he had disappeared earlier. Tony started to turn the car into the little dirt road, but Larry stopped him. "Not a good idea," he said. "Let's park and walk. If he sees our tire tracks tomorrow, he'll know someone's on to him."

Tony pulled the car to the side of the road. They got out and hiked up the long, dirt road, shining their flashlights as they went, not knowing what they were looking for, but hoping they'd know when they saw it. They followed the tiny, broken road all the way to the end, about a mile into the woods, then around a curve and further into the trees.

"Do you think this is where he was going to take her?" Tony asked.

Tony nodded. "Has to be. But it's too dark to see anything tonight. We'll have to come back tomorrow when the sun comes up."

Larry agreed. "Even if we don't find anything, at least we can get familiar with it in case we have to come this way again." He gave Tony a pensive look. "It won't be much longer now," he whispered. "He's ready. I'm just worried about the girl."

"Well, we could tell her and stop the whole thing. She could quit her job, never go home alone again, move. It would divert this attack, all right, but it wouldn't stop him from the next one."

"I want to get him," Larry whispered. "I want to get him for good."

"Then this is the only way. She'll be traumatized and terrified, but she'll be alive. We won't let him hurt her."

Larry thought about that for a long moment. "I just wish I could be sure of that."

39

IT WAS NEARLY nine in the morning by the time Tony and Larry made it back to the dirt road they had seen Pendergrast turn down the night before. They had watched his apartment for most of the night, then gone home for a little sleep before getting up and getting started again. Today, fatigued but determined, they made sure that Pendergrast was engaged at a construction site in another area before they checked out the road.

In the daylight, Highland Drive looked less threatening. Construction was going up in various places along the road, and the curb was lined with the trucks of men working. But the dirt road to which they'd followed Pendergrast last night was at least half a mile from the nearest construction site.

Again, they left the car on the street and followed the road on foot. After walking for twenty minutes or so, Tony asked, "How far do you think we've come?"

"A mile, at least," Larry said. "I didn't even know the woods back here were this thick. Where do you think it goes?"

"Nowhere," Tony said. "The next road is close to the interstate, but that's several miles from here. Listen." He slowed his step. "Do you hear that?"

Larry listened for a moment. "Water. Do you think there's a pond or something? Maybe people fish here?"

"Now that I think about it, there's a little canal that feeds into the Gulf. The road Highland runs into crosses it. It must cut through these woods."

They followed the road until they came to the canal. The Toyota's tire tracks turned onto a clearing there, and Larry muttered, "Bingo."

"This is where he came last night, anyway," Tony said, stepping into the clearing and looking around. "Well, one thing's for sure. If he's planning to bring her here at night, it's far enough back that nobody would hear her scream."

"And if he left her here, it's not likely that anybody would find her for a while, either."

He set his hands on his hips and looked around. The canopy of trees was so thick that little sun got through. It was hot, too, for little wind was able to sweep through the thick brush. He wondered how Pendergrast had found this place to begin with, then realized that the guy probably knew the land around here intimately, since his company contracted the clearing of it for new construction sites. Proffer Builders might even own it.

"What's this?"

Tony was across the small clearing, stepping through bushes and trees, getting closer to the water.

"What?" Larry asked.

"Oh, man." Tony turned back. "You've got to see this."

Larry hurried across the clearing and stepped through the brush. His breath caught in his chest when he saw what Tony was standing over. "Unbelievable."

It was a round hole about six feet deep, but the diameter of the hole was no more than three feet. The dirt that had been dug out of the hole was piled next to it, ready to be shoved back in.

Larry got down on his knees and peered into the hole. "Well, there goes the possibility that it's preparation for clearing the land. That shovel and bag you saw last night?"

Tony looked in and saw them at the bottom of the hole. "He's planning to kill her."

"Yep."

"He would have buried her here, and nobody would have found her. He could bury her in five minutes, kick a few leaves over the dirt . . ."

Larry sat down on the ground, resting his arms on his knees. "He might have buried Melissa here."

"Do you think he'll go after Karen Anderson tonight?"

"Could be. We have to be ready. Somehow, he's going to have to get her into his car, so he can get her here." Larry was beginning to look pale. "What if we don't make it in time, Tony? What if we get there too late?"

"We won't."

Larry rubbed his face. "This poor kid. She has no idea what's about to happen to her."

"We'll stop him before he hurts her, Larry."

"We *hope* we will." He looked at Tony, playing possible scenarios over in his mind. "What if we used a decoy?"

"We can't," Tony said. "Not if we want to catch him on something that'll stick. You can't really think he's going to drag some woman off and rape her without looking at her face."

"We have to catch him," Larry said. "But there has to be some other way."

"There isn't, man. She'll be all right. We'll be right there, and the minute something happens, we'll have handcuffs on that guy so fast he won't know what hit him."

"I don't like it."

"What do you mean, you don't like it? This is your case! You started the whole thing!"

"But this is somebody's life, Tony!"

"Hey, if it weren't for you, we wouldn't know anything happened until her mother reported her missing. You're saving her life, not risking it!"

"But there's a way to be more sure. First, we have to tell the captain, and get his support on this."

"Yeah, I'm with you. And then?"

Larry looked up at him. "And then we have to tell her. Maybe she can help us."

Despite Larry's absolute exhaustion, his adrenaline was pumping as he went back to the station. He was about to catch Pendergrast, and that was enough to keep him going.

It was midmorning when he and Tony finally were able to get in to talk to the captain about taking the Pendergrast case full-time until they caught him. Tony backed up what Larry had already said—adding credence to the story with his clear-headed, emotionless recitation of the things they'd observed—and the captain paced in his usual way, turning the facts over in his mind.

"Okay, I'll buy it—something's about to happen," he said. "And since we don't have any leads at the moment on the girl on the beach, I guess you can work on this for a couple of days. But if nothing happens in the very near future, I'm gonna have to take you off of it again."

Larry's relief was apparent, but he pressed on to the next question. "Thanks, man," Larry said, getting to his feet. "But there's one more thing. I want to let the woman in on it. See if we can convince her to cooperate with us."

Sam considered that for a moment. "You might blow the whole thing if she says no."

"I'll convince her."

"How?"

"I don't know," Larry said, leaning over the desk. "But her life is at risk here. If we tell her, arm her, let her know what's about to come down, she might be willing to go through with it. It's the only way we can be sure to stop it when it happens. Otherwise, something could go wrong, and she could get raped, or even killed."

The captain sat slowly down at his desk. Clasping his hands in front of his face, he gazed at Tony. "What do you think?"

Tony wasn't sure. "I'd hate to have her balk and run. Then we might never catch him. On the other hand, if anybody can convince her, Larry can."

"It might work," the captain said. "We can do a lot more to prepare if she's with us."

"All right," Larry said. "Then we'll go talk to her. But we're going to have to make some promises. Give her a sense of security. Let her know we won't abandon her."

"Let me know what you need," the captain said. "I'll make sure you get it."

Tony shook the captain's hand and started to the door, but when Larry reached for his hand, the captain held it a beat longer than necessary. "Sorry about the other day, Millsaps. I may have been too hard on you. I was a little stressed, what with this body washing up, and the mayor breathing down my neck about the drug problem."

"Don't worry about it, Captain. I have a tough skin."

"You must," he said. "How long've you been working around the clock now? A week?"

"I'll sleep when we get that jerk in jail."

"So will I," the captain said. "So will I."

40

THE CROWD OF inmates walking from the dining hall to cellblock C threaded into a single-file line that followed the yellow line down the hall and back to their cells. Melissa watched a group of correctional officers coming toward them, walking side by side. She had never realized how much she would miss the freedom to walk the way she wanted, where she wanted. Now, every step, every thought, every activity was monitored and controlled.

Some of the women talked as they walked behind each other, but most were quiet, for one never knew when the wrath of one of the "bosses" might be stirred. It didn't take much. One woman had been caught looking too long at a male officer, and it had made one of his jealous coworkers angry. She had dragged that woman out of line and put her in isolation for three days. So Melissa walked with her eyes downcast, never straying from that yellow line, for fear that she'd be cited for bad behavior and have even one extra day added to her sentence.

As they drew closer to the doors to their cellblock, instead of crossing diagonally toward it, they had to follow the yellow line to its corner, turn ninety degrees, and then follow another line toward the doors. It was degrading, humiliating.

As soon as they were in their cellblock, however, they were free to leave the line and mill about their floor. Melissa hurried toward her cell.

Something tripped her, and she stumbled, then quickly recovered her balance. She turned around. The redhead who had harassed her on her first day was walking behind her, grinning.

Melissa compressed her lips, determined not to be drawn into a fight. But when she turned to walk on, the woman tripped her again. This time, Melissa swung around. "What do you want?" she demanded.

Red shoved her then, and Melissa lashed out to defend herself. Before she knew what had happened, the woman flung herself away from Melissa across the concrete floor, slammed herself into the opposite wall, and screamed. She came up with her knee bleeding. "I'll kill you!" she shouted.

Realizing that she was watching an award-winning performance, Melissa backed away, hands raised, as the COs rushed toward them. "I didn't touch her," she said. "She was harassing me, and then she flung herself across the hall—"

"She's lying!" Red screamed. "She knocked me across the hall! Look at my knee! I think it's dislocated. I won't be able to work tomorrow because of her."

"All right," one of the COs said, grabbing Melissa's arm roughly. "I'm writing you up. You can spend a night in isolation, and see if you still want to fight tomorrow."

"But I didn't do anything! She set me up!"

But the CO didn't care. He dragged Melissa out of the cellblock and down to the isolation cell she had heard about but never seen. It was six feet by four feet; everything was metal and welded down. There were no sheets on the bed, just a two-inch-thick pad that served as a mattress on the metal bed frame. A metal sink and a metal toilet were welded to one wall. The room was sweltering.

"Listen to me, please," she told the CO. "I'm telling you—"

But the huge, sliding metal door slid shut behind him, and she was locked in.

"I didn't do it," she whispered, sitting down on the edge of the bed. "I didn't do it."

She sat there for hours, waiting for someone to come so that she could plead her case, but no one came. Unable to tell what time it was, but guessing that it was nearing midnight, she finally stretched out on the miserable excuse for a mattress and tried to sleep. Red was probably sleeping soundly in her cell, with her knee bandaged up from her self-inflicted wound, and laughing that she'd escaped a day of work at Melissa's expense.

Fantasies of revenge floated through Melissa's mind—fantasies of *really* dislocating the woman's knee—but in the wee hours of morning, she realized that she'd tried that before.

That's what had landed her here. She wasn't going to become like the others here, she told herself. Even if it killed her, she would resist.

Tears ran down her temples and into her hair. *Help me to forgive them, Lord. I'm not very good at that.*

And as she finally drifted into a fitful sleep, she knew that she could trust God to answer that prayer, in his own time.

41

LARRY AND TONY made sure that Pendergrast was working away in his office before they went to Karen Anderson's apartment. They had already learned from her license tag information her address, her name, and her age. Now all they needed was her trust.

They tried to be quiet and inconspicuous as they made their way up the stairs to her door. Larry knocked. After a moment, they heard footsteps.

"Who is it?" a woman asked through the door.

"Larry Millsaps, St. Clair Police Department. Can we talk to you for a moment?"

The door cracked open, and Karen peered beneath the chain lock. "What about?"

Larry glanced at Tony, and he stepped forward, flashing his badge. "We're detectives with the St. Clair P.D. Are you Karen Anderson?"

"Yes." She reached through the crack in the door and took both badges, read them, then peered up at the two detectives.

"We need to talk to you in private. It's very important."

Reluctantly, she closed her door, unlocked the chain, and opened it again. "You were in the store the other night," she said to Larry as they came in. "You didn't tell me you were a detective."

"No," he said. "I was hoping it wouldn't be necessary." He closed the door and glanced around the small apartment.

"Could we sit down?"

She led them into the small living room furnished with old furniture that had seen better days. A pair of shoes lay in the middle of the floor, and books and papers were scattered all over the couch and coffee table. "Excuse the apartment. I've been studying."

"You're in school?" Tony asked.

"Yes," she said. "I go to Jones College in the mornings."

Larry moved some library books out of a chair and sat down. "Don't clean up on our account. You probably have everything right where you need it. We just need to talk to you."

She stopped straightening and swept her hair behind her ears. "What's going on?"

Larry gestured for her to sit down, and finally, she did. "Miss Anderson, we're here because you're in danger. In the course of an investigation that we've been doing, it's come to our attention that you're being stalked. Were you aware of this?"

She frowned and looked from one cop to the other. "Stalked? What do you mean?"

"You're being followed by a man who has been arrested before on rape charges. He's been watching you. We believe he has every intention of making you his next victim. And soon."

"What?" The word came out in an astonished whisper, and she sprang up and went to the window. Peering out, she asked, "Is he out there now?"

"No," Larry said. "We made sure he was someplace else before we came here."

She kept staring out the window. "Why haven't you arrested him?"

"Because he hasn't done anything yet. Twice before he was arrested and got off on technicalities. We have to wait until we can catch him at something substantial enough to get him put away for a long time."

"How do you know he's following me? Maybe it's someone else."

"No, you're his target," Larry said. "He goes into the store, watches you. He's approached you once that we know of."

"Who? Who was he?"

"The one I asked you about that night. Do you remember?"

She came back to the couch, trying to remember. "No. I waited on a lot of men that night. I can't remember . . ."

"Well, that's just as well. He also parks out in the parking lot and waits for you to come out. For at least the past three nights he's followed you home."

Terror crossed her face, and she rushed to the door and turned the dead bolt, then hurried to the living-room window to see if it was locked. Desperately, she turned back to them. "The phone calls. Could he be the one making them?"

"What phone calls?"

"I've been getting a lot of hang-up calls. Like someone's just trying to see if I'm home. At all hours, day and night."

"It's him," Tony said, glancing at Larry. "Has anything else happened?"

"Well—no. I didn't know anyone was following me. I can't believe I didn't see him." She hurried around the apartment as she spoke, frantically checking window locks. "I've been taking the shortcut home, driving down Highland Drive all by myself. My mother warned me to take another route—" She swung around, confronting them. "What are you going to do about this?"

"We're going to catch him. But we need your help."

"*My* help? Are you kidding?"

"You're the only one who *can* help us right now," Larry said.

"But how? What can I do?"

"You can cooperate with us. Help us catch him."

She went back to her seat and sat on the edge. "By doing what?"

"Just what you've been doing," Tony said. "Keep going to work, driving the same way home, letting him follow you."

"Until what? He rapes me?"

"He won't rape you. We can protect you. We need for him to think everything is normal. But if you help us plan this out, we can trap him."

"So I'm the bait? Dangle me under his nose, and he'll strike?"

Larry looked down at his shoes. "I'm afraid you're the bait, anyway. We're just trying to protect you."

"No!" Beginning to cry, she shot up again. "I can't do this. I'll—I'll move. I'll go back and live with my mother."

"What about your job? School? Don't you think he'll find you?"

She thought about that for a moment. "There's a law. A stalking law, isn't there? You could arrest him just for following me."

"It wouldn't hold him any amount of time," Larry said, "if it stuck at all. He's smart. He's gotten off twice. We have to make sure that what we get him on is substantial enough to lock him up for a long time."

She shook her head again and began to pace. "Maybe—maybe he'll get discouraged if he can't find me. I mean, why is he after me, anyway?"

"He's sick. He's picked you out, Karen. He likes blondes. He's obsessed with you. If you change what you're doing, you could throw him off for a few days, but there's no guarantee that he wouldn't catch up to you eventually. By then he'll just be more desperate."

"I can't believe this!" she shouted. "I haven't done anything to anybody. All I do is go to school, work, and study. Why would this happen to me?"

Larry got up and took a couple of steps toward her. "You can turn it around, Karen. Go from being the victim to being in control."

She wiped her wet face with a trembling hand. "What would you do for me, if I did?"

"We'd have someone watching you twenty-four hours a day. We'd never let you out of our sight. When we think he's about to strike, we could wire you with a microphone so we would know what was happening every minute."

"But how far would things have to go before you arrested him?"

"At least far enough that there's no question that he was going to do you bodily harm."

Terror flooded her face as she shook her head violently. "I can't do it. You're asking too much."

"We realize it's asking a lot," Tony said. "But there's no other way."

"Karen, he's a threat to countless women out there," Larry said, getting face-to-face with her. "One woman is dead because of him. He broke into her house and brutally raped her. Almost killed her. She wound up killing herself. I don't even know how many others he's raped. But he's smart, so he's still out there on the street. We need to get him, Karen. Right now, you're the only one who can help us."

Her breath caught on a sob. "I'm twenty-one years old. I weigh 105 pounds. I can't fight him."

"We'll fight him. All you have to do is bait him."

"But I'm scared!" she cried. "Let somebody else do it, a policewoman or something."

"And what will you do?" Tony asked. "Move out of this apartment? Quit your job? Give up school? Are you going to let a maniac like this control your life?"

"I don't want to."

"Even if you did, would you ever know for sure that he wasn't stalking you again? As long as he's out there, he could come after you. He might find you, before we ever had the chance to catch him again."

"I can't do it!" she cried. "You'll have to find another way. I'll hide, if I have to. But I can't do this!"

"Then what *are* you going to do?" Tony asked.

She thought about that as she looked frantically around the apartment. "I guess I'll pack a few things and leave." She ran back to her bedroom, pulled a suitcase out of the closet.

Larry came to the door of the bedroom. "Karen, just trust us. We'll be there. We won't let anything happen to you."

"How can I know that?" she screamed. "It's my life that's at stake, not yours. If you mess up, let me down, it's no skin off your nose! I—can't—do it!"

Larry glanced over his shoulder to Tony. The look his partner gave him said this was hopeless. She was going to run, and Pendergrast would be thrown off. Sam would get impatient and close the case. On his own, Larry would have to haunt him night after night, waiting for another chance. Who knew when that would come?

Meanwhile, Melissa was sitting in jail, and Pendergrast was free, and the injustice of it all was overwhelming.

Larry leaned his forehead against the door casing as Karen ran around, grabbing the things she would take with her.

"Karen, this really good friend of mine—a woman I care a lot about—her sister was the woman who was raped and then killed herself."

Karen slowed her packing and looked up at him.

A tear stole out of Larry's eye, and he wiped it away. "He got away with it. Walked scot-free. My friend, Melissa, she's sitting in jail right now because she tried to set it up to look like he'd raped her. She figured she'd have all the evidence they needed this time. He'd never walk free again. That's desperation, Karen. She put herself in jeopardy, could have been raped or killed, to catch him. But it didn't work out, and she finally wound up confessing. She's in jail, Karen, and he's out there somewhere, terrorizing women like you. He's dangerous, and nobody's going to stop him."

She covered her face with both hands, and her shoulders shook with the force of her despair.

"If Melissa were here, she'd cooperate. She'd do anything, because she wouldn't want even one more woman to be stalked and raped like her sister was. Melissa loved Sandy. She was pretty and blonde, like you. She had a new husband, and everything was going great for her. And one night, when she didn't expect it, this man broke in and ruined her life. She couldn't live with it. And she's not the only one, Karen."

"I scream when I see a roach," Karen bit out as the tears soaked her face. "When the wind blows hard, I have nightmares. You're not looking at a brave person."

Larry took a few more steps into the room, his eyes beseeching. "Karen, the terror's not going away just because you run. Wouldn't you feel safer knowing that we're with you? Watching you?"

"No," she said, closing her suitcase and snapping it shut. "No, I wouldn't feel safer. I have to get out of here." She grabbed the suitcase up off the bed and dragged it into the living room. Leaving it at the door, she started gathering her schoolbooks. As she stacked the last one, she broke down. For a moment, she stood there with her books clutched in her arms, her eyes squeezed shut, and her shoulders rolling with the force of her sobs.

Larry touched her shoulder, but words escaped him.

"I don't want to quit school!" she cried. "I'm almost finished. It's not fair!"

"No, it isn't," he whispered.

"I like my job, and I like living here. How come he gets to ruin everything?"

"He doesn't," Larry said. "We don't have to let him."

She hesitated and looked up at him, and for a moment, Larry thought she might give in.

But instead, she opened the door and grabbed her suitcase. "I'm sorry," she said.

Tony and Larry followed her out, watched her lock the dead bolt with her key, and Larry carried her suitcase down the steps to her car.

She was still crying when she got behind the wheel and looked up at him. "I'm sorry. Call me a wimp. I just can't do it."

"I understand," Larry said. "Just be careful, okay?" He pulled a card out of his pocket. "If you need to get in touch with me, call these numbers. You'll catch me at one of them."

She took the card, looked down at it, then nodded and sucked in another sob. "I have to go," she said.

Larry backed up, and she closed the door.

She backed out of the parking space, and sped out into the street, leaving them standing there alone.

"Now what?" Tony asked.

Larry shook his head and sighed. "I don't know. I honestly have no idea."

"Maybe she'll change her mind."

Larry thought about that for a moment. Somehow, he didn't think so.

Slowly, he walked back to the car without saying a word.

42

LARRY WAS ONE of the first ones to show up Saturday for visitors' day. He waited outside for the group to be let in, and let his eyes sweep over the other family members and friends who were waiting to see loved ones. A young woman who looked no older than seventeen stood with a baby on her hip, a toddler at her knees, and a hyperactive three-year-old running up and down the sidewalk, refusing to heed her warnings to stay by her side. Larry wondered if she was the children's mother, or just keeping them while their mother served time.

A man who looked as if he'd just crawled out of bed sat on a step of the jail with two little girls—one on each side of him, holding his hands. Had they come to see their mother?

And then came a small, quiet man alone; and two women together; and more children.

Did they all feel as forlorn as he did, coming here to see what the justice system had done to the person they loved? Ironic, he thought, that he would feel like this, when he was often the one putting them behind bars. But he had never seen the pain from the other side.

The doors opened, and they all filed in. One by one, they were searched for items that were against the rules. Larry set the bag of books he'd brought Melissa on the table. As he waited for them to search him, his heart recalled the despair he'd felt yesterday when he had searched the stores for something that he could bring her—something that would lift her up, give her strength, help her to feel God's mercy and grace. He had sat in his car and wept because he'd been unable to find anything other than books—so impersonal, so benign.

"All right," the guard said, shoving the bag of books back across the table. "These are fine. Just go that way into the rec room."

Larry followed the flow of people into the big room. Since this wasn't a maximum security state penitentiary, there were no glass booths to talk through. They could sit at the same table, touch, hold hands, and he could hold her if she cried.

That, he supposed, was something he should be thankful for.

He waited with sweaty palms as one of the guards ran down a list of rules for visiting.

Most of these people were regulars, like he would be, he thought. Even the small children knew the rules and the routine.

The doors opened, and one by one the prisoners came in, some with hugs, others with cross words, others with a dull expression that said they didn't care who visited, because no one really mattered. He watched hopefully, expectantly, each time the door opened, and when Melissa didn't come right away, he began to wonder if she was going to refuse to see him. She had told him not to come. What if she'd really meant it?

His heart was sinking lower when twenty or more inmates had been brought in, and Melissa still wasn't among them. Abandoning his bag of books on the table, he walked over to the guard.

"If she didn't want to see me, would they come tell me, or would they just let me sit here and wonder?"

The guard's eyes fell on the door, and he asked, "Is that who you're looking for?"

Larry turned around and saw her at the door. She was wearing her orange jumpsuit and looking timidly around for him. He started toward her, noting how pale she was, how tired she looked. Her hair was pulled back in a ponytail and she wore no makeup—as some of the other inmates did. She looked like a fragile sixteen-year-old rather than the gutsy twenty-three-year-old who'd almost beaten Edward Pendergrast. But he'd never seen a more beautiful sight in his life.

She saw him and started toward him, and he met her halfway and threw his arms around her.

For a moment, he just held her and felt her body shaking as she began to cry. Then, quickly pulling herself together, she let him go.

"Let's go sit down," she whispered.

He led her to their table and set the books on the floor. Taking her hand, he looked into her eyes to see what he could read there. "You look great," he whispered.

"I'm okay," she said. "Really. It's not so bad."

"Are you getting along okay? With the others, I mean?"

She took in a deep, ragged breath. "Yeah."

She was holding back, he thought. She wasn't going to share much. "Do you have a cellmate?"

She nodded and looked around. Chloe was across the room with a man who must be almost six feet, but still shorter than Chloe. They were standing and talking quietly. "See that woman over there? She's my cellmate."

Larry's heart plummeted again. She looked like a linebacker—a linebacker in a bad mood. "Do you two get along okay?"

Melissa looked down at the woodgrain on the table. "I stay out of her way. Try not to make too much noise."

He was getting alarmed, and he cupped her chin and made her look at him. "Melissa, has she been harassing you?"

There was honesty in her eyes when she answered. "No. Thankfully, she's kind of left me alone."

"What about everybody else?"

Her eyes teared up, and she looked down at the wood again and tried to rub off a spot. "Well, I haven't met Miss Congeniality yet. I'm still looking for her. This isn't the best place to make friends."

He watched as she clasped her hands, and he saw the burn across her fingers. "What's this?" he asked.

She covered the burn and withdrew her hand. "I burnt myself on an iron. I work in the laundry. It's no big deal. I did it myself."

He wasn't sure she was leveling with him; carefully, he took her hand and examined the blisters. "Have you put anything on it?"

"I told you, I'm fine," she said. "Now, can we change the subject? Let's talk about you. You look tired. Are you sleeping?"

"Of course," he lied, though he couldn't remember the last time he'd had more than two hours' sleep at a time. Even though Karen had disappeared yesterday, Larry had followed Pendergrast last night to see what he would do. He had sat outside her apartment most of the night, waiting for her to come home. When she never did, Pendergrast had finally given up.

He rubbed his hand across his jaw and told himself he should have shaved for her. He had been so anxious to see her that he had only taken time to shower.

"Are you growing a beard?"

He tried to smile. "Looks like it."

She wasn't buying his "everything's fine" routine any more than he was. "Larry, tell me what's going on."

He sighed and decided there was no point in hiding the truth. "I've been following Pendergrast. Watching him."

Behind them, an inmate and her lover became embroiled in an argument, and their profanities were gaining volume. Melissa seemed not to notice. "Really? You're watching him?"

"Yeah." He lowered his voice. "He's been stalking another girl. I'm afraid to let my guard down for a minute."

"So what are you doing? Following him around the clock?"

"Something like that," he said, glancing over his shoulder at the loud couple. "But I'm thinking that may change pretty soon. The girl's onto him now, so she's kind of disappeared. As soon as he realizes it, he'll give up and look for somebody else."

"How do you know she's onto him?"

"I told her. I wanted her cooperation, so we could catch him, but she balked and ran."

Across the room a baby in a carrier wailed, and its tired mother ignored it. "What if you used somebody else?" Melissa asked. "Put another girl in her place."

"The problem is that it's a little touchy. He's watching her. We can't replace her at work, because he'll know. We could pull a switch as she gets into her car, but even then, the minute he gets close enough to see her, he could back off. I can't catch him and get enough to convict him until he does something. And if he balks and cans the whole thing, I may not be around the next time he tries this. No, the only way was to get her cooperation. Now I'm almost wishing I hadn't told her."

"You had to. You couldn't let her walk into this blindly."

"That's how I felt yesterday. Today, I'm not so sure." He looked up at her with a half-smile. "I was really hoping I could bring some good news in here today. I wanted so much to tell you he was in jail."

"Larry, I want him caught too. But I don't want you killing yourself to do it. You're exhausted." She folded both arms on the table and fixed her troubled eyes on him. "Don't let anything happen to you, okay?"

He nodded his promise.

The CO crossed the room and reprimanded the angry couple behind them. Melissa swallowed and looked around at the other inmates interacting with families she didn't know they had. The room was quickly filling up with cigarette smoke and more crying babies, and she wished she and Larry could go outside together, breathe the fresh air, feel the sunshine. But that wasn't possible. She moved her troubled, timid eyes back to his. "You know, I really didn't expect you to come today. I knew my parents were coming this afternoon, but you were a surprise."

"Why? Didn't I tell you I would?"

"I told you not to."

"Well, I had to."

"Why?" she asked.

He took her hand again and seemed to study the shape of her fingers. "Because I miss you like crazy. I've worried about you day and night. I can't stand the thought of you here."

Her lip began to tremble, and she struggled with her tears again. He hated himself for making her cry.

"I don't know how all this happened," she whispered, bending her head down to hide the tears. "I did something wrong to try and right things, and I wound up hurting so many people. I didn't want to hurt you, Larry, and the last thing I want is for you to keep coming here out of obligation. Six months is a long time. You'll forget about me. I'd hate to get used to having you come, and then start noticing that you're coming less and less. I'd hate for you to feel guilty about having fun when I'm in here, like you owe me some debt."

"That's not going to happen," he assured her. "Melissa, look at me."

She looked up, her eyes red and wet.

"I love you. It's not something I chose to do, but it happened. I really mean it. I've never felt like this about any other woman."

She sucked in a sob and covered her mouth. "I love you, too," she whispered. "But I'm so worried about you."

"*You're* worried about *me?* Why?"

"Because you're out there, and he's out there. And you're trying to catch him at something all by yourself. Larry, I've tried that. It didn't work."

"There's a difference. I'm a cop. I know what I'm doing."

"I knew what I was doing, too."

"But you manipulated what happened with you. I'm not manipulating anything. I'm just watching."

"Please don't get so tired that you get sloppy and let him see you. He might kill you, Larry. He's a vicious, violent man."

"I'm going to get him off the street. But I'm going to come and visit you on every visitors' day, too. Got that?"

She sat gazing at him for a moment, wiping her tears as fast as they came. "I have a lot to be thankful for."

"What?" he asked. "Tell me."

She tried to think. "Well, I have you. Not everybody in here has somebody. And I'm safe from Pendergrast. He can't get to me in here."

Larry smiled. "That's right. That's what Tony said. Thank God for small favors."

"That's a big one," she admitted, "and I do thank him. I thank him for other things, too. Like the fact that I'm learning to depend on God. Completely. Being this low makes me realize how high he is. But he's still here, too, even in this place. I feel him."

"I feel him, too," Larry whispered. "Sometimes when I think of you being here, and I get such dread, I feel his comfort. But I don't think I want to be comforted. I guess in a way I feel I'm doing some kind of penance by worrying myself sick about you."

"We have to have faith, Larry," she whispered. "This morning, I was reading the book of James. He said life wouldn't always be easy. He said to let your trials strengthen you. I intend to do that."

"Then I will, too," he said.

As the noise grew around them, and the chaos in the room continued, they put aside their doubts and fears, their worries and anxieties, their remorse and regrets, and lost themselves in the world they had in common.

But that night, as Larry sat in his car in the parking lot across the street from Pendergrast's, waiting for him to come out of his apartment, Larry began to worry again. Melissa had looked so tired. The burn on her hand might not have come from the iron at all. And that cellmate of hers would instill fear into the toughest of men.

He had a long talk with God, pleading with him to find her another cellmate, pleading with him to protect her with his angels, pleading with him to let something good come of all this.

And then he pleaded that he would be able to catch Pendergrast at something soon, so that he could lock him away.

But it wasn't going to happen tonight. Pendergrast didn't go out. Larry wondered if he'd realized he'd been found out.

He gave up around four A.M. and went home to get a couple hours' sleep before he had to be at church. He needed to worship today, he thought. He needed to feel God's glory. He sure hadn't seen enough of it in that rec room at the Pinellas County Correctional Facility for Women.

43

THE PRISON CHAPEL was filled with more women than Melissa had expected that Sunday morning. She had hoped it would be a sanctuary—a safe place in the midst of all this madness. But as she went in, she saw the red-haired woman who had harassed her sitting at the back, and some of the others that she feared scattered around the room.

Had they come to worship, she wondered, or had they come to break the monotony of their lives?

It didn't matter, she told herself. What really mattered was that she had the opportunity to worship here, and she was going to.

Her heart felt lighter as one of the women from the prison ministry began to play the piano and direct the inmates in some praise songs. Most of the women didn't sing, she noted, but some of them did, Melissa among them.

Next to her sat a tiny Hispanic woman with dark circles under her eyes, singing in a lovely, lilting voice, with tears running down her face. Melissa could easily picture the woman in a small evangelical church, with a cotton, flower-print dress on, and maybe a hat with a bow. Instead, she sat here in her prison-issue jumpsuit looking as out of place as Melissa felt.

The chaplain who gave his time to come here on Sunday mornings was a young man in his early twenties, probably someone who had never had a church of his own. His name was Doug Manning.

"If you have a Bible with you, please turn to John, chapter 4."

Melissa opened her Bible to John, and noticed that the woman next to her did as well. Few others had Bibles with them.

It was the passage about the woman at the well, and as he launched into his sermon about the woman with a past, the woman who stood before Christ with all her sins exposed, and was offered forgiveness freely and without cost, Melissa felt a renewal of hope.

After the sermon, the chaplain entreated the women to stay for a prayer time, but one by one, most of the women filed out. Only the woman sitting next to her, and four others in different parts of the room, stayed behind.

Melissa sat quietly, waiting for the pastor to lead them.

He looked disappointed that so many had gone. "Well—since there aren't many of us, why don't we come up to the front here, and sort of put our chairs in a circle?" As they came, he asked, "Do you all know each other?"

Melissa looked around. A couple of them knew each other, but she knew none of them. "No. I'm new."

"Then let's introduce ourselves. I'm Doug, and this is my wife, Tina."

The woman who had been sitting next to Melissa offered her a timid smile. "I'm Sonja. I'm in cellblock C. I haven't been here long, either."

The next woman, a heavyset, jolly-looking woman, spoke up. "I'm Betty. I used to be a choir director in a little mission church we belonged to."

The next one, a black woman whose Bible looked worn and used, nodded to Melissa. "I'm Keisha. In cellblock A."

And after her, the last one, another black woman with huge, almond-shaped eyes who looked like model material, said, "I'm Simone. Cellblock B."

Doug smiled, pleased, then looked at Melissa. "And you are?"

"Melissa," she said quietly.

"Do any of you have any specific prayer requests?" he asked.

Sonja spoke up as tears filled her eyes, and she groped for the tissue she carried in her pocket. "I need prayers," she said. "I don't belong here. I didn't do what they said I did."

Doug looked as if he'd heard that before, but he didn't voice it.

"I didn't know my husband was selling drugs," she went on in her heavy accent. "When he got arrested, they arrested me, too, because they had seen me driving him places and dropping him off at places where he was making deals." Her face reddened, and she covered her face. "But I didn't know what he was doing." She stopped, sniffed, and tried to steady her voice. "I have three small children. Two, three, and five. I have to serve a year, but that's an eternity to them. They'll forget all about me."

The horror of that situation gripped Melissa, and by instinct, she reached out and took Sonja's hand.

"All right," Doug said. "We'll pray about that. Anyone else?"

"Yes," Betty said. "I'm due to get out in four weeks. I need prayers that nothing happens to mess up my release."

"All right." Doug looked around, waiting, for anyone else to speak up. "Anyone else?"

"Yes," Melissa said, almost in a whisper. "I'm not like Sonja. I did something wrong to come here. But I need prayers for strength. I need to see some sense in all of this."

"You may not ever," Doug warned her. "Sometimes you just have to trust God's sovereignty."

She breathed a laugh. "I'm beginning to realize that."

"Well, let's pray for these particular requests, and then I'll pray for each of you, that you'll be safe here, and that you'll be lights in this dark place. You know, a lot of those women who walked out of here just now are hurting. They need some Christian influence here. And you may not have noticed just now, but each of the cellblocks is represented in this little group. That's no coincidence. Each one of you has the power to change this whole facility."

"I don't feel very powerful," Keisha said.

"Me, either," Betty added.

"Well, neither did the disciples after Jesus died. But they didn't understand what was ahead. God saw their future, even when they didn't. He saw the reason, and all the purpose. Maybe you're here to work on the women in this prison."

"It's hard to care about them," Sonja said. "Some of them are hateful and wicked."

"Maybe they've never known any better."

"Maybe that's just an excuse," Sonja said. She brought her remorseful eyes up to Doug's. "I'm sorry. I just haven't been feeling much love for my fellowman—or woman—lately."

"Then we'll pray about that, too."

They held hands and prayed, earnestly, openly, with tender, broken hearts, and in doing so they created a bond that Melissa hadn't felt in years. She wanted to feel it more than once a week, she thought.

When the prayer was over, she felt empowered. "We need a Bible study," she said. "More than just once a week. Would that be allowed?"

"Of course it would," he said. "But I'm in seminary during the week, about three hours from here. I can only get here on Sundays. Would you be willing to lead it?"

Melissa's eyes widened. "Me?"

"Sure, why not?"

She looked around, surprised, and saw that everyone was looking expectantly at her. "Well, the truth is—I'm not real well educated on the Bible. I haven't really been walking with God for the last few years."

"Great opportunity to learn more," he said. "Just be available, pray about it, and God will lead you."

She hesitated and looked from one woman to another. "Would you come, if we had one? Say, three times a week?"

To a woman, they all agreed that they would.

"From this core group, other women can be reached," Doug said. "One by one, you'll bring them into the group, and it'll grow. I've seen it happen before."

"When?" Sonja asked. "You're too young to have seen much."

Doug only smiled. "My mother was in prison for several years when I was a boy," he said. "She was a battered wife, and she killed my father to keep him from killing me. That's why I feel such a burden to keep this prison ministry going."

"How many years was she in?" Sonja asked.

"Seven," he said. "But I had a loving grandmother who brought me to see my mother every time she could. My mother became a light in the prison. She built up a Bible study that started with three women and grew to about 200. And Sonja, I can tell you that, even from prison, my mother had a strong influence on me. I saw her making the best of the worst situation, and I saw her taking what had been given to her, and still being available for God to use. She wrote me a lot of letters, and read me books over the telephone at night, and rocked me when I visited. It wasn't the best situation, but she made it good."

"Wow. And look how you turned out," Sonja whispered. "Maybe my babies will be all right, too."

"And so will you. You know, some of these women were drug addicts when they came in here. Now that they're clean, they're different women. Regular human beings, with feelings, and regrets, and loneliness. Think of them as being like you, even the ones who act like monsters, and love them, anyway."

He knew, Melissa thought. He understood. And she felt so blessed that God had sent him to them.

As she went back to her cell, she felt called to be the light that God had sent for this dark corridor. And she decided that Chloe needed to be the first to see that light.

That afternoon, Larry came to visit again, and this time, Melissa was brighter. As they sat and talked and watched the other inmates with their families and friends, she noted Sonja in the corner with her children. The two babies were in her lap, and she was rocking them, while the five-year-old performed some little songs she'd memorized from a videotape she had at her grandmother's.

And then she saw Chloe again with her husband. The soft look on the woman's face made her look like a different person.

Later, when they were back in their cells, Melissa tried to make conversation as she straightened her things. "Your husband seems nice, Chloe."

"Yeah. He's a prince. He's stuck by me, too. Through thick and through thin. He'll be there when I get out. And you can bet I won't wind up back in here. This is my last time. I ain't like those other women, who don't know no better than to keep doin' stupid stuff—killin' and prostitutin' and sellin' and shootin' at folks. Man, if you could get the chair for havin' the stupids, they'd be killin' ninety percent of the women in this jail."

Something about that struck Melissa as funny, and quietly, she began to laugh.

"What's so funny?" Chloe asked.

Melissa covered her mouth with her hand and tried to stop.

She heard Chloe laughing on the bunk beneath her, and felt the bed shaking with it.

"Well, it's true," Chloe said. "You can laugh, but these girls—they ain't like you and me, with our little namby-pamby crimes. Some of these women did some bad things."

Melissa came to the end of her laughter and took a deep breath. The laughter had cleansed her, relaxed her. "What did you do, Chloe?"

The woman's voice got deeper and more serious. "You won't tell nobody?"

"Of course not."

"I'm in for forgery. Forged some checks. They belonged to the woman I worked for. It was stealin', but I never shot nobody. And I never shot *up* neither. I was clean, except for forgin' checks. Never thought I'd get caught. She had plenty of money. Didn't think she'd notice if a little of it was missin'. It was what they call a victimless crime. I never hurt nobody."

That was something to be proud of, in a place like this, Melissa thought. One person's sins were worse than another's. There was always someone whose sins were worse than yours. She supposed that was why the other inmates had tried to pin child abuse and murder on her, so they could all hold her up as an example of how far they would never go.

The thing was, she wasn't sure there was a big difference in God's eyes.

"Why don't you want me to tell?" she asked.

"'Cause," Chloe said. "Some o' them might have the impression that I'm in for murder. I might have given 'em that impression."

Melissa began to laugh again. "Why, Chloe?"

"It helps for them to be scared of you."

Melissa sighed. "You have an advantage."

"You got that right. Ain't nobody much who wants to cross me here."

They were quiet for a moment, as Melissa contemplated her size.

"You married to that honey who keeps comin' to see you?" Chloe asked.

"No," Melissa said. "How long have you been married?"

"Herman and me got married three years ago. He's my man."

Something about that made Chloe seem more human. "Does Herman come often?"

"Every weekend. Never misses a one."

Melissa turned over on her back and studied the dark ceiling again. "At first I didn't want Larry to come. I didn't want him to see me like this."

"You may not have a bunch of makeup, but you don't need none. You look fine. He'll probably just be glad to see you're in one piece."

"Will I stay that way, Chloe? In one piece, I mean."

Chloe didn't answer for a while. "It ain't gon' be easy, sister, but I'll do what I can."

After a few minutes, she heard Chloe's deep, heavy breathing on the rhythmic edge of a snore, and she knew she'd gone to sleep.

44

KAREN ANDERSON SAT up abruptly in bed in her mother's guest room, and listened . . .

She could have sworn she heard a noise. But the trees outside the window were rustling too loudly, and the wind was blowing too hard—

What if he was out there?

She hadn't slept a full night since the two detectives had dropped their bomb on her. All night she heard things, and expected things, and imagined things.

She got out of bed, went to the window, and peered out into the night. There was no one there. At least, no one that she could see.

She thought of waking her mother and asking her to keep her company, but her mother would only think she was crazy. Karen hadn't been able to tell her mother about the man who was stalking her. She didn't want her to be afraid, so she'd just said that she'd had her heart broken and she didn't want to be alone. But now, in the middle of the night, listening for any and every sound, the loneliness and fear were overwhelming.

When would she stop listening? When would she be able to go back to school, or work, or anywhere, without looking over her shoulder?

Not until the man was caught, Larry had said. And he wouldn't be caught if Karen didn't help. Not until he picked another girl to attack—assuming that the police hadn't given up trying to catch him by then.

She went into her mother's room and stood in the doorway, feeling like a little girl who'd had a nightmare and needed her mother. Only the nightmare wasn't a dream—it was real. And her mother couldn't help her.

She thought of the woman who was in jail because she'd tried to get this man put away. And she thought of the woman who had killed herself. She could almost understand getting that desperate.

She went back to bed, climbed under the covers, and tried hard to go to sleep. But even with her eyes closed she saw the shadowy, mystic figure of a man who wanted to hurt her. He was still out there, even if he couldn't find her. One of these days, if he wanted to badly enough, he would. And then, just as she let her guard down, just as the police did, he would make his move. And there wouldn't be anywhere to turn.

Feeling sick, she closed her eyes and tried to sleep. But it was impossible to sleep when you were listening, waiting . . .

45

THE STEAM OF the showers hung in the air, wetting the concrete floor. Still in her stall, Melissa dressed quickly, her jumpsuit clinging to her damp skin. The thought of dressing in front of some of these violent women didn't appeal to her, so she tolerated a little discomfort for her privacy.

Hanging her towel over her arm, she pulled back the curtain and stepped out, her flip-flops squeaking as they slipped across the floor. She couldn't get out fast enough, she thought. Even though the showers were closely guarded, this was the most threatening room in the prison. She'd seen two fights break out here, for which several inmates—even the ones who'd been victims—had gotten isolation. It seemed that the high temperatures and the steam added up to boiling tempers.

She had just dropped her towel in its designated tub and headed for the door when she heard someone running toward her from behind. Before she could turn around, something walloped the back of her head, knocking her to the floor, facedown. Someone was on her instantly, her weight crushing her. She screamed as someone wrenched her arm behind her back, threatening to break it. The other inmates began to laugh and shout encouragement. "Let me go!" Melissa screamed.

"Not until you learn who's in charge around here."

"What do you want?" Melissa asked through her teeth.

"Respect. And I ain't been sensin' any from you."

The woman lifted Melissa's head by her hair, then banged it back into the concrete, bloodying Melissa's nose and scraping the skin off her forehead. She yelled again, but the guards weren't there.

She heard another set of footsteps coming, and suddenly the weight of the woman was jerked off of her.

She turned over, wiping the blood from her nose. Chloe was holding Red against the wall with her hand at her throat. Other inmates stood around, suddenly quiet.

"This is my cellmate, understand?" the big woman asked each of them. "*Nobody* touches her, or they answer to me. Any questions?" She looked around at each face in the room. When no one protested, she shook Red. "And you—I'd take great pleasure in cleanin' out the toilets with your head. If there's somethin' about what I'm sayin' that you don't understand, feel free to speak up any time."

Red didn't answer. It was clear that she feared Chloe.

Chloe let her go. "Get out of here now!" The woman leered at Melissa, silently promising to get her later, and headed out of the room.

When Chloe was satisfied that no one was going to attempt anything else, she turned on the water in the sink and began to brush her teeth, ignoring Melissa, who still lay on the floor. Melissa got to her feet and looked around at the others who were staring at her. Some of them snickered quietly. Others found other things to do. No one wanted to be the target of Chloe's wrath.

Bending over one of the sinks, Melissa washed the blood off of her nose. She fought back the tears as she looked up in the mirror. Chloe stood next to her, drying her mouth. "Thank you, Chloe," she whispered.

Chloe grunted and handed her a towel to stop the bleeding. "If it don't stop, you could go to the infirmary. Get out of a day's work."

"No, it's okay."

As she washed the rest of the blood off of her face, she wondered if God had provided this huge hulk of a woman to be the guardian angel who would protect her.

His grace amazed her. As she went back to her cell, she thanked him for disguised blessings like Chloe.

46

THE LIGHT ON his answering machine was blinking when Larry got home at four o'clock Tuesday morning, exhausted and agitated from watching Pendergrast watch Karen Anderson's empty apartment. A couple of times he'd seen another petite blonde get out of her car and trot up to another apartment, and he'd tensed up, expecting Pendergrast to go after her. But it seemed that he was waiting for Karen. For now, no one else would do.

Pendergrast had finally given up and gone back to his apartment at about 3:30. How he existed on as little sleep as he was getting, Larry couldn't imagine. He knew it was killing him.

He pulled off his shoes, sat down on the bed, and punched the button on the machine.

"Uh, Larry, this is Mrs. Nelson—Melissa's mother? We just wanted to talk to you and see how you think Melissa is doing. Please call us tomorrow if you get time."

He fell back on the bed in frustration as it beeped. What would he tell them? They wanted reassurances that she was all right, but he wasn't sure himself.

As a message from one of the guys at his church played, he tried to remember what day it was. Tuesday, he thought. Wednesday was the midweek visitation day at the jail. He could see Melissa tomorrow night. But first he had to make it through this day and the next.

The line beeped again, and the third message began to play. "Detective Millsaps," a woman's voice said. "This is Karen. Karen Anderson."

Larry sat up and lunged for the machine to turn it up.

"I—I need to talk to you. I've changed my mind. Please—no matter what time it is, call me at this number."

He grabbed the phone and dialed as she called it out. She answered on the first ring.

"Hello?"

"Karen? This is Larry Millsaps."

"Thank goodness." She breathed out a heavy sigh of relief. "I've been so scared."

"Why? Has something happened?"

"No," she said. "But I keep thinking something's going to. I can't sleep, I can't eat . . . If I help you, if I do what you ask, will this all be over soon? Will I be able to go back to my life?"

"Yes," he said. "Karen, it's really the only way to put this all to rest."

"All right, then," she whispered. "What do I have to do?"

47

IT WAS THE first time Melissa had found the pay phone in her cellblock not in use, and she hurried to it, jabbed her quarter in, and quickly dialed Larry's number.

His machine answered, and she left a tentative message that she was sorry she'd missed him, then hung up, feeling like an idiot. What made me think he'd be at home? she asked herself. Did I really believe he'd just sit around grieving over me?

Feeling that old anxiety and despair creeping in, she pulled another quarter out of her pocket and dialed the operator. "Collect to Pensacola," she said. "James Nelson. From Melissa." She wondered if the operator could tell that the call was coming from jail, if she was judging her . . .

Her mother answered the phone and accepted the call, and Melissa felt instant relief. Just to touch base with someone she loved, just to hear the voice of someone who loved her.

Her mother was telling her about the prayer chain she'd started, when Red rushed around the corner, making a beeline for the phone.

"Get off," she said. "Now!"

Melissa hesitated. Chloe wasn't around, and she knew better than to cross the woman without her. But her mother was talking, and she didn't want to frighten her by hanging up suddenly. Trying to compromise, she raised one finger, promising to get off in a minute, but Red didn't back down.

"It's an emergency," Red said. "I have to call my kid."

Melissa doubted that there was an emergency, even though she had seen emergency messages occasionally brought to the inmates. Still, there was an anxiety in Red's eyes that she didn't want to provoke. "Uh—Mom? I'll call you back in a few minutes, okay? Somebody needs to use the phone."

Melissa hung up, retrieved the quarter that had come back after the operator connected them, and turned around.

Red shoved her away from the phone, almost knocking her down, and grabbed the phone. "Give me a quarter," she said.

"I only have one," Melissa said. "I need to use it."

"I said give me the quarter!" she shouted. "Now!"

Gritting her teeth, Melissa handed her the quarter.

Red snatched it and shoved it into the machine, and Melissa thought about leaving. But something, some stoic, stubborn pride, made her stay. Maybe she was making a collect call, too, she thought, and the quarter would come back. Maybe she could still get it and call her mother back.

"This is Jean," the woman barked into the phone. "I got a message to call. Where's Johnny?"

She waited, then said, "I don't care. I want to talk to him. No, I don't want to talk to Carol. Where's my kid?"

Again, she waited, and her face began to redden. "What do you mean, an accident? Put Carol on the phone. Now!"

Something was wrong. Melissa looked up at her.

"Carol, where's Johnny?" Red yelled louder. "I want to talk to him! Put him on the phone!"

She cursed, then kicked the brick wall behind the phone, and let another curse fly. "You're lying. This is just some sick joke, isn't it? Put my kid on the phone!"

Melissa took a step forward. Red's face was twisted, and tears came to her eyes.

"He wouldn't do that! He knows to look both ways. I did teach him that!" Her voice broke and she began to sob. Letting go of the phone, she slid down the wall. The receiver dangled on its cord as Red buried her face in her knees and wailed.

Melissa stooped down next to her and took the phone. "Uh . . . they're still talking. Do you want to . . ."

Red just shook her head. "Hang up!" she sobbed. "They're liars."

Melissa slowly brought the phone to her ear. "Hello?"

"Where's Jean?" a brusque woman's voice asked.

"She's—she can't talk. She asked me to hang up."

"She thinks I'm lyin'," the woman said. "But I wouldn't lie about a thing like this. Her kid's dead. She's got to accept it."

"Dead?" Melissa looked back at the woman sitting huddled on the floor. "What happened?"

"He ran out in front of a car. It was bound to happen. He never listened to nobody. Wouldn't do nothin' I said. It wasn't my fault. And I can't pay for no funeral."

"I'll tell her to call you back when she's able." She hung up the phone, heard the quarter roll into the coin-return slot. Sitting down on the floor beside her, she tried to find the words to help her. It was strange, she thought, that until now she hadn't even known the woman's name.

"That witch. I never should have let her keep him. I should have let the state take him! He's not dead. She's a liar. Always has been."

Melissa looked around, wishing someone would come and rescue her from having to extend any compassion at all. But she was the only one here. Finally, as the woman's sobs grew deeper, she touched her shoulder. "You could have the warden find out for sure."

"No," she said. "I don't want to know. I don't want to know." Her voice got higher in pitch as she went on, until it was just a hoarse squeak.

"How old is Johnny?"

"Seven," she cried. "He's just seven. He can't be dead. He wouldn't be dead."

"If it is true, you could probably get out to go to the funeral."

"There's not gonna be any funeral for my baby!" she cried, getting to her feet. "He's not dead!" She looked at Melissa suspiciously. "You'd like it, though, wouldn't you, if he was! You'd think I deserved that!"

"No, I wouldn't," Melissa said. "I wouldn't wish that on anybody."

"Well, he's not! He's probably asleep in bed, and my sister just got drunk and thought she'd see if she could pull my string. He's a weapon she uses against me. She's always been like that."

She wanted to ask why Red was crying so hard, if that was what she believed. Instead, she watched as the woman ran back to her cell and closed herself in.

Melissa heard the soulful wailing late into the night, and when Chloe asked if she knew who it was, she didn't tell. Even Red deserved a chance to grieve her dead son.

By the next morning, word around the cellblock was that the news was true: Red was getting out that afternoon for the funeral but would be brought back right afterward.

Before she went to work that morning, Melissa wrote her a note and slipped it under her door. It said, "Please let me know if there's anything I can do for you. I'm so sorry about your son. Melissa."

Red didn't respond.

Melissa prayed for her all that day as she worked, and that evening, when Red came back to her cell, she saw the red swelling in her eyes, the purple tint to her lips, the pale cast to her cheeks. Her heart ached for her.

Again, before supper, she stuck a note under her door. "We're having a Bible study tomorrow at 4:00 in the chapel. Please come. It may be comforting to you. Melissa."

All that night, she listened to Red's wailing again, but the next morning, when she encountered the redhead at breakfast, she did nothing to acknowledge either of the notes she'd sent. Instead, she sat with the group of malcontents she usually sat with, her eyes cast down at her plate. She ate little and didn't speak at all.

That afternoon, when Melissa started to leave her cell to go to the chapel, Chloe looked up from a letter she was reading. "Where you goin'?"

"To the chapel. We've started a Bible study group. It meets at four."

"You gon' miss visitation?"

"No," Melissa said. "It'll be over by five."

"You ain't goin' by yourself, are you?"

"Well, there's another woman, Sonja, who's going from our cellblock."

"Sonja?" Chloe asked, astounded. "Goin' with her is like hangin' a rib-eye steak around your neck to swim through a school of sharks. They'll eat you alive."

"I'm going anyway," Melissa said.

Groaning, Chloe pulled her big body off the bunk. "Well, then, I guess I'll have to go with you. If I don't, you'll wind up mincemeat and I'll be stuck with another roommate. Probably one who's worse than you."

Melissa smiled. "You're welcome to come, Chloe, for whatever reason."

"I ain't got no Bible, though."

"You can look on with me."

"Whatever."

The woman followed Melissa out into the corridor, past the bubble—which wasn't really a bubble, but a booth where the guards sat—out of the cellblock and toward the chapel.

There were already three others waiting when they got there.

One of them was Red, sitting slouched in a chair with her arms crossed across her stomach.

Chloe took one look at her and said, "I'll handle this."

Melissa stopped her. "No, Chloe. I invited her."

"What? Are you crazy?"

"Her son died. She's in pain. I told her to come."

"Well, you're gon' be the one in pain, if you don't watch out. Abomination, it's a good thing I came."

Red looked up as they walked in, then quickly averted her eyes.

Both she and Chloe sat stiff and disinterested, not offering anything to the conversation about the book of John. But the group went on, each of the core members aware that a witness was being made here, that the two women, each here for different reasons, were hearing at least some of what was being said.

Red left before the meeting had entirely broken up, but as Melissa and Chloe went back to their cell, Melissa silently thanked God that progress had been made. She didn't fear the red-haired woman anymore. She'd had a glimpse into her heart, seen a little of her pain. Now she had compassion for her, and she knew that was a miracle. But she expected more miracles.

The next time she was able to get to the phone, Larry still wasn't home, and this time she left a message that she had called to see if he was coming to visitation tonight.

It was frustrating hanging up without talking to him, and she wondered again where he was. Was he still following Pendergrast? Was he getting any rest at all? Had anything happened?

When she started back to her cell, she saw Red hovering in the corridor. She tensed, wondering if Red had overcome her grief enough to go back to her old, threatening ways. Was she waiting for an opportunity?

Melissa kept walking until she was a few feet away from her.

"I need to talk to you."

Red's words were clipped and angry, and Melissa was apprehensive. Choking back her fear, she said, "Okay."

Red stepped back into her cell, and Melissa tentatively followed, wishing Chloe were nearby, instead of in the TV room. She stayed near the door, but watched as Red sat down on her bunk.

"What's wrong?"

Red just looked down at her feet and shook her head. "I was just thinkin'. You know, about hell. Wonderin' if there's one for little kids."

Suddenly all the fear rushed away, and Melissa sat down next to her. "Oh, Jean." It was the first time she'd used her name and it felt strange, but she went on. "Little children don't go to hell. They're too small for God to hold them accountable for their mistakes."

The woman looked hopefully up at her. "Then Johnny's in heaven, you think?"

"I'm sure of it. Jesus had a special place in his heart for the children."

Red pinched the bridge of her nose, fighting her tears. "I never really thought much about heaven or hell before. I pretty much assumed I'd go to hell when I died, if there was one. But Johnny—I never counted on takin' him there with me, or sendin' him ahead of me." Her stoic face cracked. "I didn't take him to church even once. What he knew about God, he never learned from me."

Melissa took her hand, squeezed it.

"I just wish . . . that the last time he visited here . . . about a month ago . . . I wish I'd known I was never gonna see him again. I'd have read him that book he likes a few more times. He wanted me to, but I got tired of it and wouldn't. I coulda read it twenty times and he wouldn't have got tired. I should have read it just one more time." She dropped her face in her hand and wept harder. "I can't believe I'll never see him again."

Melissa touched her hair, stroked it, and began to cry herself. "You can see him again, Jean. You just have to make sure you go to heaven, too."

"Too late for me," Jean said. "Some things you can't take back. I done too much."

"God can forgive anything."

"Not what I've done."

"Try him."

Jean looked up at her and saw Melissa's tears. Frowning, she asked, "What are you cryin' about?"

Melissa sniffed. "The same thing you are. I'm just so sorry."

"Why?" Red asked suspiciously. "I would have beat you to a pulp the other day if Chloe hadn't stopped me. How do you know I still won't?"

"You might," Melissa acknowledged. "I realize that."

"Then why would you cry over my baby?"

Melissa wasn't sure, but she gave it her best shot. "Because I know how I would feel if I were in your place."

They stared at each other for an eloquent moment, a moment in which anything could happen. Then Red looked away, as if uncomfortable with the thought of truly connecting with anyone.

"What did a debutante like you do to get put in here, anyway?"

The question, designed to break the intimacy and put Melissa on the defensive again, didn't daunt her. "I lied to a grand jury."

"About what?"

"I told them I'd been raped when I hadn't."

Red began to laugh. "What was it? Revenge on some guy for dumpin' you?"

Melissa looked at her feet. "Yes, it was revenge. But I was never involved with him. It's a long story."

"Looks like the joke turned out to be on you."

She felt the blow, knowing it was aimed to hurt, but she didn't let it. "You're right. It backfired. But God's forgiven me."

Red thought that over for a minute. "Bet you never thought you'd wind up in here with us losers when you were sippin' wine with all your elite little friends, plannin' out your lives and doin' lunch."

Melissa realized where this was all going, so she got slowly, sadly to her feet. "Look, if you need to talk again, I mean if you really need to talk, instead of just flinging insults, you know where I am."

Red's eyes got a dull, thoughtful gleam as she watched Melissa leave.

48

KAREN ANDERSON'S HANDS trembled as she buttoned her blouse back over the microphone and wires taped to her chest. "Are you sure they'll be able to hear me?" she asked Pam Darby, the lieutenant who was helping her.

"Positive. They'll hear every word."

"But couldn't I have some kind of ear phone so I could hear them?"

Pam shook her head. "Sorry. It might be too obvious. But as long as you're at work, they can reach you by phone."

"It's not the part at work that I'm worried about," Karen said. "It's the part where he approaches me." She raked her fingers through her hair. "See, I just can't believe that they could get to me soon enough. I mean, what if he has a gun? What if he has a knife? What if by the time they hear him hurting me, it's too late?"

"These are good cops, Karen. You have to trust them."

"Right," Karen said, flinging her hair back over her shoulder and leveling her eyes on the cop. "So you're telling me that you wouldn't be scared to death to walk into a maniac's hands like this?"

"Of course I would. It takes courage. Lots of it. You're a hero, Karen."

Karen wasn't buying it. To her, it just sounded like flattery to get her to cooperate. "Not yet, I'm not. And if I wind up getting killed in the process, am I just going to be one more statistic?"

"You're stopping the statistics, Karen," Pam said evenly. "That's why we need you."

Karen went to the window and peered out to the street, where cars passed by in a steady stream and pedestrians hurried to and from their offices. She wondered what she had ever done to wind up attracting Edward Pendergrast. Was it something she'd worn? The way she acted? Maybe it was her hair. He liked blondes, they'd said. Maybe she should dye hers after this was all over.

If she survived it.

Beginning to feel sick, she turned back to Pam. "Those other women he raped . . . do you have pictures of them?"

She thought for a moment. "Well, yeah. In his file."

Karen lifted her chin. "I want to see them."

"Why?" Pam asked.

Karen's eyes filled with tears as her face reddened. "I want to see what he did to them. I want to see what I have to expect."

Pam shook her head. "Karen, nothing like what happened to them is going to happen to you. Trust me. You don't want to see those pictures."

"That's what I thought," Karen said. "That bad." Her stomach roiled, and she set her hand on it. "I think I'm gonna be sick."

"Just take some deep breaths," Pam said, getting face-to-face with her. "In . . . out . . . in . . . out . . ."

But Karen only shoved her out of the way and headed for the bathroom. She bent over the toilet and wretched, making the tape on her chest pull with the effort, reminding her that someone was probably listening to every sound. She flushed, left the stall, and rushed to the sink. Cupping her hands, she caught some water, drank, then caught more and splashed it on her face. She looked up into the mirror, at the wet, pretty face that had caused her so much confusion over the last few years. She was too pretty to be taken seriously, and she'd fought that since high school. A woman who worked full-time and put herself through college deserved a little respect, she'd always thought. Now, that prettiness was more than a stumbling block. It was her enemy.

She began to cry as she stared past that face, to her hair, vowing to cut it off the moment this was all over, so that it wouldn't attract any more attention from sick rapists.

Pam poked her head into the bathroom. "Are you okay?" she asked. "I could get you something to settle your stomach."

Karen nodded. "Anything you have." She watched as the cop left her alone, then looked back into the mirror and began to sob. She would never make it. She would get sick the moment he spoke to her. She would throw up, ruining everything. She would slip up somehow, and he'd kill her.

Quickly, she began to unbutton her blouse, her trembling hands making it almost impossible to function. She grabbed the end of the tape with her fingertips and started to jerk it back, tear the microphone off . . .

But then what? Would she go back into hiding? Would she have to keep waiting?

She slammed both fists against the mirror, then spun around, trying to calm herself. She had to do this. She had no choice. It was the only way to find peace again.

She tried to breathe as Pam had told her . . . in . . . out . . . and slowly, she began to button her blouse again.

The door swung open, and Pam came back in. "Here's some Pepto-Bismol. Captain Richter keeps two or three bottles in his desk all the time. He has ulcers on his ulcers. Why don't you take it in your purse in case you need it while you're at work?"

Karen nodded and took it, opened the bottle, and guzzled a mouthful down. Then she shoved it into her purse.

"Do you think you're ready?" Pam asked.

Karen closed her eyes and tried to summon her strength. "I guess so," she whispered. "Ready as I'll ever be."

"Is there anything we've forgotten?" Larry peered at Tony and the captain across the table in the interrogation room.

"I don't think so," Tony said. "I think we've covered everything. As soon as she's ready, we are."

"What if she loses her nerve?"

"She can't. We've gone over and over it."

The captain stood up and peered out the window. "The van's ready. And we have enough men on the case. We can't afford to do this again. We have to bring this to a head tonight."

"I think it would have come to a head without us, Captain," Larry said. "There's a hole dug with a body bag just waiting for her. I don't think he plans to waste any time."

The door opened and Karen came in, followed by Pam Darby. Karen looked pale and more fragile than usual, but she'd dressed as she usually did for work.

"Ready?" Larry asked.

She pulled in a shaky breath. "I guess so." Her hand trembled as she ran it through her hair. "You're not going to let me down, are you? You'll be close by the whole time?"

"I promise," Larry said. "And we'll be calling you in the store every step of the way, letting you know if he's waiting, where we are, everything. And when things start happening, we'll hear every word you say."

She closed her eyes. "This is the worst thing I've ever been through in my life."

"It could have been a lot worse," the captain said.

She wasn't sure about that. "So what do I do now?"

"Get in your car," Larry told her, "go by your apartment, take your suitcase in like you just got back from a trip, just in case he's watching. We need to let him know that you're home—that things are back to normal. Then come back out, head to work. I don't think he'll strike this early. The risk is too great. He'll wait until you get off work."

"I'm gonna be sick again."

"Can't," Tony said. "There's no time."

They started out of the room, but Larry hung back. "You guys go test her mike. I'll be there in a minute."

He waited until Tony, Karen, and the captain were gone, and then he sat back down and stared at the wood grain of the table. *This is it, Lord,* he thought. *Please help us. Don't let anybody get hurt.*

He wished he'd been able to talk to Melissa when she'd called earlier, to tell her to pray for them tonight. But she hadn't called back, and now he wouldn't be able to make visitation. She would wonder where he was and convince herself that he had already lost interest. It would be Saturday before he'd be able to tell her differently.

Maybe he'd have good news.

He felt a little sick himself as he pulled up from the table and started for the door. In all his years of police work, he'd never wanted to catch anyone so much. And he'd never been more afraid that something could go wrong.

49

MELISSA TRIED TO look her best with what she had to work with as she waited to be called to the rec room for visitation. Chloe had gone over half an hour ago, as had many of the women from her cellblock, but Melissa's name hadn't been called yet. She tried to read while she waited, tried to straighten up her cell, but no one called.

Finally, she ventured out of the cell and went to the bubble at the end of the block, where two guards sat doing paperwork.

"Excuse me," she said. "No one's called me, but I'm pretty sure I was going to get a visitor tonight. Could you check the list and make sure there's no one out there for me?"

The CO scanned the list. "Sorry, honey. No enchilada."

Her heart fell, and she started back to her cell. There were still two hours left. Maybe he was just running late.

She climbed up on the top bunk and curled up into a ball. Whatever the reason he wasn't here, whatever it meant, it was his happiness that mattered. Not hers.

Closing her eyes, she began to pray for him, that whatever he was doing, God was with him. She prayed that he wouldn't feel guilty for skipping this visit, that he wouldn't be distracted from whatever he was doing or whomever he was with—that if God had another plan for him that didn't include her, that she could accept it.

But even as she prayed, despair washed over her. Loneliness as smothering as a gas seemed to suffocate her, and she began to cry. She cried for the next two hours, until Chloe came back.

"He didn't come?" Chloe asked.

"No," Melissa whispered. "He's a busy man. I'm sure he would have come if he could."

"Yeah, right." Chloe changed clothes and plopped onto the bed. "It's not a lot to ask, you know. That they come and spend a hour with us, just to break up the time."

Melissa didn't want to talk about it anymore. "I'm okay," she whispered. "Good night."

"Yeah," Chloe said.

The big woman was snoring long before Melissa fell off to sleep.

50

THE SURVEILLANCE VAN was an old purple van with no back windows, in which they had a wealth of equipment that could monitor everything that Karen said in the store, and everything that was said to her. She was nervous. Her conversations at the counter were short, brief, clipped. One of her coworkers asked her why she was in such a bad mood, and she told her she had a headache. When she spilled two bottles of cologne, then knocked another one off the counter while trying to clean them up, Larry and Tony began to wonder if she could go through with this at all.

Two rows away, they saw Pendergrast, waiting as usual for the mall to close. It was only fifteen minutes until closing time. Karen's voice was shaky, and her coworker suggested that she sit down and drink a glass of water. But she refused and tried to finish doing her job.

Tony sat in the front seat, watching with infrared binoculars through the windshield. "He's reaching for something in the backseat," he said. "What's he doing?"

Larry abandoned the tape recorder to John Hampton, their surveillance expert, who sat with headphones on in front of the tape equipment.

"He's getting out!"

Larry came to the window and watched as Pendergrast got out, looked both ways to make sure no one saw him, then sauntered over to Karen's car.

Larry grabbed his camera with the night lens and focused it. "He's got something in his hand." He clicked. "What is it?"

"Can't tell," Tony said. "He's bending over."

Larry snapped the camera again as Pendergrast stabbed something into Karen's tire, then hurried back to his car.

"Okay, this is it." Larry's heart beat wildly as he hurried back to the telephone. "I'll let her know. Tonight's definitely the night." He dialed the number for the men's cologne counter.

Through the binoculars, Tony tried to determine whether the tire was flat yet. It was hard to tell. "He's either going to try to get her into his car right here in this parking lot, or he's expecting her to drive off and not realize anything's wrong for a block or so."

"It's too risky to get her here," Larry said. "Too much could go wrong." He held up a hand to stem Tony's reply as Karen picked up the phone.

"Men's Cologne."

"Karen, it's Larry. You okay?"

"Yeah. We're getting ready to come out. I'm just waiting for the security guard who usually escorts us."

"Okay. Now, listen. He just did something to your front left tire. Looks like he punctured it—not real bad, so I don't think it's flat yet."

"What's he gonna do?" she whispered.

"We don't know yet. But get in your car like normal, and pull out, like you would if you didn't know. Stop a quarter of a mile down the road, and get out to see the tire."

"And then what?" she whispered viciously.

"He'll probably pull up behind you and approach you."

Dead silence, then in a high-pitched squeak, she said, "I can't do this."

Larry glanced back at Tony, who could hear her through the tape recorder. "Look, we're right behind you, Karen. We're not going to let anything happen to you."

"Where will he take me? What if he loses you? What if something happens before you can get to me?"

"You have to trust us, Karen. Now, just act normal."

He could tell she was crying. "The guard's coming. We're about to go."

"We're ready, Karen. Are you?"

"No, but that doesn't really matter, does it?"

Larry glanced at Tony again. "Karen, we can hear every word that's said. Remember, you're not alone. It's going to be all right."

"Here goes," she whispered, and hung up the phone.

Tony slipped into the driver's seat, keeping the binoculars to his eyes. Already, some of the employees were being escorted out. Pendergrast was sitting at attention, watching, waiting, for Karen to come through those doors.

Larry grabbed the radio mike. "All right, guys," he said into it. "We're almost to liftoff. Stand by."

The three men in the van held their breath as they watched the front door open again. Karen and a group of employees spilled out. Karen stayed with the security guard until she was almost to her car, then ventured out, as stiff as a board, and tried to jab her key into the door lock.

She dropped her keys, reached down to pick them up, then seemed to have trouble getting the car key into the keyhole in the door.

"She's shaking like a leaf," Tony muttered, watching through the binoculars.

She got the door open, then quickly slid in and locked it again. It took a moment for her to start the engine, turn on the lights, and pull out of her space.

"Is it flat?" Larry asked.

"It looks low," Tony said. "Won't last much longer, but it'll at least get her out of the parking lot."

"Here he comes." Pendergrast had cranked his car and turned on his lights like any of the other employees who'd just come out. Pulling out of his space, he took another parking lot exit, as if trying to be far enough away from Karen that she wouldn't know she was being followed. He waited until she'd pulled out, then slowly began to follow her to the barren road where he would carry out his plan.

The van pulled out as soon as he was far enough away not to see them.

"All right. She's having trouble," Tony said. "Looks like the tire's completely flat now."

"She's not stopping," Larry said as he slowed to stay far enough back to be invisible in the darkness. "When's she gonna stop?"

"She's riding on the rim," John Hampton said from behind them. "She's scared to stop."

"Well, she'll have to sooner or later. Pendergrast is getting closer."

They watched as her brake lights came on, and she pulled to the side of the road. "You guys had better be back there," she said in a hoarse voice.

"We are, baby, we are," Tony answered, though she couldn't hear him. "All right, he's pulling in behind her. Stop the van."

They stopped, and Tony watched with the binoculars as John monitored the tape. Larry began to sweat.

They heard the car door open, and saw Karen get out as Pendergrast approached.

"Hi." It was Pendergrast's voice. "You having some trouble?"

"Yeah," she said, so quietly they had to turn up the monitor to hear. "My tire's flat. Do you happen to have a jack?"

He took a look at the tire and whistled. "No, I sure don't. But I'd be happy to give you a ride somewhere."

She hesitated. "Do you have a car phone? Maybe you could just call someone for me, and I could wait."

He chuckled like anybody's big brother. "Sorry. Look, I don't want to leave a woman out on this road by herself. I wouldn't be able to sleep tonight. You never know who might come along. Let me just take you up to the nearest gas station, and you can call."

Again, hesitation.

"Come on, Karen," Larry whispered.

"Okay," she said finally. "Let me just lock it up."

She was stalling, and Larry looked over at Tony. He was sweating, too.

She locked the doors, then walked slowly back to Pendergrast's car and got in the passenger side.

Larry began to inch the van forward as he pulled the mike off its hook. "All right, boys," he told the cops who'd been planted at various spots in the woods where Pendergrast had dug the hole. "He's got her. Everybody in place. Let's not drop the ball now."

Pendergrast's car pulled slowly back onto the road.

"I can't believe it's flat," Karen said. "That tire was new."

"You probably ran over something." His voice had changed.

"I'm glad you were coming by. It sure would have been scary to stand out there alone. I've been meaning to get a car phone, but—"

From the van, they saw Pendergrast turn onto the dirt road.

"Where are we going?"

"Shortcut," he said.

Larry punched the accelerator, and the van flew toward the dirt road, its lights still off.

"On a dirt road?" she asked. "I don't think so. Look, stop the car. I'm getting out."

"You're not going anywhere," he said calmly.

The van reached the dirt road, and Larry pulled over to the curb.

"You can't go up in here with your lights off," Tony said. "Road's too rough. You'll get stuck."

Larry drew his gun and opened the van door. "I'll go the rest of the way on foot. Radio the others. Tell them not to make a move until I give them the word. As soon as you hear them get out of the car, pull in, and hurry."

Bolting out of the van, Larry took off on foot, following the dirt road. His heart pounded faster with every step, and he uttered a prayer under his breath that nothing would go wrong. He ran for what seemed an eternity, following the dirt road. He heard the water and knew he was getting close to the clearing.

A car door slammed, and he heard a blood-curdling scream, propelling him faster.

The road curved, and he saw the clearing. The Toyota was parked there.

Karen screamed again, but he didn't see her or Pendergrast. Holding his pistol out in front of him, he scanned the trees, but couldn't see where they had gone. Frantic, he followed the sound as fast as he could, into the thick brush. It was too dark to see where he was going, so he pulled his flashlight out of his pocket and almost turned it on. But he knew Pendergrast would see him.

He heard Karen pleading and crying, and he ran faster, pushing through bushes and around trees, feeling his way as he gripped the pistol in one hand and the flashlight in the other, while he groped for his radio to tell someone to intervene.

His foot sank into a hole, and he tripped and dropped both the radio and the flashlight. He reached for them frantically, feeling through leaves and dirt, but couldn't find them. She screamed again, so he left them and went on as fast as he could. He was getting closer—he could hear Pendergrast's voice, and Karen's screams were louder . . .

Karen struggled to free herself from Pendergrast's arms as he dragged her through the brush, branches and twigs tearing her clothes and scraping her skin as they went. With all her might she screamed, but he wasn't afraid. They were too isolated out here, and he knew they couldn't be heard.

It wasn't supposed to go this far! They were supposed to stop things before Pendergrast got her out of the car, she thought on a wave of terror. But here he was, dragging her off where no one could get to her, and she was going to be dead before anyone stopped him. Was catching him all they cared about? Did they need a dead body to get the conviction they wanted?

They reached another clearing where the moonlight shone through, and she could see more clearly now. If she could just break away—maybe she could run—

He grabbed her hair and flung her to the ground, and she screamed out again. They weren't going to come, she thought desperately. She looked up at him, saw the crazy look in his eye as he pulled a scarf out of his pocket and wrapped the ends around his hands. Was he going to strangle her?

Deciding her allegiance to the case wasn't as important as her life, she used the only weapon she had. "The police know you're doing this! They're all over this place! They followed us here!"

Pendergrast seemed amused by that. He grabbed her hair again, pulling her up, his fist in her hair almost drawing blood at her scalp. He crammed the scarf into her mouth, then wound it around her head until it cut into the sides of her lips, choking and cutting her at the same time. She tried to scream, but couldn't, as he knocked her to the ground again.

As the van made its way down the dark road, silence screamed through the headphones. Tony cursed. "Something happened. He must have found the wire."

"I don't know," John said, listening carefully on the headphones. "I still hear the struggle. Maybe he gagged her."

"Where's Larry? He should be there by now. He should have sent the others in."

John shook his head and clutched the headphones, as if it would help him to hear better. "Stop the van, Tony. We're getting too close. He'll hear us and we'll have a hostage situation. Maybe that's why Larry hasn't signaled us yet."

"We *already* have a hostage situation!" Tony said, continuing to drive. But as he reached the clearing, he saw the Toyota and realized he was going to have to go the rest of the way on foot anyway. "All right," he told John. "I'm going in. Get up here so you can drive if you need to."

"Negative," John said. "I can't monitor the tapes and drive the van at the same time. We need the tapes for evidence!"

"Well, we don't need a dead girl!" Tony hissed. "Or a dead cop. I'm going!"

Before John could stop him, he took off down the dirt road, desperately hoping that it wasn't too late.

Larry tried not to make a sound as he pushed through the brush toward the scuffling sounds he could still hear. He came to the end of the brush, at the clearing where they'd found the hole yesterday.

He saw the opening in the trees overhead, and moonlight shone down on a circle of ground.

Karen was on the ground in that circle, kicking and fighting with all her might, though she was gagged and couldn't scream.

Pendergrast's back was to Larry, and Larry inched closer as Pendergrast fought, struggling to grab Karen's hands to restrain her.

Larry lunged forward and shoved the barrel of his 9 mm to the back of Pendergrast's head. "Freeze!" he shouted. "Let go of the girl, step back, and put your hands behind your head!"

Stunned, Pendergrast froze, and as he let Karen go, she slid across the dirt out of his reach.

Pendergrast spun around, trying to knock the gun out of Larry's hand. He kept his grip, but Pendergrast lunged at him, trying to wrestle it from his hands.

The gun fired.

With a yelp, Pendergrast dropped, clutching his shoulder with one hand. With the other, he reached into his boot and drew his own small pistol.

"Don't even try it," Larry said through his teeth, pointing his gun between Pendergrast's eyes. "Drop the gun. Drop it! Now!"

Pendergrast looked up at him, evaluating him, testing him. Slowly, he raised the gun, holding it between his thumb and forefinger as if he were about to toss it toward Larry. But he didn't.

Instead, he flipped it up until his finger was over the trigger, and aiming it at Larry's forehead, he cocked the hammer.

"Drop—the—gun," Larry uttered through his teeth. "I'm giving you to the count of three."

Pendergrast smiled.

"One . . ."

He wasn't moving.

"Two . . ."

A *whack* split the night, and Pendergrast fell over. Behind him stood Karen, still gagged, but holding a fat branch. Pendergrast twisted on the ground, grabbed her legs, and pulled her down, shoving the barrel of his gun against her ear. "You put the gun down, Millsaps," he choked out. "Drop the gun, or she's dead."

"Killing her won't keep me from killing you, Pendergrast," Larry said. "I'll bury you in that grave you dug."

Karen bucked and twisted with all her might, making it hard for Pendergrast to keep the gun against her head. Grabbing a fistful of hair, Pendergrast slammed her head down.

He tried again. "The gun, Millsaps. Drop it, and nobody has to get hurt."

Out of the corner of his eye, Larry saw Tony stealing through the brush, the same way he had come. He knew that, by now, at least five other cops were hiding in the shadows. Slowly, he lowered his gun and dropped it on the dirt.

Pendergrast laughed out loud, letting Karen go long enough to turn the pistol on Larry.

The gunshot shrieked through the air, but it wasn't Larry who was hit. The bullet from Tony's gun hit Pendergrast in the hand that clutched the pistol.

He let out a high-pitched yell, and the gun went flying.

Larry dove for his own gun, but Pendergrast went for it, too, fighting for his life with his one good hand. His fist flew across Larry's jaw, splitting the skin, but Larry struggled to grab the pistol. Pendergrast reached it first, and Larry clamped his hand over Pendergrast's. On their knees now, each of them reached for the hammer, and both fingers grabbed for the trigger.

When the gunshot rang out this time, they both dropped to the ground, still entangled.

"Larry!" Tony shouted, and burst forward.

Sirens blared as a convoy of squad cars reached the clearing, shining their headlights into the trees.

Only then could Tony tell which one of them had survived.

Larry pushed Pendergrast off him and slowly stood up.

Tony rushed forward to the limp body lying on the ground. Turning him over, he felt his neck for a pulse. "He's dead."

Larry looked down at the gun as if it were a foreign thing. Opening his fingers, he let it fall to the ground. Then he went to Karen and untied her gag.

She was sobbing as he got it off, and she fell against him, weak and hysterical. As he held her, he looked back at the body.

Cops swarmed out of the trees, lighting the area with flashlights and headlights.

But the victory was hollow. Larry had wanted the man in jail. He had wanted him exposed, tried, locked away in a prison where he would endure the torment he deserved. He hadn't wanted him dead. That was too easy. That was too quick.

Shaking, Larry helped Karen up and walked her to one of the squad cars. Helping her in, he told one of the cops, "Get her to a hospital. Make sure she's all right."

He stood back, watching, as the car pulled away.

When it was out of his sight, he went to the hole Pendergrast had dug to hide Karen in. The shovel and bag were still there, as was the pile of dirt waiting to be pushed back in. He reached for his flashlight to better see the contents of the makeshift grave, but remembered he had dropped it, along with his radio.

The lights from the headlights made it easier for him to find his way back through the brush, and he spotted the flashlight. He reached for it, and his foot sank again, just as it had when he'd been running through earlier.

Turning the flashlight on, he shone it down on the circle of sinking dirt. It was loose and thinly covered with leaves. He stooped and brushed the leaves away.

It looked as if the dirt had been put there to fill a hole, and he scooped a handful out, then another, and another.

"Tony!" he shouted. "Over here!"

In seconds, Tony was beside him. "Get a load of this," he said. "Looks like we have another hole. Question is, what's it burying?"

They got a shovel and centered all their efforts around digging, until the beams of the flash lights revealed what was hidden there.

"Oh, no," Larry said. "It's a woman."

They pulled the dirt-encrusted body out and shone the light in her face.

"Ten to one this is Lisa," Tony said. "Our other runaway."

Larry dropped wearily down to the dirt. "So Pendergrast killed her. That means he killed the girl on the beach, too."

"Yeah," Tony said. "He must have dumped her in that canal."

"Her and who else? We might find others."

As the others photographed the hole and the body, and recorded all of the evidence they would need to close the case, Larry began to feel bone tired, sick with exhaustion. He got up and started to walk away. Tony followed him. "Look, man. I owe you an apology."

"For what?" Larry asked.

"For not taking all this as seriously as I could have. I mean, I did at the end, but in the beginning—it never crossed my mind that he was a killer—or that he had anything to do with the girl on the beach."

"Didn't cross mine, either," Larry said. He stopped and looked off into the night. "I just keep thinking. That could have been Melissa in that hole. He might have killed her, too."

"He didn't. And he didn't kill Karen Anderson. She was roughed up and traumatized, but she's in one piece. It could have been a lot worse. Karen and Melissa are both going to be fine."

"Yeah," he said. "You're right."

He walked back to the van and leaned on the hood as the flurry of activity went on around the bodies. He wanted to hold Melissa, and listen to her breathe, and thank God that it hadn't been her in one of those holes, covered with dirt . . .

Tony walked up behind him and slid his hand across his back. "Why don't you go home, buddy? It's all over. We can take it from here."

"No," Larry said. "The evidence. We have to make sure—"

"He's dead," Tony reminded him. "The evidence won't matter much now."

Larry realized wearily that Tony was right. There would be a rush of news reports, and friends and acquaintances of Edward Pendergrast would come out of the woodwork, providing glimpses of the dark side of the killer. Maybe even more bodies would be found.

But there wouldn't be a trial. Pendergrast had already been convicted. And he wasn't going to find a way to squirm out of this one.

"Come on, buddy," Tony said. "Go home. Get some sleep."

Larry didn't have the energy to argue as he got back in the van.

51

THE DEPRESSION THAT Melissa had gone to bed with had kept her awake for most of the night. She tried to tell herself that it didn't matter that Larry had skipped that visit, that she'd expected as much, that it was inevitable. But the bottom line was that she was already in love with him, and the worst part of her incarceration was that she was going to lose him.

Had God really forsaken her?

She forced herself out of bed early the next morning, dressed in the orange jumpsuit that she was beginning to hate with all her heart, and got her Bible. Chloe woke up as she opened the door that the CO had unlocked just moments before.

"Where you goin' so early?"

"Bible study," Melissa said. "We decided it would be a good way to start our day."

Chloe cursed and pulled out of bed. "Well, I guess I have to go, too, if you are."

"No, you don't. You can sleep some more."

"And let you get pulverized walkin' to the chapel?"

"Chloe, everyone's still asleep. Nobody's going to hurt me."

Chloe ignored her as she stepped into her jumpsuit. "Your blood ain't gon' be on my head."

Quietly, they started down the long hall to the door of their cellblock.

It was midmorning when one of the officers came to get her. "Put your stuff up," she said. "You have a visit from your lawyer."

"Lynda?" she asked, turning off her iron and taking off her apron. "Why?"

"Do I look like I know all the answers?" the woman barked. "She's waitin' in room B."

Sweeping her bangs back from her perspiring forehead, Melissa followed the officer out.

But it wasn't just Lynda who waited for her. It was Larry, too.

Her face lit up, and when he reached for her, she threw her arms around him.

"I missed you last night," she whispered.

"I missed you, too," he said. "But you know I wouldn't have skipped if I didn't have to, don't you? You knew that, didn't you?"

She let him go, and he saw from the look on her face that she hadn't had that faith at all.

"Melissa, something happened last night. Something really important. And Lynda agreed to get you out for an attorney's conference today so I could talk to you. She pulled a few strings to get me in."

Melissa gave Lynda a half-smile. "Thanks, Lynda." She realized then that she had no makeup on and was damp with perspiration. Her hair was pulled back in a ponytail, and she felt like a frump. But before she could apologize for her appearance, she saw the bruised cut on Larry's jaw.

"What's this?" she asked, touching his face gently. "Were you injured?"

"Melissa, Edward Pendergrast is dead."

She stared at him. "What do you mean, he's dead?"

"We were able to catch him trying to rape a woman—"

She caught her breath. "That one you told me about?"

"Yes. She cooperated with us, and we had everything we needed on him. I wanted to get him in jail, make him rot there. But things took a turn . . . and now . . ."

Lynda stood up. "There was a struggle over a gun, and—"

"And I shot him," Larry said.

She could see that they weren't easy words for Larry to utter.

"He's really dead?" she asked.

"Yes," Larry said. "He can't hurt you anymore."

She threw her arms around his neck, holding him for dear life. Together, they began to weep.

"I prayed he'd get caught and convicted," Melissa whispered. "Sometimes I didn't think God was going to answer."

"He did," Larry whispered. "He was caught *and* convicted. It just wasn't our court he was judged in."

"He's really gone," she whispered, awestruck. "When I get out, I don't have to be afraid." "He's really gone."

Lynda smiled. "I've sent a plea to the governor, Melissa, as well as the judge who sentenced you. I've asked them to pardon you, or at least consider reducing your sentence to probation, given the circumstances surrounding Pendergrast's death. Now that the story's going to be all over the news, I think we may be able to get something done."

Melissa considered that for a moment. "When?"

"I don't know. It might be a few days. Maybe even a couple of weeks. But I'm doing all I can."

"Good," Melissa said, letting go of Larry. "I need a couple of weeks, at least."

Larry shot Lynda a look, and they both looked at Melissa as if she'd lost her mind. "For what?"

She wiped her eyes and smiled, the first genuine smile Larry had seen on her in a long time. "I'm not here by accident," she said. "God needed me here. We've got this Bible study going . . . and some of the people I was terrified of . . . they're coming now, and they're listening. If you get me out, I'm coming back as often as I can, to keep the group going."

Lynda's eyes grew tearful as she began to smile. "That's one of the most amazing things I've ever heard."

Dismissing that, Melissa looked at Larry again and wiped the tears on her face. "The girl—is she all right?"

"She was pretty shaken up last night," Larry admitted.

"Can I see her when I get out?" she asked.

"I'm sure it can be arranged. Until then, you could write her a letter. I'd take it to her."

"All right," Melissa said. "I want to thank her. For myself . . . and for Sandy."

52

KAREN ANDERSON SAT in her apartment the next day, curled up in her favorite chair with a blanket over her that covered the scrapes and bruises on her legs. The ones on her arms and face were more apparent . . . but it was the ones on her heart that she worried most about.

She had spent the first night in the hospital on a sedative, and though she knew that Pendergrast was dead, she'd been afraid to come home. Her mother had threatened to sue the police department for involving her in such a dangerous situation, and Karen hadn't known whether to support the suit or discourage it. Finally, she had forced herself to return to the apartment where he'd watched her, and try to get on with her life.

She had almost refused to let Larry in when he'd shown up at her door, but when he told her that he had something to give her from his girlfriend who was in jail, she had reluctantly opened the door. She'd had little to say to him, and he had left quickly, but not before telling her that she was his idea of a true hero, a gift sent from God, and that he would do anything he could to help her heal from her trauma.

Now that he was gone, she opened the manila envelope and emptied out the contents. There was a letter there, and several pictures of a beautiful woman, with blonde hair and bright blue eyes. Beneath the snapshots was a smaller envelope.

She unfolded the letter first and began to read.

Dear Karen,

I started this letter several times, trying to find the right words, but there just aren't any. How can I tell you how much it means to me that you would risk your life to save the lives of so many potential victims? How can I explain the closure I feel at knowing that he won't be waiting when I get out of here? How can I describe my gratitude to you?

There aren't words to do it, Karen, so I decided to send you pictures. Meet Sandy, my sister . . . at her graduation, and her wedding . . . with me, and with our parents. Losing her caused pain so deep in us that we thought it would never go away. But what you did has helped to relieve that pain so much.

Thank you, Karen, and if you feel up to it when I get out, I'd love to meet you and shake the hand of the brave woman who helped me wake up from my nightmare.

God bless you,

Melissa

Karen wiped her eyes and looked at the pictures again. The beautiful, happy eyes of the woman who had killed herself smiled out at her. In comparison, what had happened to Karen seemed mild.

She picked up the smaller envelope, and opened it. It was another stack of pictures, but this time, a note from Larry was stuck to the top of the stack.

Karen,

I thought you might like to see the two women we know Pendergrast killed, and some of the other women whose lives you may have saved. Some of these were pictures we recovered from Pendergrast's apartment.

Larry

She saw the two women on top, the one who'd washed up on the beach, and the one he had buried. She flipped further through them and saw the random snapshots of women who didn't know they were being photographed. Women coming out of their homes, getting out of their cars, coming out of stores . . .

She leaned her head back on the chair and looked up at the ceiling for a moment. What she'd done was a good thing. Maybe it hadn't been so terrible, after all. It could have been so much worse. For her. For all of them.

The telephone rang, but she didn't move. The machine picked it up, and she kept looking through the pictures as her voice played its message. It beeped, and a voice said, "Miss Anderson, this is Chip Logan with the *St. Clair News.* We'd like to do a feature story on you for our paper . . ."

She smiled softly then, but didn't pick up. She wasn't ready for that just yet. But maybe later, she thought. Maybe soon.

This hero stuff was just going to take a little time to sink in.

Epilogue

AFTER THE PHONE call from the governor the following week, and the *20/20* interview with Melissa about the Pendergrast case, Judge L. B. Summerfield, who'd sentenced Melissa, agreed to release her on probation.

She had a final Bible study with her group that morning, including Chloe, who had begun to read her Bible each day so she could "argue" intelligently with the others in the circle. Melissa promised them she would be coming back with Doug to worship on Sunday mornings, and that she'd start work immediately to get permission to continue meeting with the Bible study group as part of her personal prison ministry.

Before she left her cell, she sat down on the bunk next to Chloe. "You know something, Chloe?" she asked.

Chloe grunted.

"For most of the time that I've been in here, I've considered you my personal angel, sent by God. Did you even realize you were being used by God?"

"Me? God ain't *never* used me."

"He did, Chloe. Before I came in here, my lawyer, who's also a good friend, gave me a verse of Scripture that meant a lot to me. It said that God would protect me. And it was so true. God protected me through you. Thank you . . . for being there."

Chloe smiled one of her rare smiles. "So you think God was really usin' me?"

"I sure do."

She chuckled slightly. "I'll be. Didn't even know God knew I was here."

"He does."

"Thank ya, Melissa."

"Are you going to keep coming to the Bible studies, even if you're not having to protect me?"

Chloe shrugged. "Might."

Melissa stood up and looked around the cell. "Would you like to keep all these books?"

Chloe's eyes widened. "I never been much of a reader. But I have been a little interested. Maybe I will read 'em."

"All right. They're yours. And I'm going to visit you Saturday and bring you some groceries. How's that sound? I'll bring you a box of Snickers."

Chloe laughed. "Girl, you're a saint."

She leaned over and kissed Chloe on the cheek, and the woman looked embarrassed. "Thanks, Chloe. For everything."

Then, quietly, she left the cell for the last time.

Red was lurking in the hallway, leaning against the wall. "I knew you wouldn't be here long. What did you do? Flap those blonde locks in the judge's face? Promise him somethin'?"

Melissa just looked at her. "You know what happened, Jean. You saw it on the news just like everyone else."

"Yeah, but I know what goes on behind the scenes."

"And you know me." She extended her hand to the bitter woman, but Red only slid her hands into her jumpsuit pockets and started to walk away. "I'm coming back," Melissa said to her back. "For the Bible studies."

"Right. I'll believe it when I see it."

Melissa smiled. "You've got a deal." She watched until Red had gone back into her cell, then left cellblock C for the final time.

Larry was waiting for her at the warden's office. She ran into his arms, laughing and crying. "Am I really free?"

"Completely," he whispered against her ear, holding her as if she could be snatched from him at any time. "Free to do anything you want," he whispered. "Free to go back to the life you had before. Or free to go in a new direction."

"I didn't have much of a life before," she said, looking up at him. "For the last three years, everything has revolved around my obsession to get Pendergrast."

"Then it's time for you to start over," he whispered. He handed her the bouquet of roses he'd laid on the table, and as she buried her face in them, he added, "And maybe that new beginning could include me."

She looked up at him, her eyes soft with anticipation. "What do you mean, Larry?"

"I mean that I love you," he whispered. "And I want you to be my wife."

The fragile joy and hope in her eyes slowly faded. "What will your friends say? I'm an ex-con. You're a cop."

"They'll say, 'Congratulations, Larry. She's the prettiest ex-con we've ever seen.'"

A soft smile broke through her turmoil. "No, really. What on earth will you tell them?"

He thought for a moment, then framed her face with his hands and looked into her eyes. "I'll tell them that when God shows me a treasure, I'm going to take it every time."

She wiped her tears and stared up at him with soft eyes that seemed so innocent, but she'd experienced more than she'd ever wanted to. Larry was a gift from God, something she hadn't earned, but she wouldn't refuse, either.

Throwing her arms around him, she said, "Of course I'll marry you!"

He whisked her up in his arms then, holding her in a crushing hug. Melissa laughed out loud, and he joined her, and they each realized what a new, magical lilting sound the mingling of their joy produced. It sounded like grace.

And Melissa knew why they called it amazing.

Afterword

I OFTEN THINK my life is much like that of a mouse in a maze. There's a plan and a path which is perfect for me, and it's not so hard to find. But I can convince myself that I have a better way—a shortcut, or a more interesting route to where I'm going. Sometimes, I even think the destination I choose is better than what has been ordained for me.

I picture God standing above that maze, urging me to take the turns and twists he's planned for me, luring me this way and that, showing me open doors and nudging me past the closed ones ... but so often I ignore him and go in my own direction. Sometimes I kick down the doors that would keep me out of trouble, and I forge headfirst into what lies behind them. Those are the times when God groans and slaps his forehead in frustration. But then—always—he says, "I can still work with this," and moves to Plan B, C, or D, making another path for me. It might be less wonderful because of my own careless choices, and it might be less useful to him, but he doesn't give up. He continues to work with me and guide me away from the dead ends in my life, and he opens the doors that will lead me to what he wants me to have. I have never strayed so far that he couldn't guide me back.

That's grace. That's the grace of a father who loved me—a poor, ignorant, rebellious, vagabond mouse—enough to send his Son to die so that I could get out of that maze once and for all. With my eyes on the cross, I don't have to bump into walls and turn in circles and back-track through the corridors of my life. All I have to do is follow him. And trust.

Abundant life? You bet it is.

That's why they call that grace *amazing*.

Terri Blackstock

ULTERIOR MOTIVES

This book and all those to follow it
are lovingly dedicated to
the Nazarene

Acknowledgments

I COULD NOT have written this book if I had not known what it is to be a mother or a stepmother. So I'd like to thank my children for the invaluable material they've given me.

My thanks to Michelle, my firstborn, who is so much like me that it makes her angry sometimes. But unlike me, Michelle has extraordinary gifts. She can sing like an angel, and write like a poet, and think like a philosopher. She feels things deeply, has compassion and encouragement for those who hurt, and is never afraid to share the good news with those who are lost. I can't wait to see what God does with her!

My thanks to Marie, my baby who's not a baby anymore, who has probably been used of God more than anyone else to teach me about gentleness and patience. Her sensitive side sometimes requires more care than the average child, but I suspect that that is one of God's special gifts that he intends to use in his time. She has other gifts, as well. She is an organizer and planner, and rarely forgets anything, and her fertile imagination is as well-developed as her sense of humor. She is a friend to many, even at her young age. I know God has special plans for her, too.

My thanks to Lindsey, my stepson, who is both peacemaker and jester. He has the special gift of bringing harmony wherever he goes, making people laugh, putting them at ease. He sees people through special eyes, not as others see them, but as God sees them. I see God working in him already, preparing him for something big!

None of these children has had the privilege of sailing through life without jostles or bruises. No child of divorce has that privilege. But I firmly believe that God will use each jostle, each bruise, for good in these children. He's making them into precious instruments already.

Thanks, guys, for giving me all of the emotions I needed to write this book!

1

HE HAD NEVER killed before, but it hadn't been as difficult as he'd imagined. It was a simple thing, really. The element of surprise, along with the right weapon and the adrenaline pumping through him in amazing jolts, had made it all happen rather quickly. There had been no noise, no hopeless pleading for mercy. He hadn't even had to look in his friend's eyes as he'd pulled the trigger.

With one foot on either side of the body, he bent down and probed his victim's pockets with his gloved hands. Loose change spilled out onto the floor, along with a set of keys. He took the keys and stepped away from the body, leaving it where it had dropped.

Hurrying up the stairs of the elegant art gallery—the walls accented with paintings from known and unknown artists—he reached the office. The door was locked, and he fumbled for the right key and opened it. The pungent scent of paint dominated the small studio, along with the smell of mineral oil. Canvases lay propped against the wall in varying stages of progress; in the back corner sat several framed paintings waiting to be exhibited downstairs and possibly sold. Some old, cracked, and damaged paintings by well-known artists sat in stretchers awaiting restoration so that they could be sold at European auctions for thousands of dollars.

But none of these things were what interested him.

On the other side of the studio was another door, and he unlocked it and went in. It was the office from which Dubose, who now lay dead on the floor of the gallery, had conducted his business with important clients, and as always, it was immaculate and tasteful, with antique Chippendale chairs in the corners and a Louis XIV desk at the center of the room, a throne-like leather chair behind it. On the polished desk sat a small banker's lamp, a desk diary, a Rolodex, and a calculator. Behind it, on the lavish credenza, was an eight-volume set of the *Dictionary of Painters and Sculptors,* widely known in art circles as the definitive resource on lost and stolen art across the world.

He pulled the chain on the lamp, lighting a circle beneath it, then opened the desk diary and turned to this week. There it was, written beneath tomorrow's date—the name and number of the man Dubose had kept so secret. The man Dubose was to have met with tomorrow. He tore off the page, folded it neatly, and slid it into his coat pocket. Tomorrow he would contact the man and take over the deal himself. He needed only one thing more, and he knew exactly where to find it.

He unlocked the small doorway at the rear of Dubose's office that led up to the attic. He turned on the yellow lights that lit the top floor of the building. Slowly, carefully, he made his way up the stairs.

The attic smelled of dust, and the floor creaked beneath his feet as he stepped between boxes, over stacked antique frames, past discarded sculptures and paintings. What he wanted was in a corner of the attic—in a long, wooden box built into the top corner, in which Dubose had stored what they'd worked together to hide for so many years. He opened the panel and reached inside.

It was gone.

Shock and fear made his heart race, his skin turn cold. He pulled a box over to step up and look inside. The compartment was empty.

Rage exploded like lava inside him, and he whirled around, scanning the contents of the attic. Where could it be?

He sank to the dusty planks beneath him and slid his gloved hands through his hair. Someone had taken it. But who? Had Dubose realized that he was going to be double-crossed by his partner? Surely not; he'd played it too carefully. Dubose hadn't known what was coming.

He felt himself growing dizzy with fury as he rose. He steadied himself on the rail as he made his way back down the stairs, through the office and studio and back down to the gallery. The body still lay facedown in a pool of blood. He had acted too quickly, he thought. He should have made sure he had what he wanted before he pulled the trigger. Now it was too late for Dubose to tell him where it was.

He would have to figure it out for himself.

Already, he had a good idea, and he would find it no matter what it required. It was his, and he had earned it. No one else was going to reap the profits of his labor.

He didn't care who else had to die.

2

CHRISTY ROBINSON STRETCHED as tall as her six-year-old body would allow and reached for the bottom branch of her favorite backyard tree. She could touch it with the tips of her fingers, but that wasn't good enough to pull her up.

"Use the ladder," her mother called from the screened porch of their home. "That's why I had it built."

Christy backed up from the tree and eyed the ladder that went up the tree's trunk to the tree house nestled in the branches. "No, ladders are for wimps," she called back to her mother. "Watch this, Mommy! Are you watching?"

Sharon came outside onto the patio and leaned back against the apricot stucco of her huge Florida home. She was dressed in a blue business suit and high heels, and her short, auburn hair rustled in the wind that was a little too cool even for February in St. Clair, Florida.

Satisfied that she had her mother's full attention, the little girl got a running start and leaped high to grab onto the branch.

She swung for a moment, then flipped until her feet came up between her arms. She wrapped her legs over the branch and hung upside-down, looking at her mother as her face slowly turned crimson and her foot-long cotton-colored hair flopped beneath her. "See? Told you I could reach."

"If you hurt yourself I'll kill you!" Sharon said, moving closer as if to catch her as the child righted herself and began climbing farther up. "I knew Jake was putting the tree house too high."

"No, Mommy," Christy said as she made her careful way higher. "It's perfect. Just right. Mr. Jake said I had to get used to heights if I'm gonna jump out of airplanes when I grow up."

"Over my dead body!" Sharon returned. "I need to have a little talk with Jake about putting these ideas into your head."

"They're my ideas!" Christy said. "I put them into *his* head."

Sharon tried not to be nervous as her daughter—who looked tiny so high up—reached the tree house and took the last step to the top of the ladder that went into the entrance hole at the center of the tree house's floor. Christy had insisted on the hatch in the floor, rather than a front door, and Jake had built it exactly to her specifications.

"The kid knows what she wants," he'd told Sharon. "Might as well do it her way, if she's the one who's going to use it."

When she was satisfied that Christy was safely inside, Sharon called up, "I have to go in and finish some paperwork, honey! Don't climb down until I get back here. I'll leave the window open so I can hear you."

Christy stuck her face in the square doorway. "Okay, Mommy. I'll call you when I get through making my guitar."

A guitar? Sharon thought with a smile. There was no telling what the child was making it out of. She had spent the past week collecting tissue boxes, drink cans, milk cartons, paper towel rolls, rubber bands, and heaven knew what else. All of them had been carried up in a backpack and stored like little treasures inside the tree house.

Still smiling, Sharon went back inside the huge house and looked through the front windows for any sign of her sixteen-year-old, Jenny. Sharon had told her to come straight home from school to baby-sit Christy so that Sharon could make it to the closing of the house on Lewis Street. She was only a few minutes late, but it worried Sharon nonetheless.

She went into her study and made some necessary revisions on her paperwork, frequently glancing out her open window to keep an eye on Christy. Then she loaded the papers into her briefcase, took it into the den, and set it in a chair next to a small Queen Anne table covered with framed pictures in a variety of sizes and shapes. The pictures told part of the story of their family. Sharon and her two daughters graced the table in elegant antique frames, their faces representing different ages and eras of their lives. The girls' father was conspicuously absent in the pictures on this table. But upstairs, in the children's private domain, one could find the whole story. Sharon and the two girls—Jenny and Christy—and their father and his new wife,

Anne, and the two young children that new family had produced, half-sisters to Jenny and Christy.

It was a tangled web, this modern family with all its branches and extensions, and she would have moved heaven and earth to stop it from becoming this way. But that decision had been taken out of her hands. Marriage was sacred to her, and divorce had never been an option. But her husband had not held the same sentiments.

She heard a car pull into the driveway, and rushed to the kitchen to look out the window.

Sixteen-year-old Jenny, who wore her prettiness with uncertainty, got out of her little car and headed for the door. Though her blonde hair was recently brushed and her make-up was flawlessly applied—no doubt she'd touched it up in the bathroom during her study hall—Sharon could see by the look on Jenny's face that something was wrong.

Sharon opened the door. "Hi, honey."

"Hi."

Sharon noted the despondence in Jenny's voice—and remembered that her moods were sometimes sincere, sometimes practiced. One never knew if Jenny's crises were really crises or just part of the daily drama that was the life of a teenager.

"Sorry I'm late," she said. "I had a note on my windshield from a friend in trouble, and I had to go help."

"That's okay. I'm not late—yet." Sharon rushed back into the den and grabbed her briefcase, then returned to the kitchen. Her daughter had not yet kicked off her shoes and gone to the refrigerator, her usual routine upon arriving home, which meant that something was on her mind. "Something wrong, honey?"

Jenny plopped into a chair, her long blonde hair falling into her face as she covered it dramatically with her hands. "Oh, Mom, it's just awful! This friend of mine—someone I care a lot about—is in trouble, and I've been trying to help. I really need to get back there. I can take Christy with me. It's just—I have to go. Mom, they're in such a mess!"

These were real tears, Sharon noted with surprise. She set her briefcase down and stood next to Jenny, pulling her close. "Honey, tell me. Who needs you?"

The words burst out: "Mom, these friends of mine, they're married and have these precious little kids, and yesterday he got fired from his job for no reason at all. And to make matters worse, they got evicted from their house and last night they spent the night in their car—their *whole family.* They didn't have any money, so they ate food that people had thrown away behind a fast-food restaurant."

"That's awful," Sharon said. "Who are they? Someone you know from church?"

"No. Not from church. They're friends from Westhaven."

Westhaven was an artsy area on the west side of St. Clair. It was the area where Ben lived—Sharon's ex-husband and Jenny and Christy's father. Since her children had an entire life in Westhaven on alternate weekends that she knew little about, the explanation didn't surprise her.

"Mom, can you picture those little kids sleeping in the backseat of their car?" Jenny cried. "It's not fair."

Sharon's own eyes began to well. "No, it's not. Where are they now? Can you get in touch with them?"

Jenny sniffed and looked up at her. "Yes, I know where they are."

"Then go get them and bring them back here. At least we can give them a place to sleep and some food until they get on their feet. We have plenty of room."

Jenny hesitated, but her wet eyes were hopeful. "Mom, are you sure?"

"Of course. When I bought this house, I promised myself that I'd never turn away anyone in need. I would never deliberately let some poor family sleep out on the street when we have five bedrooms. Besides, it wouldn't be the first time we've taken somebody in."

"But you don't even know who they are."

"It doesn't matter who they are. They're welcome here."

A tentative smile broke through Jenny's tears.

"What are you waiting for?" Sharon asked, getting up and heading for the refrigerator to see if she needed to make a trip to the store before their guests arrived. "Go get them. My closing won't take long. I'll hurry home, change the sheets in the guest rooms, and cook something nice for supper. Don't worry about Christy. I'll take her with me."

But Jenny kept sitting there, staring, as if she had something else to say but didn't quite know how to say it. "Mom?"

Sharon checked the pantry, distracted. "Hmm?"

"There's one more thing you should know."

"All right," Sharon said. "Shoot."

"This family . . . it's Dad and Anne and the kids."

Sharon felt the blood draining from her face. Slowly, she turned to face her daughter. "Is this a joke, Jenny?"

Jenny didn't look amused. Tears filled her eyes again, and she wiped her face as it reddened. "It's no joke, Mom. Mr. Dubose fired Daddy yesterday, just out of the blue, and took all his credit cards that the gallery had given him. Daddy was living in the apartment provided by the gallery, and Mr. Dubose told him to get out last night. They had no place to go, and Mr. Dubose refused to give Daddy his last paycheck or the paintings he still had in the studio."

"And your father didn't have any savings? Any money in his wallet?"

Jenny closed her eyes. "Mom, you know Daddy's never been good with money. He's an artist, not a banker. The gallery took care of things for him so he could paint."

"Well, what did he do to get fired?" Sharon spouted.

"Nothing!" Jenny shouted back. "He has no idea what happened."

"Right," Sharon bit out. "Just like he had no idea how Anne got pregnant while he was still married to me. Life is a big mystery to your father."

"Mom!" Jenny cried.

Sharon leaned over the kitchen counter, angry at herself for breaking her cardinal rule not to put Ben down in front of his children. She let out a ragged sigh. "I'm sorry. I shouldn't have said that."

Jenny sank down into a chair. "Mom, you offered to let them stay here. You said it didn't matter who it was."

Sharon swung around. "That was before I knew it was them! You lied to me, Jenny! You set me up!"

"I did not lie!" Jenny cried. "I just didn't tell you who they were! I knew you would refuse to help if you knew, and I wanted you to see how hypocritical that is!"

"Your father lost his job and his home, and now *I'm* a hypocrite? How do you figure that?"

"Because you'd help anyone else! The Golden Rule applies to everybody but Daddy, doesn't it, Mom? 'Doing unto the least of these' is great—unless the least of these is Daddy."

"Jenny, you can't be serious! It's crazy to think that I, of all people, would take him in, with that woman who destroyed my family, and those children that she loves to flaunt in my face!"

"Mom, I've seen you spend entire weekends working at shelters with winos and runaways. I've seen you go to prisons and teach Bible classes to inmates. If you'd do it for them, why not for my father?"

"One very good reason," Sharon said coldly. "Because he brought every bit of this on himself. He's irresponsible, and it's catching up with him!"

"But Emily and Bobby are my sister and brother! They don't deserve to eat out of a garbage dump or sleep in a car."

"They're your *half*-sister and brother. There's a big difference."

"They're my *sister* and *brother,* Mom, whether you like it or not. And if they were in the same predicament and didn't belong to Daddy, you'd be one of the first people I know to help them." She tilted her head pleadingly. "Please, Mom. Won't you let them stay here just for a few days? We have all this room—five bedrooms—and they have nothing!"

The thought of inviting the man who had cheated on her and betrayed her, not to mention the woman who had wrecked their marriage, to sleep in her home was repulsive. It had taken

Sharon five years to lose the pain, to learn not to grieve each time the kids went to spend their alternate weekends with their father. When she saw Anne, Sharon no longer seethed with hatred for this woman who had seduced her husband, then delightfully announced that she was having his child. Yes, she had grown beyond the misery. But this . . .

"They *cannot* stay here," Sharon said, setting her hands on her hips. "You can put a guilt trip on me for this if you want to, and blame me for everything, and convince yourself that this is all my fault, but I can't take that man and that woman into my home. I can't do it! It's too much to ask."

The crushing disappointment on Jenny's face made Sharon feel about an inch tall, and she found herself getting angry about her daughter's grief.

"Mom, what are they gonna do? This is my father, and my family, and I love them! Little Bobby's getting sick, and there they are out in their car. And it's cold—"

"Bobby's sick? Whatsa matter with him?" Christy stood in the doorway holding a makeshift guitar made of a tissue box with rubber bands for strings and a paper towel roll for the neck. The whole thing glistened with transparent tape.

"Christy, I told you not to come down without me!"

Christy looked apologetic. "I wanted to surprise you with my guitar." She strummed it, making a discordant sound, and danced a little. Ordinarily, Sharon and Jenny would both have laughed, but neither was able to at the moment.

Christy stopped dancing and looked up at her sister's red, wet face. "What's wrong, Jenny? What did you say about Bobby being sick?"

Jenny seized the moment to get her clout-carrying little sister involved. "He doesn't have a place to live! Neither do Daddy or Anne or Emily," she blurted. "And we have this huge house, but Mom won't let them stay here."

"Oh, for heaven's sake . . ."

The little blonde girl came farther into the kitchen, her huge eyes full of distress. "Why can't they stay here, Mommy?"

"Because!" Sharon glared at Jenny for dragging the child into this. "Jenny, you're not playing fair."

"Neither are you!" Jenny's face was growing redder as the tears came faster, and though Sharon knew she was, indeed, being manipulated, she also knew that it wasn't an act. Jenny was seriously tormented by her father's plight. "Mom, how would you feel if your father were out on the street? I know you hate Daddy and Anne, but think about the kids. Christy and Emily are close, Mom, really close—and right now Emily hasn't had a bath in two days, she hasn't slept in a bed, she hasn't eaten a full meal. Mom, she's only five years old! She shouldn't have to face this. And the baby just cries all the time. They need to take him to the doctor, but they don't have any money! Mom, just forget how you feel about him, and do this for *me*. Please!"

Sharon looked from Jenny's pleading eyes to those big blue eyes of her younger child, staring up at her with disbelief that she couldn't help her father when he was so obviously in need. She grabbed her purse and yanked out her wallet. "I'll give them some money for a hotel and food. That's all I can do."

"Really, Mom?" Jenny asked. "You'd do that? Because that would help. He'd probably even like it better."

Sharon breathed a laugh. "I'll bet he would." She jerked the money out of her billfold and began to count it. When she looked up again, she saw the hurt looks on her daughters' faces.

She took a deep breath, trying to calm down, hating herself for the feelings coursing through her. "No matter what you think, Jenny, I don't hate your father. I never wanted to see him destitute. I'll give him as much as I can." She handed her the stack of bills. "I have $150. I just went to the bank today. Give it all to him."

A smile broke through Jenny's tears. "Thank you, Mom. This means so much."

Sharon decided not to reply to that, so she leaned over and kissed Christy on the cheek. "Go get your shoes on. You and Jenny are going to take the money to Daddy while I go to my appointment."

Christy hugged her fiercely. "Bye, Mommy."

Deep love rose inside her for the small child she had raised virtually alone. "You be good, okay? And when you get back, no tree climbing. That tree is off-limits unless I'm home."

"Okay. Can I take my guitar to show Daddy?"

"Of course. Maybe you can play it for him and cheer him up."

She hugged Jenny and felt the extra squeeze her daughter gave her.

"We'll see you tonight, Mom."

"Yeah," Sharon said. She got her briefcase and headed for her car.

3

TONY DANKS STOOPED near the body. It had been found by a cleaning woman who had called the police, frightened out of her wits. Her 911 call had been almost incoherent. From the looks of things, the man had probably been dead since yesterday. Tony studied the change lying on the floor, as if it had fallen out of the victim's pocket. Something didn't ring true. Change didn't just jump out of pockets like that. He pulled out his notepad and jotted down the possibility that this had been a robbery, even though his wallet looked undisturbed in his back pocket.

Squatting beside the body, he reached into the pockets himself and found only a pair of keys. Probably the keys to the gallery, he thought. He took them out and dropped them into an evidence bag in case they were needed later.

He looked up at the photographer. "Did you get a shot of this change lying here?"

"Yeah," the cop said. "You can go ahead and tag it."

With rubber-gloved hands, Tony began to pick up the bloody change and drop it into a bag of its own. He came to a gold money clip with the initials BLR. "Hey, Jack? What did you say the victim's name is?" he asked the cop who'd been the first to arrive on the scene.

"Louis Dubose."

"Hmm," he said, and dropped the money clip into another bag. "The initials on this say BLR."

"Maybe he's our killer," the photographer said. "Maybe it fell out of his pocket."

Tony was skeptical. "If so, there were an awful lot of things falling out of pockets."

He got another bag and pulled the hairs from the victim's fingers. "On the other hand, there was probably a struggle before the killer shot him in the back. Who knows?" He carefully tagged the hairs. They would be sent to the lab today and would probably go far in helping them to identify the killer.

He stood up. "So what's the story on that apartment at the back?"

Jack checked his notes. "According to the cleaning woman, some artist named Ben Robinson lived back there until yesterday. Looks like he moved out in a rush. Left all the furniture behind, but no clothes or personal items."

"Ben Robinson," Tony repeated. "BLR. I'd say he's the first person we need to question."

"If we can find him."

"We'll find him," Tony assured him.

The front door opened and Larry Millsaps, Tony's partner, came in brandishing a bag. "You'll never guess what I found in the dumpster out behind the gallery."

"What?" Tony asked.

"The murder weapon. A .22."

"Did you run a check on it?"

"Yeah. It's registered to a Ben Robinson. At this address."

Tony looked back around the gallery, where other cops were videotaping, fingerprinting, photographing. "What do you bet that our Ben Robinson has long blonde hair?"

"Did you find some?"

"Yep. That and a money clip with his initials. Looks like he was in a hurry to leave, too. Didn't stick around long enough to clean up."

"I'd say it's time to make an arrest," Larry said.

"I'm right behind you," Tony told him.

4

BOBBY WAS SOUND asleep when Ben Robinson checked his family into the inexpensive motel room, carrying the bags of food they had picked up at the nearby fast-food restaurant. Ben laid the six-month-old baby down on one of the double beds, covered him with the blanket he was wrapped in, and felt his head. "I think his fever has gone down," he told Anne, who was ushering Christy and Emily in. "The Tylenol helped."

Jenny sat down next to him, careful not to disturb the sleeping baby. "The least Mr. Dubose could have done was give you his crib."

Anne set the bag of two-liter drinks on the table. "He said all the furniture belonged to the gallery," she said in a weary monotone.

"It did belong to the gallery," Ben said, his tone reflecting hers.

"Yeah, well, we should have seen this coming," Anne went on. "When you depend on other people, you wind up out in the street, sleeping in your car."

"Mommy, can I eat now?" Emily asked.

"Sure, sweetheart." Anne's tone softened as she looked down at the five-year-old, a couple of inches shorter than Christy, and with shorter hair, although in color it was identical to Christy's. It was obvious to anyone that they were sisters, even though they did have different mothers. She dug into the bag for Emily's burger. "Christy, here's one for you."

Christy looked questioningly at Jenny.

"I told you we don't need anything," Jenny said. "Christy and I can eat at home. You need to save your money."

"I could tell she was hungry," Anne said with a half-smile. "Besides, it wouldn't be fair for her to sit there and watch us eat and not have anything herself. Here, Chris. Your drink is in the box."

Christy smiled and went to get it.

Jenny got up from the bed and went to her father, who stood leaning against the wall, his pale eyes distant and dismal. His usually clean blonde hair was oily because he hadn't had the chance to shower since yesterday, and he had it pulled back in a pony tail, a look that her mother found disgusting, but all her friends considered cool. He was unshaven, and she noticed the tired lines under his eyes. Without those lines, he could have passed for her older brother, rather than her forty-year-old father.

She slid her arms around him from behind and laid her head against his back. At six feet, he was almost a head taller than she. "Daddy, are you okay?"

He pretended to snap out of it, and smiled. "Yeah. I was just thinking. Somehow I've got to get all my paintings out of the gallery. They're my livelihood. If I could sell them, or at least take them to another gallery . . ."

"Have you tried calling Mr. Dubose again?" Jenny asked. "Maybe he's cooled off by now, and he'll talk."

"I tried," Ben said. "There's still no answer. Besides, he had nothing to cool off from. I didn't do anything to prompt it."

"Are you *sure?*" Anne asked again, as she'd asked a thousand times since yesterday. "Ben, *think.* A man doesn't fire you from your job and evict you from your home the same afternoon, if you haven't done anything. If you could apologize, maybe—"

He stiffened. "Anne, how many times do I have to tell you? There's nothing to apologize for! When are you gonna believe me?"

She held up a hand to stem the argument, and breathing a deep sigh, turned back to the children.

"This is awful," Jenny whispered.

Ben nodded and raked his hand through his long, disheveled hair. "I never would have dreamed I'd have to take money from your mother to keep my family off the street."

"Mom didn't mind. She was happy to do it."

"Yeah, I'll bet." Catching himself, he muttered, "It really was nice of her. She didn't have to do it."

Jenny sighed and looked helplessly around the room. Little Emily was so tired that she could hardly eat, so Jenny went over and pulled the cotton-topped five-year-old into her lap. "Come on, Emily. Let me help you with this."

She began to feed the child one french fry at a time.

"She needs a nap," Anne said. "She didn't sleep very well last night. Bobby kept coughing, and the car wasn't all that comfortable."

"Anne, if Bobby gets worse, you'll take him to the emergency room, won't you?" Jenny asked.

Anne shot Ben a look that said they couldn't do even that without money. "Yeah. Somehow, we'd convince them to treat him. There's always the health department. They treat indigents."

Ben stiffened, knowing that her remark had been intended to sting. "We are not indigent."

"Right," Anne said sarcastically. "We're just homeless, penniless, and jobless. At least we're not sleeping under a bridge somewhere. I guess I should brace myself. That could be coming."

Ben went into the bathroom, the only place to which he could escape, and slammed the door behind him.

The sound woke Bobby, and he began to cry, making Ben feel even worse. He sat on the lid of the commode, rubbing his stubbled face, fighting feelings of terror and despair.

So he had come to this.

As always in times of stress, old tapes of Sharon's voice played in his mind.

You're irresponsible, Ben. When are you going to grow up and start acting like an adult?

You're selfish! You don't care about anyone but yourself. You think you've got it all figured out, with your artsy friends and your own set of rules. But this charade of a marriage is going to show everyone just how much of a loser you are.

She had been in pain when she'd said those words, reacting to his own cruelties. But knowing that didn't take away the sting of her accusations—and now he wondered whether he hadn't just proven that they were all true.

He only wished he hadn't spent every penny he made, always counting on the gallery to keep handing over monthly paychecks for his restoration work and the rights to show his work exclusively. He should have been smarter with finances, like his ex-wife was. In five short years, she'd gone from being a struggling real-estate agent to a six-figure wage earner. When she'd bought that house last year, he had convinced himself that it was intended as a slap in the face to him—a way of showing him what he could have had if he hadn't left her for greener pastures. But then he'd felt ashamed of those thoughts when he'd heard how she'd taken in a couple of unmarried pregnant women who'd needed a place to stay while they carried their babies, and then a family whose house had burned down. Her success, he'd finally realized, didn't have anything to do with him at all, one way or the other. She'd simply worked hard for herself and her daughters. His feeling that she was rubbing his nose in her wealth was his problem, not hers. He was the one who made comparisons. She had just gone on with her own life.

And he had his life with Anne. Although it had grown increasingly difficult as the infatuation had worn off and reality had set in, he had tried to make it work. He wasn't going to hurt two more children through a needless divorce. It's not as if he was a victim here. He had the power to turn this around.

But right now, he hated the feeling of Anne's disgust with him, so much like Sharon's. In fact, he realized, she had started reciting Sharon's tapes. Without using the same words, her very tone suggested that he was stupid, selfish, irresponsible, a loser . . .

But he'd prove to them that he wasn't a loser. He had to pull himself together, had to be rational. There was much to be done in the next few days.

Jenny was walking Bobby around the room, trying to make him stop crying so that Anne could eat, when a hard knock sounded on the door.

Anne, who was sitting with food balanced on her lap, sent a pleading look to Jenny. "Would you get that?"

"Sure." Still carrying the crying baby, Jenny stepped over Christy, who was sitting in front of the television, and opened the door.

Two men stood outside, one, a brunette dressed in jeans and a windbreaker and the other, a tall blonde, in khakis and a sport coat.

Bobby still cried, so the man in the sport coat had to raise his voice to be heard. "We're with the St. Clair Police Department," he said, flashing a badge. "I'm Detective Tony Danks, and this is my partner Larry Millsaps. We're looking for Ben Robinson. Is he here?"

"Sure . . . uh . . . just a minute." Anne began to put her food down, and Jenny stepped back over Christy and went to the bathroom, bouncing the crying baby on her hip. She knocked on the door. "Daddy, someone's here to see you."

Ben came out, looking more drawn and weary than she'd ever seen him.

"Someone's here," she repeated, then gave a worried glance back at the cops. "Policemen," she whispered.

Bobby's crying grew louder, and the baby reached for his mother. Anne took him, then followed Ben to the door.

"Officers," Ben said with a nod as he reached the door. "What can I do for you?"

"Ben Robinson?" one of the men confirmed.

"Yes," he said.

The one with the windbreaker pulled a pair of handcuffs out of his pocket. "I have a warrant for your arrest for the murder of Louis Dubose. You have the right to remain silent—"

"No!" Anne screamed, and Jenny rushed forward.

"Daddy!"

"Murder?" Ben asked as they got the cuffs on his hands. "What do you mean, murder?"

"He was found dead an hour ago," Tony Danks said. "You have the right to an attorney. If you can't afford an attorney—"

"There must be some mistake!" Anne cried. "My husband didn't kill anybody."

The baby was screaming louder, and now Emily and Christy abandoned their food and stood holding hands, fearfully watching the scene.

Jenny grabbed her father's arm as they tried to pull him toward their car. "Daddy, tell them you didn't do it! Tell them!"

"It's okay," Ben said hoarsely. "We'll straighten it all out."

But his family, stunned and terrified, watched as he was guided into the back seat of the squad car—and he looked anything but confident, trembling, his eyes wide. They watched wordlessly as the car pulled out of sight.

5

THE PHONE WAS ringing when Sharon walked into her house. She had just closed the deal on the house on Lewis Street, then had shown three houses to Mrs. Milford, a client who she suspected would never settle on anything. Dropping her purse and briefcase, she picked up the phone.

"Hello?"

"Oh, Mom, thank goodness you're finally home. I've been trying to reach you, but you never answered your car phone."

"I was showing houses. I must have been inside when you called. What's wrong?"

Jenny was crying, and her pain came right through the phone. "Oh, Mom!" She sobbed, caught her breath, and tried to go on. "Daddy's been arrested! They think he killed somebody!"

"What?"

"Mr. Dubose, the gallery manager, was murdered, and they think Daddy did it. Mom, he couldn't have! He was with us! But they won't listen—they don't believe us, and they say he was killed yesterday. Daddy was the last one to see him alive, so they're blaming him. Mom, I don't know what to do! My father is not a murderer!"

"I know he's not," Sharon said. "Jenny, where are you?"

"At the police station. We're all here. Anne's a basket case, and the kids are all upset . . . Christy and Emily don't understand, but they're smart enough to know that their daddy's going to jail! Mom, we've got to get him out!"

Sharon held the phone between her ear and shoulder and grabbed her purse. "Jenny, I'm coming down to the station. I'll be there in ten minutes. Does your father have a lawyer?"

"No. They can't afford one."

"I'll call Lynda," Sharon said. "She's one of the best lawyers in St. Clair."

"Yeah, I forgot she was a lawyer. Mom, ask her to hurry," Jenny said. "They're in there with him right now. Oh, and Mom? Could you stop by the store and get some cough syrup for Bobby? He's coughing his head off."

Sharon didn't like the thought of detouring on her way, but she muttered, "Sure. I'll bring it."

She hung up the phone and quickly dialed Lynda Barrett's number. They were good friends from church, and she knew the number by rote.

"Hello?"

"Oh, Lynda, I'm so glad you're home. I didn't have time to look up your office number."

"Sharon, what's wrong?"

"Ben . . . my ex-husband . . . he needs a lawyer. He's been arrested for murder."

"Murder?" Lynda repeated.

"Lynda, the man's one of my least favorite people, and he's capable of a lot. But he's not a killer. You've got to help him. I'll pay you, if he can't. He's at the police station, and they're interviewing him as we speak."

"I'll be there in five minutes," Lynda said.

Sharon hung up and breathed a sigh of relief. Then she rushed out, more concerned about the state of mind of her children than that her ex-husband was being accused of something he couldn't possibly have done.

6

BEN HADN'T HAD a shower since yesterday, and as he sat in the over-heated interrogation room—no doubt kept that way by design—sweating and trying to answer all of their questions, he wished he'd at least had time to take a quick bath before the police had come. With his oily ponytail, a two-day growth of stubble, and clothes he'd had on for two days now, he must look like a biker who wouldn't think twice about killing his boss. Now he wished he'd never let his hair grow this long. But he liked the bohemian look that said he didn't have time to worry about his appearance because he was too busy cultivating his imagination. Part of the look was for effect, he admitted, but part of it was reality. Often he got so lost in his work that he *didn't* remember to shower, shave, or eat. That was why he still didn't have the mid-life paunch that most of his contemporaries had after crossing the forty-year mark. He had crossed it last October, and still prided himself on looking ten years younger.

"Look, I told you," he said, keeping his voice even so he wouldn't appear to be losing his temper. "The last time I saw Louis he was locking himself in his office."

"But you were angry at him, weren't you?"

"Yeah, of course I was angry. You'd be angry, too, if your boss threw you and your family out into the street, and wouldn't even give you your last paycheck!"

Lynda Barrett, who had burst in just moments before and announced that the family had retained her to be his lawyer, touched his arm to shut him up.

Ben had almost told her no-thank-you when he'd realized that the aggressive brunette was Sharon's friend. But when he'd seen that she knew the two cops well, he decided to accept her services. Maybe she'd have some pull with them.

"Larry, Tony, my client has already told you everything he knows."

"He hasn't told us why we found the murder weapon in a dumpster behind the gallery—a pistol that was registered to him. And his fingerprints were all over the glass," Tony said.

"No way," Ben argued again. "I've never owned a gun in my life. I don't even know how to use one."

"Were his fingerprints on the gun?" Lynda asked, taking notes.

"No. The killer obviously wore gloves."

Lynda looked up, smiling wryly. "Larry, you said his fingerprints were all over the glass. If he was wearing gloves, how could that be? Make up your mind."

"I *did* put those fingerprints on the glass," Ben said. "We live in back of the gallery, and the day before I was fired, my little girl, Emily, was playing peek-a-boo with me outside the glass. We both got our fingerprints all over it. I meant to clean it off."

Tony pretended to be making a note. "Fingerprints due to peek-a-boo."

"I'm serious!" Ben said.

"There was obviously a struggle," Larry went on. "There was some overturned furniture."

"That doesn't mean I was there," Ben said.

"There was also a money clip next to the body. It obviously fell out of the killer's pocket. It had the initials BLR, and your fingerprints."

Ben sat straighter. "My money clip? I don't even know where that was. I haven't carried that in a couple of years."

"And there were strands of hair in Dubose's hands, like he'd gotten in a struggle and pulled it out of the killer's head. Blonde hair about your length. At first we thought it was a woman's, but now that we see you . . ."

"So I'm a killer because my hair is long?" Ben asked.

Lynda was still taking notes. She flipped her shoulder-length hair behind an ear. "Where was the entry wound, guys?"

"His back," Tony said, shooting Ben a look. "That ought to make you proud. Courage that matches the hair."

"I would never shoot someone in the back! I would never shoot anyone period!"

Lynda shot Ben a stern look, telling him to shut up. "So if he was shot in the back, then you must have figured out the range by now. How far away was the gun when it went off?"

"We're guessing a few feet."

"All right, then, how did he get a handful of Ben's hair if his back was to him and he was a few feet away?"

"They obviously fought before he turned his back."

"That's ridiculous!" Ben shouted. "I've never fought with him in my life! I don't fight with anybody! That's not my style!"

"Ben, let's go back," Larry said, playing the good guy in the good guy/bad guy routine. "Think about what you two talked about in your last few conversations. Was there anybody else there? Anyone you talked about?"

"No. He was kind of preoccupied."

"With what?" Larry asked.

"I wish I knew. Probably with his plans to throw me out. Then yesterday, out of the blue, he told me I was terminated and that my family and I had to be out of the apartment within the hour. I was stunned. I couldn't believe it."

"Angry, too, huh?" Tony asked.

"Of course I was angry. I was furious."

Lynda nudged his arm again. "That's enough, Ben."

"Not angry enough to kill him! But it was crazy. I tried to go up to my studio and get my paintings, but he said the gallery owned them—that they had paid me to paint them—and that I couldn't take them. I lost my temper when he refused to give me my last paycheck—"

"Ben, as your lawyer, I'm telling you that you've given them enough," Lynda insisted.

"But I have nothing to hide!" Ben said. "All we did was argue, and then he went up to that office of his and locked himself in. He said if I didn't leave within the hour, with my children and my wife and everything we owned, he'd have the sheriff escort me out. So I went to the apartment and started packing. We were gone an hour later. I tried calling him several times from pay phones to reason with him, but the line was busy."

"We can get the records from the phone company," Lynda told Larry and Tony.

"That'll only prove that a call was made to the gallery. It doesn't prove that Dubose was alive when he left him."

"Right," Ben snarled, slapping his hands on the table. "I got into a knock-down, drag-out fight with Dubose and shot him, then left my gun exactly where I knew you'd look for it, then called him afterward just to see if he was really dead."

The detectives both stared at him without amusement, and Lynda closed her eyes and began to massage her temples.

"I'm being sarcastic!" Ben shouted. "Why did I call the guy if I thought he was dead? And about that gun, you need to check out that registration, because I'm telling you, I have never owned one! Ask anybody. You won't find a registration with my name on it."

"We already have, pal."

Ben looked flustered. "You can't. It's impossible. I don't believe in owning guns. I have small children."

"Tell it to the judge," Larry said, jotting another note on his pad.

"People have been known to use other people's names and credentials to get guns," Lynda pointed out. "He has an alibi, Larry."

"Yeah, his wife. Big surprise."

"My children, too," Ben said. "One of them is sixteen years old. She's old enough to remember where I was when."

"Daughters are usually loyal to their fathers," Tony said.

"Then ask my ex-wife! She hates my guts and would probably love to see me rot in jail, but she'll tell you that Jenny was with me part of yesterday and this afternoon."

"We will," Larry said, getting to his feet. "But even if she corroborates what you've said, we've got enough to book you."

Ben covered his face with his hands, unable to believe what was happening. When both detectives had left the room, he turned to Lynda. "I'm gonna have to stay in jail?"

"Until morning, at least," Lynda said. "It'll be okay. You won't spend the most comfortable night of your life, but tomorrow morning I can probably convince the judge to let you out on bond. You have no prior arrests?"

"Not even a traffic ticket," Ben said wearily.

"That should play in your favor. Show up in court with your whole family in tow—all four kids—and maybe he'll show mercy and let you out pending the Grand Jury investigation."

Ben closed his eyes. "My children are all going to know I'm in jail. What kind of image is that for a father?"

"They'll also know you're innocent," she said.

"How do *you* know I'm innocent?" Ben asked angrily. "You don't even know me. If all you know of me is what my ex-wife has told you, then you probably think I'm the scum of the earth."

"Wrong. Sharon's an intelligent woman, and she was married to you for a long time. She wouldn't have married a maniac."

Ben breathed a laugh. "You haven't talked to her lately, have you?"

Actually, she had. "She says you're a good father, Ben. That tells me a lot. She just thinks you were a lousy husband."

Ben shook his head. "That's why I hate this town. You make one mistake, and everybody in town knows about it."

Lynda wore a half-smile as she got up. "Look, I believe your story, and I think I can get you out tomorrow. Then we can start working hard on your case."

"There's a killer out there," Ben said. "Nobody's even looking for him. He got away with it."

"Well, maybe we can put our heads together and figure out who it is." She stuck her notebook into her briefcase and shut it. "Ben, they're going to put you into a holding cell for the night. Just be patient. You'll probably be in a cell alone, so you'll be safe. I'll see if I can pull some strings to get them to put you in the new wing. The old one is kind of creepy. Oh, and the hearing is early tomorrow." She reached for the doorknob.

"Hey," he said before she could leave. "Tell my wife it's going to be all right. Try to make her feel better about this. She's a good person, regardless of what Sharon may have told you."

"Sharon hasn't said anything to me about her," Lynda said honestly.

"Right. Then you heard it from the famous St. Clair grapevine. All those church ladies who spend all their time exchanging gossip disguised as prayer requests."

Lynda couldn't help chuckling. "Don't worry. I'll forget whatever I've heard. See you tomorrow at the arraignment."

7

THE SMALL ST. Clair Police Department was teeming with cops, people filing complaints, criminals waiting to be booked, and friends and family members waiting to bail them out. Sharon, who was able to fit in almost anywhere from soup kitchens to inaugural balls, felt as though she stood out ridiculously in her business suit and heels. She stood uncomfortably at the door and looked around for her children. She spotted Christy sitting with Emily in the middle of a crowd of seething gang members. Jenny sat a little farther down, between two women who could have been hookers. Anne was pacing and bouncing Bobby as he screamed at the top of his lungs.

Sharon rushed across the room and grabbed Christy's hand to pull her out of the midst of the street gang. Five-year-old Emily followed as they found vacant seats at the other end of the waiting area. Jenny got up and followed as they passed her.

"Mom, thank goodness you're here," she whispered. "Anne doesn't handle a crisis very well. She's really losing it."

Sharon shot Anne a look. The woman saw her and quickly turned her head.

Sharon dug into her purse and pulled out the bag with the cough syrup. "Here, Jenny. Give her this. I also got one of those little measuring spoons I used when Christy was younger, so she can give it to him now."

"Thanks, Mom," Jenny said, then dashed to her stepmother.

Anne took the medicine reluctantly, looking more chagrined than grateful. Without acknowledging that Sharon had brought it, she headed for the bathroom to give it to the baby.

Sharon was glad she was gone. "Where's your father?"

"In that room over there. He's been there since I called you. Anne and I both signed statements saying that he couldn't have killed Mr. Dubose, because he's been with one or both of us since yesterday. But they're saying he did it when Mr. Dubose fired him. He's the only one they can prove was there yesterday, even though Anne saw him alive through the window when they were leaving their apartment."

Sharon looked toward the room. "How does your father get himself into these things?"

"Mom!" Jenny's tears had a hair trigger, and they filled her eyes now. "Daddy didn't have anything to do with this. You know that!"

She was instantly ashamed. "You're right; I'm sorry. Your father picks bugs up in his hand and takes them outside to keep from killing them."

"That's right!" Jenny said victoriously, as if that would be just the evidence she needed to clear her father. "Mom, tell them. They'll listen to you."

"I will, when I get the chance."

The door to the interrogation room opened, and Lynda Barrett came out. "Wait here with the girls," Sharon told Jenny, and hurried across the floor to meet Lynda, her heels clicking a staccato beat on the dirty tiles.

"Lynda, what's going on?" Sharon asked.

"Well, it doesn't look good," Lynda admitted. "He's going to have to spend the night in jail. His arraignment is tomorrow morning, and maybe then we can get him out on bond."

"Bond? They're not really charging him with murder, are they?"

"I'm afraid so."

Flustered, Sharon leaned toward her friend, intent on making her understand. "Lynda, I was married to the man for twelve years! He's not capable of murder! He's never even been able to bring himself to spank the kids. He's a lot of things, but he is *not* a killer."

"Sharon, the murder weapon was registered to him."

"Well, what did he say about that?"

"He said that it couldn't have been, that he's never owned a gun in his life."

"That's probably true. He wouldn't even know how to use one."

"Everybody knows how to pull a trigger. That's all the court cares about. He probably will be arraigned, Lynda, but if things go well, we can at least get him out pending an indictment."

"Excuse me!" The voice behind Sharon was Anne's, and Sharon swung around and saw the seething woman, still holding her crying baby. "This is none of her business," Anne said to Lynda. "If you're my husband's lawyer, you should be discussing my husband with me, not her! She doesn't even have the right to be here."

Sharon's teeth came together. "I'm here because I didn't want my children unattended in a police station, Anne."

"They're not unattended. They're with me."

"Forgive me if I thought you might be a little preoccupied, seeing how your husband has just been arrested for murder and all." People were starting to watch them. Sharon lowered her voice. "Look, I'll just go talk to my daughter, and you two can have a private conversation."

Her face was burning by the time she reached Jenny.

"What did she say?" Jenny asked anxiously.

"That this was none of my business. She's got so much nerve. It never fails to amaze me."

"She said that? Really? But I thought—"

"After I gave her that money, and brought the cough medicine, and hired a lawyer . . ."

Jenny's face changed. "Mom, I was talking about Lynda! What did *she* say about Daddy?"

"Oh." Sharon felt stupid and mentally kicked herself. Why was it that her dignity began slipping away bit by bit whenever she was near Anne and Ben? She tried to shift her thoughts. "Lynda said that he would have to spend the night here."

"No!" Jenny cried. "Mom, he can't! There are criminals in jail! He didn't *do* anything."

"Tomorrow is the arraignment, honey."

"What's that?"

"That's when they ask his plea and decide whether to set bond."

"Well, then he'll get out, won't he? There's not any evidence. He can tell them he wasn't there and prove it!"

"Honey, the arraignment is not really for presenting evidence. But Lynda feels sure he can get out tomorrow."

Jenny wiped her eyes. "This is like a nightmare."

"It sure is," Sharon whispered.

Anne turned away from Lynda, mascara-muddled tears staining her face, and she called Emily. Both Christy and Emily came to her, holding hands. "Come on, honey," she told the five-year-old. "We're going back to the motel."

"What about Daddy?"

"He's going to stay here tonight. We'll see him in the morning."

Sharon stood back as Jenny went to kiss Emily and Bobby good-bye. "Anne," Jenny said, "do you want me to come and help you take care of the kids?"

Anne glanced stoically at Sharon and lifted her chin, as if to hide any evidence of vulnerability. "No, thanks. We'll be fine."

"Okay," Jenny said weakly.

"You'll be here in the morning?" Anne asked.

"I sure will," she said. "Try to get some sleep, okay?"

Anne nodded and gave her a hug, then leaned down and kissed Christy on the cheek. Christy returned it easily, a gesture that bothered Sharon more than she ever would have admitted. Christy didn't follow as Anne led Emily out of the building. "Poor Anne," Jenny said, watching her go. "It's like her life is falling apart."

"I remember that feeling," Sharon muttered.

"Mom!"

Sharon took Christy's hand and started to the door. "Come on, girls. Let's get out of here."

Later that night, as Christy was changing into her pajamas, she found in her pocket the little army men that Emily had gotten in her Burger King bag. Emily had no pockets in her own pants, so she had asked Christy to hold them for her.

Christy set the little men up on her dresser and wondered if Emily had missed them. She had been so excited about them when she'd gotten them, even though Christy had found them a disappointment. Emily didn't have many toys, though, and the ones she did have were packed in a box in the back of their car. Carefully, she picked the little army men back up and held them securely in her fist. She would call Emily, she thought, and tell her she had them, so at least she'd know they weren't lost. And maybe she could offer her something else, just to make her feel better about Daddy.

Christy looked around her room for something Emily would like.

Her collection of porcelain dolls lay carefully arranged on the French provincial canopy bed, but she knew that Emily wouldn't really like those, because they broke so easily. On her shelves was a menagerie of stuffed animals. Though Emily had never been in her room before, Christy knew that she would like Simba, the little stuffed lion, better than any of the others. She climbed up on her chair and reached for it.

It was soft and good to sleep with, she thought. Maybe it would keep Emily company, and keep her mind off her troubles.

Clutching the stuffed animal in one hand and the army men in the other, Christy ran down the hall to Jenny's room. Jenny was on the phone, as usual.

"Jenny," she whispered, as if keeping her voice low would not disturb her. "Do you have the number of the motel?"

Jenny put her hand over the receiver. "Why do you need it?"

"I want to call Emily," she said. "She left her army men. They're real important."

Jenny frowned. "Christy, those aren't important. It can wait."

"She'll cry if she thinks she lost them," Christy said. "She doesn't have anything to play with. I want to tell her that she can have my Simba, too."

Jenny stared at her for a moment, then smiled. "That's sweet of you. Okay, just a minute, and I'll look up the number."

Christy waited as Jenny continued her phone conversation while simultaneously searching the phone book. "Here it is," she said. "I'll circle it for you."

Christy looked hard at the circled phone number. Then, stuffing Simba under one arm, she took the book and headed down the stairs to the study, where her mother had a separate phone line. She climbed into her mother's big chair behind the desk, laid the book open on the desktop, and set the toys down. Picking up the phone, she punched in the number slowly, checking and rechecking each digit against the phone book.

"Holiday Inn," a woman's voice said.

"Can I speak to Emily, please?" she asked.

"There's no one named Emily who works here," the woman said. "Can someone else help you?"

Christy hesitated. "No, I need Emily."

"Emily who?" the woman asked, irritated.

"Emily Robinson. She's my sister."

The woman's voice softened. "Honey, you have the wrong number."

Tears of frustration filled Christy's eyes, and she hung up the phone. Had they gone back home? she wondered. Had they forgotten to tell her where they were?

She dialed their old number and waited through three rings. Finally, an operator's voice cut in. "I'm sorry. The number you've called has been disconnected . . ."

"I want to speak to Emily!" she cried over the voice. When she realized it was a recording, she slammed the phone down and looked helplessly at the phone book again. How could she get in touch with her?

She sat at her mother's big desk, looking at Simba staring expectantly at her, and those three army men poised to strike. What if they had put Emily in jail, too? she thought. What if they had put Bobby and Anne there?

Helpless about her father's plight and about all the other things she didn't understand, she began to cry into her small hands.

Her mother came to the door. "Oh, Christy . . ."

Sharon crossed the room and pulled Christy up into a tight hug, then sat back down with the small girl in her lap.

"I miss Daddy," she squeaked. "And Emily forgot her army guys."

"We'll take Emily her army guys tomorrow when we see her, okay?"

"But she'll cry when she thinks they're lost, and I wanted to call and tell her, but she's not there."

"Honey, it'll be okay. She's probably so tired after everything that's happened that she won't even think about them. Tomorrow will be soon enough. You're going to see her first thing in the morning. And your daddy, too."

"I am?" Christy asked hopefully.

"Yes. You and Jenny are going to court, and they'll both be there."

She wiped her eyes. "Will you be there?"

Sharon thought about that for a moment. "Yes. I think I will go. I'm worried about your daddy, too. But Daddy needs for you and Jenny to sit with Anne and Emily and Bobby, so the judge can see what a beautiful family your daddy has."

The words, though delivered softly, had a little bit of a bite to them, and Christy recognized it. Wiping her eyes, she sat up on her mother's lap. "I want to sit with you. Will you sit by us, too?"

"No, honey," she said. "Anne wouldn't appreciate that. But I'll be there if you need me."

Christy suddenly felt very tired, and she began to cry again. Her mother hugged her tighter as she laid her head on Sharon's shoulder. "Mommy, can I call and talk to Daddy?"

"No, sweetheart. They don't let him have phone calls where he is."

"I know where he is," Christy said. "He's in jail. You don't have to act like I don't know."

"It's all just a mistake, honey. He'll be out soon."

"You promise?" Christy asked.

Sharon hesitated, and Christy knew that she wasn't going to promise. Sliding off her mother's lap, she grabbed up her Simba and the army men, and started for the door.

"Where are you going, honey?"

"To bed," Christy muttered.

"But it's still early, and you don't have to go to school tomorrow since we have to go to court."

"I'm tired," Christy pouted, rubbing the tears on her face. "I need my rest."

Ordinarily, Sharon would have smiled, but the words were spoken with such dejection that she didn't find them funny.

"All right. Come on, and I'll tuck you in. And we'll pray for your daddy."

Christy slept with Simba and the army men that night, eager for morning to make sure her father was all right.

8

THE CELL WAS cold and dimly lit. Ben lay on his two-inch-thick mattress stretched across sagging steel springs and tried to sleep. A few cells down, a man sang out a painful dirge in a voice that could have made him millions. How had he wound up here?

Same way I did, he thought. He watched a roach crawl across the ceiling and closed his eyes as it got directly overhead. Jail. He couldn't believe it.

He rolled onto his side and pulled the threadbare blanket up to cover him. Two voices exchanged curses down the way, and a third screamed for them to shut up. Someone closer to his cell banged out a rap beat with a spoon on the edge of his bars, a sound so annoying that he too longed to scream "Shut up!"

Anne was probably scared to death. Anne, who had once made him feel like such an important man; Anne, who had believed in his work and his dream to become a renowned painter; Anne, who had vowed that she would follow him to the ends of the earth, regardless of the consequences, if he would just make her his wife. Over the past five years, after two children and a lot of ups and downs, that deep passion had faded into a more practical (and even cynical) kind of relationship, the kind that he had fled from with Sharon. Did Anne have even an ounce of love for him left? He doubted it. Instead, she was probably wondering what she'd ever seen in him in the first place. He was wondering that himself.

Anne deserved a husband who was strong, resourceful, able to provide. Up to now he'd been none of those things. It was long past time to change that. No matter how many paintings he'd sold, no matter how many important showings he'd had, no matter how many art critics were writing positive assessments of his work, it didn't amount to anything when he was broke, homeless, and lying in a jail cell.

The roach dropped onto his chest, and he jumped up and brushed it off. He kicked it under the bars, out into the corridor, then leaned against the cold iron and looked up the darkened hall.

Would they let him out tomorrow? They had to. He couldn't bear the thought of being in jail until his Grand Jury hearing, separated from his children and his wife.

Somehow, he had to get out tomorrow. And Lynda Barrett was the only one who could get him out. She was Sharon's friend, and one of those superstitious Christians. Still, he did trust her.

After all, he had little choice. There were ways to change his family's luck. But he had to be free to pursue them.

9

IT WAS AFTER midnight when the telephone rang in Anne's motel room. She hurried to answer it before it woke her children. "Hello?"

"Anne, is that you?"

The voice sounded distant, and the static over the line made it difficult to hear. "Yes. Who is this?"

"Nelson," the voice said. "Nelson Chamberlain. I'm in London, but I've just heard about Louis's murder."

Chamberlain, who lived in St. Clair even though he traveled most of the time, was one of Ben's biggest supporters. He'd bought at least four of his paintings and sold several more for him in just the past year. He had also been one of Louis Dubose's closest friends. "It was a shock to all of us," she said, shoving her hair back from her face. "Did they tell you who's been charged with the murder?"

"I heard they'd arrested Ben. Is that true? Anne, what's going on?"

"Nelson, it's a long story, but Louis fired Ben yesterday for some unknown reason and told us to move out. The police think that Ben killed him for revenge or something. He's in jail right now." Her voice cracked, and she looked up at the ceiling, trying to fight the tears. "The arraignment is tomorrow. I don't know what we're going to do. I'm worried sick that they'll hold him until the Grand Jury investigation. Longer, if he's indicted. He's been framed, Nelson. All the evidence points to him, but I swear he didn't do it."

"This is incomprehensible," Nelson said. "I can't believe it's happening."

"Me either. And if they do set bond, I have no idea how to come up with it. A bail bondsman might not give it to us—we're not even employed."

"Don't worry about the bond, Anne," Nelson said. "I'll post it. I'm not at a number where I can be reached tomorrow, since I'm hoping to fly home to St. Clair for the funeral, but I'll phone the courthouse in the morning and have the money wired to them."

She caught her breath. "You'd do that?"

"Of course I would. I know Ben didn't kill anyone. We've got to get him out of jail."

"You're saving our lives," Anne cried. "I don't know how to thank you."

"Thanks aren't necessary. Just tell Ben to keep his chin up. I'll call you when I get back."

When she had hung up, Anne sat back against the headboard of the bed and savored the relief that she would at least be able to post bond. Nelson hadn't set a cap on the amount he was willing to pay, and she knew that he'd get his money back when Ben was acquitted. It was the one bright spot in an otherwise horrible day.

She slid back under the covers and tried to sleep. But sleep didn't come. She lay on her back, staring at the ceiling, until morning intruded on the room.

10

THE DAY WAS unusually cold for Florida, but that was no surprise. Everything else seemed out of kilter, too. Sharon walked into the courtroom and glanced around at the faces of other family members, lawyers, and accusers who had come to face the judge today. On one side of the courtroom sat the row of inmates awaiting arraignment. Ben was among them in his orange jumpsuit, looking as haggard and disheveled as she had ever seen him.

Jenny had brought Christy earlier; they were sitting with Anne. Jenny was holding little Bobby in her lap, bouncing him to keep him content, while Emily squirmed restlessly in her mother's lap—holding the army men that Christy had insisted on bringing her this morning. Christy sat beside Anne, dark circles under her eyes, dressed in her Sunday best with a big, white bow in her long hair.

Lynda Barrett was the only one among them who looked confident and unafraid, as if she knew what she was doing here. Risking Anne's wrath, Sharon approached Lynda and quietly leaned over her shoulder.

"How's it looking?" she asked.

Lynda looked up at her hopefully. "Things are moving pretty fast this morning," she said. "The judge must have a golf game this afternoon."

The judge hammered his gavel, marking the decision in the previous case, and Sharon found a seat a couple of rows back.

"St. Clair versus Robinson," the bailiff called out.

Ben got to his feet, and Lynda went to stand beside him. After hearing the charge, the judge asked, "What is your plea?"

"Not guilty," Ben said loudly.

Lynda requested that Ben be released on his own recognizance pending the Grand Jury investigation, but the prosecutor pressed to keep him in jail, citing the violent nature of the crime Ben was accused of and suggesting that the streets of St. Clair weren't safe with Ben free. Lynda refuted his points one by one, making special note of Ben's alibi.

"Your honor, since my client has no criminal record, not even a traffic violation, it would be senseless to keep him in jail. He has a wife and four children who depend on him." She gestured toward them.

The judge regarded the family. Then, taking off his glasses, he read back over the forms on his table. "Miss Barrett," he said, looking up at Lynda and shoving his glasses back on. "I see here that Mr. Robinson was evicted from his home just two days ago."

"That's right, your honor."

The judge braced his elbows on the table and leaned forward, peering at her with impatient eyes. "Explain to me how I can release him if he doesn't have an address."

Lynda didn't hesitate. "Your honor, he's going to get an address very soon, but he has to be out of jail to do so. He was just evicted the day before yesterday. Yesterday he was arrested. He hasn't had time to find a place for his family to live."

The judge shook his head. "I'm sorry, but in light of the fact that this is a murder charge, and he is homeless, I can't in good conscience release him. It's hard enough to keep up with people until a trial when they do have an address. When they don't have one, it's just impossible."

"But your honor, it's not his fault he was evicted!"

"Your honor," the prosecutor interrupted. "The fact is, the murder followed the eviction. The murdered party was his landlord. It seems obvious to me that his homelessness and the murder that took place shortly thereafter are related, so I strongly advise you not to let this man back onto the streets."

The judge nodded as he looked back over the papers. "I'm sorry, Miss Barrett, but unless a man has an address, there's no way that I can release him. I'm afraid you're going to have to stay in jail pending the Grand Jury investigation, Mr. Robinson."

"No!" Anne cried, springing up. Jenny began to wail, covering her face and shaking her head.

Suddenly, Sharon rose. "Your honor."

The outburst surprised the judge, and he looked back into the crowd, trying to figure out who had had the audacity to interrupt his court proceedings.

"Your honor," she said again, drawing his attention to her. "I am Ben Robinson's ex-wife. My name is Sharon Robinson. And he does have an address."

The judge looked back at his papers. "Well, it says here—"

"Your information is out-of-date," she said, slipping out of the row she was sitting in and heading toward the bench. "Your honor, Ben and his family are going to stay with me until he's acquitted."

Jenny caught her breath.

Ben looked at her as if she had just turned into a chicken and begun to cluck.

Sharon couldn't believe what she had just done. She looked back at her older daughter, saw the gratitude in her eyes, and hoped that, alone, would be enough to see her through this.

"Your honor, I'm absolutely certain that my ex-husband did not commit this crime. And to prove that, I'm willing to have him and his family live in my home until the hearing. They will have an address, your honor."

The judge looked dumbfounded.

"Well, uh, Mrs. Robinson—it is Robinson, isn't it?"

"Yes," she said.

"This is highly unusual, and it's against my better judgment. The man doesn't have a criminal record, though, and looking out here at his family, I don't relish the thought of locking him up for an extended period of time. In my courtroom, I prefer to think that a man is innocent until proven guilty. Therefore, if I could have Miss Barrett's word that this is not some kind of farce, and that this man will not take this opportunity to skip the country, then I suppose I could grant you your request. I'll release him on $100,000 bond."

There was no relief in the breath Sharon took. In fact, it was full of dread.

Turning, she caught the full impact of Anne's reaction. Anne's eyes were narrowed, glaring with shock and anger, as if she had no intention of doing what Sharon had suggested.

"Thank you, your honor," Lynda said.

The gavel hammered again. The next case was called. And Ben was taken back out until his bond was posted.

Lynda hurried across the floor to Anne and Jenny to explain the procedure for posting bond. Sharon stood back, watching her teenager weep with a mixture of despair and relief.

Lynda ushered them from the courtroom, and Sharon followed them to the hall, keeping her distance as if she would be flogged if she were caught hanging too close. Christy spotted her and ran toward her, her bow bouncing as it slipped lower on her hair. "Mommy! Daddy got out of jail!"

"I know, honey," she said.

She looked toward them again, and saw Lynda starting back toward her. Her friend's eyes were sympathetic and grateful. Lynda hugged her. "That was a really great thing you did," she whispered.

Sharon's eyes were filling with tears already. "You can call for the men in the white coats now. I'm ready for them."

Lynda smiled. "It was the only way he could have gotten out," Lynda said.

"But how am I going to stand this?" she whispered. "I don't get along with his wife, and I barely get along with him."

"Then why did you do it?" Lynda asked.

Sharon glanced at Jenny, still weeping openly with joy. Christy wasn't sure what was going on, but she had gone back to Emily and was holding her hands and jumping up and down. "I did it for my children," she said. "It would kill them to think of their father in jail for any length of time. I'm not going to make them go through that."

"So instead you would put yourself through this?"

Sharon breathed a deep breath and wilted. "Don't overpraise it, Lynda. I wish I could say I'm doing this out of the goodness of my heart, but I'm afraid I'm going to spend the next few weeks seething. But I know that Ben is not a murderer. And the sooner we prove it, the sooner this nightmare will be over."

11

AN HOUR LATER, Sharon watched out the window as Ben's station wagon pulled into her driveway. She could just imagine what had taken place when Ben had encountered Anne. He'd probably been lambasted. By now, the whole idea of moving in with her husband's ex-wife had probably sunk in, and Anne must be livid.

Ben got out of the car with the baby on his hip and grabbed one of the suitcases he had stuffed in the back. Anne lingered behind as if to busy herself with something—anything—to delay her entrance into the home.

Ben came tentatively to the open door and peered inside. "Hi," he said.

"Hi," Sharon returned, all business. "Come on in. I'm putting you and Anne in the bedroom at the back, third door on the left down the hall. Emily can sleep with Christy upstairs in Christy's room, and I got our old crib out of the attic for Bobby. He'll be in the room next to you."

Ben whistled under his breath. "I guess I've never been farther in than the den. I didn't realize you have two extra bedrooms."

"It's a big house," Sharon admitted.

He stood there staring at her for a moment, holding that baby on his hip. If he'd been anyone else, she would have been reaching to hold the baby by now. She had always wanted another one of her own. But now she tried not to even look his way as he came in.

"This was really nice of you, Sharon," he said. "You didn't have to do it. It was the last thing I expected."

She turned away and began chopping carrots on the big island at the center of her kitchen. "I *did* have to do it," she said. "I saw the look on my daughters' faces. And last night, Christy was so upset—I'd do anything to spare the children from the pain of seeing their father stay in jail."

"Well, whatever the motive, I appreciate it."

A moment of loud silence passed between them as Sharon continued chopping the carrots.

"I didn't kill him, Sharon."

Sharon turned back to him and looked down at the floor, studying the big, square parquet tiles. "I know you didn't, Ben."

"I'm gonna get out of this," he said. "I know it looks pretty hopeless, but I've got to fight it."

"I know."

She heard Emily and Christy giggling and chattering as they walked up to the house.

Anne, on the other hand, was still bitterly angry. She marched into the house carrying a box and wearing a sour look on her otherwise pretty face. Sharon had trouble looking at her. She always had. "Hello, Anne."

Anne's face was red as she lifted her chin and faced Sharon. "I want you to know that I'm against this," she said. "I don't like it a bit."

Sharon nodded. "That's fair."

"I don't really know why you did it," she went on, tears filling her pale blue eyes. "But I don't trust you. I don't want any favors from you."

Sharon fought the urge to rail back at her that the last thing on earth she wanted was to do Anne Robinson any favors, but instead, she turned back to the carrots. "It doesn't look like you have a choice," she bit out.

"Maybe not for now," Anne told her. "But the minute I can get into my own place, we'll be out of here."

"Come on, Anne," Ben said cautiously. "We need to be thanking her instead of badgering her."

Anne turned on him then. "Don't you dare defend your ex-wife to me!"

"I'm not defending her," he said. "I'm just trying to point out that you're being a little irrational. We don't have a place to live, so she offered us her home."

Thick silence stretched out over agonizing seconds as Anne struggled with the emotions battling on her face . . . anger, humiliation, pride, distress. Finally, Ben handed the baby to her. "We're at the back room on the left. Why don't you take Bobby and go get settled in?"

"I've got a roast in the oven," Sharon said to Anne's back as she left the room. "It's for dinner tonight."

Anne shot her a scathing look, as if about to tell her that that dinner would go uneaten, but then she looked down at Emily and her face softened. The child would have to eat, as would the baby and her husband. Anne herself might fast for as long as she was here, but not her family.

Sharon almost felt sorry for Anne as she left the room, carrying her box of meager belongings in one arm and the baby in the other.

Jenny, who must have pulled into the driveway behind Anne and Ben, came to the door, her eyes lit up like a little girl in a doll shop at Christmas. Christy and Emily were on her heels. "Oh, Mom, you are so awesome! This is gonna be so great!" She threw her arms around her mother again, almost knocking her down.

Christy took Emily's hands and began dancing with her, her long, blonde hair bouncing. "Emily gets to live with us! Emily gets to live with us! Mommy, it's gonna be so much fun! And Daddy'll be here right where we live, and we can see him all the time."

Bitterness welled back up in Sharon. If it hadn't been for Ben's recklessness with their marriage, Christy would never have had to know what it was like not to have her father living with them.

She turned back to the carrots, all her compassion for Ben slipping away. "Well, you guys have a lot of work to do," she said quickly. "Christy and Emily, why don't you go unpack? Give her some of your drawers, Christy. You two will be sharing a room."

The little girls squealed with delight, and ran up the stairs to Christy's bedroom. Ben followed them, knowing not to push Sharon any further.

When Jenny and Sharon were the only two in the kitchen, Jenny asked, "Mom, are you all right?"

"I'm fine. But Jenny, this isn't gonna be easy."

"I know," Jenny said softly. "But it'll work out. You'll see."

Sharon checked the stove, as if something might have changed in the last half hour since she'd put the roast in. If it hadn't been an electric oven, she might have considered sticking her head in it.

"Mom, I know you and Anne don't like each other."

Sharon breathed a laugh and closed the oven. "Now, there's an understatement."

"But don't you see?" Jenny asked. "That just makes it all so much greater. I mean, what you did. Letting her come live here, and Dad, and the kids. I mean, it's easy to do nice things for people you like, but when you do it for people you don't like . . ."

Sharon stiffened and turned around. "I did it, okay, Jenny? You don't have to keep on with this."

"But Mom, I mean it."

Sharon sighed and went to the medicine cabinet to look for aspirin. "I'm getting a headache."

"Maybe you and Anne will become friends," Jenny suggested. "She's really nice, most of the time. We've gotten to be kind of close, and—"

"I think the best we can hope is that we'll learn to tolerate each other," Sharon interrupted, hating the bitterness rising inside her. "And we've got a long way to go."

Jenny put her arms around Sharon's neck and forced her to look at her. She was as tall as her mother already, and it amazed Sharon that she had been as small as Christy not so long ago. Time was flying. Finding it hard to hold onto her bitterness with that sweet face smiling at her, she returned the hug.

"I love you, Mom. And you really are living your faith. I'm sorry about what I said yesterday."

"Oh, that's okay," Sharon said, letting her go. "I knew it was just manipulation."

"Hey, that's my job," Jenny said. She stepped back and gave her mother a serious look. "I'll help while they're here. It'll be good for me, too. I'll learn responsibility. I can help with Bobby and the kids. It'll be nice to have them around the house, won't it, Mom? To have the house full of kids?"

Sharon sighed. "Jenny, I know this is going to be fun for you. But I hope you'll be sensitive to the fact that some of us won't take very well to it. Not only that, but your father could still wind up in prison."

"He won't, Mom," Jenny said. "We're gonna find out who really killed Mr. Dubose. We're gonna prove he's innocent."

The determined tone in Jenny's voice alarmed her. An image flashed through Sharon's mind: Jenny out scavenging the streets in search of the real murderer. She took Jenny by the shoulders and looked straight into her eyes. "You are going to stay out of it. You are not going to pry around to find Mr. Dubose's murderer. Do you understand me? We're talking *murder* here. This is dangerous."

Jenny hesitated. "Mom, somebody's got to do something."

"I'll do everything I can," Sharon promised her. "I have as much at stake now as you do."

"What do you mean by that?"

"The sooner we clear your father, the sooner they can go back to their own lives."

Jenny's face fell so hard that Sharon thought she heard it crash. "Yeah, I guess it's not forever, is it?"

Sharon almost laughed, but she stopped herself. "No, honey, it's not forever. Now why don't you go help the girls get Emily's things put away?"

Jenny's mood changed quickly, and as she whirled to jog up the stairs, Sharon noticed the bounce in her step and the joy in her eyes that her family had finally been grafted back together again.

Anne had managed to get Bobby to sleep by the time Ben made it back to the bedroom. As he entered, she was sitting on the window seat, gazing out over the backyard. There were plenty of trees, and a swing set for Christy, and that tree house that Sharon had hired someone to build. It was clear from the way she gazed out the window that Anne envied Sharon's home.

He stood behind her and began to massage her shoulders. "You okay?"

When she looked up at him, he saw the tension on her face. "This is hard, Ben. Really hard."

"It doesn't have to be. The kids are thrilled."

"The kids don't have a clue." She jerked away from his massaging hands, got up, and went across the room to the suitcase. As she began to unpack, tears came to her eyes. "How did all this happen?"

"It'll be okay," he said. "Just trust me."

"I *have* trusted you," she snapped. "When I told you I was worried about our being so dependent on the gallery, you said to trust you. When I told you that we needed our own home for security, you said to trust you."

"Owning our own home wouldn't have helped us today, Anne. I still would have been set up for murder charges."

"Yes, but we could have gone back to our own house, instead of living off of your ex-wife." She stopped and looked up at him, her eyes tormented. "It's humiliating, Ben. It's my worst nightmare."

"You're being melodramatic," he said.

"No, I'm not!"

"Look, if you're worried about something going on between Sharon and me, it won't. I'm married to you now."

"Being married didn't stop you before, did it?"

It was a low blow, and he took a step back. "If I recall, you played a part in that, too."

She didn't like being reminded of that, so she turned back to the suitcase and jerked out a stack of his shirts.

"Anne, look at the bright side. I get to be with my kids. Emily and Christy get to be together."

"That's right," she said, swinging around again. "One big happy family, huh? Just like it was before I came into the picture. Daddy and Mommy back in the same house. The only thing wrong with this picture is me!"

He turned to the window. "Anne, it may not have occurred to you, but I'm the one who spent the night in jail. To have to come crawling to my ex-wife for help, to let my kids see me destitute and in trouble—you think I wanted it this way?"

"I don't *know* what you wanted," she said, flinging more clothes into the drawer. "I have no idea. All I know is that your name is being smeared all over the papers as a common murderer, and you've got me living in my archenemy's house. From where I stand, life with you isn't looking too good right now."

Ben looked back at her. "Anne, I need you to pull yourself together. You're my only alibi. If you start falling apart—"

"Alibi?" she almost shouted, then quickly lowered her voice. "That's another thing, Ben. I told them I was with you the whole time yesterday, but the truth is, I wasn't. When you went for that walk, you were gone over an hour."

"We needed some distance, Anne—because we were fighting, just like we are now," he said. "What do you think? That I jogged over to the gallery and killed Louis in that hour?"

"No!" she cried. "I don't think that. But *they* might if they knew!"

"Then don't tell them!"

She turned away and jerked another stack of clothes out of the suitcase. "This is a nightmare, Ben. I hate it."

"So do you want out? Is that it?"

"Out of what?"

"The marriage. The commitment to stand behind me no matter how tough things get."

"Where would I go, Ben?" she asked through compressed lips. "Whatever money I came into this marriage with is gone now. I can't even afford to take my child to the doctor. And I'm not really up to taking more money from your beloved ex!"

"Then get a job! If you're so dead set on getting away from me, then make some money and leave!"

"I'm not leaving without my kids, Ben."

"And I'm not letting you take them."

"Fine." Her face was reddening, and she crumpled over and dropped on the bed, breathing out a heavy sigh. "I'm stuck with you, then."

Ben had never been one to keep the tough-guy act going when a woman started to cry, so he sat down on the bed next to her and let out a ragged breath. Putting his arms around her, he pulled her against him. "Look, I've messed up once before, and my kids had to pay for it. I don't want another family to break up. Please, just relax and try to get through this. We can do it. We've had tough times before."

"Not like these," she cried.

"No, and neither have the kids. We have to be strong for them."

She tried to pull herself together. Wiping her face, she said, "I'm tired, Ben. I haven't slept since we left our apartment. How many days ago was that?"

"We've only been gone two nights. But I know how you feel. I haven't slept much, either. Can we just write this fight off to fatigue? Can we just forget the stuff about leaving each other for now?"

Again, she pulled away. "I don't know, Ben. I just don't know how much more of this I can take."

"You need rest," he said. "Why don't you take a nap while Bobby's asleep? It may not last long. If he wakes up, I'll take care of him."

"And what will you be doing?" she asked suspiciously. "Puttering around in the kitchen with your first wife?"

He sighed. "No, Anne. You don't have to fear Sharon. I'm the last man on earth she'd be interested in now."

"Oh, great," she said. "But if she were interested, it wouldn't be a problem for you, right?"

"Wrong. You're putting words in my mouth."

"No. I'm just interpreting them." She got up and started out of the room. "I don't think I can sleep right now. I'll go help Emily get unpacked."

Sharon decided to set the table alone, dreading the moment when everyone came to the table. When she'd finally gotten all the food into serving bowls and put them on the breakfast counter so that everyone could serve themselves, smorgasbord-style, she went to round everyone up.

Ben was on the telephone in her study talking to Lynda about the possibility of hiring a private investigator to try to find the real killer. Sharon knew that she would have to foot the bill for that, and the fact that he hadn't even asked her made her angry. On the other hand, it was worth whatever it cost to get Ben off the hook and out of her home. Jenny, who seemed not to know the purpose of chairs, sat on the floor in front of him, listening intently.

She told them both to come to the table. "Where's Anne?" she asked Jenny before she left the room.

"I think she's watching TV with the girls. I'll tell her."

"That's all right," Sharon said, determined not to let her feelings inhibit her. "I'll tell her myself."

She walked up the hall and went into the den. Christy sat on the floor next to Emily, both of them engrossed in some sleazy tabloid show that she normally didn't allow Christy to watch. Since it was just going off and a preview of the news was flashing on, she let it go. Anne sat in a recliner staring at the screen, but Sharon suspected that she didn't see any of it. Her mind seemed a million miles away.

"It's time for dinner, everybody," Sharon said in a light, upbeat voice. "Wash your hands, girls."

"Okay, Mommy." Christy got up to reach for the remote control. But just before she could turn the television off, the news came on—and a picture of her father flashed across the screen as the headline story. "A local man is the primary suspect in . . ."

"Mommy, look! It's Daddy!" Christy shouted.

Sharon froze, and Anne slowly leaned forward. "Ben Robinson, local artist, was arraigned today on murder charges. The gallery owner where he worked was found dead—" As the anchor spoke, footage showed the body covered with a sheet being wheeled out on a gurney. "And evidence points to the disgruntled artist who lived in the studio and had been fired the day of the shooting. We'll have this and other stories when we return in a moment."

Sharon rushed forward to turn off the television as Christy and Emily gaped up at her, their eyes round with horror over the image of the dead man in their father's gallery. The man the newscaster said their father had killed.

"Go wash your hands, girls," Sharon snapped.

Christy couldn't move. "Mommy, is that the man they said Daddy—"

"Your father didn't kill anyone," Sharon said quickly. She turned to Anne angrily. "I would think you'd be a little more careful about what the children watched, especially today."

Anne bristled. "I had no idea that was about to come on. You were standing there, too."

"But I never would have allowed them to watch that stupid tabloid show. Whatever happened to "Barney"?

Anne's tired face reddened. "This isn't about "Barney" or a tabloid show, Sharon. At least have the decency to say what you mean."

The girls left the room quickly, and Sharon watched them go, flustered. "You're right," she said through her teeth. "It isn't about the tabloid show. It's about them seeing their father called a murderer on television. We're going to have to be careful and monitor what they watch. Any fool would know that today of all days—"

"Oh, that does it!" Anne said, springing out of her chair and heading for the door. Sharon watched her, furious, and saw the girls still hovering together in the hall. "Girls, I said to go wash your hands!" she yelled.

Anne spun around. "Hey—you can order your kids around, but leave mine alone!"

"Fine," Sharon grated through her teeth. "Dinner's ready." She stormed out of the room, but Anne was right behind her.

"Hey, you know, this wasn't my idea. I don't like it. Like you said, I'm here because I have no choice."

"I know that," Sharon said. "But I did have a choice. I invited you to come here of my own free will."

"Why?" Anne shouted. "What's in it for you?"

Sharon stopped midstride and spun around to face Anne. "My children love their father, and it killed them to know he was in jail. I did it for them, not for either one of you!" she returned. "But that doesn't change the fact that I have rules in this house about television, and I don't want my children watching graphic images on the news about how their father murdered some guy—"

Ben walked in and Sharon stopped in midsentence.

"What are you guys talking about?" he asked.

"The news!" Sharon blurted.

"Yeah," Anne said, turning on him and beginning to cry again. "You're already all over it. Everybody we know is going to think you're a killer. You're a disgruntled employee, after all!"

"The news?" he asked.

Sharon knew she shouldn't add fuel to this fire, but she felt the need to enlist Ben's help. "Ben, your wife just let your children see Dubose's dead body being taken out of the gallery."

"Give me a break!" Anne shouted. "I had no more idea that was coming on than you did!"

"You should be more careful!" Sharon yelled.

Jenny walked into the room, carrying Bobby. "You woke him," she said quietly.

The censure in her voice stopped them both, and Sharon felt like a child being reprimanded by a teacher. Gritting her teeth, she went into the kitchen and began sticking serving spoons into the bowls. "Someone's gonna have to start eating," she said through gritted teeth. "Come on, Jenny. Eat!"

Jenny put the baby into the high chair that hooked onto the edge of the table and began to fix herself a plate. Sharon heard Anne whispering behind her to Ben, and she wanted to scream. Instead she just decided to leave the room.

"Where are you going, Mom?" Jenny asked when she was almost out of the kitchen.

"To find Christy and Emily," she said. "They ran out of the room upset."

Jenny shot a glance to her father and Anne, then silently took her plate to the table.

In her room, Sharon closed the door of her bedroom and struggled with the emotions coursing through her. She wanted to tell Anne to get herself and her family out of her house, and not to expect any more help from her. But the truth, Sharon admitted, was that she hadn't done what she'd done for Anne's sake at all—she'd done it for Jenny, and she'd done it for Christy. And she had even done it for Ben, though he was the last person she ever wanted to feel compassion for.

Her only choice now was to quickly get this murder resolved so that they could get out of her house.

She picked up the phone and dialed Lynda's number.

"Hello?"

"Lynda, it's me," Sharon said.

"How's it going?" Lynda asked knowingly.

Sharon couldn't even speak for a moment. "Lynda, you've got to help me."

"I'm doing everything I can."

"I know," Sharon said. "But I mean, *really* help me. I'll pay for the private detective you were talking to Ben about, no matter what it costs. We've got to find out who really killed Dubose and get Ben off the hook so we can get them out of my house."

Lynda was quiet for a moment. "What happened?"

"Let's just say that Anne and I rub each other the wrong way. There's so much friction that I'm afraid I'll catch fire."

Sharon could hear the smile in Lynda's voice. "Well, I had a feeling that might be a problem."

"He's being set up, Lynda. Someone's framing him. And it couldn't be that hard to figure out who."

"That's my thinking exactly," Lynda said. "Look, relax and try to get through this. I know this is hard for you, but as soon as I find out anything I'll be in touch. I know Ben's life hangs in the balance. Trust me, I'm not taking this lightly."

"I know you're not," Sharon said, falling back on her bed. "But you've been a little distracted lately with Jake and falling in love and all that kind of stuff—"

"You act like I'm a boy-crazy teenager."

"Call it jealousy," Sharon said, her tone serious. "I just can't remember what it's like."

Lynda chuckled. "Well, having Ben around might remind you a little bit."

Sharon quickly shook her head. "I'm wondering what I ever saw in the man in the first place."

"See how far you've come since the divorce? There was a time when you thought your life was over, and that you'd never get over Ben. Now you can't even remember feeling that way."

"I guess God has a way of anesthetizing us against those painful memories," she said. "And time heals. As far as I'm concerned, I wish Anne and him the utmost happiness—far, far away from here. Meanwhile, I just have to keep reminding myself that this is the right thing to do."

"It is," Lynda said. "There didn't seem to be an alternative—at least not one that would be fair to the kids. But you'll be all right. You're a sweet lady, and God can use you in this."

"You're a good friend, Lynda," Sharon said. "And a pathetic optimist."

"Let's hope I'm a good lawyer. Ben's gonna need one."

12

ERIC BOUDREAUX SAT in his opulent suite at the Tampa Biltmore, studying the stock quotes in the newspaper that had been delivered to his suite that morning. His appointment was in less than two hours, but he still hadn't heard from Louis Dubose.

The television news droned in the corner. Occasionally, he glanced up to see if anything interested him.

". . . art gallery owner Louis Dubose . . ."

Startled, Boudreaux looked up at the screen to see the face of the man he had never met before, except by phone. Leaning forward, he grabbed the remote and turned the volume up.

". . . was found dead after being shot in the back. Police sources say the gun, which was found in a dumpster near the gallery, was registered to Benjamin L. Robinson, a local artist who was residing in the gallery. According to sources, Robinson was fired and evicted the day of the murder . . ."

Eric listened, stunned, trying to follow the words, but all he was certain of was that Dubose was dead. How could that be?

He had flown from France for this very appointment, anxious to get his hands on the prize that would make him even richer than he already was. If Dubose was dead—

The phone rang, and he snatched it up. "Boudreaux," he said in his heavy French accent.

"Yes, Mr. Boudreaux," a voice said cheerily. "So nice to hear your voice. I trust your flight was a good one?"

Boudreaux frowned. "Who is this?"

"My name is John Lieber, and I'm a close friend and colleague of Louis Dubose. I'm afraid I have bad news."

Boudreaux looked back at the screen, but a commercial was playing now. "Yes. The murder."

"The murder," the man said sadly. "You've heard the news, then. Our friend was murdered brutally. A terrible thing. So unexpected."

Boudreaux was quiet. Dubose had not mentioned another contact, although Boudreaux had suspected that he wasn't involved in this business alone. He would act cautiously, he thought. It was difficult to trust Americans, and he did not like doing business with them.

"I was Dubose's partner in our little enterprise," the man said. "And I see no reason that it can't go on as planned. I'd still like to meet with you and make the exchange."

"You have it?" Boudreaux asked hopefully, his thick eyebrows arching.

"It's in a safe place," Lieber said. "It may take me a short while to secure it."

"How long?" Boudreaux asked. "I must return to France."

"Just another day or two. I give you my word it will be worth your time. After all, you didn't come all this way just to return home empty-handed."

Boudreaux considered that for a moment. He couldn't take the chance of walking into a trap. He had an impeccable reputation, and no one had ever suspected him of being involved in anything that wasn't legal. What if somehow he had come under suspicion, and international art detectives were setting him up? Things weren't going smoothly enough. Yet he wanted what he had come here for . . .

"How . . ." He tried to put the words together correctly. "How may I trust you?"

"You *have* to trust me," Lieber said, "because I have the greatest find in the art world this century. If you don't trust me, you'll lose out."

Boudreaux nodded slightly, but didn't say a word.

"Please. Just stay where you are for another day or, at the most, two. I'll be back in touch as soon as we can make the exchange. Dubose would have wanted it this way. He wouldn't have wanted this sale to be jeopardized because of some unfortunate circumstances."

Boudreaux wasn't convinced. His instincts all screamed for him to get on the plane and head back out of the country. But Lieber was right. This was the find of the century.

"I will stay until I hear from you," he said grudgingly. "If I do not hear within two days, I will leave."

"Fair enough," the man said. "I'll be in touch. And Mr. Boudreaux? You won't regret this."

13

THE CHILDREN WERE missing.

While the others were looking inside, Ben went out back to see if they were in the yard. The little tree house nestled in the oak in the backyard was a new development since he'd last been here. Sharon had hired someone to build it for Christy because she loved to climb.

But building a tree house was the father's job. He should have been the one to design and execute it, and that bothered Ben as he peered up the ladder. It looked sound enough, though. The truth is, he probably couldn't have done a better job. But it was the principle of the thing. If Sharon had asked him, he'd have built the little house.

On the other hand, Anne would have probably had a fit about his being over here at all, and it would have gotten too complicated . . .

Sharon had probably done the right thing. Christy deserved a tree house. She shouldn't have to deal with the divorce fallout every time she wanted something. Besides, her mother could afford it. Despite the financial pit Ben had left her in, Sharon had thrived since the divorce. She had a way of always bouncing back. No matter how bad things looked, good things came out of it for her. She was lucky that way.

His luck hadn't been so good.

He heard crying in the tree house. Gripping the rungs, he slowly started up the ladder. He got to the hatch at the bottom and knocked lightly on the floor of the house. "Anybody home?"

The hatch opened and Christy's wet, red face greeted him. "Come in, Daddy. We're crying."

The announcement almost amused him, but when he pulled himself in, the sight broke his heart. Christy moved back to sit by Emily. They both sat Indian style, holding hands as they wept.

"What's wrong, girls?" he asked softly.

They looked at each other. "Nothing."

Ben climbed farther up into the tree house and tested the boards to see if it would hold him. It had been well built, he admitted. But these days Sharon did everything first-class. She had the money to.

He sat down on the floor next to Christy, and Emily climbed into his lap. He pulled Christy up onto his other leg and held both of his children tight. "Now, tell Daddy what's wrong."

"It was the news, Daddy," Christy said. "They said you killed Mr. Dubose."

"You know I didn't. You do know that, don't you?"

"But we're scared."

"You know Daddy didn't kill anybody, don't you?" he asked again.

Both of the girls nodded, and fresh tears rolled down their faces. Ben buried his face in Christy's hair.

"Girls, this is the worst time in Daddy's life. Sometimes things just don't go like you plan. But I didn't kill Mr. Dubose, and I'm gonna find out who did, and it's gonna be okay. Let's look at the good side," he said, trying to cheer his daughters up. "We're all here in the same house together."

"But Mommy hates Miss Sharon," Emily said, rubbing her eyes.

Ben shook his head, saddened by the complications adults, in their weakness, throw at the children who depend on them. He kissed his youngest daughter's cheek. "Honey, it's just real hard for them. They were both married to me, and it's kind of weird, all of us living here together."

"Are they gonna fight all the time?" Emily asked.

"Let's hope not."

Christy touched Ben's face, rubbing the rough growth of stubble. He hadn't shaved since they'd been evicted. "I've been praying for you, Daddy."

"I know, sweetheart," Ben said. "You just keep right on doing that."

He looked around at the little building they sat in. "I haven't been up here before, Christy. Nice place you've got here."

"Thank you," she said, wiping her face.

"But it needs a little paint, doesn't it?"

She looked around as if she'd never noticed it before.

"I tell you what," he said. "Since I'm gonna be here with nothing to do for a little while, maybe we can start a project."

"What kind of project?" Emily asked, her face brightening. "You mean a painting project?"

Emily loved to paint, but his studio had always been off-limits to her. The idea of being involved in one of his projects now had enough appeal to distract her from her sorrow.

"Yeah," he said. "How about if we come up here tomorrow and start painting? We could paint the walls, and the floor, and the ceiling, and—"

"We could paint pictures on it," Christy piped in.

"Sure, we could paint a mural. It would be gorgeous."

"Nobody can paint a mural like you can," Emily said.

"All right, then, we have some plans to make. I want you two to go inside and eat supper, and then after supper, get some paper and draw pictures just like what you want on the walls of the house."

"Can we paint on the outside, too, Daddy?" Christy asked.

"Sure we can. We'll paint anything you want, as long as we clear it with your mom."

Christy and Emily forgot their grief as their minds reeled with possibilities. Ben wiped both their faces and kissed them on the cheeks.

"I love you guys."

"I love you, too, Daddy," they each said.

"Now, go in and eat supper. Your moms are worried about you. Then you can get started on the designs. I'm just gonna sit up here for a minute by myself."

He watched as they scurried down the ladder, and for a moment he hesitated, thinking about what had just taken place. Here he sat in the little tree house built by someone that his ex-wife had hired because Ben himself was no longer a factor in their family. And here were his two children, one from each marriage, best friends and loving each other as sisters. Now, arrested for murder, he was back in the home, but with his new wife and children . . .

Nothing about this was natural. It was as bizarre a set of circumstances as he could have imagined.

How in the world had he come to this? No job, no income, facing the possibility of going to prison . . .

The depression and anger that had been pulling him like quicksand since Dubose had fired him pulled him further under. Miserably, he slipped out of the hatch and climbed back down the ladder.

14

SHARON DIDN'T HAVE an appetite for the meal she'd cooked, so she stayed away until everyone had left the table. Then she ventured back into the kitchen to clean up. Anne was already loading the dishwasher, and when she looked up, Sharon saw that she was crying.

Sharon pretended not to notice.

"I'm cleaning up," Anne said.

"That's all right," Sharon told her. "I can do it. Why don't you go take care of the kids?"

As if Sharon's words had been an indictment, Anne dropped the pot on the counter and wiped her eyes. "Look, Sharon, the kids are being taken care of. They're playing upstairs, and Jenny's with them. Don't act like I'm neglecting them."

"I didn't say that," Sharon said. "Did I say that?"

"I know what you were thinking."

"All right," Sharon said, crossing her arms and squaring off with the woman. "What was I thinking, exactly?"

"You were thinking that you've waited six years to see us in this position," Anne said, tossing down the hand towel she was holding. "You were thinking that we deserve all this, and you're secretly delighted that we're in all this trouble."

"That's not true," Sharon said. "And I resent it."

"I can see right through all your generosity, Sharon!"

"That's enough, Anne." The words were Ben's, and both women swung around.

Anne's tears came harder now. "Don't you dare defend her!"

"I'm not defending her," Ben said. "She doesn't need defending. Now calm down." He crossed the room and cupped his wife's chin. "Anne, look at me," he said.

She looked up at him with her red, furious eyes.

"You're really stressed out, honey, and I understand that. So am I. But lashing out at Sharon is not going to help. It'll just make things worse, and we need to concentrate and keep our heads clear right now, okay? We don't have time for all this bickering."

She fell against him, and he held her for a moment, letting her cry. Sharon turned away, suddenly feeling like an intruder in her own home.

"Look, you go lie down," he whispered to Anne. "You need a break. Just go take a nap, and let Jenny look after the kids. She loves it."

"But Bobby's sick. It's almost time for his cough medicine."

"I'll give it to him," Ben said. "Go on now. I need you to be rested. There are going to be a lot of sleepless nights between now and the Grand Jury hearing."

Sharon watched her leave the room. Ben turned back to Sharon and shot her an apologetic look. "Sharon, I'm sorry. She's not herself. She's usually a sweet, warm person. Once you get to know her—"

"Spare me." Sharon turned away and started wiping the counters.

Ben's voice trailed off, as though he knew his mouth was leading him down the wrong path. "Okay, never mind. Listen, if you don't mind, I need to make some calls. Do you mind if I use your study?"

"Fine," Sharon said. "Oh, and if you need to paint, we could probably find some place around here for you to do it."

He shrugged. "Thanks a lot. I'm just not feeling real creative right now. I did promise the girls we'd do some painting in the tree house, though. You don't mind, do you?"

"No, I think it's a good idea. It's about time Christy's father got involved in her life." She turned back to the dishes and began scrubbing them with a vengeance.

Ben couldn't think of a response that wouldn't just make things worse, so he started out of the room. The phone rang, and he turned back. "I'll get it. It might be Lynda."

He picked it up. "Hello?"

He hesitated, then in an agitated voice, asked, "Who is this?"

Sharon turned around. "Who?" she whispered. He only shook his head, indicating that he didn't know.

"What are you talking about?" His face began to redden. "I have no idea what you're talking about!"

"What is it?" Sharon asked in an urgent whisper.

Ben put his hand over the phone. "Call the police," he mouthed. "Trace the call."

"It's him?" she asked in disbelief. "The killer?"

He nodded frantically and gestured for her to hurry.

As Sharon rushed to the car where she could call from her cellular phone, Ben continued the conversation. "You've got to tell me what you're looking for," she heard him say. "I can't read your mind."

She reached the garage and threw open her car door, and frantically dialed 911 on her cellular phone. After hearing what she had to say, the dispatcher transferred her. She waited, on hold, wishing someone would pick up.

After a moment, Ben burst through the door with Anne on his heels. "Do you have the police department?"

"Yes," she said. "But it takes an act of Congress to speak to the right person. I'm on hold—"

"He's looking for something," Ben cut in, raking his hand through his long hair. "I don't know what it is. He wants me to leave it at the airport at 10:30 tonight, but I have no idea what he's talking about. He threatened me. Said he'd go into the next phase of this nightmare if I didn't bring him what he wants."

"Well, what could it be?" Anne asked. "Didn't he give you a clue? Are you supposed to guess?"

"He thinks I already know," Ben said. "That's what's so bizarre."

Giving up, Sharon slammed the phone down. "Come on, Ben, we've got to go to the police station."

Anne looked stunned. "He doesn't need you to go with him."

Sharon felt reprimanded and quickly got out of the car. "You're right. Go! Somebody needs to tell somebody. Here. Take my car so you can call Lynda on the way. She probably needs to know about this."

Ben looked back toward the house. "What about the kids?"

"We'll take care of them," Sharon said. "Between Jenny and me they'll be okay."

Anne started running back into the house. "I'm not leaving Bobby. I'll take him with us."

Sharon looked as if she'd been slapped down, but she said nothing.

As they waited, Ben tried to work back through the conversation. "He said to get a black Travel-Lite garment bag from Walmart. That's what I'm supposed to deliver it in. He was very specific that it had to be that brand."

Sharon frowned, wondering why. "Well . . . all right. I'll leave Jenny with the girls and I'll run to Walmart and get one while you're gone. Who knows? Maybe it'll come to you. Maybe you'll figure out what he's looking for."

He nodded. "If the police believe me, this could clear me, Sharon. If they could catch him tonight . . . I could be off the hook."

New hope brightened her eyes. "That's right!"

Anne came back out, carrying Bobby with one arm and the diaper bag and her purse on the other. "Okay, let's go. I'm ready."

"Good luck," Sharon told him. "And don't forget to call Lynda. She probably needs to meet you at the station."

15

TONY DANKS SCRIBBLED on a legal pad as Ben related the phone conversation, every nuance of his body suggesting that he didn't believe a word of it. Larry Millsaps looked doubtful, too, though his eyes remained focused on Ben's as he spoke. Lynda sat beside Ben, occasionally prodding him with more questions that she thought might strengthen his story. Anne stood in the corner of the room, quietly swaying to keep Bobby from waking up.

"So . . . did you record this phone conversation?" Tony asked without looking up from his scribblings when Ben finished the story.

"No," Ben said. "Of course not. I didn't know he was going to call."

"He already told you that Sharon tried to get a trace started, Tony. She got put on hold," Lynda pointed out.

"Did anyone pick up on another line and hear any part of the conversation?" Tony asked.

"No, I don't think so," Ben said. "Why?"

"I just wondered if there were any witnesses."

"Sharon saw me talking to him."

"Oh, that should hold up in court," Tony said sarcastically. "'Your honor, my wife saw me on the phone.' Case closed."

"She's not his wife," Anne clipped. "I am."

"Oh, that's right," Tony said. "He lives with both of you."

The statement only further inflamed Ben, and he stood up, knocking his chair back with a clatter. Leaning over the table, he asked, "What do I have to do to prove that he called?"

Tony glanced at Larry, who seemed to be deep in thought with his hands clasped in front of his face. "Well, we checked the phone records," Tony said. "There is a record of a call that came to that house at about that time, but it was from a pay phone. It really doesn't prove anything."

"Why not?" Ben asked. "The guy obviously didn't want the call traced."

"Because it could have been anyone," Tony said. "How do we know it wasn't a salesman or something? You could have played this out to throw us off your scent."

"Then come with me tonight," Ben said. "I'll deliver a black garment bag just like he said. Someone will pick it up, and you can get him. Then you'll see."

"What will you put in the garment bag?" Tony asked. "Your story is that you don't know what he wants, remember?"

Ben wanted to break something. "It's not a story, man! This is all so crazy, why would I make it up?"

"Why?" Tony laughed and glanced at his partner, who didn't join in his amusement. "Well, let's see. You've been accused of murder. All the evidence points to you. You're probably going to spend the rest of your life in prison—I don't know, Larry, can you think of any reason he'd want to make this up?"

"It's a pretty common ploy," Larry said matter-of-factly. "Cast suspicion on someone else. Try to get the magnifying glass off you."

Ben threw up his hands. "I don't *have* to make it up! I didn't do this! And I can't believe you morons are sitting on your duffs while some murderer is walking free out there. It hasn't even occurred to you that you could be wrong—that *if* I'm telling the truth, the trail of the real killer is getting cold while you just sit there. That's what's wrong with our criminal justice system. It depends on idiots like you!"

Lynda had stood up halfway through his outburst, and now touched Ben's arm to calm him down. "Come on, Ben. This won't get you anywhere." She looked back at the two cops, who looked more stubborn and determined than ever. "Gentlemen, if we have to tell a Grand Jury that we gave you the opportunity to catch the real criminal, and you declined, it isn't going to look good. And the fact that my client just called you idiots shouldn't change the way you investigate this crime at all. His temper may be on edge right now, but I'd say ours would be, too, if we'd been accused of a murder we didn't commit." She sat back down and leaned on the table to face Larry. "What do you say, Larry? Tony? Can't you at least escort him to the airport tonight? See what happens?"

Larry glanced at Tony and shook his head. "Lynda, if we jumped every time a suspect pointed us to someone else, we'd never get any sleep. I left before dawn this morning to investigate a shooting in a bar, and I'm tired. Besides, I have a wife at home who's expecting me for dinner."

"She understands what you do for a living," Lynda said. "If I know her as well as I think I do, she wouldn't want you to pin a murder on the wrong guy just so you could be on time for dinner. And we both know that you've gone without sleep to get the job done before this. What about you, Tony?"

Tony laughed under his breath. "So let me get this straight. After working fourteen hours today, I'm supposed to go with this guy to the Tampa Airport—which is roughly an hour from here—so that he can respond to a phone call he can't prove, by leaving an empty bag by a window so that an imaginary person can pick it up?"

"Forget it!" Ben said, shoving the chair again. "Just forget it. I'll go myself."

"No, you won't, pal," Larry said. "You're not allowed to leave town until you're cleared."

"What if he's telling the truth?" Lynda shouted, making them all look at her. "What if—just what *if*—he's telling you exactly like it happened? Whoever was on that phone *threatened* him if he didn't deliver that bag! Larry, put yourself in his shoes. What if it happened to you? What if you tried to tell the police everything that had happened, but they wouldn't listen?"

Something about those words softened Larry's face. He looked up at Ben, his eyes lingering pensively on him. Tony kept scribbling.

Anne stepped forward, her eyes full of tears. "I'll go."

Everyone looked up. "What?" Lynda asked.

She cleared her throat. "Somebody has to go. I'll do it. I'll take the bag and leave it where he said, if Ben can't leave town. Maybe that would be okay. And we can stick something in the bag. Even if it's not the right thing—what he's looking for—maybe it would be enough time for the security cameras to get a picture of him as he takes it. Or maybe I could take a camera and get his picture somehow . . ."

Ben slammed his fist against the wall. "No way! This guy's a murderer! I'm not letting my wife do this."

Larry shook his head.

"I can get permission from the judge to let Ben go," Lynda said. "But to do that, I'll have to explain how the police force refuses to cooperate."

Larry looked up, rubbing his fingers down his face, leaving it red. "Forget it, Lynda. I'll go with him."

"You will?" she asked.

"Yeah. And there'd better be something to see." He looked wearily at Tony, who rolled his eyes as if he couldn't believe his partner had caved in. "Are you in, Tony?"

Tony blew out a breath heavy enough to puff his cheeks. "I guess so."

"All right," Lynda said, getting down to business. "Now, I want you two to start thinking like cops. Think you're up to that?"

Neither of them appreciated the question, and neither answered.

"What should he put inside the bag? How does the man intend to get it without being seen? And why would he want such a specific brand of garment bag?"

"It's obvious," Tony said with a sigh. "It's the most common garment bag sold. This alleged criminal is probably going to bring one just like it and make a quick exchange. If he doesn't, we'll know that our friend here was pulling our strings all along."

Ben disregarded that. "What should I put in it? He didn't give me a clue about what he's looking for. It could be anything."

"It's obviously something that would look natural in a garment bag," Lynda said. "Maybe you should just pad it with pillows or something. You're just going to have to wing it."

Ben sighed. "All right. He said to set it beside the window next to Gate C-23 just after the last flight from Atlanta lands at 10:30."

"You'd better mark the bag, so that you can prove that he took yours. And guys—" She turned back to the two cops, who looked less than enthusiastic. "At the airport, shouldn't you be watching for anyone who has a bag like this? Maybe searching them?"

"Lynda," Tony said impatiently, "if there's a guy waiting to make an exchange, the last thing we'd want to do is alert him to the fact that we're there. Besides, if we catch him before the exchange, there won't be any clues that he's the guy. We'll call Tampa PD and Airport Security and let them know what's going on, and make sure a security camera is taping in that spot. If he makes the exchange, we'll be there, and we'll see him." But he didn't sound as if he expected to see anything.

"You'll have to get him immediately after the exchange," Ben said. "Otherwise, he'll see that he's been had, and he'll retaliate."

"Retaliate how?" Larry asked grudgingly.

"I don't know," Ben said. "But frankly, I'm not real anxious to find out. He's messed my life up enough as it is."

As Ben and Anne drove back to Sharon's house, Anne was quiet, brooding, and he knew what she was thinking. She was blaming him for all of this, and he supposed she had every right to.

Christy and Emily were sound asleep when they got in, and Jenny was upstairs working on something in her room. Sharon was closed into her bedroom as if she'd had enough of them all.

Quietly, they made their way through the house and put Bobby down into the crib.

They went to their bedroom, but the tension in the room was too stiff for either of them to relax. It was like the tension before he'd left Sharon, when she'd known he was having an affair: so thick you could slice it open.

"Why don't you go on to bed?" he asked. "I'll wake you when I get home."

She shook her head and sat down on the bed with her feet beneath her, looking like a little girl. "I won't be able to sleep until I know what happened."

He sat and put his arms around her. "It's gonna be okay. Tonight we'll catch the guy who's doing this to us, and by tomorrow they'll drop all charges against me."

"Then can we move out of this place?" she asked.

"Yes. I'll get Lynda to get a court order to get my paintings out of the gallery, and I'll find another gallery to display them. We'll be back on our feet in no time, and we won't depend on anyone else."

She seemed to relax.

The doorbell rang. Ben kissed her gently and got up. "Time to go," he said.

She looked so pale and tired that he hated to leave her. "Good luck," she said. "And be careful. *Please* be careful."

"I promise." He hurried out into the hall and saw Sharon on her way to answer the door. She was wearing a long robe, and her feet were bare beneath it.

"It's for me," he said in a low voice. "Tony Danks and Larry Millsaps. We're going to make the delivery. Did you get the bag?"

"Yes," she said. "It's on the couch." She followed him to the living room and answered the door as Ben examined the garment bag.

"Hi," she said to the two men as she let them in.

Tony Danks smiled at her. "Did we get you up?"

"No," she said. "I was waiting to see what came of this. You guys have a long drive to Tampa. Are you gonna make it?"

"If we leave now," Larry said, checking his watch. "It's 9:00. We should be there by ten." They stepped into the living room and saw Ben stuffing the garment bag with some wadded paper grocery sacks.

"What are you doing?" Tony asked.

"Filling the bag up. It has to at least look like it's holding something."

The two cops just stood back, hands in pockets, looking as if they couldn't care less whether the bag looked convincing or not.

"I'll drive in my car, in case he's watching for me," Ben said. "You guys can follow me."

"You try to get on a plane, Ben, my boy, and we'll drag you off before it's even off the ground," Tony said. "Got it?"

Ben's face hardened, and he shot Sharon a look. "They don't believe me," he said. "They think this is all a hoax."

Sharon caught her breath. "Then why are you going?" she asked the cops.

"Just doing our jobs," Larry said.

She moaned. "I can promise you that it's not a hoax. Please—don't drop the ball on this."

Tony smiled reassuringly. "We'll do the right thing, Ms. Robinson. You don't have to worry."

She looked at him uneasily. "All right. I guess you'll just have to see for yourself."

Ben lifted the bag. "I marked the bag with this yellow thread on the shoulder strap, so that if we don't see him take it, we can catch him with it afterward. It shouldn't be noticeable."

"Good thinking," Larry said, obviously humoring him.

Trying not to let their obstinacy distract him, Ben headed out the door and got into his car.

The two cops started to follow, but Sharon grabbed Tony's arm and stopped him before they were out the door. He towered over her, but she looked up at him with determination in her eyes. "I'm his *ex*-wife. I haven't been a fan of his in six years. But I can promise you that he's not lying. Please take this seriously."

His blue eyes softened, and he smiled slightly as he patted her hand where it still held his arm. "Don't worry," he said.

She stood at the door and watched as both cars pulled away.

At the airport, they parked in the short-term parking area. After watching to see that Larry and Tony were behind him, Ben got out and took the garment bag from his backseat. Carrying it by the hook at the top and slung over his shoulder, he headed into the airport.

He paused at the flight schedule monitor and scanned it for the last flight coming in from Atlanta. It was ten minutes late, he saw, and coming in at Gate C-23.

Tony followed him up the stairs, then watched him stop at the security gate to lay his bag on the belt. As it made its way through the X-ray, he glanced around.

He grabbed the bag when it reached the end, headed to the C terminal, and counted off the gates.

Tony slowed his step as Ben reached the gate where a couple of dozen people milled around, waiting for the plane from Atlanta to arrive. Ben went to the window where the caller had told him to leave the bag, and keeping it hanging over his shoulder, looked out into the night for the plane.

Tony could see no sign of it yet. In the window, he saw the reflections of people behind Ben. No one looked suspicious. No one carried a bag like Ben's. Milling by, Tony went into the terminal, looking like anyone else about to catch a flight. His eyes scanned the faces there: those of women walking by with strollers, couples holding hands, tired, rumpled businessmen waiting to catch their flights home. Was one of them really a killer, or was this all some grand hoax?

He spotted lights to the north as a plane began to land. It touched down, slowed, and turned. As it taxied toward their terminal, he heard the announcement that Flight 438 from Atlanta had landed.

He could see Ben's hands trembling as he set the garment bag, doubled over, down beside the window. He looked around, then crossed the corridor and headed for the men's room. Neither Tony nor Larry followed. Tony ambled closer to the bag to peer out the window, waiting for something to happen. He knew Larry kept his eye on Ben as he came back out of the rest room.

The ramp door opened and passengers began filing off. A crowd quickly formed in the hall outside the gate, blocking Tony's view of the garment bag.

Concerned that the bag may have been switched while view was blocked, he pushed through the crowd and headed back toward the security gate, looking for anyone who carried a bag like Ben's with a yellow thread tied to the shoulder strap. He saw several similar bags, but none with the yellow thread.

He looked back up the corridor, wondering if Larry had seen anything. Slowly, the crowd by gate C-23 began to thin out, and he saw the bag still lying there, the yellow string still tied to it.

He saw Larry on the other side of the gate, still looking casual in his windbreaker and jeans. The perfect time to switch the bags would have been when the crowd was crushing in. The fact that it hadn't happened might mean that something was wrong.

Frustrated, Tony started toward the men's room, caught Ben's eye, and nodded for him to follow. Tony didn't acknowledge him as he came in. He went into a stall, pulled a notepad out of his pocket, and wrote, *No one's made the switch yet. Go home and we'll keep watch. There's another cop parked beside you in the garage. He'll follow you home. Don't try anything stupid.*

He shoved the paper into his pocket.

Ben was washing his hands when Tony took the sink next to him. He reached into his pocket, pulled out the note, and set it on Ben's sink without looking at him. Then he dried his hands as Ben read it, watching as the artist closed his eyes in frustration.

Tony found a seat next to Larry at one of the nearby gates, in perfect view of the garment bag, which lay there by itself, waiting for anyone to pick it up. It would probably be taken, all right, Tony thought, but not by the killer.

He watched as Ben came out of the rest room and trudged back down the corridor toward the main terminal.

Sharon was asleep on the couch in the living room when Ben got home. The door woke her, and she sat up. "What happened?"

"Nothing," he said. "He didn't come. At least, not while I was there. Have you heard from Larry and Tony?"

"They weren't with you?"

He shook his head and dropped into a chair. "I left them there. They had another cop follow me home. They could still be waiting, for all I know. If this guy doesn't show, they'll be convinced that I made it all up. They're pretty much convinced, already."

"Did they jeopardize anything?"

He rubbed his face. "No. Actually, they did a pretty good job. No one would have known they were cops or that they were with me." He dropped his hands and shook his head as he leaned it back on the chair. "I just can't figure out what happened."

The phone rang, and they both jumped. "I'll get it," Ben said, snatching up the extension on the table next to him.

"Hello?" His face reddened as he listened to the response, and Sharon got up and stepped toward him.

"I took the bag like you said," he insisted. "I put it exactly where you told me."

She held her breath, certain he was talking to the killer. Ben sighed heavily. "Okay, so I faked it. But you have to believe me. I have no idea what you're looking for, or I would have given it to you. There's nothing I know of that's worth a murder rap."

Sharon covered her face with her hands. The killer knew he'd been set up. Now what were they going to do?

Ben's breath was coming faster. "What do you mean, something worse?" He paused, and his face drained of color. "If you'd just tell me, straight out, what you want, I know I could get it. Why won't you just say it? Just tell me, and—" He looked up at her, his eyes dismal. "He hung up."

Sharon's eyes were as defeated as his as she watched him hang up. "What did he say?"

Ben closed his eyes. "He could tell when he saw the bag that it wasn't what he wanted. I folded it over when I laid it down, and that clued him. It must be bigger. Longer. I don't know.

Maybe it's a painting. But which one? There's nothing of mine that's valuable enough for murder. Even the pieces I was restoring weren't that important. And there were some reproductions in the gallery, but who would kill over a reproduction?" In frustration, he threw a pillow across the room. "I just don't know what he wants!"

She tried to sort it all out, but she was too tired. "Well, there's no point in hashing this out right now. I'd go to bed if I were you. There's nothing more you can do tonight."

"You go ahead," he said. "I'll call the police station and report this call. At least they can pull Larry and Tony out of there. No use having them stay there any longer for nothing." He blew out another frustrated breath. "If only I'd had time to hook up a recorder before that call. The cops still don't believe the first call ever came, and they're sure not willing to use their own resources to prove it."

Wearily, Sharon got up and padded to the doorway, then turned back. "Anne said to wake her up when you got home. She wanted to hear."

He nodded. "I'm glad she slept. It's been a while. I think I'll just let her keep sleeping."

"Whatever." She paused awkwardly for a moment, then finally whispered, "Good night."

"Good night," he said, then picked up the phone and started to dial.

16

THE CRYING BABY woke Sharon in the middle of the night, and she lay in her bed staring at the ceiling and waiting for someone to quiet him. The crying went on for fifteen minutes, and finally she got up and pulled on her robe. Someone was going to have to attend to him. His parents were so tired that they might not wake up.

Quietly, she padded up the hall toward the room where she had put his crib, stepped in—and jumped when she saw Anne rocking the screaming baby in a rocking chair.

"Oh! I didn't know you were up."

Anne shot her a contemptuous look. "You thought I was just letting my baby scream?"

Sharon sighed. She really wasn't in the mood for this. "I'll just go back to bed, then."

"I'm sorry he woke you up," Anne said. "He's sick. He's got a fever."

Sharon hesitated at the door, then turned back and bent over the baby. She touched his forehead; he was burning up. "Do you need a thermometer?"

"Yes," Anne said quietly. "If you have one."

Sharon went to the kitchen and found the thermometer, the pediatric Tylenol syrup, and an infant measuring spoon. She brought the thermometer to Anne and watched as she stuck the digital thermometer under the baby's arm. "Can you give him this?"

"What is it?"

"Tylenol," she said.

"It might help." Anne took it, and under her breath, added, "Thank you."

Sharon stood there a moment, waiting to see what the temperature was. The little thermometer beeped, and Anne took it out from under his arm. "A hundred one," she said.

"He's pretty congested," Sharon said, "so he may have an ear infection. Mine used to get them all the time."

"I've already thought of that," Anne said wearily. "I just don't know what I can do about it."

"Well, do you want to take him to the doctor?"

"I can't afford it," she said through clenched teeth, shifting the baby to hush him. "We have no money. Don't you understand?"

Sharon felt slapped down again. "Look, I'll be happy to pay the doctor bill."

"I don't want any more favors from you."

"Your child is sick!" Sharon blurted. "Besides that, no one in the house can get any sleep until he's well. Will you please take him to the doctor and let me pay the bill?"

Tears came to Anne's eyes as she stared off into the darkness. "All right," she said. "I guess I have no choice. I'll take him in the morning."

Sharon stormed back to her room and flopped onto the bed, her blood boiling. What had she done to deserve this woman's wrath? After all, it was Anne who had broken up their family, who had come between Sharon and her husband. How dare she come in here and act like Sharon was her enemy? And while Sharon was trying to help her, for pete's sake.

She tried to pray but the words wouldn't come, and as the baby continued to cry late into the night, she lay sleepless and exhausted, desperate to figure out a solution to this problem that seemed to have no end.

17

THE POLICE STATION was less chaotic than last time, Sharon thought. She stood just inside the door scanning the desks for Larry or Tony. Dark circles ringed her eyes, and she felt as though she had been beaten during the night.

As she spotted Tony slumped over his computer, looking just as tired as she felt, she resolved to do something about that situation right now. She headed for his desk, but he didn't look up from his computer as she approached. He had the weary, distracted look, yet his face reminded her of a younger version of Robert Redford.

Since the first time she'd met him, she'd been wary of him, for his good looks were like a big, red warning sign to be careful. Ben had been too handsome for his own good, too, before he'd grown his hair so long and cultivated that bohemian, too-creative-to-care image. Good-looking men needed constant affirmation and consistent hero worship—if they didn't get it, they strayed, and told themselves they were right to do so.

But Tony didn't look as if he'd spent a lot of time in front of the mirror this morning. He had shaven, but his hair looked more rumpled than usual. His eyes were bloodshot, and she suspected he'd gotten about as much sleep as she had.

She cleared her throat to get his attention, but still, he didn't look up. She stepped closer and tried again.

"Excuse me," she said. He looked up unappreciatively, but when he saw her, his face changed instantly.

"Mrs. Robinson," he said, standing up and reaching to shake her hand.

"Sharon," she corrected. "I do still use Robinson, but I dropped the 'Mrs.' six years ago. I was hoping you'd be in this morning. I was a little doubtful, since it's Saturday and you worked so late last night."

He gestured for her to sit down and sat back in his own chair. "Yeah, nothing like wasted time."

She sat down and leaned forward, trying to keep her voice low enough that others wouldn't overhear, but loud enough that he could hear her over the din in the station. "That's why I wanted to talk to you. I was worried that what happened last night might have led you to believe that . . ." Her voice trailed off, and she struggled to find the right words.

"That Ben might have been leading us on a wild-goose chase to get himself out from under the glass?"

She shrugged. "Something like that. I was afraid that you'd come back here and stop investigating—just write the murder off to an angry employee, and quit looking for the real murderer."

He leaned his elbows on his desk and took a deep breath. "Sharon, you're very loyal. That's admirable. But has it ever occurred to you that your ex-husband may really have done this?"

"No," she said with certainty. "Not for a second. It goes completely against everything I know about him. And I've known him for twenty years. Two before we were married, twelve years during, and six after."

He clasped his hands in front of his face and studied her as she spoke. When he didn't answer, she leaned back hard in her chair. "Why would I be so intent on proving him innocent if I didn't believe that?"

"Because you're the mother of his children," Tony said. "Most mothers don't want their children growing up with the stigma of having a father in prison."

"Oh, for heaven's sake," she said, leaning forward again. "It goes completely against his character, in every way. He's a make-love-not-war kind of guy. If you knew him like I did, you'd know how absurd this all is."

"I've seen his temper, Sharon. He's even admitted to losing it with Dubose." Tony's gaze didn't leave her face as he asked, "When he cheated on you, did you feel you knew him then?"

She sat slowly back and held Tony's gaze. "How do you know that's what happened?"

He nodded toward his computer screen, and she saw Ben's name in a block at the top. He had been looking into his background.

"When I count back from the birth of his next child, I don't have to be a genius to see that wife number two was pregnant already when the divorce papers were filed."

Sharon was getting angry. Was he making *her* out to be a liar now? "So you know what led to my divorce. I don't see your point."

"Point is, you don't always know people as well as you think you do."

"Okay. And?"

"And, if he lied and cheated once, maybe he could do it again. Maybe he *could* have had some motive strong enough to make him want to kill his boss. Maybe it was anger, or maybe it was something else."

"Why would he do it?" she asked him. "He'd lose his job, his home, his credit cards, his income—why would he do something so stupid?"

"He'd already lost those earlier that day." He turned back to his computer and scrolled down. "I've been looking over his history here, Sharon. He looks like a man who doesn't do a lot of planning. His financial state is a good indication that he flies by the seat of his pants. He doesn't always think things out."

"All right," she conceded. "He's definitely guilty of that. But that doesn't happen to be against the law."

"No, but it could be a clue that the man isn't always going to be predictable. That maybe sometimes he could act in a fit of passion. Artistic temperament can be very bizarre sometimes. Remember van Gogh?"

"Van Gogh was insane," she said. "Ben is not. He's a little irresponsible, a little self-absorbed, a little scatterbrained, but he is not insane. And he's not a killer. How could I let him and his family move into my house if I thought for a second that he was?"

"Instead of proving the probability of his innocence, Sharon, that could just prove the probability of your state of denial."

"Denial?" She got to her feet and leaned over his desk, putting her face close to his. "You think I'd take in the man who cheated on me and the woman who wrecked my marriage and the children she rubs in my face—all because I was in denial? Trust me, Tony, there's no denial here. Neither Ben nor Anne are my favorite people, and frankly, my first instinct is to let them sink or swim. Last night was close to the worst night of my life. This woman hates my guts for existing, and instead of being grateful that I put a roof over her head, she's spitting nails and acting like I've locked her in there by force. If I were in denial, Tony, there might be a lot more harmony around my house right now. But my only thought is to get them out of there as soon as humanly possible. The only way I see to do that is to help Ben prove his innocence. And it looks like I'm going to have to depend a lot on you to do that."

Her eyes seared into his, and he sat motionless as she unloaded.

"Now you can take the easy way out and stamp this case solved, or you can consider some other probabilities. For starters, the probability that I am an intelligent woman who wouldn't be in the position I'm in unless I had complete faith in Ben Robinson's innocence. If for no other reason than that, you should at least keep looking. Consider the probability that someone really did call him last night. That I wasn't hearing things when the phone rang. That someone threatened him and told him to make a delivery at the airport. That he doesn't have a clue what they want. Could you do that, Detective? Could you just consider it? Just in case you really don't have all this figured out, and there's some killer still out there who's laughing his head off at the St. Clair police for falling so easily for this frame-up?"

Tony took a deep breath and rubbed his eyes, then leaned back and crossed his arms over his chest. "For your information, that's why I came in today, even though it's my day off and I didn't get much sleep last night. I've already started working on locating other people who may have had vendettas against Dubose. We've been in touch with some of his other colleagues, some of his friends, some of the art dealers who frequented the gallery. We're looking for other motives, Sharon. That hasn't stopped just because Ben has been charged. But that doesn't mean that I'm optimistic about finding anything. Ben is the most obvious suspect. Those phone calls—frankly, Sharon, they prove nothing. So he has an accomplice. I'd have guessed that anyway. Probably a woman, based on his history. Sharon, everything points to Ben."

"Yeah, like a neon sign. Like big red arrows. What kind of fool would leave that much evidence behind? It's so obvious that it was a setup. And now this maniac is calling my house, making threats, and I'm afraid of what might happen next!"

"But you're not frightened of Ben?"

"No!" she said too loudly, then realized others were looking her way. Trying to calm herself, she lowered back into her chair. "How many times do I have to tell you? He can't even spank his children. He barely raised his voice to me in twelve years of marriage."

"That is some feat, considering your temper," he said with a half-grin. "Did you ever get in his face like you did in mine just now?"

She lowered her face into her hands and gently massaged her tired eyes. "Look, I'm sorry. I'm a little on edge. This may be just another case to you, but it's altering my whole life. It's serious."

He softened then and looked down at his hands. "I realize that. I didn't mean to make it seem like I was taking it lightly. I'm really not. I'm working hard on this case because I don't want to make any mistakes. Whatever you may think about the St. Clair PD, we're very thorough. Ask Lynda. She knows firsthand."

"Well, you can ask Lynda about Ben, too. We've been friends a long time, and she's heard it all." She was getting very tired, and she felt that her body showed it. She studied him for a moment. "Have you ever been married, Tony?"

He shook his head and grinned slightly. "Can't say I've had the pressure."

She lifted her eyebrows at the play on words. "Then it's no wonder that you can't understand how sure I can be that Ben is innocent."

Tony stared at her quietly for a moment. "I guess you're right. I can't understand it. But I'll respect it. And I'll keep it in mind. Fair enough?"

She nodded and got to her feet again. "It's fair as long as you find the killer. Do you think whoever did this will come after Ben? Or that he's a threat to any of us in the house?"

Tony shook his head. "Sharon, *if* Ben was set up, then he's the last one the murderer would want to touch. He wouldn't want to give himself away. And he sure wouldn't want to do away with his scapegoat."

She considered that. "I guess you're right." She reached out to shake his hand again. "I appreciate your time, Detective."

"Anytime," he said, getting to his feet and holding her hand a little longer than necessary. "In fact, if you ever feel like you need to escape the pressure for a while, just give me a call and we'll go get a cup of coffee or something."

She smiled. "I will."

"And if you think of anything else I need to know, don't hesitate to call."

"All right. Thanks."

She said good-bye and headed back across the precinct, feeling a little better than she had when she'd come in. She wasn't sure whether the visit had been merely therapeutic, or actually helpful. She got to the door and waited as several people came in, then looked quickly back over her shoulder.

Tony was still watching her.

Her heart jolted, and she told herself that she'd have to take him up on that cup of coffee soon. As she hurried out the door and back to her car, she had the gentle beginning of a smile on her face.

18

BEN UNLOCKED THE door with Jenny's key, and opened it for the girls. They had gone to the art store to buy supplies for their mural on the tree house, which Ben was determined to paint in spite of the mess he was in. The children were chattering nonstop as they bounced into the house. Then suddenly they fell silent.

Over their heads, Ben saw the open pantry, the cans that had fallen on the floor, the cabinet doors. The two little girls gasped. "What happened?"

Jenny grabbed his arm. "Dad, somebody's been in here."

Ben motioned for her to stay back and went into the den. The cushions were on the floor, and books had been pulled off the shelves. He saw that the girls had not obeyed his silent order, and had followed close behind him. He hurried into the living room, and they stood gaping at the scattered cushions and the open closet, its contents spilled out onto the floor.

"Dad, who could have done this?"

"Get the girls and go next door," he said quickly. "Then call the police. Wait there until I come for you."

"Why?" Jenny asked. "Do you think whoever did this is still here?"

"I don't know," he said. "Just do it."

She grabbed the girls' hands. "Come on, kids. We have to go."

"But who made this mess?" Christy asked. "Mommy's gonna die."

"I don't know. Just come on."

"What about Daddy?"

Jenny didn't answer as she pulled them out the door.

The police were there in ten minutes, and while Ben followed them around the house, making sure that no one was hidden there, Larry and Tony came in.

Ben looked at them with resignation as they came up the stairs.

"What's going on now?" Tony asked wearily.

"Somebody broke in," Ben said. "We were all gone, and this is what we came back to."

"Anything missing?" Larry asked, looking into the rooms he passed.

"Nothing that I can see. Sharon would know better, though. She's showing some houses this morning."

"I saw her earlier," Tony said. "She didn't mention where she was heading."

Ben raked a hand through his hair. "I think they may have been looking for something."

"Looking for what?" Tony asked skeptically.

"I don't know. Whatever I was supposed to have delivered last night, probably."

"Oh. Right." Tony blew out a heavy breath. "Ben, was there anyone with you when you discovered this?"

Ben looked insulted, but not surprised. "Yes. My kids."

"Where are they? I want to talk to them."

"They're next door. I sent them over there as soon as we saw all this. I was afraid whoever it was was still in the house."

"All right," Tony said. "Larry, I'm going over there to talk to them. You can handle it from here."

Larry nodded. "No sweat."

Tony trotted back down the stairs. Just as he reached the kitchen door, it flew open, and Sharon burst in. "I saw the police cars!" she said in a panic. "What's going on?"

"Everyone's fine," he said to calm her. "We got a burglary call. According to your ex-husband, someone broke into your house."

She looked around at the contents of the pantry on the floor, the cabinet doors—through the arched doors, she saw the mess in the den. "I'd say he's right. Is anything missing?"

"Televisions, computers, stereos are all still here. You might check your jewelry, and anything else you had that was valuable."

"Where are the kids?" she asked quickly.

"Next door. Ben sent them over when they got home."

"Good," she said, turning and rushing back for the door. "I want to go make sure they're all right."

"I'll come with you," he said. "I need to ask them some questions."

Christy watched out the window of her elderly neighbor's living room, fascinated with the police cars in her driveway and in front of her house. She saw her mother's car, which had not been there before, and she jumped up and down and yelled to her sisters. "Mommy's home! Can I go tell her what happened?"

Jenny came into the room, accompanied by Mrs. Milton, the retired schoolteacher who had gotten the girls a plate of cookies to distract them. "No, Christy. You stay here until Mom or Dad tells us to come home."

"But why? We're missing all the excitement."

Jenny pulled back the curtain and looked out the window. "I know, but—I can't believe all this. Somebody's really out to get Daddy."

"Mommy's coming!" Christy said as she saw her mother hurrying across the lawn with the cop who'd arrested her father trailing behind her. She jumped up and ran to the front door to fling it open. "Mommy, somebody robbed our house!"

Sharon bent down and hugged her younger child. "I know, honey. But it's okay." She looked up at Jenny, then at Emily hunkering in the corner, looking a little frightened. "Are you all okay?"

"Sure, Mom. We're fine," Jenny said. "Is he still in there? Did he take my computer or my stereo?"

"I don't think so," Sharon said. She looked at the widow still holding the plate of cookies. "Thanks for taking them in, Grace. I appreciate it."

"No problem," the older woman said. "Come in and relax for a minute. You look so tired."

"It's been a tough couple of days," Sharon admitted. "Grace, girls, this is Detective Tony Danks from the St. Clair Police Department. He needs to ask you a few questions."

"Me, too, Mommy?" Christy asked hopefully.

"You, too," Tony said, sitting down so he'd be eye level with the child. "Tell me how you found out the house had been broken into."

Christy's eyebrows shot up with excitement. "We came back from the art store, and there was stuff all over the place. Mommy, it's a mess!"

"I know, honey. I saw it."

"How long were you gone?" Tony asked Jenny, and she sat down across from him, much more serious than Christy.

"About an hour, I guess," she answered. "Daddy is going to help the girls paint a mural on Christy's tree house, and we went to get some art supplies. Most of his paints are still at the studio."

"All right," Tony said, pulling out the pad he kept in his pocket and making a note. "Jenny, Christy, Emily, I want you guys to think real hard when I ask you this question. When you left, who was the first one in the car?"

"I was!" Christy shouted, shooting her hand in the air.

Emily raised her hand, too. "No, it was me. We tied!"

"If we tied, then how could you be there first?" Christy asked. "I was first."

"No, I was."

"Okay, so you both got out there first," Tony said, chuckling. "Who was next?"

"I was," Jenny said, frowning. "Why?"

"So your dad was the last one out of the house?"

"Yes," Jenny said. "He locked up."

"How long was he in there before he got to the car?"

She looked disturbed at the question, and looked questioningly up at her mother. Sharon shrugged and nodded for her to answer. "Well, I don't know. A few minutes. He said he couldn't find his wallet."

"Did he find it?"

"Yes, and he came on out."

"I see." He made a note of that, then glanced up at Sharon. She was getting that look on her face that said he had a lot of nerve, but he pressed on. "Now, you went to the art store, and bought supplies, right? Did you stop anywhere else?"

"No," Christy volunteered. "We went right there and right back."

"All right. Who was the first one back in the house?"

"We all went at the same time," Jenny said. "The girls went in first, then Dad and I were right behind them."

"And which rooms did you see?"

Jenny looked confused. "Well, uh . . . I saw the kitchen, and the den, and then I went into the living room. That's when Dad sent us over here."

"So you didn't see the rest of the house?"

"No."

"Did any of you?"

"No," Jenny said. "Dad wanted us out in case he was still there."

Sharon was getting impatient. "What are you getting at, Detective?"

"I'm just asking questions," he said. "Now, your dad's wife. Emily's mom. Where is she?"

"She took Bobby to the doctor," Jenny said. "He's sick."

"And how long has she been gone?"

"Hours," Jenny said. "They had to work her in, because she didn't have an appointment."

He made another note, then looked up at Mrs. Milton. "Grace, did you see any cars over there earlier? Anybody who didn't belong there?"

"No, I'm afraid not," the woman said. "I didn't know anything was wrong until the girls came running over."

"Okay. We'll question some of the other neighbors to see if anyone saw anything."

"Good," Sharon said.

He got up and held out a hand for Christy, and she shook proudly. "Thanks for your help," he said.

"Sure. Can we go home now?"

"Stay here until the police get finished. Sharon, can I speak to you outside?"

"All right." She thanked Mrs. Milton again, then followed him out into the yard. "What is it?"

He saw Larry on his way across the yard to speak to him.

"Sharon, in light of our conversation this morning, I know you're not going to like what I have to say," Tony said as Larry approached.

"Oh, no. You're not going to blow this off like it didn't happen, are you? You're not going to ignore this! This is *my house!*"

"I'm not convinced anything happened," he said. "Ben was the last one to leave the house. He hung around in there long enough to have pulled the cushions off, opened some doors, upset some shelves. Jenny only saw the front rooms when she came back. Between the time they got home and the time the police showed up, he had plenty of time to go through the rest of the house, making it look like someone had been there. There was no sign of forced entry, no one has seen anyone who didn't belong here—"

"You haven't questioned everyone yet! You don't know!"

"And it doesn't look like anything was taken," Larry added. "It doesn't look like a robbery."

"You people are nuts. Why would Ben do this?"

"The same reason he staged that little drama last night. To throw us off. Make us think we've got the wrong guy. He's desperate, Sharon, and frankly, I'm beginning to wonder if it isn't dangerous having him in the house at all."

"So what are you saying?" she asked, keeping her voice low so her neighbors and kids wouldn't hear. "That I should send him back to jail? Just because you refuse to believe that someone actually could have broken into my house to look for whatever it is he thinks Ben has?"

"It just looks too suspicious, Sharon."

"And it may not have been Ben who did it," Larry conceded. "It could have been his wife, trying to help him out."

"No way," Sharon said. "There's a killer out there, and he's framed Ben, and he's called and threatened him, and now he's broken into my house, and you aren't going to do one thing about catching him, are you?"

"Sharon . . ."

"I had more respect for you when I left the station this morning, Tony. I thought you might really have a conscience, that you'd do a good job no matter what it cost you. That you were a good cop. But I was wrong."

He looked as if he'd been slapped across the face. "Sharon, I'm doing my job."

"No, you're not! You're passing the buck because you're too lazy to consider any other possibilities."

"We are considering them, Sharon," Larry said. "We just have to tell you what our gut instinct is. It's not unusual for someone accused of a crime to try to throw us off the track. We have to tell you if we think the man living in your house is putting your family in danger."

"We're in danger, all right," she bit out. "But I obviously can't turn to St. Clair's finest for help. The danger isn't coming from my ex-husband, detectives. It's coming from your apathy!"

She turned and fled into the house, leaving them both standing in the driveway. Tony stood there for a moment, watching her go. Finally, he turned and started walking away from the house.

"Where are you going?" Larry asked.

"To question the neighbors," he said irritably. "Might as well get started. We have a lot of ground to cover."

The police were finishing their report and clearing out as Sharon came back into the house. She found Ben sitting alone at the dining-room table, his hands covering his face.

"What was he looking for, Ben?" she asked, leaning in the doorway, suddenly feeling too weak to stand straight. "What does he want?"

"If I knew . . ." He rubbed his eyes and looked up at her. "Do you at least believe he was here? That I didn't do this?"

"Of course I do. I wish it *had* been you. I wouldn't be so scared."

"I ought to just let them take me back to jail."

"Right," Sharon said. "That should solve everything."

"Well, look at your house. He ransacked it."

She shook her head. "Actually, it doesn't look so bad. We can put it all back together. It just feels so creepy, knowing he was here."

He rubbed his temples, trying to think. "I was just going back over everything with the cops. In the second phone call, he said it was too long to fold the garment bag. That's how he knew it wasn't what he wanted. It's got to be a painting . . . something really valuable . . . maybe rolled up. I've been trying to think of all the things I was working on in the studio. There were a couple of things Dubose bought recently that I was restoring. They had some value, but not this much."

"Maybe if you could get back into the gallery and look around, you could find it."

"If that's where it is, why didn't he find it when he killed Dubose?" He looked up at her with helpless eyes. "Sharon, I know how this looks."

She heard a car pulling into the garage, and glanced out the window. "Anne's home."

"I don't know how much more she can take," he said.

Sharon knew the feeling, but she didn't voice it. "Guess I'll get busy putting Humpty Dumpty back together again."

He got up wearily. "I'll help. We'll all help."

Sharon left the room before she had to confront Anne again.

19

THE TELEPHONE IN Eric Boudreaux's elegant hotel room rang, and he picked it up quickly.

"Yes?" he said in his French-accented voice.

"Mr. Boudreaux! How are you?"

Boudreaux was quiet for a long moment. "Impatient. As a matter of fact, I was just planning to ring the airport and book a flight back tomorrow. That is, unless you have something for me."

"I, uh . . . I need another day or two. Please. I'm trying to be very careful so as not to call too much attention to us. One can't be cavalier about an exchange of this sort."

"You do not have it, do you, Monsieur Lieber?"

A pause. "Of course I have it. And you want it. Dubose showed you the snapshot of it, didn't he?"

"He did. But I have yet to touch the picture."

"You'll touch it, my friend," the voice said with a chuckle. "Very, very soon. Don't return home just yet. I want you to have it, but if you return home, I'll have to offer it to another buyer."

"This was not in the agreement," Boudreaux said. "I was to stay for two days, then return with the picture."

"No one counted on Dubose's untimely death."

"No, you are right," the Frenchman said. "And I must tell you that I am growing quite suspicious, myself. I don't relish the idea of being a—how you say—accomplice to murder."

"I had nothing to do with his death. Nothing at all. It was an unfortunate coincidence that it happened the very week you were to meet with him."

"But if his death was motivated by greed because of this picture," Boudreaux said, "I would hesitate to do business with anyone involved. My reputation is flawless, and I intend to keep it that way. My crimes have always been harmless."

"And they will continue to be, sir. Trust me."

"Then when will you deliver?" Boudreaux asked.

"Soon."

"Tomorrow," he insisted. "If I do not hear from you tomorrow, I will leave."

There was a sigh. "You'll hear from me. Please, wait until you do. I anticipate having the painting by tonight. You will have it immediately after that."

"If I do not, you will have to bring it to me in LeMans," Boudreaux said. "Smuggling it through customs will be your problem, not mine."

"I'll be in touch tomorrow, Mr. Boudreaux. You won't be sorry you waited."

"I sincerely hope not," Boudreaux said, and hung up the phone.

20

SHARON TOOK THE easy way out and ordered pizzas that night, so that they wouldn't have to subject themselves to a sit-down dinner all together. She worked into the night putting things back where they belonged. When they were finished, everyone went to their bedrooms early, and Sharon went up to tuck in Christy and Emily.

"I'm glad Bobby's better," Christy said as her mother covered her with the Laura Ashley comforter. "He had a bad ear infection."

"And an earache, too," Emily added.

Sharon smiled. "Well, he should sleep better tonight."

"Mommy, are you scared?"

Sharon's smile faltered. "Why do you ask that?"

"Because that man was in our house. What if he comes back?"

"He won't," Sharon said. "Everything's locked up tight, and we're all home now. He won't come while we're home."

"Are you sure?"

"Positive," she lied. "Emily, are you comfortable? I could get you a softer pillow if you need it."

"I like this one," Emily said, snuggling up next to Christy. "I wish I could live here all the time."

Sharon smiled in spite of herself. She took a deep breath and asked, "How about if we say prayers together?"

"Okay," Christy said, "but you lie down between us."

Sharon crawled between them on the bed and got under the covers. She put her arm around Christy, and Emily snuggled up to her as well, expecting the same affection. Sharon grinned and slid her arm around her. The children didn't understand the politics of their family, she thought. And that was good.

She prayed aloud for their father, and for the man who was out there causing so much trouble, and for Bobby's ears and his cold, and for the safety of everyone in their home. When she finished, she lay there a moment, holding both girls.

"Tell us a story, Mommy," Christy said. "Please."

"I'll tell you part of one," Sharon said. "And then you tell me part."

Christy giggled. "Okay. You start."

Sharon sighed and thought for a moment. "Once upon a time, there was a little girl named . . ."

"Named Beth," Christy said. "Can that be her name, Mommy?"

"Okay, Beth. And she lived in a beautiful little cottage with flowers all around."

"And it had this cool climbing tree in the front yard, didn't it, Mommy?"

"That's right."

"No, that's wrong!" Christy changed her mind and sat up in bed. "The cottage was *in* the tree!"

"Okay," Sharon said. "And Emily, what color do you think the flowers were?"

"Purple!" Emily cried.

"That's right," Sharon said. "How did you know?"

Emily shrugged and giggled.

"But one day, something terrible happened."

"What, Mommy?" Christy asked, her eyes growing big. "Did somebody break into her house and rob her?"

Sharon thought for a moment. "No. One day, she went ice-skating on the pond near her house, because she didn't live in Florida, she lived in . . ."

"Alaska!" Christy provided.

"That's right. And she went ice skating, and while she was gone, some mean man came and . . ."

"Picked all her flowers!" Christy said. "And he sold them at the flea market, because they had fleas!"

They all laughed and lay back down, and Sharon went on with the story.

Anne climbed the stairs and walked up the hall to say good night to Emily. As she neared the door, she could hear laughter. It was good to hear Emily giggle again, she thought, and she paused and listened. Then she heard Sharon's voice, embroidering a story that had them both enthralled.

She went to the door and looked in. Sharon lay between the two girls on the big canopy bed, an arm around each of them, giggling right along with them.

Anne stepped back, suddenly jealous again. Not only were they beholden to Sharon because of their dependence on her for shelter and money, but she feared that Emily was getting too attached to this home and this family. She was losing Ben, she was losing Emily, and she'd already lost control of her life . . .

Slowly, she went back down the stairs to Bobby's room. He was sleeping soundly now that he'd been given the medication he needed. She sat down in the rocking chair in the darkened room, trying to figure out where to turn with the anxious, dangerous emotions holding her in their vicious grip.

21

THE PHONE RANG once, and as usual, Jenny quickly answered it. After a moment, she yelled down the stairs, "Daddy! It's for you!"

Ben took the call in the study, hoping it was Lynda. "Hello?"

"Ben, it's good to hear your voice."

"Nelson?" he asked.

"Yes. I'm still in London. I had hoped to get home to attend Louis's funeral, but there was too much fog on the ground, so the planes weren't taking off."

"How did you know where I was?"

"When I had the money wired to the courthouse, the secretary there told me you had moved in with your ex. I have to admit it was a little surprising. If I'd known you really didn't have a place to live, I could have offered you the use of my house."

"Yeah, well, I appreciate it, but it's a done deal now. We have to stay until this whole thing is cleared up. Listen, thanks for the bond money. I promise you'll get it back. I'll be acquitted."

"Of course you will. Have they got any leads?"

"I seem to be the only one. Despite the fact that this guy even broke in here today."

"Broke in? Are you serious?"

"The police don't seem to think so. They think I did it."

Nelson paused a moment, as if thinking. "Look, the moment I arrive, I'll go straight to the police and vouch for you, for what it's worth. This is ludicrous. Ben, do you think Louis was involved in something we don't know about?"

"Who knows?" Ben asked dejectedly. "When do you think you'll be here, anyway?"

"Probably in the next couple of days, if the weather clears. Have you thought about what you're going to do for money?"

"Yeah, a lot," Ben said. "I didn't get my last paycheck, and my paintings are all still locked in the gallery."

"Well, I've picked up a few things here that need some restoration work. Do you feel like doing them?"

"Of course," he said. "I need the work."

"Fine. Well, just cross your fingers that I'll arrive there soon. It's all going to work out, Ben. You'll see."

22

HOME WAS A word that Tony only had a passing acquaintance with, especially these days when he spent so much time working. As he came in now, he shrugged wearily out of his sport coat and unfastened his shoulder holster. Dropping it on the counter, he carried the sport coat through the immaculate living room and into the bedroom. He hadn't slept much in the last few days, but the bed was made, anyway. Everything was in its place, perfectly in order. Normally, he found some degree of comfort in the small house he had built for himself, once he realized that he would probably never be married.

He walked across the white carpet and into the walk-in closet, where he hung his coat. Then, stepping out of his shoes, he padded back into the living room. Slumping down into his favorite chair, he pulled up his feet and stared at the vaulted ceiling.

It had been a horrendous, grueling afternoon, grilling neighbors who had seen nothing but wanted to waste his and Larry's time talking, trying to find out what was going on in the interesting and complex family that occupied the Robinson house. He'd learned more details than he'd ever intended to gather today—that Sharon Robinson rarely dated, that she was very successful on the real-estate scene, that her children were the best behaved on the street. He'd heard stories of how she'd helped elderly neighbors during the power outage last summer when the temperatures had soared to over 100 degrees. One single mother had shared how Sharon had kept her kids for an entire week while their mother was hospitalized for a ruptured appendix, then took care of her for a couple of weeks more until she had recovered.

She was too good for her own good, some of the neighbors agreed. And they all lamented the fact that she had been bamboozled into taking in her no-account ex this way, especially when everyone knew he'd killed that Dubose fellow. He suspected there would have been neighborhood complaints about his even being in the neighborhood, if it weren't for their great respect for Sharon herself.

But it wasn't those conversations that kept playing through his mind, but the one he'd last had with her. She'd said his apathy was dangerous. He worried that her generosity was.

He glanced at the phone and thought of calling her, just to let her know that he had taken it all seriously, that he had interviewed neighbors and had spent much of the early evening running down a list of people found in Dubose's Rolodex, matching them with his desk diary, and trying to determine who they needed to talk to next. But none of that mattered, he thought. He had done all that work mostly to humor Sharon. In his mind, Ben was the murderer, and all the work he did would only prove that. He just couldn't understand why it was so hard for her to see.

Maybe it was because she'd been married to the guy, he thought. She couldn't admit that she had been blind all those years. That he was ruthless and cold-blooded. That she'd had children with a man who could kill.

No one liked facing up to facts like that.

But he worried about her, and about the undying loyalty and unwavering faith that could get her into trouble. He wondered if she'd cooled down, or if, in the dark quiet of her night, she was wondering if, just maybe, Tony could be right. If Ben might have done all this, after all.

His eyes strayed to the telephone, and he started to pick it up. Then he thought better of it. He didn't need to entertain these lingering thoughts about Sharon Robinson. She had too many problems. He needed to do his job and stay away from her. Wasn't that what he'd told Larry so many times? His cardinal rule—not getting personally involved in his cases—had always stuck, even when his partner disregarded it.

But he wasn't sure why he couldn't shake her from his mind. He could pick up the phone right now and call any number of women to have dinner with him and go have a drink at the Steppin' Out across town. Or he could just show up there, and meet new ones. It was his common MO for Saturday night.

Tonight, however, his heart just wasn't in it. And he wasn't interested in meeting any other women. Tonight, only Sharon Robinson occupied his thoughts.

He tried to rationalize. He told himself that this case wasn't about her. She was only involved by virtue of her former marriage to the defendant. If he called her, it wouldn't be a conflict of interest, would it?

He looked at the phone again, and finally picked it up. Quickly, he dialed information, asked for her number, then punched it out. He waited as it rang once, twice . . .

"Hello?"

It was her older daughter's voice, and he cleared his throat and said, "May I speak to Sharon, please?"

"Yes, just a moment."

She was polite, he thought, just as the neighbors had said. He waited for a moment, then heard another extension being picked up, as the first one cut off.

"Hello?"

"Sharon? It's Tony."

"Yes?" she said coldly, obviously still perturbed at him.

He smiled. "I just wanted to see how you're doing."

"Fine, thank you."

He could see that this wasn't going to be easy, so he softened his voice and gave a stab at being contrite. "Look, I'm really sorry I made you mad today. But I spent the rest of the day interviewing neighbors. None of them saw anything, so now I'm working on friends and colleagues of Dubose who might have had a vendetta against him."

She let that sink in for a moment, then asked, "What about the fingerprints?"

"They all belonged to those of you living in the house. No one new."

She was quiet again. "Well, at least you're trying. I appreciate that."

His smile returned, then faded again. "Are you sure you're okay?"

He imagined her sinking into a chair, letting down her guard. "Yeah, I'm okay. Just tired. I don't know how well I'll sleep tonight. Tony?"

"Yeah?"

"I'm sorry about all the things I said to you today. I was under a lot of stress, but I had no right to lash out at you like that. You were just doing your job."

"You didn't think I was doing it well. You have the right to that opinion."

"Yeah, but I didn't have the right to beat you up with it. I'm sorry."

He couldn't believe he had called her to apologize, and had wound up getting one from her.

"You work really hard, don't you?" she asked. "Day and night, weekends . . ."

"It depends on what I'm working on. It's not usually so bad."

"But you and Larry are the only two detectives in the whole force, aren't you?"

"That's right," he said.

"Then you get all the junk. How do you ever have any time to yourself?"

He smiled. "I take time. I could say the same thing about you. From talking to your neighbors, I'd say that between being the best real-estate agent in town and the best neighbor on your block, not to mention the best mother and the best ex-wife, I can't imagine how you ever get time to yourself."

She laughed softly, a sound that lightened his heart.

"For instance, what were you doing when I called? I'll bet you were cleaning up the mess from the break-in."

"Wrong," she said. "I finished that earlier."

"What then?"

He could hear the smile in her voice. "If you must know, I was under the fig tree."

"Under the fig tree?" he asked. "Is that a fig tree in your backyard?"

She laughed louder now, and he couldn't help grinning. "No. That's an oak. 'Under the fig tree' is just an expression."

He let his feet down and sat up. "What does it mean?"

"Have you ever read the Bible, Tony?"

He frowned. "No. I can't say I have."

She didn't seem surprised. "Well, there's a passage in the first chapter of John, where Jesus is calling his first few disciples. He finds Philip and tells him, 'Follow me,' and then Philip goes and tells Nathaniel that he's found the Messiah. Nathaniel doesn't believe him, so Philip tells him to just come and see. Nathaniel goes with Philip to meet Jesus, and when Jesus sees him, he says, 'Here is a true Israelite, in whom there is nothing false.' And Nathaniel asks him how he knew him."

"Yeah?" Tony asked, a little surprised that a Bible story could hold his interest for this long.

"Jesus says, 'I saw you while you were still under the fig tree before Philip called you.'"

"So? He saw him under a tree. What's the big deal?"

"In those days, 'under the fig tree' meant 'seeking God.' When a man wanted to pray, often the coolest place was under a fig tree, so he'd go there to be alone and to pray. It became a common expression. Instead of saying you were praying and seeking God, you'd say you were 'under the fig tree.'"

"Oh," Tony said. "So you meant that you were praying?" The thought made him a little uncomfortable. As long as they were talking about some story in the Bible that had nothing to do with him, he was fine. But he hated it when these spiritual subjects cropped into his own comfort zone.

"Right," she said. "So you see? I do get some time to myself now and then. Sometimes I just have to take it."

"But I didn't mean praying time. I meant time that's good for you. Recreation. Something that's not an obligation, but a pleasure."

"I don't pray to fulfill an obligation, Tony. And it's pure pleasure. Even when I'm on my knees begging him for answers."

"Yeah, I know," he said, though he didn't have a clue. "But I just mean . . . well, you know, people like you . . . like us . . . they're prone to burnout. It's a big danger, you know. You have to take time out. Do things for yourself. Go to a movie. Out to dinner. Whatever."

He didn't know why he was getting so tongue-tied and nervous. He asked women out all the time, and he was smooth. Very smooth. Tonight he felt like an awkward kid asking the homecoming queen for a date.

"Well, yes," she agreed. "Those things are nice. If you have someone to do them with."

"Well, of course. I mean, not by yourself. Maybe with someone. Like me." He grinned then and winced, covering his face and kicking himself for sounding like a jerk. He leaned forward, holding the phone close to his ear. "Sharon, I'm trying to ask you for a date, but I'm doing an incredibly poor job of it."

There was a stunned silence for a moment. Finally, she said, "Well, yes. I mean, if it's okay. Not a conflict of interest or anything. I mean, you are working on Ben's case."

"It should be okay," he said.

She drew in a deep breath and let it out quickly. "Well, okay. When?"

"Well, we could wait until the case is over . . . but that could be a while. And frankly, I don't want to wait that long. How about tomorrow?"

"Tomorrow's Sunday," she said. "I go to church twice on Sundays. But you're welcome to join me."

He had walked into that one, he thought, but he could walk right back out. "Church and I don't really get along," he said. "How about after church tomorrow night? What time do you get home?"

"About seven-thirty," she said. "I guess dinner would be all right."

"Are you sure?"

"Yeah, why not?"

He smiled. "Okay. Great. I'll make reservations someplace nice. And I'll call you tomorrow afternoon and let you know what time."

"All right," she said. "I'll look forward to it."

Again, he felt like that awkward kid as he leaned back in his chair and mouthed "yes!" to the ceiling. Then trying to temper his voice, he said, "Well, I'll talk to you tomorrow then. Good night, Sharon."

"Good night."

He hung onto the phone as she hung up, then dropped it into its cradle and stared back at the ceiling again. What had he done?

He was going out with a woman who was tied up in a case he was working on, and she was a Christian, and she had kids, and she had her ex-husband who was quite possibly a killer living with her . . .

Great going, Tony, he thought. *You know how to pick 'em. The more complicated, the better. Like you don't have enough problems already.*

But it didn't matter to him as he sprang out of his chair, fully renewed, and headed for the kitchen to find something to eat.

Across town, Sharon smiled and stared at the telephone for a long moment. She had consented to going out with the cop who was trying to prove Ben's guilt. She had consented to going out with a guy who had never read word one of the Bible, a guy who was obviously uncomfortable talking about spiritual things, a guy who would never darken the doors of a church unless a crime had been committed there.

Was she crazy?

Probably, but it had been so long since she'd been attracted to any of the men who had asked her out. Maybe just one date wouldn't hurt. She could use the distraction—and the boost—after all the tension around here.

And there was no shortage of baby-sitters.

The truth was, she looked forward to it, but that anticipation only scared her. Tony was certain that Ben was a killer. Tony, who saw criminals every day, heard all their excuses, their alibis, their lies. Could it be that he saw something in Ben that she couldn't see?

She got up and pulled on her robe and padded up the dark hallway. What was Ben doing now? Where was he?

She saw a light on in her study, and went to the door. Standing back, she listened. Was he in there?

Slowly, she peered around the doorway.

Ben was there, reclining back in her leather chair, his feet propped on her desk. On his chest slept Bobby, his breathing much better now that he'd been medicated. Memories flooded through her of the same man lying on an orange bean bag with newborn Jenny on his chest. She had a snapshot of it somewhere. Could that same man have turned into a killer?

Confused by her disturbing thoughts, she turned and headed back to her room. She turned the light out and curled up on her bed. Wondering whether she'd done the right thing by agreeing to go out with the detective, she went back under the fig tree again.

23

IT DIDN'T FEEL like Sunday. To Jenny, the fact that her dad and Anne didn't care to go to church depressed her. It had felt weird, getting ready and trying not to wake them, and then there had been all the wailing when Emily had wanted to go with Christy, but her mother had awakened and tried to talk her out of it. Sharon had finally shamed Ben and Anne into letting the child go, and they had angrily gotten her dressed. The truth was, Jenny hadn't been so keen on going herself, since everyone there knew that her father had been arrested for murder. It was embarrassing, humiliating. But she needed their prayers, she thought, and she supposed that the gossip she would have to endure was worth it.

She had felt bad for her mother when she'd had to come home from church and cook a huge meal that would feed seven, since neither Ben nor Anne had shown enough initiative to start lunch before they'd gotten home. Then she had helped her mother clean up, since Anne stayed in the same room with Sharon as little as possible.

When Anne had asked Jenny to go to the store to get some more formula and diapers for Bobby, Jenny had welcomed the opportunity to get out of the tense house. She had volunteered to take Emily and Christy with her, hoping to give her mother a little reprieve from all her responsibility. Since she was going anyway, Sharon had given her a list of other things they needed.

Now, as she pulled into the parking lot of the Kroger and saw how crowded it was, Jenny almost regretted agreeing to come. She cut off the car and looked into the backseat at the two blonde girls seat-belted in and holding hands. "Now, girls, I have a list," she said. "Don't beg me for candy and stuff. It'll drive me crazy."

Christy looked crestfallen. "Not even gum? Not even Popsicles?"

"Not even Reeses?" Emily asked.

"No! Nothing! Now, come on."

In the store entryway, Jenny spotted a video game. Perfect. She pulled out some quarters and handed them to the girls. "Here. Stay and play the game for a while. When you finish, come find me."

"Will you get Popsicles?" Christy asked.

"And String Things? And Reeses?" Emily added.

"No junk. Mom said."

"That's not junk. Popsicles are not junk!"

"Okay, but just Popsicles."

"But I need String Things," Emily whined. "Mommy always puts String Things in my lunches for school. I need String Things for tomorrow."

"All right," Jenny gave in. "I'll get some. Just go play. Please!"

The two girls headed for the game. Breathing a sigh of relief, Jenny went into the store, determined to fill her mother's list as quickly as she could.

Emily was not as good at video games as Christy was, and she quickly "died." Because they had both spent their fifty cents, they began to look around for something else to do.

Spotting the bubble gum machines outside, they headed through the electric doors. Christy checked each slot to see if anyone had forgotten their candy, while Emily wound each handle to see if it would miraculously release some.

They had almost given up when a man came by and, chuckling, reached into his pocket for a quarter for each of them. "Here you go, girls. It's on me."

Christy looked up at the man who wore a straw Panama hat and dark glasses. "No, thanks, Mister. I'm not allowed to take things from strangers."

"I'm no stranger," he said with a kindly smile. "Not to Emily." He pulled his glasses off briefly and winked at the child.

Her eyes rounded. "You're Daddy's friend."

"You know my daddy?" Christy asked.

"I certainly do." The man smiled and put his glasses back on, then inserted the money into a machine, turned the knob, and caught the candy as it came out. Giving a piece to each of them, he nodded toward his car. "As a matter of fact, I have something in the car that your father needs. Would you girls mind coming with me to get it? You could take it to him." He squeezed Emily's nose. "I also have some jelly beans in the car. If you like them—"

"We do!" Emily cried. "Come on, Christy!"

The two girls bounced out behind him as he led them to his car.

Jenny pushed her loaded cart to the long line at the cash register. Thankful that her sisters had not hounded her while she was shopping, she glanced over at the play area. She didn't see them.

Sighing, she got out of line and went to the candy aisle, expecting to find them there. There were children admiring the colorful bags of treats for the Valentine season, but Christy and Emily weren't among them.

Frustrated, she decided to start at one end of the store and look down each aisle until she found them. She should have told them to stay where they were. And she should have known that they wouldn't.

She looked up every aisle in the huge store, to no avail. Again, she checked the play area, but they weren't there.

Then she remembered that Christy loved the candy machines, so she abandoned her cart and looked through the glass doors. No one was there.

She was beginning to get worried, but her anger at them overpowered it. She went to the manager's booth at the front of the store, and waited in line until it was her turn. "Could you please page my sisters over the intercom? They're somewhere in the store, but I can't find them."

They took down the little girls' names and sent out a page. When five minutes had passed with no answer, Jenny began to worry. Abandoning her cart, she went back to the first aisle; then her speed picked up as she turned a corner and ran into a stock boy, causing him to drop a box of cans. "I'm sorry!" she said, helping him pick them up. "Have you seen two little girls with blonde hair?"

"No," he said, annoyed. "I haven't."

She looked back at the front desk. The children still hadn't answered the page. Quickly, she ran back to the front. "Look," she said, breathless, "they've got to be here."

"I'll try again," the manager said. "Just hold on."

The page went out again, but there was still no answer. She headed outside, thinking they may have broken the cardinal rule of leaving the store, and she searched up and down the sidewalk for them. Beginning to get frantic, she ran out to her car and looked inside. They weren't there.

Where could they be?

Perspiring and breathless, she ran back inside and headed to the back of the store where the swinging doors led into the warehouse. She burst through and found two workers. "Have you seen two little blonde-haired girls? Five and six years old? One was wearing . . . a little red outfit with hearts on it, and the other was . . . Oh, I don't know what Emily was wearing!"

"No, they haven't been back here," one of them said.

By now her breath was coming in gasps, and she pushed out of the doors and ran up each aisle and down the next, calling out for them at the top of her voice. Store patrons were staring, and a few started to join her in the hunt.

Realizing the problem was serious, the manager got on the intercom. "If anyone has seen two little blonde girls, ages five and six, who answer to the names Emily and Christy, would you please come to the front desk?"

Jenny was in tears by the time she had searched the whole store a second time. Frantic, she made her way to the desk. A customer was standing there talking to the manager.

"Miss?" the manager said, now visibly shaken. "This woman says she saw the children getting into a car with someone. We've called the police."

"A car?" Jenny asked, breathing in a sob. "They couldn't have. They were with me. They know better than that!"

"One of the little girls had on a red tunic with hearts and some red leggings, and the other one was wearing something purple, I think," the woman said.

Jenny felt dizzy, and her heart sank. "That was them. Who were they with?"

"A man," the woman said. "He had on a straw hat and sunglasses. I think his hair was brown, but I'm not sure. He was maybe 5'9" or 5'10", average weight. They looked like they knew him and got into the car willingly. They were smiling and laughing, so I didn't think anything of it."

"They *couldn't* have!" She began to tremble, then asked, "Can I use your phone? I have to call my parents."

Her hand trembled as she tried to dial the number. The phone rang, and she closed her eyes. After a moment, her father answered. "Hello?"

"Daddy?" she said, trying to control her voice. "You didn't come and pick up Christy and Emily, did you?"

"What do you mean, did I pick them up?"

"Did you or Mom pick them up?" she shouted.

"No. No one's gone anywhere."

She sobbed again, and dropped her head on the counter. "Daddy, someone's taken them! They're gone!"

24

"WHERE ARE YOU taking us?" Christy asked tearfully as the man drove much too fast down Highway 19 leading out of St. Clair.

He didn't answer.

"He lied," Emily whispered. "He didn't have any jelly beans."

"We're gonna get in so much trouble," Christy whispered. "Jenny's gonna kill us. And Mommy will punish me for my whole life."

"Quiet back there," the man barked. "You're getting on my nerves."

They stopped talking, but continued to cry.

"Did you hear me? I told you to shut up!"

The girls put their arms around each other, trembling with fear and trying hard not to make noise.

He pulled off of the highway and turned onto a long dirt road.

"Maybe he's taking us home," Emily whispered.

"I don't think so."

"Then where is he taking us? What is he gonna do with us?"

"I don't know," Christy said. "Maybe he's not really mean. Maybe he just likes little girls."

"He doesn't act like he likes us," Emily whispered. "Maybe he's gonna hurt us."

They clung to each other as he turned down a dirt road and took them far into a patch of woods. Finally, they came to a small structure that looked like a toolshed. The car stopped.

The back door opened, and the man reached for Christy's arm. "Come on. Get out."

She slid across the seat and got out, then with a burst of adrenaline, kicked the man with all her might. "Run, Emily!"

Emily took off running, but the man grabbed Christy around the waist and bolted after the other child. He caught her before she could get far, and grabbing a fistful of hair to guide her, he pointed them toward the shack.

"See that?" he asked through his teeth. "That's where we're going."

Christy's crying grew louder, and Emily screamed and struggled to make him let go of her hair. He dragged them, writhing and trying to break free, to the door of the shed, opened it, and threw them in. They each hit the dirt floor, and Christy bumped her head on the edge of a shelf. She screamed out, but the man only slammed the door behind them.

Christy curled into a ball, holding her cut head as warm blood seeped around her fingers.

They heard him locking the door, and then going back to his car. The car door slammed, the motor roared to life, and he drove off.

Emily was sobbing and groping around, trying to find Christy. "Christy, where are you?"

"Here," she cried.

Emily's hand reached out to touch her, and they clung to each other. "I want Daddy," Emily cried.

"Me too," Christy sobbed. Blood dripped into her eyes, burning them, and she wiped it on her sleeve. On her hands and knees, she groped until she found the wall, then the door. Emily followed close behind her, her little fist clutching the back of her shirt. Christy slid her hand up the door until she found the doorknob. She jiggled it, but it had been locked from the outside.

She tried to stand up, but Emily cried, "Don't leave me! I can't see!"

"I'm right here. I'm just standing up."

Emily stood with her, still clinging to her. She pushed on the door as hard as she could, then rammed her small shoulder against the wood, like she'd seen people do on TV. It was no use.

She kicked it with all her might, then began to bang on it. "Help, somebody! Let us out!" she screamed, pounding it with her fists. Emily joined her, pounding and screaming at the top of her lungs.

"Let us out! Help! Let us *out!*"

But they could hear the car driving away on the long, gravel road.

As he drove away, Nelson Chamberlain smiled with satisfaction. Ben was probably squirming by now and preparing to make the exchange. Nelson had just provided Ben with an irresistible incentive.

He'd definitely gotten lucky. He had expected to have to take the teenager, too, which would have made the whole situation much more difficult to manage. But when she'd left the girls to fend for themselves, he'd had the perfect opportunity.

His smile faded, as he realized how deep he had gotten. Normally, he didn't like to get his hands dirty. It had been unpleasant enough working with the thug who'd had the fake IDs and credit cards made for him—one set under Ben Robinson's name so he could purchase the gun, and another set under the name of John Lieber. The murder had been even more distasteful. He had been lucky enough to find the money clip with Ben's initials; Ben had left it behind in the medicine cabinet of the gallery's apartment—along with a hairbrush, which had provided the strands of Ben's hair that Nelson had planted in Dubose's hands. Yes, all of this had been distasteful, but he'd had no choice.

He had come this far and didn't intend to stop now. Too much was invested. Too much was at stake. It wasn't easy maintaining the lifestyle he loved. A few bad investments had seriously depleted his funds. The financial injection he'd get from this transaction was essential. Things had to work out before his creditors and generous friends abroad realized he wasn't what they thought he was.

The hundred thousand dollars he'd donated for Ben's bond money had been well worth it. Ben couldn't deliver anything if he was behind bars. It would have been useful to frame Ben for Dubose's murder—that had been his original plan, and a good one. But now there was something he needed more than a fall guy, and only Ben knew where it was. This kidnapping, of course, would transfer suspicion away from Ben, even for the murder. But it couldn't be helped. Nelson was desperate to make the delivery to Boudreaux quickly. Besides, everyone thought he was still out of the country, so even if they did look earnestly for another culprit, they would never suspect him.

If things went the way he expected, he should have what he wanted and truly be out of the country, and out from under any chance of suspicion, before the sun came up tomorrow.

25

THE SOUND OF Sharon's wailing when she heard the news cut through the walls of her house and could be heard all over the neighborhood. She ran out to her car and screeched out of the driveway. Ben, Anne, and Bobby were right behind her in the station wagon.

They were at the grocery store parking lot in record time, and saw the fleet of police cars with their blue lights flashing. Sharon pulled her car up to where she saw Larry and Tony with Jenny, slammed it into park, and jumped out. Ben's car screeched to a halt behind her.

"Jenny, where are they?" she shouted. "Weren't you watching them?"

Jenny was sobbing, and Tony set his arm around the teen to steady her as she looked up at her mother. "I'm so sorry, Mom. I lost them. I let them play at the video game, and the next thing I knew they were gone!"

"What are you doing to find them?" she asked Tony. "They're so little. They must be scared to death. You've got to find them!" Her voice was rising in pitch with each word, and Larry tried to calm her. Ben was standing behind her now, and Larry faced them both.

"We have an eyewitness who saw a brown-haired man with a straw hat and sunglasses, average weight, 5'9" or 5'10". Does that sound familiar to you?"

Sharon looked helpless. "It sounds like a hundred people I know."

"We also have a description of the car. It was a blue Taurus, a rental car, but our witness didn't notice the agency. We also have an all points bulletin out on it. We've got cars at checkpoints all over St. Clair, and we've notified the state police to watch for him if he leaves town with them. But right now we need your help. I know you're upset, but we need to keep our heads clear so that we can move as fast as we can."

"What do you need?" Ben asked.

"We need pictures so we can distribute them all over the area. And we need to set up some phone lines in your house so that we can trace any ransom call you might get."

"He said he would take something of mine," Ben said. "He threatened me, the night he realized I didn't deliver what he wanted."

Furiously, Sharon stood up to face Ben. "It's him, isn't it? He took our children!" She shoved Ben back against another police car. "Give him what he wants, Ben!" she shouted. "Give him what he wants so I can get my baby back!"

"I . . . don't . . . know . . . what he wants," Ben said through his teeth. "If I knew, I'd take it in two seconds flat. I have *two* kidnapped children, Sharon. Don't you think I would do whatever I could to—"

"Stop it!" Anne commanded as she stepped between them. "We don't have time for this. We have to find them!"

Sharon swung around to Tony and grabbed the lapels of his sport coat. "If you'd listened when Ben told you! If you'd looked for the killer instead of pinning it on him—this maniac wouldn't have my child!"

She saw that television crews were beginning to gather, and one camera was aimed at her. Shaking her head, she pushed through the crowd and back to her car. "I'm going after them. I'll find them!"

Tony stopped her. "Sharon, you can't! We have people looking for them, but we need your help here."

"All right!" she screamed, shaking his hands off of her. "Tell me what to do! But don't make me just sit here while he gets farther away with the girls!"

Hours later, as it began to grow dark, there was still no word. Two cops stayed at their house, waiting for the ransom call, while Larry and Tony beat the streets trying to find any leads on who could have the children. This case took precedence over every other. There hadn't been a kidnapping in St. Clair in almost twenty years, and that one had been a parental abduction. Now the whole town of St. Clair was searching for the children. Posters were hung on every pole, every wall, every window. Church friends came to the house in a steady stream, bringing food—the only thing they knew to do—and leaving with stacks of posters with the faces of the two children.

Jenny had been sedated, and slept in her room. Bobby also slept peacefully now that he'd been medicated and was on his way to recovery. But Anne, Sharon, and Ben paced the living room waiting frantically for the phone to ring.

It was nearing dark when Tony and Larry returned to the house. Their expressions were grave, and Sharon began to feel nauseous at the thought of what they might say.

"Sharon, Anne, Ben—would you all please sit down?"

"You found them," Anne said, her face turning white with fear.

"No, no," Tony said quickly. "We haven't found any trace of them. Not yet. But we need to ask you a few questions."

"Sure," Sharon said. "Anything. What?"

Larry looked uncomfortably at Tony. "We need to know every place any of you went today, starting with the time you got up until right after the abductions."

"Oh, here it comes," Ben said. "I should have anticipated it."

Puzzled, Sharon and Anne looked at him.

"Don't you see?" he asked. "It's the parallel investigation. While they're looking for the guy who took our kids, they start to consider that we might have done it ourselves."

"What?" Anne asked, astounded.

Sharon got to her feet. "Why would we do that?"

"We're not saying you did, Sharon," Tony said. "It's a matter of protocol. Really. Just routine. For our reports."

"Now I remember," Sharon said. "A couple of years ago, that kidnapping in Virginia or somewhere. They discovered that the mother had killed them. But you don't think . . ."

"Sharon, we're not accusing anyone," Tony said. "We just have to ask a few questions."

"It's me, Sharon," Ben said. "Since I'm an alleged murderer and a pathological liar, I had to have done this, right? Another ploy to throw them off my scent!" He swung an arm and knocked a vase off the table, sending it crashing to the floor. He turned and stormed out of the room.

"Where are you going?" Larry asked loudly.

"To call my lawyer," Ben said. "I'm not saying another word until she's here."

Sharon and Anne gaped at the two detectives as Ben rushed out. "He didn't do this!" Sharon shouted. "He's their father! He was here with us the whole time! You had a witness who saw them get into the car with a man! You need to expend your energy trying to find that man, instead of wasting your time on this!"

Tony sat down, looking weary.

"Sharon, we have to ask the questions," Larry said. "You need to help us by answering them. We haven't stopped the investigation. It's still going on. But it's department policy that we cover every possibility. And with the extenuating circumstances—"

"I don't care about extenuating circumstances," Sharon cried. "This whole nightmare has been extenuating from the beginning!" She wiped her face and paced across the floor. "What about me? Am I suspect?"

"No one is suspect," Tony said.

"Why not? Maybe I had some stupid ulterior motive. Maybe I had some deep hatred against Emily, so I hired someone to kidnap both of them."

"I guess being the stepmother," Anne said, "I'm a prime suspect, too, huh?"

"We told you! We're not accusing anyone."

"You're accusing Ben!" Sharon shouted. "Admit it. You think he did it, and that would be just as absurd as either of us. They're both his kids!"

"They're just questions, Sharon! Just questions!" Tony shouted.

Ben came back into the room. "Lynda's on her way over. She said that none of us should say another word until she gets here."

"Fine," Larry said, sitting back in his chair and crossing his arms. "We'll wait."

Tony nodded. "Fair enough."

Seconds ticked by, as everyone found some spot in the room to focus on. Finally, Anne cried, "Why doesn't that phone ring?"

"He wants us to sweat," Ben said quietly.

"But what about the children? It's getting dark, and they'll be so afraid. Emily doesn't have her blankie or her little doll that she sleeps with. What if he doesn't feed them? What if they're hurt?"

"They can't be," Sharon whispered. "We just have to pray that they'll be all right. We just have to have faith."

But her faith seemed as flimsy as Anne's and Ben's as they waited for Lynda to arrive.

They waited, Tony and Larry sitting on the couch, Sharon leaning stiffly against the piano with her arms crossed, Ben pacing, and Anne in a chair watching out the window, as if the kidnapper would suddenly drive up and let the children out.

The doorbell rang. It was Lynda and Jake.

"What's going on, Tony?" Lynda asked. "Why are you badgering these people?"

"We're not badgering them, Lynda. We just want to ask some questions."

"All right," she said. "Everybody sit down."

They all took places around the room, except for Jake, who hung back in the doorway. "I'm gonna go hang some posters, guys," he said. "Lynda, are you sure you can get a ride home?"

"No problem," she said. "I think I'll be here for a while."

He touched Sharon's shoulder and squeezed hard. "Sharon, I'm praying for them. We're gonna find them. We've got hundreds of people out looking. You know that, don't you?"

Sharon touched his hand and squeezed back. "Yeah. I have more faith in you guys than I do in these so-called detectives."

Tony looked up at her, stung.

"At least somebody's doing something," she added.

Jake nodded soberly. "I'll see you later then," he said, heading out the door.

After the sound of his car died away, Lynda spoke up. "All right," she said to Larry and Tony, "ask anything you want. I know that my clients want to give you any answers that can help you find the children. But I'm not going to let you bully or badger them, and you're not going to get away with hanging this on them."

"So now they're *all* your clients?" Larry asked.

"That's right," she said defiantly.

Ben leaned forward, looking ragged and haunted. "Look, before you ask anything, can I just ask you something?"

Larry shrugged. "Go ahead."

"Think of the logic here, guys. If I really killed Dubose, why would I leave all the evidence—the gun registered to me, the money clip, the fingerprints. And it's even more illogical that I would add to that by doing something with my own children—" His voice broke off. "But think about it. If I'm being set up, and Dubose was killed because of whatever it is this maniac is looking for, then wouldn't it make sense that he'd kidnap my children to have leverage over me? He thinks I have whatever it is, so he wants to force me into handing it over."

"Sure, that would be logical," Larry said. "Logical enough for you to count on."

"What's that supposed to mean?" Lynda asked.

"It's the conspiracy theory," Sharon snapped. "Oswald didn't kill Kennedy—it was the Republicans. And this kidnapper didn't take our kids—Ben did, only he staged it so carefully that it would look like someone else did it. He was actually in two places at once, and he didn't look anything like himself, and it wasn't his car, but he was behind it, because the other way seems too blasted logical!"

Lynda touched Sharon's hand and gestured for her to be quiet.

"Just find my baby!" Sharon shouted, standing up and knocking over her chair. "Stop sitting here and find them before it's too late!"

26

THEIR EYES HAD adjusted to the dark. Above them, too far to reach, hung shelves cluttered with gardening tools. A bag of feed leaned against the corner, and a lawn mower was parked near the back. The whole space was no larger than Christy's walk-in closet at home, and the floor was made of dirt and getting colder the later it got.

"I'm hungry," Emily said, her voice hoarse from screaming.

Christy's head still throbbed, and the cut stung. Her bangs were bloody and matted to her forehead. "Me, too. But Daddy will come get us real soon. I know he will."

"What if he can't find us?"

"He will. He's real smart."

"But I want to go home *now,*" Emily whimpered.

"Me, too," Christy said.

They listened hard to the wind whistling around the corner of the building, and the raindrops pattering on the roof. Thunder cracked, and both girls screamed.

"It's just thunder," Christy said, trying to sound brave.

"I hate thunder," Emily cried.

"But it can't hurt us," Christy said, remembering what her mother had told her so many times. "We're safe in here."

Emily began to wail as thunder cracked again.

"We could pray," Christy tried.

"I don't know how."

Christy put her arm around Emily. "Just close your eyes," she whispered, "and I'll do it."

"What if God can't hear us through the thunder?"

"He will," Christy assured her. "Thunder is no big deal to God. He always hears children's prayers. Mommy told me so. Now bow your head."

"I don't want to."

"Just do it!" Christy shouted. "Bow your head now or I'll quit trying to make you feel better!"

"You're *not* making me feel better!" Emily cried. "You're making me feel worse."

"I'm the one with the hurt head!" Christy snapped. "And I'm not acting like some whiny little baby!" She started to cry even as the words came out of her mouth, and finally Emily reached over and hugged her.

"I'm sorry."

Christy sucked in a sob and wiped her eyes. "It's okay. Will you bow your stupid head now?"

Emily stuck her thumb in her mouth and bowed her head. They clung together as Christy started to pray.

"Dear God, we're really scared . . ."

The thunder and rain raged around them as Christy prayed, but before she even got to "Amen," Emily had drifted off to sleep.

Christy held her for a long time before she too finally surrendered to sleep.

27

THE STORM WAS getting more violent, as if the universe were conspiring against them. Sharon paced outside in her screened porch, while they continued questioning Ben inside. Desperately, she clutched Christy's Simba doll against her and railed mentally at God, bargaining with him, pleading with him to bring her child back. She was angry, she was frightened, she was confused.

When Tony stepped through the back door, she squelched the urge to throw something at him. "What do you want? I thought you were finished interrogating me."

"We are, for now," he said. "Sharon, are you all right?"

She breathed a despairing laugh. "Funny how things work out, isn't it? We were supposed to have had dinner tonight. Who knew that instead I'd be out of my mind with terror?"

"We'll find them. I know we will."

"Dead or alive?" she screamed at him. "Before or after it's too late?"

He looked down at his feet, and she clutched the Simba doll tighter. "I just want Christy back. I can't stand the thought of her being out there somewhere." She pressed her hands against the brick wall, staring out at the night. Lightning struck, brightening the night sky, then blackening it again. A sharp clap of thunder followed.

"That's it," she said, shoving past Tony into the house. He followed behind her as she grabbed her purse and started digging for her keys. "I'm going out there," she said through clenched teeth. "St. Clair isn't that big. I'll find them. I'll drive down the streets with my windows rolled down, and listen for their voices. I won't come back until I've gotten them."

She bolted through the kitchen and out the side door, Tony at her heels.

"You can't do this, Sharon," he argued.

"Yes, I can!" she screamed. "You can't stop me. I'm not under arrest! I can go anywhere I want to."

"You're not in any condition to drive, Sharon. And the weather's bad. If I have to, I *will* arrest you just to keep you from doing something stupid."

"But somebody has to look for the children!" she screamed. "We can't leave them out there. Do you know what it's like for a little girl in a storm? Even at home, she's terrified. She sleeps with a night-light on every night. And the hall light. And if it's damp and cold, she catches cold real easily. I've got to get to her . . ."

Feeling helpless, Tony reached for her. "You've got to leave it to the professionals, Sharon. Trust them."

"I *can't* trust them," she cried, shaking free of him. "I can't. Christy trusts me. I'm the only one. She knows I'm always there for her. I've never let her down. Never. When she's scared or tired or hungry or sick, I've always been there." Her voice broke. She was getting hoarse from crying, but she kept on. "I'll find them. I know I can. I know St. Clair better than anyone. I've sold property in every section of the town. I'll think of hiding places."

Tony glanced back toward the door. "All right, listen. I'll go with you. You're too upset to drive, so I'll drive and you can tell me where to go. Fair enough?"

She nodded and breathed another sob. "Yes, all right."

"Okay. Just let me tell Larry."

He went back to the door and saw Larry standing with Ben and Anne in the doorway. "Larry, I'm gonna take her for a ride just to make her feel better. She has a car phone, so give us a buzz if anything comes up."

Larry looked concerned. To keep Ben and Anne from overhearing, he stepped outside. "Are you sure this is a good idea? You're a cop, not a social worker. It's not your job to make her feel better."

"Larry, it's either ride with her or arrest her," Tony said in a low voice. "She's losing it, just sitting here like this. I can't blame her."

"I want to go, too," Anne said from behind Larry. "Take me with you."

Sharon heard, and swung around. "No! You and Ben have to stay here in case they call!"

"You can't go," Larry added. "I still have some questions. We aren't finished."

"But we've told you everything!" Anne cried.

"Look," Tony said, "if we find one child, we'll find both. Your husband needs you. So does your baby."

Larry coaxed Anne back into the house before she could protest further.

Feeling as if he'd been caught on the front lines of a major war, Tony hurried out to her car before Sharon could leave without him.

Sharon insisted on Tony's driving twenty miles per hour with both windows down. His left side was getting drenched as they went, and her car's interior was beginning to soak up the rain like a sponge. They had been all through the rural parts of St. Clair, up one street and down another, searching for places where a deranged kidnapper might have hidden two little girls. One time, she had been positive that an old, condemned house was where the children were, and he had been forced to follow her through the muddy yard and the pouring rain, up the broken steps of the porch, and into the rat-infested house. The children hadn't been there, though there was evidence that someone had been using it for a crack house, and he made a mental note to follow up on that later.

Now, after driving for two hours, he wondered how to broach the subject of going back to her house.

"We'll never find them, will we?" she asked.

"Not like this," he said.

She shivered as the cold rain soaked through her. "I should have dressed Christy warmer today. I should have made her wear a jacket."

"It was in the seventies earlier, Sharon. You couldn't have known."

"Yes, I could have," she said. "We knew there was a killer out there already turning our family upside-down. I should have realized the kids were in danger."

He didn't know what to say. It seemed that everything he attempted only made things worse.

"You try to teach them things, you know?" she railed. "Like, never talk to strangers. Look both ways before crossing the street. Eat your vegetables. Brush your teeth. But you never really think about teaching them how to survive in an emergency . . . how to get help . . . how to get home . . ."

Tony reached for her hand and squeezed it. It was as cold as ice. "Don't underestimate their instincts. Even children have good ones."

"But I've sheltered her so. I didn't want her to know that evil like this existed."

"You were supposed to shelter her. That's your job. Don't beat yourself up because you didn't prepare her to be kidnapped."

Quiet settled over them for a moment. Rainwater soaked her hair and trickled down her face as she gazed at him. "I almost lost it with Anne before we left. I just couldn't take any more."

"That's normal," Tony said. "And you have a lot of anger in you. For good reason. It's natural that you'd want to lash out at them."

"I thought I was different," she whispered.

He looked at her. "Different how?"

"Better," she said. "I thought I had all the biblical principles down, that I knew how to behave in any circumstance, that I could stand up to any tragedy, that trials would only make me stronger."

"And?"

"And I think I've just been fooling myself."

Tony frowned and moved his eyes back to the wet road. "You think those principles don't work, after all?"

She shook her head. "No, that's not it. I know they work. I think I've been fooling myself about what I was capable of. Christianity isn't about becoming a better actress. Hiding your feelings. *Doing* all the right things. It's about changing your heart. And I think mine has a long way to go."

Tony let those words sink in. They were foreign to him, for he couldn't fathom anyone being more self-sacrificing than this woman who had taken in her ex-husband and the woman he left her for. "You have a pretty good heart, from where I sit."

"I have a *petty* heart," she said. "Petty and angry and vindictive."

"Vindictive? How do you figure that?"

She began to cry again and shook her head with disgust. "Vindictive because I wish Emily had been taken alone. That it was just their child who'd been kidnapped. That mine was at home, safe and sound . . . because some part of me feels that they deserve that." She looked at Tony, her eyes glistening. "Isn't that terrible?"

He came to a red light and sat still for a moment, looking at her, wishing he could touch her and offer some comfort. But he knew better. He was a professional and had to maintain some detachment. Still, her tears reached straight into his heart, and he found himself doubting the logic of his own strict rules. "Sharon, there's not a mother out there who has a child kidnapped, who doesn't wish it was someone else's child. You're not horrible. And you're not vindictive. You're just distraught because something has happened to your child that you can't control. I don't have any kids, but if I did, and this happened, I'd probably have snapped and killed twenty people by now. I think you're a very special lady for analyzing your own heart at a time like this."

She dropped her forehead into her palm and wept quietly for a long moment. No other traffic was on the road as the storm raged around them, so he ignored the green light and watched her cry.

He reached across the seat and took her hand, almost tentatively. She accepted his touch, so he squeezed gently. "I want to find Christy for you," he whispered. "I'd kind of like the chance to get to know her. She's a pretty cool kid, from what I've seen. Any little girl with such a special mom is someone I'd like to make friends with."

She looked up then, and he saw the torment on her face and wished from the deepest places in his heart that he could take it from her and carry the burden for her.

"I'm gonna find her for you, Sharon."

She sucked in a sob and nodded as if she believed him. When he moved the car forward through the intersection, she leaned her head back on the wet seat. "Let's go home," she said. "Jenny might be awake by now. She's going to need me."

"Okay," he whispered. But he kept holding her hand as he drove her back to her house, where those who loved the two little girls still kept vigil through the night.

Back at Sharon's house, Ben, Anne, and Lynda still sat at the kitchen table with Larry, who had asked them a zillion questions a dozen times each. Ben had answered as patiently as he could, knowing how it looked to the police who had seen more bizarre cases than his, if not on their own turf, then in other precincts across the country. People did murder their bosses. Parents did sometimes do harm to their kids. He just didn't know how to convince them that he wasn't among them.

"All right, now, for a minute, let's assume that you're telling the truth, and that someone else killed Dubose, and wants something you have, and kidnapped your kids to force you into giving it to them. So let's go back over it all. Try to think of everyone who came into the studio to see Dubose the week leading to his death."

"I have," Ben said. "I've given you the names of everyone I could think of. None of them seemed angry at him or agitated in any way."

"Then can you think of a time in the days leading to his death when *he* was agitated or angry? Maybe after a phone call?"

Ben stared at the table, retracing the last few days. Dubose had been moody, quiet, and Ben had the feeling he was aggravated with him.

"There was something about his mood," he said, finally. "He was distant. Preoccupied. Like I had made him mad or something."

"Had you?"

"No. We usually got along real well. He was happy with my work . . . and was real generous to us. I thought he might have some personal problems."

"Then you hadn't had any blow-ups with him?"

"None."

"Wait," Anne said, her eyes widening. "There was a blow-up, Ben. Remember a few days before we were thrown out, when you found that hidden painting? You said he bit your head off about that."

Ben frowned. "Yeah, but it was so silly. I thought he was just in a bad mood."

Larry leaned forward and gazed intently at him. "Why didn't you mention this before?"

Ben threw up his hands. "I didn't think it was related. It happened days before the murder. And it was such a little thing. I had gone up to the attic looking for an old-fashioned frame for one of my paintings. I thought I might find something up there, since he stored a lot of stuff there. But I bumped my head on something, and a rolled-up canvas fell out. I unrolled it, and it looked just like the famous painting *The Multitude,* by the sixteenth-century Italian painter Marazzio. I got excited—I'd heard that that painting had been stolen several years ago. So I took it downstairs and stretched it out on a table. It looked so authentic, I could have sworn—"

"Was it the real thing?" Larry prompted.

"Well, no. Louis walked in and saw what I had, and he blew a fuse. Started yelling at me that the attic was off-limits. Which was pretty strange, because that just didn't seem like him. I apologized and told him to calm down, and I asked him if he knew that *The Multitude* had been hidden up there in a specially built compartment. Someone else owned the gallery before Louis, and I figured *they* might have hidden it there—although, when you think about it, they wouldn't have left it there. Anyway, he finally did calm down, and he looked at the painting, and quickly discovered some mistakes. They were tough to see, because the picture has a crowd of hundreds of people, supposedly at the Sermon on the Mount. But Louis said he was very familiar with all of Marazzio's work, and this wasn't real. He knew his stuff better than anyone I know, and he had a keen eye because he saw a lot of fakes that people tried to pass off as originals. Of course, he admitted his main clue that it was a fake was that the original had been recovered a couple of years ago."

"What did he do with it?"

"I don't know. I told him we should frame the picture, reproduction or not, and display it in the gallery, but he refused. He took the painting and rolled it back up, and I never saw it again."

Larry stared down at his notes now, thinking. "Why would anyone have hidden a reproduction?"

"I have no idea. It really didn't make sense, but I figure someone might have mistakenly thought it was the real thing. Who knows?"

Larry's eyes were riveted on Ben's when he asked, "Do you think there's any possibility that this Marazzio reproduction could be the painting our kidnapper wants?"

Ben frowned and considered that for a moment. "No. Why would anyone kill over a reproduction? It's practically worthless."

"What if Dubose lied, or was just wrong about that stolen painting being recovered?" Lynda asked. "What if it was the real thing? Do you think a real Marazzio could cause all this trouble?"

"A genuine Marazzio, particularly *The Multitude,* would be worth millions. Yeah, somebody might kill over it."

"But wouldn't they realize that when they sold it, they'd be sitting ducks with a murder and kidnapping attached to it?"

Ben shrugged. "It depends. The statute of limitations in Italy for stolen art is ten years. Paintings like that one disappear for a decade or more, then suddenly turn up at an auction one day, supposedly found by accident." He shook his head. "It doesn't matter, though. It was a reproduction. The real one was found a couple of years ago."

"Are you absolutely sure?" Lynda asked him.

"Yes. Louis knew his stuff. He traveled a lot, buying and selling important pieces of art, and he knew. For someone to go to all this trouble over a reproduction, they'd have to be fooled into thinking it was real. But I don't see that happening here. Anyone willing to pay what a real Marazzio is worth would check it out and find out that the real thing has been found."

"Then explain why Dubose fired you just a few days later, when you say it was completely out of his character. There must have been something else going on."

He turned his palms up and shook his head. "I don't know. I have no idea. Maybe the painting had nothing to do with it. Anyway, even if it did, I don't know where the reproduction is. I went back up there the next day to see it again, just out of curiosity, but it was gone. I don't know what he did with it."

Larry sighed. "We've got to find it. It might be what he wants."

"If I had it, and knew that was what he wanted, I'd have given it to him by now, and have my girls back in their own bed tonight."

Lynda touched Ben's hand, as if to offer some small bit of comfort, and looked beseechingly at Larry. "Larry, the man's been through enough. Leave him alone. Go look for the children."

Larry stared at them both over steepled fingers, then nodded reluctantly. "All right, Ben," he said. "That's all for now. But I may have more questions later."

28

A LIGHT RAIN pattered against the window as Lynda Barrett sat at the desk in the corner of her den, hunched over the books she had picked up from the library on her way home from Sharon's. There had to be something here. Something that might give her an idea about what to do next. She felt helpless. It had been bad enough trying to defend a man for murder when all the clues pointed to him, but the kidnapping gave it a terrible urgency. She felt sure that Ben wouldn't be a suspect much longer, since they had confirmed that he was home with Lynda and Anne when the kidnapping occurred.

Desperate to get to the bottom of this complex case, she flipped through pages and pages of art books, trying to learn more about Marazzio and the painting that Ben had discovered. If it wasn't the original, then it probably had nothing to do with the case at all. But if there was even a chance that it was, it might be the key both to clearing Ben of the murder charges and to finding the kidnapper.

Coming to a chapter on famous lost paintings, she scanned the pages for Marazzio. She found him listed halfway through and quickly began to read.

She heard a knock at the kitchen door, and before she could call "come in," the door opened. Jake, who had lived in her garage apartment since the plane crash that had changed his life, came in and peered around the doorway to the den. "Hi," he said. "I couldn't sleep and I saw your light on. Are you all right?"

She smiled up at him. He looked good, standing so tall without his cane, though he still had a slight limp. He was handsome—even more now than he'd been before the crash, because now she knew his true character. In her mind, his looks weren't marred by the scar that slashed one side of his face. That scar had special attraction for her, because it had special meaning. It was because of that scar that they had both bonded as human beings rather than adversaries. She cherished it now.

"I'm fine," she said, sitting back in her chair and holding out a hand to him. He came over to her and bent to kiss her. She reached up and touched that scar that felt so familiar beneath her fingertips.

"You sure? You were so shaken about the kidnapping."

"So were you."

"Yeah, well. That Christy's a character. I just hate the thought that . . ." His voice trailed off, and he slumped into a chair and looked at the floor.

"Yeah, me, too," she whispered. "I went to the library a while ago and got everything I could find on Marazzio—you know, the painter? I thought maybe that reproduction Ben found had something to do with all this. The police searched the gallery tonight and didn't find it. I can't help wondering—if it was just a worthless fake, where is it? Who took it?"

"Find anything?"

"No," she said, rubbing her eyes. "Well, a couple of things, but I don't know if they're important. I feel like I'm barking up the wrong tree with those kids out there somewhere. . . ." She dropped her forehead into her hand. "But then I tell myself that I have to leave the kidnapping to the police. My job is to help Ben. I have to somehow help him figure out who could be setting him up. *That* will tell us who the kidnapper is, and who the killer is."

"Not a very comforting thought, is it?" Jake asked. "That the kidnapper is the killer."

"No," she said. "It isn't."

"Well, I've been trying to think what I could do," he said. "And it came to me. As soon as it's daylight, I'm gonna head out to the airport, and Mike and I are gonna take one of the planes up and scan the landscape. See if we can spot the Taurus they were taken in. Who knows? Maybe it's parked somewhere and we can see it. It's a long shot, but it's something."

She smiled slightly. Flying was Jake's passion, but he'd lost his license after the crash due to his temporary paralysis and his blindness in one eye. He was waiting for the opportunity to get his medical release and try to get his license back, but until now, he hadn't been ready. "You gonna do the flying?" she asked.

"I might," he said. "Mike's a certified instructor. As long as he's with me, it's not a problem."

"It's been a long time. Are you sure you're ready?"

"I've never been more ready," he said. "Maybe I'll see something. You never know."

She thought about that as her smile sobered. "Even if you don't see the car, make a note of any hiding places on the outskirts of town. We could try them."

"There's not much to go on, is there?"

"No, there's not." She closed the book she was reading and stood up. "I just hope Larry and Tony will let up on the parents now that it's so obvious that they weren't involved."

"Sharon obviously couldn't have done anything like that. She's got a heart as soft as marshmallows. But what about Ben or Anne? Do you think they could have—"

"No," she said without question. "I think Ben was telling it straight from the beginning. He was framed. Somebody killed Dubose and left a trail that pointed to Ben."

"But why the kidnapping?"

"I don't know. There are still too many questions. It seems strange. If the killer wanted us to think Ben did it . . . then why would he kidnap Ben's kids? It would obviously indicate that someone else is the culprit, after all. The minute the police realize someone else is involved, Ben is out of the hot seat."

"Maybe the killer's desperate. Or maybe he's just sure he won't get caught. Maybe he's trying to manipulate Ben in some way. Needed the kids so he could work a deal."

"Yeah, but why? What does he want?"

"I'm with you. That reproduction keeps coming to mind."

Lynda looked back at the book she'd been flipping through. "But a reproduction isn't worth much. Certainly not all this."

They heard a car in the driveway, and Jake went to the kitchen and glanced out into the night. His mother sat there in the red Porsche that was once his—the toy he had cherished more than any other possession. It looked more ridiculous each time he saw her driving it. But he had given it to her free and clear. He had expected her to sell it and buy a condo or something. But she was having the time of her life driving it all over town.

"It's Mama," he said to Lynda over his shoulder. "She probably came to get some of the posters of the girls. She's working the late shift at the diner tonight and said she'd put some up and hand them out to her customers."

"Great."

Jake went to the door as his mother got out of the car, dressed in tight knit black pants, an over-frilly pink blouse, and four-inch heels. She had gotten her hair done, Lynda noted as Doris bopped in. Her roots weren't quite as black as they'd been the last time she'd seen her. Though the woman had been hard to swallow when she'd first come to St. Clair, Lynda was growing fond of her now. She was a lost soul, desperately trying to find herself. That it had taken the woman fifty-something years to do it was not her fault.

"Hey there, boys and girls!" Doris said, clicking into the kitchen and reaching up to pat her son's cheek. She took one look at Lynda and gasped. "Heavens to Betsy, girl, you look like something the cat dragged in."

Lynda's smile crashed. "I do?"

"You look like you haven't slept in a month of Sundays."

"Well, this kidnapping's got me really worried . . ."

"Of course it has!" Doris said in her Texas twang. "Those poor little sweet boys . . ."

"Girls, Mama," Jake said. "They're girls."

"Well, just imagine them out there with some awful person. It just makes my skin crawl. But honey, when this is all over, let me give you a make-over, won't you? If you're gonna keep my boy happy, you're gonna have to take better care of yourself. He's the type has to fight the ladies off with a stick, ain't you, Jake?"

Jake grinned and winked at Lynda. "No, Mama. Not really. And I think Lynda's beautiful. We're both tired, that's all."

"Well, we've got to get out there and find these kids," Doris said. "Now where are those posters you were gonna give me?"

He handed her a stack, and her face twisted as she looked at the sweet faces. "Bless their hearts. They're so little. Oh, maybe some of the truckers who come through the diner will know something. I'll give these out to everybody who comes in tonight."

"Good," Lynda said. "I've set up a television interview this morning for the parents. Maybe a personal plea from them will get people's attention."

"Television?" Doris asked, her hand immediately straying to the blonde mop piled on her head. "Why, you know, if you needed some help with that, I'll be off work at seven. I've had a little experience with this sort of thing. When my friend Spud McKinley ran for mayor of Slapout, I fixed his wife's makeup before they did their campaign ad. You remember Spud, don't you, Jake? The kid who used to shoplift cigarettes from the corner store? Lived in the trailer park across from us? Anyway, he didn't win, but his wife had the prettiest makeup job you've ever seen. If that mother looks anything like you do right now, she's gonna need a makeup job."

"That's okay, Doris," Lynda said with a smile. "We're not really concerned with makeup. Besides, there are two mothers. The children have the same father, but they're half-sisters."

"Is that so?" Doris asked, leaning back against the counter as if settling in for some juicy gossip. "Well, that's interesting. Are they all gonna go on TV together?"

"Probably."

"Hmmm. They'll probably sell that story to Hollywood and make one of them miniseries out of it."

Lynda didn't quite know how to respond to that. "Thanks for passing out the posters, Doris." She gave the woman a hug, and Jake followed his mother out the door. "You be careful now, Lynda. Messing around with murder ain't no picnic."

She smiled. "Jake's the one you should worry about. He's going to fly tomorrow for the first time since the crash."

"You're what?" Doris asked, spinning around to face Jake. "Son, are you out of your mind? After what happened to you, you would want to fly again? Lynda, you're not gonna let him do this, are you?"

Lynda laughed. "Since when have I had control over anything Jake did?"

"Honey, you've got more control than you know. You just don't use it right."

"Come on, Mama," Jake said, rolling his eyes. "I'll walk you to your car."

Lynda could hear Doris chastising Jake all the way out to her car.

29

IT WAS RAINING outside when the doorbell rang and Larry let Lynda in. Since most of the police force was looking for the girls, Larry and Tony had decided to stay at the home all night in hopes that a ransom call would come. Jenny still slept, sedated, upstairs, and Sharon paced the house, clutching Christy's Simba doll and praying. Anne stayed busy with Bobby, who was still fussy because of his cold, though the tormented, distracted expression she wore and the swelling of her eyes testified to the fact that Emily was never off her mind.

"I couldn't sleep, so I thought I might as well come on over," Lynda said as she followed Larry into the dining room of the house, where all of their tracing equipment was set up in anticipation of the phone call. "I've been doing a little homework, trying to find a motive. I got some books on Marazzio's work. I thought maybe the reproduction was a clue, somehow, and that if we could just get to the bottom of the motive, we might have some lead on who the killer and kidnapper are."

"Good. I was thinking about doing the same thing."

"Then you'll finally admit that Ben was set up?"

"I'm not admitting anything," he said wearily. "It's too soon. But while we're sitting here waiting with no leads, we can at least get a little culture."

Tony came into the room and said hello to Lynda, then picked up a Marazzio book and began flipping through. "This about that artist guy?"

"He's not just any artist," Lynda said. "According to what I've read, Marazzio's paintings have a high price tag."

"How high?"

"Millions. Three of his paintings have been stolen over the past fifteen years. Two have been recovered, and sold for millions. But this book must be outdated. At the time of its printing—three years ago—*The Multitude* still hadn't been found. The book said it was worth a whopping twenty million."

"Get outta here," Tony said. "You can't be serious."

"It's true."

Tony looked more seriously at the book in his hand, and flipped through, looking at the shots of his paintings. "Do you think the painting Ben found could have been the real thing?"

"It's possible," Lynda said. "Though I doubt it. Dubose was probably right. It probably has been recovered since this book was printed. Shouldn't be too hard to find out."

"This is ridiculous, anyway," Tony said. "People don't kill and kidnap over a picture slapped on canvas, do they? This has got to be about something else." He lowered his voice and said, "There's more here than Ben Robinson is telling. Mark my word."

"Maybe, maybe not," Larry said.

Sharon came to the doorway and looked in. It was clear that she had been crying, and she wore a fragile, haunted look. "Oh, Lynda, it's you. I thought maybe it was someone with news."

Lynda went around the table and hugged her friend. "We're working on it, Sharon."

Sharon looked down at the books on the table. "Marazzio?" She looked frustrated that they were wasting time on that. "You don't honestly think my child was kidnapped over that picture, do you?"

"No, I don't," Larry admitted. "But it's the only unusual thing that happened before Ben was fired and Dubose was killed. I don't know if there's a connection, but if there is, it might help us with the kidnapping, too."

"Instead of reading books and waiting for the phone to ring, you should be out combing the county for the girls. It's storming outside, and the whole night has passed without a phone call!" Her voice broke off, and she covered her face. "What if this maniac has hurt them?"

Tony got up and urged her to sit. Pulling his chair up close beside her, he said, "We've got people out there looking, Sharon. No one's going to get past our checkpoints with two little girls in the car. We're searching every boat and every plane that leaves St. Clair, and every man driving alone is going to have his trunk searched. We're also compiling a list of every rental car in the county with the description the witness gave. We'll find out who rented them, and that might give us some ideas."

Sharon whispered, "You think he put them in the trunk? That's horrible. Christy will be terrified. And it's thundering. She always sleeps with me when there's thunder."

"Maybe we'll find them soon. It'll be morning in a couple of hours, and we'll have the advantage of daylight."

Lynda bent over her and stroked her hair. "Sharon, as soon as the sun comes out, Jake and Mike are going up in a plane to see if they can spot the car anywhere, or get some idea where they may be. So that means all the bases are being covered. They'll be searching on the ground, in the water, and in the air."

"It's not enough!" she cried. "It won't be enough until they find them!"

The telephone rang, and they all jumped.

Ben bolted for the telephone in the kitchen, but waited and looked through the dining-room door to Tony—as he'd been instructed. Tony, who held his hand over his own phone, nodded that he was ready to begin tracing, and Ben picked it up.

"Hello?"

"Are you ready to give me what I want now?" the muffled, disguised voice asked.

"Where are my children?" Ben asked, the blood draining from his face. "Where are they?"

"I asked you a question."

Sharon rushed toward Ben. Anne already stood next to him, hanging on every word. "I don't even know what you're looking for!" he shouted.

"The painting, you con artist. You know I'm looking for the painting!"

"*What* painting?" Ben asked. "Is it . . . is it one of *my* paintings? Because Dubose didn't let me leave with any of them. But if you'll tell me which one, maybe I can get back into the gallery and get it. Please!"

"What do you want, Ben?" the voice asked. "For me to spell it out for those cops sitting there with their tape equipment, waiting for me to state it for the record?"

Ben was silent.

"I'm getting tired of these games," the voice said. "Your girls are getting tired of them, too."

"Where are they, you scumbag? Where are my children?"

"They're in a damp, dark place. Picture it, Robinson. Those two beautiful little girls screaming for their daddy. And you're the only one who can help them. All you have to do is give me what I want."

"I don't *have* what you want!" Ben said, breaking into tears and leaning his forehead against the wall. "I don't *know* what you want!"

The phone went dead in his ear.

Sharon swung back to Tony and Larry, who were each on another telephone, and were now barking orders.

"Did you trace it?" she asked, her eyes wide with hope.

"Yeah," Tony said, putting his hand over the receiver. "He was at a pay phone on the east side of town. A unit should be there by now."

"He's gone," Larry said, shaking his head and dropping his own phone. "The booth was empty when our guy got there."

"Oh, no!" Sharon cried. "I don't believe this!"

"They're combing the area. It's not too late. They could still catch him."

They all waited as moments ticked by with agonizing slowness. Finally, the officers searching for the kidnapper called to say that they hadn't found him.

Tony dropped the phone back in its cradle and looked up at Sharon, Ben, Anne, and Lynda, who were all clustered in the arched doorway of the living room.

"They lost him?" Sharon cried. "Are they looking around the area? Did they block off the neighborhood around the phone booth? Maybe he has the girls with him!"

"They're still searching the area," Larry said. "But with this storm, it's unlikely that there were any witnesses."

"But you've got to *do* something!"

Tony rewound the tape of the phone call and looked up at Ben through the door. Ben was still leaning with his forehead against the wall, weeping. Anne was staring at them with a look of shock on her face.

They played the tape again, hoping Ben would recognize the voice, but he couldn't place it. Sharon was near the breaking point. Gritting her teeth, she turned to Ben and shoved him.

"Tell him where it is!" she shouted through her teeth. "Give him what he wants!"

"I don't know what he wants!" Ben cried. "How many times do I have to say it?"

"No more times," she shouted. "Just give it to him!"

"Please, Ben!" Anne threw in, and began to sob into her hands.

He turned to her, then back to Sharon. "Do you really think that I'd put my family through this for some stupid secret?"

"Why not?" Sharon shouted. "You've done it before. Once you even *destroyed* your family over a stupid secret!"

"I have never intentionally hurt my family," he said, quieter now, though his voice trembled. "I've always tried to do the best I could."

"It was the best you could do when you left your wife and children for another woman?" she screamed. "You had no regard for them then, and I don't believe you have any regard for them now."

"Shut up!" Anne cried. "You don't know how he felt! You don't have a clue what was going on—"

Ben broke in, raising his voice over his wife's. "So what do you think is going on here now, Sharon? Do you think I have something that could ransom our children, but I'd rather sacrifice them than turn it over? Is that really what you think of me?"

"Stop it!" Lynda shouted. "All of you."

All three of them turned to look at Lynda, sobs racking them as they glared at her.

"I think I know what he wants," Lynda said. "The Marazzio, Ben. I think it's time to seriously consider that what you found may not have been a reproduction."

30

CHRISTY WOKE WITH a start and shivered from the cold. The night-light must have gone out, she thought, and Mommy must have forgotten to leave on the hall light. But as those thoughts came to her, she realized she was not at home, but lying on a dirt floor in the tool shed where the man had left them.

Emily still slept, her head resting on Christy's shoulder. For a moment, Christy didn't move, for fear of waking her. But as she sat staring into the darkness, feeling the cold creeping around them, despair fell over her. She began to cry quietly.

The feeling that she would never be found, that she and Emily would never get out, panicked her, and she suddenly felt the urgency to try to get out. She gently slid out from under Emily's weight, then helped her to lie down on the cold, dirt floor. Emily curled up in the fetal position, trying to get warm, her thumb stuck in her mouth.

Christy tried to reach the shelves to look for something to cover her with, but they were at least four feet higher than she could reach.

Her stomach ached with hunger, and she felt shaky and weak, but she went to the door and tested it again, as if hoping it had miraculously come unlocked during the night. They were still bolted in.

She sank down and listened to the sounds of the rain still pounding against the roof. Was Mommy out looking for her? Was Daddy? Had they called the police?

She wiped the tears from her face and set her hand down on the dirt by the wall. It was wet there. The rain was seeping under the walls, making the dirt floors soft. An idea came to her.

She felt around for a tool of some kind, anything she might dig with, but there was nothing. She tried using the heel of her loafer to start a hole in the dirt. It came loose, so she dug more, until she reached the softer, wetter earth underneath. Getting on her knees, she began to dig with her hands, raking away small handfuls.

"Mommy!" Emily woke, looked around, and began to scream. "Mommy!"

Christy grabbed her. "Emily, it's me. Christy. We're here, remember? In this place?"

Emily's wailing just got worse. "I want my mommy! Moooommmy!"

"She can't hear you," Christy said sullenly. "But I think I've found a way out. You have to help me. Now stop crying and look."

Emily hiccuped her sobs, but grew quieter.

"Look," Christy said, going back to the hole she'd been digging. "Help me dig under the wall, and we can get out."

"Dig with what?" Emily asked.

"Our hands," Christy told her.

Emily looked down at her hands. "I don't want to."

"Do you want to be here when that man comes back?" Christy asked her. "Or do you want to get out so we can go get help and call home?"

"Get out," Emily whimpered.

"Then help me."

Slowly, Emily moved over to the hole and began to help halfheartedly.

"If we dig deep enough, and get under the wall, we can run real fast into the woods."

"I'm scared of the woods," Emily said. "It has wolves and bobcats and alligators."

Christy hadn't thought of that. "Well . . . maybe we'll find a house. Maybe some nice grandma lives there, and she can give us some food. Maybe she has a phone."

Emily liked that idea better. "Okay, but I hope she has a heater. It's cold in here."

Together, they began to dig with their fingers, desperately trying to make a way to escape.

31

SHARON DIDN'T KNOW what to do with herself, so she set about to do something, anything, for Christy. First, she washed all her clothes. Then she pulled out a ready-made roll of dough and began to make cookies. The smell that filled the house made her feel that her child would be home by the time they were done.

But when she took them out of the oven, the children were still just as lost as they'd been before.

The house was deathly quiet, though she knew the two police officers sat in her dining room waiting for the phone to ring again. Larry and Tony had taken Ben to the gallery to look, once again, for the mystery painting, and two officers she'd never met were taking their place here while they were gone. The fact that they played a hand of cards in the dining room riled her, for she couldn't stand the thought that they were wasting time when they could be looking for the girls. It didn't matter that other cops—dozens of them—were combing the town for them.

She turned off the oven. Looking around at the clean kitchen, she realized there was nothing more to do. This busyness was crazy, anyway. It wasn't helping to give her any more peace.

She wandered upstairs to Jenny's room and checked on her. Heavily sedated, Jenny was sleeping soundly. Sharon touched her back and felt her rhythmic breathing. At least one of her children was safe. But what if something happened to Christy? Jenny would always blame herself. Her guilt over the kidnapping was overwhelming her already.

Feeling the weight of a couple of tons on her shoulders, Sharon adjusted Jenny's covers and left her bedroom. Slowly, she walked up the hall to Christy's room, trying to recover the feeling that her child was in there, tucked into bed, sleeping soundly. But as she neared the doorway, she was hit with the reality that her child was out in the cold, wet morning someplace, terrified and confused.

She burst into tears as she reached the doorway.

Anne sat there in the rocking chair in Christy's room, her knees hugged to her chest. For a moment the only sound was that of the rain pelting against the windows.

"Oh," Sharon said. "I didn't know you were in here." Anne started to get up, but Sharon stopped her. "It's okay. Stay."

Anne hugged her knees again, and Sharon could see that the misery on the woman's face reflected her own. "Where are they?" Anne asked in a whisper.

Sharon went into the room and sat down on the bed. She picked up one of the dolls propped against the pillow, and smoothed out its hair. "At least they're together."

"Yeah," Anne said. "I was just thinking that. Christy's not that much older than Emily, but she takes care of her. If either of them was alone . . ." Her voice trailed off, and she looked out the window again.

"He just wants the painting," Sharon said, trying to reassure herself more than Anne. "He has to keep them alive so he'll have something to bargain with. He can't hurt them. He just can't."

"He already has," Anne whispered. "Just by taking them, he hurt them. The trauma that they're going through . . ." She covered her face, and her voice came out in a squeak. "I know God's punishing me."

Sharon stared at her for a long moment, at a loss for what to say. There had been many times since her divorce when she had wished God would punish Anne, but in the last couple of years, those wishes had come less frequently. Why would such punishment come now, and include her own child?

Sharon grew quiet and followed Anne's gaze to the raindrops running down the window. She didn't know what to say.

"Do you remember during your and Ben's divorce, when you told him that the pain for you was bad enough, but that he had traumatized his children and robbed them of their family? That they'd never be the same because of it?"

"I said a lot of things," Sharon whispered.

"That haunted Ben," Anne went on. "And I never let it haunt me. I thought kids were resilient. That they'd recover. That it wouldn't be a big deal."

Sharon had known that was Anne's attitude. She stiffened a little, wondering where the woman was going with this.

"But sometimes, I think God punishes people by giving them more of the pain they gave somebody else." She swallowed and hiccuped a sob, then kept going. "We traumatized your children, so now he's letting us see how it feels. Only this is even worse."

Sharon stared down at the doll for a moment, running her fingertip across the porcelain face and over the pink lips. "There's one problem with your logic on this, Anne. If it's the way you say it is, why would God make me go through it?"

Anne considered that for a moment, then looked at Sharon. "I don't know. Maybe he's punishing you for something, too."

She dropped the doll and got up. "Maybe you're just wrong about all of it," she said. "Maybe God had nothing to do with any of this. Maybe he's just watching over them. Bringing them back to us."

"They're both so little," Anne said in a tormented whisper.

For a moment Sharon felt a bond with Anne that she had never felt before. The bond of one mother to another.

But she didn't want to feel that bond, and as the contagious agony caught up with her and brought her close to breaking, Sharon left the room, to suffer alone.

32

THE GALLERY WAS almost as it had been the last time Ben left it. The same paintings still graced the walls, the same sculptures stood on their pedestals.

But everything was different.

Ben let his eyes stray to the chalk mark on the floor, and realized for the first time that a man he had respected and depended on, a man he had seen every day for the last five years, was dead. Some murderer had come in here and killed him, and if Dubose had not fired and evicted him, Ben and his family might have been killed, as well. He wondered if that was why Dubose had been in such a hurry to get them out. Did he know he was in danger? Was he trying to spare Ben and his family?

Somehow, that thought made the reality seem more difficult to bear. His eyes teared up, and he turned away.

Tony looked uncomfortable with the show of emotion. "So where was this painting you told us about? How about taking us there and showing us where it was hidden?"

Ben tried to pull himself together and started up the stairs, with Larry and Tony following behind him. He cut through the studio where he'd been the most creative, and looked longingly at the work that leaned against the walls or sat on easels. Without uttering a word, he crossed the room to the office where Dubose had worked.

The little door to the attic was at the back of Dubose's office. Ben turned on the light, and the wooden stairwell lit up.

Slowly, he led them up into the attic. A few bare bulbs hung from the ceiling, casting a weak glare over wrapped and stacked canvases, over empty frames hung haphazardly on the walls.

"It was right over here," he said, and the two cops followed him. "I was up here looking for a frame." He gestured toward all of the old frames, some broken, some just dusty. "I wanted a frame that was obviously old. I was going for the antique look for one of my paintings. I'll show it to you when we go back down. Anyway, I bent down like this to look at that frame over there, and when I stood back up, my head bumped on this compartment, and the painting fell out. It had been rolled up for some time, because when I started to unroll it, the paint cracked a little."

Tony stepped forward and examined the narrow box built into the rafter at the ceiling. The door was hanging open, and he could see how the slanted compartment could have dropped its contents if it hadn't been closed properly. "Any idea where the painting is now?"

"I gave it to Dubose," Ben said. "I never saw it again."

"What might he have done with it?"

"Got me," Ben said. "He may have hidden it someplace else, though I don't really know why he'd go to all that trouble. I mean, it obviously wasn't the original."

Larry took a deep breath. "Well, maybe we'd better look around up here. It could be in a new hiding place."

"But didn't you say that the place had been rifled through? If it was here, the killer would have found it."

"We have to anyway," Tony said. So they set about examining every inch of the dusty, dark attic, moving frames and old cracked canvases, oil paintings that looked as if they'd be better suited to the dumpster outside than the attic, and broken sculptures that Dubose hadn't had the heart to throw away. There were no more hidden compartments, and very little of value there.

As they walked back through the studio, Ben showed them some of the things he'd been working on. "Pretty cushy job you had," Tony said, looking around. "Free rent, nice place to work, steady income whether you sell anything or not."

Ben's face reddened. "I sold plenty. People came from all over the country to buy my work."

"Do you think this is about one of your own paintings?" Larry asked.

Ben shook his head. "Why wouldn't he just call it by name? Describe it? Why the secrecy? Why does he think I know what he's talking about?"

They went through each of his paintings, then headed downstairs, studying each painting for something that gave it more value than the others. Nothing stood out as a work worthy of murder and kidnapping.

"All right, who can we call to find out for sure if that *Multitude* painting was recovered?" Tony asked.

Ben thought for a moment. "Come to think of it, Louis kept a set of books in his office that have information like that." He started back up the stairs, feeling excited. "I don't know why I didn't think of that before!"

They followed him back up, and he hurried into Dubose's office. "See?" he asked, pointing to the eight volumes on the credenza behind the desk. "*The Dictionary of Painters and Sculptors.* I had almost forgotten. It has information about lost and stolen art, what it's worth now, and all that kind of stuff. Louis used it extensively."

He pulled out one volume and flipped through the pages until he came to Marazzio. "There it is," he said, setting the book down and pointing to the passage so that Tony and Larry could see. "Says *The Multitude* was stolen from a museum in Palermo over ten years ago." He frowned. "I don't get it. It doesn't say it was recovered. These other two that were stolen at other times, they were recovered three years ago, but nothing about *The Multitude.*"

"How current are these books?"

"Very current. Louis kept them up-to-date. He just got this set about a month ago."

"Maybe he got *The Multitude* mixed up with one of the ones that really was recovered."

"Or he lied," Larry said.

"If the painting I found was really the original, stolen painting, then it probably is what the kidnapper wants."

"So where is it?"

"I have no idea," Ben said. "Maybe you should search his house . . . his car . . ."

"We searched it after the murder," Larry said, "but we weren't looking for a painting then."

As they drove back to Sharon's house, Tony said, "That painting is the key to whatever is going on here. This painter. Mar—"

"Marazzio," Ben said.

"Yeah, Marazzio. He was pretty famous, huh?"

Ben chuckled, almost condescendingly. "I'd say so. He's considered one of the greats. Who knows? If it was a fake, maybe Dubose was going to doctor the reproduction and try to pass it off as the original, especially if he really did know the painting was still missing. See how many millions he could get for it."

"I'm in the wrong business," Tony muttered, and Larry laughed. "No, really. I'm artistic. I used to draw a mean Bugs Bunny."

"Used to? What happened?"

"I had to trade my crayon in for a gun."

"Tough life, buddy."

"Yeah. But if I'd known the money was in those crayons . . ."

They looked in the backseat. Ben wasn't laughing. But their bantering made him realize one good thing: they no longer considered him the killer.

"So where did Dubose buy most of the original art pieces he found?" Larry asked.

Ben shrugged. "He traveled a lot, went to a lot of auctions. And there were a few dealers he did business with. Some of them spent a lot of time at the gallery."

"Who were they?"

"Well, there were several. He had dealings with people all over the world. But some of the most frequent ones, I guess, were Leon Spatika, Nelson Chamberlain, T. Z. Quarternet. All three of them have bought paintings of mine."

Tony shot Larry a look. "Would their names be in Dubose's Rolodex?"

"Sure. Why?"

"We took it as evidence. Maybe we'll give them a call."

Larry looked over his shoulder. "If Dubose was such a big-time art dealer with all these connections, what was he doing in a little town like St. Clair?"

"He had about ten galleries across the U.S.," Ben said. "They're all as small as this one. It's a good outlet for some of the lower priced paintings he sells. Plus he liked to cultivate up-and-comers. That's what he considered me."

"Then there are other galleries with artists-in-residence?"

"Sure. But I doubt there are any others where the owner has been murdered and the artist's kids have been abducted."

They pulled into Sharon's driveway, but Larry made no move to get out. "Go on in, Ben, and tell John and Nick in there that they'll have to stay a little longer. Tony and I are going to search Dubose's apartment and his car again. Maybe we can find the painting."

"All right," Ben said. "But what if the kidnapper calls back?"

"John and Nick know what to do, and they'll get in touch with us."

"All right." He got out of the car, and headed inside to face the quiet left behind by his two little girls.

33

THE HOLE THE girls had dug was deep, and though their fingers had developed blisters, they both dug with a zeal that they hadn't felt since they'd come there. At the end of the tunnel they were digging with their hands was freedom. And food. And warmth.

They heard a car pulling up to the shack, its wheels popping on the gravel road.

"Daddy's come!" Emily exclaimed, jumping to her feet. "Daddy! Daddy!"

But Christy clapped a dirty hand over Emily's mouth. "It might be him!" she hissed. "The mean man. Be quiet and help me hide the hole!"

Emily's joy crashed instantly, and she looked around for something to move over the hole. There was nothing.

"I'll sit here over it," Christy said, sitting on the edge of the hole. "You lie down with your head in my lap, and he won't see it."

"What about the pile of dirt we dug out?"

"Lie down in front of it," Christy said. "Maybe he won't see it."

Emily got into place, and Christy could feel her trembling as she laid her head in her lap. "Do I pretend I'm sleeping?" she whispered.

"If you want."

Christy's hand was trembling as she laid it over Emily's arm. "Our hands," Emily said. "When he sees them, he'll know we've been digging."

Christy considered that for a moment. "I'll put mine under you. Put yours between your legs."

Both children hid their hands as the car door slammed. Footsteps came closer to the shed, and keys jingled.

"It's not Daddy, is it?" Emily asked on a whisper.

"No. I think it's *him.*"

The door opened, and both girls stiffened. Emily closed her eyes and tried to pretend to be asleep.

The big man stepped inside holding two bags. "I brought you something to eat," he said, and thrust the bags at Christy. She took the bags, forgetting the dirt on her hands. The man didn't seem to notice.

"Thanks, Mister. Are we gonna get to go home today?"

"That depends on how much your daddy wants to keep you alive. It's up to him, kiddo."

Christy's eyes widened as she tried to understand. "It's cold in here. And dark. Real dark, and Emily's afraid of the dark." She started to cry, knowing that it wasn't the right thing to do, but she couldn't stop it. Then Emily's act crumbled, and she began to squint her eyes and cry, too.

"Please let us go home, Mister. We'll tell everybody you were nice to us. We won't tell them about this place."

The man laughed sullenly under his breath. "I told you, it's up to your father. When he gives me what I want, you can go home."

Both girls looked up at him, quiet.

"Eat your food. I don't know when I'll bring you any more."

With that, he closed the door and locked the bolt again.

"McDonald's!" Emily cried, and dug into the bag. "Drinks, too. Look, Christy!"

But Christy wasn't thinking about the food. Her mind was still hung on the fact that her father had the power to get them back, but hadn't done anything about it. More tears ran down the dirt on her face, and she wiped them away with a filthy, blistered hand, smearing mud across her face.

"Aren't you hungry, Christy?" Emily asked.

"Yeah," Christy said and took her drink out of the bag. "Emily, do you think he's ever gonna let us go home?"

Emily bit into her burger, and chewed thoughtfully as she looked at her sister. "If he doesn't, Daddy'll come get us. He'll find us. He always finds me when we play hide-and-seek."

"This isn't hide-and-seek," Christy said miserably. "He doesn't know where to look for us. And the man said it was up to him. What if we have to stay here another night?"

"We'll dig out before then," Emily said solemnly. "We'll run away and find that grandma with the telephone."

Christy wiped her eyes again and moved away from the hole. The man hadn't discovered it. Maybe Emily was right. Maybe they could escape soon.

The baby's cry woke Sharon from where she half-dozed with her head in her arms at the kitchen table, and she jumped up. It was morning. That was Christy calling her! She rushed toward the stairs.

But the crying wasn't coming from upstairs, and as the fog from her brain cleared, reality jolted her. It was Bobby, not Christy. Christy was still out there with some maniac who'd already killed at least once.

She grabbed Christy's Simba doll and wished she could at least get it to her somehow, so there would be some measure of comfort for her child.

She walked into the living room, and saw that Tony and Larry had come back and had fallen asleep on the two couches set at right angles to each other in the big living room. Tony stirred slightly, so she backed out and walked toward the sound of the crying baby.

As she grew closer, the crying stopped. She slowed her step and got to the doorway. Anne was there, holding the baby, humming to him and gently rocking him as he whimpered.

Maternal anguish washed over her, overwhelming her with pain. But it wasn't resentment this time, or jealousy. The sight just reminded her that there would be no outlet, none at all, for her emotions until Christy came back.

Then came the miserable, cruel, startling thought. *What if he's killed them? What if they're already dead somewhere? What if they cried and he got impatient? What if I never see Christy again?*

She covered her mouth to muffle her sobs. Rushing back up the hall, her head bent, she slammed right into someone coming toward her.

She caught her breath and yelped once, before she realized it was Tony.

"Are you okay?" he asked, looking down at her.

She covered her face and shook her head viciously. "What if they're dead?"

He pulled her into his arms and held her as she sobbed violently against his rumpled shirt. "They're not dead," he whispered. "You can't think like that. We're going to find them. Come on. Sit down. You're exhausted."

She let him lead her to the couch, and she sat down and allowed him to pull her against him. She laid her head on his shoulder and hiccuped sobs that wouldn't stop as he whispered soothing assurances against her ear. "Go ahead . . . it's okay to cry . . ."

The human contact helped. Slowly, her sobs subsided, and she was left under a blanket of grief. He still didn't let her go.

He stroked her hair back from her face and wiped her cheek with the back of his fingers.

"I dozed off in the kitchen," she whispered. "And the baby cried, and for a minute, I thought it was Christy. Just a split second, where I believed it had been an awful dream, and I was waking up."

"You need to get some real sleep, Sharon. You're not a superwoman."

"I can't," she said. "Some part of me thinks that if I let myself relax even for a minute, that they'll just fade away, and I'll never see my baby again."

There was nothing he could say.

After a while, she pulled out of his arms and sat upright. "I guess I should make everybody some breakfast."

"That's not necessary," Tony said. "You have enough to cope with."

"No," she said. "It's something I can do. You and Larry have been here all night. I want to feel useful somehow. I'm going to do it."

Tony stood up with her. "Are you sure you're up to it?"

"Yeah," she said. "Thanks for the shoulder. You have no idea how much I needed it."

"Any time." Tony watched her disappear back into the kitchen, then went back into the living room where he and Larry had been sleeping.

Larry was sitting up now. "You're getting a little too close to this case, don't you think, Tony?"

Tony shot him a disbelieving look. "You're kidding, right?"

"No, man. You're here to help find her child, not fall in love with her."

"Fall in love?" He almost laughed. "She was upset, and I tried to comfort her."

"Be careful. That can become a habit."

"Yeah, well, you ought to know." He raked a hand through his rumpled hair and wished for a shower.

"I'm serious, Tony. The woman's really vulnerable right now. She's going through a lot. You need to keep your distance."

Tony turned back around and glared at his partner. "That's just hilarious coming from you, Larry. In fact, I can't believe what I'm hearing."

Larry grinned. It was no secret that he had married a woman whose case he'd worked on. It was also no secret that he'd never been happier in his life. "Look, I know what you're thinking."

"I'm thinking that I was telling you the same thing just a few months ago. 'You're getting too involved. You're not being objective.'"

"I was the exception," Larry said with a grin. "But this is different."

"No, it's not different," Tony said. "But don't worry. I'm not gonna get hurt."

"Get hurt?" Larry asked. "Mr. Confirmed Bachelor? I'm not worried about *you* getting hurt!"

Tony gaped at him. "Her? You think I'll hurt her? What kind of lowlife do you think I am?"

"A noncommittal lowlife," Larry said matter-of-factly, though a twinkle of humor shone in his eye.

"Thanks a lot, pal."

Larry pulled on his shoes and got up, stretching. "Speaking of commitment, I think I'll go call my bride."

"Yeah, you do that." Tony sat down and watched his friend go out of the room. And some part of him resented that Larry had been so lucky. Tony hadn't realized he was lonely until he'd seen how happy Larry's marriage had made him. More and more lately, he had wondered if the bachelor life really had all that much to recommend it.

On the other hand, seeing the tangled web of *this* family reminded him that marriage wasn't all it was cracked up to be, either.

34

THE STORM RAGED on, tormenting those who waited. It had been two hours since the short appearance they'd all made on the news, in which they had pled for the return of their children. In her despair, Sharon had offered a $25,000 reward for information leading to their return. But still, they hadn't heard a word.

Now Sharon wandered in and out of rooms like a phantom, racking her brain for some idea that would get her child back. In her mind, her prayer for Christy and Emily's safety played like a chant, repeating itself in the same cadence over and over. She wondered whether God was even hearing it.

She stepped out onto the porch and looked up through the screen to the cloudy, angry sky. Under this same sky the children were hidden. God knew where they were, and he was the only one she could trust to keep them safe. Tears came to her eyes as she looked up to plead with him, but a voice behind her startled her.

"I thought we'd have them back by now."

She swung around and saw Ben sitting on a bench leaned back against the wall of the house. His voice was hoarse, and she could see that he'd been crying. For a moment, she thought of going back into the house, but the brief connection seemed more important. Besides Anne, Ben was the only person in the world who knew exactly how she felt.

Quietly, she turned back around and looked up at the sky.

"I never thought we'd come to this," he said. "In my worst nightmares, I wouldn't have believed . . ."

Sharon didn't look at him. A million thoughts fled through her mind, thoughts of how he'd brought it on them somehow, how he was being punished for all the cruelty he'd inflicted on her and their children, and that the kidnapped children were just caught in God's crossfire. But some part of her knew that wasn't true.

"Despite what you might think, Sharon," he went on, his voice raspy and heavy with emotion, "and despite how cruel I was, I never meant to hurt any of you."

If he'd said that two days ago, she would have laughed sarcastically, then reminded him of all the little instances in which his hurting had seemed deliberate. But the fight had left her now, and all that remained was a dull numbness.

"I thought I'd forgiven you," she whispered. "At church, I even bragged about it. Lectured to other divorced women about letting go and praying for their exes. I told them that God loved their ex-husbands as much as he loved them. Even when I invited you to move in, part of me was patting myself on the back, thinking how everyone would see how I lived out my faith. What it looked like to truly forgive. I had it all worked out. I thought I'd even gotten some peace about it. But I didn't know what a farce it all was."

A long note of silence stretched between them as the cool wind whipped around the house, whispering through the leaves.

"I can't undo what I've done, Sharon," he said from his dark corner of the porch. "This whole week, it's been like my life has passed before my eyes. But it's done."

"That's right," Sharon said. "And none of it really even matters right now. I just want my baby back."

She turned and looked at him now, and saw that his eyes were closed as he struggled to control his emotions. "I guess it would make this a little easier if I thought you and I weren't enemies," he said.

"How could we be enemies, Ben? You're in my house. You're the father of my children."

"Neither of those things qualifies for friendship."

"Oh, is that it?" she asked, her sarcasm returning. "You want to be friends?"

"It'd be nice," he said. "We have a lot in common, you know. We both love our children. And we used to love each other."

She turned away again. "Love dies, Ben. You ought to know that more than anyone."

Before he could answer, Sharon went back into the house and left him alone.

35

"LOOK, EMILY. LIGHT!"

Christy clawed at the dirt, ignoring the bloody blisters on her fingers. "We reached the other side!"

"Can we get out now?" Emily asked.

"No. We have to dig the hole bigger! Help me!"

The two girls dug faster, the skin on their fingers raw and bloody and caked with the dirt through which they would escape. More light filled the small shed, giving them hope as the hole got bigger and the pile of dirt next to it piled higher.

"I think it's big enough," Emily said. "I can slide out."

"No, you'll get stuck. It has to be bigger!"

On their knees, they both pulled and clawed at the dirt, getting closer, closer, to the point at which they could slide under the wall and embrace their freedom.

Then they heard the car.

"He's coming!" Christy cried. "He'll see the hole!"

"I'm going now!" Emily fell down on her stomach and started to crawl into the hole.

"He'll see you!"

"But I'll get away," she said. "Come on. Hurry!"

They heard his car door close, and Christy hoped he had parked on the other side of the building. His footsteps in the gravel were growing closer. He was coming around the side to the door, and probably wouldn't see Emily escaping. "Go! Hurry!" she whispered.

Emily burrowed through the hole, then up on the other side, and turned back to help Christy.

Christy went head first into the hole, slithering under the wall, but as she tried to come up on the other side, she heard the door open.

"You brats!" the man thundered. Suddenly she felt a hand grab her feet, and she was jerked backward.

"Run, Emily!" Christy screamed. "Run!" She watched as the terrified five-year-old took off into the woods, screaming in fear.

Christy fought with all her might not to be pulled back into the shed, but he yanked her up, bruising and scraping her back on the bottom of the wall as he got her back inside.

She tried to fight him as he lifted her, but he was too strong. Cursing, he held her sideways with an arm around her middle and bolted out of the building. The car parked outside was different from the one he'd taken them in, and he opened his trunk and threw her in, then slammed it shut, encompassing her in darkness once again.

Terrified, she hunkered in a little ball and covered her mouth with her hand, trying to muffle her sobs for fear he would hurt her if she made too much noise.

And then she began to pray, as hard and as fast and as deeply as she'd ever prayed in her life.

Emily had to get away. It was their only hope.

36

IT TOOK ONLY a few phone calls to confirm that the original Marazzio had never been recovered. Dubose had lied.

Larry sat over Dubose's telephone records, which he had finally managed to get from the phone company, and compared them to the names on Dubose's desk calendar. "This one guy keeps coming up," he mumbled, thinking out loud, "Eric Boudreaux. The page torn off of the desk calendar was for the day after Dubose died. From the impression on the next page, I can read the words 'Eric Boudreaux, 2:00.' The phone records show a call from Boudreaux in France the day before the murder." He looked up at Tony, who was studying some documents they'd brought from the gallery. "Have you got anything on him yet?"

"Yeah," Tony said, looking up and resting his chin wearily on the heel of his hand. He shuffled some papers around and checked his notes. "He's a museum curator in France. Nothing unusual came up. No prior arrests."

"Do you think Dubose was planning a telephone meeting, or was he going to meet him in person?"

Tony picked up the phone. "I'll call and ask."

He got the long-distance operator, placed the call, and waited. After several rings, a woman answered in French.

"Eric Boudreaux, please," Tony said.

She returned something in French that he couldn't understand, and he closed his eyes. "Excuse me. Do you speak English?"

"A little," she said in a heavy accent. "Uh . . . Monsieur Boudreaux is . . . not here . . . in town . . ."

"He's out of town? Where?"

"*Les Estats Unis.* Florida."

Tony's eyebrows shot up, and he looked up at Larry. "Do you happen to know what town?"

"Non, Monsieur. I could have him . . . phone back? Yes?"

"No, that's okay. Thank you very much." He hung up the phone and looked up at Larry. "Ten to one our boy is in St. Clair as we speak."

"Then you think the appointment was face-to-face?"

"Maybe he moved it up a little," Tony suggested.

Larry thought that over for a moment. "I'd say we need to talk to him."

"Without delay," Tony agreed, getting up. "Call for someone to relieve us while we pay him a visit, and I'll start calling the hotels until I locate him." He picked up the phone and started dialing. "Oh, and ask Ben if he knows anything about this guy. He might know something we don't know. And hurry."

Larry rushed into the kitchen, where Sharon and Ben sat stone-faced and silent over coffee that was turning cold.

"Eric Boudreaux," Larry said, leaning both hands on the table and leaning over it. "What do you know about him?"

Ben shrugged. "He's a well-known art dealer."

"Well-known how?"

"He makes some pretty amazing buys." He sat up straighter as something occurred to him. "A few years ago he found one of the lost Monets."

Larry tried to sort out what that might mean. "Where did he find it?"

"He claimed he bought it at an estate auction. That some deceased person had it, and no one knew how he'd gotten it. No one had realized it was an authentic Monet, one of the missing ones. He knew it immediately and seized the moment."

Larry went to the phone and dialed the number of the precinct. While he waited, he asked, "Did anyone ever check out that story? Confirm where he'd found it?"

"What do you mean?" Ben asked.

"I mean, to make sure he hadn't stolen it himself, or bought stolen goods, or that sort of thing?"

Ben breathed a laugh. "Actually, there was so much hoopla about finding the painting that I don't think too many people were concerned about how he'd found it. Art theft is big business, and it's rarely prosecuted, even when the people are caught. The discovery of a stolen Monet is a very big deal."

Larry turned away long enough to ask for relief officers, then hung up and turned back. He began to pace, trying to figure this out. "Okay, let's just pretend. Let's say that Dubose had some important original. And let's say that he had made contact with this Boudreaux guy to sell it. How much did the book say the original lost Marazzio would sell for?"

"Probably around twenty million."

Larry whistled.

Sharon got up, interested now. "You think this Boudreaux person is the killer? The one who has Christy and Emily?"

"No, now wait. It's a hunch. A possibility."

"But why would he kill Dubose for the painting? Why not just buy it from him?"

"Maybe the profit margin was higher if he did away with the middle man."

Ben thought that over for a long time, silently trying to work it all out in his mind. "So you think Eric Boudreaux is the one?"

"I hope so, man." He saw the squad car pull into the driveway, and Tony came into the kitchen.

"He's at the Biltmore. Let's go."

"I'm coming with you!" Sharon said, heading out the door.

Tony lassoed her with an arm and pulled her back in. "Oh, no, you don't. Let us do our work, Sharon."

"But the children could be there with him!"

"We'll call you immediately if anything breaks," he said gently. "Just trust us."

Reluctantly, she went back in. "Please. Call us if you find out anything!"

"I promise," Tony said, and they headed for their car.

37

EMILY HEARD HIS footsteps coming closer. Breathless, she kept running. She wove through trees and bushes, leapt over logs, tore through briars and thorns.

She cried as she ran, and kept looking back over her shoulder. She couldn't see him yet, which meant that he couldn't see her. Soon she would be to that grandma's house she and Christy had talked about, and she could go in and call the police, and they would come and get them so they could go home.

But the house never came into sight, only deeper, thicker woods, a forest prison that frightened Emily the farther she ran. But what came behind her frightened her more. She could hear his heavy breathing, his feet hitting the ground with weight and speed . . .

She looked back and still couldn't see him, but she could hear him getting closer. She kept running, slipping under branches and tangled vines.

Then she stopped.

She stood at the edge of a gully, looking down into the stream bubbling by. Would the stream be too deep for her if she slid down into it? No, she couldn't do that—there was no place to hide down in the gully. He would see her, slide after her, and catch her.

Panicked, she turned around and searched for a hiding place. There was a tree with low branches beside the ravine. Without thinking, she began to climb it. She climbed from one big branch to the next, knocking away smaller branches and vines entangling it, climbing higher and higher, where the man would never think to look.

Certain she was hidden by the leaves beneath her and the vines webbing through the tree, she found a sturdy branch and sat still, holding her breath.

Within seconds, the man was beneath her, searching. She saw him reach the edge of the gully and almost fall down, but he caught himself. He stood still for a minute, looking up and down the gully, but then turned back around.

She shrank into a tighter ball as he looked up into the trees. His eyes passed over where she sat, and she breathed a sigh of relief that he had not seen her.

Slowly, he walked back through the trees and brush the way he had come, and she watched until he was out of sight.

She thought she was safe—until she looked down at the branches she had climbed to get there, and didn't know if she'd ever have the nerve to go back down. Would she have to stay here, in this scary tree, even when it got dark? What if no one found her?

And where was Christy? She started to cry again. She had heard Christy scream for her to run, and she had, but then she hadn't heard anything more from her sister. What if the man had caught her? What if he had hurt her?

She put her filthy, bloody thumb into her mouth, then quickly spat it out. Wiping a smear of dirt and blood on her shirt, she tried again. The dirty thumb gave her some comfort, but only enough to make her cry harder.

Daddy would find her somehow, she told herself. This was harder than hide-and-seek, but it was more important. He had to rescue them both. He had to.

Hurry, Daddy. Hurry.

38

THERE WAS NO answer at the door to the room at the Biltmore where Eric Boudreaux was staying. Larry and Tony knocked again, then looked at the manager who had accompanied them up. "We have a warrant to search his room," Larry said, flashing the paper they had gotten from a judge on the way to the hotel. "Could you let us in, please?"

"Sure. But he isn't here. He checked out." The manager used his key to open the door. Gesturing for them to go in, he asked, "Is this guy in some kind of trouble?"

"We don't know yet," Tony said. "Thanks for your help." Tony looked around at the room. It hadn't been cleaned yet since he'd checked out, but the man had left little behind. He went to the trash can and stooped down next to it, while Larry went into the bathroom.

"At least we have some fingerprints here," Larry said.

Tony nodded as he sorted through the sundry papers that had been dropped into the can. A Delta boarding pass stub, a couple of receipts with credit card numbers, a rolled up newspaper, a small sheet of paper with a phone number on it.

"Hey, Larry," Tony said. "There's a phone number on here. You'll never guess what it is."

"The number of the gallery?" Larry asked.

"You got it."

"Well, that doesn't mean anything. We knew he had an appointment."

"This piece of paper here has the name John Lieber written on it."

"Keep it and we'll check him out." He looked around. "No evidence of any children having been here."

"Nope. If he's got them, he's got them someplace else."

Tony reached for the newspaper and shook it out. It was the edition put out on the day of the murder, and it was folded so that Dubose's picture was on top. "Well, he knows about the murder. No doubt about that."

"Where is he now?" Larry asked.

"Who knows? We'd better check out all the flights leaving in the next few hours. He could be at the airport as we speak."

"What about the children?"

Tony shook his head. "Who knows?"

39

EMILY HAD WAITED what seemed a very long time, but the longer she sat, the more afraid she got. She had seen a TV show once about snakes, and how they loved to hide in trees. Still sucking her thumb, she clung to the trunk and looked around her.

The thought that some unseen creature might be sharing this hiding place with her made her want to get down, but she was still afraid of the man, too. She hadn't heard him since he had walked away into the forest, and she hoped he had given up the search and gone back to the car.

She reached for the next branch with her foot and stepped down onto it. Trembling and perspiring, she made her way to another branch, and then another. She looked around for any sign of snakes and saw a shadow moving across the tree. Quickly, she took another step.

Branch by branch, she made her way down, propelled by fear. A small branch broke under her foot, and she slipped, but grabbed onto another branch in time. She found her footing again and continued her descent.

She breathed relief when her feet hit the ground. Quietly, she crept to the edge of the ravine again. Should she slide down it, hoping the water was shallow, and scramble up the other side? Would that take her deeper into the woods, or out to the road again? Where were those houses she and Christy had talked about, anyway?

She decided to slide into the gully, since she had no intention of going back toward the shed. She looked around for something to sit on as she slid down, but there was nothing that would work. She sat down, scooted to the edge—

Two hands grabbed her from behind, and she let out a high-pitched scream.

"I've got you, you little brat!" Chamberlain said, lifting her and squeezing her under his arm. "I'll teach you to run away from me!"

She kept screaming until he clamped his hand over her mouth and stopped her. She bit him, and he jerked his hand away, allowing her to scream some more.

When his hand came back, he shoved a handkerchief into her mouth and clamped his hand over it again. This time she couldn't bite, and she could hardly breathe as his big hand pressed against her nostrils.

He ran through the trees with no regard for the bushes and brambles tearing at her clothes and scratching her skin. When they came to the edge of the woods, she saw the shed and car, but there was no sign of Christy.

They reached the car, and he opened the trunk.

Christy sat up and looked around, eyes squinted, and started to scream. He pushed her back in, and threw Emily in on top of her. When he started to close it, Christy cried, "No, Mister! We'll be good. We promise. We won't run away again. Please don't put us in here!"

"Shut up!" he said through his teeth. "And if you make a sound as I drive through town, I'll pull over and kill you both. Do you believe me?"

Christy and Emily looked up at his searing blue eyes. "Yes," Emily whimpered, and Christy agreed.

"Lie down," he said, and they both did.

He slammed the trunk shut, and seconds later, started the car.

40

TONY AND LARRY had just returned to Sharon's house when the phone rang. The two cops who'd been waiting beside all the equipment turned on the recorder and picked up their own phone to call for a trace, then nodded for Ben to answer.

"Hello?"

"I'm losing patience, and your girls are running out of time."

Ben closed his eyes and nodded to Sharon and Anne that it was him. They both ran into the other room to hear the conversation as it played across the recorder.

"Look, you obviously want a painting of some kind," Ben said. "I'll give you anything I have. Is it the Marazzio?"

The man laughed. "You're amazing."

"If that's it, Dubose took it. I don't know what he did with it."

"You have until 11:30 tonight, Robinson. I'll call you back later with details. Just be ready."

The phone clicked, and one of the officers cursed. "It wasn't enough time! He knows we're tracing him so he's keeping the conversations short."

Ben sank down at the kitchen table. "What am I gonna do?"

"Daddy, was that the kidnapper?"

It was Jenny, standing at the door in her robe, awake for the first time since she had been sedated. Her eyes were red and swollen, and she looked pale. She hadn't eaten in two days, and he doubted she could eat now. Ben stood up and drew her into a hug. "Yes, honey, it was."

"What did he say?" she asked, beginning to cry. "Is he bringing them back?"

"Maybe tonight," he said. He turned back to the cops, hovered around the recording equipment. "It has to be the Marazzio. What if we faked it again? What if I got another painting and pretended that was it? Last time, I didn't know what size or shape the bundle in the garment bag should be. But if it's the Marazzio, I know it was a roll about four feet long. Maybe we could make a switch for the children before he realized it wasn't the right one."

Tony looked at Larry. "It depends, Ben. On a lot of things. One of them is his delivery method. We'd have to make sure that he delivered the kids before he saw the fake, otherwise it could just make him mad enough to . . . retaliate. We don't know where he wants you to take it yet."

"But don't you see, I have no choice!" Ben insisted. "I have to do something. I don't have the painting he wants, so I have to come up with something else."

"He's right, Tony."

"All right," Tony said. "Let's find a painting and get it ready."

Jenny started to cry and threw her arms around her father. "Daddy, I've been praying for you."

"Don't pray for me," he said. "Pray for your sisters."

"I have, Daddy," she said. "I'm so sorry. This is all my fault."

"Honey, I told you. It isn't."

Sharon pulled Jenny away from her dad and held her while he prepared for the next phone call.

Later, Sharon slumped on the couch alone in her den, waiting, as everyone else in the house waited, for the phone to ring. Tony found her there and sat down next to her.

"You okay?" he asked.

"Yeah," she lied. "You?"

"Just getting psyched up for the big chase tonight. We'll get the girls back, Sharon. I know we will."

She let her eyes drift to some invisible spot across the room. "You have to."

He took her hand and fondled her fingers. "You're a strong lady, you know that?"

"What choice do I have?"

"You could fall apart. Believe me, it happens all the time. Most mothers would have passed hysteria by now."

"I'm glad you have a short memory," she said.

"Well, you've had your moments, but you might have had more." He gazed at her for a moment, noting how pretty she was. Her beauty was striking, but not in the way that he usually viewed beauty. There was an intelligence about her beauty, a dignity, and if he hadn't gotten to know her in such a vulnerable state, he probably would have been intimidated by her.

"Tell me about Christy," he said. "Is she smart? Is she athletic?"

"I think she's smart," she said. "She's only in first grade, but she's been reading since she was four."

"I mean, logic smart. Clear-headed smart."

"Yeah, she's got a lot of common sense. You could say she's even a little precocious. Jenny's always been an honor student, and I have a feeling that Christy will follow in her footsteps. She can count to fifteen in Spanish, to ten in French . . . and she knows all of the states in alphabetical order, because Jenny taught her a song about it. They're working on the presidents."

"Learning them?" Tony asked, amazed. "In the first grade, they learn all the presidents?"

"No," she said. "Jenny's teaching her. She's really good at memory work."

"She sounds like a kid who could take care of herself if she had to."

Sharon's eyes misted. "I think she could," she whispered. "She's strong. She climbs all the time, getting up to her tree house. She runs really fast, and she's a strong swimmer."

Tony smiled. "Good. That's what I wanted to hear. She sounds like a real interesting kid."

"She is. You'd really like her."

"Well, I hope after all this is over, and she's back safe and sound, that you'll give me the chance to get to know her."

"Of course. If you really want to."

"I do." He looked down at her hand, laced his fingers through hers.

She gazed up at him, her eyes serious, haunted. "Who are you, Tony Danks? Are you attached? Detached?"

He breathed a laugh. "None of the above."

"Why not? Why haven't you ever married?"

"Never found the right person," he said. "Besides, marriage hasn't had much appeal to me. Every cop I know who's gotten married has wound up divorced. With the exception of Larry, but he's a newlywed. Give him time."

"Uh-oh. A cynic."

"Not really," he said, hating that she saw him that way. "I'm a realist. I don't like to believe in things that can let me down."

"And here you are asking me to believe in you."

He grinned. "Well, that's because I won't let you down. You can put your faith in me and know I'll do my very best."

"But you can't control everything," she said, her face slackening again. "There are too many factors out of your control. So I can't put any real faith in you."

He looked hurt, but she persisted. "I can't put faith in anyone who's not in control."

"Well, no one is really in control here, except for the kidnapper."

"No. He just thinks he is."

"You *have* to believe in somebody."

"I believe in God. He knows where the children are."

He let that declaration hang in the air for a moment before asking, "Then how come you still don't have any peace?"

"Because I'm weak," she whispered.

Tony got up and walked to the window. He looked out on the news truck that waited outside for some sign of drama. "I'm not much of a believer in God, Sharon," he admitted. "I've had to do too many things on my own."

"You may have thought you were doing them on your own. But God was still God, whether you believed or not."

He turned back to her. "What if we don't find the girls, Sharon? What if this ends badly? Are you still going to believe that God was in control?"

He hadn't realized how biting that remark would be, but she looked up at him with horrified eyes. "It can't end badly, Tony. You see? Already you're giving up. And you expect me to believe in you."

"No, I'm not giving up. It won't end badly. I'm just trying to make a point. What about all the other parents who've lost children? Was God in control there, too?"

She wiped away a tear. "Yes, I believe he was."

"Was he in control when that man was luring your child into his car?"

It was almost as if he wanted her to break, to scream out that God wasn't in control, that the world had fallen out of God's grasp and chaos ruled.

"I don't know what you want me to say, Tony," she said in a shaky voice. "The fact that I'm a basket case doesn't take one iota away from God's power. It just proves how fragile my faith can be. It's an indictment of me, not God."

"Fragile faith?" he asked, his voice softening as he realized he was being too harsh. "Your faith isn't fragile. It's as strong as a rock."

"No," she whispered. "If it were, I'd be asking more directly for his will to be done. But I'm not sure I can do that yet, because I don't know what his will is." She began to cry harder and covered her mouth. "I'm just not to the point where I can trust God to take my child from me, even if there's a big, divine purpose. I don't want to lose my baby!"

He sat back down and pulled her against him, holding her while she wept. For the first time since he was a kid, he thought of praying. But then he wondered what he would say. *God, I don't even think I believe in you, but Sharon does, so if you're listening . . .*

Right. As if God would be open to listening to a prayer like that. But the feeling that his prayers were no good, that there was no way he could appeal to the Creator Sharon put all her faith in, made him feel too helpless.

He dropped his chin on the crown of her head as her tears soaked the front of his shirt, and feeling more humble the harder she cried, he closed his eyes. *Give us a miracle, Lord. Bring the children back. For Sharon.*

If there was a God, wouldn't he answer a prayer for Sharon, who believed so deeply in him?

But didn't bad things happen to Christians? Didn't tragedies befall them, just like everyone else? Weren't they frequent customers at hospitals and funeral homes, just like the regular joes were? Weren't some of their prayers not being answered?

He hated the thought that her faith might not make any difference. It would be nice if it did. After all these years of going it alone, he could use something to believe in. If he just had a sign . . .

But he couldn't rely on God to bring the children home. He could rely only on himself, and his experience, and the gun he carried in the holster under his arm. He could rely only on good luck and solid planning.

Sharon pulled herself back and wiped her eyes. "I never do this."

"Do what?"

"Cry. Openly, in front of a stranger, like I have with you. It seems like every time I've been around you, I've broken down. I don't want you to think this is the real me."

"Isn't it?" he asked perceptively. "You're not really a sweet, loving, feminine beauty who loves her children more than she loves herself?"

She smiled through her tears. "You're good, you know that?" She sat up straight and shook her head. "I don't know why I feel comfortable enough with you to bare my soul like this."

"Because you have to be a tough guy for the others in the house," he said.

"Oh, is that it?" she asked, sniffing. "Why would that be?"

"Well, you can't be vulnerable around your ex-husband. That would be too painful, given your history. You have to keep that wall up, for your own protection, I would imagine."

She cocked her head and gave him a narrow look. "Is that right, Dr. Freud?"

"Yes," he said with certainty. "And you can't let your guard down around Anne, because you don't want to feel her pain. Then you'd have to be compassionate toward her, and you need to hold onto your bitterness. That's a defense mechanism, too."

She stood up. "Oh, that's ridiculous. You're forgetting that my daughter is in the house, too. Do I have deep-seated bitterness about her, too?"

"No. But around her you have to be strong, so she doesn't shrivel. I've seen you come close to cracking with Lynda Barrett, but you held back. I think it may have been because Ben and Anne and everybody were around."

"So I picked you by default? I could have fallen apart with any cop, right? It could have been Larry?"

"I'm cuter," Tony said.

She couldn't help smiling. "While I find your whole scenario to be a lot of baloney, I think you're selling yourself a little short. The fact is that you have a way about you. I've felt I could be myself with you. You've understood."

"Some of it, maybe," he said. "But I'm glad you've felt comfortable with me. Sit down."

Slowly, she sank back down with a giant sigh. He began to massage her shoulders, working out the tension that had hardened itself in her neck and upper back. "There are some things a woman just shouldn't have to face alone," he whispered.

Her face sobered again, and tears pushed to her eyes once more as she relaxed against his ministrations. It felt so good to be pampered, she thought, to be touched with gentle hands, to be spoken to in soft, masculine tones. Part of her wanted to curl up in the warmth and comfort of it, to hide in the strength of it. But another part of her told her it was a fantasy, because he was not a believer. They had little in common.

Larry came into the room, and started at the sight of them. "Excuse me," he said. "I didn't mean to interrupt anything."

"I was just massaging her shoulders," Tony said, letting her go. "No big deal."

Larry glared at him for a moment. "Can I have a word with you, Tony? In the dining room?"

"Sure." Tony stood up and winked at Sharon as he followed Larry out of the room.

Larry was fuming by the time they reached the dining room. "What in the world do you think you're doing?"

Tony looked around innocently. "What are you talking about?"

"Sitting in there with her like that, rubbing her shoulders . . ."

"She's tense and upset. I was trying to help"

"You were trying to seduce her, Tony," Larry whispered. "And I think that's reprehensible. Her child has been kidnapped, and she's not thinking straight. How could you even think of taking advantage of a woman in that state of mind?"

Tony couldn't believe his ears. He gaped at his partner as his face reddened. "You've got a lot of nerve. If I remember correctly, you're the one who gets involved with victims, not me. Check out that ring on your finger if you've forgotten!"

"I've never taken advantage of anyone, Tony. I don't hit them when they're down."

"No, but you've sure offered your shoulder for them to cry on. How come when I do it it's womanizing? Did you ever think for a minute that I might feel genuine compassion for her? That I might have some of the same instincts you've had, to comfort someone who's at her wit's end?"

"Don't get involved with the victims, Tony. That's what you've always told me."

"Yeah, and when's the last time you listened?" Tony turned around to start out of the room, but stopped at the door and turned back. "You make me sick, you know that? You think just because you're some big Christian, that your motives are pure and mine aren't. You think that if *you* comfort someone, it's because you're a good Samaritan, but if I do it, I'm trying to get them into bed." Furious, he shoved a chair under the table, then lowered his voice to a harsh whisper and went on.

"Well, here's a news flash for you, pal. I can feel the same compassion you can! And my motives can be just as pure! That woman in there is broken and hurting, and anyone who took advantage of her right now would be the scum of the earth in my book. I'm not going to let your paranoias keep me from giving her a little comfort when she needs it. Look around and tell me if there's anyone else in this house who can give it to her!"

Larry only stood there, his hands in his pockets, staring at Tony. After a moment, he looked down at his sneaker-clad feet. "All right, maybe I jumped to conclusions. This case has me in knots."

"Think how *she* feels," Tony said, and headed back to the den to find Sharon.

41

EMILY WAS WAILING, and Christy put her arms around her and pressed her sister's face against her chest. The car was going over something rough, like railroad tracks, Christy thought as they took the jarring jolts in the trunk.

"Shhh, Emily," Christy whispered. "He told us to be quiet. He'll kill us if we're not."

"He's gonna kill us anyway," Emily cried against Christy's shirt. "Christy, Daddy's not coming, is he?"

"Yes, he will," Christy said. "And if he doesn't, my mommy will. She won't let anything happen to us."

"But your mommy doesn't like me," Emily moaned.

"Who says?"

"My mom. She says your mommy hates us. That's why she didn't want me going to church with you."

"My mommy doesn't hate anybody!" Christy said.

The car came to a stop, and quickly, Christy put her hand over Emily's mouth. "He's stopping. Emily, if you get another chance, run again. We'll go in different directions. He can't come after both of us."

"But I'm scared!" she whimpered. "I want to get out of here. I want to go home."

The car started rolling again, this time on gravel, and Christy shook her sister's shoulder. "Hush! You sound like a baby!"

"But he hurt my arm when he grabbed me, and I can't move in this stupid place."

"Where did he hurt your arm? Show me."

Emily turned over on her back and, in the darkness, took Christy's hand and ran it along her arm.

"Where does it hurt?"

"All over," Emily said. "It hurts bad."

"It's probably bruised. When Daddy comes, he can look at it."

"He's not gonna come, Christy," Emily said, her panicked voice rising again. "He can't find us, anyway. Maybe he's not even looking." Her crying grew louder, and Christy searched her brain for something to quiet her sister.

"Hush," she said again. "Just listen. I'm gonna teach you a song. It's a real hard song, so you have to listen hard. And I have to whisper so he won't hear."

"I don't want to sing," Emily whined.

"You have to," Christy said. "It'll help you stop crying. Now, listen. It's a song about the states. It goes, 'Alabama, Alaska, Arizona, Arkansas . . .' Now, sing it with me. Whisper. 'Alabama, Alaska, Arizona, Arkansas . . ."

"I don't want to," said Emily.

"Do it!" Christy insisted. "Alabama, Alaska . . ."

"Arizona, Arkansas," Emily finished on a whisper.

"Good!" Christy said. "The next part is 'California, Colorado . . ."

Emily was listening, trying now to sing along. The effort of learning the song took her mind off of the cramped quarters of the trunk, the merciless way the wheels bounced on the gravel or over potholes, or the fear of what the man would do with them when they stopped.

They were up to the state of Hawaii before the car finally stopped. They heard the man slam his car door and start back to the trunk.

42

THE PHONE RANG, and everyone sprang to attention. In the kitchen, Ben put his hand on the phone and looked into the dining room, waiting for the signal. Tony nodded.

Ben picked up the phone. "Hello?"

"May I speak to Detective Danks, please?"

Everyone in the house let out a weary breath as Tony picked up and Ben hung up. "It's for them," Ben told Anne, who had run into the room with Bobby on her hip.

"He's never gonna call!" Anne said, kicking the chair. "When's he gonna call?"

Leaning wearily against the kitchen wall, Sharon watched silently.

Tony was on his feet, reaching for his coat, as he hung up. "We've had a break!" he shouted. "They found the car the girls were abducted in. It was left back at the rental company with the keys in it last night. It was paid for in advance with a credit card. You'll never guess whose name it was in."

"Whose?" Larry asked.

"Ben Robinson."

"What?" Ben asked. "I never left the house last night! Everyone saw me!"

"Don't panic. The guy who checked the car out to him gave us a description, and it matches the kidnapper, *sans* hat and glasses. He's talking our artist through a composite sketch right now." He stopped at the door and turned back. "If this pans out, Ben, then we know how he got a gun in your name."

"But none of my credit cards were stolen. He would have needed it days before the murder to get a gun."

"He probably had counterfeit IDs and credit cards made. It happens."

Sharon let out a long-held breath. "Thank goodness, we're getting somewhere."

Tony started out the door. "Larry'll stay here in case the kidnapper calls."

"I'm going with you," Ben said.

"No! You have to stay here in case he calls! As soon as we get a composite done, I'll bring it back to you."

"Fax it!" Sharon said. "Maybe Ben will recognize the guy!" She ran to grab a piece of paper and a pen. "Here's my fax number. It'll come straight into the house."

Tony grabbed the number. "I'll fax it as soon as it's done. Larry'll call me if you guys hear anything." Not waiting for an answer, Tony rushed out.

Albert Gates was a forty-two-year-old car rental agent who hadn't seen such excitement in years. He would never have dreamed that the polished gentleman who had come in here a week ago to rent a car would turn out to be a kidnapper. He couldn't wait to tell the boys at the pool hall.

Albert was suddenly important, someone whose words the cops were hanging on, someone who could make a difference, and he was enjoying every minute of it. Any minute now, the news teams would probably show up.

"The car was really dirty when we got it back," he was saying as the policemen took notes and the artist tried to sketch the description he'd already given. "It looked like he'd been driving on dirt roads. Red clay all over the fender."

The detective who'd just bolted in asked, "Is it still on the car?"

"No," Albert said apologetically. "I had it washed first thing. That's what I always do, to get it ready to go out again."

"Where is the car?" Tony asked. "I want to see it."

"It's the blue Taurus parked by the curb just outside the door."

Tony started back out of the room. "How long before that composite is ready?"

"We're almost there," the artist said, still sketching.

"All right. I'll be right back."

Tony went outside and looked the car over. Just as Albert said, the car had been washed clean. One officer was inside it, dusting for prints, so he leaned in the window. "Find anything?"

"Yeah, I'm getting some prints. But this car's been rented out four times already this month. Plus the agents here and their clean-up staff have all been through it. These prints could be anybody's."

Tony sighed and looked in the backseat. Nothing had been left. He reached through the driver's side window and punched the button to release the trunk. He walked back there and pulled the trunk open.

Nothing.

He stood back and tried to think. Dirt roads. Red clay. He got down on his knees and looked under the car. Just as he'd hoped, it was still dirty. Red clumps of clay still clung to the belly of the car. He reached under and scratched some off.

There were only a few rural places left in St. Clair. Like so much of the Tampa Bay area, it had been overbuilt. He got up and sat back on his heels, examining the red clay on his fingers.

It could be from a building site, he thought, but that was doubtful. Most of the building sites were too visible. Besides that, a single lot wouldn't be large enough to get that much mud caked on the car. It had to be a rural area.

He thought of the few farms still remaining on the east side of St. Clair, and the cover of woods that surrounded some of them. Maybe the kidnapper had taken the children there.

Dusting his hands off, he went back inside to ask about the mileage. Maybe it would give him some clue as to whether he'd left town.

"His eyes were a very pale blue," Arthur was saying. "He was a nice-looking man. And his nose was a little different than what you've done. . . ."

The artist followed the descriptions and made the necessary changes on the sketch.

"Yeah, that's real close. Only I think his lips were thinner. And his eyebrows were thicker."

Tony waited, watching, as the face emerged.

"That's it," the man said finally. "I'm sure. That's what he looked like. Isn't it amazing that you can do that just from my description? I've always wondered how that worked."

Tony leaned over the desk. "You're sure? Absolutely positive?"

"Oh, yeah," he said. "It's him."

"All right." Tony held out a hand. "Let me have it. Where's your fax machine?"

"Over there," Albert said, getting more excited. "Who are you faxing it to?"

"Somebody I hope can identify him," Tony said. He took the sketch and pulled the number out of his pocket. Quickly, he dialed Sharon's fax number, and fed the picture through.

The moment the fax machine rang in Sharon's study, they all dashed for it.

They watched, breath held, as the face slowly emerged.

Ben waited until the machine had cut the page, then inverted it and studied it. "Oh, it can't be . . ."

"You know him?" Sharon asked.

Anne pushed closer to see the picture, and her face paled. "Ben, is that . . . ?"

"Nelson Chamberlain," Ben said, turning back to Larry, who stood behind him. "It can't be him! He was Louis's best friend. He's the one who posted my bond. Why would he help get me out of jail if he's the one setting me up?"

"Because you have something he wants," Larry said. "You obviously couldn't give it to him from a jail cell."

"But he's been in England. He couldn't be the one—" He blew out a helpless breath. "He knows Emily. She knows him—"

"That's why she went with him!" Anne cried. "Ben, don't you see?"

"But I trusted him." He studied the face again. "It just doesn't make sense. If he's the one who planted all that evidence against me, he was hoping I'd take the fall for the murder. Why'd he post my bond? He stood to lose that money."

Larry picked up the phone and dialed the car agency. "That was a small investment compared to what he stands to make. And it threw us off his scent for a while." The phone was answered, and he asked for Tony.

He waited until Tony picked up. "It's Nelson Chamberlain," Larry said. "One of the art dealers we've been trying to get in touch with. He's supposed to have been in England."

Weakly, Ben lowered into a chair.

"Red clay?" Larry asked. "What do you make of that?"

Sharon stepped closer, hoping they were on to something.

"Yeah, that wouldn't hurt. We need to search his house, and any other property he owns here. Maybe it'll lead us to them."

Tony was just coming in when Larry's number rang. He snapped it up. "Yeah? All right, shoot. Okay, I'm on my way. Get somebody over here to relieve us in case the guy calls."

He grabbed his windbreaker and jumped up as he hung up the phone. "They found some property Chamberlain owns on the east side of town. It's a few acres of wooded area. I'll go over there to see if there's a building anywhere around there where he could have the kids. Then I'll check his house."

"I'm going with you!" Sharon cried.

This time, Tony knew they couldn't stop her.

"What if he calls?" Ben asked, practically chasing them to the door.

"Hopefully we'll get him before he has the chance!" Tony called back. "But if he does, just get his instructions. Play along, like you have what he wants." He saw the police car already turning into their driveway. "They're here. They know what to do if he calls."

Sharon followed Tony at a trot, and Anne ran out behind them. "Tony, Larry! I'm coming, too."

"No, it's not a good idea," Larry said.

"But my little girl could be out there!" Anne cried. "I have to be there when you find her! She'll need me!"

Sharon looked beseechingly at Tony. This time, she said, "Let her come."

He shrugged and got into the car. "All right, get in."

The ride to the other side of town was fifteen minutes or so. Sharon and Anne sat in the backseat, watching out the window, both of them tense and hopeful.

"Turn left here," Larry said. "Yeah, that's it. I think this is the edge of his property."

In the distance, Sharon heard a police siren. "Won't he hear us coming? Shouldn't they turn off the siren?"

Almost as if in answer to that, the siren hushed.

They drove up a long dirt road, and Sharon scanned the trees for any sign of a structure where the children could be. There were no buildings, no houses, only this red dirt road and the dense forest beside it.

"What's that?" Larry asked as they followed the dirt road around a cluster of trees.

Tony leaned forward. "A shed," he said. "And there are fresh tire tracks. Bingo!"

Sharon felt the blood running out of her face. The children couldn't be in there. Not in a four-by-six dirt shack out in the middle of nowhere!

"Stay here!" Tony ordered. "It doesn't look like he's here, but he could be. We'll look first."

Sharon nodded. Anne sat paralyzed, staring toward the shed as the men got out, wielding their guns, and surrounded the little building.

The men shouted something, but there was no reply.

They heard the door being kicked in, and both women jumped.

After a moment, Tony came back around the building, shaking his head.

"They're not there," Anne said, and started to cry.

Sharon, too, covered her face and tried to cope with the horror of it. She got out of the car, not knowing which way to go. "But the fresh tire tracks. It's his property, isn't it?"

Tony looked down at the tire tracks. "Somebody was here, all right. Maybe even today."

Larry came out of the little shed. "Hey, Tony. Come look at this!"

They all rushed to the door. "McDonald's bags," Larry said. "Two cups."

"They were here!" Sharon cried. "He locked them in this dark place? They must have been terrified!"

"Where are they now?" Anne almost screamed.

"It looks like they dug a hole under the wall."

Tony went back out and checked the other side. "Look, footprints," he said. "It looks like one of the kids may have gotten away."

Anne and Sharon stared down at the beloved little footprint. "It's Emily," Anne cried. "She had on tennis shoes."

"She's right," Sharon confirmed. "Christy was wearing loafers."

By now, the other cops were following the prints, trying to trace the steps of the child and the bigger steps of the man who had taken them.

Anne turned back to the woods, the direction the footsteps led. "She ran in there! She's still in there! I know it." She ran into the woods, unstoppable, calling, "Emily! Emily, it's Mommy! Honey, don't be afraid. Just tell us where you are!"

Sharon followed behind her, praying that Christy was with her. But there were no footsteps for Christy.

Frantic, Anne came to the drop-off and looked down into the gully where a stream of water ran. Had Emily tried to cross it? Had she fallen in?

She turned back, looking with horror at Sharon. "Where *is* she? Where *is* she?"

She was beginning to tremble from her head to her feet, and Sharon began to cry with her. They weren't here, and there were only two possibilities. They had either been caught by the kidnapper and taken somewhere else, or they were at the bottom of that gully somewhere, washed downstream.

"Emily!" Anne screamed. "Emily! WHERE ARE YOU?"

Feeling the same anguish Anne felt, Sharon stood motionless, fragmenting piece by piece until there was nothing left of her control.

"They're not here!" Anne screamed. "Sharon, they're not here!"

Sharon took a step toward her and put her arms around the weeping woman. Anne fell against her, heaving with sobs. "If we'd just come earlier. We could have saved them. We could have saved them."

Sharon wept, too, clinging to Anne like a sister, knowing that she was the only other woman on the face of the earth who knew exactly how Sharon felt.

Tony stood back, deeply frustrated that this lead had led nowhere. Yet this picture, of two enemies embracing, touched him in a place that he rarely visited.

Larry came up behind him and saw the women. When Tony looked up at him, Larry saw that his eyes were moist. Neither of the men wanted to look at the other.

"He must have rented another car," Larry said quietly. "I sent the others to check out all the cars that have been rented from other rental car agencies in town. We're getting the sketch printed up, so they'll be taking copies with them. Soon enough we'll know what he's driving."

Tony touched the shoulders of both women to coax them apart. "We'd better get back to Sharon's. He probably doesn't know we know who he is, so he'll be calling soon. Come on, we need to go," he said.

Sobbing, they separated and slowly made their way back to the car.

43

NELSON CHAMBERLAIN DROVE the streets of St. Clair, desperately seeking someplace else to hide the children. He couldn't take them back to the shed, not after they'd escaped from there once. His home was out of the question, since he was supposed to be out of town. He hadn't gone near his own house since before the murder. He couldn't take them to his hotel, for there was no way to get them inside without their being seen. Their pictures were posted everywhere, and he had no doubt that the St. Clair police were searching everywhere for them and the kidnapper who had abducted them. He hadn't even tried to threaten the Robinsons against involving the police—that would have been a fantasy. The police always got involved, whether overtly or covertly. The fact that they'd been camped in Sharon Robinson's home since the children disappeared was something he could watch and stay on top of.

But where should he take the children now? He couldn't leave them in the trunk all day. The fact was, even though he needed them for leverage to make Ben Robinson act, they were really more trouble than they were worth. He had counted on keeping them in the little shed until their father capitulated and handed over the painting, but the little brats had ruined that.

He saw a pay phone at a convenience store, and inched the car as close as he could so that the cord would reach inside the car. Inserting a quarter, he dialed the phone number of the Biltmore.

He asked for Boudreaux's room. When the clerk responded that Boudreaux had checked out, Nelson's heart crashed. He couldn't have left! Not without the painting!

He searched his pockets for the number of Boudreaux's museum in France, and inserted a fistful of quarters. He thought briefly about using the cellular phone he carried in his briefcase, but quickly thought better of it. If his name did ever come up as a suspect, it wouldn't do to have records on his cellular phone bill that showed he had made calls to Boudreaux, Ben Robinson, or anyone else that could incriminate him. Especially not when he was still supposed to be in England. No, he'd just have to stick with the pay phones.

A French woman answered, and he said, "Excuse me. My name is John Lieber, and I'm a friend of Monsieur Boudreaux's. I was to meet him here in St. Clair, but I'm afraid I missed him. Do you have any word on where he might be?"

"Oui, Monsieur," she said. "Monsieur Boudreaux has a message for you. He has moved to Holiday Inn downtown Tampa and is using the name Passons."

"Very good, very good," Nelson said, breathless. "Excellent. I'll call him right away."

He hung up and breathed out a gigantic sigh of relief, inserted some more quarters, and dialed information. He got the number, dialed it, then asked to be connected with Eric Passons's room.

He listened through two rings. "Hello?"

"Hello, Eric, how are you?" It was his most professional business voice, and he knew Eric recognized him immediately.

"Not well," the Frenchman said. "Very disappointed."

His temples were perspiring, and he pulled a handkerchief out of his coat pocket and dabbed at them. "Eric, has something happened?"

"Oui," the man said. "Some American phoned my secretary earlier asking where I was. I feared being drawn into this . . . uh . . . investigation. I changed my name and location."

"That was wise," Nelson said. "I'm glad you left the information for me." He paused. "Look, Eric, I can promise you that I'll have the painting by tomorrow morning. Surely you can understand how the circumstances of Dubose's death have complicated things."

Eric laughed sardonically. "Complicated things? After all this time, you still do not have the painting?"

"I know precisely where it is," Nelson countered, his face reddening. "But I don't have to tell you how delicate these matters are. I have to be very careful how and when I retrieve it. And then there's the matter of transporting it."

"You understand, do you not, that I have a buyer for it? The longer I make him wait, the less likely he is to buy it. I really must not wait any longer."

Nelson sat back hard on his seat. He could hear low, muffled voices in the trunk. The children were singing something. He looked around to make sure no one was close enough to hear it.

"Will you give me until morning, Eric? We both know that the wait will be worth it in the long run."

"Not if I am . . . how you say . . . arrested? The picture would be taken from me. And with the murder, and now the kidnapping of Ben Robinson's children, I must tell you I have grave reservations. Perhaps later, in a year or two, after the suspicions have died down."

"In a year or two I can guarantee I'll have another buyer. One who might even pay more than you're offering. Your buyer could hide it for a period of time, until he's comfortable. But unless you act now, someone else will profit from it."

That did make the man hesitate. "Very well, Monsieur Lieber. If I wait until morning, and the picture is delivered, I will proceed with our bargain. But if I do not have it by noon, I will be on my way back to LeMans."

"You'll have it by morning." Nelson cleared his throat and wiped his perspiring face again. "You do understand, now, that there will be some restoration involved? The painting has been rolled up since its theft—"

"Which often means there are cracks in the paint. I understand that, Monsieur Lieber. My price has allowed for that. But if it is an authentic Marazzio, and you do indeed deliver it to me, I am certain that it can be restored to its previous condition. Now, about this investigation."

The singing had stopped, and he heard them talking. Didn't they ever shut up? He revved his engine, hoping the noise would overpower the voices.

"I am concerned in my mind as to who killed Dubose." He hesitated, as if choosing his words carefully. "It has occurred to me that you may have been involved."

Nelson laughed too loudly. "Me? Why on earth would I be the one?"

"The money we've agreed upon is quite a lot of motive, would you not agree? Perhaps you wished to dispose of Dubose so that the money would not be divided."

"That's ludicrous," Nelson bit out. "This is a clean, painless, harmless deal. People do not murder over art."

"*Pardon,* my friend," Boudreaux said. "But there have been many murders over the last decades, precisely over art. Money is a powerful motivator."

Nelson laughed again. "I assure you that Dubose's death was as much a surprise to me as it was to anyone. He was a dear friend of mine. I don't know what I'll do without him."

"Indeed," Eric said, not convinced. "My . . . what you say . . . instincts . . . warn me to return to France."

"Then your instincts are wrong. This whole endeavor will make you a richer man," Nelson said. "I'm not a fool, Eric. I'm well aware that you could sell the painting for a third more than what you're paying me. There are museums in Italy that would sell entire roomfuls of art to raise the funds for this one picture. As for the murder and the kidnapping, I can assure you that they have nothing to do with this transaction. My theory is that Ben Robinson was involved in drug trafficking, and he was probably the real target for the murder—that is, if he didn't do it himself. Robinson is a very complex, dubious man. Very dishonest. A marvelous painter, and quite a gifted restorer. What he had going on outside of the gallery, I don't know. But I feel sure it will all come to light very soon. You'll see. And you'll be very glad you didn't miss the opportunity to find the most important piece of lost art this century."

"Do you think Robinson has any knowledge of this painting?"

"No," Nelson said, as if with certainty. "Not at all. It was very carefully hidden."

When he'd finally convinced Boudreaux to wait, he hung up the telephone and rolled his window back up. The children had grown quieter now, and he racked his brain to think of the location of a pay phone where he could call Ben Robinson and let him talk to at least one of the girls. That might remind him of the urgency here. But all of the pay phones were too public, and someone might see the child. Not only that, but one of them might do something unpredictable to call attention to herself. He couldn't take that chance.

Once again he thought longingly of his cellular, but it just wasn't worth the risk. He would wait until dark, and then take one of the children with him to make the call.

Until then, he had to find some place to put them.

A thought occurred to him as he drove across the Spanish Trail Bridge, out to the eastern edge of St. Clair, where there were still a few small farms and some old, dilapidated buildings that were boarded up. There was one in particular he remembered seeing a couple of days ago on the way to his own property. An old abandoned store. That was just the place, he thought, and headed toward it.

The car cut off, and Emily clung to Christy in fear. "We've stopped, Christy!"

"Shhh. Just be quiet."

They heard his car door slam, and braced themselves. In a moment, they heard keys jangling at the back of the trunk, and suddenly the trunk came open, letting in a harsh flood of light that made them squint.

The two grimy little girls sat up and looked fearfully at their kidnapper.

He grabbed them each by one arm and bent down close to their ears. "If either one of you so much as breathes hard while I'm moving you, I'll throw you off the St. Clair Pier into the Gulf and your parents won't find you until you wash up on shore—after the sharks are through with you."

Both children trembled and allowed him to move them out of the car.

As he herded them from the car toward the dilapidated building, Christy searched frantically, though quietly, for someone who might see them. But there was no one anywhere around.

He opened the door. This building was much bigger than the last one, and it had a concrete floor. He acted like this was the first time he had been here, and he left the front door open, providing light as he dragged them in.

"No, not here!" Emily cried. "It might have rats! Please! Not here! I want to go home! I want my daddy!"

Nelson Chamberlain squatted down in front of her, his big, threatening finger pointing at her nose. "What did I tell you about making a sound?"

She tried to keep her lips shut, but she began to cry, and the sound wouldn't be muffled easily.

"Mister, we need to go to the bathroom," Christy whispered. "Is there a bathroom here?"

That seemed to give him an idea, and he got back up, still holding each of them by their upper arms. "Up those stairs, and we'll see," he told them. "Come on now."

Emily was crying harder, biting her lip and trembling as they took each step. Some light shone in through a window that had been shot out about fifteen feet up, but it cast only enough light to show the degree of dust and filth that had accumulated since this place was last inhabited. Dead hanging plants covered with spiderwebs dangled from slimy, fungus-covered macramé hangers. The place might have been pretty once, but now it was a study in filth and decomposition.

The man nodded toward a door in the back corner of the dusty room. "There."

"No!" Emily cried again, but he jerked them toward it.

The door opened into Emily's worst nightmare. There was a filthy, cracked commode with only half a seat on it; warped and rotting boards made up the floor. The sink had long ago been torn off the wall, leaving a gaping hole that revealed rusted plumbing—the perfect place for rats to lurk. Above it all, at least ten feet up, was another broken-out window too high for them to reach, and a dozen or so dead hanging plants just like the ones on the other side, with long, brown vines laced with spiderwebs that seemed to reach down and grab for them.

"Mister, can't you leave us your flashlight?" Christy asked.

"No. The dark will keep you from trying to find some way out again."

"But . . ." Christy's voice broke, and she started to cry, but she tried to keep her voice steady. As her mother had told her more than once, whining got you nowhere. "Those dead plants have spiders, and there are rats in that wall, I can hear them. Can't you? If we're in the dark and we hear something or . . . feel something . . ." She sobbed and reached for Emily's hand. Her sister was trembling so hard she could hardly hold it still. "We might scream by accident . . . And somebody might hear us. If you want us to stay quiet, we promise we will if you'll just give us the flashlight."

The man was quiet for a moment. "All right," he said finally. "The batteries won't last long, anyway."

He handed Christy the small flashlight. "Now, go on. Get in there."

"It stinks," Emily squealed. "I'm scared."

"Mister, couldn't we stay out here, in this room?" Christy asked, crying fully now. "Please . . . We promise not to make any noise . . ."

He thrust them in and shut the door behind them.

Christy and Emily hunkered in a corner with the flashlight illuminating the nightmarish sights around them. Outside the door, they could hear him moving things to bar them in, since he didn't have a lock.

Emily buried her face against Christy's chest, and tried not to cry loudly. But Christy was having trouble herself. Her fingers, still filthy from digging, were hurting from where they'd blistered and bled as they'd dug. She knew that sores needed to be cleaned to keep them from getting infected, but she suspected that that was just one more thing she had to worry about now. She wondered what Jenny was doing. She wondered if Mommy was worried, if she and Anne were fighting. She wondered if Daddy was looking for them.

They heard something in the wall, and Emily's voice went an octave higher, though she kept her mouth muffled against Christy's shirt. Christy shone her light toward the sound, hoping to frighten whatever it was away, but she squeezed her eyes shut to keep from seeing it herself.

"Pray," she whimpered. "Pray hard. Now."

Emily only trembled, and Christy knew she couldn't count on her to pray. She'd have to do it herself. "Dear God," she squeaked. "We're so scared"

"It doesn't work!" Emily cried. "It doesn't work, Christy! We tried, remember?"

"It does work," Christy said. "It has to. Mommy said it works."

"Then why didn't it work before? Why didn't Daddy find us?"

"He will," Christy sobbed. "I know he will. We just have to pray harder. Now, either pray with me, or be quiet."

Emily chose to be quiet as Christy started praying again.

44

NELSON CHAMBERLAIN NEEDED a drink. For a while, he drove around near the abandoned store, making sure there was no reason for anyone to get close to the building where he had hidden the children. They wouldn't be discovered there, he decided finally. The building was too old and dilapidated, and those who drove past it daily would never notice that anything was different about the old building. The girls were stuck there until he went back to get them. Now all he had to do was decide what his next step would be.

He drove into town to a trendy bar called Steppin' Out and pulled into the parking lot as it filled up with happy-hour traffic. The bar was popular this time of day, he thought with relief. He could blend in, and no one would notice him. He walked into the noisy room decorated with twenties memorabilia, found a seat at the bar, and ordered a scotch. It calmed him as it went down, and he told himself that things were going to work out after all. Yes, a lot had to fall into place, but the more he drank, the more confident he became.

The music seemed to be growing louder, an unidentifiable blend of guitars and drums, drowned out by the chatter of the after-work crowd. He looked around, through the haze of cigarette smoke, at the silk suits and designer dresses, the perfectly coifed locks of young professional women, the moussed hair of lawyers and accountants and consultants of every kind. He was comfortable here, as he was in bars like it all over the world. In ways, it was his sanctuary, the place where he knew he could come at any time for sustenance or comfort. Even now, as he nursed his scotch, he felt that comfort seeping through him.

It would all work out. It had to. So much was at stake. He had held onto the painting for over ten years now, after daring to take it himself from a museum in Palermo. In Italy, the statute of limitations for art theft was ten years, so he was out of the woods as far as prosecution there was concerned. He'd finally decided a few months ago that it was time to begin searching for a buyer.

But it wasn't his style to do it himself. He liked to stay detached from the particulars of such exchanges, so that if any of his deals went sour, they couldn't be traced back to him. Dubose had been the perfect liaison. With his contacts in the art world, and his legitimate role as owner of several small galleries, he was in a good position to find a buyer. Of all the art thefts Nelson Chamberlain had been involved in, this was by far of the greatest value. It was the *coup de gras,* the one that would make world news—though his name would never be mentioned in connection with it. The fact that it would make him a fortune was enough.

But once the contact had been established, Dubose had gotten greedy. He had demanded half of what Chamberlain would be paid for the painting, though Dubose had not been involved in the theft in any way. Because Dubose already had the painting and because he needed Dubose to make the exchange with the buyer, Nelson reluctantly agreed—until he realized that Dubose was not being honest with him about the price the dealer was willing to pay. He was getting more for it than he had reported to Chamberlain, and was keeping the bigger portion for himself.

That was bad enough, but when Ben Robinson discovered the canvas, Chamberlain's concerns had grown even more inflamed. What kind of fool hid something worth millions in a wooden compartment of a cold, damp attic, where anyone could stumble upon it? There was nothing to do, he thought, except to get the middleman out of the way, and handle things himself. He had to do away with Dubose to ensure that his own interests weren't violated. What a shock, he reminded himself ruefully, after he'd gotten rid of Dubose, to discover that the painting wasn't where it was supposed to be.

There was no doubt in his mind that Ben Robinson had it; Ben was the only other person who had known that it was there. What he couldn't understand was why the man hadn't agreed to turn it over to him after the first phone call. Maybe the police were trying to make him play cat-and-mouse games with him to draw him out. He only hoped that taking his children had made Ben think better of it.

He heard a loud round of cackling laughter, and looked up to see a woman dressed in a tight red sweater and tight black jeans with four-inch heels, flirting with a group of men half her age. She was obviously in her fifties, yet here she was competing with women in their twenties.

"You are just too much!" she was saying in a deep Texas drawl to one of the men standing beside her. Her voice carried over the crowd, as if to draw attention to herself. "For heaven's sake, you have to eat!"

Was she hitting on that man who was young enough to be her son? Chamberlain wondered, amused. There was no telling, he thought. He watched her as she pretended to pout, then pranced over to the bar, pushing between two patrons, and got the bartender's attention. "Excuse me. You over there. Yes, you."

The bartender finished mixing the drinks he was mixing, and leaned toward her. "Can I help you?"

"Doris Stevens here," she said, holding out her hand with inch-long fake nails. The man shook halfheartedly. "I came in here to see if you'd let me put these posters up of those little kidnapped girls." As she spoke, she dug through her huge purse, and brought out a few copies of the posters. "Bless their hearts, they're friends of mine. Little Chrissy and Judy. The sweetest little girls you ever laid eyes on. And now somebody's kidnapped them, and well, I'm doing everything in my power to help find them."

The bartender took one of the posters. "A $25,000 reward, huh?"

Doris waved that off. "Their safe return would be payment enough."

"But the reward money wouldn't hurt, would it?"

She shrugged. "I guess I'd take it, if they insisted. Heck, if I find those kids, I'd deserve the money. And how much is that really, when you consider the value of these two beautiful little girls? Can I put 'em up or what?"

"Sure. Go ahead."

She took the posters back and clicked around the room, tacking and taping the posters, while simultaneously flirting with anyone nearby.

Chamberlain felt his body go tense as the faces of the girls stared out at him. Quickly, he turned away. No one suspected him. His plan was flawless. He was going to get the painting tonight, and he'd be out of town before anyone knew what had hit them. This was one crime the police would never solve.

But the painting was the key, and he had to have it tonight. There simply was no choice. If he didn't deliver it to Eric by tomorrow, he would have to wait another year or two before he could safely approach another buyer. This time he had no middleman. His own hands had gotten dirty for the first time, but it was worth it—as long as the deal went through.

Chamberlain downed his drink and ordered another.

A telephone rang somewhere close to him, and he watched as the man sitting on the stool next to his reached into his coat pocket and withdrew a small cellular flip phone. He answered it, and Chamberlain listened, half-interested, as the man took care of business from his bar stool.

When he hung the phone up, the man set it on the counter next to his drink, and resumed reading the stock market page of the newspaper.

The waiter brought Chamberlain his scotch, and he sipped it as he listened to conversations around him. The news was playing on a television screen up in the corner of the room, and he saw the pictures of the two Robinson girls flash across it. He tried to listen to what was being said, but it was difficult over the voices in the crowd. Nothing new, he surmised from what he could hear. They didn't have any leads yet.

He smiled. The Keystone cops of St. Clair, Florida, were going to have to get their act together if they wanted to figure him out.

Feeling almost an ecstatic energy after his two doubles and the news report that said virtually nothing, he glanced at the pay phone on the wall and wondered if he dared call Ben Robinson from here. No, he thought, someone might overhear. And if they traced the call, he might not be able to get out of the parking lot fast enough before the cops showed up to find him.

Besides, he really needed to get one of the kids to talk to their father tonight, just to drive home his point that time was running out. Robinson needed to know that he wasn't playing games. Either he turned over the painting tonight, or the kids were history.

The cellular phone rang again, and the man next to him snapped it up and answered. As he spoke, three of his colleagues came in the door, and he waved toward them. They clustered behind his stool, crowding Chamberlain as well. The man took care of the call, then hung up and set the phone back on the bar. He turned his back to Chamberlain to talk to his friends in a conspiratorial huddle.

Nelson stared at the cellular phone, unattended on the bar. He couldn't use his own cellular phone, for fear that the call would be traced, but he could use someone else's!

He looked up at the television, pretending to be absorbed in the news, and quickly put his hand over the flip phone. In one swift motion, he slipped it into his pocket. Quickly, he dropped a couple of bills onto the counter and headed for the door.

He was out of the parking lot when the phone rang again, and Chamberlain began to laugh. He wondered if the man had even noticed yet that his phone was missing. He let it ring as he headed for the building where the children were. After a moment, it stopped.

Another perfect twist in a perfect crime, he thought. All he had to do now was figure out where to have Ben Robinson drop the painting.

He headed for the old, abandoned store, but before he reached the road heading toward it, a train stopped him. It was slowing, and he watched as boxcar after boxcar passed, traveling no faster than twenty miles per hour. Slow enough to jump on, retrieve something, and get back off a few miles down the tracks.

Perfect. If Robinson put the painting on a boxcar when it was stopped, Chamberlain could be waiting a significant distance down the tracks, jump on, then jump off, and no one would ever be able to catch him.

He picked up the flip phone, called information, and asked for the number of the railroad office. Quickly, he dialed it and asked for information about when the next few trains would come through today. He was told that one was due to come through around ten o'clock. It would remain for two hours to reload, then would depart again at 12:30.

Elated and anxious, he drove the rest of the way to the abandoned store, dropped the phone into his coat pocket, got out of the car, and reached down on the seat for his other flashlight. Then, treading warily, he went back into the dark, eerie building, and headed up the stairs for the children.

He heard their voices as he came inside and went up the creaky steps. Rodents scurried and scratched in the walls and in the dark corners of the room. He kept the flashlight circle in front of him, hoping the sound of his shoes would frighten them away.

The voices hushed as they heard him coming. He reached the bathroom. Grunting from the effort, he moved aside the steel drum, old machinery, and a long, heavy bench that he'd used to block them in.

The door creaked as he pushed it open.

His light shone around the filthy bathroom, until the circle spotlighted the children, hunkered so tightly together that it was difficult to even tell that there were two of them. They both looked up at him with their grimy faces, and he remembered that he hadn't fed them since morning. He'd have to take care of that later.

"Are you going to let us out of here now, Mister?" the older one asked him in a weak, raspy voice.

"No, not yet," he said, trying not to look at them. He pulled the phone out of his pocket. "We're going to make a phone call, to your father. I want you both to talk to him, to let him know you're okay. If you do as I say, he'll come to get you tonight, and you can go home with him. But if you don't do as I say, you'll never see him again."

"We'll do what you say," the little one, the escape artist, said as her eyes got as round as quarters.

"First, you don't tell him who I am. If you do, you'll be dead in five minutes, do you understand me?"

The older one frowned. "I don't know who you are, anyway."

But the little one, Emily, piped up. "I do. You're Mr. Chamberlain. You come to the gallery sometimes and buy my daddy's paintings."

He knew that the minute she went back to her father, she'd be able to tell who he was. He couldn't let that happen. Somehow, the children would just have to disappear from the whole equation. But he needed them long enough to manipulate Ben.

"I'm going to talk to him for a minute," he said, "and I want absolute silence. When I tell you, you can say hello to your father, and that's it. You tell him that you want him to hurry and get you home, but you don't say anything about where you are, or who I am, do you understand?"

"Yes, sir."

"All right. Now, quiet. If you do this right, I'll bring you some food."

Both children sat in the corner, still huddled in fear, as he dialed the number.

45

THE PHONE RANG, and Ben bolted for it. He waited until Tony gave him the signal from the other room. Sharon, Anne, and Jenny hurried into the dining room where they could hear the conversation.

"Hello?"

"Are you ready, Ben?" the voice asked.

Ben hesitated. "Yes."

"Then tonight's the night."

In the dining room, Tony waited on the other line for the tracing to be completed.

"What have you done with my daughters?"

"They're fine, Robinson. You're lucky I haven't killed the sniveling little brats."

"How do I know you haven't?" Ben asked, his voice cracking.

"Well, you can find out for yourself. It might even give you a little more incentive. You see, if you don't deliver the painting when and where I tell you, or if you try something foolish, or if you pull what you pulled at the airport, you'll never see these girls again."

"So help me, if you hurt them, I'll find you. I'll track you down if it takes the rest of my life . . ."

Chamberlain laughed. "I'm trembling, Robinson. Say hello to your daughter."

There was a muffled sound, a shifting, and then Emily's weak, high voice on the line. "Daddy?"

Anne dropped to a seat at the table in front of the reel-to-reel tape recorder from which she could hear her child's voice. In the kitchen, Ben pressed his face against the wall. "Emily, honey, are you all right?"

"Daddy, I want to go home," she squeaked. "Please, Daddy—"

The phone was jerked from her, and then Christy was on the line. Her lower, raspy voice sounded breathy, weak. "Daddy?"

"Christy." He caught his breath on a sob. "We're looking for you, honey. We're trying to get you back. Can you tell me where you are? Any clue? Just a word?"

She hesitated. "Daddy, we're scared. It's dark and cold and there are rats . . ."

He closed his eyes. "Honey, we're going to find you. We're doing everything we can to get you back tonight. Just hold on, okay? Take care of each other."

The man's voice interrupted. "It's your choice, Robinson. Either deliver, or say good-bye."

"I'll deliver," Ben said, glancing back at Larry who was watching him as he listened to the conversation. "Just tell me where."

"Midnight," the man said. "At the railroad station. There will be a train leaving at 12:30. I'll have a red handkerchief hanging in the opening of one of the boxcars between the Franklin Street and the Alethea Street intersections. Find it and put the painting in there."

"What about the children?"

"When I have the picture, I'll let you know where they are. And I'll know it when I see it. If you try to deceive me, Robinson, the children are dead."

Tony shook his head, signaling to Ben.

"No," Ben said. "You'll have to do better than that. Why should I trust you?"

"Because you have no choice. Midnight, Robinson. I wouldn't be late, if I were you. And I mean it. If you try to put a fake past me, you'll regret it. I'll know at first glance."

The phone went dead, and Ben stood holding it for a moment, frowning and looking bewildered and despondent. He looked into the dining room where the two cops were still trying to find the source of the call, and he saw his wife slumped down on the table, sobbing into the circle of her arms. He hung up the phone and went toward her. Sharon was sitting at the table, her face in her hands, weeping.

Ben went to Anne and touched her hair. She looked up at him and fell into his arms. He held her for a long time, crying with her.

Tony longed to reach out, to at least touch Sharon's hand, to comfort her as Ben was comforting Anne. But he held himself back, waiting for Larry to finish the trace.

Larry was on another line, frowning, as though things weren't working out. "What do you mean? Well, can you get the cellular phone's number? It's got to be Chamberlain's."

He waited several more moments, then wilted. "All right. So some guy named Stu Miegel owns that phone. Find him and question him. Maybe he's working with Chamberlain." His frown got deeper. "You're kidding. Well, that's just great."

He slammed down the phone. "You're not gonna believe this."

Tony had heard most of it. "It's not his phone. So whose is it?"

"Some guy who reported his phone stolen out of a bar about half an hour ago."

Tony rubbed his forehead. "What bar?"

"Your stomping ground. Steppin' Out. He said he set it on the bar, and the next thing he knew, it was gone."

"Did anybody show him a picture of Chamberlain?"

"He said he didn't recognize him. But that he hadn't looked around much, so anybody could have been there."

Tony was getting tired. He rubbed his eyes and looked at Ben, huddled with his wife, still in tears. "All right, Ben. Looks like we're going to have to deliver something. He's got to be bluffing about recognizing it at first glance."

"He's not," Ben said. "If I know him, he'd have memorized every stroke."

"We'll just have to take that chance. Is there any place we can quickly get a close reproduction?"

Ben thought for a moment. "What did he say, exactly? Could you rewind it and let me hear?"

"Sure." Larry flicked a knob, rewound the tape, then played it again.

Ben tried hard to focus his thoughts, though the despair over his terrified daughters lingered in his mind.

He groaned and flopped back. "I can't believe Dubose was involved with him, but he must have been. That's why he was so anxious to convince me it was a fake. Then he fired me because he thought I would ruin the deal, or give his secret away! We've got to find that painting. Maybe I can give him another painting of the same size . . . and just hope it's dark enough that he can't see it right away until they catch him."

"No!" Sharon cried. "You can't do that! He'll kill them. He said so. And what if the police don't catch him? What if he gets away?"

"Sharon, what choice do we have?" Tony asked.

"I don't know!" she shouted. "But you have to do better than that!"

"She's right," Anne said.

Larry began to pace, trying to think. "Dubose moves the painting after Ben discovers it—and when Chamberlain doesn't find the painting where it's supposed to be, he naturally assumes that Ben has it."

"We've looked all over that gallery and Dubose's house."

"Could he have given it to a friend? Sent it to someone?"

Ben stared at the wall for a moment, remembering that last day, before Dubose had fired him. He had been preoccupied, busy with something.

"I remember him getting a package ready to mail out," Ben said. "It was a cylinder, about four feet long. I never thought of it then, but it could have been the Marazzio. *The Multitude* was four feet by seven feet."

Tony was practically on top of the table as he leaned over to prod Ben. "How did he mail it? U.S. Post Office, Fedex?"

"UPS," Ben said. "He always sent things UPS." His breath was short as he looked hopefully at both of them. "I know where he kept those receipts. It'll have the address he mailed it to."

Tony grabbed his sport coat. "Let's go."

Ben followed him to the door, but Sharon ran after them. "What can I do? I can't just sit here."

"Pray," Larry said over his shoulder. "Pray hard."

46

"WHY HASN'T DADDY come yet?" Emily's voice was hoarse and raspy. Her lips were getting dry from thirst. She sat close to Christy, afraid to venture too far across the floor, for fear of what might lurk there.

"He will. Didn't you hear the man? He said tonight. Daddy will come tonight."

"What if he can't find us?"

"He will. I know he will."

Hearing a scratching sound in the wall, they tensed up and huddled closer. "What's that?" Christy asked.

Emily covered her face with both hands, but then dropped them, for they hurt too badly. The dirt from all the digging was still caked on them, but the sores they'd rubbed while digging were beginning to get infected. Christy had the same problem, except that she also had that cut on her head and the scrapes on her back from where she'd been jerked out from under the wall in the shed.

"It's a rat, isn't it?" Emily asked weakly.

Christy began to cry quietly. "Let's pray some more," she said. "We have to pray that God will keep the rats from coming in here. We have to tell him how scared we are."

Emily bowed her head without protest.

"Dear God," Christy whispered, "could you please help us, please, and make those rats go away so we won't be so scared? We would appreciate it very much."

The scratching sounded again, and Christy stomped her foot on the floor and let out a loud yell, hoping to frighten whatever it was away. The sound grew quiet.

"I scared it," she whispered.

They heard a sound up above them, another scratching sound, but this one came from the window at the very top of the bathroom, probably fifteen feet up.

"What's that?" Christy asked.

Emily turned on the flashlight and shone it up. The light was weak because the battery was running out. The faint circle of light hit the window, and they saw something standing on the sill looking down at them.

"It's a—"

Before Emily could get the words out, it leaped from the windowsill to the floor.

Both girls screamed and backed further against the corner. Something furry grazed Christy's leg, and she screamed louder, harder. Then they heard a sound they hadn't expected.

"Meeeeooouw."

Emily caught her breath and shone the light on the animal. "Christy, it's a cat. Look!"

Christy opened her eyes and began to laugh with relief at the big, yellow tomcat. "A cat? Come here, kitty. You scared me."

It was a good-natured cat, and it rubbed against Christy's leg and allowed her to pick it up. "Look, Emily. He's so sweet."

Emily giggled and petted him. "How did he get in? It's so high up."

"There must be a tree outside the window. See? I told you God would answer our prayer."

"What?" Emily asked. "We didn't ask for a cat."

"No, but he'll scare the rats off. And he'll keep us company, so we won't be scared."

Emily thought about that for a moment. "Yeah. Maybe he'll stay here until Daddy comes to get us."

"He'll have to," Christy said. "He can't get back out until someone opens the door."

"He's a good answer to our prayers," Emily giggled, rubbing her face in the purring cat's fur. "How did God know?"

"God knows what we need better than we do," Christy said matter-of-factly. "My mommy always says that."

"Has God ever sent *her* a cat?"

"Nope. Other things. It's always something different."

"So praying really works?"

"It worked this time, didn't it?"

Emily smiled as the cat curled up on her lap and lay down, purring.

47

NELSON CHAMBERLAIN SAT on a small hill near the train tracks, waiting for the 10:30 train to arrive. As he sat, he wove the red handkerchief through his fingers, in and out, until it ran out. Then, unwinding it, he looked up the tracks.

He could hear the sound of a distant train, and knew that it would be here any moment. He would be glad. He didn't like getting dirty, and it wasn't his style to sit on a heap of dirt waiting for a train to come by. His work was clean—never-get-your-hands-dirty work. But lately, he'd been getting his hands dirty more and more. It made him uncomfortable, but he supposed it would all be worth it when he had exchanged the painting with Boudreaux and was on his way to England.

The train grew closer, and he saw its headlight coming up the tracks. He watched as it slowed and passed him, and he counted one boxcar after another. The train slowed even more, until it finally came to a halt, creaking and crawling by in front of him.

He sat still until he was sure it had stopped, then waited another ten minutes before picking out the car where he wanted the painting delivered. There was one not far from where he'd been sitting that had an open door and nothing inside. If they set the painting at the back right corner of that one, as he'd told them to, it would be safe.

He got to his feet, dusted off his pants, and checked to make sure no one was around who would find him suspicious. The first car, where the engineer sat, was around a curve, and no one in it was able to see him. He slipped his handkerchief over the pipe that held the door in place, and tied it there. Then he checked it, made sure it was secure and could be seen.

Jumping off the car, he looked up the tracks. He was going to drive his car to a place about two miles from here, then walk back up the tracks for about a mile. When the train left at 12:30, after Ben had delivered *The Multitude,* he would watch for that car, jump on it while the train was still moving slowly, get the painting, then jump off near where his car was parked.

It was foolproof. They could, of course, station cops on the train when Ben put the painting on board. But they wouldn't dare try to grab him before he told them where the children were. Besides that, they wouldn't know where his car was parked, and once he jumped off the train and fled, they'd never be able to find or identify him. He would be home free after he got the painting and was back in his car on the way to the airport, where Boudreaux had agreed to meet him.

He laughed as he went back over the hill to his car, which was parked behind some trees so it couldn't be seen. Just a couple more hours of this nightmare, and he would finally be on his way to ending it.

48

THE UPS RECEIPTS were exactly where Ben thought they would be. Louis Dubose had been a master organizer. He kept his office immaculate and always filed away everything so it wouldn't clutter his desk.

The receipt they were looking for was at the front of the file. Victoriously, Ben pulled it out. "It's got the address as clear as day."

Tony looked it over. "Are you sure this is the right item?"

"Positive," Ben said. "Look, he mailed it out of town, but not too far away . . . in St. Petersburg. And it says it's a cylinder. It has to be it," Ben said. "Come on. We don't have much time if we're going to get it."

They flew across St. Clair and into St. Pete, checking their map to find the street the address was on. When they found it, they saw that it was a small shop called "Home Address." A sign in the window said, "Open till 10." "It's only 9:30," Tony said. "Somebody's on our side."

Tony, Larry, and Ben burst in. "Do you have mailboxes here, where people can send things?"

"Yes," the man said, gesturing toward an entire wall of postal boxes. "Do you need one?"

"No." Tony took out his badge and flashed it to the man. "We're with the St. Clair PD. We need to confiscate the contents of Suite 320."

"It's over there. It's really a post office box, but we call them suites so it'll make people look like they have offices. Do you have a warrant?"

"No," Tony said. "But there are two children in trouble right now, and if we take the time to get one, they could wind up dead."

"But I can't hand over some other guy's mail to you."

"Look, all we want is a cylinder that's in there. It's going to save the lives of this man's two little girls, who've been kidnapped. Now, you can make me go get a warrant, but you're coming with me, got that? I'll take you in and question you for a couple of days on how you knew the guy who rented this box, and what your connection might be in his murder and the kidnapping of the two little girls."

The man looked a little stunned, then quickly reached behind the counter for the key. "All right. Open it."

Tony took the key and opened it. "It's a cylinder all right. Return address . . . your gallery."

Ben breathed out a sigh of relief. "Open it. Let's make sure it's the right painting."

Carefully, Tony opened the box and laid it on the counter, while the manager watched with awe. He opened the cylinder and slid out the contents.

"See?" Ben said. "That's it, all right." He took it with careful hands and unrolled it partially. "That's *The Multitude.*"

"All right," Larry said. "We don't have any more time to waste. We have to go by the station to report to the captain before we make the drop. We'll need a lot of help on this one."

They thanked the tense manager, then rushed out with the package and drove as fast as they could drive back to St. Clair.

49

ANNE PUT BOBBY to bed, then sat for a while in the rocking chair, thinking about her lost child. Where were Emily and Christy? Would they really get them back tonight?

Unable to sit still, she got up and walked through the house. She headed up the stairs, wanting to go into Christy's room, wanting to be among the things Emily had left there. She stepped into the doorway and saw Sharon and Jenny sitting on the bed, huddled together. They both looked up at her.

"Excuse me," she said, wiping her tears. "I didn't know you were in here." She backed away, but Sharon stopped her.

"Anne, wait."

Anne looked at her questioningly.

"We were praying for the girls, and for Ben. Would you come pray with us?"

Anne hesitated. "I'm not much of a prayer. If there's a God, I'm not sure he'd listen to a prayer that came from me."

"The fact that he ever listens to any of us is just evidence of his grace," Sharon said. "Come on."

Anne came into the room and sat down on the edge of the bed.

"Turn around, Anne," Jenny said. "Let's sit in a circle and hold hands. Jesus said that whenever two or more of us are gathered in his name, he would be among us."

"Really?" Anne asked. "He said that?"

"Yes," Sharon said. "We've got to pray for them."

"Okay," Anne whispered.

Sharon reached for Anne's left hand and held it tightly. Jenny took the other, as mother and daughter held hands, as well. And Sharon began to pray.

50

ACROSS TOWN, IN Lynda Barrett's home, she and Jake sat on the couch in her living room, with fifteen other friends of Sharon's from their church. Sharon hadn't been told they were meeting, but it didn't matter if she knew or not. Lynda had called them right after she'd gotten the call from Sharon about an exchange being made that night. Lynda had known there was only one thing to do.

The fifteen held hands and prayed one by one, earnestly, deeply . . .

It was Jake's turn, and he grew emotional as he began to speak. "Lord, you said that you would intercede for us, with groanings too deep for words . . . when we don't even know how to pray. I don't know where those little girls are, Lord, or what they need, or what danger they're in, but you can see them. You know. Lord, please take care of them. Surround them with your presence. Don't let any harm come to them. They're so little . . . And Ben . . . he's out there looking for that painting . . . something he can give to the man who has them. Let him find it, Lord. And I pray for the kidnapper, that you'll work on him, as well. Foil him, Lord. Get in his way. Convict him . . . I know you can answer this prayer, Lord. I've seen your answers before. But not our will, but thine. You know what's best . . ."

And so the prayers went on into the night as the group interceded for the family that was in such turmoil.

51

THE GIRLS FELL asleep with the cat lying across their laps. They were so exhausted that they didn't wake when the cat sprang up after hearing a scratching on the wall. His night eyes spotted the small head jerking out of the hole in the wall where the sink had been. He hissed, but the rat wasn't daunted.

His ears stretched tightly back on his head, teeth bared, back hunched, until the rat had quietly made its way out of the hole and down the wall. It had scarcely hit the floor when the cat attacked.

In seconds, the rat was dead, and the cat dragged it to the corner of the room, behind the rusty, stinking toilet. There he left it, and went back to the girls. Neither of them had stirred.

Satisfied, he crawled back onto their laps, began to purr again, and went back to sleep.

52

"ALL RIGHT," THE captain, Sam Richter, said as he paced in front of the roomful of cops waiting to spring into action. "We have men posted at the tracks already, trying to catch him when he hangs the handkerchief. If we don't get him then, we go ahead as planned. Everybody has their posts. You know what to do. The minute Chamberlain has the painting, apprehend him and bring him in."

"No!" Tony stood up and looked back at his partner for help. "Captain, that would be a mistake. We have to give him time to call about the kids."

"What if he doesn't?" Sam asked. "What if he heads straight for the airport and leaves on the next plane out?"

"He has no incentive to call," one of the cops said. "If he has the painting, he's not going to be worried about those kids."

"Maybe he'll worry because he's a human being," Tony said. "Maybe he'll keep his end of the bargain."

"The man is a criminal," Larry said. "He doesn't care about keeping his word."

Tony swung around, gaping at him. "Whose side are you on, anyway?"

"I'm on the kids' side," Larry said. "And if we go ahead and collar him, maybe we can make some kind of deal to get him to tell us where they are."

"There's one thing you're all forgetting," the captain said. "One of those little girls knows the kidnapper. He won't want her to identify him. So we face the danger of his going back to kill the kids if we don't find him right away. That is, if he hasn't already done it."

"He hasn't," Tony said. "And if he goes back, that's great. He's led us to them. We can collar him there before he has the chance to do anything. I'm not suggesting letting him go, Captain. Just give him some time after he gets the painting. Let's see if he leads us to them or calls the parents to tell them where to look."

The captain sat down on the table at the front of the room, a deep frown clefting his forehead. "All right, then what if he doesn't call or lead us to them? How far do we follow him before we take him?"

"As far as we need to."

"Even as far as the airport?"

"Yes!" Tony said. "Maybe he would call from there."

"What if he gets on a plane?" the captain asked. "Do we allow that?"

"Yes!" Tony said. "We go with him. We watch. We alert authorities at the destination to be prepared to apprehend him the minute he gets off."

The captain gave him a disbelieving look. "And what would that serve?"

"It would give him time, Captain," Tony said, his face reddening with the effort of persuasion. "Time to make a call from the plane. It might be the only place he feels safe doing it. Think about it. He'll think he got away without being followed, if we do our job right. Then when the plane takes off, he'll be breathing easier, thinking he made a clean escape. At that point, it would be logical that he would call the family from the phone on the plane."

"You have to have a credit card to make a call from the air. You really think he's going to mess up and use his own credit card to make a call, when he's gone to such lengths to keep from being traced?"

"He's resourceful. We already know he has cards in at least two other names. But if we grab him before he talks, he may *never* tell us where the girls are."

"Oh, he'll tell us," the captain assured him. "I'll see to that."

"What are you gonna do? Beat it out of him? Let him scream police brutality and get the whole case dropped for civil rights violations?" Tony dropped back into his chair. "Look, all I know is that there's a family out there who is sick with worry over their children. We're down to the wire now. Let's not mess it up."

The captain took a few deep breaths and checked his watch. It was 11:30. They would need to leave in just a few minutes to make the drop by midnight. He looked from Larry to Tony, then strolled to the window of the conference room. Outside, Ben Robinson was sitting at Larry's desk, calling his family to tell them they'd found the painting. He was crying quietly.

The captain turned back around. "All right, guys. Here's what we're gonna do. We're gonna let him get the painting, let him make his escape. Whoever gets close enough can follow him, but keep in close contact with me. If he heads for the airport, you follow him in."

Tony breathed a sigh of relief. "Thank you, Captain."

"Wait a minute. I didn't finish. Follow him in, but do not let him get on a plane. Do you hear me? Do not let him get on the plane."

"Captain, that's a mistake—"

"Apprehend him before he boards. That will give him ample time to call the family. If he hasn't done it by then, we have to assume that he's not going to. We'll play heck getting the information out of him if he's apprehended in Atlanta—or, worse yet, in Mexico City or someplace like that. We need to find those kids tonight."

Tony slammed a fist on the table and got up. "Captain—"

"You've got my orders, Danks. Don't violate them."

"Fine!" he said through his teeth, heading for the door. "I just hope those orders don't ruin any chance we have of finding those girls."

53

IT WAS NEARING midnight when Tony, Larry, and Ben went back to Sharon's house, and Ben got into his own car with the painting. The cops stationed at the track had not spotted Chamberlain or the handkerchief yet, so Larry and Tony would follow Ben at a distance to the railroad tracks, and let him look for the marking and deliver the painting to the boxcar alone. Even if they spotted Chamberlain hanging the handkerchief, the cops watching for him had been instructed not to act until he had the painting in his hand.

There were no lights in the area of the railroad tracks that Chamberlain had designated, so it was difficult for Tony and Larry to see from where their car was hidden. They quietly got out of the car. Tony watched with night glasses as Ben walked along the tracks, the multi-million-dollar painting in its cylinder clamped beneath his arm, looking for the boxcar with the red handkerchief.

"Has he found it yet?" Larry asked Tony.

Tony shook his head. "No. And I don't see it. What if he hasn't marked it yet?"

His voice stopped cold when he saw Ben hesitate. There, above the door of one of the cars, was a handkerchief flapping in the wind. Ben glanced in both directions, then jumped into the car. Seconds later, he jumped out and headed back to his car.

"All right," Tony said, shoving the night glasses back into their pouch on his belt. "If we cross here, and come up behind the train, it should be dark enough that we won't be seen. The painting's hidden on the eighth car from here. You take the one before it, number seven, and I'll take the one after it. That way we can watch from both sides."

They crossed the tracks, stepping over a joint between two boxcars, and ran hunched over, counting cars. Larry jumped into the one directly behind the marked car, and Tony ran ahead and quietly climbed into the one in front of it.

Crossing the car, he sat by the opposite door, his body carefully hidden in the darkness so that he would have a clear view when Chamberlain came to get the painting. He knew that other plain-clothed officers circled the area, searching for the rental car they had discovered Chamberlain was using now. They had been told not to act if they found it. Just to stay in place so they could follow it when he made his escape.

Tony sat so still that his muscles ached, and he wondered if Sharon was holding up all right. She was at her wit's end. And he couldn't blame her. If they messed up tonight, if the children weren't found, or if they were found but they weren't alive . . .

His heart ached, and he told himself that they just had to be alive. He couldn't accept the possibility that they weren't. He couldn't stand the thought of telling her.

Time ticked slowly by, and no one came for the painting. He began to wonder if they had put it in the wrong car, or if this was all just some kind of hoax, if maybe he was a sitting duck for Chamberlain's warped sense of humor.

He looked up at the sky. Stars sparkled with an uncanny brilliance, like white paint splattered in fine drops on a black canvas. But he doubted even Marazzio could have duplicated it tonight. It was beautiful, and seemed to testify to such peace, that for a moment he found himself wondering if there really was someone up there beyond it, keeping the earth spinning on its axis, the moon circling the planet, the stars suspended where they were.

For the first time, the thought that there was seemed infinitely more comforting than what he had always chosen to believe. If there wasn't a creator, and the earth spun on its own, and the moon controlled its own destiny, and the stars were all there by coincidence—then the world truly was formed out of chaos, and nothing could be predictable, and he might be sitting here wasting his time while those children were in grave danger.

Maybe there was a God. And maybe he did answer prayers. Intelligent people prayed to him all the time. They seemed to think he answered. Even when things went bad, as they had with Jake Stevens and Lynda Barrett, they still seemed to believe that God was with them, working it all out.

He knew that two cars back, Larry was probably praying right now. They were probably all praying. Sharon, Jenny, Lynda, Jake . . . everybody. Heck, they probably had all their church friends praying on one of those prayer chains. Half the town of St. Clair, at least those who believed, were probably praying for him and for this whole operation right now. It was a little intimidating. And a little comforting.

He looked up at the stars again. *God, is it you?* he asked silently. *Are you really there? Or are they just talking to air? I've never been one to accept things on faith. That's for dreamers. I'm a realist.*

Then why was he talking to the sky? he asked himself wryly.

The car bumped, and he sprang to attention, ready for something to happen. He looked outside, but saw no one, then wondered if he'd missed it. Had Chamberlain gotten into the car behind his, jarring the car?

But then the car bumped again, and he realized this time that the train was moving. Slowly, inch by inch, it began to creep down the tracks. He checked his watch and pushed the indiglo button to light the digital readout. It was 12:30. Time for the train to leave.

It was all right, though. He had thought of this. He and Larry had agreed that Chamberlain might be waiting a little way down the tracks, prepared to jump on the car to get the painting, then off before the train picked up any speed. It would be the most foolproof way to keep from getting caught.

He braced himself as the train began to move, the noise of the wheels grinding on the tracks sending up a roar. Knowing he wouldn't be heard now, he pulled out his walkie-talkie and turned it on. "We're moving, guys," he told the other cops who were stationed at various intervals at the intersections down the tracks. "Keep your eyes peeled."

The train moved about fifteen miles per hour down the track, slow to someone waiting to cross the tracks, but too fast for someone inside waiting to catch a killer. He stayed in the shadows, watching, watching, as they passed intersection after intersection.

Where was he? Surely he didn't plan to wait until the train's next stop. He must know they'd have people waiting there, ready to catch him. No, the best bet would be to come onto the train from some unpredictable place—anywhere but a stopping point—and jump off before anyone could be the wiser.

"Bingo." It was Larry's voice, and Tony held the walkie-talkie close to his ear.

"What?" he asked.

"I see a guy with a flashlight checking the boxcars," he said. "I think we've got our man."

Tony turned off the walkie-talkie and set it back in his coat pocket. Suddenly he saw the flashlight beam searching the doorway of his boxcar. It moved onto the next, then the beam cut off—no doubt because Chamberlain had seen the handkerchief.

He watched, carefully, as a man ran alongside the tracks, right next to his own car, looking back behind him for the perfect moment to jump on board. He fell behind, in pace with the marked car, then disappeared.

"He's on," Tony whispered to himself. He inched closer to the door, and waited for him to jump back off. Nothing happened.

What was he doing? Was he checking the painting before he got off? Was he going to ride it to the next town?

Before he had time to panic, he saw the man jump back out and roll down the bank of grass. Time for action.

Tony watched him run toward a dark intersection, where a black car was parked off the street, near some trees. He let the train take him a couple hundred feet down the tracks, then jumped off himself. Larry followed.

Tony pulled the walkie-talkie back out and turned it on. "He's at the tracks at Gray Street, guys. The black Ford Tempo."

"We see him," one of the cops radioed back.

"Don't let him see you. And keep me posted. Somebody pick Larry and me up at the same intersection in about three minutes."

Larry was dusting himself off. "Are you all right?"

"Yeah, no problem. I'm just hoping this guy has an ounce of compassion inside him. Maybe he doesn't want to abandon those kids."

"Let's hope so." They jogged back up the track to the intersection Chamberlain had left moments ago.

A car was waiting there for them, and they drove back to the car they had parked miles up the track.

54

BEN WALKED INTO the quiet house, wondering where everyone was. His hands were shaking, and he went to the cabinets, searching for something strong to drink. Something that would calm him and make the wait less excruciating.

But he found nothing, and he realized idly that Sharon never kept alcohol in the house. If ever there was a need for some, it was now. How was she coping without it?

He sat down at the table and pressed his fist against his mouth as tears came to his eyes. What had happened after he left? Had they gotten Chamberlain? Had he told them where the kids were?

He couldn't sit still, so he jumped up again and went through the house looking for his wife or his daughter—or even his ex. They weren't downstairs.

Had something happened to them? Anxious, he ran up the stairs. The world had gone haywire, and someone had come in here and taken them, too—

And then he heard voices in Christy's bedroom.

He hurried to the door. Inside, he saw his daughter Jenny, with both of the mothers of his children, sitting in a circle on Christy's bed, holding hands and praying.

He sucked in a sob, and they all looked up.

"Daddy!" Jenny lunged off the bed. "Daddy, did you see him? Did you find Christy and Emily?"

"Not yet," he said, wiping his eyes. She pulled him to the bed and he sat down next to Anne, who put her arms around him and dropped her forehead against his shoulder. "I delivered the painting. They . . . they told me to come home and wait for him to call and tell us where they are."

He felt himself losing control even as he spoke, and he collapsed against his wife and broke down completely. She got on her knees on the bed and held him, and Sharon sat back and watched her former adversary comfort the man who used to be her husband.

And it was all right.

"We were praying, Ben," Sharon whispered, reaching for his hand. "We have to keep praying. There's a phone in here. We'll hear if he calls."

He nodded, unable to speak, and kept leaning against his wife as they began to pray again.

55

NELSON CHAMBERLAIN NAVIGATED the back roads of St. Clair, making his way to the interstate where he could head for the Tampa Airport. So far, he saw no one following him, and he laughed out loud. He had gotten away with it.

He patted the long cylinder on the seat next to him. He had already checked it, back in the boxcar by flashlight, so he knew that it was just what he'd expected—*The Multitude,* a priceless masterpiece by one of the greatest Italian painters who'd ever lived.

He reached into the box on the floor. There was a fake mustache and goatee, tinted glasses, and a black fedora. As he drove, he fit the mustache above his lip, pressed the adhesive tightly, then applied the goatee. He saved the glasses and hat until he was ready to get out. The garment bag sat in the backseat. When he got to the airport, where he'd told Boudreaux to meet him, all he would have to do is slip the long tube into the garment bag, make the exchange with Boudreaux, and get on the next flight to England. Boudreaux would head back to France. No one would find the children where he'd left them, and they would probably starve to death. But that was just as well. He couldn't risk having them identify him and ruin what was turning out to be the perfect crime.

56

"WHAT HAVE YOU got, guys? Anything yet?" Larry held the walkie-talkie close to his ear as Tony drove.

"Nothing," John Hampton answered. "He's headed for the airport so fast I'm afraid the Tampa police are gonna pull him over."

"All right. We're on our way there now. If he stops to make the call, don't let him see you."

He looked at Tony as he took the ramp onto the interstate. Tony looked as tense as he'd ever seen him. "What do you think? Will he call?"

"He has to," Tony said.

57

THE PAIN IN Christy's hands woke her, and she looked down at them, barely able to see them in the darkness. They were swollen and still grimy, and the open sores from where she'd rubbed the skin off were wet and painful. Besides that, she didn't feel good. She had a bad headache, and her back was aching. And her throat burned with thirst.

She moved the cat off her lap and got on all fours to crawl to the broken pipes where the sink had been. Maybe there was a leak there. Maybe something a little wet, that she could catch on her tongue . . .

Her hand grazed something hairy, and she jumped back with a scream.

Emily jumped up. "What is it? What's wrong, Christy?"

Christy pressed back against the wall and felt around for the flashlight. Her fingers were almost in too much pain to turn the switch on, but she managed. "Over there, in the corner," she cried. "I can't look! Look and see what it is."

Emily took the flashlight, wincing as she moved the circle of light slowly across the floor. When she saw the dead rat, she yelped.

"What?" Christy asked. "What is it?"

"A rat!" Emily cried.

The cat, awakened by all the commotion, pranced over to the rat and picked it up, demonstrating that it was dead. Then he dropped it back in the corner.

"He killed it! It's dead," Christy said, still crying.

"I don't want to look anymore," Emily said weakly. She shone the flashlight on her hands. Hers, too, were oozing and swollen and grimy. "My hands hurt."

"Mine, too."

"Are they 'fected? Mommy says if you don't clean a sore, it'll get 'fected."

"I think so," Christy said.

"What will happen? What does that mean?"

"I don't know," Christy said. "All I know is it hurts. I want to get out of here. I want to go home."

They started to cry harder. Finally, Emily asked, "When do you think Daddy will come? He said tonight. He promised."

"Maybe he couldn't keep his promise."

"But Mr. Chamberlain said he would kill us if Daddy didn't do what he wanted. Do you think he's gonna kill us tonight?"

Christy thought that over for a moment. Her first instinct was to say no, that he wasn't going to kill them, but then she realized that it could be likely. He hadn't fed them all day or brought them anything to drink. He had left them here with the rats. Why wouldn't a man like that kill them?

"I wish we had a phone," Emily said matter-of-factly. "I'd call 911."

"I wish we had a ladder," Christy said. "I'd climb out that window up there."

The cat purred and rubbed up against Christy. "Well, we have a cat. And we're together. When he put me in that trunk by myself when you ran away, I was scared I'd be alone."

Emily whimpered, laying her head against Christy's shoulder. "Do you think Mommy and Daddy know we haven't eaten? Do you think they know he might kill us?"

"They know," Christy whispered. "They just can't find us."

The cat purred and snuggled deeper into their laps.

"I wish I remembered that story," Emily whispered.

"What story?"

"The one your mom told us that night. About Beth."

"Beth and her tree cottage?" Christy asked. "You don't have to remember. You just have to make it up. I'll tell it to you. You can help."

"Okay," Emily said.

"Once upon a time, a mean man came and stole Beth out of her tree house."

"And he put her in a dark, scary place," Emily added quietly.

"But Beth was very brave. And she was smart. Real smart."

"Could she read when she was four?" Emily asked on a weak whisper.

"Yes. And she knew that song with all the states."

"What happened to her?" Emily asked.

"Well, she watched and waited, and found a way to escape."

"What way?" Emily asked without much hope.

"There was a secret door in the dark place," Christy said. "A secret door that only the nice people could see. The bad man couldn't see it at all. And at first she didn't see it, because she was too upset."

"But then she saw it?" Emily whispered.

"Yes," Christy said. "And she tiptoed to it. But it needed a key to open it. And she didn't know where the key was."

"What did she do?"

Christy was getting sleepy even as she spoke. She yawned. "I don't know. I need to think about it."

Emily didn't answer, and Christy saw that her eyes had closed. Christy rested her head against the wall and surrendered to sweet, merciful sleep. Her last thought before drifting off was, *God, please help Beth find the key.*

58

THE PORTABLE LIGHT on their dashboard flashed as Tony drove at breakneck speed to the Tampa Airport. He didn't want to pass Chamberlain along the way, so he'd chosen an alternate route. Larry was on the radio with the cops who were tailing Chamberlain.

"Where are you now?"

"Nearing the airport exit," they said. "So far, nothing. There's no cellular antenna on his car. Could he be using a flip phone or something to call them?"

"No," Larry said. "I checked. They haven't heard anything yet. Just don't lose him, and don't let him see you. Let him think he's home free. Remember: There are two little girls whose lives depend on us."

59

NELSON CHAMBERLAIN PULLED off the exit ramp of the interstate and headed toward the airport. Almost there.

He turned toward the rental car return. His first instinct, to abandon the car at the curb of the Delta terminal, had been a bad idea. As far as he knew, they hadn't yet traced this crime to him. Even though he'd rented this car under the name John Lieber, he didn't want any suspicions to arise that Lieber might not be who he said he was.

Someone met him at the parking lot as he pulled his car in. "Can I help you, sir?"

"Yeah," Chamberlain said, jumping out of the car and grabbing the garment bag. "I'm late for my flight. Could you take care of this?"

"No sir. You have to go inside."

"I can't!" He reached into his pocket and pulled out a hundred-dollar bill. "This should cover whatever I might still owe. Just take care of it, and you can keep the rest."

The man hesitated. "Well, all right. The shuttle to the terminal is right over there. It's almost ready to leave."

Chamberlain leaped onto the shuttle. "Delta," he told the driver. "And hurry."

The other two passengers on the shuttle gave him indolent glances, then turned their gazes out the window. The shuttle started to leave.

"Wait!" Two men outside yelled at the bus driver, and he stopped.

They jumped on, breathless. "We almost missed you. Thanks for waiting."

One of them slid his duffel bag under the seat and sat next to Chamberlain as the shuttle started to leave; the other sat across from him, a garment bag slung over his shoulder.

Chamberlain dug his ticket out of his coat pocket and looked down to make sure that he wasn't late for his meeting with Boudreaux, and that he still had enough time to make the flight.

"What terminal?" the driver asked.

"Delta," Chamberlain said.

"Same here," one of the two men called out.

60

"SO WHERE IS he now?" Larry asked via radio as he and Tony approached the airport and took the ramp heading for the terminals.

"On the rental car shuttle," a cop said. "Nick and John are on there with him. They're plain-clothed, so he won't know who they are."

"Good going," Larry said. "We're almost at the terminals now. Any idea which one he's headed for?"

"Not yet," the cop said. "But we'll have all of them covered. We have a couple of guys going over the rental car as we speak. Maybe we'll find some clues there."

Tony pulled over to wait for the rental car shuttle to come around. Moments later, it passed them and stopped at American. One passenger got off. Then it went a few feet to the TWA terminal. Another passenger got off.

"They're stopping at Delta," Larry said into the radio seconds later. "Three men are getting off. Yep. John and Nick are two of them. The other one doesn't look like him, but it's got to be. There's nobody else on the bus. He's wearing a black mustache and a goatee, a hat, and tinted glasses. Carrying a garment bag over his shoulder. Give him a chance to check in and make the call. He still might do it."

Abandoning their car, they both followed through the door where Chamberlain had gone. They saw the man up ahead, closely followed by the two cops.

"Come on," Tony whispered. "Go to the pay phone. Make the call."

But the man headed, instead, toward the gate where his plane would soon be boarding. He checked in at the desk, and they all waited from a distance to see if he'd still turn and make that call. Instead, he turned and, still carrying the garment bag over his shoulder, went into a bar several yards down. He hesitated at the doorway, looked around, then approached a well-dressed man sitting at the back in a booth by himself.

Larry and Tony watched as the other man stood up, and the two shook hands. Chamberlain slipped into the booth, and for a moment, they could only see the back of his head.

"All right," Tony told Larry. "This must be the buyer for the painting. Let's just hang back and take it easy. If we play our cards right, we'll kill two birds with one stone. We'll get him *and* the buyer."

They waited as seconds ticked off, and as the time grew closer for Chamberlain's plane to take off.

61

IN THE BOOTH at the back of the bar, where they were hidden by two half-walls with planters full of greenery, Chamberlain unzipped the bag, pulled out the cylinder, and handed the awkward package across the table to Boudreaux. The man's eyes were huge and awestruck as he carefully removed the contents. The canvas covered the width of the table; unrolled, it extended two feet beyond the edge. Chamberlain helped him hold it uncurled as Boudreaux gazed down at *The Multitude.*

"It's magnificent," Boudreaux said, breathless. "Just as I remember it." He was beginning to perspire, and he pulled a handkerchief out of his pocket and wiped his forehead.

"Where's the money?" Chamberlain asked.

"Fifteen million," Boudreaux told him. "It is safely in a bank account in Switzerland. The account was opened under the name John Lieber." He pulled an envelope out of his breast pocket. "All of the necessary documents are here. In fact, if you wish to call the bank to make sure the funds are there—" He checked his watch. "I believe you would have no problem."

Chamberlain pulled the documents out and studied them. "Yes, I would like to call."

"All right," Boudreaux said, carefully holding the rolled canvas. "Here is the security code for that account, as well as the account number. The telephone number is on the front of the document."

"Stay here," Chamberlain said. He got up and asked the bartender if he could use his phone to make a credit card call. The man slid the phone across the counter.

62

FROM OUTSIDE THE restaurant, Tony watched Chamberlain pick up the phone. "He's calling!"

"Maybe," Larry agreed. "But we can't apprehend him until we've confirmed it. I'll go call our guys over at the Robinson's and make sure that's who he's talking to."

"All right," Tony said. "Meanwhile, I'm going to get as close as I can. He doesn't know me. Let me know the second you have confirmation, and tell all the others to stand by."

Tony couldn't get close enough to hear the telephone conversation, but he found a place at a table that Chamberlain would have to pass on his way out of the bar. He sat down and strained to hear, but the classical music playing over the sound system was too loud, and Chamberlain was turned away from him.

Let him tell them, he prayed without even realizing it.

He was on the phone longer than Tony would have imagined, but Tony sat patiently, waiting for him to finish. He saw the man turn back toward the phone, as if preparing to hang up, and Tony slipped his hand under his sport coat, ready to draw his gun.

Chamberlain hung up and turned back to the table. The other man rose again, shook his hand, and slipped the painting back into the garment bag.

Tony began to sweat. Where was Larry? It was the perfect time, the perfect place to arrest both men without drawing undue attention. If they got out of the restaurant, it would make everything more difficult.

Chamberlain checked his watch. Then he paid his bill with the credit card that probably had Ben Robinson's or John Lieber's name on it so there would still be no trace that Chamberlain had ever returned from London.

Tony got up and glanced out into the corridor, where people hurried past. Sweat began to trickle down his temples.

And then he saw Larry rush up to the doorway of the place, shaking his head and mouthing, "No."

Tony gaped at him. "No?" he mouthed back.

Chamberlain started out of the restaurant, and Tony had no choice but to follow him. Other plain-clothed cops were coming in with their eyes on Boudreaux, prepared to arrest him and confiscate the painting as soon as Chamberlain was gone.

Tony followed him through the crowds, only feet behind him. Larry caught up with him.

"What's the story?" Tony demanded in a low voice.

"He didn't call. They haven't heard from him."

Tony let a curse fly under his breath. "I still say he's going to wait until he's on the plane."

"We've got to get him *before* he gets on the plane, Tony. We have no choice. You know our orders."

Tony saw Chamberlain heading for the Delta concourse, and he hurried to stay close behind him. Chamberlain was hurrying—almost running, and the faster he went, the more people seemed to gravitate between them. Tony broke into a run, bumped into a man, and almost knocked him down. He didn't stop, just kept pushing on, no longer depending on Larry or John or Nick or any of the others who waited for his signal.

As if he sensed he was being followed, Chamberlain zigzagged through people, trying to blend. At Gate 16, the flight was already boarding, and Chamberlain shot up to the flight attendant taking the tickets.

Tony bolted forward, grabbed the man, and flung him back against the wall. "Where are they? Where did you leave them?"

Chamberlain was visibly shocked. Had this guy really thought he'd get away with it? Tony wondered. "What?" Chamberlain asked.

"Where are they?" Tony screamed.

"I don't know what you're talking about," Chamberlain bit out.

"Where are the girls, Chamberlain?" Tony's eyes stung as he took the man by the collar and shoved him again. "The ones you kidnapped?"

"I didn't kidnap anyone."

Tony flung him into the wall, face first, then ripped his goatee off and threw it down. Getting a handful of his hair, he asked, *"Where are the children?"*

Chamberlain closed his eyes. "I don't know. I had nothing to do with any children."

Tony slammed Chamberlain's face into the wall again, then Larry pulled him off. "OK, Tony, get a grip!"

"Where are they?" Tony yelled. *"What did you do with them, slimeball!"*

But it was no use. Chamberlain wasn't talking.

"Read him his rights," Larry said to the other cops as he tried to calm Tony. "We're gonna go get some air. We'll meet you back at the station."

63

"WHERE ARE THE children?" Tony Danks's question was posed with more calculated calmness now as he stood over the table where Nelson Chamberlain sat in the interrogation room of the St. Clair Police Department. But the look on his face belied that calm tone. He looked like a man who could rip Chamberlain's head off with his bare hands.

Larry sat across from Chamberlain, playing the good-guy to Tony's bad-guy routine. But tonight, Tony's behavior was no act. "Calm down, Tony," Larry said in a quieter voice. "Let the man talk."

But Chamberlain wasn't interested in talking. He studied his well-groomed fingernails, leaned back, crossed his ankle over his knee, and didn't say a word.

Larry tried again. "Look, it's not going to do you any good to leave those kids out there all alone. The jig's up, Chamberlain. You've been caught. Tell us where to find the kids, and the DA might show some leniency."

Chamberlain breathed a sardonic laugh. "I'm charged with murder, kidnapping, and theft. Do you honestly think they're just going to let me go if I talk? My reputation is already ruined. The way you Keystone cops arrested me right in public in the airport, it's guaranteed to be all over the news by morning. It might even be grounds for a lawsuit after I'm acquitted. Defamation of character."

"You bet I'll defame your character," Tony bit out. "CNN has been following the kidnapping. They're right outside this office door as we speak, waiting to get a shot of the monster they've been speculating about."

Larry gestured for Tony to calm down again. "Why won't you tell us?" he asked. "Those kids are innocent. They haven't done anything."

"Why won't I talk?" Chamberlain asked flippantly. "Because I don't know anything about a kidnapping. This is all a very stupid mistake."

Tony kicked the chair next to Larry. The sound made Chamberlain jump, and when Tony grabbed Chamberlain's collar and pulled him face-to-face, he dropped his flippant look. "You had the painting, Chamberlain. The painting that you exchanged for information about the kids. We know you know where they are."

"I told you. I don't know anything."

All three men were starting to sweat. Tony let the man go, and he jerked free and straightened his shirt, which was dirty from his roll down the hill after he jumped out of the train.

Larry leaned forward on the table and fixed his eyes on Chamberlain's. "Are they dead or alive?"

"I'm not saying anything else until I've got a lawyer sitting beside me."

Tony snapped. In one swift motion, he grabbed Chamberlain and threw him back against the wall, knocking his chair over.

"You're not in control here, Chamberlain! You got that? You're not calling the shots here. You have a choice. Either you talk, or I'll see to it that that well-groomed profile of yours is drastically altered. You like art, Chamberlain? You're gonna need an artist to repair your face when I get through with you."

"Where are the kids?" Larry asked again, louder.

Chamberlain closed his eyes but didn't answer. Tony flung him a few feet, letting him drop to the floor. "I've had it with this low-life. I'm throwing the book at him. And I'm locking him in the old wing. Let him sit in the dark, in the damp for a while, and see if he can remember where he put those kids."

Larry looked alarmed. "Tony, that wing is condemned. It's infested with rats. Captain told us not to put any more prisoners there."

Chamberlain looked up at them, wide-eyed, from his position on the floor. "I want a lawyer. Now."

"You've already called one," Tony said. "It's not my fault he's out-of-pocket. Guess your luck is just going bad." He jerked him back up off the floor and pulled him toward the door. "I'll get him processed. That's when they strip you down, Nelson, old boy, and they search you real thoroughly. And then they give you some nice prison duds. You'll like them. 'Course that bright orange seems to attract the rats, rather than repel them. But you don't have a problem with that, do you?"

Chamberlain was sweating heavily now, and trembling slightly.

Larry stood up and stopped them at the door. "Tony, let me talk to him a minute. Just the two of us. You go outside and calm down."

Tony paused a moment, then finally agreed. He shoved Chamberlain back in, and slammed the door as he stormed out.

"Anything?" the captain asked, coming out of his office into the hallway.

"Nothing yet," Tony said. He rushed around to the two-way mirror and watched as Larry kindly told Chamberlain to sit back down. He asked him if he was thirsty, then poured him some water, and waited quietly while he drank.

The captain joined Tony at the window. "So you played the insane cop about to snap and tear into him?"

Tony nodded without taking his eyes off of the criminal. "Only it wasn't an act."

Chamberlain drooped over the table, raking his hands through his short-cropped hair. "Tony's a little high-strung," Larry said in a quiet, soothing voice. "He sometimes flies off the handle. I've seen him do worse than that to a suspect before. He just loses it, somehow, and he doesn't care what the rules are, or what kind of trouble he might get into. He has a one-track mind. I apologize for his behavior."

Tony couldn't help his slight grin as the captain chuckled.

"I'm not sure I can keep him from doing any of what he threatened, though, and just between you and me, he can be pretty tough. One suspect reported him from the hospital, and Internal Affairs got hold of it—"

"Hospital?" Chamberlain asked.

Larry paused and nodded. "Yeah. It was real ugly. Anyway, I'd hate to have you be another statistic, when all you'd have to do is just come clean. Keeping those kids' hiding place secret is not going to help you at all. It's only going to hurt you."

"I'm not going to prison for kidnapping."

"Even without the kidnapping, we have murder. It's a cut-and-dried case, Chamberlain. You could get the chair for that. But if you cooperate and let us know where Christy and Emily are, maybe the judge will go easier on you. Maybe he'd even let you out on bond."

"Where's the painting?" Chamberlain asked. "What did you do with it?"

"It's being tagged as evidence."

"It's priceless, you know. And I own it. When they find me innocent, it will be returned to me, won't it?"

"Certainly. As long as we can verify that it wasn't a stolen painting, and that you indeed have proof of ownership."

Chamberlain didn't answer.

"So tell us where they are, Chamberlain. Tell me where the kids are."

"I don't know where they are. I had nothing to do with their kidnapping."

"So you're not going to tell us? You're going to leave them there? Let them die before their parents can find them? What kind of man are you?"

Chamberlain was silent.

"Did you feed them, Chamberlain? Have you taken care of them? They're only five and six years old. Did you hurt them in any way?"

Chamberlain was mute as he stared back at Larry.

Tony moaned. They weren't getting anywhere with this guy. It was going to be a long night.

64

IT WAS ALMOST morning when Tony made his way back to Sharon's house. There was no real need for him to be there anymore. They had their kidnapper, and didn't expect any more ransom calls. Larry had gone home to shower and have breakfast with his wife. But the fact that those children were still out there made it impossible for Tony to relax.

He knocked lightly on the door to the kitchen, and it was quickly opened. Lynda Barrett stood there, looking as tired as he did. "Tony. Any word?"

He shook his head. "He won't talk. I've tried everything. Boudreaux doesn't know anything about the kids. My gut tells me that Chamberlain acted alone, but he won't tell us a thing." She ushered him in. Jake was leaning against the counter next to Ben, and Sharon sat listlessly at the table, her eyes swollen from tears and exhaustion.

"He wouldn't tell you *anything?*" Sharon asked, looking up at him. "Are they alive? Are they with anyone? Are they being taken care of?"

"They said there were rats there and that it was dark!" Anne blurted from the doorway. "It didn't sound like anyone was with them. They're all alone, and he's going to let them die there!"

Sharon got up and set her hands on Tony's shoulders. "Tony, we've got to find them," she said, her voice pleading. ""We can't just leave them there. You've got to help us."

He nodded. "I was thinking. Maybe it's time to call a press conference. We need to get the whole community involved. Maybe somebody knows something."

"Good idea," Lynda said. "I'll set it up right now."

Sharon looked hopeful. "You can use my office. There's a phone book in the bottom drawer."

Lynda and Jake went into the office.

Tony looked down at Sharon, wishing he had the magic that would bring her child back. "Sharon, you need to get some sleep. You haven't slept in days."

"Neither have you."

"That's not really true," he said. "I slept on your couch while I was here. You've got to rest. There's nothing you can do right now."

"You think they're dead, don't you?" Anne asked in a raspy, breathy voice.

He frowned and turned around. "No. I don't."

"But they could be. That may be why he won't tell you. There's no urgency, because they're dead, and—"

"They're *not* dead!" Sharon cried. "I know they're not. If Christy were dead, I'd know it. I'd feel it, somehow. But she's out there!"

Ben pushed off from the counter and faced Tony squarely. "I want to talk to him. Maybe he'd listen. Maybe he'd tell me."

"Ben, I'm telling you. I've worked on him all night. I've done everything short of beating it out of him."

"Well, *I* could beat it out of him!" Ben shouted.

"No, you couldn't. He's a stubborn man. It's only going to hurt him tomorrow at his arraignment, and I'm hoping the judge will put enough fear into him to make him talk, but we can't wait. I've got him in the worst holding cell the city owns," he told them. "Not a nice place. Then again, it's not nearly as bad as I'd like for it to be, but there are laws about cruel and unusual punishment."

"You ought to have him in a cage, chained to the bars," Ben grumbled.

Sharon shook her head and went to the stove. "I made breakfast for everybody, Tony," she whispered miserably. "But no one was very hungry. Do you want some? It's still hot."

He had to admit that he was hungry. "Yeah, I'll take some, if it's not too much trouble."

Sharon seemed relieved to have something to do. She dipped out some scrambled eggs and bacon and pulled some biscuits out of the oven. Tony watched as she poured him some orange juice and set it on the table. "This is Christy's favorite breakfast," she whispered. "We have it every Saturday morning. I made it thinking . . . hoping . . . that she'd be home to eat it."

Her voice cut off, and she covered her face.

"I was thinking," Tony said quietly. "When you have your press conference, maybe we could ask anyone who's willing to help look for the children to meet at, say, ten o'clock, and with some supervised effort, we could go over St. Clair with a fine-tooth comb. Search every abandoned building in town. Every hotel room. Knock on doors, ask questions . . ."

Sharon looked hopeful. "Do you think anyone would come?"

"Are you kidding? As bad as your church friends have wanted to do something, I'd say that we'll have so many people we won't know what to do with them. Until now, all they could do was pray. Now they can start doing something useful."

Sharon's expression didn't change as she watched him for a moment. "Prayer is useful, Tony," she said quietly. "It's the most useful thing they could do. Bar none."

He looked up from his plate. "Well, I know. I mean . . . you obviously believe that . . . but I just mean . . ."

"God's listening," Sharon said. "Whether we can see what he's doing about it or not. He is listening."

Anne and Ben were stone quiet as they all looked at her, wanting some of her reassurance, desperate for the faith that she still held.

Tony ate quietly for a moment, not sure what to say. Prayer had never seemed more useful to him than action. It was a foreign concept, even though Larry had told him many times how prayer had helped him with things that were out of his control. Sharon, like Larry, seemed too intelligent to fit Tony's preconceptions of the prayer-and-Bible-study crowd.

Lynda and Jake came back into the room in a few minutes. "All right, Sharon," she said. "The press conference is set for 9:00 A.M., on your front lawn. I called Paige, my secretary, and she's going to call all of the television stations in the Tampa Bay area, as well as the newspapers and radio news directors. This is big news, so I think there will be a phenomenal turnout."

Sharon looked up at the clock, then ran her fingers through her hair. "We're going to ask people to meet at ten o'clock to start an organized search."

"Good idea," Jake said. "I was thinking about going up in the plane again. I could direct people to sparsely populated rural areas from the air. It might help."

"Right now we're going to have some new posters made," Lynda said. "These will have the girls' pictures, as well as Chamberlain's. Maybe someone has seen him, and they'll remember. Every member of the media who shows up will want a picture, and we'll need to pass them out to everyone who helps. And we'll need a number people can call to report anything they know. Are your phones still hooked up here, Tony?"

"Yeah," he said. "We can get someone to man them."

"All right. Then we're in business." She started for the door, with Jake behind her.

Sharon sighed. "Thank you, Lynda. Thanks, Jake."

"We're gonna find your kids," Jake told the three forlorn parents in the room. "Hopefully before the sun goes down today."

While the others stacked flyers and planned what to say to the press, Tony hooked up a second VCR to the television and watched a video of the girls, looking for thirty-second clips of both girls to edit out for distribution to all of the television stations. They had already distributed photographs, but now it seemed that the public needed to see the children moving, laughing. Maybe it would pull their heartstrings, as it did his. He sat on a chair right in front of the television, his elbows propped on his knees, and his chin on his clamped fists as Christy and Emily climbed on a sliding board at a park, laughing and waving to the camera.

Their size startled him, and he told himself that he had seen them before they were kidnapped, and they hadn't seemed so tiny then. But now they were in such huge danger. He watched as little Christy slid down, then turned and walked back up the slide, all the while singing, "Zacchaeus was a wee little man, a wee little man was he . . ." She stood at the top of the slide, then took a leap, and fell into sand. She looked as if she'd hurt herself and quickly got up, dusted off her knee, and looked up at the camera as though she wished her father would cut it off.

"I don't feel like performing right now," she said, lips trembling. "Turn it off."

He did, and it quickly flashed to another scene, where she was "performing," both she and Emily decked out in Anne's clothes, high heels, and jewelry as they sang a song they had made up, complete with bad choreography.

Christy seemed to be singing, or imagining, or laughing in every frame, and he sat helpless for a moment as tears sprang to his eyes. Was she singing or imagining or laughing now? What must be going through those little girls' minds?

The thought that they could already be dead hit him like a sledgehammer between the eyes, and he shook his head and swallowed hard. They couldn't be. They had to be alive. If he was any kind of cop, he'd find them.

The scene switched to a Christmas shot, when they were both sitting on the floor opening presents, with Jenny behind them. It must have been a Christmas that Sharon had spent alone. He wondered how she had filled it, and wished he had been there to help. He had been lonely last Christmas, too.

The perfect shot of the girls came when they were outside on Christmas morning, both donning their new roller blades, and trying to stand straight without falling as they wrapped their arms around each other and smiled at the camera. He pressed "pause" and froze the scene, and for a moment, just stared at those two little happy, innocent faces.

It was almost more than he could bear, and he sat still, fighting the tears in his eyes, fighting the fears in his heart.

Just hang on a little longer, girls, he told them silently. *I'm gonna find you real soon.*

Then, trying to pull himself together, he quickly turned on the second VCR and copied the scene to be splashed across television screens, both locally and nationally, until they were able to find the children.

65

Both children were getting weaker, and Christy could feel Emily's fever as she leaned her head against her. Christy, herself, was having chills, even though the cat was helping her to battle them.

Her lips felt like scabs, and she saw as the light came through the window overhead that Emily's were cracked. The five-year-old looked deathly pale. Her eyes seemed sunken in.

What had happened to Daddy? Why hadn't the man come back?

She looked around the filthy bathroom and saw the dead rat that the cat had killed last night. She turned her eyes away from it, unwilling to look at it any longer. The cat purred on her lap, and she stroked him. "You did good," she whispered weakly.

She looked up at the broken window through which the cat had come, and wished she could climb up there. She was a good climber, she thought. But both of their hands were so tender, and they didn't have much energy.

The cat meowed and looked up at the window, as if wishing he could get out.

"It's too far, boy," Christy said, though she didn't know what gender the cat was. "You can get down from there, but not back up."

But the cat got off her lap and sat back on its haunches, as if readying itself to pounce. It leaped onto the commode tank, and from there fixed its eyes on the closest plant a few feet up. He pounced, then bobbed in the hanging pot of dried leaves and dirt for a moment, shook off a spiderweb, then looked up, evaluating its next move.

It leaped again to the next plant, sending it swinging, then to the next higher one, and the one above that. In moments, the cat had reached the window.

Christy's eyes widened. She sat up, and shook Emily. "Emily, wake up."

Emily stirred slightly, but was too lethargic. "Emily! I have to show you something!"

Emily opened her eyes. "What?"

"The cat. It climbed back up and got out the window. Maybe we could climb, too." She stood up and, feeling dizzy, leaned back against the commode. After a moment, she recovered her balance and took a step toward the wall where the cat had found the first foothold. "I think I can do it. I'm a good climber. You are, too, Emily."

Emily surveyed the wide space between the plants. "I'm not that good. That's high, Christy. Besides, we're too heavy. What if they won't hold us?"

"They will," Christy said. "They have to. I can do it, and if I make it, I can come around and get you out. Or go for help."

"No," Emily whined. "Don't leave me here by myself. I'm scared."

"I promise I won't leave you," Christy said.

"But what if you can't move the stuff in front of the door?"

"I will," Christy said. "I'm strong. Daddy always says so."

"But if you get out, and you can't move the stuff, you won't be able to get back in. I'll be all by myself."

"You're what they call a pestimist," Christy said.

"I am not! What is that, anyway?"

"It's somebody who thinks of so many bad things that they become a pest."

"I am not a pest! I'm just scared!"

"Yeah, well, you're a scaredy-cat, too."

Emily started to cry, and Christy was instantly filled with remorse. She went and sat back down beside her, and put her arm around her. Emily was burning with fever. "I'm a scaredy-cat, too," she admitted. "That's why I want out. But don't worry. I won't go. I'll stay here with you."

Emily rubbed the tears from her eyes and looked up at the window. "I wish the cat could talk, and he could tell somebody we were here."

"I wish he could bring us some food and something to drink."

"I wish he would come back and keep me warm. I'm so cold."

"I wish he would come back and keep you company while I climb out."

"Maybe he will come back," Emily whispered weakly. "Maybe he just had to go to the bathroom. You promise you won't leave me?"

The conversation was exhausting Christy. Looking at the window, she wondered if she could make it even if she wanted to. "I promise not to do it right now."

Emily didn't need more. She just laid her head against her sister's shoulder, and waited. . . .

66

SHARON COULDN'T BELIEVE the number of people that had convened on her front lawn in less than an hour. Through her living-room window she saw television vans, setting up local, live broadcasts. A conglomeration of cords all led to a cluster of microphones on the front steps of her home. She turned back to Anne and Ben.

"This is a little unnerving," she said quietly. "But the publicity has to help."

"It will," Ben assured her. "Somebody has seen something. If we can just get the word out, we'll find them. I know we will."

"I guess we can each say a few words. Which one of us should go first?"

"You go first," Anne said quickly. Tears came to her eyes, and she pinched the bridge of her nose. "I don't think I can get anything out. You're the professional. You're so good at talking to people . . . you'll say the right thing."

Sharon looked at Ben. "But Ben, you'll speak, won't you?"

He nodded. "Yeah. You go first."

Lynda came in the side door. "Are you ready?"

"Yes," Sharon said. "Are they?"

"It looks like it. One of the stations told me they're doing a feed to CNN. This is going to be national news."

"Really?" Sharon asked. "Why?"

"Look at it from a news director's point of view. A kidnapper is caught before he tells where the kids are. Every heart in America will be wrenched over this, and someone will be able to tell us something. Let's get to it."

Sharon sighed and almost wished she had changed clothes and put on some make-up, but she just wasn't up to it. She called into the other room. "Jenny? Are you ready?"

Jenny came in carrying Bobby. "Mom, do we have to go out there? There are so many of them."

"Yes," Sharon said. "The whole family's doing this. We're in this together."

Sharon took a breath, bracing herself, and opened the front door. The crowd began to hush as she walked up to the cluster of microphones. Slowly, Anne and Ben came out behind her, then Jenny and Bobby, then Lynda.

Sharon stepped up to the mikes and cleared her throat. "We called you all to come here today, because . . ." She stopped, cleared her throat again. "Because our children, Christy and Emily Robinson, have been kidnapped. As you know, their kidnapper was apprehended early this morning. But he has yet to reveal the location or the condition of our little girls."

Her voice cracked, but she struggled on. "We have every reason to believe they're alive . . . and we need the help of the community to find them. If you've seen anything, please call 555-3367 and report it. If you know of any place in your area that might be a good hiding place, please call. We're depending on this community to get our little girls back. They've been missing for days now, and we don't know if they've eaten, or if they're being taken care of. But we do know that the person we believe to be the sole kidnapper is not taking care of them anymore. Time could be running out . . ." She stopped, braced herself, and got too emotional to go on.

Ben stepped up to the microphones and touched her shoulder gently as she turned away. "I'm Ben Robinson, the father of Christy and Emily. We're asking anyone who can take the time today to please meet at Roosevelt Park at 10 A.M. We're going to start a citywide search for the girls. And girls, if you can hear me, please know that Daddy is looking for you. We're going to find you . . ."

His voice broke, and he stepped back and hugged Anne, who was beside herself already.

Questions broke out from the crowd. "Mr. Robinson, does this kidnapping have anything to do with the murder charges that have been filed against you?"

"I'll take that." Tony came out of the crowd and trotted up the steps. "I'm Tony Danks with the St. Clair PD, and I can tell you that the charges against Mr. Robinson have been officially dropped as of this morning. The kidnapper is our primary suspect in this murder, and if you'll read the statement that I passed out to you, you'll see what the ransom demand was and how it fits into this kidnapping. Again, we will begin a citywide search at 10:00 A.M. this morning, at Roosevelt Park. We need everyone who can come to help us find these children."

He stepped back, and Lynda Barrett took his place. "As an added note, I've been asked to speak for the family to tell you that the $25,000 reward is still being offered to the person who finds and returns these children."

"Are you still trying to get the information out of the kidnapper?" someone asked.

"Yes, of course," Tony said. "He just isn't being very forthcoming."

"Mr. Robinson, is it true that these children are half-sisters?"

Ben stepped forward. "Yes. Christy is my daughter with Sharon. Emily is my daughter with Anne. But they're only a year apart in age. They're very close."

Sharon looked at him and saw the shame, the remorse, on his face at having to admit that their family was such a tangled web. She, too, hated the way it looked. Instantly, they would be labeled a "dysfunctional family." It was a term she hated even more than the word "divorce."

They stood there for a few moments longer as questions were fired at them from the crowd. Enlarged photographs of the girls were passed out to everyone, videos were copied and distributed to the television stations, and finally, the family went back in as Lynda and Tony fielded the rest of the questions.

Two hours later, as Larry and Jenny and Lynda manned the phone lines, Sharon, Anne, and Ben joined Tony and what looked like the rest of the town of St. Clair at Roosevelt Park. Hundreds of people had turned out to search for the children, and a mob of reporters, even more than she'd met on the front lawn of her house, recorded the event.

Sharon was so moved as they drove up that she couldn't speak. Tony saw the emotion on her face, and reached for her hand. "Are you all right?"

"Yes," she whispered. "I'm just surprised."

"St. Clair has a great community spirit," he said. "I knew they'd come."

Anne and Ben got out of the car, but Sharon held back.

"Are you sure you're all right, Sharon?" Tony asked her.

She sat there for a moment, not answering, just staring at the mob of people waiting to find her child. "I guess that . . . I'm just afraid . . . of what they might find." She wiped her tears away.

Tony scooted closer to her on the seat and wiped a tear rolling down her cheek. "Sharon, last night you said that they weren't dead. You said you would have known it. You trusted. Don't you still feel that?"

"Yes," she cried. "But maybe that's just what I *want* to feel. What if they're dead? I just don't want to know."

"They're not dead," Tony whispered. "Chamberlain is a high-brow art dealer. It would go against his nature to kill two little girls."

"It was in his nature to kill Dubose."

"But this is different. He would have no reason to kill them."

"When he left them, he knew they could identify him. He may have wanted to make sure that they didn't."

Tony grew quiet for a moment. He'd thought of that himself. "Sharon, those children need you right now. They need your faith. Now, I'm not even sure I believe in the same things you do, but I've got to tell you. Your faith has been a comfort to me during this whole thing. I may not believe in God, but I believe in your faith in God. What was it you said just yesterday, about God knowing where they are?"

She leaned her head back on the seat and closed her eyes as more tears poured out. "They're in the palm of his hand."

"Maybe he'll show us where they are," Tony whispered. "Now, come on."

They got out of the car and pushed through the crowd to the raised platform where Anne and Ben were already standing.

Jake Stevens was in the crowd, passing out flyers and pictures of the girls. His mother, Doris Stevens, who'd developed a reputation around town for being a Porsche-driving-teenager-in-a-fifty-five-year-old-woman's-body, was standing in a crowd of people telling the tidbits she knew that no one else knew.

"Jake, my boy, is good friends with the parents, ya see, and he says that the daddy and his family moved in with wife number one on account of that bum murder rap they pinned on him, so the girls were together with their older sister when she went to the grocery store . . . You know, this was all over a painting, and that man, Somebody Nelson, the kidnapper, he killed that Dupuis fella who ran the art gallery . . ."

Tony couldn't help grinning slightly, but Sharon was too focused on starting the hunt.

She stepped up on the platform, and looked at Ben. "Who's gonna do the talking?"

"I will," Ben said.

He stepped up to the microphone and tapped it. There was instant feedback, and someone adjusted it as the crowd got quiet.

"I really appreciate you all coming here today," he said, his voice wobbling. "Some pictures of my girls, Christy and Emily, are being passed out right now, along with the phone number to call if you see anything or think of anything that might help us. Uh . . ." He stopped, cleared his throat. "Christy's six, and she's real bright and real strong. And Emily is five . . . not as athletic as Christy, or as daring. But they're survivors. We . . . uh. . . . don't know how long since they've eaten. And the weather's been getting colder . . . they didn't have their coats . . ." His voice broke and he stepped back, unable to go on.

Tony gave them a few more instructions, organized the groups into sections of the city to cover, then escorted them all back to the car.

"I think the three of you should go home now," he said. "Let these people look for them."

"No," Sharon said. "I'm going to look, too. I can't sit in that house any longer doing nothing."

"But what if someone finds them? You'll need to be home."

"I can take my cellular phone with me. I'm going, Tony. Don't even try to talk me out of it."

"Take us home," Ben said. "We're going, too, but we'll take our own car."

"All right," Tony said, and headed back to Sharon's.

67

THEY SEARCHED THE town high and low, from abandoned buildings to hotel rooms. Tony spent five more hours trying to intimidate the information out of Chamberlain, but to no avail. Even at his arraignment, when the judge ordered him to tell where the children were or be held in the same cell until the Grand Jury investigation, Chamberlain maintained that he knew nothing about them.

Sharon searched in the most destitute part of town, where crack dealers and druggies and prostitutes loitered on the streets. She searched the buildings there with a vengeance, calling out the girls' names at the top of her lungs, until she was too hoarse to be heard any longer.

She had no luck, and her cellular phone never rang. Hourly, she checked at home to see if anyone had given them any leads at all, but any that had been given had already been checked out.

Finally, she drove to the beach, to her favorite spot where she often took the girls, and sat in the car, staring out across the sand and the blue waters of the Gulf.

Why aren't you answering, God? Why have you turned away?

The mighty pounding of the waves were her answer, each white-topped crest tipping toward her like an indictment. For a long while she sat, staring at those angry waves, searching her own heart and mind for the answers she needed.

She had come close to admitting the problem with Ben once, when they'd stood out on that porch and she'd told him of her ulterior motives in inviting him to live in her home. She had confessed, partially, to him, though it hadn't been a confession that sought forgiveness. It had been merely a statement, without heart, without much remorse. It had even been flung out in anger.

Now she wondered if it had been enough. God was dealing with her, she thought. He had something to teach her about her own faults, her own shortcomings, her own sins.

"Oh, God, help me to see what you see," she whispered. "I really want to be pleasing to you."

And then she knew.

She started the car and headed home. Maybe if she got her heart right, once and for all, she could pray effectively, she told herself. Maybe then she wouldn't feel this wall between herself and her Savior.

It was late afternoon when she finally returned home, not ready to give up, but desperately needing some cleansing.

The house was quiet—the phone wasn't ringing. Jenny's eyes were swollen as she sat in front of the telephone, waiting for something, anything, to happen. Lynda was studying a map of the town, trying to figure out any places that had yet to be searched.

"Have Larry or Tony called in?" Sharon asked.

"No," Lynda said. "They're apparently not having any luck with Chamberlain."

Her eyes filled with tears. "I wish they would let me at him. I'd get the information out of him!"

Sobbing quietly, Jenny lowered her face into the circle of her arms. Sharon softened and went to hug her. "Honey, have you eaten?"

"No," she said. "But neither have you. And neither have they . . . at least not since Chamberlain was found." She looked up at her mother. "Mom, why didn't he get me, too? Why didn't he just take me with them? Then I could be there taking care of them, making sure they were all right."

"You are taking care of them," Sharon said. "You're here, doing everything you can."

"Mom, I'm so afraid they're dead!" she said in a high-pitched voice. She fell into her mother's arms, and they clung to each other for a moment.

The phone rang, and Jenny jumped for it.

"I'll get it," Lynda said, but Jenny jerked it up. "Hello?"

She wilted as the caller spoke, then said, "Okay. I'll tell them."

She hung up. "It was Tony. He wanted to check on you. He said he's on his way over."

Sharon went cold. "Does he have news?"

"No," Jenny said. "He said he didn't. But they're still looking."

Sharon leaned heavily back against the wall. "Where are your father and Anne?"

"They got back about half an hour ago. Anne's taking care of Bobby, and Daddy's out on the back porch."

Sharon glanced through the den and to the back door. Sighing, she said, "I need to go talk to him."

She left them there and headed back through her house, to the back porch where Ben stood against the screen, gazing out at the tree house where he had sat with his little girls just days ago.

He heard her coming out and turned his head. She came to stand beside him and looked at it, too. "We were going to paint the tree house," he said quietly. "Since I wasn't here for the building of it, I thought I could at least do that. They wanted to paint a mural."

Sharon swallowed. "God willing, you'll still have the chance."

"Well, that's just it," Ben said. "I don't know if God is willing. I haven't done much for him."

She looked down at the tiles beneath her feet.

"You have, though," he whispered. "I guess I'm counting on him listening to you. You always did the praying for both of us."

Sharon shook her head. "It's occurred to me that maybe my prayers are worthless," she whispered on the edge of tears.

Now he looked fully at her. "Worthless? Why?"

"Because I'm still holding so much against you."

He breathed a mirthless laugh. "Yeah, well, I guess you deserve to." He turned away from the screen and went to sit down on one of the cushioned patio chairs. "You know, it's strange, looking back on what I did to you. It didn't seem so bad at the time."

Sharon couldn't look at him. She kept her eyes on the floor.

"You were doing so great professionally, and I was struggling. You weren't that naive little woman who used to look up at me like I was the one who hung the moon."

"I found out you weren't," she admitted.

"I missed having someone to look up to me," he said. "And when I met Anne—"

Sharon shook her head, unable to bear the explanation again. "Don't, Ben. You don't have to do this."

"Yes, I do," he said.

"Why? I didn't bring it up so we could salt old wounds. I came out here to forgive you."

"Is it really forgiveness, Sharon, when you can't even discuss it?" He rubbed his face and looked at her over his fingertips. "I really need to say these things to you."

She glanced at the door back into the house and wondered if she could make a clean exit. But he was right. That was no kind of forgiveness.

"My children live in two different families because of what I did, Sharon. Two of them I only get to see on weekends. Moving in here and seeing how unnatural everything is . . . well, it started me thinking about how drastically I've altered all of our lives." He looked up at her, struggling with the words. "Sharon, I never meant to hurt you. But even worse, I never meant to hurt Jenny or Christy. When I think of leaving you when she was just a little baby . . . giving up that daily experience of watching her grow . . ."

"You were the one you hurt," she whispered.

He nodded, as if he knew that was true. "I told myself that you were strong. And you prospered so over the years. I mean, look at this house. You did it yourself."

"I didn't do it myself," she whispered. "I leaned on God, and he took care of me. He does that. He makes provision."

"There have been times, over the years, when I looked back on my affair with Anne, and I realized how I deceived myself, and you, and her. There were really no winners. Everybody had to pay."

"That's divorce," Sharon said.

A long moment of silence stretched between them, and she looked down at her former husband, collapsed on the chair, in turmoil over the present, and in just as much turmoil over the past.

"I'm gonna say something that isn't easy for me," she said, sitting down opposite him and leaning her elbows on her knees as she knitted her fingers together.

"What?" he asked.

"It wasn't just you. I had a part in ending our marriage."

Wind whipped through the screen, ruffling his long hair. "How do you figure that?" he asked. "You were faithful."

"That's true. I never cheated on you. Not with a person. But with my work. And with my affections. Maybe it was my job to keep looking at you the way I had in the beginning. Maybe I set myself up for an Anne to come along." She swallowed, and made herself look at him. "All those times you wanted affection, and I was distant, cold . . . I told myself you were just a passionate artist, that your feelings didn't have to be taken seriously."

His face changed as he gazed at her. "I never in a million years thought I'd hear you say this."

"I should have said it a long time ago, Ben. Yes, you hurt our family when you left. But I hurt them, too. Maybe I left the marriage long before you did."

He struggled with the emotion twisting his face.

"I forgive you, Ben," she whispered. "I hope you can forgive me."

"I do." They were the words he'd spoken on the day they'd exchanged vows, and now they were spoken to heal them of their broken vows. He got up and hugged her, tightly, desperately, then quickly let her go.

"Now maybe God will listen to me," she whispered. "Maybe he had to bring us through this to get us to this point. Come in with me. We'll get Anne and Jenny, and start praying again."

He rubbed his red eyes and followed her in.

68

TONY PULLED INTO Sharon's driveway and sat for a moment in his car, wishing with all his heart that he had some good news for her. He hated to go in there empty-handed again, but he felt a compulsion to be here with her, as though he had some part in this loss they shared.

He got out of the car and walked to the door, but before knocking, decided to walk back to the gate that led into the backyard. He opened it and went through, and looked around the yard at all the signs of the little girl who lived here. Her Barbie bike with glittery, iridescent ribbons streaming from the handlebars stood on the patio next to a little toy stroller. Across the yard, her tire swing sat motionless, empty. He walked across the lawn to the tree house, and looked up. Something drew him up there, so he shrugged off his sport coat, dropped it on the ground, and began to climb the ladder.

He opened the hatch at the top of the ladder and went in to the little room where she'd stored so many treasures. Milk cartons and shoe boxes and rolls of string and glue . . .

He could just imagine the little rascals up here playing to their hearts' content, never worried that some stranger might come along and rock their world.

Unable to handle the emotions suddenly coursing through him, he slipped out the hatch and climbed back down. He grabbed his coat and hurried across the yard.

When he knocked on the door, Lynda let him in. "Any word?" she asked hopefully.

Tony shook his head and sighed. "No. Chamberlain's not saying a word. And now he's got this bigshot lawyer with him trying to strike a deal."

"What kind of deal?"

"Well, it's real nebulous, since the man is swearing he had nothing to do with the kidnapping, but what I'm gathering is that if we give him clemency, he might tell us where they are. But remember, all of this is being conveyed through hints—he still claims to be innocent. The DA says he's going to go for the death penalty, and the judge has done everything but torture him to make him talk. Still nothing."

She groaned.

"Where's Sharon?" he asked.

"Upstairs in Christy's room. She's a wreck. They all are."

"I'll go talk to her before I get back to the hunt," he whispered.

He went up the stairs quietly, since the house seemed so still. It felt strange disturbing it. He saw the pink walls in the room down the hall, and assumed that was Christy's room. Quietly, he went to the door.

There were Sharon, Jenny, Ben, and Anne, huddled on the bed with their arms around each other and their heads bowed, praying out loud for God's help in delivering those kids.

Something about the scene touched his heart . . . *broke* his heart. They were enemies . . . adversaries . . . Their pasts had shipwrecked their futures. Yet here they were, bound by their love for those little girls, acting as a family under the eyes of God.

Tears came to his eyes, and he stumbled backward, quietly, because he didn't want them to hear him. What if they looked up and invited him to join them? He hadn't really prayed since his "Now I lay me down to sleep" days as a boy . . . and he wasn't ready to do it now.

He rushed back down the stairs, feeling like a coward—the big, bad cop who could put the fear into everyone but Nelson Chamberlain, the one who was afraid of nothing—running from the idea of getting caught in a prayer.

He slipped out the door before Lynda could see him and got quickly into his car. He'd cranked the engine and pulled out of the driveway before the first tears stung his eyes.

He had never felt more helpless in his life. Two children were out there who he was powerless to help, and a man sat in jail who wasn't afraid enough of him to talk. Always before, there had been some way of working toward a solution. This time, however, everything seemed out of his hands.

Was Sharon right? Was God really in control? Was there even a God at all?

He drove until it began to get dark, and the stars began to appear, revealing the majesty of the Creator who was artist, astronomer, and physicist. To Sharon, he was a comforter. He was in control. He knew where those children were.

He pulled his car off the road, looked up at the dark sky, and asked himself for the first time in a very long time if he really believed. He wasn't sure. But Sharon's faith, her graciousness with her ex-husband and his wife, sure seemed real. And she was an intelligent woman, not some superstitious soul who would fall for anything. She'd been through fires and come out of them still believing.

His eyes were full of tears as he looked up through his dirty windshield. "If you're up there, God, I don't know why you'd waste any time on me," he whispered. "I'm not exactly what they call worthy. And I haven't given you more than a passing thought in about the last ten years, except when Larry has hassled me about you. You know Larry—yeah, what am I saying, of course you do."

He didn't know why he was crying. It was crazy. None of this made any sense, but as he spoke, a sense of tremendous waste, monumental loss, overtook him. "I can't believe you can even hear me, if you're there, but I figure it's worth a try, anyway. There's probably nothing that could have made me come to you, God, except maybe two little girls out there alone . . . and their grieving mother who believes in you."

He rubbed his eyes, angry at himself for losing control like this. "God, you've gotta help us. You've gotta help them. Not for me . . . not because of anything I've done . . . but do it for them. Those helpless little—"

He sobbed into his hand, then tried to pull himself together again. "I'll make a deal with you, God. If you bring them back safely to their parents . . . I'm yours. I'll be the best believer you've ever seen. I'll do anything you say . . . I'll even pray and read the Bible, even though what I've seen of it I've never understood. But I'll take classes and learn. I'll do all the stuff Larry does, and more. I'll even start being one of those people who gives money to poor people, and visits prisoners, and God, that's a big promise, because I don't have much compassion for the people I lock up . . ."

He sighed and wiped his face. "I think if you could work enough miracles to get Sharon and Ben and Anne praying together, then you can give me that kind of compassion. And you can help us find those kids."

He didn't quite know how to sign off. "Amen" seemed so trite, but "Bye" sounded too silly. So he let it hang there . . . wondering if anyone had heard.

Peace gradually washed over him as he pulled back out onto the street and started searching for the children again.

69

EMILY WASN'T ACTING right. Since the afternoon, all she had wanted to do was sleep. Her lips were cracked and bloody from thirst, and her eyes were sunken deeper into her face, casting dark circles under them. Christy had tried to wake her up, mostly from fear since darkness was beginning to close in again, but she barely stirred.

She had to get help, Christy thought, looking at the window again. She had to make her way out.

She got up and steadied herself as a wave of dizziness washed over her. After a moment, she recovered her equilibrium, and she stepped up on the rim of the commode and climbed to the broken lid. She looked up and found the plant where the cat had first jumped on its way out. The spider had repaired its web, but she shoved that thought out of her mind.

"Help me climb like a cat, God," she whispered. "Help me climb like a cat."

She was a good climber, she reminded herself. It was her favorite thing to do. She could do this, even if it was hard.

She judged the distance between where she stood and the plant, and reached out her foot. It reached, but just barely, and she pressed one hand against the wall and reached for the grimy macramé with the other. She tested her weight on it, felt the stake in the wall give slightly, but she didn't let it stop her. Quickly, she pulled her other foot up. The plant swung from its hanger, creaking with her weight, so she quickly stepped up to the next one.

Her hands throbbed and bled as she clawed at the wall for a hold, measuring her next step. When she'd gotten both feet on the next hanging pot, she began to get dizzy again.

Hold on, she told herself. *Just wait a minute.*

She waited, swinging slightly, until the dizziness passed, then looked up the wall for the next foothold.

She pulled her body up, and looked up at the window again. It was still so far up there, but she could make it, she thought. She just had to takc it easy, go slowly, be careful.

Her arms were getting tired, something that never happened, and she told herself it was weakness since she hadn't eaten. She would only get weaker if she didn't find help. She had to get out somehow.

She clawed at the bricks with each foothold, and winced at the pain in her fingers.

She was hot, but she wasn't sweating, and her throat felt as if it was on fire. If she only had some water, she thought. Just a drop . . .

She looked down, and saw her sister lying limply on the floor. She was burning with fever, and looked so weak. What if she died?

She couldn't give up now. She had to make it up.

The next plant was too high, so she grabbed its pot with her hands and tried to climb the bricks, toe hitting grout, one brick at a time, until she was able to step up to the next plant. She grabbed on to the bricks with one aching, infected hand, and held the macramé for dear life with the other.

Just above her was a wooden planter bolted to the wall, and she reached up and grabbed it. She pushed up until she was able to get her weight over it. Once she got her feet on it, she rested and looked up. The window was only a few feet away. She could make it.

She took a deep breath and calculated that three more plants would get her to the window, and she stretched her leg with all her might to reach the next one, then the next one, until finally she could reach the windowsill.

With all her strength, she pulled herself up, but the window wasn't open. The cat had come in through a broken hole in the glass. But she was too big to fit through it.

She tried to plant her feet on the windowsill, and held on to the top casing with one hand while she struggled to raise the window with the other. It was stuck.

She looked down at her sister still lying on the floor. The room was growing darker, but outside it was only dusk. She could see the big tree beside the window, the tree the cat must have climbed to get in. The branches reaching to the window were small, but she could make it, she told herself, if she could just get the window open.

Holding the casing as tightly as she could with her infected hands, she kicked at the glass. Shards fell out and crashed to the dirt outside. She looked down to see if the noise had disturbed Emily, but her sister still lay there, deep in sleep.

The hole looked big enough to get through, so she ducked through it, kicked the broken glass off of the ledge, and carefully sat down to get her bearings. The cool air against her face made her feel stronger. She tried to find a branch big enough to hold her. None of them looked secure. She grabbed the closest one and straddled it with both arms and legs, sliding toward the center.

It swayed downward as if it might break with her weight, but she grabbed the bigger one beneath her, and climbed down to it. It was stronger, and she slid in toward the trunk, then found another, stronger one, and another, until she felt secure.

It was a massive tree, a perfect climbing tree, but it didn't give her the pleasure that climbing usually did. Her hands were bleeding and sore, and she was shaking. She made her way down, one branch at a time.

When she'd made it to the bottom branch, she looked down. It was at least a six-foot jump to the ground from here, and she wasn't sure if she could manage it. But she had no choice. Emily was still in there, all alone, and she had to hurry.

She judged the distance, as the cat had done, then held her breath and leapt. She made a perfect landing.

Now what? she asked, looking around. There were no buildings, no houses, anywhere in sight. Only this lonely road with a ditch on either side, and thick woods.

She went to the road, looked up and down it, but saw nothing. No cars, no people, no houses.

She would have to get Emily out, she thought, and then they could run away as far as they needed to find help. And she had to hurry, in case the man came back.

She ran back to the front door of the dilapidated structure and pushed it open.

The building was getting dark, full of monstrous shadows and scratching noises and creaks that terrified her. But she couldn't be afraid, she told herself. Emily needed her.

She ran up the stairs, careful to avoid the holes in them, and found the bathroom. The man had slid a huge bench against the door and piled a steel drum and other pieces of rusted machinery on it to weigh it down. She tried to slide it back, but it wouldn't budge.

Christy climbed on top of it, and turned backward, pushing her back against the wall and using the force of her legs to try to slide the bench away. But she just wasn't strong enough. It was jammed tightly against the door, and there was no way she would ever get it open.

She thought of calling out to Emily, trying to wake her again, but then she realized that her sister probably needed the blessing of sleep. If she woke to find herself alone, she would fall apart. Until Christy got her help, she didn't want to wake her.

She was trembling now, both from fear and courage, both from despair and hope.

"God, you can help us," she whispered weakly. "You helped me climb like a cat. Please send somebody now."

70

DORIS STEVENS HAD been dead-set on winning that $25,000 reward money when she'd set out to look for the kidnapped children that day, but after an all-day search, she was getting discouraged. St. Clair was no huge metropolis, but it was bigger than Slapout, Texas. If she had looked for two lost children in Slapout, she could have turned the whole town upside down in two hours flat, and she would have found what she was looking for.

Now she had less than an hour to shower and change for her shift at the diner where she worked, and she wound her Porsche through the backstreets on the outskirts of St. Clair, heading for her trailer, which was parked on the only piece of land she could afford on her salary. It was far out, yes, but it was home. She'd been urged to sell the Porsche and buy a house or a condo, but she couldn't bring herself to do it. She loved that car. It was the only thing of any value she'd ever had.

It was getting dark, so she turned on her headlights and wove around the curves, ignoring the speed limit, since she rarely encountered other cars this far out. Maybe, if she was lucky, the kids wouldn't be found today, and she'd still have a shot at the grand prize tomorrow.

She turned up the radio on her favorite cry-in-your-beer country tune, something about being cheated on in the worst kind of way, something she could relate to many times over. She began to sing along in her nasal, twangy voice, as loud as the speakers blaring in her car. She had always thought she could have made it as a country singer.

A cat dashed across the road in front of her, and she barely missed hitting it, swerving only slightly to avoid losing control. Suddenly alert, she cursed and reached for her cigarette box, shook one out, pressed in the lighter, and stuck the cigarette in her mouth. She waited until the lighter was ready, then reached to get it out to light her cigarette.

From the corner of her eye, she saw something up ahead, and she dropped the lighter on the floor and looked up.

A child stood in thc middle of the road, waving her down.

She swerved, slammed on brakes, lost control. The car skidded to the right, into the ditch, kept sliding several hundred feet further, then slammed full force against a tree.

She sat still for a moment, trying to decide if anything was broken. Nothing but the car, she thought in misery. Then she screamed a curse, and slammed her hand against the steering wheel.

She saw movement outside her window and looked up, and saw that child again. Furious, she flung open the door. "You almost got me killed! What in the world were you doin' standin' out in the middle of the street? Where's your mama? I'm gonna march you right home to her and tell her what you did!" She got out and looked at her crumpled Porsche, and stamped one high-heeled foot. "Look what you did! It's ruined! The only thing decent I ever had, and you ruined it!"

The little girl looked like she'd just lost a fight, and she was shivering. "I'm sorry," she said in a hoarse, raspy voice. "But I . . . I need help. My sister's locked in that old building up the road, and I have to get her out 'cause she's sick. Please. Will you help us?"

Doris looked down at the little girl and could tell that she wasn't doing so hot herself. She had a nasty cut on her forehead, and dried blood matted her bangs. The child looked familiar, except for the dark circles beneath her eyes, the ghost-like pallor to her skin, the blistered lips. "Honey, what's your name?"

"Christy Robinson," the child said.

Doris caught her breath. "Oh, my word! You're the kidnapped kid! You're the one we've been lookin' for!"

"You have?" Christy asked.

"Yes!" Doris shouted. "And I found you! Twenty-five grand is mine! I'm goin' to Atlantic City, that's what I'm gonna do! I'm gonna get me a fancy dress and stay in some fancy room with a hot tub—"

The little girl seemed to be dizzy, and she leaned against the car to steady herself. Doris instantly shut up. "Okay, kiddo. First things first. If only I had a car phone. I mean, there's one in the car, but I couldn't afford to pay for it, so I disconnected it. Heck, I can barely afford to put gas in it, but it doesn't matter now, does it? It's gone. Well, at least it does have insurance. That's somethin'." She saw the half-bottle of Coke sitting in the drink holder, undisturbed even though the front of the car was smashed in. "Honey, you look thirsty. You want this?"

Christy's eyes widened and she took the Coke and finished most of it off in one gulp. She probably hadn't had anything to drink in a while, Doris assumed.

She stopped when there was about two inches left in the bottle. "My sister needs the rest of this," she said. "We have to hurry. The man might come back, and if he finds me gone, he might hurt Emily."

"The man?" Doris asked. "That Nelson Chamberlain fella? Oh, no. He's not comin' back. He's in jail."

Christy looked up at her with those dull, lethargic eyes. "Really?"

"That's right, and honey, your parents are sick with worry over you. They've been lookin' everywhere. Come on, let's go get your little sister."

"Do you have a flashlight?" Christy asked. "We might need it. She has one, but she's not awake. And she's locked in a bathroom, and there's all this stuff shoved in front of it, only it's too heavy and I can't move it. I climbed out the window, but Emily's not as good a climber, and she won't wake up."

"Oh, blazes," Doris said, realizing the urgency of the situation. She went to her trunk, opened it, and found the flashlight and hydraulic jack that Jake had put there. She took them both out, thinking that she might need the jack if the door was barricaded as thoroughly as Christy said.

Christy led her back up the road to the building that was encased in darkness now. It was the old country store that she passed every day. Why she hadn't thought to look there earlier, she didn't know. But the front door was always open, and windows were broken out, and she had just assumed that if anyone were hidden there, the door wouldn't be open.

She shivered at the thought of going in there, and turned on the flashlight. It lit up the downstairs. "I gotta tell you, kiddo. I ain't much of one for bravery. This ain't the kind of place I like to go."

"Me, either," Christy said. "But it's okay. Come on. We have to get to Emily."

Every muscle in her body was rigid with tension as she made her way up the creaky stairs and saw the door barricaded with that big bench, a steel drum, and some other equipment.

She set down the jack and tried to pull the bench away, but she wasn't strong enough. "All right," she said, grabbing the jack. "Never fear. This'll move it right out of the way." She wedged it the best she could between one of the pieces of machinery and the wall, then began to pump it. It immediately began to expand, pushing the bench inch by inch back from the door.

"That's good! I can open it now," Christy said. She slipped between the bench and the door, and opened it.

Emily was still sleeping deeply on the floor. "There she is!" Christy said. "I think she's sick."

Doris slipped into the filthy place and knelt next to the tiny child. She touched her head. "She's burning up with fever," she said. "Poor little thing." She picked her up in her arms, and handed the flashlight to Christy. "Here, I'll carry her, and you lead us back out with the light."

Emily didn't stir as they hurried out of the building.

"Where will we go?" Christy asked.

"My place," Doris said. "It's only about a mile up the road. I can call your mama and daddy from there, and get you somethin' to eat. Give me that Coke, will ya?"

Christy handed it to her, and watched as she poured a couple of drops on Emily's lips, then a couple more. She saw Emily swallow. "Come on, darlin'," Doris said. "Drink some of this, for Doris. It'll make you feel better."

Slowly, Emily's eyes began to open, and she raised her head enough to drink. When the bottle was empty, Doris said, "Okay, let's go."

They walked for what seemed an eternity, and her high heels began to cut into her feet, rubbing blisters and making her ankles ache. But she had the kids, she thought. That was the main thing. That and the money.

"Did that man hurt you, honey?" she asked as they trudged along.

Christy shrugged. "He locked us up."

"But did he . . . *do* anything? Are you all right?"

"I'm hungry," Christy whispered. "And my hands hurt. And I'm cold."

Emily stirred in Doris's arms. "Christy?" she whispered.

Christy looked over at Emily. "Yeah."

"Did God answer our prayers with her?" she whispered weakly.

Christy smiled. "Yeah, he did."

Doris didn't know quite what to say to that. She'd never been the answer to a prayer before.

"Is Daddy coming to get us?" Emily asked.

"You bet he is, darlin'," Doris said. "As soon as I can get us to a phone. Look. See right up there? That's my trailer."

Christy looked so relieved that she stopped for a moment and just took in the sight, before pushing herself on.

71

TONY WENT BACK to the house, unable to rest or go home until he'd found the children. Lynda had already left, and Sharon, Jenny, Anne, and Ben all sat around the kitchen table, waiting that excruciating wait that seemed almost pointless.

He joined them at the table, feeling so helpless, so ineffective as a police officer, so inept as a human being.

And then the phone rang. Jenny sprang for it. "Hello?"

"Yes . . . uh . . . is this the Robinson's residence?" a woman with a deep southern drawl asked.

"Yes, it is."

"Well, this is Doris Stevens—Jake Stevens' mama? You know my boy, don't you?"

"Yes," Jenny said.

"I've got some good news for you, honey."

"What?" Jenny asked cautiously.

"I've found your kids."

Jenny sprang out of her seat and grabbed her father's arm. "Are . . . are you sure? Christy and Emily? You have them?"

Everyone sprang up from the table, and Ben grabbed the phone away from her. "This is Ben Robinson. You've found my girls?"

"Sure have," Doris said. "Here's Christy. She can tell you for herself."

He waited a moment, then heard Christy's hoarse, weak voice. "Daddy?"

"Honey!" He burst into tears. "Where are you?"

"With Miss Doris. Daddy, will you come get us now? I want to go home."

"Of course!" he shouted. "Are you all right?"

"I don't feel good, Daddy," Christy said. "And Emily's real sick. She has fever."

"Put the lady back on."

Doris took the phone back. "Hello? I can give you directions if you've got a pencil. I'd bring 'em to you, but I'm afraid I wrecked my car to keep from hittin' your daughter."

He jotted down the directions, and they all jumped into the car.

72

CHRISTY ATE A piece of cold chicken and watched out Doris's window for any sign of her father, but it had only been a few minutes since she'd talked to him. Doris said it would be at least fifteen before he'd be here.

Doris was holding Emily like a baby and coaxing her to drink. The child's fever was too high, and she hoped with all her heart that they'd be able to stop it in time. "Come on, honey. Drink some more for Doris. You don't want your daddy to be all worried about you, do you? He's on his way, you know."

Emily's eyes fluttered open, and she drank a little more.

"My heavens, look at these hands," Doris said. "Honey, you need to go back to that pan of water and soak your hands," she told Christy. "Get some of that dirt off. They're all infected. And this child's whole hands are swollen. I'm gonna have to let the doctor clean hers. I can't bear to hurt her when she's this sick. You know, you're a hero."

"Me?" Christy asked, turning around. "What did I do?"

"You may have saved your baby sister's life."

"You did that," Christy said. "I prayed that God would send help. He sent you."

"Oh, now, I don't know about none of that superstitious stuff. I prob'ly woulda seen you anyway."

Christy smiled knowingly and shook her head. "Nope. He sent you."

"Wouldn't I know it if God had sent me?"

"Maybe not," Christy said. "But he sent you just like he sent the cat."

"What cat?"

"The cat who protected us from the rats."

Doris shivered. What had these poor children endured for the last few days? Her heart ached as she looked down at the pale, weak child in her arms. No baby should have to go through such things.

"I hope they sling that man up by his toenails and make him eat mud," she muttered. "Treatin' two beautiful little girls like this. It just breaks my heart." She dabbed at the tears in her eyes.

Christy saw headlights, and began to jump up and down. "They're here! They're here!"

Doris peered out the window and saw the station wagon, followed by two or three other cars, some of them police squad cars and a television news van. "Blazes," she muttered. "Wish I'd had time to wash my hair. Go let your daddy in, honey."

Christy ran to the door and down the steps, and straight into Ben's arms as he bolted out of the car. Then Sharon took her from him, and the child clung to her mother.

Anne ran past them and into the house, and found Emily lying weak and feverish in Doris's arms. Sobbing, Anne took her quickly from the woman, kissed the child's face, and began whispering to her.

Tony's eyes were red with emotion as he stepped into the trailer, followed by Ben and Christy and Sharon. Doris wiped her eyes at the reunion as the mothers cried over their children.

"She's burning up," Anne shouted up to Ben.

"Her hands are infected, too," Doris pointed out. "And she ain't eaten a bite. I tried to feed her, but all she'd do was drink a little."

"Christy's feverish, too," Sharon said. "We've got to get them to the hospital."

"The squad car will escort you," Tony said. "Go ahead and take them."

Photographers were gathering and cameras rolled as the children were rushed out to the car and driven away with a flashing escort. Doris ran out and grabbed Tony as he started to get in his car, ignoring the reporters who were trying to get her to stop and give them an interview about how she'd found the children. "Can you drive me to the hospital?" she asked. "I really want to know how the little things are."

Tony looked surprised. "Sure. We're going to need a statement from you, anyway. How did you find them?"

Doris started to say that it was a fluke, that the child had just appeared in her headlights. But then she thought better of it. "Well, accordin' to that little Christy, God sent me to 'em. She swears up-an'-down that I'm an answered prayer."

Tony's eyes welled with tears, and he smiled. "You know what, Doris? Christy's absolutely right."

73

THE CHILDREN WERE kept overnight in the hospital, with IVs to battle their dehydration, and antibiotics to fight the infections originating in their hands. Both girls had their hands bandaged, and Christy had a bandage over her forehead.

Anne and Sharon requested that they be allowed to share a room, so that Ben could see both children at once. Jenny came in as soon as someone from their church had come to relieve her from taking care of Bobby, and tears sprang into her eyes at the sight of her two sleeping sisters. “Oh, Mom . . . Anne . . . I’m so sorry for letting this happen to them.”

Sharon pulled her older daughter into a hug. “Honey, it’s not your fault. And they’re going to be fine.”

“Really? Are you sure?”

“Yes.”

“Were they . . . abused in any way? Molested, I mean?”

“No,” Sharon said with certainty. It was one of the first things the doctor had looked for.

She walked Jenny back out of the room, knowing that Anne would keep an eye on Christy if she woke. “Honey, I know you’re still blaming yourself for all this, but I want you to know that some good did come out of it.”

“What?” she asked. “How?”

“God used it, to make me confront the fact that I’d never really forgiven your father. Or Anne. In my heart, I think I really hated them.”

“You couldn’t have hated them, Mom. You let them move in with us.”

“Well, I had several different motives for that. One of them was to look good to you. The more generous I looked, the worse they looked. But there sure wasn’t any love involved.”

“What about now?”

She glanced back in the room. “Anne’s a mother, just like me. She loves her kids every bit as much. And she’s been a good stepmother to you and Christy. I haven’t made it easy for her. And your father . . . he’s not a bad man. He made some mistakes, and his mistakes hurt me, and you, too. But I was far from perfect myself, Jenny.”

Jenny wiped her eyes. “Me, too.”

“God forgives our mistakes,” Sharon said.

“He’s awesome,” Jenny whispered. “So awesome.”

Sharon hugged her daughter again, and saw Tony standing across the hall. He’d heard everything. “Tell you what,” she told Jenny. “Why don’t you stay with Christy for a while, and I’ll go get something to eat. I haven’t had much in the last few days, myself, and I’m starting to feel a little hungry.”

“Okay,” Jenny whispered, and went back into the room.

Sharon went out of the room and looked up at Tony—who looked as tired and relieved as she did. “You’ve been great, Tony. Really great.”

He seemed to struggle with emotion as he looked down at his feet. Unable to say what was on his mind, he nodded toward the waiting room. “Doris is the real hero. She’s in the waiting room.”

Sharon took his hand and they went to the waiting room. Doris was in there with Jake and Lynda, chattering ninety-to-nothing about how she’d found the girls. When she saw Sharon, she sprang to her feet. “How are they, hon?” she asked.

“They’re great,” Sharon said, hugging the woman who’d saved her daughter. “They’ll both get to go home tomorrow. I just don’t know how to thank you enough. The reward doesn’t even begin to cover it.” She wiped her eyes. “I’ll write you a check tonight before you leave.”

Doris glanced at Lynda and Jake, then let out a heavy sigh. “Oh, heck, I can’t take your money. At first, when I was lookin’ for ’em, I thought I could. I mean, they were just pictures on a flyer, ya know? But now that I know ’em, and I seen what they’ve been goin’ through . . . well, I can’t take money for it. It just doesn’t seem right. Not when Christy’s so sure that God was usin’ me to find ’em. I can’t imagine why. Not like he’s ever been able to use me before! Out of the mouths of babes. Who am I to dispute it? But no money.”

"But your car," Sharon said. "It's totaled. Let me at least help you . . ."

Doris raised her hand to stem the woman's offer. "My insurance will pay for the car. It was fun while it lasted, sure. But I think I'm gonna take the insurance money and get me a little secondhand car of some kind, and use the rest of the money for a down payment on a nicer place to live. That trailer's too far out. It's time I did that, anyway."

Jake hugged his mother. "Mama got a call from Oprah Winfrey a few minutes ago," he said with a grin. "She's going on her show next week."

Sharon laughed. "Really?"

"Yeah," Doris said, waving a hand as if it meant nothing. "Somethin' about modern-day heroes. Can you imagine?"

A flock of reporters rushed to the door of the waiting room and descended on Sharon, but she pointed them to Doris. "She's the one who found the children," she said. "Sacrificed her Porsche to do it."

They all surrounded her as Sharon and Tony slipped out of the room.

Downstairs, Sharon and Tony sat sipping coffee over empty plates. Neither of them had realized how ravished they had been after not eating much for several days. A feeling of utmost peace seemed to fill Tony in a way that he'd never before experienced.

"Something weird happened to me today," he said, not able to look at Sharon as he spoke.

"What?" she asked.

He shrugged. "Well, I don't know. I was . . . sort of . . . under the fig tree."

Her eyebrows shot up. "You prayed?"

He couldn't meet her eyes. "I sort of made a deal with God."

"Uh-oh," Sharon said. "You're not supposed to bargain with God."

He smiled. "He took me up on it. I told him that if he brought the girls home safely, that I'd be a believer, and that I'd be the best Christian he had ever seen."

Sharon couldn't believe her ears. "And?"

"And I'm keeping my end of the bargain," he said. "He did it, didn't he? He really answered." He swallowed and looked up at her. "See, I've been struggling with this. Some voice in my head keeps saying, well, he may have answered, but why'd he let it happen in the first place? And then I heard you and Jenny talking, and I realized that he really may have created good out of it. In a lot of ways. For one, I never dreamed Doris Stevens would turn down the money. That's a miracle in itself. And this afternoon . . ." He wiped his eyes. "I saw you and Ben and Anne praying together . . . you had just put away your problems, your differences, all that baggage . . . and you went to God. That was good, wasn't it?"

She smiled. "Yeah. It was good."

"And it worked." He propped his chin on his hand and looked at her with probing eyes. "God may not have caused the kidnapping. I don't know. But I do know that he used it to knock me in the head. He used it for a lot of things."

She smiled as tears formed in her eyes. "Then it was worth it."

Gently, he took her hand. "Sharon, would you consider going out with me when all this is over? We were supposed to have had dinner. We never got to."

She smiled poignantly. "A real date?"

He nodded, feeling like that awkward teenager again. "I would consider it an honor to spend as much time with you as you're willing to spend with me."

"I would love to," she said, squeezing his hand. "As a matter of fact, why don't you come to church with me Sunday?"

He nodded. "This time, there's nothing I'd like more."

Afterword

RECENTLY, WHEN I was reading the book of Zechariah, something jumped out at me that I had not understood before. It was in chapter 7, when the people came to the prophet and asked him to inquire of God whether they should continue observing the fast to commemorate the destruction of Jerusalem, since Jerusalem was now being rebuilt. God answered their question with a question. He asked them if they were fasting for him, or for themselves. And then he added something that seemed unrelated to their question. "Administer true justice; show mercy and compassion to one another. Do not oppress the widow or the fatherless, the alien or the poor. In your hearts do not think evil of each other." The people must have frowned at one another and thought, "Did God misunderstand the question? We asked about fasting on a particular day, and he answers us with all this stuff about justice, compassion, and our hearts."

I've read that before and it has gone right over my head, but this time, it shone in my face like a beacon illuminating my own sins. I go to God expecting a pat on the back for all the good deeds I've done, all the people I've helped, all the enemies I've forgiven, all the worship I've sacrificed my time to offer. And God says, "Get real, Terri. Who were you doing those things for? Me or yourself?"

It's as if I look up at God and say, "Well, if that's not enough, what do you want?"

And he replies, "I want your heart pure. Your good deeds amount to nothing but filthy rags if your heart isn't pure. If worshiping me is a sacrifice, and if your good deeds are nothing more than markings on the scoresheet of your life, then you still don't get it."

Like the chicken-and-the-egg question, I guess it all comes down to the question we Christians continually have to ask ourselves. Which came first, the righteous heart or the good works? Do good works give us a righteous heart, or does our righteous heart lead us to do good works? Which would God rather see?

I know the answer, and most of you do, as well. God doesn't ask for a scoresheet or a legalistic report card. He's already done all the work to save us. He sent his Son to die on the cross for all of our sins and to demonstrate our inheritance in his Resurrection. All he asks is that we give him our hearts. All of our hearts.

So many times I've run myself ragged trying to do things that I believe are pleasing to God, only to realize sometime later that I've neglected my prayer life and my Bible study—in fact, I've left God out of it entirely. "Was it really for me you fasted?" God asked. Interesting question. And a painful one, as well.

And God sits quietly, watching and shaking his head, wondering when we will learn.

Thank God that he doesn't wash his hands of us. Thank God that he asks those probing, painful questions that remind us what is important. Thank God that he never stops teaching us.

May our hearts be so pure, so full of his righteousness, so Christlike, that our good deeds burst forth as acts of worship, rather than sacrifice.

And may God never stop working on me.

God bless you all,

Terri Blackstock

PRESUMPTION
OF
GUILT

This book is lovingly dedicated to
the Nazarene

Acknowledgments

I CAN'T END this series without thanking the people who have shared my vision for it since the beginning. I'd like to thank my agent, Greg Johnson, for believing in what I was doing and sharing my enthusiasm. And I'd like to thank my Zondervan friends who have worked tirelessly beside me: Dave Lambert, the best editor I've ever worked with (and I've worked with plenty); Lori Walburg, the second best editor I've ever worked with; Sue Brower, who believed in the books enough to go to great lengths to get them into the hands of readers; and all of the others at Zondervan who have been such a pleasure to work with.

Thanks, also, to Bob Anderson from the attorney general's office in my state, for answering important law questions for me.

And thanks to you, all of the readers who have followed this series to the very end. You've been God's way of telling me over and over that this is where I'm supposed to be!

1

THE BUICK HAD been tailing Beth Wright for miles. She had first noticed it weaving in and out of traffic too closely behind her on the Courtney-Campbell Causeway, the driver making no attempt to hide the fact that he was after her. Now, nearing St. Clair, they had left most of the traffic behind, but he was still there. She pressed the accelerator harder, checking her rearview mirror.

It didn't take a genius to figure out who it was. She had known that, if word got out that she was doing the story on the St. Clair Children's Home, Bill Brandon would come after her. What he would do once he caught her was open to speculation, but she didn't want to find out.

The Buick sped up and switched lanes, cutting in front of a motorcycle, forcing it to swerve, and then pulled up beside her, as if trying to run her off the road. He must have found out somehow that she had interviewed his sister, and he didn't like it. Marlene had warned her that he wouldn't take it well, but Beth hadn't needed warning.

The Buick swerved sharply to the right, almost hitting Beth's car, and she caught her breath and rammed her right foot to the floor. Her car burst forward, leaving the Buick behind. If he ran her off the road, he would kill her. If he was desperate enough to chase her down on a state highway with other drivers watching, then he was desperate enough to commit murder.

Her hand trembled as she reached for her cellular phone. It had fallen to the floor, so she bent forward, groping for it. The Buick jolted her rear bumper, and she swerved onto the shoulder. Grabbing the wheel, she pulled it quickly back into the right lane. The few other cars on the highway had begun pulling off the roadway to let her car and the Buick go by, probably alarmed by the Buick's erratic driving. Maybe someone had already called this in to the police.

She reached again into the darkness in front of the passenger seat for the phone, and this time her hand touched it. She picked it up and dialed 911 with her thumb.

"911, may I help you?"

"There's someone after me!" she cried. "He's trying to kill me!"

"What's your address?"

"No! I'm in my car! He's following me. We're on Highway 19 between St. Petersburg and St. Clair. I just passed the Ship's End restaurant. Please hurry!"

"What is he driving, ma'am?"

"A dark Buick—I'm not sure of the color."

He bumped the rear corner of her bumper again, and she screamed as her car veered to the shoulder. "He's ramming my car! Please, have you sent someone?"

"Yes," the dispatcher said. "We have a car on its way—"

But while the woman was still talking, Beth punched the "end" button, cutting her off, so she could pay attention to Bill Brandon's Buick. The stretch of road between St. Petersburg and St. Clair wasn't as busy as the others they'd been on. If there was a patrol car in the area, he'd spot them immediately—but if not, she might be dead before they showed up. To her right, she could see the beach, the turbulent waves smashing against the sand. If he stopped her, he could easily make her disappear in the Gulf Coast—and he wouldn't think twice about it. She looked in her rearview mirror. There was a car's distance between them now, but he was gaining. No other cars were in sight behind them. Where were the police?

Nick, she thought. *I have to call Nick.* He was expecting her to come straight to his house, to let him know what she'd found out from Marlene. But with this maniac following her, she might never get there. She'd better tell him what she'd learned—just in case.

She punched out his number and waited as it rang. "Come on, Nick," she whispered.

The answering machine picked up. "Hello, you have reached the home of Nick Hutchins . . ."

The Buick bumped her again, and tears sprang to her eyes. She punched off the phone and tried to think. *Where are you, Nick? You're supposed to be waiting for me!*

A message, she thought. *He must have left a message.* Maybe he'd called to tell her to meet him somewhere else instead. Her hand trembled, making it difficult, but she managed to punch out her own number, then waited for her machine to answer so that she could punch in her code and get her messages.

"Hello?"

It was the voice of a boy.

Startled, she asked, "Who is this?"

There was a long pause. "Who do you want?"

She turned on her bright lights, looking for a road, any road, that she could turn down in hopes of losing him. "I thought I was calling my own house," she said.

"You must have the wrong number."

Confused, she punched the "end" button, and followed the road's curve along the edge of the beach. The Buick did the same, right on her bumper. *Where were the police?* And what number had she just dialed? She punched "recall" and saw the digital readout. It was her number. So who had answered the phone at her house?

Her car jolted again, and she saw the Buick in the lane next to her. He was trying to force her off the road now. She had to get help—he would kill her if she didn't lose him.

She pressed "redial" and checked the number on her readout. She had dialed right the first time. She pressed "send" and waited as her own number rang again. This time, it rang on and on. The machine, which normally picked up on the fourth ring, never answered.

What's going on?

The car edged over, pushing her toward a drop-off. She looked in her rearview mirror and saw that no one was behind her. No witnesses, no one to notice if he sent her tumbling over a seawall.

She saw a road sign up ahead, and quickly breathed a prayer. Then, waiting for just the right moment, she slammed on her brakes until she was behind the Buick and screeched into a left turn, skidding around the corner onto a side street. She stomped on the accelerator and made another turn, and another, until she was completely out of his reach, hidden by trees.

She eased up on the accelerator only slightly, checking her rearview mirror every few seconds. It was more than fifteen minutes before she was certain that she had lost him; only then did she feel that she could safely try to make it home—hoping he hadn't figured out where that was yet. She had intentionally rented the little house out in the woods because it would be hard for unwelcome guests to find. So far, she'd kept herself insulated from him, but now she knew that interviewing Marlene had been a mistake. Bill Brandon was too smart and too suspicious not to keep close tabs on the sister who had once worked with him. He must have found out about the interview somehow, and followed Beth from Marlene's house.

So maybe he still didn't know where she lived. Maybe her little house in the woods was still a safe haven.

2

THE CAR PHONE in the Buick rang, and Bill Brandon snatched it up. "Yeah, what is it?"

"Bill, it's me." The boy's voice was shaky and frightened.

"What are you doing?" the man asked. "Where are you?"

"Still in her house," the boy said in a half-whisper. "But I can't find any of the papers or any tapes. I've looked everywhere."

Bill cursed. "Does she have a desk? A file cabinet? Did you check her computer?"

"Yes. I looked in all those places, and I couldn't find anything on the computer. She has millions of directories, and I don't know what to look for."

"Well, keep trying. And hurry. You don't have much more time."

"Are you still following her?"

"No, I lost her."

There was a pause again. "She just called here."

"She *what?* What do you mean she called?" Bill's face darkened as he held the phone to his ear, taking it in. He heard the sirens, and quickly pulled off the road, cut his lights, and stopped behind a rickety-looking body shop.

"She called. I picked up the phone 'cause you told me you were gonna call and warn me when she was coming home. I thought it was you."

"You idiot! What did she say?"

"I made like she called the wrong number. She called back, and I just let it ring."

"Well, you'd better get out of there, you fool! She's on her way home!"

"I thought you were gonna stop her!"

"I didn't," he snapped. He saw the reflections of blue lights flashing against the trees and junk cars surrounding the body shop. He wiped his sweating temple as the lights continued on up the road. "You blew it already, kid. Next time I'll find someone else who can do the job without botching it up."

"But Bill, I tried—"

"That's not good enough!" Bill shouted. "I'll deal with you when we get home! Now, get out of there!"

"Where will I go?" the boy asked in a voice on the verge of tears.

"Go to the Fraser Gas Station on Banton Street. I'll pick you up."

"But that's five miles away, Bill! Will you wait for me?"

"I told you I'd pick you up, didn't I? Now don't let anyone see you. If anybody does, you don't say a word, you understand me? You don't know anything."

"Okay, Bill."

Bill slammed the phone down and cursed again as he pulled out of his hiding place and headed for the gas station.

3

AS HE HUNG up the phone, ten-year-old Jimmy Westin heard tires on the gravel outside the house. Headlights swept through the windows of the darkened house, and the small, red-haired boy froze, wondering which of the side doors she would come in, which door he could safely leave through. The little cocker spaniel at his feet yelped up at him, wanting to play. He shouldn't have given it so much attention when he'd first come in, but he'd never had a dog of his own, and he hadn't expected to find it here. Bill hadn't said anything about it.

"Shhh," he whispered, trying to quiet it. "I have to go."

He heard the car door slam in front of the house. Her keys rattled in the door.

Now it was too late to go out *any* of the doors. He would have to hide. He looked around frantically, then dashed up the stairs, leaving the fat, young puppy yelping after him. Halfway up, he looked back and saw it struggling to climb the first step. He left it behind, and hurried up to the woman's loft office, where he'd searched for the papers and tapes Bill wanted. There was a door there, next to a closet. He opened it.

It was a floored walk-in attic. He slipped in and closed the door quietly, just as he heard the door downstairs closing behind her. Instantly, he was surrounded by darkness, thicker darkness than that downstairs. Downstairs, there had been a night-light over the stove, and a small lamp she had left on. In here, the darkness was opaque, smothering . . .

He trembled as he shrugged off the black backpack he wore, unzipped it, and pulled out his flashlight. The beam revealed boxes against the walls—tall ones, short ones, empty ones, packed ones. Across the floor was a window. Perfect. He could get out that way. He walked softly, trying to make it to the window, but the floor creaked beneath him. He froze, afraid to take another step. What if she heard? What if he got caught? What would they do with him?

He was sweating, and his breath came harder. All of the heat of Florida seemed contained in this attic, locked in with no escape, just like him.

He stood there, motionless, listening. He could hear her downstairs, doors closing, footsteps moving across the floor. Was she looking for him? Had she figured out that the voice on the phone wasn't a wrong number? What if the puppy somehow led her to him?

He shone the beam around him again, looking for a hiding place, and he saw lots of them. Places where mice, too, could hide. Spiders. Snakes, even. There was no telling what could be in an attic in such an old house.

He eyed the window again, and tried taking another step. It didn't creak. Taking a deep breath, he tiptoed across the floor, walking as lightly, as quietly as he could, until he reached the window. He unlocked it and tried to slide it up, but it was stuck. With all his might he tugged, but it didn't budge.

For a panicked moment, he thought of breaking the glass and making a run for it, but it was a long way down. By the time he figured out a way to get to the ground without breaking both legs, she would have the whole police force surrounding the place.

He was stuck here. Stuck until she went to sleep. Then, if he was very careful, and the floor didn't creak, and the dog didn't bark, maybe he could get out. Bill would be furious that he hadn't made it to the gas station on time, and Jimmy would probably have to make it all the way back to the children's home on foot—unless he could get to a phone and call for someone to come get him. He reached into his empty pocket, wishing he had a quarter. Maybe the lady who lived here had one lying around somewhere. Maybe he could find it before he left.

Maybe.

He wondered what Bill would do to him for messing this up. Quickly, he shifted his thoughts. He couldn't dwell on that. He had to go back, and that was that. Lisa would bear the brunt of his punishment if he didn't. He couldn't let that happen.

He heard footsteps coming up the stairs, and quickly dove behind a box in the corner. He held his breath and listened. Her footsteps moved across the office floor; she was going to her desk. He realized that he had forgotten to turn the answering machine back on. How could he be so stupid?

He should have worn gloves. Could they trace the fingerprints of ten-year-old boys? And once they found him, would they put him in jail or send him to the detention center? Did they really have that room with the black walls and only a slit that they slid bread through—the room Bill had warned him about? Is that where they would keep him locked up until he was old enough for prison?

He closed his eyes and leaned back against the wall. He could hear her out there, doing something in her office, moving around. He heard her saying something to the puppy, heard the little animal yelp and scratch on the floor. Would the dog lead her to him?

"Please don't let her find me," he whispered. "Please . . ."

4

NICK HUTCHINS STUFFED the duffel bag full of the clothes the two frightened little boys—six and eight years old—would need, and wished they didn't have to listen to the string of expletives flying from the foul mouth of their drug-dealer father, who stood handcuffed in the corner of the living room. His wife, also involved in the family business, screamed over his curses that they couldn't take her children away. Tony Danks and Larry Millsaps, the cops who had called Nick to come take the children into state custody, ignored her pleas and continued recording the evidence they'd compiled. There was enough crack cocaine in the house to ruin the lives of everyone in St. Clair.

It wasn't an unusual event, but Nick had never gotten used to it. He zipped up the bag and went back into the living room where the two boys sat huddled together.

"My daddy didn't do anything!" the older child cried. "Neither did my mom. Why don't you just leave us alone?"

"Please don't take my kids!" their mother cried. "I didn't know nothing about what he was doing. He did it behind my back! Please!"

Nick glanced hopefully at Larry. If there was some way they could avoid arresting the mother tonight, then he could spare the children the trauma of being taken from their home, at least temporarily. But Larry shook his head.

"We caught her dealing on videotape," Larry said. "And with all the stuff we found in the back room, there's no way she didn't know what was going on."

Nick looked at the distraught woman. "Do you have any relatives we can call? Someone who can take the kids tonight?"

"No, my parents are dead," she cried. "And we don't even know where his parents are."

"Any cousins or aunts or uncles? Sisters or brothers? Anyone?"

"No!" she cried, struggling to make him understand. "So you *have* to let me stay with them. They don't have anybody to take care of them."

Wearily, Nick slid the strap of the duffel bag over his shoulder, then took the children's hands. "We'll see that they're cared for."

"But *I* can take care of them! Please don't take them."

"Come on, kids," Nick said. "Let's go."

The woman screamed and fought to get to her children, but the officers restrained her. "You're making this harder on them!" Tony shouted over her cries. "If you love them, help them through this."

"You're not—taking—my kids!" she screamed, fighting to break free.

The children pulled out of Nick's hands and ran to their mother, but with her hands cuffed, she couldn't hold them. As they screamed, Nick wrenched them away and hurried them out to his car and into the front seat. He positioned one wailing child in the middle of the bench seat, hooked his seat belt, then hooked the other one in on the passenger side. Agency policy was to put kids in the backseat, but Nick could imagine how lonely the backseat could be when you didn't know where you were going.

For a few moments after he got in, he could hardly speak. He cranked the car and pulled out of the driveway to get them away from the house as quickly as possible. Then he looked down at the kids, who were still sobbing quietly.

"My name's Nick," he said, patting the leg of the boy next to him. "And I promise you, this isn't going to be so bad, okay? We'll just find you a place to stay tonight, and you're going to be all right."

"But I want to stay at home tonight," the younger one cried. "I want my mom!"

"Are you taking them to jail?" the older child asked in a shaky voice. "For a long time?"

"I can't answer that, because I don't know," Nick said. "But you don't have to worry, because you'll be taken care of."

The children cried quietly now, tears glistening on their faces. His heart ached for them, but that voice that played like a tape in his mind reminded him not to get involved. His job was to find a place to put them tonight; tomorrow, he would try to find a more permanent temporary home. There was no rational reason for the guilt and grief that he felt; it wasn't his fault that these two boys were becoming wards of the state of Florida. He just wished their parents had thought about their kids before they'd started dealing drugs.

A few minutes later, Nick parked in front of his office. The building, a branch of the Department of Health and Rehabilitative Services, or HRS, was small, dirty, and structurally unsound, but it was all they could afford on their small budget. He dreamed of the day they could get a nicer place, with a playroom to cheer up broken-hearted kids as they waited to be processed. He unhooked the apprehensive boys and slid them across the seat and out of the car.

"Please, mister. Take us back to our mom. She's really nice." The eight-year-old wiped his face and hiccuped a sob. "She won't do anything bad or nothing."

Nick stooped in front of them and wiped the tears on both their faces. "The police have your parents," he said softly. "I can't do anything about that, and I can't make any promises about what's going to happen. But I can promise that we'll take good care of you and find you someplace nice to stay."

The boys clung together, weeping, and Nick stroked both of their heads. He couldn't mend their broken hearts or erase the trauma their parents' arrest had caused. But he could help with some of the uncertainty. "This is just my office, okay? Let's go in and see if I can find you a coke or something, maybe a couple of candy bars."

"We're not allowed to take candy from strangers."

The irony. Drug dealers for parents, and they'd managed to teach these kids not to take candy from strangers. "Then I'll give you each fifty cents and let you get it out of the vending machine yourself. And while you eat it, I'll make some phone calls and find a nice family who'll let you spend the night with them tonight. Sound fair?"

The boys shrugged.

No, you're right, Nick thought. *None of it is fair.* "Call me Nick," he said. "And I'll call you Matthew and Christopher, okay?"

"Matt and Chris," the little one corrected through his tears.

"Okay, Matt and Chris. Let's go on in. Nothing in there for you to be afraid of—just an ugly office and me." He glanced up at the other car parked next to his. "And it looks like my boss is here, too. But that's all. No big, bad wolves."

He led them in and saw Sheila Axelrod, his supervisor, sitting at her desk, talking on the telephone. In a car seat on her desktop lay a screaming baby that couldn't have been more than three months old. She hung up the phone as Nick came in. "There's got to be a better way to make a living," she said listlessly.

Nick fished some quarters out of his pockets for the vending machine. "Who've you got there?"

"Abused baby," she said. "Police intervened in a domestic fight and saw her. Cigarette burns on her little legs prove the abuse. But it'll take a miracle to find anyone to take her tonight." She nodded toward the two still-crying boys beside him. "You're lucky. At least they're old enough for SCCH. I've got to go down the list until I find a taker."

SCCH—the St. Clair Children's Home—was the only private children's home in town. It had once been Nick's first choice in cases like this, but not anymore.

"I'm not calling SCCH," he said, going to the car seat and lifting the crying baby out. Instantly, the child grew quiet and lay her head on Nick's shoulder. He felt a wave of gratification—and concern—flood through him.

"What do you mean you're not calling them? Who will you call?"

Still holding the baby, Nick ushered the two little boys to the vending machine and handed them some quarters. They took them grudgingly and chose their candy. The baby on his shoulder whimpered softly as her eyes slowly closed.

"Did that baby's mom get arrested, too?" the younger boy, Matt, asked.

"I don't know," Nick evaded. "But it looks like she's in the same boat you're in. Tell you what, guys. You're older than she is. If you'll calm down and not look like we're sending you to the dungeon, maybe she'll quit feeling like something bad is about to happen. What do you say?"

Chris shrugged. "What's SCCH? Is that where we're going?"

"No."

Sheila had the phone to her ear, but she put her hand over the receiver and asked, "Why not, Nick? They have a whole cottage just for temporaries. It's the easiest thing, and if this is long term, that's probably where they'll end up anyway."

"I told you, I have too many suspicions about some things going on at the home. Until I can give the place a clean bill of health, I'm not going to send any more kids to them."

Her face hardened, and her voice changed. "Nick, those two kids have to be placed tonight. You'll send them where I tell you to!"

He touched the baby's head again, trying to keep it calm in spite of Sheila's ranting. "Sheila, if I can find a home to take them tonight, what difference does it make to you?"

"Because I'm trying to find someone to take the baby. It's not likely that we can find more than one family this late to take them, and nobody's gonna take all three!"

"Let me try," he said. "That's all I ask, Sheila. Just give me a while to try."

She moaned. "If you don't send them to the home, you might have to split them up."

One of the boys gasped, and the other burst into tears again. "No! Please don't do that."

"We won't," Nick assured quietly. He pulled a tissue out and wiped the little boy's nose as he shot Sheila a look. "Sheila, why don't you let me take care of this, and you go on home? I can handle it."

"Really?" She looked at him as if he'd just offered her a week's vacation. Then she seemed to deflate. "I can't. Not until they're placed. I'll give you an hour to try to find a family to take them. If you don't, I'm taking them to SCCH myself. I'll work on the paperwork, and you work on the phone calling. Here, give me the baby."

"No, she's fine," he said softly. The baby was relaxing on his shoulder, and he could feel that she was close to falling asleep. "I can call while I hold her. And if I need a hand, my buddies here can help me, can't you, guys?"

The boys nodded quietly.

"All right," she said. "I'll be in here. Buzz if you need me."

He ushered them down the hall to the corner of the building he sometimes shared with two other caseworkers—except that they had both quit in the last month and hadn't yet been replaced. He looked over the baby's head to the boys. "You gonna eat that candy, or just let it melt in your hands?"

Matt put it into his mouth, but Chris just sat there. "Do we have to go anywhere with her?"

Most of the kids didn't like Sheila, which didn't surprise Nick. She could be cold sometimes, but he knew her coldness was stress-induced. She'd been at it longer than he had, and it was a job that got to you over the years. He sat down and leaned back in his chair, still stroking the baby's head. "I'll try to find a place for you myself, guys. And if I can, then I'll take you there."

"Why can't we stay with you?" the little one asked.

Nick smiled and messed up the boy's hair. "Because I'm not home much, kiddo. I couldn't watch you."

"We can watch ourselves. We'd be okay. We do it all the time."

"No can do. But trust me with this." He picked up the phone, breathed a silent prayer for help, and dialed the number of his first choice—a family he'd saddled with four new kids just this past week.

When they turned him down, he tried the next one on the list, and then the next, until he had almost given up. Little Matt had lain down on the small, garage-sale sofa against the wall, and had gone to sleep with his head in his brother's lap. The baby slept soundly, too. Chris just stared back at him with red, dismal eyes.

Not the St. Clair Children's Home, Nick prayed. *There's got to be somebody else.*

Holding the phone between ear and shoulder, he dialed the next number—a new family on their list. A retired couple who had volunteered to be foster parents, they had just today completed all the requirements to be accepted into the program. This would be their first placement call. He wondered if dumping three children on them this late at night their first time might frighten them away. He had no choice but to try.

"Hello?" The woman sounded kind—a good sign. He hadn't been the caseworker assigned to her—Sheila had done it—so he hadn't met her before. He hoped her voice wasn't deceiving.

"Mrs. Miller? This is Nick Hutchins with HRS. I have three children I need to place temporarily tonight. They're from two different families, so if you can't take all of them, we can give you one or two of them. But I'd at least like to keep the brothers together—"

"We'd be delighted to have them!" the woman said, then put her hand on the receiver and shouted, "Honey, they're bringing some children tonight." She came back to Nick. "Please, bring all three of them. What ages are they?"

Nick couldn't believe his ears. "The baby girl is probably three months, and then I have two brothers, six and eight. The baby's an abuse case, and the boys' parents are in police custody."

"Oh, the poor little things. Please, bring them right over. We'll have their beds all ready when you get here. I'll tell Vernon to get the crib out of the attic. We'll get it all dusted."

Nick mouthed "thank you" to the ceiling as he hung up the phone. He hurried to Sheila's door. "I found someone to take all three, Sheila. Grace and Vernon Miller. She's even excited about it."

Sheila didn't look impressed. "I wasn't planning to give them a trial by fire. I was going to ease them in. But I guess it can't be helped. Remind her not to get emotionally involved with them, Nick. They're new at this."

"I will," he said. But in his heart, he hoped they'd get a little involved. These kids were going to need someone who cared about them.

5

BETH IGNORED HER puppy as he whimpered and scratched at the attic door. Instead, she stared down at the answering machine. Why was it turned off? She had left it on; she was sure of it. Maybe the power had flickered, and the machine hadn't come back on.

Maybe. But that didn't explain the person who had answered the phone when she'd called.

Maybe the cellular phone company had mixed the signals. She'd heard of it happening. The fact that she was being followed at the time had made it all seem suspicious, but that didn't mean that the two events had anything to do with each other. She was probably being paranoid.

She started to turn the machine back on, but the yelping puppy distracted her. She scooped him up and stroked his head. "What's the matter, boy? You want to play?" He wiggled in her hands and reached up to lick her face. "We'll go down and play in a minute," she said, walking to the window near the apex of her roof. She peered out into the night, looking for headlights, any sign that Bill Brandon was out there, waiting, watching, ready to pounce.

No, of course he wasn't out there. She'd chosen this house very carefully. No one could just accidentally find it, and no one would be able to look her up, either. Her address was a post office box. It wasn't listed in the phone book, and it wasn't even in her files at school or the paper. Since she rented, there was no public record of where she lived. The only way to find her house would be to follow her here.

But a nagging voice in the back of her mind reminded her: *Bill Brandon has ways of finding out anything he wants. Everyone who knows him discovers that.*

Shivering, she carried the puppy back down the stairs, set him down, and went back to the phone to try Nick's office. Just as she picked up the phone, she heard a car on the gravel outside. She froze. Keeping her eyes on the door, she dropped the phone back in its cradle, pulled open a drawer in the end table, and grabbed the pistol she kept there. The doorbell rang, and the puppy erupted into a round of high-pitched barks.

He's here, she thought, holding the pistol aimed at the door. Her heart flipped into a triple-time cadence, and adrenaline pulsed through her.

The bell rang again, and a knock followed. "Beth? It's me, Nick!"

Nick. Not Bill.

She let out a huge breath of relief and lowered the gun. Feeling dizzy from the sheer terror that had gripped her, she headed for the door and opened it. "Nick, you scared me. I didn't know it was you. Where have you been? I tried to call."

Nick came in, his brown, slightly wavy hair tousled by the warm wind. His face looked tired, and the stubble on his jaw added to the picture of fatigue. "Didn't you get my message?"

"What message?"

"On your machine. Telling you I had an emergency and couldn't meet you at my house, that I would just come over here." He frowned as he saw the gun. "What's wrong?"

"I just got a little spooked, that's all." Embarrassed, she put the gun back into the drawer and closed it.

"Did something happen? Did the interview turn out badly?"

"No, no. It was fine." She shoved her hand through her short, honey-colored hair and looked up the stairs toward the answering machine that had been off when she'd checked it. "It's just . . . a little weird."

"What is?"

"That you left a message. My machine was off when I got home. Are you sure it was on when you called?"

"Positive," he said. "I left a message that the police had just done a drug bust, and there were these two boys—their parents were dealing cocaine. I had to go get the children and place them in foster care tonight until we could find some relatives."

Her face whitened. "You didn't put them at SCCH, did you?"

"No," he said. "My supervisor would have, but I put them with a retired couple new to the foster-care program. They'll be okay." He paused and studied her for a moment. "Beth, you're pale. What is it?"

She breathed a self-conscious laugh and tried to calm herself. "Nothing, really. The interview went great. Better than I could have dreamed." She sank down on her couch and covered her face, and Nick sat down next to her.

She didn't really know Nick all that well, having met him just a few days ago when she'd called to interview him about his take on the children's home. Her questions had immediately piqued his interest because he'd also had suspicions about the home. So he'd spent a lot of time with Beth since that first meeting, trying to help her put the pieces together.

Although Beth tried to deny it or, better yet, ignore it, there was something about Nick Hutchins that made her feel safe. Her life up to this point had been anything but secure—ironically, that meant she distrusted nothing more than feelings of safety and security.

Still, something about Nick invited her trust. Maybe it was that he seemed to genuinely care about the children he watched over. It had been her experience that most social workers were so overburdened that they had little time to care about the people whose lives they affected. Nick seemed different.

She drew her mind back to the conversation. "Marlene was ready to talk," she said. "I taped our conversation. It was fascinating. She confirmed everything. Bill Brandon uses some of the kids in his care in a crime ring that breaks into people's homes and businesses and steals things. He has a central warehouse where he stores things until he can sell them—or until his people can sell them. Apparently, there are more people than just Bill and the kids involved. In fact, she said he has someone big running interference for him. Like someone on the police force or in government. That's how he's gotten away with it. She didn't know any names or where the stuff is stored, but she said that he uses horrible tactics to force the kids into cooperating. Besides the abuse that you've suspected, he threatens them with harm to their sisters and brothers, their parents if they're living, or he makes them believe that they're as guilty as he is—that they're the ones breaking in, that his hands are clean, so if anyone goes down for the crime, it'll be the kids. And they have no way of knowing otherwise, so they cooperate."

Angered, Nick bolted up and paced across the floor, his fatigue evident. He needed to shave, and his light brown hair was tousled as though he hadn't given it a thought all day. Looking at his reddened eyes, she wondered if he ever got much sleep.

"We've got to put him away, Beth. We've got to get those kids out of there. Sheila, my supervisor, says I don't have enough evidence to start relocating the children. She thinks I'm nuts and Bill Brandon is a saint. I think she just can't face all the work it would take to relocate the kids. But it *has* to be done, and I don't care about the work."

Beth tried to think clearly. "First, we have to have enough evidence to convince the court. Maybe if you got some of the kids alone and told them you already knew what was going on, some of them would talk."

"I've tried. They all get this terrible look on their faces—fear, that's all I know to call it—and insist that they've never been happier and they've never been treated better."

"It's fear, all right. But we need more evidence. Marlene's statements are good, but she's just one person."

Nick frowned. "Why did she talk to you, anyway?"

Beth hesitated. "Well, I already knew she wasn't part of his organization anymore. She said that her life has changed in the past year. She seemed to genuinely care about the kids now, and she didn't want to sit by and let Bill do what he was doing."

"Are you sure you can trust her? What if she's just baiting you to see what you know?"

"She told me things I didn't know. It was real, Nick."

Nick sat slowly down and leaned forward. "Does Bill Brandon know that she talked?"

She was unsure how much to tell him. "Yes. I mean, I'm pretty sure he does. He—or someone in a dark Buick—was following me most of the way home."

"What?"

"Chasing me is more like it," she said, standing up again and setting her fists defiantly on her hips, as if the stance could erase the image of helpless victim. "It's okay. I made sure I lost him, so he couldn't follow me home. My car's got a few dents, though."

"He *hit* you? What was he trying to do?"

"Run me off the road," she said. "Near the seawalls."

"Beth, this is getting out of hand. He could have killed you!"

She went to the window, peered out through the blinds. "He almost did. I called the police, but it took them forever. By the time they came, I had lost him."

Nick went to stand behind her, and she turned around and looked up at him. "Beth, how do you know it wasn't a setup? The whole Marlene thing—all her deep confessions, and then her brother chasing you down and trying to kill you? What if they planned this together—"

"I don't think so," Beth said. "Marlene seemed scared herself. And she was sincere. She really was."

He blew out a frustrated breath. "No wonder you had a gun when you answered the door."

"It was stupid, really," she said. "He doesn't know where I live."

"Are you sure?"

"Positive," she said weakly.

"Then why do you keep looking out the window?"

"Just being careful. I mean, really, I can't even be sure it was him. I'm just assuming it was. Who else would come after me right after that interview? It had to be either him or someone who works for him."

"Beth, this is getting dangerous. You have to call the police again. Tell them who you think was following you."

She shook her head and plopped down on the couch. The puppy put its paws up on her shin, panting happily. She leaned over and picked him up. "I don't want to call them again. I did it before because I was desperate. But now that it's over, I don't think I want to bring them into this yet."

"Why not?" he asked. "Why would you wait?"

Determination tightened her features. "Because this is *my* story," she said, "and I don't want every paper in the state getting it before I can get the *whole* story out. If I call the police, it'll be public knowledge by morning. There'll be a barrage of articles, none with much meat, and Bill Brandon will clean up his act for a while and walk straight, and they won't catch him at anything, and everyone will write it off as hearsay and rumor, and go back to thinking he's the clean-cut, unsung hero who molds broken young kids into model citizens. I want to get him, Nick. And I'm not going to depend on the cops to do it."

He shook his head. "And how long will all this take?"

"I'm going to stay up late tonight transcribing the tapes of my conversation with Marlene. I'll start writing the story. Maybe tomorrow I can track down some other witnesses. If I could just find out where that warehouse is—and who he has in government working with him—"

"Beth, if you take too long, he's going to catch up with you. Then what?"

"I won't take too long," she said. "I'm as anxious to get this story out as you are. You have a list of kids in the home, don't you?"

"Yeah."

"Then start making plans to move them. I promise you, the story will be out within a week."

"I hope that's not too late. Especially now that he knows something's up."

She thought that over. "Maybe I can get it finished by tomorrow. If so, we could print it the day after—if I can convince my editor. Remember, I'm still just a grunt around there. The college kid, always looking for a front-page story. If he's going to print it, it has to be great."

Nick wasn't reassured. "What if he comes after you again? What if he *does* find where you live?"

"I can protect myself, Nick. I've done it for a long time."

He breathed a laugh. "Right. You're a junior in college. How old? Twenty?"

"Twenty-one."

"How long could you possibly have done it?"

"I'll be all right, Nick." She couldn't help the slight edge in her voice. "Now, why don't you go on home? You look really tired."

"I am tired," he said, "but I could sack out here. Make sure he doesn't show up. I'm really afraid to leave you."

She smiled slightly. "Spend the night, huh? I don't think so."

He shook his head again. "Not like that, Beth. That's not my style."

"Mine either."

"You have any objection to a guy wanting to watch out for you?"

"You have enough people to watch out for, Nick. Don't worry about me. If I can't take a little heat, I have no business being a reporter."

"That's what I figured," he said. "You're a hundred-ten-pound tough guy. What do you have for protection? Karate? Brass knuckles?"

"I have my wits," she said with a half-smile. "And the .22 in that drawer. Oh, and I have my dog." She set the puppy down, and he wagged over to Nick.

"Yeah, right." He bent down and petted the puppy, who instantly made a puddle on the floor. "Uh-oh. You're not walking him enough."

"We're working on the house-breaking thing," she said with a soft laugh as she ran to the kitchen to grab a towel. "I don't know if he's training me or if I'm training him. But he's only six weeks old. What can you expect, huh, Dodger?"

"Dodger?"

"Yeah. Like the Artful Dodger in *Oliver*."

"Any chance that name came from the story you're working on?"

She stood back up. "Yeah, I guess so. That and the fact that he loves stealing socks out of my laundry hamper. He chewed a hole in the side of it so he could get to them."

He chuckled and went to the door, opened it, and peered out into the woods surrounding the house. "It's kind of creepy out here. Are you sure you're not afraid?"

"One person's creepy is another person's refuge," she said. "He won't find me here, and very few people have the address. Reporters have to take certain precautions."

He turned back. "I guess I should feel honored that you gave it to me."

She smiled a little self-consciously, and looked down at the puppy. "Actually, you should. I don't even know why I did."

"I like to think it was my trustworthy eyes."

"They are pretty trustworthy," she said, bringing hers back to them again. For a moment, their eyes locked, and finally, she looked away, realizing her face was getting warm. "Look, I'll call you tomorrow and let you know what's happening. If you find out anything, let me know, too, okay?"

"All right."

He looked at her for a second, as if considering something else to say. "See you later."

"Yeah. Later."

She watched as he walked across the gravel, examined the dents in her car, then, shaking his head, went to his own vehicle. She checked the shadows of the trees on both sides of the house with a growing sense of unease, then shuddered and closed the door. She bolted it shut, then turned back to the puppy, who was curled up on a rug. "Yeah, that's right," she told him. "Go to sleep, just when the hard work is about to start. Never mind, I'll do it myself. Your spelling's pretty lousy, anyway."

6

NICK TRIED TO shake the uneasy feeling taking hold of him as he pulled off the dirt road leading to her property and back onto the paved street where occasional cars drove by. She was tough, that was certain, but it didn't make him feel any better. A man like Bill Brandon had ways of breaking down toughness.

On the other hand, Bill was used to dealing with children. Maybe he'd not yet met the likes of Beth Wright.

Nick knew *he* hadn't. She had blown into his life like an answered prayer, one that he was still reeling from. Just when he'd felt so helpless and frustrated that he wanted to quit his job, she had come along with some answers and the encouragement he had sorely needed.

It hadn't even been two weeks ago that he'd gotten the phone call from the distraught mother who'd had visitation with her son at the children's home that afternoon and had found him bruised from a beating that the child told her had come from Bill Brandon. Since the mother was a drug addict going through rehab, Nick hadn't taken what she said at face value. Instead, he had ordered a medical exam of the child. The doctors confirmed that he *had* suffered a beating.

Finally, Nick had confronted Bill Brandon about it. Brandon told him that the child had been fine when he'd left for visitation, but that the mother herself must have beaten him. Bill had launched from there into an impassioned argument that parental visitations were detrimental to the healthy environment he tried to provide for "his" kids.

There were obvious problems with Bill's story. Why would the mother have called attention to abuse she'd inflicted herself? Besides, Nick had heard the despair in her voice, the urgency, the worry. Yes, her child had been taken from her due to neglect and drug addiction—but now she was clean. The sound of maternal worry in her voice had been authentic. Much more authentic than Bill Brandon's arguments.

Sheila, Nick's supervisor, had blown the whole thing off, convinced that Bill Brandon was right and that the mother was just trying to cover up for something she knew would be discovered eventually. She suggested they file to revoke the mother's visitation privileges.

Nick had allowed her to believe he would take care of it, but he hadn't. Something about Bill's and Sheila's rationales didn't ring true. Something about the mother's pleas did.

He had begun to look deeper into problems at the home. He had gone to the public school where Bill Brandon's children were sent, and had studied the records of the SCCH kids. He saw a repeating pattern of children falling asleep in class, over and over and over. When he spoke to their teachers—no small feat since it was summer and some of them had been difficult to locate—he was told that they had contacted Brandon about the problem, only to be told that he would "take care of it" when the kids got home from school. Fearing what Brandon's punishment might be, and sensing the terror on the kids' faces when they thought they were being reported to him, most of the teachers had fallen into a routine of letting it slide without calling the home. They, too, suspected that things might not be all they seemed at the home, but they had little evidence to back it up. There had also been a few reports of some SCCH kids being caught committing crimes, but everyone had written those incidents off to bad parenting or to the typical rebellion of low-status, high-risk kids. None of his suspicions, none of the facts he'd compiled, added up to enough evidence to close down the home, or even to start an official investigation.

He'd been at a dead end—and then he'd gotten a phone call from a young woman who had identified herself as a reporter with the *St. Clair News* and said she was working on a story about some alleged abuses in the St. Clair Children's Home. It had been just the encouragement he'd needed to convince him he was on the right track. But when Beth had told him that she suspected Brandon was using the children in a crime ring that worked in areas within a two-hour radius of St. Clair, Nick had been stunned. Was that why the children were so sleep-deprived?

The idea had been so far-fetched that it was almost unbelievable—yet some part of him believed it. First, he had beaten himself up about placing so many children in the home. Then, he'd determined to get them all out. But first he had to get enough proof.

He'd met with Beth, told her everything he knew, and promised to help her in any way he could. Since then, she'd been busy putting together the story that would outline all of Brandon's alleged crimes. Now they could add to it his attempt to run her off the road—if they could somehow prove that he was the driver.

Nick thought back over the things she'd said tonight, the look on her face when he'd frightened her, the shakiness with which she'd revealed, little by little, how she had been followed from the interview. She hadn't looked so tough then. She was scared.

I might regret this, he told himself as he made a U-turn. But the fear in Beth's eyes haunted him.

He pulled his car into a metered space in front of the St. Clair Police Department. Larry Millsaps and Tony Danks were probably still there processing the parents of the boys Nick had placed earlier. Maybe they'd have time to give him a minute.

The station was noisy, as usual, and smelled of sweat and booze from some of those who waited in handcuffs to be booked. He scanned the desks where cops answered phones and did paperwork. Tony Danks sat tapping at his computer keys, probably getting a history on the couple who sold dope for a living. Nick ambled over.

"Man, don't you ever go home?"

Tony looked up and grinned. "Don't *you*? You look tireder than I do, Nick. How are those kids? Get them placed okay?"

"Yeah, no problem. They were a little scared, but I think they'll be all right. That's not why I'm here." He took the chair across from Tony's desk, crossed his legs and slumped back until his neck almost rested on the top back of the chair. "You got a minute?"

"Sure," Tony said, turning away from his computer and leaning on his desk. "You want Larry in on this?"

Nick glanced over at Larry's desk, saw that he was filling out reports. "Yeah, if he can spare a minute. I just need some police advice."

"You came to the right place." He half stood and yelled, "Larry!" over the din, and Larry looked up. He saw Nick sitting there and got up to head over.

"You get those kids placed?" Larry asked as he approached the desk.

"Yeah," Nick said. "But there's something else I need to ask you. Off the record."

Larry's eyebrows lifted, and he sat down on the edge of Tony's desk. "Okay, shoot."

Nick dropped his foot and leaned forward, bracing his elbows on his knees. "I have this friend. A woman. She's a reporter, and was doing an important interview tonight, and she got followed most of the way home until she lost him. She thinks she knows who it was, and she thinks it has to do with the story she's working on. Basically, he wants to shut her up, so I don't know what he might do to her. But she's convinced he doesn't know where she lives."

"You're not convinced?" Tony asked.

"Well, I can't be sure. This guy's shrewd, and he has a lot to lose. And I'm not entirely convinced that the whole interview wasn't a setup. Anyway, she didn't want to involve the police for fear of having the story come out before she breaks it—you know, the competition might get it—but I'm not sure waiting is a good idea."

"It's not illegal to follow someone," Tony said. "And it could have been a coincidence. Did he do anything to her? Ram her fender? Try to force her off the road? Anything to indicate ill intent?"

"Absolutely. She has at least two dents on her car where he tried to run her off the road."

"Then he did break a law. Would she be willing to file a complaint?"

"No, she won't. Not yet."

Larry shook his head dolefully. "Sorry, Nick. Nothing we can do."

"Officially, no," Nick said. "But what about unofficially? Could you kind of keep an eye on her tonight? Watch over her so that nothing happens?"

Larry and Tony exchanged looks. Tony rubbed his eyes. "Truth is, we're a little busy here tonight, Nick. We could send a squad car to patrol her house every hour or so, but we can't leave anyone there all night."

"Well, maybe that would be enough. Anything you could do would help. And I'd prefer that you told the cop who does it not to pull all the way down the dirt road leading to her house. Just far enough to get a look at the house and make sure no other cars are there. Seeing headlights would scare her to death. Besides, I don't want her to know I came to you. She wouldn't like it."

Larry stared at him for a moment, then broke into a sly grin. "Who is this girl, Nick? She sounds important. Something you haven't told us?"

Nick rubbed his stubbled jaw. "Actually, I just met her a few days ago. But yeah, I like her. She's a little young. Only twenty-one—"

"And you're an old man at . . . what? Thirty?"

Nick grinned. "Not quite."

Tony had to laugh. "Nick Hutchins, the guy who's too busy for a woman. Looks like he's clearing some time."

"Don't get carried away," Nick said. "I've just been trying to help her out some. She's nice. Smart. Savvy. Different than the other women I know."

"Uh-oh. Famous last words," Tony teased.

Nick got to his feet, fighting his own grin. "All right, guys. I'm just worried about the lady, that's all." He grabbed a pen off Tony's desk and jotted her address on a pad. "If you could get someone to patrol around there, just watching for anything suspicious—a dark Buick in particular—I'd really appreciate it."

Larry looked down at the pad. "All right. No guarantees, though."

"Didn't expect any."

He gave them both friendly handshakes, then walked out of the police station, wishing he could rest easy now. But he knew he wouldn't—it would be a long night for him.

And it wouldn't be any better for Beth.

7

BETH LOADED HER tape recorder and began to play back the tapes of her conversation with Marlene, quickly typing the words into her laptop computer. Beside her, Dodger slept, his little rhythmic snore making her wish she could lie down herself. But she had to get this done—and she was too tense to sleep anyway.

She heard something creak over her head. Lifting her hands from the keyboard, she looked at the ceiling. Was it her imagination, or had the floor squeaked upstairs? She cut off the tape recorder and listened.

There it was again. Quickly, she grabbed for the gun she kept in the table beside the couch. She went to the stairs and stared up at the top. Nothing there. She started to go up, then thought better of it. Still aiming at the stairs, she backed up and groped for the telephone. She snatched it up and dialed 911.

Her voice trembled as she tried to get the words out quietly. "There's someone in my house. Please—send someone right away. It's on Kramer Road, the number 343 is on the mailbox at the beginning of a long dirt road. Turn in there, and you'll see my house about a quarter of a mile in. Please hurry."

She hung up, but kept the gun aimed at the stairs. If he came down, she would shoot him. She had no choice. If Bill Brandon had found her, if he had broken into her home, then he was planning to kill her. Her only hope was to kill him first.

At the police station, one of the sergeants grabbed Tony on his way out. "Hey, Danks. That address you gave us to patrol? We just got a call from the lady who lives there. Says someone's in her house."

Surprised, Tony glanced over his shoulder at Larry, then back at the sergeant. "Have you sent a car out?"

"Yeah, there was one real close. In fact, he'd just made a swing by there and didn't see anything. Jane sent him back."

"We'll head over there, too," Larry said.

"Should we call Nick?" Tony asked as they hurried out to their car.

Larry shook his head grimly. "Let's see what's up first."

8

THE FRASER GAS Station was closed this time of night, and Bill Brandon sat in the shadows of the pumps with his headlights off, waiting for the kid to get there. It shouldn't have taken Jimmy this long to make it the five miles from her house to the gas pumps. What if he'd gotten caught? What if he'd made an even bigger mess of this?

He should have expected it. Jimmy was too soft, too young. Bill knew he should have used one of the more experienced kids. But this should have been an easy job, and Jimmy was so small for his age that slipping him in through the small bathroom window they'd found unlocked had been a snap. Besides, Jimmy was a whiz when it came to computers, and he knew that if anyone could handle the computer end of the job, it would be him.

Yeah, that was the way it was *supposed* to have gone. That was the plan. Send Jimmy in through a window, then the kid gets all the tapes and papers he can find, copies her files onto a disk, then erases her hard drive. Then everything went wrong. Bill had planned to stop her from getting home, but she'd gotten away from him. And then the stupid kid had picked up the phone. He'd pay for that.

Bill cranked his car, turned on the lights, and started back toward her house, hoping he'd see Jimmy on the road somewhere. He drove slowly, scanning the trees, watching, waiting. The kid had been trained too well to be seen easily, but Bill hoped he'd recognize the Buick and show himself.

Nothing.

He pulled over to the side of the road and thought for a moment, trying to build a strategy. Maybe he needed to go back to the house, look into the windows, see if she was home.

He pulled back onto the street and headed for her dirt road.

But before he reached it, he heard a siren, then saw a police car's lights flickering through the trees. The squad car turned onto her dirt road.

She called the police, he thought, driving quickly past. *Which means the kid got caught. Now what?*

He wiped the sweat from his brow with his sleeve and decided to return to the home. The cops would probably call him to report that they had one of his kids in custody, and he'd better be there to take the call. He'd pretend that the kid had escaped through a window when Bill thought he was sleeping, that he always had trouble with this one.

Jimmy wouldn't dare tell them differently. Bill had done too good a job preparing him for a time like this.

Upstairs in Beth's house, the boy heard the sound of a siren approaching outside, and he strained to see through the window without moving. He saw blue lights flashing against the glass, a pale flicker illuminating the shadows of the attic. Did she know he was here? Had she called the police?

He heard the front door open, the dog yelping, and the lady's voice outside. With no one downstairs to hear him, he ran across the floor to the biggest box he could find, pulled out a four-foot Christmas tree, climbed into the box, then pulled the tree in on top of him. Trying to settle his breathing, he curled into as tight a ball as he could and waited.

It didn't take long. The door opened and a light came on, a light that seemed to flood through the attic, lighting every crack, every shadow, every particle of dust. He was sure it exposed him, too. Could they see him? Could they tell where he was hiding?

He heard voices—several of them—as they filed through the attic, searching. He squeezed his eyes shut and chanted in his mind, *Don't let them find me . . . don't let them find me . . .*

"There's nobody here," one of the men said. "Maybe she heard a mouse or something."

Someone else's feet creaked as he came closer to the Christmas tree box. Jimmy braced himself. "Yeah, this house is pretty old. Probably wouldn't take more than a mouse to make the floor squeak."

"But what about the guy following her, Tony? You don't think this is a coincidence?"

"Didn't seem like it at first. But there's nobody here. Are you sure you checked thoroughly downstairs?"

"Positive."

"Well, she's probably jumpy because of what happened in the car. Maybe she just needs a little reassurance. We can tell her we'll step up our patrols of her house. Maybe that'll put her mind to rest."

"Let's look again, just in case."

He heard them shuffling boxes near him, and suddenly panicked: he had left his backpack out, lying on top of a box. They would see it and know, and then they'd empty out all of the boxes until he came tumbling out . . .

"I give up," one of the cops said, finally. "Cut the light, will you?"

The light went out, and Jimmy sat paralyzed as the door closed. He was soaked with sweat, trembling, and the tree was cutting into his arm and the back of his neck, but he didn't dare move. What if they heard him? What if they came back? Even after they left, *she* could still hear him and call them back.

A tear rolled out of his eye, a tear that Bill would not have tolerated. He managed to wipe his wet face on his shoulder. This was hopeless. He was never going to get out of here.

Downstairs, Beth tried to find comfort in Larry and Tony's assurances that no one was in her house. "I'm really sorry to bother you guys. I guess I'm just getting paranoid."

"I can understand that," Larry said. "And don't apologize. It's our job to check things like this out."

"Yeah, but I didn't expect two detectives when I called."

Larry and Tony looked at each other, and finally, Larry decided to come clean. "The truth is that Nick Hutchins was worried about you and asked us to keep an eye on you."

Her eyebrows rose. "Nick? What did he tell you?"

Tony looked apologetic. "He said you were followed home tonight—and when we drove up, we saw the dents on your car. It's no wonder you would be nervous after that."

Her face tightened, and she looked down at the puppy. "I told him I could protect myself."

"That's what he said, but since we're here—why don't you file a complaint? Give us an idea who followed you so we can arrest him."

"He'd be out by morning. Besides, I can't prove it. I can only guess who it was."

"If you give us a name and he has complementary dents in his car, that'll be proof enough."

She thought it over for a moment as she peered off into the trees surrounding her yard. There were risks either way. If they could keep him in jail for a day or two, that might help her finish her investigation. "It's Bill Brandon. He runs the St. Clair Children's Home."

Tony wrote down the name. "I've heard of him."

"Yeah. Probably as a hero and protector of children. All lies."

"Why do you say that?"

She thought of telling them everything, but she just didn't have enough evidence yet. Alerting them to part of the problem might do more harm than good. "It'll all come out in the paper in the next couple of days, detectives. Then you'll see."

"So that's why you think it was him? Because you're doing some kind of story on him?"

"You got it."

"Would you be willing to file a complaint against him tonight?"

She considered that, then shook her head. "No, I'd rather hit him with the big guns in a couple of days. There's a lot at stake."

She walked them to the door, and the little dog bounded out into the night, its tail wagging. She grabbed his leash and hurried after him, clipped it to his collar, and watched as he found a bush to do his business. "Thanks for coming," she told the cops.

Larry held back. "I'd feel better if you were locked in before we left."

"Yeah, I guess I would, too." She waited for the puppy to finish, then hustled him back inside. "Thanks again."

She locked and bolted the door, then watched out the window as the car drove out of sight. She was losing it, she told herself. Calling the police just because the house creaked. Of course it creaked. It was old. It had probably creaked every day since she'd moved in. But that was before she'd taken on Bill Brandon. Now, everything was suspect.

But she was okay, she reminded herself. He couldn't find her here.

9

MARLENE BRANDON LAY awake in bed, her mind reeling with the confessions she'd made to Beth tonight. She'd had to do it. It was the only way to set things right. Her newfound faith required it of her. It wasn't enough to simply believe; she had to put feet to that belief. Even if those feet led her into danger.

She looked at the clock and realized she had been lying here for two hours without closing her eyes. That uneasy feeling that had gripped her all day was almost strangling her now.

She turned over, fluffed her pillow, adjusted the covers, and tried to push her conversation with Beth out of her mind. Marlene had told her things that, most likely, would land her in jail, unless the prosecutor granted her immunity for testifying against her brother. The thought covered her in cold sweat.

I do not give to you as the world gives. Let not your heart be troubled, and do not be afraid. The remembered words brought her comfort, wrapping themselves around her heart. A strange, unexpected peace washed over her, and she began to think that she might sleep tonight, after all.

Her mind shifted back to Beth, so young and bright, so ambitious, so alone. She was proud of the way Beth was supporting herself through college by working at the small-town newspaper. Only twenty-one, but she'd come so far. And she was living a clean life with a pure heart, going to church faithfully and trying to follow the letter of God's law. Marlene only hoped that Beth would learn about his grace, as well. Maybe she should have made sure. Maybe she would call her tomorrow and do just that.

Her eyes began to drift shut, and her mind released its hold on her troubles as sleep pulled her under.

"Hello, Marlene."

She sat bolt upright in bed at the voice, and saw the silhouette of her brother standing in the doorway of her bedroom. "Bill!"

"Surprised?" he asked with that sinister amusement she'd heard so often when he spoke to the children. She had learned it from him, and had gotten good at using it herself over the years.

"How did you get in here?" she asked, pulling her covers up over her as though they could shield her from his wrath.

He laughed then, that condescending laugh that had crushed the spirits of young and old alike. "Marlene, Marlene. You know there isn't a lock anywhere that can keep me out." He came in and sat on the foot of her bed, gazing at her. "I'm hurt, you know. I always thought that, of all people, I could trust my sister."

"You don't trust anyone," she said, sliding back against her headboard.

His face was half lit by the hall night-light, half shadowed by the darkness in her room. "That's true, I guess. Sad, but true. It's hard to trust, Marlene, when people betray you left and right."

She swallowed, and her mind searched for the comfort of Scripture she'd recalled moments ago. *Let not your heart be troubled . . .*

"You want to talk betrayal, Bill, let's talk about what you're doing to those children."

He leaned back against the post at the foot of her bed. "I'm teaching them a trade, Marlene. One they can use all their lives."

"One that can ruin their lives and land them in prison when they're older. You're warping their minds, Bill; you're dragging them into hell. You'll pay for it. You'll be accountable for it someday."

"Is that what they tell you down at that church you've been going to? That some invisible force out there is going to swoop down and strike me dead?"

The fear seemed to have fled, and in its place was a boldness she had rarely felt around her brother. "You'll pay, Bill."

"And so will you."

"Yes, I was a part of it. I'm prepared to suffer the consequences. But I've been forgiven."

"What did you tell her, Marlene?"

His voice sliced like a knife through her words. She swallowed. "Very little that she didn't already know. She's going to expose you, Bill. She's not afraid of you."

"She should be. And so should you."

He pulled his hand out of his pocket, and she saw the shiny metal of the pistol as the hall light fell upon it. He got up and came closer; he aimed the gun at her forehead. Even so, that peace hung on, and so did the boldness. She wasn't afraid to die. "What are you going to do, Bill? Kill all of us? One by one? Me? Beth? Her editors? All the adults who grew up in your home, the ones who know the real story? The children who are working as your little slaves now?"

"Maybe," he said. "But I think for now I'll just settle for you."

10

IN COTTAGE B on the back side of the St. Clair Children's Home campus, seven-year-old Lisa Westin lay still in her bed, clutching her threadbare teddy bear with one arm. She stared up at the ceiling and forced her ears to listen hard, so hard that she'd hear her brother when he finally came home. But some long-held fear told her that he wasn't coming home.

She squeezed her eyes shut, trying to hold in the tears and block out the memories of three years ago. She had been only four, and Jimmy told her often that she was too young to remember, that she had gotten it all wrong, but she knew he was just trying to make the memories seem like a misty dream that hadn't really happened. But she knew better. They weren't her first memories—there were others, but they came more in sensations and scents, feelings that seemed warm and sad, tiny glimpses of happiness that she knew she'd felt then. The memory she had of what happened that day—the day their mother hadn't come home—was more vivid, more distinct. She remembered harsh faces of policemen, words that she didn't understand: neglect, abandonment, addiction. She remembered the realization, after two whole days of going without food, that their mother had forgotten them. And she remembered the inescapable panic, the what's-going-to-happen-to-us terror. Jimmy had seemed so much older than seven at the time; he had been the rock she had clung to, her big brother. But he had been the age then that she was now. He had promised her, as the policemen had carted them off to become wards of the state, that he wouldn't allow them to be separated—that, even though no one else in their lives had stuck around, he would never leave her.

She wiped her tears, held back the sob pulling at her throat, and slid out of bed, careful not to wake the other little girls sleeping in the beds around her. The home was supposed to look and feel like a real home, with ruffly bedspreads donated by local church groups, and frilly little dolls that no one was allowed to play with. But Lisa suspected that real homes weren't filled with fear, as this place was. Her long, white gown dragged the floor as she padded barefoot across the carpet and peered out the window. Maybe Jimmy was out with Bill, doing that job he had said was so important. But she had heard Bill's car a few minutes ago, and had gotten up then to see if Jimmy was with him. When she saw under the streetlight in front of Bill's cottage that he was alone, she had known something was wrong.

Still clinging to one last fragment of hope, she padded out of the room and into the hall, past Stella, their house mother, whose loud snores reassured Lisa that Stella was asleep, and to the big room where all the boys in this cottage stayed. She tiptoed close to Jimmy's bed. Maybe he had come in quietly, not wanting to wake anyone. Maybe he didn't know she had waited and waited . . .

But the bed was still neatly made. Jimmy wasn't there.

She looked around for some of his belongings, wondering if he'd packed them. Then she'd know if he had planned to leave her.

She got down on her knees and peered under his bed, and found the box in which he kept everything in the world he owned. As quietly as she could, she slid it out. In it, she saw his baseball glove, his ball, the Atlanta Braves cap he'd gotten somewhere . . .

And she saw the envelope with the snapshots of them taken a few years ago, snapshots he kept because he said he always wanted to remember that they were sister and brother.

Wouldn't he have taken those if he'd intended to leave? Or had he left them here for her, so she could remember even though he'd chosen to forget?

"What are you doing in here?"

The harsh whisper startled her, and she swung around and saw Brad, one of Jimmy's roommates, sitting up in bed.

She put her finger to her lips to quiet him, and quickly slid the box back under the bed. But she kept the envelope of snapshots.

"I'm telling," he whispered louder. "I'm telling Stella. And I'm gonna tell Jimmy when he comes back. You're not supposed to be in his stuff!"

Another of the boys stirred. "Will you shut up? This is the first night I've been able to sleep all week!"

"That little creep is going through Jimmy's stuff."

"I am not," she whispered back. "I was looking for something that's mine. He was keeping it for me."

"What is it?" Brad taunted. "A pacifier?"

"I don't suck a pacifier!" Lisa flung back, struggling to hold her tears back. She got to her feet and headed for the door.

"I'm still telling!" he whispered.

She ignored him and tiptoed out into the hallway and past Stella's room. Her snoring hadn't changed its rhythm, and Lisa breathed a grateful sigh of relief. Maybe Brad wouldn't tell. If he did, Stella would spank her, then send her to Bill for further punishment. She'd never been sent to Bill before, but Jimmy had. She had seen the bruises herself.

She got back into bed and lay down, staring at the ceiling as she clutched the pictures to her chest. What would she do if Jimmy didn't come back?

Now she let the tears come, heavily, deeply. She turned over and buried her face in her pillow, muffling her sobs.

A dusty ray of sunlight from the attic window woke Jimmy the next morning, and it took a moment for him to realize where he was. He was hiding at the bottom of an old Christmas tree box, and the prickly tree still covered him.

But he hadn't been found.

He reached above him to move the tree and tried to stand up. Quietly, he set it down beside the box and stretched to his full height. It felt so good to stretch after a whole night crammed into that box. He listened . . .

Was the lady home, or had she gone to work? If she had, he could escape. He could get back to the home, let Bill punish him, and get back to normal.

He heard a television downstairs, and his heart sank. She was still here.

He sank back into the box, afraid to move. He needed to go to the bathroom, and he was hungry, and his body ached, and it was getting hotter in here.

When would she ever leave?

11

BETH SAT AT her kitchen table. Spread out in front of her were the documents she'd collected from Nick about the things the children's teachers had said, as well as the statistics on the rise of burglaries in St. Clair and surrounding cities, and the few citizens who'd mentioned seeing children breaking in. She had spent most of the night transcribing Marlene's interview from the tape, and now she sat with a highlighter pen, marking off quotes she'd use in her story and trying to decide what her lead would be.

The television in the living room was on, and the Tampa news anchor droned on about last night's city council meeting, a fire in Oldsmar, a murder . . .

She tuned it all out and sipped her coffee as she reviewed the transcript of her conversation with Marlene.

"The victim was identified as fifty-one-year-old Marlene Brandon . . ."

Beth looked up, stunned. Through the doorway of the living room, the television flickered, showing footage of the police cars surrounding the house where she'd been last night. Slowly, she got to her feet.

"The murder was a result of an apparent burglary. Ms. Brandon's body was discovered early this morning by a neighbor . . ."

Gasping, Beth dove for the telephone and punched out the number of the newspaper. When her editor answered, she cried, "She was murdered, Phil! The woman I interviewed last night was murdered! Marlene Brandon. What do you know so far?"

"That was the woman you interviewed?" he asked, astounded. "Wow, Beth, all we have is that it was a burglary. The house was ransacked, according to the police."

"She was murdered because she talked to me!" Beth shouted. "Her brother did it, Phil!"

"Now, wait, Beth—unless you have proof, something we can take to the police . . ."

The floor above her squeaked again, this time twice in a row, and Dodger started barking. Catching her breath, she turned toward the staircase, the phone still clutched to her ear. "Phil, I'll call you back. No! Better yet, you hang on. I keep thinking I hear someone in my house. I'm going upstairs to look, but if I don't come back to the phone in a few minutes—"

"Beth, you're going off the deep end. You're overreacting a little, don't you think?"

"I'm not overreacting, Phil. The woman is dead. If he killed his own sister, he'll come after me next. Now, hold on, and call the police if I don't come back."

She set the phone down—and heard the squeak again. She grabbed her gun out of the drawer and, hand trembling, aimed it toward the top of the stairs as she started up.

Dodger tried to follow her, his fat stomach making it nearly impossible for him to pull himself up from one step to the next. His yelping gave her some degree of comfort, though. As long as she could hear it, she felt grounded in reality.

She swallowed as she got to the top of the stairs, crossed her little office, and flung the attic door open.

"All right," she said, beginning to sweat and tremble as she clutched the gun. "I know you're in here. I've heard you, and you're not going to get away with it, so you might as well come out and show yourself now, or I'm going to start shooting. I mean it!"

She looked around. Everything looked undisturbed. There was no sign of anyone. Mentally, she tried to calculate exactly where she'd heard the squeak. She'd been standing at the telephone, near her kitchen table; directly over that would be that back corner, where the Christmas tree box sat. Was that tree sticking further out than it had been last night?

Her heart pounded in her ears as she stepped closer to the box, breathing so loud that whoever was hiding there would know how terrified she was. *Someone* was in that box. Bill Brandon? Was he in here playing with her, trying to frighten her to death? Was she going to be his next victim?

Terror overwhelmed her, and she cocked the pistol. "I'm giving you to the count of three to come out, and then I'm going to start shooting. One. . . . two . . . three . . ."

Nothing happened, so she slipped her finger over the trigger. "I warned you," she said through her teeth. "You're underestimating me, Bill."

She heard a noise behind her and swung around. The gun went off.

The puppy yelped and squirted a puddle onto the floor. He had made it up the stairs, but now he stood there trembling just inches from the bullet hole.

She had almost shot her dog.

For a moment, she thought of dropping the gun and comforting the puppy, but someone was still here. She turned back around, took a step closer to the box, grabbed a branch of the Christmas tree, and in one quick motion jerked the tree out.

The box was empty.

Drenched in sweat now, she backed away, so relieved that she wanted to cry. The puppy got between her feet, almost knocking her over. She picked him up and gave the attic one last look around. Maybe she was losing her mind. Maybe what she'd heard was an opossum on the roof, or a squirrel, or even a rat. Any of those things would be preferable to Bill Brandon.

She left the attic and closed the door behind her, then hurried down to get a towel to clean up the dog's puddle. On her way to the kitchen, she went back to the phone. "Phil? Are you there?"

"Yeah, Beth. What's going on there? Did I hear a gunshot?"

"It was me. I thought I heard someone, but it was a false alarm. Maybe I am a little paranoid. But Marlene Brandon is still dead. I have to go to the police. Who's covering her story, Phil?"

"I don't even know if we're going to print anything about it, Beth. It was all the way in Tampa, and our St. Clair readers wouldn't be that interested. Besides, they're saying it was just a routine burglary."

"It was *not* a routine burglary, Phil!" she shouted. "She was the sister of Bill Brandon, who's the subject of the story I'm working on. She got killed right after telling me everything. You really think that's a coincidence?"

"Well—okay, no. But what do you want to do? Do *you* want to cover it?"

She hesitated and tried to slow her thoughts. "I don't know . . . yes. I guess I should go and see what I can find out."

"If what you're saying is true, Beth, then don't you think your time would be better served by finishing the story? Then the murder of Marlene Brandon will tie in and make more sense."

Confused, she sat for a moment, eyes fixed on the ceiling. "Yeah, I guess you're right. But would you put someone else on it? It's important, Phil. We have to know everything about her murder."

"All right. I'll send Todd."

"Good. Let me know everything you find out. Even if it seems insignificant."

"And you finish that story."

"I'll have it there this afternoon."

She hung up and started for the kitchen to splash water on her face, but the doorbell rang, startling her again. She snatched up the gun and peeked through the curtain. It was two police officers. Breathing a sigh of relief, she shoved the gun back into its drawer and answered it.

"Can I help you?" she asked, wondering if they noticed how badly she was still shaking.

"Yes," one of them said. "Are you Beth Wright?"

"Yes."

He introduced himself and showed her his badge. They were not from St. Clair, but from Tampa. "We'd like to come in and ask you a few questions about the murder of Marlene Brandon."

12

THE TWO POLICE officers looked around her house as she ushered them in. She wondered if they had been there when she'd fired her gun. "I just heard about the murder," she said. "On the news." Her eyes welled with tears. "I couldn't believe it."

"We understand that you were the last one to see her alive."

She sat down and gestured for them to take the couch. "Obviously someone saw her after I did. How did you know I was there, anyway?"

"Her pastor."

"Her what?"

"Her pastor spoke to her after you left. Apparently she called him. He said she seemed exhilarated, because she had confessed some things to you. What we'd like to know from you is whether you saw anyone hanging around the house, a strange car, or someone walking up the street. Anything at all."

She closed her eyes and tried to think. "I didn't see anything, at least not at her house. But I was followed most of the way home."

"Followed?"

"Yeah. Someone was after me. I called 911, but I lost him before the police got there. And when I got home, I kept thinking someone was in my house. I even had the St. Clair police come out last night to check."

One of the cops began to jot that down. "Who were the officers?"

"Well, there were several, but I remember Larry Millsaps and Tony Danks."

They jotted the names down. "What time was that?"

"Around midnight, I think."

"Miss Wright, do you have any idea who could have followed you home?"

She hesitated, glancing at the table with so much evidence waiting to be printed. If she told them too much, and word got out, the rest of the media would jump on it before she had the chance to get her story into print. Because she was the last one to see Marlene alive, other reporters would piece it together, until they discovered more than she wanted them to know. Still, if she could get Bill Brandon off the streets . . .

"She mentioned that she wasn't getting along too well with her brother, Bill Brandon. And the things she confessed to me—they had a lot to do with him. Have you questioned him?"

"Yes. Ms. Brandon's pastor indicated that she and her brother were on the outs. But he was home last night. Several people, employees of his, confirmed it."

"I'll bet they did. Officers, if I were you, I'd check his story out with someone besides his employees."

"Why? Do you have reason to believe he wasn't at home?"

"I'm just saying that she told me she was afraid of her brother. He had warned her not to talk to me."

"About what, Miss Wright? What is the story you were interviewing her about?"

She glanced at the table again and swallowed. "I'm doing a story about children's homes. She used to work with her brother at the St. Clair Children's Home, but I learned that they had parted ways, and I wondered why. They'd had some philosophical differences, and her brother was still hot over her leaving." It was part of the truth, she thought, even if it wasn't all of it.

"Hot enough to kill over?" the officer asked.

"Maybe. I'm just telling you what I think."

The two cops exchanged looks, and finally, one asked, "Miss Wright, where were you around eleven last night?"

"Right here," she said. "I got home at about ten."

"Did you talk to anyone? See anyone?"

"I told you, I saw the police around midnight."

"Before that, was there anyone?"

She couldn't believe they were asking for her alibi, but she took it seriously. "Yes, as a matter of fact. Right after I got home, Nick Hutchins stopped by. Call him and ask him. He was here about half an hour."

They didn't write the name down. "Nick Hutchins. Could you give us a number where we can reach him, please?"

"Yes," she said, anxious to clear this up. "You can call him from my phone if you want. Check me out. Then maybe you can get out of here and arrest the real murderer."

13

JIMMY HADN'T MOVED a muscle since the lady had left. He'd been sure she was going to shoot him. He had walked over to the window and had been trying desperately to open it when he'd heard her coming up the stairs. So he had jumped behind a stack of old newspapers and balled himself up as small as he could get himself, and luckily she hadn't seen him. He had heard her say that she would shoot, and then he'd heard her pull out the Christmas tree—and even though he'd braced himself, expecting the gunshot, he had still wet himself when the gun went off. He'd been sure she was about to find him, but she hadn't.

Now he wondered who was downstairs with her. He had heard the doorbell, and there were voices down there. He half expected it to be Bill—but when he got up enough courage to creep a little closer to the window and look out, he saw a Tampa police car instead. Tampa? Were *they* looking for him? Had they tied him to any of the Tampa burglaries?

He had to get out of here. Somehow, he had to make a break for it.

If only he could use her bathroom and get a drink of water.

He heard the door close downstairs, and looked out the window to see the two cops going back to their car. She was out there, too, walking the dog, and he wished she'd walk up the dirt road, far enough that he could escape. But she hung around the front door, as if afraid to get too far from it.

He slid back down the wall, hopeless, helpless.

What was Bill doing about all this? Would he try to come after him and get him out? Or would he just leave him here to rot?

And what was Lisa thinking?

He closed his eyes and tried to come up with a plan, but there wasn't one. Until she left, he was stuck here.

Outside, Beth watched the police car drive away as the puppy tugged at the leash and sprinkled every leaf and bush he could find. She didn't want to get too far from the house, for fear that Bill Brandon would jump out of nowhere.

Her eyes drifted up to the window in her attic, and she tried to tell herself that no one was there. She had searched it, and the police had searched last night. Anyone would be paranoid after the events of the last few days.

But what was that? Something moving in the darkness beyond the dusty window. She stepped further back from the house and tried to focus better. Was it a reflection from the sun through the trees, or had she seen movement?

She stepped to the side, trying to see it without the glare of sunlight on it, and stared at the glass.

Then she saw it again. The slightest, slowest movement of something rising up, then jerking back down.

Someone's in there! They're watching me!

She jerked the puppy back into the house by its leash and grabbed her gun again. This time, with bold, renewed anger, she ran up the steps and burst into the attic. She kicked at the box beside the window, knocked over the four-foot stack of newspapers in the corner, clutching the gun in front of her.

"I saw you, you sleazeball! I know you're in here!"

She was shaking so hard she could hardly hold the gun, but she swung around, knocked over more boxes, kicked at others, shoved things aside.

Then she saw, on the far wall, the shadow cast by the light coming in from the window.

She took one step cautiously closer, then another, and cocked the pistol. He was behind that box in the corner, she told herself. Crouching like a coward, waiting to pounce on her or run like the wind . . .

"Don't move!" she screamed as she trained the gun on him and kicked the box away.

A little boy with red hair looked up at her with frightened, green eyes, frozen like a doe in the glare of headlights. "Don't shoot, lady," he whimpered.

She caught her breath and stepped back, lowering the gun instantly. "You're—you're a kid! Just a kid! I almost shot you!"

"I know."

"What are you doing here?" she asked, breathless. "How did you get in?"

He slowly rose to his full height, no more than four-feet-four. The front of his black jeans were wet, and he was soaked with perspiration. "I was . . . uh . . . I was lost, and I saw your house . . . I knocked, but no one was home. I came in through a window downstairs just so I could call my mom . . . that's all I wanted to do . . . but then you came home and I got scared . . ."

"You've been here since last night?"

"Yeah."

"Why didn't you let me know you were here? I would have helped you."

"I was too scared."

She tried to stop trembling. She reached for his hand—it was dirty and rough—and pulled him around the box. "Come on, we'll call her now. She must be worried sick about you."

He grabbed up his backpack as she led him out of the attic, into the full light of her loft. "How did you get lost, anyway? What's a kid your age doing out alone at night?"

"It's a long story," he evaded. "Can I use your bathroom?"

"Of course." She glanced at the wet spot on his jeans. "If you'd like to change, you could probably wear a pair of my shorts. They'd be baggy, but—"

"That's okay," he said, embarrassed. "I don't need 'em." She led him downstairs and showed him the bathroom. He went in quickly and tried to bolt the door behind him.

"The lock's broken," she said through the door. "Tell me your number, and I'll call your mother."

There was no answer. In a moment, she heard a scraping sound, and realized he was raising the window—probably the same one he'd come through last night.

She burst through the door and caught him halfway out.

And suddenly it dawned on her. Black jeans. Black shirt. Black backpack. This child had been put here deliberately, planted in her house to rob her or spy on her or maybe even hurt her—

She grabbed him and wrestled him back in, her face reddening with escalating anger. "You lied to me," she said through her teeth. "You're not some lost kid. You're from SCCH. You're one of Bill Brandon's kids, aren't you?"

The kid looked stunned, and she knew instantly that she was right.

"Answer me," she demanded. "Did he make you break in here? What was he looking for? Papers? Tapes?"

He lowered his worried eyes to the floor, and she turned him around and yanked off his backpack.

"Answer me!" she bit out as she unzipped it and examined the contents.

"I didn't get anything!" he said. "You came home—"

"What *would* you have gotten?" she asked, jerking up his chin. "What did he tell you to get?"

The fear in his eyes was real. Instantly, she let him go, but she didn't break that lock she had on his eyes.

"He's gonna kill me," the boy whispered.

Her anger crashed. She knew that fear, understood that certainty.

"What's your name?"

"Jimmy," he muttered.

"How long have you been there, Jimmy? At the home?"

"Three years," he said. "Me and my sister. Lady, if you report me, they're gonna put me in the juvenile center, and there won't be anybody left to take care of my sister. She's only seven."

But the words weren't penetrating. She was too caught up in the realization that if this kid had gotten into her house, it was because Bill Brandon knew where she lived and how to get in. The fact that she wasn't already dead was a miracle.

"How did he know where I live?"

Jimmy shrugged. "How does he know where anybody lives? I don't know. He doesn't tell me stuff like that."

"So what *did* he tell you?"

He looked miserable as he struggled with the truth, and she knew that he wondered if any of his mission was salvageable now. He was probably hoping to get out, go back to the home, and act as though he'd never been caught.

"Come on, Jimmy. I'm not going to let that man hurt you."

"You can't stop him."

"I sure can. And he knows it. That's why he made you come here. He wants to stop me from telling what I know."

His eyes were raging as tears filled them. "He *will* stop you. He's mean, and he doesn't give up. He woulda stopped you last night if you hadn't lost him."

She caught her breath. "How do you know that?" Then her face changed as she remembered the phone call, the boy's voice . . . "That was you on the phone, wasn't it?"

He swiped at the tears spilling down his face. "He told me he'd call to warn me you were coming home. I thought it was him. It was stupid. I shouldn't have answered. Man, he's gonna kill me."

"No, he's not. Because you're not going back there."

His face began to redden now, and he looked up at her with pleading eyes. "I *gotta* go back. You don't understand. Lisa's still there. He told me the sins of the brothers are visited on the siblings. It's in the Bible."

"That's not in the Bible, Jimmy. That's something he made up."

"He'll still hurt Lisa if he thinks I ratted on him. He swore he would, and I know it's true."

"Jimmy, even if you did go back, don't you know Bill's going to go ballistic when he sees you after this botched-up break-in?"

"He hates mistakes," he whispered, leaning back against the wall and clutching his head. "But at least he'll go off on me and not Lisa. She didn't do anything. She doesn't even know about all the stuff Bill makes us do. I don't want her to know."

"But don't you want Bill stopped? Wouldn't it be great if he could get caught and arrested for what he's done?"

"No!" he shouted. "*I'll* get arrested, too. Bill didn't break into anybody's house. *I* did. I'll be the one they put in prison. Not him."

"Jimmy, that's all just a lie. He tells you that to keep you doing what he wants. He wants you to be afraid. But the truth is that they don't put little kids in prison. How old are you, anyway? Eight, nine?"

"I'm ten," he said, insulted. "I'm just . . . short for my age."

"Probably why he chose you. You can fit into small places. But Jimmy, they don't put ten-year-olds in prison. And if they stop Bill, they'll put you and Lisa and all the other kids into a decent place—"

"That *is* a decent place," he screamed. "Don't you get it?"

"Just because something is familiar, Jimmy, it doesn't mean it's good."

"It doesn't *have* to be good."

She rubbed her face, wondering what she should do. Call the police? Or Nick Hutchins? Go against this kid's will and turn him in, or let him go back?

He was afraid that he would go to prison, and she couldn't blame him. Bill had probably pounded that threat into his brain.

She took his arm and led him to the kitchen, picked up the phone, and started dialing.

"Who are you calling?" he asked.

"My friend, Nick Hutchins. He's a social worker. He'll know what to do."

"No!" The kid jerked away from her. "Are you crazy? No social workers! I'm tellin' you, he'll beat the daylights out of Lisa, just to get back at me."

"Maybe Nick can get your sister out of there."

"Nick? The one who *put* us in there? No way! Lady, you're gonna ruin everything!"

"Jimmy, I want you to call me Beth," she said. "I'm going to help you."

Tears came to his eyes, and he swatted them away. Under his breath, Jimmy muttered, "I ain't calling you nothing."

Beth heard what he said but ignored him. Of course he was angry. Of course he was afraid. So was she.

She breathed a sigh of relief when Nick answered the phone. "Nick, I was wondering if you could come over. I need to see you."

At the other end of the line, Nick hesitated. "I could get there in a couple of hours or so. I'm kind of tied up right now."

"It's really important." She glanced at the boy. "There's something I need for you to see."

"What is it? You're not going to keep me in suspense until I can get there, are you?"

"I have to," she said. "Nick, come as soon as you can."

"Is it the article? Have you finished it?"

"No," she said. "I got a little sidetracked. I'm still working on it, though."

"Are you all right?"

"Yes. For now, yes."

She could almost hear the wheels turning in Nick's head. "Beth, just hold tight. I'll be there as soon as I can tie up some loose ends here."

"All right, I'll see you then." She hung up the phone and gave Jimmy a look.

"I thought you were gonna tell him," he said, wiping his face.

"Not over the phone. I want him to see you in person. He's a nice guy, Jimmy. He cares about you."

"He doesn't care about me! None of them do! I *hate* social workers. They don't care if they separate sisters and brothers, or if they take you out of one place to put you in a worse place. They don't care about nothing."

Her heart ached for this jaded child. "Jimmy, you've obviously had some bad breaks. But Nick is going to change your opinion of social workers. I promise you."

"Yeah, I've heard promises before, too," he said. "Let's face it, lady. I'm sunk. The sooner we get this whole thing over with, the better."

14

WHILE THEY WAITED for Nick, Beth made breakfast for the boy, who attacked the food as if he'd been starving to death. She sat with him as he ate, sipping on her coffee and studying him.

"What did Bill tell you about me?" she asked.

He hesitated, then shrugged. "Nothing. Just told me to come in here and get the papers and tapes. And dump the files about us on your computer."

She frowned. "He didn't say why?"

"Said you were gonna write a story about us. That we'd all go to jail if you did."

"I'm writing a story about *him.* He's the only one going to jail—he and the other adults working with him. But not the kids, Jimmy. I'm not out to get the kids." She wiped the wet ring from his glass off her table, then looked up at him again. "Did you find anything?"

"No, nothing."

"That's because I had most of it with me, and I hadn't put anything on the computer yet. I imagine he was planning to kill me before I got home, and then he would have destroyed any evidence I had with me." She thought about that for a moment. "Why do you think he *didn't* come out here last night? If he knew where I was, and that you were still here, why didn't he come?"

"I don't know. I kept thinking he would. Maybe he thought I got away, and that you called the police after he followed you. Maybe he was too scared to come."

"Bill Brandon, scared? I don't think so."

The boy looked up and stared at her for a moment. "You know him, don't you?"

She met his eyes, then looked away. The doorbell rang, and she got up, grateful for the chance to evade the question. "Maybe that's Nick," she said.

"Or maybe it's Bill."

She stopped halfway to the door, reached into her table drawer, and pulled out her pistol. *It's not as if Jimmy doesn't know I have one,* she thought, *I almost shot him with it an hour ago.*

Peeking through the curtain, she saw Nick, and quickly put the gun away before opening the door. "Nick, you got here sooner than I thought."

"Had to. You had me so curious." He stepped into the house and saw the little freckle-faced boy with a milk mustache, his red hair tousled and unkempt. "Who's this?"

Beth drew in a deep breath. "Nick, this is Jimmy. A very interesting kid, with a very interesting story. Why don't you sit down? This could take a while."

When he'd heard Jimmy's story, Nick seemed ready to burst with excitement. "He's just what we need! A witness, from the inside."

"They're not gonna listen to me. I'm just a kid," Jimmy said. "And none of the others will talk. They're too scared."

"They *will* listen to you," Nick said. "Once we get your story into the paper, the police will be banging down the doors of that home."

"And the kids will be scattered all over the state," Jimmy added, "and brothers and sisters will be separated, and some of us will be in awful places . . ."

Nick hesitated, giving Jimmy a long look. "Jimmy, don't you want out of that home? Don't you realize what he's done to you? He's not only risking your life, he's using you to commit crimes, training you and the others to be crooks. That's child abuse."

"Can you get Lisa out? Can you keep us together? If you can't, I'm not telling anything. Nothing. You can find another witness."

"Jimmy, I can try my best to keep the two of you together. But Lisa's going to be better off no matter where we put her."

"Bull!" Jimmy shouted, his eyes filling with angry tears. "She depends on me. She's probably worried to death right now. She thinks I left her, just like—" The word fell off, and he turned away. "When can you get her out?"

"As soon as I relate all this to the police." Nick paused and shot Beth an eloquent look. "I know you want to get the story done first, but do you think you can finish it in the next couple of hours? If Brandon thinks you're ready to go public, we don't have a lot of time. I want to get those kids out of there."

She looked at all her evidence scattered across the table. "I think I might be able to pull something together by then. But then my editor—"

"Great. Beth, do you realize that this is the break I've been looking for? That we might really be able to shut down that home?"

"Yes," she said softly, touching Jimmy's shoulder, though he shook her hand away. "I realize it. It's a dream of mine, too."

"Oh, man. Jimmy," Nick said, "you could be a hero because of this. A regular celebrity. And your life of crime is over. Nobody's going to make you break into people's homes ever again."

But Jimmy didn't look so sure.

"Hey, why don't you come with me, Jimmy? We could hang out while Beth finishes the story."

"I don't want to go anywhere with you."

"He can stay here," Beth said. "He can just watch TV or something while I work. It'll be all right. He's quiet as a mouse. Proved that last night. My only fear is that Brandon will show up."

"Don't worry about that. I think I'll pay him a visit right now."

"What for?"

"I'm allowed to make impromptu inspections whenever I want. I'll just hang around there, inspecting the cottages and all. That way we can be sure he stays where he is."

"Okay," Beth said. "I'll do the best I can. But are you going to mention Jimmy? Should we call the police about finding him?"

Nick considered that. "No, I don't think so. They'd just report it to Sheila or me. Let's keep this just between us for now. I could lose my job, but I'll risk it. And I can't wait to see how Bill handles Jimmy's disappearance."

He patted Jimmy's shoulder. "Jimmy, you just relax, all right? I'll try to check on Lisa while I'm there."

"Will you tell her I'm okay? That I haven't left her?"

Nick hesitated. "I don't think that's a good idea, Jimmy. It might put her in danger. If she tells anyone, Bill could hear about it."

"She keeps secrets," he said. "She won't tell."

"She might do it without meaning to. But relax. In a little while, we can go in there and get her out for good."

That wasn't good enough for Jimmy. Brooding, he slumped on the couch.

"I'll call you in a couple of hours, Beth," Nick said, rising.

Beth walked him to the door and bolted it behind him.

15

"LOCK THE DOOR, Brad."

Bill's order was clipped and direct. The eleven-year-old boy could tell from Bill's voice and from the look on his face that this was going to be one of those meetings Brad would wish he hadn't attended. Not that he had a choice. He locked the door when the last of the dozen kids in Bill's group of "favorites" filed in, then took his seat beside his best friend, Keith.

The faces of the children were solemn—even frightened. Bill didn't often call them together in broad daylight. It drew too much attention from the other kids. But this morning he had made them all get up early, even though it was summer and they didn't have school, and file into the meeting room next to Bill's office for what he called a "briefing."

Something had happened, Brad thought, and he was sure it had something to do with Jimmy Westin.

Bill's face was angry as he paced in front of the dead-silent children, tapping a metal ruler against his palm and examining their faces one by one. "We've had a development, people," he said. "A rather upsetting development. I thought I should prepare you so you'd know what to expect." Suddenly he slammed the ruler down on a table, making all of them jump. "Jimmy Westin was arrested last night."

A collective gasp sounded in the room, and the children gaped up at him for more details.

"He got sloppy," he went on. "Let himself get caught during a mission. Now he's paying for it."

Brad whispered a curse, and anger surged inside him that his friend could be so stupid. He had always thought that Jimmy wasn't careful enough. He hadn't worked at it, like Brad had.

The boy looked up at Bill and struggled with the question weighing on his mind. "Was it adult jail, or the detention center?" Either way, it was bad, but in their room late at night, the boys sometimes speculated about what would happen if they got caught.

"I hate to say it," Bill said, "but they're holding him in the adult facility. A year ago, he may have gone to juvenile hall, but after the last election, Florida passed the Adult Crime–Adult Time Law. You do a grown-up crime—and they do include burglary—and you serve with the meanest, toughest criminals in the state.

"I wish I could tell you that I could get him out. But I'm afraid it doesn't work that way. Because he's a ward of the state, he's considered high risk, which means that—according to HRS—if I can't make something out of him, he's probably a lost cause. So they're processing him into the justice system, where he's likely to stay for at least ten or twenty years."

Brad wasn't sure he followed all of this. He often had a hard time understanding much of what Bill said. But the ten-to-twenty-years part didn't escape him. That was practically Jimmy's whole life.

"I think you all know what this means," Bill said, slapping his palm with the ruler again. "It means that every one of you is in trouble. If Jimmy Westin talks, you might go down with him."

Brad tried to imagine what Jimmy might say if he was tortured or threatened. Would he drag them all down with him? Or would he hang tough and keep his mouth shut?

"I don't think he'll talk," Bill went on, as if he'd read Brad's mind. "We have Lisa. As long as Jimmy knows that his sins will be visited on his sister, we'll be all right. And just to make sure *she* doesn't talk, I'm going to get her to replace Jimmy, and put a little fear into her myself."

Silence hung in the air as everyone imagined what he might mean by that.

"Okay, listen up. People are going to be coming around here, asking questions about Jimmy. Those people are *not* our friends; they'll be out to get us. Until I tell you differently, I want you to pretend Jimmy's still here. If HRS comes snooping around, act like he just left the cottage, or the playground, or wherever you are. You just saw him a minute ago. Got it?"

One of the girls frowned. "Won't they *know* where he is?"

Bill shook his head. "Not necessarily. 'The right hand knows not what the left hand doeth.'" None of them knew what that meant, but it sounded biblical, and thus, scary. "HRS is not in touch that much with the police. And I don't want them to know that one of *my* kids is a jailbird. Besides, they might start looking at each of you, one at a time. I don't want you to wind up where Jimmy is."

He paced the room again, this time walking between their perches on arms of sofas, tabletops, or on the floor. "But we can overcome this obstacle, if we try. Are you people up for it?"

A weak chorus of yeses sounded around the room.

"I can't hear you!"

"Yes!" they shouted.

"You're not ordinary kids! You're gifted with special skills. As the Good Book says, 'Many are called, but few are chosen.' You are the chosen. *My* chosen. You're called to a higher purpose—a mission that isn't for the faint of heart. You're called to excellence, people. And you *are* excellent. That's why I chose you. That's why you are my hands and my feet. That's why you are favored among God and men!"

It didn't matter that his words made little sense to Brad or the others. It sounded good and hopeful, and it elevated them to something more than orphaned children. It made them special.

When the children had gone back to their cottages, Bill went through his office into the room where closed-circuit television screens showed him what was happening around the campus. He watched the children going back to their cottages. Some whispered among themselves, but he knew those conversations would be harmless, so he let it go. Seeing no cause for concern, he went back into his office, sat down behind his desk, and thought over the things he'd told them. They'd believed everything. It was so easy to manipulate them. "Adult Crime–Adult Time Law"—what a laugh. There was no such thing.

He just hoped that dirty-faced brat didn't turn on him. And why had no one called him about the boy yet? If he was in police custody, wouldn't they have reported it to him?

He looked at the phone and wondered if *he* should call *them* and act like a concerned guardian worried about a missing child. But then he would have to explain why it had taken him so long to report the disappearance. He could say that he'd put the boy to bed himself—but that Jimmy had sneaked away during the night, so that he hadn't known Jimmy was missing until this morning.

It might work. And it would certainly cover him in the event that Jimmy *did* talk.

But maybe he was jumping to conclusions here. What if the kid wasn't in custody? Calling could open a whole can of worms that Bill didn't want to open. Investigations, news reports, posters all over town . . .

No, he couldn't chance it. He'd have to wait. If the police did have the boy and if they showed up to ask him about Jimmy, he could say that he'd been duped. After all, the police were always quick to assume the worst about these parentless, high-risk kids, who'd been products of alcohol, drugs, selfishness. The police, like everyone else, expected the children to continue the pattern set by their parents. As Bill himself was often quick to remind the police and others, you could take the kid out of the trash, but you couldn't take the trash out of the kid. And no one ever argued with him about it.

Yes, his best bet was to do nothing, then plead ignorance if the police called. It was the safest course.

16

THE OLD WESTERN on TV didn't hold Jimmy's attention, nor did the puppy who kept wanting to play tug-of-war with him. He could hear Beth's fingers on the keyboard upstairs as she wrote the story that would bring the walls of the St. Clair Children's Home tumbling down—exactly what Bill had sent him here to prevent.

He let the puppy win the tug-of-war with the sock, then watched him curl up on the floor to chew on it. Jimmy's eyes strayed up the open stairway. With just a slight lean, she could see him, and she'd kept a close watch on him all morning. He had kept an eye on her, too. Up there, disks were lying around. Papers. All the things that Bill wanted. If he took those things back to Bill, maybe Bill would go easy on him. Maybe Lisa wouldn't have to suffer.

But Beth wouldn't let that stop her; she would write the story anyway. Besides, she had been nice to him, and he didn't want to rip her off now. She could have reported him to the police, but she hadn't. It was like she believed he was a good person when she hardly even knew him—like she thought the bad things he had done weren't his fault. Anyone else would have hung a guilty sign on him and handed him over to the cops.

No, he couldn't turn on her now. But he still worried about Lisa. If there was just some way that he could talk to her, tell her to hold on, that he hadn't just left her.

His eyes strayed to the telephone. Could he get away with just calling her? Clicking the remote control, he turned up the television as the shoot-out raged louder. He picked up the phone, then took it to a part of the living room where he was just out of her sight. Quickly he dialed the direct number to his and Lisa's cottage. It rang, and Stella, the housemother, answered.

He tried to disguise his voice. "Can I speak to Lisa, please?"

"Who is this?" Stella asked. "Jimmy, is that you? Where in blue blazes are you?"

As if it had stung his hand, he hung up the phone quickly and backed away from it. Oh, great. Now Stella would tell Bill that he had called, and Bill would be madder than ever that he'd been near a phone and hadn't tried to reach him. When he found out Jimmy had tried to reach Lisa, Bill would fly into a rage—and when he finally found Jimmy, as he would eventually, he would get even.

The worst part was that Lisa still wouldn't know that her brother hadn't abandoned her just like every other person she'd ever loved had done.

17

BILL DIDN'T LIKE Nick Hutchins. The social worker seemed to have it in for him. Nick had been giving him too much grief lately. His monthly inspections of the home had stepped up to twice monthly, and he seemed too curious about the children, especially those who'd been caught in petty crimes. Bill had tried to explain to him that he wasn't responsible for the value systems of these kids before they came to his home, but that he did the best he could with what he got. If one of them occasionally got himself into trouble, it wasn't Bill's fault.

Now, as Bill followed the man from cottage to cottage, as if Nick expected to find some horrible violation that would warrant a severe reprimand from the state, he wondered what Nick was looking for. Did this impromptu inspection have anything to do with Jimmy's disappearance?

"Are all the kids on the premises right now?" Nick asked casually, walking into a playroom and scanning the children playing games.

So, he does know that Jimmy's missing. Bill struggled with the idea of candidly admitting to the kid's disappearance. But he couldn't understand why Nick was being so secretive. Why didn't Nick just come out and ask him where Jimmy was, and how long the boy had been missing? No, maybe he was just being paranoid. He decided not to mention it yet. "No, actually," he said. "We took a vanload to the library this morning. Some of the others had swimming lessons at the Y."

Nick peered at him skeptically.

They had just turned up the hall so that Nick could snoop in the bedrooms when Stella, the housemother of Cottage B, burst in. "Uh, Bill, could I have a word with you, please?"

"Certainly," Bill said. "Nick, you'll excuse me for a moment, won't you?"

Nick nodded but didn't say anything, and Bill felt the man's eyes on the back of his neck as he followed Stella out of earshot.

"What is it?"

"It's Jimmy. He called just now, trying to disguise his voice. He wanted to speak to Lisa."

His eyebrows shot up. "Where is he?"

"I don't know. He hung up before I could—"

"I'll find out. Go back in there and keep that jerk from doing us any harm. I have to go to my office for a minute."

He rushed out of the cottage and across the lawn to his office and bolted inside. He unlocked a closet and checked the Caller ID he kept so that he could monitor the origin of calls coming into each of the cottages. When he'd opened the home, he had had an extension to each line installed right here in his office. He also taped all of the calls made on any campus telephone, either incoming or outgoing. It was what he called quality control. You never really knew whom you could trust. And of course no one, not even his "inner circle" of staff, knew what was in this closet.

He checked the Caller ID for Cottage B—and saw the name *E. J. Wright.* Bill's heart jumped. Elizabeth Wright. Beth. Jimmy was still in her house? Was he nuts? Hadn't he told that kid to get out of there? But Jimmy hadn't asked to speak to Bill, who could come and get him, but he'd asked instead for Lisa—and in a disguised voice.

Something was wrong. Jimmy had turned on him.

What was he telling Beth? Bill rubbed his forehead and found it cool and wet with sweat. Was Jimmy giving her more fodder for her story? That little twerp knew enough to bring down his whole operation.

Bill hadn't had a lot of time to think this morning—first the cops had come to tell him about Marlene's death and ask a ton of questions, and then Nick Hutchins had shown up. But this situation didn't require a lot of thought.

He was going to have to kill both Beth and Jimmy, before she could turn that story in.

His face hardened with violent determination as he cut back across the lawn to the playground behind Cottage B. He saw Lisa, Jimmy's little sister, sitting alone on a swing, drawing figures in the dirt with the tip of her toe. Her strawberry-blonde hair strung down in her eyes, and he could see from her red eyes that she'd been crying.

He approached her, and she looked up fearfully. "Come here, darlin'," he said, taking her hand. "Come with me."

Her innocent eyes widened. "Where?"

"We got some trainin' to do. I'm about to promote you from orphan to executive. What do you think about that?"

He could see that she didn't have a clue what he was talking about. "I don't know."

"See, since Jimmy's gone and got himself in trouble, I'm giving you his job. It was a real important job. You think you're smart enough for it?"

Tears filled her eyes, but she nodded bravely. "When is Jimmy coming back?" she managed to ask through trembling lips.

"Good question," he said. "Probably never."

18

BILL DIDN'T LIKE to get his hands dirty. That was why he always used the children. It kept him nice and distant, and if the children were ever caught breaking and entering, he could throw up his hands and insist that he'd tried as hard as he could to keep tabs on them, but children would be children, and there wasn't a lot he could do about kids who'd been born among criminals—except love them and show them compassion and hope that some good would rub off on them.

Sure, Bill had compassion. So much compassion that he really wished he could see the look on Beth and Jimmy's faces as they opened the cigar box he was "doctoring" for them.

"Know what this is, darlin'?" he asked Lisa, gesturing toward the cigar box open on the desk before him.

"No, sir."

"It's a little package we're sending to a friend," he said. "A friend who's been real good to me. And I'm gonna let you deliver it for me."

She didn't say anything, just sat in the corner, trying hard not to move.

He set the explosives in carefully, then rigged up the detonator caps so that the bomb would go off the moment the box was opened. He'd never done this before, actually, but he'd read all about it in articles on the Internet about the Unabomber. It was no secret, and he and some of his partners had discussed the precise methods more than once. He couldn't believe how perfectly this would work out—except that those two traitors wouldn't get this little present until tomorrow, which could be a problem if Beth finished her story and turned it in to her editor before that. In that case, he'd have to make sure the newspaper didn't get his story out by then. In any event, if there were any questions about Bill's involvement in the explosion, he would be able to prove that he was miles away when the explosion occurred.

He closed the box carefully and wrapped it, then addressed it to Beth Wright and affixed an Express Mail waybill.

"You ready to deliver this for me, darlin'?"

Lisa hesitated. "Where?"

"The post office. You're big enough to take something in by yourself, aren't you? You don't even have to talk to anybody. Just drop it in the slot, and my friend will have it by tomorrow."

She nodded.

"If you do a good job, Lisa, honey, I'll give you a more important job, like the kind I gave Jimmy. And if you do a bad job . . . well . . ." He propped his chin on his hand and smiled. "Remember that time Jimmy had to stay in bed for two days because he couldn't walk so good? Remember those bruises?"

She seemed frozen.

"Well, just don't do a bad job, darlin'." He took the package and her hand and led her out to his pickup. He'd parked his Buick in a toolshed at the back of the property; even a stupid cop would be able to match the dents and paint scratches on it to the marks on Beth's car, so he didn't plan to drive it until some of his staff had painted it.

Across the lawn, he saw Nick coming out of one of the cottages—and heading toward him.

He cursed. "Get in, Lisa, and put the package under the seat."

She did as she was told, and Bill closed the door and walked around to the driver's side. "You about finished snooping, Nick?" he asked in a pseudo-jovial voice.

"Maybe," Nick said. "I just wondered where you're taking her."

"To a birthday party," he said. "One of her little friends at school. Don't think a kid should miss all the fun just because they're wards of the state, do you?"

Nick looked down at the little girl, and Bill wondered if he knew who she was. He wished she didn't look quite so fragile. "She's a little worried 'cause she's late. I clean forgot about it, but no harm done. She'll get there before they blow out the candles if we hurry."

Nick backed away from the truck. Bill could see that he was trying to think of a way to detain him. What was Nick up to?

"When will you be back, Bill? I want to talk to you."

"Won't be long. Haven't we talked enough? Don't you have something constructive to do? The state isn't paying you to hang around here all day, are they?"

Nick wasn't intimidated. "Get somebody else to take her, Bill. I'm not finished with you."

Bill groaned and got out of the truck. "All right, hold on. I'll get Stella, but I'll have to make sure somebody's watching the kids before she comes." He looked at Lisa with an apologetic face. "Sugar, you're gonna be a little bit late, but we'll get you there somehow."

Lisa looked perplexed.

He helped Lisa out of the truck and took her into his office to make sure that Nick didn't speak privately with her. He called over to Cottage B. "Stella, I need you to come run an errand for me. If you run into Nick, tell him that you're taking Lisa to a birthday party, but don't mention her name. Call her Susan. He might know about Jimmy, and her name might ring a bell."

"Doesn't he already know her?"

"It's been three years since he's dealt with either of them. He won't remember."

"Where am I really going?" she asked.

"To the post office. Drop Lisa off at the corner and let her put the package in the 'express' slot."

"Is Lisa going to be one of your regulars now?" she asked. "Isn't she a little young?"

"She's perfect. Just get over here. And don't botch this up. I've had enough problems lately, and I'm not in a good mood. If you mess this up, everything could blow up in our faces."

He hung up and took in a deep breath. "If that man asks your name, you tell him it's Susan. Do you hear me?"

Lisa nodded, her eyes big.

"You put the package in the Express Mail slot, and if anyone asks you what it is, you say it's a book for your grandma. Got it?"

She nodded.

"Just do as I say, and when you get back, I'll have a surprise for you."

Her eyebrows shot up. "Will Jimmy be home then?"

He decided he might need that leverage. "He might just be, darlin'."

He led her back outside as Stella hurried across the lawn. "Come on, sugar. Let's get you to that party."

19

BETH SAT BACK in her squeaky desk chair and sighed. Her article was finished—complete with the quotes by Marlene and Jimmy, along with the sad and suggestive news that Marlene had been murdered immediately after giving the interview. She wished she had another hour to tweak it, but she sensed that time was tight. Sitting forward again, she sent it by modem into the paper, then e-mailed her editor to look for it and call her back. As an afterthought, she electronically transferred the transcribed conversation with Marlene so that it would be on file at the newspaper office.

She went downstairs. Jimmy and the puppy were lying on the area rug in front of the television, curled up together as if they were old friends. She stepped around them and saw that they were both sound asleep.

She smiled. How exhausted Jimmy must be, after spending the night in terror in the attic.

The telephone rang, and she snapped it up. "Hello?"

"Beth, I got your article." It was Phil, her editor.

"Read it yet?"

"Yep. Interesting. Very interesting. Sure is going to cause a big stir."

"Phil, this is headline material. You'll print it in the Saturday edition tomorrow, won't you?"

He hesitated. "I don't know, Beth. I'm a little reluctant."

"Why?" she asked. "What's wrong with it?"

"I'd like a few more quotes. The only two people quoted are a dead woman and a little kid who might just have a vivid imagination."

"Was it my imagination that the kid broke into my house last night, Phil? I didn't make that up. He's here now."

"Still, I'd feel better if you could get another quote or two. Somebody who's not dead or a juvenile delinquent."

"Juvenile delinquent? How do you figure that?"

"Hey, don't get defensive. I'm just pointing out how it's going to look to a skeptical public. He did break into your house."

"Didn't you read the article? He was *forced* to. And Marlene's dead *because* of the article."

"The kid's story is suspect, Beth. Sorry, but that's the truth. And you *say* the woman died because of your interview; the police haven't concluded that yet. We need more. Maybe you can find someone who grew up in Brandon's home, someone who's not under his thumb anymore. Maybe they'd be willing to talk. That would be just what we need. And call the police stations in all of the towns within a two-hour radius. Find out how often there was evidence that kids had done it. You know, fingerprints, footprints, maybe they saw them but didn't catch them, that sort of thing."

She closed her eyes and started to feel sick. "If I compiled all that today, Phil, would you print it tomorrow? It's crucial. This whole thing is taking on a life of its own. Something has to be done with Jimmy, and he's worried about his little sister—with good reason—but we can't get the kids out of there until there's enough evidence. But if I turn him over to the police, *he* may suffer instead of Bill Brandon—"

"Yes, Beth," Phil cut in. "Get me what I asked for and I'll run it. You have my word."

She let out a heavy breath and dropped the phone in its cradle. What was she going to do?

She closed her eyes and asked herself if she had the guts to do what was necessary. The right thing never seemed that easy, and it had an awful lot of conditions attached.

But she had spent the last three years trying to make something of herself. She had found a church, and now she went every Sunday. She tried hard to live by the Ten Commandments—don't lie, don't covet, don't commit adultery. In fact, some people thought she followed God's laws to a fault, but she figured she had enough sin in her life that it would take fifty years of walking the straight and narrow to get to the point where she'd come close to making herself worthy of God.

But this was hard. Writing this story Phil's way meant digging deeper than she'd wanted to dig, exposing things she hadn't wanted exposed . . .

And it meant that she would need advice about the law.

She picked up the phone and dialed the number of Lynda Barrett's law office. Lynda, a devoted Christian and respected lawyer, was one of the teachers in Beth's Sunday School class. Maybe she could help.

Paige, Lynda's secretary and another friend from church, put Beth right through to Lynda.

"Hi, Beth. What's up?"

"Hi, Lynda. Uh . . . I'm sorry to bother you. I just . . . I wondered if you could come by and see me today. It's pretty important. I need some advice, and I need it quickly."

"Legal advice?"

"Yes. It has to do with a story I'm working on. It involves a little boy. I'd rather tell you about it in person, if you have time, and I'd rather not come there."

"I could come right now. I was supposed to be in court this afternoon, but it was postponed, so I'm free."

"Great. Oh, and bring Jake if you want. My little friend might like to meet him. Kids love pilots."

20

STELLA LET THE truck idle at the corner near the post office. "All right, Lisa. Take the package and go. Put it in the Express Mail slot. Then hurry back to the truck. Try not to talk to anybody."

Lisa got the package from under the seat. It was heavier than it looked, but she dared not complain. She got out of the pickup, clutching the package against her chest, and backed into the door to close it.

Walking rapidly, she hurried toward the post office door. Shifting the package to one arm, she tried to open the door, but it was heavy and she almost dropped it.

A man came to the door and opened it for her. "There you go, honey."

"Thank you," she said almost inaudibly. She stood inside the post office, looking around at the boxes and stamp vending machines and slots. Through some glass doors were the postal workers, and a dozen people waited in line.

The package was getting heavier, so she shifted it again, trying to get a more comfortable hold on it. Stella had said to put it in a slot. She saw the slots marked "local" and "stamped" and "metered." He'd said to put it in Express Mail, but she didn't see that one.

It was too heavy for her to hold any longer, so she went to the "metered" slot and tried to fit it through the small opening. It wouldn't fit.

"That's not where you want to put that, pumpkin," one of the postal workers walking through told her. "That'll have to go in Express Mail over there."

"Oh." She headed across the room to where he pointed, and looked up at the lever, which was too high for her.

"Here, sweetheart, I'll get it," the postman said. He opened the small door and took the package from her. The weight surprised him. "Boy, this is heavy. Whatcha got in here, anyway?"

She tried to speak, but her voice wouldn't come. Clearing her throat, she tried again. "A book for my grandma," she said just under her breath.

He smiled and let the door close. "I'll just take it on back, pumpkin."

She only stood staring at him for a moment, not sure what to do. Finally, she decided she'd better get back to the car before Stella left her. "Thank you," she said again, and walked quickly to the door.

Stella was still waiting at the corner. Lisa ran up the sidewalk and climbed into the pickup.

"What took you so long?" Stella demanded.

"I don't know."

"Well, did you put the package in the Express Mail slot?"

Lisa thought of telling her about the man, but a dread came over her that she might be punished for giving the package to him. "Yes," she said.

"Did you talk to anyone?"

"No."

Stella breathed out a sigh of relief as she turned the corner and headed back to the home. After a moment, she muttered, "I oughta get hazard pay for this."

Lisa turned around and looked out the back window, wondering if the man had really mailed the package, or if he'd opened it and looked inside. She hoped it wasn't anything too awful.

She sat back down and tried to console herself with the thought that Jimmy might be back when she returned to the home. Wouldn't he be proud that she was smart enough to work for Bill now, too?

21

BETH POURED TWO cups of coffee and brought them to the table where Lynda sat, filling in the notes she had made as Beth told her of the allegations she was about to make concerning the home, and what Jimmy's part had been in it. As Jimmy and Jake sat on the floor playing with the puppy, Beth quietly popped the question she had been waiting to ask.

"I wondered, Lynda, what kind of responsibility Jimmy and the other kids who've worked in Bill Brandon's crime ring will have. In other words, are they accountable for something they were forced to do?"

"You mean, can they be prosecuted?" Lynda asked.

Jimmy looked up, and she knew he'd overheard. She wished she hadn't asked.

"Well, breaking and entering is definitely a crime," Lynda said, "and under ordinary circumstances, a child Jimmy's age who committed a crime like that would be sent to the detention center, depending on the judge's disposition and the number of offenses against the child. But these are extenuating circumstances, and I find it hard to believe that any judge or jury would blame Jimmy or the other kids for being victims of Brandon's control."

Beth looked down at the coffee cup in her hand. "There's someone I know, who I might try to interview. She's someone who was in Brandon's home a few years ago. She's an adult now, and I'm hoping she'll corroborate what I've already uncovered. But she might be worried that she'll be prosecuted if she confesses. Would she?"

"Well, that depends. How old was she when she stopped committing the crimes?"

"Eighteen. She stopped when she left the home."

Lynda blew out a breath, and shook her head. "That's a tough one. A jury might say that she was old enough to know right from wrong."

"But if she'd been doing it since she was ten, and she was scared to death of him, and she knew that she had no choice but to do everything he said . . ."

"It would depend on her lawyer, Beth, and what kind of case he laid out."

"But you think she would *need* a lawyer? That there would be charges against her? Isn't the statute of limitations in Florida three years?"

"Well, yes. Has it been longer than that?"

"Just barely," Beth said. "Does that means she'd be clear?"

"Yes, she would. But any of those legal adults who stole for Bill within that three-year period would be at the judge's mercy."

"What about loopholes? Is there any way they could ignore the statute of limitations and prosecute her anyway?"

"It's possible that they could get her for something else. Something like withholding evidence or aiding and abetting."

"But she hasn't aided or abetted. Not since she left the home."

"Still, just by keeping her mouth shut she was allowing the crimes to go on."

"But that isn't fair! How much can someone be accountable when they've never had free will? When their every thought has been controlled by that man? When they're totally dependent on him for food and clothing and shelter, and they're afraid of his discipline if they don't do what he asks?"

"It may not be fair, Beth, but that's the justice system."

"Well, if that's the case, then it wouldn't be worth her while to talk, would it? Anyone would be better off keeping their mouth shut, even if they were outside the statute of limitations. And even then their reputation could be ruined—future job opportunities, credit, housing . . ."

"Technically, yes. But there's a moral issue that might outweigh all that," Lynda said. "There are children being abused and warped. Without *someone* stepping forward, it'll never end. Is it worth her reputation? I can't answer that. All I know is that God honors those who honor him by doing the right thing."

"When?" Beth asked, staring at the lines of her palm.

"When what?"

"When does God honor the person who honors him? How much of a sacrifice does he demand first?"

Lynda looked a little surprised by the question. "That depends on the person, Beth," Lynda said. "To one man Christ said to sell everything he owned. To another, he just said to go and sin no more. It all depends on what dark thing is in a person's heart, separating them from him. Mostly all he wants is confession and repentance."

"Yeah, that's the part I have trouble with," Beth said. "There are some buried things in life that you just don't want to dig up again."

Lynda's eyes lingered on her for a moment. "Confession is risky, all right. No question. But it's cleansing, Beth. Tell your source that the release that she feels afterward will overshadow anything the justice system can do to her. After repentance, she still might face consequences of some kind, but she won't be alone. God will walk with her and provide for her in all of that."

Beth tried to let it all soak in, but she wasn't sure she bought it.

"So when do you think the story will come out?" Jake asked from the floor.

"Tomorrow, if I can manage to get everything finished. It really has to be tomorrow. We can't wait any longer."

"My sister's there," Jimmy explained.

Lynda and Jake looked fully at Jimmy and saw the concern on his face. "Are you worried about your sister, Jimmy?" Lynda asked.

"Yes. He warned me. He said, 'The sins of the brothers are visited upon their siblings.' He knows the Bible real good."

"That's not in the Bible, kiddo," Jake said.

"I told him that," Beth said. "But Brandon always misquotes Scripture. He rewords verses and gives them a perverted, sinister meaning, and uses them like weapons against the children." She hesitated. "I've heard that from several people."

"Well, the more I hear, the more I think you need to get this story finished no matter what you have to do. Why don't Jake and I take Jimmy to stay with us while you work?"

Jimmy looked hopefully up at her.

"Sure," Jake said. "We could do some guy stuff."

"But we haven't reported finding him. I'm not sure what the police would do. We were just going to hide him until the arrests are made."

Jimmy sprang to his feet. "Please? It'll be all right. Nobody'll see me."

Beth gave Lynda a narrow look. "Are you sure you wouldn't feel compelled to report him?"

"Of course not," Lynda said. "I agree with you. It's best to hide him quietly for a while, as long as HRS knows."

"We could go out to the airport and take him up."

"In an airplane?" Jimmy asked, his eyes huge.

"Sure, in an airplane. Unless you know some other way to fly."

"Can I, Beth? That would be so great! None of the other kids would even believe it!"

Beth couldn't help laughing. "I guess that's all right, if Jake promises he won't crash."

"I beg your pardon," Jake said, insulted.

"It's not like you haven't done it before."

Jake gave a smirk. "It'll never happen again. Jimmy's not scared, are you, Jimmy?"

Jimmy looked a little less exuberant now. "You crashed?"

They all laughed. "It's a long story. We'll tell you about it on the way."

Beth walked them all to the door, said her good-byes to Jimmy, and watched them drive away.

For a moment, she contemplated what Lynda had said, trying to draw it into the core of her heart, her faith. It was too great a risk—yet all those children had no one fighting for them, no one to make things right. *Somebody* had to talk.

She looked through her Rolodex and found her old friend's number. All of the "graduates" of Bill Brandon's home kept unlisted phone numbers and very private addresses, so he couldn't reach them. They all continued to live in fear, to one degree or another. But Maria had trustingly shared her number with Beth, who had never expected to use it for a favor like this.

She picked up the phone and dialed Maria's number at home. Maria had gotten pregnant shortly after leaving the home, and was now the mother of twin two-year-olds. She had a sweet, supportive husband—ten years her senior. Beth hoped that Maria was happy; she hated to drag all this up now. But Maria was her best chance for getting cooperation.

"Hello?"

Beth smiled at the sound of her voice. "Maria, hi. It's Beth Wright. I mean . . . Beth Sullivan." It had been a long time since she'd used that name.

"Beth! It's good to hear from you. How are you?"

"I'm great," she said, but couldn't manage to work any enthusiasm into her voice. "Listen, I was wondering if you'd have time to meet me for lunch today. I know you have the kids and all. I could pick up hamburgers and meet you at the park or something so they could play. I just need to talk to you about something."

"Sure. I'd love to see you. But what do you need to talk to me about?"

"It's about Bill Brandon."

Dead silence hung between them for an intense moment. Finally, Maria said, "What about him?"

"There's just some stuff I need to talk to you about, but I'd rather do it in person."

"All right. What time?"

Beth didn't know what to expect Maria to look like; it had been nearly three years since she'd seen her. But the girl looked much more beautiful now than she had at eighteen. They hugged, and Beth admired the twins.

"Two babies. Wow."

"We want at least five," Maria said with a laugh as the children went to play in the sandbox. "The family I never had." They took a bench just a few feet away, so Maria could rescue them if anything happened. "You dyed your hair! I might not have recognized you if I'd seen you on the street."

"That was the point," Beth said.

Maria touched Beth's honey-colored hair. "Don't you ever miss being a brunette?"

"Sometimes. But it's worth it. Staying in St. Clair had its risks, you know."

"Tell me about it. But I was so glad to hear from you. We should stay in touch more. I didn't know how to call. I didn't know you had changed your name."

"Yeah," Beth said, watching the little girls in the sandbox. "I didn't have a husband to give me his name, like you did, so I just made one up. It made me feel more secure to have a different name."

"Maybe if we'd kept in touch, we could have supported each other."

"It's hard," Beth said. "We're both so busy. I've been working myself to death."

"I know, Beth, but I'm real proud of you. How close are you to getting your degree?"

"One more year."

"You're really going to do it, aren't you?"

"Yeah, and I've got huge student loans to prove it," Beth said.

"You always were determined. And working at the paper. I didn't expect you to get a job this soon."

"Yeah, well, they hired me as an intern my freshman year. They don't usually give bylines to interns, but I've worked so hard and dug up such good stuff, that Phil, my editor, has started treating me like a regular staff writer. During the summers, he pays me like one, but believe me, I have to work for it."

"I'm so proud of you, I guess I can forgive you for never calling me."

Beth smiled and squeezed her hand.

"So what's up, Beth? Why did you want to talk to me about Bill?"

Every muscle in Beth's body tensed as she took in a deep breath. "Maria, I've decided to expose him."

Maria's face showed no expression. She merely stared at her. "Are you sure you want to do that? He'll come after you."

"He already has."

Her face grew pale. "You're braver than I am."

Beth almost laughed. She tried to push down her own self-loathing. "It's not bravery," she said. "Not on my part. But I can't stand the thought of Bill abusing those children, training them to be thieves, preparing them for prison. Or worse. But I know that the minute this story comes out, hopefully tomorrow, Bill will be arrested. I'm not worried about him hurting me after that."

Maria stiffened. "Why are you telling me all this?"

Beth shrugged. "Well, I thought you would want to know. And—I thought you might let me interview you. My editor says I need more sources, someone who was there, who's grown now. Someone besides a dead woman and a little kid."

"Dead woman? What are you talking about?"

"Marlene," Beth said. Her mouth trembled slightly, but she managed to add, "She talked to me, and Bill killed her."

Maria threw her hand over her mouth and sprang up. With terror in her eyes, she hurried to the sandbox and picked up one of the twins, then grabbed the other by the hand and started to her car.

"Maria, where are you going?"

"Home!" Maria shouted as tears came to her eyes. "Why didn't you tell me on the phone that Bill knows you're doing this? I never would have come! If he killed Marlene for talking to you, then he'll kill me, too!"

"No, he won't! He's not following me now."

"You don't know that!" Maria shouted. She spun, her face red and raging as she glared at Beth. "I thought better of you, Beth, than to risk my life and the lives of my children. I have a family now! It took me three years to stop being afraid all the time, and now, just when I have some peace, you have to drag me into something that Bill's already killed his sister over?"

"I'm not dragging you into it, Maria. I just want to stop him."

"Then stop him yourself!" she shouted. "You don't need me. We have the same story!"

Beth froze, unable to find an argument to counter Maria's. Her story *was* the same. As much as she tried to deny it, hide it, wipe it from her mind, it was almost identical. "I can't use myself as a source," she choked out. "It wouldn't be objective."

"Are you kidding?" Maria shouted. "You'd probably win a Pulitzer Prize, if you didn't wind up in jail. Is that what you're scared of, Beth? That you'll wind up in jail?"

Beth looked down at her feet. "No. I made sure that I waited long enough. Three years. They can't try us after three years have passed."

"Oh, that's noble." Maria said with a sarcastic laugh. "You were so worried about the kids that you waited three years to make sure your own crimes were covered!"

"So did you!" Beth returned.

"That's right," she said. "Because *my* kids are more important to me right now. But I'm not the one trying to make some noble cause out of the whole thing—all that compassion and concern for those kids, while you were waiting for time to pass so you wouldn't go down with them!"

"No one but Bill is going down, Maria!" Beth bit out through her teeth. "We're not guilty! We didn't do any of it of our own free will. We were just kids."

"I was old enough to be a mother, Beth!"

"But we didn't have a choice! We were wards of the state. They put us in his care. It's *their* fault, not ours."

"Right," Maria said. "Just don't say that to a jury. When you start blaming other people for your own sins, they lose sympathy real fast. We knew that what we were doing was wrong."

Tears came to Beth's eyes, and her face was crimson as she took a step toward her old roommate. "What could we have done?"

"We could have run away," she said. "Or we could have turned him in then."

"He had us brainwashed! He wanted us to think that we would all go to jail. He *still* has us brainwashed!"

"Maybe so," Maria said. "I heard it from the time I was eight years old—that I'd be the one to go to jail, not him. I'm still hearing it. And if it's true, if any part of it is true, Beth, I can't even think about it, statute of limitations or not. I have two babies who need their mother, and I don't want them to grow up knowing I was a thief."

Beth just watched as Maria headed back to her old car. As the car drove off, she sat back down on the bench and stared ahead of her.

Maria was right. It was cowardly to expect her friend to talk, when Beth wouldn't talk herself. What kind of friend was she, anyway?

The hot breeze feathered through her hair, making little wisps stick to her face. What did God think of her, looking down from his throne that seemed so far away? Did he give her any points at all for deciding to go after Bill? Or would some of the points be taken away because she'd waited three years? Would she be docked more points for hesitating to come forward herself?

He must understand that the mere admission that she had been one of Bill's kids would immediately make people presume her guilt—not just in those crimes, but in others. She had once been branded *abandoned, orphaned, trash*—she had outgrown those labels, had overcome them. She didn't want to be known as a thief now.

Maybe she should have left town when she'd left Bill's home—gone somewhere she'd have been free to start over without constant reminders of Bill's presence nearby. But she'd spent her senior year of high school filling out forms for financial aid at St. Clair University, and when the loans and grants had been approved, it had seemed silly to go elsewhere. Now she was bound to St. Clair until she graduated, no matter how she wished she could relocate to someplace where she'd never fear Bill Brandon or think of him again.

It was too late now. She had to think of the children.

And she had to give Phil something he couldn't deny.

She got up from the bench and squinted against the sun in the direction Maria had gone. She had a decision to make. A big one. She only hoped that she had the guts to make the right one.

22

"SO YOU WERE a real pilot? The kind that flies those big planes with hundreds of people on them?" Jimmy asked as he and Jake and Lynda strolled across the tarmac to the Cessna they had rented for the afternoon.

"That's right," Jake said. "A commercial pilot. I thought I was hot stuff."

"You were!" Jimmy cried. "Go to all those cool places, whenever you wanted, and all those people trusted you—"

"And the money," Jake said, winking at Lynda. "Don't forget the money. For a bachelor with no responsibilities, I made out pretty good. I was real proud of myself."

Jimmy sighed. "I wish I could learn to fly. I'd fly me and Lisa to Brazil or somewhere far away. We'd have it made."

Lynda smiled as they reached the plane. "Look, Jimmy," she said. "See over there, on Runway 3?"

"Yeah," he said.

"That's where we crashed when our landing gear wouldn't drop."

"Right there?" Jimmy asked. "You really crashed?"

"We were trying to land."

Jimmy gazed out at the runway. "Wow," he said, awestruck. "You almost died right there."

"In a way, I did die," Jake said. "But you know what? That crash was the best thing that ever happened to me."

"Yeah, right."

"No, really. That was when I learned that God's in control of my life, not me. And once I knew that, I really started to live."

Jimmy breathed a laugh that sounded much too cynical for a boy his age. "God's not in control of *my* life. Bill is."

"Not anymore, he's not," Lynda said.

"You watch. He'll get me back, some way. And he'll make me and my sister pay."

Lynda bent down until her face was even with his. He was so small for his age, and his Opie-like expression belied the experiences he'd had. "Jimmy, I know this is easier said than done, but I want you to trust Beth and the others working on this."

But the expression that crossed his face was just the opposite of trust, and he turned away from her to peer out at Runway 3 again. "My mom said that to me once. To trust her." He didn't cry, but the tough look on his face had an amazingly fragile quality. "Are we gonna fly or what?"

Lynda looked at Jake, and silently they agreed to back off.

"All aboard," Jake said, and climbed onto the wing. Bending over, he pulled Jimmy up behind him. "Get ready, Jimmy Westin, to experience the ride of your life."

23

NICK SAT OVER the books and files on his desk, trying to find a loophole in the law that would allow him to get Lisa out of the children's home immediately so that he could satisfy Jimmy's—and his own—fears. But there was nothing. Nick's suspicions were unproven, and today's inspection had been fine, even though he'd known that Bill was tap-dancing to cover the fact that all of the children weren't accounted for.

To all outward appearances, SCCH seemed to offer the children a loving, compassionate environment. Taking the kids swimming, to the library, to birthday parties—it was all very impressive, if one didn't know better.

He got up and pulled Jimmy and Lisa's files out of the file cabinet, hoping to find some forgotten aspect of their situation that would offer him some reason to pull her out. He flipped through the file and saw a picture of the two kids. Jimmy a couple of years ago, and his little sister—

It was her. The little girl in the picture was the same one Bill had put into the car to take to the birthday party. She had looked pale, almost afraid. She was shy, Bill had said.

But that was Lisa—and if Jimmy was right, Bill was already taking his anger out on her. No wonder she'd been frightened.

He rubbed his eyes with the heels of his hands. How could he have stood there and not realized that it was her? He had placed them in SCCH, after all. But she'd been three years younger then, and her hair had been short and sparse—she'd been malnourished. No wonder he hadn't recognized her. They had driven her off right under his nose.

He grabbed his keys off the desk and rushed back out to the truck. He had to go back. He had to see if Lisa was back yet or if they were still claiming she was at the party. He had to make sure she was okay. If something had happened to her today, he would never forgive himself.

And Jimmy and Beth would never forgive him, either.

24

BILL BRANDON WAS getting angry with him, but Nick didn't care. Bill glared at him from across the lawn as Nick walked toward Cottage B, where he had learned Lisa was assigned. Some children were playing in a playground behind the cottage, and the required number of adults were on hand to supervise. He walked to the fence and scanned the faces.

Stella, the woman who had spirited Lisa off earlier, was sitting in a lawn chair watching the children. She looked up at him as he approached the fence. "Business sure must be slow at HRS, to warrant this much attention from you in one day."

"I thought I might have left something here," he said. "I can't find my favorite pen. It was a Mont Blanc that I got as a gift. You didn't happen to find it, did you?" Actually, he really *had* been given one as a college graduation gift, and it had been lost—for over two years.

"Nope. Sorry."

"So how was that birthday party?" he asked, his eyes still sweeping across the children, looking for Lisa.

"Fine," she said. Her tone was defensive, questioning.

He spotted Lisa now, sitting alone in a corner of the fenced area, leaning her head against one of the posts and peering out to the street, as if watching for someone. Was she looking for Jimmy?

"I was thinking I might have dropped my pen over there," he said, pointing to the area where Lisa was sitting. "Mind if I check?"

She got up then, and looked back over his shoulder. Bill was approaching him from behind.

"Nick, I know you're supposed to do surprise inspections," Bill Brandon said as he got closer, "but don't you think two in one day is a little ridiculous?"

"He left something," Stella said. "A pen."

"A Mont Blanc. I wanted to look around and see if I could find it." As he spoke, he started walking around the fence to where Lisa sat. "I was thinking that I might have dropped it when I came out here—"

Lisa looked up at him as he drew closer. He looked down at her legs and arms, searching for some sign of a bruise or scrape, any indication that she may have been beaten or abused.

Bill was right on his heels, trying to distract him from her. "If you'd dropped it, I'm sure we would have found it by now. If it turns up, we'll call."

Nick bent over the fence. "But I was right over here, and I may have bent over. It could have fallen out of my pocket." He pretended to look on the ground around the fence, then acted surprised as his eyes collided with Lisa's. "Hey, you're the little girl who went to the birthday party. What was your name again?"

She started to answer, but Bill interrupted. "Susan. Her name's Susan."

"Hi, Susan," Nick said. "How was that party?"

Lisa had the same pale, wide eyes as Jimmy. "Fine."

"Good. I love birthday parties. Did you have cake and ice cream?"

She glanced up at Bill, waiting for him to prompt her. Nick couldn't see him, since Bill stood behind him, but he must have signaled for her to say yes. She nodded.

There was no point in pushing it. He was obviously making Lisa uncomfortable. She was here, and she wasn't hurt—at least not that he could see.

Frustrated, he turned and started back toward his car. Bill followed. "Call if you find it, will you? It's a valuable pen. I hate to think I lost it."

"Sure. I'll call," Bill said suspiciously.

Nick headed back around the fence, his eyes scanning the other children, reading their expressions—

He froze as he saw Chris and Matt, the two little boys he'd placed in the Millers' home just last night. They sat huddled together in a corner of the yard, watching the other children with wan, miserable faces.

Nick swung back toward Bill. "Those two boys over there. When did you get them?"

Bill glanced over at them. "They're temporaries. Sheila Axelrod brought them this afternoon."

"Sheila?" Nick asked. "But I put them in a foster home last night."

"Take it up with her, Nick. She brought them to us, and we took them in."

He turned back toward the two boys, fighting the urge to leap over the fence and tell them that he hadn't meant for this to happen. The older boy, Chris, caught his gaze, and his face hardened. He muttered something to his little brother, and they both glared at him.

They think I betrayed them.

With an aching heart, Nick got back into his car and drove away.

But before he'd gone two miles, he pulled over and tried to decide what to do now. Bill and his employees were onto him. Maybe that was good. They wouldn't hurt Lisa as long as they knew he was watching. And maybe they wouldn't hurt Chris or Matt.

But that wasn't good enough. He had to get them all out.

He leaned back on the headrest and looked up at the ceiling. His eyes misted as angry sorrow rose within him. "Lord, you've got to help me. Right now I'm so mad at Sheila Axelrod I could strangle her. How could she have put those two boys there? And why? They were fine with the Millers."

He wrapped his arms around the steering wheel and rested his forehead on them. "This is too much for me," he said. "I can't handle it—without you."

A turbulent peace fell over him—peace that fighting for the kids was the right thing to do, but turbulent because he couldn't rest. God wasn't going to take that anger away from him, not yet. Maybe he was supposed to use it.

He pulled his car back out into traffic and headed to the HRS building. Sheila's car was there, and as he got out, his rage escalated.

She was at her desk, talking on the telephone. She looked up as he entered, and he strode toward her and bent over her desk. "Want to tell me what's going on with the kids I placed last night?"

She rolled her eyes. "Let me call you back, okay?" she said into the phone. She hung up and looked up at Nick, unintimidated. "You got a problem?"

"Yeah. Those kids were welcome in the Millers' home. Why did you take them out?"

"Because the Millers weren't ready for three kids. They still have the baby."

Nick's teeth came together. "I didn't want those kids in SCCH, and you know it."

"And I told you that we're not going to quit placing children there just because you don't like Bill Brandon. I am the supervisor of this office, and I have the final word. If you can't live with that, Nick, you know where the door is."

"And where would that leave you, Sheila? You can't handle this office alone."

"Watch me."

They stared each other down for a long moment. Nick thought of quitting, of insulting her, of reaching across the desk and throttling her. But if he resigned, he couldn't help Beth; he could do nothing for the kids. Working from the inside, he could help bring Bill Brandon down. When Beth's story hit the streets, Sheila would understand.

He straightened and massaged his temples. He was getting a headache. "Sheila, those kids were scared to death. The Millers were nurturing. They made them feel protected."

"It's not my job to make them feel protected, Nick. It's my job to make sure they have a secure place to stay for as long as they're wards of the state."

"It's not just about paperwork, Sheila!"

She laughed bitterly as she got up. "Don't tell me about paperwork, Nick. I've been at this longer than you've been an adult. I've seen cases that would curl your hair."

"You've seen too many," Nick said. "You've lost your compassion."

"Well, maybe it wouldn't hurt for you to do the same. That compassion will kill you, Nick. It'll turn your hair gray and keep you awake nights. And for what? For the peanuts the state pays us?"

"Then why are you still here?"

"Because this is what I was trained to do, and in case you haven't noticed, jobs aren't easy to come by in this state. After a while, you stop worrying. You stop losing sleep. Those things don't help the kids anyway—they just make you miserable. You find ways to stretch a dollar, or you supplement your income selling catalog makeup or magazine subscriptions. And you go on. You do the job, because you're the only one here to do it."

"There's got to be more to it than that, Sheila," Nick said. "I came into this because I believed it was a calling from God."

"Right," she said on a laugh. "Let me tell you something, Nick. If there were a God, there wouldn't be a need for social workers."

Nick's anger faded as he realized how little Sheila understood. "Maybe we *are* the way God's solving the problem. Maybe you and I are like angels to these miserable, abused children."

She snorted. "Yeah, well, I lost my halo a long time ago." She dropped back into her chair and picked up the phone. "This conversation is wearing me out, Nick. And I have about a million phone calls to return."

He watched as she dialed a number and began talking, ignoring him. His anger was gone, but in its place was a sad frustration, so deep that he didn't know how to combat it. Breathing out a defeated sigh, he headed out of the building and got back into his car.

There was nothing he could do for Matt and Chris right now. But there had to be something he could do for Lisa.

He pulled her file out of his briefcase. He hadn't finished studying it earlier. Now he flipped through the many forms that had been filled out to make Lisa and Jimmy wards of the state. Someone else—one of his coworkers who had long ago quit for a less stressful job—had removed them from the home. Then Nick had taken over the case, moving them from temporary foster care into SCCH, so he had never really studied their past.

They were not orphans. The forms revealed that the original social worker had been unable to locate their father. But they still had a mother.

He read intently about the woman who had voluntarily abandoned her children to the state.

Her name was Tracy, and she'd been twenty-five years old at the time. HRS had received reports of neglect, investigated, and found that she was a heavy drug abuser. Shortly after the investigation began, she had left the children, ages four and seven then, home alone for two days while she reveled in an ecstasy binge. The state had taken the children.

Nick ached for the pain those kids must have endured. He sat back in his seat. What would make a mother have such disregard for her children? That precocious little boy, that beautiful little girl—no wonder Jimmy distrusted adults. After a history of abandonment and neglect, Nick—who should have gotten things right—had dumped him from the frying pan into the fire. How many other times had he made the same mistake?

He closed his eyes and leaned his head back against his headrest. Where was that mother now? The papers said she was a resident of St. Clair, but she could have moved on since then. He wondered if her life was still controlled by drug abuse.

He closed his eyes and tried to think. He couldn't get any of the kids out of the home on his own, not until Bill was exposed tomorrow and charges filed. And plenty of things could go wrong. The state could get caught in a mire of bureaucracy and fail to act immediately. That could be a fatal mistake, because as soon as Bill Brandon read Jimmy's quotes in the article, he would be sure to take his vengeance out on Lisa.

Unless . . .

It was a long shot, but—he could at least *try* to track down their mother.

25

BETH SPENT THE afternoon writing the story of a little girl neglected and abused, then placed in what was considered the nicest, most stable home in the state. She wrote of how that child was forcefully recruited into a crime ring at the age of eight, how she was taught to pick locks, slip into small openings in windows, crawl into homes through crawl spaces with garage entrances. She told how the girl learned to unlock jewelry boxes, search for cash, unhook VCRs, TVs, computers. She explained how she had worked for hours each night in her young life of crime, only to fall asleep in class the next day and suffer punishment at the hands of teachers and principals—and then again from Bill Brandon on returning home. And she told of the "tapes" that still played in her mind, tapes of Brandon's voice telling her that *she* was the thief, not he, that she had the dirty hands, that if she ever told this story, she would have to fear not only prison, but death at his vicious hands.

The sun was low in the sky behind the trees when she finished. Just writing this anonymous confession had exhausted her. And it might not even be enough. Phil would want substantiation. He would want a name, and she wasn't ready to give hers.

Drained and depressed, she called her editor. He sounded rushed as he answered. "Yeah, Beth. What's up?"

"Phil, it's about the article. I've finished it, but—"

"But what?"

"But the other source I got. It's anonymous. It's a woman who used to live in Brandon's home and worked in his crime ring . . . but she doesn't want me to use her name."

"You realize, don't you, that we're making some fierce allegations here? If we intend to accuse an upstanding citizen of charges this serious, we have to be prepared to defend them in court, Beth. I can't take the chance of getting the paper sued, because we made allegations that we can't back up."

"We *can* back them up, Phil. It's not my fault that Marlene was murdered, and that Jimmy is a little boy."

"I know that. But you're putting me between a rock and a hard place here."

She slammed her hand on the table, waking Dodger who slept at her feet. "Phil, someone's going to get hurt if we wait! Bill Brandon already knows I'm working on the story. He's going to do everything he can to stop me. The longer we put off printing this story, the more danger I'm in, and the more danger those kids are in."

"You're asking me to ignore my legal counsel."

"I'm asking you to have a little courage, Phil. Get some guts, for heaven's sake!"

He hesitated. "Beth, are you sure that you've gotten the facts right? Are you positive?"

"Phil, I'd stake my life on it. In fact, that's exactly what I'm doing."

She could tell from his sigh that she'd made her point. "All right. Send the story in, and I'll take a look."

She closed her eyes. "Do more than take a look, Phil. Please. This could be the biggest story of the year."

"Sure, it could. It could win you an award. We could also get our pants sued off."

"Forget the awards, Phil. Don't even give me a byline. I don't care. Just print it."

"I'll read it, Beth. We'll see."

"Call me as soon as you decide," she said.

"I will."

She hung up and rested her face in her hands. She'd done her part. Now, if Phil printed the story, her career—even her life—might be ruined. Or Bill might decide to go out in a blazing act of vengeance, and come after her.

She just hoped God hadn't forgotten to record this in her scorebook.

26

NICK FOUND THE woman's apartment building, an old structure with peeling paint, busted-out windows, and trash and old furniture on the front lawn. He found it hard to believe that people lived here; it looked as if it should be torn down.

A toddler played at the bottom of a staircase, wearing nothing but a filthy diaper. As Nick walked from his car across the lawn, he looked for some sign of an adult nearby. Seeing none, he leaned down, hands on knees, and smiled at the child. The baby's face was dirty and sticky, and his nose was runny. He smiled back and reached up to hand Nick a cigarette butt that he'd, no doubt, picked up from the clutter at his feet. His fingers were crusted with filth.

"Hi there." Nick took the butt. "Where's your mommy?"

"Who wants to know?" a hoarse voice said from behind the broken staircase.

Taking a couple of steps, Nick peered around the staircase and saw a girl of no more than fifteen sitting on a cracked slab of concrete, smoking a cigarette. "Hi," Nick said. "I didn't see you there. I thought the baby was out here alone."

"What's it to you?"

He shrugged. "Just worried me, that's all. There are a lot of things around here that could hurt him."

"So what do you want, anyway?" the girl demanded.

"Uh . . ." He looked back down at the dirty toddler. His instinct was to scoop the baby up and take it away to a place where it would be cared for. But he reminded himself, as he had to several times a day, that not every child was his responsibility, and that things weren't always as bad as they seemed. "I was looking for a woman named Tracy Westin. I think she lives upstairs. Do you know her?"

"Yeah, I know her."

"Is she home?"

"I haven't seen her come out."

He looked up the broken staircase. "So she's in that apartment up there?"

"Give the man an award."

Annoyed, Nick started to respond in kind—and then realized that she was, herself, a child, unable to handle the weight of hopelessness that so obviously held her down.

He looked at the baby again, then back at the girl. Sister? Mother? One could never tell. He only hoped that she was a better caretaker than his first impression suggested. He could only hope that she *had* a better caretaker for herself.

He went up the staircase, stepping over the broken steps. A garbage bag with trash spilling out of a gnawed-out hole sat at the top of the steps, and a cat prowled in the refuse. He stepped over it, ignoring the stench, and knocked on the door.

For a moment, he heard nothing, and almost turned to go. Then he heard a voice.

He pressed his ear to the door and knocked again. He heard the voice again, but couldn't make out the words.

He checked the doorknob—unlocked. Slowly, he opened the door.

The apartment was dark and filthy. He stepped inside and looked around. There was little furniture except for an old, torn-up card table in the kitchenette, covered, as was the kitchen counter, by dishes piled on dishes, old crud dried on them. There was a mattress in the far corner of the cluttered room.

On the mattress was a woman in shorts and a dirty tank top, curled up in a fetal position, shivering. Her hair was long and red, tangled and matted. He stepped toward her. "Tracy?"

She didn't answer.

"Tracy?" he tried again.

She still didn't respond, so he stepped over the clothes lying on the floor, the sandals, the wadded sheets that had been kicked off the mattress. She looked tiny, anorexic, no more than eighty pounds. And she was sick—that was clear. He knelt beside her and reached out to touch her forehead. It was alarmingly hot.

"Tracy, can you hear me?"

Her eyes, glassy from the fever, focused on him for a second, and she moaned, "Help me."

He wasn't sure if this was drug withdrawal or a real illness, but either way she needed to be in a hospital. He looked around. "Do you have a phone?"

"No," she whispered.

He thought of rushing off to find a pay phone and call an ambulance, but decided that she would get help more quickly if he took her himself. "Tracy, can you get up?"

She only closed her eyes.

"All right," he said. "I'll pick you up. I'm going to carry you out to my car and get you to the hospital, okay?"

No answer.

He scooped her up, surprised at how light she was in his arms. She probably hadn't eaten in days—maybe even weeks. He wondered how long she had been like this.

He carried her out, stepping back over the reeking garbage, and carefully made his way down the stairs. The girl with the baby was still sitting there. She watched him blankly as he carried Tracy out.

"Can you tell me how long Tracy's been sick?" he asked her.

"Do I look like her mother?" the girl responded.

"When's the last time you saw her?"

"I don't know," she said, putting her cigarette out on the concrete. "A week maybe."

"Was she sick then?"

"How should I know?"

Frustrated, he hurried her to his car and laid her in the back seat. She curled back up in a little ball as he jumped into the front, turned on his lights, and drove away.

27

BETH DOVE FOR the phone. “Hello?”

“Beth, it’s Phil.”

She closed her eyes, bracing herself. “Phil, tell me you’re going to print the article. Please. I don’t think I can handle it—”

“Relax, I’m printing it. It was great, Beth. Thank your anonymous source for me.”

“Then it’ll be in tomorrow’s paper?”

“Absolutely.”

“Yes!” she said, punching the air. “Thank you, Phil. You may have saved my life.”

“I wish you didn’t mean that literally, but I guess you do.”

“You bet I do. Listen, Phil, I know you’re not going to go for this, but I’d like to give a copy of the story to the police department tonight.”

“No! That’s too soon!” he said. “That’s our story. I don’t want every other newspaper in the area getting it before we do, and that’s exactly what will happen if you give it to the police. You know better than that.”

“I don’t care about being scooped anymore, Phil. Jimmy’s little sister is still in that home, and so are a lot of other innocent victims. Not to mention the fact that Bill Brandon is after me. I want him locked up. Now.”

He moaned. “All right, Beth. Maybe the other papers still won’t get the whole story. Or maybe the police won’t act quickly.”

“They will. They have to.”

He hesitated, and Beth knew that all his editor’s instincts told him not to risk losing the scoop. “All right. Do what you have to do.”

“I will.”

She hung up and immediately clicked her mouse on the “print” button. Watching as the article slid out of her printer, she picked up the phone to call Nick and tell him the good news, but she only got his machine.

She grabbed the printed article, folded it in half, and headed for the door. Dodger was right behind her, begging to go out. She picked him up, clipped on his leash, and put him back down. He scurried out the door the second she opened it and made a puddle on her doorstep.

“Good boy!” she said, petting him. “You’re getting the hang of this, aren’t you?” When he was finished, she hurried him back into the house.

The sun was setting as she headed to the police station, hoping those two detectives, Larry and Tony, would be there. She wanted to make sure this didn’t fall through the cracks.

Larry was on his way out as she came in, and she grabbed his arm and stopped him. “Detective Millsaps?”

He looked down at her, and she could tell that he couldn’t place her.

“Beth Wright. You were at my house last night, remember?”

“Oh, yeah,” he said. “Nick Hutchins’s friend.”

“Right. Listen, I need to talk to you about something really important. Do you have a minute?”

He checked his watch. “Yeah, I can give you a few minutes.”

He led her back through the maze of desks in the noisy room, and offered a chair in front of his desk. Plopping into his own chair, he asked, “So what’s up? Did you hear something in your house again?”

“Yes, I did, as a matter of fact. And I found the culprit. It was a ten-year-old boy.”

“A ten-year-old boy?”

“Yes. And Bill Brandon, the man who runs the home where this little boy lives, is the one who forced him to break into my house so that he could find and destroy any evidence I had against him.”

“Oh, that’s right,” Larry said. “You were working on a story about him.” He pulled a pen out of his drawer and began to take notes. “You’re sure he was behind it?”

“Positive.” She handed him the article. “The boy is still with us—Nick knows all about it.

Don't you think it's odd that a child is missing from the St. Clair Children's Home and no one there has reported it?"

"Well, yeah . . ."

"Read the article," she said, sitting back and crossing her arms. "I'll wait."

She watched as he read the article, skimming at first, then settling in as a wrinkle of concentration and concern gradually deepened across his forehead. When he'd finished, he looked up at her and rubbed his hand across the stubble around his mouth. "That's some article."

"It's all true."

"So let me see if I got all this. Brandon has a crime ring that might explain dozens of break-ins in St. Clair over the last several years. He's abusing these kids. He probably murdered his sister to keep her quiet. And he ran you off the road—"

"Tried to," she cut in.

"Tried to run you off the road." He shook his head and looked up as he saw Tony hurrying through. "Hey, Tony. Come here."

Tony seemed a little distracted as he headed toward them.

"You got to read this," he said. "It's coming out tomorrow in the *St. Clair News.*"

They both watched as Tony read. As his interest in the article increased, he dropped the sport coat he'd been holding by one finger over his shoulder. "This is bad."

"Then you'll do something about it? Tonight?" Beth asked.

Tony glanced at Larry. "What do you think?"

"Well, we'll have to talk to the kid first . . ."

"Where is he now?" Tony asked.

"With some friends of mine," Beth said. "Lynda Barrett and Jake Stevens."

"Yeah, we know them. We'll head over there and interview him right now."

"He's scared to death that something will happen to his sister if an arrest isn't made soon. I think he has reason to be."

"I think *you* have reason to be, if what you're saying is true."

She stared at them. "Why would I lie?"

"I'm not suggesting you are," Larry said. "But we have to have more substantial proof than a newspaper article and the word of a little boy who got caught breaking the law. Kids have been known to lie their way out of tight spots."

"He isn't lying! Check the dents on my car! Check out Bill Brandon's alibi the night his sister was murdered! You think it was a coincidence that Jimmy broke into *my* house when I was working on a story about Bill?"

"We're going to check it all out, Beth," Tony said. "We aren't doubting you. We're just doing our job. Now, do you think Nick is up to placing all those kids when we arrest Brandon and take the rest of his staff in for questioning?"

"He's been ready."

"None of us may get any sleep tonight," Larry said.

Tony reached for the phone. "I'll call Sharon and cancel our date tonight."

"Yeah, I'd better call Melissa, too. Beth, if I were you, I'd wait at Lynda's until you hear from us. It's safe there. We can follow you over right now."

"All right," she said. "But you'll call me when you've got him?"

"Sure thing. Come on, Tony, we've got to get all this done so we can catch Judge Wyatt to get a warrant before he leaves for the day."

Tony shrugged on his blazer to conceal his gun. "He's the presiding judge in town," he told her. "This is worth going straight to the top."

As they hurried out ahead of her, she felt a huge weight drop from her shoulders. At last, her case was in good hands.

28

NICK KNEW ALL of the emergency room doctors and nurses, because he was called here frequently when injuries to youngsters suggested the possibility of child abuse. As soon as he'd brought Tracy in and told them how he'd found her, they'd rushed her back, intent on finding the reason for her illness. She was in good hands.

While he waited, he went to the pay phone and tried to call Beth. Her machine answered, so he left a message, hung up, and dialed his own number. Beth had left a message that she had gotten approval from the paper, that the story would be out tomorrow, and that she was giving it to the police so they could arrest Bill Brandon tonight.

He grinned and hung up, then dropped into a chair. Part of him wanted to relax, but the other part knew that he needed to be at the office finding qualified foster parents to stay with the kids tonight. He had already thought this through and decided that, instead of scattering them all over the state in private homes, it would be better, at least for the next few days, to get couples to come replace SCCH's employees so the children could stay where they were. That would be less traumatic for the kids, and less work for Sheila and him.

The emergency room physician, a guy he'd played racquetball with a few times, came out and scanned the faces in the waiting room, spotted Nick, and came to take the chair at right angles to his.

"So what is it?" Nick asked. "Drugs?"

"Actually, no. No drugs in her bloodstream at all. What your friend has is probably the worst case of double pneumonia I've ever seen."

"Pneumonia? This time of year?"

"Yeah. She's in bad shape, Nick. She may not pull through. We're admitting her into intensive care right now. Can you fill out the paperwork? Give us her insurance company, that sort of thing?"

He shook his head. "I don't know anything about her other than her name. And I seriously doubt that she has insurance. Judging from the place she lives, I'd say she's indigent. That's why I brought her here."

It was a charity hospital, so he had known that they wouldn't turn her away.

"All right. We'll take care of things," the doctor said. "Do you know if she has any next of kin?"

He thought of Jimmy and Lisa. "She has two kids that were taken away from her. They're seven and ten."

"Any adults?"

"I couldn't tell you."

The doctor suddenly looked very tired. "I'll level with you, Nick. If you hadn't brought her in here when you did, that girl wouldn't have lasted through the night. I hate to see a person that near death, without a person in the world who cares about her."

Nick rubbed his weary eyes. "Yeah, me too."

The doctor slapped his knee and got up. "We've got her on an IV, and we're starting a round of serious antibiotics. ICU doesn't allow nonfamily members to visit, but I'll pull some strings if you want to come back and see her tonight."

He nodded. "Yeah, I'll do that."

"Thanks for bringing her in, man."

Nick checked his watch as he headed out of the emergency room. He wondered if Bill Brandon had been arrested yet—and if Beth was safe.

Walking out into the night, he looked up at the stars spread by the millions across the sky like a paint-spattered canopy. God had been with him today. "Thank you," he whispered, grateful that the Holy Spirit had prompted him to find Tracy, just in the nick of time. There must have been a reason.

It wasn't all hopeless. There was a plan. There were times when Nick *did* act as an angel to a dying world. That realization gave him the energy to keep going tonight.

And he knew he wasn't working alone.

29

"I CAN'T GIVE you a warrant for Bill Brandon's arrest." Judge Wyatt said the words with such finality as he packed his briefcase that Tony and Larry only stared at him.

"Excuse me, Judge, but did you say you *can't?*" Tony asked.

"No, I can't! Not on such outlandish charges with absolutely nothing to support them."

Larry touched Tony's arm to quiet him, and tried again. "Judge, maybe we didn't make ourselves clear. There's the account given by the boy from the home who was caught breaking into this reporter's house. We just talked to him ourselves. The reporter has another source who used to live in Brandon's home, who corroborated that story. And Marlene Brandon, Bill Brandon's sister, was murdered right after she talked to the reporter. We've been in touch with the Tampa PD, and the only ones backing up Brandon's alibi are his employees, who could also be involved."

"I read the article, gentlemen," the elderly judge said. "But I'm not issuing a warrant for anybody's arrest based on some trumped-up charges by a newspaper that won't print anything unless it's painted yellow!"

"Your honor," Tony tried, hoping a little more respect might calm things a bit, "this isn't yellow journalism. This article matches the facts we do have. We have a lot of unexplained break-ins. Kids have been seen in some of the areas before or after a crime was committed. We have small unidentifiable fingerprints at the scene of some of these crimes. We didn't pursue that angle very hard in our previous investigations of the robberies because it seemed so far-fetched. But if this is a professional crime ring—"

"Then where are they keeping the stolen goods?" the judge demanded. "Where are they selling it? Have you gotten down to that, yet?"

"Well, no, not yet. But—"

"Then how do you expect me to give you a warrant for this man's arrest? This is pretty shoddy police work, gentlemen. And I'm not going to wind up with egg on my face when it comes out that a decent, upstanding citizen who provides a good home to so many children was wrongly arrested because of some cockamamie story by an overzealous reporter trying to make a name for herself! Until you come up with something I can see, something other than a kid with a strong imagination who's trying to get himself out of trouble, don't waste my time with this again."

"Judge, you can't be serious—"

"Good-bye, detectives," he said, grabbing up his briefcase and ushering them out. "I have a meeting in twenty minutes, and I don't intend to be late."

"Judge Wyatt, you're acting irresponsibly here!" Tony cried.

The judge swung around. "What did you say?"

Tony's face was red. "I said, you're acting irresponsibly. Children's lives are at stake, for Pete's sake."

"If you don't get off these premises in the next three seconds, detectives, I'll call my bailiff and have you thrown into jail yourselves."

Tony and Larry stood there, stunned, as the judge headed out of the office without another word.

"Great going," Larry bit out. "He's right. We shouldn't have been in such a hurry. We should have gotten more evidence before we came here."

"Then let's go get it now," Tony said. "Time is running out for those kids."

30

BILL BRANDON THANKED his source for the tip, hung up his phone, and stared down at his desk for a moment. So the article was scheduled to come out in tomorrow's newspaper. Beth Sullivan—alias Beth Wright, he thought with amusement—actually thought she was going to expose him. But she was so wrong.

He picked up the phone again and dialed the extension for Cottage B. One of the children answered. "Put Stella on the phone," he ordered. He waited a few seconds, then the housemother answered.

"Stella, send the team over for me, pronto. We have a job to do. Oh, and include Lisa Westin."

He went to the closet and pulled the rolled-up blueprints off the top shelf. There was one for City Hall, one for the Police Station, one for the courthouse, one for the St. Clair First National Bank . . . He pulled them out one by one, until he came to the one for the building housing the *St. Clair News.* He put the others back carefully, then went to his desk and opened the blueprint, spreading it out across his desk.

There it was: all of the rooms at the *St. Clair News,* carefully labeled with their purposes and the machinery housed there. His sources were nothing if not thorough.

A knock sounded on the door, and he called, "Come in."

Brad, an eleven-year-old he'd been grooming for the last four years, opened the door. "Bill, you called for us?"

"Yeah, guys, come on in."

Seven boys and four girls, ranging in age from eight to fifteen, filed in quietly and found places around the room. Tailing the group was little Lisa Westin, her big, green eyes looking frightened and apprehensive as she stepped into his office.

"What's she doing here?" Brad asked with contempt. "She's too little."

"She's taking Jimmy's place," Bill explained.

"Any word on Jimmy?" Brad asked.

"No. And things don't look good for him."

Bill knew that would give them all images of the child rotting in a jail cell. Enough incentive to keep them from messing things up.

He glanced at Lisa and saw that those big eyes were full of tears. "Lisa's already done one job for me, and she did such a good job that I thought I'd reward her by giving her a little more responsibility."

She didn't look all that proud.

"And she knows that if she botches anything up, Jimmy will be in even worse shape than he is now. You all know I can get to him if I have a point to make. There's not a lock made, even in a jail cell, that I can't open. You know that if you mess up, Lisa, that Jimmy will pay for it, don't you? That's how it works."

She swallowed and nodded her head.

He turned his attention back to the others. "It's come to my attention, people, that there's supposed to be a newspaper article coming out about us in the paper tomorrow. It will point fingers at each of you, exposing you as thieves, and will probably result in the police arresting all of you before daylight."

There was a collective gasp all over the room.

"Bill, what are we gonna do?"

"I don't want to go to jail!"

"Can't you tell them we're not thieves?"

Bill sat back and shrugged. "Wouldn't do any good. They have proof. Some of you have been seen, but that's not the worst of it. Jimmy Westin has turned state's evidence."

"What's that?" Brad asked.

"He's told them everything he knows about our operation."

"No! He wouldn't."

"Au contraire." He chuckled in his sinister way, and met the eyes of each individual kid

around the room. Satisfied that he had put sufficient fear in them to manipulate them into doing anything, he smiled. "But don't worry. Bill is going to take care of you. Doesn't he always?"

A few of them nodded.

"I've got a plan. But it's going to require a lot of hard work and a few risks. Somebody might even have to get hurt. But sometimes sacrifices have to be made. As the Good Book says, 'Greater courage hath no man, than to lay down a life for his cause.'"

The children all gazed somberly at him. He had them right where he wanted them.

"Oh, don't worry. I'm not asking any of *you* to lay down your lives. I just want that kind of commitment to this project—that you would if it came to it, which it won't. No, it's not your lives that'll be in danger. But the people in the building . . . well, some things are just in God's hands."

He looked down at the blueprint. "This, my friends, is the blueprint for the newspaper offices. In this big room, here at the back, is the printing press that puts out every copy of the newspaper that will be distributed all over town the first thing in the morning. Your job, should you decide to accept it," he said, drawing on the *Mission Impossible* theme, even though he knew they didn't have the option of refusing it, "is to stop the presses. Literally. That way, the story won't come out, and you won't be arrested."

Some of the kids let out huge breaths of relief, and Bill smiled and said, "I told you I'd take care of things, didn't I? Now, come on over here and get around the desk, so I can show each of you what your job will be. We've still got a few hours before we need to go. That gives us plenty of time to plan every move."

31

THE WAITING ROOM for the family members of those in the Intensive Care Unit was full of rumpled, tired people with lines on their faces and worry in their eyes. Beth followed Nick past the reception desk, where a woman stood consoling a family whose loved one had just been in a car accident. On the desk were two stacks of towels and a sign that said that toilet articles were available if anyone needed them.

"They take showers up here?" Beth asked quietly.

"Yeah. Many of these people are here twenty-four hours a day. They're afraid to leave."

"But I thought visiting hours were only thirty minutes every four hours."

"Right. They sit by the bedside for thirty minutes, then come back to the waiting room and worry for four hours until the next visit."

"Seems cruel."

"Maybe it is. But those short visiting times are usually in the best interest of the patients. They need quiet."

He led her into the huge room lined with vinyl recliners and chairs. Families had nested in certain areas of the room, surrounded by books and little bags with their belongings, Walkmans, and canned drinks. It was easy to distinguish the family members from occasional visitors. They looked more worn, more stressed, more near the breaking point. In one corner, a woman crocheted an afghan furiously, and already it was big enough to cover her legs. Beth wondered when she'd started it. Across the room, someone else worked on a laptop, and next to her, a red-eyed teenaged girl did cross-stitch as if her life depended on getting every stitch exactly in line.

The five telephones on the wall rang constantly, and they were always answered by one of those nearby. Then they would call out, "Smith family" or "Jackson family," and someone would rush to answer it.

"It's like a little community up here," Beth said.

"Yeah. My dad was in ICU for three weeks before he died. I didn't leave the unit except for meals. I ate those downstairs, and only if I had to. A lot of times, churches brought sandwiches and stuff right here to the waiting room."

"But what's the point in staying? I mean, if you can't visit them . . ."

"It's the fear that something will go wrong. That the doctor will need you to help make a decision. Even the irrational fear that if you leave, if you're not there hanging on, they'll slip away."

"I can't imagine being sick and having someone waiting out here that diligently for me."

"What about your mother?" he asked.

"She's dead." The words came so matter-of-factly that she feared Nick would think she was cold. The truth was, if Beth's mother were alive, she wouldn't have waited in the ICU waiting room for Beth anyway. The deep sadness of that fact washed over her. She was really no different than Tracy Westin, lying in there so sick with no one out here in this room, representing her and praying for her, refusing to leave because they had to stay and fight with her.

"I'm sorry."

She didn't say anything, but watched the dynamics of a family in the corner. "Poor Tracy."

Nick looked at her. "What do you mean?"

"She's all alone."

"We're here."

"Yeah, but she doesn't know us. We don't love her."

"Yes, we do. I love her because I'm a Christian. I'm ordered to love her."

Beth smiled grimly at the irony. She hadn't had much experience with love, but she knew *that* was wrong. "Love isn't something you can be ordered to do, Nick. You have to feel something."

"Love is first something you do, Beth," Nick said. "The feelings are important, yes, but love is a verb, not a noun. We're here to love her because no one else is."

Well, there was something in that. She sat quietly for a moment, looking around the room at all the people so steeped in the act of loving. She wondered what it would be like to have people like that caring for her, waiting hours to see her, not willing to leave for fear that she might need them. She couldn't even fathom it.

The crackle of the intercom quieted the room, and a voice said, "ICU visitation will begin now. The following families may go back: Anderson, Aldredge, Burton . . ." Eventually, they came to the name Westin, and Beth and Nick got up and followed the stream of visitors through the double doors into ICU. As he had promised, the doctor had bent the rules to allow Nick and Beth to visit Tracy.

There were no doorways in ICU, only three-sided rooms open to the nursing station so that the nurses could see and hear the patients at all times. Tracy lay on her bed, sitting up at a forty-five degree angle, with an IV in her hand and an oxygen mask on her face. Several cords ran out from under her sheet and hooked to monitors that kept close watch on her vital signs.

She looked so tiny, so emaciated. Beth hesitated at the foot of the bed, feeling like an intruder in this woman's private hell.

Nick went to her bedside and leaned over her. He looked carefully at her face to see if she was sleeping, but her eyes were half opened. "Tracy? Can you hear me?"

"Don't wake her up," Beth said softly.

"I don't think she's asleep," he said. "Tracy, I'm Nick. The one who found you and brought you here."

She looked up then, and met his eyes. "Thank you," she whispered.

"No problem. They're going to do everything they can for you here. Did they tell you you have double pneumonia? You're in ICU so they can watch you real closely."

She closed her eyes.

Nick looked at Beth, not sure what to do. "My friend here, Beth, knows your son. We thought—"

Her eyes fluttered back open, and she tried to rise up. "Jimmy?" she asked weakly.

"Yes," Beth said, stepping forward. "He's a great kid."

Weakly, she dropped back down. "Haven't seen him in three years. I have a little girl—"

"Lisa?" Nick asked.

Her eyes grew rounder. "You know Lisa?"

"Yes, Tracy. That's why I was coming to see you today. I'm a social worker, and I've taken an interest in your kids."

Tears began to roll down her face. "Are they all right?"

"They're good," he said. "Healthy, smart . . ."

Her face contorted in anguish, and she asked, "Do they hate me?"

Nick looked up at Beth, not sure how to answer that. Beth felt her own eyes filling, which rarely happened. She hated herself when she cried. "I don't think they hate you," she whispered.

"I left them, you know . . ." Her voice broke off, and she closed her eyes and covered her face with a scrawny hand that had the IV needle taped in place. "You should have just let me die."

Something about the heartfelt regret touched Beth in a deep place, a place of wounds that had never fully healed. She turned away, blinking back her tears, *ordering* back her tears. When she turned back to the woman on the bed, her eyes were dry. "We don't want you to die, Tracy."

Nick shook his head. "That's right. God might need you to get well so you can help your kids understand why you did it."

"*I* don't understand why," she said.

Nick leaned closer. "Tracy, are you still addicted?"

"No. Been through treatment . . . three times. Always fell back. But this last time . . . clean for two months."

"Do you work? Do you have a job?"

"No."

"Are you on welfare?"

"No. I was living with my husband . . ."

He looked up at Beth, surprised. "Husband? You're married?"

"Six months. Doomed."

"Where is your husband now?"

"Who knows? Gone. He's worse off than I was."

"Do you mean he was sick, too?"

"He's a junkie." She wiped her tear-streaked face with the hand her IV was taped to. "When I got sick, he took off. Couldn't stand to hear me hacking all the time."

"Why didn't you go to the doctor?"

"No money."

"But you could have gone to the health department."

"Too weak."

"You didn't have anyone to take you? No one?"

"No . . . no one."

The nurse came into the room and told them their visiting time was up, and Nick touched Tracy's hand. "Tracy, we have to go now, but we'll be back. You get better, okay? We're praying for you."

She nodded mutely, her face contorted with sorrow and regret.

As they stepped out into the night, Beth felt anguish gaining on her again, sneaking closer to her breaking point, pulling her under. Nick seemed to sense it. He put his arm across her shoulders and said, "Let's not go to the car just yet."

When she didn't protest, he led her down the cobblestone walkway that led through the hospital's courtyard and around the little pond. Moonlight flickered on the surface of the water, lending a sense of peace and beauty to the world that had so much ugly darkness.

"I think she's remorseful," he said. "I don't always see that."

Beth couldn't answer.

"I just hope she lives. Maybe through some miracle we could reunite the kids with her."

"Don't you think you're jumping the gun a little?" Beth asked quietly.

He shrugged. "Maybe. I guess I'm just a believer in miracles."

Beth reached a bench, sank down, and pulled her feet up to hug her knees. "I believe in miracles, too, Nick. But I've learned that you can't custom order them."

Quiet settled between them as he sat down next to her, watching her face. She couldn't look at him, for those tears were slipping up on her again, threatening her. She looked out over the water, trying to sort out the storm of emotions whirling through her mind. Anger, rage, sorrow, loneliness, rejection, frustration, fear . . .

"We sure have screwed things up, haven't we?"

"Who?" she asked.

"Us. The human race. God gave us families, such a wonderful gift, and we break them into tiny pieces, reject them, throw them away . . ."

"That's it," she whispered, still staring across the water. "Thrown away. That's how those kids feel. And no matter what happens to them, that feeling doesn't quite go away."

"And then there's Tracy."

"Yes. I wonder how Jimmy will feel when we tell him we found his mother."

Nick tried to imagine. "Well, he'll put on a tough-guy act. But deep down, kids love their mothers. Even kids who have been abused and rejected."

"Sometimes there are other things that cover that love so deeply that you can never get back down to it. I don't think we should let him see his mother like that. I don't think we should even tell him we've found her until she's better."

"That's true. Besides, she might die, and then he'd have to grieve for her all over again."

"Again?" she asked, finally looking at him. "I doubt he grieved for her at all. Being taken from her may have been a relief to some extent. And he was probably so hurt, so angry that she left him like that . . . So worried for Lisa . . ."

"He's still worried for Lisa. Like I said, this isn't the kind of thing God ever meant for a kid to have to worry about. Families are supposed to protect each other. Love each other. When I have kids, nothing in heaven or earth could force me to leave them. And the best thing I'll do for them is to love their mother."

A soft, gentle, wistful smile curved her lips. "I believe you could do that." She watched his face as he propped it on his hand and smiled at her. "Tell me about your family, Nick. Did you have a mother and father who loved you? Did you eat at the table at night, all together, talking about your day?"

He gave her a strange look that told her the question had been too revealing. "Yeah, I guess we did. I had four sisters and brothers, and my parents have been married forty-five years. It was a busy household. What about yours?"

Her smile faded and her eyes drifted back to the water. "My household was very busy, too," she said. "But not like yours. You might say I'm one of the pieces my family broke into."

He gazed at her for a moment, and she wondered if it was pity or disdain she saw on his face. Was he measuring her against himself, finding her flawed and scarred? Did he look at potential mates against a measuring stick of broken families and dysfunctional childhoods, as she sometimes did? She had broken a budding relationship recently when she'd discovered that the man had been raised fatherless. She had told herself that she desperately needed someone who had not suffered the battles she had as a child, someone who had more parts to him than she had to her.

Yet she knew it was a double standard, for if others measured her the same way, she would always be alone.

"I wondered where that tough edge came from," he whispered. "Is that where? From a broken family?"

She smiled. She liked that he'd seen a tough edge in her. She had cultivated it for years. "Maybe."

"I'm sorry if you had to go through pain as a child, Beth. But God works all things for good. And if you had to go through all you did to be who you are today, well, it turned out pretty good, didn't it?"

She sighed. "You don't really know who I am. Not really."

"Then show me."

It was a challenge, and she rarely backed down from challenges. Yet what he was asking was too intimate, too revealing, and she couldn't risk it. He couldn't know that she had once been one of those kids in the homes he monitored, one of the names in the files he kept stacked on his desk. He couldn't know that she had been a trained thief, a practiced liar . . .

"You don't have to show me," he said, finally, when he could see that she struggled with the challenge. "I've seen it. In the way you're fighting for these kids, risking your life, daring to make a change. Not many people would do that."

"Given the proper motivation," she said coolly, "people will do lots of things."

"Yeah, you're real tough," he said with a hint of amusement as he touched her soft, short hair. "But you know what I saw the first time you came to me to get information about the home?"

She looked reluctantly at him. "What?"

"I saw a woman who sent my heart stumbling in triple-time. A beautiful woman with those big, clear blue eyes, and that smile that made me want to sit and stare at it for hours . . . And then I heard you talk, heard how you cared for those kids, how passionate you were about this story . . ."

She smiled uneasily and looked down at her hands. Suddenly they were clammy. Suddenly, she was shaking.

"You cared the way I cared. I had cared about those kids for some time, had worried about them, and I felt a bond with you. I thought that maybe God had crossed our paths for a reason."

She looked at him curiously then. "You see God working in everything, don't you? Nothing's accidental. Nothing's left to chance."

"Absolutely nothing. Don't you believe that?"

"I don't know," she said honestly. "I don't think God's working in my life yet. I haven't done enough. Things are still too off balance."

"What do you mean 'off balance'?"

"You know. I'm sort of behind on this religion thing. I got a late start. I have a lot of work to do before I can expect anything from God. But I'm willing to do what it takes."

"It doesn't take work, Beth. It just takes surrender. Repentance. You just have to give all of yourself to Christ."

"I'm not sure he wants even *some* of me," she said with a self-deprecating smile.

"Trust me. He wants all of you. And you don't have to wait until your good deeds outweigh your bad ones. Look at the thief on the cross."

She looked up at him, stricken. Why had he chosen that example? Did he suspect her past? "What about him?" she asked.

"He told Jesus he believed in him. To remember him when he came into his kingdom. Did Jesus tell him to clean up his act and work hard?"

"No."

"What did he say?"

Her Bible knowledge was shaky, but she did remember that. "He said, 'Today you shall be with me in Paradise.'"

"That's right. He took him just like he was, hanging on a cross for crimes he *had* committed, while Jesus hung there for no crime at all. But that man's sins were transferred to Jesus, and when that thief got to heaven, he was clean. Not because of anything he had done, but because he believed in his heart."

Beth sighed. She had never compared herself to the thief on the cross, not until now. But she'd heard about this concept of *grace* before—they always sang and preached about it at church. Somehow, she doubted that Nick or any of them had it right. There had to be more. It had to be tied into behavior, or none of it made any sense. She couldn't believe that, after everything she'd done, God could just accept her, forgive her, welcome her into heaven—at least not without her first having to *do* something to make up for all of those sins, and that something should be substantial. Because if that was true, if God just accepted and forgave us no matter what we'd done, then . . .

Well, then, someone like Bill Brandon—who professed to believe in Christ but used Scripture for his own evils, and who had ruined the lives of hundreds of children just as he had tried to ruin hers—could be readily accepted into heaven if he made a deathbed conversion.

And that could *never* be true.

"Tell me something, Beth," Nick said. "Look ahead five years, ten years, whatever, and tell me, if you could be everything you think God wants you to be, what will you be doing? Who will you be?"

She shifted on the bench and propped her elbow on the back. "Maybe I'll be married to a wonderful man I don't deserve. And I'll have babies . . ." That smile grew across her face. "Lots of babies. And my husband will love them, and never hurt them, and I'll live my life the way a mother should, so that they'll always trust me and count on me, so that no one will ever be able to take them away."

His smile faded as she spoke, and she realized she had said too much. He was watching her with misty eyes now, hanging on every word.

But she couldn't help going on in a strange, wistful voice. "And that family will be so great. The whole world can fall apart around us, but we'll be so strong, so tightly knit, that nothing will ever break us."

"'What God has joined together let no man put asunder.'"

"Yes!" she said. "I know exactly what that means."

"Do you believe that family you described is the plan God has for you? In other words, that he has good plans for you instead of calamity?"

"Yes," she whispered. "But sometimes we bring calamity on ourselves. Sometimes other people bring it on us." She shrugged. "On the other hand, he may plan for me to be alone. Some people are supposed to be single. Some people never find the right mate."

"That thought has run through my mind a few times, too," he admitted. "But I'd prefer to think that there's a terrific family that's already a snapshot in God's mind, and that I'm standing at the head of it."

"That would be a beautiful snapshot," she said. "Send me a wallet size of it, will you?"

His smile was eloquent, but she couldn't decipher what it could mean. She was too busy wishing she could be in that snapshot.

He touched her face, feather stroking it with gentle fingertips, testing her, as if he thought she might pull away. She didn't. Their eyes met in a startling moment of awareness, and she unconsciously wet her lips.

Slowly, his face moved closer to hers, and those fingertips moved into her hair and pulled her toward him. His lips brushed hers, gently, sweetly, and she felt her heart bursting into a Fourth-of-July display as their kiss deepened.

For a moment, all time was suspended, all tragedy was held at bay, all calamity was delayed. For a moment, she saw herself in that snapshot, standing under his arm with a serene smile on her face, surrounded by children that looked like him.

The joy of that hope brought real tears to her eyes, tears that she didn't try to blink back.

He broke the kiss and pressed his forehead into hers. He wiped one of her tears away with his thumb. For a moment, neither of them could speak.

His mouth seemed engaged in the same emotional struggle as he finally tried to find words. "You're a beautiful woman, Beth. Do you know that?"

She swallowed.

"A very beautiful woman."

He pulled her into his arms then, and held her while her tough facade crumbled and she melted into tears. She didn't remember ever being held like that, not in her life, and as she reveled in that warmth, she feared the ending of it.

Finally, he let her go and stood up, taking her hand. "We'd better go. Tomorrow's going to be a big day."

"Yeah," she whispered. "I guess I do need to get home."

"I'm not taking you home," he said. "It's too dangerous. I'm taking you back to Lynda's."

"But I can't impose on her that way."

"She insisted when we left," he said. "She took me aside and made me promise not to let you go home tonight. She even invited your puppy. Besides, I want to say good night to Jimmy."

"All right, then," she whispered, leaning into him as he slid his arm around her shoulders. "If I can go by and get Dodger."

"Sure. No problem."

Smiling gently, she walked with him to his car.

32

THE PARKING LOT at the *St. Clair News* was never empty, and tonight was no exception. At least a dozen cars were parked in scattered spaces, testifying to the fact that people were in the building, working to get out the next morning's edition of the paper.

Bill Brandon had timed things just right. Earlier that day, he had phoned the paper and spoken to a building maintenance supervisor. He'd told him that he was teaching a summer class in journalism for the University of Florida—Clearwater Campus's "College for Kids" program, and that he would like to bring a group on a field trip to tour the paper. But he wanted them to see the paper actually being printed.

That was impossible, the supervisor had told him. The paper was printed after midnight, and he doubted that any children's parents would be willing to send their children on a field trip at that hour. Bill had sighed and agreed.

But by the time he got off the phone, he knew exactly where in the building the paper was printed, and what time would be best to strike. Then he'd called one of his associates, who had much to lose if the article was printed and who had agreed to help. Since his associate was a prominent member of St. Clair's government, he would show up at the paper to complain about a political editorial that had been done the week before. Before he left, he would unlock two or three windows, so that later, the kids could get in. He had called back shortly after that with the location of the windows.

The children were quiet as he drove them through the parking lot flanking the building. He pointed down a hill toward a basement door with a light on, and said, "There. You see? That's the area you want to get into. But the windows are unlocked on the other side of the building, second floor. You'll have to go through the building to the right place." He drove around until the other side was in view. Lights glowed on that side of the building, as well, but not in the area where they would break in.

"Take the ladder and go in. Remember, quiet as mice, like I taught you. Space far enough apart that if one of you is seen, everyone else won't be given away. Now, what did I tell you to say if anyone sees you?"

Brad was the first to speak up. "I'm John's boy. He brought me to work with him tonight."

"What if nobody named John works here?" one of them asked.

"Somebody named John works everywhere," Bill said. "There are people scattered all over the building, so they'll accept that without thinking about it. Now stay in the dark places, and follow the route that I gave you. Everybody got their backpacks loaded?"

The team that consisted of four rough-looking boys, and three girls, including Lisa, all clothed in black, was ready.

"Remember," Bill said as they filed out of the van. "If you botch this up, you'll go to jail tomorrow. When that article comes out—"

"We won't botch it up, Bill," one of the kids said.

"All right. Now once you've done what you came to do, you take off through that door and don't waste any time. I'll be waiting."

The kids filed out, one by one, adjusting their backpacks on their shoulders. Three of the boys unloaded the ladder that was tied to the top of the van, the ladder they would leave behind, and carried it quickly to the side of the building where the three windows on the second floor had been unlocked.

They set the ladder under the window, and two of the girls held it while Brad scurried up it and slid the window up. No one said a word as Brad stepped through. Lisa was next. She climbed the ladder carefully, not fast enough, she was sure, but she was terrified of falling, and the weight of the load on her back made it more difficult to keep her balance. She reached the window and slid under. Brad helped her down without a word. It was the quietest she'd ever seen him.

She watched as he took off through the building, exactly the direction Bill had drilled them on. She waited and helped Kevin in, then took off herself, leaving him behind to help the one behind him.

A sense of importance filled her as she took off through the dark hallway to the exit sign that was her first marker. She quietly went through the door, took the stairs down, and came out on the first floor. She saw Brad a little ahead of her, hurrying past lit offices with people working at computers, past a huge room with dozens of cluttered desks, but only two or three people working. She could hear something clicking in there, something like a fast typewriter or printer. Maybe the noise would keep the workers from hearing them.

She looked behind her and saw Kevin gaining on her. She ducked past the door and to the next exit door, and headed down to the basement.

She was big enough to do this, she thought with satisfaction. Wouldn't Bill be proud of her, that she'd taken directions so carefully and hadn't messed it up?

She heard the sound of machines running as she came out of the stairwell into the basement. It was so loud that no one was ever going to hear them. She saw Brad looking around for anyone nearby.

There were two men in one of the rooms, their skin shiny with sweat as they operated the machines. It was hot down here, even though there was air conditioning and the fans overhead hummed. The machines put out a lot of heat. But she knew that it was about to get hotter.

Brad motioned for her to follow him, and she looked behind her and gave the same gesture to the person following her. He pointed to the room where the men were. "Somebody has to go in there," he said, his voice muffled by the drone of the machinery.

"No! They'll see us. We'll get caught," one of the children protested.

"If we don't do it, we're only half doing the job, and the article will come out."

"Send Lisa. She's the littlest. They won't see her."

Lisa's eyes widened. "I'm not going."

"Yes, you are," Brad said. "If you don't, I'll tell Bill. Now go. Head under the machine, and douse it good."

She got tears in her eyes as one of the kids unzipped her backpack and pulled the hose with the trigger spray nozzle out. "We'll be in here. Now hurry."

Lisa wanted to burst into tears, but she knew that if she did, she would be punished. She had to get the job done. It's what Jimmy would have done.

Biting her lip, she went to the edge of the door and peered around the doorway. She could see the sweating men doing something with the gadgets on the machine as the pages of the paper were spat out one by one. The room smelled of sweat, mildew, ink, and paper.

She ducked out of their sight behind the machinery and began to spray the inner workings of the machine, the floor around it, and the paper behind her against the wall awaiting its turn on the printer.

She heard voices. The men were talking to each other, but she couldn't hear what they were saying. Did they smell the gas, or was the artificial wind created by the fan pushing the smell down? Would it blow the fire out as soon as it got started?

She emptied the container of gas on her back, concentrating only on that one side of the machine, since she couldn't get to the other side without the men seeing her. Then she scurried back out of the room.

The others had been busily emptying their own containers, and she smelled the acrid fumes of gasoline soaked into curtains, carpet, dripping on the machinery in every room along the darkened hallway. Brad motioned for them to follow him, and they all ran down the hall to the door through which they would escape, the last person trailing a line of gasoline behind him.

When they reached the outside door, the others sprinted toward the van. But Brad grabbed Lisa and stopped her. "You're not finished," he whispered.

"What?" she asked.

"You get to light the match," he said. "It's your initiation. Bill said."

She didn't know what an initiation was, but she didn't object to it. She took the match from his hand, struck it against the gritty side of the matchbox, and smiled at the flame dancing on the end of the matchstick.

"Throw it in, stupid!" he whispered harshly. "Don't just stand there with it."

She threw the match down in the puddle of gasoline and watched it billow into flames. She caught her breath and jumped back as the fire raced down the hall. Brad grabbed her hand and began to pull her away from the door as the rooms they had doused went up in a quiet conflagration.

Lisa felt a sudden rush of fear. Looking back at the building as Brad pulled her along, she cried, "Those men! Brad, those men were in there!"

"They'll get out," he said. "Everybody will get out as soon as the fire alarm goes off. Now hurry!"

The van was moving as they reached it, and Brad forced Lisa into it, then jumped into it himself and closed the door just as they heard the fire alarm ring out.

Lisa rolled on the van floor, unable to find her footing, as the van accelerated out of the parking lot. But she managed to claw her way up to a window and peer out in time to see people fleeing from the burning building.

33

THE TRUCKS THAT delivered Express Mail for the St. Clair area were lined up against the back of the post office, their rear doors open as graveyard shift postal workers loaded the next day's deliveries. On top of one of the stacks was the package Lisa had delivered earlier that day. The one addressed to Beth Wright, with the return address of Marlene Brandon.

As the sky began to take on the rose tints of dawn, one of the postal workers stopped for a moment to rest. He wiped his sweating brow and opened his thermos for some lukewarm coffee. "Hey, Alice," he called to the woman sitting at the front desk, "has the paper come yet?"

"Nope. Sorry. Looks like the delivery boy slept late today."

The man brooded as he slurped his coffee. Oh, well. He could always read one of the magazines before it got loaded onto a truck for delivery. He grabbed one out of a stack of mail, propped his feet up, and began to flip through.

34

ALL THAT NIGHT, Beth lay awake in Lynda's guest room, anticipating the arrival of the *St. Clair News* on the front steps of a hundred thousand readers.

She dressed as the first hints of morning began to peek through her window, put her leash on Dodger, and tiptoed past Lynda's room, then past the room where Jimmy slept, sprawled on top of his bedcovers. She went through the living room and kitchen and quietly slipped out the door into the early morning mist. She put Dodger down and walked him around to the front of the house. While he sniffed around in the bushes, she sat on the front porch steps, watching for the paperboy.

A tremendous sense of peace about what had happened with Nick last night enveloped her—only to be offset by a sense of dread about Bill Brandon.

She wondered if Bill had been arrested last night, if they'd found a way to make it stick so that he wouldn't be able to simply talk his way out of jail.

As the warm wind whipped through her hair, she pulled her feet up onto the top step of the porch. The sky was gray, but a faint pink hue crept up over the trees across the street. Maybe what happened today would wash away the sorrow and pain from the past.

Her eyes strayed up the street, where the paperboy should soon appear. She wished he would hurry.

At the end of the street she spotted a jogger dressed in black running shorts and a white tank top. She started to stand up and go inside, for she didn't trust strangers, especially not on this isolated street where no one ever came unless they were invited. And then she saw that the man was Jake.

He waved as he reached the halfway point on the block, then slowed his jog and walked the rest of the way, cooling down. When he reached the driveway, he picked up the towel he'd left on the trunk of his car, threw it around his neck, and came toward her.

"You're up awfully early," he said, his breath still coming hard. He bent down to pet Dodger, who wagged his tail stub and slobbered all over him.

"So are you. I was just waiting for the paperboy. I didn't know you jogged."

"Yeah, for about the last month or so. I'm trying to get in shape for my medical."

"Your what?"

"My medical. I have to get a medical release to get my pilot's license back. This afternoon is the moment of truth."

"Well, that shouldn't be a problem, should it?"

"No, ordinarily it wouldn't." He sat down on the steps next to her and rubbed the sweat from his face. "But this false eye could play against me, so I'm trying to overcompensate with the rest. If I can prove I'm more fit than most people, they might overlook the eye."

Beth narrowed her eyes and stared at him. "I didn't know you had a false eye, Jake. Which one?"

He chuckled. "If you can't tell, I'm not going to."

"Your eyes look just alike. And they move together. I didn't know false eyes could do that."

"They look just like ordinary eyes, but that's not what the licensing board cares about. They want to make sure that I can *see* like I'm supposed to. Half of my peripheral vision is gone now, so I can't fly for the commercial airline I used to fly for. They have pretty high standards. But if I can get my license back, I could buy a small plane and start a chartering service or something."

"That's great, Jake. They'll give it to you, won't they?"

"I think so. I'm just a little nervous. A lot is riding on this."

Thankful for the diversion, she asked, "Like what?"

He smiled and looked off in the direction from which he had just jogged. "Like . . . my relationship with Lynda."

"I thought that was pretty solid."

"It is. But I'd like for it to move forward. Have a little more permanency. I never thought I'd say this, but I don't want Lynda to just be my lady. I want her to be my wife."

Beth grinned. "Does she know this?"

"I'm sure she suspects it. But I haven't said it, straight out. Not when I have so little to offer her."

"Lynda doesn't need much."

"No, but she deserves everything." He sat down next to her on the steps. "I've been out of work and living on savings and odd jobs since the accident. I want to have an income, and be contributing something, before I ask her to marry me."

"That's admirable," Beth said. "I hope somebody will care about me like that one day."

"You're still young. No hurry."

"Yeah," she said. "And there's a lot of unfinished business I have to take care of before then." Her eyes strayed back to the end of the street. Still no paperboy.

"Unfinished business?"

"Yeah. This article is just part of it."

"Well, it should be here soon. But come to think of it, I usually see the paperboy when I'm jogging, and I didn't see him today. He must be running late. Tell you what. I'll go shower, then if it still hasn't come, I'll go pick up one at the closest newsstand. I'm anxious to see it, too." He got up and threw the towel back around his neck.

She smiled and watched him head back around the house and into the garage apartment. She wondered if Lynda had any idea how blessed she was to have a man like that in love with her.

After watching for the paperboy for a few more minutes, she decided not to wait any longer. She went back into the house and got her purse. Lynda was coming up the hall in her robe. "Beth, where are you going so early?"

"To try to find a newspaper," she said. "The paperboy is late. I'm just really anxious to see the article. There's a truck stop near my house that is always one of the earliest to get a paper. I'll go there and see if I can get one. I'll call you from home. Thanks for letting me stay here last night, okay? And tell Jimmy I'll be back to see him this afternoon."

"Okay. He'll be fine."

"Oh, and tell Jake that I'm sorry I couldn't wait."

Beth carried Dodger out to her car as that sense of uneasiness crept over her again. After she'd left Lynda's isolated street, she scanned the driveways for the rolled-up newspapers that always came with the morning. She saw none. She grabbed her car phone and dialed the number of the newspaper, planning to ask someone in circulation if there had been some delay in getting the papers out that morning.

A discordant tone came on instead of the ring, and an operator's recorded voice said that the number was temporarily out of order.

She cut the phone off, frowning, and wove her way through the neighborhood, neat little houses all lined up with no newspapers in the driveways.

Something is wrong.

She dialed the number of the police station and told the sergeant who answered the phone who she was. "I'm checking to see if Bill Brandon was arrested last night. Larry Millsaps and Tony Danks were on the case."

The sergeant checked his records, then came back to the phone. "No, I don't show an arrest made last night for a Brandon."

She closed her eyes. "All right, thanks."

She almost ran a red light, then slammed on her brakes and rubbed her forehead, trying to ease a rapidly escalating headache. What was going on? The telephone at the newspaper out of order, the arrest never carried out—

She whipped a quick U-turn at the intersection and headed back in the direction of the newspaper office.

It took her a few minutes to get to the street on which the *St. Clair News* was housed. And then she saw why the phone was out of order. The building was in shambles, half of it burned to the ground, and the other half, though still standing, only a monument of crumbling brick and slanted beams, with smoke-scalded ceilings and walls, and computer equipment and file cabinets smashed where the building had collapsed on one side.

She sat stunned, staring through her windshield at the smoldering ashes.

She hadn't realized anyone was coming toward her until a police officer knocked on her window.

"Ma'am, you'll have to move your car."

She rolled the window down. "I work here," she said. "What happened?"

"There was a fire last night," he said, as if that wasn't obvious.

"No, I mean, how did it start?"

"We suspect arson, but we're still investigating. Now, if you don't mind moving your car—"

"But the paper! The paper got out this morning, didn't it? The paper will still be delivered!"

"I don't think there's going to be an edition today, ma'am. Most of the machinery is toast."

She sat back hard on her seat and covered her mouth. The article wasn't coming out. Not today. A sense of injustice crashed over her. Familiar injustice. Predictable injustice.

"When did this happen? Did anyone see who started it?"

"No, no one saw anything. Two men who were right in the area where the fire was the most concentrated were killed."

"Killed? Oh, no! Who?"

He checked his clipboard, then asked her, "Are you asking as a member of the press, or a friend?"

"A friend!" she shouted. "Who died?"

"Off the record until we notify next of kin . . . Hank Morland and Stu Singer."

She didn't know them well, but she did know them, and now she closed her eyes and hugged herself as if she might split right down the middle and fall apart. Had her article caused someone's death? Did she have to bear that guilt now, too? She slammed her car into park, cut off the engine, and climbed out. "I need to get in touch with Larry Millsaps or Tony Danks. I need to talk to them now. Get me their home numbers, please!"

"I can't do that, ma'am. But if you have some information about who might have started this fire, you can tell me."

"Of course I know who started the fire!" she shouted. "It was Bill Brandon! You've got to tell them! Please, get in touch with them for me."

He didn't seem anxious to call in such an emotional revelation from a woman who seemed unstable, but he went to his squad car and asked the dispatcher for their home numbers.

Beth was with him when the answer was radioed back, and she bolted out of the squad car.

"Ma'am? Where are you going?"

"To call them," she said. "From my car phone."

He came to stand beside the open door as she punched out Tony's number.

He answered quickly. "Tony? This is Beth Wright."

"Yeah, Beth." His voice was gritty, as if she had awakened him. "I tried to call you last night, but you weren't home."

"What happened?" she demanded. "Why didn't you arrest him?"

"We couldn't get a warrant. Judge Wyatt was really hard-nosed about it. He said we didn't have enough evidence to arrest him."

"Not enough evidence? Are you kidding?" She looked at the building, still smoldering, and cried, "Did you show him my article?"

"I did. But he doesn't have a lot of faith in journalism. He's going to have to see more. We plan to make it our business to get him more so we can get Bill Brandon today. We're stuck with his decision because he's the presiding judge in St. Clair. There's no one higher up to go to."

"Well, if you're looking for evidence that Bill Brandon is too dangerous to be running loose, I've got it right in front of me."

"What do you mean, Beth?"

"I mean that the newspaper article is not going to come out today, Tony, because there's not going to *be* a newspaper today, because Bill Brandon burned the blasted place down last night. He killed two people in the process!"

"What?"

She was about to cry, and she fought it, hating herself for it. "He did it, Tony. You know he did. Somebody told him about the article—he's got lots of connections. So he took care of it."

"You're sure it was him?"

"He didn't sign his name, if that's what you want. He probably didn't even get within fifty feet of the building himself. He probably used his kids to do it, like he does everything. Think of that, Tony—such a dangerous thing, and the kids are so young . . ."

His pause told her she was getting too emotional, giving herself away, so she tried to rein in her emotions. "Look, you've got to arrest him before he does anything else. He stopped the presses last night, kept the article from coming out today. Now he has to get to the source of that article, and that, we both know, is me."

"You're right," he said. "Beth, stay there. Larry and I will be there in twenty minutes. Maybe we can find something to prove definitively that Bill Brandon or his kids were behind this. Something we can show Judge Wyatt."

"All right," she said. She glanced at the police officer's name tag. Lt. J.T. Mills. "Tell your friend Lt. Mills, so he'll let me stay."

"Okay. Hand him the phone."

She did, then got out of her car and took a few steps toward the building. Flashes came back to her, flashes of those late-night planning sessions with Bill and the rest of his kids, memorizing of blueprints, the endless drilling on which way they were to turn when they broke in, what they were to take, how they were to escape. She remembered the feel of her heightened senses as he'd let them out of his dark van, the urgency and adrenaline rush as they'd climbed into windows or cut glass out to unlock back doors, the smothering fear as they'd stolen through dark hallways . . .

Bill had never asked her to start a fire or take someone's life. But he was getting desperate now, and his crimes were more catastrophic. What guilt those children would live with! She hoped they didn't know they had killed someone last night.

She heard the officer close her car door and come toward her. "You can stay, ma'am, but please stay back. Danks and Millsaps will be here soon."

She nodded her head. Leaning against her car, she watched the smoke softly swirling above the rubble, like prayers that would never find their way to heaven.

35

THE TELEVISION NEWS woke Jimmy. He sat up in bed and looked around, trying to figure out where he was. Oh, yeah. Lynda Barrett's house. Today was the day that Beth's article would come out, and Bill would be arrested, and he'd see Lisa again.

He quickly got dressed, then walked barefoot into the den. Lynda and Jake were glued to the television, and neither of them saw him.

". . . suspected arson. The building went up in flames at approximately one A.M. Fire crews were on the scene within five minutes of the alarm going off, but it was too late to save the millions of dollars worth of equipment . . . or the lives of the two men who were trapped in the flames . . ."

"What building is that?" Jimmy asked, startling them. They both turned around.

"Good morning, Jimmy," Lynda said. "Did you sleep well?"

"Sure, but what building is that?"

"It's the building for the *St. Clair News.*"

"The newspaper building," Jimmy said, staring at the footage of the building engulfed in flames. He felt as if a fist had just whopped him in the stomach, knocking the wind out of him.

Bill's fist. His face reddened, and he tightened his lips to keep them from trembling with the emotion gripping him. "So he did it."

"Who?" Lynda asked.

"Bill. I told you he'd never let it come out." He knew his expression belied his matter-of-fact tone, but he couldn't seem to control it.

Lynda stepped toward him, but he backed away.

"I told you he'd never let Lisa out, either. They're never gonna hang anything on him. He's just gonna keep doing what he does, and now I've blown it and I can't go back, and Lisa's trapped there—"

"Jimmy, we don't know for sure that he was behind this. Even if he was—"

"*I* know for sure," he cut in. "*I* know!"

He ran out of the room, back to the bedroom where he had slept last night, and slammed the door. He sat down on the bed, trying to think. Somehow, he had to reach Lisa.

He went to the phone extension that sat on his bed table and put his trembling hand on it, wondering if he should risk calling her again. Then he wondered if he could risk *not* calling her.

Lisa wasn't safe.

He picked up the phone, punched in the number of Cottage B at the St. Clair Children's Home, and waited, holding his breath.

In Cottage B, Stella stood like a sentry over the children, making sure they all finished every last bite of their cereal. Some of the children woke up more easily than others, but all were awakened at the same time. Those who'd gone out with Bill last night, and had come in smelling of gasoline fumes, could barely hold their heads up, but they could have no one sleeping because that Nick fellow might pop in for an inspection again, and it wouldn't do to have children sleeping in the daylight. To keep up appearances, everyone had to be out of bed at the same time. It was good for them. It would make them tough.

The telephone rang, and Stella picked it up. "Hello?"

Click.

Annoyed, she hung it back up just in time to see Lisa's little head bobbing toward her cereal bowl, as though she might fall asleep right in the milk. "Lisa!" she shouted, startling the child. "Get a grip, would ya?"

The child propped her chin and tried to make her eyes stay open.

Frustrated, Jimmy admitted to himself that he'd never get to talk to Lisa—at least, not by phone. He closed his eyes and tried to think of a way to communicate with her. He wished she had a computer, that he could e-mail her as easily as he did the friends he corresponded with across the country on one of the computers that had been donated to the children's home. Bill had always encouraged Jimmy's interest in computers—after all, he'd been able to use the boy's knowledge on a number of occasions. That was why Jimmy'd been chosen to break into Beth's house; Bill had needed someone who could find Beth's files on SCCH.

No, Lisa didn't have access to the home's computers—but others did. Was there someone he could trust?

Brad. He was Jimmy's best friend, and there was nothing Brad liked more than keeping a secret. It made him feel important. That was why he seemed to thrive on the jobs Bill sent him to do. They were all secrets, and Brad went on all his missions like a miniature spy sent out into the night to risk his life to save his country.

Yes, Brad would keep Jimmy's secret. As loyal as Brad was to Bill, he'd been beaten enough to harbor the same smoldering hatred for him that Jimmy had.

Jimmy found Lynda in the kitchen. "Lynda, do you care if I play on your computer?"

She grinned. "Well, I don't mind, Jimmy, but I don't have any games on there."

"Do you have access to the Internet?"

Lynda couldn't help chuckling. "Yes, as a matter of fact. My modem is hooked to a second phone line, so you can use it all you want. You can probably find some good games on the network I subscribe to."

She told him the name of the network she used, and he smiled. It was the same one they used at the home.

"You're not an Internet addict, are you?" she asked.

"I just like to surf around and see what's there."

"Okay. Sure. I'll show you how to turn it on."

"No, I already know how," he said.

He went into the area of the great room where the computer sat, and turned it on. He found the icon for her network, registered himself as Lynda's guest, and entered his own screen name from the home's system. Quickly, he got on-line and clicked the "compose mail" button.

He sat there a moment, trying to remember what Brad's screen name was. It was something weird, some combination of letters from his name. Darb? Arbd? Drab? Yes, that was it. Drab and some numbers. His age. That was it. Drab11.

He addressed the letter, under "Subject" put "Secret," and then tabbed his cursor down to the body of the letter.

Brad,

It's me, Jimmy. Don't tell anybody you saw me here. I don't know what Bill told you, but I'm okay and I'm staying with a friend. I got caught on my mission the other night, but they were nice and didn't turn me in. If Bill finds me, he'll kill me. You know he will. Please don't tell.

Get a message to Lisa. Tell her I'm okay, and I'm trying to get her out of there. Tell her to be ready. I don't know how I'll do it yet, but I will. She can write me back if she wants. I think I can get my e-mail here.

Don't touch any of my stuff, and don't let anybody else get it. Especially my baseball cards. And if you tell, I'll tell the police everything you've ever done. If you keep my secret, maybe I'll try to get you out, too, and we can all find a boxcar to live in like the kids in that book and have fun from now on. Wouldn't that be cool?

Your friend,

Jimmy

He clicked the "send" button, and sat back. *Please let him see it. Please let him see it.*

"So how's it going?" Lynda asked.

"Good," he said, clicking the network off-line, and cutting the computer off.

"Hungry?"

"Sure."

She led him into the kitchen where a huge breakfast waited. He wished Lisa was here to share it with him.

36

BRAD SAT DOWN at the computer, too tired to go outside where it was hot and muggy. Instead, he'd gotten permission to stay inside and play on the computer. It was one of the perks that the kids in Bill's "inner circle" got.

He turned on the network, got on-line, and checked his e-mail for a message from one of his pen pals in another part of the country, a pen pal who didn't know that he was an orphan, or that he lived in a children's home, or that he was a thief.

There was only one message from someone named JWMan. JWMan? It was familiar, but he couldn't remember who used that name. He clicked "read mail," and saw instantly that it was from Jimmy.

He sat up straighter as he read.

When he was finished, he looked out the window and saw Lisa sitting on a swing on the playground, leaning her head against the chains, as though she might fall asleep and come tumbling off. He went to the door and called out for her. "Lisa!"

She looked up.

"Come here. I have to show you something."

She looked like she didn't want to, but she got up and shuffled to the door. "What?" she asked belligerently.

"I've got a message for you from Jimmy," he whispered, taking her hand and pulling her to the computer.

Her eyebrows popped up. "Where?"

"Here. Look."

Lisa sat down in front of the screen and began to slowly read the letter. She had made A's in reading her first-grade year, but she still had to read slowly and concentrate very hard. Her finger followed the words, and she whispered them as she sounded them out, while Brad stood guard making sure no one came in.

Her eyes widened as she got to the part about him seeing her soon. "He's coming to get me!" she said. "We're gonna live in a boxcar! I want to write him back."

"All right," Brad said. "Hit 'reply' and type it in. It'll be under my screen name, but that's okay."

"Will you type it for me?" she asked.

He glanced toward both doors, then sat back down and put his fingers on the keyboard. "Okay. Tell me what to say."

"Say, 'Dear Jimmy, I miss you.'"

"I'm not typing that," Brad said. "That's gross."

"You said you would. It's my letter. I can say it if I want."

He moaned and typed the words. "What else?"

"Please hurry to get me. Bill gave me your job, and I don't like it."

"Not so fast," Brad said, still hunting and pecking on the word h-u-r-r-y. He made his way through the rest of the sentence.

"I guess that's all," she said, her lips beginning to quiver as tears filled her eyes. "I'm glad he's okay. I thought he wasn't coming back. I thought he left me here."

Brad didn't tell her that he had believed Bill's story about Jimmy being in jail. He might have known it was a lie. The boxcar thing sounded good—real good. They could get somewhere where Bill would never find them. They could get jobs—and until they did they could steal enough to get by. He hoped it would happen soon, before the police tried to arrest all of them.

"Tell me if he writes back," Lisa said.

Typing his own note now, Brad nodded. "Yeah, don't worry, I will."

In his secret room, Bill Brandon scanned the closed-circuit television monitors that kept him informed of everything that went on at SCCH. He watched with mild curiosity as Brad played in the computer room—then with suspicious puzzlement, watched as Brad called Lisa

Westin in. They weren't good friends—in fact, Brad could hardly tolerate the girl. So why the sudden camaraderie?

He saw Lisa sit down and read something on the computer; Brad shuffled around the door, seeming to stand guard. Whatever was going on here, Bill didn't like it.

He waited, stiff, until the boy had turned off the computer and left the room. Then Bill headed across the campus to the computer room. A couple of kids had drifted in since Brad had left. Bill said loudly, "Outside, kids. It's too pretty a day to be playing inside."

They quickly turned off the computers and headed outside, leaving him alone. He locked the doors, then sat down at the computer Brad had been using. He turned it on, opened the online network he allowed them to use, and typed in Brad's screen name. His list of recent mail came up, but there were only three letters. One from some kid who was under the impression that Brad was the son of a congressman and lived in a mansion with a pool. Bill chuckled with disdain.

He clicked the next message, saw that it was part of a stupid conversation that didn't interest him.

Then he clicked the third. It was from someone going by the name of JWMan. He read the first line and knew that JWMan was Jimmy Westin.

His face reddened, and he clicked open the "Read Mail You've Sent" area, where outgoing messages were held. When Brad's log of messages appeared, Bill clicked the most recent one.

Lisa's letter came up, along with Brad's addition.

After he'd read them, he sat staring at the screen, trying to decide what to do. There was no question that Lisa and Brad should be punished for communicating with Jimmy, but he had to do more. He had to put the fear in them, so that they wouldn't tell the other kids what they'd learned. He hoped it wasn't too late. He looked out the window, saw Brad and Lisa talking quietly together at the back of the playground. Lisa was more animated than he'd seen her in days.

He looked back at the screen. Besides punishing the two of them, he had to find a way to make Jimmy come to him, so that he could put him out of commission. Too much was going wrong; there were too many people out there who knew too much. HRS people sniffing around, reporters trying to write exposes of his operation, cops trying to get warrants for his arrest . . . Bill's whole world was in danger unless he could do some quick damage control, and Jimmy, little Jimmy, was right in the middle of it all. He had to lure Jimmy in somehow.

He clicked "unsend" on the letter the two kids had sent Jimmy, and waited anxiously to see if it was too late. If Jimmy had already opened it, he couldn't get it back. But if he hadn't . . .

The computer said that the letter had been unsent, and he grinned. He clicked "edit," then made a few changes. He deleted Lisa's portion, then on Brad's typed in, "Lisa's hurt real bad from the beating Bill gave her. Jimmy, you need to come get her before he kills her. I'll leave Stella's window unlocked so you can get in. Please hurry!"

He grinned as he sent the letter across cyberspace. Now all he had to do was be ready when Jimmy came.

He cut off the computer, then went to the back door and called for Brad and Lisa. Reluctantly, apprehensively, they both came in.

He locked the door behind them, then turned around to Brad. His arm swung and he backhanded the boy with a fist across the chest, knocking him down. Then he kicked him twice, once in each side, until the child was balled up in fetal position, moaning and crying and begging Bill to stop.

When he was satisfied that he'd done enough damage, he turned to Lisa. She shrank back against the wall, tears in her eyes and her face as red as the shirt she wore. "I didn't do anything."

"You've been communicating with your brother, and so has Brad," he said in a surprisingly gentle voice. "And I can't have that."

He grabbed her shoulders, shook her violently, then flung her across the room. But he didn't kick her, like he had Brad. Nick or someone else might come around asking about her, and she'd better not have a mark on her. He left Brad lying on the floor, and grabbed Lisa up.

Marching her out of the computer room, he dragged her across the campus to another specially built room near his office. This one had been designed for discipline. It had no windows, no lights, and no furniture. Just a bare floor and darkness.

He flung her in there as she screamed in protest, and he locked the door behind her, blocking out the sound of her cries.

Then he sat down behind his desk and tried to catch his breath. No, there wouldn't be a mark on her—at least not on her body. Just on her mind. And if anyone came asking about either of the Westin kids . . . he could get her out of his "special room" quickly and no one would be the wiser.

As for Brad—no one cared about Brad anyway, so he didn't expect anyone to ask. He only hoped the beating had taught the kid a lesson.

He couldn't wait for Jimmy to get his message and show up at the home. With a grin, Bill jumped up and hurried across campus to Cottage B, where he unlocked Stella's window.

37

A FEW MINUTES after he got up that morning, Nick saw the news reports about the burning of the newspaper building, and quickly phoned Lynda's house to see if Beth had heard. When he didn't catch her there or at her own house, he decided to drive to the newspaper building itself. Just as he'd suspected, she stood there in the parking lot, leaning on the fender of her car, staring, stunned, at the smoldering ruins.

He pulled up beside her and got out of the car. "Beth, are you all right?"

She shrugged, then said in a dull monotone, "He stopped us. I knew he would."

"You really think Bill Brandon did this?"

She sighed. "They just found footprints of children's sneakers. They came in that window." She pointed to the part of the building that had not burned to the ground. "There was a ladder left behind, and children's fingerprints all over it."

"But I thought Brandon was arrested last night."

"The stupid judge refused to give them a warrant." Her voice was so flat, so calm, that he could hear the defeat there. "Now two people are dead, and those poor kids have this guilt on their heads."

He looked around. "Have Larry and Tony been out here?"

"Yeah, but they've gone back to try again to get a warrant." She looked up at him. "Nick, I'm worried about the kids. What if one of them was burned in the fire? What if they got too close?"

"I'll go back to SCCH today," he said.

"What good can you do there? They already know you're onto them."

"So I've got nothing to lose. If I'm there, he can't do anything to foil the police's arrest attempts."

"All right," she said. "Do it. Do whatever you have to."

"And you go back to Lynda's."

"No, I can't. I've still got the article on computer. I'm going to take it to the *St. Petersburg Times* today. Somehow, I'll convince them to print it."

"But you can't go to your house, now that Bill knows where it is. It's not safe."

"Nick, I have to. I have to get the disks that the story is on."

"Then I'll go with you."

She sighed. "All right. Follow me. It'll just take a minute."

She climbed into her car, took a moment to greet Dodger, who had been asleep on the front seat, and cranked her engine. Nick followed her closely all the way home.

"It's almost over, Dodger," she said to the puppy. "The article will still come out, regardless of the fire, and Bill will still get arrested, and Jimmy and Lisa and the other kids will be put in safe homes . . ." She tried to believe what she said as she reached the dirt road leading through the trees to her house—but the truth was, Bill had beaten them all. As, deep down, she had known he would.

The house looked undisturbed as she pulled up to it and parked. She got out, put Dodger on the ground, and waited as Nick pulled to a halt beside her car.

Nick insisted on going in first, but Dodger beat him to it. The puppy sniffed around, wagging his tail, and headed for the chew toy lying on the floor. As though he'd never ceased to work on it, he began to chew with his little tail stub wagging.

"It looks all right," Nick said. "Then again, somebody could be hiding in your attic and we'd never know. Is your computer upstairs?"

"Yeah," she said. "I'll just go up and get the disk . . ."

"I'll go first." He went up the stairs, checked around the corner, then motioned for her to follow. He stood with her as she found the disk and her briefcase, in which she had put a hard copy of the article. "Here it is."

"All right, let's go."

She followed him down. "I'll leave Dodger here, I guess. We can come back for him later." She checked the puppy's food supply and water, then locked the door and followed Nick back to her car.

He leaned over and dropped a kiss on her lips. "I'll head over to the home, and you call me when you get back from St. Pete. Go to Lynda's first—not home, okay?"

"All right. Be careful, Nick."

"You too."

With Beth's car in the lead, they headed down the dirt road leading to the street. They were almost to the end of the road when a postal truck turned in. Since the mailman always left Beth's mail in her box out by the street, she assumed he must have a package for her, so she did a quick U-turn and rolled her window down as she came next to Nick. "It's a package. I'd better get it."

He turned his car around and followed her back.

She got out just as the postman began to knock on her door.

"Hi," she called up to the house. "Is that for me?"

"Beth Wright?" he asked.

"Yes."

"It's an overnight delivery." He stepped down the porch steps and handed her his clipboard. "Sign here."

She could hear Dodger inside, whimpering and scratching to get out. He didn't like being left any more than she did. She signed the clipboard, then took the package, surprised at the weight of it.

"Thanks," the postman said. "You have a nice day."

"You too."

Dodger began to howl and whine, and rolling her eyes, she shoved the package under one arm. Nick had rolled his window down so he could hear the exchange, and she called back to him, "I have to get Dodger, Nick. He's having a fit in there."

Before he could respond, she stuck the key back into the door and opened it. Dodger panted and jumped up on her calves, as if he hadn't seen her in weeks. "I was coming back, you silly little thing," she said, bending down to pet him. "I wasn't leaving you forever. Come on, let's put your leash back on and you can go with me."

She headed for the kitchen to get the leash. Dodger took the opportunity to dash outside, and she heard Nick's car door slam. "I'll get him!" After a second, he brought the squirming puppy back to the door. "Throw me the leash and I'll walk him. Who's the package from?"

"I'm trying to see." In the kitchen, she took the leash off its hanger and tossed it to Nick. Nick stooped in the doorway and tried to clip it to Dodger's collar, but he slipped free and bolted into the kitchen, his feet sliding on the hardwood floor.

She knelt down to make him quit jumping on her, still looking for the return address. She froze as her eyes located the "From" square. "It can't be."

"What?" Nick asked, leaning against the doorjamb to block it if the dog decided to make a break for it again.

"It's from Marlene Brandon. The woman who was murdered after she talked to me. But it's postmarked in St. Clair." Quickly, she got a knife and began to tear open the wrapping paper as she walked back into the living room. She tore off a strip of it, but the package was heavily taped. The dog frolicked beside her, trying to reach the torn strip hanging down.

"But this was an overnight package," Beth said, puzzled. "How could Marlene have mailed it yesterday? She was dead the night before."

"Maybe she mailed it before you talked. Maybe the post office just took longer than they should have."

She sat down on the couch, and Dodger tried to jump up onto it. She helped him, then slid the box halfway out of the envelope. Had Marlene sent her more documents? Photographs? Tapes?

Before she had the chance to slide it all the way out, Dodger rammed his nose against it, sniffing, and it slipped out of her hands. Dodger slipped off the couch with it as it hit the floor and, playfully, he grabbed a corner of the thick wrapping, the cigar box still held half inside, and dragged it across the room, inviting a game of hide-and-seek or tug-of-war.

Beth stood up as he scurried away from her, his tail wagging. "Dodger, stop that!"

The box slid all the way out of the express envelope, landing on its side, and the top fell open.

The explosion sounded like the end of the world. The last thing that crossed Beth's mind before she blacked out was that Bill had kept his word. He had gotten her. And now she would never be able to tell her story.

38

WHEN BETH WOKE she was lying on the dirt outside. She had no idea how long she had been unconscious. Smoke poured through the charred door of her house. Nick crouched over her, his face stained with soot.

"It's okay, Beth," he was whispering. "Just hang on. They're on their way."

She heard a siren and tried to sit up. Her head hurt, and she felt dizzy. She began to cough, calling, "Dodger! Dodger! Nick, where's Dodger?"

But the look on Nick's face was a clear enough answer even without words. Distraught, she sank back against the ground.

"Hang on," he said. "An ambulance is coming."

She became gradually aware that he wasn't simply touching her to reassure her, but rather that he was pressing hard on her chest because she was bleeding. She closed her eyes, feeling nauseous. The fire truck wailed toward her house, getting louder and louder, and she opened her eyes just in time to see it jerk to a halt and the fire crew leap off and begin unwinding the hose. Behind the fire truck came an ambulance, and two EMTs rushed to her. Nick moved aside as the two began to check her vitals.

In minutes, she was in an ambulance racing to the hospital.

When the ambulance reached the hospital and she was whisked inside, she again saw Nick's worried face as he jogged along beside the gurney. Then darkness closed over her.

In the waiting room, Nick stood at the window, staring out at the pond they had sat at just last night. How could he have let her open that package? Why hadn't he realized what it was and snatched it out of her hands? Why hadn't he been clued by the return address of the dead woman?

Smoke inhalation, burns, a chest wound—but Beth could have been killed. If the puppy hadn't knocked the box off the couch, if she'd had it in her lap as Bill Brandon had intended, she would have been. Instead, the dog was blown apart, and she'd been knocked back.

He had dived toward her the moment the bomb had exploded, had dragged her out of the fire started by whatever incendiary device Brandon had included in the box. Then he had scrambled to her car where he knew she kept a phone. He'd been shaking so hard he almost hadn't been able to dial 911.

Thank God she was alive.

The sliding doors to the emergency room opened, and Lynda and Jake burst in, with Jimmy on their heels. He had asked a nurse to call them, for he hadn't had the composure to do it himself.

"How is she?"

"She's in surgery," he said. "She has a pretty bad chest wound. I don't know . . . how bad it is."

"I got hold of Larry Millsaps in his car," Lynda said. "He's heading out to Beth's house with a bomb inspector, and he's determined to get definitive evidence against Bill Brandon. He'll need it—he said they tried again today to get an arrest warrant for Brandon, and Judge Wyatt refused again."

"What is wrong with that judge?" Nick shouted, slamming the heel of his hand against the windowsill. "If he'd issued it last night, there wouldn't have been a fire at the paper, and Beth wouldn't have . . ." He stopped, unable to continue.

"I don't know, Nick. Judge Wyatt is really hard-nosed. I always try to avoid him in the courtroom if I can. He's not the most reasonable man in the world."

"Then what's he doing on the bench?"

"He's a lifetime appointee. Plus, he's the presiding judge. There's no one higher to appeal to unless they go to the prosecutor. He has great job security."

"Even if he's an idiot?"

She sighed. She was still trying to find an answer when the doctor came out and looked around for Nick. "Mr. Hutchins? She's out of surgery, and she looks good. We were able to clean all the fragments out of her wound—it wasn't as bad as it looked, and her stitches should heal quickly. Thanks to you, her blood loss wasn't bad, nor did she inhale much smoke. You just may have saved her life."

"The dog saved her life," he said.

Jimmy's eyebrows rose. "Dodger saved her? Where is he?"

Nick swallowed. "Jimmy, I'm sorry, but Dodger's—" He stopped, gesturing hopelessly, trying to think of a way to break the news.

Jimmy's face fell. "He's dead, isn't he?"

Nick looked at Lynda and Jake, wishing for someone to say it for him. But there were no takers.

"I'm afraid so. If he hadn't done what he did, Beth might be the one dead instead."

Jimmy tried to plaster on his tough-kid look, and nodded stoically. He turned away from them and went to look out the window. Jake followed him, laying a hand on his shoulders, but the boy shrugged him away.

Nick turned back to the doctor. "When can I see her?"

"In a little while. We've put her in a room, and she should be waking up soon. We'll be keeping her until we're satisfied that there aren't any complications. Maybe she can go home tomorrow."

Home, Nick thought. Her home was in bad shape. She wouldn't be going there.

Lynda patted his back. "We'll wait here, Nick. You go on in and see her."

Nick was grateful that they didn't make him wait.

There was a nurse standing over her bed when she woke up. "Beth, how do you feel?" the nurse asked.

Beth had to think for a minute. "Okay," she whispered, but realized instantly that that wasn't exactly true. "Where is this?"

"The hospital," the nurse said. "You were in an explosion. Do you remember it?"

It started to come back to her in film-clip images . . . the package . . . the tape that was too tough to tear . . . Dodger getting it away from her . . .

"You've had some injuries, but you're going to be fine. I'm going to run out for just a minute and let the doctor know that you're awake, okay?"

She watched the nurse leave the room, and lay there for a moment, looking around at the cold, barren room, with nothing in it that belonged to her, and realized how alone she was. Just like Tracy.

She closed her eyes, her mind moving slowly through disjointed images until it called up a time when she was ten, when she'd broken into a huge home of a wealthy businessman. No one had been home, but he'd had a bird that she hadn't been told about. The bird had fluttered in its cage, spooking her, and she'd taken off running. She'd been so spooked that she had run through the sliding glass door to his patio. It had shattered around her, knocking her out and cutting her in a million places. The other kids had quickly carried her out and thrown her into the van.

Bill had refused to take her to the hospital because he was afraid someone would make the connection between the glass door shattered in a robbery attempt and the little girl covered in glass fragments. Then they'd be caught for sure. So he'd kept her in a room by herself at the home, where he had tweezed the fragments out one by one. It had been a slow torture, one he had seemed to enjoy, and he had followed each withdrawal with a swab of alcohol that had stung worse than any pain she'd ever felt before or since. She still had small scars in some places to remind her.

She'd had bruises all over her body from that incident, and must have had a concussion as well, for she'd slept at least three days following the accident.

Lying here in this room alone reminded her of the week she'd spent in bed in that room at SCCH as a child, wondering if anyone out there cared at all about her, wondering if anyone even gave her a thought.

Bill had told her as he picked glass out of her that they had ways of identifying the blood on glass shards, and that he expected them to arrest her at any moment. It was her fault she was in this position, he'd told her, because she shouldn't have panicked. He was trying to protect her by keeping her here, he'd told her, but Bill's kind of caring wasn't the kind she craved. His was a sick, self-centered concern that frightened her to death.

Funny that Bill was behind this injury, as well. He had almost succeeded at keeping her quiet. He had almost killed her along with her story.

Tears rolled down her face. Lying here, alone, she felt like a wasted, discarded, useless body—the way Tracy probably felt. Was God really there, watching out for her, or was he just disgusted by her?

She thought of the lies she'd told about this story, the anonymous confession, the sneaky way she'd tried to get Maria to confess so that she, Beth, wouldn't have to. She thought of the secrets she'd kept from Nick, from Phil, from the law enforcement officers who needed to know the name of the only available adult witness. The secrets she had kept from little Jimmy, who needed to know that there was someone who truly understood his plight as no one else could, someone who had been there and suffered as he was suffering, someone who had survived it—maybe even grown through it.

Could God see through those sins and walk with her now? The consequences of confessing those sins loomed ever bigger in her consciousness, reminding her that there would be a price to pay. But all those children were still paying. Paying and paying, and they would continue to pay as they grew older and broke free of Bill Brandon. They would pay like she was paying until someone broke the cycle.

And that's what she'd been trying to do. But she'd been trying to do it the easy way, the cheap way. Maybe there was no cheap way. Maybe the only way was to accept the possibility of losing her job and her reputation, and to tell the truth. Maybe then she could have a chance with God.

To do that, she'd have to forget the story she'd written so neatly and remotely, and instead offer herself as a witness who could put Bill Brandon away for life. The buck had to stop somewhere, and it was going to stop here. Unless he stopped her first.

She heard a knock on the door, and then it opened. Nick stood there, looking as fragile and shaken as she'd felt lying out on the dirt with her house burning behind her. He tried to smile, but she could see that the effort was almost too great for him.

He came and leaned over her. "Are you all right?" he asked.

Her voice was hoarse, weak. "Yes. Amazingly, I am. I wasn't supposed to be, though. He intended to kill me."

She could see that Nick agreed with her.

"If I could have just gotten the package away from you before you opened it," he whispered. "I should have realized right away . . . I should have taken it and—"

"Shhh," she whispered, reaching up to touch his lips. "Don't. He set us up. He knew I wouldn't be able to resist a package with Marlene's name on it. He's smart, Nick. I told you how smart he is." She closed her eyes, fighting the tears. "Poor Dodger. He didn't know what hit him."

Nick clearly didn't know what to say. He just stroked her hair back from her face, and she closed her eyes.

A memory, white-hot and miserable, came back to her, a memory of another little dog they had found at the home. It had wandered up onto the lawn one day, and they had played with it, then asked Bill if they could keep it. He'd told them no.

She wasn't sure why that little dog had created such a fierce longing in them, why the children had wanted him badly enough to risk Bill's wrath, but someone had suggested that they hide it and keep it anyway, that they could keep it a secret from Bill. They had all agreed.

They had hidden the little dog in a storage shed at the back of the grounds at night, then moved him wherever he was least likely to be found during the day. He had been a kind, gentle secret that bound the children, so unlike the dark, ugly secrets they had shared before.

But one night, when they'd come in from robbing the home of the president of the local college, Bill told them that he'd discovered the puppy, and that he realized how much they must love the dog to work so hard to hide him for so long. He told them that they had worked hard for him, too, and that they deserved something of their own for their labors. He told them they didn't have to hide the puppy anymore.

Eagerly, they had all run out to the shed to get the puppy and bring him in, each of them arguing about which one of them the dog would sleep with that night. They had reached the shed, thrown open the door, flicked on the light—

The puppy lay dead on the floor, shot through the head.

Bill had taught them a valuable lesson.

She wondered how many more "valuable lessons" he had taught to Jimmy and Lisa and all those other children at the home—lessons that might twist and scar them for life. How many times over the years had she fantasized about a rescuer who would come and save them all from Bill. Maybe that was why she had suffered the childhood she had. Maybe God was grooming Beth to be the rescuer of these children. Maybe she was going to be their Esther, groomed "for such a time as this."

"I have to go," she said weakly, trying to sit up. "I have to get out of here."

"You can't leave, Beth. You have to stay, at least overnight."

"No, I can't. I have to talk to Phil, my editor. I have to tell him what happened. I have to tell him some other things."

"I've put too much pressure on you," Nick said, his eyes misting over. "I've made this seem like the most important thing in the world, and you almost got killed. It's not worth it."

"Of course it is! Until I get that story printed, I'm in danger. Once the story's out, it would be too obvious if anything happened to me. He wouldn't dare try anything." She looked up at him. "Nick, tell them I'm okay. That I can go. Please?"

"No," he said. "You're not as strong as you think. You have to lie still, Beth. You have to stay here."

"Then make Phil come to me," she said. "And call Lynda, and Larry Millsaps and Tony Danks at the St. Clair Police Department."

"Lynda's already here," he said. "With Jake and Jimmy. But I'll call the others. I'll tell them to come tomorrow."

"No, not tomorrow. Now! I have something I have to tell all of you, Jake and Jimmy, too. Something important, Nick. Please. It really can't wait."

"Okay," he said finally. "Just calm down. Be still. I'll go call them now."

39

THE DOCTORS WERE at first strongly opposed to having such a group in her room so soon after her injuries, but when Beth convinced them that her long-term safety depended on a quick arrest of the one who'd injured her, they finally allowed it.

Phil was the first one in when the group came quietly into her room. "Beth, are you all right?" he asked.

"Yes, for now," she said. "But I need to talk to you. All of you."

Lynda rushed forward and hugged her. "I'm so glad you're okay. And what a miracle that Jimmy wasn't there."

"Yeah," she said. "Where is he?"

"I'm right here," Jimmy said from behind Lynda. He came up to the bed, hands in his pockets, and glanced awkwardly at her. "Bill did this, you know."

She swallowed hard and nodded. "I know."

"But he'll get away with it. He always does."

"Not this time, Jimmy."

Jake bent over the bed and pressed a kiss on her cheek, and she saw Tony and Larry coming in. Nick was last to enter the room, and she held out a hand to him. He came to the bed and held her hand, lending her support he didn't even know she was going to need.

"Thanks for coming, everybody," she said. "I won't keep you long. You've probably all figured out by now that someone's trying to kill me, to keep me from finishing the story I'm working on, about the St. Clair Children's Home. Last night, the *St. Clair News* building was burned down, and this morning, the explosion—Bill Brandon doesn't want it printed." She cleared her throat and looked at her editor.

"Phil, you kept saying you wanted one more quote. Yesterday, I gave you one, but it was from an anonymous source." She hesitated, then forced herself to go on. "But it's time to tell who that source is. The reason this story is such a passion for me is that . . . I was the anonymous witness who grew up at SCCH."

Nick looked more stunned than anyone. His mouth fell open. "You what?"

Jimmy gasped, then narrowed his eyes and studied her closely. The others looked first at one another, then at her, shock evident on their faces.

"I didn't want to tell anyone because . . . being in Bill's home brings with it some degree of . . . guilt."

"Wait a minute," Phil said, scratching his head. "Are you telling me that you've seen these abuses firsthand?"

She closed her eyes again, and Nick tightened his hold on her hand. "I'm telling you that I've been involved in them."

Larry and Tony got up from their chairs and came closer to the bed. "So you were one of the kids in his crime ring? He actually used you to break into homes and steal things?"

"That's right. From the time I was eight years old until I left the home at eighteen." She lifted her chin high, to fight the tears pushing into her eyes, and met Nick's stunned gaze. "I'm sorry, Nick. I should have told you—"

Nick took a few steps closer, his face twisting as he tried to understand. "You were in that home? But I worked for HRS then. I would have seen you."

"No, Sheila Axelrod is the one who processed my release when I turned eighteen. And actually, we did cross paths a couple of times. But I've changed my hair color and cut it, and I changed my name. But I came to you when I decided to expose Bill, because I knew you seemed like someone who would listen. I knew that from the way you treated some of my housemates."

Nick was still gaping, disbelieving, and she turned back to Larry and Tony. "I realize that this confession could get me into trouble, and that's why I've tried not to expose myself in this story. But Bill Brandon has got to be stopped. An old friend of mine from the home told me yesterday that if I wouldn't even talk, what made me think anyone else would? Well, now I'm talking." She looked at Phil. "You wanted a reliable adult's word? Well, here it is. She's got a name and everything."

"Awesome!" Jimmy said. "No wonder you knew so much about Bill. No wonder he knew so much about you!"

"Wow." Phil slumped back in his chair. "I can't believe this."

"Believe it. It's true. Bill Brandon trained me to be a thief, and for ten years, that's what I was. And as we speak, he's training other kids to be thieves. Maybe worse. Kids were involved in the arson last night. They could have been killed."

"There's more," Tony said, glancing back at Larry. "After the explosion at your house, Nick told us where the package was postmarked, so we went by that post office to see what they could remember about the package. Turns out that one of the postal workers saw a little girl bringing it in."

"A little girl, delivering a bomb?" Beth asked.

"He described her as six or seven, reddish-blonde, shoulder-length hair, big eyes, very polite."

"Lisa," Jimmy said. "It's Lisa."

Nick clenched his jaw. "Tony, Larry, you've got to get this guy. Somebody else is gonna get killed if you don't."

Jimmy's face was reddening, and his lips trembled. "You've got to get Lisa out of there. She doesn't know any better. She's just seven. He's so mean . . ."

"All right," Larry said. "We have ample evidence now to arrest Bill Brandon. If Judge Wyatt refuses us a warrant this time, we'll go over his head to the prosecutor. We'll have Brandon locked up by the end of the day."

"I wish the article hadn't been destroyed," Phil said.

"It wasn't," Nick said. "She has a copy in her car, with a disk."

"I was taking it to the *St. Petersburg Times*."

"Good idea. They'll print it, if we can't. If you'll give it to me, I'll make sure of it, Beth."

"I want to make some changes, first. I want to put my own name in there, and write down what I just told you."

"You can dictate it over the phone. I'll call you here when I get to St. Pete."

"What about me?" Jimmy's rough voice surprised them all. "What about Lisa, and all the other kids? Are we gonna go to jail?"

"You leave that to me," Lynda told him. "I'll take care of everything."

"Can either of you lead us to where he warehouses all of the things he steals?"

"No," Beth said. "He never shared that part of the business with us. He just gave us our orders, and we followed them."

"Do you know who else was involved?"

"All of the adults who work for him, according to Marlene. But not all of the kids. Sometimes I didn't even know what other kids were involved. He seemed to pick out the ones he could control the best. The ones who would fear him and try to please him."

"Was there physical abuse involved?"

"Yes. Always. That was how he controlled us."

"Sexual abuse?"

She shook her head. "No, thank God. I was never molested, and I didn't hear about it happening to anyone else. I think Bill considers himself a fine, upstanding, normal citizen who happens to have an unusual hobby."

"How about you, Jimmy? Has Bill ever molested you or any of the other kids?"

"Not me, and not the others as far as I know."

"Just beatings."

"Yeah, and other things."

Other things. She thought about the plate-glass window, and the alcohol, and the puppy with a bullet hole through his head. Bill's cruelties knew no bounds. She wondered what horrors Jimmy had experienced.

"What other things, Jimmy?"

He looked down at his worn sneakers. "One time, Keith Huxtin fell from a ladder when he was breaking into a house, and he broke his leg. We didn't think anybody was home, but somebody was, and they came out and saw us. We had to carry Keith down the street to the van, running as fast as we could to keep from getting caught. Bill wouldn't take him to the hospital because he knew they were looking for a kid who'd been hurt. He made him sweat the pain out for two days. Then he took us to school early and made us carry him in and lay him in the hall. We had to pretend he had fallen at school, so Bill wouldn't be blamed and it would seem like it had happened two days after the break-in. Those idiots bought the whole story, even though his scrapes had already scabbed over."

"This van. What does it look like, and where does he keep it?"

"In the shed at the back of the campus. It's dark green."

Larry's eyebrows rose. "Can *you* take us to the warehouse?"

"No. I don't know where it is. It was always dark, and I was always in the back of the van. Sometimes there was a truck there, loading up. I don't know where they took all the stuff. Somewhere to sell it, I guess."

"There are a lot more people than Bill and the kids involved," Beth said. "I don't know who they are, but there are others."

"All right," Larry said. "We need to take Jimmy down to the station to make another statement, and we'll send someone in here to get Beth's. We'll also post a guard here for protection."

"I'm going with Jimmy," Lynda told Beth. "I'll be back as soon as they're finished with him."

"Nick, we need everything you've already compiled about the home," Tony said. "We're going to throw the book at this guy, and make sure no one drops the ball. We also need you to be there for Jimmy's statement. As long as a representative of HRS is with us, we won't have to get any other bureaucrats involved."

"All right." Nick's voice was distant, and he seemed distracted, preoccupied, as he looked down at Beth. "I'll be back as soon as I get them what they need, okay?"

"Yeah," she said, touching his face. "Just one thing."

"What?"

"Are you disappointed in me?"

"Why would I be disappointed?" he asked.

"Because I lied about my interest in the case. And you didn't know that I was raised breaking into people's homes. You thought I was a normal, healthy woman."

"Hush," he said, stroking her hair back from her face. "Enough of that. You are a normal, healthy woman. And you're courageous. You could have let it all go. But you cared enough about those kids to tell the truth."

"Took me long enough."

He leaned over and kissed her forehead, but she could still see the troubled expression in his eyes. "I'll be back."

When the room had cleared out, Beth lay on her back, staring at the ceiling and wondering what would happen next. Wouldn't there be consequences? Wouldn't the media ask when she'd been old enough to know right from wrong, and to do something about it? Why she hadn't turned Bill in years ago? Maybe the media wouldn't ask—but *she* still had those questions. She pictured that little boy, Keith, who'd broken his leg and suffered for two days. The plate-glass-window incident could have been the last time, if she had found some way to turn Bill in then. Then Keith wouldn't have had to suffer. But no, she'd kept her mouth shut, and gone along, and even after she was out, she'd been so grateful and relieved to be away from Bill Brandon that she hadn't thought much about the kids she'd left behind. Jimmy had come only shortly after she'd left. Because of her silence, he'd suffered.

Now she wondered what her own personal consequences would be. While Nick was too kind to condemn her, did this revelation change the way he felt about her? It wasn't as if she was looking toward marriage, but the thought that Nick might reject her because of this filled her with despair. What if Nick, who dealt with troubled pasts and presents all day every day, decided that he didn't need all her baggage—that she just wasn't the one for him?

She wouldn't blame him at all if he did.

40

JAKE WAS IN the Police Department waiting room when Jimmy, Nick, and Lynda came out of the interrogation room. Jimmy had just spent two hours answering questions, and he looked worn out.

Jake stood up as they approached. "How'd it go?"

"Okay, I guess," Jimmy said. "I think I told them what they wanted."

"All they wanted was the truth."

"Well, that's what I gave them." He looked up at Nick. "What now?"

"Nothing yet. We just have to keep you safe until we get Brandon off the streets and start moving the kids from the home. I'll spend the rest of the day trying to line up places to relocate them."

"You'll keep me and Lisa together, won't you?"

"Of course. I'll move heaven and earth to do that, Jimmy."

"Hey, Nick," Jake cut in. "Since you'll be so busy, and Lynda needs to go to the office, how about letting Jimmy spend the afternoon with me? I have some errands to run, and he can help me."

Nick looked down at the kid. "Want to, Jimmy?"

"Sure," he said. "It's better than nothing."

Jake chuckled at the under-enthusiastic response. He kissed Lynda good-bye and ushered him out to his car.

"So where are we going?" Jimmy asked.

"Someplace really important," he said. "Remember I told you I was going to try to get my medical release so I could get my pilot's license back?"

"Yeah."

"Well, it's this afternoon. I thought you might like to come with me."

He shrugged. "Yeah, okay."

"You can't go into the examination room, but you can wait outside, and if they turn me down, you can help carry me out to the car. I'll be too depressed to walk."

"Nervous?" Jimmy asked.

"Were you nervous in there with the cops?"

Jimmy nodded.

"That's about how nervous I am," Jake said. "I have a lot riding on this. I have a flying job lined up that I really want. But no license, no job."

"And you won't ask Lynda to marry you?"

He thought that one over for a moment. "I'm not sure, Jimmy. All I know is that I want to get back on my own two feet before I ask her."

"They'll give you your license back. Why wouldn't they?"

"Well, one of their concerns is my reflexes. Whether my legs have healed enough to react as they should. I think I've got that one in the bag. But the eye thing . . . Sometimes they'll overlook a false eye, if the pilot can convince them that his vision is fine anyway, that he can compensate with the other eye. But it all depends. Sometimes they decide it's just too risky, and they ground you for life."

Jimmy just looked up at him. "I hope you get it, Jake."

"Yeah, me too."

Jimmy sat by the window in the Federal Aviation Administration offices, staring down at the parking lot just in case Bill managed to find him and come after him here. If Bill only knew what he'd told the police, he'd kill him for sure. And if he couldn't kill Jimmy, he'd kill Lisa.

The door opened, startling him, and Jake came out, his face solemn and pale. Jimmy got to his feet. "They turned you down?"

A slow grin stole across Jake's lips. "No! They gave me my license back!"

"All right!" Jimmy said, jumping up and slapping Jake's hand. They both danced a little jig, and then Jake pulled him into a tight hug and almost knocked him over. "I'm glad you were here to share this moment with me, buddy. I don't think I could have done it if I hadn't known you were out here for moral support."

"I didn't do anything."

"You did plenty. You were here!"

Jake practically floated back out to his car, alternately walking fast, then punching the air, then dancing again.

"Wait till you tell Lynda," Jimmy said.

Jake shook his head as he got into the car. "No way. I still don't want her to know. I want to spring the whole thing on her when I ask her to marry me."

"So when will that be?"

"Soon, my boy. Very soon. Let's just hope she says yes."

"She'd be stupid not to."

Jake laughed. "You're a good friend, pal-o-mine. And just as a reward, I think I'll take you for my first post-crash flight without another licensed pilot tagging along. Are you up for it?"

"Yes!" Jimmy said. "Let's go."

At the airport, Mike, the owner, celebrated with Jake over the return of his license, and offered him free use of a rental plane for the afternoon. Jake took Jimmy up, and they flew out over the Gulf, where Jimmy had a bird's-eye view of St. Clair.

The familiar serenity washed over Jake, calming his spirit and making him feel close to Jimmy. "Isn't this beautiful?" he asked.

"Yeah," Jimmy said. "When I grow up, I want to be a pilot."

"I'll teach you myself," he said. "The job I'm hoping for is as a flight instructor. I'll do that part-time, and fly for several ministries around this area on the side. But I'm sure I could make time to teach a bright kid like you how to fly."

"It depends," Jimmy said. "I don't really know where I'll be. I may not even be in St. Clair anymore."

How pressing this worry must be for Jimmy, Jake realized. The low hum of the engine accompanied the thoughts going through both their minds.

"Tell me something," Jake said quietly. "Tell me about your parents."

"They're dead," Jimmy said quickly.

Jake knew that wasn't true, but he wasn't sure that Jimmy knew it. "Do you remember them?"

He shrugged and looked out the window. "My dad was a spy who was killed in France during the war," he said. That was impossible, Jake knew, but it didn't matter—it was a fantasy he could identify with. He'd never known his father either, and had made up similar stories.

"I didn't have a dad," Jake said. "Never knew him." Jimmy didn't change his answer, so Jake pressed on. "What about your mom?"

Jimmy took a little longer to answer that. "She died almost three years ago. That's why they put us in the home."

"What did she die of?" Jake asked.

"Cancer," Jimmy said. "She had cancer."

"I'm sorry, Jimmy. What kind of cancer?"

Jimmy thought for a moment. "Prostate cancer, I think it was."

Jake's eyebrows shot up. "Prostate cancer, huh?"

"Yeah."

"Oh." He almost smiled. "That's rare in women."

"Yeah."

"Do you remember much about her?"

"Sure. She was the greatest mom in the world. She made our lunches, and cooked these great suppers, and we'd all sit at the table and talk about our days. And we always had plenty to eat and warm beds to sleep in and clean clothes . . . and she loved us."

Tears came to Jake's eyes. The memories were sweet, yet the boy thought his mother was dead. What if he found out that she was alive? What if they reintroduced him to her?

He looked at the boy, and saw the solemn, dreamy look that had passed over his face. "Do you ever miss her?"

Jimmy swallowed and shrugged. He couldn't seem to answer, so he only nodded. "Lisa misses her most," he said. "She can't remember her too good. I tell her stories about her. Good stories, about all the things she used to do."

Jake had heard enough from Nick to know that none of those stories were true. But maybe they could be, if they reintroduced the boy to his mother . . .

The thought wouldn't leave his mind, and after they landed, he left Jimmy alone and made a couple of phone calls—to Lynda first, and then to Nick.

Jake didn't mention his phone calls to Jimmy when they got back into the car. Instead, he told him that they were going to the hospital to check on Beth, and that Nick would meet them there. But as he drove, he prayed silently that he was doing the right thing.

41

TRACY HAD BEEN moved out of ICU, Jake learned when he got to the hospital and found Nick waiting for him. Nick spoke to Jimmy, then stepped aside with Jake. "Look, if he gets upset or anything . . ."

"He's out of there. No problem."

"All right."

They went back to where Jimmy waited, and Nick leaned down to Jimmy. "Jimmy, before we go see Beth, while you're here at the hospital, I think there's somebody here you might like to see."

His eyes widened. "Lisa?"

"No, not Lisa. Someone else. A patient who's in here with pneumonia. I found her real sick the other day and brought her here."

Jimmy hesitated. "I'm not too good with sick people."

"It's okay. You don't have to do anything. You don't even have to say anything."

"Then why am I going?"

The elevator doors opened, and Nick led him on. "You'll see. Just wait."

Jake was quiet as he followed Nick and Jimmy off the elevator.

They reached the open door, and Nick peered in. It was a semiprivate room, but the other bed was unoccupied. Tracy lay in bed, IVs still attached to her and an oxygen mask over her face.

Jake touched the back of Jimmy's neck, and followed Nick in. As they came closer to the bed, Nick leaned over her. "Hi," he said. "How're you feeling?"

"Okay," she said weakly.

He looked back at Jimmy, who stood awkwardly back. "Recognize her?"

Jimmy shook his head. "No. Do I know her?"

Nick shot a concerned look at Jake. "I have someone here I wanted you to see, Tracy," he said.

Jimmy froze at the name. "No. Not her." His mouth tightened, tears sprang to his eyes, and he began to back out of the room. "I don't want to see her."

Tracy rose up slightly and saw her son. "Jimmy?"

"No!" he shouted, and the nurse came running. Jake grabbed him, but he shook free and fled from the room. Jake followed him out.

"Jimmy, wait!"

The boy ran to the elevators and began punching the down button, waiting for one to open. His face was crimson and covered with tears, and he turned his face away so Jake couldn't see. Jake squatted in front of him and held him by the shoulders. "Son, you don't have to go back in there. It was a bad idea, okay? We didn't know it would upset you. We thought you'd be happy. Will you forgive us?"

"So you proved I lied. You coulda just told me you knew!"

"I didn't know you lied, Jimmy. I thought you might really think she was dead."

"I know what you're all up to. You're gonna take Lisa out of the home and give us back to her. And it'll be even worse than it was at the home." His voice broke off, and he bent over, weeping, and covered his face with both hands. "I should have known."

"Jimmy, nobody's giving you or Lisa back to your mom."

"Lisa's better off where she is than with that sorry excuse for a mother in there!" Jimmy raged. "At least she has a chance where she is. I can take care of my sister better than she can. I was the one who did it, anyway, when we lived with her."

"Jimmy, you've got to trust us."

Jimmy's eyes flashed. "I don't believe anything you say. You're all a bunch of liars! You don't care who gets stuck with who, or what things are like there."

"Jimmy, listen to me, please—"

"I'm not listening anymore," he said. "Just let me go, and I'll handle things myself."

The elevator doors came open, and Jake grabbed Jimmy's shoulder and followed him on. *What a terrible move*, he thought. *What a mistake.*

"Look, son, you don't have to talk to me, but you do have to come with me. And you can just listen, okay?"

Jimmy didn't answer.

"We'll go for a ride. Maybe out to the beach."

Jimmy didn't respond.

The doors opened on the first floor, and Jimmy darted off. Jake caught up to him and grabbed his shoulder. "This way, little buddy," he said, and directed him to his car.

Back in Tracy's room, Nick tried to apologize to her, but the sight of her son had shaken her. She was crying and gasping for breath, and he wanted to kick himself for making such a stupid error in judgment.

"I'm sorry, Tracy," he said. "I thought—I don't know what I thought. That it would help Jimmy to see you, I guess. To know that he still has a mother. That he's not all alone in the world."

"I'm not his mother," she wheezed. "The state took him away. He hates me, and I don't blame him, 'cause I hate myself."

"Don't say that, Tracy," Nick told her. "How can you hate someone God loves?"

"God doesn't love me," she said. "Why would he love me?"

"Because he created you."

"Yeah, and then I destroyed myself."

"Not yet. It's not too late to turn around, Tracy. It's not too late to make your kids love you again, either."

She turned her head to the side and wiped at her eyes. "You don't even know what you're talking about," she said. "Just leave me alone."

Nick started to protest, then thought better of it. "All right," he said quietly. "Listen—if you decide you want to talk in the next hour or so, call me up in Beth Wright's room."

She didn't answer, and he felt a deep self-loathing. He shouldn't have tried it. So stupid. Defeated, he walked out of the room.

42

TONY DIDN'T EVEN bother to sit down when they returned to Judge Wyatt's office. All he wanted was to snatch the warrant and run as fast as he could to SCCH so he could arrest Bill Brandon. "The evidence is overwhelming and conclusive, your honor," he told Judge Wyatt. "We have an adult who was raised in the home who has given us a statement. We have a child who's been participating in Brandon's crime ring recently. We have the murder of Bill Brandon's sister, and we have two attempts on Beth Wright's life—including a package bomb that almost killed her, and we have the arson at the newspaper the night before the article exposing Brandon would have come out."

Judge Wyatt adjusted his glasses and looked over the charges, a deep wrinkle clefting his forehead. He seemed to study it too hard, as if it required much thought, and Larry, who was sitting, shot Tony a disturbed look.

The judge started to get up, almost distractedly, as if he'd forgotten they were in the room. "I'll spend some time looking over these charges tonight," he muttered. "I'll take all of it under advisement and get back to you tomorrow."

"Tomorrow?" Larry sprang out of his chair. "Judge, tomorrow's too late. He's a killer, and he's trying to take out our main witness. She's in the hospital as we speak."

"She'll be safe until tomorrow," the judge said. "No idiot would attempt murder in as public a place as a hospital."

"Give me a break!" Tony cried. "What is the deal here? You've stood in the way every step of this investigation!"

The judge banged his fist down. "It's my job to ensure that you do your job within the bounds of the law, so that my courtroom doesn't fill up with a bunch of lawyers who waste my time with technicalities and loopholes. I will not issue arrest warrants for every Tom, Dick, and Harry you *think* may have committed a crime!"

"Think? What does all this evidence spell, Judge? Witnesses, bodies—what do you want? You want him to come after you? Would you give us an arrest warrant then?"

The judge's dagger eyes pierced Tony. "Get out of my office. Now, or I'll hold you in contempt!"

"We're not in court, Judge!"

The judge snatched up the phone. "I'm calling security."

"No need," Tony said, jerking the door open. "I get the picture."

Larry covered his face. This was going from bad to worse. "We need this warrant," he said, in a voice he hoped would appease. "There are children in danger, your honor. Every minute counts. Brandon knows we're bearing down on him, and he's going to get desperate. Please let us know the minute you decide to issue the warrant."

"You'll hear from me."

Larry followed Tony out, and Tony slammed the door behind them.

"Good going," Larry said. "That ought to change his mood."

"He's either senile or dirty," Tony said. "He doesn't want us to arrest Brandon, and there's a reason. We're going to the prosecutor's office right now. We'll get the warrant from him."

"Whoa—we can't just go over Wyatt's head without talking to the captain," Larry said.

"Fine. Then let's do it."

An hour later, they sat in Captain Sam Richter's office at the police station, watching him pace, clearly disturbed, as he processed the facts they had given him. "Did he say why the evidence wasn't sufficient?" he asked. "Did he tell you what he would need to give you the warrant?"

"No," Tony said. "He's not interested in helping us on this, Captain. If we handed him videotapes of Brandon beating and maiming the kids, the man would still have to take it under advisement. Something stinks."

"Yeah, I'd say so. But I don't like making enemies of our judges. There's got to be another way."

"What, then?" Tony asked. "We need to get this guy locked up tonight!"

Sam sank into his chair and leaned back, staring at the ceiling. "But if we go to the prosecutor, and it turns out that Judge Wyatt has just taken a conservative turn and isn't really doing anything wrong, we'll have made an enemy out of the person who's supposed to be our number-one ally in this game."

"He's a judge because he's supposed to have good judgment," Larry pointed out. "If he's lost that judgment, for whatever reason, then he needs to be removed from the bench."

Sam opened a drawer and dug around, then came up with a roll of antacids. He broke the roll of tablets in half and put four into his mouth. As he chewed, he leaned forward on his desk, studying both men. "Here's what I want you to do. I want you to follow Judge Wyatt tonight. Just tail him and see what he does. If he's dirty, maybe you'll get evidence of that. Tomorrow, if he still hasn't issued the warrant, you can go to the prosecutor's office—I'll even go with you—and we'll try to get the warrant from them."

"What about Brandon?" Larry asked. "Captain, he's a killer, and there are people that he needs dead."

"You follow him, Larry. Watch every move he makes. Don't lose him for a second. In fact, we might be able to set up a stakeout in that hardware store across the street from the home."

Larry shot Tony a frustrated look. "Captain, that may not be good enough."

"It'll have to be," Sam said. "I'm not willing to bring a judge down until I know for sure that I have an excellent reason. It sounds like somebody tipped Brandon off about the article, right after you showed it to Judge Wyatt. Maybe it was the judge."

"I'd bet my life on it," Tony said.

They went back to their car, then just sat there for a moment before Tony started the ignition. "How do you do it, Larry? How do you stay calm when the top of your head is about to blow off? This whole Christianity thing is new to me, I know, but I don't think I'll ever get to the point where I don't want to throw a man like Judge Wyatt against the wall and beat some sense into him."

"It's not a sin to be angry, Tony. Christ got angry."

"It wouldn't be so bad if I could trust that the work we do out here, on the streets, is going to count for something, that it was a partnership. We nab the bad guys, and the judges and courts put them away. Now the courts won't even let me nab the bad guys."

"What do you think Brandon's next move will be?"

"Whatever he wants," Tony said, throwing up his hands. "He can blow up the police station, for all Judge Wyatt cares. Get an automatic weapon and mow down every kid in his home. You think Wyatt would give us a warrant then?"

"He'd take it under advisement."

Tony's face reddened as he jabbed the key into the ignition and cranked the old car. "Sometimes I think I need to find another job."

"You couldn't leave this, even if you wanted to."

"Don't count on it. It sounds better and better every day."

He headed out into traffic. "You can take this car tonight. I'll use my car to follow Judge Bozo around."

"Take your cell phone so we can stay in touch."

"Nick and Beth are gonna keel over and die when they find out that we can't get that scumbag today. Not to mention Jimmy."

"We'll just have to do the next best thing."

"What's that?"

"Make sure no one else gets hurt before we can get him behind bars."

43

ST. CLAIR BEACH was busy this time of year, but Jake found a parking space. Jimmy got out before Jake could say anything and headed for the long pier shooting out into the Gulf.

The wind blustered through the boy's hair, making him look small and vulnerable. Jake followed him down the pier.

When they got to the end, Jimmy leaned over the rail and looked out toward the horizon. Jake sat down on a bench next to where Jimmy stood and looked up at him. "Want to talk now?"

"No."

"Then will you listen?"

Jimmy ignored him.

"Jimmy, I know how you feel."

"No, you don't."

"Yes, I do. There was a time when I pretty much despised my mother, too. And I was embarrassed by her, and I never wanted to see her again."

Jimmy gave him a reluctant glance. "What did she do to you?"

He sighed. "It wasn't so much what she did. It was more what she didn't do. She wasn't exactly June Cleaver."

"Who?"

He regrouped and tried to find a more modern reference point. "She wasn't a storybook mom. She had a lot of problems. She caused me a lot of problems. And while I was growing up, I remember always thinking that the minute I was old enough, I'd be out of there and never look back."

"I didn't have to wait that long."

"No, you didn't." He looked up at the kid. "What did she do, Jimmy? Did she hurt you in some way?"

"Hurt me? No. She didn't pay enough attention to hurt me. Unless you call leaving us without food for three days hurting us. She was so strung out on dope that she didn't know where she was half the time."

"Pretty messed up, huh?"

"Yeah."

"So when you went to the home, I guess it seemed like an improvement."

He sighed. "I didn't have so much responsibility."

"How old were you?"

"Seven."

Jake thought it over. He almost couldn't blame the kid for hating his mother. No seven-year-old should have responsibility for his home, himself, and his four-year-old sister.

"What about when you realized the home wasn't what it seemed to be?"

"It was okay," he said. "As long as I did what Bill said, I didn't worry too much. He took care of us. And he never touched Lisa. I knew I could take whatever heat there was to take, if they'd just leave her alone. While I was there, they did. Now, everything's all messed up. I don't know where we're gonna live, I don't know if Lisa's all right—and if they give us back to . . ." His voice trailed off. He didn't seem to know how to refer to Tracy.

Jake understood. "Mother" didn't seem to apply, and neither did "Mom." "Jimmy, I want you to understand that when Nick went looking for your mom, it wasn't to reunite you, necessarily. He just wanted to see if she was still in bad shape. He wanted to see if there was any hope there."

"Well, there's not."

"Maybe not. Not in human terms, anyway."

"What's that supposed to mean?"

"It means that when we think something's impossible, or someone's impossible to change,

God sometimes comes along and does something really awesome, and the next thing you know, you've got a bona fide human being there with morals and a heart and a conscience."

"You talking about your mother?"

Jake smiled. "No. I'm talking about myself, kiddo."

Jimmy leaned his shoulder into the rail and looked at Jake, grudgingly interested.

"Have you ever heard the term 'morally bankrupt'?" Jake asked.

Jimmy shrugged.

"It's a term used to describe a person who doesn't have any morals. Someone who lives for today, and only cares about the pleasures of the moment. Someone who doesn't care who he hurts or what he has to do to get what he wants." He stood up next to the boy and leaned on the rail, looking out over the ocean. "That's what I was, Jimmy. I may not have been a junkie, and I may not have had a couple of kids to neglect, but I was morally bankrupt. And God taught me a few things."

"I don't know if I believe in God," Jimmy said matter-of-factly. "But if he was real, what did he teach you?"

"He taught me that I was no better than your mom, or my mom, or any other morally bankrupt person out there. Some of us wear it prettier than others, some of us are masters at hiding it, but the bottom line is that sin is sin. We've all got it. And until we trust in someone bigger than ourselves, it'll do every one of us in. Me, my mom, your mom, you, Lisa—"

"We're already done in," Jimmy said.

"No, you're not. Because God can turn things around. He turned things around for me, and made a new person out of the sorry slug I was. He can do that for your mom. He could even do it for you."

"You calling me a sorry slug?"

"No. But I'm telling you that it doesn't matter that you didn't have a father to bring you up and take care of and protect you. I didn't, either. It doesn't matter that your only other parent failed you. It doesn't matter that the adults in your life, for the most part, have been morally bankrupt and even abusive. What matters is that there's someone more important than them, someone who has a lot more authority over you than they do, someone who loves you more than you can even love yourself—even more than you love Lisa."

The little boy considered that as the wind ruffled his hair. "Well, you can believe that if you want to. I'm not gonna make fun of you. I just don't believe it."

"That's fine, kiddo. I'm no preacher, and I'm not trying to shove a sermon down your throat. But take it from me, one homeless, fatherless guy to another: God is taking care of you, whether you believe in him or not."

"I don't want him to take care of me. I'll be all right. I want him to take care of Lisa."

"Her, too. If I'm lyin', I'm dyin'. God loves you both."

"We'll see," Jimmy said.

Jake smiled and messed up his hair. "Yeah, we'll see. What do you say we go back to my place and chill for a while? See what Lynda's found out."

He sighed. "Whatever."

"Okay. Come on." He started walking back up the pier, and Jimmy followed behind him a few paces. After a moment, he caught up. "Jake, why'd you say 'one homeless guy to another'? You have a home."

"Not really. It isn't mine. See, when I was where you are, homeless and broke, feeling like I didn't have a single soul to love me, with no idea where I would live, God sent Lynda to help me. And she did, man. I've been living in her garage apartment ever since. But it's not really mine, and even though I'm paying rent now, I still feel like I'm mooching."

"When you marry her, you won't be a freeloader anymore."

The choice of words both stung and amused Jake. "I guess not. Listen, I've been thinking. If she says yes, I'm gonna need a best man. You think you might be up for the job?"

Jimmy's eyes widened. "Really? Me?"

"Yeah, you."

"Well, I guess so."

"Good. But I may be jumping the gun. Maybe I need to wait until the bride says yes before I start planning the wedding, huh?"

By the time they got to the car, Jimmy's mood had lifted, and he was a kid again.

44

BETH DIDN'T KNOW if it was sheer boredom or genuine concern that made her decide to slip out of her room to visit Tracy Westin. Without asking permission of the nurses, she pulled on the robe she had borrowed from Lynda and walked weakly to the elevators.

It was only one floor up. Fortunately, Tracy's room wasn't far from the elevators, so the walk wasn't long.

Tracy was sitting upright in her bed, still weak, and still connected to an IV and a monitor.

Beth knocked lightly on the door and went in.

Tracy looked up. Her eyes were red, wet, and swollen, and it was clear that she'd been crying. Something about that fragility touched Beth.

"Hi," she said. "I'm Beth Wright. Do you remember when I was here yesterday, with Nick?"

Tracy nodded, her expression holding more than a little suspicion.

Beth looked down at her robe. "As you can see, I'm a patient here, too. I had a little accident, but I'm okay."

She was babbling, she thought, and so far the woman hadn't said a word to her. She wished she hadn't come. Tracy wiped the wetness from her face, and Beth wondered how to comfort her. "Want to talk about it?" she asked.

Tracy shook her head.

"Okay." Beth pulled up a chair and gingerly sank into it. "You look better. You have more color in your face." She realized, kicking herself, that that might only be because she was crying. Didn't everyone's face turn red when they cried? She looked down at her hands. "Look, I know you don't know me from Adam. And you probably don't feel like spilling your guts to a complete stranger. I don't blame you. So if you want me to, I'll just go back to my room." She started to get back up.

"What kind of accident?" The woman's question startled her, and she turned back around.

"What?"

"What kind of accident did you have?"

"Oh. I was kind of in an explosion. Somebody sent me a package bomb, and I made the mistake of opening it."

Tracy's face twisted. "Really?"

"Yeah, really. Pretty awful, huh? You think I look bad, you should see my house."

Tracy drew in a deep cleansing breath, and wiped her face. "No wonder there was blood on Nick's shirt."

"You saw him?" she asked.

Tracy nodded slightly, and tears filled her eyes again. "He brought Jimmy."

Beth stepped closer. "He brought *Jimmy?* He didn't tell me he was going to do that. He came by a little while ago, but I was sleeping, so he just left a note."

"Apparently it was . . . spur of the moment. It turned out to be a . . . really bad idea."

"Why?"

Tracy's face twisted again as she relived the scene. "My kid took one look at me and took off running. I told you, he hates me. He has every right."

"I'm sorry." But Beth didn't know if she was sorrier for Tracy or Jimmy.

"Yeah, me too. Too late."

Beth stood there awkwardly, watching her cry for a moment before it occurred to her to hand her a tissue. "I wondered why they didn't bring Lisa," Tracy said, wiping her nose. "Is she dead?"

"Dead?" Beth asked, surprised by the question. "No, she's not dead. She's just . . . she's still at the children's home."

"Does she hate me, too? I was hoping . . . that she was too little . . . when she left . . ."

"I don't know," Beth whispered. "I've never met Lisa. Just Jimmy."

"Ohhh," Tracy moaned on a weak breath. "Why didn't I just die when I had the chance?"

"Maybe it wasn't your time."

"Why not?" she asked. "I've seen it all. I've done it all. I'm just so tired."

"There's lots more, Tracy. And just because Jimmy doesn't want to see you now doesn't mean there won't be a chance later. And speaking of chances, Tracy, you've got another one yourself—to pull your life back together."

"Yeah, right." She looked Beth over. "Easy for you to say. You have people you can trust. You probably have a job, money—and you don't have a monkey riding your back, so hard that no matter how you fight him, he's still there, reminding you, threatening you, pulling you . . ."

"Addictions can be overcome, Tracy. Think about it—it's been weeks since you've had any drugs. You could walk out of here and never touch the stuff again. Nick found you for a reason. Someone up there was looking out for you."

"Why now? He never has before."

"Maybe he was, but you just didn't notice."

"Yeah, right." She looked up at the ceiling. "If there's a God in heaven, he wouldn't waste his time on somebody like me."

Beth understood that sentiment. She had uttered it herself. "Nick wasted his time on you. Do you think God isn't at least as compassionate as Nick?"

"I don't know," she whispered.

"He is, Tracy."

"I abandoned my kids. I was a lousy mother. I shouldn't have even been allowed to have kids."

The old bitterness from childhood reared its head in Beth's soul, and she tried to argue. "Don't say that."

But Tracy had more to say, and she sobbed out the bitter words. "You want to know what I was thinking that last time I left them alone? I knew they were there without any food or anyone to watch them. But all I kept thinking was that I needed a fix. That was the most important thing. And I did whatever I needed to do to get one." She shook her head and covered her eyes. "I don't even think I was that upset when I got home and found them gone. I was too high by then, and I didn't want to come down. Somebody told me a few days later that the state had taken them, but I never did anything about it. I let them take my kids, and the truth is, I didn't even care."

Tears stung Beth's eyes, and she wondered if her own mother had had the same attitude. Had anyone cried when she'd been taken from her home? Had anyone felt any remorse? Did it change anyone's life, one way or another?

"So don't tell me about God loving me," Tracy went on. "If God loved me, he would have let me die before Nick found me. Then it would all be over, and I wouldn't have to deal with all this."

Beth tried to harden herself, so she wouldn't fall apart. "I'll see that Jimmy isn't brought back up here. Then you won't have to deal with him."

"No, that's not what I mean!" Tracy cried. "I *want* to see him. It just hurts . . . The past . . ."

The past did hurt. Beth knew that more than anyone. And it was hard having compassion for a woman who had left her children to be cared for by an indifferent and impersonal bureaucracy, to be turned over to a thief and child abuser.

"Tracy, you can change if you want. But you have to want to. Nobody can force you."

"I *do* want to. I just don't know if I'm strong enough."

Beth sat there for a long moment, wishing she had some strength to give her. But she didn't think she could spare any. Her throat tightened until she felt as if she were choking. She had to get out of here. She had to go somewhere where the memories didn't rush up to smother her. She had to get away from Tracy Westin. "I've got to go."

Tracy accepted that without a response.

When Beth reached the door, she turned back. "Maybe I'll come back by tomorrow. See how you're doing." But she had no intention of doing that, and she suspected that Tracy knew it.

45

LYNDA WAS HOME when Jimmy and Jake pulled up. She came outside to meet them, looking a little apprehensive, and Jimmy realized that Nick must have filled her in about the fiasco at the hospital. He hoped they all felt real bad about it.

He got out of the car. "Has Bill been arrested yet? Can they get Lisa out?"

Lynda shot a look to Jake. "Uh—no, Jimmy. Not yet."

Jake stiffened. "Why not?"

She sighed. "Judge Wyatt is still giving them a hard time. He's taken the matter under advisement."

"You're kidding me!" Jake said.

"What does that mean?" Jimmy asked.

Lynda didn't want to say it, but she bent down to get even with his face and tried to find the words. "It means that it may be tomorrow before they're able to arrest Bill."

"Oh, man!" Jimmy cried, backing away as his face darkened. "No way! *No way!* They can't wait."

"Larry and Tony are tailing him tonight, Jimmy. They'll make sure he doesn't do anything. They'll know where he is at all times."

"But they can't see into the home!" he shouted. *"If he beats Lisa, they won't know!"* He was crying now, and he hated himself for it.

Lynda reached out to hug him, but he shook her off. "I told you! I told all of you!" He ran into the house and back to his room.

He threw himself on the bed and cried into the pillow, cursing Bill Brandon, cursing the police, cursing his mother, cursing Lynda and Jake. His little sister's safety depended on them, and they were stupid, all of them.

He had to talk to her. He had to call Lisa and make sure she was all right. Wiping his face, he sat up on the bed and tried to calm himself so that he could talk clearly. He reached for the phone and started to dial the number, then thought better of it. He'd tried that before.

The computer. He hadn't checked to see if he had any messages from her or Brad.

He heard Jake and Lynda in the kitchen, and he went into the bathroom and blew his nose, splashed water on his face, and dried it off. He went into the living room, and they both saw him through the door into the kitchen.

"Jimmy? You want to talk now?"

"No," Jimmy said. "Can I play on your computer?"

The question seemed to surprise them, but he knew it was partial relief he saw in their faces. They thought he'd be playing games or something and were glad for the distraction. "Sure, Jimmy. That's fine."

He went to the computer and turned it on, navigated his way to the network, registered himself as a guest user, and signed on. In moments, the computer told him he had mail.

Lisa had gotten his message!

He clicked "read incoming mail," and found Brad's screen name posted at the top.

He opened the letter, and read as the color drained slowly from his face.

> Lisa's hurt real bad from the beating Bill gave her. Jimmy, you need to come get her before he kills her. I'll leave Stella's window unlocked so you can get in. Please hurry!

Jimmy stared at the words, his heartbeat slamming against his chest. Then he sat back and closed his eyes in horror, trying to think. He'd known this would happen. He'd tried to tell them all, and they hadn't listened, because they didn't know Bill Brandon. He couldn't depend on them. He had to do something. He had to do something *now.*

His heart pounded so hard that he almost couldn't think. He had to get Lisa out of there. But he needed a weapon.

Beth's gun. He knew just where she kept it.

He navigated his way on the network to a game that had sound effects, and started it running. The sound would make them think he was still in there.

Then, leaving the computer on, he went to the back of the house. He knew that one of the bedrooms had an outside door. Quietly, he unlocked it and slipped out.

The backyard was fenced, but he climbed it and leaped down. Night had fallen, and no one was around to see him. Lynda's closest neighbors lived on the other side of the cluster of trees up the street. He ran through the woods until he came out on the street that ran parallel to Lynda's.

He was home free. All he had to do was figure out how to get to Beth's house to get the gun, and then get to the children's home from there without being caught. Then he had to figure out how to get Lisa out. He didn't know how he would do it, but whatever he did, it would be better than what all these grown-ups were doing.

46

WHEN NICK GOT to Beth's hospital room, she was standing at her window, peering out. For a moment, he didn't knock, just stood at the door without letting her know he was there. She must be doing well, he thought with a rush of relief, to be standing and walking without help. This morning, after the explosion, he had wondered if she'd even live to see another day.

He knocked lightly on the wall, and she turned around.

"Hi," he said.

"Hi." She had more color in her face than she'd had earlier, but the light was still gone from her eyes.

"Are you okay?"

"Yeah. They said they would probably let me go home as soon as the doctor came by one last time."

"Really?"

"Yeah. The thing is, I don't *have* a home."

"That's just temporary. You can rebuild."

She turned halfway back to the window and gazed out again. "What do you think of me now, Nick?"

He came further into the room and joined her at the window. "What do you mean?"

"Now that you know I'm a criminal." She couldn't look at him as she uttered the words.

"You're not a criminal. You're a hero."

She breathed a mirthless laugh. "Yeah, right."

"You are. If it weren't for you, no one would have ever figured out what Bill Brandon was doing with those kids."

"You would have. You already had a feeling."

"Feelings don't change things. They don't give you evidence. You came up with that."

"I *am* the evidence."

"That's not your fault."

She sat down on the edge of her bed, and Nick grabbed a chair and pulled it up to her bedside. Straddling it, he got close to her. "Beth, you can't blame yourself. You're a good person, no matter what Bill Brandon spent years trying to make you believe."

She didn't want to face him, didn't want to meet his eyes, but she forced herself to. "I'm not really a good person," she said. "I went up there to visit Tracy today, and I've got to tell you, Nick. I have a hard time with her."

Nick waited, then prompted her. "Tell me."

Beth sighed. She got up and went to the window, putting her back to him. "She brings back a lot of memories, Nick. A lot of really bad ones."

"Your mother?" he asked.

She closed her eyes.

"You know, I'd really like to hear about her," he said softly. "I want to know everything about you."

"My mother was like Tracy," she said, "only she wasn't a junkie. She was an alcoholic. My father got disgusted and left her—and me, too. I guess the Invisible Daughter wasn't important enough to take along. Eventually, the state took me away from her and put me in Bill Brandon's home."

He was quiet for a moment, then asked, "Have you heard from your mother since then?"

She gazed out the window for a moment, one side of her face cast in shadow, the other side in light. "She died a couple of years ago. Those distant relatives who were nowhere to be found when the state took me into custody managed to get in touch with me to tell me about the funeral arrangements. I didn't go."

Nick looked down at his hands. As many kids as he'd taken out of homes himself, as many as he'd seen neglected or abused by their parents, he would never have guessed that Beth had been one of them.

"All my life I kept thinking that something would happen, that she'd sober up and remember she had a child and come back and get me. She'd be this wonderful, perfect mom. But she never did. And then one day she was dead."

Nick got up from the chair and came to stand behind her. He touched her shoulder and leaned his forehead on the crown of her head. "Beth, I'm so sorry."

She swallowed back the emotion in her throat. "It wasn't that hard. It wasn't hard at all. I hardly knew the woman, and what I did know of her, I hated." When she turned around to face him, her eyes were blazing with tears. "I know we're not supposed to hate, Nick. I know that with all my heart, and I've asked God to help me with it. But I can't help it, I still hate. And the worst part is that the person I hate is dead, and there's nothing I could ever do to change it."

"You can forgive a dead woman, Beth."

She shook her head. "I don't think I can. Maybe after I've read through the whole Bible and learned all the things that I'm supposed to learn, maybe then I'll have the strength to forgive my mother. But right now, it doesn't seem possible. She doesn't deserve forgiveness."

"Probably not," he agreed. "But you do. You deserve to be able to let it go. Sometimes forgiveness does more for us than it does for the ones we forgive. Besides, God told us to forgive."

She shook free of him and walked across the room again, picked up a water glass from the bed table, turned it over in her hand, then set it back down hard. "You don't know anything about it, Nick. You've never been thrown away like a piece of trash. You've never been dumped into an orphanage under someone who's going to turn you into a thief for his own selfish gain."

"No, you're right. I never have."

"That's the thing with Tracy. Her life—her attitude—it reminds me so much of my mother's."

"She had some bad breaks, Beth. Maybe it's not too late for her."

"Bad breaks?" she asked with an angry laugh. "She *chose* to abandon her children. She got herself hooked on drugs. She was a junkie, and probably a prostitute, and you're telling me that she just had some bad breaks?"

"You don't know what her life was like, Beth."

"I know what *my* life has been like, Nick. I know that if everybody turned to drugs because of a horrible past, then I'd be the worst junkie in town."

"You're right. You have more strength. More character. You've risen above your past. There's something about you, Beth, that some people just don't have. It's what's so attractive about you."

She looked as if she didn't know how to respond to such a compliment. Nick sighed and rubbed his eyes. "But God's grace covers people like Tracy, too. When I found her, she was lying there helpless, almost dead. I don't know why God put it in my head to go look for her that day, of all days, but I did, and if I hadn't, she'd be dead now. That means that God loves her, for some reason that you and I may not be able to fathom. And she has the same opportunity for heaven that we have."

"That's absurd," she said. "God doesn't send junkies and child abusers to heaven. Tracy Westin has never done anything for God or anyone else. Even if she were to repent now and turn into Mother Theresa for the rest of her life, all the junk in her life up until now would still outweigh any good she could do. Even God's grace couldn't balance all that out."

"But that's the great thing about grace. It doesn't have anything to do with a balance sheet," he said with a smile. "How do you think that thief on the cross came out when God looked at his balance sheet?"

Beth tried to think. "I don't know. I still say he hadn't done that much wrong."

"He was *crucified,* Beth. Whatever he did wrong was bad enough to get him executed. The Bible calls him a thief."

She was getting confused. "But God wouldn't take someone like Tracy—or even me, for that matter—and give us the same reward he gives someone like you or Lynda! You've done good things all your life, Nick. You've probably never really done anything displeasing to God."

"Don't bet on it," Nick said. "In God's eyes, there's no real difference between your life and mine. The only thing either of us has ever done that would win us admission to heaven is to believe in and trust in Christ."

Her face paled again, and she sank down into the chair. "That's not enough. Not for someone like me. It wouldn't be fair to people like you."

He knelt in front of her, his eyes riveting into hers. "Yes, it is." He grabbed the Gideon's Bible off her bed table and flipped through the pages. "Here," he said. "Matthew 20:1." He read to her the parable of the landowner who paid the same wages to those hired at the end of the day as he paid those who had worked all day. Those who had worked all day complained.

Nick read, "'"I want to give the man who was hired last the same as I gave you. Don't I have the right to do what I want with my own money? Or are you envious because I am generous?" So the last will be first and the first will be last.'"

He handed her the Bible so that she could see it for herself.

Tears came to her eyes. "But what about redemption? I'm not stupid, Nick. There's a price for the secrets I've kept all these years."

"Christ redeemed you when he gave his life for you, Beth."

She just couldn't buy it. Not the Messiah, dying for her, leaving her blameless. It was too unbelievable. "I'm not sure I agree with your theology, Nick."

"All right," he said. "Just promise me you'll think about it. Pray about it, too."

"I will." She took in a deep, shaky breath. "Faith is a hard thing for me, Nick. Sometimes I feel like I've got holes punched in me. If I walk carefully, I can keep everything in, but if the slightest thing shakes me, it all comes pouring out. All the putrid, ugly things about me that I don't want anyone to see."

"Well, we'll see what we can do about patching up those holes."

47

DARKNESS SEEMED INVITING to Tracy Westin. She watched lethargically out her window as the sun went down and twilight overwhelmed the sky. It would be night soon. But she needed more darkness than this; she needed enough to hide in.

She looked around her cold, sterile hospital room. It was better than anything she'd had in a long time, but she hated it. She didn't belong here. She didn't belong anywhere. Her life was hopeless, futile, and she didn't know where she had gone wrong.

Liar, she told herself. That was just one of the myths she'd been clinging to for years. She knew where she'd gone wrong—she'd gone wrong the first time she'd taken crack. It wasn't as if she hadn't known better. She had just wanted to be a part of things. She had wanted to fit in, to be a part of that group of people she admired who seemed so glamorous and exciting.

She'd never forget her first experience with the drug. It had been a high like she'd never experienced, yet afterwards she'd felt so low, so hungry for more, that it had changed her thinking. While she was pregnant, she had managed to stay off it, though she had occasionally smoked marijuana. She had told herself that she would clean up her act as soon as the baby was born. But it hadn't happened either time.

For years, she had blamed Jimmy and Lisa's fathers, the men who had wooed, then abandoned her when she'd needed them most. For years, she had told herself that she wasn't really to blame; she was just a victim, after all. But right now she didn't feel much like a victim. She felt like a monster who had ruined two young lives for no good reason. And that was hard to live with. So hard, in fact, that she really didn't want to live at all.

She was angry that Nick had found her lying in her room. If he'd just left her alone, she'd be at peace now. Or would she?

Was there really an afterlife? Was there a god cruel enough to prolong what she wanted so desperately to end? Would she pay the price for the sins she'd committed during her unhappy life? No, she told herself. If there was a god, he couldn't be that cruel.

Desperate enough to gamble that death meant an end to her existence and peace at last, she tore the IV needles out of her hands, peeled off the monitors glued to her chest, and threw down the oxygen mask that was making it so much easier for her to breathe. She didn't need this. She didn't need life. She didn't need another moment of it.

She pulled herself to the edge of the bed, sitting, trying to balance. If she got on the elevator and went straight up, would there be a window at the top from which she could hurl herself? It would be so easy. Just one step, and there would be an end to it all. And she couldn't get in anyone's way again, and she couldn't hurt anyone else, least of all herself. It would be the greatest act of kindness she had ever done for herself.

She touched the floor with her bare feet and tried to stand. Her legs wobbled beneath her, and she remembered how weak she had been when Nick had found her. She had thought she'd been getting stronger during these days in the hospital, but she knew now she was mistaken. She took a step, reached out to hold onto the bed table, then another step. She began to sweat and grow dizzy. How would she ever make it all the way to the elevator?

Finally, she backed up to the bed and sat again. She was too weak to kill herself, she thought bitterly. Wasn't that the way it always went? Finally had the courage, and now she didn't have the strength.

She wilted into tears and pulled her wobbly, bony knees up to her chest and hugged them tightly. She was sickened by her own frailty.

"What are you doing?" came the voice at the doorway. It was a stern nurse, and Tracy didn't have the energy to argue. "What do you mean taking that IV out of your hand? Girl, get that mask back on your face and get back under those covers!"

Tracy did as she was told. She didn't want to talk. She just closed her eyes, wishing to shut out the reality around her. The voices. The guilt. The demands.

She lay still as the woman reinserted the IV. It hurt—but that was fair. It was comfort that she couldn't endure. Never comfort.

"Where were you going, honey?" the nurse asked.

Tracy still couldn't talk, and as the woman put the mask back over her face, she felt sleep pulling her under. But not far enough.

48

IT WAS ALREADY six-thirty, and Judge Wyatt hadn't yet left the courthouse. Tony sat at the wheel of his car, tapping his fingers impatiently.

The telephone on his seat rang, and he picked it up. "Hello?"

"Tony, it's me." Larry sounded excited.

"You got anything?"

Larry, who had been staking out the children's home from the hardware store across the street, began to chuckle. "He just came out and headed to a storehouse at the back of the campus. He opened the door, and voila! Inside sits a green van. I'm in my car; as soon as he hits the street, I'll be on his tail."

"Up to no good?" Tony asked.

"Definitely no good."

"Any kids with him?"

"No," he said. "He's alone."

The door to the side of the courthouse opened, and a cluster of people spilled out. At the back of the group, he saw Judge Wyatt walking regally, carrying his briefcase. He wondered if the briefcase contained the evidence they had given him, and if he indeed planned to "take it under advisement."

"Well, guess what. Our boy just came out, too. Call me if Brandon does anything."

"Yeah, you do the same," Larry said.

Tony clicked off the telephone and cranked his engine, waiting inconspicuously as the judge got into his Lexus and backed out. Tony waited until two or three cars got between them, then pulled out and followed the judge out into the downtown traffic. He had looked up the judge's home address, so he knew his likely route home—but that wasn't the direction that Wyatt headed. Curious, Tony followed at a distance, keeping a mental record of their exact route.

The judge slowed as they came to a gas station with a convenience store attached. Tony braked as the Lexus pulled into the parking lot next to a pay phone. He didn't follow, only pulled to the side of the road far enough away that the judge wouldn't spot him, and watched as Wyatt got out of his car and stood at the pay phone.

Who was he calling? Tony wondered. There was a cellular antenna on Wyatt's car, so Tony knew the judge had a car phone. The only reason he would have for calling from a pay phone was that he didn't want any record of the phone call—or didn't want it traced. Tony grabbed his phone, punched out the number of the police station, and asked for one of the cops that he knew would be around this time of day. "Hey, Mac, I need you to do me a favor. Find out the phone number for a pay phone on the corner of Lems Boulevard and Stone Street, and see if you can get a record of the last few numbers called from that phone. There's a call taking place right now; I want to know who's on the other end of the line."

"Okay, Tony, I'll try."

"Call me back on my cell phone. I'm keeping my radio off so my cover isn't blown."

He hung up as Judge Wyatt finished the call and jumped back into his car. When the judge pulled back onto the street, Tony let a couple of other cars get between them before he began to follow.

He still wasn't heading home, and he wasn't going back to the courthouse. Tony recorded every turn; the route had gotten too complicated to remember, so he scribbled the information without looking on a piece of paper on the seat next to him.

The phone rang, and he clicked it on. "Yeah?"

"Tony, I got the number of the latest phone call from that phone. It was a cellular phone number. 555-4257. It's registered to the St. Clair Children's Home."

Tony's heart tripped. "Are you serious?"

"That's right."

He watched the judge make another turn, and he followed. "Then my hunch seems to be right on the mark. Thanks, Mac."

The Lexus turned down a road that looked as if it was rarely traveled. Tony waited until the judge had rounded a curve before he turned in behind him. The road curved like an S, cutting through a dense forest. Tony passed an abandoned warehouse here and an old, dilapidated structure there. He started to get suspicious—was this some kind of trap? Had the judge spotted him?

No, not likely. Whatever Wyatt was doing, it had nothing to do with Tony. But Tony suspected that it had everything to do with Bill Brandon.

As he slowly rounded the final curve, a big warehouse came into view. Adrenaline pulsed through Tony, and he pulled off the road and into a cluster of bushes where he wouldn't be seen. He got out and pushed through the brush until he had a clear view of the warehouse.

"Bingo," he muttered. "Just what we've been looking for!"

Tony peered through his binoculars and read the sign on the building. He wrote down the name Winrite, Inc., along with the address, and waited for the judge to come back out.

He would look up the owner of the building when he got back to the station to determine what kind of business operated from here. A light went on in one of the rooms. After a few minutes, the light went out, and the judge reappeared in the doorway, locked up, and got back into his Lexus.

Tony got back in his car but kept his engine off as the judge pulled out of the parking lot and back onto the street.

Again, the judge headed away from home, and Tony found his heart beating faster as he tailed him. His gut told him something was going on. The judge was going to lead him someplace that he didn't want anyone to see.

The Lexus turned onto a street that took them near the underside of a bridge on the outskirts of town. It was hard to stay close enough to the Lexus without losing him and still not be seen, but Tony was good at this; he'd done it often enough.

When the judge pulled his car over near the bridge, Tony pulled his car off the road behind a grove of trees. After a minute or two, he saw another car approaching. It pulled alongside the Lexus and idled there a moment.

The phone rang again.

"Yeah?"

"It's me," Larry said. "Looks like Brandon's meeting with somebody. It's a light-colored Lexus."

"A Lexus?" Tony's heart pounded.

"That's right."

"Larry, I've been following the Lexus."

"You *what?* Who is it?"

"One guess."

There was a brief silence, then: "Bingo."

"Looks like we figured out why we can't get our warrant," Tony said.

"You were right all along, buddy."

"Wish I could hear what they're saying."

"I'll tell you what they're saying. Judge Wyatt's filling him in on the gory details of our meeting this afternoon. And Brandon's trying to figure out a way to get out of this whole mess. More buildings to burn down. More people to try to kill."

"No," Tony said. "Just one. Beth Wright."

"Don't forget the kid."

"Jimmy's safe. He's with Jake and Lynda."

"Called the hospital lately to see if Beth's all right?"

"I called earlier. She's getting out tonight as soon as the doctor makes his rounds."

"So where's she going?" Larry asked.

"Not sure yet, but I'll find out."

"Do that," Larry said. "I'd feel better if we had somebody watching her."

"We're low on manpower, buddy. With us watching these two, I don't know who's going to do it."

"Somebody'll have to," Larry said. "I'll take care of it."

49

LYNDA AND JAKE had talked through everything—the injustice of the judge's delays in issuing a warrant for Bill Brandon, the difficulty of Jimmy's reaction to his mother, the feelings of rejection that reaction must have caused in Tracy, their worry for Lisa, still in Brandon's clutches . . .

But they would solve nothing sitting at Lynda's kitchen table, so after a while Lynda went into the living room to check on Jimmy. Although the noise from the computer game had been consistent for the past hour, Jimmy wasn't sitting there. Shrugging, Lynda walked on past the living room, down the hall, and to the bedroom where he had been staying. There was no sign of him.

"Jimmy," she called. "Jimmy!"

When she got no answer, she went to the back door and looked out into the yard. He wasn't there. "Jake!"

Jake came from the kitchen. "What is it?"

"Jimmy's gone!"

"I thought he was playing on the computer."

"He's not." Growing alarm sent her running from one room to another, searching for the boy and calling for him at the top of her lungs, but there was no answer.

"Where could he be?" she asked Jake.

"I don't know. You don't think—"

"He's run away." Lynda headed for the telephone. "We have to call Larry and Tony."

Jake got to the phone first and punched out the number of the St. Clair Police Department. Larry and Tony were out, he was told, so he left a message and hung up. He didn't want to report the runaway, not yet, not until he'd consulted with Larry and Tony, and even Nick, on how to proceed. So far, Jimmy hadn't been officially reported missing. Reporting it now to people who didn't know the case might do more harm than good; if Jimmy were found, he'd probably be taken back to SCCH.

"I'm calling Nick," he said. "Then I'll call Beth. Maybe he went there, to the hospital."

"Do you think he may have gone to see his mother?" she asked.

"Doubtful," he said, "judging from the way he reacted today. On the other hand, sometimes our first reactions aren't what we really mean. Maybe he did go back to finally confront her."

"Why didn't he just ask us to take him? He knew we would."

"He was pretty upset," Jake said. "I guess we underestimated how much."

"But he seemed content in there playing on the computer."

"It was a ruse," Jake said. "He was just trying to distract us so we wouldn't see him when he ran away."

Lynda paced across the floor, running her fingers through her hair. "We should have kept an eye on him. We should have been watching him."

"We thought he was safe, Lynda. Who would have thought he'd leave here, knowing that Bill Brandon is still out there?"

"That's no excuse!"

Sighing, Jake dialed the number for Nick's house, but there was no answer, so he quickly dialed the hospital and connected with Beth's room.

"Hello?"

"Beth, thank goodness you're still there. I thought you may have checked out by now."

"No, I'm still waiting for the doctor."

"Beth, Jimmy's missing."

"What?"

"He's run away. He's gone."

"Weren't you watching him?"

"We thought he was playing on the computer. We were just in the next room. We're thinking maybe he went there to see you, or maybe even his mother."

Beth paused for a moment, thinking. "All right, I'll be on the lookout for him. But aren't you going to call the police?"

"We put a call in to Larry and Tony, but we're reluctant to report this to anyone else."

"Do it anyway!" she said. "Bill Brandon is out there, Jake. If he gets his hands on Jimmy, we'll never see him alive again!"

"But Brandon may have a police scanner. If he hears about the disappearance, he may find Jimmy before we do."

"Call anyway. *Please,* Jake. Maybe the police can find him."

In the hospital room, Beth hung up the phone and turned back to Nick. "He's gone."

"Where did he go?"

"They think he may be coming here. Maybe to see me, or you—maybe even Tracy."

"No way," Nick said. "Not after his reaction today. He wouldn't come to see Tracy."

"But, Nick," Beth said, "what if he thought it over and decided he does want to see her after all?"

Nick shrugged. "Well, maybe we'd better go warn her," he said.

"Yeah, maybe."

They told the nurse where they'd be in case the doctor came, then headed to the elevator. They got off on the floor above Beth's and walked quickly to Tracy's room. Tracy's eyes were swollen and red, and she looked as dismal as she'd looked when Beth had left her earlier.

"Tracy?"

She looked up, but her expression was lifeless.

"Tracy, we need to talk to you."

"About what?"

"About Jimmy."

She closed her eyes. "There's nothing you can say to me about Jimmy."

"Yes, there is. He's disappeared."

"What?" Her eyes came open fully, and she sat partially up.

"Tracy, I want you to listen to me, and I want you to listen carefully," Nick said. "Jimmy's been in trouble. The reason I came looking for you is that he and Lisa were in a children's home and Jimmy was being used in a crime ring. We're about to have the operator of the home arrested, but meanwhile, Jimmy's been hiding with us."

"And you let him run away?" Tracy asked. "How could you do that?"

"He's smart," Nick said. "He duped the people who were watching him by setting up a distraction, and he slipped out of the house without anyone realizing it."

"Well, is anyone looking for him?"

"Yes. But Tracy, we wanted to tell you, in case he comes here."

"Here? Why would he come here?" Tears spilled over her lashes, and she smeared them across her face. "I can't think of a reason in the world he would come to me."

"You're his mother."

"I'm *not* his mother!" she shouted. "He doesn't have a mother!"

Beth moved closer to the bed. "Tracy, you *are* his mother, whether you like it or not. Whether *he* likes it or not."

Tracy fell back on her pillows. "What if something happens to him?"

"We'll find him," Beth said. "They'll find him. He couldn't have gotten far on foot."

Tracy looked skeptical. "Like you said, he's a smart kid. He was smart when he was seven years old. He can go anywhere he wants to go."

"Not if people are looking for him," Beth said. "But Tracy, if he comes here, you have to tell us, okay? You have to call this number." She wrote down Larry and Tony's number at the station and set it on the bed table. "Do you hear me? You have to call."

"What if he doesn't want me to?"

"Do it anyway. He's in danger. The man who runs the home isn't in jail yet. If he finds Jimmy before we do, he may kill him."

"Oh, terrific," Tracy said. "So my son went from a bad situation with me to a worse one with some guy who could kill him, is that what you're saying?"

Nick leaned over her bed and touched Tracy's hand. "Tracy, look at me."

Tracy looked up at him with wet eyes that looked too big for her face.

"Tracy, there's a purpose in all this, whether you believe it or not."

"I *don't* believe it," Tracy said.

Beth felt her cheeks growing hot, and she tightened her lips. "Well, you'd better believe it, because maybe that purpose is to save and protect your son."

Tracy shook her head as if to rid it of the cobwebs. "What about Lisa? Is she in danger, too?"

"We're trying to get her out of the home," Nick said, "but we have to wait until the guy's arrested."

She closed her eyes, taking in the horror of it all. "What have I done to my kids?" she whispered.

More tears ran down the sides of her face, and Beth sat there staring at her for a long moment, feeling the pain that she didn't want to feel, because she didn't want to empathize with this woman who had abandoned her children. She wanted to hate her like she hated her own mother, but something about Tracy's pain touched her, and she leaned over the bed and touched the woman's hand.

"Tracy, it's not too late."

"What isn't?"

"It's not too late to become somebody to your kids. It's never too late until you're dead." Her voice cracked on the last word. "Take it from a kid who's been there."

Tracy brought both forearms up to cover her face. "I don't want to do this!" she cried. "I don't want to be here. I don't want to see my kids. I don't want to face them, and they sure don't want to face me!"

"If Jimmy comes, we'll help you," Beth said.

"And what if he doesn't?" Tracy cried. "What if he gets into more trouble? What if someone grabs him? What if—"

"Shhh," Nick cut in, trying to calm her. "Jimmy's a tough kid. He'll be all right."

"What if he isn't?" she screamed.

The silence in the wake of her question lay heavy over the room. "He will," Nick said finally. "Take my word for it. We'll find him within the hour."

"What if he went back to that orphanage?" she demanded.

"He would never go back there," Beth said. "He knows how dangerous that would be."

Tracy's sobs were deep, wrenching, soul-rending. "Are you sure I didn't die?"

Nick's own eyes were filling with tears. "What do you mean, Tracy?"

"When you found me lying there on that mattress, are you sure I wasn't already dead?"

"I'm sure," he said, glancing uneasily at Beth. "You're very much alive. Why would you ask a thing like that?"

"Because," Tracy choked out, "this feels like some kind of hell."

50

IT WAS GETTING darker. Jimmy knew that he couldn't hitchhike, since police were probably already out looking for him. For all he knew, his face could be on the screen of every television in St. Clair by now.

So he ran, as fast and as hard as he could, cutting through yards and plowing through woods, trying to get to Beth's house. His body was covered with sweat, and his shirt stuck to him, but he was glad that he had these running shoes. Bill hadn't skimped on shoes for the kids who "worked" for him. They had to be black, and they had to be quiet—for quick getaways.

His navigational skills were pretty good, just as his computer skills were, and he tried to remember where Bill had taken him the night he'd dropped him off at Beth's house. He had turned here, and passed that railroad crossing, then turned again . . .

By the time Jimmy found the long road that connected to Beth's dirt road, two hours had passed since he'd left Lynda's, and it was growing dark. He cut through the woods and hit the dirt road leading up to her house. He slowed to a walk as he headed up the dirt road, trying to catch his breath.

Because there were no streetlights on Beth's little dirt road, Jimmy was on the driveway before he saw that the house wasn't there anymore.

He squinted through the darkness at the gutted structure where he had hidden for so long, where he'd met the first adult who'd really cared about him in a long time, where he'd gotten to know the little puppy. He had known about the explosion, of course, but he had imagined it like one of those cartoon explosions, where one corner of a room gets soot on the walls, but nothing else is hurt. The condition of the house now stunned him, and he leaned back against a tree and slid down to the ground, almost dizzy with the reality of how close Beth had come to death.

And with that chilling thought came another: Bill had probably expected Jimmy to be at Beth's house, too. Had the bomb been as much for him as for Beth?

He felt that familiar pain in his stomach at the thought that his sister could have been killed delivering the bomb or setting the newspaper building on fire. He grew nauseous at the thought of her beaten up and awaiting rescue. He had to hurry.

But first he needed the gun.

There was nothing left of her living room. If the gun had been there, it was ruined now. Then again, she might have taken it with her in the car when she'd tried to go to St. Petersburg the day of the explosion, knowing that Bill was after her.

But where was the car?

He tried to think. It wasn't at Lynda's. It could be at Nick's. Or someone could have taken it to the hospital for her . . .

Yes. The hospital. It wasn't far from here. It shouldn't take long to get there.

He jogged back to the main road again, then cut through the trees skirting the street, hidden by the trees as well as the darkness.

Forty-five minutes later, drenched with sweat and panting, he reached the hospital. He went from one row to another, ducking between cars, until he spotted Beth's car. He closed his eyes and tried to concentrate on the gun being there as he approached it, as if wishing could make it so. Please be there . . . please be there . . .

The car was locked.

He looked toward the front doors of the hospital. Would anyone recognize him if he went in? He had no choice. Sliding his hands into his jeans pockets, the same black ones he'd been wearing since Beth had found him, he ambled up to the doors and slipped into the lobby. There was a coat rack in the corner of the room, so he checked to see if anyone was looking, then went over and grabbed a coat hanger. He shoved it into the front of his jeans, then pulled his T-shirt out to hang over it.

Quickly, he headed back out to Beth's car. Just as Bill had taught him, he stretched the coat hanger into the shape he needed, then maneuvered it between the rubber and the top of the window. In seconds, he had hooked the hanger onto the lock and popped it open.

When he opened the door, the light came on, making him feel vulnerable and exposed. He closed the door quickly, encasing himself in darkness.

He felt around on the seat. No gun. He bent and felt under it. Nothing.

Then he saw the glove compartment, and he punched the button and slowly pulled it open.

The gun lay there on its side, filling him with bittersweet relief.

His hands trembled as he took it. Quickly, he pulled his tee shirt up again. He stuck the barrel into his pants, as he'd seen it done on television, then tucked his shirt back over it.

He was ready. He could face a standoff with Bill Brandon now. He could rescue his sister, and maybe some of the others. He was ready to do whatever he had to do. And if he had to go to jail—whether for burglary or for murder—to see Lisa freed from Bill's bondage, then it would be worth it.

He got back out of the car and started walking in the direction of SCCH. His courage rose with every step, until finally he was running again. He knew the way to the home from here. And those who were looking for him would never even think to look there.

51

THE PARTY THAT Bill Brandon had insisted on having at the home was a first. He had never had one before—though occasionally local churches had given them Christmas parties—but this afternoon, he'd told the children that he was throwing a birthday party to celebrate all of the birthdays that occurred throughout the year. Everyone would be the guest of honor. He had let Lisa out of the back room for the occasion. Though Stella had dressed her up in her newest dress, she was pale and drawn. Weak from the fear of further punishment, she sat in a corner as the festivities unfolded around her.

This was some kind of trick, she thought wearily. He had called the television stations, and cameras went around the room, filming the happy faces of the children as they ate cake or tore into their presents—rag dolls for the girls and plastic race cars for the boys. It was as if he was trying to make the world think that they always did this, that he cared about the children, that he wanted them to be happy. She wondered what the reporters and cameramen would think if they knew where she'd been for the last day and a half, or if they could see the injuries under Brad's clothes. He, too, sat very still against the wall, pale and quiet, as if the effort of speaking might cause too much pain.

She got up, holding her rag doll by one arm, and went to the cluster of boys talking near Brad. She wasn't welcome among them, she knew, especially since Jimmy wasn't here anymore, but she wanted to hear what they were saying.

"I heard Stella say he was expecting someone."

"Someone like who?"

"Somebody from HRS, or cops, maybe. Probably what he warned us of the other day, after Jimmy got busted."

The faces in the circle changed, and Lisa couldn't hold her silence anymore. "Are they gonna arrest us? Did we get caught?"

"Shhhh," Brad ordered. "Are you crazy? Somebody could hear you."

"I told you she was too little to keep a secret."

"I am not too little," she returned. "I have kept the secret. But I don't want to go to jail."

"That's where Jimmy is," Kevin said.

"He is not! They don't have computers in jail!"

"Lisa, shut up!" Brad warned.

"Well, they don't!"

"What's that got to do with anything?" Kevin asked.

"Because Jimmy e-mailed me—"

Brad grabbed her wrist and jerked her to shut her up, when the other boys' eyes widened to the size of quarters. "You heard from him?"

"I'm not saying nothing," Brad said. "And neither is she. Are you, Lisa?" She didn't answer. "I can just tell you that Jimmy's not in jail."

"Well, what if he snitched on us? What if that's why the cops are coming?"

"It might be why," Brad said, looking back over the festive children and the cameras still going. "But I don't think so."

The door opened, and Bill came in, all smiles and laughter. He tried to act as if he genuinely loved all of the children in the home, bending over them and hugging them, wishing them happy birthday for the sake of the cameras.

"Why would Bill want cameras here if the cops are coming?"

"Maybe to show the world that he's really a nice guy, and that we're all happy kids who love it here, so that whatever Jimmy told them won't seem true," Keith said. "I wonder if he told them about my leg."

"He should have," Lisa whispered.

Brad hugged himself around the ribs that were probably broken. “I don’t really care what he told them. I don’t even care what happens to me. I just want them to get Bill. And I hope he tries to escape and they shoot him, just bad enough for him to hurt and see what it feels like. Then I hope he dies.”

The other children only gazed at him, caught up in the terrors they wished on their keeper.

52

"WEIRD," LARRY TOLD Tony via cell phone. Tony had followed the judge home and was now watching the house. Larry had set up his equipment on the second floor of the hardware store across the street, a vantage point from which he could see most of the buildings on the campus of SCCH. "Brandon just made it back to the home, and it looks like there's a party going on here. Television vans, music . . . I can see into the game room through a window, and I see balloons and streamers. Not exactly what I would have expected from a man who's desperate and knows we're coming after him."

"Sure it is. It's brilliant PR," Tony said. "He's trying to make the press think he's a wonderful guy. Get them all psyched up, so that when they get the real story, they won't believe it. Either that, or he can use it in court. 'Well, to be perfectly honest, Judge, I was just minding my own business giving a party for my beloved children, when the gestapo cops broke the doors down and arrested me in front of all of them. I only hope they're not traumatized for life.'"

"He knows we can't touch him tonight. Not until Judge Wyatt gives us the warrant, and you and I both know he won't do it."

"Well, I've been thinking. What if we went to the judge and told him what we know?"

"Like blackmail, Tony?"

"More like cutting a deal. We tell him that we saw him talking to Brandon, then he gives us that warrant, hoping we'll forget what we saw."

"No way," Larry said. "He's going down with Brandon. No deals."

Tony got quiet for a moment, thinking. "Then call the captain at home," he said. "Tell him about Wyatt's meeting with Brandon. Then try to get him to go to the prosecutor for two warrants tonight—for both of them."

"All right," Larry said. "But I don't want to leave for a while yet. I want to see how this party pans out. It could get interesting."

"At least the kids are safe while the cameras are there."

"Yeah. It's after they leave that I'm worried about. Any word on Jimmy?"

"Not yet. Lynda and Jake are basket cases. They've been out looking for him since he left."

"I hope that kid's all right," Larry said. "I just wonder what he's got up his sleeve."

"I'm just hoping he left of his own free will, and didn't get abducted without anyone knowing it."

"Well, we know Brandon and Wyatt didn't get him. I'd say he's just out there hiding somewhere, trying to figure out who he can trust."

"Let's hope it's not the wrong person."

53

LARRY'S CAR WAS the first thing Jimmy saw when he approached the children's home from the woods behind the hardware store. Larry must be in there, watching Bill. The fact that they'd put so much effort into watching him—yet couldn't arrest him—only reinforced the idea that Bill would get off scot-free. Nothing ever happened to Bill Brandon.

Jimmy stayed back in the shadows of the trees, trying to figure out how to get close to the cottages without Larry seeing him. He peered through the trees at the activity building. Something was going on at the home. It looked like a party. And television vans were outside.

He crossed the street a block down the road, then stole through the woods, staying in the shadows so Larry wouldn't see him. He came up on the other side of the building, out of Larry's sight, and peered through the window of the activities building. He saw Stella being interviewed by a local reporter, and across the room, Bill and some of the other employees of SCCH were also talking to reporters, smiling, laughing, gesturing at the balloons, the crepe paper, the happy children.

But not all the children were happy. Jimmy saw his sister Lisa sitting alone, holding a Raggedy Ann doll that she didn't seem interested in. She didn't look good. Near her, Brad sat hugging himself with a pallid, pained expression. Some of the guys around Brad whispered among themselves.

Jimmy turned from the window and looked across the lawn toward the cottages. The lights were all turned off. Maybe if he went in now and hid in the cottage where Lisa stayed, he could get her out tonight before anyone realized he was around. Brad had said he'd leave Stella's window open. He hoped he hadn't forgotten.

Stealing through the trees, he came up on the back door of Cottage B. He went to Stella's room and tried the window. It slid open easily. Quietly, he climbed in, shut the window behind him, and headed farther into the house. A strange mixture of sensations overwhelmed him as he walked through the building he had lived in for so long—homesickness and fear, familiarity and terror. Had any of this been worth it? Maybe everyone would have been better off if he had just found a way to get out of that attic and back to Bill . . .

No, that wasn't right. Eventually, Bill would have used Lisa in his little schemes, anyway. Eventually, Jimmy would not have been able to protect her. Eventually, Bill would have gone too far and killed one of the children. Eventually, they would have been caught. No, he had done the right thing. And what he was about to do was even more right—he had to save Lisa from Bill Brandon.

He went into the bedroom where he and Brad and Keith had slept, along with five other boys, in the bunk beds lined against the walls. Going to the bed that used to be his, he looked under it for the box of his belongings. They were gone; now another boy's shoes were there. Had Bill already replaced him? A sinking feeling began to pull him under. The feeling surprised him. He didn't live here anymore—didn't want to. But he didn't want to be forgotten, either.

He went to Lisa's room. He found his box hidden under her bed, and felt relieved that his sister had protected his things. *She* hadn't forgotten him.

He sat down on her bed, feeling so helpless, so dismal, so confused.

"It's not fair," he whispered to the darkness. "It's just not fair." He had done little to deserve all of this: the risks, the danger, the sadness. And Lisa had done even less. He closed his eyes and wished he had been able to protect her from the past few days. She was tiny, helpless—just the way Bill liked them.

Jimmy hoped he was getting to her in time. He knew she would expect him to rescue her, to make all the evil go away, to set everything right. She had always thought he was some kind of superkid, and he hadn't minded it. She'd looked up to him like he was her father. But he wasn't—and didn't have any more idea of how a father acted than she did.

He thought of the few men he knew that he admired. He admired Nick—the way he had gotten Beth out of the fire after her explosion and taken care of her. Nick had rescued Jimmy's mother, too—although part of Jimmy wished she had died. But then Nick was also the one who had placed him and Lisa in this home.

Tears came to Jimmy's eyes, and he wiped them away. Maybe Nick wasn't the one he wanted to be like. Maybe someone else. Someone like . . .

Jake Stevens. The name came to him with a warmth that burned in his heart. Jake was someone he could look up to. What would Jake do in this situation? How would he get Lisa out?

Lynda had told him how Jake had saved her from some murderer while he was still in his wheelchair. Even that hadn't stopped Jake. And Jimmy didn't plan to let anything stop him, either.

He heard car doors closing outside, and he peered through the window. The television crews were loading up, and Bill was standing outside with them, giving one last interview before they packed their equipment and disappeared. The children were still inside the rec room, and Jimmy guessed that Bill had them all doing cleanup detail before they could return to the cottages.

Just in case someone came back early, he slipped into the closet. He sat down in the corner and closed the door in front of him. It was stifling in there. There was no ventilation, and the hot Florida air was sweltering there where the air conditioner failed to blow. He reached into the waist of his jeans and felt for the pistol. It was there. If he needed it, he would use it. He wouldn't hesitate.

Across the street, Larry watched inconspicuously as the party broke up. Bill seemed to be trying to delay the television crew's departure. It was his last-ditch effort to appear to be a pillar of the community. He wanted to make friends with these people who, tomorrow, would have to condemn him on the news. He was running scared, Larry thought with satisfaction. He only wished he could walk up there right now, while the cameras were rolling, and slap some cuffs on the man's wrists. He wished he could expose him as a murderer, thief, and child abuser, and drag him away in front of all the children. Now *that* would be a party they could appreciate.

He picked up the phone and dialed Tony's car. Tony picked up. "Yeah?"

"The party's breaking up," Larry said. "Camera crews are going home. Has the judge moved?"

"Not an inch. He's tucked safely into his house. Doesn't look like he's going anywhere else tonight."

"Don't take your eyes off him, anyway," Larry said.

"I won't. I'm still trying to track the captain down. Call me if anything happens."

54

JAKE PULLED HIS old car into the driveway at Lynda's house, hoping to see Jimmy sitting beside the door, waiting to be let in. They hadn't found him, and their only hope now was that he had decided to come back home.

"He's not here," Lynda said, defeated.

"Maybe he came in through a back door or something. It's possible. He went out one."

Lynda's dull expression didn't change. "He couldn't trust us anymore. I can't believe we let this happen."

"We didn't *let* anything happen, Lynda," Jake said. "It just did. It couldn't be helped."

In the house, Lynda searched every room, hoping, praying that he was there, sitting in the dark, brooding. But he wasn't. "Where could he be?" she asked, fighting tears. "Oh, Jake, he could be in real trouble."

She saw the glow from the computer screen still on in the darkened living room, and went in to shut it off. "If he had just said something—" She realized the computer was still on-line, so she moved the mouse to exit the game. "We could have taken him ourselves, helped him if he needed it . . ."

When the game window closed, the mail window was still on the screen, and she started to close it, too—then froze when she saw the letter on the screen, from someone with the screen name Drab11. "Jake—Jake, this is e-mail! Jimmy's been communicating with someone from the home."

Jake rushed over and read the letter signed "Brad." "You're right. And he didn't like what he heard."

"I don't think we have to wonder where anymore, do you?"

"No, I sure don't. Come on, let's go. Maybe we can stop him before he does something stupid."

"Wait. First we have to call Larry and Tony. Maybe they can get to him before we can." Lynda ran to the phone and punched out the number to Tony's car.

"Yeah?" Tony answered.

"Tony, this is Lynda," she blurted. "We've figured out where Jimmy is."

"Where?"

"He's gone back to SCCH to get Lisa out."

"No. He wouldn't do that."

"He's doing it. I'm telling you, that's where we're going to find him. We're headed over there."

"No way. Let us take care of it, Lynda."

"You said yourself that you aren't authorized to do anything! Tony, there's a child's life at stake here. Somebody has to do something besides sitting around watching!"

"Lynda, we know what's at stake! If you get in the way of what we're doing, I'll gladly arrest you myself. Now stay out of the way!"

Lynda's face reddened. "I'm a lawyer, Tony. You just try and arrest me! I'll drag you into court for false arrest, police brutality, and anything else I can come up with!"

"Go ahead," Tony said, undaunted. "I'll arrest you anyway. It would keep you out of the way tonight while we're trying to get to Bill Brandon. After that, you can do anything you want to me."

Lynda grew quiet, and she covered her eyes with a trembling hand. "So help me, Tony, if anything happens to that kid . . ."

"Let us do our job, Lynda. That's the best way to make sure nothing will."

55

IT WAS AT least an hour before the children began coming back into the cottage. Jimmy heard their voices as they approached the bedroom. The girls who shared a room with Lisa were laughing and talking about their rag dolls, as if they'd been given some precious gift they'd never forget. He couldn't hear Lisa's voice.

He heard the sounds of them getting ready for bed, then Stella's voice barking out orders. He waited until the light went out and everyone had quieted down, then opened the door slightly so that he could see where everyone was. There was Lisa, lying in her bed on her side, still awake, staring dismally into the dark. Her rag doll had been discarded on the floor beside her bed, but she clutched her old teddy bear tightly.

Why had they gotten presents tonight? What was Bill up to?

He felt for the gun again, and it gave him courage to wait. He sat there for what seemed an eternity, hoping the others would go to sleep. But it didn't matter if they didn't. He had the gun, and that gave him power. He could take Lisa anywhere he wanted to, as long as he had the gun.

When silence had prevailed for a half hour or more, he opened the door ever so slightly. It creaked, but no one moved.

He crawled out on his hands and knees, staying down in case anyone's eyes were still open. But they all seemed to be asleep, which surprised him. In his room, which was an older group, that didn't happen. They often argued long after lights out, or they were up getting ready to do some dirty deed of Bill's.

He crawled to Lisa's bed, then got to his feet and bent over her. He shook her shoulder, and her eyes came open with a flash of fear, making him wonder if she'd expected Bill.

He held his finger to his mouth, hushing her, but she couldn't help the gasp that escaped. *"Jimmy!"*

He put his hand over her mouth, but it was too late—a little girl named Jill opened her eyes and sat up. "What are you doing here?" she whispered in surprise.

"Shhh." He waved frantically for her to be quiet. "Come on, Lisa," he whispered. "Come with me."

"Can I come, too?" Jill asked.

"You don't want to go where we're going," Jimmy said.

"I might."

"Just *hush.* I came to get my sister, that's all. And if you tell—" He pulled his shirt up, showing the gun.

She caught her breath and lay back down quickly. "I won't tell."

Lisa shrank back onto her pillow, horrified. "Jimmy, where'd you get that?" she whispered.

He shook his head and put his fingers over her lips. "Come on, we've got to get out of here."

She got up and ran to the shelves where all of their clothes were piled in little cubbyholes. She pulled out a pair of shorts and slipped on her shoes. "Wait," she whispered. "I've got to get the box."

"Leave it," he said. "It doesn't matter. We can't carry it."

"Yes, we can," she said. "We have to. It has pictures of our mama. I don't want to forget what she looks like."

She ran to the closet and pulled out a black backpack—which Jimmy recognized immediately as the kind that Bill issued to all the kids who worked under him. His heart sank. So Bill had gotten to her, too. She stuffed the contents of the box into the backpack, along with her teddy bear, and slipped it onto her small shoulders. "I'm ready," she whispered with a smile. "I knew you'd come to get me, but he told us you were in jail."

"He's the one who's going to jail," Jimmy said. "Not me."

"But we've all broken laws," she said. "He said if we get caught—"

"He lied," Jimmy said. "He's a liar and a murderer and a thief and you can't believe a word he says. Especially all that Bible stuff."

"He said the sins of the brother are visited on the sister. Jimmy, what does that mean?"

"It means that if I see him face-to-face, I might just use this gun on him." He went to the window and tried to open it. It wouldn't budge.

"It's nailed shut," Jill whispered. "Bill did it yesterday."

He breathed out a ragged sigh. "Okay, then we'll have to go up the hall." He turned with a menacing look toward Jill, who still followed them with her eyes, though she lay quietly. "Jill, if you make one sound or tell anyone Lisa's gone before morning, so help me, I'll come back here and get revenge. Got it?"

"Okay," she whispered. "Bye, Lisa. Are you coming back?"

Lisa looked at her brother, and he shook his head no. The little girl's face changed to an expression of deep sadness, and she lay back down. "Are you sure I can't come?"

"Yes," Jimmy said. "Not right now. Maybe later."

He took Lisa's hand and tiptoed with her up the hall, desperately silent. He heard Stella moving around in her own room, so he knew that he couldn't go back out the same way he had come in. They were going to have to sneak through the den. He could only hope that no one was there. But he'd been trained in walking through people's homes while they slept and not getting caught. They cut through the dark kitchen, heading for the den, when the sound of the front door startled him. He heard Stella dash from her room into the den to meet her guest.

"I think that was a success, don't you?" It was Bill's voice, and Jimmy almost panicked. He motioned frantically for Lisa to head back to her room, and he followed.

"Absolutely. You've got them eating out of your hand," Stella said.

"Let's just hope they keep eating out of it," he said. "Judge Wyatt is fighting hard, but they may find a way to go over his head by tomorrow. It might be time for me to get out of town."

"And what about me?" Stella asked. "I'll be implicated, too. We all will."

"Just say you didn't know what was going on. That you weren't actually involved."

"But according to the paper, they know that it was a little girl who delivered the package bomb to the post office—and that she was seen with a woman in a pickup truck."

"That was me!" Lisa whispered. She and Jimmy were standing in the doorway to her room now, trying to listen. Jimmy put his hand over her mouth to silence her.

"They can't prove that woman was you," Bill told Stella.

"Bill, I'm not taking the heat for attempted murder. You know I didn't know what was in that package—"

"You knew it wasn't a box of chocolates."

"What about Jimmy?" she demanded. "He's still out there somewhere, telling his story."

Jimmy moved his hand from Lisa's face, and they both listened hard.

"Don't worry about Jimmy," Bill said. "He's not going to be a factor."

"Bill, you'll never get to him without getting caught."

"I won't have to," he said. "He'll come to us, before we know it. Maybe even tonight."

Lisa's eyes rounded with terror. Bill was *expecting* Jimmy!

But Jimmy only stared into space, trying to figure out how Bill had known he was coming—and how he and Lisa would get past him now.

56

LARRY'S PHONE RANG, and he snatched it up.

"We've got a problem," Tony said before Larry could speak.

"What?"

"Lynda and Jake think Jimmy's headed over there."

"Here? To the home?"

"That's what they said. Seen any evidence of it?"

"No," Larry said. "Why in the world would he come here?"

"Apparently, he got a desperate e-mail note from some kid there to come get Lisa out before Bill killed her."

Larry's hand slid down his face. "Tell me you're kidding."

"No, and Jimmy must have taken off to rescue her."

"But he's a kid! He can't take on Bill Brandon by himself."

"Well, let's hope Jake and Lynda are wrong. But just in case, keep your eyes peeled and let me know if you see anything."

57

BY NOW, ALL of the girls in Lisa's room had awakened. They all looked at Jimmy as he and Lisa turned and came back into the room. "Don't anybody say a word," he whispered. He pulled out his gun again, just for good measure, and waved it in the air. "I'm not afraid to use this."

All the girls lay back down, their eyes wide as they watched to see what he was going to do next. Then Jimmy noticed that their eyes darted suddenly toward the door behind him.

"Jimmy?"

Jimmy swung around to see his friends Brad and Kevin standing in the doorway.

"What are you doing here?" Brad whispered harshly.

"Shut up!" Jimmy mouthed. "Bill's out there."

"I know he is," he said. "He came to get us. He wants Lisa, too."

"No," Jimmy said through his teeth. "He's not taking her." He stepped closer to the boys, keeping his voice as low as he could. "Cover for her. Distract him until we get out of here."

"I want to go, too," Brad returned. "Take me with you."

"No! Just Lisa. That's all I can handle."

"But you *gotta* take me, too," Brad whispered, starting to cry, something Jimmy had never seen him do before. "Bill's got it in for me lately. If you don't take me, you're gonna have to come visit me in the graveyard."

"No!" Jimmy cried. He reached out to push the boy away, but Brad winced and doubled over in pain.

Only then did Jimmy notice that Brad was wearing a long-sleeved shirt and jeans, rather than the shorts and T-shirt he usually wore in the summer. He remembered that he had done that, despite the heat, to cover bruises after Bill's beatings. "What happened?" he asked.

"Bill beat him up because of the e-mail," Lisa said.

A sense of dread washed over Jimmy. "What e-mail?"

"The one we sent you."

Jimmy's face went cold as the blood drained from it. "Bill found it?"

"Yeah, and was he mad."

The little girls were all sitting up now, and Lisa was on the edge of her bed, not sure what to do next.

Jimmy touched Brad's shoulder. "I'm sorry I shoved you, man. No wonder you wanted to leave so bad."

Brad wiped the tears off his face.

"The e-mails," he said. "You were the one who told me to hurry because Lisa had been beaten, weren't you? You're the one who left Stella's window unlocked?"

"No, man. That's not what I wrote. Bill must have sent that."

Jimmy felt such rage that his head threatened to burst. "It was a trap." His face grew hot and mottled, and he pulled the gun out of his pocket. "He knows I'm here. He set this whole thing up. Even left the window open for me."

One of the little girls buried her face in her pillow and began to cry, and the others sat huddled on their beds, eyes wide with fear.

"What's gonna happen?" Lisa asked.

"I'm gonna get you out of here, that's what," Jimmy told her. "All we have to do is get out the door. There's a cop across the street. As soon as he sees us, we'll be home free."

"Is that so?" The deep voice startled them all, and Jimmy turned and saw Bill standing in the doorway, leaning indolently against the frame. "Hello, Jimmy. Long time, no see. I've been expecting you."

With shaky hands, Jimmy raised the gun and pointed it at Bill. "All I want is my sister. Let us go, and nobody'll get hurt."

Bill laughed. "You don't know how to use a gun, Jimmy. And even if you did, you wouldn't."

"Watch me," Jimmy said through his teeth.

Bill started walking toward him, his hand outstretched. "Give me the gun, Jimmy, and then we'll go to my office and talk this thing out, man-to-man."

"Yeah? Like you talked to Brad?"

"Brad knows he deserved what he got. Don't you, Brad?"

"Yes, sir."

Bill got too close, and Jimmy shouted, "Don't take another step or I'll shoot!"

Bill laughed again. "Go ahead, Jimmy. You're not even holding the gun right."

Jimmy trembled as his finger tried to close over the trigger. It didn't budge. He squeezed harder. It was locked, and he didn't have a clue how to release it.

"Just give it to me," Bill said calmly. "I'm not mad at you, Jimmy. In fact, I've missed you. Things haven't been the same around here without you."

"Yeah? Is that why you've already put somebody else in my bed?" It was a stupid, irrational thing to say, and Jimmy knew it.

Bill shook his head. "Your bed is still empty. I put another kid's shoes there in case of an inspection. I didn't want them to know you were gone. I was afraid they'd come after you, lock you up. I was just protecting you." He leaned over, still reaching for the gun. "Jimmy, give me that thing."

"No." Jimmy backed away, and Brad backed with him.

"You have to cock it," Brad mumbled. Suddenly Bill's hand came down across Brad's face, knocking him down. The little girls screamed, and the others came running from down the hall to crowd around the door. Bill jerked Brad up off the floor and flung him back against the wall, and his fist came back to deliver another blow.

Jimmy cocked the gun and fired it.

58

BETH WAS WATCHING Nick load her things onto a cart so that he could roll them out of the hospital when Lynda and Jake came in.

"Did you find him?" Beth asked the moment she saw them.

Nick swung around. "Is he all right?"

"No, we didn't find him, but we think we know where he is," Lynda said.

"Where?"

"We think he went back to the home to try to get Lisa out."

"No!" Nick cried.

"Apparently, he did." Lynda quickly recounted the story of the e-mail.

"Well, we've got to get over there!" Beth said.

"No, Tony and Larry are working on it. They made us promise to stay away."

"But we *can't* stay away. What if they mess things up?"

"They won't. We just have to have faith. Tony's been trying to track down the prosecutor to get a warrant. As soon as he gets it, we can go in there and get Jimmy and Lisa out. Until then, Beth, you can come back to my house. Your things are there from the other night, anyway. You can stay until your house is rebuilt."

A few minutes later, as Nick started the engine of Beth's car in the hospital parking lot, she looked uneasily at the shadows around them. "It's getting down to the wire," she said.

"Yeah, it's getting pretty hairy."

"He's going to kill somebody tonight," she said. "Might be Jimmy. Might be me." Beth closed her eyes. "What in the world have I started?"

"You didn't start it. Bill Brandon did."

"But I could have let it go. And the worst those kids ever would have been guilty of was robbing people's houses and businesses. They might have been beaten a time or two, but they wouldn't have been killed."

"Stop it. You're believing the lie that you did the wrong thing. You did the *right* thing, Beth."

He pulled out of the parking space and shifted into drive. They drove slowly past a van, and she jumped as she noticed someone standing on the other side of it. *Just a hospital visitor,* she realized with relief—but it could just as easily have been Bill, or one of his cohorts. He could ambush her at any second, and he wouldn't hesitate if he got the chance.

She was trembling now, and she reached into her glove compartment to get her gun.

"Oh, no."

"What?"

"My gun. It was here, but it's gone. Somebody's taken it."

"But the doors were locked. It didn't look broken into."

"Jimmy," she said. "Bill taught us how to break into cars as well as buildings. Sometimes there were valuable things in cars. Laptop computers, stereos, cellular phones, money—guns. Jimmy knew I had the gun. He came after it. He was here."

Nick braked and sat there for a moment, staring at her. Then he drove to the other side of the parking lot, where Lynda and Jake were standing and talking near Nick's car, which Jake had agreed to drive home for him. Nick rolled his window down.

"Jimmy was here," Nick told them. "And he's got Beth's gun."

59

WHEN NICK RUSHED through Tracy's hospital room door, panting and sweating as if he'd run all the way up, she knew that something was wrong.

"I started to leave, but I thought you should know," he said. "We figured out where Jimmy is. We think he went back to the home to rescue Lisa."

She sat up abruptly and jerked the oxygen mask off her face. "Somebody's got to stop him."

"That's what we plan to do," he said. "I just thought you should know. He could still come here, if we're wrong, and if he does, you have to call us, okay?" When she'd promised, he nodded and ran out.

It took Tracy less than a minute to get the IV out of her hand and pull off the other monitors and cords. She got to her feet and wobbled to the window. Down in the illuminated parking lot, three cars caravanned out—probably Nick and his friends. What if they couldn't stop him?

She stood there for a moment, feeling totally helpless, completely alone, realizing just how badly she had failed her children so many years ago. But she hadn't been herself then. She hadn't understood what was happening. She hadn't cared.

She cared now.

In the closet of her room, she found the dirty clothes she had worn into the hospital. They were filthy, but they were all she had, so holding the counter to steady herself, she pulled them on.

When she'd dressed, she sat abruptly on the edge of her bed because she was so dizzy. It didn't matter. She was determined to get out of here. She had to find her son and her daughter and save them if she could. Maybe then she could redeem herself with them. Maybe for once in their young lives, they could believe that their mother cared about them.

How she would get there she had no idea, but she made her way to the elevator, punched the button, then flopped against the corner and waited for it to hit the first floor, feeling as if she would pass out at any moment. Her lungs felt as if a great weight sat on them, keeping her from breathing, but she pressed on. When the doors opened, she stumbled off and walked out into the parking lot.

Where would she go? How would she get there?

She looked around at the hundreds of cars lining the parking lot and wished one of them was hers. She did have one, sitting out in front of her apartment, though all but one seat was torn out and it had a rusted fender and was missing a door. If she could just get to it, she could drive it. The engine was one of the few things that still worked.

She saw two people walking out to their car, and she made her way toward them. "Excuse me," she said, then had a fit of coughing, which caught their attention. She struggled to catch her breath, supporting herself against the fender of a car.

"Are you all right?" the elderly lady asked her.

"Yes. I've just got a cold," she said, breathless. "Listen, I have a flat tire, and I really need to get home. Could you give me a ride?"

The woman set a maternal hand on Tracy's forehead. "Honey, you're burning up! Have you seen a doctor?"

"Yes, just now. I'm fine, really. I just have asthma—probably the stress of the flat tire brought it on. I have to get home. I don't live that far, I don't think."

"Certainly we can give you a ride," the man said.

"I don't have any money."

"We don't need any," he said. "Come on, dear. Let's get you out of this night air."

She tried to look stronger than she was as she sat in the backseat, but they kept looking over their shoulders with concern. They were nice people. Grandparent types. She wished Jimmy and Lisa could have people like them in their lives.

She gave them directions until they came to her corner, and she started to get out.

"Thank you very much."

The old man reached back across the seat to stop her. "Miss, are you sure you want me to let you off here? It doesn't look very safe."

"It's better than it looks," she said. "Bye now."

She closed the door and headed for her apartment steps.

The couple sat in their car, watching her. She knew they wouldn't leave until she had gone in. But she had no intention of trying to climb those stairs. Instead, she just stepped into the shadows and stood still until, apparently assuming she was safe inside a downstairs apartment, they pulled away.

She made her way slowly and with great effort down the block to where her car was parked on the road. The key was where she had left it, hidden between the vinyl and foam rubber of the torn visor. She pulled it out and jabbed it into her ignition. It coughed, then died. She tried again; finally, on the third try, it caught.

She sat behind the wheel, trying to wait out the dizziness. *Jesus, help me. My children need me. Let me act like a mother just once in this pathetic life of mine.*

The vertigo seemed to clear, and she pulled the car forward, trying to remember where the children's home was located.

60

THE GUNSHOT STILL rang in the air, and everyone froze. Jimmy had shot at the floor, but now he raised the gun toward Bill. "I told you I could do it," he said in a high-pitched voice that sounded as if it came from someone else. "Next time my aim is gonna be better." He looked down at the boy lying on the floor of the girls' room, half-propped against the wall where Bill had dropped him. "Are you all right, Brad?"

Brad stumbled to his feet, holding his ribs with one hand and his face with the other. "You gotta take me with you, Jimmy," he pleaded. "Please!"

Visibly shaken by the gunshot, Bill pointed at Jimmy with one hand and with the other gestured around the room at everyone else. "Everybody out," he said quietly, his voice trembling slightly. "Now!"

The ones clustered in the doorway scattered, and the girls in the room slid off their bunks and ran crying into the hall. Lisa stayed in her room hunkered behind her brother, and Brad stood next to Jimmy, facing Bill.

Jimmy kept the gun trained on the man who had exploited and abused him.

"You know, Jimmy, you may think I'm some terrible person," Bill said, trying to speak in gentle, soothing tones, "but that's only because they've brainwashed you, wherever you've been. Probably Beth Wright has been working her evil on you. But there's something you should know about Beth, Jimmy. That's not even her real name. She's really Beth Sullivan, and she killed my sister. But her wickedness will catch up with her. The Good Book even describes her in detail. It says, 'She has haughty eyes, a lying tongue, hands that shed innocent blood, a heart that devises wicked schemes, feet that are quick to rush into evil. She is a false witness who pours out lies and stirs up dissension among brothers.' She's like that, Jimmy, and the Lord finds those things detestable. But he knows my heart, and so do you. I forgive you for straying, Jimmy, because you're young and easily influenced. But in your heart, you know I've always thought of you as a son. My son."

Jimmy's cheeks mottled red, and he kept the gun aimed. Bill took a step toward him, but he backed up.

"Jimmy, if you do this, every child here will be farmed out to foster homes. Some of those homes are bad, Jimmy. Really bad. And those of you who have committed crimes will be locked up until you're so old that you'll never have kids of your own, or families. There won't be any hope for any of you. You kids are spoiled by all the nice things here, but you won't have that there. You and Lisa will be split up, for sure—since they don't jail men and women together—and you may never see her again."

"No!" Lisa cried. "Jimmy, is that true?"

Jimmy held his breath for a moment. "I don't know."

"But Jimmy! I thought we were gonna be together! I thought you said—"

"Listen to her, Jimmy," Bill cut in. "Do you want to hear your sister's screams as they drag her away from you? Do you want to wonder every night whose care she's in—and just what they're doing to her?"

Jimmy swallowed. He was getting confused. The thought of Lisa being placed in some foster home—or worse, a juvenile detention center or jail—where he didn't know who would be taking care of her, made him sick. Sure, Beth and the others had assured him that he and the other kids wouldn't go to jail, but he couldn't really trust what they'd said. They'd been wrong about other things. Still—"At least she won't be raised a thief or an arsonist or a bomb smuggler," Jimmy said. "Or even a murderer!"

"You've been watching too much television, Jimmy. You have a very loose grasp on reality."

"Like Beth?" he asked through lips stretched thin. "You almost killed her! And you did kill her dog. Dodger never did anything to you."

"It was just a warning, son," Bill said. "It wasn't meant to hurt anyone. I just wanted to put a scare into her to keep her from telling those lies." He bent over, his face too close to Jimmy's. "Jimmy, listen to me. All this time you were gone, I didn't report it, because I didn't want you to have to go to jail. Now you can just come back and pick up like you never left. No one will know. We'll just go on like we were . . ."

Bill's voice was mesmerizing, and Jimmy wanted so much to believe that he meant the things he said. Suddenly all that was familiar about Jimmy's life at the home began to call out to him—spending time with Brad and Kevin, his own bed, being able to watch over Lisa and protect her . . .

He lowered the gun slightly . . .

Bill lunged for him and wrestled the gun from his hand as Lisa screamed. He flung Jimmy to the floor, then turned the gun on them and laughed. Jimmy, Lisa, and Brad shrank back.

"I'm going to call a news conference tomorrow," he said, "and I'm going to tell the world that you three were responsible for the murder of my sister, the arson at the paper, and a hundred other crimes that haven't been solved. I'm going to tell them that you had a twenty-one-year-old cohort named Beth Wright who drove you, and every night you sneaked out to wreak havoc on the town. They'll have you locked in a cage in no time." He laughed cruelly, then regarded them tauntingly for a moment. "Or maybe I'll just decide to kill you first and dump your remains off a bridge somewhere. They'd never find you, not until the sharks had gotten their fill."

Lisa pressed herself into the corner of her room, trying to get smaller and farther away from the man who looked so natural with a gun. Brad stood next to her, a defeated, desperate look on his bruised face. Jimmy got up and stood in front of them both. "You'll have to kill me to get to them."

"I can do that." Bill backed to the doorway of the room and called out to Stella. She waddled into view, looking a little frightened herself.

"Go to the shed and get my Buick out," he said. "I'm gonna take these kids for a ride. After I get the stuff in the warehouse shipped and collect what's due me, then I'm going on a long vacation."

Stella dashed out, and they heard the door close behind her.

No one spoke until the car pulled up to the front door of the house and Stella came back in. "It's there, Bill. Just one thing before you go. What about us?"

"What about you? You're on your own. I'm getting out of here."

61

"I'M EXHAUSTED," BETH said, getting slowly to her feet. She looked around Lynda's living room at Lynda, Jake, and Nick, who looked back at her with sympathy and understanding. "I need to lie down for a while."

"We'll wake you up the minute we get any word from Tony," Lynda said, with a weary smile.

Beth nodded and plodded down the hallway, apparently barely able to put one foot in front of the other. But as soon as she got into the guest room, her eyes brightened and her movements became quick and sure. She slipped out the back door of the guest room onto the patio and stole around the house to her car.

She prayed, as she started the car and pulled out of the driveway, that the others wouldn't hear her; she breathed a sigh of relief as no one followed. Then she headed for the children's home, determined to do something to keep Jimmy from getting killed. Even with a gun, she knew the boy was no match for Bill Brandon. Neither was she. But she might at least be able to distract Bill long enough for Jimmy and his sister to escape.

Her bandaged chest hurt as she drove to the home as fast as she could, knowing that Nick or Lynda or Jake might discover at any time that she was gone and come after her. She took every shortcut she knew to cover the short distance to the compound where she had grown up. After she pulled up to the front of the compound, she sat for a moment, letting the car idle with the headlights off as she stared up into the buildings where all those children slept at night, trying to forget the heartache and terror of their pasts—even though the present might be worse. Tears came to her eyes, and she covered her face with her hands. She hadn't seen Bill face-to-face since she'd walked out of the home on her eighteenth birthday. Just seeing him now would bring back a flood of despair and resentment and hatred. In truth, she might not come out of this alive. Bill wanted her dead, and wouldn't be likely to just sit back and watch her walk out.

She wished she had her gun. She couldn't go in there to face her enemy unarmed, not if she expected to help Jimmy.

She scanned the cottages. She wasn't even sure which one to try. And what would she do? Break in? Knock? What would she say when she came face-to-face with Bill? Was she really as tough as she thought, or would she melt in fear, as she had done as a child, the moment Bill's angry eyes had turned on her?

Hatred so real and vibrant that it seemed to have a life of its own welled inside her, and she suddenly realized that she didn't need a weapon. Her hatred of Bill Brandon was enough. It would propel her, drive her, protect her . . .

She wilted. That was a lie. Hatred wasn't going to get her anything. There had to be another way.

The words of an old favorite passage of Scripture came back to her, and she chanted them in a whisper. *The Lord is my shepherd, I shall not be in want. He makes me lie down in green pastures, he leads me beside quiet waters, he restores my soul.*

Her soul didn't feel restored yet, but that was her fault. There was a price that had to be paid, a sacrifice that must be offered . . .

He guides me in paths of righteousness for his name's sake.

She didn't feel righteous, either, but she wasn't finished trying.

Even though I walk through the valley of the shadow of death, I will fear no evil, for you are with me; your rod and your staff, they comfort me.

This was the valley of the shadow of death—it always had been for her. Now she tried to imagine walking into this valley with that rod and staff as her only weapons—and found confidence that they would be enough.

Armed with new courage, she got out of the car and slammed the door, not even caring if Bill heard her. She *wanted* him to see her, wanted him to forget whatever he was doing and come out to confront her. That might give Jimmy a window of opportunity to escape with Lisa.

As she entered the compound, she saw a cluster of crying children standing in front of one of the cottages, huddled together. The Buick that had tried to run her off the road days ago was parked in front of the door with the driver's door open. Across the compound, she saw Stella hurrying into a shed. The big woman backed a van out of it, and sped through the yard and away.

Beth approached the kids. "What's going on?" she asked.

"Bill's gonna kill them!" one of the children cried. "We heard a gunshot, but Bill's still in there yelling. He must have shot Jimmy or Lisa or Brad!"

Beth thought she might faint, but she forced herself through it. "Are there any other adults on the campus?"

"There were, but they all left!"

"Go over to the rec room," she ordered. "Get down on the floor and don't come out until I tell you. Do you hear me?"

She watched as they fled to the building across the campus.

Taking a deep breath, she tested the knob, then opened it. "Your rod and your staff, they comfort me," she muttered under her breath as she stepped inside.

She heard voices in the back room. Taking a deep breath, she held it for a moment, marshaling her courage and steadiness of mind. This was it. Then she yelled: "Bill Brandon!"

The voices stopped. "That's right," she called. "It's me. Beth Sullivan. You wanted me dead. Well, now's your chance."

62

THE MOMENT HE had heard the gunshot, Larry had called Tony, explaining even as he pounded down the stairs and out the door what he'd heard. As he rushed across the street and toward the home, he said, "What the—Tony, you're not going to believe this."

"What!" Tony prompted.

"Beth. She's heading onto the compound—too far away for me to stop. Her car's out front here. Looks like she's heading for a group of children."

"What's she thinking of? If Brandon finds her, he'll kill her—he's already tried it twice."

"I'm right behind her," Larry said into the cell phone. "Send me some backups."

He tucked the phone into his belt pouch as the children fled to the rec room. As he rounded the corner, he could see Beth heading into the cottage where a Buick was parked out front. He pulled his gun out of his shoulder holster. Praying under his breath, he ran in a crouch the remaining distance to the cottage, went to the window, and looked through. Bill stood with a pistol pointed at three children—Jimmy and two others. The little girl had to be Lisa. The gunshot he'd heard hadn't wounded any of these people, apparently.

He heard Beth call out. Bill swung around . . .

63

BILL STEPPED SLOWLY into the hallway, grinning at Beth. Then he motioned with the gun in his hand—her own gun, Beth realized—and Jimmy and two other children stepped out into the hallway with him, huddled together. Beth choked back her fear. "Let them go, Bill," she said. "Let it be just you and me, face-to-face."

He chuckled. "Well, well. Been a long time, darlin'. How are you?"

"Better than you expected," she said. "I'm just fine."

"Well, it was nice of you to drop in tonight. You missed the party, though. It was a good one. Made me some friends, I'll wager. You can never have too many friends in the media."

"Let them go, Bill," she said again. "You don't need them."

"Oh, I need them, all right," he said, slowly herding the children down the hallway toward her. "And as much as I'd like to finish the job I started a couple of days ago, I need you. I'm not stupid. I know the cops have been trying to get a warrant. I know that as soon as they do, they'll be out here to arrest me. But I won't be here. And neither will you. We're gonna be taking a little trip. I'll take all of you along for insurance."

"Just me," she said. "Let them go and take me."

"Let them go?" He threw his head back and laughed. "Beth, Beth, you know better than that." He was almost within arm's reach now. Could she grab the gun? No, too dangerous. If it went off and hit one of the kids . . .

"There are too many of us," she said. "We'll be too conspicuous. If it's just me . . ."

"Just you and me, Beth? Think about it. They'd shoot us as soon as look at us. You're nothing but trash, and you don't have family that'll sue them later. They'd be safe taking risks with a hostage like you. But with these cute little kids, they wouldn't dare take a chance, or they'd have the whole country coming down on them the minute they pulled the trigger. No, the kids are my ticket out of here."

"Where will you go?" she asked through her teeth. "Somewhere to ruin more lives? Are you going to keep killing everybody who gets in your way?"

"I might," he said with a grin. He grabbed her hair by the roots, and swung her back toward the door. "But right now, I need to keep you alive." He scowled at the three children huddled together. "Come on, kids. Into the car. All of you."

Jimmy held his sister close to him; tears ran down both their cheeks. "Beth, I'm sorry. I shouldn't have taken your gun. Now he's got it and—"

"It's okay, Jimmy," she said, her face reddening with pain as he jerked her by her hair. "Just do what he says."

Bill kept the gun trained on them as the children climbed into the backseat of the car. He shoved Beth into the passenger seat and said, "Scoot over. You'll do the driving."

He was just about to climb in after her when a voice cut through the night: *"Freeze!"*

Bill froze, then slowly turned to see Larry with his gun trained on him.

"Drop the gun and get down on the ground!"

Bill leaned down slowly, the gun still in his hand. His arm swung out, apparently to toss the gun, but instead he raised the pistol and pulled the trigger.

The children screamed as Larry dropped to the ground.

Bill dove into the car. "Let's go!" he told Beth. "Turn that key and get us out of here! Move!"

"You killed him!" she cried as she cranked the car and pulled across the lawn. "You killed him!"

"Yeah, and you're next! Now shut up!"

The children tried to muffle their sobs of horror as Beth tore down the dark street.

"Where are we going?" she asked.

"We're just gonna drive," he said. "Until I get far enough away that I don't need you anymore."

"And then what?"

"Then I'll find a bridge to throw you over. Every last one of you."

64

TRACY WAS NEARLY to the children's home when she was overcome with dizziness. She pulled the car to the side of the road and tried to gather what little strength she had left. She was almost there. She had to make it.

Just when her head seemed a little clearer, a coughing fit hit her. It was getting harder to breathe. Her lungs felt heavy and full of fluid, as if they didn't have room for anything as mundane as oxygen.

She was still struggling to catch her breath when she saw a car race across the children's home lawn and shoot the curb onto the street.

The car sped toward her, and as it passed under a streetlight she saw Jimmy sitting in the backseat with a little girl next to him.

A little girl! Was it Lisa? Tracy sucked a huge gulp of air, despite the pain. Her kids were in danger. She was their mother; it was her job to stop him. Ignoring her weakness, she shoved her car into a tight U-turn, tires squealing, and followed the other car until she'd caught up with it. Then, stepping on her accelerator, she pulled up beside them and tried to pass.

The other car began to zigzag, to keep her from staying on the road next to it. But she wouldn't give up. Tears streamed down her face as she urged the old rattletrap ahead and, finally, almost through sheer force of will, she inched ahead of them. *This was it,* she told herself. Her last chance to do something for her children. Something important. Something that mattered. It was her last chance to show her children she loved them.

She cranked the wheel as hard as she could, throwing her car into a power turn, spinning out of control just a few feet in front of the other car.

Tracy felt the impact of the collision almost immediately, heard the crunching metal. She only hoped Jimmy and Lisa were wearing their seatbelts. Her car had none, nothing to hold her in, and the last thing she was aware of before she lost consciousness was the sensation of being thrown out of the car into the night air.

65

THERE WAS A moment of shocked silence just after the two mangled cars ground to a halt. Then the inside of the Buick erupted in frightened screams. But the loudest was Jimmy's—because he had seen, behind the wheel of the rusty old car that had passed them and then pulled spinning in front of them, the face of his mother.

With no regard for Bill or any further danger, Jimmy bolted from the Buick and ran to the other car, which now lay on its side. But there was no one in that car. He looked up then, frantic—and saw his mother, several yards ahead, lying motionless on the concrete like a discarded rag doll. "Mom!" he yelled through his tears. "Mom!" He fell down beside her, wailing at the sight of the blood oozing from her nose and mouth.

But she opened her eyes slowly and looked up at him. "Run!" she whispered. "Take your sister and run!"

Jimmy was crying so hard he could barely speak. "Why did you do it?" he asked. "Why?"

"Because I . . . love you," she whispered. "Run, Jimmy! Please run . . ." Her voice trailed off, and Jimmy watched her eyes go dead and empty.

He wanted to stay with her, but her words echoed in his mind: *Take your sister and run.* He looked back toward the car. Lisa and Brad had gotten out, too. Bill had hit his head, and was holding it with one hand as he tried to crank the car with the other. Jimmy couldn't see Beth.

Jimmy ran to his sister and took her hand. "Come on, Brad," he whispered. "Let's hide in the woods."

He pulled Lisa after him, and Brad followed in a painful, stumbling run. Then he heard a yell. Looking back over his shoulder, Jimmy felt a surge of panic as he saw Bill throw open the car door and leap out. But with Bill's first step toward them, Beth dove from the car, landing on Bill's back, and wrestled him to the ground.

"Come on!" Jimmy urged, and pulled Lisa toward the safety of the trees.

It only took Bill a moment to regain his equilibrium, throw Beth off of him, and get the upper hand, but by then, the children were gone.

He grabbed her by the throat and lifted her to her feet. "Back in the car," he said through gritted teeth.

He threw her in on the driver's side, then pushed her across to the passenger seat. She gasped in pain as she moved, and he saw blood seeping onto her blouse from some wound he couldn't see on her chest. He jumped in beside her, cranked the car, and it started. He'd noticed some significant damage to the front of the car, but it looked driveable.

"Are you just going to leave her on the road?" Beth screamed.

"Shut up!" he shouted, bringing his fist hard across her jaw. "Don't say another word or it'll be the last thing you'll say!"

Furious, he drove around the wrecked car and the body lying in the street, and flew as fast as he could out of the area.

66

JIMMY URGED LISA and Brad through the woods at a run, trying to make it to the road on the other side where they might find help. Maybe a police car would come by, and they could flag it down.

Not long ago, Jimmy realized suddenly, a policeman would have been the last person he would have turned to when he was in trouble. For that matter, he wouldn't have trusted any other adults, either. But since then, he'd learned something: Adults weren't all bad. Beth had come here tonight, despite her fears of Bill, for the sole purpose of rescuing the children. And then there was his mother. A lump rose in his throat again, and he swallowed it down.

He still didn't understand why she had done it. She had already proven she didn't care about them. She had let the state take them and dump them somewhere. Why come back now, sick and weak, and risk her life to stop Bill from taking them away?

It didn't make sense. But it changed things, somehow.

"Why are you crying?" Lisa asked him breathlessly as they fought the vines and bushes in their way. "Aren't you happy we got away?"

Jimmy wiped his face. "Yeah, I'm happy. I was just thinking about the cop and that lady in the street." He couldn't tell her the lady had been her mother. Not yet. Maybe someday.

Brad was panting and wheezing, and Jimmy wondered if he was going to make it through the woods. He needed to get Brad to a hospital; they couldn't just hide someplace. Somehow, he needed to find help. Besides, they had to get help for Beth. They were the only ones who knew that Bill had taken her.

And he had to get help for all those children back at the home, who wouldn't know what to do or what was going to happen to them next.

The trees thinned, and suddenly they came to the road. Not far away was a gas station with a convenience store attached. Jimmy reached into his pocket for the change that Jake had let him keep when they'd gone for a Coke earlier. He fished out a quarter. "Come on, let's go call for help."

"Who are we gonna call?" Lisa asked.

He thought about it for a moment. "Jake," he said. "We'll call Jake."

Lynda answered on the first ring. "Lynda Barrett," she said.

"Lynda, it's me. Jimmy."

"Jimmy! Where are you? We've been worried sick—"

Jimmy cleared the emotion from his throat and tried to speak clearly. "I need to speak to Jake," he said.

"Oh . . . okay." Lynda gave the phone to Jake.

"Jimmy, are you all right?" he asked.

"I'm okay," he said. "But Bill's got Beth."

"What do you mean he's got Beth? Beth's here," Jake said. "She's asleep in the guest room."

"No. She came here. Bill's got her in a car, and he's taking her away. I think he's gonna kill her! Jake, you've got to stop him!"

"Jimmy, where are you?"

Jimmy was crying again. He stopped and wiped his eyes. "At the gas station about a mile from the home. I think it's called Quik Stop. It's on—" He checked the street signs near the phone booth. "The corner of Jefferson and Third Street."

"Jimmy, we're coming after you. You stay there. We'll be there in ten minutes."

"No! Don't worry about us! Lisa and Brad and me will be okay. You gotta worry about Beth. He'll kill her. And there's something else."

"Yeah? What?"

"My . . . my . . ." Jimmy lowered his voice to keep Brad or Lisa from hearing.

"What? I can't hear you."

"My m—" He choked on the word, then tried again. "Tracy. She needs an ambulance. And so does that cop—Larry, I think it was. He was shot."

"Shot? Are you sure?"

"Hurry, Jake! They may not be dead yet."

"But Tracy's in the hospital, Jimmy. You're confused—"

"No!" he shouted. "She came here, too. We'd still be in the car with Bill if she hadn't. But first he shot Larry, and then he ran over her, and she's lying in the road . . ." His voice broke off, and he couldn't go on.

"Jimmy, stay right where you are. We'll be there in ten minutes."

Jake drove faster than he'd ever driven in his life. In the passenger seat, Lynda was on the cellular phone, trying to locate Tony or Nick. She heard sirens, but they were coming from the opposite direction.

She found Nick in his office. "Nick, it's Lynda."

"Hi. I've been working on what to do with all the children. It's not going to be easy, but I think—"

"Nick, listen to me," Lynda said. "Jimmy just called."

"Oh, that's great! You've found him?"

"Yes. He went to the home, and something went wrong. We're headed to get him. He says that Bill's got Beth."

She heard something crash on Nick's end. "He can't. She's at your house! She was asleep—"

"No, she snuck out to go to the home to rescue the children. But apparently it backfired, and he's got her now."

"Oh, no."

"Nick, you've got to—" Her voice stopped as Jake slammed on the brakes and skidded to a halt. Lynda dropped the phone and looked through the windshield.

The headlights shone on something in the road, and Jake whispered, "Oh, God, please don't let this be."

"Tracy," Lynda whispered.

67

THE POLICE RADIO report of an officer down at the St. Clair Children's Home stunned Tony, but before he could call in to ask for details, his cellular phone rang. He grabbed it as he turned a corner on two wheels, on his way to SCCH. "Larry?" he asked.

"No, Tony, it's Lynda!" She was choked and could hardly speak. "I'm sitting on Tenth about a mile from the children's home. Tracy Westin is lying in the middle of the road—she was thrown from her car. I checked her pulse, but there isn't one—she's dead, Tony. Bill Brandon ran her down. And Jimmy said he shot Larry!"

Tony went cold. "Larry?"

"Yeah. I don't have details, but I hear sirens. They may have gotten to him by now, but they're coming from the other direction and they don't know about Tracy. Jake's gone to get Jimmy. Apparently Bill had him, but Jimmy escaped. Bill's still got Beth, though! Jimmy said he's in the Buick. Tony, he's holding her hostage!"

Tony's heart lurched. He longed to check on Larry, but he knew that Beth's safety had to come first. "Lynda, I'm on my way."

It took only a few minutes to put an all-points bulletin out on the Buick, and soon roadblocks had been set up on the outskirts of town, and the policemen in other parts of the county were alerted. Additional ambulances and squad cars were dispatched to the children's home. As soon as the prosecutor had been informed of the circumstances, officers were sent to check out the warehouse. When they tallied over a hundred thousand dollars' worth of stolen goods, the prosecutor issued warrants for the arrest of Judge Wyatt, Sheila Axelrod, and her husband—in whose names the warehouse was listed—and all of the employees of the children's home, who had fled.

At the home, Nick paced the lawn in front of the cottages as they loaded Larry into an ambulance. He was still alive, thank God; Nick had no idea how badly he was injured. All he knew was that Beth was in danger of the same fate. In a few moments, when he saw Tony's car barreling into the parking lot, he bolted toward him.

Tony got out of the car and met him halfway. "How's Larry?"

"Alive," Nick said. "But unconscious. He's lost a lot of blood. It doesn't look good."

Tony fought the panicked rage and the furious despair threatening to smother him, and looked toward the ambulance, on its way off the property with its lights flashing. He was halfway back to his car, intending to follow it, when a cop shouted, "They've spotted Brandon's car! It's heading up Highway 18 toward St. Pete. There's a high-speed chase underway." Tony hopped behind the wheel and cranked the engine, knowing there was nothing more he could do for Larry, but maybe he could help save Beth.

"He's going to kill her!" Nick shouted. "Please, Tony, let me come with you."

"Who'll take care of placing these children for the night?"

"My colleagues," Nick answered. "I've already called in every social worker in the county. They're on their way. They can handle it."

"Nick, listen—we just learned that Sheila Axelrod is involved. She's probably being arrested as we speak. That leaves you. You're the only one who can take care of these kids right now. We're counting on you."

"Sheila?" he asked, then backed away, trying to sort it all out. He shook the information from his head and decided he could only deal with one thing at a time. "But what about Beth?"

"We'll take care of Beth. That's our job."

Nick kicked at some invisible wall in the air. "How could she do this? How could she confront him? She's *terrified* of him—and she *knew* he would kill her!"

"She did it for the kids," Tony said. "And right now she would want you to think of the kids, too."

Nick hesitated. "All right," he said. "I'll stay. But call me the minute you hear anything!"

68

IN THE BUICK, Bill cursed as the flashing lights grew closer behind him. He turned off onto a little country road, then slammed his accelerator to the floor, flying around corners and curves. But the police stayed close behind him.

He kept one arm clamped around Beth's neck, with the cold barrel of the gun pressed against her cheek. Beth sat as still as she could, frightened that the slightest provocation might cause him to pull the trigger. He had nothing to lose. Nothing except his hostage.

As he drove, she prayed. Prayed that he wouldn't lose the police. Prayed that they would manage to set up a roadblock ahead of him. Prayed that she would find an opportunity to escape. Tears streamed down her face, born of all the confusing emotions whirling through her heart.

"You've sure caused a lot of trouble," Bill said through his teeth, clamping his arm tighter. "Unbelievable."

Beth tried to lift her head enough to see the squad cars in the rearview mirror, but Bill let go of the wheel, grabbed a handful of hair, and jerked her head back against the seat. "Be still," he said. "I didn't tell you to move. I'm not ready to kill you yet."

Only then did he notice the tears running down her face. "I've never seen you cry, Beth, darlin'," he mocked, his eyes back on the twisting road again. "Tears become you."

She stiffened her lips, determined not to shed another tear in front of him.

"Funny how scared you are now," he said. "You weren't scared at all when you were coming after me with both barrels for that newspaper of yours, hiding Jimmy from me, putting the police on my tail, turning HRS against me. But you know what? It didn't matter. I have friends in high places. Nothing you did could have gotten me. Even now, I'll probably get out of this scot-free."

"If they don't kill you first," she muttered.

"They *can't* kill me," he said. "They won't even aim a gun at me as long as I've got this one pointed at your head. You're my ticket out of here."

She didn't respond. And as the road emerged from the woodland and led them through a complex of industrial buildings, she watched his eyes dart, searching for something. "We're gonna find us a building," he said, glancing at the rearview mirror to gauge the distance between himself and the nearest cop behind them. "If I drive up to the front door, we'll have just enough time to get inside before they catch up."

"And then what?"

"Then I can negotiate."

"For what?"

"For a plane. I'm leaving the country, and you're coming with me."

"I'm not going anywhere."

"Yes, you are," he chuckled. "If I have to drag your dead body with me, you're going. Like I said, you're my ticket, and I'm not letting you go."

He swerved into a gravel parking lot in front of a building with light coming through the windows. Through the glass, they could see a man heading for the front window, probably alerted by the sirens. Bill skidded to a stop in front of the door. Grabbing Beth's hair, he pulled her behind him as he bolted from the car and, putting his shoulder to the door, broke through into the building.

The man who'd been working there backed into a stack of boxes, knocking them over. "What the—"

"Get out!" Bill screamed. "Get out or I'll kill you!"

The man stumbled to the door and ran out into the night. By now the parking lot was filling with police cars—skidding in the gravel, sirens blaring, their doors flying open as the officers leaped out to crouch next to the cars, guns drawn.

Bill threw Beth down on the floor behind a desk, reached to the wall behind him to turn off all the lights in the room, and grabbed the phone.

Wincing in pain, Beth looked down. The front of her shirt was spotted with blood where her wound was bleeding through the bandages. She tried to push back the pain and concentrate, instead, on finding some means of escape.

"Now we wait for them to call," he said. "Should be just a matter of minutes."

Beth jumped when the telephone rang almost on cue. He picked it up confidently, wiping sweat out of his eyes with the back of his gun hand. "One wrong move and she's dead," he said.

"What do you want, Brandon?" Beth could hear the voice from the phone's ear piece.

"A plane," Bill said. "I want a plane to take me to Cozumel."

"We're not going to get you a plane, Brandon."

"Then you'd better start calling her next of kin." He chuckled and glanced down at her. "Not that she has any."

"If you let her go, we'll talk about a plane."

Bill laughed. "You think I'm stupid? She's the only reason you haven't killed me yet. I'm not letting her go."

Bill hung up, sat down, and tried to catch his breath. Beth leaned back against a file cabinet. He kept the gun leveled at her, just inches from her face. Desperately, her eyes searched the darkened room, lit only by the flashing lights coming through the windows. This appeared to be a small accounting office. She looked for a knife, a letter opener, anything she could use as a weapon if she needed one. She saw nothing.

Bill got down onto the floor next to her and dragged her face close to his. His breath smelled stale, and she turned her face. "You know, Beth, I always liked you. Sure will be a shame when I have to kill you."

She glared back into his eyes. "Go ahead, Bill. Kill me." But she knew he wouldn't. Not yet.

Bill chuckled. "In good time, darlin'. In good time. How do you feel about being buried in Cozumel? 'Course, we could work out a burial at sea, if you'd prefer that. I could rent a boat and take you out over the Caribbean."

The phone rang again, and he jerked it up. "You got the plane?"

"This is Tony Danks," Beth heard the voice say. "I'm a detective with the St. Clair Police Department. I'm on my way over, and I think we can work something out."

"A plane is all I want worked out," Bill said. "I want a plane to get me out of the country. You have one hour, and then I'm gonna kill her."

"The minute you pull the trigger, we'll be on you like fleas on a mutt. I'd think twice before I tried that," Tony said.

"Get me the plane," Bill said, "and nobody else has to die."

Tony punched "end" on his cell phone, then punched in the number of the hospital emergency room. Concentrating on high-speed, one-handed steering down this curving road through the woods, he asked the nurse about Larry's condition. He was put on hold for what seemed an eternity, and finally, the nurse came back on the line and told him that they weren't allowed to give out any information until Larry's family was contacted. Tony slammed the phone down on the seat next to him and kept driving. Was Larry dead? Was that why they couldn't give him any information? He breathed a prayer that it wasn't so, rubbed the mist stinging his eyes, and pushed his car even faster.

Moments later, he skidded into the parking lot of the building where Bill was holding Beth. He grabbed his cell phone, made a quick call to the airport, then called the children's home and asked for Jake, who was still waiting there with Lynda and all the children.

"Jake, I need a favor," he shouted into the phone. "We've found Brandon. He's holed up in a building, holding Beth hostage. He wants a plane and a pilot. We're running out of time, Jake. We've got a plane, but we need a pilot. Do you have your license back yet?"

"You bet I do," Jake said.

"All right, get to the airport as fast as you can. We're trying to come up with a plan."

Suddenly Tony heard Nick's voice on the line. "Tony, where's Beth?"

"He's holding her hostage, Nick. He's demanding a plane."

"Don't let him take her out of the country!" Nick cried. "You've got to stop him!"

"We're going to."

"I'm coming over there right now," Nick said.

Tony thought about that for a second. "The other social workers are there to take care of the kids?"

"They are."

"All right. If you promise to stay out of the way and not do anything stupid, I'll give you the address."

69

LESS THAN FIFTEEN minutes later, Nick found himself crouching with Tony behind the squad cars in front of the building where Bill held Beth. Beside him, Tony dialed the number of the phone inside.

"We got you a plane," Tony said when Brandon answered. "And a pilot. How do you want to be transported to the airport?"

Bill hesitated. "My car," he said.

"You know we're not gonna let you drive off without an escort."

"Fine," Bill said. "Escort me. But once I hit the airport tarmac you stay back. I'm getting on that plane and out of here, and if anybody tries to stop me, Beth will be history."

Nick held his breath as the building's front door opened and Bill Brandon stepped out with an arm around Beth's neck. He opened the car's passenger door and climbed in, pulling her with him, then slid across to the steering wheel. He was obviously trying to keep Beth between him and the police, so that they wouldn't be able to get a clear shot at him without endangering Beth, too.

Nick watched as Bill's car started and pulled out on the street. The police jumped into their cars and Nick into his, following at the end of the procession.

"Lord, you've got to save her," he said as he drove. "I don't know why you brought her into my life, but I haven't felt like this about a woman in a long time, maybe never." His voice cracked as he drove at breakneck speed behind the procession of police cars, with a killer at the front of the caravan who seemed to be in control of it all.

When they reached the airport, the squad cars stayed back as Bill headed for the waiting plane. Nick stopped his car back beyond the fence and got out, standing with the cops to watch.

Bill pulled Beth out of the car and dragged her toward the plane. The only way into the plane was to climb up onto the wing and go in from there, but to do that, Bill had to let Beth go for a moment. Nick watched, holding his breath, as he lifted her up onto the wing, then quickly followed her before she could balk and run.

Nick let out a heavy, disappointed breath as the plane began to taxi out toward the runway.

"What now?" Nick asked Tony.

"Pray," Tony said. "Pray hard."

70

IN THE PLANE, Jake tried to stay calm as Bill panted on the seat behind him, still holding Beth in a wrenching grip with one hand and pressing the barrel of the gun to her temple with the other. Jake didn't know whether she had noticed that he was the one flying the plane. When Bill had searched him after getting on, he thought Beth may have realized it was him. "Come on! Get moving," Bill said, "before they pull something."

"St. Clair Unicom," Jake said into the microphone. "Cessna 3-0-2-2 Delta requesting takeoff."

There was a crackling on the other end. "Cessna 3-0-2-2 Delta, go ahead. All's clear. Runway 3."

It was the same runway where Jake and Lynda had crashed, but he had overcome the fear of crashing months ago. Still, he had never flown at gunpoint before, and he'd never had a man like Bill Brandon in his plane. He glanced back at the couple entangled on the seat behind him. "Cozumel, huh? Nice place. I've been there."

"Shut up and fly the plane," Bill said. "And turn the light on back here. I don't want any surprises."

Jake cut on the dim light over their seats. Instantly, the light cast a reflection of the two onto the windshield in front of Jake, offering him a clear view of the backseat. He taxied the rest of the way to the runway, straightened the plane, and increased power to the engine. Beth wasn't fighting, and Bill had relaxed his hold on the gun. From the expression on his face and the way he was sweating, Jake had the feeling that Bill Brandon didn't like to fly.

The accelerating plane approached the end of the runway and lifted off, and Bill's face seemed to grow paler. His hold on Beth was looser now, and he seemed distracted—as though airsickness was assaulting him now.

Jake met Beth's eyes in the glass, hoping she was thinking what he was thinking. With a little help from Jake, Beth might be able to knock the gun out of his hand.

He thought of that first trip with Lynda, when he'd played the hotdogger and dipped and zigzagged all over the sky like a Thunderbird. Even Lynda, a seasoned pilot, had gone pale at that. A good dip might just push Bill over the edge.

Jake took a deep breath, braced himself—then shoved the control yoke forward, making the plane drop, them quickly pulled it back up.

Bill fell backward against the seat, but Beth was ready. With a quick swing, she knocked the gun from his hand. "You sniveling piece of trash!" he shouted, bringing his backhand across her face as he dove for the gun. She slid to the floor on her knees, and just before he grabbed the pistol, she reached it herself. His grip on her wrist made her drop it, but she managed to knock it with her elbow, sending it sliding under the seat.

"Jake, help!" she screamed as Bill hit the floor, grabbing her hair and banging her head into the floor, while he groped under the seat for the gun.

Jake couldn't abandon the controls and felt helpless as he tried to find something that could be used as a weapon. "Get the gun, Beth. You have to get the gun!" He looked back and saw the blood seeping through the side of her shirt around the edges of the bandage on her chest. Still, she lurched under the seat, reaching, stretching . . .

Jake pulled the plane up, made a steep climb, then dove suddenly, making Bill slide toward the front of the plane. "*Now,* Beth!" Jake shouted.

Twisting her body sideways, Beth dropped onto her stomach and pushed further under the seat until, at last, with a desperate, painful lunge, she reached the gun. Sliding backwards out from under the seat, she put her back to the plane's side wall and pushed with her feet until she was as near upright as she could get in the small plane. She pointed the gun at Bill's forehead.

"I got it, Jake!" she shouted.

Jake glanced back at her. Blood was dripping down her temple where Bill had slammed her head into the floor, and more blood soaked through her shirt. Her eyes were venomous as she aimed the gun at the man who had tormented her for most of her life. Her hands trembled as she clutched the pistol in a life-or-death grip.

"Don't shoot, Beth," Jake said. "I'm turning around."

"I won't shoot," she said. "Not until we're on the ground."

There were strings of wet hair plastered to Bill's forehead, and beads of sweat rolling down his face. He looked up at her. "Come on, Beth. You couldn't pull that trigger. You know I didn't raise you to be a killer."

She cocked the hammer and through her teeth said, "You raised me to do what has to be done."

"Beth, don't do it! You may shoot the plane," Jake said. "I don't want to crash again!"

"He'll finagle a way out of this," she said in a dull voice. "He could go free, get off without even a fine. They're all in it with him."

"All who?" Bill asked.

"All your friends. They're all making a mint off what you're doing to those kids. You'll keep on doing it. You'll find a way. Unless I kill you. And I can do that. All I have to do is wait until we touch down, then pull this trigger and watch your whole world end. Then it'll all be over."

"Let him go to jail, Beth," Jake said. "Let him see what it feels like to be locked up in a place he can't leave. Let him see what it feels like to live the way he made you live, Beth."

"It's different," she said. "He's not a child. There's no way to show him how much worse it is for a little, innocent kid who can't defend himself."

"Then let God teach him that, Beth."

Bill latched onto that idea. Breathless and beginning to shake, he said, "That's right, Beth. If I've made mistakes, if I've hurt anyone, the Creator will deal with me. 'Vengeance is mine, saith the Lord.' It's not yours, Beth."

"Don't you dare quote Scripture to me!" she screamed. "I've heard enough of your filthy distortions and your twisted paraphrases. Maybe God will get his vengeance on all those kids through me. Maybe he wants a bullet in your head for defiling his Word."

"Don't believe it!" Jake shouted. "That's twisted thinking, Beth!"

"That's right, Beth, darlin'. You don't want to pull that trigger."

The plane touched down with a bump, and Jake slowed the plane to a stop.

Bill was looking up at her, as though he knew she would never shoot. Her finger trembled over the trigger. She thought of all the ways she'd tried to purify her life, the score sheet she'd been keeping. But all of that meant nothing if she could still contemplate murder for revenge. If she could still hate, after all she'd learned about God, maybe she didn't have it in her to be a child of God. That reality filled her with choking despair, and for a split second, she thought of turning the gun on herself.

But something stopped her. Some still, soothing voice from the center of her soul: *You don't have it in you, but I have it in me.*

She had a quick, fleeting memory of the discussion she and Nick had had about the thief on the cross, and the grace that God had extended to him. For the first time, it made sense.

Beth's law-keeping was worthless. Her good works were empty. It was only through Christ's power that she could have any righteousness at all.

Nick was right.

She moved her finger from the trigger, keeping the gun pointed at Bill Brandon. Murder—even if some would consider it justified—would only destroy it all.

"Radio in and tell them I've got him. Tell them to come get him."

In moments, police had surrounded the plane. Nick jogged up just as they helped Bill Brandon, handcuffed, down from the plane's wing and led him away.

As soon as Beth stepped down from the wing, Nick caught her in a crushing hug. "Are you all right? You're bleeding."

"Not much," she said. "I popped a few stitches, but I'm all right."

"Don't be such a tough guy," he said. "I know you're in pain." He wrapped his arms tighter around her, and in a moment, he felt her body quaking with tears. She stood on her toes and wrapped her arms so tightly around his neck that he felt tears burning his own eyes. She was sobbing now, sobbing out her heart and her soul, sobbing in a way he'd never seen her do before.

Somehow, he didn't have to ask what she was crying for. He knew she was crying for the children in that home who had robbed all night and then studied all day, those children who had been deprived of their ability to trust, those children who would carry the guilt of what they'd done all their lives. He knew she was crying for herself, for the child she had been, the child who'd had no one to protect her from evils such as Bill Brandon. He knew she was crying for a lifetime of loneliness, a lifetime of wishing she could belong somewhere.

And he vowed that, if it was the last thing he ever did, he would give her that place to belong.

He lifted her and began to carry her back, and she kept her face buried against his neck. "Where are you taking me?" she asked him.

"Back to the hospital," he said. "So they can make sure you're all right."

"I don't want to spend the night at the hospital," she said. "I don't want to be alone."

"I have no intention of leaving you alone. I'm going to sit with you all night long."

"Why?" she asked.

"Because I don't think I could tear myself away from you if I wanted to," he whispered.

71

TONY BURST THROUGH the ER doors and bolted to the desk. Someone was talking to the receptionist, but he couldn't wait. "My partner was brought in here with a gunshot—Larry Millsaps!"

The receptionist shot him an annoyed look. "I'll be with you in a moment, sir."

"No, I have to know now! Is he dead or alive?"

"He's alive," she said. "Now if you'll wait . . ."

Tony sank back in relief, feeling as if he could finally breathe. "Alive? You're sure?"

"Yes, I'm sure."

"I have to see him, then." He started toward the double swinging doors leading to the examining rooms, and the woman stood up.

"Sir, I'm sorry, but you aren't supposed to go in there." When he kept walking, she picked up the phone. "I'll call security!"

Breathing a weary sigh, he turned around and flashed his badge at her. "I'm a police officer, and my partner was shot tonight. I'm going in there, and if security would like to try and stop me, they're welcome to."

She sat back down, and he pushed through the doors.

He went from room to room, looking for Larry, hoping that he wouldn't find him comatose or on the verge of death. His heart pounded as he rounded the corner in the hall, looking into every room—

"Tony?"

He swung around and saw Melissa Millsaps, Larry's wife, looking pale and fatigued, standing in a doorway across the hall.

"Melissa!" he said, stepping toward her. "How is he?"

She nodded without speaking, and led him into Larry's room.

Larry lay on a gurney, his left shoulder bandaged and his arm in a sling.

"It just missed his heart," she said as tears came to her eyes—tears that didn't look as if they were the first she had cried tonight. "Angels were watching over him."

"Then he's . . . gonna be all right?"

Larry opened his eyes, and looked up at his partner. "'Course I'm gonna be all right. Takes more than a bullet to stop Larry Millsaps."

Tony began to laugh with such relief that tears filled his own eyes. Larry reached up to take his hand, and Tony grabbed it and squeezed it hard. "Thought I'd lost you there, buddy."

Melissa went to the other side of the table and stroked his forehead gently. "Me, too," she said.

Larry looked up at Tony, his eyes heavy. Tony knew they had probably given him something strong for the pain. "You get Brandon?"

"Locked up tight," Tony said. "Right where he's gonna be for a long time. Him and Sheila Axelrod and the good Judge Wyatt."

Larry grinned. "What about the kids? And Beth?"

"When you're feeling better, I'll tell you about how everything happened. But Beth's fine. They're still processing the kids, though," Tony said. "But they'll be all right. Nick's looking out for them."

Larry closed his eyes and smiled, and Melissa leaned over him and pressed a soft kiss on his eyelid. He reached up with his good arm and held her face against his. "Sorry I scared you," he whispered to his wife.

"It's okay," she said. "I've given you a few scares, too. You owed me one."

Tony told Larry to get some rest, then went back out into the hall. Emotion overwhelmed him as he realized how close he had come to losing his best friend. And how close Melissa had come to losing her husband.

He felt a sudden urge to talk to Sharon, the woman who had meant so much to him for the past several months. He wanted to hold her and tell her that he loved her, to ask her if they had a future together, to take care of her and her children. There was so much ugliness out there, so much horror—and Tony just didn't want to stand alone anymore in a world like that. He went through the emergency room doors, picking up purpose with every step.

He got into his car and sat there for a moment, looking up at the sky as he had done months earlier, when he had opened his heart to Jesus Christ. Tony knew that he wasn't really alone now—his Lord knew all of the weariness in Tony's soul, all the wounds in his heart—and all the reasons that this man who never committed, wanted to commit now.

Tony began to smile as he cranked his car and headed to Sharon's house.

72

BETH SLEPT BETTER than she'd ever slept that night, knowing that Bill was in jail, along with all of those who'd worked with him, including Judge Wyatt, Sheila Axelrod, and a number of others whose names and fingerprints they'd gotten from examining the warehouse.

When she woke the next morning, still in the hospital, Nick was sitting beside her bed, where he'd been when she'd fallen asleep last night. He looked sleepy as he smiled at her. "Hi."

"Hi," she said. "You really did stay all night, huh?"

"Right here in this chair." He handed her the newspaper. "Thought you might want to see this."

"What?"

"The *St. Petersburg Times*. Phil did it. He got them to print your article this morning, along with several sidebars about last night, and the arson at the paper, and the bomb in your house, and even Tracy Westin."

She sat up slowly in bed and read her headline. "I don't believe it. I had given up."

"Whatever Brandon and Judge Wyatt may have planned for squirming their way out of this, it isn't likely to work now—not with all this publicity. I think the media will dive into this story today. Maybe even the national networks. Better get ready to be a hero."

"I'm no hero," she said. "I'll never shake the stigma of being one of Bill's kids." She sighed. "What about Jimmy and the rest of them? Will they be punished?"

"Nope," he told her. "There's a quote right here by the prosecutor. 'We have no plans to prosecute any of the children who participated in these crimes, nor any of those who participated as children and are now adults.' All he wants is for you to be witnesses in the trial."

She closed her eyes in relief, whispering, "Then they aren't presuming we're all guilty until we're proven innocent?"

"Not at all," he said. "You're altogether innocent."

"Not altogether," she whispered. "But I believe in the power of Christ's forgiveness now."

"Wanna talk about it?" he asked.

She swallowed and tried to sort through her feelings. An image of Tracy, weak and sick, trying to stop the car that was carrying off her children, offering her life in exhange for theirs, overwhelmed her. No matter what Tracy had done in the past, in the end, she had loved her children enough to die for them.

Beth closed her eyes as tears streamed down her face. "I can't quit thinking of Tracy," she whispered. "What she did—I think that's the kind of love you tried to tell me about. The kind that could ransom those little kids."

"That's right," Nick said, stroking her forehead. "The same kind of love that could ransom a woman with a painful past."

She breathed in a shaky sob. "And no score sheet can ever outshine that kind of love, can it?"

Nick shook his head, and she saw the tears in his eyes. She covered her face as her tears fell harder, as her soul swelled within her.

"Oh, Jesus, I believe you," she prayed aloud through her tears. "Ransom me. Not just from Bill, but from myself. From all the lies I've believed. From all the pain I've hardened myself to . . ."

Nick held her hand tightly as she prayed, encouraging her prayer with words of his own.

When she opened her eyes, she was smiling, but the tears continued nonetheless. Nick was crying, too. For a moment, they just looked at each other and laughed through their tears. When Nick took in a deep, cleansing breath and began to wipe her tears, her smile faded. "I just thought of something," she said. "You remember how I compared Tracy to my own mother?"

"Yeah," Nick said.

"Well, I wonder—would she have done what Tracy did? I mean, if Tracy had the capacity for that kind of love in her, maybe, in the end, my mother could have cared, too. If she'd been put to the test—who knows?"

"God knows," Nick said. "That's why you're thinking of it right now. Maybe God can help you forgive her."

A light of realization dawned behind Beth's eyes. "Yeah, I think I can," she whispered in wonder. "I think, if God can forgive me for all that I've done—yeah, I can forgive my mom."

Nick pulled her up into his arms and held her as tightly as he could without hurting her. For the first time in her life, she belonged. Right here, in his arms. Together, they cried and clung together until there were no more tears, and laughter joined their hearts.

When he let her go, she reached out and touched his stubbled jaw. "I guess you'll be getting Sheila Axelrod's job, huh?"

He looked thoughtful. "I've had a lot of time to think tonight—about my job, about all these problems we've seen, about how hard it's going to be to place those kids. And I think I've come to a decision."

"What?"

"I want to apply to take over the home. I want to give those kids a chance to see what God's grace is like. I want to bring them to him—to the real Lord, not some perverted version like Bill had. I want to be a father to all those kids."

Her heart burst. "Oh, Nick, you'd be wonderful at it, and you have such a heart for them."

"I'd need helpers," he said. "I was thinking about that nice couple, the Millers, who wanted so badly to be in the foster parent program. Maybe they could be cottage parents, and I can think of other retired couples who'd be good, too. And I thought that, well—maybe you could help."

"I'm too young to be a cottage mother."

"You're not too young to be my wife."

She stared at him for a long moment, stricken with disbelief. He took her hand, kissed it, and set her palm against his jaw. "What do you think, Beth? Would you make me the happiest man in the world and be my wife? Have my children? Let me be your family, and then we can be the family for all those kids."

Beth threw her arms around his neck, too choked up to answer. Somehow, Nick was pretty sure that she was going to say yes.

73

TWO WEEKS LATER, Lynda bought Lisa a new bathing suit and got special permission to take her and Jimmy out to the beach that morning. But Jimmy and Jake were cooking something up, and they were late arriving.

"What do you think those two boys are doing?" she asked the little girl.

"I don't know," Lisa said. "Can we build a castle while we wait?"

"Of course we can. Come on. Let's go down to the water."

"But we'll get wet."

"It doesn't matter. A little water never hurt anybody." Lynda got down on her knees just out of reach of the waves, and began helping the child pile the sand into a castle.

"When I grow up," Lisa said with a self-conscious smile, "I want to live in a castle."

Lynda laughed. "I thought that, too, when I was a little girl. And when I grew up, I got something just as good as a castle. But you know what? It didn't make me happy."

The little girl hung on every word. "What made you happy?" she asked.

"People," she said. "People I love. People who love me."

"I have people who love me," Lisa said. "Jimmy loves me. And my mom."

Lynda's smile slowly faded. "Do you remember your mom, Lisa?"

She shook her head and looked across the water. The breeze blew her hair back from her face. "Not really," she said. "But Jimmy's been telling me about her. He told me how much she loved us."

"She did," Lynda agreed.

"She died, though." Her wistful eyes focused on the half-formed castle, and she started patting the sand again. "Do you love Jake?"

Lynda grinned. "Very much."

They heard a plane overhead, and Lisa looked up as Lynda dug up more sand.

"Look, Lynda! What does it say?"

Lynda looked up. It was a skywriting plane, and it was writing something across the sky. Lisa stood up and waved, jumping up and down. "It looks like . . . M-a-r-r-y . . . Marry . . . me . . ." Lisa read. "L-y-n—"

Lynda got to her feet and shaded her eyes as she stared up in disbelief. "Marry me, Lynda." She caught her breath. "It's Jake, Lisa! He's asking me to marry him! What should I say?"

Lisa began to dance and wave her arms with delight. "Tell him yes! Hurry!"

The cellular phone in Lynda's beach bag rang, and she pulled it out and, with a big grin, answered, "Yes, I'll marry you!"

Jake laughed out loud. "Will you, really?"

"Of course I will! Now get down here so I can kiss you!"

74

THAT NIGHT, AFTER they had taken Jimmy and Lisa back to the home—which Nick was already running on a temporary basis until the state approved him to take it over permanently—Lynda and Jake sat out on the swing in her backyard, moving slowly back and forth.

"There's something I want to talk to you about," Jake said. "Something important."

"More important than marriage?" she asked, smiling down at the ring sparkling on her finger.

"Not really. But maybe *as* important."

"What?"

"It's about children."

"I want them," Lynda said. "Lots of them. And I hope they look just like you."

He laughed. "I'd rather they look like you. But I was thinking of a head start, kind of. I was thinking of adoption."

Her eyes caught his grin, and she sat up straight and cocked her head to look at him. "Jake, you're not thinking what I think you're thinking, are you? Because I've thought it myself, only I didn't think you'd think—"

"Jimmy and Lisa," he said.

"Yes!" she shouted. "Yes! We can be the best parents anybody ever had, and—"

"Let's call Nick," he said. "I don't want to waste any time!"

75

SIX MONTHS LATER The plane Jake had named *Trinity* circled the airfield, to the cheers of the dozens of children—most of them residents of the St. Clair Children's Home—then descended for a landing on the long dirt runway. Nick and Beth watched from a crowd of children as Jake Stevens rolled the plane to a stop, and Lynda Barrett Stevens turned back to the crowd with her bullhorn.

"All right, guys! Who hasn't been up yet?"

"Me, Mommy! I wanna go!" Lisa jumped up and down in front of her, waving her arm in front of her face so she wouldn't be missed.

"You can go anytime!" Jimmy said. "Let Dad take *them,* Lisa!"

"But I wanna go too! I wanna see their faces!"

Lynda laughed and hugged the child that had brought so much joy to the home she and Jake were making together. "All right, sweetie. You're in the next group."

Melissa and Larry Millsaps counted off the next group of kids Jake would take up for a flight, then herded them over to the wing, where Tony Danks and his fiancée, Sharon Robinson, stood waiting to pull them up and help them into the plane.

The children roared and cheered as Jake turned the plane around and taxied back up the airstrip.

Nick slid his arm around his wife and pulled her close. "They're loving this," he said.

Beth laughed and ran her fingers through her hair. She had let it grow out some and had returned it to its natural color. "Yeah, it was a good idea. And you know he's not just showing them the clouds. He's got a captive audience up there to tell them all about Jesus."

"The way things have been going at the home, they might just tell *him* about Jesus. You're a great influence for them, Beth. You never let an opportunity go by—"

"When they lie down, and when they rise up. I wish someone had explained it all to me earlier. Then I would have known that I was loved. That I wasn't just some throwaway kid that nobody wanted."

"Not one of these kids feels like a throwaway," Nick said. "They're happy, aren't they?"

"Yeah, I think they are. Bill Brandon's brainwashing goes deep, but Christ's grace is deeper."

"Way deeper," Nick said. He leaned over and kissed his wife, then pulled her into a crushing hug as the plane circled over their heads, and the burgers sizzled on the grills, and the children laughed and squealed and ran across the grass.

And the joy they all felt was a divine gift that couldn't be doused or destroyed by men, because God had chosen to bestow it on them like a beautiful package under a Christmas tree—

Or a marriage that blossomed brighter with each passing day—

Or an eternity without threat or malice.

Miracles, they were, all shining and bright beneath the warm rays of God's smile.

Afterword

RECENTLY, I WAS sitting in the Green Room at CBN Headquarters in Virginia Beach, waiting to go on *The 700 Club,* when God taught me one of those lessons that he often teaches when we least expect it. The producer had just come in and told me that I'd be squeezed on at the end of the program, and that I might get six minutes.

My heart sank, because I wanted so much to give my whole testimony about how God had convicted me to leave my career in the secular market and write Christian fiction only. There were so many miracles God had performed in my life, so many things I wanted the *700 Club* viewers to know about. But there was no way I could tell them all of it in six minutes.

The guest coordinator of the show and the executive producer were in the Green Room with me, and when the producer who had delivered the startling news retreated, I looked at the other two and confessed that I was nervous. That was an understatement. The truth was that I was in a state of sheer panic.

Without batting an eye, Jackie, the guest coordinator, began praying for me. She asked God to remind me that he had brought me here for a reason, and that he wasn't going to forsake me now. Immediately afterward, the two were called away, and I was left in the room alone.

Instantly, I began to pray again. I asked God not to let Terry Meeuwsen, the interviewer, waste time with fluffy talk about writing and publishing, but that the Lord would give her the exact questions that would move the story forward rapidly enough that I could get out the most important parts of my testimony. I asked him to give me peace about going out there under such time constraints, as well as a clear head so that my thoughts and my words would flow smoothly. And I prayed for the hearts of those viewers who needed to hear what God had done for me.

Peace fell over me, and when the producer came for me, I was calm. Terry asked pertinent and intelligent questions that jumped the story forward when it needed to jump forward, and I was able to get my testimony out. The interesting thing is that some parts of the story which I might have left out, God saw fit to leave in. Terry's questions prompted me to answer them.

What was the lesson I learned that day? I learned that when we do anything by our own strength, we have the potential of failing. But when we empty ourselves of our own intentions, our own plans, our own goals, God will fill us up with his Holy Spirit. When we're directed by the Creator of the universe, how can we fail?

God gives us everything we need. Christian friends, teachers, churches, pastors, the Bible . . . But if we just use those things to get us to some end—whether it be a successful interview or salvation itself—they're nothing more than tools. Without the Father to guide us, the Christ to motivate us, and the Holy Spirit to empower us, we have the potential to fail.

But thanks be to God, through Jesus Christ our Lord, that "he who began a good work in you will carry it on to completion until the day of Christ Jesus" (Philippians 1:6). And thanks to our Father for giving us not just the tools, but the reason and the power to go along with them. And thanks to him, especially, for giving us the outcome—success, always, pure and divine, the way he designed it.